REEDS
NAUTICAL ALMANAC

CARIBBEAN
1994

Publisher: Jerald D. Knopf
Editor: John J. Kettlewell
Assistant Editor: Leslie Kettlewell

First Edition 1994

THOMAS REED
PUBLICATIONS, INC.

LONDON ● BOSTON

NAUTICAL PUBLISHERS SINCE 1782

© 1993 Thomas Reed Publications Inc.
122 Lewis Wharf
Boston MA 02110
U.S.A.
Tel: (617) 248-0084 Fax: (617) 248-5855

ISBN 1-884666-01-9

Composition and Layout by:
DeNee Reiton Skipper
24 Essex Road
Belmont, MA 02178

Printed in the U.S.A. by:
Courier E.P.I.C., Inc.
15 Wellman Avenue
North Chelmsford, MA 01863

CONTENTS

PREFACE

This is the first edition of *Reed's Nautical Almanac: Caribbean Edition*. As with our East Coast, Pacific Northwest, North European and South European editions, we have created the most complete navigation guide available for the area. For the first time, boaters have a Nautical Ephemeris, a Coast Pilot, a light list, complete tide and current tables, electronic navigation information and communication data all in one easy-to-use volume. The tidal data created for this almanac is the most complete available from any source — we have actually created new tables, not previously available, to make this information much easier to use.

As with our other editions, this annual almanac is designed to be used in conjunction with the information found in *Reed's Nautical Companion*. The *Companion* is your on-board reference source for the many topics that do not change each year. This combination provides you with a complete nautical reference library — in only two compact volumes! To get the most out of your almanacs, order your copy of *Reed's Nautical Companion*, or pick one up at your local chandler.

All of our almanacs are the result of extensive research by our editorial staff, but, particularly in the Caribbean, currently available information and data may be found to be out-of-date. In order to provide the best product possible, we welcome your input, advice and contributions.

To keep your almanac up-to-date send for your FREE SUPPLEMENT — this list of the latest navigational changes will be shipped in mid-1994.

We sincerely hope this almanac helps you plan and execute a safe and enjoyable voyage — may all your landfalls be expected!

Editor: John J. Kettlewell
Assistant Editor: Leslie Kettlewell

ACKNOWLEDGEMENTS

The publisher and editors would like to thank the many people, government agencies and businesses that have helped us in the preparation of this almanac. Without their assistance, this project would not have been possible. Here are a few of the many contributors:

Micronautics Inc., Rockport, ME: Jim Mays and Ben Ellison; U.S. Customs Service; U.S. Coast Guard; L.J. Harri Nautical Booksellers, Boston, MA; Bluewater Books, Ft. Lauderdale, FL; The Armchair Sailor Bookstore, Charleston, SC; The National Oceanic and Atmospheric Administration, NOAA; the Defense Mapping Agency, DMA; AT&T High Seas Radio Telephone Service; WLO Radio, Alabama; Virgin Islands Radio; Bermuda Harbour Radio; Voice of America, VOA; The British Broadcasting Corporation, BBC; The Radio Technical Commission; Lady's Island Marina: Jack Ford; Jim and Tricia Johnston; Kent Brokenshire; Ralph Johnson

Mexican hydrographic and cartographic information is courtesy of the Secretaría de Marina, Dirección de Oceanografía Naval, of Mexico.

GOVERNMENT PUBLICATIONS

Government publications for the waters covered in this almanac:

U.S. Government Printing Office: Light List Volume III: Atlantic and Gulf Coasts; The Nautical Almanac

Defense Mapping Agency: Pub. 110, List of Lights, Radio Aids and Fog Signals; Pub. 117, Radio Navigational Aids; Pub. 140, Sailing Directions North Atlantic Ocean; Pub. 147, Sailing Directions for the Caribbean Sea, Volume I; Pub. 148, Sailing Directions for the Caribbean Sea, Volume II; Pub. 150, World Port Index; Pub. 151, Distances Between Ports; Notices to Mariners

U.S. Coast Guard: Local Notices to Mariners, District 7

National Oceanic and Atmospheric Administration: United States Coast Pilot, Volumes 4 and 5; Selected Worldwide Marine Weather Broadcasts; Tide Tables, East Coast of North and South America; Tidal Current Tables, Atlantic Coast of North America

Data given in the Ephemeris has been supplied by the Nautical Almanac office of the Science and Engineering Research Council, and is reproduced with the permission of the Controller of HM Stationery Office.

REED'S

NAUTICAL ALMANAC

CARIBBEAN 1994

Here is the most complete, compact, easy-to-use onboard reference covering the entire Caribbean Basin

- The only nautical almanac compiled exclusively for the entire Caribbean
- Includes complete information on transiting the Panama Canal
- More than $300 worth of vital information from government & private resources in one handy volume

> Bermuda • Southeast Florida • Bahamas • Turks & Caicos • Cuba
> Cayman Islands • Jamaica • Haiti • Dominican Republic • Puerto Rico
> US & British Virgin Islands • Leewards • Windwards • Barbados
> Trinidad & Tobago • Venezuela • Aruba, Bonaire, Curaçao • Colombia
> Panama • Costa Rica • Nicaragua • Western Caribbean (offshore islands)
> Honduras • Guatemala • Belize • Mexico

- Coast pilot information — organized geographically for 42 Caribbean regions
- Tide tables and current information
- Aids to navigation — all major aids to navigation with latitude/longitude positions
- Selected harbor chartlets — more than 200, with descriptions for the most popular ports and anchorages
- Communication and weather service information — VHF, SSB, high-seas radiotelephone, NOAA weather radio, and weatherfax broadcast services
- Celestial navigation tables — a complete nautical ephemeris for 1994

A valuable Caribbean resource that no mariner should be without!

REED'S NAUTICAL COMPANION

Table of Contents

To get your **REED'S NAUTICAL COMPANION,** call 1-800-995-4995 and ask for the **REED'S** dealer nearest you!

Notices to Mariners

NAVTEX COMMENCEMENT

Commencing August 1, 1993, NAVTEX service of Maritime Safety Information (MSI) broadcasts under the Worldwide Navigational Warning Service will be operational worldwide. For a listing of stations, schedule times and types of information provided consult DMA Publication 117, Radio Navigational Aids and Chapter 6 of *Reed's Nautical Almanac, Caribbean.* These internationally coordinated broadcasts on medium frequency 518kHz will provide mariners with distress, urgent and safety messages, and weather forecasts and warnings. The coverage of NAVTEX will be reasonably continuous out to 200 nautical miles from the transmitting station. In the U.S., the Coast Guard is the responsible agency for NAVTEX operation.

The U.S. NAVTEX area of coverage will reduce the number of NAVAREA IV and XII messages sent out by DMA, since most of these warnings fall within the 200 nautical mile limit. It is estimated that NAVAREA IV and XII traffic will be reduced by more than half. NAVAREA IV and XII traffic will also be used to cover gaps in U.S. NAVTEX coverage and to allow for messages that traverse the 200 nautical mile border so as to provide full MSI coverage in these two areas. In addition, the Coast Guard will forward to DMA those NAVTEX messages that are within the 200 nautical mile limit, but which are significant enough that they should be sent by NAVAREA broadcast as well (as an example, a closure of port).

DISCONTINUE WATCH-KEEPING OF DISTRESS FREQUENCY 500KHZ

Effective August 1, 1993, all United States Coast Guard communication stations and cutters will discontinue watchkeeping on the distress frequency 500kHz, and will cease all morse code services in the medium frequency radiotelegraphy band. More efficient telecommunication systems are now available to provide the mariner with options for initiating or relaying distress alerts, and passing and receiving maritime safety information. These options include INMARSAT, radio telex (SITOR), MF/HF single sideband and VHF radiotelephone, satellite EPIRBS, INMARSAT Safetynet, NAVTEX and HF NAVTEX (SITOR). NAVTEX broadcasts include the same Notice to Mariners, weather, search and rescue and fixed fishing gear location products that have been provided by the MF morse broadcasts. Distress and other calls to any U.S. Coast Guard communication station can also be made on any of the following HF single sideband radiotelephone channels: 424 (4134kHz), 601 (6200kHz), 816 (8240kHz), or 1205 (12242kHz). Meteorological broadcasts are also made on these channels. These options are believed to provide sufficient redundancy to ensure that adequate distress and safety communication capabilities are available. Questions or comments regarding this discontinuance of MF morse telegraphy services can be sent to any Coast Guard communications station or direct to U.S. Coast Guard Headquarters:

COMMANDANT (G-TTM)
U.S. Coast Guard
Washington, DC 20593
TELEFAX: (202) 267-4106 or 267-4662

WARNING ON USE OF FLOATING AIDS TO NAVIGATION TO FIX A NAVIGATIONAL POSITION

The aids to navigation depicted on charts comprise a system consisting of fixed and floating aids with varying degrees of reliability. Therefore, prudent mariners will not rely solely on any single aid to navigation, particularly a floating aid.

The buoy symbol is used to indicate the approximate position of the buoy body and the sinker which secures the buoy to the seabed. The approximate position is used because of practical limitations in positioning and maintaining buoys and their sinkers in precise geographical locations. These limitations include, but are not limited to, inherent imprecisions in position fixing methods, prevailing atmospheric and sea conditions, the slope of and the material of the seabed, the fact that buoys are moored to sinkers by varying lengths of chain, and the fact that buoy and/or sinker positions are not under continuous surveillance but are normally checked only during periodic maintenance visits which often occur more than a year apart. The position of the buoy body can be expected to shift inside and outside the charting symbol due to the forces of nature. The mariner is also cautioned that buoys are liable to be carried away, shifted, capsized, sunk, etc. Lighted

buoys may be extinguished or sound signals may not function as the result of ice or other natural causes, collisions or other accidents.

For the foregoing reasons, a prudent mariner must not rely completely upon the position or operation of floating aids to navigation, but will utilize bearings from fixed objects and aids to navigation on shore. Further, a vessel attempting to pass close aboard always risks collision with a yawing buoy or with the obstruction the buoy marks.

AREAS TO BE AVOIDED (ATLAS MOORINGS) IN THE EQUATORIAL PACIFIC

The National Oceanic and Atmospheric Administration (NOAA) is in the process of placing buoys called Autonomous Temperature Line Acquisition System (ATLAS) reaching from the Galapagos to New Guinea along the Equator.

The ATLAS buoys are Q type 2 to 3 meter toroid buoys with orange and white bands. Mariners are advised to give the following mooring positions a 6 nautical mile berth:

2 00N, 095 00W
0 00, 095 00W
2 00S, 095 00W

8 00N, 110 00W
5 00N, 110 00W
2 00N, 110 12W
2 00S, 110 00W
5 00S, 110 00W
8 00S, 110 00W

8 00N, 125 00W
5 00N, 125 00W
2 00N, 125 00W
0 00, 124 24W
2 00S, 124 54W
5 00S, 124 54W
8 00S, 125 00W

9 00N, 140 18W
5 00N, 140 00W
2 00N, 140 00W
2 00S, 140 00W
5 00S, 140 00W

8 00N, 155 00W
5 00N, 154 54W
2 00N, 155 00W
0 00, 155 00W
2 00S, 155 00W
5 00S, 155 00W
0 10S, 155 00W

8 00N, 170 00W
5 00N, 170 00W
2 00N, 170 00W
0 00, 170 00W
2 12S, 170 00W
5 00S, 170 00W
8 00S, 170 00W

5 00N, 179 54W
2 00N, 179 54W
0 00, 179 54W
2 00S, 179 48W
5 00S, 179 54W

8 00N, 165 00E
5 00N, 165 00E
2 00N, 165 00E
2 00S, 164 30E
5 00S, 165 12E
8 00S, 165 00E

5 00N, 156 00E
2 00N, 156 00E
2 00S, 156 00E
5 00S, 156 00E

5 00N, 147 00E
2 00N, 147 00E

5 00N, 137 00E
2 00N, 137 00E

SPECIAL WARNING FOR CUBA

Cuba claims a 12 mile territorial sea extending from straight baselines drawn from Cuban coastal points. The effect is that Cuba's claimed territorial sea extends in many areas well beyond the 12 miles from Cuba's physical coastline. These claims are not in conformance with international law and are not recognized by the United States. Nonetheless, United States vessels have been stopped and boarded by Cuban authorities more than 20 miles from the Cuban coast in some cases. Within the limits of prudence and good judgment, mariners

are advised to protest (but not physically resist) any improper attempt to stop, board or seize U.S. vessels in international waters. Notify the U.S. Coast Guard of your status so that they can relay information about your situation to the Department of State for diplomatic attention.

On September 1, 1990, seven Traffic Separation Schemes, approved by the International Maritime Organization, were implemented off the eastern, western and northern coasts of Cuba. The government of Cuba has unilaterally established a mandatory ship reporting system within the Old Bahama Channel to govern vessel movement within the area. While it is the U.S. Position that the mandatory provisions of the ship reporting system are inconsistent with International Law, vessels should exercise caution while transiting the Old Bahama Channel.

The Traffic Separation Schemes are in the following areas:

Off Cabo San Antonio
Off La Tabla
Off Costa de Matanzas
In the Old Bahama Channel
Off Punta Maternillos
Off Punta Lucrecia
Off Cabo Maysi

CHANNEL 9 VHF-FM CALLING CHANNEL

In an effort to eliminate traffic congestion on channel 16 VHF-FM, the Federal Communications Commission (FCC) has recently designated channel 9 VHF-FM as the nationwide *Recreational Calling Channel* for use by non-commercial boaters within the United States. Use of this channel by recreational boaters is strictly voluntary, but is strongly encouraged by the Coast Guard and the FCC.

It is important to note though, **the Coast Guard will not — repeat will not — monitor channel 9 VHF-FM for distress calls.** Vessels in distress should make their calls on channel 16 VHF-FM. Further information can be obtained from your nearest Coast Guard facility.

PROPER USE OF CHANNEL 16 VHF-FM

Channel 16 VHF-FM (156.8 MHz) is designated by the Federal Communications Commission (FCC) as the National Distress, Safety and Calling frequency. It must be monitored at all times by vessels underway. Calls to other vessels are normally initiated on channel 16 (except by recreational vessels, see above), and except in an emergency, vessels should shift to another channel to communicate. If a vessel cannot be raised on channel 16 for communications concerning navigational safety, an attempt can be made on channel 13.

The Coast Guard has received complaints concerning the failure of vessels to answer calls from other vessels on channel 16 VHF-FM. Incidents of failure to respond on channel 16 involving safety communications should be reported to the nearest Coast Guard Marine Safety Office.

FCC Regulations prohibit radio checks with the Coast Guard on channel 16 VHF-FM except when conducted by FCC representatives, qualified radio technicians installing or repairing equipment, or when requested by the Coast Guard.

COAST GUARD DROP/FLOAT PUMPS

The Coast Guard often provides vessels in distress with emergency pumps by parachute drop, helicopter hoist, or by vessel. The most commonly used type of pump comes complete in a sealed aluminum drum about half the size of a 55 gallon drum.

A single lever on the top opens the drum. **Do not allow smoking or open flames in the vicinity while opening, as there may be gas fumes inside the can.** The pump will draw about 90 gallons of water per minute. There should be a waterproof flashlight on top of the pump for night use. Operating instructions are provided inside the pump container.

FCC STATION LICENSE CHECK

In an effort to improve maritime safety, the Federal Communications Commission (FCC) and the U.S. Coast Guard are jointly enforcing existing radio regulations to help reduce the growing problem of hoaxes, and other violations interfering with distress operations.

Because of evidence that many boaters and operators of uninspected vessels disregard FCC maritime radio licensing and usage rules, or are unaware of such rules, the Coast Guard will check a FCC Ship Station License or radio equipped vessels during boarding inspections.

Recreational boaters with a VHF-FM radio, EPIRB, Radar, HF-Single Sideband radio or portable radio installed aboard their vessels are required to have a Ship Station License to operate their radio. If you plan to visit a foreign port you must also have a Restricted Radiotelephone Operator's Permit. You are required to post the original or a clearly legible copy of the Ship Station License at the principal control point of each station. A copy must indicate the location of the original. If you cannot post the license it must be kept where it will be readily available for inspection.

To obtain a Ship Station License you should request FCC Form 506. The license is valid for 5 years and the cost is currently $35.00. To obtain a Restricted Radiotelephone Operators Permit you should request FCC Form 753. This license is valid for your lifetime and the cost is currently $35.00. Forms may be obtained by visiting your FCC Field Operations Bureau or by phoning (202) 632-3676.

Those who have failed to obtain an FCC authorization to operate such maritime equipment are liable for a criminal misdemeanor penalty of up to $1,000, one year in prison, or both. CB radios, cellular telephones and receive-only equipment are exempted.

CLARIFICATION OF RULES ON DIVERS FLAGS

There has been some confusion over the status of the traditional sport divers flag because of a change to the U.S. Inland Navigation rules concerning the use of a one meter rigid replica of the International Code Flag ALFA (a blue and white swallow tailed flag).

The ALFA flag is to be flown on small vessels engaged in diving operations whenever the vessels are restricted in their ability to maneuver. However, in sport diving, where divers are usually free swimming, the ALFA flag does not have to be shown and the Coast Guard encourages the continued use of the traditional sports diver flag. Divers should also review state laws as these may have different requirements for dive flags and operations.

The distinction the Coast Guard wants to make clear is: the ALFA is a navigational signal intended to protect the vessel from collision. The sport diver flag is an unofficial signal that, through custom, has come to be used to protect the diver in the water. It is the responsibility of the operator of a diving vessel to determine if his craft's movements are restricted. To be most effective, the sport diver flag should be exhibited on a float in the water to mark the approximate location of the diver.

Chapter 1

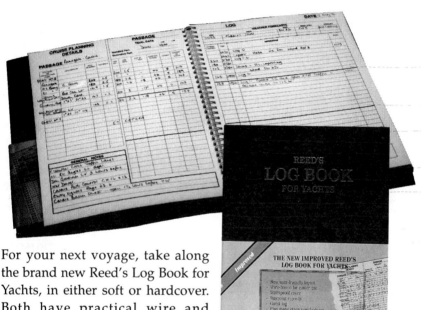

COAST PILOT

2

COAST PILOT INTRODUCTION

The Coast Pilot is organized geographically, beginning with Bermuda, then proceeding clockwise around the Caribbean from southeast Florida and the Bahamas. The north coast of South America, Central America and the East Coast of Mexico are included. Refer to the chapter table of contents, or the Index to find a particular region. Each region contains information on Entry Procedures, selected major lights, buoys, daymarks and harbors. Harbor descriptions for selected ports and harbor chartlets for reference purposes are included. The harbor chartlets are located in each regional section.

WAYPOINTS
Whenever available, we have listed the latitude and longitude of major aids to navigation. The listings are in degrees, minutes and tenths of a minute. These positions have been obtained from the government light lists, and are for reference only. Many navigators will be tempted to use these as waypoints in their LORAN or GPS units. If doing so, the listed position should be plotted on a large scale chart of the area to ascertain its relationship to navigational hazards in the vicinity. It must be kept in mind, that floating aids to navigation, such as buoys, will move about on their anchor rodes. The positions of buoys should be regarded as approximate. Reed's can not guarantee the accuracy of any latitude/longitude positions. The prudent navigator will use these waypoints with caution, and will not rely upon them as his sole means of position fixing.

HARBOR DESCRIPTIONS
A new feature of this almanac are the many brief harbor descriptions. This information has been gathered from a variety of sources, including actual visits by our editors. Individual harbors may be found by locating them in the index, or by referring to the geographic section appropriate for that harbor. Whenever possible, the harbors have been placed near the buoys and lights leading to the harbor.

CHARTLETS
As a further aid to the mariner we have added over 200 chartlets of major harbors. Each chartlet coincides with a harbor description, and a listing of the major aids to navigation in the area. Though in many cases these chartlets are actual reproductions of government charts,

the prudent mariner will not use these for navigation. Every vessel should be equipped with up to date charts of their intended route. These chartlets can be very useful in planning your trip, and familiarizing yourself with the area.

LIGHTS, BUOYS AND DAYMARKS
Items listed as "Lights" may vary from simple poles to major stone towers over 100 feet high. We've included a brief description of many lights, which can often help identify them during the day. In general, a "Light" is a fixed structure that is lighted at night. Some major "Lights" remain lit 24 hours a day - this is generally noted in the listings.

Buoys are floating aids to navigation. Within the United States and Canada, all even numbered buoys (ie. 2, 4, 6, 8 etc.) are colored red. All odd numbered buoys (ie. 1, 3, 5, 7, 9 etc.) will be green in color. In some parts of the Caribbean you may encounter a few black buoys that have not been given a coat of green paint yet. The color of the light shown by the buoy will usually match the color of its hull. Center of channel buoys will often be red and white. Buoys marking hazards will often be yellow.

Large navigational buoys are designated as LNBs in the listings. These are 40 feet in diameter and were designed to replace lightships. They are red in color to aid their visibility. They are equipped with lights, radiobeacons, sound signals and racons.

An unlit red buoy will usually be a nun, while an unlit green buoy will be a can. If this is not the case, there will be an indication in the list.

Daymarks are signs on posts, lighthouses and buildings that can be seen during the day — or sometimes at night if illuminated with a spotlight. There are many types of daymarks, which can be very confusing to even the most informed navigators. The following list of abbreviations should help alleviate some of the confusion.

Most lighted aids will include a listing of visible range, and in the case of Lights, a listing of the height of the light. Range will always be listed in nautical miles (abbreviated M), unless noted otherwise. Heights will be in feet (above High Water). Feet is abbreviated ft. and meters is abbreviated m. When bearings are given (usu-

ally for ranges) they will be true bearings, not adjusted for magnetic variation. Limits of light sectors and arcs of visibility *as observed from a vessel* are given in clockwise order.

A standard order is used for all listings of aids to navigation. The sequence is as follows: *Light or buoy name and designation, Latitude and longitude, Light characteristics, Height of Light, Range of Light, Description of Aid, other characteristics or features.*

An example of a typical listing is for **HARRISON POINT LIGHT:**

HARRISON POINT LIGHT, NW side of island, 13 18.3N, 59 39.0W, Fl (2) W 15s, 193ft., 22M, W stone tower.

The name of the aid to navigation is HARRISON POINT LIGHT. Its location is 13 18.3N, 59 39.0W. The light characteristic is 2 white flashes every 15 seconds. The light is located 193 feet above sea level. Its range is 22 nautical miles. The light is located on a white stone tower.

Tables describing various types of lights and daybeacons will be found on the following pages.

ABBREVIATIONS

The following is a list of abbreviations as used in the Coast Pilot:

N=north S=south W=west E=east
R=red G=green W=white B=black
Y=yellow Or=orange

Al=alternating
F=fixed
Fl=flashing
Gp=group
IQ=interrupted quick flashing
Iso=isophase
IVQ=interrupted very quick flashing
Km=kilometer
L Fl=long flashing
Lt=light
M=nautical mile
Mo=Morse code
min=minute (or minimum in Tidal Current Tables)
m=meters
obsc=obscured
Oc=occulting
Q=quick
s=seconds
UQ=ultra quick flashing

vert=vertical
vis=visible
VQ=very quick flashing

DAYMARKS

The first letter of the daymark listing indicates it's basic purpose.
S=Square. Used to mark the port (left) side of channels when entering from seaward.
T=Triangle. Used to mark the starboard (right) side of channels when entering from seaward.
J=Junction. May be a square or a triangle. Used to mark channel junctions or bifurcations in the channel. May be used to mark wrecks, or other obstructions, which may be passed on either side. The color of the top band has lateral significance for the preferred channel.
M=Safe Water. Octagonal. Used to mark the fairway, or middle of the channel.
K=Range. Rectangular. When the front and rear daymarks are aligned on the same bearing, you are on the azimuth of the range - this usually marks safe water.
N=No lateral significance. Diamond or rectangular shaped. Used for special purposes as a warning, distance or location marker.

Additional information after a - :

-I=Intracoastal Waterway. A yellow reflective strip will be oriented horizontally on the daymark.

-SY=Intracoastal Waterway. A yellow reflective square will be on the daymark. This indicates a port hand marker. This may appear on a red triangular daymark, in places where the Intracoastal Waterway coincides with another channel's markings.

-TY=Intracoastal Waterway. A yellow reflective triangle will be on the daymark. This indicates a starboard hand marker. This may appear on a green square daymark, in places where the Intracoastal Waterway coincides with another channel.

These abbreviations are combined in the list of aids to navigation. The following list gives many of the major designations:

SG=Square green daymark with a green reflective border.

SG-I=Square green daymark with a green reflective border, and a yellow reflective horizontal strip.

Chapter 2

SG-SY=Square green daymark with a green reflective border, and a yellow reflective square.

SG-TY=Square green daymark with a green reflective border, and a yellow reflective triangle.

SR=Square red daymark with a red reflective border.

TG=Triangular green daymark with a green reflective border.

TR=Triangular red daymark with a red reflective border.

TR-I=Triangular red daymark with a red reflective border, and a yellow reflective horizontal strip.

TR-SY=Triangular red daymark with a red reflective border, and a yellow reflective square.

TR-TY=Triangular red daymark with a red reflective border, and a yellow reflective triangle. JG=Daymark with horizontal bands of green and red, green band topmost, with a green reflective border.

JG-I=Daymark with horizontal bands of green and red, green band topmost, with a green reflective border, and a yellow reflective horizontal strip.

JG-SY=Daymark with horizontal bands of green and red, green band topmost, with a green reflective border, and a yellow reflective square.

JG-TY=Daymark with horizontal bands of green and red, green band topmost, with a green reflective border, and a yellow reflective triangle.

JR=Daymark with horizontal bands of green and red, red band topmost, with a red reflective border.

JR-I=Daymark with horizontal bands of green and red, red band topmost, with a red reflective border, with a yellow horizontal strip.

JR-SY=Triangular daymark with horizontal bands of green and red, red band topmost, with a red reflective border, and a yellow reflective square.

JR-TY=Triangular daymark with horizontal bands of green and red, red band topmost,

with a red reflective border, and a yellow reflective triangle.

MR=Octagonal daymark with stripes of white and red, with a white reflective border.

MR-I=Octagonal daymark with stripes of white and red, with a white reflective border and a yellow reflective horizontal strip.

CG=Diamond shaped green daymark bearing small green diamond shaped reflectors at each corner.

CR=Diamond shaped red daymark bearing small red diamond shaped reflectors at each corner.

KBG=Rectangular black daymark bearing a central green stripe.

KBG-I=Rectangular black daymark bearing a central green stripe and a yellow reflective horizontal strip.

KBR=Rectangular black daymark bearing a central red stripe.

KBR-I=Rectangular black daymark bearing a central red stripe and a yellow reflective horizontal strip.

KBW=Rectangular black daymark bearing a central white stripe.

KBW-I=Rectangular black daymark bearing a central white stripe and a yellow reflective horizontal strip.

KGB=Rectangular green daymark bearing a central black stripe.

KGB-I=Rectangular green daymark bearing a central black stripe and a yellow reflective horizontal strip.

KGR=Rectangular green daymark bearing a central red stripe.

KGR-I=Rectangular green daymark bearing a central red stripe and a yellow reflective horizontal strip.

KGW=Rectangular green daymark bearing a central white stripe.

KGW-I=Rectangular green daymark bearing a central white stripe and a yellow reflective horizontal strip.

KRB=Rectangular red daymark bearing a central black stripe.

KRB-I=Rectangular red daymark bearing a central black stripe and a yellow reflective horizontal strip.

KRG=Rectangular red daymark bearing a central green stripe.

KRG-I=Rectangular red daymark bearing a central green stripe and a yellow reflective horizontal strip.

KRW=Rectangular red daymark bearing a central white stripe.

KRW-I=Rectangular red daymark bearing a central white stripe and a yellow reflective horizontal strip.

KWB=Rectangular white daymark bearing a central black stripe.

KWB-I=Rectangular white daymark bearing a central black stripe and a yellow reflective horizontal strip.

KWG=Rectangular white daymark bearing a central green stripe.

KWG-I=Rectangular white daymark bearing a central green stripe and a yellow reflective horizontal strip.

KWR=Rectangular white daymark bearing a central red stripe.

KWR-I=Rectangular white daymark bearing a central red stripe and a yellow reflective horizontal strip.

NB=Diamond shaped daymark divided into four diamond shaped colored sectors, with the sectors at the side corners white, and the sectors at the top and bottom corners black, with a white reflective border.

NG=Diamond shaped daymark divided into four diamond shaped colored sectors, with the sectors at the side corners white, and the sectors at the top and bottom corners green, with a white reflective border.

NR=Diamond shaped daymark divided into four diamond shaped colored sectors, with the sectors at the side corners white, and the sectors at the top and bottom corners red, with a white reflective border.

NW=Diamond shaped white daymark with an orange reflective border and black letters describing the information, or regulatory nature, of the mark.

ND=Rectangular white mileage marker with black numerals indicating the mile number.

NL=Rectangular white location marker with an orange reflective border and black letters indicating the location.

NY=Diamond shaped yellow daymark with a yellow reflective border.

LIGHT CHARACTERISTICS

Abb.	Old Abb		Period shown
F		FIXED a continuous steady light	
		OCCULTING total duration of light more than dark and total eclipse at regular intervals.	
Oc	Occ	SINGLE OCCULTING steady light with eclipse regularly repeated.	
Oc (2)	Gp Occ (2)	GROUP OCCULTING two or more eclipses in a group, regularly repeated	
Oc (2+3)	Gp Occ (2+3)	COMPOSITE GROUP OCCULTING in which successive groups in a period have different number of eclipses.	
Iso		ISOPHASE a light where duration of light and darkness are equal.	
		FLASHING single flash at regular intervals. Duration of light less than dark.	
Fl		SINGLE FLASHING light in which flash is regularly repeated at less than 50 flashes per minute	
L Fl		LONG FLASHING a flash of 2 or more seconds, regularly repeated	
Fl (3)	Gp Fl (3)	GROUP FLASHING successive groups, specified in number, regularly repeated.	
Fl (2+1)	Gp Fl (2+1)	COMPOSITE GROUP FLASHING in which successive groups in a period have different number of flashes	
		QUICK usually 50 or 60 flashes per minute.	
Q	Qk Fl	CONTINUOUS QUICK in which a flash is regularly repeated	
Q (3)	Qk Fl (3)	GROUP QUICK in which a specified group of flashes is regularly repeated.	
IQ	Int Qk Fl	INTERRUPTED QUICK sequence of flashes interrupted by regularly repeated eclipses of constant and long duration.	
		VERY QUICK usually either 100 or 120 flashes per minute.	
VQ	Q Qk Fl	CONTINUOUS VERY QUICK flash is regularly repeated.	
VQ	V Qk (3)	GROUP VERY QUICK specified group of flashes regularly repeated.	
IVQ	Int V Qk Fl	INTERRUPTED VERY QUICK FLASH in groups with total eclipse at regular intervals of constant and long duration.	
		ULTRA QUICK usually not less than 160 flashes per minute.	
UQ		CONTINUOUS ULTRA QUICK in which flash is regularly repeated.	
IUQ		INTERRUPTED ULTRA QUICK in groups with total eclipse at intervals of long duration.	
Mo (K)		MORSE CODE in which appearances of light of two clearly different durations are grouped to represent a character(s) in the Morse code.	
F Fl		FIXING AND FLASHING steady light with one brilliant flash at regular intervals.	
Al WR	Alt WR	ALTERNATING a light which alters in color in successive flashing.	R W R W R W

U.S. CUSTOMS

The harbor descriptions indicate when a port is a designated Customs Port of Entry. When a pleasure boat arrives in the United States for the first time (or returns from a foreign destination), the first landfall must be at a designated Customs Port of Entry. If you must make an emergency stop at some other port first, Customs should be notified immediately via telephone. Nothing should be allowed ashore from the vessel, and no person should be allowed ashore (other than the master), until the authorities have been notified.

When U.S. documented, or registered, vessels depart the United States for foreign destinations, they need not report their departure.

Pleasure boats of certain countries may obtain a Cruising License for the United States. This license exempts them from formal reporting and clearance procedures at every port of call. They can be obtained from the District Director of Customs at the first port of arrival in the United States. The licenses are issued for no more than a one year period. They do not exempt a vessel from applicable duties. The following countries are eligible to obtain a Cruising License:

Argentina
Australia
Austria
Bahamas
Belgium
Bermuda
Canada
Denmark
Germany
France
Greece
Honduras
Ireland
Jamaica
Liberia
Netherlands
New Zealand
Norway
Sweden

Great Britain is also eligible (including Turks and Caicos, St. Vincent, Northern Grenadine Islands, Cayman Islands, British Virgin Islands, St. Christopher-Nevis-Anguilla islands).

In the absence of a Cruising License, vessels must report at each U.S. port, and must obtain clearance for the next port. When these vessels depart the U.S., they must clear Customs.

There is no charge for Customs inspection during normal working hours (8AM to 5PM, Monday through Saturday, except holidays). After hours, Sundays and holidays, inspection service will cost a maximum of $25.00 per boat.

Effective July 6, 1986, pleasure craft must pay an annual $25.00 user fee when clearing Customs. This fee is good for one year, and an annual sticker will be issued for the vessel.

For more information on U.S. Customs procedures contact:

U.S. Customs Service
Washington, D.C. 20229
(202) 927-1310

The following is a partial list of U.S. Customs Offices where you may report your arrival:

Maine: Portland, (207) 780-3328, (800) 343-2840.
Massachusetts: Boston, (617) 565-4657, (800) 343-2840.
Connecticut: Bridgeport, (203) 579-5606, (800) 343-2840.
New York: New York City, (212) 466-5605, (800) 522-5270.
Albany, (518) 472-3456, (800) 522-5270.
New Jersey: Newark, (201) 645-3760, (800) 221-4265.
Perth Amboy, (201) 442-0415, (800) 221-4265.
If you arrive in New Jersey south of Manasquan Inlet, contact the Customs office in Philadelphia.
Pennsylvania: Philadelphia, (215) 597-4605, (800) 343-2840.
Maryland: Baltimore, (301) 962-2666, (800) 343-2840.
Virginia: Alexandria, (703) 557-1950, (301) 953-7454, (202) 566-2321.
Newport News, (804) 245-6470.
Norfolk, (804) 441-6741.
Richmond, (804) 925-2552.
North Carolina: Morehead City, (919) 726-5845, (919) 726-3651, (919) 726-2034.
Wilmington, (919) 343-4616.
South Carolina: Charleston, (803) 727-4468.
Georgia: Brunswick, (912) 262-6692, (800) 877-7816 (pager #9763). Savannah, (912) 652-4400, (912) 652-4430, (912) 232-7507
Florida: Jacksonville, (904) 291-2775. Port Canaveral, (407) 783-2066

All pleasure vessels arriving in the Miami District, in southern Florida, must report to a

Chapter 2

designated reporting station. This reporting requirement extends from Sebastian Inlet, FL, on the east coast, to Naples, FL, on the west coast. This area includes the Florida Keys. At the designated locations will be a special phone, which will dial the Customs Service automatically, or you may call (800) 432-1216. After answering several Customs service questions you will either be issued a clearance number, or asked to await a formal inspection. Only the person designated to report the arrival may leave the vessel until clearance is made. Failure to report to a designated station may result in a fine of up to $5000 for the first violation, and $10,000 for subsequent violations. Any questions regarding this procedure should be directed to:

U.S. Customs Service
Southeast Region
Office of Inspection and Control
Suite 710
Miami, FL 33131
(305) 536-5283

The designated reporting stations in the Southeast Region (in geographic order) are:

Sebastian Inlet Marina
2580 U.S. 1
Sebastian, FL

Harbortown Marina
25 N. Causeway Drive
Ft. Pierce, FL

Sailfish Marina
3565 Southeast Street
Stuart, FL

Jupiter Marina
97 Lake Drive
Jupiter, FL

Sailfish Marina
98 Lake Drive
Palm Beach Shores

Spencers Boat Yard
4000 Dixie Highway
West Palm Beach, FL

Lake Worth Boating Center
7848 S. Federal Highway
Hypoluxo, FL

Delray Harbour Club Marina
1035 S. Federal Highway
Delray, FL

Cove Marina
1755 SE 3rd Court
Deerfield Beach, FL

Sands Harbor Marina
125 N. Riverside Drive
Pompano Beach, FL

Lighthouse Point Marina
2830 NE 29th Avenue
Pompano Beach, FL

Pier 66
2301 SE 17th Street
Ft Lauderdale, FL

Lauderdale Marina
1800 SE 15th Street
Ft Lauderdale, FL

Bahia Mar
801 Sea Breeze Blvd.
Ft. Lauderdale, FL

Bakers Haulover Marina
10800 Collins Avenue
Miami Beach, FL

Sunset Harbour Marina
1982 Purdy Avenue
Miami Beach, FL

Miamarina
401 Biscayne Blvd.
Miami, FL

Phillips 66 Marina
1050 MacArthur Causeway
Watson Island
Miami, FL

Crandon Park Marina
Miami, FL

Matheson Hammock Marina
Matheson Hammock Park
(open sunrise to sunset)
Biscayne Bay, FL

Ocean Reef Club
Key Largo, FL

Tavernier Creek Marina
Tavernier, FL

Holiday Isle Marina
Mile Marker 85, US 1
Islamorada, FL

Boot Key Marina
1000 15th Street
Marathon, FL

Oceanside Marina
5950 Maloney Avenue
Key West, FL

A & B Marina
700 Marina Street
Key West, FL

O'Shea's Restaurant
1081 Bald Eagle Drive
Marco Island, FL

Naples City Dock
880 12th Avenue South
Naples, FL

Florida: Ft. Myers, (813) 768-4318, (813) 826-2385 after 5PM.
St. Petersburg, (813) 536-7311.
Tampa, (813) 826-2385.
Panama City, (904) 785-4688, (904) 291-2775.
Pensacola, (904) 432-6811, (904) 291-2775.

Alabama: Mobile, (205) 690-2111, (800) 432-1216.

Mississippi: Gulfport, (601) 864-1274, (504) 589-3771.
Pascagoula, (601) 762-7311, (504) 589-3771.

Louisiana: New Orleans, (504) 589-6804.
Texas: Port Arthur, (409) 727-0285, (800) 392-3142.
Galveston, (409) 766-3624, (800) 392-3142.
Houston, (713) 443-3883, (800) 392-3142.
Freeport, (409) 233-3004, (800) 392-3142.
Port Lavaca, (512) 987-2722, (800) 392-3142.
Corpus Christi, (512) 888-3352, (800) 392-3142, (512) 888-7019 (Saturday).
Brownsville, (512) 542-4232.

Puerto Rico: Mayaguez, (809) 831-3342, (809) 831-3343.
San Juan, (809) 253-4533, (809) 253-4534 (0800-2300, Mon.-Sun.).
Ponce, (809) 841-3130, (809) 841-3331, (809) 841-3132.
Fajardo, (809) 863-0950, (809) 863-0811, (809) 863-4075.
Vieques, (809) 741-8366.
Culebra, (809) 742-3531.
Note: In Puerto Rico all vessels arriving after 1700 hours, or on Sundays and holidays, must report to the San Juan station via telephone. All vessels arriving from the U.S. Virgin Islands

must report to Customs. Vessels traveling from Puerto Rico to the U.S. Virgin Islands need not clear Customs.

U.S. Virgin Islands: St. Croix, (809) 773-1011.
St. Thomas, (809) 774-6755, (809) 774-5539.
St. John, (809) 776-6741.

TIDE AND TIDAL CURRENT TABLES

Sir Charles Darwin wrote in the *Admiralty Manual of Tides* in 1891:
"When we consider that the incessant variability of the tidal forces, the complex outlines of our coasts, the depth of the sea and the earth's rotation are all involved, we should regard good tidal prediction as one of the greatest triumphs of the theory of universal gravitation."

Reed's tide and current tables are now computed independently by Micronautics Inc, Micronautic's predictions apply a slightly more accurate algorithm to the same harmonic constituent information used by the U.S. National Ocean Service. Hence, there are small differences between the times, heights and current velocities cited in these tables and those published by NOS. The mariner will not find these differences to be of navigational significance, and should, in fact, find these tables to be a slightly more accurate representation of the real world phenomenon. Above all, the prudent mariner understands that all tide and current predictions are approximations, and are also subject to weather influences that can not be predicted in the long term.

The primary tide and tidal current tables are located in the chapter near the other navigational information for a particular locality. Tide predictions for many other locations are provided in a supplemental chapter of Tide and Tidal Current Differences. The Tidal Differences are listed in geographic order in Chapter 3. The Tidal Difference may be applied to the reference station to obtain an estimate of the tidal situation in a desired location. Use the Index to locate a particular Tidal Difference.

For instructions on how to use Tide and Current Differences, see Chapter 3.

CAUTION:
The time and height differences are average differences derived from comparisons of simultaneous tide observations at the subordi-

nate location and its reference station. Because these figures are constant, they may not always provide for the daily variations of the actual tide; especially if the subordinate station is some distance from the reference station. Therefore, it must be realized that although the application of the time and height differences will generally provide fairly accurate approximations, they cannot result in predictions as accurate as those at the reference station. The reference stations are based upon much larger periods of analyses.

For more information on tides and tidal currents, see Chapter 10 in *Reed's Nautical Companion.*

THE GULF STREAM

The region where the Gulf of Mexico narrows to form the channel between Florida Keys and Cuba may be regarded as the head of the Gulf Stream. From this region the stream sets eastward and northward through the Straits of Florida and after passing Little Bahama Bank it continues northward and then northeastward, following the general direction of the 100-fathom curve as far as Cape Hatteras. The flow in the Straits is frequently refered to as the Florida Current.

Shortly after emerging from the Straits of Florida, the stream is joined by the Antilles Current, which flows northwesterly along the open ocean side of the West Indies before uniting with the water which has passed through the straits. Beyond Cape Hatteras the combined current turns more and more eastward under the combined effects of the deflecting force of the Earth's rotation and the eastwardly trending coastline, until the region of the Grand Banks of Newfoundland is reached.

Eastward of the Grand Banks the whole surface is slowly driven eastward and northeastward by the prevailing westerly winds to the coastal waters of northwestern Europe. For distinction, this broad and variable wind-driven surface movement is sometimes referred to as the North Atlantic Drift or Gulf Stream Drift.

In general, the Gulf Stream as it issues into the sea through the Straits of Florida may be characterized as a swift, highly saline current of blue water whose upper stratum is composed of warm water.

On its western or inner side, the Gulf Stream is separated from the coastal waters by a zone of rapidly falling temperature, to which the term "cold wall" has been applied. It is most clearly marked north of Cape Hatteras, but extends, more or less well defined, from the Straits to the Grand Banks.

Throughout the whole stretch of 400 miles in the Straits of Florida, the stream flows with considerable speed. Abreast of Havana, the average surface speed in the axis of the stream is about 2.5 knots. As the cross-sectional area of the stream decreases, the speed increases gradually, until abreast of Cape Florida it becomes about 3.5 knots. From this point within the narrows of the straits, the speed along the axis gradually decreases to about 2.5 knots off Cape Hatteras, N.C. These values are for the axis of the stream where the current is a maximum, the speed of the stream decreases gradually from the axis as the edges of the stream are approached. The speed of the stream, furthermore, is subject to fluctuations brought about by variations in winds and barometric pressure.

The following tables give the mean surface speed of the Gulf Stream in two cross sections in the Straits of Florida:

GULF STREAM MEAN SURFACE SPEED			
Between Rebecca Shoal and Cuba		Between Fowey Rocks and Gun Cay	
Distance south of Rebecca Shoal	Mean surface speed observed	Distance east of Fowey Rocks	Mean surface speed observed
Nautical miles	Knots	Nautical Miles	Knots
20	0.3	8	2.7
35	0.7	11.5	3.5
50	2.2	15	3.2
68	2.2	22	2.7
86	0.8	29	2.1
		36	1.7

Crossing the Gulf Stream at Jupiter or Fowey Rocks, an average allowance of 2.5 knots in a northerly direction should be made for the current.

Crossing the stream from Havana, a fair allowance for the average current between 100-fathom curves is 1.1 knots in an east-north-easterly direction.

From within the straits, the axis of the Gulf Stream runs approximately parallel with the 100-fathom curve as far as Cape Hatteras. Since this stretch of coast line sweeps northward in a sharper curve than does the 100-fathom line, the stream lies at varying distances from the shore. The lateral boundaries of the current within the straits are fairly well fixed, but when the stream flows into the sea the eastern boundary becomes somewhat vague. On the western side, the limits can be defined approximately since the waters of the stream differ in color, temperature, salinity, and flow from the inshore coastal waters.On the east however, the Antilles Current combines with the Gulf Stream, so that its waters here merge gradually with the waters of the open Atlantic. Observations of the National Ocean Service indicate that, in general, the average position of the inner edge of the Gulf Stream as far as Cape Hatteras lies inside the 50-fathom curve. The Gulf Stream, however, shifts somewhat with the seasons, and is considerably influenced by the winds which cause

fluctuations in its position, direction, and speed; consequently any limits which are assigned refer to mean or average positions. For the approximate mean positions of the inner edge and axis (point where greatest speed may be found) see the table below.

At the western edge of the Straits of Florida the limits of the Gulf Stream are not well defined, and for this reason the location of the inner edge has been omitted for Havana, Cuba, and Key West Fla., in the above table. Between Fowey Rocks and Jupiter Inlet the inner edge is deflected westward and lies very close to the shore line.

Along the Florida Reefs, between Alligator Reef and Dry Tortugas, the distance of the northerly edge of the Gulf Stream from the edge of the reefs gradually increases towards the west. Off Alligator Reef it is quite close inshore, while off Rebecca Shoal and Dry Tortugas it is possibly 15 to 20 miles south of the 100-fathom curve. Between the reefs and the northern edge of the Gulf Stream the currents are ordinarily tidal and are subject at all times to considerable modification by local winds and barometric conditions. This neutral zone varies in both length and breadth; it may extend along the reefs a greater or lesser distance than stated, and its width varies as the northern edge of the Gulf Stream approaches or recedes from the reefs.

APPROXIMATE MEAN POSITION OF THE GULF STREAM

Locality	Inner Edge Nautical miles	Axis Nautical miles
North of Havana, Cuba		25
Southeast of Key West, Fl		45
East of Fowey Rocks, Fl		10
East of Miami Beach, Fl		15
East of Palm Beach, Fl		15
East of Jupiter Inlet, Fl		20
East of Cape Canaveral, Fl	10	45
East of Daytona Beach, Fl	25	75
East of Ormond Beach, Fl	25	75
East of St. Augustine, Fl (coast line)	40	85
East of Jacksonville, Fl (coast line)	55	90
Southeast of Savannah, GA (coast line)	65	95
Southeast of Charleston, SC (coast line)	55	90
Southeast of Myrtle Beach, SC	60	100
Southeast of Cape Fear, N C (light)	35	75
Southeast of Cape Lookout, N C (light)	20	50
Southeast of Cape Hatteras, N C	10	35
Southeast of Virginia Beach, VA	85	115
Southeast of Atlantic City, N J	120	
Southeast of Sandy Hook, N J	150	

The approximate position of the axis of the Gulf Stream for various regions is shown on the following National Ocean Srevice Charts: No. 11013, Straits of Florida; No. 411, South Carolina to Cuba; No. 11460, Cape Canaveral to Key West; No. 11420, Alligator Reef to Havana. Chart No. 11009 shows the axis and the position of the inner edge of the Gulf Stream from Cape Hatteras to Straits of Florida.

AREA DESCRIPTIONS

FLORIDA, EAST COAST

Florida's east coast varies in character from north to south. North of St. Lucie there are open sounds and rivers interspersed with short stretches of canal. Sailors can often raise sail, and enjoy a good run. Anchorages are not frequent, but they are well spaced. South of St. Lucie the character of the waterway changes. High rise buildings begin to intrude upon the natural landscape. Anchorages are infrequent, and often restricted by local laws. Most boats will have to proceed under power. The many opening bridges have restricted schedules. However, here the marine facilities are top notch — the finest, and most frequent in the country.

Many boaters will want to make the crossing of the Gulf Stream to the Bahamas. Palm Beach is a favorite spot to depart for West End, and the Abacos. Fort Lauderdale and Miami are good departure points for Bimini, Cay Cay or Nassau.

FLORIDA, THE KEYS

The Keys are Florida's answer to the Bahamas. They are an archipelago of tropical islets surrounded by beautiful, but shallow, water. For those drawing less than 4 or 5 feet, the inside route is possible. For deeper draft boats, the often boisterous Hawk Channel route is preferred. To pass between the two you are restricted to a few good openings. For sailors, Channel Five near Long Key, and the Moser Channel near Marathon, are your only choices.

You encounter your first coral reefs here. The John Pennekamp Park, near Key Largo, is an undersea coral reef park. Everywhere, the coral is protected, and should not be anchored upon, or even touched. Those who go aground in coral, are liable for fines.

Key West is the end of the line for most boaters. The adventurous make the 60 mile passage to the Dry Tortugas, to find a true "out island". Fort Jefferson guards a beautiful sandy lagoon, sheltered by coral reefs. The nesting ground of the Frigate bird is on aptly named Bird Key. There are no facilities for boaters — you must even remove your own trash.

BERMUDA

This is a favorite offshore destination for U.S. boaters. Whether as a stopover on your way to the Caribbean, or a cruising ground of its own, Bermuda is a favorite port of call. It is just under 700 miles from either Newport, Rhode Island or Norfolk, Virginia. It's approximately 900 miles north of St. Thomas in the Virgin Islands.

The major consideration voyaging to Bermuda is always the weather. Routes to the islands cross the major hurricane tracks. In addition, the Gulf Stream must be crossed to get there from the U.S.

The approaches to Bermuda are generally well marked. You will be beyond the range of reliable LORAN coverage, but the island does have several powerful radiobeacons, and long range lights. Bermuda Harbor Radio is always standing by to aid those in trouble.

It is wise to stand well off Bermuda in heavy weather. Many vessels have encountered severe seas when deep ocean waves began tumbling on the Bermuda shelf waters. It is often hard to spot the edge of the reefs surrounding Bermuda. Keep in mind, the major beacons are situated on the reef itself — they should be given a wide berth in bad weather.

Bermuda offers a warm welcome to the visiting cruiser. The island is beautiful and safe. Most boating supplies are readily available. This is a great place to break up an offshore trip, and recoup for the next leg.

THE BAHAMAS

Cruising in the Bahamas is very different than in the United States. The waters are shallow, and filled with shifting sands and coral reefs. Aids to navigation are few and far between, and none should be trusted in the Bahamas. LORAN is unreliable, at best.

The tools of Bahama navigation are simple — a good depthsounder, and your eyes. Most boaters will learn to quickly read the water depth ahead, utilizing the beautiful colors visible through the crystal clear water. Experienced Bahamas cruisers learn to travel when the sun is high — to prevent glare on the water.

The VHF radio can be a handy tool. If you leave it on channel 16 while entering an unfamiliar harbor, advice will often be radioed out to you from a boater inside. During storms boaters relay information on location, wind speeds and wind direction. In the evenings an informal chat hour invariably commences around 5PM.

Working your way from Island to Island you will encounter wild places with few people. The island chain is around 500 miles long, and most of the islands are uninhabited. Despite a few, often repeated, horror stories you are much safer here than in your home town. Bahamians are friendly and helpful people.

THE CARIBBEAN

The islands of the Caribbean are many and varied. From the gorgeous reef diving of the Caymans, to the old world charm of San Juan, to the crowded harbors of the Virgins to the boisterous sailing of the Grenadines, this is an area of contrasts. You will encounter many new cultures. Some people will speak Spanish, others French but most will know at least a smattering of English. You must be more self-sufficient to travel here. You may have to travel 200 miles to get fuel (Bahamas to Dominican Republic), and you may have to jug your water from an inland spigot. You will learn to stock up when the food is plentiful and low priced (Puerto Rico, the Dominican Republic and Venezuela). You will want to carry lots of heavy ground tackle, with plenty of anchor chain, to resist the chafe on coral bottoms.

Many of the harbors are not geared strictly for transient boaters. Of course, charter areas do have marinas with stateside type facilities. But,

many of the islands cater to boaters only as a courtesy - the harbors are designed for the handling of commercial ships and cruise liners. You may have to tie to a crumbling concrete wharf while clearing customs, or you may have to anchor out for weeks at a time. Of course, this is part of the great charm. Despite decades of tourism, Caribbean people have often maintained their own cultures, in the face of mounting pressures to change.

Navigation in the Caribbean often involves simply sailing to the next island. Visibility is usually excellent. There is often plenty of wind — in the winter, 20 to 30 knots almost every day. The trades blow from the east day after day, week after week, month after month. When the wind switches, many harbors become uncomfortable for a few days. There are many harbors that are simply coves on the leeward side of an island.

The currents of the Caribbean tend to be the result of the constant northeast trade winds. However, they do vary with the strength of the wind, its direction and the season. See the following current charts for an indication of the general pattern to be expected.

Hurricanes are the scourge of the Caribbean. Experienced boaters plan to be south in the Grenadines or Venezuela, from August through October. After years with few problems, Hugo destroyed large numbers of boats, before heading off to pound the U.S. mainland. If you must stay in the islands during the hurricane season, plan your strategy well ahead of time. Find your hurricane hole, and retreat to it early — before the crowd takes up all the good spots.

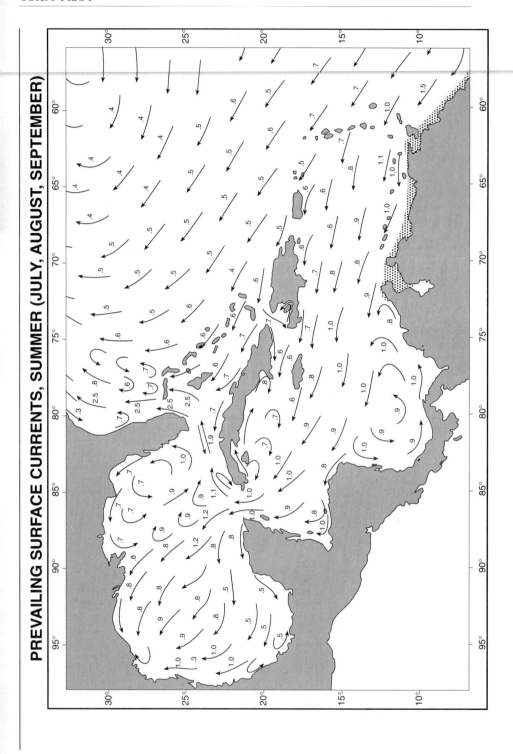

PREVAILING SURFACE CURRENTS, SUMMER (JULY, AUGUST, SEPTEMBER)

PREVAILING SURFACE CURRENTS, WINTER (JANUARY, FEBRUARY, MARCH)

Chapter 2

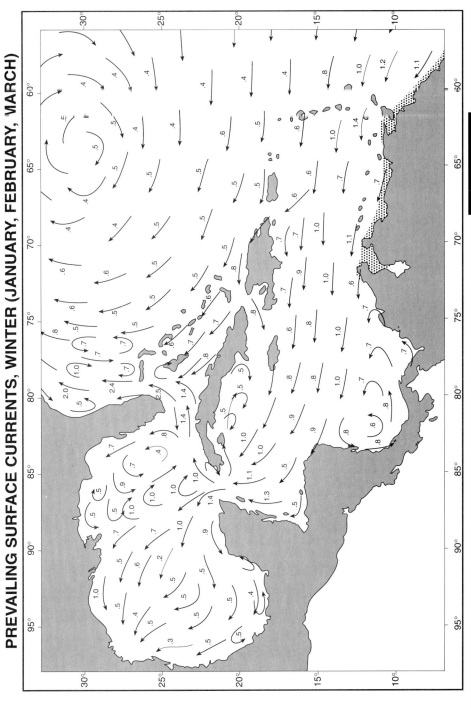

BERMUDA

APPROACHES

NOTE: In Bermuda, offshore light towers are referred to as beacons.

NORTH ROCK BEACON, 32 28.5N, 64 46.0W, Fl (4) W 20s, 70 ft., 12M, Black over yellow tower, Radar reflector, Worded NORTH ROCK in white letters on black background near the top of the tower.

NORTH EAST BREAKER BEACON, 32 28.7N, 64 40.9W, Fl W 2.5s, 45 ft.,12M, Red tower on red tripod base, Worded NORTH EAST in red letters on a white background near the base of the tower, RACON: N(−·).

KITCHEN SHOAL BEACON, 32 26.0N, 64 37.6W, Fl (3) W 15s, 45 ft., 12M, Red and white horizontal striped tower on a tripod, Radar reflector, Worded KITCHEN in red letters on a white background at the base of the tower.

Mills Breaker Buoy, 32 23.9N, 64 36.8W, V Q Fl (3) 5s, Black with a single horizontal yellow band, Topmark 2 black cones base to base, Worded MILLS in black on a yellow background.

Spit Buoy, 32 22.6N, 64 38.4W, Q Fl (3) W 10s, Black with a single horizontal yellow band, Topmark 2 black cones base to base, Worded SPIT in black on a yellow background.

ST. DAVIDS ISLAND LIGHTHOUSE, 32 21.8N, 64 39.0W, Fl (2) W 20s on top, F R+G sectored light below, 212 ft., White range 15M, R+G range 20M, W tower with red band, R from 135° to 221°, G from 221° to 276°, R from 276° to 044°, R from 044° to 135°, W+R partially obscured from 044° to 135°.

ST. DAVIDS RADIOBEACON, 32 22.0N, 64 38.9W, BSD (−··· ··· −··), 323kHz A2A, 150M.

KINDLEY FIELD AVIATION LIGHT, 32 21.9N, 64 40.5W, Al Fl W W G 10s, 140 ft., 15M, On control tower at airport.

GIBBS HILL LIGHTHOUSE, 32 15.1N, 64 50.0W, Fl W 10s, 354 ft., 26M, White tower, Obscured from 223° to 228° and from 229° to 237°, F R obstruction light shown on top of lantern.

GIBBS HILL RADIOBEACON, 32 15.1N, 64 50.0W, BDA (−··· −·· ·−), 295kHz A2A, 130M.

CHUBB HEADS BEACON, 32 17.3N, 64 58.6W, V Q Fl (9) 15s, 60 ft., 12M, Yellow and black horizontal striped tower on tripod, Worded CHUB HEADS in white letters on black central band, RACON: C(−·−·).

EASTERN BLUE CUT BEACON, 32 24.0N, 64 52.6W, Fl W Morse U(··−) 10s, 60 ft., 12M, Black and white horizontal striped tower on black tripod, Worded EASTERN BLUE CUT in black letters on white central band, Radar reflector.

TOWN CUT CHANNEL

GATES FORT LIGHT, 32 22.7N, 64 39.7W, F R, 46 ft., 8M, White metal framework tower with black and white checkered daymark, Visible 250° to 080°, On NE end of channel.

HIGGS ISLAND LIGHT, 32 22.6N, 64 39.7W, F G, 48 ft., 8M, R+W checkered square on red metal framework tower, White bands, On SE end of channel, FR lights shown from Fort George flagstaff 1 mile W.

CHALK WHARF LIGHT, 32 22.7N, 64 39.9W, F R 52 ft., 8M, White metal framework tower with black and white checkered daymark, Visible 250° to 095°, On NW end of channel.

HORSESHOE ISLAND LIGHT, 32 22.6N, 64 39.8W, F G, 8M, On west corner of Horseshoe Island, Marks SW end of channel.

ST. GEORGE'S HARBOUR

THREE SISTERS SHOAL BEACON, 32 22.6N, 64 40.0W, V Q G (80 Per minute), 4M, White beacon with green band.

HEN ISLAND BEACON, 32 22.5N, 64 40.5W, Fl G 1.5s, 16 ft., 4M, White metal framework tower with green band, Red and white checkered daymark.

ST. GEORGE'S

Bermuda Harbour Radio: Contact BHR on VHF channel 16 (working 27) or 2182kHz (working 2582kHz) when approaching the islands and when moving vessels within Bermuda. They are the Airsea Rescue Coordination Center for the Bermuda area, and are in contact with the U.S. Coast Guard 24 hours a day.

Weather Reports: Available from the Bermuda Yacht Reporting Service on Ordnance Island. A dedicated phone line connects directly to the Naval Oceanography Command Facility for recorded weather and special warnings. Departure weather packages may be obtained. BHR transmits local and high seas weather on VHF channel 27 at 1235 and 2035 GMT.
Bermuda Radio VRT: VHF channel 26 or 28 for marine phone calls.
H.M. Customs: Contact on VHF channel 16 (working channel 68). Pleasure vessels should clear at the Customs wharf located on the NE end of Ordnance Island. All firearms must be declared and will be held by the officials for the duration of your stay. This regulation includes flare guns. A fee of $30.00 per person is levied on arriving yachtsmen. Fruit and vegetables from other countries are prohibited.
Dockage: The concrete wharves on the north side of Ordnance Island provide side-to dockage. Rafting boats several deep is common. More dockage is available at bulkheads west of the island. St. George's Dinghy Club may have some space at their docks near Town Cut.
Anchorage: There are designated yacht anchorages east of Ordnance Island and west of Hen Island. H.M. Customs will supply a map of the harbor area.
Fuel: Available at the bulkhead west of Ordnance Island and at the west end of St. George's Harbour. Vessels must register in advance to obtain duty free fuel upon departure.
Repairs: Good services are available. There are some haulout facilities near the west end of the harbor, in the Dockyard, in Hamilton and in other locations. There are several sail repair agents, a rigger and an electronics specialist. Most marine supplies are available. BHR may be able to assist in locating repair services.
Supplies: A small, but well stocked, grocery is located in St. George's. Larger supermarkets are a short drive away.
Currency: The Bermuda dollar is on a par with the U.S. dollar. U.S. currency is accepted everywhere, and credit cards are widely accepted. The Bank of Bermuda has 13 ATM machines linked to the Visa/Plus system.

Entering St. George's after dark is not recommended. If in any doubt, it is wise to stand off until daylight. Bermuda Harbour Radio will usually contact you on VHF channel 16 when they pick you up on radar. If they do not, you should contact them before approaching the island. BHR can provide valuable navigational and traffic safety advice. Keep in mind the possibility of encountering a large cruise ship or commercial vessel when approaching, or transiting Town Cut Channel. The anchorages in St. George's are secure in most conditions, but there are other sheltered harbors nearby if severe weather threatens. Most hurricanes pass to the west of Bermuda, with the peak season being August 15th to October 15th. For the latest information sheet on Bermuda contact: Bermuda Department of Tourism, P.O. Box HM 465, Hamilton, Bermuda, HM BX.

THE NARROWS

Buoy 1, Fl R 2.5s.
Buoy 2, Fl G 2.5s.
BEACON 10, 32 23.4N, 64 39.9W, Fl G 4s.
Buoy 15, Fl R 4s.
Buoy 16, Fl (2) G 7.5s.

SOUTH CHANNEL

BEACON 20, 32 20.9N, 64 44.4W, Fl G 2.5s, Green column.
Buoy 21, Fl R 2.5s, To be replaced with a beacon.
BEACON 22, Fl G 4s.
SHELLY BAY SHOAL BEACON, Fl (2) W 7.5s, Black beacon with one broad horizontal red band, Topmark is 2 black spheres, Middle ground mark.
GIBBET ISLAND LIGHT, 32 19.3N, 64 44.6W, Fl R 4s, 24 ft., 2M, Wood column, White base.
DEVONSHIRE DOCK LIGHT, West side of entrance, 32 18.4N, 64 46.3W, FG, 27 ft., 2M, White post.
BEACON 26, 32 18.7N, 64 47.5W, Fl G 2.5s, Green column.
Elbow Buoy, Q Fl W (6) plus one long every 10s, Yellow and black pillar, Two cones point down, Worded ELBOW.
BEACON 30, 32 19.1N, 64 48.7W, Fl G 4s, 16ft., Green.
HOGFISH BEACON, 32 18.6N, 64 49.3, Fl (2) Y 10s, 16 ft., 5M, White masonry structure with black band, F R on radio mast 1.07 mile 290°.

THE DOCKYARD

NORTH BREAKWATER LIGHT, 32 19.3N, 64 50.0W, Fl R 4s, 12 ft., 2M, Black structure on white bollard.
SOUTH BREAKWATER LIGHT, 32 19.2N, 64 49.9W, Fl G 4s, 12 ft., 3M, Black structure on white bollard.

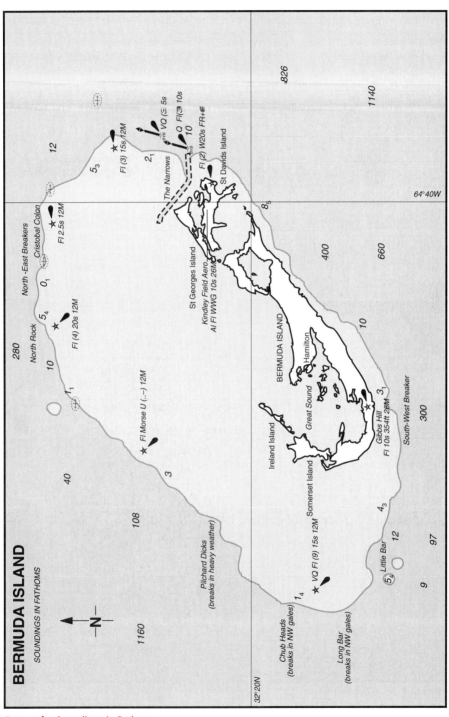

BERMUDA ISLAND
SOUNDINGS IN FATHOMS

Bermuda, Soundings in Fathoms

Chapter 2

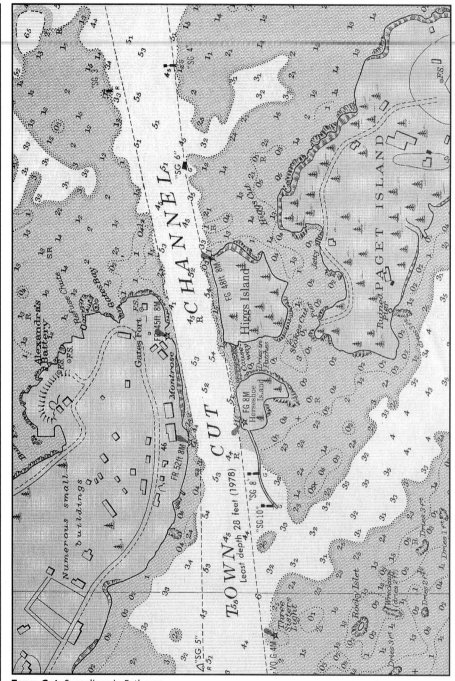

Town Cut, Soundings in Fathoms

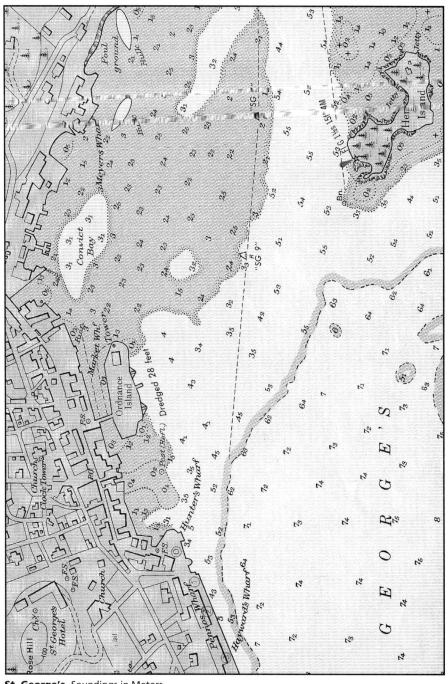

St. George's, Soundings in Meters

Chapter 2

WEST CORNER OF SOUTH BASIN LIGHT,
Dockyard gate, 32 19.2N, 64 50.3W, F G, 27 ft.,
2M, Visible 322° to 350°.
IRELAND ISLAND WHARF LIGHT, On pier in
front of captain-in-charge residence, 32 19.1N,
64 50.4W, F R, 11 ft., 2M.

DUNDONALD CHANNEL

Buoy 33, Fl R 2.5s.
BEACON 35, 32 18.8N, 64 49.7W, Fl R 4s,
White column with a red band.
Buoy 38, Fl G 2.5s.
Buoy 40, V Q Fl W (9) 15s, Yellow with a broad
black band, Topmark 2 black cones point to
point.
Buoy 99, Fl R 2.5s.
Buoy 102, Fl G 4s.
PEARL ISLAND LIGHT, 32 17.5N, 64 50.2W,
Fl Y 4s, 20 ft., 5M, White beacon.
Buoy 103, Fl R 4s.

GREAT SOUND

PLAICES POINT LIGHT, Somerset Island,
32 17.8N, 64 51.5W, F R, 20 ft., 2M, Iron column, A F R light is shown from the center of
Watford Bridge.
TWO ROCKS PASSAGE LIGHT, On north side
of channel, On islet off SW point of Agars
Island, 32 17.5N, 64 48.6W, V Q G (80 per
minute), 21 ft., 5M, White structure with a
green band.
TWO ROCKS PASSAGE SOUTH SIDE LIGHT,
32 17.4N, 64 48.6W, V Q R (80 per minute),
21ft., 5M, White structure with a red band.

HEAD OF THE LANE CHANNEL NORTH SIDE,
32 17.3N, 64 48.8W, Fl W 4s, 15 ft., 1M, Black
circular stone beacon with a white base.
TEE ROCK LIGHT, SW of RBYC dock in
Hamilton, 32 17.3N, 64 47.2W, Fl G 4s, 8ft.,
3M, White circular concrete tower.
HINSON ISLAND LIGHT, NW Point of island,
32 17.0N, 64 48.3W, F R, 12ft., 5M, White
structure with a red band.
DAGGER ROCK LIGHT, 32 16.5N, 64 48.8W,
Fl R 4s, 13 ft., 4M, White column with red band.
RICKETTS ISLAND LIGHT, 32 16.5N,
64 49.7W, Fl R 2.5s, 18 ft., 4M, White column
with red top.
RIDDELLS BAY LIGHT, North side of point,
32 15.7N, 64 49.8W, Fl R 4s, 12ft., 1M, White
circular stone tower with red band.
PEROTS ISLAND LIGHT, SW end, 32 15.5N,
64 49.9W, F W, Occasional.

HOGFISH CUT CHANNEL

*NOTE: This channel is not recommended.
Boaters should not attempt it without
local knowledge. All arriving yachts must
report to customs in St. Georges.*

POMPANO BEACON, 32 15.0N, 64 52.6W,
V Q G (80 per minute), Green square on bea-
con, Turning mark for entrance into Hogfish
Channel.
HOGFISH TRIPOD, 32 15.3N, 64 52.7W, Fl G 4s.
HOGFISH CUT BEACON, 32 15.5N, 64 52.9W,
Fl R 4s, 13 ft., 5M, Post.
WRECK HILL BEACON, 32 16.8N, 64 53.3W,
V Q R, Red triangular daymark on beacon.

ST GEORGE'S, BERMUDA

HIGH & LOW WATER 1994 32°23'N 64°42'W

ATLANTIC STANDARD TIME, ADD 1 HOUR DAYLIGHT SAVING APRIL 3 - OCTOBER 29

JANUARY

Day	Time	ft	Time	ft		Day	Time	ft	Time	ft
1 Sa	0416	0.8	1041	3.8		**16** Su	0502	1.0	1114	3.3
	1702	0.8	2307	3.4			1731	0.9	2343	3.2
2 Su	0508	0.9	1124	3.7		**17** M	0547	1.1	1153	3.1
	1749	0.8	2356	3.4			1812	0.9		
3 M	0606	1.0	1212	3.5		**18** Tu	0028	3.1	0637	1.3
	1840	0.8					1233	2.9	1857	1.0
4 Tu	0052	3.4	0710	1.1		**19** W	0117	3.0	0732	1.4
	1305	3.3	1935	0.8			1320	2.7	1944	1.1
5 W	0154	3.5	0819	1.1		**20** Th	0213	2.9	0832	1.4
	1406	3.1	2034	0.8			1415	2.5	2036	1.1
6 Th	0302	3.5	0930	1.1		**21** F	0314	3.0	0935	1.4
	1515	2.9	2135	0.8			1520	2.5	2131	1.1
7 F	0410	3.6	1040	1.1		**22** Sa	0414	3.1	1037	1.4
	1628	2.9	2235	0.8			1628	2.5	2225	1.1
8 Sa	0512	3.7	1145	0.9		**23** Su	0510	3.2	1132	1.3
	1733	2.9	2334	0.7			1739	2.6	2318	1.0
9 Su	0609	3.9	1244	0.8		**24** M	0601	3.4	1221	1.1
	1831	3.0					1822	2.8		
10 M	0030	0.6	0701	4.0		**25** Tu	0008	0.9	0649	3.6
	1336	0.7	1922	3.2			1305	1.0	1910	3.0
11 Tu	0122	0.6	0749	4.0		**26** W	0055	0.8	0733	3.8
	1422	0.7	2010	3.3			1347	0.8	1955	3.2
12 W	0209	0.6	0834	4.0		**27** Th	0142	0.7	0816	3.9
	1504	0.6	2055	3.3			1429	0.7	2038	3.4
13 Th	0254	0.6	0917	3.9		**28** F	0228	0.6	0858	4.0
	1541	0.7	2137	3.3			1511	0.6	2121	3.5
14 F	0336	0.7	0958	3.8		**29** Sa	0315	0.6	0940	3.9
	1617	0.7	2219	3.3			1553	0.5	2204	3.6
15 Sa	0418	0.8	1037	3.6		**30** Su	0404	0.6	1021	3.8
	1653	0.8	2301	3.3			1637	0.5	2249	3.6
						31 M	0456	0.7	1105	3.6
							1722	0.5	2338	3.6

FEBRUARY

Day	Time	ft	Time	ft		Day	Time	ft	Time	ft
1 Tu	0552	0.8	1152	3.4		**16** W	0556	1.2	1152	2.8
	1812	0.6					1804	1.0		
2 W	0033	3.6	0655	0.9		**17** Th	0030	3.1	0645	1.3
	1244	3.1	1907	0.7			1234	2.6	1843	1.1
3 Th	0134	3.5	0804	1.1		**18** F	0120	3.0	0744	1.4
	1346	2.9	2008	0.8			1325	2.5	1932	1.2
4 F	0242	3.5	0916	1.1		**19** Sa	0219	2.9	0849	1.4
	1459	2.7	2114	0.9			1430	2.4	2038	1.2
5 Sa	0352	3.5	1028	1.1		**20** Su	0326	3.0	0953	1.4
	1615	2.7	2222	0.9			1548	2.4	2145	1.2
6 Su	0458	3.5	1135	1.0		**21** M	0431	3.1	1051	1.3
	1722	2.8	2327	0.8			1656	2.6	2247	1.1
7 M	0557	3.6	1233	0.9		**22** Tu	0529	3.3	1144	1.1
	1819	3.0					1753	2.8	2343	0.9
8 Tu	0026	0.8	0648	3.7		**23** W	0620	3.5	1231	0.9
	1322	0.8	1908	3.1			1843	3.1		
9 W	0117	0.7	0734	3.8		**24** Th	0035	0.7	0707	3.7
	1404	0.7	1952	3.3			1316	0.7	1929	3.4
10 Th	0201	0.7	0816	3.8		**25** F	0124	0.6	0752	3.8
	1439	0.7	2033	3.4			1359	0.6	2014	3.6
11 F	0239	0.7	0854	3.7		**26** Sa	0213	0.5	0835	3.9
	1510	0.7	2113	3.4			1443	0.4	2058	3.8
12 Sa	0316	0.8	0930	3.6		**27** Su	0302	0.4	0918	3.8
	1541	0.7	2151	3.4			1526	0.4	2143	3.9
13 Su	0354	0.8	1005	3.4		**28** M	0352	0.4	1001	3.7
	1615	0.8	2228	3.4			1610	0.3	2230	3.9
14 M	0432	0.9	1039	3.3						
	1651	0.8	2306	3.3						
15 Tu	0513	1.0	1114	3.1						
	1727	0.9	2346	3.2						

MARCH

Day	Time	ft	Time	ft		Day	Time	ft	Time	ft
1 Tu	0444	0.5	1046	3.5		**16** W	0446	1.0	1045	3.0
	1651	0.4	2320	3.9			1647	0.9	2312	3.3
2 W	0541	0.7	1135	3.3		**17** Th	0020	1.1	1121	2.8
	1747	0.5	2352	3.2			1718	1.0		
3 Th	0015	3.7	0643	0.8		**18** F	0610	1.2	1202	2.7
	1230	3.0	1843	0.7			1752	1.1		
4 F	0115	3.6	0750	1.0		**19** Sa	0037	3.1	0704	1.3
	1334	2.8	1948	0.9			1250	2.5	1839	1.2
5 Sa	0222	3.4	0900	1.1		**20** Su	0130	3.0	0807	1.4
	1448	2.7	2100	1.0			1351	2.5	1949	1.3
6 Su	0334	3.3	1011	1.1		**21** M	0235	3.0	0911	1.4
	1603	2.7	2213	1.0			1507	2.5	2111	1.2
7 M	0443	3.4	1117	1.1		**22** Tu	0347	3.1	1010	1.3
	1709	2.9	2321	1.0			1620	2.7	2218	1.1
8 Tu	0542	3.4	1213	1.0		**23** W	0452	3.2	1105	1.1
	1803	3.1					1720	3.0	2318	0.9
9 W	0019	0.9	0631	3.5		**24** Th	0548	3.4	1155	0.9
	1259	0.9	1849	3.2			1813	3.3		
10 Th	0108	0.9	0714	3.5		**25** F	0014	0.7	0638	3.6
	1336	0.9	1931	3.4			1243	0.7	1902	3.6
11 F	0148	0.8	0753	3.5		**26** Sa	0106	0.5	0725	3.7
	1406	0.8	2010	3.5			1329	0.5	1950	3.9
12 Sa	0223	0.8	0829	3.5		**27** Su	0158	0.4	0811	3.7
	1434	0.8	2047	3.6			1414	0.3	2036	4.1
13 Su	0257	0.8	0903	3.4		**28** M	0249	0.3	0856	3.7
	1506	0.8	2123	3.6			1459	0.3	2124	4.2
14 M	0331	0.9	0936	3.3		**29** Tu	0341	0.3	0942	3.6
	1539	0.8	2159	3.5			1545	0.3	2212	4.1
15 Tu	0408	0.9	1010	3.2		**30** W	0434	0.4	1031	3.4
	1614	0.8	2235	3.4			1634	0.4	2303	4.0
						31 Th	0530	0.6	1122	3.2
							1726	0.5	2357	3.8

APRIL

Day	Time	ft	Time	ft		Day	Time	ft	Time	ft
1 F	0630	0.7	1219	3.0		**16** Sa	0548	1.2	1142	2.7
	1825	0.7					1725	1.1		
2 Sa	0036	3.6	0733	0.9		**17** Su	0006	3.2	0637	1.2
	1323	2.8	1933	0.9			1229	2.6	1816	1.2
3 Su	0201	3.4	0839	1.0		**18** M	0055	3.1	0733	1.3
	1433	2.8	2045	1.1			1326	2.6	1925	1.2
4 M	0311	3.2	0946	1.1		**19** Tu	0154	3.1	0833	1.2
	1544	2.8	2158	1.1			1432	2.7	2043	1.2
5 Tu	0419	3.2	1048	1.1		**20** W	0302	3.1	0932	1.1
	1648	3.0	2304	1.1			1542	2.9	2152	1.1
6 W	0517	3.2	1141	1.0		**21** Th	0410	3.2	1028	1.0
	1740	3.1					1646	3.2	2254	0.9
7 Th	0002	1.0	0605	3.2		**22** F	0511	3.3	1120	0.8
	1224	1.0	1825	3.3			1743	3.5	2353	0.7
8 F	0049	1.0	0647	3.2		**23** Sa	0606	3.4	1210	0.6
	1257	0.9	1905	3.5			1836	3.8		
9 Sa	0129	0.9	0725	3.3		**24** Su	0048	0.5	0657	3.4
	1327	0.9	1943	3.6			1258	0.4	1926	4.0
10 Su	0204	0.9	0800	3.3		**25** M	0143	0.4	0747	3.5
	1358	0.9	2020	3.6			1346	0.3	2015	4.2
11 M	0237	0.9	0835	3.2		**26** Tu	0236	0.3	0836	3.5
	1432	0.8	2056	3.6			1434	0.2	2104	4.2
12 Tu	0312	0.9	0910	3.2		**27** W	0329	0.3	0926	3.4
	1507	0.9	2133	3.6			1523	0.3	2154	4.2
13 W	0348	0.9	0947	3.0		**28** Th	0423	0.4	1017	3.3
	1541	0.9	2210	3.5			1614	0.4	2246	4.0
14 Th	0426	1.0	1024	2.9		**29** F	0518	0.5	1110	3.1
	1614	1.0	2247	3.4			1709	0.5	2339	3.8
15 F	0505	1.1	1102	2.8		**30** Sa	0613	0.6	1206	3.0
	1646	1.0	2325	3.3			1809	0.8		

TIME MERIDIAN 60°W

0000h is midnight, 1200h is noon.

Heights in feet are referred to the chart datum of sounding.

ST GEORGE'S, BERMUDA

HIGH & LOW WATER 1994   32°23'N 64°42'W

ATLANTIC STANDARD TIME, ADD 1 HOUR DAYLIGHT SAVING APRIL 3 - OCTOBER 29

MAY

Day	Time	ft	Day	Time	ft
1 Su	0036	3.5	16 M	0615	1.1
	0711	0.8		1212	2.8
	1306	2.9		1805	1.1
	1914	0.9			
2 M	0136	3.3	17 Tu	0031	3.2
	0810	0.9		0705	1.1
	1410	2.9		1304	2.8
	◐ 2022	1.1		1910	1.1
3 Tu	0240	3.1	18 W	0124	3.2
	0909	1.0		0800	1.0
	1516	2.9		1403	2.9
	2129	1.1		◑ 2020	1.1
4 W	0343	3.0	19 Th	0224	3.1
	1004	1.0		0857	0.9
	1616	3.0		1508	3.1
	2234	1.2		2127	1.0
5 Th	0439	3.0	20 F	0328	3.1
	1053	1.0		0952	0.8
	1709	3.1		1614	3.3
	2332	1.1		2231	0.9
6 F	0529	2.9	21 Sa	0433	3.1
	1134	1.0		1047	0.6
	1755	3.3		1715	3.6
				2333	0.7
7 Sa	0021	1.1	22 Su	0534	3.1
	0612	3.0		1139	0.5
	1210	1.0		1811	3.8
	1836	3.4			
8 Su	0102	1.0	23 M	0032	0.5
	0652	3.0		0631	3.2
	1246	0.9		1231	0.3
	1915	3.5		1904	4.0
9 M	0139	1.0	24 Tu	0129	0.4
	0730	3.0		0725	3.2
	1323	0.9		1322	0.2
	1953	3.6		1956	4.2
10 Tu	0215	0.9	25 W	0223	0.3
	0809	3.0		0818	3.2
	1401	0.8		1413	0.2
	● 2031	3.6		O 2046	4.2
11 W	0252	0.9	26 Th	0317	0.3
	0848	3.0		0910	3.2
	1437	0.9		1505	0.3
	2109	3.6		2137	4.1
12 Th	0329	0.9	27 F	0409	0.4
	0927	2.9		1001	3.2
	1513	0.9		1558	0.4
	2148	3.6		2227	4.0
13 F	0408	1.0	28 Sa	0500	0.5
	1007	2.9		1053	3.1
	1549	0.9		1652	0.5
	2226	3.5		2319	3.7
14 Sa	0447	1.0	29 Su	0551	0.6
	1047	2.8		1146	3.1
	1627	1.0		1749	0.7
	2305	3.4			
15 Su	0529	1.0	30 M	0011	3.5
	1128	2.8		0641	0.7
	1711	1.1		1240	3.0
	2345	3.3		1848	0.9
			31 Tu	0105	3.2
				0732	0.8
				1337	2.9
				1948	1.1

JUNE

Day	Time	ft	Day	Time	ft
1 W	0200	3.0	16 Th	0059	3.2
	0821	0.9		0730	0.8
	1437	2.9		1338	3.2
	◑ 2048	1.2		◐ 1958	1.0
2 Th	0255	2.8	17 F	0154	3.1
	0909	1.0		0824	0.8
	1535	3.0		1440	3.3
	2149	1.2		2105	1.0
3 F	0350	2.7	18 Sa	0254	3.0
	0956	1.0		0921	0.7
	1629	3.1		1546	3.5
	2247	1.2		2211	0.9
4 Sa	0441	2.7	19 Su	0400	3.0
	1041	1.0		1017	0.6
	1717	3.2		1650	3.6
	2340	1.2		2315	0.8
5 Su	0529	2.7	20 M	0507	3.0
	1125	0.9		1113	0.5
	1802	3.3		1749	3.8
6 M	0027	1.1	21 Tu	0016	0.7
	0615	2.7		0609	3.0
	1208	0.9		1209	0.4
	1844	3.4		1845	4.0
7 Tu	0109	1.0	22 W	0114	0.6
	0659	2.8		0707	3.1
	1250	0.9		1303	0.4
	1925	3.5		1938	4.1
8 W	0149	1.0	23 Th	0209	0.5
	0742	2.8		0800	3.2
	1330	0.9		1357	0.4
	2006	3.6		O 2029	4.1
9 Th	0228	0.9	24 F	0300	0.5
	0825	2.9		0852	3.2
	1410	0.9		1449	0.4
	● 2047	3.6		2118	4.0
10 F	0307	0.9	25 Sa	0349	0.5
	0908	2.9		0941	3.3
	1449	0.9		1541	0.5
	2127	3.6		2207	3.9
11 Sa	0346	0.9	26 Su	0435	0.5
	0949	2.9		1030	3.2
	1530	0.9		1632	0.6
	2207	3.6		2254	3.7
12 Su	0426	0.9	27 M	0519	0.6
	1030	3.0		1118	3.2
	1612	0.9		1723	0.8
	2246	3.5		2340	3.4
13 M	0507	0.9	28 Tu	0602	0.7
	1110	3.0		1207	3.1
	1700	0.9		1814	0.9
	2327	3.4			
14 Tu	0551	0.9	29 W	0026	3.2
	1153	3.0		0645	0.8
	1753	1.0		1258	3.1
				1907	1.1
15 W	0010	3.3	30 Th	0112	3.0
	0638	0.9		0730	0.9
	1242	3.1		1350	3.0
	1853	1.0		◑ 2002	1.2

JULY

Day	Time	ft	Day	Time	ft
1 F	0201	2.8	16 Sa	0129	3.1
	0817	1.0		0755	0.8
	1445	3.0		1418	3.5
	2059	1.3		◐ 2047	1.1
2 Sa	0252	2.7	17 Su	0230	3.0
	0906	1.0		0854	0.8
	1541	3.0		1524	3.6
	2156	1.3		2154	1.0
3 Su	0347	2.6	18 M	0339	2.9
	0955	1.0		0954	0.7
	1634	3.1		1630	3.7
	2253	1.3		2300	1.0
4 M	0443	2.6	19 Tu	0449	3.0
	1043	1.0		1055	0.7
	1724	3.2		1732	3.8
	2345	1.2			
5 Tu	0537	2.6	20 W	0002	0.9
	1131	1.0		0553	3.0
	1811	3.4		1155	0.7
				1829	3.9
6 W	0033	1.2	21 Th	0100	0.8
	0628	2.7		0650	3.2
	1217	1.0		1252	0.6
	1856	3.5		1922	4.0
7 Th	0116	1.1	22 F	0152	0.7
	0715	2.9		0742	3.3
	1302	0.9		1345	0.6
	1940	3.6		O 2011	4.0
8 F	0158	1.0	23 Sa	0239	0.7
	0800	3.0		0831	3.4
	1345	0.9		1435	0.6
	● 2022	3.7		2058	3.9
9 Sa	0238	1.0	24 Su	0322	0.7
	0844	3.1		0917	3.5
	1428	0.9		1522	0.7
	2104	3.8		2142	3.8
10 Su	0318	0.9	25 M	0401	0.7
	0926	3.2		1002	3.5
	1512	0.8		1607	0.8
	2145	3.8		2224	3.7
11 M	0359	0.9	26 Tu	0439	0.8
	1007	3.3		1046	3.4
	1557	0.8		1651	0.9
	2225	3.7		2305	3.5
12 Tu	0440	0.8	27 W	0518	0.9
	1048	3.3		1130	3.4
	1645	0.9		1737	1.0
	2305	3.6		2344	3.3
13 W	0524	0.8	28 Th	0559	0.9
	1132	3.4		1214	3.3
	1738	0.9		1825	1.2
	2348	3.5			
14 Th	0610	0.8	29 F	0024	3.0
	1221	3.4		0642	1.0
	1836	1.0		1301	3.2
				1916	1.3
15 F	0036	3.3	30 Sa	0108	2.9
	0700	0.8		0729	1.1
	1316	3.5		1353	3.1
	1940	1.0		◐ 2012	1.4
			31 Su	0158	2.7
				0818	1.2
				1448	3.1
				2110	1.5

AUGUST

Day	Time	ft	Day	Time	ft
1 M	0256	2.6	16 Tu	0328	3.0
	0911	1.2		0941	1.0
	1547	3.1		1616	3.7
	2208	1.5		2247	1.2
2 Tu	0400	2.6	17 W	0438	3.1
	1004	1.2		1046	1.0
	1644	3.2		1719	3.8
	2303	1.4		2348	1.1
3 W	0501	2.7	18 Th	0540	3.2
	1057	1.2		1149	1.0
	1737	3.4		1815	3.9
	2353	1.3			
4 Th	0556	2.9	19 F	0043	1.1
	1147	1.1		0634	3.4
	1826	3.6		1245	0.9
				1906	3.9
5 F	0040	1.2	20 Sa	0131	1.0
	0646	3.1		0723	3.6
	1235	1.0		1335	0.9
	1912	3.7		1951	4.0
6 Sa	0123	1.1	21 Su	0212	1.0
	0732	3.3		0808	3.7
	1321	1.0		1419	0.9
	1956	3.9		O 2034	3.9
7 Su	0205	1.0	22 M	0248	1.0
	0816	3.4		0851	3.8
	1407	0.9		1500	0.9
	● 2039	3.9		2114	3.8
8 M	0246	0.9	23 Tu	0322	1.0
	0859	3.6		0932	3.8
	1453	0.8		1540	1.0
	2120	3.9		2151	3.7
9 Tu	0328	0.8	24 W	0358	1.0
	0941	3.7		1012	3.7
	1540	0.8		1620	1.1
	2201	3.9		2228	3.5
10 W	0411	0.8	25 Th	0435	1.1
	1024	3.8		1052	3.6
	1630	0.8		1702	1.2
	2242	3.7		2304	3.4
11 Th	0455	0.8	26 F	0515	1.1
	1111	3.8		1133	3.5
	1723	0.9		1746	1.3
	2326	3.6		2343	3.2
12 F	0542	0.8	27 Sa	0555	1.2
	1202	3.8		1217	3.4
	1822	1.0		1834	1.5
13 Sa	0016	3.4	28 Su	0026	3.0
	0634	0.9		0639	1.3
	1258	3.8		1305	3.3
	1925	1.1		1929	1.6
14 Su	0111	3.2	29 M	0115	2.9
	0732	0.9		0732	1.4
	1400	3.7		1359	3.2
	◐ 2033	1.2		◐ 2027	1.6
15 M	0216	3.1	30 Tu	0214	2.8
	0835	1.0		0826	1.5
	1508	3.7		1500	3.3
	2140	1.2		2126	1.7
			31 W	0321	2.8
				0927	1.5
				1603	3.3
				2222	1.6

TIME MERIDIAN 60°W   0000h is midnight, 1200h is noon.
Heights in feet are referred to the chart datum of sounding.

ST GEORGE'S, BERMUDA

HIGH & LOW WATER 1994 | **32°23'N 64°42'W**

ATLANTIC STANDARD TIME, ADD 1 HOUR DAYLIGHT SAVING APRIL 3 - OCTOBER 29

SEPTEMBER

Day	Time	ft	Time	ft	Time	ft	Time	ft
1 Th	0426	2.9	1025	1.4	1701	3.5	2314	1.5
16 F	0526	3.5	1142	1.2	1759	3.8		
2 F	0520	0.1	1119	1.3	1754	3.7		
17 Sa	0022	1.3	0617	3.7	1236	1.2	1846	3.9
3 Sa	0002	1.4	0615	3.4	1210	1.2	1842	3.8
18 Su	0105	1.3	0702	3.8	1322	1.2	1928	3.9
4 Su	0047	1.2	0702	3.6	1258	1.0	1927	4.0
19 M	0140	1.2	0745	3.9	1402	1.2	2007	3.9
5 M	0131	1.1	0747	3.9	1346	0.9	2011	4.0
20 Tu	0211	1.2	0825	4.0	1438	1.2	2044	3.8
6 Tu	0214	0.9	0832	4.1	1435	0.8	2053	4.1
21 W	0244	1.2	0903	4.0	1514	1.2	2119	3.7
7 W	0257	0.8	0916	4.2	1524	0.8	2136	4.0
22 Th	0320	1.2	0941	3.9	1552	1.3	2154	3.6
8 Th	0341	0.8	1002	4.2	1615	0.9	2220	3.8
23 F	0357	1.2	1019	3.8	1632	1.4	2231	3.4
9 F	0427	0.8	1051	4.2	1710	1.0	2308	3.7
24 Sa	0434	1.3	1058	3.7	1714	1.5	2310	3.3
10 Sa	0517	0.9	1144	4.1	1809	1.1		
25 Su	0512	1.4	1140	3.6	1759	1.6	2353	3.1
11 Su	0000	3.5	0612	1.0	1242	4.0	1913	1.2
26 M	0550	1.5	1225	3.5	1851	1.7		
12 M	0100	3.3	0715	1.1	1345	3.9	2020	1.3
27 Tu	0042	3.0	0637	1.6	1317	3.4	1948	1.7
13 Tu	0208	3.2	0823	1.2	1453	3.8	2127	1.4
28 W	0140	3.0	0742	1.6	1417	3.4	2047	1.7
14 W	0320	1.3	0933	1.3	1602	1.4	2232	1.4
29 Th	0245	3.0	0851	1.6	1522	3.4	2144	1.7
15 Th	0427	3.3	1041	1.3	1705	3.8	2331	1.4
30 F	0350	3.2	0954	1.5	1624	3.6	2236	1.5

OCTOBER

Day	Time	ft	Time	ft	Time	ft	Time	ft
1 Sa	0450	3.4	1050	1.1	1719	3.7	2326	1.4
16 Su	0557	3.8	1221	1.3	1822	3.7		
2 Su	0543	3.7	1145	1.2	1810	3.8		
17 M	0031	1.3	0640	3.9	1305	1.3	1902	3.7
3 M	0013	1.2	0633	3.6	1237	1.0	1857	4.0
18 Tu	0103	1.3	0721	4.0	1343	1.3	1940	3.7
4 Tu	0058	1.0	0720	4.2	1328	0.9	1942	4.0
19 W	0136	1.2	0759	4.1	1418	1.3	2016	3.6
5 W	0143	0.8	0807	4.4	1418	0.8	2027	4.0
20 Th	0211	1.2	0837	4.1	1453	1.3	2052	3.6
6 Th	0228	0.8	0854	4.5	1510	0.8	2113	4.0
21 F	0248	1.2	0914	4.0	1530	1.3	2128	3.5
7 F	0315	0.7	0943	4.5	1603	0.8	2201	3.8
22 Sa	0324	1.3	0952	3.9	1609	1.4	2207	3.4
8 Sa	0404	0.8	1034	4.4	1659	0.9	2253	3.7
23 Su	0400	1.4	1031	3.8	1649	1.5	2247	3.2
9 Su	0456	0.9	1127	4.3	1757	1.1	2349	3.5
24 M	0436	1.4	1111	3.7	1732	1.5	2329	3.1
10 M	0555	1.1	1225	4.1	1859	1.2		
25 Tu	0514	1.5	1153	3.6	1819	1.6		
11 Tu	0051	3.4	0701	1.2	1328	3.9	2003	1.3
26 W	0016	3.1	0602	1.6	1241	3.5	1912	1.7
12 W	0158	3.3	0812	1.4	1436	3.8	2108	1.4
27 Th	0109	3.1	0706	1.6	1336	3.5	2009	1.6
13 Th	0307	3.4	0922	1.4	1543	3.7	2210	1.4
28 F	0209	3.1	0818	1.6	1437	3.4	2105	1.6
14 F	0411	3.5	1029	1.4	1644	3.7	2305	1.4
29 Sa	0313	3.3	0925	1.5	1541	3.5	2159	1.4
15 Sa	0508	3.6	1129	1.4	1736	3.7	2353	1.4
30 Su	0416	3.5	1025	1.4	1641	3.6	2250	1.2
31 M	0513	3.8	1123	1.2	1735	3.7	2340	1.0

NOVEMBER

Day	Time	ft	Time	ft	Time	ft	Time	ft
1 Tu	0606	4.1	1218	1.0	1827	3.8		
16 W	0028	1.2	0657	3.9	1324	1.3	1913	3.3
2 W	0028	0.8	0656	4.3	1312	0.8	1916	3.8
17 Th	0105	1.2	0735	4.0	1359	1.2	1951	3.3
3 Th	0116	0.7	0746	4.5	1405	0.7	2006	3.8
18 F	0143	1.2	0813	4.0	1435	1.2	2029	3.3
4 F	0204	0.6	0836	4.6	1458	0.7	2056	3.8
19 Sa	0220	1.2	0851	4.0	1511	1.2	2109	3.3
5 Sa	0253	0.6	0926	4.6	1551	0.7	2147	3.7
20 Su	0257	1.2	0930	3.9	1549	1.3	2149	3.2
6 Su	0344	0.7	1017	4.5	1646	0.8	2240	3.6
21 M	0334	1.2	1008	3.9	1628	1.3	2229	3.2
7 M	0439	0.8	1110	4.3	1742	0.9	2336	3.5
22 Tu	0411	1.3	1047	3.8	1709	1.4	2309	3.1
8 Tu	0539	1.0	1207	4.1	1840	1.1		
23 W	0451	1.4	1127	3.6	1751	1.4	2352	3.1
9 W	0035	3.4	0644	1.2	1307	3.8	1939	1.2
24 Th	0539	1.4	1209	3.5	1838	1.4		
10 Th	0138	3.3	0752	1.3	1410	3.6	2039	1.3
25 F	0040	3.1	0638	1.5	1258	3.4	1930	1.4
11 F	0244	3.4	0900	1.4	1513	3.5	2136	1.3
26 Sa	0135	3.2	0747	1.5	1353	3.3	2026	1.3
12 Sa	0348	3.4	1006	1.5	1612	3.4	2228	1.3
27 Su	0237	3.3	0856	1.4	1454	3.3	2122	1.2
13 Su	0444	3.5	1107	1.4	1705	3.3	2313	1.3
28 M	0342	3.5	1001	1.3	1558	3.3	2216	1.0
14 M	0533	3.7	1201	1.4	1752	3.3	2351	1.3
29 Tu	0445	3.8	1103	1.1	1701	3.3	2310	0.8
15 Tu	0616	3.8	1246	1.3	1833	3.3		
30 W	0542	4.1	1202	0.9	1800	3.4		

DECEMBER

Day	Time	ft	Time	ft	Time	ft	Time	ft
1 Th	0002	0.6	0636	4.3	1258	0.8	1856	3.5
16 F	0007	1.1	0712	3.7	1339	1.2	1928	3.0
2 F	0053	0.6	0728	4.4	1353	0.6	1949	3.5
17 Sa	0118	1.0	0751	3.8	1415	1.1	2010	3.1
3 Sa	0144	0.5	0819	4.5	1446	0.6	2041	3.6
18 Su	0157	1.0	0830	3.9	1452	1.1	2051	3.1
4 Su	0236	0.5	0909	4.5	1538	0.6	2133	3.6
19 M	0236	1.0	0909	3.9	1528	1.1	2131	3.2
5 M	0329	0.6	1000	4.4	1630	0.6	2224	3.5
20 Tu	0313	1.1	0948	3.8	1606	1.1	2210	3.2
6 Tu	0424	0.7	1051	4.2	1721	0.7	2317	3.4
21 W	0352	1.1	1025	3.7	1643	1.1	2249	3.2
7 W	0521	0.9	1143	3.9	1813	0.9		
22 Th	0434	1.1	1102	3.6	1723	1.1	2328	3.2
8 Th	0012	3.4	0620	1.1	1237	3.6	1905	1.0
23 F	0521	1.2	1141	3.5	1805	1.1		
9 F	0110	3.3	0722	1.2	1332	3.3	1957	1.1
24 Sa	0012	3.2	0615	1.2	1225	3.3	1853	1.0
10 Sa	0211	3.3	0826	1.3	1430	3.1	2048	1.2
25 Su	0104	3.3	0720	1.2	1316	3.2	1947	1.0
11 Su	0313	3.3	0931	1.4	1529	3.0	2138	1.2
26 M	0205	3.3	0830	1.3	1414	3.1	2045	0.9
12 M	0412	3.3	1035	1.4	1625	2.9	2226	1.2
27 Tu	0312	3.5	0939	1.2	1521	3.0	2145	0.8
13 Tu	0504	3.4	1133	1.4	1716	2.9	2311	1.2
28 W	0420	3.7	1046	1.0	1633	3.0	2244	0.7
14 W	0550	3.5	1221	1.4	1803	2.9	2354	1.1
29 Th	0523	3.9	1149	0.9	1741	3.1	2341	0.6
15 Th	0632	3.6	1302	1.2	1846	3.0		
30 F	0620	4.1	1247	0.7	1841	3.2		
31 Sa	0037	0.5	0713	4.2	1342	0.6	1935	3.3

TIME MERIDIAN 60°W | 0000h is midnight, 1200h is noon.
Heights in feet are referred to the chart datum of sounding.

FLORIDA

NOTE: This section is excerpted from REED'S NAUTICAL ALMANAC: NORTH AMERICAN EAST COAST. For more complete information on Florida, or other areas in the United States, refer to the EAST COAST almanac. For more information on U.S. Customs and Immigration procedures refer to the introduction to this chapter.

FORT PIERCE INLET

Fort Pierce Inlet Lighted Whistle Buoy 2, 27 28.5N, 80 16.2W, Fl R 4s, 4M, Red.
ENTRANCE RANGE (Front Light), 27 28.1N, 80 18.2W, Q R, 15ft., KRW on skeleton tower on piles, Visible 2° each side of rangeline.
(Rear Light), 1,285 yards, 259.6° from front light, Iso R 6s, 50ft., KRW on skeleton tower on piles, Visible 2° each side of rangeline.
Buoy 3, Green can.
Buoy 4, Red nun.
Buoy 4A, Red nun.
Buoy 5, Green can.
Buoy 6, Red nun.
Lighted Buoy 7, Fl G 4s, 4M, Green.
INNER RANGE (Front Light), 27 28.3N, 80 17.8W, Q W, 20ft., KRW on skeleton tower on piles, Obscured from 129° to 355°, Higher intensity on rangeline. **(Rear Light),** 266 yards, 061.6° from front light, Iso W 6s, 32ft., KRW on skeleton tower on piles, Visible all around, Higher intensity on rangeline.
CENTER RANGE (Front Light), 27 27.5N, 80 19.4W, F R, 53ft., On warehouse, Visible 2° each side of rangeline. **(Rear Light),** 630 yards, 242° from front light, F R, 90ft., On telephone pole, Visible 2° each side of rangeline.
Buoy 8, Red nun.
Buoy 9, Green can.
Buoy 10, Red nun.
Buoy 11, Green can.
Buoy 12, Red nun with yellow square.
LIGHT 13, 27 27.6N, 80 19.1W, Fl G 4s, 12ft., 4M, SG-SY on pile.

FORT PIERCE

27 28N, 80 19W

Customs Reporting Station: Harbortown Marina.

U.S. Coast Guard: Station located just inside Ft. Pierce inlet.
Dockage. Extensive selection of marinas both north and south on the ICW. Care should be used when approaching the marinas due to the strong currents on the beam.
Anchorage: This city is attempting to outlaw anchoring through local ordinances.
Fuel: Available at marinas.
Repairs: Extensive. Haulout facilities.
Supplies: Extensive.

Ft. Pierce Inlet is considered to be navigable by most craft under ordinary conditions. Caution should be used when an ebb current meets heavy seas outside. Contact the Coast Guard if unsure of conditions. The boatyards and marinas in this area can provide any marine service. The city is a major sportfishing center. The nearby inlet provides easy access to the Gulf Stream.

FORT PIERCE TO ST. LUCIE

Capron Shoal Buoy 10A, East side of 18 foot shoal, 27 26.6N, 80 13.3W, Red nun.
Fort Pierce Yacht Club Race Course Buoy, 27 26.4N, 80 16.1W, Orange and white bands, Nun, Private aid.
St. Lucie Shoal Lighted Whistle Buoy 12, 27 23.3N, 80 08.0W, Fl R 6s, 4M, Red.
St. Lucie Power Plant Ocean Discharge Pipeline Obstruction Lighted Buoy, 27 21.3N, 80 13.8W, Q Y, Yellow, Worded DANGER SUBMERGED DISCHARGE STRUCTURE, Private aid.
St. Lucie Power Plant Intake Pipe North Obstruction Lighted Buoy, 27 20.9N, 80 14.0W, Q Y, Yellow, Worded DANGER SUBMERGED INTAKE STRUCTURE, Private aid.
St. Lucie Shoal Buoy 14, Near southeast end of shoal, 27 18.3N, 80 08.9W, Red nun.

ST. LUCIE INLET

St. Lucie Entrance Lighted Whistle Buoy 2, 27 10.0N, 80 08.4W, Fl R 4s, 3M, Red.
Buoy 3, Green can.
Buoy 4, Red nun.
Lighted Buoy 5, Fl G 2.5s, 3M, Green.

Chapter 2

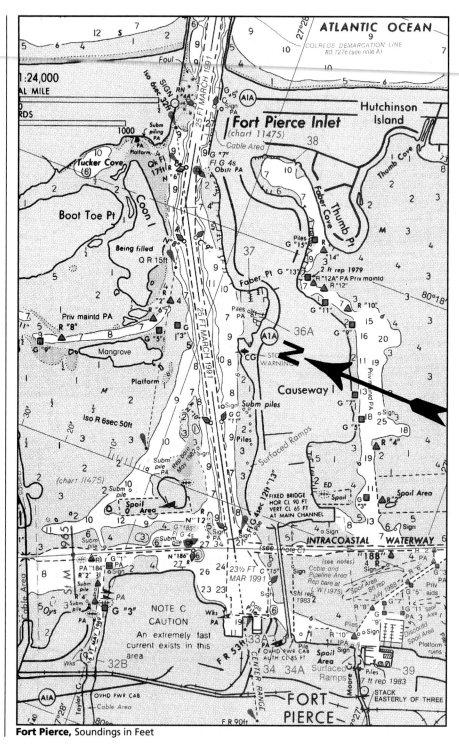

Fort Pierce, Soundings in Feet

Buoy 6, 27 10.1N, 80 09.6W, Red nun.
Buoy 8, Red nun.
Buoy 9, Green can.
Daybeacon 10, TR on pile.
Daybeacon 12, TR on pile.
Daybeacon 14, TR on pile.
Daybeacon 16, TR on pile.
Daybeacon 17, SG on pile

ST. LUCIE
27 10N, 80 10W

Customs Reporting Station: Sailfish Marina, Stuart.
U.S. Coast Guard: Ft. Pierce station.
Dockage: Large number of marinas in Manatee Pocket.
Anchorage: Excellent, well sheltered anchorage in Manatee Pocket. The Coast Pilot considers this a Hurricane Hole.
Fuel: At marinas in Manatee Pocket or further up river at Stuart.
Repairs: Extensive. Haulout facilities. More repairs at Stuart.
Supplies: Good.

St. Lucie Inlet is another "local knowledge" only entrance. Sportfishermen use the inlet constantly - it may be possible to follow one if you are trying to locate the best channel. Buoys are shifted frequently to match the changing conditions. Use care when negotiating the ICW in the vicinity of the inlet. Strong currents hit boats on the beam and the area is prone to shoaling. Manatee Pocket is a pleasant anchorage well away from the traffic of the ICW. The St. Lucie River is the eastern end of the cross Florida Okeechobee Waterway.

STUART
27 12N, 80 14W

Customs Reporting Station: Sailfish Marina.
U.S. Coast Guard: Ft. Pierce station.
Town Dock: Concrete dock is located before the railroad bridge.
Dockage: Marinas on both the North and South Forks.
Anchorage: Good anchorage on both the North and South Forks. The city is trying to restrict anchoring with local ordinances.
Fuel: Several fuel docks.
Repairs: Extensive.
Supplies: Good.

The Stuart area is well serviced by a variety of marinas and repair facilities. There are good anchoring opportunities, which are rare from

here south to Miami. The beginning of the Okeechobee Waterway passes down the South Fork. If you can clear the 49 foot bridge, this is an excellent way to voyage to the west coast of Florida.

JUPITER INLET TO LAKE WORTH

JUPITER INLET LIGHT, 26 56.9N, 80 04.9W, Fl (2) W 30s, 146ft., 25M, Red brick tower, Obscured from 231° to 234° when within 5.5 miles.
JUPITER INLET RADIOBEACON, 27 04.5N, 80 07.1W, J (·———), 110M, 294kHz.
Jupiter Inlet South Jetty Daybeacon 1, 26 56.6N, 80 04.3W, SG on pile on jetty, Private aid.
Jupiter Inlet North Jetty Daybeacon 2, TR on pile on jetty, Private aid.
Palm Beach Sailing Club Race Course Buoy B, 26 49.6N, 80 00.3W, Orange and white bands, Nun, Private aid.
Palm Beach Sailing Club Race Course Buoy D, 26 42.0N, 80 01.7W, Orange and white bands, Nun, Private aid.

LAKE WORTH INLET

Lake Worth Lighted Whistle Buoy LW, 26 46.3N, 80 00.6W, Mo (A) W, 6M, Red and white stripes with red spherical topmark.
Lighted Bell Buoy 2, 26 46.4N, 80 01.5W, Fl R 2.5s, 4M, Red.
LAKE WORTH ENTRANCE RANGE (Front Light), 26 46.3N, 80 02.5W, Q W, 30ft., KRW on skeleton tower on dolphin, Visible 4° each side of rangeline. **(Rear Light),** 440 yards, 271.5° from front light, Iso W 6s, 55ft., KRW on skeleton tower, Visible 4° each side of rangeline.
Lighted Buoy 3, Fl G 4s, 3M, Green.
Buoy 4, Red nun.
LIGHT 5, Fl G 6s, 19ft., 4M, SG on dolphin.
Lighted Buoy 7, Fl G 2.5s, 3M, Green.
LIGHT 8, Fl R 4s, 16ft., 3M, TR on pile.
Palm Beach Channel Daybeacon 2, TR on pile.
Palm Beach Channel Daybeacon 4, TR on pile.
Palm Beach Channel Daybeacon 6, TR on pile.
LIGHT 9, Fl G 6s, 16ft., 3M, SG on dolphin.
LIGHT 10, Fl R 6s, 16ft., 3M, TR on dolphin.
LIGHT 11, Fl G 4s, 16ft., 3M, SG on pile.
LIGHT 12, Fl R 4s, 12ft., 3M, TR on pile.
LIGHT 13, Fl G 2.5s, 16ft., 3M, SG on pile.
LAKE WORTH SOUTH LIGHT 1, Q G, 12ft., 4M, SG-SY on pile.

Chapter 2

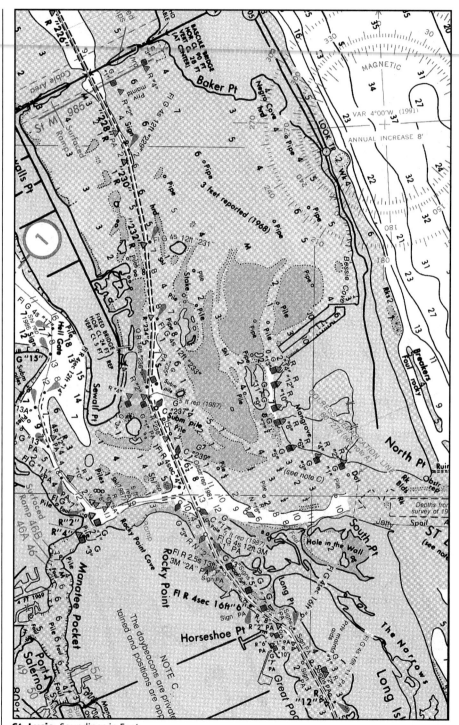

St. Lucie, Soundings in Feet

Chapter 2

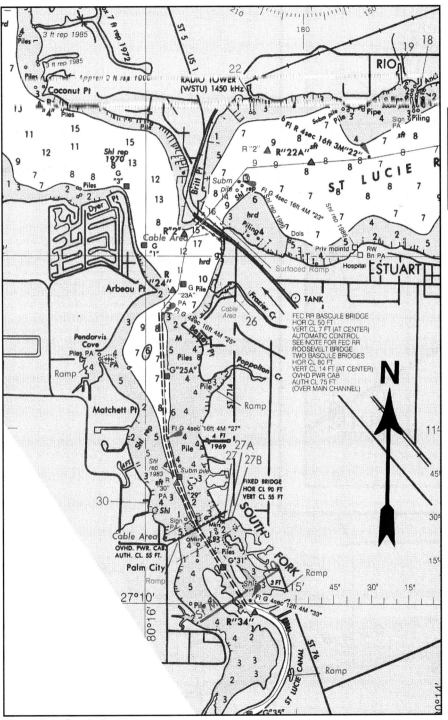

Stuart, Soundings in Feet

PALM BEACH
26 46N, 80 03W

Customs Reporting Stations: Sailfish Marina, Spencers Boat Yard and Lake Worth Boating Center in Hypoluxo.
U.S. Coast Guard: Lake Worth Inlet station south side of Peanut Island.
Customs: Port of Entry
Dockage: Many luxurious marinas.
Anchorage: Good anchorage in the northern-most portion of Lake Worth. Possible to anchor just east of Peanut Island.
Fuel: Many fuel docks.
Repairs: Extensive. Haulout facilities.
Supplies: Extensive.

The Palm Beach and West Palm Beach area form one of the wealthiest and most luxurious communities in the United States. Every con-ceivable marine service is available for yachts of any size. The shopping on Palm Beach is absolutely top notch in both quality and price. Lake Worth Inlet is one of the best on Florida's coast. This is a favorite jumping off spot for those heading to West End in the Bahamas.

BOCA RATON INLET

NORTH JETTY LIGHT 2, 26 20.1N, 80 04.2W, Q R, 14ft., TR on pile, Private aid.
SOUTH JETTY LIGHT 1, Q G, 14ft., SG on pile, Private aid.

HILLSBORO INLET

HILLSBORO INLET LIGHT, 26 15.6N, 80 04.9W, Fl W 20s, 136ft., 28M, Octagonal pyramidal iron skeleton tower with central stair cylinder, Lower third of structure white, Upper two-thirds black, Obscured from 015° to 186°.
HILLSBORO INLET RADIOBEACON, 26 15.6N, 80 04.9W, Q (–·–·–), 25M, 299kHz, Antenna 75 feet, 357° from Hillsboro Inlet Light Tower.
Hillsboro Inlet Entrance Lighted Buoy HI, 26 15.1N, 80 04.5W, Mo (A) W, 5M, Red and white stripes with red spherical topmark.
ENTRANCE LIGHT 1, 26 15.3N, 80 04.8W, Fl G 4s, 8ft., 4M, SG on dolphin.
ENTRANCE LIGHT 2, Fl R 4s, 16ft., 4M, TR on dolphin.
Entrance Daybeacon 3, SG on pile.

PORT EVERGLADES

APPROACH LIGHT, 26 05.7N, 80 06.4W, Fl W 5s, 349ft., 17M, On building, Obscured from 030° to 180°.

Lighted Whistle Buoy PE, 26 05.5N, 80 04.8W, Mo (A) W, 7M, Red and white stripes with red spherical topmark.
Spoil Bank Daybeacon, 26 05.8N, 80 06.0W, NW on pile worded DANGER SHOAL.
Spoil Bank West Daybeacon, 26 05.8N, 80 06.2W, NW on pile worded DANGER SHOAL.
Lighted Buoy 2, Fl R 2.5s, 3M, Red.
Lighted Buoy 3, Fl G 2.5s, 3M, Green.
ENTRANCE RANGE (Front Light), 26 05.6N, 80 07.5W, F G, 85ft., KRW on skeleton tower, Visible 2° each side of rangeline. **(Rear Light),** 924 yards, 269.5° from front light, F G, 135ft., KRW on skeleton tower, Visible 2° each side of rangeline.
LIGHT 4, 26 05.7N, 80 06.1W, Fl R 4s, 16ft., 3M, TR on pile.
LIGHT 5, Fl G 4s, 21ft., 4M, SG on dolphin.
LIGHT 6, Fl R 2.5s, 16ft., 4M, TR on dolphin.
LIGHT 7, 26 05.5N, 80 06.7W, Fl G 4s, 28ft., 4M, SG on triangular skeleton tower on piles.
LIGHT 9, Fl G 6s, 16ft., 4M, SG on piles.
TURNING BASIN LIGHT 11, Fl G 4s, 16ft., 4M, SG-SY on pile.
TURNING BASIN LIGHT 12, Q R, 16ft., 3M, TR-SY on dolphin.
Stranahan River Lighted Buoy 30, Fl R 4s, 3M, Red with yellow triangle.

FT. LAUDERDALE
26 06N, 80 07W

Customs Reporting Stations: Pier 66, Laud-erdale Marina and Bahia Mar.
City Dockmaster: Contact him at the city docks up the New River. Try VHF channel 09. Dockmaster in charge of the mooring area near the Las Olas Boulevard bridge.
U.S. Coast Guard: On the east side of the ICW at mile 1066.8.
Customs: Port of Entry
Dockage: Very extensive for any size pleasure boat.
Moorings: Near Las Olas Boulevard bridge. The city regulates the moorings and collects the fees. A dinghy dock and fresh water are provided.
Anchorage: Possible near moorings by Las Olas Boulevard bridge. You'll probably be asked to move, or pick up a mooring if available.
Fuel: Large fueling docks can handle any request.
Repairs: Very extensive. Large haulout facilities.
Supplies: Very extensive.
Fort Lauderdale provides the most complete marine facilities on the U.S. east coast. The marinas accommodate the largest luxury yachts alongside the ordinary. Despite the huge num-ber of berths, reservations are always recom-

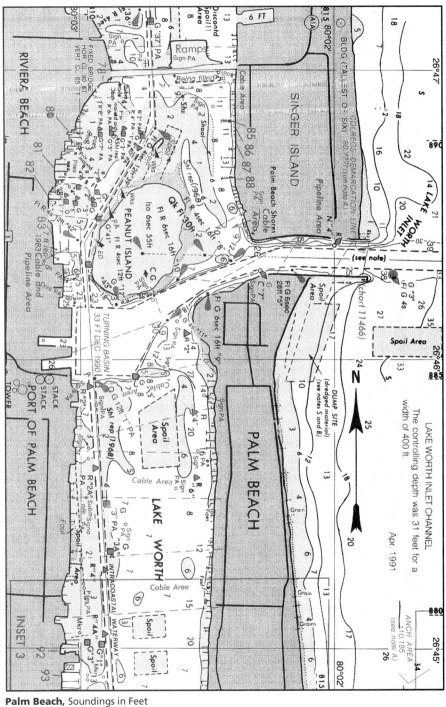

Palm Beach, Soundings in Feet

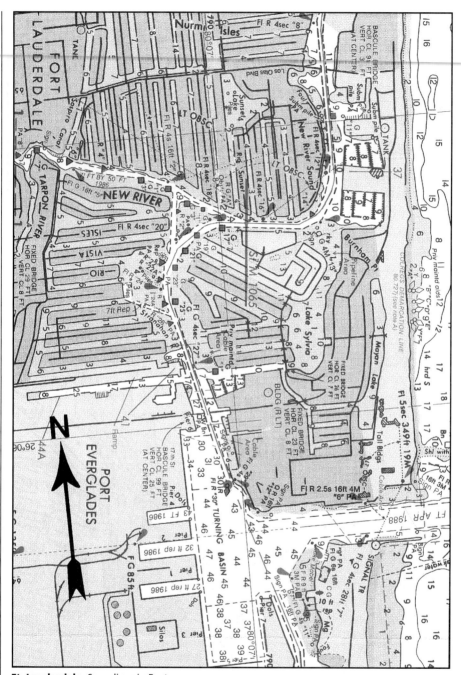

Ft. Lauderdale, Soundings in Feet

mended. Ashore are many luxury hotels, restaurants and endless shops. Port Everglades is a safe and well marked inlet. This is an excellent departure port for trips to the Bahamas.

PORT EVERGLADES TO MIAMI

Parker Dorado Association Obstruction Daybeacon, 25 58.5N, 80 07.1W, NW on pile worded DANGER SUBMERGED OUTFALL, Private aid.

BAKERS HAULOVER INLET JETTY LIGHT, 25 53.9N, 80 07.2W, Q W, 13ft., NW on pile worded DANGER JETTY, Private aid.

MIAMI ENTRANCE

Miami Anchorage Buoy A, 25 48.3N, 80 05.7W, Yellow nun, Marks anchorage area east of Miami Beach.

Miami Anchorage Buoy B, 25 46.4N, 80 06.2W, Yellow nun, Marks anchorage area east of Miami Beach.

MIAMI APPROACH LIGHT, 25 46.0N, 80 08.0W, Fl (2) W 30s, 240ft., 17M, On building, Obscured from 065° to 195°.

Miami Lighted Whistle Buoy M, 25 46.1N, 80 05.0W, Mo (A) W, 7M, Red and white stripes with red spherical topmark, RACON: M (– –).

MIAMI RADIOBEACON, 25 43.9N, 80 09.6W, U (· ·–), 100M, 322kHz.

ENTRANCE RANGE (Front Light), 25 45.1N, 80 07.7W, Q G, 25ft., Fl W 4s, 27ft., 5M, KRB on skeleton tower on piles, Visible 4° each side of rangeline, Passing light visible around horizon. **(Rear Light),** 670 yards, 249.5° from front light, Iso G 6s, 49ft., KRB on skeleton tower on piles, Visible 4° each side of rangeline.

Lighted Buoy 1, Fl G 6s, 4M, Green.

Lighted Bell Buoy 2, Fl R 4s, 4M, Red.

Lighted Buoy 3, Fl G 4s, 3M, Green.

Lighted Buoy 4, Q R, 3M, Red.

Lighted Buoy 5, Fl G 2.5s, 4M, Green.

Lighted Buoy 6, Fl R 2.5s, 4M, Red.

Lighted Buoy 7, Q G, 4M, Green.

GOVERNMENT CUT RANGE (Front Light), 25 45.2N, 80 06.5W, Q W, 25ft., Fl W 4s, 28ft., 5M, KRW on tower on piles, Visible 2° each side of rangeline, Passing light visible around horizon. **(Rear Light),** 785 yards, 114.8° from front light, Iso W 6s, 50ft., Fl W 4s, 25ft., 5M, KRW on tower on piles, Visible 2° each side of rangeline, Passing light visible around horizon.

Lighted Buoy 6A, Fl R 2.5s, 4M, Red.

Lighted Buoy 7A, Fl G 2.5s, 4M, Green.

Lighted Buoy 8, Q R, 4M, Red.

Lighted Buoy 9, Q G, 4M, Green.

Lighted Buoy 10, Fl R 4s, 4M, Red.

NORTH JETTY FISHING PIER EAST OBSTRUCTION LIGHT, 25 45.8N, 80 07.8W, F W, 17ft., On jetty, Private aid.

NORTH JETTY FISHING PIER WEST OBSTRUCTION LIGHT, F W, 17ft., On jetty, Private aid.

LIGHT 11, Fl G 4s, 16ft., 4M, SG on dolphin.

Buoy 12, Red nun.

Lighted Buoy 14, Fl R 4s, 4M, Red.

LIGHT 15, Fl G 2.5s, 16ft., 3M, SG on dolphin.

MIAMI HARBOR

INTERNATIONAL YACHT HARBOR BREAKWATER SOUTH LIGHT, 25 46.0N, 80 08.4W, Q W, 12ft., On pile, Private aid.

INTERNATIONAL YACHT HARBOR BREAKWATER BARRIER SOUTH LIGHT, Q W, 12ft., On pile, Private aid.

INTERNATIONAL YACHT HARBOR BREAKWATER BARRIER NORTH LIGHT, Q W, 12ft., On pile, Private aid.

Lighted Buoy 16, 25 46.0N, 80 08.5W, Fl R 4s, 4M, Red.

MIAMI

25 46N, 80 08W

Customs Reporting Stations: Bakers Haulover Marina, Sunset Harbour Marina, Miamarina, Phillips 66 Marina, Crandon Park Marina and Matheson Hammock Marina on Biscayne Bay.

U.S. Coast Guard: Miami Beach Coast Guard on Causeway Island.

Customs: Port of Entry

Dockage: Extensive dockage available at Miami Beach just inside Government Cut. Be careful in the strong currents running through the marina. Many marinas and repair facilities along the ICW and in the Miami River.

Anchorage: Good anchorage possibilities exist north of the MacArthur Causeway. Beware of cable and pipeline areas marked on the charts.

Fuel: Many fuel docks. Beware strong currents in the marina just inside Government Cut.

Repairs: Extensive. Haulout facilities.

Supplies: Extensive.

Miami is the largest city in Florida and has become the de-facto capital of the Caribbean in recent years. A large volume of commercial traffic steams through Government Cut day and night. The channel is safe and almost too well marked. The profusion of buoyage and lights can be confusing at night. From the marina at Miami Beach you can walk to museums, restaurants and shops. The downtown marina complex

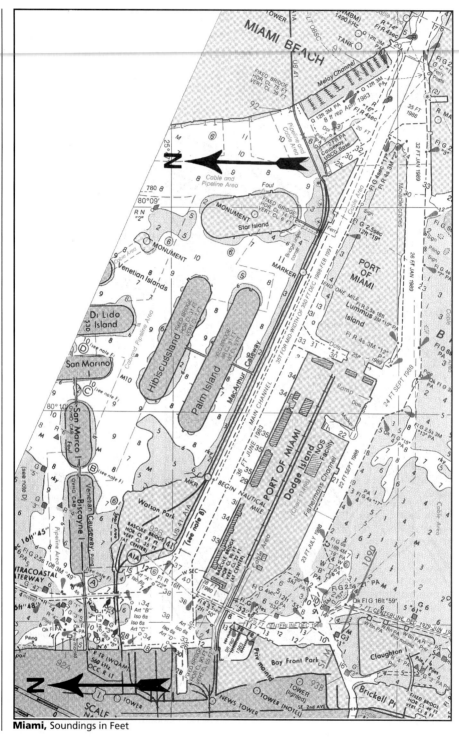

Miami, Soundings in Feet

is in the heart of Miami's revitalized waterfront. Shops and restaurants overlook the harbor. Visitors should be careful where they walk, especially at night.

MIAMI TO FOWEY ROCKS

Bear Cut Daybeacon 2, 25 43.5N, 80 08.0W, TR on pile.
CASA DEL MAR LIGHT, 25 41.1N, 80 09.4W, Fl W 6s, 350ft., 8M, On building, Obscured from 017° to 180°.
Cape Florida Daybeacon 2, TR on pile.
CAPE FLORIDA LIGHT 4, 25 41.1N, 80 11.0W, Fl R 2.5s, 16ft., 4M, TR on pile.
Biscayne National Park North Lighted Buoy N, 25 38.7N, 80 05.4W, Fl Y 2.5s, 4M, Yellow.
FOWEY ROCKS LIGHT, On outer line of reefs, 25 35.4N, 80 05.8W, Fl W 10s (2R sectors), 110ft., 16M white, 12M red, Brown octagonal, Pyramidal skeleton tower, Enclosing white stair cylinder and octagonal dwelling, Pile foundation, White from 188° to 359° and from 022° to 180°, Red in intervening sectors.

BISCAYNE CHANNEL

LIGHT, 25 38.3N, 80 07.9W, Fl W 4s, 37ft., 5M, NG on skeleton tower on piles.
LIGHT 1, 25 38.7N, 80 08.0W, Fl G 2.5s, 16ft., 4M, SG on dolphin.
LIGHT 2, Fl R 2.5s, 16ft., 4M, TR on dolphin.
LIGHT 3, Fl G 4s, 12ft., 3M, SG on pile.
Daybeacon 4, TR on pile.
LIGHT 6, Fl R 4s, 12ft., 3M, TR on dolphin.
Daybeacon 7, SG on pile.
Daybeacon 8, TR on pile.
Daybeacon 10, TR on pile.
Daybeacon 12, TR on pile.
Daybeacon 14, TR on pile.
LIGHT 15, 25 39.1N, 80 10.5W, Fl G 4s, 16ft., 4M, SG on pile.
Daybeacon 16, TR on pile.
Daybeacon 18, TR on pile.
Daybeacon 19, SG on pile.
Daybeacon 20, TR on pile.
LIGHT 21, Fl G 2.5s, 12ft., 3M, SG on pile.

FOWEY ROCKS TO ALLIGATOR REEF

TRIUMPH REEF LIGHT 2TR, 25 28.6N, 80 06.7W, Fl R 2.5s, 19ft., 6M, TR on dolphin.
PACIFIC REEF LIGHT, 25 22.2N, 80 08.5W, Fl W 4s, 44ft., 9M, Black skeleton tower on piles.

Turtle Harbor Lighted Whistle Buoy 4, Marks entrance between shoal patches, 25 17.5N, 80 09.9W, Fl R 6s, 5M, Red.
CARYSFORT REEF LIGHT, On outer line of reefs, 25 13.3N, 80 12.7W, Fl (3) W 60s (3R sectors), 100ft., 15M white, 15M red, Brown octagonal pyramidal skeleton tower enclosing stair cylinder and conical dwelling, Pile foundation, White from 211° to 018°, 049° to 087° and 145° to 184°, Red in intervening sectors.
ELBOW REEF LIGHT 6, 25 08.7N, 80 15.5W, Fl R 2.5s, 36ft., 6M, TR on skeleton tower on piles.
Dixie Shoal Buoy 8, On seaward edge of reef, 25 04.6N, 80 18.7W, Red nun.

MOLASSES REEF BOUNDARY
Northwest Buoy, 25 00.7N, 80 22.4W, Yellow nun worded NO ANCHOR ZONE, Private aid.
Northeast Buoy, 25 00.6N, 80 22.4W, Yellow nun worded NO ANCHOR ZONE, Private aid.
Southwest Buoy, 25 00.6N, 80 22.4W, Yellow nun worded NO ANCHOR ZONE, Private aid.
Southeast Buoy, 25 00.6N, 80 22.4W, Yellow nun worded NO ANCHOR ZONE, Private aid.

MOLASSES REEF LIGHT 10, 25 00.7N, 80 22.6W, Fl R 10s, 45ft., 13M, TR on square brown pyramidal skeleton tower, Pile foundation.
Conch Reef Buoy 12, Near seaward edge of reef, 24 57.0N, 80 27.5W, Red nun.
DAVIS REEF LIGHT 14, 24 55.5N, 80 30.2W, Fl R 4s, 20ft., 6M, TR on dolphin.
Crocker Reef Buoy 16, 24 54.5N, 80 31.5W, Red nun.
ALLIGATOR REEF LIGHT, On outer line of reef, 24 51.1N, 80 37.1W, Fl (4) W 60s (2R sectors), 136ft., 16M white, 13M red, White octagonal pyramid skeleton tower enclosing stair cylinder and square dwelling, Black pile foundation, Red from 223° to 249° and 047° to 068°.

HAWK CHANNEL: SOLDIER KEY TO CHANNEL FIVE

Soldier Key Daybeacon 2, 25 35.8N, 80 07.6W, TR on pile.
Fowey Rocks Daybeacon 3, 25 35.7N, 80 06.9W, SG on pile.
Soldier Key Daybeacon 4, 25 34.2N, 80 07.9W, TR on pile.
Ragged Key Daybeacon 7, 25 31.0N, 80 08.3W, SG on pile.
BOWLES BANK LIGHT 8, 25 30.4N, 80 08.7W, Fl R 4s, 16ft., 3M, TR on pile.

Bache Shoal Daybeacon 9, SG on pile.
BACHE SHOAL LIGHT 11BS, On southwest edge of shoal, 25 29.2N, 80 08.9W, Fl G 6s, 18ft., 5M, SG on dolphin.
Bache Shoal Daybeacon 13, SG on pile.

ELLIOT KEY
Daybeacon 14, TR on pile.
Daybeacon 15, SG on pile.
Daybeacon 16, 25 26.8N, 80 10.2W, TR on pile.
Daybeacon 17, SG on pile.
Daybeacon 18, TR on pile.
Daybeacon 19, SG on pile.
Pacific Reef Daybeacon 2, TR on pile.
Pacific Reef Daybeacon 3, 25 22.4N, 80 09.6W, SG on pile.
Pacific Reef Daybeacon 4, TR on pile.
LIGHT 20, 25 23.1N, 80 11.5W, Fl R 4s, 16ft., 3M, TR on pile.

CAESAR CREEK
Caesar Creek Buoy 1, 25 23.1N, 80 11.7W, Black can, Maintained by National Park Service.

NOTE: A series of 36 black cans and red nuns, maintained by the National Park Service, mark Caesar Creek to the Junction Buoy, which is a black and red can. Then West Buoys 1 through 4 mark the remainder of the channel.

OLD RHODES KEY
Daybeacon 21, SG on pile.
LIGHT 22, Fl R 2.5s, 12ft., 4M, TR on pile.
Daybeacon 23, SG on pile.
Daybeacon 24, TR on pile.

ANGELFISH CREEK
LIGHT 2, 25 19.7N, 80 15.0W, Fl R 4s, 12ft., 3M, TR on pile.
Daybeacon 1, SG on pile.
Daybeacon 2A, TR on pile.
Daybeacon 3, SG on pile.
Daybeacon 3A, SG on pile.
Daybeacon 4, TR on pile.
Daybeacon 5, SG on pile.
LIGHT 6, Fl R 4s, 12ft., 3M, TR on pile.
Daybeacon 8, TR on pile.
Daybeacon 10, TR on pile.
Daybeacon 12, TR on pile.
LIGHT 14, 25 20.1N, 80 16.8W, Fl R 4s, 12ft., 3M, TR on pile.

VILLA CHANNEL
Daybeacon 1, 25 18.8N, 80 15.9W, SG on pile, Private aid.

NOTE: A series of 21 daybeacons, alternating red triangles and green squares on pilings, mark the Villa Channel. These are private aids.

OCEAN REEF HARBOR ENTRANCE LIGHT 2, 25 18.5N, 80 16.0W, Fl R 4s, 18ft., 3M, TR on dolphin.

DISPATCH CREEK CHANNEL
Daybeacon 3, 25 18.3N, 80 16.2W, SG on pile, Private aid.

NOTE: A series of 20 daybeacons, alternating red triangles and green squares on pilings, mark the Dispatch Creek Channel. These are private aids.

HARBOR COURSE CREEK
Daybeacon 1, 25 18.6N, 80 17.0W, SG on pile, Private aid.
Daybeacon 2, TR on pile, Private aid.

TURTLE HARBOR
West Shoal Daybeacon 2, 25 19.4N, 80 12.7W, TR on pile.
WEST SHOAL PREFERRED CHANNEL LIGHT, 25 18.3N, 80 12.8W, Fl (2 + 1) G 6s, 16ft., 3M, JG on pile.
Daybeacon 1, SG on pile.
Daybeacon 3, SG on pile.
Daybeacon 4, TR on pile.
Daybeacon 5, SG on pile.
Daybeacon 6, TR on pile.

Key Largo Daybeacon 25, SG on pile.
Key Largo Daybeacon 27, SG on pile.
Key Largo Daybeacon 29, 25 14.3N, 80 17.0W, SG on pile.

WORLDS BEYOND MARINA
Daybeacon 1, SG on pile, Private aid.
Daybeacon 2, TR on pile, Private aid.
Daybeacon 3, SG on pile, Private aid.
Daybeacon 4, TR on pile, Private aid.
Daybeacon 6, TR on pile, Private aid.
Daybeacon 7, SG on pile, Private aid.

BASIN HILLS LIGHT 31BH, Fl G 4s, 27ft., 4M, SG on skeleton structure on piles.
KEY LARGO LIGHT 32, 25 10.6N, 80 20.3W, FL R 2.5s, 16ft., 3M, TR on pile.

BASIN HILLS CHANNEL
Daybeacon 2, 12ft., TR on pile, Private aid.
Daybeacon 3, 12ft., SG on pile, Private aid.

Daybeacon 5, 12ft., SG on pile, Private aid.
Daybeacon 7, 12ft., SG on pile, Private aid.
Daybeacon 9, 12ft., SG on pile, Private aid.
Daybeacon 11, 12ft., SG on pile, Private aid.

GARDEN COVE
Daybeacon 1, SG on pile, Private aid.

NOTE: A series of 18 daybeacons, alternating red triangles and green squares on pilings, mark the Garden Cove channel. These are private aids.

North Largo Yacht Club Marina Daybeacon 18A, 25 10.2N, 80 22.0W, TR on pile, Private aid.
North Largo Yacht Club Marina Daybeacon 18B, TR on pile, Private aid.

NORTH SOUND CREEK
Daybeacon 21, SG on pile, Private aid.
Daybeacon 22, TR on pile, Private aid.
Daybeacon 24, TR on pile, Private aid.
Daybeacon 25, SG on pile, Private aid.
Daybeacon 26, TR on pile, Private aid.
Daybeacon 27, SG on pile, Private aid.
Daybeacon 29, SG on pile, Private aid.

Key Largo Daybeacon 32A, TR on pile.
Key Largo Daybeacon 33, SG on pile.

JOHN PENNEKAMP
CORAL REEF STATE PARK
Buoy D, 25 07.4N, 80 18.0W, Orange and white bands, Barrel, Private aid.
Buoy E, 25 06.7N, 80 18.5W, Orange and white bands, Barrel, Private aid.
Buoy F, 25 06.6N, 80 20.7W, Orange and white bands, Barrel, Private aid.
Buoy G, 25 03.2N, 80 20.2W, Orange and white bands, Barrel, Private aid.
Carysfort North Reef North Obstruction Daybeacon, 25 13.5N, 80 12.5W, NW on pile worded DANGER SHOAL, Private aid.
Carysfort North Reef South Obstruction Daybeacon, 25 13.2N, 80 12.7W, NW on pile worded DANGER SHOAL, Private aid.
Carysfort South Reef North Obstruction Daybeacon, 25 12.8N, 80 13.1W, NW on pile worded DANGER SHOAL, Private aid.
Carysfort South Reef South Obstruction Daybeacon, 25 12.4N, 80 13.3W, NW on pile worded DANGER SHOAL, Private aid.
Key Largo Dry Rocks Obstruction Daybeacon, NW on pile worded DANGER SHOAL, Private aid.

Grecian Rocks Obstruction Daybeacon, NW on pile worded DANGER SHOAL, Private aid.
Cannon Patch Obstruction Daybeacon, NW on pile worded DANGER SHOAL, Private aid.
Mosquito Bank Obstruction Daybeacon, NW on pile worded DANGER SHOAL, Private aid.
White Banks Obstruction Daybeacon, 25 02.4N, 80 22.3W, NW on pile worded DANGER SHOAL, Private aid.
French Reef Obstruction Daybeacon, 25 02.1N, 80 21.1W, NW on pile worded DANGER SHOAL, Private aid.
Sand Island Obstruction Daybeacon, 25 01.1N, 80 22.0W, NW on pile worded DANGER SHOAL, Private aid.
Molasses Reef North Obstruction Daybeacon, 25 00.8N, 80 22.4W, NW on pile worded DANGER SHOAL, Private aid.
Molasses Reef South Obstruction Daybeacon, 25 00.6N, 80 22.7W, NW on pile worded DANGER SHOAL, Private aid.

LARGO SOUND CHANNEL
LIGHT 2, 25 05.6N, 80 23.8W, Fl R 4s, 16ft., 4M, TR on dolphin.
Daybeacon 3, SG on pile.
Daybeacon 4, TR on pile.
Daybeacon 5, SG on pile.
Daybeacon 6, TR on pile.
Daybeacon 6A, TR on pile.
Daybeacon 7, SG on pile.
Daybeacon 7A, SG on pile.
Daybeacon 8, TR on pile.
LIGHT 9, Fl G 4s, 16ft., 3M, SG on pile.
Daybeacon 10, TR on pile.
Daybeacon 11, SG on pile.
Daybeacon 12, TR on pile.
Daybeacon 13, SG on pile.
Daybeacon 14, TR on pile.
Daybeacon 16, TR on pile.
Daybeacon 17, SG on pile.
Daybeacon 19, SG on pile.
Daybeacon 20, TR on pile.
Daybeacon 21, SG on pile.
Daybeacon 22, TR on pile.
Daybeacon 23, SG on pile.
MARVIN D. ADAMS WATERWAY LIGHT A, 25 08.2N, 80 23.7W, Fl W 6s, 12ft., 4M, NR on pile.
MARVIN D. ADAMS WATERWAY LIGHT B, Fl W 6s, 12ft., 4M, NR on pile.

MOSQUITO BANK LIGHT 35, 25 04.3N, 80 23.6W, Fl G 4s, 37ft., 5M, SG on triangular pyramidal skeleton structure on piles.

Chapter 2

MOSQUITO BANK LIGHT 2, Fl R 2.5s, 16ft., 4M, TR on pile.
PORT LARGO PROPERTY OWNERS LIGHT, 25 05.3N, 80 25.9W, F G, 16ft., On pile, Private aid.
Hidden Bay Daybeacon 2, 25 04.8N, 80 26.2W, TR on pile, Private aid.
Hidden Bay Daybeacon 4, TR on pile, Private aid.
KAWAMA MARINA AND YACHT CLUB LIGHT, 25 04.6N, 80 26.4W, Q R, 25ft., On roof of thatched hut, Private aid.
HARBORAGE YACHT CLUB ENTRANCE LIGHT 2, 25 04.1N, 80 27.7W, Fl R 4s, 12ft., TR on steel tower, Private aid.
Key Largo Daybeacon 37, SG on pile.
Key Largo Daybeacon 39, Northwest of shoal, SG on pile.

KEY LARGO

25 06N, 80 26W

Customs Reporting Stations: Ocean Reef Club, Tavernier Creek Marina and Holiday Isle Marina on Islamorada.
U.S. Coast Guard: Islamorada Station at the SW end of Plantation Key.
Dockage: The marinas are in a series of canals NW of Mosquito Bank on Key Largo. Four to five foot approach depths.
Anchorage: Good anchorage in the lee of Rodriguez Key.
Fuel: At marina up the canal.
Repairs: Good. Haulout facilities.
Supplies: Good.

The big attraction on Key Largo is the John Pennekamp Coral Reef State Park. Dive boats take visitors out to the reefs — anchoring is forbidden on the reefs. Ashore are many restaurants and shops strung out along Route 1. The marinas are small and low key, but provide most services. When approaching any docks do so at slow speed — shoaling occurs frequently.

MOLASSES REEF

Daybeacon 1, On south side of passage between shoals, 25 01.6N, 80 23.7W, SG on pile.
Daybeacon 3, SG on pile.
Daybeacon 5, SG on pile.

KEY LARGO OCEAN RESORT LIGHT 2, 25 02.5N, 80 29.3W, Fl R 4s, TR on pile, Private aid.

BLUE WATERS TRAILER VILLAGE LIGHT 1, 25 00.8N, 80 30.3W, Fl G 6s, 12ft., SG on pile, Private aid.
Daybeacon 2, TR on pile, Private aid.
Daybeacon 3, SG on pile, Private aid.
Daybeacon 4, TR on pile, Private aid.
Daybeacon 5, SG on pile, Private aid.
Daybeacon 6, TR on pile, Private aid.

TAVERNIER KEY LIGHT 2, 25 00.2N, 80 29.0W, Fl R 4s, 16ft., 3M, TR on pile.
Tavernier Key Daybeacon 3, SG on pile.
Tavernier Key Daybeacon 4, TR on pile.
Tavernier Ocean Shores Daybeacon 2, TR on pile, Private aid.
Tavernier Ocean Shores Daybeacon 4, TR on pile, Private aid.

TAVERNIER CREEK

LIGHT, 24 59.2N, 80 31.4W, Fl W 6s, 16ft., 5M, NR on pile.
Daybeacon 1, SG on pile.
Daybeacon 2, TR on pile.

NOTE: Tavernier Creek is marked by a series of red and green daymarks, numbered to 18. These are private aids.

Coral Harbor Club Daybeacon 1, SG on pile, Private aid.
Coral Harbor Club Daybeacon 2, TR on pile, Private aid.
HEN AND CHICKENS SHOAL LIGHT 40, Southeast of shoal, 24 55.9N, 80 32.9W, Fl R 2.5s, 35ft., 5M, TR on triangular pyramidal structure on piles.

SNAKE CREEK

LIGHT 2, 24 56.5N, 80 34.8W, Fl R 4s, 16ft., 4M, TR on pile.
Daybeacon 1, SG on pile.
Daybeacon 3, SG on pile.
Daybeacon 4, TR on pile.
Daybeacon 4A, TR on pile.
Daybeacon 5, SG on pile.
Daybeacon 6, TR on pile.
Daybeacon 6A, TR on pile.
Daybeacon 7, SG on pile.
Daybeacon 7A, SG on pile.
Daybeacon 8, TR on pile.
Daybeacon 9, SG on pile.
Daybeacon 10, TR on pile.
LIGHT 12, Fl R 2.5s, 16ft., 3M, TR on pile.

WHALE HARBOR

LIGHT 1, 24 55.8N, 80 35.8W, Fl G 2.5s, 14ft., 3M, SG on pile.

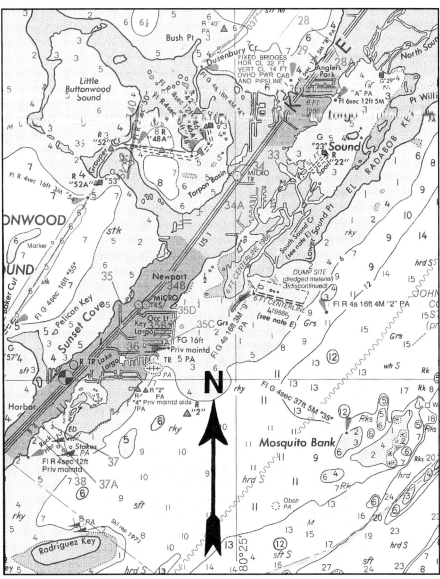

Key Largo, Soundings in Feet

Daybeacon 2, TR on pile.
Daybeacon 3, SG on pile.
Daybeacon 4, TR on pile.
Daybeacon 4A, TR on pile.
Daybeacon 5, SG on pile.
Daybeacon 6, TR on pile.
Daybeacon 7, SG on pile.

Daybeacon 8, TR on pile.
Daybeacon 9, SG on pile.

WINDLEY PASS
Daybeacon 11, SG on pile, Private aid.
Daybeacon 12, TR on pile, Private aid.
Daybeacon 13, SG on pile, Private aid.

Daybeacon 15, SG on pile, Private aid.
Daybeacon 16, TR on pile, Private aid.

HOLIDAY ISLE MARINA
Daybeacon 1, 24 56.3N, 80 36.5W, SG on pile, Private aid.

NOTE: A series of red and green day-beacons, numbered 1 through 6, mark the Holiday Isle Marina channel. These are private aids.

BEACON REEF PIER LIGHT, 24 55.8N, 80 37.0W, Q W, 10ft., On pile, Private aid.
Upper Matecumbe Daybeacon 41, SG on pile.

LA SIESTA RESORT
Daybeacon 1, SG on pile, Private aid.
Daybeacon 2, TR on pile, Private aid.
Daybeacon 3, SG on pile, Private aid.
Daybeacon 4, TR on pile, Private aid.

BUD AND MARY'S FISHING MARINA
Daybeacon 1, 24 53.5N, 80 39.2W, SG on pile, Private aid.

NOTE: A series of red and green day-beacons, numbered 1 through 14, mark Bud and Mary's Fishing Marina channel. These are private aids.

Teatable Key Daybeacon 42, TR on pile.
Alligator Reef Daybeacon 43, SG on pile.

INDIAN KEY CHANNEL
Daybeacon 2, 24 52.6N, 80 40.2W, TR on pile.
Daybeacon 4, TR on pile.
Daybeacon 6, TR on pile.
Daybeacon 7, SG on pile.
Daybeacon 8, TR on pile.
Daybeacon 9, SG on pile.
Daybeacon 10, TR on pile.

CALOOSA COVE CHANNEL
LIGHT 2, 24 50.1N, 80 44.8W, Fl R 6s, 10ft., TR and NL on dolphin, NL worded CALOOSA COVE, Private aid.

NOTE: A series of red and green daybea-cons, numbered 4 through 21, mark the Caloosa Cove channel. These are private aids.

CHANNEL FIVE
Channel Five Daybeacon 1, SG on pile.
CHANNEL FIVE LIGHT 2, 24 49.6N, 80 46.4W, Fl R 4s, 16ft., 4M, TR on pile.

ALLIGATOR REEF TO SOMBRERO KEY

Tennessee Reef East Lighted Buoy 18, 24 47.5N, 80 41.6W, Fl R 2.5s, 5M, Red.
TENNESSEE REEF LIGHT, On west side of shoal, 24 44.7N, 80 46.9W, Fl W 4s, 49ft., 8M, Small black house on hexagonal pyramidal skeleton tower on piles.
COFFINS PATCH LIGHT 20, 24 40.5N, 80 57.4W, Fl R 6s, 20ft., 6M, TR on dolphin.
SOMBRERO KEY LIGHT, 24 37.6N, 81 06.6W, Fl (5) W 60s (3R sectors), 142ft., 15M white, 12M red, Brown octagonal pyramidal skeleton tower enclosing stair cylinder and square dwelling, Pile foundation, White from 222° to 238°, 264° to 066° and 094° to 163°, Red in intervening sectors.

HAWK CHANNEL: LONG KEY TO MARATHON

LONG KEY LIGHT 44, Fl R 6s, 4M, TR on pile.
Layton Canal Channel Daybeacon 1, SG on pile, Private aid.
Layton Canal Channel Daybeacon 2, TR on pile, Private aid.
Layton Canal Channel Daybeacon 3, SG on pile, Private aid.

DUCK KEY INLET CHANNEL
LIGHT 1, Fl W 4s, SG on pile, Private aid.

NOTE: A series of red and green day-beacons, numbered 2 through 8, mark the Duck Key Inlet channel. These are private aids.

Duck Key Channel Daybeacon 2, TR on pile, Private aid.
Duck Key Channel Daybeacon 4, TR on pile, Private aid.

LITTLE CRAWL KEY CHANNEL
Daybeacon 1, 24 44.4N, 80 58.2W, SG on pile, Private aid.
NOTE: A series of red and green day-beacons, numbered 1 through 15, mark the Little Crawl Key Channel. These are private aids.

EAST TURTLE SHOAL LIGHT 45, 24 43.5N, 80 56.0W, Fl G 4s, 27ft., 5M, SG on tower.
West Turtle Shoal Daybeacon 47, SG on pile.
Coco Plum Channel Daybeacon 1, SG on pile, Private aid.

Coco Plum Channel Daybeacon 3, SG on pile, Private aid.

KEY COLONY BEACH
East Channel Daybeacon 2A, TR on pile, Private aid.
East Channel Daybeacon 3A, SG on pile, Private aid.
West Channel Daybeacon 1, SG on pile, Private aid.
West Channel Daybeacon 3, SG on pile, Private aid.
West Channel Daybeacon 6, TR on pile, Private aid.

Fat Deer Key Daybeacon 48, 24 41.5N, 81 01.5W, TR on pile.
EAST WASHERWOMAN SHOAL LIGHT 49, On north side of shoal, 24 40.0N, 81 04.0W, Fl G 4s, 36ft., 5M, SG on black triangular pyramidal structure on piles.

SISTER CREEK
LIGHT 2, 24 41.2N, 81 05.2W, Fl R 4s, 16ft., 3M, TR on pile.
Daybeacon 3, SG on pile.
Daybeacon 4, TR on pile.
Daybeacon 6, TR on pile.
Daybeacon 8, TR on pile.

BOOT KEY HARBOR
LIGHT 1, 24 42.0N, 81 07.3W, Fl G 4s, 16ft., 4M, SG on pile.

NOTE: A series of red and green daybeacons, numbered 2 through 21, mark the Boot Key Harbor channel. A series of Private daybeacons, numbered 1 through 9, mark the channel in the eastern part of the harbor.

MARATHON
24 42N, 81 06W

Customs Reporting Station: Boot Key Marina.
U.S. Coast Guard: Marathon station on the north side of Vaca Key, east of Knight Key Channel.
Dockage: Many marinas line the shores of Boot Key Harbor.
Anchorage: Good anchorage in Boot Key Harbor. Beware of the local authorities conducting surprise boat inspections.
Fuel: Many fuel docks.
Repairs: Extensive.
Supplies: Extensive. Haulout facilities.

This is one of the few sheltered harbors on the Hawk Channel side of the Keys. Elaborate marine facilities provide most services. Nearby Moser Channel is one of only two high level bridges allowing access to the waters of Florida Bay. This is a possible route for those headed north to the west coast of Florida. Ashore are many stores and restaurants. This is your last bout for restocking in the keys. Unfortunately, in recent years the authorities have made a practice of mass boat inspections in the harbor.

SOMBRERO KEY TO KEY WEST
BIG PINE SHOAL LIGHT 22, On seaward edge of reef, 24 34.1N, 81 19.6W, Fl R 2.5s, 16ft., 6M, TR on dolphin.
LOOE KEY LIGHT 24, 24 32.8N, 81 24.2W, Fl R 4s, 20ft., 6M, TR on dolphin.
AMERICAN SHOAL LIGHT, 24 31.5N, 81 31.2W, Fl (3) W 15s (2R sectors), 109ft., 13M white, 10M red, Brown octagonal pyramidal skeleton tower enclosing white stair cylinder and brown ocagonal dwelling, Pile foundation. White from 270° to 067°, Red from 067° to 090°, Obscured from 090° to 125°, White from 125° to 242°, Red from 242° to 270°.
PELICAN SHOAL LIGHT 26, On seaward edge of reef, 24 30.3N, 81 36.0W, Fl R 6s, 20ft., 7M, TR on dolphin.
Eastern Sambo Daybeacon 28, 24 29.5N, 81 39.8W, TR on pile.
Western Sambo Daybeacon 30, 24 28.9N, 81 42.3W, TR on pile.
STOCK ISLAND APPROACH CHANNEL LIGHT 32, 24 28.4N, 81 44.5W, Fl R 2.5s, 19ft., 6M, TR on dolphin.
Key West Entrance Lighted Whistle Buoy KW, 24 27.7N, 81 48.1W, Mo (A) W, 6M, Red and white stripes with red spherical topmark.

HAWK CHANNEL: MOSER CHANNEL TO KEY WEST

MOSER CHANNEL
South Daybeacon 2, 24 41.1N, 81 10.0W, TR on pile.
South Daybeacon 4, TR on pile.
South Daybeacon 5, SG on pile.
South Daybeacon 6, TR on pile.

BAHIA HONDA KEY LIGHT 49A, 24 37.5N, 81 14.2W, Fl G 6s, 20ft., 6M, SG on piles.

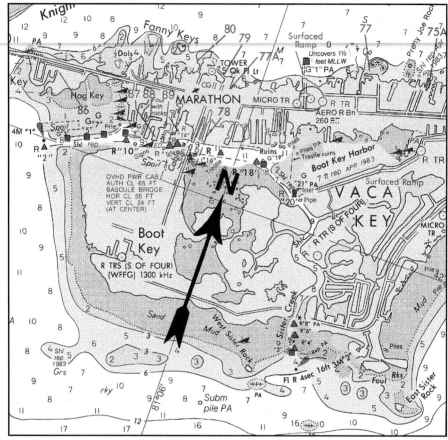

Marathon, Soundings in Feet

NEWFOUND HARBOR KEYS LIGHT 50,
24 36.8N, 81 23.6W, Fl R 2.5s, 16ft., 4M, TR on
pile.

NEWFOUND HARBOR CHANNEL
ENTRANCE LIGHT 2, 24 37.1N, 81 24.4W,
Fl R 4s, 16ft., 3M, TR on dolphin.
Daybeacon 3, SG on pile.
Daybeacon 4, TR on pile.
Daybeacon 5, SG on pile.
Daybeacon 6, TR on pile.
Daybeacon 8, TR on pile.

RAMROD KEY
Approach Daybeacon 2, TR on pile, Private
aid.
Shoal Daybeacon, 24 31.5N, 81 23.7W, NW
on pile worded SHOAL, Private aid.
Channel Daybeacon 1, SG on pile, Private aid.

Channel Daybeacon 2, TR on pile, Private aid.
Channel Daybeacon 3, SG on pile, Private aid.
Channel Daybeacon 5, SG on pile, Private aid.

NILES CHANNEL
Daybeacon 4, TR on pile.
Daybeacon 5, SG on pile.
Daybeacon 6, TR on pile.
North Shoal Daybeacon, NW on pile.
South Shoal Daybeacon, 24 39.7N, 81 25.9W,
NW on pile worded SHOAL.

TROPICAL MARINA
Daybeacon 2, TR on pile, Private aid.
Daybeacon 4, TR on pile, Private aid.
Daybeacon 6, TR on pile, Private aid.
Daybeacon 8, TR on pile, Private aid.
LOGGERHEAD KEY LIGHT 50A, 24 35.8N,
81 27.3W, Fl R 6s, 16ft., 4M, TR on pile.

KEMP CHANNEL
This channel is marked by a series of red and green private daymarks, numbered from 1 through 25. Near the end of the channel is an Obstruction Daybeacon, worded DANGER SUBMERGED PILES.

SUMMERLAND KEY
Daybeacon 1, 24 36.5N, 81 30.7W, SG on pile, Private aid.
Daybeacon 2, TR on pile, Private aid.
Daybeacon 4, TR on pile, Private aid.
Daybeacon 5, SG on pile, Private aid.

PIRATES COVE AND CUDJOE KEY
This channel is marked by a series of red and green daymarks numbered from 1 through 24. Numbers 11 through 24 are private aids.

NINEFOOT SHOAL LIGHT, 24 34.1N, 81 33.1W, Fl W 2.5s, 18ft., 6M, NG on dolphin.
West Washerwoman Daybeacon 51, 24 33.3N, 81 33.8W, SG on pile.
West Washerwoman Daybeacon 53, SG on pile.
Pelican Key Daybeacon 55, SG on pile.

SADDLEBUNCH HARBOR
Daybeacon 1, 24 34.5N, 81 37.6W, SG on pile, Private aid.

NOTE: This channel is marked by a series of red and green daymarks numbered from 1 through 18. These are private aids.

TAMARAC PARK CHANNEL
Obstruction East Daybeacon, NW on pile, Private aid.
Obstruction West Daybeacon, NW on pile, Private aid.
Daybeacon 1, SG on pile, Private aid.
Daybeacon 2, TR on pile, Private aid.
Daybeacon 3, SG on pile, Private aid.
Daybeacon 4, TR on pile, Private aid.
Daybeacon 6, TR on pile, Private aid.

BOCA CHICA LIGHT 56, 24 33.1N, 81 41.2W, Fl R 4s, 14ft., 3M, TR on pile.

STOCK ISLAND
APPROACH CHANNEL
LIGHT 32, 24 28.4N, 81 44.5W, Fl R 2.5s, 19ft., 6M, TR on dolphin.
Daybeacon 2, TR on pile.
HAWK CHANNEL LIGHT 57, 24 31.9N, 81 45.5W, Fl G 4s, 16ft., 4M, SG on dolphin.

BOCA CHICA CHANNEL
LIGHT 1, 24 32.8N, 81 43.6W, Fl G 4s, 16ft., 4M, SG on pile.
Daybeacon 2, TR on pile.
Daybeacon 3, SG on pile.
Daybeacon 4, TR on pile.
Daybeacon 5, SG on pile.
Daybeacon 6, TR on pile.
Daybeacon 7, SG on pile.
LIGHT 8, Fl R 4s, 16ft., 3M, TR on pile.
Daybeacon 9, SG on pile.
Daybeacon 10, TR on pile.
Daybeacon 11, SG on pile.
Daybeacon 12, TR on pile.
Daybeacon 13, SG on pile.
Daybeacon 14, TR on pile.
Daybeacon 15, SG on pile.
LIGHT 16, Fl R 4s, 16ft., 3M, TR on pile.
Daybeacon 17, SG on pile.

STOCK ISLAND EAST CHANNEL
A **Daybeacon 1A,** 24 33.3N, 81 43.4W, SG on pile, Private aid.
A **Daybeacon 3A,** SG on pile, Private aid.
A **Daybeacon 4A,** TR on pile, Private aid.
A **Daybeacon 5A,** SG on pile, Private aid.
B **Daybeacon 1B,** 24 33.7N, 81 43.1W, SG on pile, Private aid.
B **Daybeacon 2B,** TR on pile, Private aid.
B **Daybeacon 3B,** SG on pile, Private aid.
B **Daybeacon 4B,** TR on pile, Private aid.
B **Daybeacon 5B,** SG on pile, Private aid.
B **Daybeacon 6B,** TR on pile, Private aid.
B **Daybeacon 7B,** SG on pile, Private aid.

SAFE HARBOR CHANNEL
LIGHT 2, 24 32.5N, 81 43.9W, Fl R 4s, 16ft., 3M, TR on dolphin.
LIGHT 3, Fl G 6s, 16ft., 4M, SG on dolphin.
LIGHT 4, Fl R 2.5s, 16ft., 3M, TR on pile.
Daybeacon 5, SG on pile.

KEY WEST OCEANSIDE MARINA
This channel is marked by alternating red and green daybeacons numbered 1 through 9. These are private aids.

COW KEY CHANNEL
Daybeacon 1, 24 33.3N, 81 44.7W, SG on pile, Private aid.
This channel is marked by red and green daybeacons, with numbers from 1 to 20. These are private aids.

COW KEY WEST CHANNEL
Daybeacon 1A, 24 33.9N, 81 45.0W, SG on pile, Private aid.

Daybeacon 3A, SG on pile, Private aid.

CASA MARINA
Daybeacon 1, 24 32.4N, 81 47.4W, SG on pile, Private aid.
Daybeacon 2, TR on pile, Private aid.
Daybeacon 3, SG on pile, Private aid.
Daybeacon 4, TR on pile, Private aid.

KEY WEST HARBOR
MAIN CHANNEL
Entrance Lighted Whistle Buoy KW,
24 27.7N, 81 48.1W, Mo (A) W, 6M, Red and white stripes with red spherical topmark.
Lighted Bell Buoy 2, Fl R 4s, 3M, Red.
Lighted Buoy 3, Fl G 4s, 4M, Green.
RANGE (Front Light), 24 32.2N, 81 48.4W, Q G, Fl R 4s, 32ft., 3M red, KRW on skeleton tower on piles, Visible 2° each side of range-line, Passing light obscured from 326° to 026°. **(Rear Light),** 1,310 yards, 356° from front light, Iso G 6s, 75ft., KRW on skeleton tower on piles, Visible 2° each side of rangeline.
Lighted Bell Buoy 3A, 24 29.8N, 81 48.3W, Fl G 6s, 4M, Green.
EASTERN TRIANGLE LIGHT, 24 30.5N, 81 48.2W, Fl R 2.5s, 36ft., 5M, Red skeleton tower on piles.
Western Triangle Lighted Bell Buoy 5, At edge of shoal, Fl G 4s, 4M, Green.
Lighted Buoy 7, Fl G 4s, 4M, Green.
CUT A RANGE (Front Light), 24 33.2N, 81 50.0W, Q G, 44ft., KRW on tower on piles, Visible 2° each side of rangeline. **(Rear Light),** 1,000 yards, 325° from front light, Iso G 6s, 70ft., KRW on tower on piles, Visible 2° each side of rangeline.
Lighted Buoy 8, Q R, 3M, Red.
North Spoil Bank Buoy A, Yellow can.
Lighted Buoy 9, Fl G 4s, 4M, Green.
CUT B RANGE (Front Light), 24 33.6N, 81 48.9W, Q R, 25ft., KRW on tower, Visible 4° each side of rangeline. **(Rear Light),** 300 yards, 003° from front light, Iso R 6s, 40ft., KRW on tower, Visible 4° each side of rangeline.
Lighted Buoy 12, 24 32.0W, 81 48.9W, Q R, 3M, Red.
Lighted Buoy 13, Fl G 4s, 4M, Green.
Lighted Buoy 14, Q R, 3M, Red.
Lighted Buoy 15, Fl G 4s, 4M, Green.
KEY WEST HARBOR RANGE (Front Light), 24 34.7N, 81 48.0W, Q W, 16ft., KRW on dolphin, Visible all around, Higher intensity on range-line. **(Rear Light),** 775 yards, 024° from front light, Iso W 6s, 36ft., KRW on piles, Visible 4° each side of rangeline.
Buoy 17, Green can.

Buoy 19, Green can.
TRUMAN ANNEX BARRIER PIER LIGHT,
24 33.4N, 81 48.5W, F W, 5ft., On pier, Private aid.
Daybeacon 21, SG on pile.
Lighted Buoy 23, Fl G 2.5s, 3M, Green.
Lighted Buoy 24, Fl R 4s, 3M, Red.
Lighted Buoy 25, Fl G 4s, 3M, Red.
TURNING BASIN LIGHT 27, 24 34.0N, 81 48.5W, Fl G 4s, 16ft., 4M, SG on dolphin.
Turning Basin Lighted Buoy 29, Fl G 4s, 4M, Green.
Turning Basin Daybeacon 31, SG on pile.

KEY WEST
24 34N, 81 48W

Customs Reporting Station: A & B Marina.
U.S. Coast Guard: Key West Station located at Pier D2, N of main waterfront.
Customs: Port of Entry
Dockage: There is a marina in the old Truman Annex basin, and a couple in Key West Bight. Others are located in Garrison Bight.
Anchorage: The best anchorage is just east of Wisteria Island. There may be some room near Light 2, but the holding is poor and the area crowded with moorings. A public dinghy land-ing is SW of Light 2.
Fuel: Garrison Bight has fuel.
Repairs: Good. Haulout facilities.
Supplies: Good. Walking distance to most shops.

Key West is the final stop for boats cruising the Keys. It has several well marked approaches. The southern channel is the easiest. The NW channel is shallower and has several hazards, including a submerged breakwater. Study the chart well if using the NW channel after dark. The anchorage off of Wisteria Island offers poor shelter and holding, but is within dinghy distance of town. If bad weather threatens, you are better off in a marina or some other harbor. This is no place to be in a hurricane. Ashore is a collage of everything touristy and entertaining. Live music, tie-die shirts, open air bars and the Hemingway house all vie for your attention. There is always something interest-ing happening in Key West.

FLEMING KEY
RANGE (Front Daybeacon), 24 34.5N, 81 47.8W, KRW on dolphin, Maintained by U.S. Navy. **(Rear Daybeacon),** 45 yards, 256° from front daybeacon, KRW on dolphin, Main-tained by U.S. Navy.
Daybeacon 2, TR on pile, Maintained by U.S. Navy.

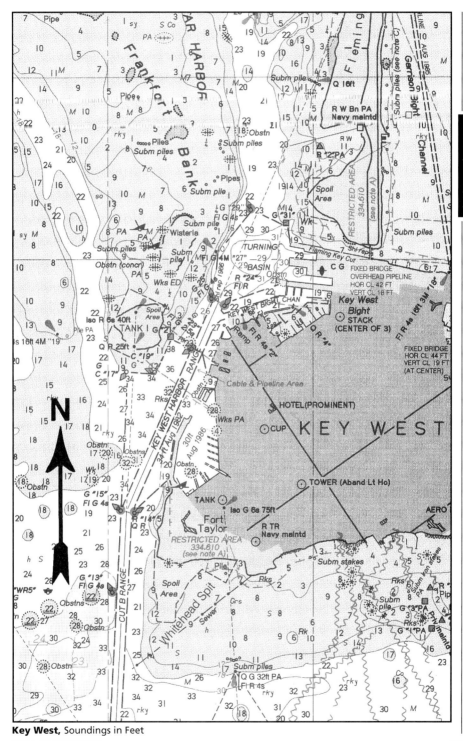

Key West, Soundings in Feet

KEY WEST BIGHT CHANNEL LIGHT 2, 24 33.7N, 81 48.3W, Fl R 4s, 16ft., 4M, TR on dolphin.
KEY WEST BIGHT CHANNEL LIGHT 4, Q R, 16ft., 4M, TR on dolphin.

GARRISON BIGHT CHANNEL
APPROACH LIGHT 2, 24 35.0N, 81 48.3W, Fl R 4s, 16ft., 3M, TR on pile.
LIGHT 3, Fl G 4s, 16ft., 4M, SG on pile.
Daybeacon 4, TR on pile.
Daybeacon 6, TR on pile.
LIGHT 8, Fl R 4s, 12ft., 3M, TR on pile.
Daybeacon 10, TR on pile.
Daybeacon 12, TR on pile.
LIGHT 13, Fl G 4s, 16ft., 4M, SG on dolphin.
Daybeacon 14, TR on pile.
LIGHT 16, Fl R 4s, 16ft., 3M, TR on pile.
LIGHT 17, Fl G 4s, 13ft., 4M, SG on pile.
LIGHT 18, Fl R 4s, 16ft., 3M, TR on pile.
Daybeacon 19, SG on pile.
Daybeacon 20, TR on pile.
LIGHT 21, Fl G 4s, 16ft., 4M, SG on pile.
Daybeacon 22, TR on pile.

GARRISON BIGHT CHANNEL TURNING BASIN
Daybeacon 24, 24 33.7N, 81 47.0W, TR on pile.
Daybeacon 25, SG on pile.
Daybeacon 26, TR on pile.
Daybeacon 27, SG on pile.
Daybeacon 29, SG on pile.

KEY WEST NORTHWEST CHANNEL
Entrance Lighted Bell Buoy 1, 24 38.8N, 81 54.0W, Fl G 2.5s, 4M, Green.
ENTRANCE RANGE (Front Light 6), 24 37.9N, 81 53.8W, Q R, 22ft., 5M, TR and KRW on piles, Visible all around. **(Rear Light),** 787 yards, 166° from front light, Iso R 6s, 36ft., KRW on triangular pyramidal structure on piles, Visible all around, Higher intensity on rangeline.
JETTY LIGHT, 24 38.4N, 81 53.6W, Fl W 6s, 18ft., 5M, NW on pile worded DANGER SUBMERGED JETTY.
Buoy 2, Red nun.
Buoy 3, Green can.
Buoy 4, Red nun.
Buoy 5, Green can.
Daybeacon 8, TR on pile.
Buoy 9, Green can.
LIGHT 10, 24 36.9N, 81 52.6W, Fl R 4s, 12ft., 3M, TR on pile.
Daybeacon 11, SG on pile.

LIGHT 12, 24 36.1N, 81 51.8W, Fl R 2.5s, 16ft., 3M, TR on pile.
LIGHT 14, Fl R 6s, 16ft., 3M, TR on pile.
Daybeacon 15, SG on pile.
LIGHT 15A, Fl G 4s, 14ft., 4M, SG on pile.
Daybeacon 16, TR on pile.
LIGHT 17, Fl G 2.5s, 16ft., 3M, SG on pile.
LIGHT 18, On east point of shoals, 24 33.4N, 81 49.7W, Fl R 2.5s, 36ft., 4M, TR on red triangular pyramidal skeleton structure on piles.
LIGHT 19, On southeast end of middle ground, Fl G 4s, 16ft., 4M, SG on pile.

LAKE PASSAGE CHANNEL
Daybeacon 1, 24 34.2N, 81 50.5W, SG on pile, Private aid.
NOTE: This channel is marked by a series of private red and green daymarks, with numbers between 1 and 18.

CALDA CHANNEL
LIGHT 1, 24 37.8N, 81 49.6W, Fl G 4s, 16ft., 4M, SG on pile.
Daybeacon 3, SG on pile.
Daybeacon 5, SG on pile.
Daybeacon 6, TR on pile.
Daybeacon 6A, TR on pile.
Daybeacon 8, TR on pile.
Daybeacon 9, SG on pile.
Daybeacon 11, SG on pile.
Daybeacon 12, TR on pile.
Daybeacon 13, SG on pile.
Daybeacon 14, TR on pile.
Shoal Daybeacon, 24 36.7N, 81 48.3W, NW on pile worded SHOAL.
Daybeacon 16, TR on pile.
Daybeacon 17, SG on pile.
Daybeacon 18, TR on pile.
Daybeacon 20, TR on pile.
Daybeacon 21, SG on pile.
Daybeacon 22, TR on pile.
Daybeacon 24, TR on pile.
Daybeacon 25, SG on pile.

SAND KEY CHANNEL
Daybeacon 2, 24 27.6N, 81 52.8W, TR on pile.
Middle Ground Daybeacon 3, 24 29.0N, 81 52.9W, SG on pile.
Preferred Channel Buoy, Red and green bands, Nun.

KEY WEST SOUTHWEST CHANNEL
Buoy A, 24 26.6N, 81 58.8W, Red and white stripes, Spherical buoy.
Buoy B, Red and white stripes, Spherical buoy.
Buoy C, Red and white stripes, Spherical buoy.

Buoy D, Red and white stripes, Spherical buoy.
Buoy 2, Red nun.
Buoy 3, Green can.
Buoy 4, Red nun.
Buoy E, Red and white stripes, Spherical buoy.
Buoy F, Red and white stripes, Spherical buoy.
Buoy G, Red and white stripes, Spherical buoy.
Wreck Lighted Buoy WR3, 24 32.8N, 81 49.6W, Q G, 3M, Green.

KEY WEST TO THE DRY TORTUGAS

SAND KEY LIGHT, 24 27.2N, 81 52.6W, Fl (2) W 15s, 40ft., 13M, NR on square skeleton tower.
Western Dry Rocks Daybeacon K, 24 26.8N, 81 55.6W, NB on pile.
Boca Grande Channel Daybeacon 1, 24 37.4N, 82 04.2W, SG on pile.
Boca Grande Channel Daybeacon 2, TR on pile.
Coalbin Rock Buoy CB, On south side of shoal, 24 27.0N, 82 05.3W, Red and green bands, Nun.
COSGROVE SHOAL LIGHT, 24 27.5N, 82 11.1W, Fl W 6s, 49ft., 9M, Small black house on red hexagonal skeleton tower on piles.
Marquesas Rock Buoy MR, On south side of reef, Red and green bands, Nun.
Twenty-Eight Foot Shoal Lighted Bell Buoy, On southwest side of shoal, 24 25.6N, 82 25.5W, Fl (2+1) R 6s, 4M, Red and green bands.
HALFMOON SHOAL LIGHT WR2, 24 33.5N, 82 28.5W, Fl R 6s, 19ft., 4M, TR on dolphin.
REBECCA SHOAL LIGHT, 24 34.7N, 82 35.2W, Fl W 6s, (R sector), 66ft., 9M white, 6M red, Square skeleton tower on brown pile foundation, Red from 254° to 302°.
DRY TORTUGAS LIGHT, 24 38.0N, 82 55.2W, Fl W 20s, 151ft., 24M, Conical tower, Lower half white, Upper half black, Emergency light of reduced intensity when main light is extinguished.
DRY TORTUGAS RADIOBEACON, 24 37.9N, 82 55.3W, OE (--- ·), 110ft., 286kHz, Whip antenna on platform 269 yards, 144° from Dry Tortugas Light.

NORTHWEST CHANNEL TO THE DRY TORTUGAS
SMITH SHOAL LIGHT, On northeast end of shoal, 24 43.2N, 81 55.0W, Fl W 6s, 47ft., 9M, Small black house on white hexagonal pyramidal skeleton tower on piles.

ELLIS ROCK LIGHT, 24 39.2N, 82 11.2W, Fl W 2.5s, 16ft., 3M, NB on dolphin.
NEW GROUND ROCKS LIGHT, 24 40.1N, 82 26.7W, Fl W 4s, 19ft., 7M, NB on pile.

DRY TORTUGAS

Lighted Buoy A, 24 34.0N, 82 54.0W, Fl Y 2.5s, 4M, Yellow.
Buoy B, Yellow can.
Lighted Buoy C, 24 34.0N, 82 58.0W, Fl Y 4s, 4M, Yellow.
Buoy D, Yellow can.
Lighted Buoy E, 24 39.0N, 82 58.0W, Fl Y 6s, 5M, Yellow.
Buoy F, Yellow can.
Buoy G, Yellow can.
Lighted Buoy H, 24 43.0N, 82 54.0W, Fl Y 2.5s, 4M, Yellow.
Lighted Buoy I, 24 43.5N, 82 52.0W, Fl Y 4s, 4M, Yellow.
Buoy J, Yellow can.
Lighted Buoy K, 24 43.5N, 82 48.0W, Fl Y 6s, 5M, Yellow.
Lighted Buoy L, 24 42.0N, 82 46.0W, Fl Y 2.5s, 4M, Yellow.
Lighted Buoy M, 24 40.0N, 82 46.0W, Fl Y 4s, 4M, Yellow.
Buoy N, Yellow can.
Lighted Buoy O, 24 37.0N, 82 48.0W, Fl Y 6s, 5M, Yellow.
Buoy P, Yellow can.
Buoy Q, Yellow can.
PULASKI SHOAL LIGHT, On east side of shoal, 24 41.6N, 82 46.4W, Fl W 6s, 49ft., 9M, Small black house on hexagonal pyramidal skeleton tower on piles.

SOUTHEAST CHANNEL
Daybeacon 1, SG on pile.
Lighted Buoy 2, Fl R 4s, 3M, Red.
LIGHT 3, 24 38.3N, 82 51.7W, Fl G 4s, 16ft., 4M, SG on dolphin.
Daybeacon 4, TR on pile.
Middle Ground Daybeacon, On east side of shoal, JR on pile.

EAST CHANNEL
Daybeacon 2, 24 38.1N, 82 52.5W, TR on pile.
Daybeacon 3, SG on pile.
Daybeacon 5, SG on pile.
Daybeacon 6, TR on pile.
Daybeacon 7, SG on pile.
Daybeacon 8, TR on pile.
Daybeacon 9, SG on pile.

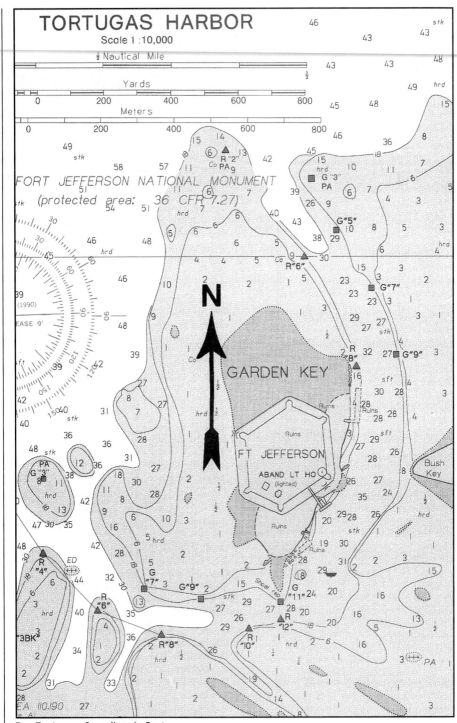

Dry Tortugas, Soundings in Feet

SOUTHWEST CHANNEL
Buoy 1, Green can.
Daybeacon 3, 24 37.6N, 82 54.5W, SG on pile.
Daybeacon 4, TR on pile.
Daybeacon 6, TR on pile.
White Shoal North Daybeacon 7, SG on pile.

WEST CHANNEL
Daybeacon 2, 24 37.7N, 82 52.9W TR on pile.
Daybeacon 3, SG on pile.
Daybeacon 4, TR on pile.
Daybeacon 6, TR on pile.
Daybeacon 7, SG on pile.
Daybeacon 8, TR on pile.
Daybeacon 9, SG on pile.
Daybeacon 10, TR on pile.
Daybeacon 11, SG on pile.
Daybeacon 12, TR on pile.

BIRD KEY HARBOR
Daybeacon 2BK, TR on pile.
Daybeacon 3BK, SG on pile.
Daybeacon 5BK, SG on pile.

DRY TORTUGAS
24 38N, 82 52W

U.S. Coast Guard: Key West station. Lighthouse keepers on Loggerhead Key on VHF channel 16.

National Park Service: Station located in Fort Jefferson. Call on VHF channel 16. They are in charge of the Fort Jefferson National Monument and surrounding waters.
Dockage: Temporary landings may be made at the National Park Service dock. No overnight dockage.
Anchorage: Directly east of Fort Jefferson and south of Bird Key. The surrounding shallows are not marked, but may be easily seen when the sun is high. The holding is good. Though there is no protection from high ground the shoals break up most seas. Dinghy ashore near the Park Service dock.
Fuel, Repairs, Supplies: None. There is no water available. All trash must be taken away.

The Dry Tortugas are a small slice of the Bahamas brought to the U.S. Beautiful sandy beaches and crystal clear water are your reward for the often rough 65 mile trip from Key West. The approaches are best made in daylight due to the many surrounding shoals that may be easily seen. Large areas of coral reef should be carefully avoided. A Coast Guard mooring may be available for those wishing to visit the 151ft. lighthouse on Loggerhead Key. Check ahead with the Coast Guard personnel stationed at the lighthouse.

Chapter 2

MIAMI, FLORIDA

HIGH & LOW WATER 1994 25°46'N 80°08'W

EASTERN STANDARD TIME, ADD 1 HOUR DAYLIGHT SAVING APRIL 3 - OCTOBER 29

JANUARY

Day	Time ft	Time ft	Time ft	Time ft
1 Sa	0405 -0.2	1023 2.8	1635 -0.1	2243 2.7
2 Su	0454 -0.1	1109 2.8	1725 -0.1	2337 2.6
3 M	0547 0.0	1200 2.7	1819 -0.1	
4 Tu	0037 2.6	0646 0.1	1256 2.6	1919 -0.1
5 W	0142 2.5	0749 0.2	1356 2.5	2022 -0.2
6 Th	0249 2.5	0857 0.3	1501 2.5	2127 -0.2
7 F	0357 2.6	1004 0.3	1605 2.5	2230 -0.3
8 Sa	0500 2.7	1107 0.2	1707 2.6	2329 -0.4
9 Su	0557 2.8	1205 0.1	1804 2.6	
10 M	0024 -0.5	0649 2.8	1257 -0.0	1857 2.6
11 Tu	0114 -0.5	0738 2.9	1346 -0.1	1947 2.7
12 W	0201 -0.5	0822 2.9	1432 -0.2	2033 2.7
13 Th	0246 -0.4	0905 2.8	1515 -0.2	2118 2.6
14 F	0329 -0.3	0946 2.7	1558 -0.2	2202 2.5
15 Sa	0411 -0.2	1026 2.6	1639 -0.1	2246 2.4
16 Su	0453 -0.0	1105 2.5	1721 -0.0	2331 2.3
17 M	0536 0.2	1145 2.3	1804 0.1	
18 Tu	0018 2.2	0621 0.3	1228 2.2	1850 0.1
19 W	0109 2.1	0710 0.4	1315 2.1	1940 0.2
20 Th	0205 2.0	0806 0.5	1406 2.0	2033 0.2
21 F	0303 2.0	0905 0.6	1502 2.0	2129 0.1
22 Sa	0401 2.1	1004 0.5	1558 2.0	2223 0.0
23 Su	0454 2.2	1058 0.4	1652 2.1	2314 -0.1
24 M	0543 2.3	1148 0.3	1743 2.2	
25 Tu	0002 -0.3	0628 2.5	1234 0.1	1832 2.4
26 W	0048 -0.4	0711 2.6	1318 -0.1	1918 2.5
27 Th	0133 -0.5	0753 2.7	1401 -0.3	2004 2.6
28 F	0218 -0.6	0835 2.8	1444 -0.4	2051 2.7
29 Sa	0303 -0.6	0918 2.8	1529 -0.5	2138 2.8
30 Su	0350 -0.5	1002 2.8	1615 -0.5	2228 2.7
31 M	0438 -0.4	1049 2.7	1705 -0.5	2322 2.6

FEBRUARY

Day	Time ft	Time ft	Time ft	Time ft
1 Tu	0530 -0.3	1139 2.6	1759 -0.5	
2 W	0019 2.5	0627 -0.1	1234 2.5	1857 -0.4
3 Th	0123 2.4	0730 0.1	1335 2.3	2002 -0.3 ☽
4 F	0231 2.4	0839 0.2	1442 2.3	2109 -0.3
5 Sa	0341 2.3	0949 0.2	1551 2.2	2216 -0.3
6 Su	0446 2.4	1055 0.1	1656 2.3	2317 -0.4
7 M	0544 2.5	1153 0.0	1754 2.4	
8 Tu	0012 -0.4	0635 2.5	1244 -0.1	1846 2.4
9 W	0101 -0.5	0721 2.6	1329 -0.2	1933 2.5
10 Th	0146 -0.5	0802 2.6	1411 -0.3	2016 2.5 ●
11 F	0227 -0.4	0840 2.6	1450 -0.3	2057 2.5
12 Sa	0305 -0.3	0917 2.6	1528 -0.3	2136 2.5
13 Su	0343 -0.2	0952 2.5	1604 -0.3	2215 2.4
14 M	0420 -0.1	1027 2.4	1641 -0.2	2255 2.3
15 Tu	0458 0.1	1103 2.2	1720 -0.1	2336 2.2
16 W	0539 0.2	1142 2.1	1801 -0.0	
17 Th	0022 2.1	0624 0.3	1225 2.0	1848 0.1
18 F	0113 2.0	0716 0.5	1315 1.9	1941 0.1 ☽
19 Sa	0212 2.0	0815 0.5	1413 1.9	2040 0.1
20 Su	0313 2.0	0918 0.5	1516 1.9	2142 0.1
21 M	0413 2.1	1019 0.4	1618 2.0	2240 -0.1
22 Tu	0507 2.2	1113 0.2	1715 2.2	2334 -0.2
23 W	0555 2.4	1203 -0.0	1808 2.4	
24 Th	0024 -0.4	0641 2.6	1250 -0.3	1857 2.6
25 F	0112 -0.5	0726 2.7	1335 -0.5	1945 2.8
26 Sa	0158 -0.6	0810 2.9	1421 -0.6	2033 2.9 ○
27 Su	0245 -0.6	0855 2.9	1507 -0.7	2122 3.0
28 M	0332 -0.6	0940 2.9	1555 -0.8	2212 2.9

MARCH

Day	Time ft	Time ft	Time ft	Time ft
1 Tu	0422 -0.5	1028 2.8	1645 -0.7	2305 2.8
2 W	0514 -0.3	1119 2.7	1739 -0.6	
3 Th	0002 2.7	0611 -0.1	1216 2.5	1838 -0.4
4 F	0104 2.5	0714 0.1	1318 2.3	1943 -0.2 ☽
5 Sa	0213 2.4	0823 0.2	1428 2.2	2053 -0.1
6 Su	0323 2.3	0934 0.2	1539 2.2	2201 -0.1
7 M	0429 2.3	1040 0.2	1645 2.3	2304 -0.1
8 Tu	0526 2.4	1137 0.1	1743 2.4	2358 -0.2
9 W	0615 2.5	1225 -0.1	1832 2.4	
10 Th	0044 -0.2	0658 2.5	1307 -0.2	1916 2.5
11 F	0126 -0.2	0736 2.6	1345 -0.2	1955 2.6
12 Sa	0204 -0.2	0811 2.6	1421 -0.3	2033 2.6 ●
13 Su	0240 -0.1	0845 2.5	1456 -0.2	2109 2.6
14 M	0315 -0.1	0918 2.5	1530 -0.2	2145 2.5
15 Tu	0350 0.0	0952 2.4	1605 -0.2	2222 2.4
16 W	0426 0.2	1026 2.3	1641 -0.1	2301 2.4
17 Th	0504 0.3	1103 2.2	1720 0.0	2343 2.3
18 F	0547 0.4	1144 2.1	1804 0.1	
19 Sa	0031 2.2	0636 0.5	1234 2.0	1857 0.2
20 Su	0126 2.1	0733 0.6	1333 2.0	1957 0.2
21 M	0227 2.1	0837 0.5	1440 2.1	2103 0.2
22 Tu	0329 2.2	0940 0.4	1547 2.2	2206 0.1
23 W	0427 2.3	1038 0.2	1648 2.4	2304 -0.1
24 Th	0520 2.5	1131 -0.1	1744 2.7	2358 -0.2
25 F	0610 2.7	1221 -0.3	1836 2.9	
26 Sa	0048 -0.4	0657 2.9	1309 -0.6	1926 3.1
27 Su	0137 -0.5	0744 3.0	1357 -0.7	2015 3.2
28 M	0225 -0.5	0831 3.1	1445 -0.8	2104 3.2
29 Tu	0314 -0.5	0919 3.1	1535 -0.8	2155 3.2
30 W	0405 -0.3	1009 2.9	1626 -0.6	2248 3.0
31 Th	0458 -0.2	1102 2.8	1720 -0.5	2345 2.8

APRIL

Day	Time ft	Time ft	Time ft	Time ft
1 F	0555 0.0	1159 2.6	1819 -0.2	
2 Sa	0046 2.7	0658 0.2	1303 2.4	1924 -0.0
3 Su	0152 2.5	0806 0.3	1413 2.3	2033 0.1 ☽
4 M	0259 2.4	0915 0.3	1524 2.3	2141 0.2
5 Tu	0403 2.4	1018 0.3	1629 2.4	2242 0.2
6 W	0458 2.4	1112 0.2	1724 2.4	2335 0.2
7 Th	0546 2.5	1158 0.1	1811 2.5	
8 F	0020 0.1	0627 2.5	1238 -0.0	1853 2.6
9 Sa	0100 0.1	0704 2.6	1315 -0.1	1931 2.7
10 Su	0137 0.1	0738 2.6	1350 -0.1	2007 2.7
11 M	0213 0.1	0812 2.6	1424 -0.1	2042 2.7 ●
12 Tu	0248 0.2	0845 2.5	1457 -0.1	2117 2.7
13 W	0323 0.2	0919 2.5	1532 -0.1	2154 2.6
14 Th	0359 0.3	0954 2.4	1608 -0.1	2231 2.5
15 F	0437 0.4	1032 2.3	1647 0.1	2312 2.5
16 Sa	0518 0.5	1116 2.2	1732 0.2	2358 2.4
17 Su	0606 0.6	1205 2.2	1823 0.3	
18 M	0050 2.3	0701 0.6	1304 2.2	1923 0.3
19 Tu	0148 2.3	0802 0.5	1411 2.2	2028 0.3
20 W	0249 2.4	0905 0.4	1519 2.4	2134 0.3
21 Th	0349 2.5	1005 0.1	1622 2.6	2235 0.1
22 F	0445 2.7	1100 -0.1	1719 2.8	2331 -0.0
23 Sa	0538 2.8	1153 -0.4	1814 3.1	
24 Su	0024 -0.2	0629 3.0	1244 -0.6	1906 3.2
25 M	0116 -0.3	0719 3.1	1334 -0.7	1957 3.3
26 Tu	0206 -0.3	0809 3.1	1425 -0.8	2047 3.4
27 W	0257 -0.3	0859 3.1	1515 -0.7	2139 3.3
28 Th	0349 -0.2	0951 3.0	1607 -0.6	2231 3.1
29 F	0442 -0.1	1045 2.8	1702 -0.4	2327 3.0
30 Sa	0539 0.1	1143 2.7	1800 -0.1	

TIME MERIDIAN 75°W
Heights in feet are referred to the chart datum of sounding.

0000h is midnight, 1200h is noon.

MIAMI, FLORIDA

HIGH & LOW WATER 1994

EASTERN STANDARD TIME, ADD 1 HOUR DAYLIGHT SAVING APRIL 3 - OCTOBER 29

MAY

Day	Time ft	Time ft	Time ft	Time ft
1 Su	0025 2.8	0639 0.2	1246 2.5	1902 0.1
2 M	0125 2.6	0743 0.3	1352 2.4	◑ 2007 0.3
3 Tu	0227 2.5	0846 0.3	1500 2.4	2111 0.4
4 W	0327 2.4	0946 0.3	1602 2.4	2211 0.4
5 Th	0420 2.4	1038 0.2	1656 2.4	2303 0.4
6 F	0507 2.4	1123 0.1	1743 2.5	2349 0.4
7 Sa	0549 2.5	1204 0.1	1824 2.6	
8 Su	0030 0.3	0628 2.5	1242 -0.0	1903 2.7
9 M	0108 0.3	0704 2.5	1317 -0.1	1940 2.7
10 Tu	0145 0.3	0740 2.5	1353 -0.1	● 2016 2.7
11 W	0222 0.3	0815 2.5	1428 -0.1	2052 2.7
12 Th	0258 0.2	0851 2.5	1505 -0.1	2129 2.7
13 F	0335 0.4	0929 2.4	1542 0.0	2207 2.6
14 Sa	0414 0.4	1009 2.4	1623 0.1	2247 2.6
15 Su	0456 0.4	1053 2.3	1708 0.2	2331 2.5
16 M	0543 0.4	1144 2.3	1758 0.2	
17 Tu	0000 2.4	0643 0.3	1243 2.3	1856 0.2
18 W	0115 2.4	0733 0.3	1347 2.4	◐ 1959 0.3
19 Th	0214 2.5	0834 0.2	1453 2.5	2104 0.3
20 F	0314 2.5	0934 -0.0	1557 2.7	2206 0.2
21 Sa	0412 2.7	1033 -0.2	1657 2.9	2306 0.1
22 Su	0509 2.8	1129 -0.4	1753 3.0	
23 M	0002 -0.1	0604 2.9	1222 -0.6	1847 3.2
24 Tu	0056 -0.2	0657 3.0	1315 -0.7	1940 3.3
25 W	0149 -0.2	0749 3.0	1407 -0.7	○ 2031 3.3
26 Th	0241 -0.2	0841 3.0	1458 -0.7	2122 3.2
27 F	0333 -0.2	0934 2.9	1550 -0.5	2213 3.1
28 Sa	0425 -0.1	1028 2.8	1643 -0.3	2305 2.9
29 Su	0519 -0.0	1124 2.6	1737 -0.1	2358 2.7
30 M	0615 0.1	1213 2.5	1834 0.1	
31 Tu	0053 2.6	0712 0.2	1323 2.4	1932 0.3

JUNE

Day	Time ft	Time ft	Time ft	Time ft
1 W	0148 2.4	0809 0.2	1425 2.3	◑ 2032 0.4
2 Th	0242 2.3	0904 0.2	1524 2.3	2129 0.6
3 F	0334 2.3	0956 0.2	1619 2.3	2223 0.5
4 Sa	0423 2.3	1043 0.1	1707 2.4	2311 0.5
5 Su	0507 2.3	1126 0.1	1752 2.5	2356 0.4
6 M	0550 2.3	1205 -0.0	1833 2.5	
7 Tu	0037 0.4	0630 2.4	1246 -0.1	1912 2.6
8 W	0117 0.3	0709 2.4	1324 -0.1	1950 2.7
9 Th	0156 0.3	0748 2.4	1403 -0.2	● 2028 2.7
10 F	0234 0.3	0828 2.4	1442 -0.2	2106 2.7
11 Sa	0313 0.2	0908 2.4	1521 -0.1	2145 2.6
12 Su	0353 0.2	0951 2.4	1603 -0.1	2225 2.6
13 M	0435 0.2	1037 2.4	1649 0.0	2308 2.6
14 Tu	0521 0.1	1128 2.4	1738 0.1	2355 2.5
15 W	0612 0.1	1224 2.4	1833 0.2	
16 Th	0047 2.5	0707 0.0	1325 2.4	1934 0.2
17 F	0144 2.5	0807 -0.1	1430 2.5	2038 0.2
18 Sa	0244 2.5	0909 -0.2	1535 2.6	2142 0.2
19 Su	0346 2.6	1010 -0.3	1638 2.7	2245 0.1
20 M	0446 2.7	1109 -0.5	1736 2.9	2344 -0.0
21 Tu	0544 2.7	1205 -0.6	1832 3.0	
22 W	0040 -0.1	0640 2.8	1259 -0.7	1925 3.1
23 Th	0133 -0.2	0734 2.9	1351 -0.7	○ 2015 3.1
24 F	0225 -0.2	0826 2.9	1442 -0.6	2105 3.0
25 Sa	0315 -0.2	0918 2.8	1532 -0.5	2153 2.9
26 Su	0405 -0.2	1009 2.7	1621 -0.3	2240 2.8
27 M	0454 -0.1	1101 2.6	1710 -0.1	2327 2.7
28 Tu	0543 -0.0	1153 2.4	1800 0.1	
29 W	0014 2.5	0634 0.1	1247 2.3	1852 0.3
30 Th	0103 2.4	0725 0.1	1342 2.2	◑ 1946 0.4

JULY

Day	Time ft	Time ft	Time ft	Time ft
1 F	0152 2.2	0816 0.2	1439 2.2	2041 0.5
2 Sa	0243 2.2	0908 0.2	1535 2.2	2137 0.6
3 Su	0334 2.1	0959 0.1	1627 2.2	2230 0.5
4 M	0424 2.1	1047 0.1	1716 2.3	2320 0.5
5 Tu	0512 2.2	1132 -0.0	1801 2.4	
6 W	0006 0.4	0558 2.3	1216 -0.1	1843 2.5
7 Th	0048 0.3	0641 2.3	1258 -0.2	1924 2.6
8 F	0129 0.2	0724 2.4	1339 -0.2	● 2003 2.7
9 Sa	0209 0.1	0806 2.5	1419 -0.3	2042 2.7
10 Su	0249 0.1	0849 2.5	1502 -0.3	2121 2.7
11 M	0330 -0.0	0934 2.6	1545 -0.2	2202 2.7
12 Tu	0413 -0.1	1020 2.6	1631 -0.1	2245 2.7
13 W	0459 -0.1	1111 2.6	1720 -0.0	2331 2.6
14 Th	0549 -0.1	1206 2.5	1813 0.1	
15 F	0023 2.6	0644 -0.2	1306 2.5	1912 0.3
16 Sa	0119 2.5	0744 -0.2	1410 2.5	2016 0.3
17 Su	0221 2.5	0848 -0.2	1517 2.0	2123 0.3
18 M	0326 2.5	0952 -0.3	1622 2.6	2229 0.2
19 Tu	0430 2.6	1054 -0.4	1723 2.8	2330 0.1
20 W	0531 2.7	1152 -0.4	1819 2.9	
21 Th	0027 0.0	0628 2.7	1247 -0.5	1911 2.9
22 F	0119 -0.1	0721 2.8	1338 -0.5	○ 1959 3.0
23 Sa	0208 -0.2	0812 2.8	1426 -0.4	2044 3.0
24 Su	0255 -0.2	0900 2.8	1512 -0.3	2128 2.9
25 M	0339 -0.2	0946 2.7	1556 -0.2	2210 2.8
26 Tu	0423 -0.1	1032 2.6	1640 -0.0	2251 2.7
27 W	0506 -0.0	1118 2.5	1724 0.2	2333 2.5
28 Th	0550 0.1	1206 2.4	1809 0.4	
29 F	0016 2.4	0636 0.2	1256 2.3	1858 0.5
30 Sa	0102 2.3	0725 0.3	1350 2.2	◑ 1951 0.6
31 Su	0152 2.2	0818 0.3	1447 2.2	2049 0.7

AUGUST

Day	Time ft	Time ft	Time ft	Time ft
1 M	0246 2.1	0912 0.3	1544 2.2	2148 0.7
2 Tu	0342 2.2	1007 0.3	1646 2.3	2242 0.6
3 W	0437 2.2	1058 0.2	1727 2.4	2332 0.5
4 Th	0528 2.3	1146 0.1	1812 2.6	
5 F	0018 0.4	0615 2.5	1232 -0.0	1854 2.7
6 Sa	0100 0.2	0701 2.6	1315 -0.1	1934 2.8
7 Su	0142 0.1	0745 2.8	1358 -0.2	● 2014 2.9
8 M	0223 -0.1	0830 2.9	1442 -0.2	2055 3.0
9 Tu	0305 -0.2	0915 2.9	1526 -0.2	2137 3.0
10 W	0350 -0.2	1003 3.0	1612 -0.1	2221 2.9
11 Th	0436 -0.2	1053 2.9	1701 0.0	2309 2.9
12 F	0527 -0.2	1147 2.9	1755 0.2	
13 Sa	0001 2.8	0623 -0.1	1247 2.8	1854 0.3
14 Su	0100 2.7	0725 -0.0	1353 2.7	◑ 2000 0.4
15 M	0205 2.6	0831 0.0	1502 2.7	2110 0.5
16 Tu	0314 2.6	0939 0.0	1609 2.7	2210 0.4
17 W	0421 2.7	1044 -0.0	1711 2.8	2320 0.3
18 Th	0523 2.8	1143 -0.1	1805 2.9	
19 F	0014 0.2	0619 2.9	1235 -0.1	1854 3.0
20 Sa	0103 0.1	0709 2.9	1323 -0.1	1939 3.0
21 Su	0148 0.0	0756 3.0	1407 -0.1	○ 2020 3.0
22 M	0230 0.0	0839 3.0	1448 0.0	2059 3.0
23 Tu	0310 0.0	0921 3.0	1528 0.1	2136 2.9
24 W	0349 0.1	1001 2.9	1607 0.3	2213 2.8
25 Th	0427 0.2	1042 2.8	1647 0.4	2251 2.7
26 F	0507 0.3	1125 2.7	1728 0.6	2330 2.6
27 Sa	0549 0.4	1210 2.5	1813 0.8	
28 Su	0014 2.5	0635 0.5	1301 2.4	1905 0.9
29 M	0104 2.4	0728 0.6	1358 2.4	◑ 2003 1.0
30 Tu	0201 2.3	0826 0.6	1458 2.4	2105 1.0
31 W	0303 2.2	0926 0.6	1556 2.5	2204 0.9

TIME MERIDIAN 75°W

Heights in feet are referred to the chart datum of sounding.

0000h is midnight, 1200h is noon.

MIAMI, FLORIDA

HIGH & LOW WATER 1994

25°46'N 80°08'W

EASTERN STANDARD TIME, ADD 1 HOUR DAYLIGHT SAVING APRIL 3 - OCTOBER 29

SEPTEMBER

Day	T1	ft	T2	ft	T3	ft	T4	ft
1 Th	0403	2.5	1023	0.5	1649	2.6	2257	0.7
2 F	0459	2.6	1116	0.4	1736	2.8	2344	0.5
3 Sa	0549	2.8	1204	0.2	1821	3.0		
4 Su	0029	0.3	0637	3.0	1250	0.1	1903	3.1
5 M	0112	0.1	0723	3.2	1335	0.0	1945	3.3
6 Tu	0156	-0.0	0809	3.4	1420	-0.0	2028	3.3
7 W	0240	-0.1	0856	3.4	1506	0.0	2112	3.3
8 Th	0326	-0.0	0944	3.4	1553	0.1	2159	3.3
9 F	0415	-0.1	1035	3.4	1644	0.3	2249	3.2
10 Sa	0507	-0.0	1130	3.4	1739	0.4	2343	3.1
11 Su	0604	0.1	1230	3.1	1840	0.6		
12 M	0045	2.9	0708	0.3	1337	3.0	1948	0.7
13 Tu	0153	2.8	0817	0.4	1447	2.9	2059	0.7
14 W	0305	2.8	0928	0.4	1554	2.9	2207	0.7
15 Th	0414	2.9	1033	0.4	1655	3.0	2306	0.6
16 F	0515	3.0	1130	0.4	1747	3.1	2358	0.5
17 Sa	0608	3.1	1220	0.4	1833	3.1		
18 Su	0043	0.4	0654	3.2	1305	0.4	1914	3.2
19 M	0124	0.3	0737	3.2	1345	0.4	1952	3.2
20 Tu	0202	0.3	0816	3.2	1423	0.4	2027	3.2
21 W	0239	0.3	0853	3.2	1500	0.5	2102	3.1
22 Th	0314	0.3	0931	3.2	1536	0.6	2137	3.0
23 F	0350	0.4	1008	3.1	1613	0.8	2212	2.9
24 Sa	0427	0.5	1048	3.0	1652	0.9	2250	2.8
25 Su	0506	0.6	1130	2.8	1735	1.0	2332	2.7
26 M	0551	0.8	1218	2.8	1824	1.1		
27 Tu	0022	2.6	0642	0.9	1312	2.7	1921	1.2
28 W	0120	2.6	0742	0.9	1412	2.7	2023	1.2
29 Th	0225	2.6	0845	0.9	1511	2.8	2123	1.0
30 F	0330	2.7	0947	0.8	1607	2.9	2219	0.9

OCTOBER

Day	T1	ft	T2	ft	T3	ft	T4	ft
1 Sa	0429	2.9	1043	0.7	1658	3.0	2310	0.6
2 Su	0522	3.2	1135	0.5	1745	3.2	2357	0.4
3 M	0612	3.4	1224	0.4	1831	3.4		
4 Tu	0044	0.2	0700	3.6	1311	0.0	1917	3.5
5 W	0130	-0.0	0748	3.8	1358	0.2	2002	3.6
6 Th	0216	-0.1	0837	3.8	1446	0.2	2049	3.6
7 F	0305	-0.1	0926	3.8	1535	0.3	2138	3.6
8 Sa	0355	-0.1	1018	3.7	1628	0.4	2231	3.4
9 Su	0449	0.1	1113	3.5	1724	0.6	2328	3.3
10 M	0547	0.3	1213	3.4	1826	0.7		
11 Tu	0031	3.1	0651	0.5	1319	3.2	1933	0.8
12 W	0141	3.0	0801	0.7	1427	3.1	2043	0.9
13 Th	0254	3.0	0911	0.7	1532	3.1	2149	0.8
14 F	0401	3.0	1015	0.8	1631	3.1	2246	0.7
15 Sa	0500	3.1	1111	0.7	1722	3.1	2335	0.6
16 Su	0551	3.2	1200	0.7	1806	3.2		
17 M	0018	0.5	0634	3.3	1242	0.7	1845	3.2
18 Tu	0057	0.5	0714	3.3	1321	0.7	1921	3.2
19 W	0133	0.4	0751	3.4	1357	0.7	1956	3.2
20 Th	0208	0.4	0827	3.3	1433	0.8	2030	3.1
21 F	0242	0.5	0903	3.3	1508	0.8	2104	3.1
22 Sa	0317	0.5	0939	3.2	1545	0.9	2140	3.0
23 Su	0353	0.6	1017	3.1	1623	1.0	2218	2.9
24 M	0432	0.7	1057	3.0	1705	1.1	2300	2.8
25 Tu	0515	0.8	1142	2.9	1751	1.2	2348	2.7
26 W	0605	0.9	1232	2.9	1844	1.2		
27 Th	0046	2.7	0702	1.0	1327	2.8	1943	1.1
28 F	0151	2.7	0806	1.0	1426	2.9	2043	1.0
29 Sa	0257	2.9	0910	0.9	1524	3.0	2141	0.8
30 Su	0358	3.1	1010	0.8	1619	3.1	2235	0.5
31 M	0455	3.3	1105	0.6	1711	3.3	2327	0.3

NOVEMBER

Day	T1	ft	T2	ft	T3	ft	T4	ft
1 Tu	0519	3.5	1157	0.5	1801	3.4		
2 W	0017	0.1	0639	3.7	1248	0.4	1850	3.6
3 Th	0106	-0.1	0729	3.8	1338	0.3	1939	3.6
4 F	0156	-0.2	0819	3.9	1428	0.2	2029	3.6
5 Sa	0246	-0.2	0910	3.8	1519	0.3	2121	3.6
6 Su	0338	-0.1	1002	3.7	1613	0.4	2215	3.4
7 M	0432	0.1	1057	3.6	1709	0.5	2313	3.3
8 Tu	0530	0.4	1154	3.4	1809	0.6		
9 W	0016	3.1	0632	0.5	1255	3.2	1913	0.7
10 Th	0123	3.0	0738	0.7	1359	3.1	2018	0.7
11 F	0232	2.9	0845	0.8	1500	3.0	2121	0.7
12 Sa	0338	2.9	0948	0.8	1557	2.9	2217	0.6
13 Su	0436	3.0	1044	0.8	1648	2.9	2305	0.6
14 M	0526	3.0	1132	0.8	1732	2.9	2348	0.5
15 Tu	0610	3.1	1215	0.8	1812	3.1		
16 W	0027	0.4	0649	3.1	1255	0.8	1850	3.0
17 Th	0104	0.4	0727	3.2	1332	0.7	1926	3.0
18 F	0139	0.3	0803	3.2	1408	0.7	2001	2.9
19 Sa	0215	0.3	0838	3.2	1444	0.8	2037	2.9
20 Su	0250	0.4	0915	3.1	1521	0.8	2114	2.8
21 M	0327	0.4	0952	3.1	1559	0.8	2153	2.8
22 Tu	0406	0.5	1030	3.0	1639	0.8	2235	2.7
23 W	0448	0.6	1112	2.9	1723	0.8	2323	2.7
24 Th	0535	0.7	1157	2.8	1812	0.8		
25 F	0018	2.6	0629	0.8	1248	2.8	1907	0.7
26 Sa	0119	2.7	0729	0.8	1344	2.8	2005	0.6
27 Su	0224	2.8	0833	0.8	1443	2.8	2105	0.5
28 M	0328	2.9	0937	0.7	1542	2.9	2204	0.2
29 Tu	0429	3.1	1037	0.5	1639	3.1	2300	0.0
30 W	0526	3.3	1133	0.4	1734	3.2	2354	-0.2

DECEMBER

Day	T1	ft	T2	ft	T3	ft	T4	ft
1 Th	0620	3.5	1228	0.2	1828	3.3		
2 F	0047	-0.4	0712	3.6	1320	0.1	1921	3.4
3 Sa	0139	-0.4	0803	3.6	1412	0.1	2013	3.4
4 Su	0231	-0.4	0854	3.6	1504	0.1	2106	3.3
5 M	0323	-0.3	0946	3.5	1557	0.1	2200	3.2
6 Tu	0416	-0.2	1038	3.3	1651	0.2	2256	3.0
7 W	0510	0.0	1131	3.1	1747	0.3	2355	2.9
8 Th	0607	0.3	1226	3.0	1844	0.3		
9 F	0057	2.7	0706	0.5	1322	2.8	1943	0.4
10 Sa	0200	2.6	0808	0.6	1419	2.7	2042	0.4
11 Su	0303	2.6	0909	0.7	1514	2.6	2137	0.4
12 M	0402	2.6	1006	0.7	1606	2.5	2228	0.4
13 Tu	0454	2.6	1058	0.7	1654	2.5	2314	0.3
14 W	0540	2.7	1145	0.7	1738	2.5	2356	0.2
15 Th	0622	2.7	1227	0.6	1819	2.6		
16 F	0035	0.1	0701	0.0	1307	0.6	1858	2.6
17 Sa	0114	0.1	0739	2.8	1345	0.5	1937	2.6
18 Su	0151	0.0	0816	2.9	1422	0.4	2015	2.6
19 M	0228	0.2	0852	2.8	1459	0.4	2054	2.6
20 Tu	0306	0.1	0928	2.8	1537	0.4	2134	2.6
21 W	0345	0.1	1006	2.8	1615	0.4	2216	2.6
22 Th	0427	0.2	1045	2.7	1657	0.3	2302	2.5
23 F	0512	0.3	1127	2.6	1743	0.3	2354	2.5
24 Sa	0602	0.3	1215	2.6	1835	0.2		
25 Su	0051	2.5	0659	0.4	1309	2.6	1932	0.1
26 M	0155	2.5	0801	0.4	1408	2.6	2034	0.0
27 Tu	0301	2.6	0907	0.4	1510	2.6	2136	-0.1
28 W	0405	2.7	1012	0.3	1613	2.7	2238	-0.3
29 Th	0506	2.9	1113	0.2	1714	2.8	2336	-0.5
30 F	0604	3.0	1211	0.0	1812	2.9		
31 Sa	0032	-0.6	0658	2.6	1306	-0.1	1907	3.0

TIME MERIDIAN 75°W
Heights in feet are referred to the chart datum of sounding.

0000h is midnight, 1200h is noon.

MIAMI HARBOR ENTRANCE, FL

CURRENT TABLES 1994   FLOOD 293° EBB 112°

EASTERN STANDARD TIME, ADD 1 HOUR DAYLIGHT SAVING APRIL 3 - OCTOBER 29

JANUARY

Day	Slack time	Max time	Fld knots	Ebb knots
1 Sa		0203		1.8
	0554	0821	2.1	
	1157	1433		1.8
	1824	2049	2.0	
2 Su	0018	0251		1.8
	0643	0913	2.1	
	1242	1520		1.9
	1915	2144	2.0	
3 M	0111	0343		1.7
	0738	1004	2.0	
	1331	1609		1.8
	2010	2236	2.0	
4 Tu	0209	0437		1.5
	0835	1054	1.9	
	1424	1702		1.7
	2107	2329	1.9	
5 W ◐	0310	0549		1.4
	0934	1147	1.7	
	1521	1829		1.6
	2205			
6 Th		0041	1.8	
	0413	0815		1.4
	1034	1257	1.5	
	1621	2025		1.7
	2304			
7 F		0237	1.9	
	0519	0915		1.5
	1136	1456	1.5	
	1723	2126		1.8
8 Sa	0005	0341	2.0	
	0624	1018		1.6
	1238	1603	1.6	
	1825	2232		1.9
9 Su	0103	0441	2.1	
	0721	1120		1.7
	1335	1703	1.8	
	1921	2334		2.0
10 M	0157	0534	2.2	
	0813	1212		1.9
	1428	1754	1.9	
	2014			
11 Tu ●		0025	2.0	
	0247	0620		2.3
	0901	1258	2.0	
	1518	1839		1.9
	2104			
12 W		0110	2.0	
	0335	0702		2.3
	0946	1341	2.0	
	1604	1921		1.9
	2153			
13 Th		0152	2.0	
	0420	0743		2.2
	1029	1423	1.9	
	1648	2004		1.9
	2240			
14 F		0234	1.8	
	0504	0825		2.0
	1109	1503	1.8	
	1731	2051		1.8
	2324			
15 Sa		0313	1.7	
	0546	0906		1.9
	1147	1536	1.7	
	1813	2133		1.7
16 Su	0007	0344		1.5
	0629	0916	1.7	
	1225	1552		1.6
	1857	2148	1.7	
17 M	0051	0351		1.4
	0715	0942	1.6	
	1305	1552		1.5
	1943	2210	1.6	
18 Tu	0138	0407		1.2
	0805	1019	1.5	
	1349	1617		1.4
	2032	2247	1.5	
19 W ◐	0228	0440		1.1
	0856	1100	1.4	
	1436	1654		1.3
	2122	2330	1.5	
20 Th	0321	0751		0.9
	0948	1145	1.2	
	1526	1742		1.2
	2050			
21 F		0022	1.4	
	0418	0844		0.9
	1043	1240	1.1	
	1620	2038		1.1
	2307			
22 Sa		0128	1.3	
	0345	0933		1.0
	1140	1343	1.1	
	1718	2114		1.2
23 Su	0003	0340	1.4	
	0615	1029		1.1
	1236	1446	1.1	
	1815	2219		1.2
24 M	0057	0436	1.5	
	0706	1123		1.2
	1328	1652	1.3	
	1908	2323		1.4
25 Tu	0147	0522	1.7	
	0753	1206		1.4
	1417	1732	1.5	
	1957			
26 W		0001	1.6	
	0234	0555		1.9
	0838	1237	1.5	
	1502	1750		1.7
	2045			
27 Th ○		0026	1.7	
	0320	0611		2.1
	0922	1257	1.7	
	1547	1818		1.9
	2135			
28 F		0050	1.9	
	0406	0639		2.2
	1007	1316	1.9	
	1631	1856		2.1
	2224			
29 Sa		0121	2.0	
	0451	0717		2.2
	1051	1345	2.0	
	1716	1941		2.2
	2313			
30 Su		0201	2.0	
	0536	0803		2.2
	1135	1424	2.1	
	1802	2033		2.2
31 M	0003	0248	1.9	
	0624	0855		2.2
	1220	1509	2.1	
	1852	2129		2.2

FEBRUARY

Day	Slack time	Max time	Fld knots	Ebb knots
1 Tu	0054	0338		1.8
	0717	0947	2.1	
	1308	1557		2.0
	1917	2201	2.1	
2 W	0149	0430		1.6
	0814	1036	1.9	
	1401	1648		1.8
	2044	2313	2.0	
3 Th ◐	0249	0545		1.4
	0912	1127	1.7	
	1458	1820		1.6
	2143			
4 F		0034	1.8	
	0351	0801		1.4
	1012	1238	1.5	
	1559	2018		1.7
	2243			
5 Sa		0221	1.8	
	0458	0903		1.5
	1115	1445	1.5	
	1704	2119		1.7
	2345			
6 Su		0324	1.8	
	0606	1002		1.6
	1218	1549	1.5	
	1809	2222		1.8
7 M	0045	0423	1.9	
	0705	1102		1.7
	1317	1648	1.7	
	1908	2322		1.9
8 Tu	0140	0517	2.0	
	0755	1155		1.8
	1410	1739	1.8	
	2001			
9 W		0012	1.9	
	0230	0603		2.1
	0840	1241	1.9	
	1457	1823		1.9
	2049			
10 Th ●		0056	2.0	
	0316	0644		2.1
	0922	1321	1.9	
	1542	1904		1.9
	2135			
11 F		0136	1.9	
	0359	0722		2.0
	1001	1359	1.9	
	1623	1941		1.9
	2218			
12 Sa		0214	1.8	
	0440	0755		1.9
	1039	1432	1.8	
	1702	2014		1.8
	2259			
13 Su		0246	1.7	
	0520	0759		1.8
	1115	1452	1.7	
	1741	2015		1.8
	2339			
14 M		0259	1.5	
	0600	0821		1.7
	1152	1444	1.6	
	1821	2047		1.8
15 Tu	0019	0258	1.4	
	0642	0901		1.6
	1230	1502	1.6	
	1904	2129		1.7
16 W	0102	0324		1.3
	0728	0944	1.6	
	1310	1535		1.5
	1930	2211	1.7	
17 Th	0148	0400		1.2
	0817	1026	1.5	
	1355	1614		1.4
	2041	2254	1.6	
18 F ◐	0239	0441		1.1
	0910	1111	1.3	
	1445	1659		1.3
	2133	2341	1.5	
19 Su	0334	0532		0.9
	0804	1201	1.2	
	1540	1754		1.2
	2228			
20 M		0038	1.4	
	0433	0852		0.9
	1101	1300	1.1	
	1640	1916		1.1
	2327			
21 Tu		0144	1.4	
	0534	0941		1.0
	1200	1406	1.2	
	1743	2040		1.2
22 W	0025	0346	1.4	
	0631	1039		1.2
	1256	1514	1.3	
	1841	2230		1.4
23 Th	0119	0448	1.7	
	0722	1129		1.4
	1346	1703	1.6	
	1934	2336		1.6
24 F	0209	0530	1.9	
	0808	1205		1.6
	1434	1740	1.9	
	2025			
25 Sa		0013	1.8	
	0257	0559		2.1
	0854	1233	1.9	
	1521	1810		2.2
	2116			
26 Su ○		0046	2.0	
	0345	0626		2.2
	0940	1259	2.1	
	1607	1845		2.3
	2206			
27 M		0119	2.1	
	0431	0702		2.3
	1026	1332	2.2	
	1653	1927		2.4
	2256			
28 Tu		0158	2.1	
	0517	0745		2.3
	1112	1411	2.2	
	1740	2017		2.4
	2346			

TIME MERIDIAN 75°W

0000h is midnight, 1200h is noon.

MIAMI HARBOR ENTRANCE, FL

CURRENT TABLES 1994 **FLOOD 293° EBB 112°**

EASTERN STANDARD TIME, ADD 1 HOUR DAYLIGHT SAVING APRIL 3 - OCTOBER 29

MARCH

Day	Slack time	Max time	Fld knots	Ebb knots
1 W		0245	2.0	
	0605	0836	2.2	
	1159	1458		2.2
	1830	2115	2.3	
2 Th	0036	0336		1.9
	0657	0931	2.1	
	1247	1547		2.0
	1924	2211	2.2	
3 F	0130	0429		1.7
	0753	1022	1.9	
	1340	1639		1.8
	2022	2304	2.0	
4 Sa ◑	0228	0605		1.4
	0852	1114	1.6	
	1438	1839		1.6
	2122			
5 Su		0041	1.8	
	0329	0745		1.4
	0952	1315	1.4	
	1540	2007		1.6
	2222			
6 M		0202	1.7	
	0434	0846		1.5
	1054	1429	1.4	
	1646	2107		1.6
	2323			
7 Tu		0304	1.7	
	0542	0942		1.6
	1157	1530	1.5	
	1755	2205		1.7
8 W	0024	0401	1.8	
	0643	1039		1.7
	1256	1627	1.6	
	1856	2303		1.8
9 Th	0120	0455	1.9	
	0731	1132		1.8
	1347	1719	1.8	
	1946	2354		1.8
10 F	0209	0542	1.9	
	0813	1218		1.9
	1433	1803	1.9	
	2031			
11 Sa		0038		1.9
	0254	0623	1.9	
	0852	1257		1.9
	1515	1842	2.0	
	2113			
12 Su ●		0117		1.8
	0336	0658	1.9	
	0929	1332		1.8
	1554	1915	1.9	
	2154			
13 M		0152		1.8
	0416	0726	1.8	
	1006	1359		1.7
	1632	1935	1.9	
	2233			
14 Tu		0219		1.6
	0454	0719	1.7	
	1043	1400		1.7
	1710	1935	1.9	
	2312			
15 W		0217		1.5
	0533	0745	1.7	
	1120	1357		1.6
	1748	2009	1.9	
	2350			
16 Th		0220		1.5
	0612	0825	1.6	
	1157	1423		1.6
	1828	2052	1.8	
17 F	0031	0250		1.4
	0655	0910	1.6	
	1237	1500		1.6
	1912	2138	1.8	
18 Sa	0114	0328		1.3
	0743	0956	1.5	
	1320	1542		1.5
	2002	2223	1.7	
19 Su	0203	0410		1.2
	0835	1042	1.4	
	1410	1627		1.4
	2057	2310	1.6	
20 M ◐	0256	0457		1.1
	0930	1131	1.3	
	1507	1719		1.2
	2153			
21 Tu		0002	1.5	
	0354	0557		1.0
	1026	1228	1.3	
	1608	1828		1.2
	2252			
22 W		0105	1.4	
	0454	0753		1.0
	1124	1334	1.3	
	1713	2010		1.2
	2352			
23 Th		0214	1.5	
	0553	0905		1.2
	1222	1444	1.5	
	1816	2124		1.4
24 F	0050	0330	1.6	
	0647	1016		1.5
	1315	1618	1.7	
	1912	2259		1.6
25 Sa	0143	0454	1.8	
	0737	1121		1.7
	1405	1719	2.1	
	2005	2353		1.9
26 Su	0233	0537	2.1	
	0824	1203		2.0
	1454	1759	2.4	
	2056			
27 M ○		0033		2.1
	0322	0612	2.2	
	0912	1239		2.2
	1542	1835	2.5	
	2147			
28 Tu		0111		2.2
	0410	0647	2.3	
	1000	1317		2.3
	1630	1915	2.6	
	2238			
29 W		0153		2.2
	0458	0729	2.3	
	1049	1358		2.3
	1718	2003	2.5	
	2328			
30 Th		0242		2.1
	0547	0819	2.2	
	1138	1447		2.2
	1808	2106	2.4	
31 F	0018	0336		1.9
	0638	0920	2.0	
	1228	1542		2.0
	1902	2210	2.2	

APRIL

Day	Slack time	Max time	Fld knots	Ebb knots
1 Sa	0110	0434		1.7
	0734	1020	1.8	
	1321	1641		1.8
	2000	2307	2.0	
2 Su	0206	0558		1.5
	0833	1123	1.6	
	1419	1828		1.6
	2059			
3 M ◐		0023	1.8	
	0305	0724		1.5
	0932	1259	1.5	
	1522	1950		1.5
	2158			
4 Tu		0137	1.6	
	0406	0824		1.5
	1032	1408	1.5	
	1628	2048		1.6
	2258			
5 W		0238	1.6	
	0509	0917		1.6
	1131	1507	1.5	
	1736	2142		1.6
	2358			
6 Th		0334	1.6	
	0609	1010		1.6
	1228	1602	1.6	
	1838	2238		1.6
7 F	0054	0427	1.7	
	0658	1103		1.7
	1318	1653	1.8	
	1927	2330		1.7
8 Sa	0143	0515	1.7	
	0739	1150		1.7
	1403	1738	1.9	
	2009			
9 Su		0015		1.7
	0228	0557	1.7	
	0817	1230		1.8
	1444	1817	1.9	
	2048			
10 M		0055		1.7
	0310	0633	1.7	
	0855	1304		1.7
	1524	1850	1.9	
	2127			
11 Tu ●		0129		1.7
	0350	0659	1.7	
	0933	1329		1.7
	1602	1905	1.9	
	2206			
12 W		0156		1.6
	0429	0650	1.6	
	1011	1321		1.6
	1640	1906	1.9	
	2245			
13 Th		0150		1.5
	0508	0716	1.6	
	1050	1325		1.6
	1718	1938	1.9	
	2324			
14 F		0152		1.6
	0547	0755	1.6	
	1128	1352		1.6
	1758	2020	1.9	
15 Sa	0004	0222		1.4
	0628	0840	1.5	
	1209	1431		1.6
	1840	2108	1.8	
16 Su	0046	0301		1.4
	0714	0929	1.5	
	1253	1515		1.5
	1929	2156	1.7	
17 M	0132	0345		1.3
	0805	1017	1.5	
	1343	1602		1.4
	2024	2243	1.7	
18 Tu	0223	0432		1.3
	0900	1106	1.5	
	1440	1653		1.3
	2122	2334	1.6	
19 W	0319	0527		1.2
	0955	1201	1.4	
	1542	1757		1.2
	2220			
20 Th		0032	1.5	
	0416	0647		1.2
	1051	1305	1.5	
	1647	1943		1.3
	2320			
21 F		0139	1.5	
	0515	0820		1.4
	1149	1417	1.7	
	1751	2102		1.5
22 Sa	0020	0247	1.6	
	0612	0917		1.6
	1245	1536	1.9	
	1850	2219		1.6
23 Su	0116	0403	1.8	
	0705	1026		1.8
	1337	1654	2.2	
	1944	2330		1.9
24 M	0208	0512	2.0	
	0755	1134		2.1
	1428	1744	2.5	
	2036			
25 Tu ○		0019		2.0
	0259	0557	2.2	
	0845	1221		2.2
	1518	1826	2.6	
	2128			
26 W		0103		2.1
	0349	0635	2.2	
	0936	1304		2.3
	1608	1907	2.6	
	2220			
27 Th		0147		2.2
	0439	0716	2.2	
	1027	1349		2.3
	1658	1955	2.5	
	2310			
28 F		0239		2.1
	0528	0808	2.1	
	1118	1442		2.2
	1748	2102	2.4	
	2400			
29 Sa		0335		1.9
	0619	0925	1.9	
	1209	1541		2.0
	1840	2204	2.2	
30 Su	0050	0432		1.8
	0714	1028	1.8	
	1302	1643		1.7
	1936	2258	2.0	

TIME MERIDIAN 75°W

0000h is midnight, 1200h is noon.

REED'S NAUTICAL ALMANAC

MIAMI HARBOR ENTRANCE, FL

CURRENT TABLES 1994   **FLOOD 293° EBB 112°**

EASTERN STANDARD TIME, ADD 1 HOUR DAYLIGHT SAVING APRIL 3 - OCTOBER 29

MAY

Day	Slack time	Max time	Fld knots	Ebb knots
1 M	0142	0538		1.6
	0811	1126	1.7	
	1400	1806		1.5
	2054	2337	1.7	
2 Tu ◐	0237	0655		1.5
	0900	1224	1.5	
	1500	1925		1.4
	2131			
3 W		0106	1.6	
	0333	0757		1.5
	1005	1341	1.5	
	1603	2024		1.5
	2228			
4 Th		0207	1.5	
	0429	0848		1.6
	1059	1438	1.5	
	1708	2115		1.5
	2325			
5		0302	1.5	
	0525	0937		1.6
	1153	1531	1.6	
	1809	2207		1.5
6 Sa	0021	0353	1.5	
	0616	1028		1.6
	1244	1622	1.7	
	1859	2300		1.5
7 Su	0112	0443	1.5	
	0701	1117		1.6
	1330	1709	1.8	
	1941	2349		1.6
8 M	0158	0529	1.5	
	0741	1201		1.6
	1412	1751	1.9	
	2021			
9 Tu		0031		1.6
	0241	0607	1.5	
	0820	1237		1.6
	1453	1825	1.9	
	2100			
10 W ●		0107		1.6
	0323	0635	1.5	
	0900	1303		1.6
	1534	1845	1.9	
	2140			
11 Th		0137		1.5
	0404	0626	1.5	
	0941	1257		1.5
	1614	1842	1.9	
	2220			
12 F		0141		1.4
	0444	0651	1.6	
	1022	1300		1.6
	1653	1913	1.9	
	2300			
13 Sa		0133		1.4
	0524	0729	1.6	
	1103	1329		1.6
	1733	1954	1.9	
	2340			
14 Su		0200		1.5
	0605	0814	1.6	
	1146	1408		1.6
	1815	2041	1.8	
15 M	0022	0240		1.5
	0649	0905	1.6	
	1231	1453		1.6
	1903	2131	1.8	
16 Tu	0106	0325		1.5
	0739	0956	1.6	
	1322	1542		1.5
	1937	2220	1.8	
17 W	0155	0413		1.5
	0000	1010	1.0	
	1419	1634		1.4
	2054	2310	1.7	
18 Th ◑	0248	0505		1.4
	0927	1138	1.6	
	1520	1734		1.3
	2152			
19 F		0004		1.6
	0343	0612	1.4	
	1022	1239		1.7
	1623	1916	1.3	
	2250			
20 Sa		0107		1.6
	0441	0747	1.6	
	1119	1352		1.8
	1727	2046	1.5	
	2351			
21 Su		0215		1.6
	0539	0850	1.8	
	1216	1514		2.0
	1828	2154	1.6	
22 M	0049	0326		1.8
	0636	0952	1.9	
	1312	1634		2.2
	1924	2310	1.8	
23 Tu	0144	0451		1.9
	0729	1111	2.1	
	1405	1731		2.4
	2017			
24 W		0007	2.0	
	0237	0546		2.0
	0821	1210	2.2	
	1457	1818		2.6
	2109			
25 Th ○		0055	2.1	
	0329	0631		2.1
	0914	1258	2.3	
	1548	1902		2.6
	2201			
26 F		0142	2.1	
	0420	0714		2.1
	1007	1345	2.2	
	1638	1951		2.5
	2252			
27 Sa		0233	2.1	
	0510	0810		2.0
	1059	1439	2.1	
	1728	2051		2.3
	2340			
28 Su		0326	2.0	
	0600	0919		1.9
	1151	1536	1.9	
	1818	2149		2.1
29 M	0027	0418	1.8	
	0651	1016		1.8
	1242	1632	1.7	
	1910	2238		2.0
30 Tu	0115	0511	1.7	
	0746	1106		1.7
	1336	1735	1.5	
	2005	2326		1.7
31 W	0204	0617	1.5	
	0840	1202		1.6
	1433	1851	1.4	
	2100			

JUNE

Day	Slack time	Max time	Fld knots	Ebb knots
1 Th ◐		0024	1.5	
	0254	0722		1.5
	0932	1305	1.5	
	1531	1954		1.3
	2154			
2 F		0128	1.4	
	0445	0813		1.3
	1023	1404	1.5	
	1629	2045		1.3
	2248			
3 Sa		0224	1.3	
	0437	0902		1.5
	1115	1456	1.5	
	1728	2134		1.3
	2343			
4 Su		0316	1.3	
	0529	0949		1.5
	1206	1547	1.6	
	1822	2227		1.3
5 M	0036	0407	1.3	
	0619	1040		1.5
	1255	1637	1.7	
	1909	2319		1.4
6 Tu	0126	0457	1.3	
	0705	1129		1.5
	1341	1723	1.8	
	1951			
7 W		0006		1.4
	0212	0540	1.4	
	0748	1211		1.5
	1424	1801	1.8	
	2032			
8 Th		0045		1.5
	0256	0613	1.4	
	0830	1242		1.5
	1507	1829	1.8	
	2114			
9 F ●		0118		1.4
	0339	0608	1.4	
	0913	1247		1.5
	1549	1825	1.9	
	2156			
10 Sa		0137		1.4
	0420	0631	1.5	
	0957	1246		1.5
	1630	1853	1.9	
	2237			
11 Su		0124		1.5
	0501	0708	1.6	
	1042	1314		1.6
	1712	1932	1.9	
	2318			
12 M		0146		1.5
	0542	0752	1.6	
	1127	1352		1.6
	1754	2018	1.9	
	2359			
13 Tu		0224		1.6
	0626	0843	1.7	
	1213	1437		1.6
	1840	2109	1.9	
14 W	0042	0308		1.6
	0714	0936	1.8	
	1303	1527		1.6
	1932	2159	1.9	
15 Th	0129	0356		1.7
	0807	1027	1.8	
	1359	1619		1.5
	2029	2248	1.8	
16 F ◐	0220	0446		1.7
	0901	1118	1.8	
	1458	1716		1.4
	2126	2339	1.7	
17 Sa	0314	0545		1.6
	0956	1216	1.8	
	1600	1850		1.3
	2224			
18 Su		0038	1.6	
	0411	0720		1.7
	1053	1330	1.9	
	1704	2039		1.4
	2324			
19 M		0148	1.6	
	0511	0836		1.8
	1152	1507	2.0	
	1807	2144		1.6
20 Tu	0025	0311	1.7	
	0611	0942		1.9
	1250	1620	2.2	
	1906	2257		1.7
21 W	0123	0439	1.8	
	0708	1103		2.0
	1346	1719	2.3	
	2000	2356		1.9
22 Th	0218	0538	1.9	
	0802	1204		2.1
	1438	1809	2.4	
	2052			
23 F ○		0046		2.0
	0310	0626	2.0	
	0855	1254		2.2
	1530	1854	2.5	
	2143			
24 Sa		0132		2.1
	0401	0712	2.0	
	0949	1341		2.1
	1620	1940	2.4	
	2232			
25 Su		0220		2.0
	0450	0802	2.0	
	1041	1431		2.0
	1707	2031	2.2	
	2317			
26 M		0309		2.0
	0538	0900	1.9	
	1131	1522		1.9
	1754	2125	2.1	
27 Tu	0001	0355		1.9
	0625	0953	1.8	
	1219	1610		1.7
	1842	2211	1.9	
28 W	0044	0438		1.7
	0714	1039	1.7	
	1308	1658		1.5
	1933	2250	1.7	
29 Th	0128	0525		1.5
	0805	1122	1.6	
	1359	1802		1.3
	2025	2306	1.5	
30 F ◐	0214	0631		1.4
	0855	1213	1.5	
	1452	1915		1.2
	2117	2330	1.3	

TIME MERIDIAN 75°W

0000h is midnight, 1200h is noon.

Chapter 2

MIAMI HARBOR ENTRANCE, FL

CURRENT TABLES 1994   FLOOD 293° EBB 112°

EASTERN STANDARD TIME, ADD 1 HOUR DAYLIGHT SAVING APRIL 3 - OCTOBER 29

JULY

Day	Slack time	Max time	Fld (knots)	Ebb (knots)
1 F	0302	0735		1.3
	0945	1319	1.4	
	1547	2012		1.2
	2209			
2 Sa	0057	0135	1.2	
	0351	0826		1.3
	1035	1417	1.4	
	1643	2101		1.2
3 Su		0234	1.1	
	0444	0911		1.3
	1127	1509	1.5	
	1740	2151		1.2
	2358			
4 M		0328	1.1	
	0538	0959		1.3
	1219	1602	1.5	
	1834	2246		1.2
5 Tu	0052	0422	1.2	
	0630	1054		1.3
	1309	1653	1.6	
	1921	2338		1.3
6 W	0141	0511	1.3	
	0718	1144		1.4
	1356	1737	1.7	
	2004			
7 Th		0021		1.4
	0227	0550	1.4	
	0804	1221		1.5
	1441	1810	1.8	
	2047			
8 F ●		0056		1.4
	0312	0607	1.5	
	0849	1242		1.5
	1525	1817	1.9	
	2130			
9 Sa		0119		1.5
	0355	0615	1.6	
	0935	1244		1.6
	1608	1837	2.0	
	2212			
10 Su		0119		1.6
	0437	0651	1.7	
	1022	1306		1.7
	1651	1913	2.0	
	2254			
11 M		0135		1.7
	0519	0733	1.8	
	1109	1342		1.7
	1734	1957	2.0	
	2335			
12 Tu		0209		1.8
	0602	0822	1.9	
	1156	1426		1.7
	1820	2046	2.0	
13 W	0018	0253		1.8
	0649	0916	2.0	
	1246	1515		1.7
	1910	2138	2.0	
14 Th	0104	0339		1.9
	0741	1008	2.0	
	1339	1606		1.6
	2005	2227	1.9	
15 F	0154	0428		1.8
	0836	1059	2.0	
	1437	1700		1.5
	2103	2317	1.8	
16 Sa ◑	0248	0524		1.7
	0933	1154	1.9	
	1538	1847		1.3
	2201			
17 Su		0013	1.6	
	0346	0709		1.7
	1031	1317	1.8	
	1642	2036		1.4
	2301			
18 M		0128	1.5	
	0448	0841		1.7
	1131	1502	1.9	
	1748	2138		1.5
19 Tu	0004	0321	1.6	
	0551	0948		1.8
	1232	1607	2.0	
	1849	2245		1.6
20 W	0104	0430	1.7	
	0652	1059		1.9
	1329	1706	2.2	
	1944	2344		1.8
21 Th	0200	0527	1.9	
	0747	1158		2.0
	1422	1756	2.3	
	2034			
22 F ○		0033		2.0
	0252	0616	2.0	
	0840	1247		2.1
	1512	1841	2.3	
	2122			
23 Sa		0118		2.0
	0342	0700	2.0	
	0932	1331		2.1
	1600	1923	2.3	
	2208			
24 Su		0201		2.0
	0428	0744	2.0	
	1022	1416		2.0
	1645	2007	2.1	
	2251			
25 M		0244		2.0
	0512	0832	1.9	
	1108	1500		1.8
	1729	2053	2.0	
	2331			
26 Tu		0324		1.8
	0556	0921	1.8	
	1153	1541		1.7
	1813	2135	1.8	
27 W	0010	0357		1.7
	0640	1002	1.8	
	1237	1614		1.5
	1859	2148	1.6	
28 Th	0051	0412		1.5
	0726	1021	1.7	
	1323	1628		1.3
	1948	2210	1.5	
29 F	0133	0418		1.4
	0815	1039	1.6	
	1412	1640		1.1
	2041	2247	1.4	
30 Sa ◐	0219	0445		1.3
	0905	1117	1.5	
	1504	1809		0.9
	2131	2329	1.2	
31 Su	0309	0648		1.1
	0955	1204	1.4	
	1558	2028		1.0
	2223			

AUGUST

Day	Slack time	Max time	Fld (knots)	Ebb (knots)
1 M		0020	1.1	
	0402	0835		1.1
	1048	1349	1.3	
	1656	2117		1.0
	2319			
2 Tu		0123	1.0	
	0346	0921		1.2
	1143	1524	1.4	
	1755	2210		1.1
3 W	0016	0340	1.1	
	0557	1015		1.2
	1238	1619	1.5	
	1848	2305		1.2
4 Th	0109	0439	1.2	
	0650	1113		1.3
	1329	1708	1.6	
	1934	2352		1.3
5 F	0158	0524	1.4	
	0739	1156		1.5
	1416	1747	1.8	
	2018			
6 Sa		0027		1.5
	0243	0554	1.6	
	0826	1226		1.6
	1501	1807	1.9	
	2101			
7 Su ●		0051		1.6
	0327	0604	1.8	
	0914	1242		1.7
	1546	1821	2.0	
	2144			
8 M		0101		1.7
	0410	0636	2.0	
	1002	1303		1.8
	1630	1855	2.1	
	2227			
9 Tu		0121		1.9
	0453	0716	2.1	
	1050	1335		1.9
	1714	1936	2.1	
	2310			
10 W		0154		2.0
	0537	0802	2.2	
	1138	1417		1.9
	1759	2024	2.1	
	2354			
11 Th		0236		2.0
	0624	0856	2.2	
	1227	1505		1.8
	1849	2117	2.0	
12 F	0041	0323		2.0
	0716	0950	2.1	
	1320	1555		1.7
	1943	2208	1.9	
13 Sa	0131	0413		1.9
	0813	1042	2.1	
	1417	1649		1.5
	2042	2258	1.8	
14 Su ◑	0227	0508		1.7
	0912	1137	1.9	
	1518	1915		1.3
	2141	2354	1.6	
15 M	0327	0733		1.6
	1011	1338	1.8	
	1622	2030		1.4
	2242			
16 Tu		0203	1.5	
	0430	0845		1.7
	1113	1451	1.8	
	1729	2129		1.5
	2346			
17 W		0315	1.5	
	0537	0947		1.8
	1215	1552	1.9	
	1833	2229		1.7
18 Th	0047	0417	1.7	
	0640	1050		1.9
	1312	1649	2.0	
	1927	2327		1.8
19 F	0143	0513	1.9	
	0736	1146		2.0
	1405	1739	2.1	
	2014			
20 Sa		0016		1.9
	0233	0601	2.0	
	0826	1234		2.0
	1453	1823	2.2	
	2058			
21 Su ○		0059		2.0
	0319	0643	2.0	
	0914	1316		2.0
	1539	1903	2.1	
	2140			
22 M		0138		2.0
	0403	0722	2.0	
	1000	1356		1.9
	1622	1939	2.0	
	2220			
23 Tu		0214		1.9
	0444	0800	2.0	
	1043	1434		1.8
	1703	2009	1.8	
	2258			
24 W		0245		1.8
	0524	0831	1.9	
	1124	1505		1.6
	1744	2011	1.7	
	2336			
25 Th		0255		1.6
	0604	0837	1.8	
	1205	1514		1.5
	1826	2046	1.6	
26 F	0014	0257		1.6
	0647	0915	1.7	
	1247	1520		1.3
	1911	2128	1.5	
27 Sa	0055	0324		1.5
	0733	0956	1.6	
	1332	1550		1.2
	2001	2211	1.4	
28 Su	0140	0401		1.4
	0824	1038	1.6	
	1422	1628		1.1
	2054	2255	1.3	
29 M ◐	0230	0443		1.2
	0917	1124	1.4	
	1516	1853		0.9
	2147	2343	1.2	
30 Tu	0324	0534		1.1
	0855	1217	1.3	
	1614	2044		0.9
	2243			
31 W		0040	1.1	
	0423	0846		1.1
	1108	1324	1.3	
	1710	2131		1.0
	2340			

TIME MERIDIAN 75°W   0000h is midnight, 1200h is noon.

MIAMI HARBOR ENTRANCE, FL

CURRENT TABLES 1994   **FLOOD 293°   EBB 112°**

EASTERN STANDARD TIME, ADD 1 HOUR DAYLIGHT SAVING APRIL 3 - OCTOBER 29

SEPTEMBER

Day	Slack time	Max time	Fld knots	Ebb knots
1 F		0148	1.1	
	0524	0931		1.2
	1205	1537	1.4	
	1811	2222		1.1
2 Sa	0036	0329	1.3	
	0623	1030		1.3
	1259	1631	1.5	
	1901	2312		1.3
3 Su	0126	0450	1.5	
	0715	1123		1.5
	1349	1715	1.7	
	1946	2349		1.5
4 M	0213	0527	1.8	
	0804	1201		1.7
	1436	1743	1.9	
	2030			
5 Tu ●		0015		1.7
	0258	0551	2.0	
	0852	1228		1.8
	1522	1803	2.1	
	2114			
6 W		0035		1.9
	0342	0621	2.2	
	0941	1255		2.0
	1607	1836	2.2	
	2159			
7 Th		0102		2.1
	0427	0659	2.4	
	1030	1328		2.0
	1653	1916	2.2	
	2245			
8 F		0137		2.2
	0513	0744	2.4	
	1119	1408		2.0
	1739	2003	2.2	
	2331			
9 Sa		0220		2.2
	0601	0836	2.3	
	1209	1457		1.9
	1829	2056	2.1	
10 Su	0019	0309		2.1
	0654	0934	2.2	
	1301	1550		1.7
	1923	2151	1.9	
11 M	0111	0402		1.9
	0751	1029	2.1	
	1357	1650		1.5
	2023	2244	1.7	
12 Tu ◑	0208	0503		1.7
	0852	1128	1.9	
	1458	1907		1.4
	2124	2344	1.5	
13 W	0310	0733		1.6
	0953	1326	1.7	
	1602	2017		1.5
	2225			
14 Th		0158	1.5	
	0416	0838		1.6
	1054	1434	1.7	
	1708	2113		1.6
	2328			
15 F		0302	1.6	
	0525	0936		1.7
	1156	1533	1.8	
	1812	2209		1.7
16 Sa	0028	0400	1.7	
	0630	1034		1.8
	1254	1628	1.9	
	1905	2304		1.8
17 Su	0122	0454	1.9	
	0725	1128		1.9
	1346	1718	2.0	
	1950	2353		1.9
18 M	0210	0541	2.0	
	0811	1216		1.9
	1432	1802	2.0	
	2030			
19 Tu O		0036		2.0
	0253	0622	2.1	
	0855	1257		1.9
	1516	1840	2.0	
	2109			
20 W		0113		1.9
	0334	0659	2.1	
	0936	1334		1.8
	1557	1912	1.9	
	2147			
21 Th		0144		1.8
	0414	0728	2.0	
	1016	1407		1.7
	1637	1920	1.7	
	2225			
22 F		0201		1.7
	0452	0727	1.9	
	1055	1428		1.6
	1716	1930	1.7	
	2303			
23 Sa		0152		1.6
	0531	0752	1.9	
	1134	1417		1.5
	1756	2007	1.6	
	2341			
24 Su		0210		1.6
	0611	0833	1.8	
	1215	1437		1.4
	1839	2051	1.5	
25 M	0021	0244		1.5
	0655	0919	1.7	
	1258	1513		1.3
	1926	2138	1.4	
26 Tu	0104	0325		1.4
	0745	1005	1.6	
	1345	1554		1.2
	2019	2225	1.3	
27 W	0154	0409		1.3
	0840	1052	1.5	
	1438	1639		1.1
	2114	2313	1.3	
28 Th ◐	0250	0459		1.2
	0936	1142	1.4	
	1534	1735		1.0
	1921			
29 F		0007	1.2	
	0351	0603		1.1
	1033	1241	1.3	
	1632	2047		1.0
	2305			
30 Sa		0111	1.2	
	0453	0844		1.1
	1131	1350	1.4	
	1730	2117		1.2

OCTOBER

Day	Slack time	Max time	Fld knots	Ebb knots
1 Su	0000	0223	1.4	
	0555	0927		1.3
	1228	1501	1.5	
	1824	2149		1.4
2 M	0053	0347	1.6	
	0651	1015		1.5
	1321	1623	1.7	
	1912	2246		1.6
3 Tu	0142	0453	1.9	
	0742	1129		1.7
	1410	1708	1.9	
	1958	2332		1.9
4 W	0229	0532	2.2	
	0831	1209		1.9
	1457	1743	2.1	
	2044			
5 Th ●		0008		2.1
	0316	0607	2.5	
	0920	1244		2.1
	1545	1819	2.2	
	2132			
6 F		0044		2.2
	0403	0645	2.6	
	1011	1320		2.1
	1632	1858	2.3	
	2220			
7 Sa		0123		2.3
	0451	0727	2.6	
	1101	1403		2.1
	1720	1944	2.2	
	2310			
8 Su		0207		2.2
	0540	0819	2.4	
	1151	1455		1.9
	1810	2038	2.0	
	2400			
9 M		0300		2.1
	0633	0924	2.3	
	1242	1554		1.8
	1905	2142	1.9	
10 Tu	0053	0400		1.9
	0730	1029	2.1	
	1337	1705		1.6
	2004	2245	1.7	
11 W ◑	0151	0520		1.6
	0831	1140	1.8	
	1436	1848		1.5
	2105			
12 Th		0020		1.5
	0254	0718	1.5	
	0932	1305		1.7
	1537	1957	1.6	
	2206			
13 F		0140		1.5
	0401	0823	1.6	
	1032	1411		1.7
	1640	2052	1.7	
	2305			
14 Sa		0241		1.6
	0510	0917	1.7	
	1132	1508		1.7
	1742	2144	1.7	
15 Su	0003	0337	1.7	
	0615	1012		1.7
	1230	1602	1.7	
	1835	2236		1.8
16 M	0056	0429	1.9	
	0708	1105		1.8
	1322	1652	1.8	
	1919	2326		1.8
17 Tu	0143	0517	2.0	
	0752	1154		1.8
	1408	1737	1.8	
	1958			
18 W		0010		1.8
	0225	0559	2.0	
	0832	1236		1.8
	1451	1816	1.8	
	2036			
19 Th O		0047		1.8
	0305	0635	2.0	
	0911	1313		1.7
	1532	1848	1.7	
	2114			
20 F		0117		1.7
	0344	0702	2.0	
	0950	1345		1.6
	1612	1851	1.6	
	2153			
21 Sa		0127		1.6
	0423	0658	1.9	
	1028	1402		1.5
	1651	1901	1.6	
	2232			
22 Su		0117		1.6
	0502	0722	1.9	
	1107	1346		1.4
	1730	1936	1.6	
	2311			
23 M		0138		1.6
	0541	0801	1.8	
	1147	1407		1.4
	1811	2020	1.5	
	2352			
24 Tu		0212		1.5
	0623	0847	1.7	
	1228	1443		1.4
	1856	2108	1.4	
25 W	0035	0255		1.5
	0710	0936	1.7	
	1313	1526		1.3
	1947	2158	1.4	
26 Th	0124	0342		1.4
	0804	1023	1.6	
	1403	1612		1.2
	2041	2247	1.4	
27 F ◐	0220	0431		1.3
	0901	1112	1.5	
	1456	1703		1.2
	2135	2338	1.2	
28 Sa	0321	0529		1.2
	0958	1206	1.4	
	1552	1809		1.2
	2229			
29 Su		0039	1.4	
	0423	0702		1.1
	1056	1309	1.4	
	1649	1955		1.3
	2325			
30 M		0148	1.6	
	0526	0845		1.3
	1155	1416	1.5	
	1746	2049		1.5
31 Tu	0020	0259	1.8	
	0626	0942		1.5
	1251	1519	1.7	
	1839	2140		1.7

TIME MERIDIAN 75°W   0000h is midnight, 1200h is noon.

MIAMI HARBOR ENTRANCE, FL

CURRENT TABLES 1994 **FLOOD 293° EBB 112°**

EASTERN STANDARD TIME, ADD 1 HOUR DAYLIGHT SAVING APRIL 3 - OCTOBER 29

NOVEMBER

Day	Slack time	Max time	Fld knots	Ebb knots
1 W	0112	0415	2.1	
	0719	1056		1.7
	1343	1627	1.9	
	1928	2247		1.9
2 Th	0202	0514	2.3	
	0810	1151		1.9
	1433	1723	2.1	
	2017	2346		2.2
3 F ●	0251	0557	2.5	
	0901	1234		2.1
	1523	1805	2.2	
	2107			
4 Sa		0032		2.3
	0341	0636	2.6	
	0952	1316		2.1
	1612	1845	2.2	
	2158			
5 Su		0115		2.3
	0431	0718	2.6	
	1043	1402		2.1
	1702	1931	2.2	
	2250			
6 M		0203		2.2
	0521	0811	2.4	
	1133	1458		2.0
	1752	2029	2.0	
	2342			
7 Tu		0301		2.1
	0613	0926	2.3	
	1223	1558		1.9
	1846	2153	1.9	
8 W	0036	0406		1.8
	0708	1029	2.1	
	1315	1701		1.7
	1944	2257	1.8	
9 Th	0133	0522		1.6
	0807	1127	1.9	
	1411	1819		1.6
	2043			
10 F ◐		0003	1.6	
	0235	0653		1.5
	0906	1235	1.7	
	1507	1930		1.6
	2141			
11 Sa		0114	1.6	
	0339	0759		1.5
	1004	1341	1.6	
	1604	2026		1.6
	2237			
12 Su		0215	1.6	
	0445	0853		1.5
	1102	1438	1.5	
	1701	2115		1.7
	2332			
13 M		0309	1.7	
	0549	0945		1.6
	1159	1531	1.5	
	1756	2205		1.7
14 Tu	0024	0401	1.8	
	0643	1038		1.6
	1252	1622	1.5	
	1843	2255		1.7
15 W	0112	0450	1.9	
	0727	1129		1.6
	1340	1710	1.6	
	1925	2342		1.7
16 Th	0155	0534	1.9	
	0807	1214		1.6
	1424	1752	1.6	
	2004			
17 F		0022		1.7
	0237	0612	1.9	
	0845	1253		1.6
	1506	1826	1.5	
	2043			
18 Sa ○		0055		1.6
	0317	0642	1.9	
	0924	1327		1.6
	1547	1840	1.5	
	2124			
19 Su		0111		1.6
	0357	0641	1.9	
	1004	1351		1.5
	1627	1839	1.5	
	2205			
20 M		0057		1.5
	0437	0659	1.9	
	1043	1334		1.4
	1707	1912	1.5	
	2246			
21 Tu		0116		1.6
	0516	0735	1.9	
	1123	1347		1.4
	1747	1954	1.5	
	2328			
22 W		0150		1.5
	0557	0819	1.8	
	1203	1421		1.4
	1830	2042	1.5	
23 Th	0012	0232		1.5
	0642	0909	1.8	
	1245	1503		1.4
	1918	2133	1.5	
24 F	0100	0319		1.5
	0733	0958	1.7	
	1331	1549		1.4
	2009	2223	1.6	
25 Sa	0154	0409		1.4
	0829	1046	1.7	
	1421	1638		1.4
	2103	2313	1.6	
26 Su ◑	0253	0503		1.3
	0926	1136	1.6	
	1515	1734		1.4
	2156			
27 M		0009	1.6	
	0355	0614		1.2
	1023	1234	1.5	
	1611	1853		1.5
	2251			
28 Tu		0115	1.7	
	0458	0810		1.3
	1122	1339	1.6	
	1709	2013		1.6
	2348			
29 W		0228	1.9	
	0600	0914		1.5
	1221	1445	1.7	
	1807	2110		1.8
30 Th	0045	0349	2.1	
	0657	1030		1.6
	1318	1556	1.8	
	1901	2219		2.0

DECEMBER

Day	Slack time	Max time	Fld knots	Ebb knots
1 F	0138	0500	2.3	
	0750	1137		1.8
	1411	1712	2.0	
	1954	2335		2.1
2 Sa ●	0231	0551	2.5	
	0842	1228		2.0
	1503	1802	2.1	
	2046			
3 Su		0028		2.3
	0322	0635	2.6	
	0934	1313		2.1
	1554	1845	2.2	
	2140			
4 M		0115		2.3
	0413	0719	2.6	
	1026	1401		2.1
	1644	1932	2.1	
	2233			
5 Tu		0205		2.2
	0503	0812	2.4	
	1115	1454		2.1
	1735	2039	2.0	
	2326			
6 W		0303		2.1
	0553	0917	2.3	
	1203	1548		2.0
	1826	2147	1.9	
7 Th	0018	0402		1.9
	0645	1013	2.1	
	1251	1641		1.8
	1920	2242	1.8	
8 F	0112	0501		1.6
	0740	1102	1.9	
	1340	1742		1.7
	2015	2336	1.7	
9 Sa ◐	0209	0617		1.4
	1431	1156	1.6	
	2110	1853		
10 Su		0038	1.6	
	0308	0729		1.4
	0932	1302	1.5	
	1523	1953		1.6
	2202			
11 M		0141	1.6	
	0408	0825		1.4
	1026	1403	1.4	
	1616	2043		1.5
	2254			
12 Tu		0236	1.6	
	0509	0915		1.4
	1122	1457	1.3	
	1710	2131		1.5
	2347			
13 W		0328	1.6	
	0608	1007		1.4
	1217	1549	1.3	
	1802	2221		1.5
14 Th	0038	0419	1.7	
	0657	1100		1.4
	1309	1640	1.3	
	1850	2313		1.5
15 F	0125	0507	1.8	
	0739	1149		1.5
	1356	1726	1.4	
	1934	2359		1.5
16 Sa	0209	0550	1.8	
	0820	1232		1.5
	1440	1806	1.4	
	2016			
17 Su		0036		1.5
	0252	0625	1.8	
	0900	1309		1.5
	1523	1833	1.5	
	2058			
18 M ○		0102		1.5
	0334	0643	1.8	
	0940	1339		1.5
	1604	1825	1.5	
	2142			
19 Tu		0057		1.5
	0415	0643	1.9	
	1020	1341		1.4
	1645	1853	1.6	
	2225			
20 W		0105		1.6
	0455	0715	1.9	
	1100	1336		1.5
	1725	1933	1.6	
	2309			
21 Th		0135		1.6
	0536	0756	1.9	
	1139	1404		1.6
	1806	2019	1.7	
	2353			
22 F		0215		1.6
	0618	0844	1.9	
	1220	1444		1.6
	1850	2110	1.7	
23 Sa	0039	0301		1.6
	0706	0933	1.8	
	1303	1528		1.7
	1939	2201	1.8	
24 Su	0131	0350		1.5
	0759	1021	1.8	
	1350	1615		1.7
	2032	2250	1.8	
25 M ◑	0227	0441		1.4
	0856	1110	1.7	
	1442	1707		1.6
	2126	2343	1.8	
26 Tu	0328	0543		1.3
	0953	1204	1.6	
	1538	1812		1.6
	2222			
27 W		0045	1.8	
	0430	0740		1.3
	1052	1307	1.6	
	1637	1945		1.7
	2321			
28 Th		0202	1.9	
	0535	0903		1.4
	1154	1417	1.6	
	1739	2056		1.8
29 F	0021	0340	2.0	
	0637	1018		1.6
	1254	1548	1.7	
	1839	2214		1.9
30 Sa	0118	0450	2.2	
	0733	1127		1.8
	1351	1708	1.9	
	1935	2334		2.1
31 Su	0213	0544	2.4	
	0826	1220		2.0
	1445	1801	2.0	
	2030			

TIME MERIDIAN 75°W 0000h is midnight, 1200h is noon.

KEY WEST, FLORIDA

HIGH & LOW WATER 1994 24°33′N 81°49′W

EASTERN STANDARD TIME, ADD 1 HOUR DAYLIGHT SAVING APRIL 3 - OCTOBER 29

JANUARY

Day	Time ft	Time ft	Time ft	Time ft
1 Sa	0547 -0.2	1227 1.3	1735 0.2	
16 Su	0004 1.5	0619 -0.0	1241 1.3	1854 0.1
2 Su	0008 1.7	0626 -0.1	1307 1.4	1835 0.2
17 M	0046 1.3	0653 0.1	1318 1.3	1931 0.2
3 M	0103 1.5	0708 0.0	1350 1.5	1945 0.2
18 Tu	0132 1.1	0727 0.2	1355 1.3	2035 0.2
4 Tu	0207 1.3	0753 0.2	1438 1.6	2103 0.1
19 W	0226 0.9	0805 0.3	1440 1.3	2147 0.2
5 W	0326 1.1	0844 0.3	1534 1.7	2223 0.0
20 Th	0337 0.8	0850 0.4	1533 1.4	2300 0.1
6 Th	0501 0.9	0942 0.4	1636 1.7	2338 -0.1
21 F	0509 0.7	0946 0.5	1634 1.4	
7 F	0631 0.9	1044 0.4	1742 1.8	
22 Sa	0004 0.0	0636 0.7	1047 0.5	1737 1.5
8 Sa	0044 -0.3	0739 0.9	1146 0.4	1845 1.9
23 Su	0058 -0.1	0735 0.8	1145 0.4	1835 1.6
9 Su	0140 -0.4	0832 1.0	1245 0.3	1942 2.0
24 M	0142 -0.2	0819 0.9	1237 0.4	1927 1.7
10 M	0229 -0.4	0917 1.0	1339 0.3	2034 2.0
25 Tu	0221 -0.3	0857 0.9	1326 0.3	2014 1.8
11 Tu	0314 -0.4	0956 1.1	1431 0.2	2121 2.0
26 W	0257 -0.4	0933 1.0	1412 0.2	2100 1.8
12 W	0355 -0.4	1032 1.1	1520 0.1	2204 1.9
27 Th	0332 -0.4	1007 1.1	1459 0.1	2144 1.8
13 Th	0433 -0.4	1106 1.2	1607 0.1	2245 1.8
28 F	0406 -0.4	1041 1.2	1547 -0.1	2229 1.8
14 F	0510 -0.3	1138 1.2	1655 0.1	2325 1.6
29 Sa	0441 -0.4	1116 1.3	1637 -0.2	2316 1.7
15 Sa	0545 -0.2	1209 1.3	1743 0.1	
30 Su	0517 -0.3	1151 1.4	1731 -0.2	
31 M	0005 1.5	0554 -0.2	1229 1.5	1829 -0.2

FEBRUARY

Day	Time ft	Time ft	Time ft	Time ft
1 Tu	0059 1.3	0633 -0.1	1311 1.6	1934 -0.2
16 W	0103 1.0	0632 0.2	1302 1.4	1945 0.0
2 W	0201 1.0	0717 0.1	1400 1.6	2047 -0.2
17 Th	0150 0.9	0703 0.3	1341 1.4	2049 0.1
3 Th	0318 0.8	0807 0.2	1458 1.6	2207 -0.2
18 F	0251 0.7	0740 0.4	1435 1.3	2205 0.1
4 F	0454 0.7	0908 0.3	1609 1.6	2326 -0.2
19 Sa	0416 0.7	0835 0.4	1539 1.3	2319 0.0
5 Sa	0624 0.7	1020 0.4	1727 1.6	
20 Su	0555 0.7	0952 0.5	1652 1.4	
6 Su	0034 -0.3	0730 0.8	1132 0.3	1839 1.7
21 M	0020 -0.1	0702 0.7	1109 0.4	1803 1.5
7 M	0130 -0.3	0819 0.9	1238 0.2	1940 1.7
22 Tu	0108 -0.2	0747 0.8	1213 0.3	1904 1.6
8 Tu	0216 -0.4	0859 1.0	1335 0.1	2031 1.7
23 W	0148 -0.3	0824 1.0	1309 0.2	1957 1.7
9 W	0256 -0.4	0933 1.1	1426 0.0	2115 1.7
24 Th	0224 -0.3	0858 1.1	1401 -0.0	2047 1.7
10 Th	0331 -0.3	1003 1.2	1513 -0.1	2155 1.7
25 F	0258 -0.4	0931 1.3	1450 -0.2	2135 1.7
11 F	0404 -0.3	1032 1.2	1557 -0.1	2232 1.6
26 Sa	0333 -0.3	1004 1.4	1540 -0.3	2223 1.7
12 Sa	0436 -0.2	1058 1.3	1640 -0.1	2308 1.4
27 Su	0408 -0.3	1039 1.6	1631 -0.5	2311 1.5
13 Su	0506 -0.1	1126 1.3	1722 -0.1	2344 1.3
28 M	0444 -0.2	1115 1.7	1724 -0.5	
14 M	0535 -0.0	1154 1.4	1806 -0.1	
15 Tu	0022 1.2	0604 0.1	1226 1.4	1852 -0.1

MARCH

Day	Time ft	Time ft	Time ft	Time ft
1 Tu	0002 1.3	0522 -0.1	1155 1.8	1820 -0.5
16 W	0003 1.2	0520 0.2	1144 1.5	1821 -0.1
2 W	0055 1.1	0602 0.0	1250 1.7	1921 -0.4
17 Th	0043 1.0	0547 0.3	1220 1.3	1907 -0.1
3 Th	0156 0.9	0647 0.2	1330 1.7	2031 -0.3
18 F	0128 0.9	0618 0.4	1300 1.5	2003 0.0
4 F	0310 0.8	0740 0.3	1432 1.6	2148 -0.2
19 Sa	0226 0.8	0655 0.5	1349 1.4	2111 0.1
5 Sa	0441 0.7	0848 0.4	1549 1.6	2307 -0.2
20 Su	0342 0.7	0751 0.5	1451 1.4	2225 0.1
6 Su	0607 0.8	1011 0.4	1717 1.5	
21 M	0510 0.8	0915 0.5	1609 1.4	2329 0.0
7 M	0014 -0.1	0709 0.9	1130 0.3	1834 1.5
22 Tu	0616 0.9	1043 0.5	1730 1.4	
8 Tu	0108 -0.0	0754 1.0	1237 0.2	1934 1.6
23 W	0020 -0.0	0702 1.0	1155 0.3	1840 1.5
9 W	0150 -0.1	0830 1.1	1333 0.1	2024 1.6
24 Th	0103 -0.1	0740 1.2	1256 0.1	1941 1.6
10 Th	0226 -0.1	0900 1.2	1422 -0.0	2106 1.5
25 F	0141 -0.1	0815 1.4	1350 -0.1	2035 1.6
11 F	0259 -0.1	0927 1.3	1505 -0.1	2143 1.5
26 Sa	0218 -0.1	0850 1.6	1441 -0.4	2127 1.6
12 Sa	0329 -0.1	0953 1.4	1545 -0.2	2218 1.4
27 Su	0255 -0.1	0926 1.8	1531 -0.5	2216 1.5
13 Su	0358 -0.0	1018 1.5	1623 -0.2	2252 1.3
28 M	0333 -0.0	1004 1.9	1622 -0.6	2306 1.4
14 M	0426 0.1	1044 1.5	1701 -0.2	2326 1.3
29 Tu	0412 0.0	1044 2.0	1714 -0.6	2356 1.3
15 Tu	0453 0.1	1113 1.6	1740 -0.2	
30 W	0452 0.1	1127 2.0	1808 -0.5	
31 Th	0050 1.1	0535 0.2	1214 2.0	1907 -0.4

APRIL

Day	Time ft	Time ft	Time ft	Time ft
1 F	0148 1.0	0624 0.3	1308 1.8	2013 -0.2
16 Sa	0116 1.0	0546 0.5	1227 1.6	1930 -0.0
2 Sa	0258 0.9	0723 0.4	1401 1.7	2124 -0.1
17 Su	0211 0.9	0630 0.6	1310 1.0	2028 0.1
3 Su	0418 0.9	0840 0.5	1530 1.5	2236 0.0
18 M	0315 0.9	0731 0.6	1415 1.5	2132 0.1
4 M	0534 1.0	1008 0.5	1700 1.5	2338 0.1
19 Tu	0424 1.0	0857 0.6	1532 1.4	2232 0.1
5 Tu	0632 1.1	1129 0.4	1819 1.4	
20 W	0523 1.1	1026 0.5	1658 1.4	2325 0.1
6 W	0029 0.1	0716 1.2	1234 0.2	1921 1.4
21 Th	0610 1.3	1141 0.3	1818 1.4	
7 Th	0110 0.1	0751 1.3	1327 0.1	2011 1.4
22 F	0012 0.1	0652 1.5	1243 0.0	1926 1.4
8 F	0146 0.1	0820 1.5	1412 -0.0	2052 1.4
23 Sa	0055 0.1	0731 1.7	1339 -0.2	2025 1.4
9 Sa	0218 0.2	0846 1.6	1452 -0.1	2129 1.4
24 Su	0136 0.2	0811 1.9	1431 -0.4	2119 1.5
10 Su	0249 0.2	0912 1.6	1530 -0.1	2203 1.3
25 M	0218 0.2	0852 2.1	1522 -0.6	2210 1.4
11 M	0318 0.2	0939 1.7	1606 -0.2	2237 1.3
26 Tu	0259 0.2	0935 2.2	1612 -0.6	2259 1.3
12 Tu	0346 0.3	1008 1.7	1641 -0.2	2312 1.2
27 W	0342 0.2	1019 2.2	1703 -0.6	2349 1.2
13 W	0414 0.3	1038 1.7	1718 -0.2	2349 1.2
28 Th	0427 0.3	1106 2.2	1756 -0.5	
14 Th	0442 0.4	1111 1.7	1757 -0.2	
29 F	0040 1.2	0515 0.3	1156 2.1	1852 -0.3
15 F	0030 1.1	0512 0.4	1147 1.7	1840 -0.1
30 Sa	0135 1.1	0609 0.4	1250 1.9	1950 -0.2

Chapter 2

TIME MERIDIAN 75°W
Heights in feet are referred to the chart datum of sounding.

0000h is midnight, 1200h is noon.

KEY WEST, FLORIDA

HIGH & LOW WATER 1994

24°33'N 81°49'W

EASTERN STANDARD TIME, ADD 1 HOUR DAYLIGHT SAVING APRIL 3 - OCTOBER 29

MAY

Day	Time ft	Time ft	Time ft	Time ft
1 Su	0236 1.1	0714 0.5	1352 1.7	2052 -0.0
16 M	0153 1.1	0618 0.6	1254 1.7	1952 0.0
2 M ◑	0342 1.1	0833 0.5	1504 1.5	2153 0.1
17 Tu	0245 1.1	0725 0.6	1352 1.5	2045 0.1
3 Tu	0447 1.2	1000 0.5	1629 1.4	2249 0.2
18 W ◐	0338 1.2	0847 0.6	1506 1.4	2138 0.2
4 W	0542 1.3	1118 0.4	1751 1.3	2339 0.3
19 Th	0429 1.3	1012 0.4	1633 1.3	2231 0.2
5 Th	0627 1.4	1222 0.3	1858 1.2	
20 F	0519 1.5	1127 0.2	1759 1.2	2321 0.3
6 F	0021 0.3	0703 1.5	1313 0.1	1951 1.2
21 Sa	0606 1.7	1231 -0.1	1914 1.2	
7 Sa	0059 0.4	0735 1.6	1357 -0.0	2034 1.2
22 Su	0010 0.3	0653 1.9	1328 -0.3	2016 1.3
8 Su	0134 0.4	0804 1.7	1437 -0.1	2112 1.2
23 M	0057 0.3	0739 2.1	1421 -0.5	2111 1.3
9 M	0206 0.4	0835 1.8	1513 -0.2	2148 1.2
24 Tu	0144 0.3	0827 2.2	1513 -0.6	2202 1.2
10 Tu ●	0238 0.4	0906 1.8	1549 -0.2	2223 1.2
25 W O	0231 0.3	0914 2.3	1602 -0.6	2250 1.2
11 W	0309 0.4	0938 1.9	1624 -0.2	2259 1.2
26 Th	0318 0.3	1003 2.3	1652 -0.5	2337 1.2
12 Th	0339 0.5	1012 1.9	1700 -0.2	2338 1.2
27 F	0408 0.3	1052 2.2	1741 -0.4	
13 F	0412 0.5	1047 1.9	1738 -0.2	
28 Sa	0024 1.2	0500 0.3	1141 2.1	1831 -0.3
14 Sa	0019 1.1	0447 0.5	1125 1.8	1819 -0.1
29 Su	0112 1.2	0557 0.4	1233 1.9	1921 -0.1
15 Su	0104 1.1	0528 0.6	1206 1.8	1904 -0.1
30 M	0203 1.2	0702 0.5	1328 1.6	2012 0.0
31 Tu	0255 1.3	0818 0.5	1431 1.4	2103 0.2

JUNE

Day	Time ft	Time ft	Time ft	Time ft
1 W ◑	0348 1.3	0939 0.5	1544 1.2	2153 0.3
16 Th ◐	0252 1.4	0837 0.4	1449 1.3	2050 0.2
2 Th	0440 1.4	1054 0.6	1707 1.1	2242 0.4
17 F	0341 1.6	0958 0.3	1615 1.1	2142 0.3
3 F	0527 1.5	1159 0.3	1824 1.1	2327 0.5
18 Sa	0433 1.7	1114 0.1	1747 1.1	2236 0.4
4 Sa	0609 1.6	1252 0.1	1925 1.1	
19 Su	0528 1.9	1220 -0.1	1906 1.0	2331 0.4
5 Su	0009 0.5	0648 1.7	1338 0.0	2012 1.1
20 M	0624 2.0	1319 -0.3	2010 1.1	
6 M	0048 0.5	0726 1.8	1418 -0.1	2053 1.1
21 Tu	0026 0.4	0719 2.2	1413 -0.4	2104 1.1
7 Tu	0126 0.5	0803 1.9	1456 -0.2	2130 1.1
22 W	0119 0.4	0812 2.3	1504 -0.5	2151 1.1
8 W	0201 0.5	0840 1.9	1532 -0.2	2207 1.1
23 Th O	0211 0.3	0904 2.3	1551 -0.5	2235 1.2
9 Th ●	0236 0.5	0917 2.0	1608 -0.2	2245 1.1
24 F	0303 0.3	0953 2.3	1637 -0.4	2317 1.2
10 F	0312 0.5	0954 2.0	1643 -0.2	2323 1.1
25 Sa	0355 0.3	1041 2.1	1720 -0.3	2358 1.3
11 Sa	0350 0.5	1031 1.9	1719 -0.2	
26 Su	0448 0.3	1127 2.0	1803 -0.2	
12 Su	0002 1.2	0431 0.5	1111 1.9	1757 -0.2
27 M	0039 1.3	0544 0.3	1214 1.8	1845 -0.0
13 M	0042 1.2	0518 0.5	1154 1.8	1836 -0.1
28 Tu	0120 1.4	0644 0.4	1302 1.6	1926 0.1
14 Tu	0124 1.2	0614 0.5	1242 1.7	1917 -0.0
29 W	0201 1.4	0751 0.4	1354 1.3	2009 0.3
15 W	0207 1.3	0720 0.5	1339 1.5	2002 0.1
30 Th ◑	0245 1.5	0904 0.4	1454 1.2	2053 0.4

JULY

Day	Time ft	Time ft	Time ft	Time ft
1 F	0331 1.5	1017 0.4	1609 1.0	2140 0.5
16 Sa ◐	0259 1.8	0943 0.2	1606 1.1	2101 0.4
2 Sa	0421 1.6	1125 0.3	1736 0.9	2229 0.5
17 Su	0358 1.9	1101 0.1	1741 1.0	2201 0.5
3 Su	0513 1.6	1224 0.2	1851 0.9	2318 0.6
18 M	0503 2.0	1211 -0.1	1901 1.0	2305 0.5
4 M	0604 1.7	1314 0.1	1946 1.0	
19 Tu	0609 2.1	1312 -0.2	2002 1.1	
5 Tu	0005 0.6	0652 1.8	1358 0.0	2030 1.0
20 W	0007 0.5	0711 2.2	1405 -0.2	2051 1.1
6 W	0049 0.6	0737 1.9	1437 -0.1	2109 1.1
21 Th	0107 0.4	0807 2.2	1452 -0.3	2134 1.2
7 Th	0131 0.5	0819 2.0	1513 -0.1	2146 1.1
22 F O	0202 0.4	0859 2.2	1535 -0.2	2212 1.3
8 F	0212 0.5	0859 2.0	1547 -0.2	2222 1.2
23 Sa	0255 0.3	0945 2.2	1614 -0.2	2249 1.4
9 Sa	0253 0.4	0939 2.0	1620 -0.2	2257 1.2
24 Su	0346 0.3	1029 2.1	1652 -0.1	2323 1.5
10 Su	0336 0.4	1020 2.0	1654 -0.2	2333 1.3
25 M	0436 0.3	1112 1.9	1728 0.0	2357 1.5
11 M	0422 0.4	1102 1.9	1728 -0.1	
26 Tu	0527 0.3	1153 1.7	1803 0.1	
12 Tu	0009 1.4	0512 0.3	1146 1.8	1804 -0.1
27 W	0030 1.6	0619 0.3	1234 1.6	1838 0.3
13 W	0046 1.5	0608 0.3	1236 1.6	1842 0.1
28 Th	0105 1.6	0716 0.4	1319 1.4	1914 0.4
14 Th	0125 1.6	0712 0.3	1332 1.4	1923 0.2
29 F	0144 1.6	0819 0.4	1410 1.2	1951 0.5
15 F	0209 1.7	0825 0.2	1440 1.2	2008 0.3
30 Sa ◐	0228 1.6	0930 0.4	1513 1.1	2034 0.6
31 Su	0320 1.7	1043 0.4	1638 1.0	2127 0.7

AUGUST

Day	Time ft	Time ft	Time ft	Time ft
1 M	0420 1.7	1150 0.4	1810 1.0	2228 0.7
16 Tu	0450 2.1	1201 0.2	1852 1.1	2254 0.7
2 Tu	0523 1.8	1247 0.3	1915 1.0	2327 0.7
17 W	0605 2.1	1301 0.1	1947 1.2	
3 W	0622 1.8	1333 0.2	2001 1.1	
18 Th	0003 0.6	0710 2.2	1350 0.1	2031 1.3
4 Th	0020 0.7	0713 1.9	1411 0.1	2040 1.2
19 F	0105 0.5	0806 2.2	1432 0.1	2108 1.5
5 F	0109 0.6	0800 2.0	1445 0.0	2115 1.3
20 Sa	0200 0.4	0854 2.2	1510 0.1	2142 1.6
6 Sa	0155 0.5	0844 2.1	1517 -0.0	2148 1.4
21 Su O	0250 0.3	0937 2.1	1544 0.2	2213 1.7
7 Su ●	0240 0.4	0926 2.1	1549 -0.0	2222 1.5
22 M	0337 0.3	1017 2.0	1617 0.2	2242 1.8
8 M	0326 0.3	1009 2.1	1621 0.0	2255 1.6
23 Tu	0422 0.3	1055 1.8	1649 0.3	2311 1.8
9 Tu	0414 0.2	1054 2.0	1655 0.1	2329 1.7
24 W	0506 0.3	1132 1.8	1720 0.4	2340 1.9
10 W	0505 0.2	1141 1.9	1730 0.2	
25 Th	0551 0.3	1209 1.6	1750 0.5	
11 Th	0005 1.8	0600 0.2	1231 1.7	1807 0.3
26 F	0013 1.9	0639 0.4	1249 1.5	1821 0.6
12 F	0045 1.9	0701 0.2	1328 1.4	1847 0.4
27 Sa	0050 1.9	0732 0.5	1335 1.3	1853 0.7
13 Sa	0131 2.0	0810 0.2	1436 1.2	1934 0.5
28 Su	0133 1.8	0837 0.6	1432 1.2	1932 0.8
14 Su ◑	0226 2.0	0928 0.2	1602 1.1	2031 0.6
29 M ●	0225 1.8	0953 0.6	1550 1.1	2026 0.9
15 M	0333 2.1	1049 0.2	1737 1.1	2140 0.7
30 Tu	0329 1.8	1108 0.6	1725 1.1	2141 0.9
31 W	0441 1.8	1209 0.6	1837 1.2	2255 0.9

TIME MERIDIAN 75°W

0000h is midnight, 1200h is noon.

Heights in feet are referred to the chart datum of sounding.

REED'S NAUTICAL ALMANAC

KEY WEST, FLORIDA

HIGH & LOW WATER 1994

24°33'N 81°49'W

EASTERN STANDARD TIME, ADD 1 HOUR DAYLIGHT SAVING APRIL 3 - OCTOBER 29

SEPTEMBER

Day	Time / ft	Time / ft	Time / ft	Time / ft
1 Th	0550 1.9	1256 0.4	1924 1.3	2358 0.8
16 F	0007 0.7	0707 2.1	1324 0.4	2002 1.7
2 F	0009 1.0	1334 0.3	2001 1.4	
17 Sa	0107 0.6	0801 2.1	1402 0.4	2036 1.8
3 Sa	0052 0.7	0740 2.1	1407 0.3	2035 1.6
18 Su	0158 0.5	0847 2.1	1436 0.5	2106 1.9
4 Su	0141 0.5	0828 2.2	1439 0.3	2107 1.7
19 M	0243 0.4	0927 2.1	1508 0.5	2133 2.0
5 M	0229 0.4	0914 2.2	1511 0.3	2140 1.9
20 Tu	0325 0.3	1003 2.0	1539 0.6	2200 2.1
6 Tu	0316 0.2	1000 2.1	1545 0.3	2214 2.0
21 W	0405 0.3	1038 1.9	1609 0.6	2227 2.1
7 W	0405 0.1	1047 2.0	1619 0.4	2249 2.2
22 Th	0445 0.3	1112 1.8	1638 0.7	2256 2.1
8 Th	0455 0.1	1135 1.9	1656 0.5	2328 2.3
23 F	0524 0.4	1148 1.7	1706 0.8	2329 2.1
9 F	0549 0.1	1226 1.7	1734 0.6	
24 Sa	0606 0.4	1227 1.6	1735 0.8	
10 Sa	0011 2.3	0649 0.1	1324 1.5	1818 0.7
25 Su	0006 2.1	0653 0.5	1311 1.5	1807 0.9
11 Su	0102 2.3	0756 0.2	1432 1.4	1908 0.8
26 M	0048 2.0	0749 0.6	1405 1.4	1845 1.0
12 M	0202 2.2	0912 0.3	1556 1.3	2013 0.9
27 Tu	0139 2.0	0858 0.7	1516 1.3	1940 1.1
13 Tu	0316 2.2	1032 0.4	1723 1.3	2134 0.9
28 W	0242 1.9	1013 0.7	1641 1.3	2103 1.1
14 W	0442 2.1	1142 0.4	1832 1.4	2256 0.8
29 Th	0357 1.9	1116 0.7	1750 1.4	2229 1.0
15 Th	0602 2.1	1239 0.4	1922 1.5	
30 F	0514 1.9	1205 0.6	1837 1.5	2339 0.9

OCTOBER

Day	Time / ft	Time / ft	Time / ft	Time / ft
1 Sa	0622 2.0	1245 0.6	1916 1.7	
16 Su	0104 0.6	0751 2.0	1324 0.7	1958 2.0
2 Su	0037 0.7	0700 2.1	1321 0.5	1950 1.9
17 M	0152 0.5	1358 0.7	2027 2.1	
3 M	0128 0.5	0813 2.1	1356 0.5	2024 2.1
18 Tu	0233 0.4	0915 2.0	1430 0.7	2054 2.2
4 Tu	0217 0.3	0903 2.1	1431 0.5	2059 2.3
19 W	0312 0.3	0949 1.9	1501 0.8	2122 2.2
5 W	0306 0.1	0951 2.1	1507 0.6	2136 2.4
20 Th	0349 0.3	1023 1.8	1531 0.8	2151 2.2
6 Th	0354 -0.0	1039 2.0	1545 0.6	2216 2.5
21 F	0425 0.3	1056 1.7	1600 0.8	2222 2.2
7 F	0445 -0.1	1129 1.9	1625 0.7	2259 2.6
22 Sa	0502 0.3	1131 1.7	1629 0.9	2256 2.2
8 Sa	0538 0.0	1220 1.7	1708 0.7	2347 2.5
23 Su	0541 0.4	1210 1.6	1700 0.9	2333 2.2
9 Su	0636 0.1	1317 1.6	1755 0.8	
24 M	0624 0.5	1254 1.5	1734 1.0	
10 M	0041 2.4	0740 0.3	1422 1.4	1853 0.9
25 Tu	0014 2.1	0712 0.5	1346 1.4	1815 1.0
11 Tu	0144 2.3	0851 0.4	1538 1.4	2006 1.0
26 W	0102 2.0	0809 0.6	1447 1.4	1914 1.1
12 W	0301 2.1	1003 0.3	1655 1.5	2134 1.0
27 Th	0201 1.9	0911 0.7	1553 1.4	2037 1.1
13 Th	0429 2.0	1109 0.6	1758 1.6	2259 0.9
28 F	0315 1.9	1011 0.7	1653 1.5	2206 1.0
14 F	0551 2.0	1203 0.6	1846 1.7	
29 Sa	0437 1.8	1104 0.7	1743 1.7	2320 0.8
15 Sa	0008 0.7	0658 2.0	1246 0.7	1925 1.9
30 Su	0555 1.8	1149 0.7	1825 1.9	
31 M	0021 0.5	0702 1.9	1231 0.7	1904 2.1

NOVEMBER

Day	Time / ft	Time / ft	Time / ft	Time / ft
1 Tu	0115 0.3	0800 1.9	1312 0.7	1944 2.0
16 W	0220 0.2	0901 1.6	1353 0.7	2009 2.1
2 W	0206 0.0	0853 1.9	1352 0.6	2025 2.5
17 Th	0258 0.2	0935 1.6	1426 0.7	2052 2.2
3 Th	0255 -0.1	0943 1.8	1434 0.6	2107 2.6
18 F	0334 0.1	1008 1.6	1458 0.7	2125 2.2
4 F	0345 -0.2	1032 1.8	1516 0.6	2152 2.7
19 Sa	0409 0.1	1042 1.5	1529 0.7	2159 2.2
5 Sa	0435 -0.2	1121 1.7	1600 0.6	2240 2.6
20 Su	0445 0.1	1118 1.5	1601 0.8	2234 2.1
6 Su	0527 -0.1	1211 1.6	1648 0.7	2330 2.5
21 M	0521 0.2	1156 1.4	1635 0.8	2311 2.1
7 M	0621 0.0	1303 1.5	1741 0.7	
22 Tu	0600 0.2	1238 1.4	1714 0.8	2352 2.0
8 Tu	0026 2.4	0719 0.2	1401 1.5	1844 0.8
23 W	0641 0.3	1323 1.4	1801 0.8	
9 W	0127 2.2	0820 0.4	1505 1.5	2001 0.9
24 Th	0037 1.9	0726 0.4	1412 1.4	1901 0.8
10 Th	0240 1.9	0923 0.5	1611 1.6	2128 0.8
25 F	0132 1.8	0816 0.5	1503 1.4	2018 0.8
11 F	0404 1.8	1022 0.6	1710 1.7	2251 0.7
26 Sa	0240 1.6	0908 0.5	1555 1.5	2142 0.7
12 Sa	0529 1.7	1114 0.7	1800 1.8	2359 0.6
27 Su	0404 1.5	1001 0.6	1645 1.7	2259 0.5
13 Su	0640 1.6	1200 0.7	1842 1.9	
28 M	0531 1.5	1053 0.6	1734 1.9	
14 M	0054 0.4	0737 1.6	1241 0.7	1917 2.1
29 Tu	0005 0.2	0647 1.5	1143 0.6	1823 2.1
15 Tu	0140 0.3	0818 1.6	1318 0.7	1949 2.1
30 W	0102 -0.0	0751 1.5	1231 0.6	1911 2.3

DECEMBER

Day	Time / ft	Time / ft	Time / ft	Time / ft
1 Th	0155 -0.2	0846 1.5	1319 0.6	2000 2.4
16 F	0243 -0.0	0920 1.2	1355 0.6	2030 2.0
2 F	0246 -0.3	0936 1.5	1401 0.6	2049 2.5
17 Sa	0319 -0.1	0953 1.2	1401 0.5	2107 2.0
3 Sa	0336 -0.4	1023 1.5	1455 0.5	2139 2.5
18 Su	0354 -0.1	1027 1.3	1506 0.5	2143 2.0
4 Su	0425 -0.4	1108 1.4	1544 0.4	2229 2.5
19 M	0428 -0.1	1102 1.3	1542 0.5	2220 2.0
5 M	0513 -0.3	1154 1.4	1636 0.4	2320 2.3
20 Tu	0501 -0.1	1137 1.3	1621 0.5	2258 1.9
6 Tu	0602 -0.2	1241 1.4	1732 0.5	
21 W	0535 -0.1	1214 1.3	1703 0.5	2338 1.8
7 W	0012 2.1	0651 0.0	1329 1.4	1835 0.5
22 Th	0611 -0.0	1252 1.3	1752 0.5	
8 Th	0108 1.9	0742 0.2	1420 1.5	1948 0.6
23 F	0022 1.7	0648 0.1	1331 1.3	1851 0.4
9 F	0211 1.6	0833 0.3	1514 1.5	2108 0.5
24 Sa	0114 1.5	0729 0.2	1413 1.4	2001 0.4
10 Sa	0325 1.4	1609 1.6	2227 0.5	
25 Su	0218 1.3	0814 0.3	1459 1.5	2120 0.3
11 Su	0451 1.3	1018 0.6	1702 1.6	2337 0.4
26 M	0338 1.1	0905 0.4	1552 1.6	2238 0.1
12 M	0613 1.2	1108 0.6	1750 1.7	
27 Tu	0512 1.0	1001 0.4	1650 1.8	2349 -0.1
13 Tu	0034 0.2	0717 1.2	1155 0.6	1834 1.8
28 W	0637 1.0	1100 0.5	1750 1.9	
14 W	0123 0.1	0806 1.2	1208 0.6	1914 1.9
29 Th	0051 -0.3	0744 1.0	1159 0.4	1850 2.1
15 Th	0205 0.0	0845 1.2	1318 0.6	1953 1.9
30 F	0147 -0.4	0839 1.1	1255 0.4	1947 2.2
31 Sa	0238 -0.5	0926 1.1	1349 0.3	2041 2.2

TIME MERIDIAN 75°W
Heights in feet are referred to the chart datum of sounding.

0000h is midnight, 1200h is noon.

KEY WEST, FLORIDA (.3M W of Fort Taylor)

CURRENT TABLES 1994

FLOOD 022° EBB 194°

EASTERN STANDARD TIME, ADD 1 HOUR DAYLIGHT SAVING APRIL 3 - OCTOBER 29

JANUARY

Day	Slack time	Max time	Fld	Ebb
1 Sa		0307		2.2
	0646	0923	1.4	
	1228	1539		2.0
	1917	2141	1.1	
2 Su	0031	0357		2.0
	0736	1008	1.2	
	1308	1627		2.0
	2011	2236	1.0	
3 M	0132	0451		1.8
	0833	1058	1.0	
	1353	1721		1.9
	2113	2340	1.0	
4 Tu	0243	0553		1.6
	0939	1156	0.8	
	1444	1820		1.9
	2220			
5 W ◑	0401	0059	0.9	
		0703		1.4
	1053	1306	0.6	
	1544	1926		1.9
	2330			
6 Th	0519	0231	1.0	
		0824		1.3
	1211	1431	0.6	
	1650	2036		1.9
7 F	0037	0350	1.2	
	0631	0943		1.4
	1321	1551	0.6	
	1757	2144		2.0
8 Sa	0137	0452	1.4	
	0734	1049		1.5
	1420	1655	0.7	
	1859	2245		2.1
9 Su	0231	0544	1.5	
	0827	1142		1.6
	1509	1747	0.9	
	1956	2337		2.3
10 M	0319	0631	1.6	
	0914	1227		1.8
	1553	1833	1.0	
	2047			
11 Tu ●	0404	0023		2.3
		0712	1.6	
	0956	1306		1.8
	1633	1913	1.1	
	2134			
12 W	0446	0105		2.3
		0749	1.5	
	1034	1342		1.9
	1712	1950	1.1	
	2218			
13 Th	0526	0144		2.2
		0822	1.4	
	1109	1415		1.9
	1750	2024	1.1	
	2300			
14 F	0605	0222		2.1
		0851	1.3	
	1142	1449		1.9
	1829	2058	1.0	
	2341			
15 Sa	0644	0259		2.0
		0920	1.1	
	1214	1524		1.8
	1910	2134	0.9	
16 Su	0022	0339		1.8
	0725	0951	1.0	
	1246	1603		1.7
	1954	2213	0.8	
17 M	0105	0421		1.6
	0810	1027	0.8	
	1318	1645		1.6
	2044	2259	0.7	
18 Tu	0155	0509		1.4
	0902	1109	0.6	
	1353	1732		1.5
	2141	2354	0.6	
19 W ◑	0254	0603		1.2
	1005	1159	0.4	
	1433	1826		1.5
	2245			
20 Th	0404	0107	0.5	
		0708		1.1
	1119	1302	0.3	
	1525	1927		1.4
	2349			
21 F	0518	0245	0.6	
		0822		1.0
	1234	1421	0.3	
	1632	2032		1.5
22 Sa	0047	0357	0.8	
	0625	0936		1.1
	1334	1542	0.3	
	1741	2133		1.6
23 Su	0137	0448	1.0	
	0723	1034		1.3
	1420	1637	0.5	
	1842	2227		1.8
24 M	0222	0530	1.2	
	0812	1119		1.5
	1458	1720	0.7	
	1936	2315		2.0
25 Tu	0303	0606	1.3	
	0855	1159		1.7
	1533	1759	0.9	
	2026	2359		2.2
26 W	0343	0639	1.5	
	0934	1237		1.9
	1608	1837	1.1	
	2113			
27 Th O	0422	0041		2.4
		0712	1.6	
	1012	1314		2.0
	1645	1916	1.3	
	2200			
28 F	0502	0124		2.5
		0747	1.6	
	1048	1353		2.2
	1724	1957	1.4	
	2247			
29 Sa	0544	0207		2.4
		0824	1.6	
	1124	1433		2.3
	1806	2040	1.4	
	2335			
30 Su	0628	0252		2.3
		0903	1.5	
	1201	1516		2.3
	1853	2127	1.4	
31 M	0027	0340		2.1
	0716	0946	1.3	
	1239	1602		2.2
	1945	2219	1.3	

FEBRUARY

Day	Slack time	Max time	Fld	Ebb
1 Tu	0124	0432		1.8
	0810	1033	1.0	
	1321	1653		2.1
	2045	2319	1.1	
2 W	0228	0530		1.6
	0914	1127	0.8	
	1409	1751		1.9
	2153			
3 Th ◐	0341	0036	1.0	
		0639		1.3
	1031	1236	0.5	
	1508	1858		1.8
	2309			
4 F	0500	0216	0.9	
		0805		1.2
	1158	1415	0.4	
	1622	2016		1.8
5 Sa	0024	0340	1.0	
	0614	0935		1.2
	1316	1548	0.5	
	1738	2135		1.8
6 Su	0130	0444	1.2	
	0717	1042		1.4
	1415	1652	0.7	
	1847	2240		1.9
7 M	0226	0535	1.3	
	0810	1133		1.6
	1500	1743	0.9	
	1947	2332		2.1
8 Tu	0313	0619	1.4	
	0854	1214		1.7
	1539	1826	1.0	
	2038			
9 W	0354	0016		2.1
		0658	1.4	
	0932	1248		1.8
	1614	1903	1.1	
	2124			
10 Th ●	0431	0053		2.2
		0730	1.4	
	1006	1319		1.9
	1648	1935	1.2	
	2205			
11 F	0507	0127		2.2
		0758	1.3	
	1037	1348		2.0
	1721	2003	1.2	
	2243			
12 Sa	0540	0200		2.1
		0821	1.2	
	1107	1417		2.0
	1755	2031	1.2	
	2320			
13 Su	0615	0233		2.0
		0845	1.1	
	1135	1449		1.9
	1831	2101	1.1	
	2356			
14 M	0651	0308		1.8
		0912	1.0	
	1203	1525		1.9
	1910	2135	1.0	
15 Tu	0034	0347		1.7
	0730	0945	0.8	
	1229	1604		1.8
	1954	2215	0.9	
16 W	0116	0430		1.5
	0816	1023	0.7	
	1256	1647		1.7
	2046	2302	0.7	
17 Th	0207	0520		1.2
	0913	1108	0.5	
	1326	1738		1.5
	2148			
18 F ◐	0312	0001	0.6	
		0619		1.1
	1026	1204	0.3	
	1408	1838		1.4
	2258			
19 Sa	0430	0121	0.5	
		0730		1.0
	1149	1317	0.2	
	1523	1946		1.5
20 Su	0007	0307	0.6	
	0545	0849		1.1
	1258	1449	0.3	
	1659	2056		1.6
21 M	0106	0414	0.8	
	0647	0957		1.2
	1346	1606	0.5	
	1816	2200		1.8
22 Tu	0156	0500	1.1	
	0739	1048		1.5
	1426	1657	0.8	
	1919	2253		2.0
23 W	0240	0539	1.3	
	0823	1131		1.8
	1503	1740	1.1	
	2014	2340		2.3
24 Th	0322	0615	1.5	
	0904	1211		2.0
	1540	1821	1.3	
	2104			
25 F	0403	0025		2.4
		0650	1.6	
	0942	1250		2.3
	1619	1901	1.6	
	2152			
26 Sa O	0444	0108		2.5
		0726	1.6	
	1019	1329		2.4
	1700	1943	1.7	
	2240			
27 Su	0526	0152		2.5
		0803	1.6	
	1056	1410		2.5
	1743	2026	1.7	
	2328			
28 M	0611	0237		2.4
		0842	1.4	
	1133	1453		2.5
	1830	2112	1.6	

TIME MERIDIAN 75°W

0000h is midnight, 1200h is noon.

REED'S NAUTICAL ALMANAC

KEY WEST, FLORIDA (.3M W of Fort Taylor)

CURRENT TABLES 1994 **FLOOD 022° EBB 194°**

EASTERN STANDARD TIME, ADD 1 HOUR DAYLIGHT SAVING APRIL 3 - OCTOBER 29

MARCH

Day	Slack time	Max time	Fld knots	Ebb knots
1 Tu	0019	0323		2.1
	0658	0924	1.2	
	1212	1539		2.4
	1921	2203	1.5	
2 W	0113	0414		1.8
	0752	1011	1.0	
	1254	1629		2.2
	2021	2301	1.2	
3 Th	0213	0511		1.5
	0856	1105	0.7	
	1342	1726		1.9
	2130			
4 F ◑		0018	1.0	
	0321	0619		1.3
	1016	1217	0.4	
	1444	1835		1.7
	2249			
5 Sa		0201	0.9	
	0436	0749		1.1
	1147	1412	0.4	
	1604	2000		1.6
6 Su	0011	0324	0.9	
	0549	0921		1.2
	1306	1540	0.5	
	1727	2126		1.6
7 M	0121	0427	1.0	
	0651	1025		1.4
	1401	1641	0.7	
	1838	2232		1.8
8 Tu	0216	0517	1.2	
	0742	1113		1.5
	1442	1729	0.9	
	1936	2322		1.9
9 W	0301	0559	1.2	
	0823	1151		1.7
	1517	1810	1.1	
	2026			
10 Th		0002		2.0
	0339	0635	1.2	
	0900	1222		1.8
	1549	1845	1.2	
	2109			
11 F		0036		2.0
	0413	0705	1.2	
	0932	1250		1.9
	1620	1914	1.3	
	2148			
12 Sa ●		0106		2.0
	0445	0729	1.2	
	1002	1316		2.0
	1651	1939	1.3	
	2224			
13 Su		0136		2.0
	0516	0749	1.1	
	1030	1345		2.0
	1723	2004	1.3	
	2259			
14 M		0207		1.9
	0548	0811	1.0	
	1056	1416		2.0
	1757	2031	1.2	
	2333			
15 Tu		0241		1.8
	0622	0838	0.9	
	1121	1451		2.0
	1833	2104	1.1	
16 W	0009	0318		1.7
	0659	0910	0.8	
	1145	1528		1.9
	1914	2141	1.0	
17 Th	0048	0359		1.5
	0742	0947	0.7	
	1011	1311		1.7
	2002	2226	0.9	
18 F	0134	0447		1.3
	0836	1031	0.5	
	1241	1701		1.6
	2100	2320	0.7	
19 Sa	0232	0543		1.1
	0944	1126	0.3	
	1325	1759		1.5
	2210			
20 Su ◑		0028	0.6	
	0345	0650		1.1
	1103	1237	0.3	
	1442	1908		1.5
	2324			
21 M		0158	0.6	
	0459	0805		1.1
	1213	1406	0.3	
	1630	2022		1.5
22 Tu	0030	0324	0.8	
	0604	0914		1.3
	1306	1531	0.6	
	1755	2130		1.7
23 W	0126	0420	1.0	
	0658	1010		1.6
	1350	1630	0.9	
	1902	2229		2.0
24 Th	0214	0505	1.2	
	0745	1057		1.9
	1431	1718	1.3	
	1959	2319		2.2
25 F	0259	0545	1.4	
	0827	1141		2.2
	1512	1802	1.6	
	2052			
26 Sa		0006		2.4
	0342	0623	1.5	
	0908	1223		2.4
	1553	1845	1.8	
	2141			
27 Su ○		0051		2.4
	0425	0702	1.5	
	0947	1304		2.6
	1636	1928	1.9	
	2230			
28 M		0136		2.4
	0508	0741	1.5	
	1026	1347		2.6
	1721	2012	1.9	
	2318			
29 Tu		0221		2.3
	0554	0822	1.3	
	1106	1431		2.6
	1809	2059	1.8	
30 W	0008	0308		2.1
	0643	0906	1.1	
	1148	1518		2.4
	1902	2149	1.5	
31 Th	0100	0358		1.8
	0738	0954	0.9	
	1232	1608		2.2
	2001	2247	1.2	

APRIL

Day	Slack time	Max time	Fld knots	Ebb knots
1 F	0156	0455		1.5
	0843	1050	0.6	
	1324	1706		1.9
	2109			
2 Sa		0001	1.0	
	0259	0602		1.3
	1001	1208	0.0	
	1430	1815		1.6
	2227			
3 Su ◑		0136	0.8	
	0407	0726		1.2
	1127	1401	0.4	
	1551	1941		1.5
	2349			
4 M		0257	0.8	
	0513	0851		1.2
	1241	1521	0.6	
	1712	2107		1.5
5 Tu	0100	0358	0.9	
	0612	0953		1.4
	1333	1619	0.8	
	1822	2212		1.6
6 W	0156	0448	0.9	
	0702	1040		1.6
	1414	1707	1.0	
	1919	2300		1.7
7 Th	0240	0530	1.0	
	0744	1117		1.7
	1448	1747	1.1	
	2007	2340		1.8
8 F	0317	0606	1.0	
	0820	1148		1.8
	1520	1821	1.2	
	2049			
9 Sa		0013		1.9
	0350	0635	1.0	
	0854	1216		1.9
	1551	1850	1.3	
	2128			
10 Su		0043		1.9
	0421	0658	1.0	
	0924	1244		2.0
	1622	1915	1.3	
	2204			
11 M ●		0112		1.9
	0453	0718	0.9	
	0952	1314		2.0
	1654	1939	1.3	
	2239			
12 Tu		0143		1.8
	0525	0741	0.9	
	1019	1346		2.1
	1727	2007	1.3	
	2314			
13 W		0217		1.8
	0559	0809	0.8	
	1044	1421		2.0
	1803	2039	1.2	
	2350			
14 Th		0254		1.6
	0636	0842	0.8	
	1110	1500		1.9
	1843	2116	1.1	
15 F	0028	0335		1.5
	0718	0920	0.6	
	1139	1543		1.8
	1929	2200	1.0	
16 Sa	0111	0422		1.4
	0809	1006	0.5	
	1216	1632		1.7
	2025	2251	0.9	
17 Su	0203	0516		1.3
	0911	1101	0.4	
	1310	1700		1.0
	2130	2352	0.7	
18 M	0305	0617		1.2
	1021	1210	0.4	
	1432	1836		1.5
	2242			
19 Tu ◑		0106	0.7	
	0412	0725		1.3
	1128	1332	0.5	
	1611	1949		1.6
	2351			
20 W		0226	0.8	
	0515	0831		1.5
	1224	1456	0.7	
	1735	2059		1.7
21 Th	0052	0332	0.9	
	0612	0930		1.8
	1314	1601	1.1	
	1844	2202		1.9
22 F	0145	0425	1.1	
	0702	1023		2.1
	1401	1655	1.4	
	1944	2257		2.1
23 Sa	0234	0512	1.2	
	0749	1110		2.3
	1446	1743	1.7	
	2038	2347		2.2
24 Su	0320	0556	1.3	
	0833	1156		2.5
	1531	1829	1.9	
	2129			
25 M ○		0034		2.3
	0406	0638	1.3	
	0917	1241		2.7
	1616	1915	2.0	
	2218			
26 Tu		0121		2.2
	0452	0721	1.3	
	1000	1326		2.7
	1703	2000	1.9	
	2307			
27 W		0207		2.1
	0539	0805	1.2	
	1043	1412		2.6
	1752	2047	1.8	
	2355			
28 Th		0254		2.0
	0630	0851	1.0	
	1128	1459		2.4
	1845	2137	1.5	
29 F	0045	0344		1.8
	0725	0941	0.9	
	1217	1550		2.1
	1942	2233	1.3	
30 Sa	0137	0438		1.6
	0827	1040	0.7	
	1312	1647		1.8
	2046	2339	1.0	

TIME MERIDIAN 75°W   0000h is midnight, 1200h is noon.

Chapter 2

KEY WEST, FLORIDA (.3M W of Fort Taylor)

CURRENT TABLES 1994 **FLOOD 022° EBB 194°**

EASTERN STANDARD TIME, ADD 1 HOUR DAYLIGHT SAVING APRIL 3 - OCTOBER 29

MAY

Day	Slack time	Max time	Fld Ebb knots
1 Su	0231 0938 1417 2158	0539 1157 1752	1.4 0.5 1.6
2 M ◑	0329 1052 1532 2314	0059 0650 1333 1909	0.8 1.3 0.5 1.4
3 Tu	0427 1200 1648	0215 0803 1449 2030	0.7 1.3 0.6 1.4
4 W	0024 0523 1254 1755	0318 0906 1548 2137	0.7 1.4 0.8 1.4
5 Th	0123 0613 1338 1853	0410 0955 1637 2228	0.7 1.5 0.9 1.5
6 F	0209 0657 1415 1942	0454 1036 1719 2310	0.8 1.7 1.1 1.6
7 Sa	0249 0737 1450 2026	0531 1110 1755 2346	0.8 1.8 1.2 1.6
8 Su	0324 0813 1523 2106	0601 1142 1826	0.8 1.9 1.3
9 M	0358 0846 1556 2144	0018 0626 1213 1853	1.7 0.8 2.0 1.3
10 Tu ●	0431 0917 1629 2221	0050 0649 1245 1919	1.7 0.8 2.0 1.3
11 W	0505 0946 1704 2257	0122 0715 1320 1948	1.7 0.8 2.1 1.3
12 Th	0540 1015 1740 2334	0157 0745 1357 2020	1.7 0.8 2.0 1.3
13 F	0617 1046 1821	0235 0821 1437 2058	1.6 0.7 2.0 1.2
14 Sa	0012 0659 1123 1906	0316 0901 1521 2140	1.6 0.7 1.9 1.1
15 Su	0053 0746 1209 1957	0401 0948 1610 2228	1.5 0.6 1.8 1.0
16 M	0139 0842 1309 2057	0452 1043 1706 2323	1.5 0.6 1.7 0.9
17 Tu	0230 0943 1428 2204	0548 1148 1809	1.5 0.6 1.6
18 W ◐	0327 1047 1554 2312	0026 0649 1303 1918	0.8 1.5 0.7 1.6
19 Th	0427 1147 1715	0136 0752 1424 2029	0.8 1.7 0.9 1.6
20 F	0017 0525 1242 1825	0245 0853 1535 2135	0.8 1.9 1.2 1.7
21 Sa	0117 0620 1334 1928	0347 0950 1635 2235	0.9 2.1 1.4 1.9
22 Su	0211 0712 1424 2024	0442 1043 1728 2329	1.0 2.4 1.7 2.0
23 M	0301 0802 1513 2117	0532 1133 1817	1.1 2.5 1.8
24 Tu	0350 0851 1601 2206	0020 0620 1221 1905	2.0 1.2 2.6 1.9
25 W ○	0438 0938 2254	0108 0707 1309 1951	2.1 1.2 2.6 1.8
26 Th	0526 1026 1738 2340	0154 0753 1356 2038	2.0 1.1 2.5 1.7
27 F	0616 1114 1829	0241 0840 1444 2125	1.9 1.0 2.3 1.5
28 Sa	0026 0708 1204 1922	0328 0930 1533 2214	1.8 0.9 2.1 1.3
29 Su	0111 0804 1258 2019	0416 1025 1625 2307	1.7 0.7 1.8 1.0
30 M	0157 0904 1358 2120	0508 1129 1722	1.5 0.6 1.6
31 Tu	0245 1008 1503 2227	0007 0604 1246 1826	0.8 1.5 0.6 1.4

JUNE

Day	Slack time	Max time	Fld Ebb knots
1 W ◑	0335 1110 1612 2335	0113 0704 1403 1936	0.0 1.4 0.6 1.3
2 Th	0427 1208 1718	0222 0804 1507 2046	0.6 1.4 0.7 1.3
3 F	0038 0517 1257 1819	0320 0900 1601 2146	0.5 1.5 0.8 1.3
4 Sa	0132 0606 1341 1912	0410 0948 1648 2235	0.6 1.6 1.0 1.4
5 Su	0218 0651 1420 2000	0452 1030 1728 2317	0.6 1.7 1.1 1.4
6 M	0258 0732 1457 2044	0527 1108 1804 2354	0.6 1.8 1.2 1.5
7 Tu	0335 0810 1533 2125	0557 1145 1835	0.6 1.9 1.3
8 W	0411 0847 1608 2204	0029 0625 1221 1904	1.6 0.7 2.0 1.3
9 Th ●	0445 0922 1645 2241	0103 0654 1259 1933	1.6 0.7 2.1 1.3
10 F	0520 0958 1722 2317	0139 0728 1338 2006	1.7 0.8 2.1 1.3
11 Sa	0557 1036 1802 2354	0217 0805 1419 2042	1.7 0.8 2.1 1.3
12 Su	0637 1120 1846	0257 0847 1503 2122	1.7 0.8 2.0 1.2
13 M	0032 0721 1210 1934	0340 0933 1552 2206	1.7 0.8 1.9 1.1
14 Tu	0112 0812 1309 2029	0427 1026 1645 2256	1.7 0.8 1.8 1.0
15 W	0156 0909 1420 2130	0519 1127 1744 2352	1.7 0.8 1.7 0.9
16 Th ◐	0010 1011 1538 2238	0616 1237 1850	1.9 0.9 1.5
17 F	0342 1115 1656 2347	0055 0717 1356 2000	0.8 1.9 1.0 1.5
18 Sa	0442 1216 1808	0205 0821 1514 2112	0.7 2.0 1.2 1.5
19 Su	0053 0543 1314 1913	0316 0923 1621 2219	0.8 2.1 1.4 1.6
20 M	0153 0643 1409 2011	0421 1022 1719 2317	0.8 2.3 1.6 1.7
21 Tu	0248 0739 1500 2104	0518 1116 1810	0.9 2.4 1.7
22 W	0338 0833 1550 2152	0009 0610 1208 1858	1.8 1.0 2.5 1.8
23 Th ○	0425 0924 1638 2237	0057 0658 1256 1943	1.9 1.1 2.5 1.7
24 F	0511 1013 1725 2319	0141 0744 1342 2025	1.9 1.1 2.4 1.6
25 Sa	0557 1101 1811 2359	0223 0829 1427 2106	1.9 1.1 2.3 1.4
26 Su	0643 1149 1858	0305 0913 1512 2146	1.9 1.0 2.1 1.2
27 M	0039 0731 1238 1947	0347 0959 1558 2226	1.8 0.9 1.8 1.0
28 Tu	0118 0823 1330 2038	0430 1049 1646 2309	1.7 0.8 1.6
29 W	0157 0918 1426 2136	0516 1146 1739 2357	1.6 0.7 1.4 0.6
30 Th ◑	0239 1017 1528 2239	0606 1255 1838	1.5 0.6 1.2

TIME MERIDIAN 75°W

0000h is midnight, 1200h is noon.

KEY WEST, FLORIDA (.3M W of Fort Taylor)

CURRENT TABLES 1994   FLOOD 022° EBB 194°

EASTERN STANDARD TIME, ADD 1 HOUR DAYLIGHT SAVING APRIL 3 - OCTOBER 29

JULY

Day	Slack time	Max time	Fld knots	Ebb knots
1 F	0326, 1117, 1634, 2347	0056, 0702, 1412, 1944	0.5, 0.6	1.5, 1.1
2 Sa	0417, 1214, 1100	0207, 0800, 1519, 2034	0.4, 0.7	1.5, 1.1
3 Su	0052, 0512, 1306, 1839	0315, 0858, 1615, 2156	0.4, 0.8	1.5, 1.2
4 M	0147, 0605, 1351, 1933	0411, 0951, 1702, 2248	0.4, 1.0	1.7, 1.3
5 Tu	0233, 0655, 1432, 2020	0455, 1038, 1742, 2330	0.5, 1.1	1.8, 1.4
6 W	0312, 0741, 1511, 2103	0532, 1121, 1817	0.6, 1.2	1.9
7 Th	0347, 0825, 1549, 2142	0008, 0605, 1201, 1847	0.7, 1.3	1.5, 2.0
8 F ●	0421, 0907, 1626, 2219	0043, 0638, 1241, 1917	0.8, 1.4	1.6, 2.1
9 Sa	0456, 0949, 1704, 2255	0119, 0713, 1321, 1949	0.9, 1.4	1.7, 2.2
10 Su	0532, 1032, 1744, 2330	0156, 0751, 1403, 2024	1.0, 1.4	1.8, 2.2
11 M	0611, 1118, 1826	0235, 0833, 1446, 2102	1.1, 1.3	1.9, 2.2
12 Tu	0005, 0654, 1208, 1912	0316, 0918, 1533, 2143	1.1, 1.2	2.0, 2.1
13 W	0042, 0743, 1304, 2003	0402, 1009, 1624, 2229	1.1, 1.1	2.0, 1.9
14 Th	0123, 0838, 1408, 2102	0451, 1106, 1721, 2322	1.1, 0.9	2.0, 1.7
15 F	0209, 0941, 1521, 2210	0546, 1213, 1824	1.0	1.9, 1.5
16 Sa ◐	0303, 1049, 1638, 2325	0022, 0647, 1335, 1937	0.7, 1.0	1.9, 1.4
17 Su	0407, 1157, 1753	0135, 0754, 1503, 2056	0.6, 1.1	1.9, 1.4
18 M	0038, 0516, 1302, 1900	0258, 0904, 1615, 2209	0.6, 1.3	2.0, 1.5
19 Tu	0144, 0624, 1400, 1958	0414, 1009, 1714, 2310	0.7, 1.4	2.1, 1.6
20 W	0239, 0726, 1453, 2049	0515, 1108, 1804	0.8	2.2, 1.6
21 Th	0327, 0822, 1541, 2133	0000, 0607, 1159, 1849	1.0	1.7, 2.3, 1.6
22 F ○	0410, 0914, 1626, 2214	0044, 0652, 1246, 1930	1.1	1.9, 2.3, 1.6
23 Sa	0452, 1002, 1709, 2252	0123, 0734, 1328, 2007	1.2	1.9, 2.3, 1.5
24 Su	0532, 1047, 1750, 2327	0200, 0812, 1408, 2040	1.2	1.9, 2.2, 1.4
25 M	0612, 1130, 1830	0235, 0849, 1447, 2111	1.1, 1.2	1.9, 2.0
26 Tu	0001, 0654, 1213, 1912	0311, 0926, 1527, 2142	1.0, 1.0	1.9, 1.9
27 W	0034, 0738, 1257, 1956	0349, 1005, 1609, 2217	0.9, 0.8	1.8, 1.6
28 Th	0107, 0827, 1345, 2047	0430, 1049, 1654, 2256	0.8, 0.6	1.7, 1.4
29 F	0141, 0922, 1440, 2147	0516, 1142, 1747, 2344	0.7, 0.5	1.6, 1.2
30 Sa ◐	0221, 1024, 1545, 2257	0608, 1251, 1848	0.6	1.5, 1.1
31 Su	0310, 1129, 1655	0044, 0707, 1425, 2000	0.3, 0.6	1.4, 1.0

AUGUST

Day	Slack time	Max time	Fld knots	Ebb knots
1 M	0012, 0414, 1230, 1803	0203, 0811, 1539, 2115	0.3, 0.7	1.5, 1.1
2 Tu	0117, 0522, 1300, 1902	0328, 0914, 1551, 2216	0.3, 0.8	1.6, 1.2
3 W	0205, 0625, 1408, 1952	0426, 1010, 1717, 2303	0.4, 1.0	1.7, 1.4
4 Th	0244, 0719, 1449, 2035	0509, 1058, 1753, 2342	0.6, 1.2	1.9, 1.6
5 F	0318, 0809, 1528, 2115	0545, 1141, 1825	0.8, 1.3	2.1
6 Sa	0352, 0855, 1606, 2151	0018, 0621, 1223, 1855	1.0, 1.4	1.8, 2.2
7 Su ●	0427, 0940, 1644, 2226	0054, 0657, 1304, 1927	1.2, 1.5	1.9, 2.3
8 M	0503, 1025, 1724, 2300	0131, 0735, 1346, 2001	1.3, 1.5	2.1, 2.3
9 Tu	0543, 1112, 1806, 2335	0210, 0817, 1429, 2039	1.4, 1.4	2.2, 2.3
10 W	0626, 1201, 1851	0251, 0901, 1515, 2119	1.4, 1.3	2.2, 2.1
11 Th	0011, 0715, 1255, 1941	0335, 0950, 1604, 2204	1.3, 1.1	2.2, 1.9
12 F	0051, 0811, 1356, 2040	0424, 1046, 1700, 2255	1.2, 0.8	2.1, 1.6
13 Sa	0136, 0916, 1505, 2151	0519, 1153, 1803, 2357	1.1, 0.6	2.0, 1.4
14 Su ◐	0232, 1028, 1621, 2312	0622, 1321, 1920	1.0	1.9, 1.2
15 M	0343, 1144, 1736	0118, 0735, 1457, 2048	0.5, 1.0	1.8, 1.2
16 Tu	0033, 0502, 1254, 1843	0300, 0854, 1608, 2204	0.5, 1.2	1.8, 1.4
17 W	0138, 0616, 1354, 1940	0416, 1006, 1705, 2301	0.7, 1.3	2.0, 1.6
18 Th	0229, 0720, 1446, 2027	0513, 1104, 1753, 2347	0.9, 1.4	2.1, 1.7
19 F	0312, 0815, 1531, 2108	0601, 1152, 1834	1.1, 1.4	2.2
20 Sa	0351, 0904, 1612, 2145	0025, 0642, 1234, 1910	1.2	1.9, 2.2, 1.4
21 Su ○	0427, 0948, 1649, 2218	0059, 0718, 1311, 1942	1.3	2.0, 2.2, 1.3
22 M	0503, 1029, 1726, 2250	0131, 0750, 1346, 2008	1.3	2.0, 2.1, 1.2
23 Tu	0539, 1108, 1801, 2320	0202, 0820, 1420, 2033	1.2	2.0, 2.0, 1.1
24 W	0616, 1146, 1838, 2348	0234, 0851, 1455, 2100	1.2	2.0, 1.8, 1.0
25 Th	0655, 1224, 1918	0309, 0924, 1533, 2132	1.0, 0.8	1.9, 1.7
26 F	0016, 0740, 1306, 2004	0348, 1003, 1616, 2209	0.9, 0.6	1.8, 1.5
27 Sa	0045, 0831, 1355, 2101	0431, 1049, 1704, 2254	0.7, 0.5	1.7, 1.3
28 Su	0116, 0932, 1457, 2213	0521, 1147, 1802, 2349	0.6, 0.3	1.5, 1.1
29 M ◐	0200, 1042, 1610, 2334	0620, 1307, 1912	0.5	1.4, 1.0
30 Tu	0313, 1151, 1723	0103, 0728, 1453, 2031	0.2, 0.6	1.4, 1.0
31 W	0042, 0444, 1250, 1825	0241, 0838, 1558, 2139	0.3, 0.8	1.5, 1.2

Chapter 2

TIME MERIDIAN 75°W   0000h is midnight, 1200h is noon.

KEY WEST, FLORIDA (.3M W of Fort Taylor)

CURRENT TABLES 1994

FLOOD 022° EBB 194°

EASTERN STANDARD TIME, ADD 1 HOUR DAYLIGHT SAVING APRIL 3 - OCTOBER 29

SEPTEMBER

Date	Slack time	Max time	Fld knots	Ebb knots
1 Th	0131	0355	0.5	
	0559	0942		1.7
	1340	1644	1.0	
	1916	2229		1.4
2 F	0209	0443	0.7	
	0700	1034		1.9
	1423	1721	1.2	
	2000	2310		1.7
3 Sa	0245	0522	1.0	
	0754	1120		2.1
	1504	1755	1.3	
	2040	2348		1.9
4 Su	0320	0600	1.2	
	0843	1203		2.3
	1543	1827	1.4	
	2117			
5 M		0026		2.2
	0356	0638	1.5	
	0929	1245		2.4
	1622	1901	1.5	
	2152			
6 Tu		0104		2.3
	0435	0718	1.6	
	1016	1327		2.4
	1703	1937	1.5	
	2228			
7 W		0144		2.4
	0516	0800	1.7	
	1103	1411		2.3
	1745	2015	1.4	
	2304			
8 Th		0226		2.5
	0601	0844	1.7	
	1152	1457		2.1
	1831	2056	1.2	
	2342			
9 F		0311		2.4
	0651	0933	1.5	
	1244	1546		1.9
	1923	2142	1.0	
10 Sa	0023	0400		2.2
	0748	1029	1.3	
	1343	1641		1.6
	2024	2234	0.8	
11 Su	0111	0456		2.0
	0854	1137	1.1	
	1449	1746		1.4
	2139	2340	0.5	
12 M	0211	0601		1.8
	1011	1312	0.9	
	1602	1907		1.2
	2305			
13 Tu		0120	0.4	
	0331	0721		1.7
	1132	1446	0.9	
	1715	2039		1.2
14 W	0026	0303	0.5	
	0456	0849		1.7
	1245	1554	1.0	
	1820	2151		1.4
15 Th	0127	0411	0.7	
	0610	1001		1.8
	1345	1648	1.2	
	1913	2243		1.6
16 F	0213	0503	1.0	
	0713	1056		1.9
	1435	1733	1.2	
	1958	2325		1.8
17 Sa	0252	0547	1.2	
	0805	1140		2.0
	1516	1812	1.3	
	2036	2400		1.9
18 Su	0327	0625	1.3	
	0851	1218		2.1
	1553	1845	1.2	
	2111			
19 M		0030		2.0
	0401	0658	1.3	
	0932	1250		2.0
	1627	1912	1.2	
	2142			
20 Tu		0059		2.0
	0433	0726	1.3	
	1009	1321		2.0
	1700	1935	1.1	
	2211			
21 W		0128		2.1
	0506	0751	1.3	
	1045	1353		1.9
	1733	1957	1.0	
	2239			
22 Th		0159		2.0
	0541	0819	1.2	
	1120	1426		1.8
	1808	2023	0.9	
	2305			
23 F		0234		2.0
	0618	0850	1.1	
	1156	1502		1.7
	1846	2055	0.8	
	2330			
24 Sa		0311		1.9
	0659	0927	1.0	
	1235	1543		1.5
	1930	2131	0.6	
	2356			
25 Su		0354		1.7
	0747	1010	0.8	
	1320	1630		1.3
	2024	2215	0.5	
26 M	0026	0443		1.6
	0845	1103	0.7	
	1415	1726		1.1
	2133	2310	0.3	
27 Tu	0109	0541		1.4
	0954	1210	0.6	
	1524	1831		1.1
	2251			
28 W		0020	0.2	
	0226	0648		1.4
	1107	1341	0.6	
	1636	1945		1.1
	2359			
29 Th		0152	0.3	
	0412	0801		1.5
	1212	1507	0.7	
	1740	2053		1.3
30 F	0050	0316	0.5	
	0535	0909		1.6
	1307	1600	0.9	
	1833	2148		1.5

OCTOBER

Date	Slack time	Max time	Fld knots	Ebb knots
1 Sa	0101	0410	0.8	
	0641	1007		1.9
	1354	1642	1.1	
	1919	2234		1.8
2 Su	0210	0456	1.2	
	0737	1056		2.1
	1437	1720	1.2	
	2001	2315		2.1
3 M	0249	0538	1.5	
	0828	1142		2.3
	1519	1757	1.4	
	2040	2356		2.4
4 Tu	0328	0619	1.7	
	0917	1226		2.4
	1600	1834	1.4	
	2119			
5 W		0037		2.6
	0410	0701	1.9	
	1004	1310		2.4
	1643	1913	1.4	
	2157			
6 Th		0119		2.6
	0454	0744	1.9	
	1052	1355		2.3
	1727	1953	1.3	
	2237			
7 F		0203		2.6
	0541	0830	1.8	
	1141	1441		2.1
	1815	2037	1.2	
	2318			
8 Sa		0250		2.5
	0632	0919	1.6	
	1233	1531		1.9
	1909	2124	1.0	
	2323			
9 Su	0003	0340		2.2
	0729	1015	1.4	
	1328	1626		1.6
	2011	2220	0.7	
10 M	0055	0437		2.0
	0835	1123	1.1	
	1430	1730		1.4
	2126	2332	0.5	
11 Tu	0200	0543		1.7
	0951	1255	0.9	
	1537	1850		1.3
	2250			
12 W		0121	0.4	
	0322	0706		1.5
	1113	1422	0.9	
	1644	2016		1.3
13 Th	0007	0250	0.6	
	0445	0835		1.5
	1228	1529	0.9	
	1744	2124		1.4
14 F	0104	0353	0.8	
	0558	0945		1.6
	1328	1622	1.0	
	1836	2215		1.6
15 Sa	0149	0444	1.0	
	0659	1039		1.7
	1417	1707	1.0	
	1921	2256		1.8
16 Su	0227	0527	1.2	
	0750	1122		1.8
	1457	1745	1.0	
	1959	2330		1.9
17 M	0301	0604	1.3	
	0834	1157		1.9
	1532	1817	1.0	
	2034	2359		2.0
18 Tu	0334	0636	1.3	
	0913	1228		1.9
	1605	1843	1.0	
	2105			
19 W		0028		2.0
	0406	0703	1.4	
	0950	1258		1.8
	1637	1904	0.9	
	2135			
20 Th		0057		2.1
	0439	0728	1.3	
	1025	1328		1.8
	1709	1926	0.9	
	2202			
21 F		0129		2.1
	0512	0754	1.3	
	1100	1401		1.7
	1744	1954	0.8	
	2229			
22 Sa		0204		2.0
	0548	0824	1.2	
	1135	1438		1.6
	1821	2026	0.7	
	2254			
23 Su		0242		1.9
	0627	0900	1.1	
	1212	1518		1.5
	1903	2103	0.6	
	2323			
24 M		0324		1.8
	0712	0941	1.0	
	1254	1603		1.4
	1954	2147	0.5	
	2358			
25 Tu		0412		1.6
	0805	1030	0.8	
	1342	1655		1.3
	2055	2240	0.4	
26 W	0047	0508		1.5
	0909	1129	0.7	
	1440	1754		1.2
	2203	2347	0.4	
27 Th	0204	0612		1.4
	1019	1239	0.6	
	1545	1900		1.3
	2309			
28 F		0108	0.4	
	0344	0723		1.4
	1128	1358	0.7	
	1647	2006		1.4
29 Sa	0004	0232	0.6	
	0510	0834		1.6
	1229	1505	0.8	
	1744	2105		1.7
30 Su	0053	0338	1.0	
	0619	0937		1.8
	1322	1559	0.9	
	1834	2156		2.0
31 M	0137	0431	1.3	
	0719	1031		1.9
	1410	1645	1.1	
	1921	2244		2.3

TIME MERIDIAN 75°W

0000h is midnight, 1200h is noon.

REED'S NAUTICAL ALMANAC

KEY WEST, FLORIDA (.3M W of Fort Taylor)

EASTERN STANDARD TIME, ADD 1 HOUR DAYLIGHT SAVING APRIL 3 - OCTOBER 29

NOVEMBER

Day	Slack time	Max time	Fld knots	Ebb knots
1 Tu	0221	0518	1.6	
	0813	1121		2.1
	1455	1728	1.2	
	2005	2329		2.5
2 W	0305	0603	1.8	
	0904	1208		2.2
	1540	1810	1.3	
	2140			
3 Th ●		0014		2.7
	0350	0648	2.0	
	0953	1254		2.2
	1625	1853	1.3	
	2131			
4 F		0059		2.7
	0436	0733	2.0	
	1041	1341		2.2
	1712	1937	1.2	
	2215			
5 Sa		0145		2.7
	0525	0819	1.9	
	1130	1428		2.0
	1801	2023	1.1	
	2301			
6 Su		0233		2.5
	0616	0908	1.7	
	1219	1517		1.9
	1855	2113	0.9	
	2350			
7 M		0324		2.2
	0712	1002	1.4	
	1310	1611		1.7
	1956	2210	0.8	
8 Tu	0045	0419		2.0
	0814	1105	1.1	
	1405	1710		1.5
	2105	2322	0.6	
9 W	0150	0523		1.7
	0925	1222	0.9	
	1502	1819		1.4
	2219			
10 Th ◐		0057	0.5	
	0306	0638		1.5
	1041	1343	0.8	
	1601	1933		1.4
	2331			
11 F		0221	0.6	
	0423	0803		1.4
	1156	1452	0.7	
	1658	2041		1.5
12 Sa	0031	0326	0.8	
	0535	0915		1.4
	1300	1548	0.7	
	1750	2135		1.6
13 Su	0119	0418	1.0	
	0636	1012		1.5
	1351	1635	0.8	
	1837	2219		1.7
14 M	0159	0503	1.1	
	0728	1057		1.6
	1434	1715	0.8	
	1918	2256		1.8
15 Tu	0236	0542	1.2	
	0813	1135		1.6
	1510	1749	0.8	
	1956	2329		1.9
16 W	0310	0616	1.3	
	0853	1208		1.7
	1544	1816	0.8	
	2031			
17 Th		0000		2.0
	0343	0645	1.3	
	0931	1239		1.7
	1617	1839	0.8	
	2103			
18 F ○		0032		2.0
	0416	0711	1.3	
	1008	1309		1.7
	1650	1903	0.8	
	2133			
19 Sa		0105		2.1
	0450	0737	1.3	
	1043	1342		1.7
	1725	1932	0.8	
	2203			
20 Su		0141		2.0
	0526	0807	1.3	
	1118	1418		1.6
	1801	2005	0.7	
	2233			
21 M		0219		2.0
	0604	0841	1.2	
	1154	1457		1.6
	1841	2043	0.7	
	2307			
22 Tu		0301		1.9
	0646	0920	1.1	
	1232	1540		1.5
	1926	2127	0.6	
	2348			
23 W		0348		1.8
	0734	1004	1.0	
	1313	1627		1.5
	2018	2218	0.6	
24 Th	0041	0440		1.6
	0830	1055	0.8	
	1400	1720		1.4
	2117	2318	0.6	
25 F	0152	0540		1.5
	0934	1153	0.7	
	1453	1819		1.5
	2219			
26 Sa ◐		0029	0.6	
	0319	0646		1.5
	1042	1259	0.7	
	1551	1921		1.6
	2320			
27 Su		0149	0.8	
	0443	0757		1.5
	1149	1409	0.8	
	1651	2023		1.8
28 M	0017	0305	1.0	
	0557	0905		1.6
	1250	1515	0.8	
	1748	2121		2.0
29 Tu	0109	0408	1.3	
	0701	1008		1.7
	1345	1612	0.9	
	1843	2216		2.3
30 W	0159	0502	1.6	
	0759	1103		1.9
	1436	1704	1.1	
	1934	2307		2.5

DECEMBER

Day	Slack time	Max time	Fld knots	Ebb knots
1 Th	0248	0552	1.8	
	0852	1154		2.0
	1524	1753	1.1	
	2024	2356		2.6
2 F ●	0336	0639	1.9	
	0942	1243		2.1
	1612	1840	1.2	
	2113			
3 Sa		0044		2.7
	0424	0726	1.9	
	1030	1329		2.1
	1659	1927	1.2	
	2202			
4 Su		0132		2.6
	0512	0812	1.8	
	1116	1416		2.0
	1748	2015	1.1	
	2251			
5 M		0219		2.5
	0602	0858	1.7	
	1201	1503		1.9
	1839	2104	1.0	
	2341			
6 Tu		0309		2.2
	0654	0946	1.4	
	1247	1551		1.8
	1933	2157	0.9	
7 W	0035	0400		2.0
	0750	1037	1.1	
	1332	1641		1.7
	2032	2258	0.7	
8 Th	0133	0456		1.7
	0850	1135	0.9	
	1420	1736		1.5
	2137			
9 F ◑		0013	0.6	
	0238	0558		1.4
	0957	1243	0.7	
	1510	1836		1.5
	2243			
10 Sa		0135	0.6	
	0348	0710		1.3
	1109	1356	0.6	
	1602	1941		1.5
	2347			
11 Su		0247	0.7	
	0458	0827		1.2
	1219	1501	0.5	
	1655	2042		1.5
12 M	0042	0346	0.8	
	0603	0934		1.2
	1320	1556	0.5	
	1747	2136		1.6
13 Tu	0129	0437	1.0	
	0659	1027		1.3
	1409	1643	0.6	
	1835	2221		1.7
14 W	0211	0520	1.1	
	0749	1111		1.4
	1450	1722	0.6	
	1920	2300		1.8
15 Th	0248	0558	1.2	
	0833	1148		1.5
	1526	1755	0.6	
	2000	2337		1.9
16 F	0324	0631	1.3	
	0913	1222		1.6
	1600	1822	0.7	
	2030			
17 Sa		0012		2.0
	0358	0650	1.0	
	0951	1254		1.6
	1633	1848	0.7	
	2113			
18 Su ○		0047		2.1
	0433	0725	1.3	
	1027	1326		1.7
	1706	1917	0.8	
	2148			
19 M		0124		2.1
	0509	0753	1.3	
	1101	1400		1.7
	1740	1951	0.8	
	2224			
20 Tu		0202		2.1
	0546	0825	1.3	
	1135	1437		1.7
	1817	2028	0.9	
	2303			
21 W		0243		2.0
	0625	0900	1.2	
	1209	1517		1.7
	1857	2110	0.9	
	2347			
22 Th		0327		1.9
	0709	0940	1.1	
	1244	1600		1.7
	1943	2157	0.9	
23 F	0038	0416		1.8
	0758	1025	1.0	
	1322	1648		1.7
	2036	2252	0.8	
24 Sa	0141	0511		1.6
	0855	1115	0.9	
	1406	1742		1.7
	2136	2356	0.8	
25 Su ◐	0256	0613		1.5
	1000	1214	0.7	
	1459	1841		1.8
	2240			
26 M		0111	0.9	
	0417	0722		1.4
	1112	1321	0.6	
	1600	1945		1.9
	2345			
27 Tu		0235	1.0	
	0535	0836		1.4
	1222	1436	0.6	
	1706	2051		2.0
28 W	0047	0351	1.3	
	0645	0948		1.5
	1326	1548	0.7	
	1811	2153		2.2
29 Th	0143	0453	1.5	
	0746	1051		1.7
	1422	1651	0.9	
	1912	2251		2.4
30 F	0236	0546	1.7	
	0840	1145		1.8
	1513	1746	1.0	
	2009	2344		2.5
31 Sa	0326	0635	1.8	
	0929	1234		2.0
	1601	1835	1.1	
	2102			

TIME MERIDIAN 75°W   0000h is midnight, 1200h is noon.

Chapter 2

CAUTION: Our information on aids to navigation comes from official government sources. The latitudes and longitudes of these marks may not correspond to the readings from GPS or LORAN receivers. Some aids have been reported as unreliable, missing, off position or showing incorrect characteristics. No single aid to navigation, or waypoint, should be relied upon as a sole means of fixing your position.

ENTRY PROCEDURES

Bahamas Customs and Immigration require proof of birth and citizenship for each person, preferably in the form of a passport. You should also have proof of ownership of the vessel. You may stay in the country for up to one year without paying duty on your boat. Extensions for additional years are available for $500 per year. A duty of 7.5% is applicable to boats from 30 to 100 feet long that remain in the Bahamas for periods longer than three years. Duties vary for other types of boats, equipment and repair materials. All firearms should be declared. For more information contact the Bahamas Sports Promotion Office at (800) 327-7678.

Fishing licenses for the boat should be obtained when entering the country. They are available at $10.00 per vessel for the duration of your stay, or $50.00 per calendar year for those who make several trips to the islands. There are stiff fines for fishing without a license.

Language spoken: English.

WEST END AND LITTLE BAHAMA BANK

MEMORY ROCK LIGHT, 26 56.8N, 79 06.8W, Fl W 3s, 37ft., 11M, Metal tower.
INDIAN CAY LIGHT, 26 43.0N, 79 00.1W, Fl W 6s, 40ft., 8M, Aluminum tower.
SETTLEMENT POINT LIGHT, 26 41.5N, 78 59.9W, Fl W 4s, 44ft., 6M, W steel tower.

LITTLE SALE CAY LIGHT, 27 02.5N, 78 10.5W, Fl W 3s, 47ft., 9M, Metal tower, Unreliable.

WEST END
26 42N, 78 59W
Emergencies: Call the Bahamas Air Sea Rescue Association (BASRA) on VHF Channel 16, or on 2182kHz. The Nassau headquarters can be reached at (809) 325-8864 or at (809) 322-3877
Port of Entry: The office is located in the yacht basin, near the marina docks. You may tie up in the marina and walk to the customs office.
Dockage: Available at the Jack Tar Marina in the Yacht Basin. They monitor VHF channel 16. Entering the marina after dark may be difficult.
Anchorage: Possible between North Point and Settlement Point. This is a good anchorage if arriving after dark. Most vessels anchor outside the channel into the marina.
Services: Fuel and water are available. There are some groceries available in town. More extensive supplies are available in Freeport.

This is a convenient port of entry for many vessels traveling to the northern Bahamas. At night the tall television tower makes a good leading light. When approaching the marina the first channel to the south is for the commercial harbor. The second channel leads into the marina. The passages onto the Little Bahama Bank are very shoal here. Depths of less than 5 feet have been reported in the channel north of Indian Cay. Deeper draft boats should enter the bank near Memory Rock.

WALKERS CAY
27 16N, 78 24W
Emergencies: Call the Bahamas Air Sea Rescue Association (BASRA) on VHF Channel 16, or on 2182kHz. The Nassau headquarters can be reached at (809) 325-8864 or at (809) 322-3877
Port of Entry: The custom officer may be at the airstrip. He may be contacted through the marina.

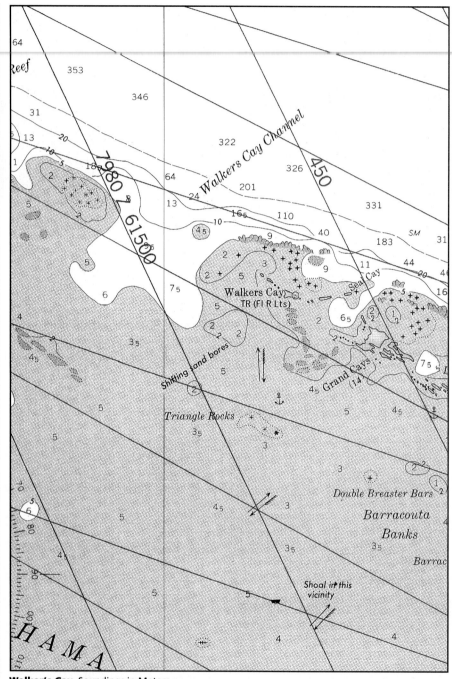

Walker's Cay, Soundings in Meters

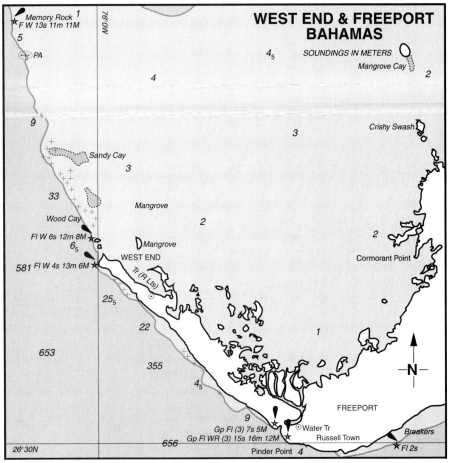

West End and Freeport Approaches, Soundings in Meters

Dockage: Available at Walkers Cay Marina which fills the protected basin on the south side of the island. Call them from the U.S. at (800) 432-2092, or on VHF channel 16. Dock space fills quickly during fishing tournaments, and reservations are advised.

Anchorage: There may be some room to anchor west of the western breakwater forming the marina. This area is shallow.

Services: Fuel, water, fishing supplies and some limited groceries are available. The resort has accommodations and a restaurant.

This island and resort are dedicated to sport fishing. The entry channel is very shoal and shifting. Stakes are moved to mark the deep water, but an approach in good light is recom-

mended. Approach depths have been reported as less than 5 feet from the banks side.

GREAT ABACO

CRAB CAY LIGHT, Angel Fish Point, 26 55.6N, 77 36.3W, Fl W 5s, 33ft., 8M, Metal tower.

GREEN TURTLE CAY

26 46N, 77 20W

Emergencies: Call the Bahamas Air Sea Rescue Association (BASRA) on VHF Channel 16, or on 2182kHz. The Nassau headquarters can be reached at (809) 325-8864 or at (809) 322-3877

Dockage: In White Sound there is the Bluff House Marina (809) 365-4247 and the Green Turtle Club (809) 365-4460. The Other Shore

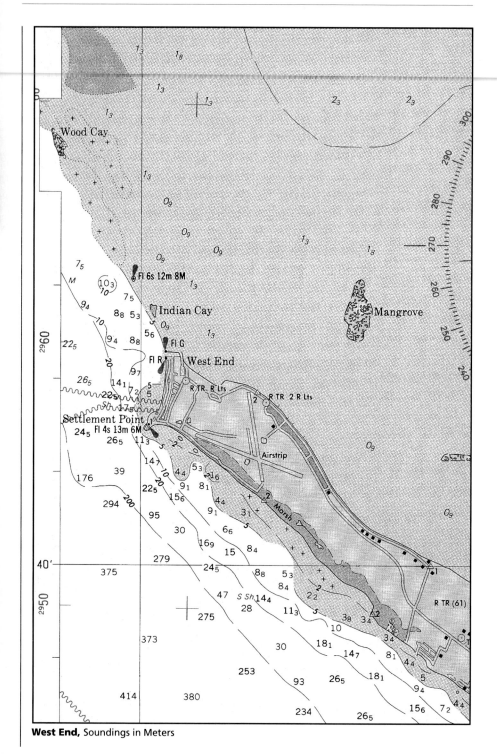

West End, Soundings in Meters

GAMEFISH OF THE BAHAMAS

The following table will give you a general idea of the fishing prospects in the Bahamas. Check with Bahamian officials for the latest bag limits and other restrictions.

E = Excellent   **G** = Good   **F** = Fair   **O** = Occasional   **N** = None

	Jan	Feb	Mar	Apr	May	June	July	Aug	Sept	Oct	Nov	Dec
Blue Marlin	O	O	G	G	E	E	E	G	F	O	O	O
White Marlin	O	F	G	E	E	G	F	F	F	F	F	O
Sailfish	F	F	G	E	G	F	F	O	O	F	F	F
Swordfish	F	F	F	F	G	E	F	E	E	F	F	F
Dolphin	F	F	G	E	G	E	E	G	G	G	E	F
Wahoo	E	E	E	F	O	F	O	O	O	F	E	E
Kingfish	F	F	F	F	F	O	O	O	F	F	F	F
Mackeral	G	G	E	E	F	G	G	F	F	F	F	F
Allison Tuna	O	O	E	E	E	F	F	O	O	O	O	O
Blackfin Tuna	F	F	F	F	G	E	E	F	O	F	F	F
Bluefin Tuna	N	N	O	G	E	G	N	N	O	N	N	N
Bonito	F	F	F	F	G	E	E	F	N	F	F	F
Bonefish	G/E	G/E	E	E	G/E	G/E	G/E	G/E	G/E	G/E	G/E	G/E
Permit	F	F	G	E	E	E	E	G	F	F	G	G
Tarpon	O	O	O	F	G	G	F	F	O	O	O	O
Amberjack	F	F	E	E	E	E	E	E	F	F	F	F
Grouper	E	E	G	G	G	G	G	G	G	G	G	G
Snapper	G	G	G	E	E	E	E	G	G	G	G	G
Barracuda	G	G	G	G	G	E	E	E	E	G	G	G
Shark	G	G	G	E	E	G	G	G	G	G	G	G

Chapter 2

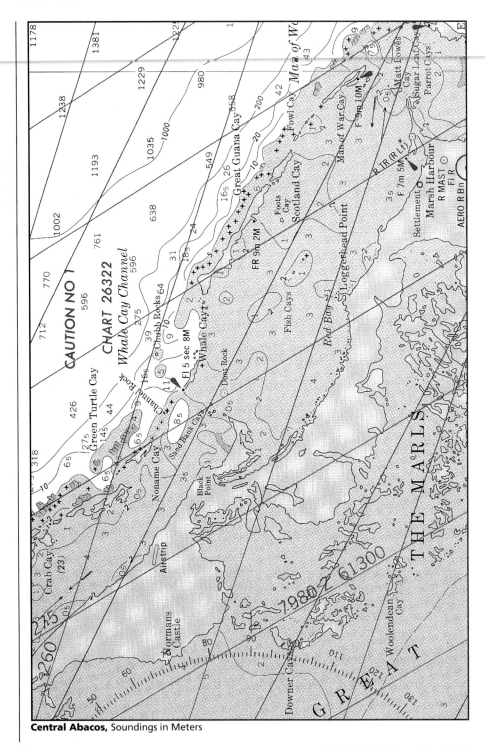

Central Abacos, Soundings in Meters

Club (809) 365-4195 and Green Turtle Shipyard (809) 365-4033 are located in Black Sound. All marinas monitor VHF channel 16. Contact the marinas for the latest channel depths.

Anchorage: Good anchorage is available in both Black Sound and White Sound. Some boats anchor west of New Plymouth or in shallow Settlement Creek to the east of town.

Services: Fuel, water and repairs are available. There are haulout facilities in Black Sound. Plymouth has a good selection of shops and restaurants.

WHALE CAY LIGHT, Western point, 26 42.9N, 77 14.8W, Fl W 5s, 40ft., 8M, Black and aluminum structure.

WHALE CAY PASS

26 42N, 77 14W

Emergencies: Call the Bahamas Air Sea Rescue Association (BASRA) on VHF Channel 16, or on 2182kHz. The Nassau headquarters can be reached at (809) 325-8864 or at (809) 322-3877

CAUTION: This is a dangerous passage during periods of heavy onshore seas and winds. These conditions are known locally as a "rage". Large vessels have been capsized during these conditions.

A marked ship channel used by cruise ships leads in the direction of Guana Cay. Several large spoil banks have been created south of the channel from dredged material. The shallow "Don't Rock Passage" leads across the banks inside of Whale Cay, but it is very poorly defined. Depths are reported to be less than 3 feet.

TREASURE CAY

26 40N, 77 17W

Emergencies: Call the Bahamas Air Sea Rescue Association (BASRA) on VHF Channel 16, or on 2182kHz. The Nassau headquarters can be reached at (809) 325-8864 or at (809) 322-3877

Dockage: Treasure Cay Marina can be reached at (809) 365-2570 or on VHF channel 16. Luxurious dockage, with all amenities, is available.

Anchorage: Anchor outside of the channel before reaching the marina. There may be some moorings available for rent.

Services: Fuel, water and basic supplies are available. The resort has several restaurants and shops.

GREAT GUANA CAY LIGHT, 26 39.8N, 77 06.8W, F W, 30ft., 2M, W pole.
MARSH HARBOR, N. side, 26 33.1N, 77 03.4W, Fl W 4s, 23ft., 5M, W mast.
MAN OF WAR CAY LIGHT, 26 35.2N, 77 00.0W, Q W, 30ft., 5M, W pole.

MARSH HARBOUR

26 33N, 77 03W

Emergencies: Call the Bahamas Air Sea Rescue Association (BASRA) on VHF Channel 16, or on 2182kHz. The Nassau headquarters can be reached at (809) 325-8864 or at (809) 322-3877

Port of Entry: Use the Government Wharf at the western end of the harbor. A separate channel leads to the wharf.

Dockage: Several marinas offer many possibilities for dockage here. Boat Harbour (809) 367-2736. Conch Inn Marina (809) 367-2800. Harbour View Marina (809) 367-2175. Marsh Harbour Marina (809) 367-2700. Triple J Marina (809) 367-2163. All marinas monitor VHF channel 16.

Anchorage: Anchor anywhere depths permit, without blocking the marked channels.

Services: All services available. Nearby Man of War Cay has haulout facilities. This is the commercial center of the Abacos, and is your best port for major stocking of groceries, doing laundry, obtaining parts, receiving mail and making travel arrangements. Fresh water is available in large quantities.

Marsh Harbour is one of the largest towns in the Bahamas. It is often the best port for restocking your boat when in the Abacos. There's also a good selection of shops, restaurants and night-life ashore.

MAN OF WAR CAY

26 35N, 77 00W

Emergencies: Call the Bahamas Air Sea Rescue Association (BASRA) on VHF Channel 16, or on 2182kHz. The Nassau headquarters can be reached at (809) 325-8864 or at (809) 322-3877

Dockage: Contact Man-O-War Marina at (809) 365-6008 or on VHF channel 16. They are located in the western arm of the harbor. Approach depths are reported to be about 5 feet.

Anchorage: A popular anchorage is in Eastern Harbour. There may be some moorings available here. It may be possible to anchor among the moored boats in the main harbor to the west. Beware of shoal spots.

Chapter 2

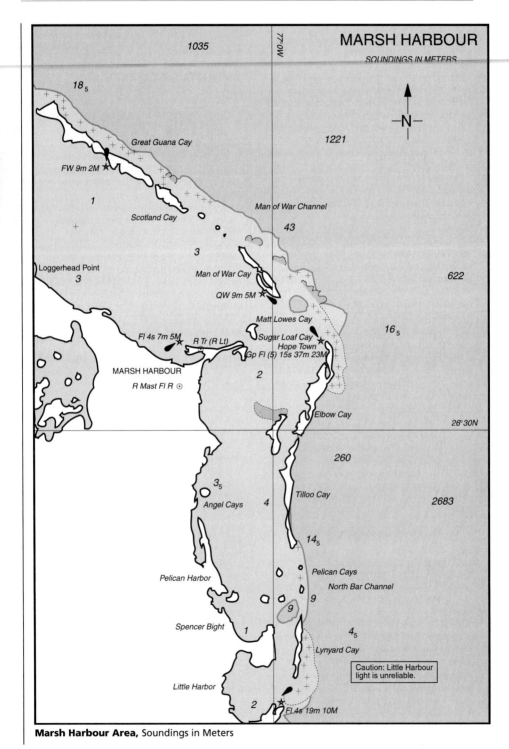

1035

77°0'W

MARSH HARBOUR

SOUNDINGS IN METERS

N

18₅

Great Guana Cay

1221

FW 9m 2M ★

1

Scotland Cay

Man of War Channel

43

3

Loggerhead Point

3

Man of War Cay

QW 9m 5M ★

622

Matt Lowes Cay

16₅

Fl 4s 7m 5M ★

R Tr (R Lt)

Sugar Loaf Cay
Hope Town
Gp Fl (5) 15s 37m 23M

MARSH HARBOUR

R Mast Fl R ⊙

2

Elbow Cay

26°30'N

260

3₅

Angel Cays

4

Tilloo Cay

2683

14₅

Pelican Harbor

Pelican Cays

North Bar Channel

9

9

Spencer Bight

1

4₅

Lynyard Cay

Caution: Little Harbour
light is unreliable.

Little Harbor

2

Fl 4s 19m 10M

Marsh Harbour Area, Soundings in Meters

Services: All boat services are available. This is one of the best places for major repairs in the Bahamas. There are haulout facilities and services for major repairs of all sorts. The boat yards are expert in wood repairs, and there is a sail loft and a well stocked hardware store. Most groceries are available, though the selection is not as great as in Marsh Harbour.

ELBOW CAY LIGHT (Hope Town), 26 32.4N, 76 58.0W, Fl (5) W 15s, 120ft., 23M, W tower, R bands, W lantern.

HOPE TOWN

26 33N, 76 58W

Emergencies: Call the Bahamas Air Sea Rescue Association (BASRA) on VHF Channel 16, or on 2182kHz. The Nassau headquarters can be reached at (809) 325-8864 or at (809) 322-3877

Dockage: Contact Hope Town Marina at (809) 366-0003, or Lighthouse Marina at (809) 366-0154. The marinas monitor VHF channel 16. Approach depths have been reported as about 5 feet.

Moorings: A profusion of moorings now cover most of Hope Town harbor. Contact one of the marinas for mooring assignment. Hope Town Marina has red moorings.

Anchorage: It may be possible to find some room among the moored boats, but be prepared for poor holding and limited swinging room.

Services: Fuel, water and a good selection of groceries are available. There is a bakery and several restaurants.

SANDY CAY BEACON, 26 24.0N, 76 59.1W, Fl G 3s, Beacon.

LITTLE HARBOR LIGHT, S. side of entrance, 26 19.7N, 76 59.6W, Fl W 4s, 61ft., 10M, W building.

LITTLE HARBOUR

26 20N, 77 00W

Emergencies: Call the Bahamas Air Sea Rescue Association (BASRA) on VHF Channel 16, or on 2182kHz. The Nassau headquarters can be reached at (809) 325-8864 or at (809) 322-3877

Moorings: Contact Pete's Pub at the dock on the western side of the harbor. The channel depths have been reported to be 3 to 4 feet.

Anchorage: Anchor off the docks, or wherever depths allow.

Services: Meals and drinks are available at Pete's Pub. No other services.

This is the location of the famous Johnston Studios, where Randolph Johnston has created his famous lost wax process bronzes. A visit to the studios is a must stop. There are bronzes and jewelry available for sale. This harbor is well sheltered in most weather, but the entrance channel is quite shoal. The pass from the ocean is rather tricky, and should only be attempted in good light. North Bar Channel is a better pass if conditions are not ideal.

CHEROKEE SOUND LIGHT, On Duck Cay, 26 16.0N, 77 04.0W, F R, 29ft., 6M, W stone building, Visible 229° to 094° except where obscured to the E by the high land of Cherokee Point.

ABACO LIGHT, HOLE IN THE WALL, 25 51.5N, 77 11.2W, Fl W 10s, 168ft., 23M, W tower, R top, W lantern.

ROCKY POINT LIGHT, 25 59.9N, 77 24.3W, Fl W 6s, 33ft., 10M, Black metal framework.

SANDY POINT LIGHT, 26 01.6N, 77 24.0W, F W, 25ft., 5M, Pole.

CHANNEL CAY LIGHT, 26 15.0N, 77 37.8W, Fl W 2.5s, 38ft., 7M, Black steel lattice structure.

GRAND BAHAMA ISLAND

SWEETINGS CAY LIGHT, 26 36.7N, 77 54.0W, Fl W 6s, 23ft., 8M, Black tower.

RIDING POINT AVIATION LIGHT, 26 42.7N, 78 09.5W, Oc R 3s, 269ft., R+W tower.

SOUTH RIDING POINT HARBOR RANGE, (Front Light) 26 37.5N, 78 13.1W, Oc G 3s, 39ft., Orange triangle on framework tower. **(Rear Light)** 60 meters, 340° from front, Oc G 3s, 52ft., Orange diamond on framework tower.

COMMUNICATIONS TOWER LIGHTS, 26 37.7N, 78 14.3W, 2 F R, 239ft., R + W tower, Lights in vertical line on tower.

PLATFORM LIGHT, 26 36.8N, 78 13.7W, Fl R 3s, Control building, Two Q R lights on east and west dolphins.

HIGH ROCK LIGHT, S. side of Grand Bahama, 26 37.3N, 78 16.1W, F W, 25ft., 6M, W pole.

IONOSPHERIC TOWER AVIATION LIGHT, 26 37.1N, 78 18.8W, Fl R, Oc R 8s, 210ft.

BASSETT COVE TOWER AVIATION LIGHT, 26 36.8N, 78 19.4W, Q R, 2 F R, 407ft., R + W tower, Lights in vertical line.

BORE SITE TOWER AVIATION LIGHT, 26 36.7N, 78 20.9W, F W, 2 F R, Oc R 4s, 174ft., R+W tower, Lights in vertical line.

GRAND LUCAYAN WATERWAY LIGHT, W breakwater head, 26 32.4N, 78 33.4W, Fl (3) G 10s, 13ft., 3M, Concrete column.

GRAND LUCAYAN WATERWAY LIGHT, E breakwater head, 26 32.4N, 78 33.3W, Fl (3) R 10s, 13ft., 3M, Concrete column.

BAHAMIA MARINA LIGHT, Xanadu Marina, E breakwater head, 26 29.3N, 78 42.1W, Q R, 3M, Concrete pedestal.

BAHAMIA MARINA LIGHT, Xanadu Marina, W breakwater head, 26 29.3N, 78 42.2W, Q G, 3M, Concrete pedestal.

XANADU, RUNNING MON, OCEAN REEF, LUCAYA

26 29N 78 42W

Emergencies: Call the Bahamas Air Sea Rescue Association (BASRA) on VHF Channel 16, or on 2182kHz. The Nassau headquarters can be reached at (809) 325-8864 or at (809) 322-3877

Ports of Entry: Pleasure boats may clear at Xanadu in the first marked channel east of Freeport. You may also clear at the two marinas in the Bell Channel area.

Harbormasters: Contact Xanadu, Running Mon, Ocean Reef, Port Lucaya and the Lucayan Marina on VHF Channel 16 or at the following phone numbers: Xanadu – (809) 352-6782, Running Mon – (809) 352-6834, Ocean Reef – (809) 373-4662, Port Lucaya – (809) 373-9090, Lucayan Marina – (809) 373-8888.

Dockage: Available at all of the marinas mentioned above.

Services: All services available in this area. A short bus or taxi ride will take you to Freeport proper. Many tourist shops and restaurants are located near the marinas.

The first marked channel east of Freeport leads to the Xanadu marina. This area is listed as Bahamia Marina on the charts. A little further east is the entrance to Running Mon Marina, and the entrance to the Ocean Reef Club is located about 2.2 miles further east at about 78 39.6W. The waterway labeled Bell Channel is the home of the Port Lucaya and Lucayan Marinas. The entrance to the Lucayan Waterway is located about 5 miles east of the Bell Channel. The waterway provides a protected inside route to the Little Bahama Bank for those who can clear a 27 foot fixed bridge. Controlling depth is reported to be about 4 or 5 feet.

FREEPORT INTERNATIONAL AIRPORT AVIATION LIGHT, 26 32.9N, 78 42.3W, Alt W G 10s, 98ft., 40M.

FREEPORT LIGHT, Pinder Point, 26 30.4N, 78 45.9W, Fl (3) W R 15s, 54ft., 12M, W structure, Black bands, W 301° to 113°, R 113° to 301°, Occasional, Reported obscured to seaward by jetties and ships.

BORCO OIL TERMINAL LIGHT, No. 1 Jetty SE end, 26 30.0N, 78 46.2W, Q W.

BORCO OIL TERMINAL LIGHT, No. 1 Jetty NW end, 26 30.3N, 78 46.7W, Fl (3) W 7s, 5M, Dolphin.

BORCO OIL TERMINAL LIGHT, No. 2 Jetty NW end, 26 30.5N, 78 46.7W, Q W, Dolphin.

FREEPORT WEST BREAKWATER LIGHT, 26 31.1N, 78 46.7W, Fl W 4s, 23ft., 2M, Metal structure.

FREEPORT CHANNEL ENTRANCE, W side, 26 31.2N, 78 46.6W, Fl G 4s, 12ft., 2M, Metal structure.

FREEPORT CHANNEL ENTRANCE, E side, 26 31.2N, 78 46.5W, Fl R 4s, 12ft., 2M, Metal structure.

FREEPORT

26 31N 78 47W

Emergencies: Call the Bahamas Air Sea Rescue Association (BASRA) on VHF Channel 16, or on 2182kHz. The Nassau headquarters can be reached at (809) 325-8864 or at (809) 322-3877

Port of Entry: Vessels may clear customs here, though the harbor is oriented to serving large commercial vessels. Pleasure boats usually clear at one of the marinas to the east of Freeport.

Freeport Harbour Control: Call on VHF channel 16 when approaching the harbor.

Dockage: Contact Freeport Harbour Control for details. Most pleasure boats dock at one of the marinas to the east of Freeport.

Anchorage: None in harbor.

Services: Fuel and water are available at the marinas to the east. Freeport has a good selection of supplies including a variety of tourist oriented shops. The town is located well to the northeast of the harbor, and will be a cab ride away for most boaters.

Freeport is one of the leading commercial harbors in the Bahamas. Large cruise ships, cargo vessels and oil tankers call here.

PINDER POINT RANGE, (Front Light) 26 31.5N, 78 46.4W, F G, 26ft., 3M, Orange and W diamond shaped daymark on beacon. **(Rear Light)** 255 meters, 021°47' from front, 26 31.6N, 78 46.4W, F G, 45ft., 3M, Orange and W diamond shaped daymark on beacon.

SETTLEMENT POINT LIGHT, 26 41.5N, 78 59.9W, Fl W 4s, 44ft., 6M, W steel tower.

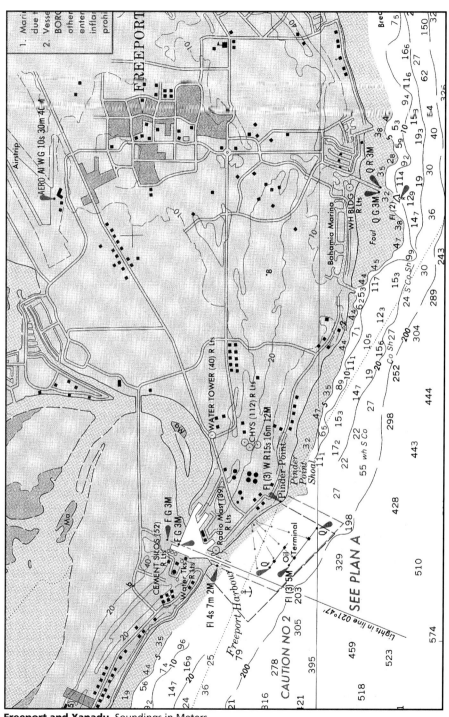

Freeport and Xanadu, Soundings in Meters

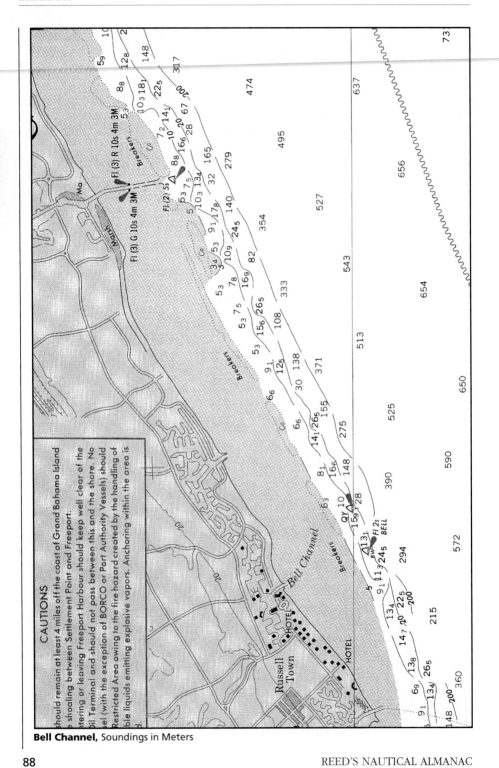

Bell Channel, Soundings in Meters

BIMINI AND CAT CAY APPROACHES

GREAT ISAAC LIGHT, 26 01.8N, 79 05.4W, Fl W 15s, 152ft., 23M, W tower.
NORTH ROCK LIGHT, 1.9 km N of North Bimini, 25 48.2N, 79 16.7W, Fl W 3s, 40ft., 8M, W skeleton steel tower, Visible 022° to 343°.
NORTH BIMINI ISLAND LIGHT, Head of wharf, 25 43.7N, 79 19.1W, F W, 20ft., 5M, Gray steel framework tower, Two F R range lights indicate channel through reef on South Bimini, These lights are considered unreliable.
BIMINI AVIATION LIGHT, 25 42.5N, 79 16.3W, Mo (B) R 20s, 284ft., 23M, Steel framework tower.

BIMINI

25 43N, 79 18W
Emergencies: Call the Bahamas Air Sea Rescue Association (BASRA) on VHF Channel 16, or on 2182kHz. The Nassau headquarters can be reached at (809) 325-8864 or at (809) 322-3877.
Port of Entry: You may clear customs after securing your boat in a marina. Check with the dockmaster for the location of the customs office.
Dockage: Contact Bimini Blue Water at (809) 347-3166 or on VHF channel 68; Bimini Big Game Fishing Club at (809) 347-3391 or on VHF channel 16; Weech's Bimini Dock at (809) 347-3028. Care should be taken when approaching any slip due to the strong currents running through the harbor.
Anchorage: Good anchorage is available off of the marina docks. Be careful not to block access to the marinas or the seaplane ramp. There are strong currents and the bottom shoals rapidly to the east and north.
Services: Fuel, water, groceries, liquor, hardware and limited marine supplies available. Any supplies needed may be flown in from Miami or Ft. Lauderdale, but import duties will apply.

Bimini is only 45 miles from Miami, and makes a convenient first port of call for boaters. The entrance channel is frequently shifted to follow the deepest water. There is usually a range on the South Bimini beach directing boaters over the bar. The channel then parallels the beach running north into the harbor. If in any doubt, call one of the marinas on the VHF radio for directions. It is best to arrive with good light, when the shoals will be most visible.

GUN CAY LIGHT, 25 34.5N, 79 18.8W, Fl W 10s, 80ft., 23 M, Tower, Upper red, Lower white, Obscured by Bimini between 176° and 198° when 8 miles distant.

GUN CAY CAT CAY

25 34N, 79 18W
Emergencies: Call the Bahamas Air Sea Rescue Association (BASRA) on VHF Channel 16, or on 2182kHz. The Nassau headquarters can be reached at (809) 325-8864 or at (809) 322-3877.
Port of Entry: In the past boaters cleared customs at the docks on the east side of North Cat Cay. The marina was severely damaged in Hurricane Andrew and may not be open until after July 1993. Boaters are advised to clear customs in Bimini. Call the Cat Cay Yacht Club at (305) 359-8272 for the latest information.
Dockage: The Cat Cay Yacht Club will be out of operation for non-members until at least July 1993 due to hurricane damage. Call Cat Cay Yacht Club at (305) 359-8272 for the latest information.
Anchorage: The best anchorages are on either side of Gun Cay, depending upon the weather. Honeymoon Harbor, on the north end of Gun Cay, is another favorite spot, but be careful not to get caught there in a north wind.

This is a good place to anchor before crossing the Great Bahama Bank. The channel between Gun Cay and North Cat Cay is easy when the sun is high. Hug the shore of Gun Cay closely until past the bar extending north from North Cat Cay. You can receive NOAA weather radio from Florida; it is advisable to cross the banks with a favorable forecast.

GREAT BAHAMA BANK

NORTH CAT CAY, Head of breakwater, 25 34.0N, 79 18.3W, Fl W 2s, 10ft., 5M, Beacon, Not visible W or SW of Cat Cay.
SOUTH RIDING ROCK LIGHT, 25 13.8N, 79 10.0W, Fl W 5s, 35ft., 11M, W framework structure.
SYLVIA BEACON, 25 28.0N, 79 01.0W, FL W 5s, 33ft., 8M, Beacon on piles.
MACKIE SHOAL LIGHT, 25 41.2N, 78 39.2W, Fl W 2s, 15ft., 10M, W tripod, Yellow top.
RUSSELL BEACON, 25 28.6N, 78 25.5W, Beacon has been destroyed, Use caution as the remains are dangerous.

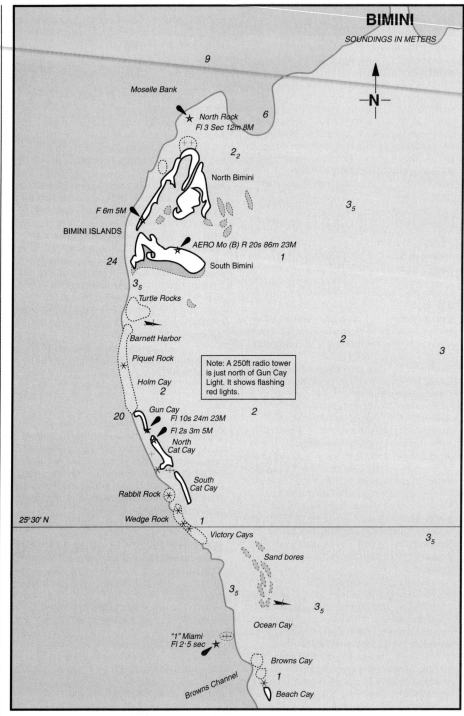

BIMINI

SOUNDINGS IN METERS

-N-

9

Moselle Bank

★ North Rock
Fl 3 Sec 12m 8M

6

2 2

North Bimini

3 5

F 6m 5M

BIMINI ISLANDS

AERO Mo (B) R 20s 86m 23M

24

1

South Bimini

3 5

Turtle Rocks

Barnett Harbor

2

3

Piquet Rock

Note: A 250ft radio tower
is just north of Gun Cay
Light. It shows flashing
red lights.

Holm Cay
2

Gun Cay
Fl 10s 24m 23M

2

20

Fl 2s 3m 5M

North
Cat Cay

South
Cat Cay

Rabbit Rock

25° 30' N

Wedge Rock

1

Victory Cays

3 5

Sand bores

3 5

3 5

Ocean Cay

"1" Miami
Fl 2·5 sec

Browns Cay

1

Browns Channel

Beach Cay

Bimini and Cat Cay Approaches, Soundings in Meters

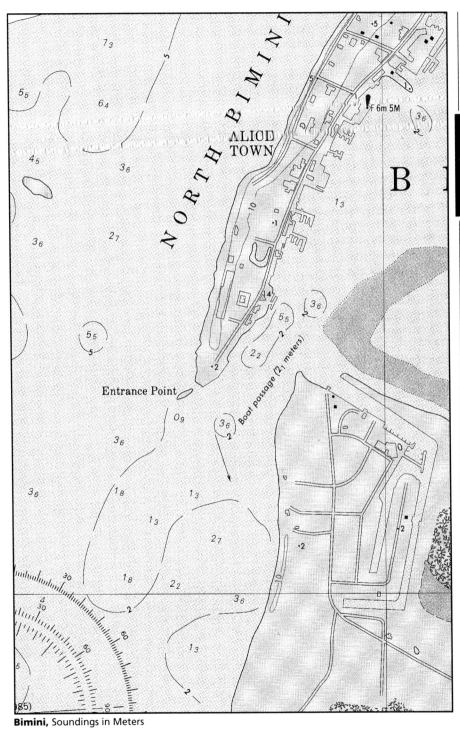

Bimini, Soundings in Meters

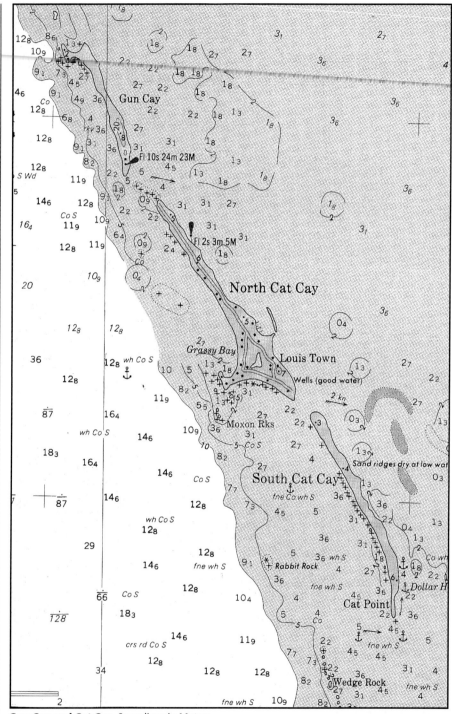

Gun Cay and Cat Cay, Soundings in Meters

Russell Lighted Buoy, 25 28.6N, 78 25.5W, Replaces Russell Beacon, Vessels anchor here at night, Use caution when approaching after dark. *Reported missing 1993.*
NORTHWEST CHANNEL LIGHT, 25 27.2N, 78 09.8W, Fl W 5s, 33ft., 8M, W skeleton tower. *Reported destroyed 1993.*

GREAT BAHAMA BANK

Emergencies: Call the Bahamas Air Sea Rescue Association (BASRA) on VHF Channel 16, or on 2182kHz. The Nassau headquarters can be reached at (809) 325-8864 or at (809) 322-3877.
Pilotage: Many boaters cross the banks from Gun Cay Light (25 34.5N, 79 18.8W) to the remains of Northwest Channel Light (25 27.2N, 78 09.8W), a distance of about 62 miles. At this writing, in early 1993, none of the aids to navigation on the banks can be considered reliable. They may be missing, off station or showing incorrect characteristics due to hurricane damage.

When leaving Gun Cay you will encounter a series of sand ridges within the first 10 miles. The controlling depth of this route has been reported as 6 feet. The water depths improve approximately 10 miles east of Gun Cay. Deeper draft vessels may want to travel from North Rock Light (25 48.2N, 79 16.7W) to Northwest Channel, taking care to avoid Mackie Shoal in approximate position 25 41.2N, 78 39.2W. On the southern route, Russel Beacon and buoy are reported as missing. Vessels anchoring on the banks are advised to show an anchor light.

Good depths have been reported on the route from South Riding Rock Light (25 13.8N, 79 10.0W) to the vicinity of the Russel Beacon, then on to Northwest Channel. Vessels may get some protection anchoring between South Riding Rock and Castle Rock.

THE BERRY ISLANDS

CHUB POINT LIGHT, 25 23.8N, 77 54.2W, Fl W R 10s, 44ft., 7M, Aluminum colored lattice structure, W from 320° to 054°, R 054° to 320°, Fl W and Fl G on water tower .8M to the NE.
FRAZERS HOG CAY AVIATION LIGHT, 25 25.0N, 77 53.7W, Fl W G, Radiobeacon.

CHUB CAY

25 24N, 77 54W
Emergencies: Call the Bahamas Air Sea Rescue Association (BASRA) on VHF Channel

16, or on 2182kHz. The Nassau headquarters can be reached at (809) 325-8864 or at (809) 322-3877.
Port of Entry: Tie up in Chub Cay Club Marina to clear customs. The officials may have to travel from the airstrip, adding an extra charge to your bill.
Dockage: Chub Cay Club Marina (809) 325-1490, or on VHF channel 68, has re-opened, having sustained damage in Hurricane Andrew. They have a protected boat basin with a reported 6 feet of water in the entrance channel.
Anchorage: Boats crossing the banks, and headed to Nassau, often anchor in the bight just south of the marina entrance channel. This area is subject to a surge, and depths run less than 6 feet in some spots. Shallow draft boats can get good protection between Mama Rhoda Cay and Chub Cay. Controlling depth in this channel is reported to be about 3 feet. Good anchorage is found in the channel along the eastern shore of Frazier's Hog Cay.
Services: Fuel and water are available in the marina. Some groceries are sold in the marina store and there is a restaurant.
This is a good spot to break up the long journey from Nassau across the banks. From here it is about 50 miles to Nassau and 76 miles to Gun Cay. The main anchorage may become untenable in strong winds due to the large swell that rolls through it.

WHALE POINT LIGHT, SW Point of Whale Cay, 25 23.0N, 77 47.8W, Fl W 4s, 70ft., 7M, Stone tower, W steel superstructure.
LITTLE HARBOR CAY LIGHT, 25 33.6N, 77 42.4W, Fl W 2.2s, 94ft., 9M, B + W banded pipe.

LITTLE HARBOUR CAY

25 34N, 77 43W
Anchorage Only: Anchor between Little Harbour Cay and Cabbage Cay. A shallow channel leads north to a private dock on Little Harbour. This channel has a reported depth of less than 3 feet.

BULLOCK HARBOR LIGHT, 25 45.8N, 77 52.1W, Fl R 6s, 36ft., 7M, Iron pyramidal structure, Upper half W, Lower half black.

GREAT HARBOUR CAY

25 45N, 77 52W
Emergencies: Call the Bahamas Air Sea Rescue Association (BASRA) on VHF Channel 16, or on 2182kHz. The Nassau headquarters

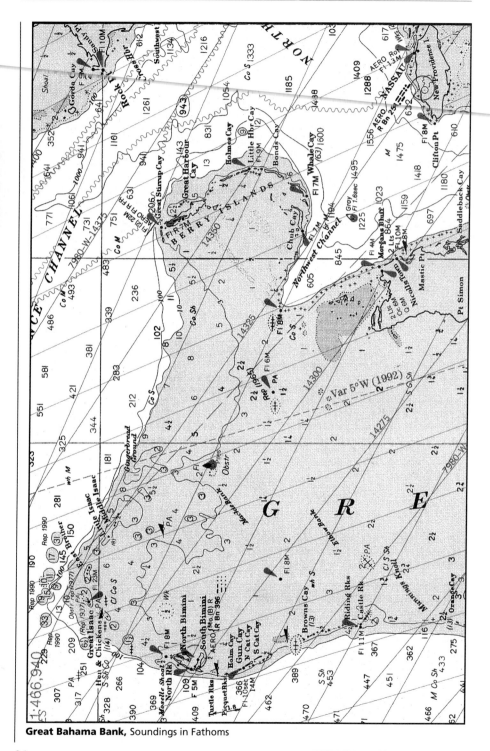

Great Bahama Bank, Soundings in Fathoms

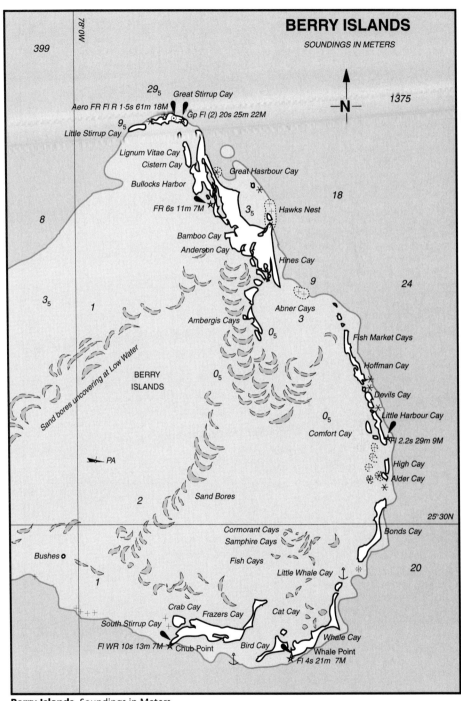

BERRY ISLANDS

SOUNDINGS IN METERS

399

78·0W

29_5 Great Stirrup Cay

Aero FR Fl R 1·5s 61m 18M

Gp Fl (2) 20s 25m 22M

9_5
Little Stirrup Cay

1375

–N–

Lignum Vitae Cay
Cistern Cay

Great Hasrbour Cay

Bullocks Harbor

18

FR 6s 11m 7M

3_5

Hawks Nest

8

Bamboo Cay

Anderson Cay

Hines Cay

3_5

1

9

24

Abner Cays

Ambergis Cays

3

0_5

Fish Market Cays

Hoffman Cay

BERRY
ISLANDS

0_5

Devils Cay

Sand bores uncovering at Low Water

0_5

Little Harbour Cay

Comfort Cay

Fl 2.2s 29m 9M

PA

High Cay

Alder Cay

2

Sand Bores

25° 30N

Cormorant Cays

Samphire Cays

Bonds Cay

Bushes o

Fish Cays

Little Whale Cay

20

1

Crab Cay

Frazers Cay

Cat Cay

South Stirrup Cay

Whale Cay

Fl WR 10s 13m 7M

Chub Point

Bird Cay

Whale Point

Fl 4s 21m 7M

Berry Islands, Soundings in Meters

Chapter 2

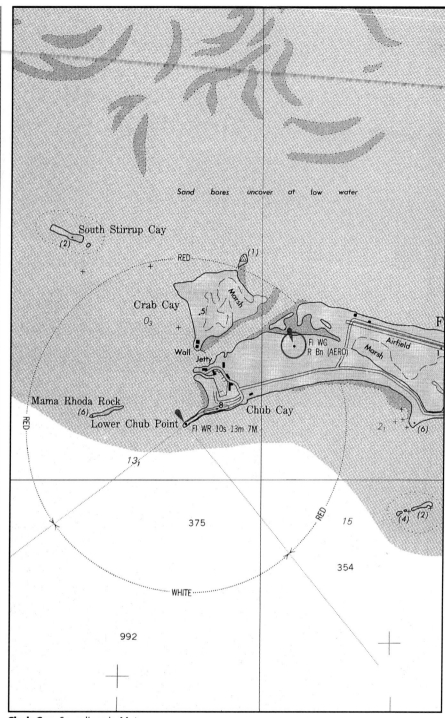

Sand   bores   uncover   at   low   water

South Stirrup Cay
(2)

RED

(1)

Crab Cay
.5
0₃

Marsh

FI WG
R Bn (AERO)

F

Airfield

Marsh

Wall
Jetty

Mama Rhoda Rock
(6)

Lower Chub Point
FI WR 10s 13m 7M

8

Chub Cay

RED

2₇

(6)

13₇

375

RED

15

(4) (2)

354

WHITE

992

Chub Cay, Soundings in Meters

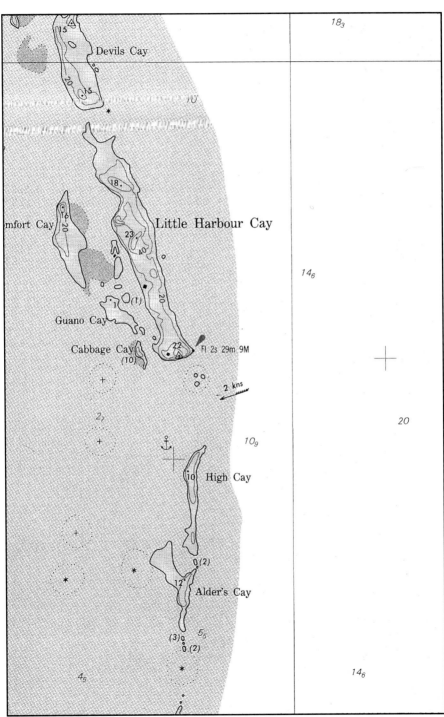

Little Harbour Cay, Soundings in Meters

can be reached at (809) 325-8864 or at (809) 322-3877.

Port of Entry: Tie up in Great Harbour Cay Marina, and call customs via telephone. They must come in from the airstrip.

Dockage: Contact Great Harbour Cay Marina at (809) 367-8114, (800) 343-7256 or on VHF channel 68. A staked channel leads from an unlit mark about 2 miles south of the west end of Little Stirrup Cay. Call the marina, or the toll free number for the latest information.

Anchorage: Anchor west of Bullock's Harbour, or south of the marina channel.

Services: Fuel, water, groceries and restaurants are available.

GREAT STIRRUP CAY LIGHT, 640 meters from E end, 25 49.7N, 77 54.0W, Fl (2) W 20s, 82ft., 22M, W circular tower. *Reported extinguished 1993.*

GREAT STIRRUP CAY AVIATION LIGHT, 1189 meters from E end, 25 49.8N, 77 54.4W, Fl R 1.5s, 200ft., 18M, Radio mast, Obstruction light.

GREAT STIRRUP CAY

25 50N, 77 54W

Anchorage Only: Enter the anchorage at the eastern end of the cay. Cruise ships discharge passengers in the coves on the north side of the island. Caution: The light has been reported as unreliable.

NASSAU AND APPROACHES

CLIFTON TERMINAL LIGHT, Commercial harbor on SW end of New Providence Island, 25 00.4N, 77 32.5W, 2 Q R (horiz.), 121ft., 13M, 2 F R (horiz.), 59ft., 10M, Orange mast w/white bands.

GOULDING CAY LIGHT, Off W end of New Providence Island, 25 01.6N, 77 35.8W, Fl W 2s, 36ft., 8M, Gray structure.

FORT FINCASTLE AVIATION LIGHT, 25 04.4N, 77 20.3W, Fl W 5s, 219ft., 28M, Gray concrete tower.

PARADISE ISLAND LIGHT, W point, 25 05.2N, 77 21.1W, Fl W or R 5s, 68ft., 13M white, White conical stone tower, *Changed to Fl R 5s when bar is dangerous,* Obscured 334° to 025°.

NASSAU EAST BREAKWATER HEAD LIGHT, 25 05.3N, 77 21.2W, Fl G 5s, 29ft., Reported destroyed February 1991.

NASSAU WEST BREAKWATER HEAD LIGHT, 25 05.1N, 77 21.3W, Fl R 5s, 29ft., Tower.

NASSAU HARBOR RANGE, (Front Light) 25 04.7N, 77 21.0W, F G, 37ft., 7M, R framework tower. **(Rear Light)** 260 meters, 151°36' from front, F G, 61ft., 7M, R framework tower.

GOVERNMENT HOUSE LIGHT, 25 04.5N, 77 20.7W, Fl R 3s, 122ft., 10M, Green cupola on building.

THE NARROWS LIGHT, Between Paradise Island and Athol Island, 25 05.0N, 77 18.5W, Fl R 5s, 12M, 2M, R post.

PORGEE ROCKS LIGHT, 25 04.3N, 77 15.8W, Fl W 3s, 25ft., 5M, Gray structure.

CHUB ROCKS LIGHT, 25 06.9N, 77 15.6W, Fl W 5s, 32ft., 4M, W framework tower.

EAST END POINT LIGHT, On point S of East End Point on New Providence Island, 25 02.3N, 77 16.8W, Fl W 6s, 57ft., 8M, W square stone building, Visible 180° to 056°.

NASSAU

25 05N, 77 21W

Emergencies: Call the Bahamas Air Sea Rescue Association (BASRA) on VHF Channel 16, or on 2182kHz. The Nassau headquarters can be reached at (809) 325-8864 or at (809) 322-3877. BASRA headquarters is located just west of the Paradise Island Bridge and Potter's Cay. They have a dock which is a favorite dinghy landing site. For more information contact BASRA, P.O. Box SS-6247, Nassau, Bahamas.

Nassau Harbour Control: All vessels must report on VHF channel 16 when entering the harbor, or when moving within the harbor.

Port of Entry: The office is located on the cruise ship docks. You may tie up here (use lots of fenders) or call customs from one of the marinas.

Dockage: Contact East Bay Marina at (809) 322-3754, or on VHF channel 16; Hurricane Hole at (809) 326-3600; Nassau Yacht Haven at (809) 393-8173, or on VHF channel 16; Nassau Harbour Club at (809) 393-0771, or on VHF channel 16. All of the marinas are located east of the Paradise Island Bridge, except East Bay Marina. The latter is located in the basin just west of the bridge.

Anchorage: The holding ground in most of Nassau Harbour has been reported to be very poor. Boats must stay clear of the cruise ship docks, the marinas and the seaplane landing area. Some boats anchor south of Paradise Island near the docks of Club Med, or at the eastern end of the harbor. There are also charted shoal areas and cable areas to be avoided.

Services: All services are available. Major repairs and haulouts may be done here. There

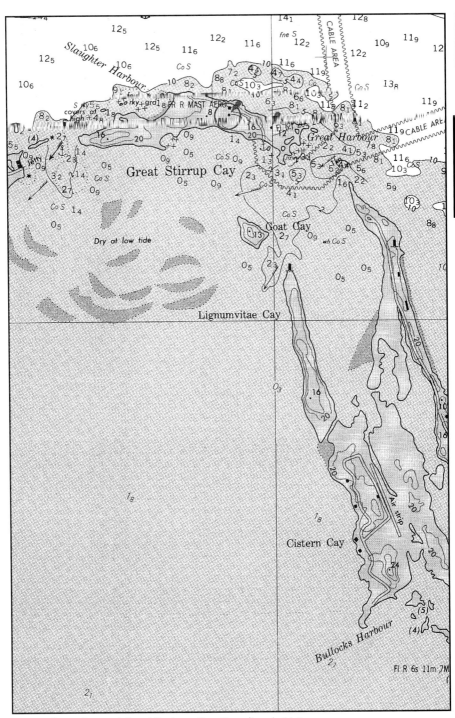

Great Stirrup Cay and Great Harbour Cay, Soundings in Meters

Chapter 2

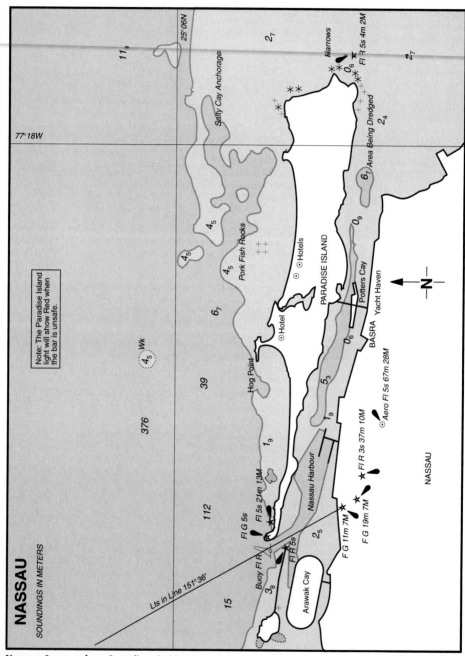

Nassau Approaches, Soundings in Meters

Within the chart:

NASSAU

SOUNDINGS IN METERS

Note: The Paradise Island light will show Red when the bar is unsafe.

25°06N

77°18W

11₃

2₇

2₇

Salty Cay Anchorage

Narrows

Fl R 5s 4m 2M

0₆

Area Being Dredged

2₄

6₇

0₉

4₅

4₅

4₅

Pork Fish Rocks

4₅

6₇

Hotels

Hotels

PARADISE ISLAND

Potters Cay

Yacht Haven

N

Wk

4₅

39

Hotel

0₆

BASRA

376

6₇

5₃

Hog Point

Aero Fl 5s 67m 28M

1₉

Fl R 3s 37m 10M

1₉

Fl 5s 21m 13M

NASSAU

112

Fl G 5s

Nassau Harbour

F G 11m 7M

F G 19m 7M

Buoy Fl R

Fl R 5s

2₅

15

Lts in Line 151°36'

3₈

Arawak Cay

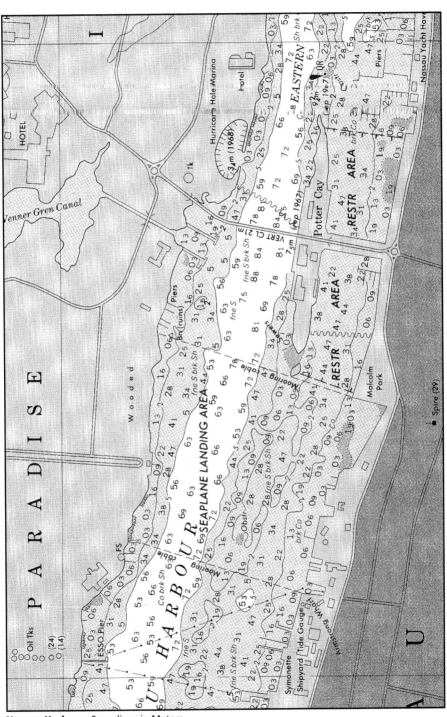

Nassau Harbour, Soundings in Meters

are several large grocery stores, hardware stores, marine supply stores and many restaurants, bars, casinos, shops and modern services of all types.

Nassau Harbor has a bar across the entrance channel. If the Paradise Island bar light shows red, the channel is considered dangerous. In general, approaching the harbor after dark is not considered safe due to the difficulty of spotting the navigation aids against the background of the city lights. Boaters should be prepared to encounter large cruise ships, freighters and barges in the harbor. Nassau Harbour Control will advise you of any traffic problems.

This is the capital of the Bahamas and is an exciting port of call. There are many historic sights and interesting attractions to see ashore. This is also a good place to conduct banking, place phone calls and make travel arrangements.

PORT NEW PROVIDENCE MARINA LIGHT, 25 00.2N, 77 15.7W, Fl W 4s, 7 ft, 4M, Wooden Pile.
MARINA CHANNEL NO. 1, 25 00.3N, 77 15.7W, Fl W 4s, 7 ft., 4M, Wooden Pile.
MARINA CHANNEL NO. 2, 25 00.4N, 77 15.8W, Fl W 4s, 7 ft., 4M, Wooden Pile.

ANDROS

MORGANS BLUFF RANGE, (Front Light) 25 10.5N, 78 02.1W, Q W, 29ft., 6M. Intensified on range line, **(Rear Light)** 223°44′ from front, Oc W 4s, 60ft., 6M. Intensified on range line.
MORGANS BLUFF DOCK LIGHT, 25 10.8N, 78 01.6W, Fl W 4s, 20ft., 4M.
NICOLLS TOWN RANGE, (Front Light) 25 07.8N, 78 00.5W, Fl W 5s, 60ft., 8M, R and aluminum colored structure. **(Rear Light)** 24 meters, 247° from front Fl W 5s, 65ft., 10M, R and aluminum colored structure.
STANIARD ROCK LIGHT, 24 51.1N, 77 52.5W, Fl W 4s, 18ft., 6M, Gray structure.
STANIARD CREEK LIGHT, 24 50.8N, 77 54.0W, F R, 26ft., 6M, Wooden framework structure.
FRESH CREEK ISLET LIGHT, S side, 24 44.3N, 77 46.9W, Fl W 6s, 10ft., 5M, Metal mast.
ANDROS TOWN LIGHT, S side of entrance, 24 43.7N, 77 47.8W, F W, 27ft., 6M, W quadrangular stone building.
SITE 1 N ITT TOWER, 24 43.9N, 77 46.3W, Fl Y 4s, 5M, Steel skeleton tower.

SITE 1 S ITT TOWER, 24 42.4N, 77 45.3W, Fl Y 4s 5M, Steel skeleton tower.
OHDF TOWER LIGHT, 24 43.7N, 77 45.7W, Q W, 5M, 51ft.
AVIATION LIGHT, 24 42.3N, 77 46.4W, Al Fl W G Y 2s, 136ft., Tower.
AUTEC SITE 1 RANGE, (Front Light) 24 42.3N, 77 45.9W, Q W, 25ft., 10M, W tower, R daymark w/white stripe. **(Rear Light)** 335 meters, 223°48′ from front, Iso W 6s, 33ft., 10 M, W tower, R daymark w/white stripe.
HIGH CAY LIGHT, 24 39.3N, 77 42.6W, Fl W 4s, 70ft., 6M, Metal Mast.
AUTEC SITE 1 LIGHT 5, 24 42.8N, 77 45.3W, Fl G 4s, 18ft., 4M, Dolphin, Green square daymark w/green reflective border, Fl G and Fl R lights mark channel.
AUTEC SITE 2 RANGE, (Front Light) 24 29.9N, 77 43.1W, Q W, 22ft., 10M, W skeletal tower, R daymark w/white stripes. **(Rear Light)** 745 meters, 269°54′ from front, Iso W 6s, 42ft., 10M, W skeletal tower, R daymark w/white stripes.
AUTEC SITE 2 LIGHT 3, 24 29.9N, 77 42.1W, Fl G 4s, 19ft., 4M, Dolphin, Green square daymark w/green reflective border, Fl G and Fl R lights mark channel.
SITE 3 ITT TOWER, 24 20.9N, 77 40.4W, Fl Y 4s, 33ft., 5M.
AUTEC SITE 3 LIGHT 3, 24 20.1N, 77 40.4W, Fl G 4s, 19ft., 4M. Dolphin, Green square daymark w/green reflective border, Fl G and Fl R lights mark channel.

NOTE: AUTEC (ATLANTIC UNDERSEA TEST AND EVALUATION CENTER) SITES ARE OFF LIMITS TO BOATERS, EXCEPT IN AN EMERGENCY.

MIDDLE BIGHT LIGHT, On rock S side of channel, 24 18.8N, 77 40.3W, Fl W 5s, 17ft., 7M, W steel framework tower.
MANGROVE CAY PEATS WHARF LIGHT, 24 14.8N, 77 39.2W, F R, 20ft., 7M.
SIRIOUS ROCK LIGHT, 24 13.5N, 77 37.0W, Fl W 3s, 29ft., 7M, B+W mast on W cylindrical structure.
SITE 4 ITT TOWER, 24 13.3N, 77 36.0W, Fl Y 4s, 33ft., 5M.
AUTEC SITE 4 LIGHT 1, 24 13.3N, 77 36.3W, Fl G 4s, 23ft., 4M.
AUTEC SITE 4 LIGHT 2, 24 13.3N, 77 36.2W, Fl R 4s, 22ft., 3M.
GREEN CAY LIGHT, W end, 24 02.2N, 77 11.2W, Fl W 3s, 33ft., 7M, Black structure, W house.
AUTEC SITE 6 RANGE, (Front Light) 24 00.4N, 77 31.7W, Q W, 34ft., 10M Skeleton

tower. **(Rear Light)** 760 meters, 257° from front, Iso W 6s, 68ft., Skeleton tower.
AUTEC SITE 6 LIGHT 4, 24 00.5N, 77 30.1W, Fl R 4s, 16ft., 3M, Fl G and Fl R lights mark channel.
TINKER ROCKS LIGHT, 23 59.0N, 77 29.6W, Fl W (14 flashes per minute), 32ft., 8M, Black mast on W cylindrical housing.
HIGH POINT CAY LIGHT, 23 55.6N, 77 29.0W, Fl W 5s, W building on piles.
BILLY ISLAND LIGHT, N end of Williams Island, 24 39.3N, 78 28.7W, F W, 22ft., 5M, Mast, Fishing light.
SITE 7 ITT TOWER, 23 54.5N, 77 28.5W, Fl Y 4s, 33ft., 5M.
AUTEC SITE 7 LIGHT 4, 23 53.9N, 77 28.7W, Fl R 4s, 20ft., 3M.
AUTEC SITE 7 LIGHT 5, 23 53.9N, 77 28.7W, Fl G 4s, 20ft., 4M.

NASSAU TO ELEUTHERA

SIX SHILLING CHANNEL LIGHT, 4.3 km, 235°30' from Six Shilling Cays Light. 25 15.1N, 76 56.4W, Fl R 4s, 16ft., 8M, R + Yellow structure.
SIX SHILLING CAYS LIGHT, 25 16.7N, 76 55.1W, Fl W 8s, 32ft., 10M, Gray steel framework tower.
CURRENT ROCK LIGHT, 25 25.0N, 76 52.0W, Fl W 8s, 41ft., 7M, Framework structure.
EGG ISLAND LIGHT, On summit of island, Northeast Providence Channel, 25 30.0N, 76 53.0W, Fl W 3s, 112ft., 12M, W metal tower.

ELEUTHERA

MAN ISLAND LIGHT, 25 32.8N, 76 38.5W, Fl (3) W 15s, 93ft., 12M, Aluminum framework tower.

HARBOUR ISLAND

25 30N, 76 38W
Emergencies: Call the Bahamas Air Sea Rescue Association (BASRA) on VHF Channel 16, or on 2182kHz. The Nassau headquarters can be reached at (809) 325-8864 or at (809) 322-3877.
Port of Entry
Dockage: You may tie up temporarily to the Government Dock at Dunmore Town. South of the dock is Valentine's Yacht Club and Marina (809) 333-2142, or VHF channel 16. Further

south is Harbour Island Club and Marina (809) 333-2427, or VHF channel 16.
Services: There is fuel, water and ice at the marinas. There are several good grocery stores and, in general, a very good selection of supplies. The town's resorts have a variety of bar's, restaurants and nightclubs.

The approaches to Harbour Island from Spanish Wells through Devil's Backbone are notoriously difficult. See the section on Spanish Wells for information on obtaining a local pilot to guide you. This route should not be attempted in strong north winds.

SPANISH WELLS LIGHT, 25 53.0N, 76 46.0W, F W, 6ft., 1M, Concrete column.

SPANISH WELLS

25 33N, 76 45W
Emergencies: Call the Bahamas Air Sea Rescue Association (BASRA) on VHF Channel 16, or on 2182kHz. The Nassau headquarters can be reached at (809) 325-8864 or at (809) 322-3877.
Dockage: Contact Spanish Wells Yacht Haven at (809) 333-4255 or on VHF channels 9 and 16.
Anchorage: A few boats manage to squeeze into the small pocket of deep water near the east end of town. Do not block the channel. Good anchorage is found in nearby Royal Harbour.
Services: Fuel, water, groceries, hardware, and restaurants are ashore. Fresh fish and lobster is usually on sale at the town docks. Pilots may be hired to assist vessels headed to Harbour Island. For information and rates contact "A-1 Broadshad" on VHF channel 16, or at (809) 333-4427. Other guides are "Cinnabar" and "Dolphin", on VHF channel 16, or at (809) 333-4079, 4209.

THE BLUFF LIGHT, 25 31.0N, 76 45.0W, F W, 20ft., 1M, Mast.
CURRENT ISLAND LIGHT, W side of island, 25 23.0N, 76 49.0W, F W, 20ft., 1M, Mast.
CURRENT LIGHT, At town of Current, 25 25.0N, 76 48.0W, F W, 12ft., 1M, Mast.
STAFFORD LIGHT, GREGORY TOWN, 25 23.5N, 76 34.5W, F W, 41ft., 9M, Mast.
HATCHET BAY LIGHT, W side of entrance, 25 20.5N, 76 29.8W, Fl W 15s, 57ft., 8M, Tapered cast iron pipe mast, 2 F R range lights in line on 022° are shown from the E side of the bay.

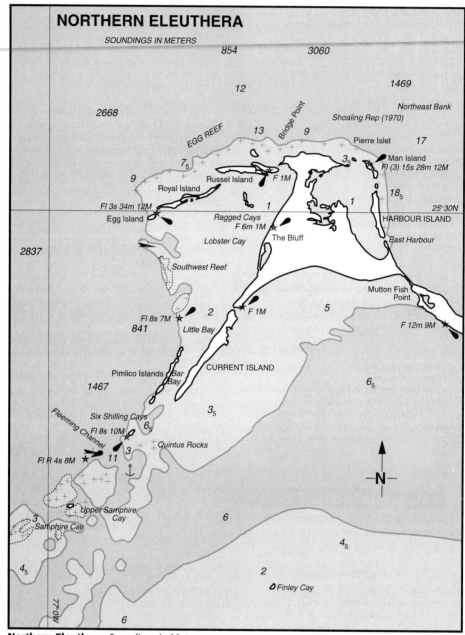

NORTHERN ELEUTHERA

SOUNDINGS IN METERS

854 3060

12 1469

2668 Northeast Bank
Shoaling Rep (1970)

EGG REEF 13 Bridge Point 9 Pierre Islet 17

7₅ 3₅ Man Island
Fl (3) 15s 28m 12M

9 Russel Island F 1M

Royal Island 18₅

Fl 3s 34m 12M 1 1 25°30N

Egg Island Ragged Cays HARBOUR ISLAND
F 6m 1M

Lobster Cay The Bluff East Harbour

2837

Southwest Reef

Mutton Fish
Point

Fl 8s 7M 2 F 1M 5
841 Little Bay F 12m 9M

Pimlico Islands Bar
Bay CURRENT ISLAND

1467 6₅

Fleeming Channel 3₅

Six Shilling Cays
Fl 8s 10M 6₅

Quintus Rocks 3

Fl R 4s 8M 11 3

–N–

3 Upper Samphire
Cay 6

Samphire Cay

4₅ 4₅

6 2

77°0W Finley Cay

6

Northern Eleuthera, Soundings in Meters

HATCHET BAY

25 21N, 76 30W

Emergencies: Call the Bahamas Air Sea Rescue Association (BASRA) on VHF Channel 16, or on 2182kHz. The Nassau headquarters can be reached at (809) 325-8864 or at (809) 322-3877.

Dockage. Contact Eleuthera Bahamas Charters on VHF channel 16, or at (508) 255-8930 in the U.S. They have a concrete bulkhead that may be available for transient dockage.

Moorings: Contact Eleuthera Bahamas Charters.

Anchorage: This harbor offers notoriously poor holding, though there is good shelter from the wind and seas. Stay clear of the commercial docks in the northwest portion of the bay.

Services: Fuel, water and some supplies are available. There are several small grocery stores. You can probably organize transport to other towns on Eleuthera, if necessary.

AVIATION LIGHT, 25 16.1N, 76 19.1W, Iso R 3s, Radio Mast.
CUPID CAY LIGHT, Governors Harbor, 25 12.0N, 76 16.0W, Fl W 4s, 40ft., 8M, Aluminum colored steel tower.

GOVERNOR'S HARBOUR

25 12N, 76 15W

Emergencies: Call the Bahamas Air Sea Rescue Association (BASRA) on VHF Channel 16, or on 2182kHz. The Nassau headquarters can be reached at (809) 325-8864 or at (809) 322-3877.

Anchorage Only: The holding ground is reported to be poor here. There may be some moorings available, but their holding power is also uncertain.

Services: Groceries, stores and restaurants are ashore.

NORTH PALMETTO POINT LIGHT, 25 10.8N, 76 11.4W, Iso W 4s, 73ft., 12M, White tower w/black top and dwelling.
TARPUM BAY LIGHT, S end, 25 00.0N, 76 13.1W, F W, 35ft., 7M, Mast.
POISON POINT LIGHT, 24 52.4N, 76 13.7W, Fl W 15s, 29ft., 7M, W mast.
ROCK SOUND SETTLEMENT LIGHT, 24 54.4N, 76 12.3W, F R, 25ft., Mast.

ROCK SOUND

24 52N, 76 10W

Emergencies: Call the Bahamas Air Sea Rescue Association (BASRA) on VHF Channel 16, or on 2182kHz. The Nassau headquarters can be reached at (809) 325-8864 or at (809) 322-3877.

Dockage: You may be able to tie up temporarily to the government wharf. Check your depths carefully as you approach.

Anchorage: Anchor wherever depths permit. There are many shallow spots sprinkled throughout the harbor. Some of these shoal areas are hard coral.

Services: There is a good selection of groceries and shops ashore. You may be able to obtain water via jugs or hose at the wharf. Fuel may be jugged from a service station.

POWELL POINT LIGHT, 24 52.4N, 76 21.9W, Fl W 3s, 38ft., 8M, Aluminum colored steel framework tower.
FREE TOWN LIGHT, 24 48.1N, 76 18.2W, F W, 19ft., 7M, W pole.
WEMYSS BIGHT LIGHT, 24 45.0N, 76 14.1W, F W, 27ft., 2M, W pole.

DAVIS HARBOUR

24 44N, 76 14W

Emergencies: Call the Bahamas Air Sea Rescue Association (BASRA) on VHF Channel 16, or on 2182kHz. The Nassau headquarters can be reached at (809) 325-8864 or at (809) 322-3877.

Dockage: A privately marked channel leads to a marina in a small dredged basin. They are reported to have fuel, water, a restaurant and limited supplies. The Cotton Bay Club has a golf course and accommodations. The marina monitors VHF channel 16.

ELEUTHERA POINT, SE extremity of island, 24 36.8N, 76 08.8W, Fl W 4.6s, 61ft., 6M, Light colored framework structure on white house.

LITTLE SAN SALVADOR

LITTLE SAN SALVADOR LIGHT, 24 35.0N, 75 56.0W, Fl W 2.4s, 69ft., 13M, Aluminum colored steel skeleton structure, Visible 240° to 110°, Obscured 110° to 130°, Visible 130° to 140°, Obscured 140° to 170°, Visible 170° to 190°, Obscured 190° to 200°, Visible 200° to 220°, Obscured 220° to 240°.

LITTLE SAN SALVADOR

24 34N, 75 56W

Emergencies: Call the Bahamas Air Sea Rescue Association (BASRA) on VHF Channel 16, or on 2182kHz. The Nassau headquarters can be reached at (809) 325-8864 or at (809) 322-3877.

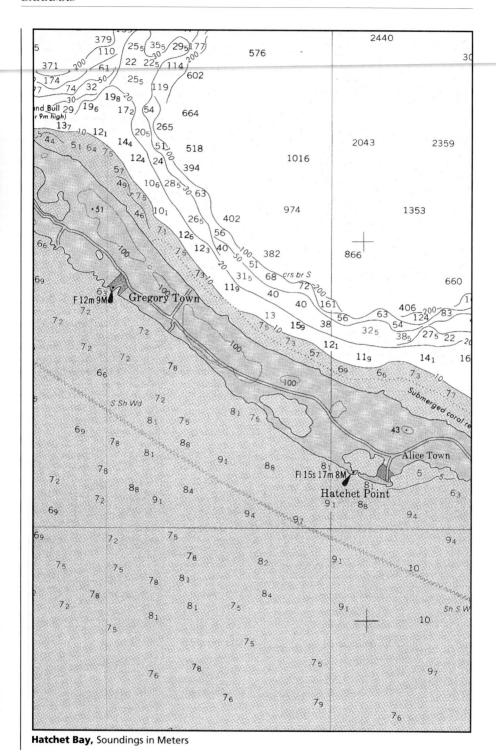

Hatchet Bay, Soundings in Meters

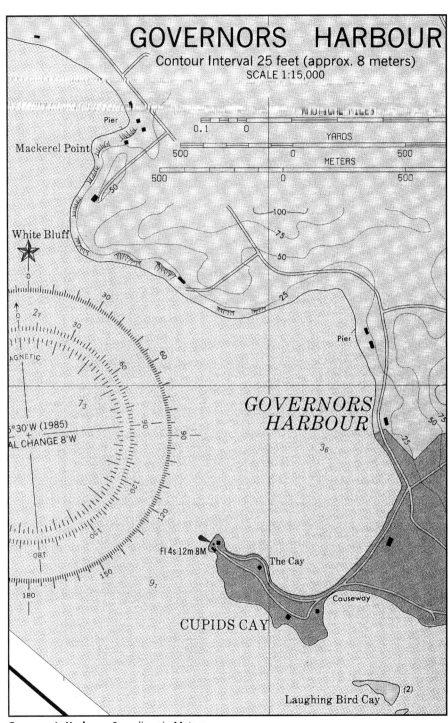

GOVERNORS HARBOUR

Contour Interval 25 feet (approx. 8 meters)
SCALE 1:15,000

Governor's Harbour, Soundings in Meters

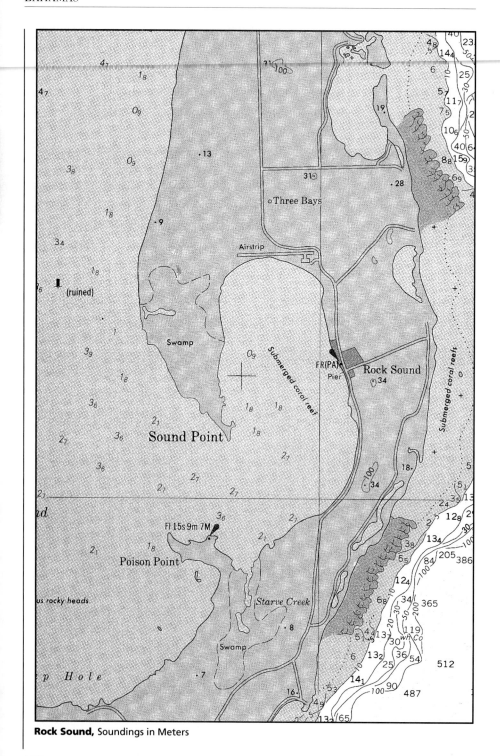

Rock Sound, Soundings in Meters

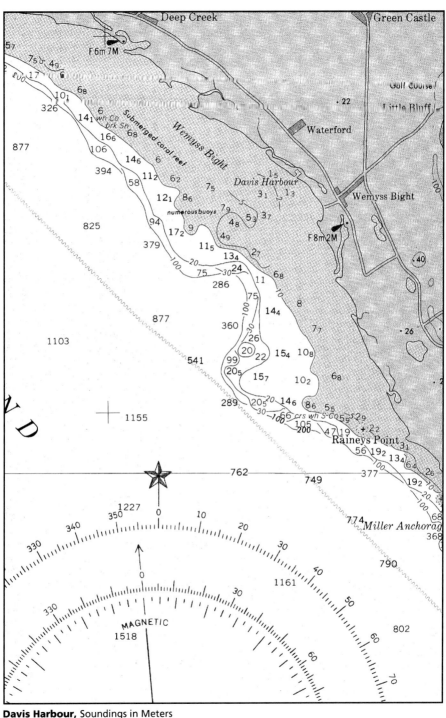

Davis Harbour, Soundings in Meters

Chapter 2

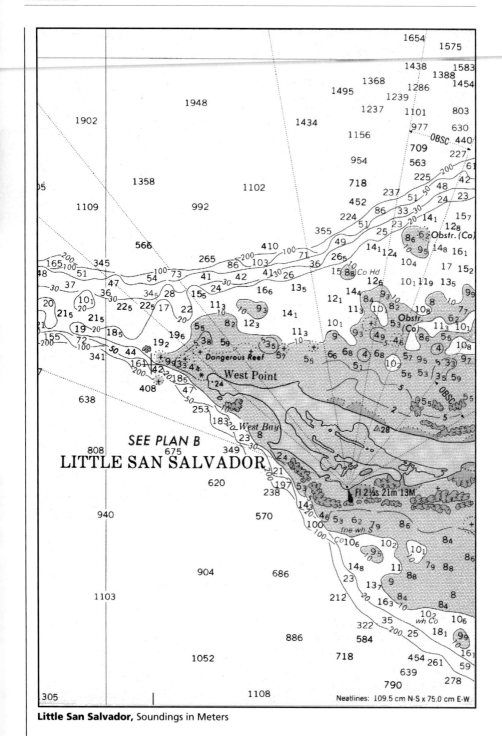

Little San Salvador, Soundings in Meters

Anchorage Only: The anchorage in West Bay, with its spectacular crescent shaped beach, is a popular one.

EXUMAS

BEACON CAY LIGHT, North Rock, Ship Channel, 24 52.4N, 76 49.8W, Fl W R 3s, 58ft., 8M, Gray structure, Red from 292° to 303°, White from 303° to 292°, Partially obscured by neighboring islands from 319° to 006°.
HIGHBORNE CAY AVIATION LIGHT, 24 42.9N, 76 49.3W, Oc R 2s, 216ft., F R, 161ft., Radio mast.

ALLAN'S CAY

24 45N, 76 50W
Emergencies: Call the Bahamas Air Sea Rescue Association (BASRA) on VHF Channel 16, or on 2182kHz. The Nassau headquarters can be reached at (809) 325-8864 or at (809) 322-3877.
Anchorage Only: This is a popular stop at the northern end of the Exumas chain of islands. The easiest approach is from the west. As there are no aids to navigation, the approach should be made in good light. Some coral will be spotted in the entrance channel at the south end of Allan's Cay. Once inside, most boats anchor on either side of the shallow sand bar that runs up the middle of the harbor. It is possible to anchor in the bight on the north end of S.W. Allan's Cay. The small cay to the east of Allan's is famous for the many large iguanas wandering its beaches.

HIGHBORNE CAY

24 42N, 76 49W
Emergencies: Call the Bahamas Air Sea Rescue Association (BASRA) on VHF Channel 16, or on 2182kHz. The Nassau headquarters can be reached at (809) 325-8864 or at (809) 322-3877.
Dockage: There is some dockage available in the basin at the south end of the cay. Contact "Wee Watin" on VHF channel 16. A range on the hill may lead you clear of the coral shoals to the west of the marina. An approach in good light is recommended.
Anchorage: There is some room to anchor in the small basin off the docks. Be careful to limit your swinging room if a wind shift is expected.
Services: Fuel, water and some groceries are available.
ELBOW CAY LIGHT, W end, 24 31.0N, 76 49.0W, Fl W 2s, 46ft., 11M, Gray structure.

WARDERICK WELLS

24 24N, 76 38W
Emergencies: Call the Bahamas Air Sea Rescue Association (BASRA) on VHF Channel 16, or on 2182kHz. The Nassau headquarters can be reached at (809) 325-8864 or at (809) 322-3877.
Exuma Cays Land and Sea Park. The Bahamas National Trust administers the park which has its headquarters here in Warderick Wells. The park rangers monitor VHF channel 16, and you may see the park warden's boat "Moby" nearby. The park has several moorings available to visitors. All fishing and collection of wildlife is prohibited within the park. For more information contact The Bahamas National Trust, P.O. Box 4105, Nassau, Bahamas.
Anchorage: Only approach in good light to find the narrow deep water channel. Boats can anchor all along the channel, but should use two anchors to limit swinging room. This is where the classic Bahamian Moor is desirable.
Services: The park headquarters provides maps of the trails ashore, and descriptive information on the flora and fauna to be seen.

SAMPSON CAY

24 13N, 77 29W
Emergencies: Call the Bahamas Air Sea Rescue Association (BASRA) on VHF Channel 16, or on 2182kHz. The Nassau headquarters can be reached at (809) 325-8864 or at (809) 322-3877.
Dockage: Contact Sampson Cay Club at (809) 355-2034 or via VHF channel 16. They have very protected dockage available in the lagoon for those leaving their boats for extended periods.
Anchorage: Anchor west of the docks in good holding, but be wary of several shoal spots, and do not block access to the docks.
Services: The club has fuel, water, ice, some groceries, liquor, diving supplies, air refills and a restaurant. Reservations are recommended for the restaurant. A seaplane is available for chartered flights and emergencies. This is also the headquarters of a salvage operation complete with a mobile crane.

STANIEL CAY

24 10N, 76 27W (Charted as Staniard Cay)
Emergencies: Call the Bahamas Air Sea Rescue Association (BASRA) on VHF Channel 16, or on 2182kHz. The Nassau headquarters can be reached at (809) 325-8864 or at (809) 322-3877.

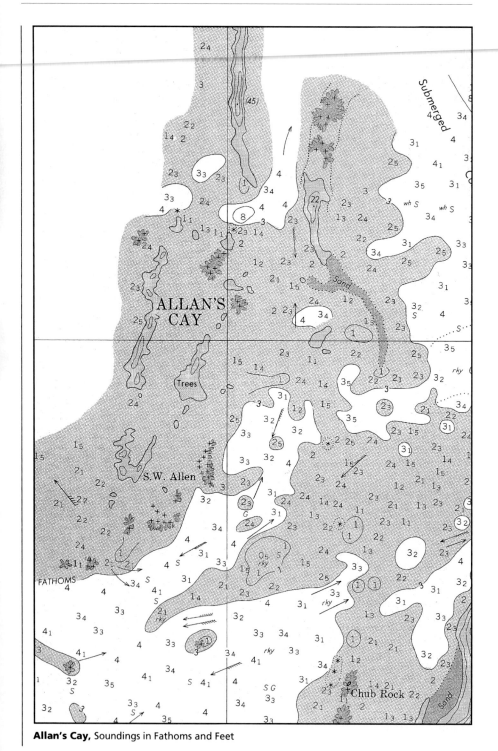

Allan's Cay, Soundings in Fathoms and Feet

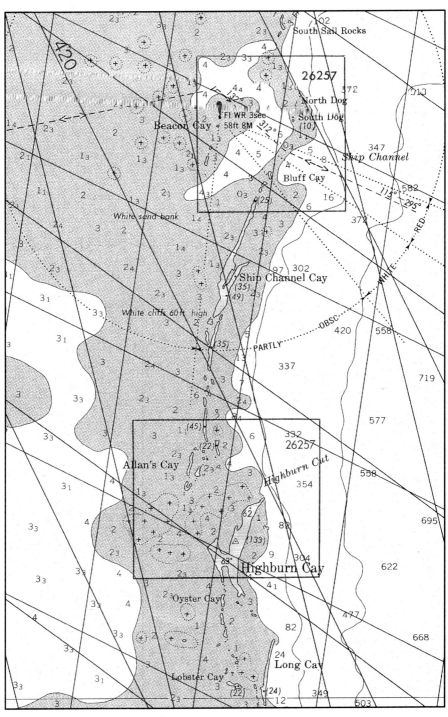

Highborne Cay, Soundings in Fathoms

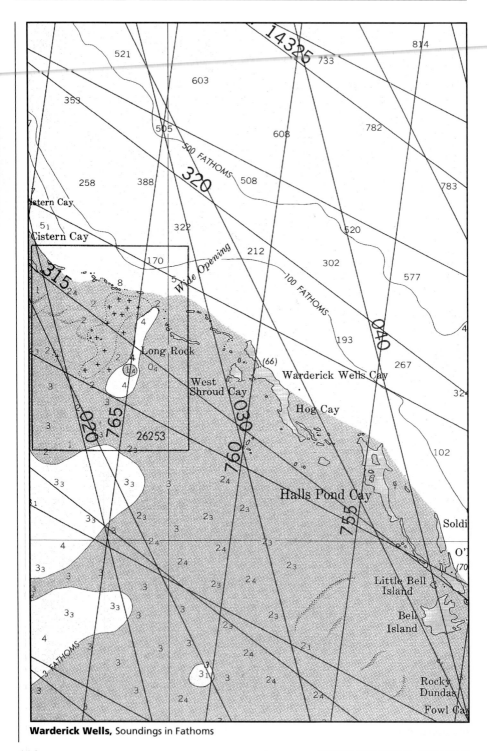

Warderick Wells, Soundings in Fathoms

Chapter 2

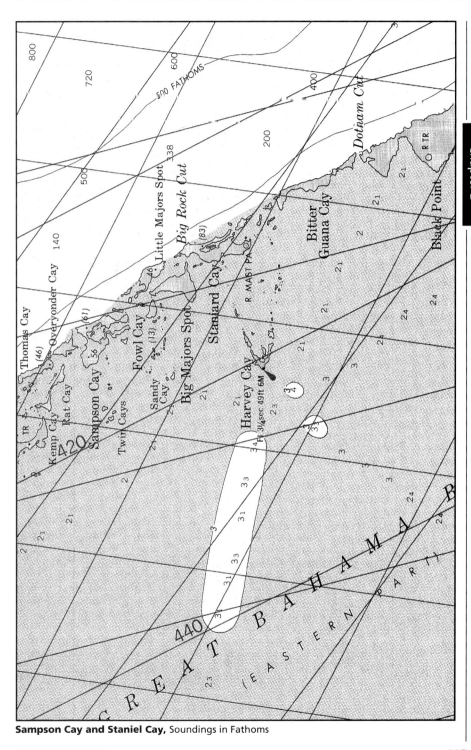

Sampson Cay and Staniel Cay, Soundings in Fathoms

Dockage: Contact the Staniel Cay Yacht Club (809) 355-2024 or the Happy People Marina (809) 355-2008. Both monitor VHF Channel 16. Strong currents run parallel to the yacht club docks.

Anchorage: Boats anchor in several places here. A favorite bad weather spot is in the narrow channel east of Big Majors Spot. Some boats anchor east of the yacht club docks or in the shallow basin south of the docks. Be wary of old moorings and coral south of the docks. The approach depths to all areas are reported to be around 6 feet.

Services: Fuel, water, limited groceries, some marine supplies and a telephone are available. There are several general repair people available. If you can't find something, just ask anyone on the street. For instance, ask around to get baked goods to order.

HARVEY CAY LIGHT, 24 09.0N, 76 28.0W, Fl W 3.3s, 49ft., 6M, Gray beacon.
BITTER GUANA CAY LIGHT, N side of Dotham Cut, 24 07.0N, 76 23.0W, Fl W 5s, 33ft.

LITTLE FARMER'S CAY

23 57N, 76 19W
Emergencies: Call the Bahamas Air Sea Rescue Association (BASRA) on VHF Channel 16, or on 2182kHz. The Nassau headquarters can be reached at (809) 325-8864 or at (809) 322-3877.
Dockage: Contact Farmer's Cay Yacht Club.
Anchorage: Make your approach in good light as this area is loaded with shoals and coral areas. There is a narrow strip of deep water along the shore of Great Guana Cay and one along the east side of Little Farmer's. The mouth of the cove on the end of Big Farmer's is a good anchorage. Farmer's Cay Cut is a good passage to the deeper waters of Exuma Sound. The passage on the banks side gets quite shallow south of Little Farmers.
Services: There are a couple of small restaurants and bars. The well known Ocean Cabin may be reached at (809) 355-4006 or via VHF channel 16. There's a telephone, air strip and a diver available.

GALLIOT CUT, N end of Cave Cay, 23 54.0N, 76 14.0W, Fl W 4s, 49ft., 7M, Aluminum colored steel framework tower.
CONCH CAY LIGHT, Approach to George Town, 23 34.0N, 75 49.0W, Fl W 5s, 40ft., 8M, Aluminum and steel framework structure, Housing at base.
SIMON POINT LIGHT, Approach to George Town, 23 32.0N, 75 48.0W, F W, 40ft., 5M, Mast.

GEORGETOWN

23 31N, 75 47W
Emergencies: Call the Bahamas Air Sea Rescue Association (BASRA) on VHF Channel 16, or on 2182kHz. The Nassau headquarters can be reached at (809) 325-8864 or at (809) 322-3877.
Port of Entry: Customs is located in the government building near the head of the government wharf. You may tie to the wharf temporarily.
Dockage: Available at Exuma Docking Services in Kidd Cove. Contact them on VHF channel 16, or at (809) 336-2578. Their call sign is "Sugar One". The approaches to the dock have been reported to have depths under 6 feet.
Anchorage: Hundreds of cruising boats may be found here during the winter. A popular spot is off the "holes" at Stocking Island, or in one of the "holes" themselves. Drafts of around 6 feet may enter the holes with local knowledge. It is wise to scout the channels with your dinghy. Many boats anchor off the Peace and Plenty Hotel, where there is a convenient dinghy dock.
Services: Fuel, water, ice, propane, groceries, some marine supplies, a telephone, restaurants and bars are available. Good air connections can be made via Nassau. During the regattas many open air snack bars line the streets.

Georgetown is the southern terminus of many Bahamas cruisers. A large gathering of boats is bound to be here, but there always seems to be room for more. The popularity of this port has promoted the development of a good selection of shops oriented towards boaters. This is the best restocking port in the southern Bahamas.

HAWKSBILL ROCKS, On banks side, 23 26.0N, 76 07.0W, Fl W 3.3s, 32ft., 6M, W conical metal structure, Black bands.
JEWFISH CUT, On banks side, 23 27.0N, 75 58.0W, Fl W 2.5s, 38ft., 8M, W metal conical structure, Black bands.

CAT ISLAND

BENNETS HARBOR, Entrance to Harbor Creek, 24 33.5N, 75 38.3W, Fl W 4s, 53ft., 12M, Light gray structure, Visible 350° to 130°.

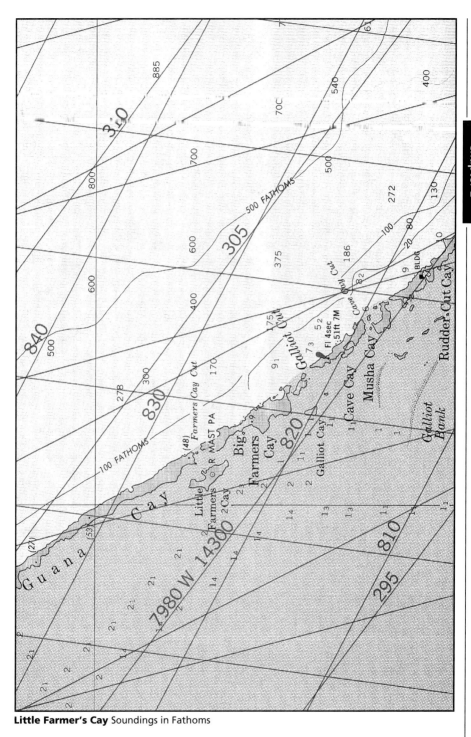

Little Farmer's Cay Soundings in Fathoms

Chapter 2

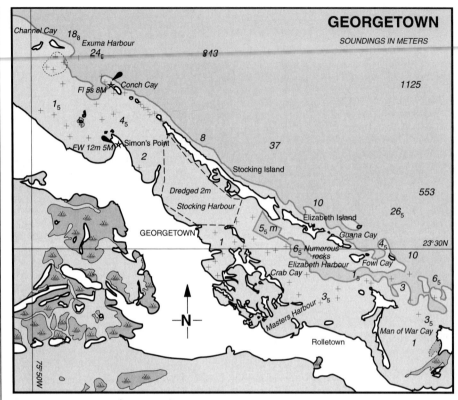

Georgetown Approaches, Soundings in Meters

BENNETT'S HARBOR

24 33N, 75 38W

Emergencies: Call the Bahamas Air Sea Rescue Association (BASRA) on VHF Channel 16, or on 2182kHz. The Nassau headquarters can be reached at (809) 325-8864 or at (809) 322-3877.

Dockage: You may be able to tie up temporarily to the government wharf.

Anchorage: There is not a lot of shelter off the west coast of Cat Island. Some of the creeks may offer shelter to shallow draft boats.

Services: Very limited.

SMITH TOWN, 24 19.8N, 75 28.5W, Fl W 3.3s, 38ft., 7M, Light gray steel structure.

DEVILS POINT LIGHT, On summit, 823 meters NW of point, 24 08.0N, 75 29.0W, Fl W 5s, 143ft., 12M, Aluminum colored steel skeleton structure.

HAWKSNEST CREEK

24 09N, 75 32W

Emergencies: Call the Bahamas Air Sea Rescue Association (BASRA) on VHF Channel 16, or on 2182kHz. The Nassau headquarters can be reached at (809) 325-8864 or at (809) 322-3877.

Dockage: Contact the Hawks Nest Club Marina on VHF channel 16. Depths are reported to be about 6 feet.

Anchorage: You can anchor in the narrow channel between the shoals. Don't block the channel to the marina.

Services: Fuel, water and ice are available.

CONCEPTION ISLAND

CONCEPTION ISLAND LIGHT, 23 50.0N, 75 08.0W, Fl W 2s, 84ft., 6M, Gray structure.

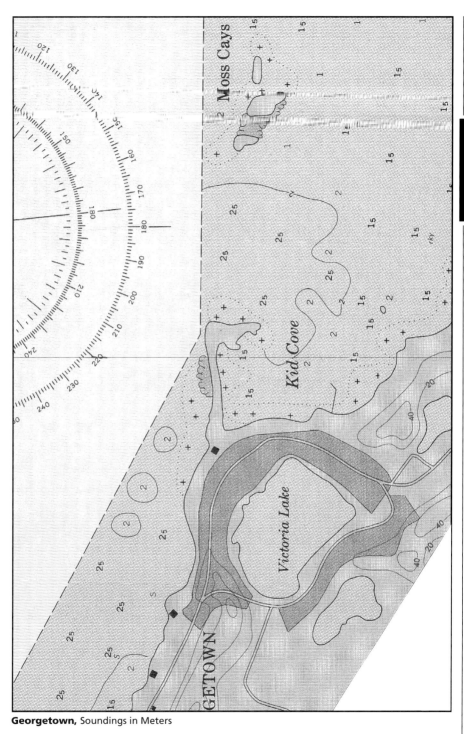

Georgetown, Soundings in Meters

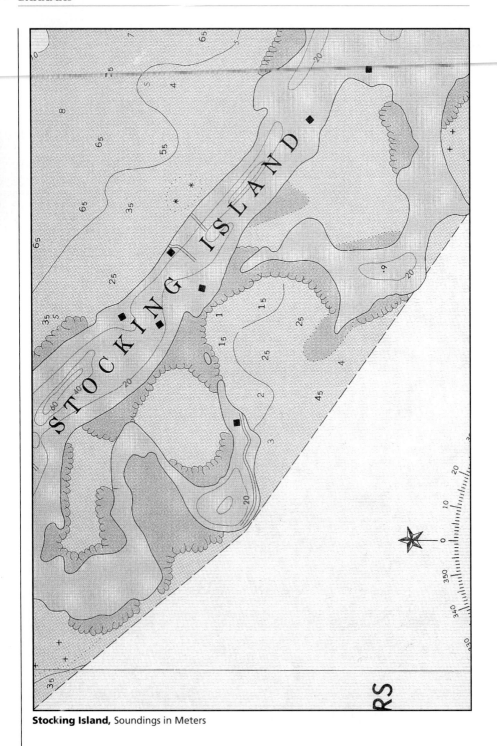

Stocking Island, Soundings in Meters

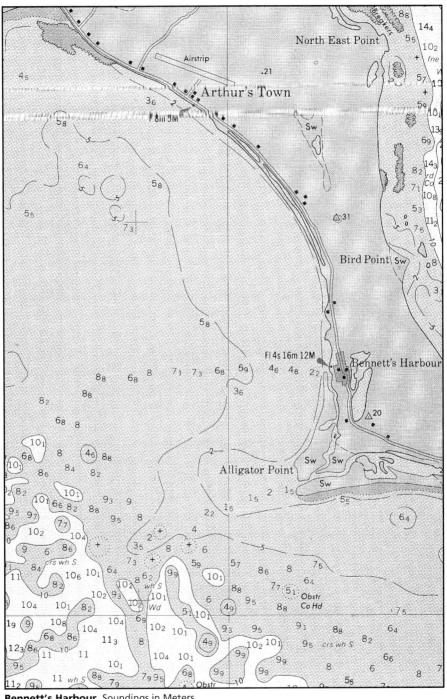

Bennett's Harbour, Soundings in Meters

Chapter 2

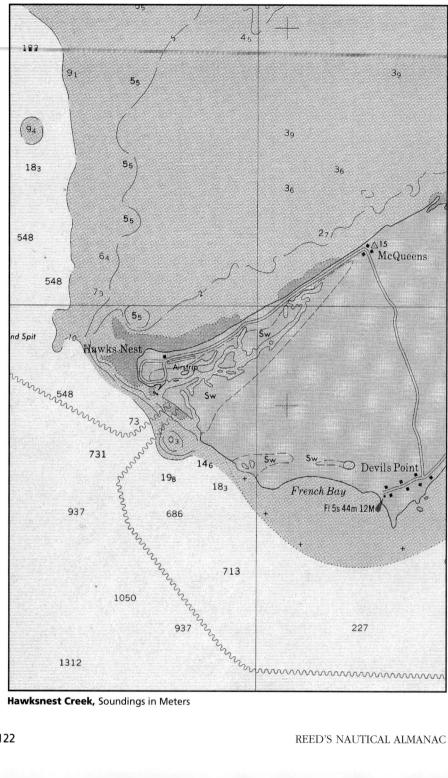

Hawksnest Creek, Soundings in Meters

Chapter 2

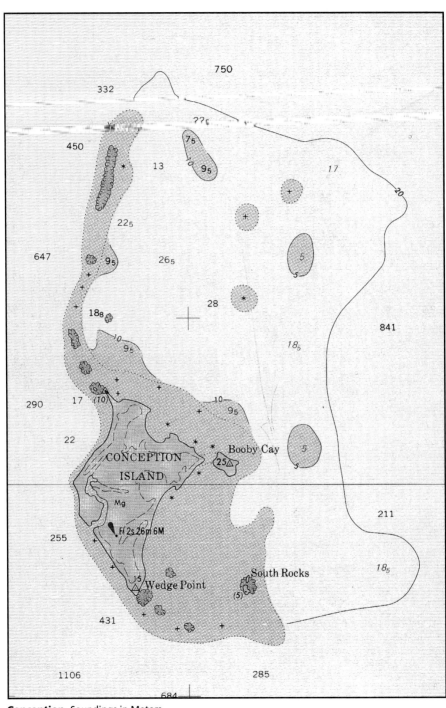

Conception, Soundings in Meters

BAHAMAS

CONCEPTION

23 50N, 75 07

Emergencies: Call the Bahamas Air Sea Rescue Association (BASRA) on VHF Channel 16, or on 2182kHz. The Nassau headquarters can be reached at (809) 325-8864 or at (809) 322-3877.

Bahamas National Trust: This uninhabited island is a land and sea park, with similar regulations to the Exumas park. For more information contact: The Bahamas National Trust, P.O. Box 4105, Nassau, Bahamas.

Anchorage Only: Anchor in the bay at the northwest end of the island. Proceed in slowly as coral heads have been reported in here. The coral becomes thicker within 1/4 mile of the beach.

RUM CAY

COTTON FIELD POINT LIGHT, 23 39.2N, 74 51.6W, L Fl W Y R 10s, 75 ft., 10M, R 083°30' to 006°30' W 006°30' to 014°30', Y 014°30' to 075°30', W 075°30' to 083°30'.
PORT NELSON LIGHT, Near wharf, 23 38.4N, 74 49.8W, F W, 18ft., 5M, Pole.

PORT NELSON

23 40N, 74 50W

Emergencies: Call the Bahamas Air Sea Rescue Association (BASRA) on VHF Channel 16, or on 2182kHz. The Nassau headquarters can be reached at (809) 325-8864 or at (809) 322-3877.

Dockage: You may be able to tie up temporarily to the government dock. Depths are reported to be less than 6 feet.

Anchorage: Anchor west of town, as depths permit. The charted approach takes you through a deep passage between several coral reefs. A bearing of 013° T on Cotton Field Point will bring you safely across the reef. When the dock at Port Nelson bears 081° T, steer for the dock.

Services: There's a bar, restaurant and some limited supplies. The town has less than 100 residents.

SAN SALVADOR

DIXON HILL LIGHT, Near NE point, 24 05.4N, 74 27.0W, Fl (2) W 10s, 163ft., 23M, W stone tower, Dwelling each side, Partially obscured from 001° to 008°, 010° to 068° and 076° to 095°.
COCKBURN TOWN LIGHT, Near landing, 24 03.0N, 74 32.0W, F W, 23ft., 1M, W mast.

COCKBURN TOWN

24 03N, 74 32W

Emergencies: Call the Bahamas Air Sea Rescue Association (BASRA) on VHF Channel 16, or on 2182kHz. The Nassau headquarters can be reached at (809) 325-8864 or at (809) 322-3877.

Port of Entry

Dockage: There may be some space at the tiny Riding Rock Marina (809) 367-2106. It is located about halfway between town and Riding Rock Point. There is reported to be a range (about 075°) leading boats safely into the marina basin. Call them on VHF channel 16.

Anchorage: In good weather boats can anchor in the bay off of town. Be prepared to leave if bad weather threatens.

Services: Fuel, water, a telephone and some supplies available.

This island is considered to be the first landing place of Columbus in the New World. A monument has been erected on the eastern side of the island. Its charted location makes a good landmark.

LONG ISLAND

CAPE ST. MARIA, Near N extremity of island, 23 41.0N, 75 21.0W, Fl W 3.3s, 99ft., 14M, Light gray iron framework structure, Obscured 240° to 340°.

STELLA MARIS

23 33N, 75 16W

Emergencies: Call the Bahamas Air Sea Rescue Association (BASRA) on VHF Channel 16, or on 2182kHz. The Nassau headquarters can be reached at (809) 325-8864 or at (809) 322-3877.

Port of Entry

Dockage: The Stella Maris Inn and Marina has all facilities. Contact them at (809) 336-2106, at (800) 426-0466 in the United States or on VHF channel 16. The approach depths are reported to be about 3 1/2 feet at low tide and 6 feet at high tide. Tides run approximately 2 hours after Nassau. Boaters should head south about 1 1/2 miles past Dove Cay, until the sand bar to the east ends. Then turn to the east and head toward the bright yellow sign at the marina entrance.

Services: A marine railway makes Stella Maris the only full repair facility south of Nassau in the Bahamas. They also have fuel, water, ice, supplies, banking, a post office and a restau-

Chapter 2

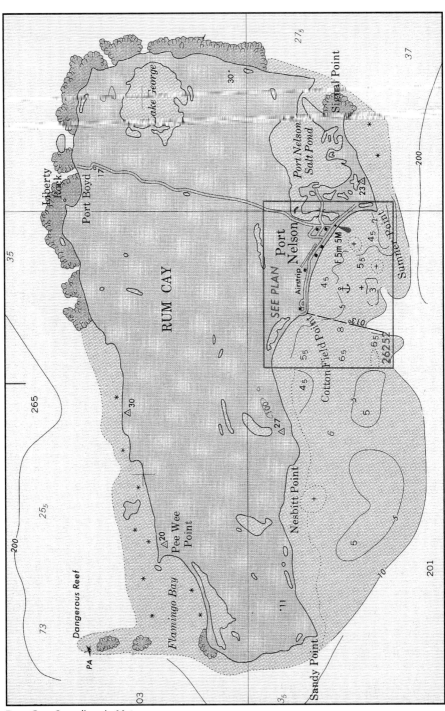

Rum Cay, Soundings in Meters

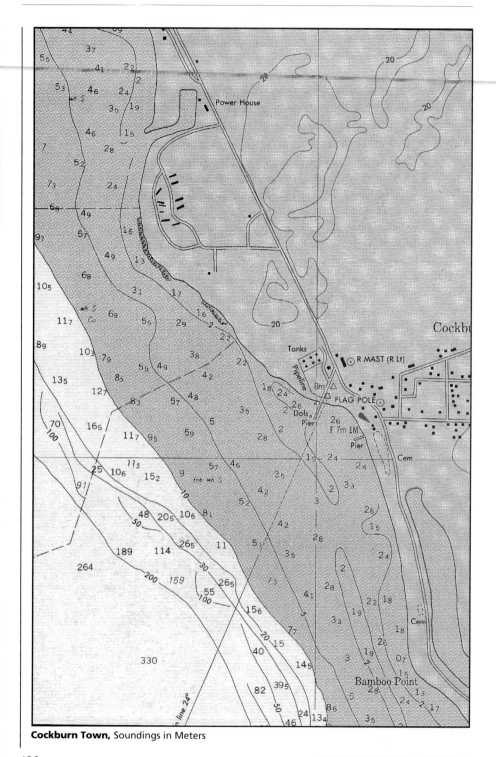

Cockburn Town, Soundings in Meters

rant. There are car and bicycel rentals for those who want to explore the island.

SIMMS LIGHT, 23 29.0N, 75 14.0W, F W, 23ft., 4M, Mast.
BOOBY ROCK LIGHT, Approach to Clarence Town, 23 07.0N, 74 58.3W, Fl W 2s, 39ft., 8M, R+W structure.
HARBOR POINT LIGHT, Approach to Clarence Town, 23 06.2N, 74 57.5W, F W, 25ft., 3M, W mast and hut.

CLARENCE TOWN

23 06N, 74 58W

Emergencies: Call the Bahamas Air Sea Rescue Association (BASRA) on VHF Channel 16, or on 2182kHz. The Nassau headquarters can be reached at (809) 325-8864 or at (809) 322-3877.
Dockage: You may be able to tie up temporarily to the government wharf.
Anchorage: Anchor off of town, avoiding the charted cables. This area is wide open to north and west winds. It may be untenable in bad weather.
Services: Fuel, water, groceries, ice, a telephone and a restaurant are available.

The best approach is from the north, passing west of Booby Rocks. Approach in good light to avoid the many reefs and shoals in the area. This is the administrative center of Long Island, and consequently has a good variety of services.

SOUTH POINT LIGHT, Turbot Hill, 22 51.3N, 74 51.2W, Fl W 2.5s, 61ft., 12M, Gray metal structure, Partially obscured 140° to 245°.
GALLOWAY LANDING LIGHT, 23 04.0N, 75 00.0W, F W, 14ft., 2M, W post and lantern, Marks landing place for small boats.

JUMENTOS CAYS

NUEVITAS ROCKS LIGHT, On eastern Jumentos Cays, 23 09.0N, 75 23.0W, Fl W 4s, 38ft., 10M, Gray structure.
FLAMINGO CAY LIGHT, On hill, 22 53.0N, 75 52.0W, Fl W 6s, 138ft., 8M, Aluminum colored steel tower.
RAGGED ISLAND LIGHT, Duncan Town, Man-O-War Hill, 22 11.0N, 75 44.0W, Fl W 3s, 118ft., 12M, Black pipe, Platform, F W light shown from settlement wharf, Unreliable.

RAGGED ISLAND HARBOR

22 14N, 75 44W

Emergencies: Call the Bahamas Air Sea Rescue Association (BASRA) on VHF Channel 16, or on 2182kHz. The Nassau headquarters can be reached at (809) 325-8864 or at (809) 322-3877.
Dockage: The narrow, shallow channel to Duncan Town should be attempted with local knowledge only.
Anchorage: Anchor in a sandy spot away from the coral. The sailing directions recommend an anchoring spot in a position where the south extremity of Little Ragged Island bears 097° T and Point Wilson, on Ragged Island, bears 004° T. The latter anchorage is not shown on the chartlet in this book.
Services: There's a bar, restaurant and some limited supplies.

Ragged Island is at the southern end of the Jumento's Cays, in one of the most remote areas of the Bahamas.

CAY SANTO DOMINGO LIGHT, 21 42.0N, 75 44.0W, Fl W 5s, 29ft., 7M, Aluminum and R steel structure, Reported extinguished 1990.

OLD BAHAMA CHANNEL

CAY LOBOS, Near W end, 22 22.9N, 77 35.9W, Fl (2) W 20s, 145ft., 22M, W round metal tower, Reported extinguished 1991.

CROOKED AND ACKLINS ISLAND

WINDSOR POINT LIGHT, 22 34.0N, 74 22.5W, Fl W 3s, 36ft., 8M, Black structure.
BIRD ROCK LIGHT, On summit, 22 50.9N, 74 21.5W, Fl W 15s, 112ft., 23M, W conical stone tower.
MAJORS CAY LIGHT, 22 45.0N, 74 09.0W, F W, 30ft., 4M, Mast, Unreliable.
ATTWOOD HARBOR LIGHT, W of NE point of Acklins Island, 22 44.2N, 73 52.6W, Fl W 4.5s, 20ft., 5M, Metal tower.
ACKLINS ISLAND NORTHEAST POINT LIGHT, Hell Gate, 22 43.8N, 73 50.8W, Fl W 6s, 56ft., 10M, Gray steel tower.
CASTLE ISLAND LIGHT, Near SW point, 22 07.3N, 74 19.6W, Fl (2) W, 20s, 131ft., 22M, W cylindrical tower.
SPRING POINT LIGHT, 22 28.5N, 73 57.7W, F W, 19ft., 7M, W pole.

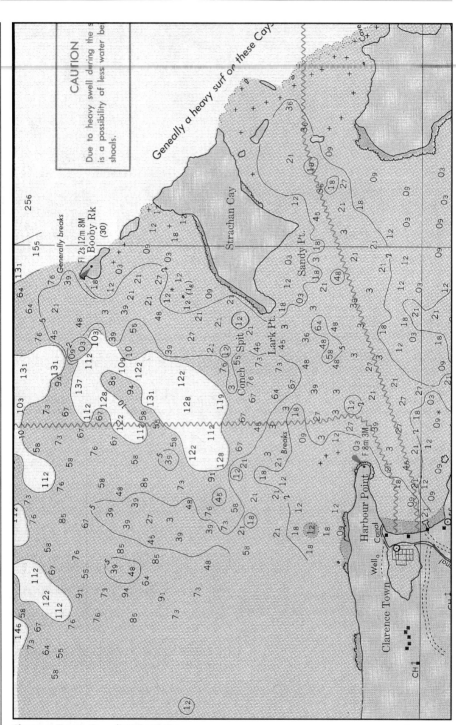

Clarence Town, Soundings in Meters

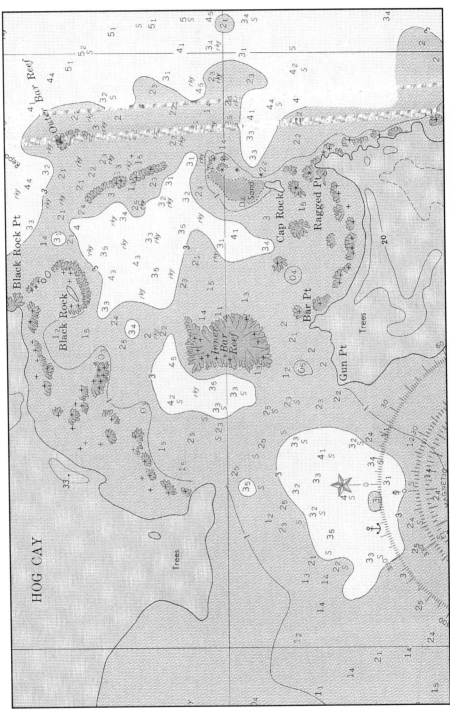

Ragged Island Harbour, Soundings in Fathoms and Feet

LONG CAY LIGHT, E side of cay, 22 37.0N, 74 19.3W, F W, 60ft., 4M, W post.

MAYAGUANA

NORTHWEST POINT LIGHT, 22 27.8N, 73 07.6W, Fl W 5s, 70ft., 12M, W framework tower, R lantern.

GUANO POINT LIGHT, Abraham Bay, 22 21.1N, 72 57.9W, Fl W 3s, 14ft., 8M, Gray structure.

ABRAHAM BAY

22 21N, 73 00W

Emergencies: Call the Bahamas Air Sea Rescue Association (BASRA) on VHF Channel 16, or on 2182kHz. The Nassau headquarters can be reached at (809) 325-8864 or at (809) 322-3877.

Anchorage: The best area is in Abraham Bay, southwest of the settlement. There are two channels through the reef. One is near Guano Point, and the other is southeast of Low Point. An approach in good light is recommended. Keep a good lookout for coral throughout Abraham Bay.

Services: There is a telephone and limited supplies. You can jug fuel or water to your boat.

HOGSTY REEF

HOGSTY REEF LIGHT, On Northwest Cay, 21 41.4N, 73 50.8W, Fl W 4s, 29ft., 8M, R mast, W bands.

GREAT INAGUA ISLAND

MAN OF WAR BAY RANGE, (Front Light)
21 03.3N, 73 39.2W, F Y, B+W square daymark.

(Rear Light) 320 meters 087° from front, F Y, B + W square daymark.

MAN OF WAR BAY RANGE, (Front Light)
21 03.3N, 73 39.3W, F Y, B + W square daymark.

(Rear Light) 120 meters 130° from front, F Y, B + W square daymark.

MATTHEW TOWN LIGHT, 20 56.5N, 73 40.2W, Fl (2) W 10s, 120ft., 22M, W cylindrical stone tower, Partially obscured 165° to 183°.

MATTHEW TOWN

21 00N, 73 30W

Emergencies: Call the Bahamas Air Sea Rescue Association (BASRA) on VHF Channel 16, or on 2182kHz. The Nassau headquarters can be reached at (809) 325-8864 or at (809) 322-3877.

Port of Entry: Located in Matthew Town at the southwest corner of the island.

Bahamas National Trust: The Inagua Park is the home of a huge colony of flamingoes. For more information contact: The Bahamas National Trust, P.O. Box 4105, Nassau, Bahamas.

Anchorage: There is anchorage in Man of War Bay on the western side of the island. The wharf, extending 400 yards seaward, is owned by the Morton Salt Co. and is private. Vessels up to 35,000 tons call here. The terminal call sign is "Morton Salt", and they may be contacted on 2182kHz, or on VHF channel 16. Matthew Town is the administrative center of the island, and an open roadstead anchorage is available off of town.

Services: Some supplies and a telephone are available. There is an airstrip with flights available to Nassau.

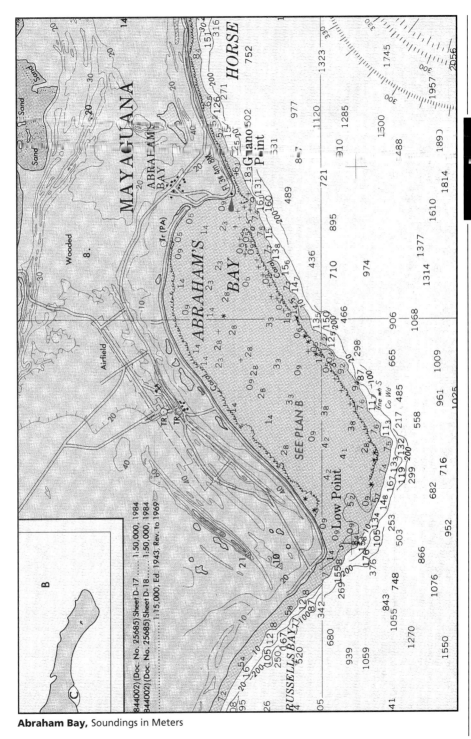

Abraham Bay, Soundings in Meters

Chapter 2

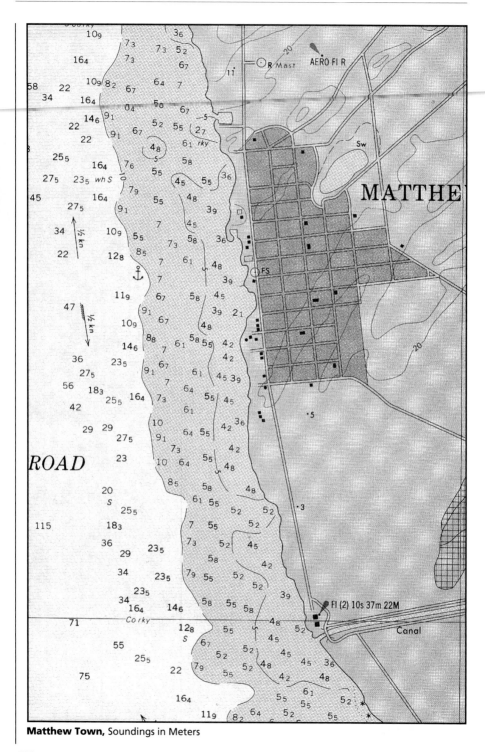

Matthew Town, Soundings in Meters

NASSAU, BAHAMAS

HIGH & LOW WATER 1994 25°05′N 77°21′W

EASTERN STANDARD TIME, ADD 1 HOUR DAYLIGHT SAVING APRIL 3 - OCTOBER 29

JANUARY

Day	Reading 1	Reading 2	Reading 3	Reading 4
1 Sa	0337 1.0	1000 4.2	1636 1.0	2229 3.7
2 Su	0430 1.1	1047 4.1	1711 0.9	2324 3.8
3 M	0527 1.2	1138 3.9	1800 0.9	
4 Tu	0021 3.9	0629 1.3	1232 3.8	1852 0.9
5 W	0122 4.0	0735 1.4	1330 3.6	◑1948 0.9
6 Th	0225 4.1	0843 1.4	1432 3.5	2046 0.9
7 F	0328 4.2	0951 1.4	1535 3.4	2144 0.8
8 Sa	0428 4.3	1054 1.3	1637 3.4	2242 0.8
9 Su	0525 4.4	1153 1.2	1736 3.4	2338 0.8
10 M	0618 4.4	1247 1.1	1832 3.4	
11 Tu	0031 0.9	0708 4.4	1336 1.1	●1924 3.5
12 W	0122 0.9	0755 4.4	1422 1.0	2014 3.5
13 Th	0210 1.0	0838 4.2	1504 1.0	2101 3.5
14 F	0257 1.1	0920 4.1	1545 1.1	2146 3.5
15 Sa	0343 1.2	1000 3.9	1623 1.1	2231 3.5
16 Su	0428 1.4	1038 3.7	1707 1.2	2316 3.5
17 M	0514 1.5	1117 3.5	1739 1.2	
18 Tu	0002 3.5	0603 1.7	1157 3.4	1819 1.2
19 W	0051 3.5	0655 1.7	1241 3.2	◑1902 1.3
20 Th	0141 3.6	0752 1.8	1331 3.1	1948 1.3
21 F	0233 3.6	0851 1.8	1425 3.1	2038 1.2
22 Sa	0326 3.7	0948 1.7	1522 3.1	2129 1.2
23 Su	0417 3.9	1043 1.6	1618 3.1	2222 1.1
24 M	0506 4.0	1132 1.4	1712 3.2	2313 1.0
25 Tu	0553 4.2	1219 1.2	1804 3.4	
26 W	0004 0.9	0639 4.3	1303 1.1	1853 3.5
27 Th	0054 0.8	0724 4.4	1346 1.0	O 1941 3.7
28 F	0143 0.8	0809 4.4	1429 0.8	2030 3.8
29 Sa	0233 0.8	0854 4.3	1513 0.8	2119 3.9
30 Su	0325 0.8	0940 4.2	1558 0.7	2210 4.0
31 M	0418 0.9	1028 4.1	1645 0.7	2304 4.1

FEBRUARY

Day	Reading 1	Reading 2	Reading 3	Reading 4
1 Tu	0515 1.0	1119 3.9	1735 0.8	
2 W	0001 4.1	0615 1.2	1213 3.7	1828 0.8
3 Th	0102 4.1	0721 1.3	1313 3.5	◑1926 0.9
4 F	0207 4.1	0830 1.4	1417 3.3	2028 1.0
5 Sa	0312 4.1	0939 1.4	1524 3.3	2131 1.0
6 Su	0415 4.1	1043 1.4	1628 3.3	2232 1.0
7 M	0513 4.2	1140 1.3	1728 3.4	2329 1.0
8 Tu	0605 4.2	1230 1.2	1821 3.4	
9 W	0022 1.0	0652 4.2	1315 1.1	1910 3.5
10 Th	0110 1.0	0735 4.1	1355 1.1	●1954 3.6
11 F	0155 1.1	0814 4.0	1433 1.1	2036 3.6
12 Sa	0237 1.2	0851 3.9	1508 1.1	2116 3.7
13 Su	0318 1.3	0926 3.8	1541 1.1	2155 3.7
14 M	0358 1.4	1001 3.6	1615 1.2	2234 3.7
15 Tu	0440 1.5	1036 3.5	1650 1.2	2316 3.7
16 W	0524 1.6	1114 3.3	1728 1.3	
17 Th	0001 3.6	0612 1.7	1157 3.2	1810 1.3
18 F	0050 3.7	0707 1.8	1247 3.1	◐1859 1.4
19 Sa	0144 3.7	0806 1.8	1344 3.1	1954 1.4
20 Su	0240 3.8	0906 1.7	1446 3.1	2053 1.3
21 M	0337 3.9	1003 1.6	1547 3.3	2152 1.2
22 Tu	0430 4.0	1055 1.4	1645 3.4	2250 1.1
23 W	0522 4.2	1143 1.2	1738 3.7	2344 0.9
24 Th	0610 4.3	1229 1.0	1829 3.9	
25 F	0037 0.8	0658 4.4	1314 0.9	1919 4.1
26 Sa	0128 0.7	0745 4.4	1358 0.7	O 2008 4.3
27 Su	0219 0.7	0831 4.3	1443 0.7	2058 4.4
28 M	0311 0.8	0919 4.2	1530 0.7	2149 4.4

MARCH

Day	Reading 1	Reading 2	Reading 3	Reading 4
1 Tu	0405 0.9	1008 4.1	1618 0.7	2243 4.4
2 W	0501 1.0	1101 3.9	1710 0.9	2340 4.3
3 Th	0602 1.2	1157 3.7	1806 1.0	
4 F	0042 4.2	0707 1.4	1300 3.5	◐1908 1.1
5 Sa	0148 4.1	0816 1.5	1407 3.4	2014 1.2
6 Su	0254 4.1	0924 1.5	1516 3.4	2120 1.3
7 M	0358 4.1	1026 1.5	1620 3.4	2224 1.3
8 Tu	0455 4.1	1119 1.4	1717 3.5	2321 1.3
9 W	0546 4.0	1205 1.3	1807 3.7	
10 Th	0011 1.3	0630 4.0	1246 1.3	1850 3.8
11 F	0056 1.3	0709 3.9	1322 1.3	1930 3.9
12 Sa	0138 1.3	0746 3.9	1355 1.3	●2008 3.9
13 Su	0217 1.4	0820 3.8	1427 1.3	2044 4.0
14 M	0254 1.4	0853 3.7	1459 1.3	2119 4.0
15 Tu	0332 1.5	0926 3.6	1531 1.3	2156 4.0
16 W	0411 1.6	1001 3.5	1605 1.4	2235 3.9
17 Th	0453 1.7	1039 3.4	1643 1.4	2318 3.9
18 F	0539 1.8	1123 3.3	1727 1.5	
19 Sa	0005 3.9	0630 1.8	1214 3.3	1818 1.5
20 Su	0059 3.9	0727 1.8	1313 3.3	◑1917 1.6
21 M	0157 3.9	0825 1.7	1417 3.4	2022 1.5
22 Tu	0257 4.0	0922 1.6	1520 3.5	2126 1.4
23 W	0354 4.1	1015 1.4	1619 3.8	2227 1.2
24 Th	0449 4.2	1105 1.2	1714 4.1	2324 1.1
25 F	0540 4.3	1153 1.0	1805 4.3	
26 Sa	0019 0.9	0630 4.4	1240 0.9	1856 4.6
27 Su	0112 0.8	0719 4.4	1327 0.7	O 1946 4.8
28 M	0204 0.8	0808 4.3	1414 0.7	2037 4.8
29 Tu	0257 0.8	0858 4.2	1503 0.7	2129 4.8
30 W	0351 1.0	0949 4.1	1554 0.9	2223 4.7
31 Th	0448 1.1	1044 3.9	1647 1.0	2320 4.6

APRIL

Day	Reading 1	Reading 2	Reading 3	Reading 4
1 F	0548 1.3	1143 3.7	1746 1.2	
2 Sa	0021 4.4	0652 1.4	1248 3.6	1850 1.4
3 Su	0125 4.2	0757 1.5	1357 3.5	◑1958 1.5
4 M	0231 4.1	0901 1.6	1505 3.6	2107 1.6
5 Tu	0332 4.0	0958 1.6	1606 3.7	2210 1.6
6 W	0428 4.0	1048 1.5	1659 3.8	2306 1.6
7 Th	0517 3.9	1131 1.5	1745 3.9	2354 1.6
8 F	0559 3.9	1208 1.4	1826 4.1	
9 Sa	0038 1.5	0637 3.8	1242 1.4	1903 4.1
10 Su	0117 1.5	0713 3.8	1315 1.4	1938 4.2
11 M	0156 1.6	0747 3.7	1347 1.4	●2013 4.3
12 Tu	0232 1.6	0821 3.6	1419 1.4	2048 4.3
13 W	0309 1.6	0856 3.6	1452 1.5	2124 4.2
14 Th	0348 1.7	0932 3.5	1528 1.5	2202 4.2
15 F	0429 1.7	1012 3.4	1607 1.6	2244 4.2
16 Sa	0513 1.8	1059 3.4	1653 1.6	2330 4.1
17 Su	0601 1.8	1151 3.4	1747 1.7	
18 M	0022 4.1	0654 1.7	1250 3.5	1849 1.7
19 Tu	0119 4.0	0749 1.7	1353 3.6	◑1956 1.7
20 W	0219 4.0	0844 1.5	1455 3.8	2103 1.6
21 Th	0318 4.1	0938 1.4	1554 4.1	2206 1.4
22 F	0415 4.2	1029 1.2	1650 4.4	2305 1.2
23 Sa	0509 4.2	1119 1.0	1743 4.7	
24 Su	0001 1.1	0602 4.3	1209 0.9	1835 4.9
25 M	0056 1.0	0654 4.3	1258 0.8	O 1926 5.1
26 Tu	0149 1.0	0745 4.2	1348 0.8	2018 5.1
27 W	0243 1.0	0838 4.2	1439 0.9	2110 5.0
28 Th	0337 1.1	0932 4.0	1531 1.0	2204 4.9
29 F	0433 1.2	1028 3.9	1627 1.2	2259 4.7
30 Sa	0531 1.3	1128 3.8	1726 1.4	2357 4.5

Chapter 2

TIME MERIDIAN 75°W
Heights in feet are referred to the chart datum of sounding.

0000h is midnight, 1200h is noon.

NASSAU, BAHAMAS

HIGH & LOW WATER 1994

25°05'N 77°21'W

EASTERN STANDARD TIME, ADD 1 HOUR DAYLIGHT SAVING APRIL 3 - OCTOBER 29

MAY

Day	Time	ft	Time	ft		Day	Time	ft	Time	ft
1 Su	0630	1.5	1233	3.7		16 M	0536	1.7	1132	3.6
	1830	1.6					1726	1.8	2353	4.2
2 M ☽	0057	4.3	0730	1.5		17 Tu	0624	1.6	1230	3.7
	1339	3.7	1937	1.8			1827	1.8		
3 Tu	0158	4.1	0828	1.6		18 W	0047	4.1	0716	1.6
	1443	3.8	2044	1.8			1331	3.9	1933	1.8
4 W	0256	3.9	0920	1.6		19 Th	0145	4.1	0809	1.4
	1540	3.9	2146	1.9			1431	4.1	2040	1.7
5 Th	0349	3.8	1007	1.6		20 F	0245	4.1	0903	1.3
	1631	4.0	2242	1.8			1531	4.4	2145	1.6
6 F	0437	3.7	1048	1.6		21 Sa	0343	4.1	0957	1.1
	1715	4.1	2330	1.8			1628	4.6	2247	1.4
7 Sa	0520	3.7	1126	1.5		22 Su	0441	4.1	1050	1.0
	1755	4.2					1723	4.9	2345	1.3
8 Su	0014	1.8	0600	3.7		23 M	0537	4.1	1142	0.9
	1201	1.5	1833	4.3			1816	5.1		
9 M	0054	1.7	0638	3.6		24 Tu	0041	1.2	0632	4.1
	1235	1.5	1909	4.4			1234	0.9	1909	5.2
10 Tu ●	0133	1.7	0715	3.6		25 W ○	0135	1.1	0726	4.1
	1310	1.5	1944	4.5			1326	0.9	2001	5.2
11 W	0211	1.7	0752	3.6		26 Th	0229	1.1	0820	4.1
	1345	1.5	2020	4.5			1419	1.0	2053	5.1
12 Th	0249	1.7	0830	3.5		27 F	0322	1.2	0915	4.0
	1421	1.5	2057	4.5			1512	1.1	2145	4.9
13 F	0328	1.7	0910	3.5		28 Sa	0416	1.3	1011	3.9
	1500	1.6	2136	4.4			1607	1.3	2237	4.7
14 Sa	0408	1.7	0953	3.5		29 Su	0509	1.4	1110	3.9
	1543	1.6	2218	4.4			1705	1.6	2330	4.5
15 Su	0450	1.7	1040	3.5		30 M	0602	1.5	1209	3.8
	1631	1.7	2303	4.3			1805	1.8		
						31 Tu	0023	4.2	0654	1.5
							1310	3.8	1907	1.9

JUNE

Day	Time	ft	Time	ft		Day	Time	ft	Time	ft
1 W ☽	0117	4.0	0745	1.6		16 Th	0021	4.2	0645	1.6
	1409	3.9	2010	2.0			1308	4.1	1914	1.8
2 Th	0210	3.8	0833	1.6		17 F	0117	4.1	0738	1.4
	1504	4.0	2111	2.1			1409	4.3	2021	1.8
3 F	0301	3.7	0918	1.6		18 Sa	0216	4.0	0833	1.3
	1554	4.1	2207	2.1			1509	4.5	2127	1.7
4 Sa	0350	3.6	1000	1.6		19 Su	0317	4.0	0929	1.2
	1639	4.2	2258	2.0			1609	4.7	2231	1.6
5 Su	0436	3.6	1041	1.6		20 M	0417	4.0	1026	1.1
	1721	4.3	2344	1.9			1706	4.9	2331	1.5
6 M	0520	3.5	1120	1.5		21 Tu	0517	4.0	1121	1.0
	1801	4.4					1801	5.0		
7 Tu	0027	1.9	0603	3.5		22 W	0028	1.4	0614	4.0
	1159	1.5	1839	4.5			1216	1.0	1855	5.1
8 W	0108	1.8	0644	3.6		23 Th	0123	1.4	0710	4.0
	1238	1.5	1918	4.6			1310	1.1	1946	5.1
9 Th ●	0148	1.7	0726	3.6		24 F	0214	1.3	0805	4.0
	1318	1.5	1956	4.6			1403	1.4	2036	5.0
10 F	0227	1.7	0808	3.6		25 Sa	0304	1.3	0858	4.0
	1359	1.5	2035	4.6			1456	1.3	2125	4.8
11 Sa	0306	1.6	0851	3.6		26 Su	0353	1.4	0952	4.0
	1441	1.5	2115	4.6			1548	1.5	2212	4.6
12 Su	0346	1.6	0936	3.7		27 M	0440	1.4	1044	4.0
	1527	1.6	2157	4.5			1640	1.7	2259	4.4
13 M	0427	1.6	1023	3.8		28 Tu	0526	1.5	1138	4.0
	1616	1.7	2241	4.4			1734	1.9	2345	4.2
14 Tu	0510	1.5	1114	3.9		29 W	0611	1.6	1231	4.0
	1710	1.7	2329	4.3			1830	2.0		
15 W	0556	1.5	1209	4.0		30 Th ☽	0031	4.0	0656	1.6
	1810	1.8					1325	4.0	1927	2.2

JULY

Day	Time	ft	Time	ft		Day	Time	ft	Time	ft
1 F	0118	3.8	0740	1.7		16 Sa	0053	4.1	0711	1.4
	1417	4.0	2026	2.2			1347	4.5	2004	1.9
2 Sa	0208	3.6	0825	1.7		17 Su	0154	4.0	0809	1.4
	1508	4.1	2124	2.2			1451	4.6	2112	1.9
3 Su	0258	3.6	0911	1.7		18 M	0257	4.0	0909	1.3
	1557	4.2	2218	2.2			1553	4.7	2219	1.8
4 M	0350	3.5	0956	1.7		19 Tu	0402	3.9	1009	1.3
	1643	4.3	2309	2.1			1653	4.9	2320	1.7
5 Tu	0440	3.5	1042	1.6		20 W	0504	3.9	1108	1.3
	1727	4.5	2355	2.0			1749	4.9		
6 W	0529	3.6	1127	1.6		21 Th	0017	1.6	0603	4.0
	1810	4.6					1205	1.3	1842	5.0
7 Th	0039	1.9	0616	3.6		22 F ○	0108	1.5	0658	4.1
	1212	1.5	1851	4.7			1259	1.3	1931	5.0
8 F	0120	1.8	0702	3.7		23 Sa	0156	1.5	0750	4.1
	1256	1.5	1932	4.7			1350	1.4	2018	4.9
9 Sa	0200	1.7	0746	3.8		24 Su	0241	1.5	0840	4.2
	1341	1.5	2013	4.7			1440	1.5	2102	4.7
10 Su	0239	1.6	0831	3.9		25 M	0324	1.5	0927	4.2
	1427	1.5	2054	4.7			1527	1.6	2144	4.5
11 M	0319	1.5	0916	4.0		26 Tu	0405	1.6	1014	4.2
	1514	1.5	2137	4.6			1614	1.8	2224	4.3
12 Tu	0400	1.5	1004	4.1		27 W	0444	1.6	1100	4.2
	1604	1.6	2221	4.5			1701	2.0	2304	4.1
13 W	0443	1.4	1054	4.2		28 Th	0523	1.7	1146	4.1
	1657	1.7	2307	4.4			1750	2.1	2345	4.0
14 Th	0528	1.4	1148	4.3		29 F	0604	1.8	1235	4.1
	1755	1.8	2358	4.2			1841	2.3		
15 F	0618	1.4	1246	4.4		30 Sa ☽	0028	3.8	0646	1.8
	1857	1.8					1325	4.1	1937	2.3
						31 Su	0116	3.7	0732	1.9
							1417	4.2	2036	2.4

AUGUST

Day	Time	ft	Time	ft		Day	Time	ft	Time	ft
1 M	0210	3.6	0822	1.9		16 Tu	0247	3.9	0856	1.6
	1510	4.2	2134	2.3			1539	4.7	2207	2.0
2 Tu	0307	3.6	0914	1.9		17 W	0354	3.9	1000	1.5
	1602	4.4	2229	2.2			1641	4.8	2307	1.9
3 W	0404	3.6	1007	1.8		18 Th	0457	4.0	1102	1.6
	1651	4.5	2318	2.1			1737	4.8		
4 Th	0458	3.7	1058	1.7		19 F	0001	1.8	0554	4.1
	1738	4.6					1158	1.6	1827	4.8
5 F	0004	1.9	0549	3.9		20 Sa	0049	1.7	0646	4.3
	1148	1.6	1822	4.7			1250	1.6	1913	4.8
6 Sa	0046	1.8	0636	4.0		21 Su ○	0132	1.7	0733	4.4
	1237	1.5	1906	4.8			1338	1.6	1956	4.7
7 Su ●	0127	1.6	0722	4.2		22 M	0212	1.6	0817	4.4
	1325	1.4	1948	4.8			1423	1.7	2035	4.6
8 M	0208	1.5	0808	4.4		23 Tu	0249	1.7	0859	4.4
	1412	1.4	2031	4.8			1506	1.8	2112	4.4
9 Tu	0249	1.4	0855	4.5		24 W	0325	1.7	0940	4.4
	1501	1.4	2115	4.7			1547	1.9	2149	4.3
10 W	0331	1.4	0943	4.6		25 Th	0400	1.8	1020	4.4
	1551	1.5	2200	4.6			1629	2.1	2225	4.1
11 Th	0415	1.4	1033	4.7		26 F	0435	1.8	1101	4.3
	1644	1.6	2248	4.5			1713	2.2	2302	3.9
12 F	0502	1.4	1127	4.7		27 Sa	0513	1.9	1145	4.3
	1741	1.8	2339	4.3			1800	2.3	2344	3.8
13 Sa	0553	1.4	1225	4.7		28 Su	0554	2.0	1233	4.3
	1844	1.9					1852	2.4		
14 Su ☽	0036	4.1	0649	1.5		29 M	0033	3.7	0642	2.0
	1328	4.7	1951	2.0			1326	4.3	1950	2.4
15 M	0139	4.0	0751	1.6		30 Tu	0129	3.7	0736	2.1
	1434	4.7	2100	2.0			1422	4.3	2049	2.4
						31 W	0230	3.7	0835	2.1
							1518	4.4	2145	2.2

TIME MERIDIAN 75°W
Heights in feet are referred to the chart datum of sounding.

0000h is midnight, 1200h is noon.

NASSAU, BAHAMAS

HIGH & LOW WATER 1994 25°05'N 77°21'W

EASTERN STANDARD TIME, ADD 1 HOUR DAYLIGHT SAVING APRIL 3 - OCTOBER 29

SEPTEMBER

Day	Time	ft	Time	ft		Day	Time	ft	Time	ft
1 Th	0331	3.8	1612	4.5		16 F	0449	4.2	1719	4.6
	0935	1.9	2237	2.1			1055	1.8	2338	1.8
2 F	0438	4.0	1702	4.6		17 Sa	0510	1.0	1807	4.6
	1032	1.8	2324	1.9			1150	1.8		
3 Sa	0521	4.2	1750	4.7		18 Su	0022	1.8	1239	1.8
	1126	1.7					0630	4.4	1850	4.5
4 Su	0008	1.7	1217	1.5		19 M	0101	1.7	1323	1.8
	0610	4.4	1836	4.8			0712	4.5	1929	4.4
5 M ●	0051	1.6	1307	1.4		20 Tu	0137	1.7	1404	1.8
	0657	4.6	1921	4.8			0752	4.6	2005	4.3
6 Tu	0133	1.4	1356	1.4		21 W	0211	1.7	1444	1.9
	0744	4.8	2006	4.8			0830	4.6	2040	4.2
7 W	0217	1.3	1446	1.4		22 Th	0244	1.8	1522	2.0
	0832	5.0	2052	4.8			0906	4.6	2114	4.1
8 Th	0301	1.3	1537	1.4		23 F	0317	1.8	1601	2.1
	0921	5.0	2140	4.6			0943	4.5	2149	4.0
9 F	0348	1.3	1631	1.6		24 Sa	0351	1.9	1642	2.2
	1012	5.0	2230	4.5			1021	4.5	2227	3.8
10 Sa	0438	1.4	1729	1.7		25 Su	0428	2.0	1726	2.2
	1107	5.0	2324	4.3			1102	4.4	2310	3.8
11 Su	0532	1.5	1832	1.9		26 M	0510	2.0	1816	2.3
	1206	4.9					1148	4.4		
12 M ◑	0025	4.1	1310	4.8		27 Tu	0000	3.7	1239	4.3
	0632	1.7	1939	2.0			0600	2.1	1910	2.3
13 Tu	0131	4.0	1417	4.7		28 W ◐	0057	3.7	1335	4.3
	0738	1.8	2047	2.0			0657	2.1	2006	2.2
14 W	0241	4.0	1523	4.6		29 Th	0159	3.8	1434	4.3
	0847	1.8	2151	2.0			0801	2.1	2101	2.1
15 Th	0349	4.0	1624	4.6		30 F	0301	3.9	1530	4.4
	0954	1.8	2248	1.9			0905	2.0	2153	1.9

OCTOBER

Day	Time	ft	Time	ft		Day	Time	ft	Time	ft
1 Sa	0359	4.2	1624	4.5		16 Su	0524	4.3	1739	4.2
	1006	1.8	2242	1.7			1136	1.9	2347	1.7
2 Su	0452	4.4	1715	4.6		17 M	0000	1.1	1223	1.8
	1103	1.7	2328	1.5					1820	4.1
3 M	0543	4.7	1804	4.6		18 Tu	0024	1.7	1305	1.8
	1156	1.5					0648	4.5	1858	4.0
4 Tu	0014	1.4	1248	1.4		19 W O	0059	1.7	1344	1.8
	0632	5.0	1853	4.7			0725	4.6	1934	3.9
5 W ●	0100	1.2	1339	1.3		20 Th	0132	1.7	1422	1.9
	0721	5.1	1941	4.7			0800	4.6	2008	3.9
6 Th	0146	1.2	1431	1.3		21 F	0205	1.7	1500	1.9
	0810	5.3	2030	4.6			0836	4.6	2044	3.8
7 F	0231	1.1	1524	1.3		22 Sa	0238	1.7	1538	1.9
	0901	5.3	2120	4.5			0911	4.5	2120	3.7
8 Sa	0324	1.2	1618	1.4		23 Su	0314	1.8	1617	2.0
	0953	5.2	2214	4.3			0948	4.5	2200	3.6
9 Su	0416	1.3	1717	1.6		24 M	0352	1.9	1659	2.0
	1049	5.1	2312	4.2			1028	4.4	2244	3.6
10 M	0514	1.5	1818	1.7		25 Tu	0436	1.9	1745	2.0
	1148	4.9					1112	4.3	2335	3.6
11 Tu ◑	0015	4.0	1251	4.7		26 W	0527	2.0	1834	2.0
	0617	1.7	1923	1.8			1201	4.2		
12 W	0123	4.0	1356	4.5		27 Th	0031	3.6	1254	4.2
	0725	1.8	2027	1.8			0626	2.0	1926	1.9
13 Th	0232	4.0	1506	4.4		28 F	0131	3.8	1351	4.2
	0836	1.9	2127	1.8			0730	2.0	2019	1.8
14 F	0337	4.1	1559	4.3		29 Sa	0232	4.0	1449	4.2
	0943	1.9	2220	1.8			0836	1.9	2111	1.6
15 Sa	0434	4.2	1652	4.2		30 Su	0329	4.2	1546	4.2
	1043	1.9	2306	1.7			0939	1.7	2201	1.4
						31 M	0424	4.5	1640	4.3
							1039	1.6	2251	1.2

NOVEMBER

Day	Time	ft	Time	ft		Day	Time	ft	Time	ft
1 Tu	0517	4.8	1733	4.3		16 W	0620	4.4	1824	3.6
	1135	1.4	2340	1.1			1243	1.8		
2 W	0608	5.0	1825	4.3		17 Th	0021	1.5	1323	1.7
	1229	1.2					0657	4.4	1900	3.6
3 Th ●	0030	1.0	1323	1.2		18 F	0056	1.5	1401	1.7
	0659	5.2	1917	4.3			0733	4.4	1940	3.5
4 F	0119	0.9	1416	1.1		19 Sa	0132	1.5	1439	1.7
	0750	5.3	2009	4.3			0809	4.4	2018	3.5
5 Sa	0210	0.9	1510	1.1		20 Su	0208	1.5	1517	1.7
	0842	5.2	2103	4.2			0845	4.4	2057	3.4
6 Su	0303	1.0	1605	1.2		21 M	0246	1.6	1555	1.7
	0936	5.1	2200	4.1			0922	4.4	2139	3.4
7 M	0358	1.2	1702	1.3		22 Tu	0327	1.6	1635	1.7
	1031	4.9	2259	4.0			1001	4.3	2224	3.4
8 Tu	0457	1.4	1800	1.4		23 W	0412	1.7	1717	1.6
	1128	4.7					1044	4.2	2313	3.5
9 W	0002	3.9	1227	4.5		24 Th	0503	1.7	1802	1.6
			1859	1.5			1129	4.1		
10 Th ◑	0108	3.9	1328	4.2		25 F	0007	3.6	1220	4.0
	0708	1.7	1958	1.5			0601	1.8	1849	1.5
11 F	0214	3.9	1428	4.1		26 Sa	0104	3.7	1314	3.9
	0816	1.8	2053	1.6			0704	1.7	1940	1.4
12 Sa	0315	4.0	1524	3.9		27 Su	0203	3.9	1412	3.9
	0922	1.9	2143	1.6			0809	1.7	2032	1.2
13 Su	0409	4.1	1616	3.8		28 M	0301	4.2	1510	3.9
	1021	1.9	2228	1.5			0914	1.6	2125	1.1
14 M	0458	4.2	1702	3.7		29 Tu	0358	4.4	1608	3.9
	1114	1.8	2308	1.5			1016	1.4	2218	0.9
15 Tu	0541	4.3	1745	3.6		30 W	0454	4.7	1705	3.9
	1201	1.8	2345	1.5			1115	1.3	2312	0.8

DECEMBER

Day	Time	ft	Time	ft		Day	Time	ft	Time	ft
1 Th	0548	4.9	1801	3.9		16 F	0628	4.2	1832	3.2
	1212	1.1					1258	1.6		
2 F ●	0005	0.7	1308	1.0		17 Sa	0023	1.3	1337	1.5
	0641	5.0	1856	3.9			0706	4.2	1911	3.2
3 Sa	0058	0.7	1402	1.0		18 Su	0105	1.2	1415	1.4
	0734	5.0	1952	3.9			0744	4.3	1955	3.3
4 Su	0152	0.7	1455	1.0		19 M	0145	1.3	1453	1.4
	0826	5.0	2048	3.9			0822	4.2	2037	3.3
5 M	0246	0.8	1548	1.0		20 Tu	0226	1.3	1530	1.3
	0919	4.9	2144	3.8			0900	4.2	2119	3.3
6 Tu	0342	1.0	1642	1.0		21 W	0310	1.3	1608	1.3
	1011	4.7	2242	3.8			0939	4.1	2204	3.4
7 W	0440	1.2	1735	1.1		22 Th	0356	1.4	1648	1.2
	1105	4.4	2342	3.7			1020	4.0	2251	3.5
8 Th	0540	1.4	1828	1.2		23 F	0446	1.4	1730	1.2
	1159	4.2					1103	3.9	2342	3.6
9 F ◐	0043	3.7	1253	3.9		24 Sa ◑	0541	1.5	1816	1.1
	0642	1.6	1920	1.3			1151	3.8		
10 Sa	0143	3.7	1347	3.7		25 Su ◐	0037	3.7	1243	3.7
	0747	1.7	2011	1.3			0641	1.5	1905	1.0
11 Su	0241	3.8	1441	3.5		26 M	0135	3.9	1340	3.6
	0850	1.8	2058	1.3			0745	1.5	1959	1.0
12 M	0335	3.9	1532	3.4		27 Tu	0235	4.1	1440	3.6
	0950	1.8	2143	1.3			0851	1.4	2055	0.9
13 Tu	0424	3.9	1620	3.3		28 W	0336	4.3	1542	3.5
	1044	1.8	2226	1.3			0957	1.3	2153	0.8
14 W	0508	4.0	1706	3.2		29 Th	0434	4.5	1643	3.6
	1133	1.7	2306	1.3			1059	1.2	2250	0.7
15 Th	0549	4.1	1750	3.2		30 F	0531	4.6	1743	3.6
	1217	1.6	2346	1.3			1158	1.1	2347	0.6
						31 Sa	0626	4.7	1841	3.7
							1253	1.0		

TIME MERIDIAN 75°W

0000h is midnight, 1200h is noon.

Heights in feet are referred to the chart datum of sounding.

Chapter 2

TURKS AND CAICOS

ENTRY PROCEDURES

You may obtain temporary permission to stay for 7 days from the harbormaster at the Turtle Cove Marina on Providenciales. To obtain permission for a stay of 30 days, you must go to the immigration office in town. Temporary permission is also granted at the Provo Aquatic Centre in Sapodilla Bay (on the south side of the island), at Caicos Marina and Shipyard (also on the south banks side) and at Leeward Marina in the Leeward Going Through Cut.

Other ports of entry are Cockburn Harbour on South Caicos and at Cockburn Town on Grand Turk, which is the capital of the islands. Boaters will need passports, but no visas. Firearms should be declared and you should check on the latest sportfishing regulations. There are restrictions regarding the use of all types of fishing spears.

There is reported to be a departure tax and possibly other fees. U.S. dollars are legal tender in the islands.

For the latest information on procedures contact Customs at (809) 946-4776, and Immigration at (809) 946-4776. The Immigration office on Grand Turk may be reached at (809) 946-2972. Call the Turks and Caicos Tourist Board at (809) 946-2321.

Language spoken: English.

CAICOS

NORTHWEST POINT LIGHT, On NW point of Providenciales Island, 21 51.9N, 72 20.0W, Fl (3) W 15s, 14M.
WEST CAICOS LIGHT, S end, 21 37.9N, 72 27.9W, Q R, 52ft., Pillar.
PROVIDENCIALES ISLAND LIGHT, E end, 21 48.6N, 72 07.8W, Fl W 10s, 12M.
FRENCH CAY LIGHT, 21 30.3N, 72 12.1W, Fl R, 10ft., Pillar.
CAPE COMETE LIGHT, East Caicos Island, 21 43.4N, 71 28.3W, Fl (2) W 20s, 12M.
SOUTH CAICOS ISLAND LIGHT, Cockburn Harbor on Government Hill, 21 29.9N, 71 30.7W, F W, 50ft., 9M, W building, Flat roof, Visible 180° to 090°.
LONG CAY LIGHT, E end, 21 29.0N, 71 32.1W, Fl R 2.5s, 5M.
DOVE CAY LIGHT, W end, 21 29.0N, 71 32.1W, Fl G 2.5s, 5M, W tower.
BUSH CAY LIGHT, 21 11.0N, 71 38.0W, Fl (2) W 10s, 14M.

PROVIDENCIALES

21 47N, 72 17W
Port of Entry: Contact the harbormasters at Turtle Cove Marina, Provo Aquatic Centre or at the Leeward Marina. The harbormasters stand by on VHF channel 16.
Dockage: Located on the north side of Providenciales are Turtle Cove Marina (809) 946-4232 and the Leeward Yacht Club and Marina (809) 946-5553. Located on the south side are the Provo Aquatic Centre on VHF channel 68 and Caicos Marina and Shipyard (809) 946-5600. All marinas monitor VHF channel 16. Turtle Cove offers guides to bring vessels in safely through the reefs.

The approach to Turtle Cove through the reef is made via Sellers Cut. The marina advises new visitors to call ahead for a paid guide for this passage. The approach to Leeward Marina is also through the reef, and is reported to be marked with a red and white striped buoy. The channel from the cut to the marina is marked by red and green buoys. Both marinas report approach depths of over 6 feet. The

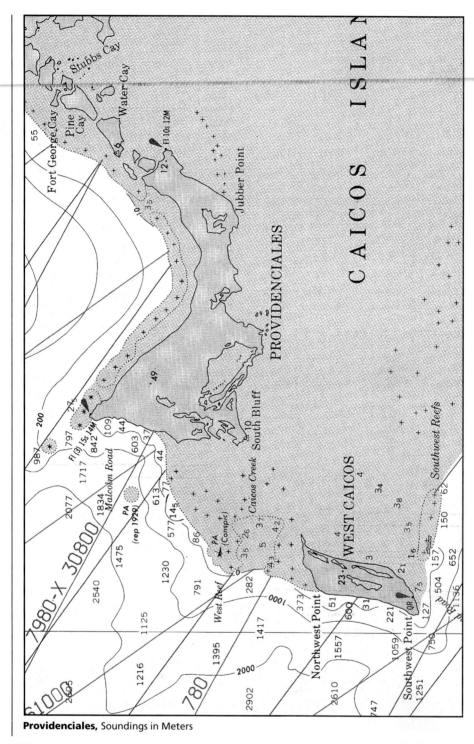

Providenciales, Soundings in Meters

approaches to the marinas on the south side are mentioned in the Anchorage section.
Anchorage: A popular spot is off the Sand Bore Channel, which takes you into the harbors on the south side of Providenciales. Enter the Sand Bore Channel through West Reef via a break south of a visible wreck. The channel then runs about 103° T towards the southern point of Providenciales. If in doubt, contact one of the marinas on the VHF.

You can also make the approach to the south side of Providenciales via the Clear Sand Road. This channel is reported to run about 068° from the southern end of West Caicos. You can anchor in Clear Sand Road on the edge of the banks.

Sapodilla Bay is located west of the Caicos Marina. It has up to 8 feet of water for anchoring. The Government Dock is nearby.
Services: All services are available, including haulouts and major repairs. There is a good selection of parts and supplies. Regular air service to the U.S. can bring in special items. There is good telephone service.

Providenciales has become a tourist, dive and boating destination in recent years. The expansion of all facilities has made this a good stop for those traveling to, or from, the Caribbean.

COCKBURN HARBOR, SOUTH CAICOS

21 29N, 71 32W
Port of Entry
Dockage: Contact Sea View Marina at (809) 946-3219 or on VHF channel 16. It may be possible to tie up at the government wharf.
Anchorage: Anchor off of the town, or north of Long Cay. Be wary of shallow spots, and the charted reef north of Long Cay. The protection is good in most conditions.
Services: The marina can provide fuel at either their docks or the government wharf. They also have water, laundry service and

some provisions. There are telephones and some restaurants.

TURKS

GRAND TURK LIGHT, 21 30.9N, 71 07.9W, Fl W 7.5s, 108ft., 18M, W cylindrical iron tower, Signal station.
SALT CAY LIGHT, NW point, 21 20.2N, 71 12.7W, Fl (4) W 20s, 8M.
SAND CAY LIGHT, 21 11.9N, 71 14.0W, Fl W 2s, 85ft., 10M, R steel framework structure.

COCKBURN TOWN, GRAND TURK

21 28N, 71 09W
Port of Entry
Pilotage: There are reported to be two lighted ranges on the west coast of the island. The northern range leads through the reef on a course of 084° T to Cockburn Town, while the southern range leads on a course of 056° T to a large government wharf. Boaters are urged to attempt their approach in good light.
Anchorage: The best anchorage is reported to be north of the wharf at the southern end of the island. A cut has been made through the reef at the north end of the island. This allows access to North Creek, which is very sheltered. The entrance is marked by a pile of black stones on the east. Local knowledge is recommended for those attempting this pass. The Hawks Nest anchorage is at the south end of the island, but requires local knowledge.
Services: Most supplies are available and there is good telephone service. There are small shops, restaurants and hotels. Call Sheila and Robin Laing on VHF channel 16 (call sign Flagstaff) for information on the area. They also run a radio net on 21.4MHz from 1300 to 1400 GMT.

This is the administrative headquarters of the Turks and Caicos, though the anchorages are not as sheltered as some in the Caicos area.

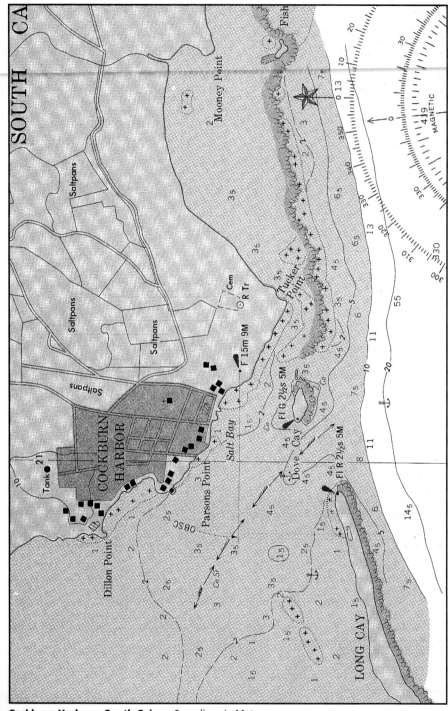

Cockburn Harbour, South Caicos, Soundings in Meters

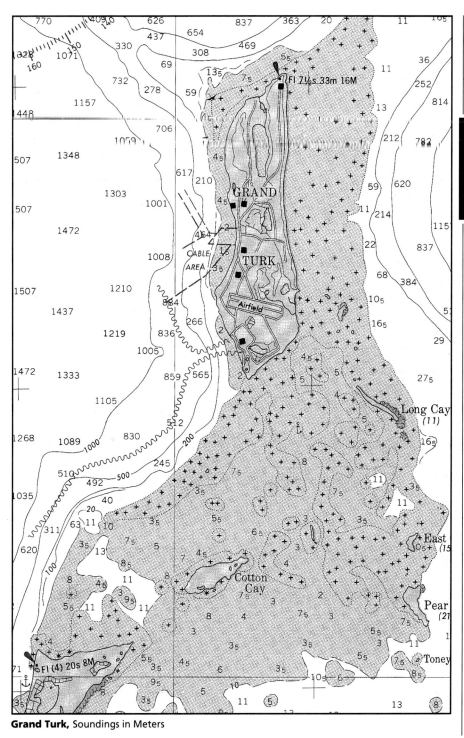

Grand Turk, Soundings in Meters

Chapter 2

REED'S
NAUTICAL ALMANACS & COMPANIONS

1994

CARIBBEAN
The only almanac which covers the entire Caribbean basin including Bermuda, the Bahamas, Caribbean islands, the north coast of South America, Central America, Panama and Mexico. Contains 200 harbor chartlets, complete tide and celestial tables, coast pilot with aids to navigation, weather and communication information.   800 pages $29.95(US) Retail

NORTH AMERICAN: EAST COAST
Now in its 21st year of publication, it includes over 200 harbor chartlets, tide and current tables from Nova Scotia to the Bahamas, light and buoy lists, waypoints, radio and communication information, a complete nautical ephemeris and lots more.
900 pages $29.95(US) Retail

NORTH AMERICAN: PACIFIC NORTHWEST
The only almanac to include US and Canadian Hydrographic information in a single volume, and covers from the head of the Columbia River to the Gulf of Alaska and Kodiak Island, including Puget Sound and the British Columbia coastline. More than 170 harbor charts, tide and current tables, nautical ephemeris, aids to navigation, communication and weather information.   900 pages $29.95(US) Retail

NORTHERN EUROPEAN
Our flagship almanac, now enjoying its 63rd year of publication. Its coverage ranges from Skagen, on the northern coast of Denmark, to the French-Spanish border and Biarritz. This extensive European coverage includes 450 chartlets and illustrations, 2000 ports and complete tidal information for each area.   1,200 pages $45.00(US) Retail

SOUTHERN EUROPEAN
A completely reorganized and updated version of our Mediterranean almanac, featuring the Atlantic-European coast and islands, as well as the complete coastline of one of the world's most popular cruising areas, the Mediterranean sea. This edition is an excellent reference book for those planning a transatlantic voyage including stopovers in the Azores and entry via Gibraltar to the Mediterranean.   800 pages $45.00(US) Retail

NAUTICAL COMPANION
The COMPANION is designed to complement the Caribbean, North American East Coast and Pacific Northwest REED'S ALMANACS, and is full of practical information for the cruising boater. It includes extensive chapters on seamanship, rules of the road, coastal passage making, signaling, first aid and more.   444 pages $19.95(US) Retail

NAUTICAL COMPANION (European edition)
An outstanding nautical reference with essential information on subjects similar to those included in our US COMPANION. Designed to complement our European editions.
450 pages $24.95(US) Retail

Call 1-800-995-4995 for your nearest dealer!

CUBA

*WARNING: Cuba claims a 12 mile territori
al sea extending from straight baselines
drawn from Cuban coastal points. The
effect is that Cuba's claimed territorial
sea extends in many areas well beyond
the 12 miles from Cuba's physical coastline. These claims are not in conformance
with international law and are not recognized by the United States. Nonetheless,
United States vessels have been stopped
and boarded by Cuban authorities more
than 20 miles from the Cuban coast in
some cases. Within the limits of prudence
and good judgment, mariners are advised
to protest (but not physically resist) any
improper attempt to stop, board or seize
U.S. vessels in international waters. Notify the U.S. Coast Guard of your status so
that they can relay information about
your situation to the Department of State
for diplomatic attention.*

TRAFFIC SEPARATION SCHEMES: On September 1, 1990, seven Traffic Separation
Schemes, approved by the International Maritime Organization, were implemented off the
eastern, western and northern coasts of Cuba.
The government of Cuba has unilaterally
established a mandatory ship reporting system
within the Old Bahama Channel to govern vessel movement within the area. While it is the
U.S. Position that the mandatory provisions of
the ship reporting system are inconsistent with
International Law, vessels should exercise caution while transiting the Old Bahama Channel.

The Traffic Separation Schemes are in the following areas:

Off Cabo San Antonio
Off La Tabla
Off Costa de Matanzas
In the Old Bahama Channel
Off Punta Maternillos
Off Punta Lucrecia
Off Cabo Maisi

*CAUTION: Our information on aids to nav-
igation comes from official government
sources. The latitudes and longitudes of
these marks may not correspond to the*

*readings from GPS or LORAN receivers.
Some aids have been reported as unreliable, missing, off position or showing
incorrect characteristics. No single aid
to navigation, or waypoint, should be
relied upon as a sole means of fixing your
position.*

CUBAN ASSETS CONTROL REGULATIONS

The Cuban Assets Control Regulations were
issued by the U.S. Government on July 8, 1963
under the Trading With the Enemy Act in
response to certain hostile actions by the
Cuban government. They are still in force
today and affect all U.S. citizens and perma-
nent residents wherever they are located, all
people and organizations physically in the
United States and all branches and subsidiaries
of U.S. organizations throughout the world.
The regulations are administered by the U.S.
Treasury Department's Office of Foreign
Assets Control. The basic goal of the sanctions
is to isolate Cuba economically and deprive it
of U.S. dollars. Penalties for violating the sanctions range up to 10 years in prison, $500,000
in corporate and $250,000 in individual fines.
The regulations require those dealing with
Cuba to maintain records, and, upon request
from the U.S. Treasury Department, to furnish
information regarding such dealings.

Spending money in connection with tourist,
business, or recreational trips is prohibited,
whether travelers go directly to Cuba or via a
third country. In April 1992 the Treasury
Department further tightened these sanctions
with a new regulation. Vessels are prohibited
entry into any U.S. port if they are carrying
passengers or goods to or from Cuba. There
are certain exceptions to these rules for family
visitors, official government travelers, news
gatherers, professional researchers and spon-
sored travelers. Certain types of humanitarian
assistance may be carried to Cuba.

When in Cuba U.S. citizens should contact and
register with the United States Interests Section, Embassy of Switzerland, Calzada

between L&M, Vedado Section, Havana, telephone: 320551, 320543.

For the latest information on these regulations contact:

Office of Foreign Assets Control
U.S. Department of the Treasury
1500 Pennsylvania Avenue NW
Washington, DC 20220
(202) 622-2520

ENTRY PROCEDURES

Yachtsmen are advised to enter the country at a marina where the officials will be familiar with the procedures for pleasure boats. Ports of Entry (circling the island in a clockwise direction) include Santa Lucía, the Marina Hemingway in Barlovento, the marinas in Veradero, Bahía Naranjo Marina, Punta Gorda in Bahía de Santiago de Cuba, Trinidad, Cienfuegos, Cayo Largo and Isla de Pinos. You must clear in and out whenever moving the boat from one point to another, and you should always check with the authorities ashore, whether or not in a Port of Entry. Havana is a commercial port only, and has no facilities for clearing yachts.

You should have passports, a clearance from your last port, crew lists and ship's papers. Make sure the crew list has everyone's birth date and nationality. When approaching the coast of Cuba you must notify the authorities on VHF channel 16. You should do this when within the 12 mile limit of Cuba, and don't be surprised if a patrol boat comes out to meet you. You will be met by many officials, usually including an armed member of the national guard.

Most visitors will be granted a temporary tourist card for a 3 day visit, which can be renewed for periods of up to several months. For more information on traveling to Cuba contact the Cuba Intrasection at 16th Street NW, Washington, DC 20009, (202) 797-8518.

You will be issued a coastwise clearance stating where you can go — be careful to avoid unplanned intermediate stops.

When telephoning Cuba from the U.S. you must use an International Operator. Recent restrictions have been placed on companies routing calls through Canada to avoid the congestion on the limited number of circuits available. In general, the phone system is reported to be slow and cumbersome.

The official currency is the Cuban peso, but U.S. dollars are accepted in many places — in fact U.S. currency is preferred by many. There are special stores for visitors which only take dollars. The official exchange rate is 1 peso per 1 U.S. dollar, though in reality, dollars can buy much more in Cuba. U.S. citizens should check the restrictions on spending money discussed previously. You will probably not be able to use any U.S. credit cards, and you should change all Cuban currency before leaving the country. Non- U.S. citizens may be able to use their credit cards and traveler's checks.

Spanish is the main language, but visitors report many people can speak some English or French. English is taught to all students in school. Marina personnel, and tourist offices, can be helpful with language problems.

Visitors to Cuba can obtain official Cuban charts, pilots and other information at the Marina Hemingway.

THE YUCATAN CHANNEL

21 30N, 86 00W

Pilotage: This channel is about 108 miles wide between Cabo San Antonio on Cuba and Isla Contoy off the Mexican coast. It serves as the main route for shipping between the Gulf of Mexico and the Panama Canal. The east side of the channel is deep, shoaling gradually toward the Mexican coast.

There is a tremendous flow of water from the Caribbean Sea through the Yucatan Channel toward the Gulf of Mexico. Currents reach velocities of up to 4 knots on the stream's axis. The eastern border of the flow is about 20 miles off Cabo San Antonio, which is just beyond Cuba's 12 mile territorial limit. Twenty to thirty-five miles from Cabo San Antonio the rate is 1 knot; at 50 miles, 2 knots; at 65 miles, 3 knots; at 78 miles, 4 knots, and at 90 miles, or about 25 miles from Yucatan, 1 knot. The current axis is located about 35 miles off the Yucatan coast, or about 6 miles beyond the 100 fathom curve. The mean rate during April, May and June along the axis is about 4 knots.

The current increases in the summer, and decreases in the winter. When the current is stronger, the width of the flow is wider, and when the flow is weaker, the width shrinks. There is also a noticeable daily variation in flow, particularly on the west side. The flow has been known to increase or decrease by as much as 3 knots in 5 hours time.

Within 20 miles of Cabo San Antonio the flow is either northeast toward the Straits of Florida, or southeast along the south coast of Cuba. At times the east setting current can reach velocities of 4 knots, especially during southerly winds.

CAUTION: During periods of southerly winds it is advisable to avoid the coast of Cuba from Cabo San Antonio to Cabo Corrientes, due to dangerous currents.

NORTH COAST: CABO SAN ANTONIO TO BAHIA HONDA

CABO SAN ANTONIO LIGHT, W extremity of Cuba, 21 52.0N, 84 57.2W, Fl (2) W 10s, 103ft., 40M, Yellow tower, Marked RONCALI, Masonry house, Radiobeacon, Radar reflector, Aeromarine light.

CABO SAN ANTONIO
21 52N, 84 57W

Pilotage: This is the western extremity of Cuba. It is low and covered by trees from 69 to 79 feet in height. The trees will be visible before the land, frequently having the appearance of vessels under sail. The curve of the coast is so gradual that the position of the cape can only be determined by the lighthouse. The area is reported to be radar conspicuous at a distance of 15 miles. Currents near the outer edge of the bank are confused, while near shore they flow north on a rising tide and south on a falling tide. Tide rips are also present.
Anchorage: Temporary anchorage is available south of the lighthouse, with the southeast extremity of the land bearing 135°, and the west extremity 023°.

BANCO SANCHO PARDO, 22 09.6N, 84 45.0W, Fl W 8s, 36ft., 11M, Yellow aluminum skeleton tower.
LA TABLA, 22 18.3N, 84 40.1W, Fl W 5s, 33ft., 11M, Metal framework tower on white concrete base. RACON: **M (– –)**, 30s, 12M.

ZORRITA, 22 23.2N, 84 34.8W, FL W 7S, 33ft., 11M, Metal framework tower on white concrete base.
EL PINTO, 22 25.0N, 84 31.2W, Fl W 15s, 33ft., 11M, Metal framework tower, yellow and red bands on white concrete base.
CAYO BUENAVISTA, 22 24.1N, 84 26.7W, Fl W 5s, 100 ft., 0M, White metal framework tower.
QUEBRADO DE BUENAVISTA, 22 28.1N, 84 28.0W, Fl W 7s, 33ft., 11M, Metal framework tower on white concrete base.
CABEZO SECA, 22 32.0N, 84 20.0W, Fl W 12s, 33ft., 11M, Metal framework tower, red and white bands on concrete platform on piles.
PUERTO DE LOS ARROYOS, BAJA LA PAILA, 22 21.4N, 84 22.8W, Fl G 5s, 16ft., 4 M, Port Green beacon, topmark.

GOLFO DE GUANAHACABIBES
22 08N, 84 35W

Pilotage: This area is located just to the northeast of Cabo San Antonio. The area is much encumbered with shoals and cays, and the intricate channels indicate local knowledge may be necessary.

LA FE
22 03N, 84 16W

Pilotage: This is a small port situated on the east bank 2 miles from the Río Guadiana, in the southeast part of Golfo de Guanahacabibes. Drafts of up to 9 feet can anchor here. The area is marked with navigational aids, but they are considered unreliable. There is a wharf with fresh water available.

FONDEADERO LOS ARROYOS
22 22N, 84 26W

Pilotage: This anchorage is located in the extreme northeast part of Golfo de Guanahacabibes. The holding ground is reported to be good, and there is shelter from the prevailing winds. It is a loading place for the inland community of Mantua.

PUNTA TABACO, 22 34.7N, 84 15.3W, Fl W 8s, 33ft., 11M, Yellow metal framework tower on concrete platform on piles.
RONCADORA, 22 38.3N, 84 11.6W, Fl W 10s, 33ft., 15M, Yellow metal framework on concrete platform on piles.

ARCHIPIELAGO LOS COLORADOS

Pilotage: This group of sunken dangers fronts about 100 miles of the northeastern coast of Cuba from Golfo de Guanahacabibes to Bahía Honda. It consists of an almost uninterrupted series of reefs rising steeply from seaward. The shallow area between the reefs and the coast is also full of hazards and low-lying islets. The shore beyond the dangers is low and the dangers rarely marked by breakers, except during heavy weather. Needless to say, boaters should approach this coast with extreme caution. Those with local knowledge can use some shallow channels to proceed to towns along the coast. The coast becomes generally steep-to when east of the archipelago.

CAYO JUTIAS LIGHT, NE point, 22 42.9N, 84 01.4W, L Fl W 15s, 138ft., 36M, Octagonal skeleton steel tower, Yellow and black bands, Lower part enclosed, Masonry structure to S. **Bahia de Santa Lucia, Buoy 1,** 22 45.7N, 83 59.1W, L Fl W 10s, SAFE WATER, RW, pillar w/topmark.

BAHÍA SANTA LUCIA
22 42N, 83 58W

Pilotage: This shallow water bay is located about 73 miles northeast of Cabo San Antonio. It is fronted by fields of mangroves and a low-lying terrain that rises gradually to hills in the interior. Seaward of the bay are the many dangers of the Archipielago Los Colorados. The island of Cayos Jutias is marked by a light, and the intricate entrance channel, Pasa Honda, begins 2 1/2 miles northeast of it. Many sunken dangers are scattered in this area, and a radar conspicuous wreck lay on the reef about 2 1/2 miles northeast of Pasa Honda.

This port is under the jurisdiction of Bahía de Mariel, located about 72 miles to the east-northeast. Ore is lightered out to larger vessels from the town of Santa Lucia.

PUNTA BANO, offshore on W side of entrance to channel, 22 41.2N, 83 58.2W, Fl R 4s, 16ft., 4M, Starboard Red, beacon w/topmark.
CAYO ARENAS LIGHT, 22 50.2N, 83 39.3W, Fl W 10s, 46ft., 12M, Aluminum framework tower.
PUNTA GOBERNADORA LIGHT, 3 miles W of Bahía Honda entrance, 22 59.6N, 83 12.9W, Fl W 5s, 108ft., 16M, R+W banded conical tower, Radar reflector, Aeromarine light.

BAHÍA HONDA

BAHIA HONDA, N of old fort on Punta del Morillo, 22 58.9N, 83 09.2W, Fl (2) W 10s, 89ft., 12M, White iron skeleton.
BAHIA HONDA RANGE, (Front Light), W end of Cayo del Muerto, 22 57.4N, 83 09.8W, Q W, 16ft., 9M, Yellow diamond with black border on white skeleton structure on piles. **(Rear Light),** W end of Cayo del Muerto, Head of Bay, 3.9 km, 183° from front, 22 55.3N, 83 10.0W, Fl W 6s, 46ft., 16M, White diamond with black border on white skeleton structure on piles, Visible 6° each side of range line.

BAHÍA HONDA
22 58N, 83 10W

Pilotage: This "pocket bay" is located about 120 miles northeast of Cabo San Antonio, and 45 miles west of Havana. The saddle-shaped 2,270 foot summit of El Pan de Guajiaibon (22° 47'N, 83° 10'W) is a conspicuous landmark when making your approach to the bay from offshore.

The deep entrance channel leads through a coral reef into the bay. The port is part of the jurisdiction of Bahía de Mariel, located 23 miles to the east. There are several deep water (up to 27 foot draft) docks and anchorages within the bay.

BAHÍA CABANAS LIGHT, Cerro Frias W side of entrance, 22 59.7N, 82 58.9W, Fl W 6s, 174ft., 19M, Aluminum skeleton tower, Gray hut.

CABANAS
23 00N, 82 58W

Pilotage: This is another sub-port of Mariel, which is located about 12 miles to the east. Puerto Cabanas is divided into east and west parts by the Peninsula Juan Tomas. The Canal Orozco leads into the western part and the Canal Cabanas into the eastern part. Fuerte Reina Amalia stands in ruins on the north extremity of the peninsula and serves as a conspicuous landmark when approaching these channels from the sea.

Tidal currents in the entrance have a flow of about 1 1/2 knots during the ebb, with a somewhat stronger flow during the rainy season. There is a bulk sugar pier within the bay.

PUNTA ARENAS, edge of shoal S of Punta Arena (No.2A), 22 59.2N, 82 59.0W, Fl R 6s, 16ft., 4M, Starboard Red, beacon w/topmark.
PUNTA AFRICANA, NE point of Cayo Juan Tomas (No. 6), 22 59.2N, 82 58.4W, Fl R 4s, 16ft., 4M, Starboard Red, beacon w/topmark.
PIEDRA GLORIA lighted Beacon No. 8. 22 59.5N, 82 56.7W, Fl R 6s, 16ft., 4M, Starboard Red beacon w/topmark.

BAHÍA DEL MARIEL

Puerto Mariel, Buoy 1, E side of entrance. 23 01.7N, 82 45.4W, Fl G 5s, Green buoy.
PUERTO DEL MARIEL LIGHT, W side of entrance, 23 01.3N, 82 45.6W, Fl W 12s, 134ft., 15M, Metal framework tower.
PUNTA REGULA ENTRANCE RANGE, (Front Light), 23 00.9N 82.45.5W, Q W, 16ft., 9M, Black diamond w/white border on triangular structure. **(Rear Light),** 620 meters 182°54' from front. Q Y, 29ft., 8M, Black diamond w/white border on triangular structure, Visible 6° each side of range line.

MARIEL

22 59N, 82 45W

Pilotage: This is one of the major "pocket bays" found along the north coast of Cuba. The terrain on either side of the narrow entrance channel is low-lying, except for the east side of the bay where hills slope steeply upward directly from the water's edge. The west face of these hills has been quarried into a conspicuous white cliff.

Mesa del Mariel is a conspicuous plateau located about 8 miles east-northeast of the entrance to Bahía del Mariel. There is a distinctive terrace at the high elongated plateau's eastern end, and a remarkable steep slope at its west extremity. It has been reported as radar conspicuous.

There are several tall chimneys in a cement works on the east side of the bay — they may be seen up to 12 miles offshore. The light-colored smoke forms a dense distinctive cloud, which can be sighted from up to 25 miles. This is the best landmark on the north coast of Cuba.

The Cuban Naval Academy, a large group of white buildings, is located on the southeast side of the bay on the slopes behind the community of Mariel. This serves as a good land-mark for the approach to the bay's entrance channel. Line up the center of the academy with a large white tower on the bay's entrance point. Range lights also mark the channel.

Mariel is an important port, particularly for cement and sugar cargoes. The harbor pilots, "Mariel Practice", may be contacted by VHF radio.

BOCA DEL RÍO BANES

23 02N, 82 38W

Pilotage: This small inlet is about 6 1/2 miles east of Bahía del Mariel. The channel is short and unencumbered. On its eastern shore there is a small sugar loading facility.

RÍO SANTA ANA, 23 03.7N, 82 32.3W, Fl W 12s, 30 ft., 11M, White framework tower.
RÍO SANTA ANA, BEACON NO. 5, 23 03.5N, 82 31.9W, Fl G 3s, 9ft., Port G beacon w/topmark.
RÍO SANTA ANA, BEACON NO. 6, 23 03.5N, 82 32.0W, Fl R 4s, 9ft., Starboard R beacon w/topmark.
RÍO SANTA ANA, BEACON NO. 8, 23 03.5N, 82 32.0W, Fl R 6s, 9ft., Starboard R beacon w/topmark.
DARSENA DE BARLOVENTO, 23 05.5N, 82 29.6W, Fl W 7s, 118ft., 17M, W skeleton tower on building.
BOCA DE JAIMANITAS BEACON, 23 05.6N, 82 29.4W, Fl G 3s, 16ft., 4M, Round concrete structure, green square topmark.

MARINA HEMINGWAY

23 04N, 82 30W

Pilotage: The entrance to the marina is located about 8 miles west of the entrance to Havana, and about 90 miles south-southwest of Key West, Florida. The light at Barlovento is a good position indicator. An entrance range of 140.1° will help guide you in. You should contact the harbor authorities on VHF channels 12 or 16 when within the 12 mile territorial limit. They may send out a patrol boat to escort you in.
Port of Entry: The officials are located right in the marina. This is reported to be one of the best places for pleasure vessels to enter the country.
Dockage: Contact Marina Hemingway on VHF channel 12 or 16, or at telephone 22 5590-3. The dockage rate at Cuban marinas is reported to be $0.35 (U.S.) per foot, per day.

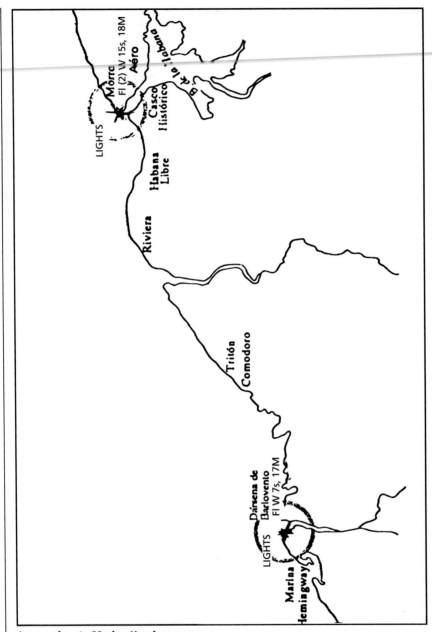

Approaches to Marina Hemingway

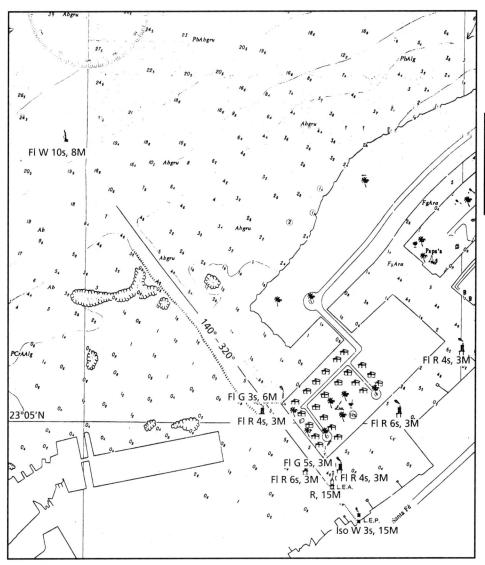

Marina Hemingway, Soundings in Meters

CUBA

Facilities: There is a special market for visitors with U.S. dollars, and there are supermarkets nearby, or in Havana. Repair facilities for yachts may be available, but services tend to be geared toward fishing and commercial vessels. Cuban charts, publications and guides are available at the marina.

This is the first stop for many boaters in Cuba, and is a good place to clear with the officials and collect information. The city of Havana is a short bus or taxi ride away.

LA HABANA (HAVANA)

BAHÍA CHORRERA, W side of entrance (No. 2). 23 08.0N, 82 24.6W, Fl R 6s, 33ft., 7M, Starboard Red, beacon w/topmark.
BAHÍA CHORRERA, NO. 3 BEACON, on mole., 23 07.9N, 82 24.7W, Fl G 3s, 10ft., 4M, Port Green, beacon w/topmark.

BAHÍA DE LA CHORRERA
23 08N, 82 25W

Pilotage: This inlet is about 3 miles west of the entrance to Bahía de La Habana. The Río Almenderes flows into the harbor. The coast in the vicinity is low and ragged, with blackened coral honeycombed by the sea. Depths in the bay average 20 to 30 feet over coral sand, in a position just within the entrance. With winds from the northeast through northwest, through north, the anchorage would be subject to a surge.

CASTILLO DEL MORRO, E side of entrance, 23 09.0N, 82 21.4W, Fl (2) W 15s, 144ft., 18M, W truncated conical tower, Storm signals, Signal station, Aeromarine light.
PIER HEAD (PILA DE NEPTUNO), 23 08.5N, 82 20.9W, Fl R 4s, 26ft., 4M, Starboard Red, beacon w/topmark. F R and F G lights are shown from various piers within the harbor.
RANGE, (Front Light), 23 07.9N, 82 19.8W, Q Y, 42ft., 12M, White pyramidal framework tower, yellow diamond daymark. **(Rear Light),** 300 meters 124.8° from front, 23 07.8N, 82 19.7W, Iso Y 6s, 62ft., 13M, White pyramidal framework tower, yellow diamond daymark.

LA HABANA
23 08N, 82 20W

Pilotage: This is one of the largest sugar shipping ports in the world, and is the commercial and shipping center for all of Cuba. Castillo

Del Morro is east of the entrance and La Punta Castle is located to the west. A powerful light is shown from Castillo Del Morro. The land east of Castillo Del Morro is about 197 feet high and flat, with a prominent ridge, Sierras de Jaruco, located about 19 miles further east. About the same distance west of the entrance is a distinctive notch in the east end of Mesa de Mariel. At night, the loom of the metropolis is reported visible up to 25 miles offshore.

CAUTION: Occasionally, powerful lights are displayed from the dome of the capitol in La Habana — these lights may be confused with the navigation light on Castillo Del Morro.

The pilot station's call sign is "Habana Practicos", and they may be contacted on VHF channels 13 and 16. The port signal station is located in Castillo Del Morro, and they may be contacted by calling "Morro Habana" on VHF channels 13, 16 and 68. The port authorities, call sign "Habana Capitonia", may be reached on VHF channels 16 and 68.

NOTE: Pleasure vessels should enter at Marina Hemingway, where facilities are geared to their needs.

BOCA DE COJIMAR BEACON, E side of entrance, 23 10.0N, 82 17.6W, Fl G 5s, 36ft., 4M, Square concrete structure, green square topmark.
BOCA DE GUANABO BEACON, E side of entrance, 23 10.4N, 82 07.4W, Fl G 3s, 26ft., 4M, Port Green, beacon w/topmark.
BOCA DE JARUCO LIGHT, Located 914 meters W of the entrance to Río Jaruco, 23 11.1N, 82 01.0W, Fl W 10s, 72ft., 15M, Concrete tower on white hut. Reported extinguished (1985).
RÍO JARUCO BEACON, W side of entrance, 23 10.8N, 82 00.6W, Fl R 4s, 23 ft., 4M, Starboard Red, beacon w/topmark.

SANTA CRUZ DE NORTE
23 09N, 81 55W

Pilotage: This is a small community located about 24 miles east of Bahía de La Habana. A distillery has a tall chimney and two storage tanks, which can be clearly seen from sea. Central Hershey sugar mill is located 2 miles southwest of Santa Cruz del Norte, and has three tall chimneys standing on an elevation of 387 feet, which make an excellent landmark. Between January and June the sugar mill is brightly lit for nighttime operations.

150

REED'S NAUTICAL ALMANAC

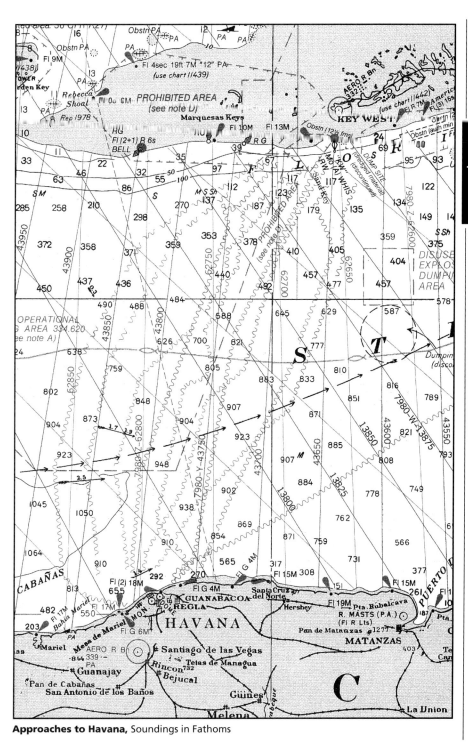

Approaches to Havana, Soundings in Fathoms

CANASI LIGHT, 23 08.8N, 81 48.0W, Fl W 7s, 374ft., 19M, R framework tower on platform.
PUNTA SEBORUCO LIGHT, 23 09.1N, 81 36.4W, Fl W 15s, 115ft., 15M, Round concrete tower, R + W bands.
PUNTA MAYA LIGHT, E side of entrance to Bahía de Matanzas, 23 05.6N, 81 28.5W, Fl W 8s, 112ft., 17M, W cylindrical tower, A F W light is shown from a wharf on the N side of port.

MATANZAS
23 03N, 81 35W

Pilotage: This is an important port and city located about 45 miles east of La Habana. It is situated near the head of one of the north coast's largest bays. Two aeronautical lights shown from the high ground on the west side of the bay are visible for distances up to 35 miles.

Bajo Nuevo, a shoal with a least depth of 10 feet, and Bajo La Laja, with a least depth of 6 feet, lie offshore near the head of Bahía de Matanzas. Several deepwater passages lead in from the sea around and between these rocky dangers.

The pilots, call sign "Matanzas Practicos", may be contacted on VHF channels 13, 16 and 68.

CANALIZO PASO MALO

KAWAMA WEST JETTY, 23 08.8N, 81 18.8W, Fl R 4s, 23ft., 4M, Starboard Red, beacon w/topmark.
EAST JETTY, 23 08.0N, 81 18.7W, Fl G 3s, 23ft., 4M, Port Green, beacon w/topmark.
RANGE, (Front Light), 23 07.8N, 81 18.6W, Q W, 9ft., 7M, White concrete tower, square base. **(Rear Light),** 108 meters 152°36′ from front. Iso W 6s, 23ft., 7M, White concrete tower, square base.
LAGUNA DE PASO MALO, NO. 3, 23 07.8N, 81 18.3W, Fl G 3s, 20ft., 4M, Port Green, beacon w/topmark.
LAGUNADE PASO MALO, NO. 6, 23 07.8N, 81 18.1W, Fl R 6s, 20ft., 4M, Starboard Red, beacon w/topmark.
LAGUNA DE PASO MALO, NO. 9, 23 07.8N, 81 17.7W, Fl G 5s, 20ft., 4M, Port Green, beacon w/topmark.
CAYO MONITO, 23 13.8N, 81 08.6W, Fl (2) W 10s, 20ft., 7M, ISOLATED DANGER BRB, beacon w/topmark.

LAGUNA DE PASO MALO, NO. 11, 23 07.8N, 81 17.6W, Fl G 3s, 20ft., 4M, Port Green, beacon w/topmark.
LAGUNA DE PASO MALO, NO. 21, 23 07.0N, 81 16.7W, Fl G 3s, 20ft., 4M, Port Green, beacon w/topmark.
LAGUNA DE PASO MALO, NO. 22, 23 07.8N, 81 16.7W, Fl R 4s, 7ft., 4M, Starboard Red, beacon w/topmark.

BAHIA DE CARDENAS

CAYO PIEDRAS LIGHT, Entrance to bay, 23 14.5N, 81 07.2W, Fl W 10s, 79ft., 15M, W cylindrical masonry tower.
Cabezo del Coral Buoy, 23 15.1N, 81 06.3W, Fl G 3s, Port Green, pillar w/topmark. Radar reflector.
Buoy 1, 23 13.6N, 81 05.3W, Fl G 5s, Port Green, pillar w/topmark.
CAYO DIANA, S side, 23 09.9N, 81 06.2W, Fl W 8s, 49ft., 12M, White framework tower.

PUNTA HICACOS
23 12N, 81 09W

Pilotage: This is the northern extremity of Peninsula de Hicacos which guards the northern border of Bahía De Cardenas. It is low and sandy, but can be identified by the buildings of a salt works near it. Punta de Molas is the low-lying eastern extremity of the peninsula. The seaward side of the peninsula is a long fine beach, broken only in a few places by low cliffs. The highest cliff is situated 4 1/2 miles southwest of Punta Hicacos and is named Bernardino.

VARADERO

23 08N, 81 15W (approx.)

Pilotage: This resort community is located on a low part of the Peninsula de Hicacos, near where it connects with the mainland. It is about 7 1/2 miles southwest of Punta Hicacos. This is one of the premier boating areas on the north coast of Cuba. From seaward this community is identified by its tall trees, houses, windmills, a club house and a large white building with a red roof. At night, the lights of the settlement are conspicuous.
Port of Entry: This is a recommended place for pleasure boats to clear in.
Dockage: Cayo Largo Marina is located just outside Veradero. Marina Veradero has more complete repair facilities, including a crane for

hauling. Marina Chapelin is in a mangrove protected basin.

Facilities: This being a tourist area, there are nightclubs, restaurants and shops for entertainment.

CARDENAS
23 02N, 81 12W

Pilotage: This is the second biggest sugar exporting port in Cuba, and also the location of a significant fishing industry. It is the northernmost port in Cuba. The port is located on the western side of Bahía de Cardenas, which lies under the shelter of Peninsula de Hicacos to the northwest. The bay is scattered with low-lying mangrove-fringed islands, but there are several deep water passages among them. The tall buildings in the resort of Varadero are prominent when approaching the bay from the north. The lighthouse on the low reef-fringed islet Cayo Piedras de Norte marks the entrance to the bay.

CAUTION: The lights and other navigational aids in Bahía de Cardenas have been reported as unreliable.

CAYO DIANA, BEACON NO. 2, 23 10.8N, 81 07.7W, Fl R 6s, 13ft., 3M, Starboard Red, beacon w/topmark.
CAYO DIANA, BEACON NO. 3, 23 11.5N, 81 07.8W, Fl G 3s, 13ft., 3M, Port Green, beacon w/topmark.
CAYO DIANA, BEACON NO. 4, 23 11.2N, 81 07.7W, Fl R 4s, 13ft., 3M, Starboard Red, beacon w/topmark.
CHANNEL BEACON 4A, PUNTA GORDA, 23 10.0N, 81 10.3W, Fl R 4s, 13ft., 4M Starboard Red, beacon w/topmark.
BEACON NO. 6A, 23 09.9N, 81 11.2W, Fl R 6s, 13ft., 4M, Starboard Red, beacon w/topmark.
CANAL DE LA MANUY, NO. 1, 23 08.6N, 81 01.2W, Fl G 3s, 16ft., Port Green, beacon w/topmark.

CANAL DE LA MANUY, NO. 2, 23 08.3N, 81 01.1W, Fl R 4s, 16ft., Starboard Red, beacon w/topmark.
CANAL DE LA MANUY, NO. 3, 23 08.2N, 81 00.8W, Fl G 5s, 16ft., Port Green, beacon w/topmark.
CANAL DE LA MANUY, NO. 4, 23 07.8N, 81 00.6W, Fl R 6s, 16ft., Starboard Red, beacon w/topmark.
CANAL DE LA MANUY, NO. 7, 23 07.1N, 80 59.8W, Fl G 3s, 16ft., Port Green, beacon w/topmark.
CANAL DE LA MANUY, NO. 9, 23 05.2N, 80 57.8W, Fl G 5s, 16ft., Port Green, beacon w/topmark.
CANAL DE LOS BARCOS, NO. 2, 23 11.8N, 80 42.2W, Fl R 4s, 16ft., Starboard Red, beacon w/topmark.
CANAL DE LOS BARCOS, NO. 3, 23 10.1N, 80 42.1W, Fl G 5s, 16ft., Port Green, beacon w/topmark.
CAYO CRUZ DEL PADRE LIGHT, 23 16.9N, 80 53.9W, Fl W 7s, 82ft., 14M, W concrete tower on square base, RACON: **C** (– · – ·), 16M.

CAYO CRUZ DEL PADRE
23 16N, 80 55W

Pilotage: This small mangrove-fringed piece of land is located about 13 miles east-northeast of Punta Hicacos, making it the northernmost islet along the north coast of Cuba. To seaward of it is a dangerous partially-drying reef, which can be distinguished in calm weather by discoloration in the surrounding water. In heavy weather, waves break over it.

CAYO BAHÍA DE CADIZ LIGHT, N side of cay, 23 12.3N, 80 28.9W, Fl (3) W 15s, 177ft., 19M, Pyramidal tower w/white + black stripes.

CAYO BAHÍA DE CADIZ
23 12N, 80 29W

Pilotage: This flat islet is located about 24 miles east-southeast of Cayo Cruz del Padre. It is rocky on its north side and somewhat higher than other islets in the vicinity.
Anchorage: Bahía de Cadiz is a shoal bay located close southwest of the islet. Vessels with local knowledge can anchor here with some protection from the prevailing northeast winds. The anchorage is open to winds from the north.

Megano de Nicolas Buoy, 23 13.2N, 80 19.3W, Fl (2) W 6s, ISOLATED DANGER BRB, pillar w/topmark.

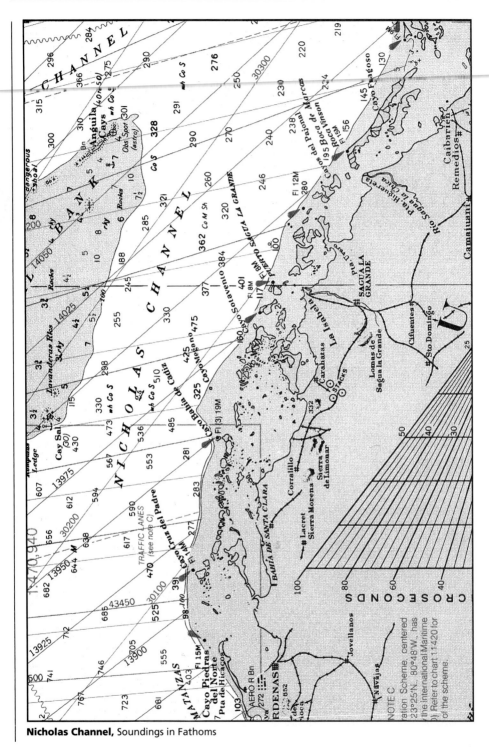

Nicholas Channel, Soundings in Fathoms

SAGUA LA GRAND

CAYO HICACAL, ON PUNTA DE LA RAN-CHERIA, 23 04.3N, 80 05.2W, Fl W 8s, 36ft., 8M, White framework tower.

NO. 4, 23 03.5N, 80 07.4W, Fl R 6s, 13ft., 4M, Starboard Red beacon w/topmark.

CAYO DEL CRISTO, ON PUNTA DE LOS PRACTICOS, 23 02.0N, 79 59.4W, Fl W 10s, 50ft., 12M, White framework tower.

RÍO SAGUA ENTRANCE BEACON, E side, 22 56.8N, 80 00.0W, Fl G 3s, 13ft., Port Green, w/topmark.

RÍO SAGUA, NO. 21, 22 56.9N. 80 00.6W, Fl G 5s, 13ft., Port Green, beacon w/topmark.

RÍO SAGUA, NO. 22, 22 56.9N. 80 00.6W, Fl R 6s, 13ft., Starboard Red, beacon w/top-mark.

RÍO SAGUA, NO. 26, 22 56.8N. 80 01.0W, Fl R 6s, 13ft., Starboard Red, beacon w/top-mark.

PUERTO SAGUA LA GRANDE

22 58N, 80 03W

Pilotage: The main entrance to this port, which fronts the Río Sagua la Grande, is through Canal Boca de Maravillas. The dredged channel passes between Cayo dela Cruz and Cayo Maravillas. Cayo del Cristo light, located about 6 miles north of Río Sagua la Grande, is the major identifying mark along this coast. The area off the coast consists of small mangrove-covered islands.

Being open to the northeast, there is frequently a very heavy sea in the entrance channel.

CAUTION: Dredged material has been deposited on each side of the channel where it lies uncharted, and built up in the form of partially drying banks.

LA ISABELLA

22 57N, 80 00W

Pilotage: This small community is located at the entrance to Río Sagua la Grande. It is a sugar shipping center for Sagua la Grande, a well populated community located about 12 miles upstream. The pilot may be contacted on VHF channel 16.

CANAL DEL SERON BEACON, E side, 22 58.0N, 79 55.6W, Fl G 5s, 10ft., 3M, Port Green, topmark.

BOCA DE JUTIAS BEACON, 22 58.0N, 79 51.9W, Fl G 5s, 16ft., 3M, Port Green, w/topmark.

CANAL DE CILINDRIN BEACON, 22 56.3N 79 49.0W, Fl G 5s, 16ft., 4M, Port Green, w/topmark.

CANAL DE LAS BARZAS BEACON, 22 54.0N, 79 45.6W Fl G 3s, 16ft., 4M, Port Green, w/topmark.

CAYO ALTO BEACON, 22 51.9N, 79 46.5W, Fl G 5s, 16 ft., 5M, Port Green, w/topmark.

CAYO LA VELA, 22 56.6N, 79 45.4W, Fl W 12s, 39ft., 14M, White round metal column.

CAYO FRAGOSO, NW end, 22 48.4N, 79 34.6W, Fl W 15s, 68ft., 15M, W framework tower.

CAYO FRAGOSO, BEACON NO. 2, 22 44.6N, 79 36.9W, Fl R 6s, 19ft., 4M, Starboard Red, w/topmark.

CAYO FRAGOSO, BEACON NO. 3, 22 42.6N, 79 36.2W, Fl G 5s, 16ft., 4M, Port Green, w/topmark.

CAYO FRAGOSO, BEACON NO. 5, 22 41.0N, 79 35.0W, Fl G 3s, 16ft., 4M, Port Green, w/topmark.

CAYO FRAGOSO, BEACON NO. 8, 22 40.1N, 79 34.2W, Fl R 4s, 16ft., 4M, Starboard Red, w/topmark.

CAYO FRANCES, W end at entrance to Caibarien, 22 38.5N, 79 13.8W, Fl W 10s, 32ft., 9M, White square concrete tower.

Buoy 1, West of Cayo Frances Light, 22 38.3N, 79 15.1W, Fl G 5s, 13ft., Port Green, pillar w/topmark.

Cayo Frances Anchorage, 22 37.8N 79 13.2W, Fl G 5s, 13ft., 4M, Port Green, w/topmark.

CAYO FRANCES, BEACON NO. 4, 22 35.6W, 79 17.4W, Fl R 4s, 16ft., 4M, Starboard Red, w/topmark.

CAYO FRANCES, BEACON NO. 6, 22 34.4W, 79 18.5W, Fl R 6s, 16ft., 4M, Starboard Red, w/topmark.

CAYO FRANCES, BEACON NO. 8, 22 33.4W, 79 22.8W, Fl R 4s, 16ft., 4M, Starboard Red, w/topmark.

PUERTO DE CAIBARIEN

22 37N, 79 15W

Pilotage: This is the sugar port for the city of Caibarien, located 16 miles to the west-south-west. It is located about 46 miles east-south-east of Puerto Sagua La Grande, with its seaward entrance near Cayo Frances (22° 38'N, 79° 13'W).

PUNTA BRAVA BEACON, NO. 9, 22 31.9N, 79 26.7W, Fl G 5s, 39ft., 4M, Port Green, w/topmark.

Chapter 2

PUNTA BRAVA BEACON, NO. 11, 22 31.9N, 79 28.5W, Fl G 5s, 16ft., 4M, Port Green, w/topmark.
CAYO FIFA BEACON, SE, 22 35.5N, 79 28.5W, Fl R 6s, 16ft., 4M, Starboard Red, w/topmark.
CAYO FIFA BEACON, NE, 22 36.1N, 79 27.9W, Fl G 3s, 13ft., 3M, Green square daymark on concrete tower.
CANAL DEL REFUGIO, E BEACON, NO. 1, 22 31.8N, 79 27.5W, Fl G 5s, 16ft., 4M, Port Green, w/topmark.
CANAL DEL REFUGIO, W BEACON, NO. 2, 22 31.5N, 79 27.3W, Fl R 6s, 16ft., 4M, Starboard Red, w/topmark.
CANAL DE LAS PIRAGUAS BEACON, 22 37.0N, 79 13.2W, Fl R 4s, 13ft., 4M, Starboard Red, w/topmark.
CANALIZO DE LOS BARCOS BEACON, NO. 2, 22 31.7N, 79 18.8W, Fl R 4s, 13ft., 4M, Starboard Red, w/topmark.
CANALIZO DE LOS BARCOS BEACON, NO. 3, 22 31.0N, 79 18.9W, Fl G 3s, 19ft., 4M, Starboard Red, w/topmark.
BAJO DEL MEDIO BEACON, NO. 5, off SW end, 22 29.8N, 79 17.4W, Fl G 5s, 16ft., 4M, Port Green, w/topmark.
BAHIA DE BUENAVISTA BEACON, NO. 6, 22 27.4N, 78 56.7W, Fl R 4s, 13ft., 4M, Starboard Red, w/topmark.
CAYO BORACHO BEACON, W END, 22 39.0N, 79 09.4W, Fl G 5s, 28ft., 4M, Port Green, w/topmark.
CAYO CAIMAN GRANDE DE SANTA MARIA LIGHT, 22 41.1N, 78 53.0W, Fl W 5s, 158ft., 19M, Conical tower, Black + white bands, Radiobeacon, Aeromarine light.

OLD BAHAMA CHANNEL

Pilotage: This channel separates the Great Bahama Bank from the north coast of Cuba, and allows passage from the Atlantic via Crooked Island Passage to the Straits of Florida or the Gulf of Mexico. An IMO Traffic Separation Scheme has been established in the channel, which can best be seen on the appropriate chart.

The government of Cuba has unilaterally established a mandatory ship reporting system to govern vessel movement in the area. See Chapter 2 for more information on this.

Two hours before entering the Scheme vessels should contact the appropriate shore station in Cuba. The message should be prefixed "OLDBACHA" and should include information

on the type of vessel, nationality, position, course, speed etc. For the western approach call "CLG-50 CAIMAN". For the eastern approach call "CLG-60 CONFITES". Communication with the stations is conducted on VHF channel 13, which should be monitored continuously while within the Traffic Separation Scheme. Vessels may contact the station in English or Spanish

The southwest side of the channel is composed of low-lying islands and other dangers. There are a number of small lagoons suitable for exploration by small craft only. The southwest side of the channel from Cayo Paredon Grande Light (22° 30'N, 78° 10'W) to Cayo Confites (22° 11'N, 77° 40'W) is considered quite dangerous. For this 34 mile stretch vessels are recommended to stay in the middle of the channel and proceed with caution.

PASO MANUY WEST BEACON, 22 24.9N, 78 41.4W, Fl R 6s, 13ft., 4M, Starboard Red, w/topmark.
CAYO JAULA, 22 34.2N, 78 30.9W, Fl W 10s, 68ft., 14M, Aluminum skeleton tower, white concrete base. *Reported extinguished (1983).*
BOCO DE MANATI, E SIDE MANATI CHANNEL ENTRANCE, 22 15.7N, 78 29.8W, Fl G 5s, 13ft., 4M, Port Green, w/topmark.
CAYO PAREDON GRANDE LIGHT, N side, 22 29.0N, 78 09.9W, Fl (3) W 15s, 157ft., 19M, Black + yellow checkered iron column.
CAYO CONFITES, 22 11.4N, 77 39.7W, Fl W 7.5s, 75ft., 14M, Gray metal framework tower.
CAYO CONFITES, NO. 2, 22 10.3N, 77 39.2W, Fl R 6s, 13ft., 3M, Starboard Red, w/topmark.
CAYO CONFITES, NO. 3, 22 10.2N, 77 38.6W, Fl G 5s, 13ft., 3M, Port Green, w/topmark.
CAYO CONFITES BEACON, 22 08.7N, 77 41.6W, Fl Y 7s, 13ft., 5M, Special Yellow w/topmark.

CAYO CONFITES
22 10N, 77 40W

Pilotage: This low islet lies close within the outer edge of the bank along the south side of the Old Bahama Channel. A drying reef extends 1 mile south-southeast from the cay, and a channel 300 yards wide separates the cay from a reef that dries, which extends from it. A light is shown from a 66 foot high tower standing on the north side of the cay.
Anchorage: Proceed to a position on the coastal edge of the bank where the light of Cayo

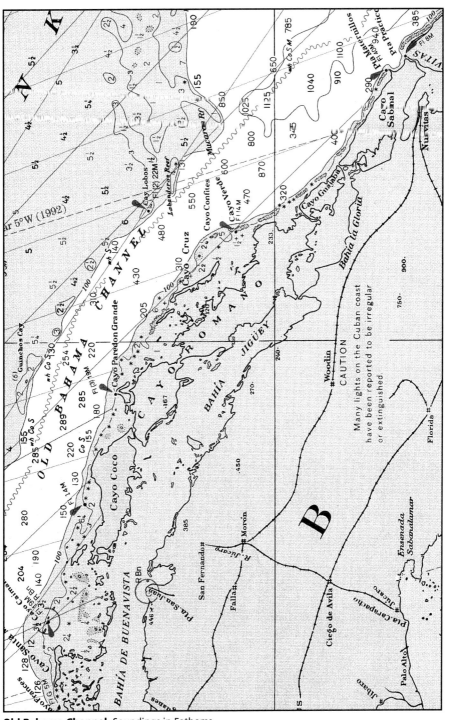

Old Bahama Channel, Soundings in Fathoms

Verde bears 191° and Cayo Confites' extremity bears 314°. From this point a vessel steers 270° until the south extremity of Cayo Confites bears 344°. The vessel then hauls to starboard and takes a heading of about 323° until Cayo Confites' extremity bears 030°, distant 1/2 mile. Anchor in a charted depth of 22 feet.

BAHÍA DE NUEVITAS

PUNTA MATERNILLOS LIGHT, 21 39.8N, 77 08.5W, Fl W 15s, 174ft., 40M, W conical tower, Aeromarine light.
PUNTA PRACTICOS, E side of entrance, 21 36.3N, 77 05.9W, Fl W 10s, 32ft., 8M, White concrete tower.

NUEVITAS

21 33N, 77 16W

Pilotage: The coast from Cayo Confites to Cayo Sabinal consists of sandy beaches, punctuated by numerous lagoons and swamps, with broken reefs adding to the dangers. Punta Maternillos light is about 4 miles northwest of the entrance to Puerto de Nuevitas, and is the principal landmark in the area.

Bahía de Nuevitas is entered through a narrow deepwater channel 7 miles long. The bay is divided by a somewhat hilly and heavily scrub-covered peninsula extending 3 miles east from the southwest side of the bay. Bahía Nuevitas lies southeast of the peninsula and Bahía de Mayanabo lies northwest of it. The towns of Pastelillo and Puerto Tarafa, sub-ports of Nuevitas, lie respectively on the southeast and northwest sides of the peninsula. The terminal of Bufadero lies on the northeast side.

The surrounding coastal terrain is low-lying, flat and without distinguishing features, except for the hills on the dividing peninsula and the nearby conical islets Cayo Ballenatos which, rising above the lowland, are visible from the sea.

The entrance channel to Nuevitas has four right angle turns in it, and has a tidal current reaching 3 to 4 1/2 knots about 2 to 3 hours after high or low water. There is about a 20 minute slack.

The ports in Bahía de Nuevitas are the major sugar shipping centers of Cuba. There is an IMO Traffic Separation Scheme in the waters off Bahía de Nuevitas.

ENTRANCE RANGE, (Front Light), 21 35.5N, 77 06.4W, Q W, 6ft., 7M, White diamond with black border on triangular concrete structure. **(Rear Light),** 175 meters 185°36' from front, Iso W 3s, 22ft., 10M, White diamond with black border on triangular concrete structure, Visible 6° each side of range line.
PUNTA SALTEADORES LIGHTED BEACON, NO. 3, 21 35.8N, 77 06.2W, Fl G 3s, 13ft., 4M, Port Green, w/topmark.
PENA REDONDA BEACON NO. 4, 21 35.7N, 77 06.4W, Fl R 4s, 16ft., 4M, Starboard Red, w/topmark.
PLAYA CHUCHU RANGE, (Front Light), 21 35.6N, 77 06.9W, Q W, 20ft., 9M, White diamond with black border on triangular concrete structure. **(Rear Light),** 195 meters 000°54' from front, Iso W 3s, 33ft., 9M, White diamond with black border on square concrete structure, Visible 6° each side of range line.
LAS CALABAZAS RANGE, (Front Light), 21 33.9N, 77 06.9W, Q W, 23ft., 9M, White diamond with black border on triangular concrete structure. **(Rear Light),** 190 meters 180°54' from front, Iso W 3s, 33ft., 12M, White diamond with black border on triangular concrete structure.
BAJO DEL MEDIO RANGE, (Front Light), 21 34.2N, 77 08.3W, Q W, 20ft., 10M, White diamond with black border on triangular concrete structure on pilings. **(Rear Light),** 265 meters 269°30' from front, Iso W 3s, 33ft., 11M, White diamond with black border on triangular concrete structure, Visible 6° each side of range line.
CAYO CAYITA, COMMON, (Front Light), 21 32.8N, 77 08.1W, Q W, 16ft., 5M, White diamond with black border on triangular concrete structure. **(Rear Light),** 290 meters 179°30' from common front, Iso W 3s, 22ft., 10M, White diamond with black border on square concrete column on pilings, Visible 6° each side of range **(Rear Light),** 225 meters 057°48' from common front, Iso W 3s, 33ft., 11M, White diamond with black border on square concrete column, Visible 6° on each side of range line.
BAJO DEL RÍO LIGHT BEACON, NO. 7A, 21 31.2N, 77 14.8W, Fl G 5s, 16ft., 4M, Port Green, column w/topmark.

BAHÍA DE MANATI

BAHIA DE MANATI, PUNTA ROMA, 21 23.4N, 76 48.8W, Fl W 12s, 43ft., 12M, Iron conical tower, aluminum and red bands.

Buoy 1, E side of entrance channel, 21 23.5N, 76 48.5W, Fl G 3s, Green pillar buoy, can w/topmark.

PUERTO MANATI
21 22N, 76 50W

Pilotage. This small community is located on the west side of the "pocket bay" called Bahía de Manatí. The bay is located about 21 miles southeast of Puerto de Nuevitas and 165 miles west-northwest of Cabo Maisi. The light structure is reported to be visible by day up to 8 miles, and there is a gray brick chimney in the port. The port is a major sugar shipping center.

PUERTO PADRE, PUNTA MASTERLERO, W side of entrance, 21 16.5N, 76 32.2W, Fl W 8s, 50ft., 12M, White round metal tower.
Puerto Padre Buoy 1, 21 16.5N, 76 31.9W, Fl G 5s, Green pillar buoy, can w/topmark.

PUERTO PADRE
21 12N, 76 36W

Pilotage: This community is at the head of Bahía de Puerto Padre, and is another major sugar shipping point. Punta Mastelero light structure stands at the seaward entrance to the bay, and is reported visible during the day at a distance of 6 miles. The entrance itself is reported radar conspicuous at a distance of 5 miles.

PUNTA PIEDRA DEL MANGLE, 21 15.0N, 76 18.7W, Fl W 10s, 76ft., 15M, White metal framework tower.
PUNTA RASA LIGHT, 21 09.0N, 76 07.8W, Fl W 15s, 112ft., 16M, White cylindrical concrete tower, red bands.
PUERTO GIBARA, ON PUNTA PEREGRINA, E side of entrance, 21 06.7N, 76 06.7W, Fl G 5s, 26ft., 5M, Green square on round green tower.

GIBARA
21 07N, 76 08W

Pilotage: This is the port for Holguin — the third largest city in Cuba. Silla de Gibara (21° 02'N, 76° 05'W) lies about 6 miles south-southeast of the entrance to Puerto Gibara. This saddle-shaped hill has a gray rocky summit rising to over 1000 feet. Cerro Colorado (834 feet) and Cerro Yabazon (808 feet) are two conspicuous hills lying within miles west-southwest of Silla de Gibara. Lomas de Cupeicillo are a series of forested hills and conspicu-

ous ridges rising to heights of 492 to 805 feet. They extend up to 10 miles west of Puerto Gibara.

Tidal currents are negligible in the entrance, but the flow from rivers in the rainy season can sometimes create a 1/4 knot current setting north.

BAHÍA DE BARIAY AND BAHÍA DE JURURU
21 05N, 76 01W

Pilotage: Bahía de Bariay is entered between Punta La Mula (Desiree) and a point 3/4 mile southwest. It is a shoal water bay providing temporary anchorage for vessels with local knowledge in about 30 feet of water over white sand and coral.
Anchorage: Anchor close inshore off the second sandy beach south of Punta La Mulla. This anchorage is fully open to the north, and is considered dangerous in the winter. Bahía de Jururu is located west of Bahía de Bariay, and is completely sheltered. It is entered through a narrow channel blocked by a bar, and is only suitable for small craft.

PUERTO DE VITA, PUNTA BARLOVENTO, E side of entrance, 21 05.8N, 75 57.7W, Fl W 10s, 115ft., 14M, White cylindrical tower.

PUERTO VITA
21 05N, 75 57W

Pilotage: The "pocket bay" of Bahía Vita is located about 9 miles east of Puerto Gibara and 115 miles west-northwest of the eastern extremity of Cuba. A narrow and intricate channel leads to a deepwater berthing facility at Puerto Vita. Because of the flat terrain in the area, vessels at Puerto Vita are discernible from sea.

The port is a sub-port of Gibara, and another in the string of sugar shipping centers. An excellent landmark on the approach is the tall white chimney of Central Rafael Friere sugar mill located about 4 miles south-southwest of the entrance. An isolated 397 foot high hill, with a conspicuous outcropping of white rock on its top, is another good mark. The white rock looks like a vertical white stripe. The summit is reported to be visible 10 to 12 miles at sea. At night the Punta Barlovento light, on the east side of the port entrance, can be seen up to 10 miles.

BAHIA NARANJO, E side of entrance, 21 06.8N, 75 52.6W, Fl W 6s, 59ft, 8M, White metal framework tower.

BAHÍA DE NARANJO
21 06N, 75 53W

Pilotage: This is another "pocket bay" with no facilities except for a well sheltered anchorage. The west side of the bay is marked by a high flattened wooded hill rising to 344 feet. On the east side there is an isolated sugarloaf hill. About 3 miles southeast of the entrance is a high flat-topped ridge having a white, precipitous west slope. A conspicuous red scarp at Punta Barlovento marks the entrance. The drying coastal reef north-northeast of Punta Barlovento extends almost 3/4 mile offshore.

BAHIA SAMA, ON PUNTA BOTA FUERTE, E side of entrance, 21 07.5N, 75 46.1W, Fl W 8s, 98ft., 10M, White metal framework tower.

SAMA
21 07N, 75 46W

Pilotage: This small community is located on the west side of Bahía Sama, which is about 11 miles east of Bahía Vita. The inlet is shoal, allowing vessel of less than 14 1/2 foot draft to enter. The mean tidal range here is about 2 feet. Pan de Sama, a rounded hill about 4 miles south-southwest of Bahía Sama, stands out well against a terrain of wooded flats and small undulations. This anchorage is open to winds from the north.

CABO LUCRECIA LIGHT, Near extremity, 21 04.3N, 75 37.2W, Fl W 5s, 132ft., 18M, White stone tower on octagonal base, Aeromarine light, RACON: **G** (−−·) 14M.

CABO (PUNTA) LUCRECIA
21 04N, 75 37W

Pilotage: This is one of the principal landfalls for vessels proceeding along the north coast of Cuba. For a mile or two either side of the point the coast has a low profile and consists of a low white scarp partially interrupted by sandy beaches. Trees and mangroves are inland. A light is shown from a prominent stone tower standing 121 feet in height. A stone dwelling stands behind the light tower. In 1990 a RACON was reported at the tower. There is an IMO Traffic Separation Scheme off Cabo Lucrecia.

BAHIA DE BANES, ON CARACOLILLO BEACH, S side of entrance, 20 52.6N, 75 39.7W, Fl W 8s, 43ft., 8M, White cylindrical tower.
BAHIA DE BANES, BEACON NO. 2, 20 52.9N, 75 39.8W, Fl R 4s, 13ft., 3M, Starboard Red, Column w/topmark.
BAHIA DE BANES, BEACON NO. 3, 20 52.8N, 75 39.8W, Fl G 5s, 13ft., Port Green, Column w/topmark.
BAHIA DE BANES, BEACON NO. 5, 20 52.8N, 75 39.9W, Fl G 3s, 13ft., 4M, Port Green, Column w/topmark.
BAHIA DE BANES, BEACON NO. 7, 20 52.7N, 75 40.1W, Fl G 5s, 13ft., 3M, Port Green, Column w/topmark.
BAHIA DE BANES, BEACON NO. 9, 20 52.4N, 75 40.3W, Fl G 3s, 10ft., 3M, Port Green, Column w/topmark.
BAHIA DE BANES, BEACON NO. 10, 20 52.5N, 75 40.3W, Fl R 6s, 13ft., 3M, Starboard Red, Column w/topmark.
BAHIA DE BANES, BEACON NO. 11, 20 52.9N, 75 40.6W, Fl G 3s, 13ft., 3M, Port Green, Column w/topmark.
BAHIA DE BANES, BEACON NO. 12, 20 52.8N, 75 40.8W, Fl R 4s, 15ft., 4M, Starboard Red, Column w/topmark.
BAHIA DE BANES, BEACON NO. 15, 20 53.0N, 75 41.1W, Fl G 5s, 15ft., 3M, Starboard Red, Column w/topmark.
BAHIA DE BANES, BEACON NO. 16, 20 53.4N, 75 41.4W, Fl R 4s, 20ft., 3M, Starboard Red, Column w/topmark.
BAHIA DE BANES, BEACON NO. 23, 20 54.6N, 75 42.5W, Fl G 3s, 15ft., 4M, Port Green, Column w/topmark.

PUERTO BANES
20 55N, 75 42W

Pilotage: The deepwater "pocket bay" called Bahía de Banes is well sheltered and almost totally landlocked. The entrance channel is one of the most intricate on the Cuban coast. The bay is difficult to recognize from the sea, but from a position about 12 miles to the west three grouped hills, equal in elevation, can be seen. They are serrated in appearance and steep-to on the northeast side, but sloping on the southwest. Close northeast of the hills is a conspicuous rounded, or somewhat saddle-shaped, hill.

The entrance channel is marked by a light, but it should not be confused with the nearby light marking Bahía de Nipe. The sharp hairpin turns of the channel are crucial and the seaward end is open to the northeast. Tidal currents run up

to 6 knots, so vessels are advised to enter only at slack water during the day. The currents continue to run along the sides of the channel 40 to 45 minutes after high and low water.

Traffic signals are flown from Boca de la Bahía de Banor seaward entrance on the south side. A white flag means the channel is clear; a red flag means anchor and wait; a gray flag means wait, a vessel is outbound.

BAHÍA DE NIPE

PUNTA MAYARI LIGHT, E side of entrance, 20 47.5N, 75 31.5W, Fl W 6s, 115ft., 16M, White metal framework tower.
PUNTA MAYARI RANGE, (Front Light), 20 46.3N, 75 32.8W, Q W, 25ft., 8M, Aluminum skeleton tower, red daymark yellow border.
(Rear Light), 230 meters 201°36' from front, Fl W 4s, 90ft., 9M, White skeleton tower enclosing gray box on concrete base, Visible 6° on each side of range line.

BAHÍA DE NIPE
20 47N, 75 42W

Pilotage: This is one of the largest "pocket bays" on the entire Cuban coast. The bay is extensive, well sheltered and almost landlocked. The entrance channel is deep and easy, though strong tidal currents continue to run up to 45 minutes after high or low water. From the east the entrance appears as a steep-sided notch, while from the north it cannot be distinguished at any great distance. The Río Mayari empties into the bay and has cut a notch into Sierra de Cristal. This notch is visible well out at sea.

PUNTA PIEDRA, NO. 4, 20 47.7N, 75 35.2W, Fl R 6s, 15ft., 4M, Starboard Red, w/topmark.
PUNTA BERRACO, NO. 6, 20 48.5N, 75 36.0W, Fl R 8s, 16ft., 4M, Starboard Red, w/topmark.
BAJO LA ESTRELLA, NO. 9, 20 47.5N, 75 36.7W, Fl G 5s, 15ft., 4M, Port Green, w/topmark.
BAJO SALINA GRANDE, NO. 10, S end, 20 48.5N, 75 41.8W, Fl R 4s, 13ft., 4M, Starboard Red, w/topmark.

ANTILLA CHANNEL

LENGUA TIERRA BEACON, NO. 11, 20 48.7N, 75 42.6W, Fl G 5s, 13ft., 4M, Port Green, w/topmark.
BAJO MANATI, NO. 12, S end, 20 49.0N, 75 43.2W, Fl R 8s, 13ft., 4M, Starboard Red, w/topmark.

BAJO LENGUA DE TIERRA, NO. 13, N end, 20 48.9N, 75 43.8W, Fl G 5s, 13ft., 4M, Port Green, w/topmark.
BAJO MARABELLA, NO. 14, S end, 20 49.1N, 75 43.8W, Fl R 6s, 13ft., 4M, Starboard Red, w/topmark.
BAJO MARABELLA, NO. 15, 20 48.9N, 75 44.8W, Fl G 5s, 13ft., 4M, Port Green, w/topmark.
BAJO MARABELLA, NO. 17, 20 49.1N, 75 45.2W, Fl G 7s, 13ft., 4M, Port Green, w/topmark.
CANAL A, BEACON NO. 1A, 20 46.0N, 75 34.7W, Fl G 7s, 13ft., 4M, Port Green, w/topmark.
BAJO PLANACA BEACON, NO. 3A, 20 44.7N, 75 34.6W, Fl G 5s, 13ft., 4M, Port Green, w/topmark.
PUNTA LIBERAL, 20 44.8N, 75 28.8W, Fl W 10s, 56ft., 9M, White framework tower.

ANTILLA
20 50N, 75 44W

Pilotage: This is the principal shipping center for Bahía de Nipe, and is located on the north side of the bay.

PRESTON
20 46N, 75 39W

Pilotage: This is another important sugar port located about 7 1/2 miles west-southwest of Punta Mayari. It is a sub-port of Antilla. The Río Miyari discharges near the berthing facilities causing a great deal of silting.

FELTON
20 45N, 75 36W

Pilotage: This small community is on the west side of Bahía de Cajinaya, and about 1 mile east of the mouth of the Río Mayari. This is another sub-port of Antilla specializing in iron-ore.

SAETIA
20 47N, 75 34W

Pilotage: This is the site of a small banana plantation and shipping facility.

BAHÍA DE LEVISA

BAHIA DE LEVISA BEACON, NO. 17, 20 43.2N, 75 29.3W, Fl G 3s, 13ft., 3M, Port Green, w/topmark.

BAHÍA DE LEVISA BEACON, NO. 19, 20 43.4N, 75 29.8W, Fl G 5s, 13ft., 3M, Port Green, beacon w/topmark.
BAHÍA DE LEVISA BEACON, NO. 22, 20 43.6N, 75 30.4W, Fl R 4s, 13ft., 3M, Starboard Red, beacon w/topmark.
BAHÍA DE LEVISA BEACON, NO. 23, 20 43.4N, 75 30.7W, Fl G 3s, 13ft., 3M, Port Green, beacon w/topmark.
BAHÍA DE LEVISA BEACON, NO. 27, 20 43.2N, 75 31.8W, Fl G 5s, 13ft., 3M, Port Green, w/topmark.
BAHÍA DE LEVISA BEACON, NO. 28, 20 43.4N, 75 31.8W, Fl R 4s, 13ft., 3M, Starboard Red, w/topmark.
BAHÍA DE LEVISA BEACON, NO. 29, 20 43.1N, 75 32.2W, Fl G 3s, 13ft., 3M, Port Green, beacon w/topmark.
BAHÍA DE LEVISA BEACON, NO. 32, 20 43.2N, 75 32.9W, Fl R 4s, 13ft., 3M, Starboard Red, w/topmark.
CAYO GRANDE, 20 43.1N, 75 29.4W, Fl G 5s, 13ft., 3M, Framework tower.

BAHÍA DE LEVISA
20 43N, 75 31W

Pilotage: This "pocket bay" is entered about 5 miles southwest of Bahía de Nipe. It is well sheltered and almost totally landlocked. It is entered by a very narrow and intricate channel. Nicaro (20° 43'N, 75 33'W) is the main shipping port in the bay — it is another sub-port of Antilla in Bahía de Nipe. Sugar and nickel ore are handled here.

BAHÍA DE SAGUA DE TANAMO

PUNTA BARLOVENTO, E point of entrance, 20 43.2N, 75 19.2W, Fl W 8s, 42ft., 12M, White conical skeleton tower.
BAHÍA DE SAGUA DE TANAMO RANGE, (Front Light), 20 43.6N, 75 19.5W, Q W, 22 ft., 6M, Aluminum skeleton structure on concrete base. **(Rear Light),** 210 meters 180° from front, Iso W 6s, 39ft., 6M, White shield with black border on silver three-faced lattice tower on concrete base.
BAHÍA DE SAGUA DE TANAMO, NO. 3, West point, 20 42.6N, 75 19.8W, Fl G 3s, 15ft., Port Green, beacon w/topmark.
BAHÍA DE SAGUA DE TANAMO, NO. 5, Cayo Juanillo, West side, 20 42.3N, 75 20.2W, Fl G 5s, 15ft.,Port Green, beacon w/topmark.
BAHÍA DE SAGUA DE TANAMO, NO. 8, Cayo Alto, East side, 20 41.7N, 75 20.2W,

Fl R 6s, 15ft., Starboard Red, beacon w/topmark.
BAHÍA DE SAGUA DE TANAMO, NO.11, Cayo Medio, West side, 20 41.1N, 75 19.4W, Fl G 3s, 15ft., Port Green, beacon w/topmark.

DE SAGUA DE TANAMO
20 42N, 75 19W

Pilotage: Bahía de Sagua de Tanamo is located about 9 1/2 miles east-southeast of Bahía de Levisa. It is entered via a deep, but intricate channel. The surrounding terrain is hilly and rises inland in a succession of uneven hills to Sierra del Cristal, a conspicuous mountain range some 13 miles to the south. The entrance is concealed and difficult to identify from offshore. The light at the east entrance point is difficult to see by day at a distance greater than 3 miles. The tidal current runs over 3 knots in the channel.

The port is a shipping center for sugar and molasses.

PUERTO CAYO MOA

CAYO MOA GRANDE, 20 41.6N, 74 54.4W, Fl W 10s, 76ft., 13M, Aluminum framework tower.
Buoy 1, E side of entrance channel, 20 41.0N, 74 52.0W, Fl G 5s, 13ft., Port Green, w/topmark.
BAJO GRANDE RANGE, (Front Light), Entrance, 20 40.1N, 74 52.9W, Q W, 13ft., 7M, Red + yellow checkered rectangular daymark on aluminum framework tower on concrete piles. **(Rear Light),** 615 meter 211° from front, Iso W 6s, 26ft., 7M, Red + yellow checkered redctangular daymark on aluminum framework tower on concrete piles.

PUERTO CAYO MOA
20 41N, 74 52W

Pilotage: Between Bahía de Sagua de Tanamo and Puerto Cayo Moa are several shallow inlets suitable for small craft with local knowledge. An unbroken barrier of drying reefs and sand flats extends about 2 miles offshore, and is marked by breakers. There is a shoal water lagoon between the reefs and the coastline. Behind the coastline the terrain rises rapidly to lofty interior mountains known as Cuchillas de Toa.

This port lies inshore of the outer barrier and is somewhat sheltered by it. An extremely deep gut passes east of the low-lying mangrove-covered islet Cayo Moa Grande, and leads to the deepwater port facilities at Darsena de Yaguasey and Punta Gorda. Tidal currents seaward of the entrance set southwest on a rising tide at a velocity of about 1 knot, and north on a falling tide. In the anchorage area south of Cayo Moa the currents set basically east and west.

PUNTA GORDA

20 38N, 74 51W

Pilotage: This small mining community is located about 2 3/4 miles southeast of Puerto Cayo Moa. Ships load chromium ore from lighters while on moorings. Punta Gorda is a sub-port of Bahía de Barocoa.

BAHÍA DE YAMANIQUEY

20 34N, 74 43W

Pilotage: This bay is located about 3 miles south of Punta Guarico. It is approached via a break in the offshore reefs, and is suitable for small craft only. The entrance is dangerous, except in very calm weather. This is a sub-port of Baracoa.

BAHÍA DE TACO

20 31N, 74 40W

Pilotage: This another miniature "pocket bay", providing anchorage for small vessels with local knowledge. A short dog-legged channel has depths of about 30 feet. The sea breaks with considerable force on the rocky coast to the west of the entrance, and tends to obscure the channel. Approaching vessels steer for the conspicuous south extremity of Punta Sotavento (20° 32'N, 74° 40'W) on a heading of 240°, then proceed in mid channel to the anchorage.

PUNTA GUARICO, 20 37.1N, 74 43.9W, Fl W 6s, 37ft., 11M, Aluminum tower.

BAHÍA (PUERTO) NAVAS

Pilotage: This "pocket bay" is located about 10 1/2 miles southeast of Punta Guarico. It has an easy deepwater entrance and provides anchorage protected from the prevailing winds. The bay is open to the north.

BAHÍA DE (PUERTO) MARAVI

Pilotage: This deepwater estuary is located about 15 miles southeast of Punta Guarico. Anchorage is available in calm conditions, but the bay is open to the prevailing winds.

BAHIA DE BARACOA, S entrance point, 20 21.1N, 74 29.9W, Fl W 6s, 63ft., 14M, Concrete pedestal on mansonry structure.

BARACOA

20 21N, 74 30W

Pilotage: Bahía de Baracoa is located about 21 miles west-northwest of Cabo Maisi. It is a very small but deep "pocket bay", open to the east and directly accessible from the open sea. The surrounding terrain is hilly and heavily scrub covered. Baracoa, on the east side of the bay, is one of the oldest communities in Cuba. Bahía Miel is a deepwater cove east of Baracoa, backed inland by a broad flat river valley, leading to high interior hills.

Loma El Yunque, located 4 miles to the west, is the best approach landmark to the bay. It is a conspicuous steep-sided flat-topped high hill, rising to 1,932 feet. It is remarkable in its profile and can be seen for distances of 40 miles in clear weather. It is particularly visible from the northeast. Testas de Santa Teresa, two hills about 3 3/4 miles south-southeast of the bay, and Loma Majayara, close southeast of Bahía Miel, are three conspicuous hills, remarkable at a distance of 24 miles, with clear visibility.

CAUTION: This anchorage is subject to a heavy swell sent in by the prevailing winds, particularly during strong north and northeast winds in the winter.

Bahía Miel has anchorage somewhat sheltered from east winds, where vessels can anchor if they do not want to enter Baracoa.

BAHÍA DE MATA

20 18N, 74 23W

Pilotage: This bay will accommodate vessels up to about 300 feet, with drafts less than 15 feet. It has a deepwater entrance, and is the first anchorage west of Cabo Maisi. Small vessels commonly drop anchor when abeam Punta Cuartel, tying their sterns to moorings further in the bay. This is not a well sheltered

anchorage, particularly during the winter when a heavy sea can set in.

ROCA BUREN, 20 21.3N, 74 30.1W, Fl G 5s, 39ft., 4M, Port Green, w/topmark.
QUEBRADO DEL MANGLE, 20 15.2N, 74 08.6W, Fl G 5s, 13ft., 4M, Green beacon, square daymark.
PUNTA MAISI LIGHT, On Punta de la Hembra, 20 14.6N, 74 08.6W, Fl W 5s, 122ft., 17M, W conical masonry tower and dwelling, RACON: **K** (–·–) 16M.

CABO MAISI

20 13N, 74 08W

Pilotage: This is the eastern extremity of Cuba. It has a low-lying shore of white sand and is rounded. The land within the cape begins to rise 3/4 mile from the coast, and when viewed from the north, appears to form three steps, making useful landmarks. The terrain southwest of Punta Pintado becomes progressively steeper and more abrupt.

CAUTION: Cabo Maisi is a lee shore open to the effects of the sea and the prevailing east wind. Vessels navigating in the vicinity are cautioned to stand well offshore, and are reminded that, if proceeding at night from the south, Cabo Maisi light is obscured to the west of a line bearing 359°.

An IMO Traffic Separation Scheme is in effect off Cabo Maisi.

WINDWARD PASSAGE

Pilotage: This passage lies between the eastern end of Cuba and the western part of Hispaniola, 45 miles to the east-southeast. An IMO Traffic Separation Scheme lies off Cabo Maisi, and the appropriate chart should be consulted when in the area. Vessels not using the traffic separation scheme should avoid it by as wide a margin as possible.

The current set through the middle of the channel is to the southwest at a rate usually less than 3/4 knot, but may attain speeds of up to 2 knots. Near the coasts on either side of the passage, tidal currents are strong and irregular.

On the east side of the passage (near Haiti) the current sets north at about 3/4 knot around

Pearl Point (19° 40'N, 73° 25'W), but 6 miles offshore the current will be found to set west or west-southwest. North of Cap du Mole, on Haiti, there are ripples where the northerly flow meets the current running west along the north shore of the island.

On the west side of the passage (near Cuba) a north current sets around Cabo Maisi. This flow is affected by the tides and the wind. During the summer months, and with southerly winds, an east set is experienced. With northerly winds a southerly set is found. Frequently, especially during the winter, a westerly current of considerable strength will be experienced.

SOUTH COAST

PUNTA CALETA LIGHT, 20 04.0N, 74 17.8W, Fl W 10s, 149ft., 15M, White skeleton tower.
BAHIA DE BAITIQUIRI, N, 20 01.5N, 74 51.2W, Fl W 6s, 29ft., 11M, Red metal framework tower.

PUERTO BAITIQUERI

20 01N, 74 51W

Pilotage: This very well sheltered "pocket bay" is located about 42 miles west of Cabo Maisi. It is clearly indicated by the opening between the hills on either side of the entrance. The entrance channel has a least depth of about 10 feet and is only 49 feet wide between the reefs on either side. The sea breaks heavily over these reefs, and can be seen from 1/4 mile away.

PUERTO ESCONDIDO

19 55N, 75 03W

Pilotage: This port is located about 6 miles east of Bahía de Guantanamo. The entrance is quite deep, but narrow, and the bay is landlocked. The coast on either side of the entrance appears as a continuous jagged bluff, and the entrance itself cannot be distinguished until very close in. A tower is situated on the summit of Mogate Peak, a hill that rises to 520 feet about 1 3/4 miles northwest of the entrance. A hill to the east of the entrance has a well defined saddle-shaped summit. Vessels entering the port steer 336°, and head for the extremity of a rocky scarp that lines up with the middle of the entrance channel.

Inside, the bay branches into numerous mangrove-fringed deep water inlets that lead off into surrounding fields of drying tidal flats.

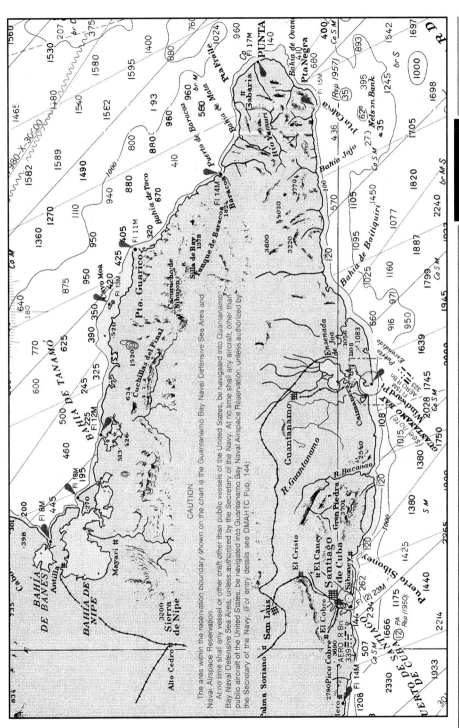

CAUTION

The area within the reservation boundary shown on the chart is the Guantanamo Bay Naval Defensive Sea Area and Naval Airspace Reservation.

At no time shall any vessel or other craft other than public vessels of the United States, be navigated into Guantanamo Bay Naval Defensive Sea Area, unless authorized by the Secretary of the Navy. At no time shall any aircraft, other than public aircraft of the United States, be navigated into Guantanamo Bay Naval Airspace Reservation, unless authorized by the Secretary of the Navy. (For entry details see DMAHTC Pub. 144.)

Southeast End, Soundings in Fathoms

Chapter 2

GUANTANAMO BAY

PUNTA BARLOVENTO, WINDWARD POINT LIGHT, On 110 meters peak, E side of entrance to bay, 19 53.6N, 75 09.6W, Fl W 5s, 378ft., 15M, Gray building.

WINDWARD POINT LIGHT HOUSE, 19 53.6N, 75 09.8W, Fl W 2.5s, 90ft., 5M, White conical steel tower, Obscured 270° to 110°.

HICACAL BEACH RANGE, (Front Light), N side of entrance to bay, 19 56.5N, 75 09.9W, Q W, 57ft., 13M, Red rectangular daymark, white stripe on skeleton tower, Higher intensity on range line. **(Rear Light),** 405 meters 021°30′ from front, Iso W 6s, 80ft., 15M, Red rectangular daymark, white stripe on skeleton tower, Higher intensity on range line.

LEEWARD POINT, AVIATION LIGHT, 19 54.2N, 75 12.3W, Alt Fl W Green, 118ft., On NE corner of hangar.

FISHERMAN POINT LIGHT, E side of entrance to bay, 19 55.2N, 75 09.7W, Fl W 4s, 28ft., 5M, Red skeleton tower on pyramidal base, red + white diamond-shaped daymark. Marks point for leaving Hicacal Range. Various lights mark the channel in the cove south of Deer Light. A F R light is shown at each end of fuel berth N of Deer Point.

CORINASO POINT LIGHT, 19 55.1N, 75 09.3W, Fl G 6s, 42ft., 3M, Red skeleton steel tower, red + white diamond-shaped daymark.

McCALLA HILL, 19 54.9N, 75 09.6W, F R, 175ft., 4M, Black steel framework tower, yellow bands, Private light.

RADIO POINT LIGHT, NO. 1, 19 55.3N, 75 09.0W, Fl G 4s, 15ft., 3M, Green square on black piling, Obscured 240° to 310°.

RADIO POINT LIGHT, NO. 2, Q R, 14ft., 3M, Red triangular daymark on piles, Obscured 310° to 050°.

RADIO POINT LIGHT 4, FL R 4s, 11ft., 3M, Red triangular day mark on dolphin, Obscured 334° – 139°.

DEER POINT LIGHT, NO. 1, 19 55.4N, 75 08.8W, Fl G 4s, 10ft, 3M, Green square daymark on dolphin.

DEER POINT LIGHT, NO. 3, Q G, 12ft., 2M, Green square daymark on dolphin.

DEER POINT LIGHT, NO. 5, Fl G 4s, 14ft., 3M, Green square daymark on dolphin.

JUNCTION LIGHT, I Q W, 13ft., 4M, Triangular-shaped daymark with red + green bands, on piles.

EVANS POINT LIGHT, NO. 8, Fl R 4s, 14ft., 3M, Red triangular daymark on piles.

MARINE SITE TWO CHANNEL LIGHT, NO. 3, 1.9 kilometers SE of Hospital Cay South–Light,

19 55.9N, 75 08.1W, Fl G 4s, 10ft., 3M, Green square daymark on dolphin.

BAHÍA DE GUANTANAMO
19 56N, 75 10W

Pilotage: This bay is located about 62 miles west-southwest of Cabo Maisi. It is spacious, well sheltered, easily entered and largely landlocked. The bay is about 11 miles long and divides into Outer and Inner harbors. It is deep enough for any vessel.

REGULATIONS: Most of the bay is leased by the United States Government, and is part of the Guantanamo Bay Naval Defensive Sea Area. This area is closed to the public. Full details concerning entry control and application requirements will be found in Title 32, Code of Federal Regulations, Part 761.

Harbor Control Post: The U.S. Navy maintains a Harbor Entrance Control Post which challenges and identifies all vessels approaching Guantanamo Bay. Permission to enter the U.S. Naval Reservation boundaries should be secured in advance of your arrival. Vessels sailing to Boqueron should forward their ETA and request permission to transit the waters of the Naval Reservation. Such passage is only permitted in daylight.

The Harbor Entrance Control Post operates from the signal station atop a building on McCalla Hill (19ª 55′N, 75° 09′ 5W). Their call sign is "Port Control", and they monitor VHF channel 12. The pilots stand by on VHF channel 74.

MARINE BOAT CHANNEL LIGHT, NO. 2, 457 meters S of Caravela Point, 19 56.0N, 75 08.0W, Fl R 4s, 13ft., 3M, Triangular-shaped red daymark on dolphin.

GRANADILLO POINT WEST, NO. 8, 19 56.8N, 75 07.5W, Fl R 4s, 13ft., 3M, Red box on dolphin.

GRANADILLO BAY, EAGLE CHANNEL, 19 56.9N, 75 07.9W, Fl R (2 + 1) 6s, 14ft., 3M, Preferred Channel, RGR dolphin, with topmark.

HOSPITAL CAY, Watergate Channel No. 2, 19 56.5N, 75 08.7W, Q R, 13ft., 3M, Starboard, Red with topmark.

WATERGATE CHANNEL NO. 4, 19 57.1N, 75 08.7W, FL R 4S, 11ft., 5M, Starboard Red with topmark.

PALMA POINT SHOAL, NO. 13, 19 57.8N, 75 08.9W, Fl G 4s, 14ft., 4M, 3-pile cluster, black battery box.

BAHÍA DE SANTIAGO DE CUBA

MORRO DE CUBA LIGHT, On El Morro E side of entrance to Santiago de Cuba, 19 58.0N, 75 52.1W, Fl (2) W 10s, 269ft., 23M, White cylindrical concrete tower, Aeromarine light.

SANTIAGO DE CUBA
20 01N, 75 50W

Pilotage: This is one of the oldest and most important port cities in Cuba. The bay is well sheltered and land locked. A number of coves and inlets indent this natural harbor, which is entered via a 263 foot wide channel. The entrance is marked by the fortifications of El Morro on the east side. Lower-lying fortifications at Punta Estrella are below the fort. When entering, head for Punta Estrella on a course of 043° and proceed in mid-channel through most of the entrance fairway. The pilot's call sign is "Santiago Practicos", and they monitor VHF channels 13 and 16.

A signal mast at the fortifications of El Morro indicates traffic conditions in the channel. International Code Flag P (See **Reed's Nautical Companion**) indicates a power-driven vessel is outbound; Flag P under a red pennant indicates a sailing vessel is outbound; and Flag P over a red pennant indicates the outbound vessel has anchored. **CAUTION: When a signal is displayed indicating a vessel is outbound, inbound vessels must not attempt to enter.** Contact the harbor authorities on VHF channel 16 before entering the harbor.
Port of Entry
Dockage: The yacht club Bases Nautico is in nearby Punta Gorda.

PUNTA ROMPE CANILLAS, 19 59.2N, 75 53.1W, Fl Y 7s, 13ft., 3M, Special Yellow beacon, w/topmark.

PUERTO NIMA NIMA
19 57N, 75 59W

Pilotage: This port is located about 1 1/4 miles west-northwest of Punta Cabrera. There are numerous mooring buoys and a pier, which connects to the mines inland. A good mark on this part of the coast is a red hill excavated in terraces located about 1 1/2 miles west of Puerto Nima Nima.

Bahía Aserradero indents the coast 9 miles west-northwest of Puerto Nima Nima. Río Aserradero flows into this bay. The wreck of the Spanish cruiser Vizcaya is located on the west side of the bay.

ASERRADERO, 19 59.0N, 76 10.3W, Fl W 19s, 107ft., 11M, White framework tower.
PUERTO DE CHIRIVICO RANGE, (Front Light), 19 58.2N, 76 23.8W, Q W, 13ft, 4M, Aluminum painted triangular skeleton structure on ruins of pier. **(Rear Light),** 255 meters 337° from front, Fl W 4s, 33ft., 5M, Aluminum painted skeleton structure, Visible 6° each side of range line.

PUERTO DE CHIVIRICO
19 58N, 76 24W

Pilotage: This port is located about 30 miles west of Bahía de Santiago de Cuba. It is west of Punta Tabacal, a 425 foot high wooded conical hill with a grassy summit, which is easily identified from the east. The coast in this area is dominated by the rugged mountainous Sierra Maestra, which rise steeply. Pico Turquino (20° 00'N, 76° 50'W) is the culminating summit of the mountain range, and is the highest summit in Cuba at 6,560 feet. In clear weather the summit can be seen in Jamaica, 93 miles away.

The entrance to Puerto de Chivirico is between Cayo de Damas to the east and a peninsula that extends 600 yards from the coast to the west. The entrance channel is narrow. An abandoned ore loading facility is in the harbor.

PUERTO PILON RANGE, (Front Light), 19 54.0N, 77 17.2W, Q W, 16ft., 6M, White quadrangular daymark with yellow border on black metal framework tower. **(Rear Light),** on shore 1.5 kilometers 355°30' from front, L Fl W 10s, 26ft., 8M, White quadrangular daymark with yellow border on metal framework tower.
PUERTO PILON BEACON, NO. 11, 19 54.0N, 77 19.0W, Fl G 5s, 13ft., 4M, Port Green, w/topmark.

PILON
19 54N, 77 19W

Pilotage: This is the small town on the west side of Ensenada de Mora where the sugar mill is located. The maximum draft for this sub-port of Manzanillo is 20 feet.

ENSENADA MAREA DEL PORTILLO, NO. 4,
19 54.7N, 77 11.2W, Fl R 6s, 10ft, 3M, Starboard
Red, beacon w/topmark.

PUERTO PORTILLO

19 55N, 77 11W

Pilotage: The harbor is 45 miles west of Puerto de Chivirico. It is entered between Punta de
Piedras and Punta de Los Farallones, 1/2 mile
to the west-southwest. Puerto Portillo can be
identified by low, swampy mangrove-covered
land on its east side, and by the three perpendicular white cliffs on its west point. The bay is
small, and much encumbered.

BAJO PUNTA DEL MEDIO, 19 54.6N, 77 11.4W,
Fl (2) W 6s, 10ft., 4M, ISOLATED DANGER BRB,
beacon w/topmark.
PUNTA RASA, 19 54.8N, 77 11.1W, Fl Y 7s,
10ft., 3M, Special Yellow beacon w/topmark.

ENSENADA DE MORA

19 54N, 77 18W

Pilotage: This break in the coast is located
about 5 miles west of Puerto Portillo. Its
entrance is between Cayo Blanco on the east,
and Punta Icacos, 2 miles to the west-southwest. The bight consists of deep water indenting the low-lying coastal plain, with the westernmost part of the Sierra Maestra backing it.
Close to the northeast is 1,248 foot high Loma
Aguada, which provides an excellent landmark.
There are prominent cane fields west of the
peak and a sugar mill on the northwest shore
of the bay. The white spire of a church and a
water tower with a red tank are north and
northwest of the sugar mill.

The entrance is rather intricate, with a fairway
partially blocked by rocky heads. The bay is encumbered with dangers. Head for Loma Aguada
on a heading of 005°, then when abeam of
Punta Icacos, the low mangrove-covered west
entrance of the bight, ease to port and steer
for the light charted northeast of Cayo Pajaro.
Pass north and east of Cayo Pajaro, then proceed to your destination.

Río Toro cuts a remarkable gorge through the
coastal terraces 7 miles west of Ensenada de
Mora. Just west of the river Ojo del Toro rises
to a height of 1,750 feet. This is the westernmost peak of the Sierra Maestra and is very
prominent. When viewed from the southwest,

the summit of this mountain appears as two
or three hummocks.

CABO CRUZ LIGHT, 914 meters E of SW
extremity of cape, 19 50.4N, 77 43.6W, Fl W 5s,
111ft., 37M, Yellow stone tower and dwelling,
Aeromarine light.

CABO CRUZ

19 51N, 77 44W

Pilotage: The point is low and sandy, backed
by a relatively level, somewhat forested, plain.
The plain continues inland as flat tableland,
eventually rising into the foothills of the Sierra
Maestra to the east. There is a pilot station at
the village located on the sandy spit of Cabo
Cruz, which consists of a few huts and a
flagstaff. The light is about 1/2 mile east of
the cape's extremity, on the rear of a large
rectangular building. East of Punta Del Ingles
the light is obscured by high land when bearing less than 285°. It is reported the light is
also beamed for use by aircraft. The sea breaks
heavily on an awash reef located 1 1/2 miles
west of the lighthouse. A light marks the
outer end of the reef.
Anchorage: Anchorage is available in a depth
of 24 feet over sand, northwest of Cabo Cruz.

Pilots: Contact the pilot station on VHF channels 13 and 16.

RESTINGA CABO CRUZ BEACON, 19 50.1N,
77 44.9W, Fl R 4s, 20ft., 5M, Starboard Red,
w/topmark.
RESTINGA CABO CRUZ BEACON, NO. 2,
19 50.3N, 77 44.7W, Fl R 6s, 10ft., 2M, Starboard Red, beacon w/topmark.
RESTINGA CABO CRUZ BEACON, NO. 3,
19 50.4N, 77 44.5W, Fl G 3s, 10ft., 3M, Port
Green, beacon w/topmark.

GOLFO DE GUACANAYABO

20 28N, 77 30W

Pilotage: This large gulf on the south coast of
Cuba lies between Cabo Cruz and Punta de las
Angosturas, about 66 miles to the north-
northwest. The gulf is interrupted by many
shoals, reefs and cays, including Bajo de Buena
Esperanza in the center. Numerous channels
lead through the groupings of above and

BANCO VIBORA BEACON, 20 33.8N, 77 41.5W, Fl R 6s, 13ft., 4M, Starboard Red, w/topmark.
BANCO VIBORA BEACON, NO. 2, 20 41.7N, 77 58.1W, Fl R 4s, 16ft., 4M, Starboard Red, w/topmark.
PUNTA BONITA, NO. 3, 20 41.8N, 77 58.6W, Fl G 5s, 16ft., 4M, Port Green, beacon w/topmark.
PUNTA BONITA, NO. 4, 20 41.9N, 77 58.5W, Fl R 6s, 16ft., 4M, Starboard Red, beacon w/topmark.

MEDIA LUNA CHANNEL
CAYO GUIZASA BEACON, 20 35.8N, 77 49.6W, Fl G 5s, 13ft., 3M, Port Green, w/topmark.
CAYO CULEBRA BEACON, 20 33.6N, 77 50.0W, Fl R 4s, 16ft., 4M, Starboard Red w/topmark.
CAYO MEDIO LUNA BEACON, 20 33.0N, 77 53.5W, Fl G 5s, 13ft., 4M, Port Green, w/topmark.
CAYO JUAN SUAREZ BEACON, NO. 2, 20 32.5N, 78 01.8W, Fl R 6s, 13ft., 3M, Starboard Red, beacon w/topmark.
CAYO JUAN SUAREZ BEACON, NO. 3, 20 33.5N, 78 04.1W, Fl G 5s, 13ft., 3M, Port Green, beacon w/topmark.
CAYO JUAN SUAREZ BEACON, NO. 4, 20 36.3N, 78 06.2W, Fl R 4s, 16ft., 4M, Starboard Red, beacon w/topmark.
CAYO JUAN SUAREZ BEACON, NO. 5, 20 35.9N, 78 06.8W, Fl G 5s, 13ft., 3M, Port Green, beacon w/topmark.

CANAL DE CUATRO REALES
CAYO CARAPACHO, 20 26.9N, 78 02.5W, Fl W 10s, 47ft., 9M, Red iron skeleton structure enclosing gray hut with red band.

SANTA CRUZ DEL SUR
20 42N, 77 59W

Pilotage: This community is located on the northwest shore of Golfo de Guacanayabo. The entrance channel is between La Ceiba bank and Carapacho Cay Lighthouse.

MUELLE MANOPLA
20 43N, 77 52W

Pilotage: This sub-port of Santa Cruz is located about 6 1/2 miles to the east. It is approached via Canal Media Luna and Bayameses Passage.

Cayo Carapacho, Buoy 2, 20 25.0N, 78 01.0W, Fl R 4s, Red buoy.
CAYO CARAPACHO BEACON, NO.5, 20 28.5N, 77 59.7W, Fl G 5s, 13ft., 6M, Port Green, w/topmark.

CAYO CARAPACHO BEACON, NO.8, 20 28.6N, 77 58.9W, Fl R 4s, 13ft., 6M, Starboard Red, w/topmark.
CAYO CARAPACHO BEACON, NO.9, 20 29.2N, 77 58.8W, Fl G 5s, 13ft., 4M, Port Green, w/topmark.
CANAL DE CABEZA DEL ESTE, W side of entrance on Cabeza del Este Cay, 20 31.0N, 78 19.8W, Fl W 12s, 47ft., 13M, Aluminum skeleton structure.
MEDANO DE MANUEL GOMEZ, 21 01.5N, 78 51.8W, Fl R 6s, 13ft., 4M, Starboard Red, beacon w/topmark.
CAYO CUERVO, 21 04.2N, 78 58.1W, Fl G 3s, 16ft., 4M, Port Green, beacon w/topmark.
CAYO MANUEL GOMEZ, NW extremity of reef, 21 04.5N, 78 50.8W, Fl R 4s, 13ft., 7M, Starboard Red, beacon w/topmark.
CAYO SANTA MARIA, SW part of the bank, 21 11.0N, 78 39.2W, Fl W 5s, 43ft., 10M, Aluminum skeleton tower.
PUERTO VERTIENTES LIGHTED BEACON, 21 24.5N, 78 34.5W, Fl G 3s, 13ft., 4M, Port G beacon w/topmark.

CANAL BALANDRAS
CANAL BALANDRAS LIGHT BEACON NO. 1, 21 25.6N, 78 45.0W, Fl G 5s, 13ft., 4M, Port Green, beacon w/topmark.
CANAL BALANDRAS LIGHT BEACON NO. 3, 21 26.4N, 78 46.1W, Fl G 3s, 13ft., 5M, Port Green, beacon w/topmark.
MEDANO DE BALANDRAS, 21 26.0N, 78 49.0W, Fl G 5s, 13ft., 4M, Port Green, beacon w/topmark.
CANAL BALANDRAS LIGHT BEACON NO. 6, 21 27.8N, 78 47.0W, Fl R 6s, 16ft., 4M, Starboard Red, beacon w/topmark.
BAJO LAS CHARCAS, 21 27.5N, 79 04.3W, Fl G 5s, 10ft., 4M, Port Green, beacon w/topmark.
CAYUELO SABICU, NO. 9, 21 30.1N, 78 50.1W, Fl G 5s, 13ft., 4M, Port Green, beacon w/topmark.
CABEZO DEL FLAMENCO, 21 24.8N, 78 53.2W, Fl R 6s, 10ft., 4M, Starboard Red, beacon w/topmark.

GOLFO DE ANA MARIA
21 25N, 78 40W

Pilotage: This is part of a broad coastal indentation lying between Punta de Las Angostura and Punta Maria Aguilar about 112 miles to the west-northwest. The coast is similar to the

below-water dangers. These channels may be affected by silting caused by the rivers flowing into the gulf.

NIQUERO

20 03N, 77 35W

Pilotage: Bahía de Niquero is entered about 15 miles northeast of Cabo Cruz. Niquero is a sugar port, and the tall chimney of the sugar mill is an outstanding landmark. The pier is reported to be 525 feet long, taking a maximum draft of 23 feet alongside.

MEDIA LUNA

20 09N, 77 26W

Pilotage: This port lies about 25 miles northeast of Cabo Cruz. It is composed of a community and a sugar mill with several prominent chimneys. The sugar loading pier is connected by rail to the town 1 1/4 miles inland. There is an anchorage northwest of the pier, with poor holding in soft mud reported. This bay is wide open to the northwest.

SAN RAMON

20 13N, 77 22W

Pilotage: This port is located 31 miles northeast of Cabo Cruz. The sugar mill is marked by a prominent chimney. There is a 660 foot wooden pier with a minimum depth of 21 feet alongside.

CANAL DE PALOMINO
CANAL DE PALOMINO BEACON, NO. 9, 20 10.0N, 77 44.9W, Fl G 5s, 13ft., 4M, Port Green, w/topmark.
CANAL DE PALOMINO BEACON, NO. 10, 20 09.2N, 77 45.1W, Fl R 6s, 13ft., 4M, Starboard Red, w/topmark.
CANAL DE PALOMINO BEACON, NO. 12, 20 09.5N, 77 40.9W, Fl R 4s, 13ft., 4M, Starboard Red, w/topmark.
CANAL DE PALOMINO BEACON, NO. 13, 20 09.8N, 77 39.8W, Fl G 5s, 13ft., 4M, Port Green, w/topmark.
BANCO FUSTETE BEACON, 20 11.3N, 77 35.6W, Fl G 3s, 13ft., 4M, Port Green, w/topmark.
CANAL DE CEIBA HUECA, NO. 5, 20 14.0N, 77 19.6W, Fl G 3s, 13ft., 4M, Port Green, beacon w/topmark.

CIEBA HUECA

20 13N, 77 19W

Pilotage: This sugar loading port is located _ _ miles northeast of Cabo Cruz. A conspicuous chimney marks the location of a large sugar mill. Small tankers also use a pier here. Vessels anchor northwest of the pier.

CAMPECHUELA

20 14N, 77 17W

Pilotage: This is another sugar loading town, located about 35 miles northeast of Cabo Cruz. There are berthing facilities for small craft only.

PUNTA GUA, 20 17.3N, 77 15.5W, Fl R 6s, 13ft., 4M, Starboard Red, beacon w/topmark.
ENSENADA GUA, 20 18.4N, 77 10.2W, Fl Y 7s, 13ft., 7M, Yellow framework tower on piles.

CAYOS MANZANILLO
CAYO PERLA, on South point, approach to Manzanillo, 20 21.4N, 77 14.6W, Fl W 5s, 36ft., 9M, Aluminum skeleton structure enclosing gray hut, gray wooden house.
PUNTA SOCORRO, 20 20.8N, 77 12.9W, Fl G 5s, 12ft., 5M, Square concrete pile.
PUNTA CAIMANERA, 20 19.8N, 77 09.4W, Fl R 4s, 5M, Red concrete tower.
CAYITA, 20 22.2N, 77 08.7W, Fl G 3s, 12ft., 5M, Square concrete pile.
BAJO CUCHARILLAS, SW of Medano de Cauto, 20 31.6N, 77 17.3W, Fl R 4s, 13ft., 6M, Starboard R, beacon w/topmark.
CHINCHORRO BANK, 20 32.7N, 77 22.5W, Fl R 6s, 13ft., 6M, Starboard Red, beacon w/topmark.

MANZANILLO

20 21N, 77 07W

Pilotage: This small metropolis, and sugar shipping center, is located in Bahía de Caimanera, about 40 miles northeast of Cabo Cruz. It is the port for Bayamo, one of the oldest cities in Cuba. The bay is fronted offshore by several low-lying reef-fringed, mangrove-covered islets known as Cayos Manzanillo. The light colored buildings of Manzanillo, at the head of the bight, may be seen over the cays at distances up to 20 miles under favorable conditions.

PASO DE CHINCHORRO
BAJO DE SANTA CLARA, NE side of shoal, 20 31.6N, 77 24.0W, Fl G 3s, 4M, Port Green, beacon w/topmark.

Golfo de Guacanayabo in that it is low-lying and consists of a muddy shore, overgrown by mangroves. Behind the shore is a coastal plain largely cultivated for sugar cane. In the far west-northwest the coast gradually rises into the foothills of the mountainous Sierra de Saneti Spiritus and Sierra de Trinidad. Conspicuous on this coast is Loma de Banao, one of the highest peaks in the chain of the Sierra de Sancti Spiritus. Also conspicuous is Pico Porterillo, the summit peak of Sierra de Trinidad

The 70 mile islet chains, Jardines de la Reina and Laberinto de Las Doce Leguas, form the south side of the area. These islets are steepto, reef-fringed and mangrove-covered. A line of sunken dangers continues to Punta Maria Aguilar, and more islets string along to Punta de las Angosturas. Inside these barriers the area is somewhat obstructed by a considerable scattering of above and below-water dangers, particularly in the east-southeast and westnorthwest portions. The muddy bottom often discolors the water, making it difficult to see the dangers.

PASA ANA MARIA, S side, 21 30.7N, 78 46.4W, Fl G 5s, 13ft., 5M, Port Green, beacon w/topmark.

FUERA CHANNEL
Fuera Channel Buoy 3, 21 32.0N, 78 53.0W, Fl W 4s, Black buoy.
BOCA GRANDE INLET, E side of entrance, 21 33.0N, 78 40.6W, Fl G 5s, 13ft., 5M, Port Green, beacon w/topmark.
CAYO ENCANTADO, 21 33.6N, 78 49.7W, Fl G 3s, 12ft., 5M, Port Green, beacon w/topmark.
CAYO ENCANTADO, NO. 6, 21 36.9N, 78 51.4W, Fl R 6s, 7ft., 3M, Starboard Red, beacon w/topmark.
JUCARO, W side of channel, 21 36.6N, 78 51.2W, Fl G 5s, 13ft., 4M, Port Green, beacon w/topmark.

JUCARO
21 37N, 78 51W

Pilotage: This port is located about 123 miles northwest of Cabo Cruz. It is a sugar shipping port and the harbor for the larger community of Ciego de Avila. The shipping anchorage (21° 31'N, 78° 53'W) lies west of the low-lying, mangrove-covered Cayo Guinea. This anchorage is about 40 miles northeast of the entrance to Canal de Breton.

ENSENADA DE SANTA MARIA
21 16N, 78 31W

Pilotage: This is a shoal coastal indentation located about 28 miles southeast of Jucaro. Vessels have sugar lightered out to them from the harbor.

PALO ALTO
21 36N, 78 58W

Pilotage: This is a sub-port of Jucaro. It is marked by a conspicuous chimney that stands near the commercial pier. There are also four prominent gray molasses tanks.

Arrecife Palo Alto lies about 2 1/4 miles south of Palo Alto. It is awash near its south end, and a light marks its southeast side.

MUELLE DE MAMBISAS, 21 36.9N, 78 51.2W, Fl R 4s, 13ft., 3M, Starboard Red, w/topmark.
TOMEGUIN, N end of shoal, 21 19.1N, 79 13.0W, Fl R 6s, 13ft., 4M, Starboard Red, w/topmark.
CAYO CACHIBOCA LIGHT, 20 40.7N, 78 45.0W, Fl W 15s, 111ft., 15M, Aluminum framework tower on piles.

CANAL DE BRETON
21 10N, 79 30W

Pilotage: This is the primary deepwater access to the Golfo De Ana Maria area. It is entered about 127 miles northwest of Cabo Cruz. The east side of the entrance is marked by Cayo Breton, which is low and mangrove covered. There is a barely awash reef to seaward that breaks in heavy seas, but is hard to see in calm weather. The conspicuous remains of a white concrete tower stand on the west of the reef.

Vessels bound for Jucaro steer for the summit of Sierra de Sancti Spiritus on a heading of 354°, and proceed so as to avoid the dangerous reef fronting Cayo Breton. When the light bears 098°, distant 4 miles, haul to starboard and proceed through Canal de Breton. It was reported in 1990 that a RACON was on the light at Cayo Breton.

CAYO BRETON, on W side, 21 07.3N, 79 26.9W, Fl W 10s, 108ft., 13M, White metal skeleton tower, concrete base. RACON: **K (– · –)** 12M.

Canal de Breton, Buoy 2, 21 08.3N,
79 30.5W, Fl R 6s, Starboard Red, pillar w/top-
mark.
Canal de Breton, Buoy 3, 21 11.4N,
79 29.0W, Fl G 5s, Port Green, pillar w/top-
mark.
MEDANOS DE LA VELA, 21 13.3N, 79 33.3W,
Fl R 4s, 16ft., 4M, Starboard Red, beacon
w/topmark.
MEDANOS DE LA VELA BEACON, NO. 6,
21 13.8N, 79 26.3W, Fl R 4s, 13ft., Starboard
Red, w/topmark.
MEDANOS DE LA VELA BEACON, NO. 8,
21 24.1N, 79 22.1W, Fl R 4s, 10ft., 4M, Starboard Red, w/topmark.

CANAL TUNAS
21 31N, 79 40W

Pilotage: This access to Golfo de Ana Maria is
located about 148 miles northwest of Cabo
Cruz. This is the most direct route to the port
of Tunas de Zaza. Cayo Zaza de Fuera is the
first above-water landmass southeast of Canal
Tunas. It is low-lying, heavily wooded and
sandy. Cayos Machos de Fuera lie northwest of
the passage, and are equally low and wooded.
A sunken danger, with visible boulders, is
reported to lie about 6 3/4 miles west-southwest of Cayo Zaza de Fuera.

Vessels proceed to a position about 9 1/2 miles
west-northwest of Cayo Zaza de Fuera, then
steer east-northeast until Cayo Blanco de Zaza
light bears 351°, distant about 3 miles. If heading for Tunas de Zaza, steer for Central Siete
de Noviembre chimney and proceed until Cayo
Blanco de Zaza light bears 305°, before heading toward town.

BOCA ESTERO DE TUNAS, NO. 8, 21 37.9N,
79 33.6W, Fl R 6s, 13ft., 4M, Starboard Red,
column w/topmark.
CAYO BLANCO DE ZAZA, 21 35.9N, 79 35.9W,
Fl W 12s, 48ft., 11M, Skeleton tower on concrete base.

CANAL MULATAS
ESTERO TUNAS DE ZAZA, NO. 6, 21 36.4N.
79 33.0W, Fl R 4s, 13ft., 3M, Starboard Red,
beacon w/topmark.
Landfall Buoy, 21 30.9N, 79 41.4W, Fl R 4s,
Starboard Red, pillar w/topmark.
Buoy 4, 21 31.8N, 79 37.5W, Fl R 6s, Starboard
Red, pillar w/topmark.

TUNAS DE ZAZA
21 38N, 79 33W

Pilotage: This town is located about 149 miles
northwest of Cabo Cruz, and is a sugar shipping port.

CANAL DE JOBABO
21 38N, 79 52W

Pilotage: This is the principal passage to Casilda. The entry is easy, and the passage deep,
but intricate. Cayo Blanco de Casilda is on the
west side of the entrance. It is a reef-fringed
wooded islet of white rock and sand, which
has the appearance of a wedge when seen
from the southwest. A largely uninterrupted
line of awash and sunken dangers extends from
the islet northwest to Punta Maria Aguilar.
Banco Cascajal, a shoal water sandbank, continues the islet northeast to the mainland.

CASILDA
21 45N, 79 59W

Pilotage: This port is located just east of Punta
Maria Aguilar, and is entered by the previously mentioned Canal de Jobabo. This is the port
for the inland city of Trinidad. Sugar is the main
product being shipped here. The quay is about
650 feet long with depths of 24 feet alongside.

CAYO BLANCO DE CASILDA, E end,
21 38.3N, 79 53.0W, Fl W 7s, 46ft., 12M, White
metal framework tower.
Les Guairos Channel Buoy 1, 21 38.8N,
79 52.4W, Fl G 3s, 21ft., 5M, Port Green, pillar
w/topmark.
BAJO LOS GUAIROS BEACON, 21 40.3N,
79 53.4W, Fl G 5s, 14ft., 4M, Port Green, column w/topmark.
BAJO JOBABOS BEACON NO.4, 21 40.5N,
79 53.2W, Fl R 4s, 14ft., 4M, Starboard Red,
w/topmark.
CANAL DE LOS GUAIROS BEACON, NO. 5,
21 40.7N, 79 53.8W, Fl G 3s, 20ft., 4M, Port
Green, column w/topmark.
CANAL DE LOS GUAIROS BEACON, NO. 9,
21 40.7N, 79 54.0W, Fl G 3s, 21ft., 4M, Port
Green, column w/topmark.
CANAL DE LOS GUAIROS BEACON, NO. 11,
21 40.6N, 79 54.1W, Fl G 5s, 20ft., 4M, Port
Green, w/topmark.

CANAL DE LOS GUAIROS BEACON, NO. 12, 21 40.7N, 79 54.2W, Fl R 6s, 13ft., Starboard Red, beacon w/topmark.
Canal Las Mulatas, Buoy 2, 21 41.7N, 79 58.6W, Fl R 4s, Starboard Red, pillar w/topmark.
BANCO DERRIBADA, 21 42.0N, 79 57.9W, Fl G 5s, 13ft., 4M, Port Green, beacon w/topmark.
BANO DEL GUEYO BEACON, NO. 14, 21 42.3N, 79 56.6W, Fl R 6s, 20ft, Starboard Red, w/topmark.
BANO DEL MEDIO BEACON, NO. 17, 21 42.6N, 79 57.7W, Fl G 3s, 20ft., 4M, Port Green, column w/topmark.
PUNTA CASILDA BEACON, NO. 21, 21 43.8N, 79 58.2W, Fl G 3s, 14ft., 4M, Port Green, column w/topmark.
Punta Lastre Beacon, No. 25, 21 44.4N, 79 59.2W, 14ft., Port Green, w/topmark.
BASE NAUTICA ANCON, NO. 2, 21 44.4N, 79 59.7W, Fl R 4s, 13ft., 3M, Starboard pile w/topmark.
BASE NAUTICA ANCON, NO. 3, 21 44.3N, 79 59.6W, Fl G 3s, 13ft., 3M, Port pile w/topmark.
BASE NAUTICA ANCON, NO. 5, 21 44.3N, 79 59.6W, Fl G 5s, 13ft., 3M, Port pile w/topmark.
CAYO RATON BEACON, NO. 26, 21 44.4N, 79 59.1W, 14ft., Starboard Red, column w/topmark.
CAYO RATON BEACON, NO. 28, 21 44.5N, 79 59.2W, 14ft., 4M, Starboard Red, column w/topmark.
CAYO RATON BEACON, NO. 31, 21 45.5N, 79 59.5W, Fl G 3s, 14ft., 4M, Port Green, w/topmark.
CAYO RATON BEACON, NO. 32, 21 44.9N, 79 59.4W, Fl R 4s, 14ft., 4M, Starboard Red, column w/topmark.
CAYO RATON BEACON, NO. 37, 21 45.1N, 79 59.6W, 14ft., 4M, Port Green, w/topmark.
ANCON, PUNTA MARIA ANGUILAR, 21 44.6N, 80 01.3W, Fl W 5s, 56ft., 25M, Pedestal on white water tank.
RÍO YAGUANABO LIGHT, E entrance point, 21 51.4N, 80 12.4W, Fl W 10s, 190ft., 15M, White round concrete tower with hut at base.
CIENFUEGOS, PUNTA DE LOS COLORADOS LIGHT, E side of entrance, 22 02.0N, 80 26.6W, Fl W 5s, 83ft., 15M, White conical masonry tower, Radiobeacon.
CIENFUEGOS, PUNTA DE LOS COLORADOS RANGE, (Front Light), 22 03.5N, 80 27.5W, F R, 14M, White concrete structure. **(Rear Light),** 220 meters, 350°12' from front, F R, 14M, White concrete structure.
CIENFUEGOS, PUNTA DE LOS COLORADOS RANGE, NO. 2, (Front Light), 22 03.8N,

80 27.9W, Fl W 1.5s, 11M, White concrete structure. **(Rear Light),** 60 meters 322°48' from front, Fl W 1.5s, 11M, White concrete structure.
JURAGUA LIGHT, NO. 5, 22 03.6N, 80 27.9W, Fl G 3s, 22ft., 4M, White triangular pyramidal tower, square house.
PASA CABALLOS, 22 03.7N, 80 27.7W, Fl R 2s, 33ft., 4M, Starboard Red, beacon w/topmark
CIENFUEGOS, PUNTA DE LOS COLORADOS RANGE, NO. 3, (Front Light), 22 03.6N, 80 27.8W, F W, 11M, White concrete structure. **(Rear Light),** 50 meters 204°54' from front, F W, 11M, White concrete structure.
CAYO ALCATRAZ, SSW side, 22 04.3N, 80 26.6W, Fl G 5s, 16ft., 8M, Black square concrete tower on platform on piles.
CIENFUEGOS, PUNTA DE LOS COLORADOS RANGE, NO. 4, ON CAYO CARENAS, (Front Light), 22 05.1 N, 80 27.5W, Fl W 1.5s, 11M, White concrete structure. **(Rear Light),** 60 meters 358°30' from front, Fl W 1.5s, 11M, White concrete structure.

CIENFUEGOS
22 09N, 80 27W

Pilotage: This harbor is located about midway along the eastern side of Bahía de Cienfuegos. The bay is surrounded by level or undulating land, which is heavily cultivated with sugar cane, especially to the east. This is considered one of the most important cities on Cuba. Punta Colorados light marks the east side of the entrance to the bay. Pico Cuevita, 15 1/2 miles east-southeast, is an excellent landmark, with its sharp conspicuous crest, which seen from the west, appears as the highest peak of Sierra de San Juan. Loma Guamo, about 6 miles north-northwest, is an irregular peak and useful mark for determining position offshore when plotted together with Pico La Cuevita and the light at Punta Colorados.

Tidal currents average 1 to 2 knots during the dry season, but can increase to 4 knots during the wet season. The ebb can be particularly strong when runoff adds to the flow. Entry on an ebb tide is recommended. Range lights mark the channel.
Port of Entry

PASA BAJO DE LA CUEVA, NO. 1, 22 05.8N, 80 27.3W, Fl G 3s, 13ft., 4M, Port Green, pile w/topmark.
PASA BAJO DE LA CUEVA, NO. 2, 22 05.7N, 80 27.3W, Fl R 4s, 13ft., 3M, Starboard Red, pile w/topmark.

Chapter 2

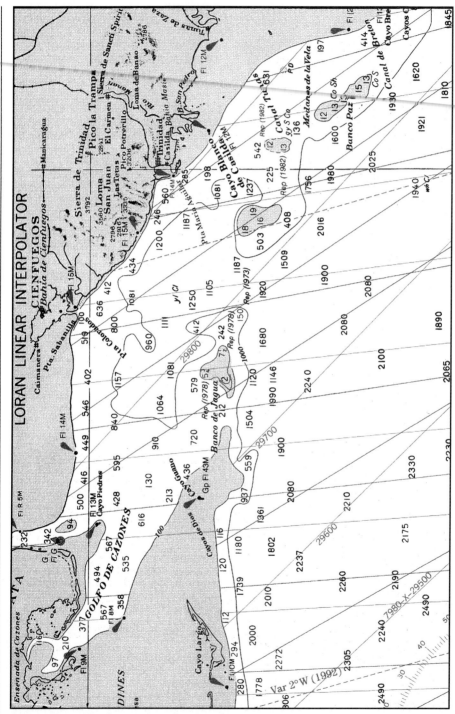

Approaches to Cienfuegos, Soundings in Fathoms

PASA BAJO DE LA CUEVA, NO. 3, 22 05.7N, 80 27.2W, Fl G 5s, 13ft., 3M, Port Green, pile w/topmark.
PASA BAJO DE LA CUEVA, NO. 4, 22 05.6N, 80 27.2W, Fl R 6s, 13ft., 3M, Starboard Red, pile w/topmark.
JUNCO SUR, 22 06.6N, 80 26.3W, Fl G 5s, 13ft., 3M, Port Green, beacon w/topmark.
PUNTA DE LA MAJAGUA, SSW of point 22 07.5N, 80 28.0W, Fl (2 + 1) R 10s, 16ft., 8M, PREFERRED CHANNEL RGR, beacon w/topmark.
ENSENADA DE COTICA, NO. 5B, 22 09.3N, 80 27.9W, Fl G 5s, 30ft., Port Green, column w/topmark.
ENSENADA DE COTICA, NO. 6B, 22 09.4N, 80 27.8W, Fl R 4s, 14ft., 4M, Starboard Red, column w/topmark.
ENSENADA DE COTICA, NO. 7B, 22 09.3N, 80 27.5W, Fl G 3s, 14ft., 4M, Port Green, column w/topmark.
ENSENADA DE COTICA, NO. 8B, 22 09.1N, 80 27.4W, Fl R 4s, 14ft., 4M, Starboard Red, column w/topmark.

BANCO DE JAGUA

21 35N, 80 40W

Pilotage: This bank lies well offshore and to the east of Banco de los Jardines. It is an isolated shoal water patch of coral that rises steepto. During the day, it can be seen at a distance of about 1 mile, but at night it is hard to spot.

CAYO PIEDRAS, W side of entrance to Bahía de Cochinos, 21 58.2N, 81 07.4W, Fl W 10s, 55ft., 13M, Aluminum framework tower.

BAHÍA DE COCHINOS
22 07N, 81 10W

Pilotage: This is the deepest and most extensive of all the sleeve-like inlets indenting the Cuban coastline. Depths of over 100 fathoms are found over most of its area. Its west entrance point is Punta Palmillas, which is extended seaward to Cayo Piedras by a shoal water spit that forms the only known danger in the immediate approaches. Playa Buenaventura lies at the head of the bay, and is the only community of significance here. Anchorage near the inlet is not considered safe.

MUELLE, 21 58.0N, 81 07.5W, Fl G 3s, 13ft., 3M, Port Green, beacon w/topmark.
CAYO PIEDRAS, 21 58.1N, 81 07.6W, Fl G 5s, 4M, Port Green, beacon w/topmark.

REEF, SW side, 21 57.7W, 81 09.4W, Fl R 4s, 4M, Starboard Red, beacon w/topmark.
CAYO GUANO DEL ESTE LIGHT, Near E extremity of Banco los Jardines, 21 39.7N, 81 02.5W, Fl (2) W 15s, 177ft., 43M, White cylindrical concrete tower w/red bands on building, Aeromarine light.
CALETA DE TORO, 22 02.4N, 80 53.6W Fl W 15s, 72ft., 14M, White metal framework tower.
BEACON NO. 1, 22 13.5N, 81 08.8W, Fl G 3s, 23ft., 4M, Port Green, w/topmark.
NO. 2, 22 13.6N, 81 08.7W, Fl R 6s, 13ft, 3M, Starboard Red, beacon w/topmark.
BEACON NO. 2, 22 12.6N, 81 08.4W, Fl R 4s, 26ft., 4M, Red framework tower, concrete base.
CABETA DE BUENAVENTURA, NO. 1, 22 12.6N, 81 08.4W, Fl G 3s, 13ft, 4M, Port Green, beacon w/topmark.
CABETA DE BUENAVENTURA, NO. 2, 22 16.7N, 81 12.5W, Fl R 4s, 13ft, 3M, Starboard Red, beacon w/topmark.
CABETA DE BUENAVENTURA, NO. 5, 22 16.9N, 81 12.6W, Fl G 5s, 13ft, 3M, Port Green, beacon w/topmark.
CABETA DE BUENAVENTURA, NO. 6, 22 16.9N, 81 12.6W, Fl R 4s, 13ft, 3M, Starboard Red, beacon w/topmark.
CAYO SIGUA, 21 53.4N, 81 25.1W, Fl W 7s, 28ft., 8M, Aluminum-colored skeleton structure.
PASA DE DIEGO PEREZ, on reef at entrance, 22 01.4N. 81 30.9W, Fl W 5s, 38ft., 9M, Red iron skeleton structure enclosing gray hut with red stripe.
CABEZO DEL VAPOR, 22 01.5N, 81 36.5W, Fl G 5s, 13ft., 4M, Port Green, beacon w/topmark.
CABEZO DEL CARBONERO, 22 05.9N, 81 46.0W, Fl G 3s, 13ft., 4M, Port Green, beacon w/topmark.
MEDANO DON CRISTOBAL, 22 07.3N, 81 49.2W, Fl R 6s, 13ft., 3M, Starboard Red, beacon w/topmark.
CAYOS BALLENATOS (LOS BALLENATOS), 21 34.7N, 81 38.3W, Fl W 10s, 31ft., 9M, Red iron skeleton structure enclosing gray hut with red stripe.
CAYOS BALLENATOS BEACON 25, 22 03.8N, 81 59.6W, Fl G 5s, Port Green, beacon w/topmark.
CAYOS BALLENATOS BEACON 28, 22 08.5N, 82 05.4W, Fl R 6s, Starboard Red, beacon w/topmark.
BAJO LAS GORDAS, off SW side, 22 13.0N, 82 08.7W, Fl R 6s, 13ft., 3M, Red, on column, on platform on piles w/topmark.
CAYO AMBER, off SE side, 22 19.1N, 82 09.6W, Fl G 5s, Port Green, beacon w/topmark.

Chapter 2

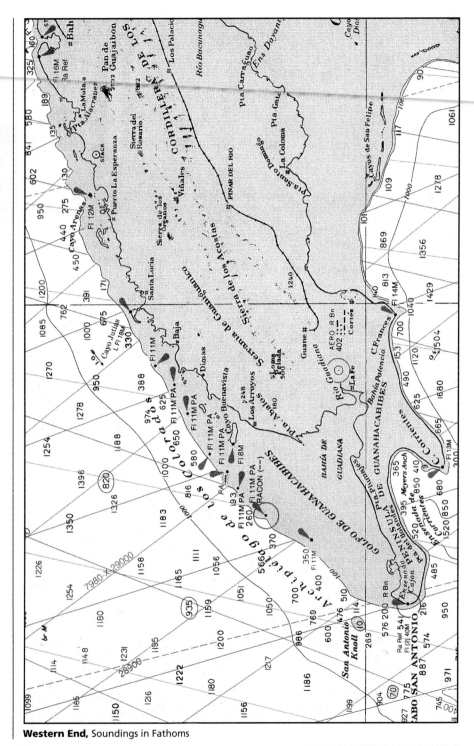

Western End, Soundings in Fathoms

PUNTA GORDA, 22 23.6N, 82 09.5W, Fl R 4s, Starboard Red, beacon w/topmark.
CAYO LARGO, 21 38.4N, 81 33.9W, Fl W 6s, 42ft., 11M, White concrete tower.
CAYO LARGO, NO. 6, 21 36.2N, 81 34.4W, Fl R 4s, 13ft., 4M, Starboard Red, beacon w/topmark.
CAYO LARGO, NO. 11, 21 37.5N, 81 34.2W, Fl G 3s, 13ft., 3M, Port Green, beacon w/topmark.
CAYO AVALOS, S end, 21 32.3N, 82 09.9W, Fl W 8s, 71ft., 12M, Aluminum-colored iron skeleton structure enclosing gray hut with red stripe.

CAYO AVALOS
21 33N, 82 10W

Pilotage: This small sandy islet is located about 22 miles east of Isla de Pinos. It has good anchorage in 27 feet over sand and rock, when Cayo Avalos light bears northeast, distant about 1 3/4 miles. Vessels make their approach with the light bearing between 045° and 070°, so as to pass northwest of the drying rock Sambo Head.

CALETA DE CARAPACHIBEY LIGHT, S side of Isla de la Juventud, 21 26.9N, 82 55.5W, Fl W 7.5s, 184ft., 29M, W cylindrical concrete tower, Yellow band, Aeromarine light.

GOLFO DE BATABANO
PETATILLOS DEL NORTE, 22 28.0N, 82 39.8W, Q W, 20FT., 4M, North Cardinal Black + Yellow beacon w/topmark.
BAJO LA PIPA, 22 09.5N, 82 58.0W, Fl R 5s, 13ft., 4M, Starboard Red, beacon w/topmark.
CAYO HAMBRE, 22 10.2N, 82 51.6W, Fl G 5s, 13ft., 4M, Port Green, beacon w/topmark.
PUNTA DO LOS BARCOS, 21 56.3N, 82 59.7W, Fl R 5s, 13ft., 3M, Starboard Red, beacon w/topmark.
PUNTA BUENAVISTA, 21 46.9N, 83 05.7W, Fl R 6s, 13ft., 4M, Starboard Red, beacon w/topmark.
DARSENA DE SIGUANEA, N entrance, 21 37.0N, 82 59.1W, Fl G 5s, Red structure.
DARSENA DE SIGUANEA, S entrance, Fl R 6s, Red structure.
CAYOS LOS INDIOS, 21 43.1N, 83 10.0W, Fl G 12s, 13ft., 5M, Port Green, beacon w/topmark.
Ensenade de la Siguanea Buoy, 21 41.0N, 83 12.0W, Fl W 7.5s, Black + white striped buoy.

LOS COYUELOS, 21 38.4N, 83 11.2W, Q W, 16ft., 4M, North Cardinal Black + Yellow beacon w/topmark.
GOLFO DE BATABANO LIGHT, NO. 1, 21 59.5N, 82 43.4W, Fl G 3s, 13ft., Port G beacon.
GOLFO DE BATABANO BEACON, NO. 2, 21 59.7N, 82 43.2W, Fl R 4s, 13ft., 4M, Starboard Red, beacon w/topmark.
GOLFO DE BATABANO LIGHT, NO. 13, 22 00.3N, 82 42.8W, Fl G 5s, 3M, Black skeleton tower
GOLFO DE BATABANO LIGHT, NO. 14, 22 00.2N, 82 42.7W, Fl R 4s, 7ft,. 4M, Red skeleton tower.
GOLFO DE BATABANO LIGHT, NO. 21, 22 01.2N, 82 42.4W, Fl G 3s, 13ft., Port G beacon.
GOLFO DE BATABANO LIGHT, NO. 22, 22 01.3N, 82 42.3W, Fl R 4s, 13ft., 3M, Port Green, beacon w/topmark.
GOLFO DE BATABANO BEACON, NO. 2, 21 55.7N, 82 39.4W, Fl R 4s, 13ft., 3M, Starboard Red, beacon w/topmark.
GOLFO DE BATABANO BEACON, NO. 30, 21 56.0N, 82 37.3W, Fl R 4s, 13ft., 3M, Starboard Red, beacon w/topmark. Pasa Quitasol marked by lights and beacons between "2" and "30".
CANAL DEL INGLES, NE of Pasa de Quitasol, 21 57.2N, 82 36.5W, Fl G 5s, 19ft., 4M, Port G w/topmark.
SURGIDERO DE BATABANO LIGHT, 22 41.1N, 82 17.8W, Fl W 3s, 101ft., 10M, White water tank.

SURGIDERO DE BATABANO
22 41N, 82 18W
Pilotage: This city on the north side of the Golfo de Batabano has a partially sheltered roadstead anchorage. The area is exposed to southeast winds, which are common between July and October. The Golfo de Batabano lies between the mangrove-fringed island Cabo Diego Perez and Cabo Frances, 142 miles to the west. The numerous islets east and west of Isla de Pinos form the southern boundary of the relatively shallow gulf. Tidal action here is slight, but currents and water levels are strongly influenced by the wind direction. A northeast wind lowers water levels, while a southeast wind raises them. Extreme lows occur with a northwest wind, while extreme highs occur with a southwest breeze. Currents outside the gulf can be of concern as they tend to set vessels to the northwest, which is toward the dangers between Banco de Jardinillos and Isla de Pinos. This is particularly the case with southeast winds.

Chapter 2

ISLA DE PINOS

21 40W, 82 50W

Pilotage: This is the largest of the islands lying off the Cuban coast. It is quite flat, with the south part being very low, swampy and densely wooded. The north two-thirds of the island has a wide, very flat, coastal plain, that merges with a scattering of high, often heavily forested, interior hills and mountains. Loma la Canada (1017 feet) is the highest, and the first sighted when coming from the south. From the west it appears as a domed summit flanked by two sharp peaks. Loma Daguilla is the highest peak (612 feet) on the east side of the island — from the southeast it appears as a steep-sided isolated hill.

The Cayos Jardines are the numerous islets lying scattered east of Isla de Pinos for a distance of about 67 miles to the heavily wooded islet Cayo Largo. They continue on to Cayo Guamo del Este, a group of high, closely spaced barren rocks, which form the easternmost above-water dangers fronting this section of the coast.

Ensenada de la Siguanea (21° 38'N, 83° 05'W) is a spacious deepwater inlet on the west side of Isla de Pinos. It is entered between Punta Frances, the low-lying mangrove covered west extremity of the island, and Cayos los Indios, a group of low-lying heavily wooded islets that give a measure of shelter from the west. If approaching from the west, steer for Loma la Canada on a heading of 084°. When approaching from the south or southwest, pass no less than 2 1/4 miles northwest of Punta Frances before turning into the entrance.

Nueva Gerona (21° 53'N, 82° 48'W) is a small riverine community lying somewhat inland on the north coast of Isla de Pinos. This is the principal community on the island. Vessels can approach this area by passaging around the west side of Isla de Pinos, via Ensenada de la Siguanea.

REFUGE CANAL, E breakwater, 22 40.6N, 82 17.9W, Fl R 6s, 19ft., 4M, Red concrete pyramid.
REFUGE CANAL, W side, 22 40.8N, 82 17.9W, Fl G 3s, 13ft., 4M, Port Green, column w/topmark.
SUR BAJO BOQUERON, 22 21.1N, 82 25.7W, Fl G 5s, 14ft., 3M, Port Green, beacon w/topmark.

MONTERREY, 22 20.2N, 82 20.5W, Fl R 6s, 14ft., 7M, Starboard Red, beacon w/topmark.
CAYO CRUZ, 22 28.1N, 82 16.8W, Fl G 3s, 13ft., 6M, Port Green, beacon w/topmark.
BUENAVISTA, 22 30.0N, 82 21.2W, Fl R 6s, 13ft., 3M, Starboard Red, beacon w/topmark.
CAYO CULEBRA, 22 24.1N, 82 33.8W, Fl R 6s, 13ft., 4M, Starboard Red, beacon w/topmark.
CAYO CARABELA, 22 29.2N, 82 28.7W., Fl G 3s, 13ft., 4M, Port Green, beacon w/topmark.
BOQUERON DEL HACHA, 22 29.3N, 82 27.8W, Fl R 4s, 13ft., 4M, Starboard Red, beacon w/topmark.

ENSENADA DE COLOMA

SANTO DOMINGO, APPROACH BEACON, 22 09.5N, 83 36.5W, L Fl W 10s, 19ft., 5M, Red metal tower, white stripes, on platform on piles, ball topmark.
ENSENADA DE COLOMA, NO. 1, W side, 22 11.9N, 83 35.6W, Fl G 3s, 13ft., 4M, Port Green, beacon w/topmark.
ENSENADA DE COLOMA, NO. 4, E side, 22 12.4N, 83 35.3W, Fl R 4s, 13ft., 4M, Starboard Red, beacon w/topmark.
ENSENADA DE COLOMA, NO. 5, W side, 22 13.0N, 83 34.9W, Fl G 5s, 13ft., 4M, Port Green, beacon w/topmark.
ENSENADA DE COLOMA, NO. 8, E side, 22 13.5N, 83 34.6W, Fl R 4s, 13ft., 4M, Starboard Red, beacon w/topmark.
ENSENADA DE COLOMA, NO. 10, E side, 22 14.1N, 83 34.2W, Fl R 6s, 13ft., 4M, Starboard Red, beacon w/topmark.

ENSENADA DE CORTES

Pilotage: This coastal bight is located in the far western part of Golfo de Batabano. The approaches are obstructed by a string of dangers extending west from Isla de Pinos to the mainland. It is entered by means of a narrow passage west of a partially emerged sunken wreck charted about 12 1/2 miles north-northeast of Cabo Frances.

CABO FRANCES, 21 54.4N, 84 02.1W, Fl W 10s, 28ft., 15M, Aluminum framework tower.
CABO CORRIENTES, 21 45.7N, 84 31.0W, Fl W 5s, 88ft., 13M, Aluminum-colored iron skeleton structure enclosing gray hut with red band.

CAYMAN ISLANDS

ENTRY PROCEDURES

All vessels should anchor off George Town, or tie up to the government wharf, to clear customs and immigration. You should call the Port Authority on VHF channel 16, and they will alert customs to your arrival. If you cannot anchor off of George Town due to bad weather, contact the Port Authority for information on an alternate harbor. The harbor is wide open to northwest winds.

Information required includes a clearance from your last port of call, the ship's documents, proof of ownership and passports. There is a $40.00 fee for vessels arriving after 4:30 PM weekdays, on Sundays, or after 12:30 PM on Saturdays. All guns, spear guns, pole spears and Hawaiian slings will be held for the duration of your stay. There are strict environmental rules and regulations that must be complied with while in the islands.

The Cayman dollar is the official currency, but U.S. dollars are accepted everywhere. Credit cards are widely accepted, and there are over 500 banks to do business with.

For more information contact the customs office at (809) 949-2473.

Language spoken: English.

GRAND CAYMAN

GRAND CAYMAN LIGHT, Georgetown near church, 19 17.8N, 81 23.0W, Q R, 41ft., 7M, Black steel tower, W base.
BOATSWAIN POINT LIGHT, NW end of island, 19 23.1N, 81 24.6W, Fl W 15s, 90ft., 15M, W steel tower, Black base, Partially obscured from 241° to 257°, Obscured 257° to shore.
GORLING BLUFF LIGHT, At SE end of island, 19 18.0N, 81 06.3W, Fl (2) W 20s, 72ft., 12M, W steel tower, Black base.
GEORGETOWN AVIATION LIGHT, 19 17.5N, 81 21.5W, Al W G, 40ft., 20M.

GEORGE TOWN

19 18N, 81 23W
Port of Entry: Contact the Port Authority on VHF channel 16 upon arrival. See Entry Procedures for more information.

Dockage: You may be able to tie up temporarily to the government wharf while clearing customs. There are three marinas in North Sound. Contact Morgan's Harbour at (809) 949-3948, or on VHF channel 16. They are located in West Bay, on the western side of North Sound. Contact Harbour House Marina at (809) 947-1307, or on VHF channel 16. They are located at the south end of the sound. Contact Kaibo in North Side at (809) 947-1307.
Anchorage: There are sheltered anchorages in North Sound. In good weather you can anchor west of West Bay. Boats anchored off of George Town move around the south end of the island when a norther threatens.
Services: Fuel, water, repairs and haulouts to 70 tons are available at Harbour House Marina. Fuel and water are available at Morgan's Harbour. There are good chandlers and grocery stores on the island. The offshore banking industry has promoted the development of modern facilities of all sorts.

Being situated well off the normal trade wind routes of the Caribbean, the Caymans are less visited by transient yachts then other islands. For those who do make it the islands have world famous diving opportunities, and good shoreside facilities. The Lesser Caymans are over 60 miles northeast of Grand Cayman. They are only sparsely inhabited, with few possibilities for shelter without local knowledge.

LITTLE CAYMAN

SOUTH WEST POINT LIGHT, 19 15.7N, 81 23.2W, Fl (2) W 10s, 30ft., 15M, W metal tower and base, Visible 253° to 150°.
LITTLE CAYMAN LIGHT, South West Point, 19 39.5N, 80 06.8W, Fl W 5s, 30ft., 10M, W steel tower, Black base.
EAST POINT LIGHT, 19 42.4N, 79 58.2W, Fl W 10s, 36ft., 10M, W tower and base.

CAYMAN BRAC

CAYMAN BRAC LIGHT, SW point, 19 41.0N, 79 53.5W, Fl (2) W 15s, 41ft., 15M, Mast.
CAYMAN BRAC LIGHT, North East Point, 19 45.0N, 79 44.0W, L Fl W 20s, 150ft., 12M, W steel tower, Black base.

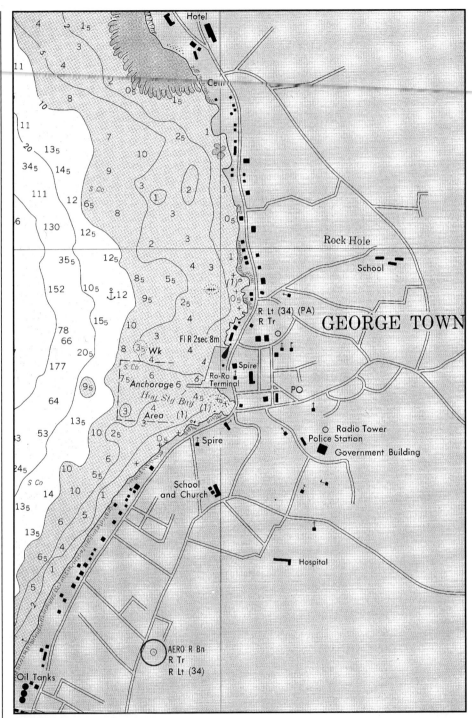

George Town, Soundings in Meters

JAMAICA

CAUTION: Our information on aids to navigation comes from official government sources. The latitudes and longitudes of these marks may not correspond to the readings from GPS receivers. Some aids have been reported as unreliable, missing, off position or showing incorrect characteristics. No single aid to navigation, or waypoint, should be relied upon as a sole means of fixing your position.

Customs will hold all firearms and ammunition for the duration of your stay.

For more information contact the Customs office at Port Royal (809) 924-8633.

The official currency is the Jamaican dollar. Credit cards are widely used in tourist areas.

Language spoken: English.

ENTRY PROCEDURES

Arriving yachts should proceed to a Port of Entry for Customs and Immigration clearance. Ports of Entry include Port Royal, Kingston Harbour; Port Antonio; Montego Bay; and Ocho Rios. In Port Royal you should tie up to the customs dock or anchor out with the Q flag flying. The Customs people will come out to see you. After Customs, you will be visited by Immigration and Quarantine Officials.

You should have a clearance from your last port of call, passports or identification for the crew, documentation and proof of ownership for the boat. You may apply for a 3 month stay in the country, with another 3 month extension possible. Further 3 month extensions may be granted depending upon the circumstances. Normal working hours are 8:00AM to 4:00PM, Monday through Friday. Overtime charges will apply (double time) for clearance on Saturdays, Sundays and Public Holidays. Charges are based upon the number of officials involved and the amount of time needed.

To move about the island you will need a Coastwise Clearance stating your itinerary and schedule. You must report to Customs upon arriving in your next port of call, and then get another Coastwise Clearance for the next leg of your trip.

When leaving the country you can wait for up to 24 hours after receiving your clearance if you do not have any firearms being held.

NORTH COAST: LUCEA HARBOR TO OCHOS RIOS BAY

LUCEA HARBOR LIGHT, On Flagstaff Reef, 18 27.1N, 78 09.8W, Fl R 4s, 12ft., 5M, Triangular steel skeleton structure.
MONTEGO BAY LOWER RANGE, (Front Light) 18 28.1N, 77 55.4W, F R, 22ft., 5M, Cylindrical iron structure triangular shaped, Visible 108° to 128°, **(Rear Light)** 323 meters 118.5° from front, F R, 57ft., 5M, Black structure, Visible 108° to 128°.
MONTEGO BAY UPPER RANGE, (Front Light) 18 28.7N, 77 55.6W, F R 44ft., 5M, Cylindrical iron structure, Ball topmark, Visible 026° to 046°, Stopping lights, Reported destroyed 1991. **(Rear Light)** 104 meters 035.2° from front, F R, 113ft., 5M, Cylindrical iron structure, Ball topmark, Visible 026° to 046°, Stopping lights.
MONTEGO BAY ENTRANCE CHANNEL RANGE, (Front Light) 18 27.5N, 77 56.3W, Oc W 2s, 26ft., Post, R triangle daymark. **(Rear Light)** 300 meters 200.8° from front, Oc W 3s, 43ft., Post, R triangular daymark.
AVIATION LIGHT, 18 29.9N, 77 55.1W, Fl W 4s, 59ft., 10M, Control tower.
MONTEGO PORT LIGHT 2, W Side, 18 27.8N, 77 56.2W, Fl R 5s, 16 ft., Red pile.
MONTEGO PORT LIGHT 3, W Side, 18 27.8N, 77 56.3W, Fl R 3s, 16 ft., Red pile.
MONTEGO PORT LIGHT 4, 18 27.7N, 77 56.5W, Fl R 5s, 16 ft., R steel column on pile.
MONTEGO PORT LIGHT 5, 18 27.6N, 77 56.5W, Fl R 3s, 16 ft., R steel column on pile.
MONTEGO PORT LIGHT 6, 18 27.7N, 77 56.2W, FG, 20 ft., G steel column.

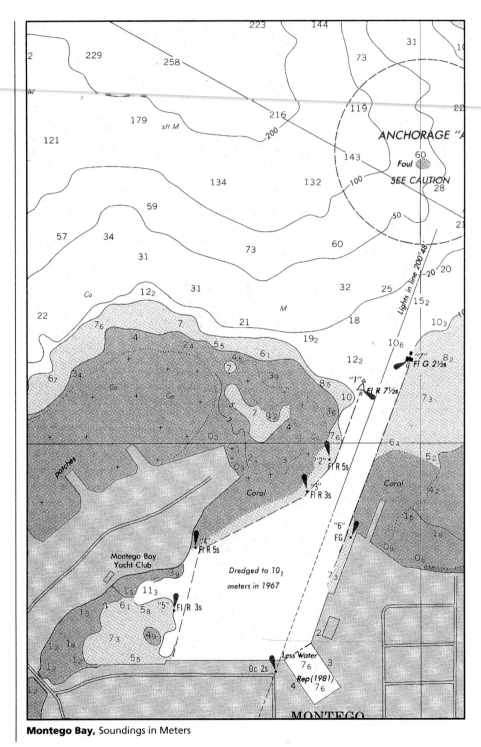

Montego Bay, Soundings in Meters

MONTEGO BAY

18 28N, 7756W

Port of Entry: If you anchor off or dock at the Montego Bay Yacht Club they will call the officials for you.

Dockage: The Montego Bay Yacht Club is located in the bay west of town that forms the commercial port. Contact them at (809) 979 8038 or on VHF channel 10. Their wharf will take up to 30 foot draft at the outer end, but depths vary as you progress toward shore. There is a fee for anchoring off the club and using their facilities.

Services: At this writing only diesel fuel is available at the Yacht Club, but they may get gasoline soon. You can order ice in large quantities for delivery the next day. There is a bar, restaurant, showers, tennis and swimming. Minor repairs may be carried out at the docks, but the lift is not working at this time. You may be able to get hauled near Pier 1 in the commercial area. There are all sorts of tourist diversions available at the club, in town and nearby.

Though the Yacht Club is situated several miles from downtown, it is a popular stop for boaters. There are good facilities at the club, which is more like a small resort. This is a well sheltered harbor.

ROSE HALL LIGHT, 18 32.1N, 77 49.2W, Fl (5) W 30s, 106ft., 22M, Metal framework tower.
FALMOUTH HARBOR LIGHT, 18 29.3N, 77 39.1W, F R, 37ft., W structure, Circular shaped.
DISCOVERY BAY RANGE (Front Light) (DRY HARBOR), 18 27.7N, 77 24.6W, F R, 25ft., Post, W triangular daymark, Point up. **(Rear Light)** 220 meters 193.9° from front, F R, 40ft., Framework tower, W triangular daymark, Point down.
ST. ANNS BAY RANGE, (Front Light) On Custom House, 18 26.1N, 77 12.1W, F R, 59ft., 11M, Roof of Custom House, Visible 186° to 206°, Destroyed 1966. **(Rear Light)** 580 meters 193.5° from front, F R, 275ft., 11M, W iron column, Visible 186° to 206°.

OCHOS RIOS BAY

Buoy, 18 25.0N, 77 07.0W, Fl R 3s, R buoy w/triangular topmark, Radar reflector.
RANGE, (Front Light) 18 24.5N, 77 06.9W, Oc R 5s, 42ft., 10M, R + W triangular daymark, Shown when vessels are expected. **(Rear Light)** 384 meters 169° from front, Oc R 5s, 150ft., 10M, Steel column, R + W triangular daymark, Synchronized with front, Shown when vessels are expected.
BEACON, 18 24.7N, 77 06.7W, Fl G 5s, 16 ft., Square topmark on three pile beacon.
BEACON, 18 24.6N, 77 06.6W, Fl G 1.5s, 16 ft., Square topmark on three pile beacon.

ORACABESSA BAY

RANGE, (Front Light) E side of bay, 18 24.3N, 76 56.0W, Fl W 2.5s, 23ft., 7M, W circular iron column, W circular daymark. **(Rear Light)** 46 meters 093.2° from front, Q W, 41ft., 7M, W circular iron column, W circular daymark.
RANGE, (Front Light) S part of bay, 18 24.0N, 76 57.1W, Fl W 5s, 12ft., 7M, W circular iron column, W diamond daymark. **(Rear Light)** 55 meters 175.7° from front, Q W, 18ft., 7M, W circular iron column, W diamond daymark.
GALINA POINT LIGHT, 18 25.2N, 76 55.1W, Fl W 12s, 62ft., 22M, W round concrete tower and hut, F R on radio masts close W.

PORT ANTONIO

FOLLY POINT LIGHT, 18 11.3N, 76 26.6W, L Fl W 10s, 54ft., 23M, Concrete tower, R+W bands, Obscured by Wood Island.
FOLLY POINT RANGE, (Front Light) 18 11.2N, 76 26.6W, F R, Beacon, When required. **(Rear Light)** 146 meters 068.8° from front, F R, Beacon, When required.
WEST HARBOR RANGE, (Front Light) On the shore, 18 10.9N, 76 27.6W, F R, 25ft., W structure. **(Rear Light)** 1271 meters 249° from front, F R, 277ft., W structure.
TITCHFIELD LIGHT, 18 11.0N, 76 27.1W, Q G, Beacon.

PORT ANTONIO

18 11N, 76 27W
Port of Entry
Dockage: Navy Island Marina and Resort has dock space at the south end of Navy Island. You can take a ferry into the market area of town. Contact them at (809) 993-2667 or on VHF channel 1. Port Antonio Marina and Huntress Marina are located near the Boundbrook Wharf area. Contact Port Antonio at (809) 993-3209 or on VHF channel 16. Contact Huntress at (809) 993-3053 or on VHF channel 16.

Services: All three marinas have water and electricity. Huntress has fuel and Port Antonio can order fuel. There is a bar and restaurant at Port Antonio Marina. There are grocery stores and general supplies available in town.
Port Antonio is one of the most beautiful towns on the island, and the marinas are a

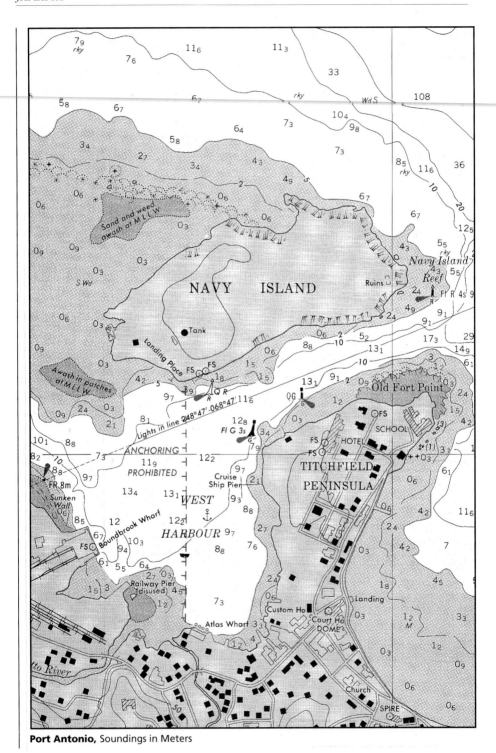

Port Antonio, Soundings in Meters

popular stop for cruisers. The mountain scenery is spectacular and makes a visit inland worthwhile. This is also a good place to clear customs when coming down from the north through the Windward Passage.

MORANT POINT LIGHT, SE extremity of Jamaica, 17 54.9N, 76 11.1W, Fl (3) W 20s, 115ft., 22M, W metal tower, R bands, Obscured when bearing more than 067°, Reported L Fl W 10s 1991.

SOUTH COAST: MORANT POINT TO KINGSTON

MORANT CAYS LIGHT, Northeast Cay, 17 25.0N, 75 59.2W, L Fl W 10s, 75ft., 12M, Aluminum framework tower, Radar reflector.
PORT MORANT RANGE, (Front Light) 17 53.3N, 76 19.4W, F R, 34ft., 5M, W beacon. **(Rear Light)** 418 meters 005.8° from front, F R, 95ft., 5M, W beacon.
HARBOR SHOAL SOUTH LIGHT, 17 52.4N, 76 19.6W, Fl G 5s, Beacon.
MORANT BAY LIGHT, 17 53.0N, 76 24.0W, Fl W 5s, 244ft., 14M, R framework tower, Visible 283° to 078°, Only top of tower is visible above trees.
HARBOR SHOAL NORTH, Fl G 1.5s, Beacon.
COTTON TREE SPIT, Fl R 1.5s, Beacon.
LEITH HALL SPIT, Fl G 3s, Beacon.
WATSON SPIT, Fl G 5s, Beacon.

KINGSTON AND APPROACHES

PLUMB POINT LIGHT, 17 55.6N, 76 46.7W, Fl W R 9s, 70ft., 19M, W tower, W 297° to 010°, R 010° to 136°, W 136° to 181°, Obscured elsewhere.
NORMAN MANLEY AVIATION LIGHT, 17 56.1N, 76 46.8W, Al Fl W G 8s, 55ft., Tower, Occasional.
Lime Cay Buoy, 17 55.0N, 76 49.0W, QR, R buoy.
East Middle Ground Buoy, 17 55.0N, 76 47.0W, Fl R, R buoy, Radar reflector.

PORT ROYAL

GUN CAY LIGHT, S end of shoal, 17 55.6N, 76 50.2W, Fl R 4s, 20ft., 5M, W triangular topmark on pile structure.
RACKHAMS CAY RANGE, (Front Light) N extremity of shoal, 17 55.5N, 76 50.3W, Fl G 5s, 28ft., 8M, Green beacon. **(Rear Light)**

Lazaretto, 3.9 km 284° from front, 17 56.0N, 76 52.5W, Fl W 3s, 92ft., W cairn, Lights mark the boat channel off Gallows Point when required.
BEACON SHOAL LIGHT, S extremity, 17 55.7N, 76 50.8W, Q R, 18ft., W tripod structure, Black base.
HARBOR SHOAL LIGHT, SW edge of shoal, 17 55.9N, 76 51.0W, Fl W 3s,16ft., 5M, W triangular topmark on pile structure.
CHEVANNES BEACON, 17 56.2N, 76 50.8W, Q W.

PORT ROYAL
17 56N, 76 50W
Emergencies: Call the Jamaican Coast Guard on VHF channel 16.
Port of Entry: Tie up to the Customs wharf or anchor out with the Q flag flying. See Entry Procedures for more information.
Dockage: Morgan's Harbour Club is located in Port Royal and can be reached at (809) 924-8464. The Royal Jamaica Yacht Club is located east of the airport on the north side of the Palisadoes Peninsula. They can be called at (809) 924-8685. They both offer the necessities of fuel, water and some repairs. Haulouts may be available.
Services: From Port Royal take the ferry to Pier 2 in Kingston. It is about 12 miles to town by taxi. All services available in Port Royal or Kingston.

Kingston Harbour is a busy commercial port and boaters should be aware of the possibility of encountering large ships in the channels. It is a good idea to monitor VHF channel 16 when underway here. Port Royal is the former hangout of Captain Morgan, the pirate, and other nefarious characters. The area was subsequently converted to a naval base and features a maritime museum and a castle. The vibrant streets of Kingston are but a ferry ride away.

PELICAN SPIT, N side of Port Royal Harbor, 17 56.6N, 76 50.7W, Fl W 5s, 21ft., 4M, W tripod, Black base.
BUSTAMENTE LIGHT, SW of Gallows Point, 17 56.6N, 76 50.3W, Q G, Black structure, W top.

KINGSTON HARBOUR

CURREYS GATE LIGHT, 17 57.0N, 76 50.9W, Fl W 4s, W triangular topmark on pile structure, Destroyed and replaced temporarily with buoy.

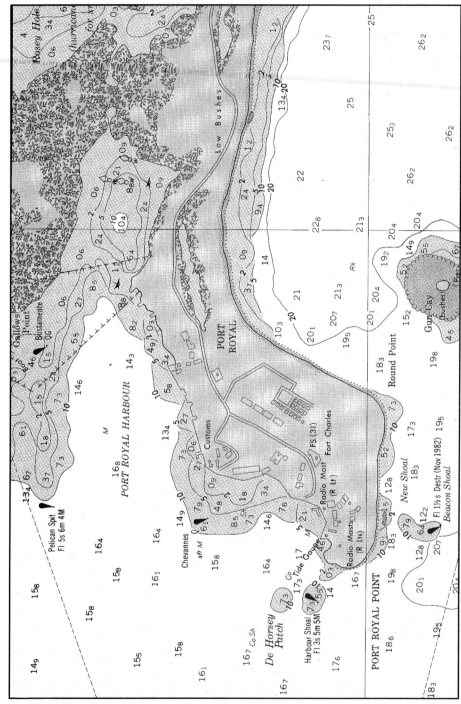

Port Royal, Soundings in Meters

DELBERT SICARD, 17 56.7N, 76 51.5W, Fl R 4s, Beacon, Destroyed 1985.
MORTON BEACON, Fl R 1.5s, 22ft., 6M, Concrete pile, R square topmark, Destroyed 1985.
BLOOMFIELD BEACON, 17 56.8N, 76 50.0W, Q G, In range 249.5° with Lazaretto.
ANGEL BEACON, 17 57.0N, 76 49.6W, Q W, Beacon.
TWO SISTERS LIGHT, Near W extremity of Middle Ground, E side of ship channel, 17 57.5N, 76 50.7W, Fl W 3s, 18ft., 3 pile tripod beacon, W topmark, Reported Fl R 3s (T).
BURIAL GROUND LIGHT, W side of channel, 17 57.5N, 76 50.9W, Fl R 3s, 22ft., R tripod structure on 2 pile base.
SPHINX LIGHT, 17 57.6N, 76 50.6W, Fl W 5s, 18ft., 3 pile tripod beacon, W topmark, Reported destroyed 1988.
AUGUSTA, Fl R 5s, Beacon.
MAMMEE, E side of Ship Channel, Fl W 1.5s, 18 ft., W tripod on black base.
ST. ALBANS, W side of Ship Channel, Q R, 22ft., R square pile beacon, Reported destroyed, Marked by green buoy 38 meters NNE.
EAST HORSESHOE, N extremity of Middle Ground, Fl W 3s, 26 ft., W tower.
HUNTS BAY BEACON, 17 57.9N, 76 49.9W, Fl R 3s, Three pile beacon, R square topmark.
GREENWICH BEACON, 17 58.3N, 76 49.6W, Fl G 3s, 17 ft., Two pile concrete structure, W topmark.
NEWPORT A, Fl G 5s, Two pile structure, W topmark.
NEWPORT B, Fl G 1.5s, Single pile beacon, W topmark.
MIDDLE GROUND LIGHTED BEACON, 17 57.6N, 76 49.5W, Fl W 5s, 17 ft., W triangular topmark on pile structure.
PONDMOUTH, S extremity of bank, W of railway wharf, Fl R 1.5s, 22 ft., R square pile beacon.
PICKERING BEACON, 17 57.0N, 76 48.4W, Fl W 1.5s, Black beacon, W triangular topmark.
TUPPER BEACON, 17 56.9N, 76 47.9W, Fl W 3s, Black beacon, W triangular topmark.
ROYAL JAMAICAN YACHT CLUB MARINA LIGHT, E side of entrance, 17 56.6N, 76 46.5W, Fl G 3s, Pile.
SHELL PIER LIGHTS, On each end of pier, 17 57.8N, 76 44.7W, 2 QR, QR shown from eastern dolphin.
WRECK REEF, 17 49.7N, 76 55.3W, Fl R 5s, 25ft., 6M, R+W banded iron column, Radar reflector.

PORTLAND BIGHT

Approach Buoy, 17 46.0N, 77 01.0W, Q W, Conical shaped, B+W checkered buoy.
BARE BUSH CAY LIGHT, 17 45.2N, 77 02.0W, Fl R 10s, 28ft., 6M, W metal column, R bands, Radar reflector.
PIGEON ISLAND RANGE, (Front Light) Common front, 17 47.5N, 77 04.4W, Fl W 3s, 25ft, 9M, W Iron column, Circular daymark for East Channel, W triangle point up for South Channel. **(Rear Light)** On pumping station 11.3 km 294.7° from common front, 17 50.1N, 77 10.2W, Oc W 5s, 131ft., 16M, W steel structure, Marks East Channel. **(Rear Light)** 878 meters 343.3° from common front, L Fl W 6s, 80ft., 10M, W lattice tower, Daymark W triangle, Point down, Visible 004.25° either side of range line, Marks South Channel.
ROCKY POINT PIER LIGHT, 17 49.1N, 77 08.4W, 2 F R, 1 light shows from each end.
RANGE, (Front Light) 17 53.4N, 77 08.4W, Fl R 3s, 26ft., W conical beacon, A Q W and a Q R are shown in harbor. **(Rear Light)** 677 meters 300° from front, 17 53.5N, 77 08.8W, Q R, 41ft., W conical beacon.
SALT ISLAND LIGHT, N end, 17 50.0N, 77 08.2W, Fl W 5s, 21ft., 7M, W iron column, W disk topmark.
SALT RIVER LIGHT, Near mouth, 17 50.0N, 77 09.7W, Q W, 31ft., 7M, W iron column.
PORTLAND RIDGE LIGHT, Summit, 17 44.4N, 77 09.5W, Fl (2) W 15s, 650ft., 20M, Steel framework tower, Reported Fl (2) W 27s.

SOUTH COAST: PORTLAND BIGHT TO SOUTH NEGRIL POINT

KAISER PIER RANGE, (Front Light) Outer end of pier, 17 51.5N, 77 36.2W, F R, 34ft. **(Rear Light)** 690 meters 347.5° from front, F R, 138ft., Framework tower.
LOVERS LEAP LIGHT, 17 52.0N, 77 39.7W, Fl W 10s, 530 meters, 40M, W round tower, R bands, Reported Fl W 18.5s 1985.
SAVANNA LA MAR LIGHT, N extremity at Boat Stag Reef, 18 11.6N, 78 07.8W, Fl R 5s, 23ft., 9M, Iron column on concrete base.
Southeast Channel Buoy, 18 12.0N, 78 08.0W, F W, Black Buoy, W bands.
SAVANNA LA MAR RANGE, (Front Light) On S side of ruined fort, 18 12.4N, 78 08.1W, F R, 13ft., Occasional. **(Rear Light)** 1006 meters 032.2° from front, F R, 40ft., Occasional.

SOUTH NEGRIL POINT LIGHT, W end of Jamaica, 18 14.7N, 78 21.7W, Fl W R 2s, 100ft., 15M, W tower, R 297° to 305°, W 305° to 161°, R thence to the coast to the north, Partially obscured by trees in the latter sector.

PEDRO BANK LIGHT, Northeast Cay, NW extremity of Cay, 17 03.1N, 77 45.8W, Fl W 5s, 35ft., 11M, Beacon, Square topmark, R + W bands.

NAVASSA ISLAND, U.S.A

NAVASSA ISLAND LIGHT, Summit, 18 23.8N, 75 00.8W, Fl W 10s, 395ft., 9M, Light gray tower.

NAVASSA ISLAND, U.S.A.

18 24N, 75 01W
Navassa Island lies about 30 miles W of the W extremity of Haiti and is reported to be radar conspicuous at a distance of 20 miles. It is about 1.9 miles long and 1.1 miles wide. The island's shores are white cliffs that rise as much as 50 feet directly from the sea. The lighthouse is on the SE side of the island.

The U.S. claimed possession of the island in 1857, and it was formally annexed in January 1916 by presidential proclamation. It is un-inhabited, except for a few goats, and there is no water.

Lulu bay is a small indentation on the SW side of the island, and is the safest place to make a landing. This was the sight of a phosphate mining operation. Small craft can anchor here, but should be careful due to frequent surge. Vessels can also anchor about .4 mile WSW of Lulu Bay with the light bearing about 080° T. The bottom is sand and coral in depths of around 85 feet.

A current with a rate of 1 to 2 knots sets along the SW side of the island, in a NW direction, changing to W at the last of the E-going tidal current.

The island is a reservation administered by the U.S. Coast Guard. Entry and landing are prohibited, except by permit. Contact the Commander, Seventh Coast Guard District, 909 Southeast First Avenue, Miami, FL, 33131.

USE NOTICES TO MARINERS!

Your 1994 almanac is up-to-date at the time of publication, but prudent mariners will always use Notices to Mariners and Local Notices to Mariners to keep abreast of the latest navigational changes. To obtain these notices contact the Coast Guard District Commanders for the areas where you travel. See *Reed's Nautical Companion* for more information, and send in the post-paid reply card to receive your *FREE 1994 Supplement* for this almanac.

HAITI

ENTRY PROCEDURES

The U.S. State Department has issued several warnings to visitors planning a trip to Haiti. The country is the poorest in the Western Hemisphere, and visitors may be targeted by criminals, especially in urban areas. Those involved in legal problems may find the police and other officials not responsive to their problems. Tourists are advised to avoid areas of unrest, especially during demonstrations.

As sanitation may not be up to standards, visitors are advised to drink only bottled water and bottled drinks. Medical facilities are generally substandard. Those seeking medical treatment should be prepared to pay in cash, as medical insurance may not be honored. Tropical diseases are prevalent, including malaria, typhoid and dengue fever. There is a special alert concerning AIDS.

A trade embargo by the United States, and other nations, is in effect. Contact the U.S. Treasury Department at (202) 622-2480 for more information.

The best ports of entry are Port-au-Prince and Cap-Haitién. Cruising permits issued at other ports may, or may not, be honored by Haitian officials. You should be able to obtain a cruising permit, which allows you to visit other ports in the country. You must have a clearance from your last port of call, ship's papers, crew lists and passports. All firearms should be declared, and they may be held for the duration of your stay.

Clearing in at other places has been reported as difficult and dangerous. Ports on the south coast of Haiti are reported to be particularly poor, and boaters are advised not to cruise the area. Jacmel and Les Cayes are ports of entry, but are not recommended due to difficulties encountered by private yachts. Other possible places to enter are Fort Liberté, Port-de-Paix, Gonaives, St. Marc, Petit Goave, Miragoane and Jérémie. Penalties for failing to comply with regulations are reported to be severe.

U.S. citizens over the age of eighteen need proof of identification to enter Haiti. Those under 18 years old must have a passport, which is the preferred means of identification for everyone. Upon departure there is a tax of $20.00 per person.

Boats should not be left unattended if at all possible. During periods when large numbers of "boat people" are leaving, private yachts become possible targets of theft.

For assistance in Haiti contact the American Citizens Service Officer at the U.S. Embassy, Harry Truman Boulevard, P.O. Box 1761, Port-au-Prince, (509) 220 200, 220 354, 220 368 or 220 612. Within the country you need only the last six digits, and from the United States dial 011 first, as this is an international call. For information on Haiti contact the Haitian Consulate, 2311 Massachusetts Avenue, Washington, D.C. 20008, (202) 332-4090.

The official currency is the gourde, which is equal to 5 U.S. dollars. A "Haitian Dollar" is actually 5 gourdes. Carrying large amounts of cash and valuables is not recommended. Banks can cash travelers checks, and some businesses will take U.S. dollars, though it is against the law.

French is the official language, but Haitian Creole is widely spoken.

CAP-HAITIÉN

19 46N, 72 12W

Emergencies: Contact the American Citizens Service Officer at the U.S. Embassy (509) 220 200. Within the country dial 220 200.

Pilotage: The marked channel runs along the shore southward from Point Picolet. South of the main pier is an area where small craft and yachts can tie up. There are shoals east of the marked channel. The Pilot boats monitor VHF channel 16, and may be able to assist.

Port of Entry: Customs is located on the main wharf.

Dockage: There may be some dockage available at the south side of the main docking basin.

Anchorage: Though the anchorage off of town is unsheltered, Baie de L'Acul, 10 miles to the west of Pointe Picolet, is reported to be a good hurricane hole. Also, see Fort Liberté.

Services: There may be fuel and water available, but you may have to carry jugs from ashore. There are groceries and general stores, but no marine supplies.

Somewhere between Cap-Haitién and Passe Caracol, to the east, Columbus put the Santa Maria on the reefs. This area has many unmarked shoals and reefs, and should be transited in good light if possible. A visit to San Souci and the Citadelle, King Christophe's palace and fort, are a must. The Citadelle is an enormous fort; built at the cost of many lives to protect Christophe from an imagined attack by Napoleon's legions.

FORT LIBERTÉ

19 40N, 71 50W

Emergencies: Contact the American Citizens Service Officer at the U.S. Embassy (509) 220 200. Within the country dial 220 200.

Pilotage: The coast between Baie de Fort Liberte entrance and Pointe Jacquezy, about 8 miles W, is low with a sandy beach, fringed with reefs and backed by mangroves. A long reef then extends another 8 miles in a WNW direction. The entrance to the bay is in position 19 43N, 71 50.8W.

Port of Entry: You can clear customs in the town, but there are reports your cruising permit may not be honored in Cap Haitian, or other ports. Boaters are advised to obtain a cruising permit in Cap Haitién before visiting other ports on the north coast.

Dockage: Depths are reported as shallow off the town docks.

Anchorage: This area is a good hurricane hole, with excellent holding ground reported.

Services: Fuel, water and general supplies are available. You will probably have to carry everything in the dinghy out to your anchored boat.

NORTH COAST

ILE DE LA TORTUGA LIGHT, E point, 20 01.0N, 72 38.0W, Fl (2) W 6s, 77ft., 14M, White metal framework tower, Triangular base.
ILE DE LA TORTUGA LIGHT, W point, 20 04.4N, 72 58.2W, V Q W.
PORT-DE-PAIX, W side of pier, 19 57.1N, 72 50.1W, F R, 7M, On second story of building, A F R light is shown from a post on NW corner of pier.
CAP DU MOLE ST. NICOLAS LIGHT, 19 50.0N, 73 25.0W, Oc W 3s, 15M, White tower.

WEST COAST

POINT LAPIERRE LIGHT, N side of entrance to Gonaives Bay, 19 27.0N, 72 46.0W, Fl W 6s, 318ft., 11M, W square stone tower.
POINTE DE ST. MARC LIGHT, 19 02.7N, 72 49.0W, Q (9) W 15s, 96ft., 9M, W framework tower.
LES ARCADINS LIGHT, NW point, 18 48.4N, 72 38.9W, Fl (2) W 5s, 41ft., 9M, Circular W iron tower, Obscured from 358 to 012.

PORT-AU-PRINCE AND APPROACHES

LAFITEAU RANGE, (Front Light) On head of pier, 18 41.7N, 72 21.2W, F R, B+W beacon on structure. **(Rear Light)** 304 meters 044.5 degrees from front, F R, B + W beacon on building.
RANGE, (Front Light) Head of navy yard dock, 18 32.3N, 72 22.7W, F R. **(Rear Light)** Inner end of dock, 120 meters 183 degrees from front, F G.
RANGE, (Front Light) N tower of cathedral, 18 32.9N, 72 20.3W, Oc W 3s, 12M, F R on Port Captains office 0.5 mile WNW. **(Rear Light)** Near SW corner of Fort Alexander, 823 meters 104 degrees from front, Oc W 3s, 12M.
POINTE DU LAMENTIN LIGHT, 18 33.4N, 72 24.5W, Fl W 3s, 106ft., 16M, W circular iron tower, Obscured by trees from 109 to 126.

PORT-AU-PRINCE

18 33N, 72 21W

Emergencies: Contact the American Citizens Service Officer at the U.S. Embassy (509) 220 200. Within the country dial 220 200.

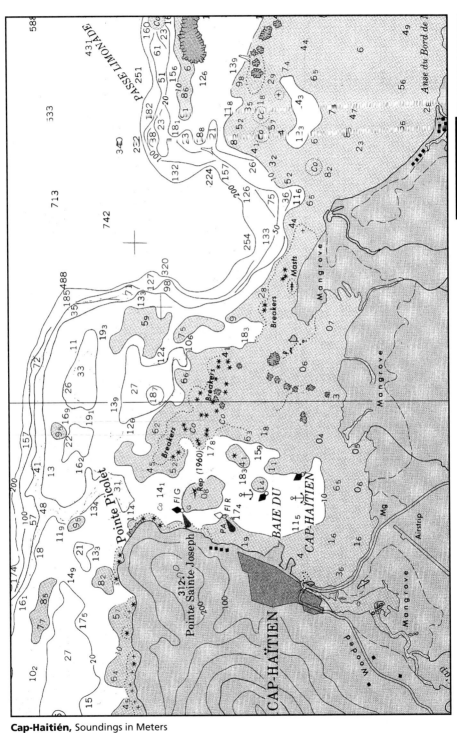

Cap-Haïtién, Soundings in Meters

HAITI

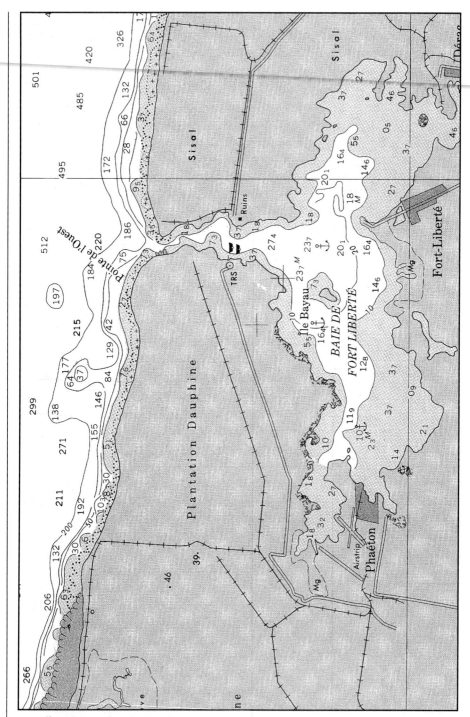

Fort Liberté, Soundings in Meters

192 REED'S NAUTICAL ALMANAC

Chapter 2

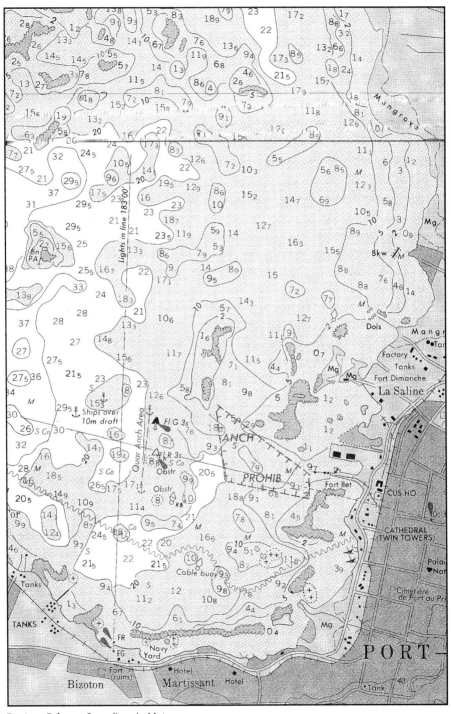

Port-au-Prince, Soundings in Meters

Pilotage: Mariners are warned that numerous fishing vessels may be encountered between Ile de Gonave and the SE head of Baie de Port-au-Prince. The forenoon haze may obscure the inner entrance range at distances greater than 4 miles. The most favorable time to enter port is in the afternoon, or at dawn. Aids to navigation have been reported extinguished, missing or showing incorrect characteristics.

Port of Entry: Tie up at the commercial wharf, or anchor out as directed by port control.

Port Control: Contact them on 2182kHz or on VHF channel 16. The pilot boats can also be reached on these channels, and they are reported to respond to three whistle blasts.

Dockage: There is a small marina near the main wharf in Port-au-Prince. They may be able to furnish dockage. There is a marina at Ibo Beach about 10 miles north of Port-au-Prince. The marina is located on the north side of Ile á Cabrit, also known as Carenage Island. The island is surrounded by reefs, and must be approached with care — call Captain Ron on VHF channel 6 for advice.

Anchorage: Anchoring is possible, but not recommended off of Port-au-Prince. There are good spots to anchor on the north side of Ibo Beach.

Supplies: Groceries, fuel and water is available. There are no marine supplies or repair facilities.

Port-au-Prince is the capital, and principal city of Haiti. Though it has many political and economic problems, there are many fascinating things to see. A visit to some of the galleries, with their distinctive "primitivist" Haitian art, is a must. Visitors should be prepared for lots of haggling and requests for handouts — you may be carrying more cash then an average Haitian's yearly wages!

PORT-AU-PRINCE TO CAP DAME MARIE

POINTE FANTASQUE LIGHT, SE end of Ile de la Gonave, 18 41.8N, 72 49.2W, Q (6) + L Fl W 15s, 50ft., 9M, Skeleton tower, B + W bands.

Baie de Miragoane Lighted Buoy, 18 29.0N, 73 05.0W, Fl W 3s, Red buoy.

Miragoane Approach Buoy, 18 29.0N, 73 04.0W, Fl W 5s, Red buoy w/topmark.

MIRAGOANE LIGHT, 18 27.2N, 73 06.4W, F R, 20ft., Corner of loading chute.

BANC DE ROCHELOIS LIGHT, In Canal de Sud, On Les Pirogues, 18 38.9N, 73 12.0W, Mo (A) W 10s, 30ft., 9M, W framework tower, Black band, Red lantern, Hut on S side.

POINTE OUEST (WEST POINT) LIGHT, W end of Ile de la Gonave, 18 55.6N, 73 18.0W, Fl (4) W 15s, 279ft., 20M, W iron framework tower.

GRANDE CAYEMITE LIGHT, N. Point, 18 38.6N, 73 45.5W, V Q W 3s, 54ft., 12M, W iron tower, Triangular base.

CAP DAME MARIE LIGHT, 18 36.3N, 74 25.7W, Iso W 5s, 123ft., 9M, W square concrete structure surmounted by skeleton framework.

SOUTH COAST

ILE VACHE LIGHT, 18 03.5N, 73 34.0W, Q (6) + L Fl W 15s, W square tower.

CAP JACMEL LIGHT, 18 10.0N, 72 32.0W, F W 6s, 127ft., 9M, W skeleton tower, R lantern.

DOMINICAN REPUBLIC

CAUTION: Our information on aids to navigation comes from official government sources. The latitudes and longitudes of these marks may not correspond to the readings from GPS or LORAN receivers. Some aids have been reported as unreliable, missing, off position or showing incorrect characteristics. No single aid to navigation, or waypoint, should be relied upon as a sole means of fixing your position.

ENTRY PROCEDURES

Arriving yachts must enter the Dominican Republic at an official port of entry. Ports of entry on the north coast are Pepillo Salcedo, in Manzanillo Bay; Luperon in Puerto Blanco; Puerto Plata; and Samaná. On the south coast they are La Romana, San Pedro de Macoris, Santo Domingo and Haina. Boats should fly the Q flag, and await the arrival of the officials. It is illegal to go ashore before you have cleared into the country.

You should have a clearance from your last port of call and the usual identification for all crewmembers and the boat. Firearms should be declared, and will most likely be held until your departure. Each person will have to purchase a tourist card for $10.00 U.S. if they do not have a visa. Tourist cards are good for 60 days, and are renewable.

You should obtain clearance to your next port of call, whether or not it is within the country.

The U.S. State Department is warning tourists of the danger of petty street crime. There is also some danger from Malaria, particularly near the Haitian border. AIDS is also a growing health problem.

For U.S. citizens in need of assistance contact the U.S. Embassy in Santo Domingo at (809) 541-2171, or in Puerto Plata at (809) 586-4204. Information on the Dominican Republic may be obtained from the Consulate of the Dominican Republic, 1715 22nd St. NW, Washington, DC 20008, (202) 332-6280.

The official currency is the peso, and the language spoken is Spanish. Travelers are advised to have at least a rudimentary knowledge of the language.

NORTH COAST: CAYO ARENAS TO PUERTO PLATA

CAYO ARENAS LIGHT, On Bahía de Monte Cristi, 19 52.9N, 71 52.0W, L Fl W 6s, 65ft., 13M, R tower, Black lantern.
PUERTO LIBERATADOR LIGHT, On head of steel pier, 19 43.2N, 71 44.7W, Iso R 20s, 50ft., 10M, W tower, R lantern, Reported removed 1992.

PEPILLO SALCEDO

19 43N, 71 45W
Port of Entry
Pilotage: A light is shown from the end of the pier. A water tank, 3/4 mile SW of the pier, and two oil tanks 600 yards SE of the pier are good landmarks.
Dockage: If the surge is not too bad, you may be able to obtain permission to tie to the pier. It is about 740 ft. long, with depths reported of 34 ft. alongside. The pier is reported to be a good radar target for up to 15 miles. There is reported to be a marina under development in Estero Balsa.
Anchorage: With local knowledge you can bring boats into Estero Balsa, which is reported to be a good hurricane hole.
Services: Fuel should be available by truck. Water and groceries are available in limited quantities.

CABRA ISLAND LIGHT, NW side of Bahía de Monte Cristi, 19 54.1N, 71 40.3W, L Fl W 12s, 110ft., 13M, W pyramidal steel tower.
EL MORRO DE MONTE CRISTI LIGHT, 19 54.2N, 71 39.1W, L Fl W 8s, 860ft., 25M, W metal tower, Square base, Reported destroyed 1992.
PUNTA RUCIA AVIATION LIGHT, 19 52.3N, 71 12.7W, Al Fl W G 10s.

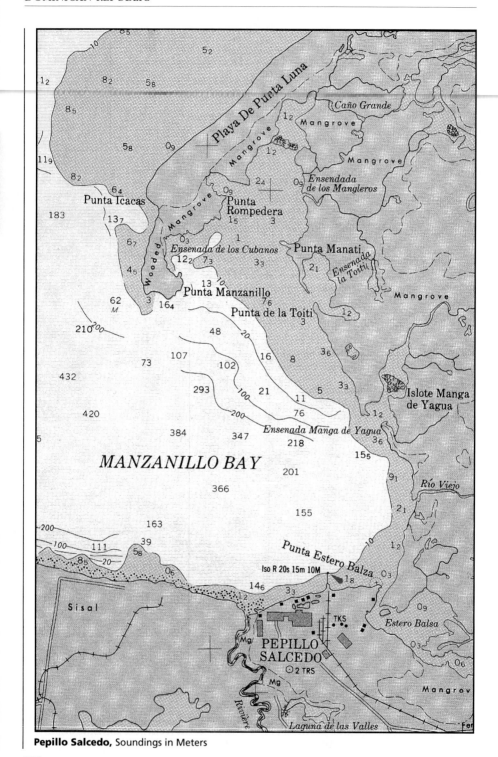

Pepillo Salcedo, Soundings in Meters

LUPERON

19 54N, 70 57W
Port of Entry
Pilotage: The town of Luperon is situated in the southwestern arm of Puerto Blanco. The entrance to Puerto Blanco is about 4 miles ESE of Cabo Isabela, which is the northernmost point of Hispaniola. A coastal reef extends 1,200 yards seaward from the NW side of the cape. Punta Patilla, about 5 miles east of Puerto Blanco, has a light and a reef extending 1 mile W of the point.
Anchorage: Excellent protection and holding ground reported to be excellent.

Services: Fuel and water will have to be jugged to the boat. Other supplies limited.

PUNTA PATILLA LIGHT, 19 54.8N, 70 49.9W, Mo (A) W 10s, 80ft., 12M, Yellow and black concrete tower, Reported extinguished 1992.
PUERTO PLATA LIGHT, On hill near signal station, 19 40.8N, 70 41.5W, L Fl W 6s, 137ft., 18M, Yellow steel skeleton tower, Black lantern, Signal station occasional.
PUERTO PLATA RANGE, (Front Light) 19 48.6N, 70 42.0W, Fl R, W concrete tower, R lantern. **(Rear Light)** 230 meters 218° from front, Fl R, W concrete tower, R lantern.

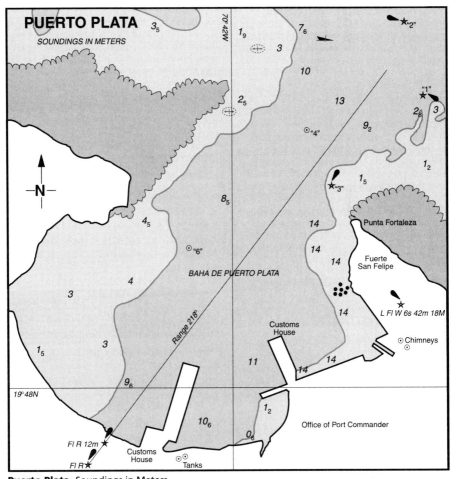

Puerto Plata, Soundings in Meters

PUERTO PLATA AVIATION LIGHT, 19 46.2N, 70 33.5W, Al Fl W G 10s, 10M.

PUERTO PLATA

19 48N, 70 42W
Port of Entry
Pilotage: A set of range lights stand at the head of the bay and when in line bearing 218° T, lead through the entrance channel. The pilot boat's call sign is HIW 8, and they may be contacted on VHF channel 16. The pilot boat is black and flies a blue flag with a white "P".
Dockage: The yacht dock is on the western side of the wharf to the east. Boats usually use a "Mediterranean Moor" here, to avoid damage from the surge.
Anchorage: There is some room to anchor near the yacht dock.
Services: This is the best place to restock along the north coast of the Dominican Republic. Fuel, water and all groceries should be available. You may have to jug your fuel. General repairs may be possible, but marine supplies are not available. There is a U.S. consulate here - call them at (809) 586-4204.

Puerto Plata is a popular stop for those trying to beat into the headwinds down the "Thorny Path" to the islands. The coastline is high (up to 3000 feet), and the water deep close to shore. There are few official ports of entry on this coast, so you should plan your passage carefully. A good selection of charts is necessary to avoid the many reefs - it is wise to keep a good offing until sure of your position. The docking situation is rather rough, and requires careful placement of your anchors and heavy gear. Once you get the boat settled, you'll find an interesting city ashore, with further exploring possibilities inland.

NORTH COAST: PUERTO PLATA TO CABO ENGANO

CABO VIEJO FRANCES LIGHT, Near edge of cliff, 19 40.5N, 69 54.6W, L Fl W 10s, 163ft., 18M, W pyramidal steel tower, Visible 132° to 304°.
PORT SANCHEZ LIGHT, At end of pier, 19 13.6N, 69 36.6W, Fl R 6s, 30ft., 6M, W pyramidal tower, Reported removed 1992.
CABO SAMANA LIGHT, 19 18.5N, 69 08.6W, Fl W 5s, 463ft., 10M, W pyramidal skeleton tower, R lantern.
PUNTA BALANDRA LIGHT, On the bluff, 19 11.2N, 69 13.4W, Fl W 4s, 155ft., 10M,

W tower, Black lantern, Reported extinguished 1992.
CAYO VIGIA LIGHT, 19 11.7N, 69 19.6W, Fl R, 23ft., 8M, W pyramidal metal tower, Reported extinguished 1992.

SAMANA

19 12N, 69 20W
Charted Name: Santa Bárbara de Samaná.
Port of Entry: Tie up to the wharf and await the arrival of the officials. Approach carefully, as we have received unconfirmed reports of depths less than 6 feet in the area.
Dockage: You may be able to tie up to the wharf for refueling, water and loading supplies.
Anchorage: There is reported to be good holding in depths of 12 to 25 feet. Stay clear of the channel to the main wharf.
Services: Fuel, water, ice, water and groceries are available. There is a farmer's market for obtaining fresh fruits and vegetables. There is a telephone station for placing calls. There is a ferry from Samana to Sabana de la Mar.

This is a good spot to plan your passage across the notorious Mona Passage, or to clear in to the Dominican Republic if coming from Puerto Rico. The scenery is reported to be spectacular, and a trip outside of town is recommended. Los Haitises National Park, on the other side of the bay, is reported to be quite interesting.

PUNTA NISIBON LIGHT, 18 58.5N, 68 46.2W, Fl (2) W 10s, 50ft., 12M, W pyramidal tower, R lantern, Reported extinguished 1992.
CABO ENGANO LIGHT, E point of island, 18 36.8N, 68 19.5W, Fl W 5s, 141ft., 11M, R+W steel tower.

SOUTH COAST: CABO ENGANO TO PUERTO DE ANDRES

PUNTA BARRACHANA LIGHT, 18 32.7N, 68 21.3W, Iso R 2s, Tower.
BOCA DE YUMA LIGHT, 18 23.1N, 68 35.5W, Fl R 11s, 30ft., 10M, R pyramidal steel tower, Reported extinguished 1992.
ISLA SAONA LIGHT, E end on Punta Cana, 18 06.6N, 68 34.5W, Fl W 10s, 105ft., 16M, W concrete tower, Reported destroyed 1992.
PUNTA LAGUNA LIGHT, 18 08.3N, 68 44.8W, Fl W 4s, 45ft., 10M, W concrete tower.

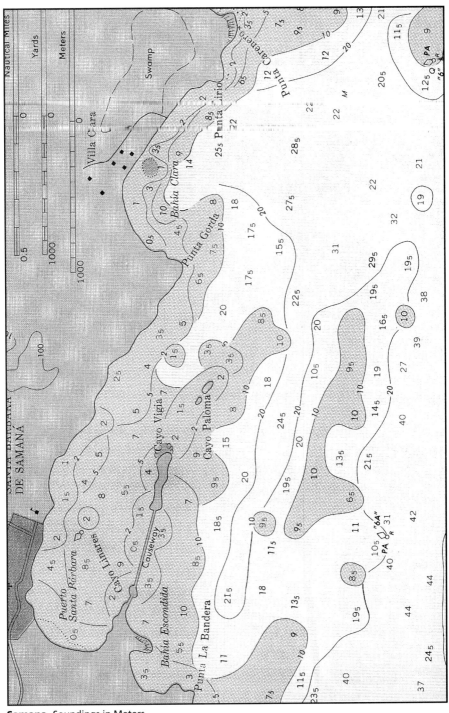

Samana, Soundings in Meters

LA ROMANA LIGHT, E point at entrance to river, 18 24.8N, 68 57.1W, Fl W 6s, 90ft., 15M, Yellow metal tower, R lantern.

LA ROMANA

18 25N, 68 57W
Pilotage: The sugar mill on the west side of the mouth of the Río Dulce is conspicuous day or night. Its lights have been reported to be visible at up to 20 miles, and the smokestacks will be visible during the day. A navigation light is shown on the east side of the entrance to the river. The first large wharf to the west is for the sugar plant. The next wharf north is the government dock. Pilot boats monitor VHF channel 16 - call sign "HIW 9".
Bridge Height: Reported as 28 feet.
Port of Entry: The government wharf is on the west side of the river before the bridge. Depths are reported as 5 to 6 feet alongside.
Dockage: There is a shipyard and a marina near the bridge on the eastern side of the river. There is a yacht club north of the bridge, on he eastern shore.
Anchorage: There is a possible anchorage in the small cove on the eastern side of the river about 200 yards inside the mouth.
Services: The shipyard can haul your boat and has a fuel dock. Most supplies are available.

SAN PEDRO DE MACORIS LIGHT, E point, 18 26.1N, 69 17.7W, L Fl W 10s, 49ft., 12M, W+R tower, Reported extinguished 1992.

SAN PEDRO DE MACORIS

18 27N, 69 19W
Port of Entry
Pilotage: Entry is recommended before 1100, as there is decreased swell in the channel entrance. The pilot boat monitors VHF radio - call sign "HIW 19".
Dockage and Anchorage: This is primarily a commercial harbor, serving the needs of the sugar industry. Possible anchorage, but no dockage reported. Visiting yachtsmen might be better off visiting Club Nautico, in Boca Chica, 17 miles to the west.

ISLA CATALINA LIGHT, Punta Berroa, 18 20.5N, 68 59.3W, L Fl W 8s, 40ft., 10M, Yellow and black concrete tower, Reported destroyed 1992.

PUERTO DE ANDRES

LA CALETA AVIATION LIGHT, 18 25.9N, 69 40.2W, Al Fl W G 5s, 14M, On Aero Radiobeacon tower, On request.

RANGE, (Front Light) 18 26.1N, 69 38.0W, Fl R, 6M, Yellow metal tower, Reported extinguished 1992. **(Rear Light)** 118 meters 300° from front, Fl R, 6M, Yellow metal tower, Reported extinguished 1992.

BOCA CHICA

18 26N, 69 38W
Pilotage: Boca Chica is also called Andrés on the chart. The harbor is about 18 miles east of Santo Domingo at the head of a small bay. The port consists of a basin 500 yards long and 200 yards wide with wharves on its NW and NE sides, and protected on its SW side by a reef which has been reinforced to form a breakwater. The village of Andrés has a sugar factory with a conspicuous chimney, marked by a red obstruction light with the name BOCA CHICA painted prominently on it. Range lights located on the S side of the port lead to the entrance channel when in line bearing 300° T. Vessels can enter only during the day. The port is under the jurisdiction of the Commander of the Port, Santo Domingo.
Dockage: Club Nautico yacht club has dockage, repair facilities and luxurious facilities.
Services: Haulouts, fuel, water, repairs and most supplies available. This is not a port of entry.

PUNTA TORRECILLA LIGHT, 18 27.8N, 69 52.6W, L Fl (2) W 10s, 135ft., 13M, W tower, Black diagonal bands.

PUERTO DE SANTO DOMINGO

Approach Buoy, 18 27.0N, 69 53.0W, Fl R.
ENTRANCE RANGE, (Front Light) E side of harbor, 18 28.3N, 69 52.6W, F R, W concrete tower. **(Rear Light)** 155 meters 047° from front, F R, W concrete tower.

SANTO DOMINGO

18 28N, 69 53W
Pilotage: The port of Santo Domingo lies at the mouth of the Río Ozama. West of the river the coast is low and rocky, with foothills rising 4 or 5 miles inland. East of the river, a coastal plain extends for 15 or 20 miles. Strong onshore winds can cause a rise in sea level considerably above normal in the bay. Currents in the river average 1 1/2 knots, however during the rainy season (May to September) the current is reported to reach rates of 4 1/2 knots. The port may be entered from 0600 to 2100. Harbor authorities may be reached on the VHF radio.

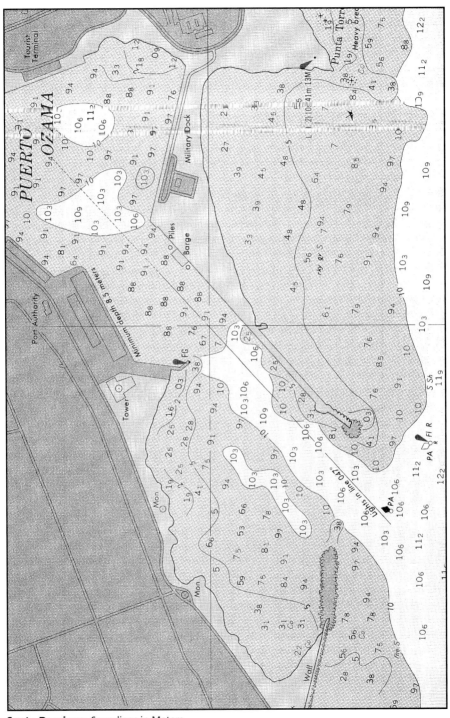

Santo Domingo, Soundings in Meters

Port of Entry
Dockage and Anchorage: This is primarily a commercial harbor. Boaters may be better off at Boca Chica, which is 18 miles by highway to the east.

Santo Domingo is one of the oldest cities in the Caribbean, and one of the largest, with a population of around 2 million. The son of Christopher Columbus, Don Diego, began building a palace and a fort in 1510, and started the first church in the New World, which is the supposed final resting place of the "Navigator" himself.

PUERTO DE HAINA TO CABO ROJO

PUERTO DE HAINA ENTRANCE RANGE, (Front Light) 18 25.4N, 70 01.2W, Fl Y, Yellow framework tower, Bearing is not reliable, Reported extinguished 1989. **(Rear Light)** 150 meters 349.8° from front, Fl Y, Yellow framework tower, Reported extinguished 1989.

PUERTO DE HAINA

18 25N, 70 01W
Pilotage: Two conspicuous chimneys, which show red lights, stand 450 yards NNW of the root of the W breakwater. The lights on the chimneys are visible for about 20 miles. There is an obstruction about 3/4 mile SE of the harbor entrance. The river currents increase to 2 1/2 knots during the rainy season (May to September). The pilot boat may be contacted on VHF channel 16, or on 2182kHz. Their call sign is "HIW 20".
Port of Entry

Dockage and Anchorage: This is primarily a commercial harbor.

PUNTA PALENQUE LIGHT, 18 13.5N, 70 09.0W, Fl W 7s, 45ft., 12M, W pyramidal concrete tower, R lantern.
BOCA CANASTA LIGHT, 18 14.4N, 70 19.6W, F R, Fl R vertical, 22M.
PUNTA SALINAS LIGHT, Bahía de las Calderas, 18 12.3N, 70 31.8W, Fl W 3s, 98ft., 10M, R pyramidal steel tower, Reported extinguished 1992.
PUERTO VIEJO DE AZUA LIGHT, 18 19.5N, 70 49.1W, L Fl (2) W 10s, 75ft., 15M, Black steel tower on concrete base, Reported destroyed 1992.
BARAHONA HARBOR RANGE, (Front Light) 18 12.1N, 71 04.5W, F R, 6M, W pyramidal tower, Occasional. **(Rear Light),** 85 meters 243° from front, F R, W pyramidal tower, Occasional.
ISLA ALTO VELO, Summit, 17 28.3N, 71 38.5W, Fl (2) W 10s, 535ft., 13M, Yellow truncated concrete tower, Black triangular projections on each side, Reported extinguished.
PUNTA BEATA LIGHT, 17 36.1N, 71 25.2W, Fl W 9s, 80ft., 14M, Concrete tower, Extinguished.
LOS FRAILES LIGHT, 17 38.0N, 71 40.9W, Q R, 32ft., 5M, Reported removed 1992.
ANSE JOSEPH LIGHT, Head of jetty, 17 55.2N, 71 39.0W, F R, 8M.
PEDERNALES LIGHT, 18 02.2N, 71 44.9W, L Fl W 12s, 40ft., 11M, W pyramidal steel tower, R lantern.
Cabo Rojo Entrance Buoy, 17 56.0N, 71 40.0W, Fl W 4s, Red buoy, Radar reflector.

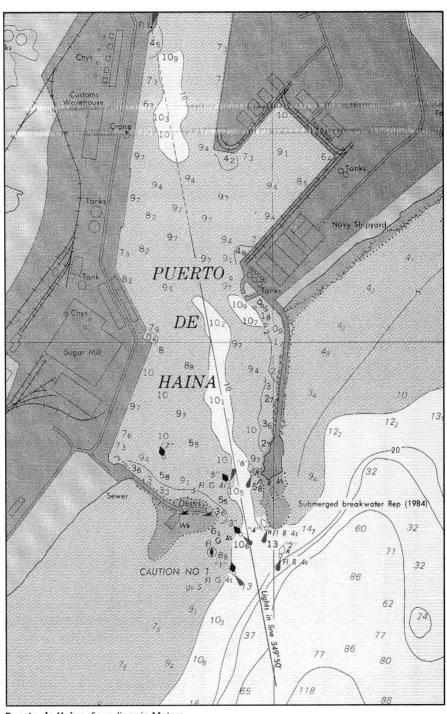

Puerto de Haina, Soundings in Meters

PUERTO RICO

CAUTION: Our information on aids to navigation comes from official government sources. The latitudes and longitudes of these marks may not correspond to the readings from GPS or LORAN receivers. Some aids have been reported as unreliable, missing, off position or showing incorrect characteristics. No single aid to navigation, or waypoint, should be relied upon as a sole means of fixing your position.

ENTRY PROCEDURES

The Commonwealth of Puerto Rico is voluntarily associated with the United States. Many of the laws, rules and regulations are similar to those in effect in the U.S.

Entering Puerto Rico is similar to entering the continental U.S. See the introduction to the Coast Pilot for more information. Ports of entry are Aguadilla, Mayagüez, Guánica, Ponce, Puerto de Jobos, Humacao, Fajardo and San Juan. There is also a customs station in Culebra at the airport. Call (809) 831-3342 or 831-3343 in Mayagüez; (809) 841-3130, 841-3331 or 841-3132 in Ponce; (809) 863-0950, 863-0811 or 863-4075 in Fajardo; (809) 253-4533 or 253-4534 in San Juan; and (809) 742-3531 in Culebra.

Vessels arriving after 1700 hours, or on Sundays and holidays, must report to the San Juan station via telephone. All vessels arriving from the U.S. Virgin Islands must report to customs. Vessels traveling from Puerto Rico to the U.S. Virgin Islands need not clear customs.

The U.S. dollar is the official currency.

Language spoken: Spanish. English is widely spoken as a second language.

WEST COAST

PUNTA BORINQUEN LIGHT, 18 29.8N, 67 08.9W, Fl (2) W 15s, 292 Ft., 24M, Gray cylindrical tower.

AGUADILLA

18 26N, 67 09W
Emergencies: Contact the U.S. Coast Guard on VHF channel 16, or on 2182kHz. A Coast Guard air station is at Borinquen Airport, north of Aguadilla.
Pilotage: There is a 1,208 foot high naval communication tower south of town which is quite prominent. Large vessels load raw sugar and molasses at the pier 1.1 miles north of town, and an Air Force pier is 1.8 miles north of town. The bay is exposed to north and west winds, and experiences a frequent surge.
Port of Entry
Dockage: None for pleasure craft.
Anchorage: Anchor off of town, but be prepared for rough conditions if the wind is in the north.
Services: No yacht facilities. General supplies available ashore.

PUNTA HIGUERO LIGHT, 18 21.7N, 67 16.2W, Oc W 4s, 90 ft., 9M, Gray cylindrical tower.
RINCON SEWER EXTENSION LIGHT, On seaward side of sewer outfall, 18 20.1N, 67 15.4W, Q R, 12 ft., On pile, Private aid.

BAHÍA DE MAYAGÜEZ

Manchas Exteriores Buoy 1, 18 14.6N, 67 12.7W, Green can.
Entrance Lighted Buoy 3, Fl G 4s, 4M, Green.
Entrance Lighted Buoy 4, Fl R 4s, 4M, Red.
RANGE (Front Light), 18 13.3N, 67 09.8W, Q G, 54 ft., KRW on tower on roof of warehouse, Visible 4° each side of rangeline.
(Rear Light) 310 yards, 092° from front light, Oc G 4s, 87 ft., KRW on tower on building, Visible 4° each side of rangeline.
Lighted Buoy 5, Fl G 4s, 4M, Green.
NORTH BREASTING DOLPHIN ONE OBSTRUCTION LIGHT, Fl W 2.5s, 13M, On dolphin, Private aid.
SOUTH BREASTING DOLPHIN SIX OBSTRUCTION LIGHT, Fl W 2.5s, 13M, On dolphin, Private aid.
Lighted Buoy 6, Fl R 4s, 3M, Red.

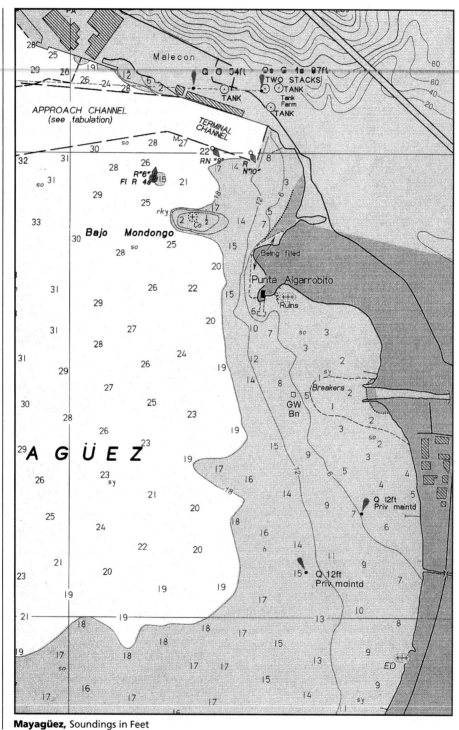

Mayagüez, Soundings in Feet

Buoy 8, Red nun.
Buoy 10, Marks southeast end of 18 foot spot, Red nun.
Mayagüez Harbor Daybeacon, 18 12.6N, 67 09.5W, NG on tower on house.
NORTH SEWER EXTENSION LIGHT, Marks edge of sewer outfall, QW, 12 ft., On pile, Private aid.
SOUTH SEWER EXTENSION LIGHT, Marks end of sewer outfall, 18 12.2N, 67 09.4W, Q W, 12M, On pile, Private aid.

MAYAGÜEZ
18 12N, 67 09W
Emergencies: Contact the U.S. Coast Guard on VHF channel 16, or on 2182kHz.
Pilotage: At Punta Guanajibo, 2 miles south of Mayagüez, is a 165 foot high flat-topped ridge with a prominent reform school on top. Cerro Anterior is a 433 foot-high saddle-shaped hill 1.5 miles inshore of the city. The city hall clock tower and a church are conspicuous above the other buildings. Several red and white radio towers are visible along the south shore of the bay.
Port of Entry: Call (809) 831-3342 or 831-3343. Boats should tie to the commercial wharf north of town to clear customs and immigration.
Dockage: None for pleasure craft in town. Club Deportivo marina is located about 6.5 miles south of Mayagüez. Contact them at (809) 851-8880.
Anchorage: Pleasure boats anchor south of the charted private lights off of town.
Services: There are no pleasure boat facilities in Mayagüez. The large city has all general supplies, good transportation, banking and communications.

Mayagüez is primarily commercial in orientation, but makes a convenient first port of call if arriving from the west. The city is one of Puerto Rico's major ports and commercial centers.

CANAL DE GUANAJIBO
Punta Arenas Buoy 6, At northwest edge of shoal point, Red nun.
Punta Ostiones Buoy 4, At southwest edge of shoal spot off point, Red nun.
Punta Melones Shoal Buoy 1, Green can.

PUERTO REAL
18 04N, 67 12W
Emergencies: Contact the U.S. Coast Guard on VHF channel 16, or on 2182kHz.
Pilotage: The harbor is located about two miles north of the Bahía de Boquerón. It is a circular basin 0.7 miles in diameter used by local fishing vessels and small pleasure craft. Depths in the basin are 6 to 15 feet with shoal water toward the eastern end. The town of Puerto Real is on the north shore of the basin.
Dockage: There are a couple of small marinas with dockage and most services.
Anchorage: A well protected spot.
Services: Water, fuel, some marine supplies and groceries are available. There are haulout facilities for fishing boats, which you may be able to use. Take a publico (small bus) to Cabo Rojo for more extensive shopping.

BAHÍA DE BOQUERÓN
Bajo Enmedio South Lighted Buoy 1, At south end of shoal, 18 00.8N, 67 12.5W, Fl G 4s, 3M, Green.

BOQUERÓN
18 01N, 67 11W
Emergencies: Contact the U.S. Coast Guard on VHF channel 16, or on 2182kHz.
Pilotage: For boats coming from the west the primary obstruction is Bajo Enmedio, stretching for about a mile across the entrance to the bay. It is marked by a buoy at its south end.
Dockage: The Club Nautico de Boquerón may have some space at the docks near the north end of the waterfront. Call them at (809) 851-1336.
Anchorage: Anchor south of the yacht club docks. Hurricane protection among the mangroves is available in the Cano Boquerón a mile south of town. Depths are reported to be 10 feet in the channel.
Services: Fuel, water, general supplies, and some marine supplies are available.

MONA PASSAGE
ISLA DE MONA LIGHT, 18 16.6N, 67 54.5W, Fl W 5s, 323 ft., 14M, On steel tower, Light may be obscured by land masses when viewed from approximate bearings 140° and 270°.

Chapter 2

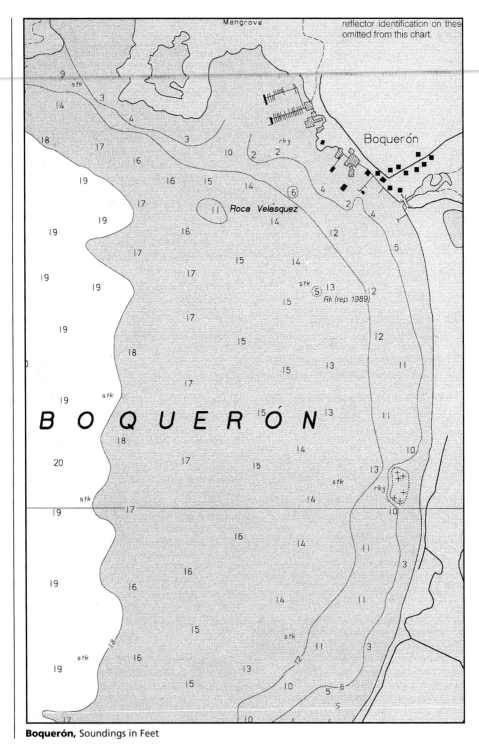

Boquerón, Soundings in Feet

Arrecife Tourmaline Lighted Buoy 8,
18 09.7N, 67 20.7W, Fl R 6s, 4M, Red.
Canal de la Mona East Shoal Lighted Buoy 6, 18 05.3N, 67 25.4W, Fl R 6s, 4M, Red.
Canal de la Mona East Shoal Lighted Buoy 4, 18 00.4N, 67 23.1W, Fl R 6s, 4M, Red.
Canal de la Mona East Shoal Lighted Buoy 2, Fl R 6s, 4M, Red.
CABO ROJO LIGHT, 17 56.0N, 67 11.6W, Fl W 20s, 121ft., 20M, Gray hexagonal tower attached to flat roofed dwelling, Emergency light when main light is extinguished shows Fl W 6s, 9M.

ISLA MAGUEYES

Buoy 1, Black can, Private aid.
Buoy 2, Red nun, Private aid.
Buoy 4, Red nun, Private aid.
Buoy 6, Red nun, Private aid.
Buoy 7, Black can, Private aid.

BAHÍA DE GUÁNICA

Entrance Lighted Buoy 2, 17 55.2N, 66 54.6W, Fl R 4s, 4M, Red.
Buoy 3, Green can.
GUÁNICA LIGHT, 17 57.1N, 66 54.3W, Fl W 6s, 132 ft., 7M, White skeleton tower, Obscured by Punta Brea to seacoast traffic westward to 044°.
Lighted Buoy 4, On west end of shoal, 17 56.2N, 66 54.4W, Fl R 4s, 3M, Red.
Buoy 5, Marks 27 foot shoal, Green can.
RANGE (Front Light), 17 57.9N, 66 54.6W, Q R, 27 ft., 4M, KRW on skeleton tower, Visible 4° each side of rangeline. **(Rear Light),** 560 yards, 354.5° from front light, Iso R 6s, 48 ft., 5M, KRW on skeleton tower, Visible 4° each side of rangeline.
Lighted Buoy 6, Fl R 6s, 3M, Red.
Buoy 7, Green can.
Buoy 8, Red nun.
Buoy 9, 17 57.6N, 66 54.6W, Green can.
Buoy 10, At south end of shoal, Red nun.
Buoy 11, Green can.
Buoy 12, Red nun.
SUGAR PIER LIGHTS (2), 17 57.9N, 66 55.5W, F R, 16 ft., On pier, Private aids.

GUÁNICA

17 58N, 66 56W
Emergencies: Contact the U.S. Coast Guard on VHF channel 16, or on 2182kHz.
Pilotage: A range of 354° 30' leads up the main dredged channel to the town.

Port of Entry: The Captain of the Port is located near Playa de Guánica.
Anchorage: Anchor outside of the dredged ship channels in well protected waters. Depths become quite shallow in the north end of the bay off Playa de Guánica.
Services: General supplies available ashore.

BAHÍA DE GUAYANILLA

CAYO MARIA LANGA LIGHT, 17 58.0N, 66 45.2W, Fl W 2.5s, 42 ft., 8M, NR on skeleton tower.
ENTRANCE RANGE (Front Light), 17 58.6N, 66 45.8W, Q Y, 16 ft., KRW on dolphin, Visible all around, Higher intensity on rangeline.
(Rear Light), 1,000 yards, 358° from front light, Iso Y 6s, 36 ft., KRW on tower on piles, Visible 15° each side of rangeline.
Lighted Buoy 1, Fl G 2.5s, 3M, Green.
Lighted Buoy 2, 17 58.0N, 66 45.8W, Fl R 4s, 3M, Green.
Lighted Buoy 3, Fl G 4s, 4M, Green.
PUNTA GOTAY SOUTH MOORING DOLPHIN LIGHT, 17 58.8N, 66 45.8W, F R, 15 ft., On square concrete deck, Private aid.
PUNTA GOTAY NORTH MOORING DOLPHIN LIGHT, 17 58.9N, 66 45.8W, F R, 15 ft., On square concrete deck, Private aid.
Lighted Buoy 5, Fl G 6s, 4M, Green.
Lighted Buoy 6, Marks end of shoal, Fl R 4s, 4M, Red.
Buoy 7, Green can.
Buoy 8, Marks end of shoal, Red nun.
Buoy 9, Green can.
COMMONWEALTH OIL REFINING COMPANY SOUTH LOADING DOCK LIGHT, 17 59.6N, 66 46.0W, F R, 12 ft., Private aid.
COMMONWEALTH OIL REFINING COMPANY NORTH LOADING DOCK LIGHTS (3), 17 59.8N, 66 45.9W, F R, 19 ft., On pile, Private aids.

PPG INDUSTRIES

RANGE (Front Light), 18 00.3N, 66 46.0W, Q W, 20 ft., Visible 4° each side of rangeline, Private aid. **(Rear Light),** 158 yards, 014° from front light, Oc W 4s, 40 ft., Visible 2° each side of rangeline, Private aid.
Lighted Buoy 1, 17 57.8N, 66 46.2W, Fl G 2.5s, Black, Private aid.
Lighted Buoy 2, Fl R 2.5s, Red, Private aid.
Lighted Buoy 3, Fl G 2.5s, Black, Private aid.
Lighted Buoy 4, Fl R 2.5s, Red, Private aid.

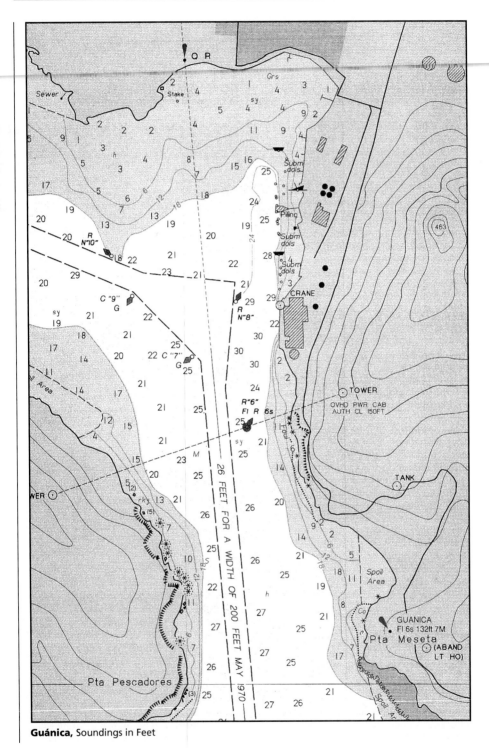

Guánica, Soundings in Feet

PIER LIGHT, F R, 13 ft., On dolphin, Private aid.

TEXACO WEST MOORING DOLPHIN ONE LIGHT, 18 00.0N, 66 45.9W, Fl R 6s, 15 ft., On dolphin, Private aid.

TEXACO LOADING DOCK LIGHT, F R, 30 ft., On pile, Private aid.

TEXACO EAST MOORING DOLPHIN FOUR LIGHT, 18 00.0N, 66 45.8W, Fl R 6s, 15 ft. On dolphin, Private aid.

BAHÍA DE TALLABOA

Lighted Buoy 1, 17 57.7N, 66 44.3W, Fl G 4s, 4M, Green.

Buoy 2, Red nun.

Lighted Buoy 4, Fl R 4s, 3M, Red.

Lighted Buoy 5, 17 58.2N, 66 44.3W, Fl G 2.5s, 4M, Green.

Lighted Buoy 6, Q R, 2M, Red.

LIGHT 7A, 17 58.8N, 66 44.2W, Fl G 2.5s, 15 ft., SG on pile, Private aid.

Buoy 7, Green can.

LOADING PLATFORM LIGHTS (4), 17 59.0N, 66 44.5W, F W, Platform, Private aids.

Union Carbide Canal Buoy 1, Black can, Private aid.

Union Carbide Canal Buoy 2, Red nun, Private aid.

Buoy 8, 17 58.7N, 66 43.7W, Red nun, Private aid.

Lighted Buoy 10, 17 59.0N, 66 43.8W, Fl R 2.5s, Red, Private aid.

PIER LIGHT, 17 59.2N, 66 43.9W, F R, 20 ft., On pier, Private aid.

Buoy 12, 17 59.3N, 66 43.8W, Red nun, Private aid.

Side Channel Lighted Buoy 2, 17 58.7N, 66 44.7W, Q R, Red, Private aid.

Side Channel Lighted Buoy 3, Fl G 6s, Black, Private aid.

Side Channel Lighted Buoy 4, Fl R 6s, Red, Private aid.

UCCI Cayo Río Buoy 2, 17 58.5N, 66 45.4W, Red nun, Private aid.

UCCI Cayo Río Buoy 4, Red nun, Private aid.

BAHÍA DE PONCE AND APPROACHES

ISLA DE CARDONA LIGHT, 17 57.4N, 66 38.1W, Fl W 4s, 46 ft., 8M, White cylindrical tower on center of front of flat-roofed dwelling.

Lighted Buoy 1, Fl G 4s, 4M, Green.

RANGE (Front Light), 17 58.8N, 66 37.2W, Q G, 49 ft., KRW on pyramidal skeleton tower, Visible 15° each side of rangeline. **(Rear Light),** 305 yards, 015° from front light, Iso G 6s, 75 ft., KRW on roof of building, Visible 4° each side of rangeline.

Lighted Buoy 3, Fl G 4s, 3M, Green.

Buoy 4, On southwest side of shoal, Red nun.

MUELLE MUNICIPAL PIER LIGHTS (2), 17 58.0N, 66 37.3W, F W, 10ft., On pier, Private aids.

PONCE HARBOR PIER 4 OBSTRUCTION LIGHT, 17 58.1N, 66 37.3W, F W, 5ft., Square white case, Light is not visible 360°, Light may be obscured by vessels moored at pier, Private aid.

TRAILER WHARF OBSTRUCTION LIGHT, 17 58.4N, 66 37.1W, F W, 10 ft., On steel pile, Private aid.

Lighted Buoy 5, Fl G 4s, 4M, Green.

SEWER EXTENSION LIGHT, Marks end of sewer outfall, 17 58.9N, 66 37.8W, F W, 12 ft., White rectangular framework on piles, Private aid.

ISLA CAJA DE MUERTOS LIGHT, 17 53.6N, 66 31.3W, Fl W 30s, 297 ft., 12M, Gray cylindrical tower on center of flat-roofed dwelling.

RÍO BUCANA EAST JETTY LIGHT, 17 58.0N, 66 36.0W, Fl W 5s, 19 ft., On a tripod, Private aid.

RÍO BUCANA JETTY LIGHT, 17 58.1N, 66 36.0W, Fl W 5s, 19 ft., On a tripod, Private aid.

PONCE

17 59N, 66 37W

Emergencies: Contact the U.S. Coast Guard on VHF channel 16, or on 2182kHz.

Pilotage: Prominent from offshore are the stacks of the cement factory west of Ponce, the large microwave tower in Ponce and the hotel on the hill back of Ponce. The charted radio towers can be seen from well offshore. The eastern entrance channel is marked by a lighted range running 015° T, which takes you right up to the waterfront.

Port of Entry: You can tie up at the yacht club on Isla de Gata. Call (809) 841-3130, 841-3331 or 841-3132 in Ponce.

Dockage: The Ponce Yacht and Fishing Club is located on Isla de Gata. You can contact them on VHF channel 16 or at (809) 842-9003, and they have all facilities. Anchored boats can use the club for a small fee.

Anchorage: There is a designated anchorage shown on the chartlet. Many cruisers prefer to anchor off of the yacht club, where they can dinghy in to use the club facilities.

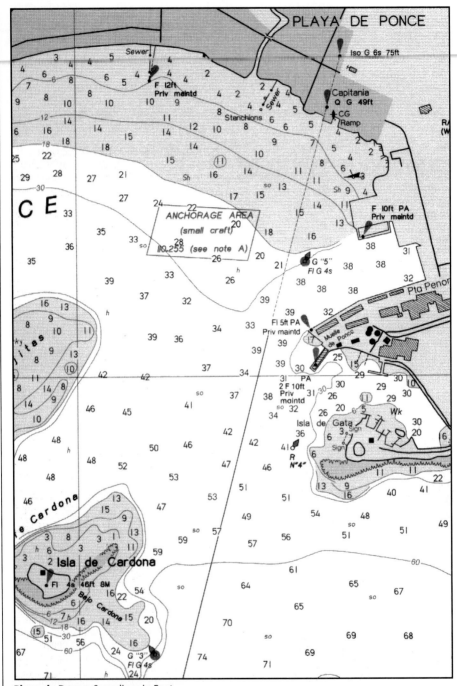

Playa de Ponce, Soundings in Feet

Services: All facilities are available. Haulouts up to 50 tons can be handled, and repairs are readily available. Fuel, water and ice are available at the yacht club, and good grocery stores are in town. There is good transportation to any point on the island.

Ponce is the second largest city in Puerto Rico, and one of its most important ports. There are art museums, historic buildings, shops and restaurants, and excellent transportation facilities. You might want to leave your boat here while taking a visit to San Juan, or use this as a crew transfer point. This is your best bet for marine supplies and repairs on the south coast.

BAHÍA DE JOBOS AND APPROACHES

CAYOS DE RATONES LIGHT, 17 56.0N, 66 17.0W, Fl W 2.5s, 48 ft., 5M, NR on triangular skeleton tower.

Buoy 2, Red nun.

SALINAS
17 58N, 66 18W
Emergencies: Contact the U.S. Coast Guard on VHF channel 16, or on 2182kHz.
Pilotage: Enter the small bay east of Cayo Mata from the south.
Dockage: The Marina de Salinas may be able to offer some space. Contact them at (809) 824-6647.
Anchorage: Good protection, and good holding reported. Anchor anywhere off of Playa de Salinas and dinghy in to the marina.
Services: Fuel, water, ice, canvas work and general supplies are available. Take the publico (local bus) to the town of Salinas one mile away, or to Ponce for major shopping.

This is a favorite anchorage on the south coast. Cruisers stop here for rest, repairs and protection from the weather.

Cayo Puerca Buoy 3, Green can.
Punta Colchones Cut Buoy 5, Green can.
Punta Colchones Cut Buoy 6, Red nun.
DISCHARGE PIPE EAST OBSTRUCTION LIGHT, On rock mound, 17 56.0N, 66 13.7W, Q R, 12 ft., On piles, Private aid.
DISCHARGE PIPE WEST OBSTRUCTION LIGHT, On rock mound, Q R, 12 ft., On piles, Private aid.

AGUIRRE POWER PLANT

Lighted Buoy 1, 17 56.6N, 66 13.5W, Q G, Black, Private aid.
Lighted Buoy 2, Q R, Red, Private aid.
Lighted Buoy 3, Fl G 4s, Black, Private aid.
Lighted Buoy 4, Fl R 4s, Red, Private aid.
Lighted Buoy 5, Fl G 4s, Black, Private aid.
Lighted Buoy 6, Fl R 4s, Red, Private aid.

PUERTO DE JOBOS
17 57N, 66 12W
Emergencies: Contact the U.S. Coast Guard on VHF channel 16, or on 2182kHz.
Pilotage: The main buoyed entrance leads to the commercial wharves at Central Aguirre. The stacks of the sugar plant show up well from offshore. The southern channel through the reefs is known as Boca del Inferno.. There is 11 feet of water over the bar, which breaks in heavy weather.
Port of Entry
Dockage: There may be some dockage at a small yacht club in the indentation about 0.7 miles east of Punta Rodeo.
Anchorage: Good anchorage throughout the bay. Avoid the commercial area of Central Aguirre.

LAS MAREAS TO PUNTA TUNA

Lighted Buoy LM, 17 54.1N, 66 10.6W, Mo (A) W, Red and white stripes with red spherical topmark, Private aid.
RANGE (Front Light), 17 56.4N, 66 09.4W, Q W, 86 ft., KRW on tower, Visible on rangeline only, Private aid. **(Rear Light),** 635 yards, 017.7° from front light, Iso W 6s, 124 ft., KRW on tower, Visible on rangeline only, Private aid.
Lighted Buoy 1, 17 55.6N, 66 09.9W, Fl G 4s, Black, Private aid.
Lighted Buoy 2, Fl R 2.5s, Red, Private aid.
LIGHT 3, Fl G 4s, 25 ft., SG on pile, Private aid.
LIGHT 4, Fl R 2.5s, 50 ft., TR on tower, Private aid.
ARTICULATED LIGHT 5, Q G, On mast, Private aid.
LIGHT 6, Q R, 25 ft., TR on pile, Private aid.
PIER LIGHTS (3), F R, 10 ft., On dolphin, Private aids.
PUNTA TUNA LIGHT, 17 59.4N, 65 53.1W, Fl (2) W 30s, 111 ft., 16M, White octagonal tower on square flat-roofed dwelling.

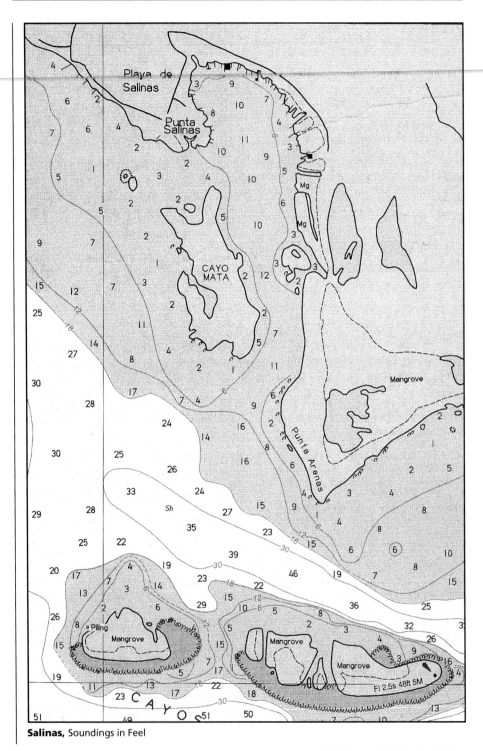

Salinas, Soundings in Feet

Chapter 2

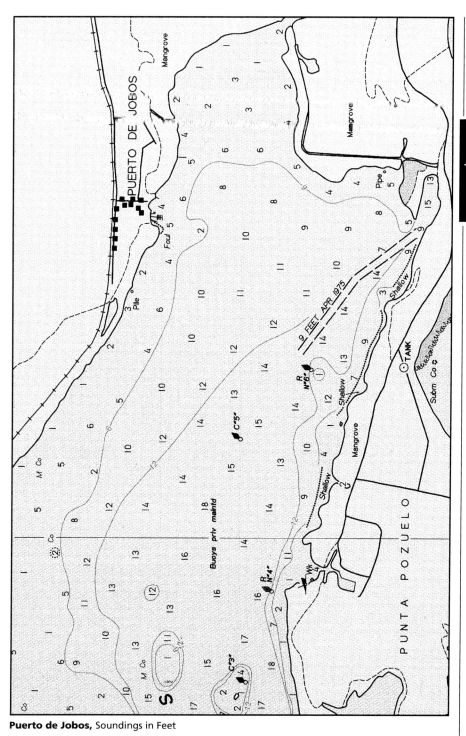

Puerto de Jobos, Soundings in Feet

PUERTO YABUCOA

CHANNEL RANGE (Front Light), 18 03.4N, 65 50.2W, Q W, 75 ft., KRW on tower, Visible 1° each side of rangeline, Private aid. **(Rear Light),** 910 yards, 296.8° from front light, Iso W 6s, 140 ft., KRW on tower, Visible 1° each side of rangeline, Private aid.
Channel Lighted Buoy 2, 18 02.7N, 65 48.6W, Fl R 4s, Red, Private aid.
Channel Lighted Buoy 3, Q G, Black, Private aid.
CHANNEL LIGHT 5, Fl G 4s, 15 ft., SG on dolphin, Ra. ref., Private aid.
CHANNEL LIGHT 6, Fl R 4s, 15 ft., TR on dolphin, Ra. ref., Private aid.
CHANNEL LIGHT 7, Fl G 4s, 15 ft., SG on pile, Ra. ref., Private aid.
CHANNEL LIGHT 8, Fl R 4s, 15 ft., TR on pile, Ra. ref., Private aid.
CHANNEL BREAKWATER LIGHT, 18 03.3N, 65 49.7W, F R, 51 ft., Ra. ref., Private aid.
CHANNEL LIGHT 9, Fl G 4s, 15 ft., SG on pile, Ra. ref., Private aid.
CHANNEL LIGHT 10, Fl R 4s, 15 ft., TR on pile, Ra. ref., Private aid.

PALMAS DEL MAR

LIGHT 1, Fl G 6s, 12 ft., SG on pile, Private aid.
LIGHT 2, Q W, 16 ft., TR on pile, Red from 203.5° to 295°, Private aid.
LIGHT 3, Q G, 6 ft., SG on pile, Private aid.
LIGHT 4, Q W, 6 ft., TR on pile, Private aid.

PALMAS DEL MAR

18 05N, 65 48W
Emergencies: Contact the U.S. Coast Guard on VHF channel 16, or on 2182kHz.
Pilotage: The harbor entrance is marked by private lights. The marina is on the south side of the harbor. It is reported that strong easterly winds cause breaking seas in the harbor entrance and surge inside the harbor.
Dockage: Available at the marina with all facilities. Contact them on VHF channel 16.
Anchorage: Anchor in the small basin north of the marina.
Services: All services available, including haulouts.

This artificial harbor is formed by a group of luxurious resorts clustered around a small dredged basin.

RADAS ROOSEVELT PASSAGE

Lighted Buoy 9, Fl G 4s, 1M, Green.
Lighted Buoy 8, Fl R 4s, 3M, Red.
Lighted Buoy 7, Fl G 4s, 3M, Green.
Lighted Buoy 6, Fl R 2.5s, 2M, Red.
Lighted Buoy 5, Fl G 6s, 4M, Green.
Lighted Buoy 4, Q R, 3M, Red.
Lighted Buoy 3, Q G, 3M, Green.
Lighted Buoy 2, Fl R 4s, 3M, Red.
Lighted Buoy 1, On west end of shoal, 18 13.6N, 65 28.2W, Fl G 6s, 4M, Green.
Sonde de Vieques Obstruction Lighted Buoy LAE, Marks end of sewer outfall, IQ W, Black and red bands, Private aid.

ISLA DE VIEQUES

VIEQUES NAVAL PIER LIGHTS (2), 18 08.9N, 65 30.9W, F R, 15 ft., On pier, Maintained by U.S. Navy.
VIEQUES NAVAL BREAKWATER LIGHT, 18 09.1N, 65 30.9W, Q R, 10 ft., On pile, Maintained by U.S. Navy.
PUNTA MULAS LIGHT, 18 09.3N, 65 26.6W, Oc R 4s, 68 ft., 7M, White octagonal tower on top of flat-roofed dwelling.
PUNTA ESTE LIGHT, 18 08.2N, 65 16.1W, Fl W 6s, 43 ft., 7M, NR on tower.
PUNTA CONEJO LIGHT, 18 06.6N, 65 22.6W, Fl W 6s, 58 ft., 7M, NR on tower.
PUERTO FERRO LIGHT, 18 05.9N, 65 25.4W, Fl W 4s, 56 ft., 7M, NR on skeleton tower.
Puerto Real Shoal Buoy 1, On west end of shoal, 18 05.0N, 65 29.0W, Green can.
Puerto Real Shoal Buoy 2, On west end of shoal, Red nun.

PASAJE DE VIEQUES

RANGE (Front Light), 18 12.7N, 65 36.0W, Q W, 70 ft., KWR on skeleton tower, Visible all around, Higher intensity on rangeline. **(Rear Light),** 1,715 yards, 025.4° from front light, Iso W 6s, 142 ft., KWR on tower, Visible 4° each side of rangeline.
NAVY PIER LIGHTS (2), West of Punta Puerca, 18 13.6N, 65 36.1W, F R, Maintained by U.S. Navy.
Lighted Buoy 2, Fl R 2.5s, 4M, Red.
Lighted Buoy 3, Fl G 2.5s, 4M, Green.
Buoy 4, Red nun.
Lighted Buoy 6, Fl R 2.5s, 3M, Red.

Chapter 2

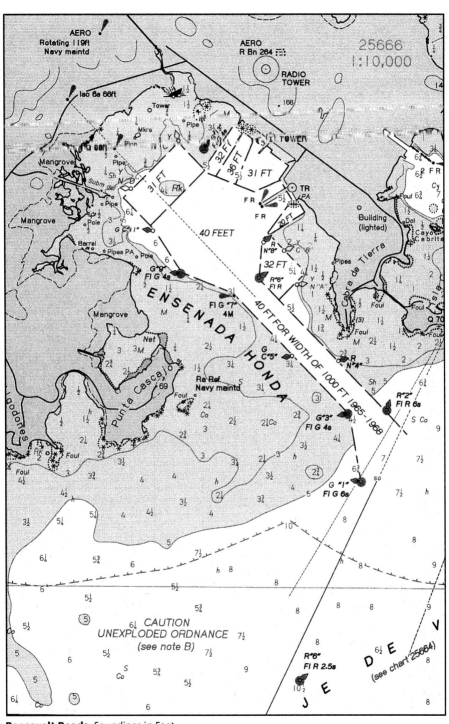

Roosevelt Roads, Soundings in Feet

ROOSEVELT ROADS HARBOR

Channel Lighted Buoy 1, 18 11.8N, 65 36.6W, Fl G 6s, 4M, Green.

Channel Lighted Buoy 2, Fl R 6s, 3M, Red.

ENTRANCE CHANNEL RANGE (Front Light), 18 13.7N, 65 38.1W, Q W, 36 ft., KWR on skeleton tower on piles, Visible 2° each side of rangeline. **(Rear Light),** 800 yards, 315° from front light, Iso W 6s, 66 ft., KWR on tower, Visible 2° each side of rangeline.

Channel Lighted Buoy 3, Fl G 4s, 3M, Green.

Channel Buoy 4, Red nun.

Channel Buoy 5, Green can.

Channel Lighted Buoy 6, Fl R 2.5s, 2M, Red.

CHANNEL LIGHT 7, Fl G 4s, 16 ft., 4M, SG on dolphin.

ROOSEVELT ROADS PIER 3 LIGHTS (2), F R, 10 ft., On pier, Maintained by U.S. Navy.

Turning Basin Buoy 8, Red nun.

Anchorage Buoy A, Yellow nun.

Anchorage Buoy B, Yellow can.

Turning Basin Lighted Buoy 9, Fl G 4s, 3M, Green.

Turning Basin Buoy 11, Green can.

Turning Basin Lighted Buoy 13, Fl G 4s, 4M, Green.

Anchorage Buoy C, Yellow nun.

Anchorage Buoy D, Yellow nun.

ROOSEVELT ROADS

18 13N, 65 37W

Emergencies: Contact the U.S. Coast Guard on VHF channel 16, or on 2182kHz.

Pilotage: Note the charted Restricted Area extending about 1 mile to 1 1/2 miles offshore from the naval base. No vessel shall enter or remain within the restricted areas at any time unless on official business. Fishing is not permitted in the restricted areas. Naval personnel may obtain permission to use the small craft facilities of the base. You should contact the Roosevelt Roads Marina by calling the base at (809) 865-2000. Obtain permission, and make reservations before approaching the area.

Port Control: Contact them on VHF channel 12 before entering the naval base.

Dockage: The Roosevelt Roads marina monitors VHF channel 16. They may be contacted via the base telephone number (809) 865-2000. There is also a Roosevelt Roads Yacht Club.

Services: Fuel, water and general supplies are available.

The Roosevelt Roads United States Naval Station is a convenient and safe port for those in the military, retired military personnel and those able to obtain a sponsor on the base. This would be a good place to leave your boat for an extended trip back to the U.S.

ROOSEVELT ROADS TO FAJARDO

Cabeza de Perro Lighted Buoy 7, 18 13.6N, 65 33.7W, Fl G 6s, 4M, Green.

BAJOS CHINCHORRO DEL SUR LIGHT, 18 14.1N, 65 31.2W, Fl W 4s, 25 ft., 8M, NR on tower on piles.

CABEZA DE PERRO LIGHT, 18 15.0N, 65 34.6W, Fl W 6s, 80 ft., 8M, Red sector 6M, Red from 021° to 031° and 066° to 161°, Obscured from 031° to 066°.

Roca Lavandera del Oeste Buoy 5, Green can.

Punta Figueras Buoy 4, On shoal, Red nun, Buoy edge of red sector of Cabeza de Perro Light.

Bajos Largo Buoy 3, Green can.

Isla de Ramos Buoy 2, Red nun.

Cayo Largo Lighted Buoy 1A, Midway of westerly shoal, 18 18.9N, 65 35.3W, Fl G 4s, 3M, Green.

Cayo Largo Buoy 1, North side of shoals, Green can.

Isla Palominos Lighted Buoy 2, 18 21.1N, 65 33.6W, Fl R 4s, 3M, Red.

FAJARDO

Fifteen-foot Spot Lighted Buoy 1, Fl G 2.5s, 3M, Green.

Bajo Onaway Buoy 3, Green can.

PUERTO CHICO MARINA BREAKWATER LIGHT, 18 20.8N, 65 38.0W, F R, 13 ft., On pile, Private aid.

SEA LOVERS PIER A EAST LIGHT, 18 20.8N, 65 38.1W, F R, 10 ft., On pier pile, Private aid.

SEA LOVERS PIER A WEST LIGHT, F R, 10 ft., On pier pile, Private aid.

SEA LOVERS PIER B EAST LIGHT, F R, 10 ft., On pier pile, Private aid.

SEA LOVERS PIER B WEST LIGHT, F R, 10 ft., On pier pile, Private aid.

FAJARDO HARBOR PIER OBSTRUCTION LIGHTS (2), 18 20.1N, 65 37.8W, F R, 10 ft., On pile, Private aids.

ISLETA MARINA, FAJARDO

PIER A LIGHT, 18 20.4N, 65 37.3W, Q W, 12 ft., On pile, Private aid.

PIER B LIGHT, F G, 12 ft., On pile, Private aid.

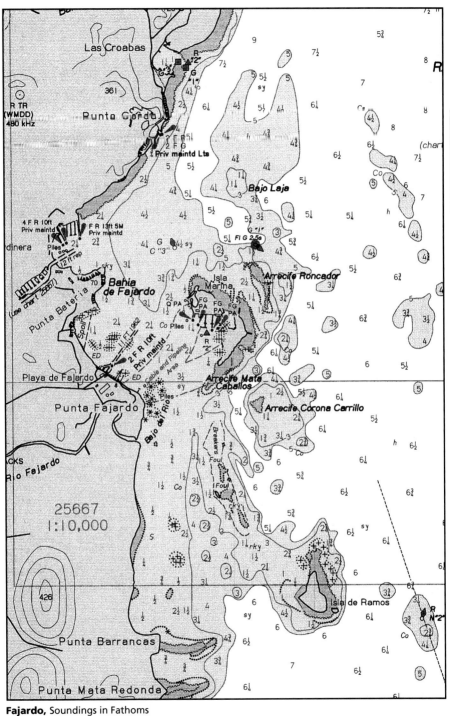

Fajardo, Soundings in Fathoms

PIER C LIGHT, F G, 12 ft., On pile, Private aid.
PIER D LIGHT, F G, 12 ft., On pile, Private aid.
Daybeacon 2, TR on pile, Private aid.

FAJARDO

18 20N, 65 38W

Emergencies: Contact the U.S. Coast Guard on VHF channel 16, or on 2182kHz.

Pilotage: The easiest entrance is from the north, via the unmarked ferry channel. There are some fixed red lights, privately maintained, on the ferry dock. The controlling depth is 11 feet to the public wharf. Depths at the dock are 12 feet at the outer end, and 8 feet alongside. The southern approach has more hazards and less marks, but should have about 9 to 11 feet of water.

Port of Entry: There is a customs office on the waterfront near the ferry dock. Contact them at (809) 863-0950, 863-0811 or 863-4075. Boaters arriving from the Virgin Islands should clear here, if they haven't done so in Culebra. If you tie up to the public wharf be prepared to move at a moments notice upon the arrival of a ferry.

Dockage: This area has a profusion of repair yards, marinas and boating services. At Las Croabas, about 1 1/2 miles south of Cabo San Juan, is Marina Lanais. It is entered via a marked channel through the reef. At the north end of Playa Sardinera is the Puerto Chico marina for smaller, local boats. Villa Marina is located in a small dredged basin behind a breakwater just north of the public wharf. They can be contacted at (809) 863-5131, or on VHF channels 16 and 68. Isleta Marina is on the island across from town. Puerto del Rey marina is behind a protective breakwater in Bahía Demajagua, about 3 miles south of the main waterfront. Call them at (809) 860-1000, or on VHF channel 71.

Anchorage: There is good anchorage south of the island with the marina. Note the charted cable and pipeline areas between the island and Fajardo.

Services: All services available. This is one of the best places in Puerto Rico to obtain supplies, and accomplish repairs on your boat.

LAS CROABAS

Daybeacon 1, 18 21.8N, 65 37.3W, SG on pile.
Daybeacon 2, TR on pile.
Daybeacon 3, SG on pile.

FAJARDO TO CULEBRA

Isla Palominos Lighted Buoy 2, 18 21.1N, 65 33.6W, Fl R 4s, 3M, Red.
Bajo Blake South Buoy 3, 18 20.5N, 65 31.9W, Green can.
CAYO LOBITO LIGHT, 18 20.1N, 65 23.5W, Fl W 6s, 110 ft., 8M, NR on skeleton tower.

CULEBRA

PUNTA MELONES LIGHT, 18 18.1N, 65 18.7W, Fl W 6s, 45 ft., 6M, NR on tower.
PUNTA DEL SOLDADO LIGHT, 18 16.7N, 65 17.2W, Fl W 2.5s, 65 ft., 5M, NR on tower.
Bajo Amarillo Lighted Buoy 2, 18 16.7N, 65 16.5W, Fl R 4s, 3M, Red.
Canal del Este Buoy 2, 18 16.6N, 65 15.1W, Red nun.
Cabezas Crespas Lighted Buoy 3, 18 16.8N, 65 15.4W, Fl G 4s, 4M, Green.
Cabezas Puercas Buoy 4, Red nun.
ISLA DE CULEBRA OUTER RANGE (Front Daybeacon), 18 17.7N, 65 17.0W, KRW on skeleton tower. **(Rear Daybeacon),** 750 yards, 296° from front daybeacon, KRW on skeleton tower.
Bajo Grouper Buoy 5, Green can.
Bajo Camaron Buoy 6, Red nun.
Bajo Snapper Lighted Buoy 8, 18 17.4N, 65 16.3W, Q R, 3M, Red.
ISLA DE CULEBRA INNER RANGE (Front Daybeacon), On Punta Cemeterio, 18 18.6N, 65 17.3W, KRW on skeleton tower. **(Rear Daybeacon),** 1,200 yards, 323° from front daybeacon, KRW on skeleton tower.
Punta Colorada Lighted Buoy 9, Fl G 4s, 3M, Green.
Punta Caranero Buoy 10, Red nun.
Punta Caranero Buoy 12, Red nun.
Punta Caranero Buoy 14, Red nun.

CULEBRA

18 18N, 65 18W

Emergencies: Contact the U.S. Coast Guard on VHF channel 16, or on 2182kHz.

Pilotage: The area charted as Bahía de Sardinas is the location of the town's waterfront and ferry dock. You can anchor in the bay and dinghy in to the ferry wharf or the small creek just south of the wharf. This area is prone to a surge, or roll, under certain conditions. Most boaters prefer to enter Ensenada Honda, and anchor west or southwest of Cayo Pirata. A large bay on the eastern side of Ensenada Honda has good hurricane anchorage among the mangroves at its head.

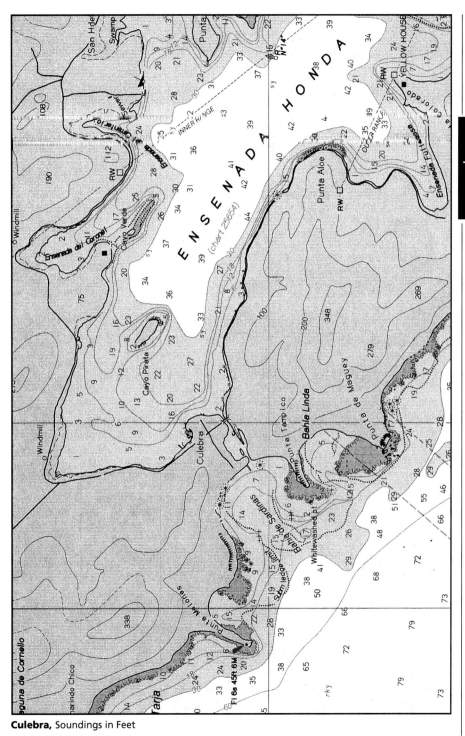

Culebra, Soundings in Feet

Chapter 2

Customs Station: The office in town has closed, and boaters should call the airport office at (809) 742-3531. Hours are 9:00AM to Noon and 1:00PM to 4:00PM, Monday through Saturday. All boats coming from the U.S. Virgin Islands must clear customs when entering Puerto Rico.

Dockage: You may be able to tie temporarily to the ferry wharf to get fuel and supplies. There is no dockage for large boats in Ensenada Honda.

Anchorage: Excellent anchorages abound in Culebra. The most popular spot is east of town in Ensenada Honda. Dinghy ashore near the head of the small creek that passes through town. Anchorage can also be found in any of the bays along the shores of Ensenada Honda. A cool spot is west of the reef blocking the entrance to Ensenada Honda.

Services: There is fuel and water (via jugs), a hardware store, a canvas shop, a dive shop, several small restaurants, groceries, a post office, a bank and telephones. Supplies can be limited. A ferry runs daily to Fajardo for those in need of something special.

Culebra is only 20 miles west of St. Thomas, yet it is in another cruising world. The island is only quietly interested in tourists, but offers marvelous gunkholing and peaceful anchorages.

CULEBRA TO ST. THOMAS

ISLA CULEBRITA LIGHT, 18 18.8N, 65 13.7W, Fl W 10s, 305 ft., 13M, Stone colored cylindrical tower with red trim on flat-roofed dwelling, Obscured by Cayo Norte from 125° to 142°.

CULEBRITA

18 19N, 65 14W

Emergencies: Contact the U.S. Coast Guard on VHF channel 16, or on 2182kHz.

Pilotage: A powerful light marks the summit of Isla Culebrita. When approaching from the northeast, large seas may become steep breakers on the bar. Be prepared to leave if a norther threatens.

Anchorage: This is a lovely anchorage, off of a crescent shaped sandy beach. The island is all park land preserved in its natural state. There are no facilities here.

Bajos Grampus South Lighted Buoy 2, Southerly side of shoals, 18 14.3N, 65 12.5W, Fl R 4s, 3M, Red.

Sail Rock Lighted Buoy 1, 18 17.1N, 65 06.5W, Fl G 6s, 4M, Green.

SAVANA ISLAND LIGHT, 18 20.4N, 65 05.0W, Fl W 4s, 300 ft., 7M, White tower.

CABO SAN JUAN TO SAN JUAN HARBOR

CABO SAN JUAN LIGHT, 18 22.9N, 65 37.1W, Fl W 15s, 260 ft., 26M, Cylindrical tower on front of white rectangular dwelling, Black band around base.

LAS CUCARACHAS LIGHT, 18 24.0N, 65 36.7W, Fl W 6s, 38 ft., 7M, NG on skeleton tower.

Punta Picua Lighted Buoy WR2, Northeast of 2 1/2 fathom shoal, 18 26.6N, 65 45.6W, Fl R 4s, 4M, Red.

Lighted Buoy BC, 18 28.1N, 66 00.6W, Mo (A) W, 5M, Red and white stripes with red spherical topmark, Use only with local knowledge.

CABALLO CHANNEL RANGE (Front Lights), 2 lights, 18 26.9N, 65 59.9W, F R, 20 ft., Red and orange diamond daymark, Private aids. **(Rear Lights),** 2 lights, 29 yards, 146.5° from front light, F R, 25 ft., Red and orange round daymark, Private aids.

PLATFORM LIGHT, 18 27.1N, 65 59.2W, F W, 12 ft., On pile, Maintained by Federal Aviation Administration.

SAN JUAN HARBOR

PUERTO SAN JUAN LIGHT, 18 28.4N, 66 07.4W, Fl (3) W 40s, 181 ft., 24M, Buff colored square tower, Octagonal base, On Morro Castle, Obscured from 281° to 061°.

CABRAS LIGHT, 18 28.5N, 66 08.4W, Iso W 6s, 44 ft., 9M, NR on tower.

RANGE (Front Light), 18 27.3N, 66 07.8W, Q G, 23 ft., KRW on skeleton tower on piles, Visible 2° each side of rangeline. **(Rear Light),** 1,335 yards, 187.7° from front light, Oc G 4s, 56 ft., KRW on skeleton tower, Visible 2° each side of rangeline.

Lighted Buoy 1, 18 28.3N, 66 07.6W, Fl G 4s, 4M, Green.

Lighted Buoy 2, Fl R 6s, 3M, Red.

Lighted Buoy 3, 18 28.2N, 66 07.6W, Q G, 3M, Green.

Lighted Buoy 4, Fl R 4s, 3M, Red.

Lighted Buoy 5, 18 28.1N, 66 07.6W, Fl G 2.5s, 3M, Green.

Lighted Buoy 6, Fl R 2.5s, 2M, Red.

Buoy 6A, Red nun.

Lighted Buoy 7, Fl G 4s, 4M, Green.

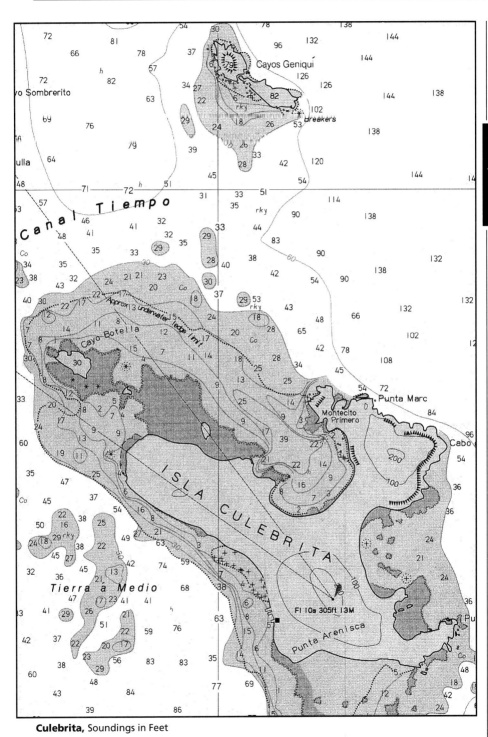

Culebrita, Soundings in Feet

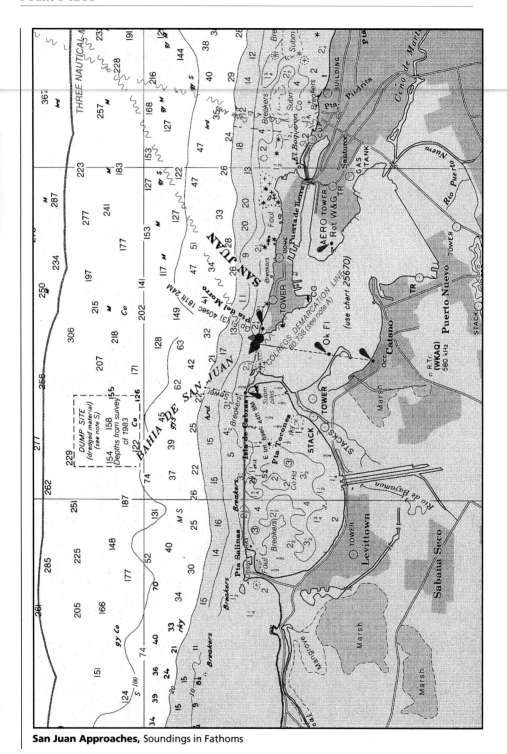

San Juan Approaches, Soundings in Fathoms

Chapter 2

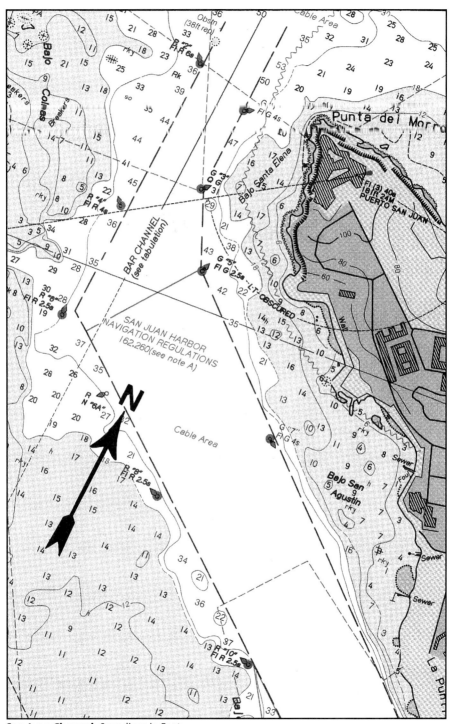

San Juan Channel, Soundings in Feet

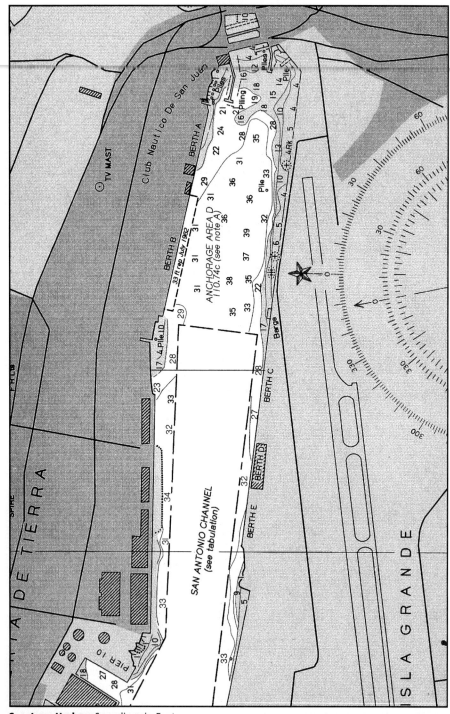

San Juan Harbor, Soundings in Feet

Lighted Buoy 8, Fl R 2.5s, 4M, Red.
Lighted Buoy 10, Fl R 2.5s, 4M, Red.
Lighted Buoy 11, Q G, 2M, Green.
Lighted Buoy 13, Fl G 4s, 3M, Green.
San Juan Harbor Anchorage F Buoy A,
18 27.0N, 66 07.0W, Yellow can.
Lighted Buoy 14, Q R, 2M, Red.
TMT OUTER DOLPHIN OBSTRUCTION LIGHT,
18 27.1N, 66 06.2W, Q W, 12 ft., On mooring
dolphin, Private aid.
**TMT MIDDLE DOLPHIN OBSTRUCTION
LIGHT,** Q W, 12 ft., On mooring dolphin,
Private aid.
San Juan Harbor Anchorage E Buoy A,
Yellow can.
San Juan Harbor Anchorage E Buoy B,
18 27.0N, 66 06.1W, Yellow nun.

SAN ANTONIO CHANNEL
LA PUNTILLA FINGER PIER B LIGHT, 18 27.6N,
66 06.9W, F G, 10 ft., On pier.
LA PUNTILLA FINGER PIER A LIGHT, F G,
10 ft., On pier.
PIER 1 LIGHTS (3), 18 27.6N, 66 06.8W, F G,
10 ft., On dolphins, Private aids.
PIER 3 LIGHTS (3), F G, 13 ft., On dolphins,
Private aids.

SAN JUAN
18 28N, 66 07W
Emergencies: Contact the U.S. Coast Guard
on VHF channel 16, or on 2182kHz.
Pilotage: The harbor entrance is deep and
well marked. When approaching from offshore, be careful to stay well off the land until
you are sure of your position, as there are
many hazardous reefs along the coast. It can
be hard to spot the charted landmarks from
offshore, but you may be lucky enough to see
a cruise ship entering or leaving. Steep seas
can pile up on the bar at the entrance to the
harbor.
Puerto Rico Ports Authority: The signal station at Fort San Cristobal is manned 24 hours a
day, and boaters should contact the authorities on VHF channel 16 (switching to channel
14) for permission to enter or leave the harbor.
Port of Entry: Call (809) 253-4533 or 253-4534
to reach customs and immigration. You can
dock at one of the marinas at the eastern end
of the San Antonio Channel. Vessels arriving
from the U.S. mainland, with no other intermediate stops, do not have to clear in. Vessels
arriving from the U.S. Virgin Islands, and other
foreign ports, must clear customs.
Dockage: There are two marinas at the eastern end of the San Antonio Channel. The Club

Nautico de San Juan is on the north side. Contact them at (809) 722-0177. Across the channel is the San Juan Bay Marina offering both
slips and some moorings. Both marinas monitor VHF channel 16. These marinas tend to
have limited room for transients.
Anchorage: There is some room to anchor
west of the marinas, among the moorings.
Small white buoys with orange markings limit
the anchoring area. The bottom is poor holding, and the area swept by strong currents.
You can dinghy in to the marina to the south.
Services: All services available. Haulouts can
be done and there are facilities for major
repairs of engines, electronics and hulls. There
are several good chandlers, and nearby grocery
stores. This is a good place for major restocking
of the ship's larder.

San Juan was founded in 1421, and is a delight
for historically minded boaters. The approach
to the harbor takes you dramatically below
the ramparts of El Morro castle, and past the
walls of Old San Juan. Though limited in its
cruising amenities, this is a fascinating port of
call.

ARMY TERMINAL CHANNEL
Lighted Buoy A, Fl (2+1) G 6s, 3M, Green and
red bands.
Lighted Buoy 2, Fl R 4s, 3M, Red.
Lighted Buoy 3, Fl R 4s, 3M, Red.
Buoy 4, Red nun.
RANGE (Front Light), 18 25.7N, 66 06.5W,
Q R, 28 ft., KRW on tower, Visible 2° each side
of rangeline. **(Rear Light),** 380 yards, 175.6°
from front light, Oc R 4s, 43 ft., KRW on
tower, Visible 2° each side of rangeline.
Lighted Buoy 5, Fl G 4s, 3M, Green.
Lighted Buoy 6, Fl R 4s, 3M, Red.
Lighted Buoy 7, Fl G 4s, 3M, Green.
Turning Basin Lighted Buoy 9, Fl G 2.5s,
3M, Green.

PUERTO NUEVO CHANNEL
Lighted Buoy 1, Fl G 4s, 4M, Green.
RANGE (Front Light), 18 26.5N, 66 05.2W,
Q G, 45 ft., KRW on tower on piles, Visible 2°
each side of rangeline. **(Rear Light),** 610
yards, 058.4° from front light, Oc G 4s, 60 ft.,
KRW on tower, Visible 2° each side of range-
line.
LIGHT 3, Fl G 4s, 16 ft., 4M, SG on dolphin.
LIGHT 5, Q G, 16 ft., 2M, SG on dolphin.
Turning Basin Buoy 7, Green can.
Turning Basin Lighted Buoy 9, Q G, 3M,
Green.

TURNING BASIN LIGHT 10, Fl R 4s, 19 ft., 2M, TR on dolphin.

GRAVING DOCK CHANNEL
RANGE (Front Light). 18 26.5N, 66 05.2W, Q R, 25 ft., KRW on piles, Visible all around, Higher Intensity on rangeline. **(Rear Light),** 535 yards, 111.1° from front light, Oc R 4s, 60 ft., KRW on tower, Visible 2° each side of rangeline.
Buoy 1, Green can.
Lighted Buoy 2, Fl R 4s, 3M, Red.
Lighted Buoy 3, Fl G 4s, 4M, Green.
Buoy 5, Green can.
Turning Basin Buoy 6, Red nun.

SAN JUAN TO PUNTA BORINQUEN

ARECIBO LIGHT, 18 29.0N, 66 41.9W, Fl W 5s, 120 ft., 14M, White hexagonal tower attached to square flat-roofed dwelling.

Puerto Arecibo Buoy 1, Green can.
Puerto Arecibo Buoy 2, Red nun.

ARECIBO
18 29N, 66 42W
Emergencies: Contact the U.S. Coast Guard on VHF channel 16, or on 2182kHz.
Pilotage: This is one of the few places to obtain shelter along the north coast of Puerto Rico, other than San Juan. It is located about 33 miles west of San Juan, and is marked by a powerful light. A 600 foot wharf projects from Punta Morrillos, providing some protection. Depths range from 5 to 20 feet around the wharf.
Anchorage: Anchor south of the breakwater.

PUNTA BORINQUEN LIGHT, 18 29.8N, 67 08.9W, Fl (2) W 15s, 292 ft., 24M, Gray cylindrical tower.

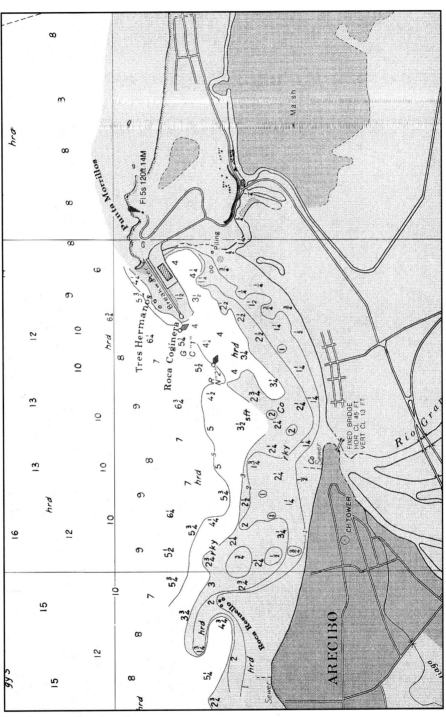

Arecibo, Soundings in Fathoms

SAN JUAN, PUERTO RICO

HIGH & LOW WATER 1994 18°28'N 66°01'W

ATLANTIC STANDARD TIME (GMT -4H)

JANUARY

Day	Time ft	Time ft	Time ft	Time ft
1 Sa	0431 -0.2	1127 1.6	1759 0.2	2330 1.0
16 Su	0539 0.1	1206 1.2	1838 0.0	
2 Su	0526 -0.0	1205 1.5	1838 0.0	
17 M	0043 0.9	0628 0.2	1238 1.1	1914 -0.0
3 M	0036 1.1	0627 0.1	1246 1.4	1922 -0.1
18 Tu	0139 1.0	0723 0.3	1312 1.0	1952 -0.1
4 Tu	0147 1.2	0736 0.3	1330 1.2	2009 -0.2
19 W	0238 1.0	0825 0.6	1349 0.9	2032 -0.1
5 W	0259 1.3	0854 0.4	1418 1.1	2101 -0.3
20 Th	0339 1.1	0936 0.5	1429 0.8	2116 -0.1
6 Th	0411 1.5	1017 0.5	1512 1.0	2156 -0.4
21 F	0438 1.2	1050 0.5	1515 0.7	2201 -0.2
7 F	0518 1.6	1137 0.5	1612 0.9	2253 -0.5
22 Sa	0533 1.2	1200 0.5	1605 0.7	2248 -0.2
8 Sa	0621 1.7	1249 0.4	1715 0.9	2350 -0.5
23 Su	0624 1.3	1258 0.4	1658 0.7	2336 -0.3
9 Su	0718 1.8	1350 0.4	1817 0.8	
24 M	0710 1.4	1345 0.4	1752 0.7	
10 M	0046 -0.5	0810 1.8	1443 0.3	1918 0.8
25 Tu	0023 -0.4	0751 1.5	1424 0.3	1845 0.7
11 Tu	0139 -0.5	0858 1.7	1530 0.3	2015 0.9
26 W	0110 -0.4	0830 1.5	1458 0.3	1938 0.8
12 W	0230 -0.4	0942 1.7	1612 0.2	2110 0.9
27 Th	0157 -0.4	0907 1.5	1531 0.2	2032 0.8
13 Th	0319 -0.3	1022 1.6	1651 0.2	2203 0.8
28 F	0246 -0.4	0944 1.5	1605 0.1	2127 0.8
14 F	0406 -0.2	1059 1.5	1728 0.1	2256 0.9
29 Sa	0336 -0.4	1020 1.4	1640 0.1	2224 1.0
15 Sa	0452 -0.1	1133 1.4	1803 0.1	2349 0.9
30 Su	0429 -0.2	1057 1.3	1719 -0.2	2324 1.1
31 M	0526 -0.1	1136 1.2	1801 -0.3	

FEBRUARY

Day	Time ft	Time ft	Time ft	Time ft
1 Tu	0027 1.2	0628 0.0	1218 1.1	1847 -0.4
16 W	0055 1.0	0656 0.3	1223 0.8	1851 -0.1
2 W	0134 1.3	0737 0.2	1304 1.0	1939 -0.5
17 Th	0148 1.0	0752 0.3	1258 0.8	1933 -0.2
3 Th	0244 1.4	0852 0.3	1355 0.9	2035 -0.5
18 F	0246 1.1	0857 0.4	1338 0.7	2020 -0.2
4 F	0355 1.4	1013 0.3	1455 0.8	2136 -0.5
19 Sa	0347 1.1	1007 0.4	1427 0.7	2112 -0.2
5 Sa	0504 1.5	1130 0.3	1601 0.7	2239 -0.5
20 Su	0446 1.2	1114 0.4	1525 0.6	2207 -0.3
6 Su	0607 1.5	1237 0.3	1710 0.7	2341 -0.5
21 M	0540 1.2	1209 0.4	1629 0.7	2303 -0.3
7 M	0704 1.5	1333 0.2	1816 0.8	
22 Tu	0628 1.3	1253 0.3	1732 0.7	2359 -0.4
8 Tu	0040 -0.5	0754 1.5	1420 0.2	1917 0.8
23 W	0712 1.3	1331 0.2	1832 0.8	
9 W	0134 -0.4	0839 1.5	1501 0.1	2012 0.8
24 Th	0053 -0.4	0752 1.4	1406 0.1	1930 0.9
10 Th	0225 -0.4	0918 1.4	1537 0.1	2103 0.9
25 F	0146 -0.4	0830 1.4	1442 -0.0	2026 1.1
11 F	0311 -0.3	0953 1.3	1610 0.0	2150 0.9
26 Sa	0240 -0.3	0908 1.3	1519 -0.2	2121 1.2
12 Sa	0356 -0.2	1025 1.2	1641 -0.0	2236 1.0
27 Su	0334 -0.3	0947 1.3	1558 -0.3	2217 1.3
13 Su	0438 -0.1	1055 1.1	1711 -0.1	2321 1.0
28 M	0429 -0.2	1026 1.2	1640 -0.4	2314 1.4
14 M	0521 0.1	1123 1.0	1742 -0.1	
15 Tu	0006 1.0	0606 0.2	1152 0.9	1815 -0.1

MARCH

Day	Time ft	Time ft	Time ft	Time ft
1 Tu	0527 -0.1	1109 1.1	1726 -0.5	
16 W	0552 0.2	1109 0.8	1719 -0.1	
2 W	0014 1.5	0629 0.1	1154 1.0	1816 -0.5
17 Th	0017 1.2	0637 0.3	1139 0.8	1755 -0.1
3 Th	0118 1.5	0736 0.2	1245 0.9	1912 -0.5
18 F	0105 1.2	0729 0.4	1214 0.7	1838 -0.1
4 F	0225 1.5	0848 0.3	1343 0.8	2013 -0.4
19 Sa	0158 1.2	0826 0.4	1258 0.7	1928 -0.1
5 Sa	0334 1.4	1003 0.3	1450 0.8	2119 -0.4
20 Su	0255 1.2	0927 0.4	1353 0.7	2025 -0.1
6 Su	0442 1.4	1113 0.3	1603 0.8	2228 -0.4
21 M	0353 1.2	1025 0.4	1501 0.7	2129 -0.1
7 M	0545 1.4	1213 0.2	1715 0.8	2334 -0.4
22 Tu	0448 1.3	1114 0.3	1614 0.8	2234 -0.1
8 Tu	0640 1.4	1303 0.2	1820 0.9	
23 W	0538 1.3	1157 0.2	1722 0.9	2338 -0.2
9 W	0035 -0.3	0728 1.3	1345 0.1	1918 0.9
24 Th	0623 1.3	1237 0.1	1825 1.1	
10 Th	0131 -0.2	0810 1.2	1421 0.1	2008 1.0
25 F	0040 -0.2	0706 1.3	1316 -0.0	1923 1.3
11 F	0220 -0.2	0846 1.2	1453 0.0	2053 1.1
26 Sa	0138 -0.2	0748 1.2	1356 -0.2	2018 1.4
12 Sa	0306 -0.1	0918 1.1	1522 -0.0	2135 1.1
27 Su	0236 -0.1	0829 1.2	1437 -0.3	2113 1.6
13 Su	0348 0.0	0947 1.0	1550 -0.0	2214 1.2
28 M	0332 0.1	0912 1.1	1521 -0.4	2207 1.7
14 M	0429 0.1	1014 0.9	1618 -0.1	2253 1.2
29 Tu	0429 -0.0	0956 1.1	1607 -0.5	2302 1.7
15 Tu	0509 0.2	1041 0.9	1647 -0.1	2334 1.2
30 W	0527 0.1	1043 1.0	1656 -0.5	2359 1.7
31 Th	0627 0.2	1134 0.9	1749 -0.4	

APRIL

Day	Time ft	Time ft	Time ft	Time ft
1 F	0059 1.7	0731 0.2	1231 0.9	1848 -0.4
16 Sa	0031 1.4	0712 0.4	1139 0.7	1753 -0.1
2 Sa	0202 1.6	0837 0.3	1337 0.8	1952 -0.3
17 Su	0118 1.4	0800 0.4	1230 0.7	1845 -0.1
3 Su	0307 1.5	0944 0.3	1450 0.8	2102 -0.2
18 M	0209 1.4	0850 0.4	1336 0.8	1947 0.0
4 M	0410 1.4	1045 0.2	1606 0.9	2215 -0.1
19 Tu	0300 1.3	0937 0.4	1451 0.8	2056 0.1
5 Tu	0510 1.4	1138 0.2	1718 1.0	2325 -0.0
20 W	0352 1.3	1022 0.3	1606 1.0	2210 0.1
6 W	0603 1.3	1223 0.1	1819 1.1	
21 Th	0442 1.3	1106 0.1	1715 1.2	2321 0.1
7 Th	0028 0.0	0649 1.2	1302 0.1	1912 1.2
22 F	0530 1.2	1149 -0.0	1817 1.4	
8 F	0125 0.1	0729 1.1	1336 0.0	1959 1.3
23 Sa	0029 0.1	0618 1.2	1233 -0.2	1915 1.6
9 Sa	0215 0.1	0804 1.0	1406 0.0	2040 1.3
24 Su	0132 0.1	0705 1.1	1317 -0.3	2009 1.8
10 Su	0300 0.2	0835 1.0	1434 -0.0	2117 1.4
25 M	0232 0.1	0752 1.1	1404 -0.4	2103 1.9
11 M	0342 0.2	0904 0.9	1501 -0.4	2153 1.4
26 Tu	0330 0.1	0840 1.0	1451 -0.5	2156 2.0
12 Tu	0422 0.3	0932 0.8	1529 -0.1	2229 1.4
27 W	0426 0.2	0929 1.0	1540 -0.5	2249 2.0
13 W	0502 0.3	0959 0.8	1559 -0.1	2307 1.4
28 Th	0523 0.2	1022 1.0	1632 -0.5	2343 1.9
14 Th	0543 0.4	1028 0.8	1632 -0.1	2347 1.4
29 F	0620 0.2	1118 0.9	1727 -0.4	
15 F	0626 0.4	1100 0.7	1709 -0.1	
30 Sa	0039 1.8	0718 0.2	1221 0.9	1826 -0.2

TIME MERIDIAN 60°W

Heights in feet are referred to the chart datum of sounding.

0000h is midnight, 1200h is noon.

SAN JUAN, PUERTO RICO

HIGH & LOW WATER 1994   18°28'N 66°01'W

ATLANTIC STANDARD TIME (GMT -4H)

MAY

Day	Time	ft	Time	ft	Time	ft	Time	ft	Day	Time	ft	Time	ft	Time	ft	Time	ft
1 Su	0136	1.7	0817	0.2	1330	0.9	1930	-0.1	16 M	0044	1.5	0729	0.4	1217	0.8	1817	0.1
2 M ◑	0233	1.5	0904	0.2	1446	0.9	2041	0.1	17 Tu	0127	1.5	0810	0.3	1328	0.9	1920	0.1
3 Tu	0329	1.4	1007	0.2	1601	1.0	2155	0.2	18 W ◑	0212	1.4	0852	0.2	1444	1.0	2033	0.2
4 W	0423	1.3	1055	0.1	1709	1.1	2307	0.3	19 Th	0300	1.3	0937	0.1	1558	1.2	2151	0.3
5 Th	0512	1.2	1137	0.1	1808	1.2			20 F	0349	1.2	1022	-0.1	1706	1.4	2309	0.4
6 F	0014	0.3	0557	1.1	1214	0.0	1858	1.3	21 Sa	0440	1.2	1110	-0.2	1808	1.6		
7 Sa	0113	0.3	0638	1.0	1248	0.0	1942	1.4	22 Su	0022	0.4	0532	1.1	1158	-0.4	1906	1.8
8 Su	0205	0.3	0715	0.6	1320	-0.0	2021	1.5	23 M	0128	0.3	0625	1.0	1247	-0.5	2000	1.9
9 M	0252	0.4	0748	0.9	1350	-0.1	2058	1.6	24 Tu	0229	0.3	0719	1.0	1338	-0.5	2053	2.0
10 Tu ●	0335	0.4	0819	0.8	1420	-0.1	2134	1.6	25 W ○	0325	0.3	0813	1.0	1429	-0.5	2145	2.0
11 W	0416	0.4	0849	0.8	1450	-0.1	2209	1.6	26 Th	0420	0.3	0908	1.0	1520	-0.5	2235	2.0
12 Th	0455	0.4	0919	0.8	1522	-0.1	2246	1.6	27 F	0513	0.3	1005	1.0	1613	-0.4	2326	1.9
13 F	0533	0.4	0952	0.7	1558	-0.1	2324	1.6	28 Sa	0604	0.2	1105	0.9	1708	-0.3		
14 Sa	0612	0.4	1030	0.7	1637	-0.1			29 Su	0015	1.8	0656	0.2	1209	0.9	1805	-0.1
15 Su	0003	1.6	0650	0.4	1118	0.8	1723	-0.0	30 M	0104	1.7	0746	0.2	1318	1.0	1906	0.1
									31 Tu	0153	1.5	0835	0.2	1430	1.0	2013	0.3

JUNE

Day	Time	ft	Time	ft	Time	ft	Time	ft	Day	Time	ft	Time	ft	Time	ft	Time	ft
1 W ◑	0240	1.3	0922	0.1	1541	1.1	2100	0.4	16 Th ◑	0131	1.4	0811	0.1	1435	1.2	2010	0.4
2 Th	0327	1.2	1006	0.1	1647	1.2	2240	0.5	17 F	0215	1.3	0857	0.1	1547	1.4	2140	0.5
3 F	0413	1.1	1047	0.0	1744	1.3	2350	0.5	18 Sa	0305	1.2	0947	-0.2	1655	1.5	2301	0.5
4 Sa	0458	1.1	1126	-0.0	1834	1.4			19 Su	0358	1.1	1039	-0.4	1758	1.7		
5 Su	0054	0.5	0541	0.9	1203	-0.1	1918	1.5	20 M	0016	0.5	0456	1.0	1133	-0.4	1857	1.9
6 M	0149	0.5	0622	0.8	1238	-0.1	1959	1.6	21 Tu	0123	0.5	0556	1.0	1227	-0.5	1951	2.0
7 Tu	0238	0.5	0700	0.8	1312	-0.1	2037	1.6	22 W	0223	0.4	0656	1.0	1321	-0.5	2043	2.0
8 W	0322	0.5	0736	0.8	1346	-0.1	2114	1.7	23 Th ○	0316	0.4	0755	1.0	1414	-0.5	2133	2.0
9 Th ●	0402	0.5	0811	0.8	1421	-0.1	2150	1.7	24 F	0406	0.3	0854	1.0	1507	-0.4	2220	1.9
10 F	0438	0.5	0848	0.8	1457	-0.2	2225	1.7	25 Sa	0453	0.3	0953	1.0	1559	-0.3	2305	1.8
11 Sa	0512	0.5	0928	0.8	1536	-0.1	2300	1.7	26 Su	0539	0.2	1052	1.0	1652	-0.1	2347	1.7
12 Su	0545	0.4	1014	0.8	1619	-0.1	2336	1.6	27 M	0623	0.2	1153	1.0	1745	0.1		
13 M	0617	0.4	1109	0.9	1707	-0.0			28 Tu	0029	1.6	0705	0.2	1256	1.1	1841	0.2
14 Tu	0012	1.6	0651	0.3	1212	0.9	1802	0.1	29 W	0109	1.4	0748	0.1	1401	1.1	1942	0.4
15 W	0050	1.5	0729	0.2	1321	1.0	1906	0.2	30 Th ◐	0149	1.3	0830	0.1	1507	1.2	2050	0.5

JULY

Day	Time	ft	Time	ft	Time	ft	Time	ft	Day	Time	ft	Time	ft	Time	ft	Time	ft
1 F	0229	1.2	0912	0.1	1610	1.3	2202	0.6	16 Sa	0141	1.2	0824	-0.2	1532	1.6	2134	0.6
2 Sa	0312	1.0	0954	0.0	1708	1.3	2316	0.6	17 Su	0233	1.2	0919	-0.3	1641	1.7	2255	0.6
3 Su	0357	1.0	1037	0.0	1801	1.4			18 M	0331	1.1	1017	-0.3	1746	1.8		
4 M	0024	0.6	0444	0.9	1119	-0.0	1848	1.5	19 Tu	0010	0.6	0436	1.0	1116	-0.4	1846	1.9
5 Tu	0123	0.6	0532	0.8	1200	-0.1	1932	1.6	20 W	0115	0.6	0543	1.0	1215	-0.4	1941	1.9
6 W	0213	0.6	0617	0.8	1240	-0.1	2012	1.7	21 Th	0210	0.5	0648	1.0	1313	-0.4	2031	1.9
7 Th	0255	0.6	0700	0.8	1320	-0.1	2050	1.7	22 F ○	0259	0.5	0749	1.1	1407	-0.3	2117	1.9
8 F ●	0331	0.5	0744	0.8	1400	-0.2	2125	1.7	23 Sa	0343	0.4	0848	1.1	1459	-0.2	2159	1.8
9 Sa	0403	0.5	0828	0.8	1441	-0.1	2159	1.7	24 Su	0424	0.3	0944	1.2	1550	-0.1	2238	1.7
10 Su	0433	0.5	0916	0.9	1524	-0.1	2232	1.7	25 M	0502	0.3	1038	1.2	1639	0.1	2315	1.6
11 M	0503	0.4	1008	1.0	1610	-0.0	2306	1.6	26 Tu	0540	0.2	1132	1.2	1728	0.2	2350	1.5
12 Tu	0534	0.3	1104	1.1	1701	0.1	2340	1.6	27 W	0616	0.2	1226	1.3	1818	0.4		
13 W	0609	0.2	1206	1.2	1758	0.2			28 Th	0024	1.4	0654	0.2	1322	1.3	1912	0.5
14 Th	0017	1.5	0649	0.1	1312	1.3	1902	0.4	29 F	0058	1.3	0733	0.2	1421	1.3	2013	0.6
15 F	0056	1.4	0734	-0.1	1421	1.4	2014	0.5	30 Sa ◐	0135	1.2	0815	0.2	1521	1.4	2121	0.7
									31 Su	0216	1.1	0900	0.2	1621	1.4	2234	0.7

AUGUST

Day	Time	ft	Time	ft	Time	ft	Time	ft	Day	Time	ft	Time	ft	Time	ft	Time	ft
1 M	0303	1.0	0947	0.1	1718	1.5	2344	0.8	16 Tu	0322	1.2	1002	-0.1	1731	1.9	2358	0.7
2 Tu	0355	1.0	1036	0.1	1810	1.0			17 W	0434	1.2	1108	0.1	1838	1.8		
3 W	0044	0.7	0450	1.0	1125	0.1	1857	1.7	18 Th	0057	0.7	0545	1.2	1211	-0.1	1924	1.9
4 Th	0131	0.7	0544	1.0	1212	0.0	1939	1.7	19 F	0147	0.6	0651	1.3	1310	-0.0	2011	1.9
5 F	0210	0.7	0636	1.0	1258	0.0	2017	1.8	20 Sa	0230	0.5	0750	1.3	1404	0.0	2054	1.8
6 Sa	0243	0.6	0727	1.1	1344	-0.0	2052	1.8	21 O	0309	0.5	0844	1.4	1455	0.1	2132	1.7
7 Su ●	0313	0.5	0817	1.2	1430	0.0	2126	1.7	22 M	0345	0.4	0934	1.5	1543	0.2	2206	1.6
8 M	0344	0.4	0909	1.3	1518	0.1	2159	1.7	23 Tu	0418	0.4	1022	1.5	1629	0.4	2238	1.5
9 Tu	0415	0.3	1002	1.4	1608	0.1	2233	1.6	24 W	0451	0.3	1108	1.5	1714	0.5	2309	1.4
10 W	0450	0.2	1057	1.5	1701	0.5	2309	1.5	25 Th	0523	0.3	1153	1.6	1759	0.6	2340	1.4
11 Th	0529	0.1	1156	1.6	1759	0.4	2347	1.5	26 F	0557	0.3	1241	1.6	1848	0.7		
12 F	0612	0.0	1258	1.7	1903	0.5			27 Sa	0012	1.3	0635	0.3	1332	1.6	1941	0.8
13 Sa	0030	1.4	0701	-0.1	1405	1.7	2013	0.7	28 Su	0048	1.2	0716	0.3	1428	1.6	2043	0.8
14 Su ◐	0119	1.3	0756	-0.1	1515	1.8	2131	0.7	29 M	0129	1.2	0804	0.3	1527	1.6	2151	0.9
15 M	0216	1.2	0857	-0.1	1624	1.8	2248	0.7	30 Tu	0219	1.1	0856	0.3	1627	1.6	2257	0.9
									31 W	0317	1.1	0953	0.3	1722	1.7	2353	0.9

TIME MERIDIAN 60°W   0000h is midnight, 1200h is noon.

Heights in feet are referred to the chart datum of sounding.

SAN JUAN, PUERTO RICO

HIGH & LOW WATER 1994 18°28'N 66°01'W

ATLANTIC STANDARD TIME (GMT -4H)

SEPTEMBER

Day	Time ft	Day	Time ft
1 Th	0421 1.1 / 1049 0.3 / 1811 1.7	16 F	0029 0.7 / 0553 1.4 / 1208 0.3 / 1857 1.9
2 F	0037 0.8 / 0523 1.2 / 1145 0.3 / 1854 1.8	17 Sa	0114 0.6 / 0655 1.3 / 1309 0.3 / 1942 1.8
3 Sa	0113 0.7 / 0621 1.3 / 1238 0.2 / 1933 1.8	18 Su	0153 0.6 / 0750 1.6 / 1403 0.4 / 2022 1.7
4 Su	0147 0.6 / 0716 1.4 / 1330 0.2 / 2010 1.8	19 M	0228 0.5 / 0838 1.7 / 1453 0.5 / ○ 2057 1.6
5 M	0219 0.5 / 0808 1.6 / 1422 0.3 / ● 2045 1.7	20 Tu	0301 0.5 / 0922 1.8 / 1539 0.6 / 2129 1.5
6 Tu	0253 0.4 / 0900 1.7 / 1514 0.3 / 2121 1.7	21 W	0331 0.5 / 1003 1.8 / 1622 0.6 / 2159 1.5
7 W	0330 0.3 / 0952 1.9 / 1607 0.4 / 2159 1.6	22 Th	0401 0.4 / 1043 1.8 / 1703 0.7 / 2227 1.4
8 Th	0409 0.2 / 1046 2.0 / 1702 0.5 / 2239 1.6	23 F	0431 0.4 / 1122 1.8 / 1745 0.8 / 2257 1.3
9 F	0453 0.1 / 1143 2.0 / 1800 0.6 / 2322 1.5	24 Sa	0504 0.4 / 1204 1.8 / 1830 0.8 / 2329 1.3
10 Sa	0541 0.0 / 1243 2.0 / 1903 0.7	25 Su	0540 0.5 / 1250 1.8 / 1919 0.9
11 Su	0011 1.4 / 0634 0.0 / 1347 2.0 / 2012 0.8	26 M	0005 1.3 / 0622 0.5 / 1340 1.8 / 2014 0.9
12 M	0107 1.3 / 0734 0.1 / 1454 2.0 / ◑ 2124 0.8	27 Tu	0050 1.2 / 0710 0.6 / 1435 1.8 / 2112 1.0
13 Tu	0213 1.3 / 0841 0.1 / 1602 2.0 / 2234 0.8	28 W	0145 1.2 / 0806 0.5 / 1531 1.8 / 2208 0.9
14 W	0327 1.3 / 0951 0.2 / 1707 2.0 / 2336 0.8	29 Th	0251 1.2 / 0909 0.5 / 1625 1.8 / 2256 0.9
15 Th	0443 1.4 / 1102 0.2 / 1805 1.9	30 F	0402 1.3 / 1015 0.5 / 1714 1.8 / 2337 0.8

OCTOBER

Day	Time ft	Day	Time ft
1 Sa	0508 1.4 / 1119 0.5 / 1759 1.8	16 Su	0035 0.5 / 0653 1.7 / 1306 0.6 / 1903 1.6
2 Su	0015 0.7 / 0609 1.6 / 1220 0.5 / 1841 1.7	17 M	0112 0.5 / 0743 1.8 / 1401 0.7 / 1941 1.5
3 M	0052 0.5 / 0704 1.8 / 1319 0.5 / 1921 1.7	18 Tu	0145 0.5 / 0827 1.9 / 1450 0.7 / 2016 1.4
4 Tu	0129 0.4 / 0757 2.0 / 1415 0.5 / 2002 1.7	19 W	0216 0.4 / 0907 2.0 / 1535 0.7 / 2048 1.4
5 W	0209 0.3 / 0849 2.1 / 1510 0.5 / 2043 1.6	20 Th	0246 0.4 / 0944 2.0 / 1616 0.8 / 2117 1.3
6 Th	0251 0.1 / 0941 2.2 / 1605 0.6 / 2126 1.6	21 F	0316 0.4 / 1020 2.0 / 1656 0.8 / 2146 1.3
7 F	0336 0.1 / 1034 2.3 / 1701 0.6 / 2212 1.5	22 Sa	0346 0.4 / 1057 2.0 / 1736 0.8 / 2217 1.2
8 Sa	0424 0.0 / 1129 2.3 / 1759 0.7 / 2302 1.5	23 Su	0419 0.4 / 1135 2.0 / 1817 0.9 / 2250 1.2
9 Su	0516 0.1 / 1227 2.3 / 1900 0.7 / 2358 1.4	24 M	0455 0.4 / 1216 1.9 / 1901 0.9 / 2330 1.2
10 M	0613 0.1 / 1327 2.2 / 2003 0.8	25 Tu	0537 0.5 / 1300 1.9 / 1947 0.9
11 Tu	0102 1.4 / 0716 0.2 / 1430 2.1 / ◑ 2108 0.8	26 W	0020 1.2 / 0626 0.5 / 1347 1.8 / 2033 0.9
12 W	0215 1.4 / 0825 0.4 / 1533 2.0 / 2209 0.7	27 Th	0122 1.2 / 0724 0.6 / 1435 1.8 / ◑ 2118 0.8
13 Th	0334 1.4 / 0940 0.5 / 1633 1.9 / 2304 0.7	28 F	0234 1.3 / 0831 0.6 / 1524 1.7 / 2200 0.7
14 F	0449 1.5 / 1054 0.5 / 1729 1.8 / 2352 0.6	29 Sa	0347 1.4 / 0943 0.7 / 1612 1.7 / 2241 0.6
15 Sa	0556 1.6 / 1203 0.6 / 1819 1.7	30 Su	0455 1.6 / 1056 0.7 / 1659 1.6 / 2322 0.4
		31 M	0556 1.8 / 1205 0.7 / 1746 1.6

NOVEMBER

Day	Time ft	Day	Time ft
1 Tu	0005 0.3 / 0652 2.0 / 1309 0.7 / 1832 1.5	16 W	0104 0.3 / 0810 1.9 / 1443 0.7 / 1931 1.2
2 W	0048 0.1 / 0746 2.2 / 1408 0.6 / 1919 1.5	17 Th	0136 0.3 / 0849 1.9 / 1528 0.7 / 2005 1.1
3 Th	0134 -0.0 / 0838 2.3 / 1505 0.6 / ● 2007 1.4	18 F	0208 0.2 / 0925 1.9 / 1609 0.7 / 2037 1.1
4 F	0221 -0.1 / 0930 2.4 / 1601 0.6 / 2057 1.4	19 Sa	0239 0.2 / 1000 1.9 / 1648 0.7 / 2109 1.1
5 Sa	0310 -0.1 / 1022 2.4 / 1656 0.6 / 2150 1.4	20 Su	0312 0.2 / 1036 1.9 / 1725 0.7 / 2142 1.0
6 Su	0402 -0.1 / 1115 2.4 / 1752 0.6 / 2247 1.3	21 M	0346 0.2 / 1111 1.9 / 1801 0.7 / 2220 1.0
7 M	0456 -0.0 / 1209 2.3 / 1848 0.6 / 2349 1.3	22 Tu	0424 0.3 / 1148 1.9 / 1838 0.7 / 2306 1.0
8 Tu	0555 0.1 / 1304 2.2 / 1946 0.6	23 W	0506 0.3 / 1226 1.8 / 1914 0.7
9 W	0058 1.3 / 0658 0.3 / 1400 2.0 / 2042 0.6	24 Th	0001 1.1 / 0556 0.4 / 1305 1.7 / 1950 0.6
10 Th	0214 1.3 / 0808 0.4 / 1456 1.9 / ◑ 2136 0.5	25 F	0107 1.1 / 0654 0.5 / 1345 1.6 / 2029 0.5
11 F	0331 1.4 / 0923 0.6 / 1550 1.7 / 2225 0.4	26 Sa	0219 1.2 / 0802 0.5 / 1429 1.6 / ◑ 2109 0.4
12 Sa	0443 1.5 / 1040 0.6 / 1642 1.6 / 2311 0.4	27 Su	0331 1.4 / 0918 0.6 / 1515 1.5 / 2153 0.2
13 Su	0547 1.6 / 1152 0.7 / 1730 1.4 / 2352 0.3	28 M	0439 1.6 / 1037 0.7 / 1604 1.4 / 2239 0.1
14 M	0641 1.7 / 1257 0.7 / 1814 1.3	29 Tu	0541 1.8 / 1152 0.7 / 1655 1.3 / 2327 -0.1
15 Tu	0029 0.3 / 0728 1.8 / 1354 0.7 / 1854 1.3	30 W	0639 2.0 / 1300 0.6 / 1749 1.2

DECEMBER

Day	Time ft	Day	Time ft
1 Th	0017 -0.2 / 0734 2.1 / 1401 0.6 / 1844 1.2	16 F	0102 -0.0 / 0828 1.7 / 1513 0.6 / 1925 0.9
2 F	0108 -0.3 / 0827 2.2 / 1458 0.5 / ● 1939 1.2	17 Sa	0137 -0.0 / 0905 1.7 / 1553 0.6 / 2002 0.8
3 Sa	0200 -0.4 / 0918 2.3 / 1552 0.5 / 2036 1.2	18 Su	0212 -0.1 / 0940 1.7 / 1628 0.5 / 2039 0.8
4 Su	0253 -0.4 / 1009 2.2 / 1645 0.5 / 2135 1.2	19 M	0248 -0.1 / 1014 1.7 / 1701 0.5 / 2118 0.8
5 M	0346 -0.3 / 1059 2.2 / 1736 0.4 / 2236 1.2	20 Tu	0325 -0.0 / 1047 1.7 / 1731 0.5 / 2202 0.9
6 Tu	0442 -0.2 / 1149 2.1 / 1827 0.4 / 2340 1.2	21 W	0405 0.0 / 1120 1.6 / 1800 0.4 / 2253 0.9
7 W	0539 0.0 / 1237 1.9 / 1917 0.3	22 Th	0449 0.1 / 1152 1.6 / 1831 0.3 / 2350 1.0
8 Th	0049 1.2 / 0641 0.2 / 1326 1.7 / 2006 0.3	23 F	0539 0.2 / 1226 1.5 / 1904 0.2
9 F	0201 1.2 / 0747 0.4 / 1413 1.6 / 2054 0.2	24 Sa	0054 1.0 / 0638 0.3 / 1302 1.4 / 1942 0.1
10 Sa	0314 1.3 / 0900 0.5 / 1501 1.4 / ◑ 2141 0.1	25 Su	0203 1.2 / 0746 0.4 / 1342 1.3 / ◑ 2025 -0.1
11 Su	0423 1.4 / 1016 0.6 / 1548 1.2 / 2225 0.1	26 M	0313 1.3 / 0902 0.5 / 1428 1.2 / 2113 -0.2
12 M	0525 1.5 / 1131 0.6 / 1635 1.1 / 2307 0.1	27 Tu	0422 1.5 / 1023 0.5 / 1519 1.1 / 2205 -0.3
13 Tu	0619 1.6 / 1239 0.6 / 1721 1.0 / 2347 0.0	28 W	0526 1.6 / 1141 0.5 / 1617 1.0 / 2300 -0.4
14 W	0706 1.6 / 1338 0.6 / 1805 0.9	29 Th	0626 1.8 / 1250 0.5 / 1718 1.0 / 2356 -0.5
15 Th	0025 0.0 / 0749 1.7 / 1428 0.6 / 1846 0.9	30 F	0722 1.9 / 1351 0.4 / 1821 0.9
		31 Sa	0052 -0.6 / 0815 2.0 / 1446 0.4 / 1923 1.0

TIME MERIDIAN 60°W

Heights in feet are referred to the chart datum of sounding.

0000h is midnight, 1200h is noon.

VIEQUES PASSAGE, PUERTO RICO

CURRENT TABLES 1994 **FLOOD 250° EBB 057°**

ATLANTIC STANDARD TIME (GMT -4H)

JANUARY

Columns per entry: Slack time | Max time | Fld / Ebb (knots)

Date	Slack time	Max time	Fld	Ebb
1 Sa	0436 1013 1818 2312	0131 0725 1322 1847	0.6 · 0.7 ·	· 0.5 · 0.5
2 Su	0801 1118 1705 2349	0214 0910 1415 2031	0.7 · 0.6 ·	· · · 0.8
3 M	0615 1227 1755	0259 0916 1512 2118	0.8 · 0.5	· 0.7 · 0.8
4 Tu	0028 0708 1338 1848	0347 1016 1613 2208	0.8 · 0.5	· 0.7 · 0.7
5 W ◑	0111 0804 1452 1946	0439 1117 1717 2302	0.9 · 0.4	· 0.8 · 0.6
6 Th	0157 0900 1605 2050	0533 1220 1824 2359	0.9 · 0.4	· 0.8 · 0.6
7 F	0248 0956 1713 2158	0629 1321 1931	0.9 0.9 ·	· · 0.4
8 Sa	0342 1052 1815 2307	0100 0726 1420 2035	· 0.9 0.9	0.5 · · 0.4
9 Su	0439 1146 1910	0202 0823 1516 2136	· 0.9 1.0	0.5 · · 0.4
10 M	0015 0538 1237 1958	0303 0918 1609 2231	· 0.9 1.0	0.5 · · 0.5
11 Tu ●	0117 0637 1325 2042	0403 1012 1657 2321	· 0.8 1.0	0.5 · · 0.5
12 W	0215 0736 1411 2122	0459 1103 1742	· 0.8 1.0	0.5 · ·
13 Th	0308 0834 1454 2159	0008 0553 1152 1825	· · 0.7	0.6 0.5 · 0.9
14 F	0358 0931 1535 2234	0051 0645 1239 1905	· · 0.6	0.6 0.5 · 0.9
15 Sa	0445 1028 1615 2307	0133 0734 1326 1944	· · 0.6	0.7 0.5 · 0.8
16 Su	0530 1125 1804 2340	0213 0823 1413 2022	· 0.5 ·	0.7 · 0.5 0.7
17 M	0616 1224 1735	0253 0912 1501 2102	· 0.6 0.4	0.7 · · 0.7
18 Tu ◐	0014 0658 1325 1818	0334 1002 1551 2143	0.7 · 0.3	· 0.6 · 0.6
19 W ◑	0048 0742 1428 1905	0415 1052 1645 2226	0.7 · 0.3	· 0.6 · 0.5
20 Th	0125 0827 1532 1958	0459 1144 1742 2313	0.7 · 0.3	· 0.6 · 0.5
21 F	0203 0912 1633 2058	0544 1236 1841	0.7 0.7 ·	· · 0.2
22 Sa	0245 0958 1729 2201	0004 0631 1328 1940	· 0.7 0.7	0.4 · · 0.3
23 Su	0332 1044 1819 2303	0057 0719 1417 2034	· 0.7 0.8	0.4 · · 0.3
24 M	0422 1130 1902	0152 0809 1504 2124	· 0.7 0.8	0.4 · · 0.3
25 Tu	0001 0516 1216 1940	0246 0858 1549 2210	· 0.7 0.9	0.4 · · 0.4
26 W	0054 0614 1301 2016	0340 0948 1633 2253	· 0.7 0.9	0.4 · · 0.5
27 Th ○	0143 0712 1347 2050	0432 1038 1715 2335	· 0.8 0.9	0.5 · · 0.6
28 F	0231 0811 1432 2124	0524 1128 1757	0.6 0.7 0.9	· · ·
29 Sa	0318 0911 1518 2159	0017 0616 1218 1839	· 0.6 0.7	0.7 · · 0.7
30 Su	0407 1012 1604 2236	0100 0708 1310 1923	· 0.7 0.7	0.7 · · 0.8
31 M	0457 1115 1652 2316	0145 0802 1404 2008	· 0.8 0.6	0.8 · · 0.8

FEBRUARY

Date	Slack time	Max time	Fld	Ebb
1 Tu	0549 1220 1742 2359	0232 0858 1500 2056	· 0.8 0.5	0.9 · · 0.7
2 W	0640 1328 1836	0322 0957 1559 2148	· 0.8 0.5	0.9 · · 0.7
3 Th ◐	0045 0739 1437 1934	0415 1057 1702 2244	0.9 · 0.4	· 0.8 · 0.6
4 F	0136 0846 1546 2038	0511 1159 1808 2343	0.9 · 0.4	· 0.8 · 0.5
5 Sa	0231 0935 1651 2147	0610 1301 1914	0.9 0.9 ·	· · 0.4
6 Su	0330 1033 1750 2256	0047 0709 1401 2017	· 0.8 0.9	0.5 · · 0.4
7 M	0432 1128 1842	0151 0809 1456 2116	· 0.8 0.9	0.5 · · 0.4
8 Tu	0001 0535 1219 1928	0254 0906 1548 2208	· 0.8 0.9	0.5 · · 0.5
9 W	0100 0637 1307 2009	0352 0959 1634 2255	· 0.7 0.8	0.5 · · 0.6
10 Th ●	0153 0736 1352 2045	0446 1050 1717 2339	· 0.7 0.8	0.5 · · 0.6
11 F	0241 0831 1434 2119	0536 1137 1757	0.6 0.6 0.7	· · ·
12 Sa	0325 0924 1513 2152	0019 0623 1221 1835	· 0.6 0.6	0.6 · · 0.7
13 Su	0407 1015 1551 2223	0057 0708 1305 1911	· 0.6 0.5	0.7 · · 0.7
14 M	0447 1107 1630 2255	0134 0752 1348 1948	· 0.6 0.5	0.7 · · 0.6
15 Tu	0528 1159 1710 2328	0211 0836 1433 2026	· 0.6 0.4	0.7 · · 0.6
16 W	0609 1253 1753	0250 0921 1521 2106	· 0.6 0.4	0.7 · · 0.5
17 Th	0003 0651 1349 1839	0330 1000 1611 2149	0.7 · 0.3	· 0.7 · 0.5
18 F ◑	0041 0736 1446 1931	0413 1059 1705 2237	0.7 · 0.3	· 0.7 · 0.4
19 Sa	0123 0823 1543 2028	0500 1150 1801 2329	0.7 · 0.3	· 0.7 · 0.4
20 Su	0211 0913 1636 2129	0551 1242 1857	0.7 0.7 ·	· · 0.3
21 M	0305 1004 1724 2229	0025 0644 1334 1951	· 0.7 0.7	0.4 · · 0.3
22 Tu	0405 1055 1807 2325	0124 0739 1424 2041	· 0.7 0.8	0.5 · · 0.4
23 W	0507 1146 1847	0222 0834 1512 2129	· 0.7 0.8	0.5 · · 0.5
24 Th	0018 0610 1237 1924	0318 0929 1558 2214	· 0.7 0.8	0.5 · · 0.6
25 F	0109 0711 1326 2001	0412 1022 1643 2258	· 0.7 0.8	0.6 · · 0.7
26 Sa ○	0158 0811 1414 2039	0505 1114 1728 2343	0.7 0.7 0.8	· · · 0.8
27 Su	0247 0910 1503 2119	0558 1206 1813	0.8 0.7 0.8	· · ·
28 M	0337 1009 1551 2200	0029 0650 1259 1859	· 0.9 0.7	0.8 · · 0.8

TIME MERIDIAN 60°W   0000h is midnight, 1200h is noon.

VIEQUES PASSAGE, PUERTO RICO

CURRENT TABLES 1994   **FLOOD 250° EBB 057°**

ATLANTIC STANDARD TIME (GMT -4H)

MARCH

Day	Slack time	Max time	Fld/Ebb knots
1 Tu	0429, 1109, 1641, 2245	0117, 0744, 1353, 1947	0.9, 0.9, 0.6, 0.7
2 W	0521, 1209, 1733, 2332	0206, 0839, 1448, 2038	0.9, 0.9, 0.6, 0.7
3 Th	0616, 1312, 1829	0258, 0936, 1546, 2132	0.9, 0.9, 0.5, 0.6
4 F ◑	0024, 0712, 1415, 1929	0353, 1034, 1648, 2231	0.9, 0.9, 0.5, 0.6
5 Sa	0120, 0811, 1518, 2034	0451, 1135, 1751, 2334	0.8, 0.8, 0.4, 0.5
6 Su	0222, 0910, 1618, 2141	0552, 1236, 1854	0.8, 0.8, 0.4
7 M	0328, 1009, 1713, 2245	0039, 0654, 1335, 1954	0.5, 0.7, 0.8, 0.5
8 Tu	0435, 1105, 1801, 2345	0144, 0756, 1430, 2049	0.5, 0.7, 0.8, 0.5
9 W	0541, 1158, 1845	0245, 0854, 1520, 2138	0.5, 0.6, 0.7, 0.6
10 Th	0038, 0642, 1246, 1924	0341, 0947, 1605, 2223	0.6, 0.6, 0.7, 0.6
11 F	0125, 0738, 1331, 1959	0431, 1036, 1647, 2303	0.6, 0.6, 0.7, 0.6
12 Sa ●	0208, 0830, 1413, 2032	0517, 1121, 1725, 2340	0.6, 0.5, 0.6, 0.7
13 Su	0248, 0918, 1453, 2104	0559, 1204, 1802	0.7, 0.5, 0.6
14 M	0326, 1004, 1532, 2135	0016, 0640, 1246, 1838	0.7, 0.7, 0.5, 0.6
15 Tu	0403, 1050, 1612, 2207	0052, 0720, 1328, 1915	0.7, 0.7, 0.4, 0.5
16 W	0441, 1136, 1653, 2242	0128, 0801, 1410, 1953	0.7, 0.7, 0.4, 0.5
17 Th	0520, 1223, 1736, 2319	0206, 0843, 1455, 2033	0.7, 0.7, 0.4, 0.4
18 F	0601, 1312, 1823	0247, 0928, 1542, 2118	0.7, 0.7, 0.4, 0.4
19 Sa	0001, 0646, 1401, 1913	0331, 1015, 1631, 2207	0.6, 0.7, 0.4, 0.4
20 Su ◑	0049, 0735, 1450, 2008	0420, 1104, 1723, 2302	0.6, 0.7, 0.4, 0.4
21 M	0146, 0827, 1538, 2104	0514, 1156, 1816	0.6, 0.7, 0.6
22 Tu	0249, 0922, 1623, 2200	0001, 0612, 1249, 1908	0.4, 0.6, 0.7, 0.4
23 W	0357, 1019, 1706, 2255	0102, 0713, 1341, 1958	0.5, 0.6, 0.7, 0.5
24 Th	0504, 1115, 1748, 2347	0202, 0812, 1432, 2047	0.6, 0.6, 0.7, 0.6
25 F	0609, 1210, 1829	0259, 0910, 1522, 2135	0.6, 0.6, 0.7, 0.7
26 Sa	0039, 0711, 1303, 1911	0354, 1006, 1610, 2223	0.8, 0.7, 0.7, 0.8
27 Su ○	0129, 0810, 1356, 1955	0447, 1101, 1658, 2311	0.9, 0.7, 0.7, 0.9
28 M	0220, 0907, 1447, 2040	0540, 1154, 1747, 2400	1.0, 0.7, 0.7, 0.9
29 Tu	0310, 1003, 1539, 2126	0632, 1247, 1837	1.0, 0.7, 0.7
30 W	0402, 1059, 1632, 2216	0049, 0725, 1341, 1928	1.0, 1.0, 0.6, 0.7
31 Th	0454, 1155, 1727, 2309	0141, 0818, 1436, 2022	0.9, 1.0, 0.6, 0.6

APRIL

Day	Slack time	Max time	Fld/Ebb knots
1 F	0548, 1251, 1825	0234, 0913, 1532, 2119	0.9, 1.0, 0.6, 0.6
2 Sa	0007, 0643, 1348, 1926	0331, 1009, 1631, 2221	0.8, 0.9, 0.5, 0.5
3 Su ◐	0109, 0740, 1443, 2029	0430, 1107, 1730, 2325	0.7, 0.8, 0.5, 0.5
4 M	0218, 0838, 1536, 2131	0533, 1205, 1829	0.6, 0.8, 0.5
5 Tu	0329, 0937, 1625, 2230	0031, 0637, 1301, 1925	0.5, 0.6, 0.7, 0.6
6 W	0440, 1034, 1711, 2323	0134, 0739, 1354, 2016	0.5, 0.5, 0.6, 0.6
7 Th	0545, 1129, 1752	0232, 0837, 1444, 2102	0.6, 0.5, 0.6, 0.6
8 F	0011, 0645, 1220, 1830	0324, 0931, 1529, 2144	0.6, 0.5, 0.6, 0.6
9 Sa	0054, 0738, 1307, 1905	0411, 1020, 1611, 2223	0.7, 0.5, 0.5, 0.7
10 Su	0133, 0826, 1352, 1939	0454, 1105, 1650, 2300	0.7, 0.5, 0.5, 0.7
11 M ●	0210, 0910, 1434, 2012	0534, 1147, 1728, 2336	0.8, 0.4, 0.5, 0.7
12 Tu	0246, 0952, 1516, 2045	0613, 1228, 1805	0.8, 0.4, 0.4
13 W	0321, 1034, 1558, 2120	0011, 0651, 1309, 1844	0.7, 0.4, 0.4, 0.4
14 Th	0358, 1115, 1641, 2157	0048, 0729, 1350, 1923	0.7, 0.8, 0.4, 0.4
15 F	0436, 1156, 1724, 2240	0126, 0809, 1432, 2006	0.7, 0.8, 0.4, 0.4
16 Sa	0517, 1237, 1810, 2328	0208, 0851, 1516, 2053	0.6, 0.8, 0.4, 0.4
17 Su	0602, 1319, 1858	0254, 0935, 1601, 2144	0.6, 0.8, 0.4, 0.4
18 M	0025, 0650, 1400, 1949	0346, 1022, 1649, 2241	0.6, 0.7, 0.5, 0.4
19 Tu ◑	0130, 0743, 1442, 2042	0443, 1112, 1738, 2341	0.5, 0.7, 0.5, 0.5
20 W	0241, 0840, 1525, 2136	0545, 1205, 1829	0.5, 0.7, 0.6
21 Th	0353, 0941, 1608, 2229	0043, 0648, 1258, 1919	0.6, 0.5, 0.6, 0.7
22 F	0503, 1041, 1652, 2321	0143, 0751, 1352, 2010	0.7, 0.5, 0.6, 0.8
23 Sa	0608, 1141, 1738	0241, 0852, 1445, 2101	0.8, 0.6, 0.6, 0.8
24 Su	0013, 0709, 1239, 1825	0336, 0950, 1538, 2152	0.9, 0.6, 0.6, 0.9
25 M ○	0105, 0806, 1336, 1914	0430, 1046, 1630, 2242	1.0, 0.6, 0.6, 1.0
26 Tu	0155, 0901, 1432, 2004	0522, 1141, 1723, 2333	1.1, 0.6, 0.6, 1.0
27 W	0246, 0954, 1527, 2057	0614, 1234, 1816	1.1, 0.6, 0.6
28 Th	0337, 1046, 1623, 2151	0025, 0705, 1328, 1911	1.0, 1.1, 0.6, 0.6
29 F	0428, 1137, 1720, 2250	0117, 0757, 1421, 2007	0.9, 1.1, 0.6, 0.6
30 Sa	0520, 1227, 1819, 2352	0212, 0849, 1516, 2107	0.8, 1.0, 0.6, 0.5

TIME MERIDIAN 60°W   0000h is midnight, 1200h is noon.

VIEQUES PASSAGE, PUERTO RICO

CURRENT TABLES 1994 **FLOOD 250° EBB 057°**

ATLANTIC STANDARD TIME (GMT -4H)

MAY

Day	Slack time	Max time	Fld knots	Ebb knots
1 Su	0010	0308	0.7	
	1316	1610	0.6	0.9
	1918	2208		0.5
2 M	0100	0408	0.6	
	0705	1035		0.8
	1404	1705	0.6	
	2017	2312		0.5
3 Tu	0212	0509	0.5	
	0800	1128		0.7
	1450	1758	0.6	
	2114			
4 W		0015		0.5
	0326	0613	0.4	
	0856	1220		0.6
	1534	1849	0.7	
	2207			
5 Th		0115		0.6
	0437	0715	0.4	
	0954	1311		0.6
	1616	1937	0.7	
	2255			
6 F		0211		0.6
	0542	0814	0.4	
	1050	1400		0.5
	1655	2022	0.7	
	2339			
7 Sa		0301		0.7
	0640	0909	0.4	
	1145	1447		0.5
	1733	2103	0.7	
8 Su	0020	0346		0.8
	0731	0959	0.4	
	1238	1530		0.4
	1810	2143	0.7	
9 M	0058	0428		0.8
	0816	1045	0.4	
	1327	1613		0.4
	1846	2221	0.7	
10 Tu	0134	0507		0.8
	0858	1128	0.4	
	1415	1654		0.4
	1921	2258	0.7	
11 W	0210	0546		0.9
	0938	1210	0.4	
	1500	1734		0.4
	1959	2335	0.7	
12 Th	0246	0623		0.9
	1016	1250	0.4	
	1544	1815		0.3
	2038			
13 F		0013	0.7	
	0323	0701		0.9
	1052	1330	0.4	
	1627	1858		0.3
	2122			
14 Sa		0054	0.7	
	0401	0739		0.9
	1128	1409	0.5	
	1710	1943		0.4
	2211			
15 Su		0138	0.6	
	0442	0819		0.8
	1204	1450	0.5	
	1754	2032		0.4
	2307			
16 M		0226		0.6
	0526	0901		0.8
	1239	1532	0.5	
	1840	2125		0.4
17 Tu	0011	0010	0.7	
	0613	0946		0.7
	1316	1617	0.6	
	1929	2223		0.5
18 W	0121	0417	0.5	
	0706	1034		0.7
	1354	1704	0.7	
	2020	2323		0.6
19 Th	0235	0520	0.5	
	0802	1125		0.7
	1435	1754	0.7	
	2113			
20 F		0024		0.7
	0349	0626	0.4	
	0904	1219		0.6
	1519	1846	0.8	
	2206			
21 Sa		0124		0.8
	0500	0731	0.4	
	1008	1315		0.6
	1606	1939	0.9	
	2259			
22 Su		0223		0.9
	0605	0834	0.5	
	1112	1412		0.6
	1656	2032	0.9	
	2352			
23 M		0319		1.0
	0704	0935	0.5	
	1215	1509		0.6
	1748	2125	1.0	
24 Tu	0044	0413		1.1
	0800	1032	0.5	
	1317	1605		0.6
	1842	2218	1.0	
25 W	0135	0505		1.1
	0852	1127	0.6	
	1416	1702		0.6
	1937	2311	1.0	
26 Th	0225	0556		1.1
	0941	1220	0.6	
	1514	1758		0.6
	2034			
27 F		0003	0.9	
	0315	0646		1.1
	1029	1312	0.7	
	1612	1855		0.5
	2133			
28 Sa		0057	0.8	
	0404	0735		1.0
	1114	1404	0.7	
	1709	1952		0.5
	2234			
29 Su		0150	0.8	
	0452	0824		1.0
	1158	1454	0.7	
	1805	2051		0.5
	2339			
30 M		0245		0.6
	0540	0912		0.9
	1241	1544	0.7	
	1901	2151		0.5
31 Tu	0047	0342		0.5
	0628	0959		0.8
	1322	1634	0.7	
	1955	2251		0.5

JUNE

Day	Slack time	Max time	Fld knots	Ebb knots
1 W	0159	0441	0.4	
	0718	1047		0.7
	1402	1722	0.7	
	2046	2350		0.6
2 Th	0012	0512	0.4	
	0810	1136		0.6
	1442	1809	0.7	
	2135			
3 F		0047		0.6
	0422	0643	0.3	
	0906	1225		0.5
	1522	1855	0.7	
	2221			
4 Sa		0140		0.7
	0527	0742	0.3	
	1004	1313		0.4
	1600	1939	0.7	
	2304			
5 Su		0230		0.7
	0624	0839	0.3	
	1104	1402		0.4
	1639	2022	0.7	
	2344			
6 M		0316		0.8
	0714	0932	0.3	
	1203	1449		0.4
	1719	2104	0.7	
7 Tu	0023	0359		0.8
	0758	1020	0.3	
	1259	1536		0.3
	1759	2144	0.7	
8 W	0101	0439		0.8
	0839	1105	0.4	
	1350	1621		0.3
	1840	2224	0.7	
9 Th	0139	0518		0.9
	0916	1147	0.4	
	1438	1705		0.3
	1923	2305	0.7	
10 F	0217	0557		0.9
	0951	1226	0.4	
	1522	1750		0.3
	2010	2346	0.7	
11 Sa	0255	0634		0.9
	1025	1304	0.5	
	1604	1836		0.4
	2101			
12 Su		0030	0.7	
	0335	0712		0.5
	1056	1342	0.5	
	1646	1923		0.4
	2156			
13 M		0116	0.6	
	0416	0751		0.7
	1128	1422	0.6	
	1730	2013		0.5
	2257			
14 Tu		0205	0.6	
	0459	0832		0.8
	1201	1503	0.6	
	1816	2107		0.5
15 W	0003	0259	0.5	
	0546	0915		0.8
	1236	1547	0.7	
	1905	2204		0.6
16 Th	0114	0357	0.5	
	0637	1002		0.7
	1314	1634	0.8	
	1956	2304		0.7
17 F	0228	0500	0.4	
	0702	1050		0.7
	1356	1725	0.8	
	2050			
18 Sa		0005		0.8
	0341	0605	0.4	
	0833	1148		0.6
	1442	1818	0.9	
	2144			
19 Su		0106		0.8
	0452	0712	0.4	
	0939	1246		0.6
	1532	1913	0.9	
	2239			
20 M		0205		0.9
	0556	0817	0.4	
	1046	1346		0.5
	1625	2009	1.0	
	2333			
21 Tu		0302		1.0
	0655	0919	0.4	
	1154	1446		0.5
	1722	2104	1.0	
22 W	0026	0357		1.1
	0748	1017	0.5	
	1259	1546		0.5
	1820	2159	1.0	
23 Th	0117	0449		1.1
	0837	1111	0.6	
	1401	1645		0.5
	1920	2253	0.9	
24 F	0207	0538		1.1
	0922	1203	0.6	
	1459	1743		0.5
	2020	2346	0.9	
25 Sa	0255	0626		1.0
	1005	1253	0.7	
	1555	1839		0.5
	2120			
26 Su		0038	0.8	
	0341	0712		1.0
	1046	1340	0.7	
	1649	1935		0.5
	2222			
27 M		0130	0.7	
	0426	0756		0.9
	1125	1427	0.7	
	1741	2030		0.6
	2325			
28 Tu		0222	0.6	
	0509	0840		0.8
	1203	1512	0.7	
	1832	2125		0.6
29 W		0314	0.5	
	0553	0923		0.7
	1240	1557	0.7	
	1921	2220		0.6
30 Th	0137	0409	0.4	
	0638	1006		0.6
	1317	1641	0.7	
	2009	2315		0.6

Chapter 2

TIME MERIDIAN 60°W 0000h is midnight, 1200h is noon.

VIEQUES PASSAGE, PUERTO RICO

CURRENT TABLES 1994 **FLOOD 250° EBB 057°**

ATLANTIC STANDARD TIME (GMT -4H)

JULY

Day	Slack time	Max time	Fld knots	Ebb knots
1 F	0245	0505	0.3	
	0727	1051		0.6
	1354	1726	0.7	
	2055			
2 Sa		0009		0.6
	0353	0604	0.3	
	0820	1139		0.5
	1432	1811	0.7	
	2140			
3 Su		0102		0.7
	0457	0704	0.2	
	0919	1228		0.4
	1512	1856	0.7	
	2224			
4 M		0153		0.7
	0554	0803	0.3	
	1022	1319		0.4
	1554	1942	0.7	
	2307			
5 Tu		0241		0.8
	0644	0858	0.3	
	1125	1411		0.3
	1638	2027	0.7	
	2349			
6 W		0326		0.8
	0729	0948	0.3	
	1224	1502		0.3
	1724	2112	0.7	
7 Th	0030	0408		0.9
	0808	1034	0.4	
	1317	1551		0.3
	1813	2156	0.7	
8 F	0111	0449		0.9
	0844	1115	0.4	
	1405	1640		0.4
	1904	2241	0.7	
9 Sa	0152	0528		0.9
	0917	1155	0.5	
	1449	1727		0.4
	1958	2326	0.7	
10 Su	0233	0607		0.9
	0948	1233	0.5	
	1532	1815		0.5
	2053			
11 M		0012	0.7	
	0314	0645		0.9
	1019	1311	0.6	
	1615	1904		0.5
	2152			
12 Tu		0100	0.6	
	0357	0725		0.8
	1050	1351	0.7	
	1700	1955		0.6
	2253			
13 W		0151	0.6	
	0441	0806		0.8
	1124	1433	0.7	
	1748	2048		0.6
	2358			
14 Th		0244	0.5	
	0527	0850		0.8
	1200	1518	0.8	
	1838	2145		0.7
15 F	0106	0341	0.5	
	0617	0937		0.7
	1241	1607	0.9	
	1931	2244		0.8
16 Sa ☽	0216	0443		0.4
	0712	1028		0.6
	1326	1659	0.9	
	2026	2345		0.8
17 Su	0328	0547		0.4
	0813	1124		0.6
	1415	1755	0.9	
	2123			
18 M		0046		0.9
	0437	0654		0.4
	0919	1225		0.5
	1510	1853	0.9	
	2220			
19 Tu		0147		0.9
	0540	0800		0.4
	1029	1328		0.5
	1608	1951	0.9	
	2316			
20 W		0245		0.9
	0637	0902		0.4
	1138	1432		0.5
	1710	2049	0.9	
21 Th	0010	0339	1.0	
	0727	0959		0.5
	1244	1534		0.5
	1812	2146	0.9	
22 F ○	0101	0431	1.0	
	0813	1052		0.6
	1344	1633		0.5
	1914	2240	0.8	
23 Sa	0150	0518	1.0	
	0855	1141		0.6
	1440	1730		0.6
	2015	2332	0.8	
24 Su	0236	0603		0.9
	0934	1227	0.7	
	1532	1823		0.6
	2114			
25 M		0022	0.7	
	0320	0646		0.9
	1011	1311	0.7	
	1621	1915		0.6
	2212			
26 Tu		0110	0.6	
	0401	0726		0.8
	1047	1353	0.7	
	1708	2004		0.6
	2310			
27 W		0158	0.5	
	0442	0806		0.7
	1121	1434	0.7	
	1753	2054		0.6
28 Th	0008	0246	0.4	
	0523	0846		0.7
	1156	1516	0.7	
	1838	2143		0.6
29 F	0108	0336	0.4	
	0606	0927		0.6
	1232	1558	0.7	
	1923	2234		0.6
30 Sa ☾	0209	0429	0.3	
	0653	1011		0.5
	1309	1641	0.7	
	2008	2326		0.6
31 Su	0312	0525	0.3	
	0745	1058		0.5
	1348	1727	0.7	
	2054			

AUGUST

Day	Slack time	Max time	Fld knots	Ebb knots
1 M		0018		0.7
	0413	0624	0.3	
	0843	1148		0.4
	1431	1814	0.7	
	2140			
2 Tu		0110		0.7
	0509	0722	0.3	
	0946	1242		0.4
	1518	1903	0.7	
	2227			
3 W		0200		0.7
	0600	0818	0.3	
	1048	1338		0.3
	1609	1953	0.7	
	2313			
4 Th		0248		0.8
	0644	0908	0.3	
	1147	1432		0.4
	1704	2043	0.7	
	2359			
5 F		0333		0.8
	0723	0954	0.4	
	1239	1525		0.4
	1800	2133	0.7	
6 Sa	0045	0416		0.8
	0758	1036	0.5	
	1326	1616		0.5
	1857	2221	0.7	
7 Su ●	0129	0457		0.8
	0831	1116	0.5	
	1412	1706		0.5
	1954	2310	0.7	
8 M	0213	0537		0.8
	0903	1156	0.6	
	1456	1755		0.6
	2052	2358	0.7	
9 Tu	0257	0617		0.8
	0936	1236	0.7	
	1541	1845		0.7
	2150			
10 W		0047	0.6	
	0341	0658		0.8
	1011	1319	0.8	
	1628	1936		0.7
	2249			
11 Th		0138	0.6	
	0427	0742		0.8
	1048	1403	0.8	
	1718	2028		0.8
	2350			
12 F		0232	0.5	
	0515	0828		0.7
	1129	1451	0.9	
	1810	2124		0.8
13 Sa	0054	0328	0.5	
	0606	0917		0.7
	1214	1542	0.9	
	1905	2222		0.8
14 Su ☽	0200	0428	0.4	
	0702	1011		0.6
	1304	1637	0.9	
	2002	2323		0.8
15 M	0307	0532	0.4	
	0804	1110		0.6
	1359	1736	0.9	
	2101			
16 Tu		0025		0.8
	0412	0637	0.4	
	0911	1213		0.5
	1500	1837	0.8	
	2200			
17 W		0126		0.9
	0513	0742	0.4	
	1020	1319		0.5
	1604	1938	0.8	
	2257			
18 Th		0224		0.9
	0607	0842	0.5	
	1127	1425		0.5
	1711	2039	0.8	
	2353			
19 F		0319		0.9
	0655	0937	0.5	
	1229	1526		0.5
	1816	2136	0.7	
20 Sa	0045	0409		0.8
	0739	1028	0.6	
	1324	1623		0.6
	1917	2229	0.7	
21 Su ○	0133	0454		0.8
	0818	1113	0.6	
	1415	1716		0.6
	2016	2319	0.6	
22 M	0218	0537		0.8
	0855	1156	0.7	
	1502	1804		0.6
	2110			
23 Tu		0007	0.6	
	0300	0617		0.7
	0930	1236	0.7	
	1545	1851		0.7
	2203			
24 W		0052	0.5	
	0340	0655		0.7
	1003	1315	0.7	
	1627	1935		0.7
	2254			
25 Th		0136	0.5	
	0419	0733		0.6
	1037	1353	0.7	
	1708	2020		0.7
	2345			
26 F		0221	0.4	
	0500	0811		0.6
	1111	1432	0.7	
	1750	2104		0.7
27 Sa	0037	0307	0.4	
	0543	0852		0.5
	1147	1513	0.7	
	1832	2151		0.7
28 Su	0131	0356	0.3	
	0630	0935		0.5
	1226	1556	0.7	
	1916	2240		0.7
29 M ☾	0226	0449	0.3	
	0721	1023		0.4
	1309	1643	0.7	
	2003	2330		0.7
30 Tu	0321	0544	0.3	
	0818	1115		0.4
	1358	1733	0.6	
	2052			
31 W		0022		0.7
	0413	0639	0.3	
	0917	1212		0.4
	1452	1827	0.6	
	2143			

TIME MERIDIAN 60°W 0000h is midnight, 1200h is noon.

VIEQUES PASSAGE, PUERTO RICO

CURRENT TABLES 1994 **FLOOD 250° EBB 057°**

ATLANTIC STANDARD TIME (GMT -4H)

SEPTEMBER

Day	Slack time	Max time	Fld knots	Ebb knots
1 Th		0114		0.7
	0502	0733	0.4	
	1015	1310		0.4
	1552	1922	0.6	
	2235			
2 F		0204		0.7
	0545	0823	0.4	
	1110	1407		0.4
	1654	2017	0.6	
	2326			
3 Sa		0252		0.7
	0624	0909	0.5	
	1201	1502		0.5
	1756	2111	0.6	
4 Su	0016	0337		0.7
	0701	0953	0.6	
	1249	1554		0.6
	1855	2203	0.7	
5 M ●	0105	0421		0.7
	0737	1036	0.7	
	1335	1645		0.7
	1953	2254	0.7	
6 Tu	0153	0505		0.8
	0813	1118	0.7	
	1422	1735		0.8
	2050	2344	0.7	
7 W	0240	0548		0.7
	0851	1202	0.8	
	1510	1825		0.9
	2146			
8 Th		0035		0.7
	0327	0633	0.7	
	0931	1248		0.9
	1559	1916	0.9	
	2243			
9 F		0127	0.6	
	0416	0719		0.7
	1014	1335	0.9	
	1649	2009		0.9
	2340			
10 Sa		0220	0.6	
	0507	0809		0.7
	1101	1426	0.9	
	1742	2103		0.9
11 Su	0039	0316	0.5	
	0601	0902		0.6
	1152	1520	0.9	
	1838	2200		0.9
12 M ◑	0140	0415	0.5	
	0659	0959		0.6
	1249	1618	0.8	
	1936	2300		0.9
13 Tu	0241	0517	0.5	
	0802	1102		0.5
	1351	1719	0.8	
	2035			
14 W		0001		0.8
	0340	0619	0.5	
	0908	1208		0.5
	1459	1823	0.7	
	2136			
15 Th		0101		0.8
	0436	0720	0.5	
	1014	1315		0.5
	1610	1927	0.7	
	2235			
16 F		0158		0.8
	0527	0818	0.5	
	1115	1419		0.6
	1719	2029	0.6	
	2332			
17 Sa		0252		0.7
	0613	0910	0.6	
	1211	1517		0.6
	1824	2126	0.6	
18 Su	0025	0340		0.7
	0655	0957	0.6	
	1301	1610		0.7
	1923	2218	0.6	
19 M ○	0113	0425		0.7
	0733	1040	0.7	
	1346	1659		0.7
	2017	2306	0.5	
20 Tu	0158	0506		0.6
	0808	1120	0.7	
	1428	1743		0.7
	2106	2351	0.5	
21 W	0240	0545		0.6
	0842	1158	0.7	
	1507	1825		0.7
	2153			
22 Th		0034		0.5
	0321	0623	0.6	
	0915	1234		0.7
	1545	1905	0.8	
	2238			
23 F		0116		0.5
	0402	0700	0.5	
	0949	1311		0.7
	1623	1946	0.8	
	2323			
24 Sa		0158		0.4
	0444	0739	0.5	
	1025	1349		0.7
	1702	2027	0.8	
25 Su	0008	0242		0.4
	0528	0820	0.4	
	1103	1430		0.7
	1742	2110	0.7	
26 M	0054	0328		0.4
	0615	0905	0.4	
	1146	1514		0.6
	1826	2156	0.7	
27 Tu	0141	0416		0.4
	0705	0954	0.4	
	1235	1602		0.6
	1913	2244	0.7	
28 W ◑	0228	0507		0.4
	0758	1048	0.4	
	1331	1655		0.6
	2003	2334	0.7	
29 Th	0314	0558		0.4
	0852	1146	0.4	
	1435	1752		0.5
	2057			
30 F		0026		0.7
	0359	0648	0.5	
	0945	1246		0.5
	1542	1852	0.5	
	2153			

OCTOBER

Day	Slack time	Max time	Fld knots	Ebb knots
1 Sa		0117		0.7
	0441	0737	0.5	
	1037	1344		0.5
	1649	1952	0.5	
	2250			
2 Su		0207		0.7
	0521	0821	0.8	
	1127	1439		0.7
	1752	2049	0.6	
	2345			
3 M		0256		0.7
	0601	0911	0.7	
	1216	1533		0.8
	1853	2144	0.6	
4 Tu	0039	0344		0.7
	0642	0957	0.8	
	1304	1624		0.9
	1950	2238	0.6	
5 W ●	0131	0432		0.7
	0724	1043	0.9	
	1353	1715		1.0
	2045	2330	0.6	
6 Th	0222	0519		0.7
	0808	1131	0.9	
	1442	1806		1.0
	2139			
7 F		0022		0.6
	0314	0608	0.7	
	0855	1220		0.9
	1532	1857	1.1	
	2233			
8 Sa		0114		0.6
	0406	0659	0.6	
	0944	1310		0.9
	1623	1949	1.0	
	2327			
9 Su		0208		0.6
	0500	0753	0.6	
	1038	1403		0.9
	1716	2042	1.0	
10 M	0021	0303		0.6
	0558	0850	0.6	
	1136	1459		0.8
	1811	2138	0.9	
11 Tu ◑	0115	0400		0.6
	0658	0951	0.6	
	1239	1559		0.7
	1907	2234	0.9	
12 W	0209	0459		0.6
	0800	1055	0.6	
	1348	1702		0.5
	2006	2332	0.8	
13 Th	0302	0558		0.6
	0903	1202	0.6	
	1502	1807		0.5
	2106			
14 F		0030		0.7
	0352	0654	0.6	
	1002	1307		0.6
	1616	1912	0.5	
	2206			
15 Sa		0125		0.6
	0439	0748	0.6	
	1058	1408		0.6
	1726	2014	0.5	
	2304			
16 Su		0217		0.6
	0523	0837	0.7	
	1148	1503		0.7
	1829	2111	0.5	
	2358			
17 M		0306		0.6
	0608	0906	0.7	
	1233	1553		0.7
	1924	2203	0.5	
18 Tu	0049	0350		0.5
	0641	1003	0.7	
	1315	1638		0.8
	2014	2251	0.4	
19 W ○	0137	0432		0.5
	0717	1042	0.7	
	1353	1719		0.4
	2100	2335	0.4	
20 Th	0221	0511		0.5
	0751	1119	0.7	
	1430	1759		0.8
	2142			
21 F		0017		0.4
	0305	0550	0.4	
	0826	1155		0.7
	1506	1837	0.8	
	2222			
22 Sa		0058		0.4
	0348	0630	0.4	
	0902	1232		0.7
	1542	1915	0.8	
	2302			
23 Su		0138		0.4
	0432	0710	0.4	
	0941	1310		0.7
	1619	1954	0.8	
	2342			
24 M		0220		0.4
	0516	0753	0.4	
	1024	1352		0.6
	1658	2034	0.8	
25 Tu	0021	0302		0.4
	0602	0840	0.4	
	1112	1436		0.6
	1741	2117	0.8	
26 W	0100	0346		0.5
	0649	0930	0.5	
	1208	1526		0.5
	1827	2202	0.7	
27 Th ◑	0140	0431		0.5
	0737	1025	0.5	
	1312	1621		0.5
	1917	2249	0.7	
28 F	0219	0518		0.5
	0827	1123	0.5	
	1422	1721		0.5
	2012	2339	0.6	
29 Sa	0259	0606		0.6
	0917	1222	0.5	
	1533	1823		0.5
	2110			
30 Su		0030		0.6
	0340	0655	0.7	
	1007	1321		0.7
	1643	1926	0.5	
	2210			
31 M		0123		0.6
	0423	0744	0.7	
	1058	1417		0.7
	1748	2027	0.5	
	2311			

TIME MERIDIAN 60°W 0000h is midnight, 1200h is noon.

VIEQUES PASSAGE, PUERTO RICO

CURRENT TABLES 1994 **FLOOD 250° EBB 057°**

ATLANTIC STANDARD TIME (GMT -4H)

NOVEMBER

Day	Slack time	Max time	Fld Ebb knots
1 Tu	0507 / 1148 / 1848	0215 / 0833 / 1511 / 2125	0.6 / 0.8 / 0.9 / 0.5
2 W	0010 / 0553 / 1238 / 1944	0308 / 0923 / 1604 / 2221	0.6 / 0.9 / 1.0 / 0.6
3 Th ●	0107 / 0642 / 1328 / 2038	0400 / 1013 / 1656 / 2315	0.6 / 1.0 / 1.1 / 0.6
4 F	0203 / 0732 / 1418 / 2130	0453 / 1104 / 1747	0.6 / 1.0 / 1.1
5 Sa	0259 / 0825 / 1509 / 2220	0008 / 0547 / 1155 / 1838	0.6 / 0.6 / 1.0 / 1.1
6 Su	0356 / 0921 / 1600 / 2310	0101 / 0642 / 1248 / 1929	0.6 / 0.6 / 0.9 / 1.1
7 M	0453 / 1020 / 1651 / 2359	0154 / 0739 / 1343 / 2021	0.7 / 0.6 / 0.9 / 1.0
8 Tu	0551 / 1123 / 1744	0248 / 0838 / 1440 / 2113	0.7 / 0.6 / 0.8 / 1.0
9 W	0047 / 0651 / 1232 / 1837	0342 / 0941 / 1540 / 2206	0.7 / 0.6 / 0.7 / 0.9
10 Th ◑	0135 / 0750 / 1345 / 1933	0437 / 1045 / 1642 / 2300	0.7 / 0.6 / 0.5 / 0.8
11 F	0221 / 0848 / 1500 / 2030	0531 / 1149 / 1746 / 2353	0.7 / 0.6 / 0.5 / 0.7
12 Sa	0306 / 0943 / 1615 / 2128	0623 / 1251 / 1851	0.7 / 0.6 / 0.4
13 Su	0349 / 1033 / 1724 / 2226	0046 / 0713 / 1349 / 1953	0.6 / 0.7 / 0.7 / 0.4
14 M	0430 / 1120 / 1825 / 2324	0137 / 0800 / 1442 / 2050	0.5 / 0.7 / 0.7 / 0.4
15 Tu	0510 / 1203 / 1918	0225 / 0844 / 1530 / 2143	0.5 / 0.7 / 0.8 / 0.4
16 W	0019 / 0548 / 1242 / 2005	0311 / 0925 / 1613 / 2231	0.4 / 0.7 / 0.8 / 0.4
17 Th	0112 / 0626 / 1319 / 2048	0355 / 1004 / 1654 / 2316	0.4 / 0.7 / 0.9 / 0.4
18 F O	0201 / 0703 / 1356 / 2127	0438 / 1042 / 1732 / 2358	0.4 / 0.7 / 0.9 / 0.4
19 Sa	0248 / 0742 / 1431 / 2204	0520 / 1120 / 1810	0.3 / 0.7 / 0.9
20 Su	0333 / 0822 / 1507 / 2239	0038 / 0602 / 1159 / 1847	0.4 / 0.3 / 0.7 / 0.9
21 M	0417 / 0906 / 1545 / 2314	0117 / 0645 / 1239 / 1924	0.5 / 0.3 / 0.6 / 0.9
22 Tu	0500 / 0955 / 1624 / 2348	0156 / 0730 / 1321 / 2003	0.5 / 0.3 / 0.6 / 0.8
23 W	0543 / 1050 / 1705	0235 / 0817 / 1407 / 2043	0.5 / 0.4 / 0.6 / 0.8
24 Th	0021 / 0626 / 1151 / 1749	0315 / 0908 / 1458 / 2124	0.5 / 0.4 / 0.5 / 0.7
25 F	0055 / 0712 / 1259 / 1838	0357 / 1002 / 1553 / 2209	0.6 / 0.5 / 0.5 / 0.7
26 Sa ◐	0130 / 0800 / 1524 / 1931	0442 / 1100 / 1653 / 2257	0.6 / 0.5 / 0.4 / 0.6
27 Su	0208 / 0849 / 1524 / 2030	0529 / 1159 / 1756 / 2349	0.7 / 0.6 / 0.4 / 0.6
28 M	0250 / 0940 / 1634 / 2132	0618 / 1257 / 1901	0.8 / 0.7 / 0.4
29 Tu	0335 / 1032 / 1739 / 2237	0043 / 0709 / 1355 / 2004	0.6 / 0.9 / 0.9 / 0.4
30 W	0423 / 1124 / 1839 / 2341	0139 / 0802 / 1451 / 2105	0.6 / 0.9 / 1.0 / 0.5

DECEMBER

Day	Slack time	Max time	Fld Ebb knots
1 Th	0515 / 1216 / 1934	0236 / 0855 / 1545 / 2203	0.5 / 1.0 / 1.0 / 0.5
2 F ●	0044 / 0609 / 1307 / 2026	0334 / 0949 / 1638 / 2259	0.5 / 1.0 / 1.1 / 0.6
3 Sa	0145 / 0706 / 1358 / 2115	0431 / 1042 / 1729 / 2353	0.6 / 1.0 / 1.1 / 0.6
4 Su	0245 / 0804 / 1449 / 2202	0529 / 1136 / 1820	0.6 / 1.0 / 1.1
5 M	0343 / 0905 / 1538 / 2248	0045 / 0627 / 1230 / 1909	0.7 / 0.6 / 0.9 / 1.1
6 Tu	0440 / 1007 / 1628 / 2332	0137 / 0725 / 1325 / 1959	0.7 / 0.6 / 0.8 / 1.0
7 W	0538 / 1113 / 1717	0228 / 0825 / 1421 / 2047	0.7 / 0.6 / 0.7 / 0.9
8 Th	0016 / 0634 / 1222 / 1807	0318 / 0925 / 1518 / 2136	0.7 / 0.6 / 0.6 / 0.8
9 F ◐	0058 / 0729 / 1334 / 1857	0409 / 1026 / 1618 / 2224	0.7 / 0.6 / 0.5 / 0.7
10 Sa	0139 / 0822 / 1448 / 1949	0458 / 1126 / 1719 / 2313	0.8 / 0.6 / 0.4 / 0.6
11 Su	0220 / 0913 / 1601 / 2044	0547 / 1225 / 1821	0.8 / 0.6 / 0.3
12 M	0300 / 1001 / 1708 / 2143	0003 / 0634 / 1321 / 1922	0.5 / 0.8 / 0.7 / 0.3
13 Tu	0340 / 1046 / 1808 / 2244	0053 / 0720 / 1412 / 2021	0.5 / 0.7 / 0.7 / 0.3
14 W	0420 / 1129 / 1900 / 2344	0142 / 0805 / 1500 / 2116	0.4 / 0.7 / 0.8 / 0.3
15 Th	0501 / 1209 / 1946	0232 / 0848 / 1544 / 2206	0.4 / 0.7 / 0.8 / 0.3
16 F	0042 / 0542 / 1247 / 2026	0320 / 0929 / 1626 / 2251	0.3 / 0.7 / 0.9 / 0.4
17 Sa	0136 / 0625 / 1325 / 2104	0406 / 1010 / 1705 / 2334	0.3 / 0.7 / 0.9 / 0.4
18 Su O	0225 / 0710 / 1403 / 2138	0452 / 1051 / 1743	0.3 / 0.7 / 0.9
19 M	0310 / 0756 / 1440 / 2210	0013 / 0537 / 1132 / 1820	0.4 / 0.3 / 0.7 / 0.9
20 Tu	0352 / 0846 / 1518 / 2241	0051 / 0622 / 1215 / 1857	0.5 / 0.3 / 0.6 / 0.9
21 W	0433 / 0940 / 1558 / 2311	0128 / 0708 / 1259 / 1934	0.5 / 0.4 / 0.6 / 0.8
22 Th	0514 / 1038 / 1639 / 2342	0204 / 0756 / 1346 / 2012	0.6 / 0.4 / 0.6 / 0.8
23 F	0556 / 1141 / 1722	0243 / 0846 / 1436 / 2052	0.6 / 0.5 / 0.5 / 0.7
24 Sa ◑	0014 / 0642 / 1248 / 1809	0324 / 0940 / 1531 / 2136	0.7 / 0.6 / 0.4 / 0.7
25 Su ◐	0048 / 0730 / 1358 / 1900	0408 / 1036 / 1630 / 2223	0.7 / 0.6 / 0.4 / 0.6
26 M	0127 / 0821 / 1510 / 1958	0456 / 1135 / 1732 / 2315	0.8 / 0.7 / 0.4 / 0.6
27 Tu	0211 / 0915 / 1620 / 2101	0547 / 1234 / 1838	0.9 / 0.8 / 0.4
28 W	0300 / 1009 / 1725 / 2208	0011 / 0641 / 1334 / 1943	0.6 / 0.9 / 0.9 / 0.4
29 Th	0353 / 1103 / 1825 / 2317	0111 / 0737 / 1431 / 2046	0.5 / 1.0 / 1.0 / 0.4
30 F	0450 / 1157 / 1919	0213 / 0834 / 1527 / 2145	0.5 / 1.0 / 1.0 / 0.5
31 Sa	0550 / 1250 / 2008	0024 / 0315 / 0930 / 1620 / 2241	0.5 / 1.0 / 1.1 / 0.5

TIME MERIDIAN 60°W   0000h is midnight, 1200h is noon.

U.S. VIRGIN ISLANDS

CAUTION: Our information on aids to navigation comes from official government sources. The latitudes and longitudes of these marks may not correspond to the readings from GPS or LORAN receivers. Some aids have been reported as unreliable, missing, off position or showing incorrect characteristics. No single aid to navigation, or waypoint, should be relied upon as a sole means of fixing your position.

ENTRY PROCEDURES

The U.S. Virgin Islands are a territory of the United States, but constitute a separate customs district. U.S. vessels should clear customs if arriving from a foreign port, but need not if arriving directly from Puerto Rico or the U.S. mainland. All vessels arriving from the British Virgin Islands must clear in. All foreign vessels, and U.S. vessels arriving from another country, must check in with the authorities at Charlotte Amalie, St. Thomas (809-774-6755); Christiansted, St. Croix (809-773-1011); Frederiksted, St. Croix; or Cruz Bay, St. John (809- 776-6741). Most foreign yachts will have to obtain a cruising permit. See the introduction to the Coast Pilot for more information on U.S. Customs and Immigration procedures.

Normal working hours are 8:00AM to 5:00PM, Monday through Saturday. Their is an overtime charge for Sundays, holidays and after-hours arrivals. U.S. registered vessels do not necessarily need to obtain a clearance upon leaving the U.S. Virgin Islands, but they may need one when checking in with the authorities in another country.

The local currency is the U.S. dollar, and credit cards or traveler's checks are widely accepted.

The language spoken is English.

APPROACHES TO ST. THOMAS

Sail Rock Lighted Buoy 1, 18 17.1N, 65 06.5W, Fl G 6s, 4M, Green.
SAVANA ISLAND LIGHT, 18 20.4N, 65 05.0W, Fl W 4s, 300 ft., 7M, White tower.

WEST GREGERIE CHANNEL

Lighted Buoy 2, Fl R 4s, 3M, Red.
Buoy 3, Green can.
Lighted Buoy 4, Fl R 2.5s, 3M, Red.
Lighted Buoy 5, Fl G 4s, 3M, Green.
LIGHT 6, 18 19.9N, 64 56.9W, Fl R 4s, 16 ft., 4M, TR on dolphin.
CROWN BAY MOORING CELL LIGHT, 18 19.9N, 64 57.1W, F R, On dolphin, Private aid.

KRUM BAY

SOUTH DOLPHIN OBSTRUCTION LIGHT, 18 19.6N, 64 57.7W, Q W, On dolphin, Sychronized with Krum Bay Pier Obstruction Light, Private aid.
PIER OBSTRUCTION LIGHT, 18 19.6N, 64 57.7W, Q W, On end of pier, Synchronized with Krum Bay North Mooring Dolphin Obstruction Light, Private aid.
NORTH MOORING DOLPHIN OBSTRUCTION LIGHT, 18 19.6N, 64 57.7W, Q W, On dolphin, Synchronized with Krum Bay Pipeway Obstruction Light, Private aid.
PIPEWAY OBSTRUCTION LIGHT, 18 19.6N, 64 57.7W, Q W, On end of pipeway, Synchronized with Krum Bay Pier Obstruction Light, Private aid.

EAST GREGERIE CHANNEL

East Gregerie Channel Lighted Buoy WR1, 18 18.7N, 64 56.1W, Q G, Green.
Lighted Buoy 2, Westerly side of shoal, Fl R 2.5s, 3M, Red.
Lighted Buoy 3, Fl G 4s, 3M, Green.

ST. THOMAS HARBOR

Entrance Lighted Buoy 2, South of rocks, Fl R 6s, 4M, Red.
BERG HILL RANGE (Front Light), 18 20.6N, 64 56.0W, Q G, 197 ft., KRW on skeleton tower, Visible 2° each side of rangeline.
(Rear Light), 125 yards, 344° from front light, Oc G 4s, 302 ft., KRW on skeleton tower, Visible 2° each side of rangeline.
Lighted Buoy 3, On shoal about center of entrance to harbor, Fl G 4s, 4M, Green.

Buoy 4, West of bank, Red nun.
Rupert Rock Daybeacon, NW on pile worded DANGER.
Lighted Buoy 6, Off east side of entrance to harbor, Fl R 4s, 3M, Red.

HARBOR AREA BOUNDARY

Buoy B, 18 20.3N, 64 55.9, Yellow sphere, Private aid.
Buoy C, Yellow sphere, Private aid.
Buoy D, Yellow sphere, Private aid.
Buoy E, Yellow sphere, Private aid.
Buoy F, Yellow sphere, Private aid.
Buoy G, Yellow sphere, Private aid.

CHARLOTTE AMALIE

18 20N, 64 56W

Emergencies: Contact the U.S. Coast Guard on VHF channel 16, or on 2182kHz. There is a vessel documentation office in town, and a patrol vessel is often based at Kings Wharf. Virgin Islands Radio can assist in emergencies.
Pilotage: When approaching the Virgin Islands from the north, the prominent mountains rising over 1500 feet make the islands highly visible. At night, the "loom" is visible for many miles. The western approach to the harbor passes through the Savana Passage, marked by a light on Savana Island. At night, it is safer to pass west of the light to avoid the unlit rocks in the passage. Several other unlit rocks clutter the approach from the west, but a safe bearing can be taken on the lights of the airport. Many boats will often be anchored in West Gregerie Channel, while the channel east of Hassel Island is kept clear for the many cruise ships calling at the West Indian Docks. The entrance range of 344° will bring you safely into the main harbor.
Port of Entry: See Entry Procedures and the introduction to the Coast Pilot. You may tie up in a marina and call customs at (809) 774-6755. The Customs Office is in the Post Office building downtown.
Virgin Islands Radio: This private station provides an important communication link in the islands. They broadcast weather reports, make telephone calls and provide emergency assistance. Contact them on VHF channel 16. For more information refer to the Communications and Weather Services chapter.
Dockage: There are several marinas in St. Thomas, and all services are available. On the west side of Crown Bay contact the Crown Bay Marina at (809) 774-2255. Sugar Reef Marine

Services at (809) 777-7100, is located on the east side of Crown Bay. Avery's Marine Inc. at (809) 776-0113, is located on the west side of Haulover Cut. Yacht Haven Marina is located in the head of Long Bay, east of the cruise ship docks. Contact them at (809) 774-9700. The Haulover Marine Yachting Center is a service facility located in West Gregerie Channel. Contact them at (809) 776-2078. Contact any of the marinas on VHF channel 16, or through Virgin Islands Radio.
Moorings: There are numerous moorings scattered around the harbor, though most of them are privately owned. A few rental moorings may be available from Yacht Haven Marina.
Anchorages: There is usually room to anchor among the moored boats in Long Bay, taking care to stay clear of the cruise ship docks, the approaches to the marina and the turning basin. The holding is good, though the harbor can be rough from wakes and a surge rolling in from the south. Many boats anchor all along the West Gregerie Channel; at times practically blocking passage. Other spots to anchor include Hassel Island and the cove on the west side of Water Island known locally as Honeymoon Harbor. A crowded dinghy dock is available at Yacht Haven. Locking your tender is recommended.
Services: All services available. Large supermarkets, banks, a post office, hardware stores, marine stores, drug stores, and liquor stores are all within easy walking distance. A major airport has good connections to all points. If it is not available here, U.S. mail can get it to you quickly.

St. Thomas is the capital of commerce, and the biggest city in the Virgin Islands. It is the place to take care of major repairs, stock up and conduct your business affairs. The harbors are crowded with cruisers and charter boats from all over the world, bringing to the waterfront a fascinating variety of sights. Ashore are all of the pleasures of a major tourist destination, including interesting historical sights and good restaurants. When you're in St. Thomas, you're in the center of the action.

SOUTHEAST COAST OF ST. THOMAS

BUCK ISLAND LIGHT, 18 16.7N, 64 53.6W, Fl W 4s, 125 ft., 8M, White square tower.
Packet Rock Buoy 2, On south side of rock, 18 17.8N, 64 53.4W, Red nun.
Red Point Buoy 1, 18 18.4N, 64 51.7W, Green can.

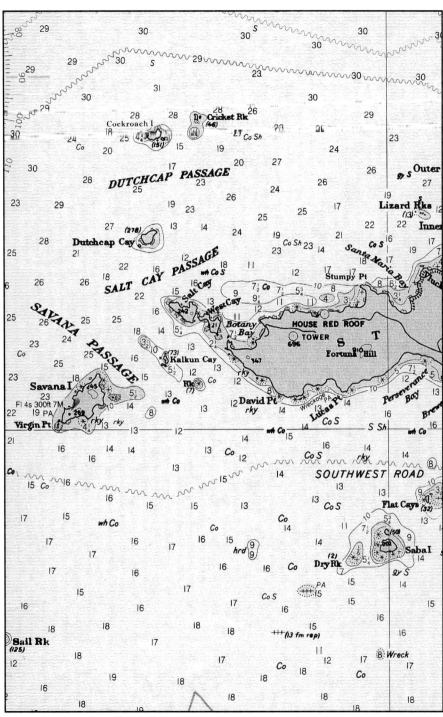

Savana Passage, Soundings in Fathoms

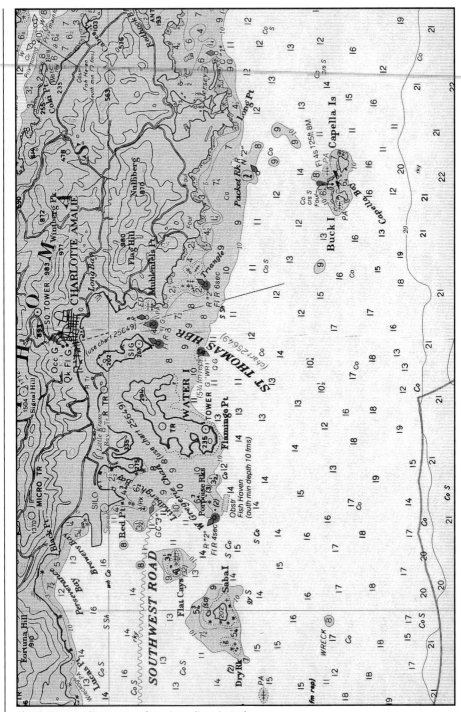

Charlotte Amalie Approaches, Soundings in Fathoms

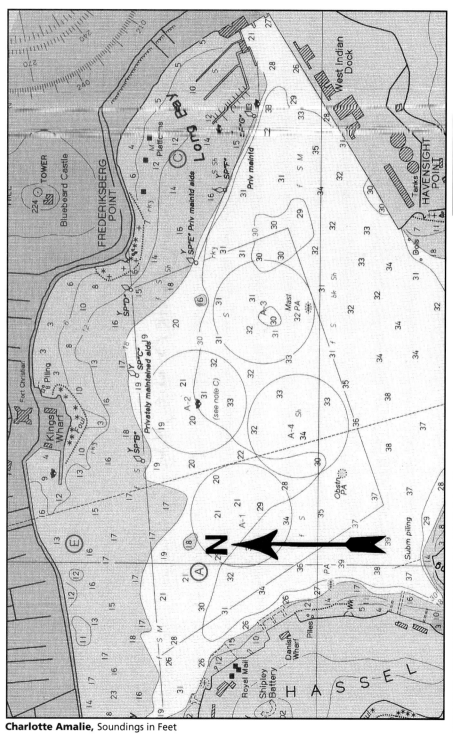

Charlotte Amalie, Soundings in Feet

Chapter 2

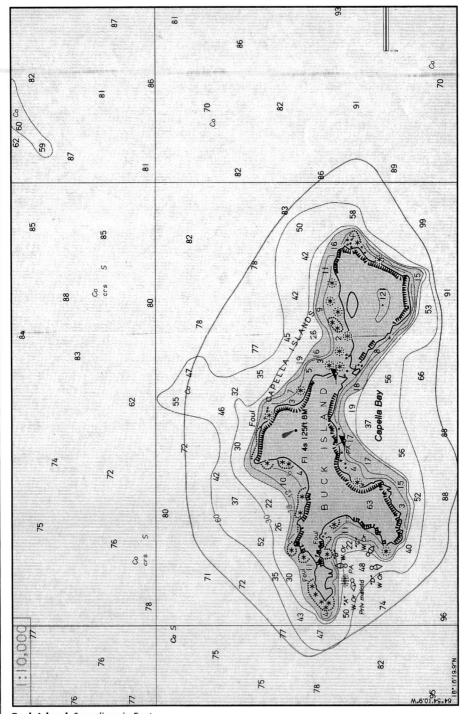

Buck Island, Soundings in Feet

BENNER BAY CHANNEL

Lighted Buoy 1, 18 19.0N, 64 52.1W, Fl G 2s, Green, Private aid.
Lighted Buoy 2, Fl R 2s, Red, Private aid.
Buoy 3, Green can, Private aid.
Buoy 4, Red nun, Private aid.
Buoy 5, Green can, Private aid.
Buoy 6, Red nun, Private aid.
Buoy 7, Green can, Private aid.
Buoy 8, Red nun, Private aid.
Buoy 9, Green can, Private aid.
Buoy 10, Red nun, Private aid.
Buoy 12, Red nun, Private aid.
Buoy 13, Green can, Private aid.
Buoy 14, Red nun, Private aid.
Buoy 15, Green can, Private aid.
Buoy 16, Red nun, Private aid.
Buoy 18, Red nun, Private aid.

BENNER BAY

18 19N, 64 52W

Emergencies: Contact the U.S. Coast Guard on VHF channel 16, or on 2182kHz. Virgin Islands Radio can assist in emergencies.
Pilotage: Do not pass between Cas Cay and Patricia Cay. The green can off the east end of Cas Cay is your main entrance mark. The channel into Benner Bay (known locally as the Lagoon) is privately marked by red and green buoys. The channel is reported to be shoal in places, with possible broken off pilings outside of the deeper water. You might want to call ahead for the latest depth information if you draw over 6 feet.
Virgin Islands Radio: This private station provides an important communication link in the islands. They broadcast weather reports, make telephone calls and provide emergency assistance. Contact them on VHF channel 16. For more information refer to the Communications and Weather Services chapter.
Dockage: This area features several marinas and repair yards. Contact La Vida Marina at (809) 775-6901, Tropical Marine at (809) 775-6595 and Ruan's Marine at (809) 775-6346. For repairs contact Independent Boat Yard at (809) 776-0466.
Anchorage: There may be some room to anchor along the channel leading into Benner Bay. The water shoals rapidly outside of the dredged area, and broken off pilings have been reported.
Services: All services are available here, or nearby on the island. This is a good place for major repairs or storing your boat, being more sheltered then Charlotte Amalie or Red Hook.

CURRENT CUT TO RED HOOK

CURRENT ROCK LIGHT, 18 18.9N, 64 50.1W, Fl W 6s, 20 ft., 6M, NR on skeleton tower, Higher intensity beams towards Buck Island and Two Brothers.
Cabrita Point Buoy 1, Green can.
Vessup Bay Buoy 1, 18 19.7N, 64 50.6W, Black can, Private aid.
Buoy 2, Red nun, Private aid.
Buoy 3, Black can, Private aid.
Buoy 4, Red nun, Private aid.
Buoy 5, Black can, Private aid.
Buoy 6, Red nun, Private aid.

RED HOOK

18 20N, 64 51

Emergencies: Contact the U.S. Coast Guard on VHF channel 16, or on 2182kHz. Virgin Islands Radio can assist in emergencies.
Virgin Islands Radio: This private station provides an important communication link in the islands. They broadcast weather reports, make telephone calls and provide emergency assistance. Contact them on VHF channel 16. For more information refer to the Communications and Weather Services chapter.
Dockage: Contact American Yacht Harbor at (809) 775-6454 or the St. Thomas Sport Fishing Center at (809) 775-7990. The Sapphire Beach Resort and Marina is in a small bay just north of Redhook Point. Call them at (809) 775-6100, or on VHF channel 16.
Anchorage: Many moorings limit the available anchoring area, but some boats find room in Muller Bay. There is heavy boat traffic, and many wakes from the ferries running to St. John.
Services: Most services are available here, except for haulouts. Any supplies can be found near the docks, or elsewhere on the island.

PILLSBURY SOUND

TWO BROTHERS LIGHT, 18 20.6N, 64 49.0W, Fl W 6s, 23 ft., 6M, NR on skeleton tower.
STEVENS CAY LIGHT, 18 19.9N, 64 48.5W, Fl W 4s, 14 ft., 5M, NR on skeleton tower.
Mingo Rock Lighted Buoy 2, 18 19.4N, 64 48.2W, Fl R 4s, 4M, Red.

CRUZ BAY

CRUZ BAY LIGHT, 18 20.0N, 64 47.9W, Fl W 4s, 12 ft., 5M, NR on pile.

Chapter 2

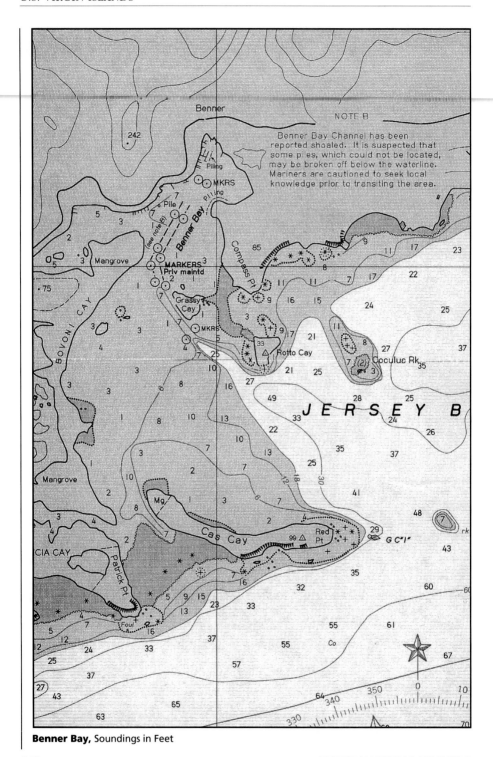

Benner Bay, Soundings in Feet

Chapter 2

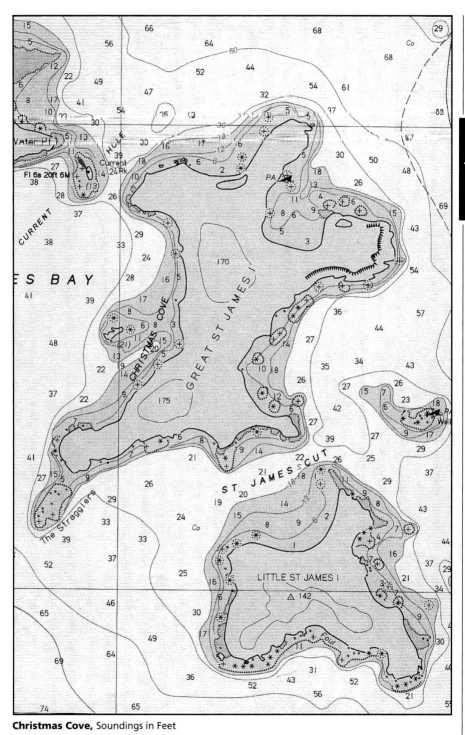

Christmas Cove, Soundings in Feet

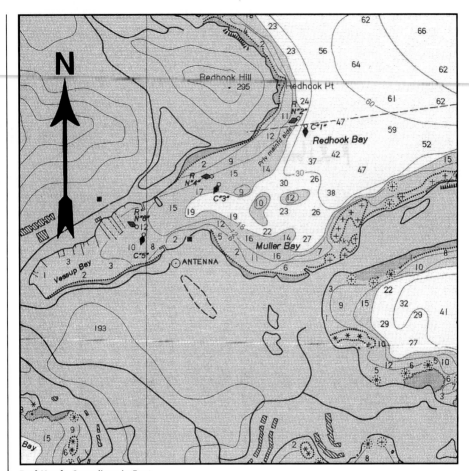

Red Hook, Soundings in Feet

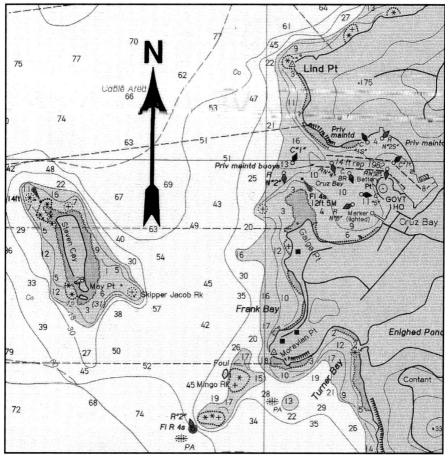

Cruz Bay, Soundings in Feet

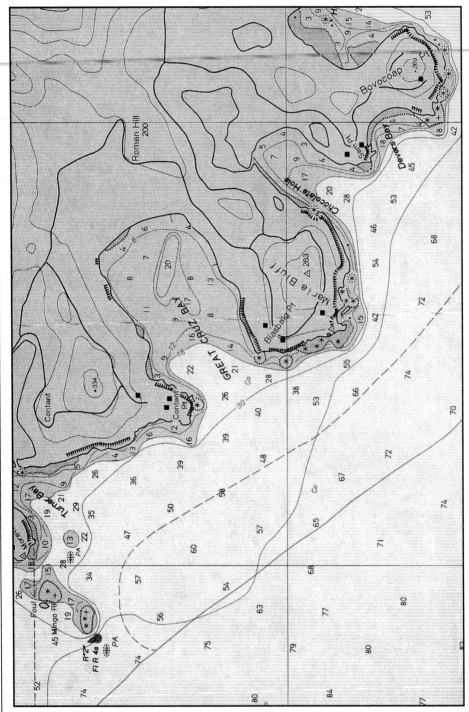

Great Cruz Bay, Soundings in Feet

Buoy 1, 18 20.0N, 64 47.9W, Black can, Private aid.

Buoy 2, Red nun, Private aid.

Buoy 4, Red nun, Private aid.

Junction Buoy, Black and Red Bands, Private aid.

Buoy 5, Black can, Private aid.

Buoy 6, Red nun, Private aid.

Viss Channel Buoy 1S, 18 20.1N, 64 47.8W, For Seaplane Ramp, Black can, Private aid.

Viss Channel Buoy 2S, Red nun, Private aid.

Battery Point Buoy 1, North of point, 18 20.0N, 64 47.7W, Black can, Private aid.

Battery Point Buoy 2, North of point, Red nun, Private aid.

CRUZ BAY

18 20N, 64 48W

Emergencies: Contact the U.S. Coast Guard on VHF channel 16, or on 2182kHz. Virgin Islands Radio can assist in emergencies.

Virgin Islands Radio: This private station provides an important communication link in the islands. They broadcast weather reports, make telephone calls and provide emergency assistance. Contact them on VHF channel 16. For more information refer to the Communications and Weather Services chapter.

Port of Entry: Dinghy in to the customs dock in the northern arm of the harbor. They may be contacted at (809) 776-6741. Vessels arriving from the British Virgin Islands must check in with customs.

National Park Service: They have a dock, and a visitors center located in the northern arm of the harbor. Contact the office at (809) 776-6201 for the latest regulations on boating in the park. Currently there is a 2 week limit (per year) on anchoring in the park. There are currently 4 park moorings in Little Lameshur Bay, 5 in Great Lameshur Bay, 1 in Leinster Bay and 1 in Hawksnest Bay. They are available on a first come/first served basis.

Dockage: You might be able to tie up temporarily to the National Park Service dock in the cove off the northern channel in the harbor.

Anchorage: The anchorage areas are very small, crowded and swept by wakes from the frequent ferries. Boats anchor both north and south of the main ferry channel in the southern arm of the harbor. Stay clear of the marked channels and the reef extending north from Galge Point. Temporary anchorage is available south of Lind Point. You may find there is not enough room to safely anchor in any of these spots. Dinghies may be landed

north of the ferry wharf in the southern arm of the harbor.

Services: Caneel Bay Shipyard provides haul-outs, fuel, water, supplies and repairs. Contact them at (809) 776-6111. Limited groceries and general stores are available from several small shops in town. Connections specializes in providing communication services for boaters. Contact them at (809) 776-6922. There are lots of small specialty shops, boutiques and informal eateries.

Many people prefer the calmer pace of St. John to the big city rush of Charlotte Amalie. Unfortunately, Cruz Bay is tiny, crowded and constantly stirred up by ferries. With much of the island being national park, the natural beauty of St. John is spectacular. It is well worth a climb to the top of one of the 1000 foot high peaks to catch a glimpse of the Virgin Islands spread before you.

CANEEL BAY

Buoy 1, 18 20.6N, 64 47.3W, Black can, Private aid.

Buoy 2, Red nun, Private aid.

Buoy 3, Black can, Private aid.

Buoy 4, Red nun, Private aid.

Buoy 5, Black can, Private aid.

Buoy 6, Red nun, Private aid.

HAWKSNEST BAY

Buoy 1, 18 20.8N, 64 46.7W, Black can, Private aid.

Buoy 2, Red nun, Private aid.

TRUNK BAY

Buoy 1, 18 21.1N, 64 46.2W, Black can, Private aid.

Buoy 2, Red nun, Private aid.

WINDWARD PASSAGE

Johnson Reef Lighted Buoy 1JR, 18 21.9N, 64 46.4W, Fl G 4s, 4M, Green.

Johnson Reef South Buoy 2, 18 21.5N, 64 46.4W, Red nun.

FRANCIS BAY

Buoy 1, 18 21.9N, 64 44.7W, Black can, Private aid.

Buoy 2, Red nun, Private aid.

Chapter 2

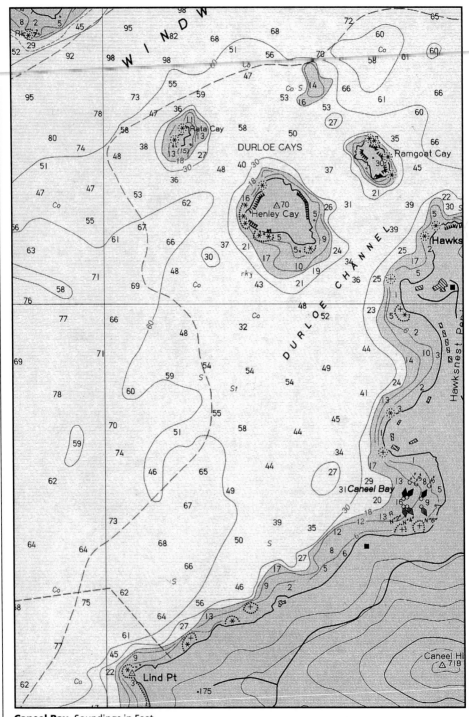

Caneel Bay, Soundings in Feet

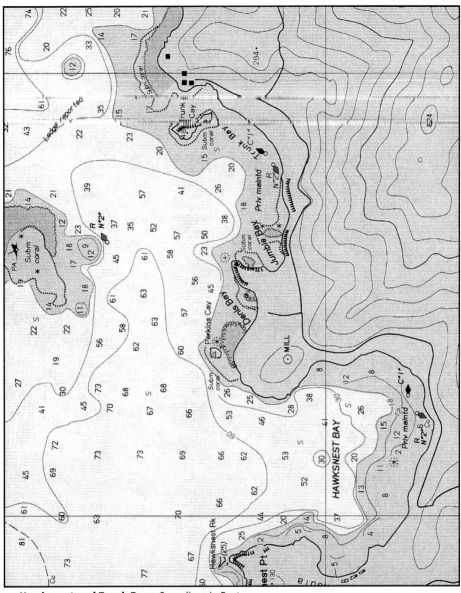

Hawksnest and Trunk Bays, Soundings in Feet

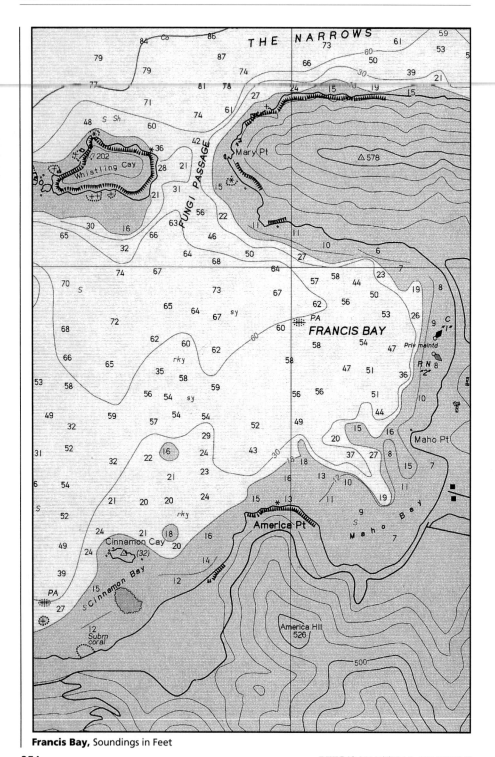

Francis Bay, Soundings in Feet

FRANCIS BAY

18 22N, 64 45W

Emergencies: Contact the U.S. Coast Guard on VHF channel 16, or on 2182kHz. Virgin Islands Radio can assist in emergencies.

Virgin Islands Radio: This private station provides an important communication link in the islands. They broadcast weather reports, make telephone calls and provide emergency assistance. Contact them on VHF channel 16. For more information refer to the Communications and Weather Services chapter.

National Park Service: See the section on Cruz Bay for more information on the park headquarters. Anchoring is limited to two weeks per year within the park. NPS boats patrol this area regularly.

Anchorage: This is an excellent anchorage area, with wonderful swimming, snorkeling and beaching. Several private buoys mark an area where dinghies may proceed in to the beach. From here you can hike the road to the Annaberg Sugar Mill ruins near Leinster Bay.

Services: You might be able to purchase a few basic supplies, or make a phone call at the resort in nearby Maho Bay.

CORAL HARBOR CHANNEL

Buoy 1, 18 20.6N, 64 42.7W, Green can, Private aid.
Buoy 2, Red nun, Private aid.
Buoy 3, Green can, Private aid.
Buoy 4, Red nun, Private aid.
Buoy 5, Green can, Private aid.
Buoy 6, Red nun, Private aid.
Buoy 7, Green can, Private aid.
Buoy 8, Red nun, Private aid.

CORAL BAY AND HURRICANE HOLE

18 20N, 64 42W

Emergencies: Contact the U.S. Coast Guard on VHF channel 16, or on 2182kHz. Virgin Islands Radio can assist in emergencies.

Virgin Islands Radio: This private station provides an important communication link in the islands. They broadcast weather reports, make telephone calls and provide emergency assistance. Contact them on VHF channel 16. For more information refer to the Communications and Weather Services chapter.

Anchorage: There are many excellent possibilities for anchoring in any of the arms of the harbor. The area to the north is known as Hur-

ricane Hole, due to the excellent protection available among the mangroves. The small boat wharf, at the head of the bay, is reported to have 3 feet of depth alongside.

Services: Coral Bay Marine at (809) 776-6859 and Coral Bay Sails at (809) 776-6665 can offer some repairs. There are a few small shops, a grocery, a laundry and casual eateries. There are buses and taxis that run to Cruz Bay if you need something.

ST. CROIX

HAMS BLUFF LIGHT, West end of island, 17 46.3N, 64 52.3W, Fl (2) W 30s, 394 ft., 16M, White cylindrical tower, Visible from 053° to 265°, Partially obscured from 053° to 062°.

National Undersea Research Habitat Lighted Buoy, Off entrance to Salt River Bay, 17 47.5N, 64 45.3W, Q W, Large white hull lettered NOAA, Maintained by NOAA.

CHRISTIANSTED APPROACHES

Lighted Buoy 1, 17 45.8N, 64 41.8W, Fl G 2.5s, 3M, Green.
ENTRANCE RANGE (Front Light), 17 45.4N, 64 41.7W, Q W, 45 ft., KRW on skeleton tower, Visible all around, Higher intensity on rangeline. **(Rear Light),** 735 yards, 164° from front light, Iso W 6s, 93 ft., KRW on skeleton tower, Visible all around, Higher intensity on rangeline.
Buoy 2, At northeast point of shoal, Red nun.
Buoy 3, At west point of bank, Green can.
Lighted Buoy 4, Q R, 2M, Red.
Buoy 5, At southwest point of bank, Green can.
Buoy 6, Red nun.
LIGHT 7, Fl G 4s, 16 ft., 4M, SG on dolphin.
Round Reef Northeast Junction Buoy, At northeast point of reef, Green and red banded can.
Round Reef Southwest Daybeacon 2, TR on dolphin.
Buoy 8, Red nun.
LIGHT 9, Fl G 2.5s, 16 ft., 5M, SG on dolphin.
Daybeacon 10, TR on pile.
LIGHT 11, Q G, 10 ft., 2M, SG on dolphin.
Buoy 12, Red nun.
LIGHT 13, Fl G 4s, 16 ft., 4M, SG on pile.
Buoy 15, Green can.
Daybeacon 16, TR on pile.
CHRISTIANSTED HARBOR WHARF LIGHTS (2), F W, 12 ft., Private aids.

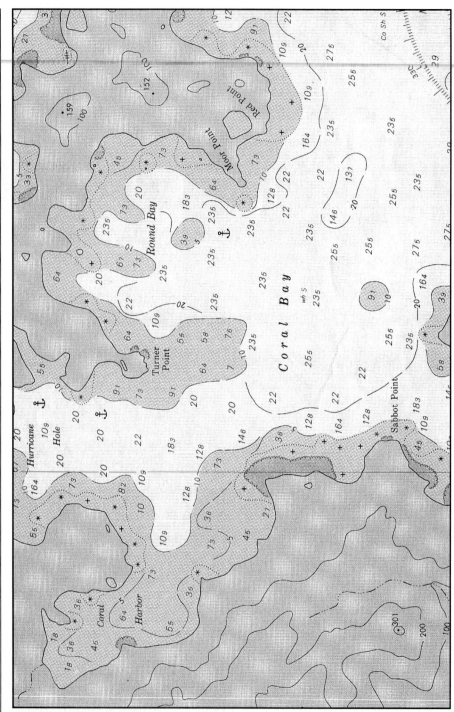

Coral Bay and Hurricane Hole, Soundings in Meters

Chapter 2

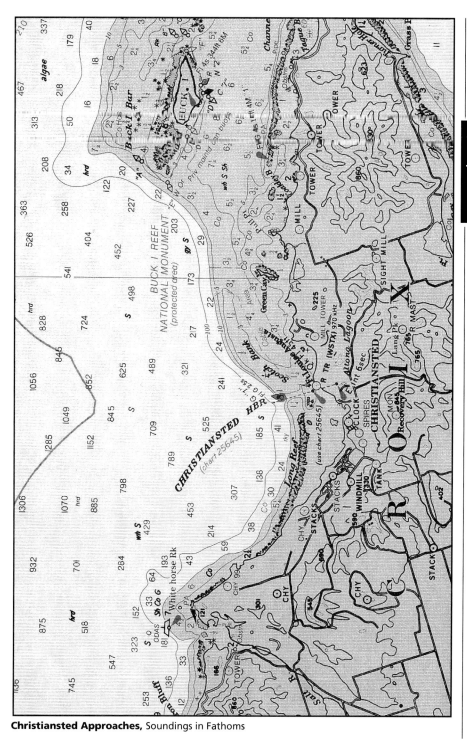

Christiansted Approaches, Soundings in Fathoms

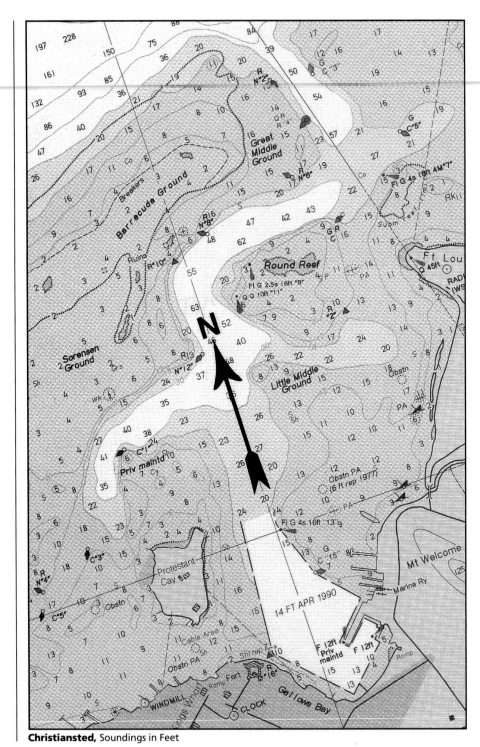

Christiansted, Soundings in Feet

SCHOONER CHANNEL

This privately marked channel runs from east of Round Reef to the main harbor area.

Lighted Buoy 5, 17 45.3N, 64 41.8W, Q G, Green, Private aid.
Lighted Buoy 6, Q R, Red, Private aid.
Lighted Buoy 7, Q G, Green, Private aid.
Lighted Buoy 8, Q R, Red, Private aid.
Lighted Buoy 9, Fl G 4s, Green, Private aid.
Lighted Buoy 10, Fl R 4s, Red, Private aid.
Lighted Buoy 11, Fl G 4s, Green, Private aid.
Lighted Buoy 14, Fl R 4s, Red, Private aid.

CHRISTIANSTED

17 45N, 64 42W
Emergencies: Contact the U.S. Coast Guard on VHF channel 16, or on 2182kHz. Virgin Islands Radio can assist in emergencies.
Virgin Islands Radio: This private station provides an important communication link in the islands. They broadcast weather reports, make telephone calls and provide emergency assistance. Contact them on VHF channel 16. For more information refer to the Communications and Weather Services chapter.
Pilotage: St. Croix is located about 37 miles south of St. Thomas. Due to extensive off lying reefs, boaters should stay a mile or two offshore until sure of their position. When crossing from St. Thomas, you should allow for a westerly set to the current of about 1/2 knot - it is often prudent to lay your course for the east end of the island, to avoid a final slog to windward. The initial entrance range is 164°, and gets you through the reef. Then the channel zig-zags to the west and south to get to the waterfront.
Port of Entry: Contact customs at (809) 773-1011.
Dockage: St. Croix Marine is a full-service yard northeast of the main wharf. Contact them at (809) 773-0289, or on VHF channel 16. East of Christiansted is Green Cay Marina. Enter via the channel west of Green Cay. They may be contacted at (809) 773-1453, or on VHF channel 16. The Salt River Marina is located in Salt River Bay, 4 miles west of Christiansted. Contact them at (809) 778-9650.
Anchorage: In Christiansted anchor southwest of Protestant Cay, avoiding the charted cable area. Salt River is a hurricane hole, with about 6 feet of water in the tricky reef entrance. Call ahead for the latest directions before entering. Private marks help to define the channel.

Services: All services are available, including haulouts and repairs.

Christiansted is less visited by cruisers, due to its location 37 miles south of the beaten track. There are many historic buildings worth seeing, and there is more open countryside outside of the cities. The combination of Danish, British and West Indian heritage is more visible here than in other parts of the U.S. Virgins.

PUERTO RICAN CEMENT COMPANY

This channel begins north of Protestant Cay and runs west to the industrial plant.

Channel Buoy 1, 17 45.3N, 64 42.2W, Black can, Private aid.
Channel Buoy 3, Black can, Private aid.
Channel Buoy 4, Red nun, Private aid.
Channel Buoy 5, Black can, Private aid.
Channel Buoy 6, Red nun, Private aid.
Channel Buoy 7, Black can, Private aid.
Channel Buoy 8, Red nun, Private aid.
Channel Buoy 9, Black can, Private aid.
Channel Buoy 10, Red nun, Private aid.
CHRISTIANSTED WATER INTAKE LIGHTS (4), 17 45.2N, 64 42.8W, F W, 12 ft., On Pile, Private aids.
CHRISTIANSTED WATER INTAKE SOUTH LIGHTS (4), 17 45.1N, 64 42.8W, F W, On piles, Private aids.

ST. CROIX: NORTHEAST COAST

COAKLEY BAY LIGHT 1, 17 46.1N, 64 38.2W, Fl G 4s, 16 ft., 3M, SG on pile.
BUCK ISLAND LIGHT, 17 47.3N, 64 37.1W, Fl W 4s, 344 ft., 6M, Red pyramidal skeleton tower.
Buck Island Channel Buoy 1, Black can, Private aid.
Buck Island Channel Buoy 2, Red nun, Private aid.

BUCK ISLAND REEF NATIONAL MONUMENT

Buoy A, 17 48.0N, 64 38.3W, Orange and white banded can, Private aid.
Buoy B, Orange and white banded can, Private aid.
Buoy C, Orange and white banded can, Private aid.

Buoy D, Orange and white banded can, Private aid.
Buoy D1, Orange and white banded can, Private aid.
Buoy E, Orange and white banded can, Private aid.
Buoy F, Orange and white banded can, Private aid.
Buoy G, 17 47.3N, 64 37.7W, Orange and white banded can, Private aid.

LIME TREE BAY

CHANNEL RANGE (Front Light), 17 42.2N, 64 45.0W, F G, 165 ft., KRW on skeleton tower, Visible 4° each side of rangeline, Private aid.
(Rear Light), 500 yards, 334° from front light, F G, 195 ft., KRW on skeleton tower, Visible 4° each side of rangeline, Private aid.
CHANNEL EAST AUXILIARY RANGE (Front Light), 17 42.2N, 64 45.0W, F R, 55 ft., Black and yellow bands, Pole, Visible 4° each side of rangeline, Private aid. **(Rear Light),** 303 yards, 334° from front light, F R, 70 ft., Black and yellow bands, Pole, Visible 4° each side of rangeline, Private aid.
Channel Lighted Buoy 1, 17 40.7N, 64 44.3W, Q G, Green, Spar station buoy, Private aid.
Channel Lighted Buoy 2, Q R, Red, Spar station buoy, Private aid.
Channel Lighted Buoy 3, Fl G 5s, Green, Private aid.
Channel Lighted Buoy 4, Fl R 5s, Red, Private aid.

Note: The following lights are located 35 feet outside the channel limits.

CHANNEL LIGHT 5, Fl G 4s, 14 ft., SG on pile, Private aid.
Channel Lighted Buoy 6, Fl R 4s, Red, Private aid.
CHANNEL LIGHT 7, Fl G 2.5s, 14 ft., SG on pile, Private aid.
CHANNEL LIGHT 8, Fl R 2.5s, 14 ft., TR on pile, Private aid.
CHANNEL LIGHT 9, Fl G 2.5s, 14 ft., SG on pile, Private aid.
CHANNEL LIGHT 11, Fl G 2.5s, 14 ft., SG on pile, Private aid.
CHANNEL JUNCTION LIGHT LK, Fl (2+1) G 6s, 14 ft., JG on pile, Obscured from 296° to 026°, Private aid.
CONTAINER PORT BASIN LIGHT 13, Fl G 5s, 14 ft., SG on pile, Private aid.

CONTAINER PORT BASIN LIGHT 15, Fl G 4s, 14 ft., SG on pile, Private aid.
CONTAINER PORT BASIN LIGHT 17, Fl G 2.5s, 14 ft., SG on pile, Private aid.

KRAUSE LAGOON CHANNEL

Entrance Lighted Buoy 1, 17 40.7N, 64 45.2W, Fl G 4s, Black, Private aid.
Entrance Lighted Buoy 2, Fl R 6s, Red, Private aid.
LIGHT 3, Fl W 4s, 18 ft., SG on pile, Private aid.
LIGHT 4, Fl R 4s, 18 ft., TR on pile, Private aid.
LIGHT 4A, Q R, 14 ft., TR on pile, Obscured from 227° to 317°, Private aid.
LIGHT 5, Q G, 14 ft., SG on pile, On same structure as Krause Lagoon Cross Channel Range Front Light, Private aid.
LIGHT 6, Q W, 14 ft., TR on pile, Private aid.
LIGHT 7, Fl G 4s, 15 ft., SG on pile, Private aid.
LIGHT 8, Fl R 2.5s, 15 ft., TR on pile, Private aid.
LIGHT 9, Fl G 4s, 16 ft., SG on pile, Private aid.
LIGHT 10, Fl R 2.5s, 16 ft., TR on pile, Private aid.
LIGHT 11, Fl G 4s, 16 ft., SG on pile, Private aid.
LIGHT 12, Fl R 2.5s, 16 ft., TR on pile, Private aid.
LIGHT 13, Fl W 4s, 16 ft., SG on pile, Private aid.
LIGHT 14, Fl R 2.5s, 16 ft., TR on pile, Private aid.
LIGHT 16, Fl R 2.5s, 16 ft., TR on pile, Private aid.
LIGHT 17, Fl G 4s, 16 ft., SG on pile, Private aid.
EAST MOORING DOLPHIN SIX LIGHT, Fl R 5s, 12 ft., On dolphin, Private aid.
WEST TURNING DOLPHIN LIGHT, Fl W 5s, 12 ft., On dolphin, Private aid.

KRAUSE LAGOON CROSS CHANNEL

RANGE (Front Light), 17 41.4N, 64 45.6W, Q G, 14 ft., KWB on pile, On same structure as Krause Lagoon Channel Light 5, Private aid.
(Rear Light), 153 yards, 244° from front light, Oc G 4s, 28 ft., KWB on pile, Private aid.
LIGHT 1, Fl G 4s, 14 ft., SG on pile, Private aid.
LIGHT 2, 17 41.4N, 64 45.5W, Fl W 4s, 14 ft., TR on pile, Obscured from 260° to 350°, Private aid.

Note: The following lights are located 35 outside the channel limits.

LIGHT 3, Fl G 2.5s, 14 ft., SG on pile, Private aid.
LIGHT 4, Fl R 2.5s, 14 ft., TR on pile, Obscured from 288° to 018°, Private aid.
LIGHT 5, Q G, 14 ft., SG on pile, Private aid.

TEXACO CARIBBEAN

Buoy 1, 17 39.6N, 64 52.1W, Black can, Private aid.
Buoy 2, Red nun, Private aid.
Buoy 3, Black can, Private aid.
Buoy 4, Red nun, Private aid.
Buoy 5, Black can, Private aid.
Buoy 6, Red nun, Private aid.
Buoy 7, Black can, Private aid.
Buoy 8, Red nun, Private aid.

FREDERIKSTED ROAD

SOUTHWEST CAPE LIGHT, 17 40.8N, 64 54.0W, Fl W 6s, 45 ft., 7M, Gray skeleton tower.
Southwest Cape Shoal Buoy 2, Marks shoal off cape, Red nun.
U.S. Navy Radar Reflector Buoy, 17 41.3N, 64 54.2W, Platform of 3 yellow spherical buoys, Orange radar reflector. Maintained by U.S. Navy.
FREDERIKSTED HARBOR LIGHT, 17 43.0N, 64 53.1W, Fl W 4s (2 red sectors), 42 ft., 8M white, 6M red, NR on skeleton tower, Red from 000° to 044.5° and from 137° to 180°.
FREDERIKSTED PIER LIGHTS, F R, 12 ft., Private aids.

Chapter 2

CHARLOTTE AMALIE, U.S.V.I.

HIGH & LOW WATER 1994 18°20'N 64°56'W

ATLANTIC STANDARD TIME (GMT -4H)

JANUARY

Day	Time ft	Day	Time ft
1 Sa	0339 -0.2 / 1152 0.6 / 1940 0.0 / 2307 0.1	**16** Su	0402 -0.0 / 1149 0.3 / 1939 -0.1
2 Su	0442 -0.1 / 1228 0.5 / 1953 -0.0	**17** M	0230 0.1 / 0434 0.1 / 1149 0.3 / 1953 -0.1
3 M	0113 0.1 / 0605 0.0 / 1301 0.4 / 2016 -0.1	**18** Tu	0506 0.2 / 0609 0.2 / 1119 0.2 / 2012 -0.2 ◐
4 Tu	0304 0.2 / 0806 0.1 / 1330 0.3 / 2046 -0.2	**19** W	0533 0.3 / 2035 -0.3 ◯
5 W	0429 0.4 / 1044 0.2 / 1346 0.2 / 2121 -0.2 ◖	**20** Th	0559 0.3 / 2104 -0.3
6 Th	0534 0.5 / 2159 -0.3	**21** F	0626 0.4 / 2137 -0.4
7 F	0629 0.6 / 2240 -0.4	**22** Sa	0653 0.5 / 2214 -0.4
8 Sa	0719 0.7 / 2323 -0.4	**23** Su	0722 0.5 / 2254 -0.4
9 Su	0806 0.7	**24** M	0753 0.6 / 2337 -0.4
10 M	0006 -0.4 / 0850 0.7	**25** Tu	0825 0.6
11 Tu ●	0049 -0.4 / 0931 0.7	**26** W	0023 -0.4 / 0859 0.6
12 W ○	0131 -0.4 / 1009 0.7	**27** Th ○	0111 -0.4 / 0933 0.6 / 1743 -0.0 / 1848 -0.0
13 Th	0212 -0.3 / 1043 0.6	**28** F	0203 -0.3 / 1008 0.5 / 1730 -0.0 / 2035 0.0
14 F	0251 -0.2 / 1112 0.5 / 1935 0.0 / 2140 -0.0	**29** Sa	0258 -0.3 / 1041 0.4 / 1742 -0.1 / 2206 0.1
15 Sa	0328 -0.2 / 1135 0.4 / 1931 -0.1 / 2352 0.0	**30** Su	0400 -0.2 / 1114 0.3 / 1803 -0.0 / 2339 0.1
		31 M	0515 -0.1 / 1142 0.2 / 1830 -0.2

FEBRUARY

Day	Time ft	Day	Time ft
1 Tu	0116 0.2 / 0654 0.0 / 1204 0.2 / 1904 -0.3	**16** W	0254 0.2 / 1839 -0.3
2 W	0248 0.3 / 0917 0.1 / 1209 0.1 / 1944 -0.3	**17** Th	0358 0.3 / 1913 -0.3
3 Th ◐	0407 0.4 / 2030 -0.4	**18** F ◐	0445 0.4 / 1954 -0.3
4 F	0513 0.5 / 2119 -0.4	**19** Sa	0525 0.4 / 2042 -0.4
5 Sa	0609 0.6 / 2210 -0.5	**20** Su	0601 0.5 / 2133 -0.4
6 Su	0659 0.6 / 2301 -0.5	**21** M	0637 0.5 / 2228 -0.4
7 M	0745 0.6 / 2352 -0.5	**22** Tu	0712 0.5 / 2324 -0.4
8 Tu	0826 0.6	**23** W	0748 0.5 / 1545 0.0 / 1714 0.0
9 W	0041 -0.4 / 0903 0.5 / 1725 -0.0	**24** Th	0022 -0.4 / 0823 0.5 / 1529 0.0 / 1851 0.0
10 Th ●	0128 -0.4 / 0935 0.5 / 1708 -0.0 / 1955 -0.0	**25** F	0121 -0.3 / 0858 0.4 / 1537 -0.0 / 2006 0.1
11 F	0214 -0.3 / 1002 0.4 / 1711 -0.1 / 2114 0.0	**26** Sa ○	0222 -0.3 / 0930 0.3 / 1554 -0.1 / 2118 0.2
12 Sa	0300 -0.2 / 1000 0.3 / 1720 -0.1 / 2233 0.1	**27** Su	0327 -0.2 / 1000 0.3 / 1616 -0.1 / 2230 0.2
13 Su	0346 -0.1 / 1032 0.2 / 1733 -0.1 / 2358 0.1	**28** M	0440 -0.1 / 1026 0.1 / 1645 -0.2 / 2346 0.3
14 M	0440 0.0 / 1031 0.2 / 1750 -0.2		
15 Tu	0129 0.2 / 0602 0.1 / 1009 0.1 / 1812 -0.2		

MARCH

Day	Time ft	Day	Time ft
1 Tu	0608 -0.0 / 1045 0.1 / 1719 -0.3	**16** W	0037 0.3 / 1644 -0.2
2 W	0104 0.4 / 0810 0.0 / 1046 0.1 / 1759 -0.3	**17** Th	0135 0.4 / 1717 -0.3
3 Th	0222 0.4 / 1847 -0.3	**18** F	0232 0.4 / 1757 -0.3
4 F ◐	0336 0.5 / 1941 -0.4	**19** Sa	0325 0.5 / 1847 -0.3
5 Sa	0441 0.5 / 2041 -0.4	**20** Su ◯	0414 0.5 / 1948 -0.3
6 Su	0538 0.6 / 2144 -0.4	**21** M	0500 0.5 / 2058 -0.2
7 M	0628 0.5 / 2246 -0.3	**22** Tu	0543 0.5 / 2212 -0.2
8 Tu	0712 0.5 / 1516 0.0 / 1703 0.0 / 2347 -0.3	**23** W	0624 0.5 / 1346 0.0 / 1711 0.1 / 2325 -0.2
9 W	0750 0.5 / 1506 0.0 / 1832 0.1	**24** Th	0702 0.4 / 1347 0.0 / 1828 0.2
10 Th	0045 -0.2 / 0821 0.4 / 1510 -0.0 / 1942 0.1	**25** F	0036 -0.2 / 0739 0.4 / 1359 -0.0 / 1934 0.3
11 F	0141 -0.2 / 0847 0.3 / 1518 -0.1 / 2044 0.2	**26** Sa	0146 -0.1 / 0812 0.3 / 1418 -0.1 / 2035 0.3
12 Sa ●	0236 -0.1 / 0904 0.3 / 1528 -0.1 / 2143 0.2	**27** Su	0257 -0.1 / 0841 0.2 / 1442 -0.1 / 2136 0.4
13 Su	0332 -0.0 / 0912 0.2 / 1541 -0.1 / 2241 0.3	**28** M	0412 -0.0 / 0905 0.1 / 1510 -0.2 / 2237 0.5
14 M	0436 0.1 / 0910 0.2 / 1558 -0.2 / 2338 0.3	**29** Tu	0538 0.0 / 0921 0.1 / 1543 -0.2 / 2341 0.6
15 Tu	0600 0.1 / 0846 0.1 / 1618 -0.2	**30** W	0734 0.1 / 0914 0.1 / 1620 -0.3
		31 Th	0046 0.6 / 1704 -0.3

APRIL

Day	Time ft	Day	Time ft
1 F	0153 0.6 / 1753 -0.3	**16** Sa	0128 0.6 / 1656 -0.2
2 Sa	0258 0.6 / 1852 -0.3	**17** Su	0217 0.6 / 1750 -0.2
3 Su	0359 0.6 / 2001 -0.2	**18** M ◐	0307 0.6 / 1901 -0.1
4 M	0454 0.6 / 2119 -0.2	**19** Tu ◯	0356 0.5 / 1236 0.1 / 1442 0.1 / 2033 -0.1
5 Tu	0541 0.5 / 1327 0.0 / 1700 0.1 / 2239 -0.1	**20** W	0443 0.5 / 1210 0.0 / 1643 0.1 / 2211 -0.0
6 W	0622 0.4 / 1326 0.0 / 1819 0.2 / 2355 -0.0	**21** Th	0526 0.4 / 1216 0.0 / 1758 0.3 / 2343 -0.0
7 Th	0654 0.4 / 1332 0.0 / 1921 0.2	**22** F	0606 0.4 / 1231 -0.0 / 1858 0.4
8 F	0107 0.0 / 0718 0.3 / 1342 -0.0 / 2014 0.3	**23** Sa	0108 0.0 / 0640 0.3 / 1253 -0.1 / 1954 0.5
9 Sa	0215 0.1 / 0733 0.2 / 1353 -0.1 / 2102 0.4	**24** Su	0228 0.1 / 0710 0.2 / 1318 -0.2 / 2047 0.6
10 Su	0324 0.1 / 0737 0.2 / 1407 -0.1 / 2146 0.4	**25** M ○	0350 0.1 / 0732 0.2 / 1348 -0.2 / 2141 0.7
11 M ●	0441 0.1 / 0726 0.2 / 1424 -0.2 / 2229 0.5	**26** Tu	0521 0.1 / 0742 0.1 / 1421 -0.3 / 2235 0.7
12 Tu	1445 -0.2 / 2312 0.5	**27** W	1457 -0.3 / 2329 0.7
13 W	1509 -0.2 / 2355 0.5	**28** Th	1536 -0.3
14 Th	1539 -0.2	**29** F	0025 0.7 / 1619 -0.3
15 F	0040 0.6 / 1614 -0.2	**30** Sa	0121 0.7 / 1706 -0.2

TIME MERIDIAN 60°W

0000h is midnight, 1200h is noon.

Heights in feet are referred to the chart datum of sounding.

CHARLOTTE AMALIE, U.S.V.I.

HIGH & LOW WATER 1994   18°20'N 64°56'W

ATLANTIC STANDARD TIME (GMT -4H)

MAY

Day	Time	ft	Day	Time	ft
1 Su	0215 / 1803	0.7 / -0.1	16 M	0124 / 1713	0.6 / -0.1
2 M ☾	0308 / ???? / 1354 / 1917	0.6 / ??? / 0.0 / -0.0	17 Tu	0209 / ???? / 1331 / 1834	0.6 / ??? / 0.1 / -0.0
3 Tu	0355 / 1159 / 1639 / 2057	0.5 / 0.0 / 0.1 / 0.1	18 W ☽	0255 / 1041 / 1554 / 2028	0.5 / 0.0 / 0.2 / 0.1
4 W	0435 / 1159 / 1802 / 2247	0.4 / 0.0 / 0.0 / 0.1	19 Th	0339 / 1050 / 1716 / 2232	0.4 / -0.0 / 0.3 / 0.1
5 Th	0507 / 1206 / 1858	0.4 / -0.0 / 0.3	20 F	0419 / 1109 / 1816	0.4 / -0.1 / 0.4
6 F	0029 / 0527 / 1217 / 1943	0.3 / 0.3 / -0.1 / 0.4	21 Sa	0022 / 0454 / 1134 / 1909	0.2 / 0.2 / -0.1 / 0.6
7 Sa	0203 / 0535 / 1230 / 2023	0.2 / 0.2 / -0.1 / 0.5	22 Su	0202 / 0522 / 1202 / 1959	0.1 / 0.2 / -0.2 / 0.7
8 Su	0346 / 0517 / 1246 / 2100	0.2 / 0.2 / -0.2 / 0.6	23 M	0339 / 0537 / 1235 / 2049	0.1 / 0.1 / -0.3 / 0.8
9 M	1305 / 2135	-0.2 / 0.6	24 Tu	1310 / 2137	-0.3 / 0.8
10 Tu ●	1327 / 2209	-0.2 / 0.7	25 W ○	1347 / 2225	-0.3 / 0.8
11 W	1353 / 2244	-0.3 / 0.7	26 Th	1426 / 2313	-0.3 / 0.8
12 Th	1422 / 2320	-0.3 / 0.7	27 F	1506	-0.3
13 F	1455 / 2359	-0.3 / 0.7	28 Sa	0000 / 1547	0.8 / -0.2
14 Sa	1533	-0.2	29 Su	0046 / 1630	0.7 / -0.1
15 Su	0040 / 1617	0.7 / -0.2	30 M	0129 / 1717	0.6 / -0.0
			31 Tu	0207 / 1033 / 1551 / 1825	0.5 / 0.0 / 0.1 / 0.1

JUNE

Day	Time	ft	Day	Time	ft
1 W ☽	0239 / 1034 / 1741 / 2048	0.4 / 0.0 / 0.2 / 0.2	16 Th	0156 / 0921 / 1609 / 2056	0.5 / 0.0 / 0.3 / 0.2
2 Th	0301 / 1043 / 1831 / 2339	0.4 / -0.0 / 0.4 / 0.3	17 F	0230 / 0945 / 1719 / 2322	0.4 / -0.1 / 0.5 / 0.2
3 F	0304 / 1057 / 1910	0.3 / -0.1 / 0.5	18 Sa	0258 / 1015 / 1816	0.3 / -0.1 / 0.6
4 Sa	1113 / 1943	-0.1 / 0.5	19 Su	0145 / 0306 / 1048 / 1907	0.2 / 0.2 / -0.2 / 0.7
5 Su	1132 / 2015	-0.2 / 0.6	20 M	1125 / 1955	-0.3 / 0.8
6 M	1154 / 2044	-0.2 / 0.7	21 Tu	1204 / 2041	-0.3 / 0.9
7 Tu	1219 / 2114	-0.3 / 0.7	22 W	1245 / 2126	-0.3 / 0.9
8 W	1247 / 2144	-0.3 / 0.8	23 Th ○	1326 / 2210	-0.3 / 0.9
9 Th ●	1318 / 2215	-0.3 / 0.8	24 F	1408 / 2252	-0.3 / 0.8
10 F	1353 / 2249	-0.3 / 0.8	25 Sa	1449 / 2331	-0.2 / 0.8
11 Sa	1431 / 2324	-0.3 / 0.7	26 Su	1530	-0.1
12 Su	1514	-0.2	27 M	0006 / 0906 / 1029 / 1611	0.7 / 0.1 / 0.1 / 0.0
13 M	0001 / 1603	0.7 / -0.1	28 Tu	0036 / 0850 / 1333 / 1652	0.6 / 0.1 / 0.2 / 0.1
14 Tu	0040 / 0908 / 1152 / 1706	0.6 / 0.1 / 0.1 / 0.0	29 W	0058 / 0857 / 1640 / 1755	0.5 / 0.1 / 0.3 / 0.3
15 W	0118 / 0905 / 1424 / 1840	0.6 / 0.1 / 0.2 / 0.1	30 Th ☽	0105 / 0911 / 1748 / 2149	0.4 / 0.0 / 0.4 / 0.4

JULY

Day	Time	ft	Day	Time	ft
1 F	0029 / 0929 / 1823	0.4 / -0.0 / 0.5	16 Sa ☽	0109 / 0847 / 1704	0.4 / -0.1 / 0.7
2 Sa	0950 / 1854	-0.1 / 0.6	17 Su	0928 / 1802	-0.1 / 0.8
3 Su	1014 / 1923	-0.1 / 0.7	18 M	1011 / 1853	-0.2 / 0.9
4 M	1041 / 1950	-0.2 / 0.7	19 Tu	1057 / 1941	-0.2 / 0.9
5 Tu	1111 / 2017	-0.2 / 0.8	20 W	1144 / 2026	-0.2 / 1.0
6 W	1144 / 2045	-0.2 / 0.8	21 Th	1230 / 2108	-0.2 / 0.9
7 Th	1220 / 2114	-0.2 / 0.8	22 F ○	1317 / 2147	-0.2 / 0.9
8 F ●	1258 / 2145	-0.2 / 0.8	23 Sa	1402 / 2223	-0.1 / 0.8
9 Sa	1340 / 2218	-0.2 / 0.8	24 Su	0638 / 0803 / 1447 / 2254	0.3 / 0.3 / 0.0 / 0.7
10 Su	1426 / 2251	-0.1 / 0.8	25 M	0634 / 0948 / 1533 / 2319	0.3 / 0.3 / 0.1 / 0.7
11 M	0715 / 0830 / 1516 / 2325	0.2 / 0.2 / -0.1 / 0.7	26 Tu	0644 / 1134 / 1620 / 2335	0.2 / 0.2 / 0.2 / 0.6
12 Tu	0703 / 1038 / 1616 / 2358	0.2 / 0.2 / 0.1 / 0.6	27 W	0700 / 1336 / 1718 / 2336	0.2 / 0.2 / 0.4 / 0.5
13 W	0717 / 1235 / 1732	0.1 / 0.3 / 0.2	28 Th	0719 / 1538 / 1921 / 2300	0.1 / 0.5 / 0.5 / 0.5
14 Th	0029 / 0740 / 1425 / 1923	0.5 / 0.1 / 0.4 / 0.3	29 F	0743 / 1654	0.1 / 0.6
15 F	0055 / 0811 / 1555 / 2158	0.5 / 0.0 / 0.5 / 0.3	30 Sa ☾	0810 / 1738	0.1 / 0.7
			31 Su	0840 / 1812	0.0 / 0.7

AUGUST

Day	Time	ft	Day	Time	ft
1 M	0915 / 1842	-0.0 / 0.8	16 Tu	0940 / 1830	-0.0 / 1.0
2 Tu	0953 / 1911	-0.0 / 0.9	17 W	1036 / 1918	-0.0 / 1.0
3 W	1034 / 1939	-0.1 / 0.9	18 Th	1132 / 2001	0.0 / 1.0
4 Th	1118 / 2009	-0.1 / 0.9	19 F	1226 / 2040	0.1 / 1.0
5 F	1204 / 2040	-0.1 / 0.9	20 Sa	0417 / 0639 / 1319 / 2115	0.4 / 0.5 / 0.1 / 0.9
6 Sa	1252 / 2111	-0.0 / 0.9	21 Su ○	0420 / 0758 / 1411 / 2143	0.4 / 0.5 / 0.2 / 0.8
7 Su ●	0501 / 0647 / 1344 / 2143	0.4 / 0.4 / 0.0 / 0.8	22 M	0430 / 0911 / 1504 / 2205	0.4 / 0.5 / 0.3 / 0.7
8 M	0454 / 0821 / 1439 / 2215	0.4 / 0.4 / 0.1 / 0.8	23 Tu	0444 / 1024 / 1559 / 2218	0.4 / 0.6 / 0.4 / 0.7
9 Tu	0505 / 0945 / 1540 / 2245	0.3 / 0.5 / 0.2 / 0.7	24 W	0500 / 1141 / 1703 / 2217	0.3 / 0.6 / 0.5 / 0.6
10 W	0525 / 1110 / 1652 / 2312	0.3 / 0.5 / 0.3 / 0.6	25 Th	0519 / 1302 / 1840 / 2146	0.3 / 0.7 / 0.6 / 0.6
11 Th	0552 / 1238 / 1824 / 2334	0.2 / 0.6 / 0.4 / 0.6	26 F	0542 / 1422	0.3 / 0.7
12 F	0626 / 1407 / 2035 / 2341	0.2 / 0.7 / 0.5 / 0.5	27 Sa	0610 / 1530	0.2 / 0.8
13 Sa	0707 / 1528	0.1 / 0.8	28 Su	0644 / 1623	0.2 / 0.9
14 Su ☽	0753 / 1637	0.1 / 0.9	29 M ☽	0725 / 1706	0.2 / 0.9
15 M	0845 / 1737	0.1 / 1.0	30 Tu	0812 / 1743	0.2 / 0.9
			31 W	0906 / 1817	0.2 / 1.0

TIME MERIDIAN 60°W   0000h is midnight, 1200h is noon.

Heights in feet are referred to the chart datum of sounding.

Chapter 2

CHARLOTTE AMALIE, U.S.V.I.

HIGH & LOW WATER 1994 18°20'N 64°56'W

ATLANTIC STANDARD TIME (GMT -4H)

SEPTEMBER

Day	Time ft	Day	Time ft
1 Th	1003 0.2 / 1851 1.0	16 F	0226 0.5 / 0505 0.6 / 1130 0.3 / 1923 1.0
2 F	1102 0.2 / 1925 1.0	17 Sa	0226 0.5 / 0628 0.6 / 1235 0.3 / 1958 0.9
3 Sa	0312 0.5 / 0513 0.5 / 1202 0.2 / 1958 0.9	18 Su	0234 0.5 / 0736 0.7 / 1337 0.4 / 2025 0.9
4 Su	0258 0.5 / 0643 0.6 / 1302 0.3 / 2031 0.9	19 M	0245 0.5 / 0837 0.8 / 1439 0.5 / 2045 0.8
5 M ●	0305 0.5 / 0754 0.6 / 1404 0.3 / 2102 0.8	20 Tu	0259 0.4 / 0935 0.8 / 1543 0.5 / 2055 0.7
6 Tu	0320 0.4 / 0900 0.7 / 1510 0.4 / 2131 0.8	21 W	0315 0.4 / 1031 0.9 / 1655 0.6 / 2050 0.7
7 W	0342 0.4 / 1007 0.8 / 1622 0.4 / 2156 0.7	22 Th	0333 0.4 / 1126 0.9 / 1846 0.6 / 2004 0.6
8 Th	0410 0.3 / 1117 0.9 / 1747 0.5 / 2215 0.6	23 F	0354 0.3 / 1221 0.9
9 F	0443 0.3 / 1229 0.9 / 1940 0.6 / 2218 0.6	24 Sa	0419 0.3 / 1316 1.0
10 Sa	0523 0.2 / 1343 1.0	25 Su	0449 0.3 / 1409 1.0
11 Su	0609 0.2 / 1455 1.0	26 M	0525 0.3 / 1500 1.0
12 M ◑	0704 0.2 / 1602 1.1	27 Tu	0610 0.3 / 1547 1.0
13 Tu	0805 0.2 / 1702 1.1	28 W ◐	0708 0.3 / 1632 1.0
14 W	0913 0.2 / 1755 1.1	29 Th	0820 0.3 / 1714 1.0
15 Th	1022 0.2 / 1842 1.0	30 F	0940 0.4 / 1754 1.0

OCTOBER

Day	Time ft	Day	Time ft
1 Sa	0121 0.6 / 0505 0.6 / 1100 0.4 / 1831 0.9	16 Su	0102 0.5 / 0710 0.8 / 1302 0.5 / 1853 0.8
2 Su	0119 0.5 / 0620 0.7 / 1216 0.4 / 1906 0.9	17 M	0115 0.4 / 0804 0.8 / 1419 0.6 / 1909 0.7
3 M	0130 0.5 / 0722 0.8 / 1329 0.5 / 1939 0.9	18 Tu	0130 0.4 / 0853 0.9 / 1537 0.6 / 1913 0.6
4 Tu	0148 0.4 / 0819 0.9 / 1441 0.5 / 2007 0.7	19 W ○	0146 0.3 / 0938 1.0 / 1714 0.6 / 1848 0.6
5 W ●	0211 0.4 / 0916 1.0 / 1557 0.5 / 2031 0.7	20 Th	0205 0.3 / 1021 1.0
6 Th	0239 0.3 / 1014 1.1 / 1722 0.6 / 2048 0.6	21 F	0226 0.2 / 1102 1.0
7 F	0312 0.3 / 1113 1.1 / 1914 0.6 / 2041 0.6	22 Sa	0249 0.2 / 1143 1.0
8 Sa	0349 0.2 / 1214 1.1	23 Su	0316 0.2 / 1224 1.0
9 Su	0431 0.2 / 1316 1.2	24 M	0347 0.2 / 1306 1.0
10 M	0520 0.2 / 1419 1.1	25 Tu	0424 0.2 / 1350 1.0
11 Tu ◐	0617 0.3 / 1520 1.1	26 W	0510 0.3 / 1435 1.0
12 W	0726 0.3 / 1617 1.1	27 Th ◐	0613 0.3 / 1521 1.0
13 Th	0119 0.5 / 0229 0.5 / 0848 0.4 / 1707 1.0	28 F	0024 0.5 / 0223 0.5 / 0744 0.4 / 1605 0.9
14 F	0049 0.5 / 0446 0.6 / 1017 0.4 / 1751 0.9	29 Sa	2348 0.5 / 0436 0.6 / 0933 0.4 / 1648 0.8
15 Sa	0053 0.6 / 0607 0.7 / 1142 0.5 / 1826 0.8	30 Su	2350 0.4 / 0549 0.7 / 1117 0.5 / 1727 0.8
		31 M	0004 0.4 / 0646 0.8 / 1249 0.5

NOVEMBER

Day	Time ft	Day	Time ft
1 Tu	1801 0.7 / 0025 0.3 / 0738 0.9 / 1414 0.5	16 W	0029 0.1 / 0851 0.9
2 W	1830 0.6 / 0051 0.2 / 0829 1.0 / 1538 0.5	17 Th	0050 0.1 / 0927 0.9
3 Th ●	1852 0.5 / 0121 0.2 / 0919 1.1 / 1711 0.5	18 F ○	0112 0.0 / 1001 1.0
4 F	1901 0.4 / 0154 0.1 / 1011 1.1	19 Sa	0137 0.0 / 1034 1.0
5 Sa	0231 0.1 / 1103 1.1	20 Su	0204 0.0 / 1107 1.0
6 Su	0311 0.1 / 1155 1.1	21 M	0234 0.0 / 1141 1.0
7 M	0354 0.1 / 1249 1.1	22 Tu	0308 0.0 / 1217 0.9
8 Tu	0441 0.1 / 1342 1.0	23 W	0348 0.1 / 1255 0.9
9 W	0537 0.2 / 1433 1.0 / 2351 0.4	24 Th	0436 0.1 / 1335 0.8 / 2246 0.3
10 Th ◐	0122 0.4 / 0649 0.3 / 1521 0.9	25 F	0051 0.3 / 0544 0.2 / 1416 0.7
11 F	2323 0.4 / 0410 0.5 / 0830 0.4 / 1603 0.8	26 Sa ◐	2217 0.3 / 0338 0.4 / 0735 0.3 / 1457 0.7
12 Sa	2328 0.3 / 0540 0.6 / 1029 0.5 / 1636 0.7	27 Su	2224 0.2 / 0502 0.5 / 0954 0.4 / 1535 0.6
13 Su	2339 0.3 / 0641 0.7 / 1223 0.5 / 1658 0.6	28 M	2242 0.1 / 0601 0.6 / 1159 0.4 / 1608 0.5
14 M	2353 0.2 / 0730 0.8 / 1410 0.5 / 1704 0.5	29 Tu	2307 0.1 / 0652 0.7 / 1349 0.4 / 1634 0.4
15 Tu	0010 0.2 / 0813 0.8	30 W	2336 -0.0 / 0740 0.9

DECEMBER

Day	Time ft	Day	Time ft
1 Th	0009 -0.1 / 0827 0.9	16 F	0005 -0.2 / 0906 0.8
2 F ●	0046 -0.2 / 0914 1.0	17 Sa	0033 -0.2 / 0934 0.8
3 Sa	0124 -0.2 / 1001 1.0	18 Su ○	0103 -0.3 / 1003 0.8
4 Su	0205 -0.2 / 1048 1.0	19 M	0136 -0.2 / 1033 0.8
5 M	0247 -0.2 / 1134 0.9	20 Tu	0212 -0.2 / 1104 0.7
6 Tu	0331 -0.1 / 1219 0.9	21 W	0252 -0.2 / 1137 0.7
7 W	0417 -0.0 / 1301 0.8 / 2217 0.2	22 Th	0337 -0.1 / 1211 0.6 / 2041 0.1
8 Th	2334 0.2 / 0509 0.1 / 1340 0.7 / 2153 0.2	23 F	2315 0.1 / 0434 0.0 / 1245 0.5 / 2036 0.1
9 F	0251 0.2 / 0621 0.2 / 1412 0.6	24 Sa ◑	0149 0.2 / 0557 0.1 / 1318 0.5
10 Sa	2201 0.1 / 0457 0.4 / 0832 0.3 / 1435 0.5	25 Su ◐	2051 -0.0 / 0342 0.3 / 0808 0.2 / 1347 0.4
11 Su	2215 0.1 / 0604 0.5 / 1129 0.4 / 1435 0.4	26 M	2115 -0.1 / 0456 0.4 / 1048 0.2 / 1410 0.3
12 M	2233 0.0 / 0650 0.6 / 2254 -0.1	27 Tu	2145 -0.2 / 0553 0.5 / 2220 -0.3
13 Tu	0729 0.6 / 2316 -0.1	28 W	0644 0.7 / 2259 -0.3
14 W	0804 0.7 / 2340 -0.2	29 Th	0732 0.7 / 2340 -0.4
15 Th	0836 0.8	30 F	0818 0.8
		31 Sa	0023 -0.4 / 0903 0.8

TIME MERIDIAN 60°W
Heights in feet are referred to the chart datum of sounding.

0000h is midnight, 1200h is noon.

REED'S NAUTICAL ALMANAC

BRITISH VIRGIN ISLANDS

ENTRY PROCEDURES

The British Virgin Islands (B.V.I.) include the islands of Jost Van Dyke, Tortola, Norman, Peter, Salt, Cooper, Ginger, Virgin Gorda, Guana, Great Camanoe, Anegada, and numerous small cays. The country is a British dependency.

Ports of Entry are Jost Van Dyke, West End (Soper's Hole), Road Town, and Virgin Gorda Yacht Harbour. Normal working hours are 0830 to 1530, Monday through Friday, and 0830 to 1230 on Saturdays. An overtime charge applies after these hours, and on Sundays and holidays. Boats must clear customs and immigration when traveling between the U.S. Virgin Islands and the B.V.I.

You should have a clearance from your last port of call, though this is not strictly necessary when arriving from the U.S. Virgin Islands. You should also obtain a clearance before departing the B.V.I.s.

Immigration clearance will be given for 30 days, with extensions possible for $10.00 per person. You can generally get permission for visits of up to six months, provided you can prove adequate finances. Visitors from some countries may need a visa. For the latest information contact Road Town Customs at (809) 494-3475, and Road Town Immigration at (809) 494-3471.

There is a small fee for private cruising boats, and a per diem charge for charter boats. From December 1 to April 30 B.V.I. registered charter boats pay $2.00 per person, per day. Boats registered elsewhere pay $4.00 per person, per

day. From May 1 through November 30 the rates are $0.75 and $1.00 per person, per day.

Dive boats, sport fishing boats and day charter boats should contact the B.V.I. Customs department regarding Cruising Permits. All non B.V.I. residents must have a recreational fishing permit. Call the Fisheries Division at (809) 494-3429.

Their are National Parks Trust Moorings located near many dive sites. You must have a permit to use these moorings, which is available from Customs or from the Trust at (809) 494-3904.

The currency of the B.V.I. is the U.S. dollar, and major credit cards are widely accepted, especially in tourist areas. The language spoken is English.

GREAT HARBOUR

18 27N, 64 45W
Emergencies: Contact Virgin Islands Search and Rescue, VISAR, on VHF channel 16, at (809) 494-4357, or dial 999 on the telephone. Call Tortola Radio on VHF channel 16.
Pilotage: This bay is easy to enter with depths of 15 to 20 feet. A reef extends across most of the head of the bay, so don't venture too far in. A gap in the middle of the reef creates a safe route for dinghies traveling to the wharf. When anchoring, check your set well, as the holding is not all good, and the wind tends to swing the boats in strange ways.
Port of Entry: Dinghy in to the main dock. The Customs and Immigration offices are located near the wharf.
Dockage: None on Jost Van Dyke.
Anchorage: Good anchorage in White Bay, Great Harbour, Little Harbour and south of Little Jost Van Dyke. Green Cay and Sandy Cay are favorite day stops.
Services: There are several well known restaurant/bars, famous for their pig roasts and entertainment. Probably the best known "yachty" hangout is "Foxy's", where you'll be serenaded by Foxy himself. There are a few small stores, some groceries and a couple of telephones.

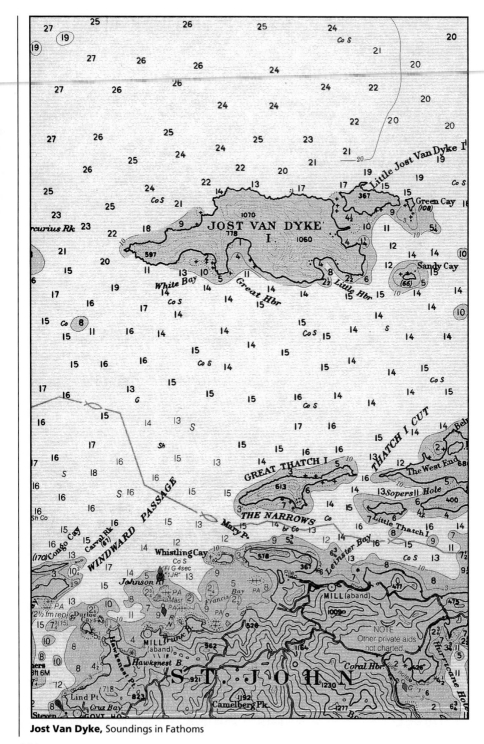

Jost Van Dyke, Soundings in Fathoms

Jost Van Dyke is famous for its watering holes and its relaxed atmosphere. This is probably the easiest place to clear customs in the B.V.I.

TORTOLA

SOPERS HOLE LIGHT, Passenger terminal, SW end, 18 23.4N, 64 42.2W, F R, 16ft.

WEST END

18 23N, 64 43W

Emergencies: Contact Virgin Islands Search and Rescue, VISAR, on VHF channel 16, at (809) 494-4357, or dial 999 on the telephone. Call Tortola Radio on VHF channel 16.

Pilotage: This popular harbor is charted as Soper's Hole, and both names are used interchangeably. The entrance is deep and free of obstructions, except close to shore. Be prepared for currents up to 3 or 4 knots in the mouth of Soper's Hole, in Thatch Island Cut and in the pass between Little Thatch and Frenchman's Cay. Stay clear of the docking ferries at the wharf on the north side of the harbor.

Port of Entry: The officials are located in the building on the ferry wharf. Due to the constant flow of traffic at the wharf, it is best to dinghy over from your moored boat.

Dockage: Contact Soper's Hole Marina at (809) 495-4553 or on VHF channel 16. Next door is Sunsail at (809) 495-4740.

Moorings: There are so many moorings here, you may have trouble finding room to anchor. Generally, you can pick up a free mooring and a boat will come to collect the fee. Short term rates are available for those just wishing to clear customs.

Anchorage: With depths of 25 to 65 feet, lots of moorings and frequent crowds of boats, anchoring is problematic at best. Many people try it, before picking up a rental mooring for the night.

Services: West End Slipway has a 200 ton marine railway and complete repair facilities for boats of all types. Contact them at (809) 495-4353. The Wood Works Ltd. is a wooden boat specialty shop. Contact them at (809) 495-4813. There are other repair shops, and most marine supplies can be obtained from Road Town via taxi. Pusser's Rum and the Jolly Roger have popular bars and restaurants, and the Ample Hamper can supply most food and liquor needs. Call Ample Hamper at (809) 495-4684 for provisioning information if you are on a bareboat charter. Baskin in the Sun is a full service dive shop—(809) 495-4582, or on VHF channel 16.

West End, or Soper's Hole, is a popular and busy spot. The yacht facilities are good, and the entertainment ashore is geared to the many charter boats visiting here. The presence

Chapter 2

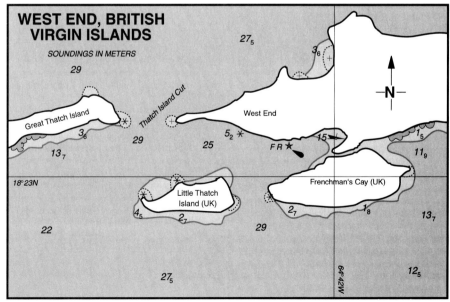

WEST END, BRITISH VIRGIN ISLANDS
SOUNDINGS IN METERS

West End, Soundings in Meters

of first class wooden boat specialists and repair facilities of all sorts makes this a unique harbor. The Sweethearts of the Caribbean race features classic yachts racing in these beautiful waters.

ROAD TOWN RANGE, (Front Light)
18 25.3N, 64 37.1W, F R, 37ft., 3M, Administration building, F R lights on radio mast 1.5M WNW, Aero F R, F W (occasional) 3M east.
(Rear Light) About 40 meters 290° from front, F R 52ft., 3M, Administration building.

ROAD TOWN
18 26N, 64 37W
Emergencies: Contact Virgin Islands Search and Rescue, VISAR, on VHF channel 16, at (809) 494-4357, or dial 999 on the telephone. Call Tortola Radio on VHF channel 16.
Pilotage: The range of 290° T will take you in to the government wharf safely. There are several shoal areas within the harbor that may, or may not, be marked . There is shallow water both north and south of the main wharf, off Baugher's Bay, and all along the shore north of the Fort Burt Marina area. Note the central harbor area where anchoring is prohibited.
Port of Entry: You may tie up temporarily to the main passenger wharf while clearing customs and immigration, but there may be a surge. The Office is located just across the street from the wharf. Contact Road Town Customs at (809) 494-3475, and Road Town Immigration at (809) 494-3471.
Dockage: The Nanny Cay Resort and Marina is located about 2 miles southwest of Road Harbor on the south coast of Tortola. Contact them at (809) 494-2512. Prospect Reef Resort and Marina is entered through a reef just a bit southwest of Fort Burt Point. Depths are reported to be less than 6 feet in the entrance channel. Fort Burt Marina can be contacted at (809) 494-2393 or at (809) 494-3870. Road reef Marina is located in the small cove south of Fort Burt Marina. Contact them at (809) 494-4537. In the Wickhams Cay basin are Village Cay Marina (809) 494-2771 and Inner Harbour Marina (809) 494-4502.
Anchorage: Most boaters find room north of the Fort Burt Marina, where there is a dinghy dock. Check your depths carefully, as the bottom shoals rapidly towards shore. There may be some room among the many moored boats in the Wickham's Cay basin. There is a dinghy dock near the Village Cay Marina. It is also possible to anchor south of the charter boat marina in Baugher's Bay. Most of the harbor is subject to surge and swells; especially when the wind comes in south of east.

Services: Tortola Yacht Services, on Wickham's Cay 2, is a full service boat yard. Contact them at (809) 494-2124. Nanny Cay also has hauling and repair services. There are several chandlers. Fuel, water and ice are available in Nanny Cay, Road Reef Marina, Village Cay Marina, and Inner Harbour Marina. There is a propane plant near the marina in Baugher's Bay. Road Town is the capital, and commercial center, of the British Virgin Islands. There are good telephone connections, banks, a post office, several grocery stores, many eateries and good shopping. Everything is available in a compact area, easily accessible for those on foot.

Road Town is a delightful Caribbean city, of small winding streets, with colorful wooden buildings leaning over the narrow sidewalks. This is a pleasant place to stock up on supplies, while avoiding the hectic pace of St. Thomas. The small bars and restaurants are often full of cruisers from around the world. Try a visit to the botanical garden, or a trip into the hills via taxi or rental car.

FAT HOGS BAY LIGHT, 18 26.1N, 64 33.6W, Fl W 8s, 25ft., 5M.
BELLAMY CAY LIGHT, Off Beef Island, 18 27.0N, 64 31.9W, F W, 25ft., White mast.

TRELLIS BAY
18 27N, 64 32W
Emergencies: Contact Virgin Islands Search and Rescue, VISAR, on VHF channel 16, at (809) 494-4357, or dial 999 on the telephone. Call Tortola Radio on VHF channel 16.
Pilotage: Entering from the north there are some rocks off Sprat Point, on the east side of Trellis Bay, and a 3 foot deep reef extending north from Conch Shell Point on the west side of the bay. There is a cable extending from Bellamy Cay west to shore, and a small shallow patch south of the cay.
Anchorage: Good anchorage is available throughout the bay. The airport is within walking distance from the docks on the west side of the bay.
Services: The famous Last Resort Island Restaurant offers a huge buffet and an evening of laughs when the owner parodies the foibles of visitors to the islands.

NORMAN ISLAND
18 19N, 64 37W
Emergencies: Contact Virgin Islands Search and Rescue, VISAR, on VHF channel 16, at (809) 494-4357, or dial 999 on the telephone. Call Tortola Radio on VHF channel 16.

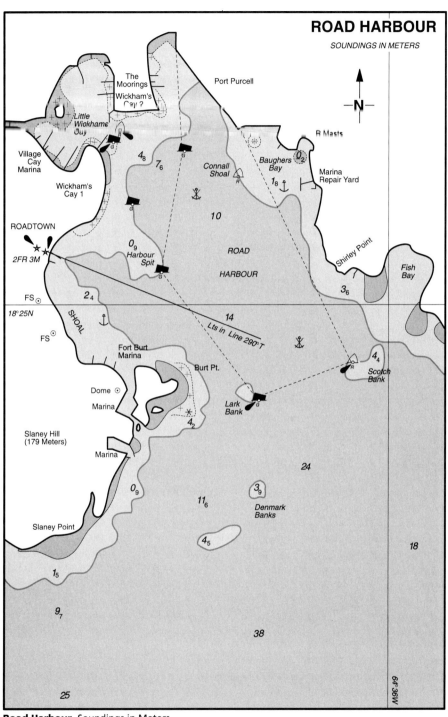

Road Harbour, Soundings in Meters

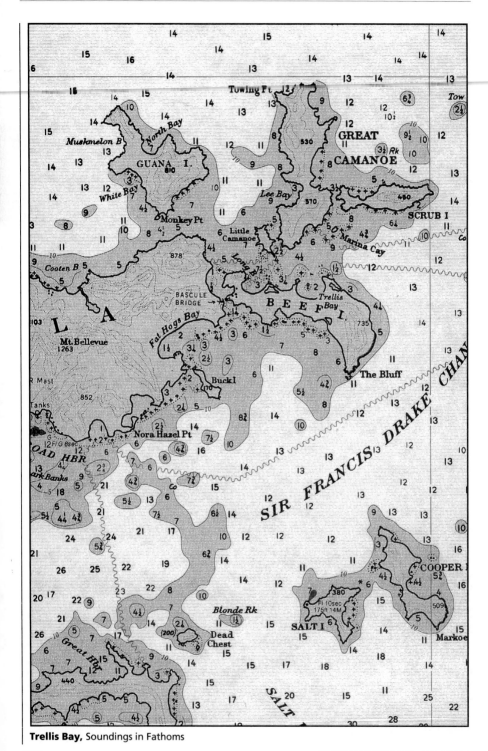

Trellis Bay, Soundings in Fathoms

Pilotage: The tall rocks west of Pelican Island are known as the Indians. This is a favorite dive site, and the National Parks Trust has placed moorings here to avoid damage to the coral. You must have a permit to use the moorings. South of Treasure Point is another reef, and a series of caves, which are also a dive site. Use the moorings if possible.

Anchorage: Anchor as far in the Bight as you can, to avoid the over 30 foot depths further out. You can dinghy in to the small beach at the head of the cove. This anchorage is often crowded with charter boats in the winter. In settled weather, Benures Bay, on the north coast of the island, is a pleasant anchorage. You should pass west of the reefs before looping up inside the hook of land.

Services: An anchored boat serves as a bar and restaurant. Contact the "William Thornton" on VHF channel 16.

PETER ISLAND

18 21N, 64 35W

Emergencies: Contact Virgin Islands Search and Rescue, VISAR, on VHF channel 16, at (809) 494-4357, or dial 999 on the telephone. Call Tortola Radio on VHF channel 16.

Pilotage: The only yacht facility on the island is located east of the spit of land forming the eastern boundary of Great Harbour. This body of water is called Sprat Bay.

Dockage: Peter Island Resort and Yacht Harbour offers dockage for yachts up to 170 feet, with 12 foot draft. Contact them at (809) 494-2561 or on VHF channel 16.

Moorings: Peter Island Resort has some rental moorings in Sprat Bay.

Anchorage: Anchorages include Sprat Bay, Great Harbour and Little Harbour. In settled weather you can anchor in White Bay on the south shore, or west of Key Cay.

Services: Diesel, water, ice and electricity are available at the Peter Island Resort docks. Their restaurant serves lunch, dinner and cocktails (jackets required for dinner).

SALT ISLAND

SALT ISLAND LIGHT, NW corner of island, 18 22.5N, 64 32.1W, Fl W 10s, 175ft., 14M.

SALT ISLAND

18 22N, 64 32W

Emergencies: Contact Virgin Islands Search and Rescue, VISAR, on VHF channel 16, at (809) 494-4357, or dial 999 on the telephone. Call Tortola Radio on VHF channel 16.

Pilotage: Salt Island rises to a height of 380 feet. There is a rock awash off the northeast point of the island. There is a small settlement in Salt Island Bay on the north shore where workers once mined the salt ponds on the island. The Wreck of the Rhone is a favorite dive site located southwest of the island. Boaters can anchor in Lee Bay to dinghy over to the dive site, which is located in over 20 feet of water. No anchoring is allowed, and visitors must use the National Trust moorings

Anchorage: Anchor in Salt Island Bay or Lee Bay.

COOPER ISLAND

18 23N, 64 31W

Emergencies: Contact Virgin Islands Search and Rescue, VISAR, on VHF channel 16, at (809) 494-4357, or dial 999 on the telephone. Call Tortola Radio on VHF channel 16.

Pilotage: Cooper Island is 1.7 miles long and rises to 530 feet high at its south end. The passage between Salt and Cooper is constricted by a rock awash off the northeast point of Salt. A small islet off the west coast of Cooper forms the southern boundary of Manchioneel Bay.

Moorings: Available in Manchioneel Bay.

Anchorage: The swirling winds, deep waters and crowded moorings make this anchorage uncomfortable at times. You can dinghy in to the beach club dock.

Services: A small beach club, with bar and restaurant, is often the site of lively charter boat parties.

GINGER ISLAND

GINGER ISLAND LIGHT, NE end of island, 18 23.6N, 64 28.3W, Fl W 5s, 498ft., 14M Yellow tower.

VIRGIN GORDA

PAJAROS POINT LIGHT, 18 30.2N, 64 19.5W, Fl (3) W 15s, 200ft., 16M.

THE BATHS AND VIRGIN GORDA YACHT HARBOUR

18 26N, 64 27W

Emergencies: Contact Virgin Islands Search and Rescue, VISAR, on VHF channel 16, at (809) 494-4357, or dial 999 on the telephone. Call Tortola Radio on VHF channel 16.

Pilotage: The Baths are located about 1/2 mile north of the southern tip of Virgin Gorda. Virgin Gorda Yacht Harbour is located about 1 1/2 miles further north. The marina has a

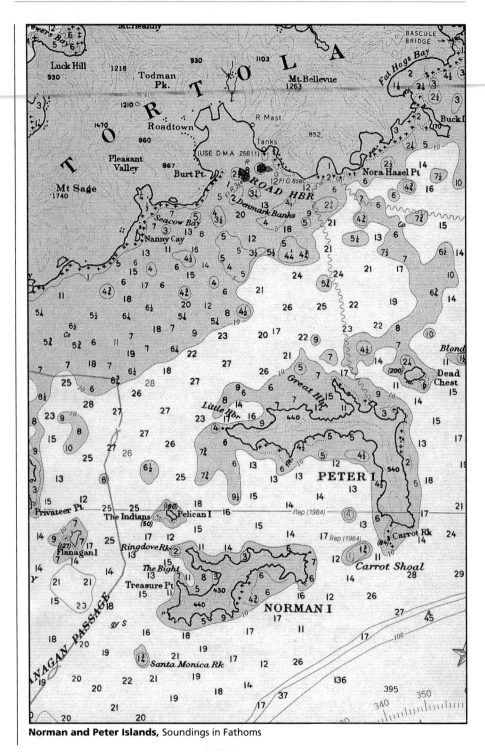

Norman and Peter Islands, Soundings in Fathoms

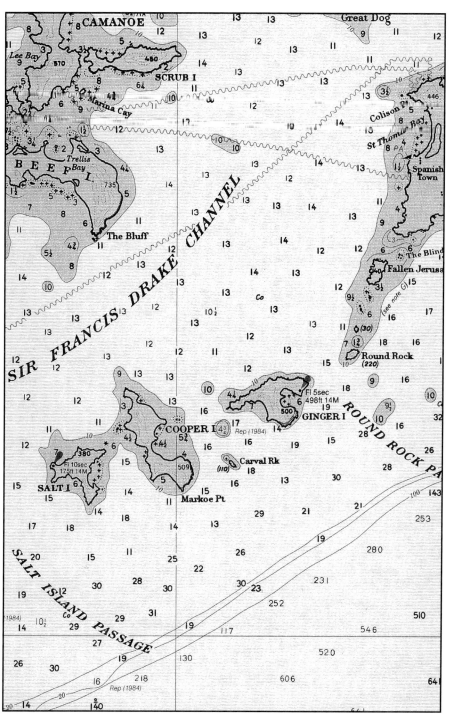

Salt, Cooper and Ginger Islands, Soundings in Fathoms

Chapter 2

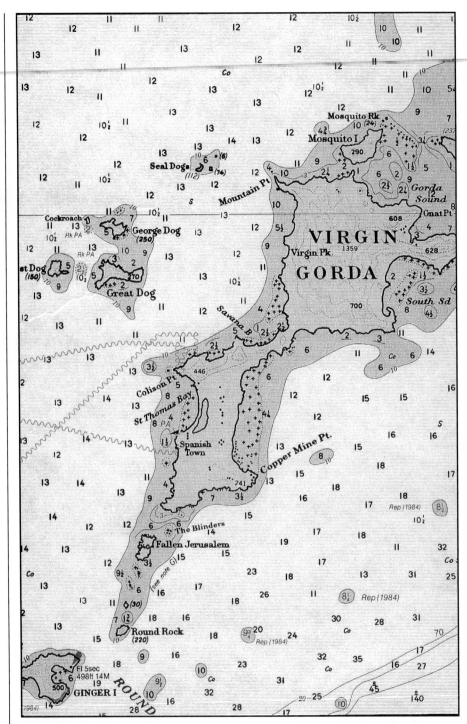

The Baths, Soundings in Fathoms

privately marked channel that takes you safely through the reef.

Port of Entry: Contact the officials in the marina.

Dockage: Contact Virgin Gorda Yacht Harbour at (809) 495-5555, or on VHF channel 16.

Anchorage: Anchor off the huge boulders that form the Baths. Be very careful to avoid the many snorkelers if you motor in to the beach in your dinghy. There is a marked dinghy channel. This anchorage can be very rolly, and is only a day stop.

Services: Virgin Gorda Yacht Harbour is a full service marina with fuel, water, ice, haulouts, repairs and a chandlery. A shopping center, a grocery store, a post office and several restaurants are nearby. You can take a taxi to other parts of the island, including the Baths.

GORDA SOUND

18 30N, 64 22W

Emergencies: Contact Virgin Islands Search and Rescue, VISAR, on VHF channel 16, at (809) 494-4357, or dial 999 on the telephone. Call Tortola Radio on VHF channel 16.

Pilotage: The west entrance to the sound passes through a narrow channel south of Mosquito Island. Just east of the narrowest part (175 yards wide) is a shallow bar to the north. Controlling depth is about 5 or 6 feet. You should only attempt this passage in good light. The northern entrance passes east of Colquhoun Reef, and is marked by a red and green buoy at the narrowest point. Least depth is about 17 feet on this route.

Dockage: Pusser's Leverick Bay has dockage and moorings in Leverick Bay along the south shore of Gorda Sound. They give you a free bottle of Pusser's Rum with every 25 gallon fuel purchase. Contact them on VHF channel 16. The Bitter End Yacht Club is located on the eastern side of the sound, and offers moorings and dockage. Contact them at (809) 494-2746, or on VHF channel 16. The Biras Creek Marina is south of the Bitter End. Contact them at (809) 495-5455.

Moorings: Rental moorings are available at Pusser's, the Bitter End, Biras Creek and at Drake's Anchorage on Mosquito Island. Contact Drake's Anchorage at (809) 494-2254.

Anchorage: There are many excellent places to anchor in Gorda Sound. In addition to anchorage's off of the establishments mentioned above, favorite spots include west of Prickly Pear Island, In Gun Creek, and near Saba Rock. Choose your spot depending upon the wind direction, and watch for coral heads in the shallows.

Services: All of the marinas and resorts have excellent bars and restaurants. Fuel, water and ice are available at Pusser's and the Bitter End. Some provisions are available at the Bitter End. There are interesting shops at Pusser's and the Bitter End. Kilbride's Underwater Tours leads snorkeling and diving expeditions from the Bitter End. Contact them at (809) 495-9638, or on VHF channel 16. Pirates Pub, on Saba Rock, is a favorite "yachty" hangout. Contact them on VHF channel 16.

Gorda Sound is a miniature cruising ground all by itself. There are interesting anchorages, good restaurants and beautiful views in all directions. Despite its popularity, there always seems to be room for everyone to find a good anchoring spot.

ANEGADA

ANEGADA LIGHT, W end, 18 44.8N, 64 24.7W, Fl W 10s, 62ft., 10M, Caution: This light may be inoperative.

ANEGADA

18 44N, 64 23W

Emergencies: Contact Virgin Islands Search and Rescue, VISAR, on VHF channel 16, at (809) 494-4357, or dial 999 on the telephone. Call Tortola Radio on VHF channel 16.

Pilotage: Anegada is only 30 feet high and very difficult to spot from a distance. It is surrounded by coral reefs and shoals You should never approach the island after dark, or in poor visibility. The direct course from Gorda Sound to the west end of Anegada is about 352° True. With the west end of Anegada lined up on your bow, and with Gorda Sound on your stern, you should clear all the coral heads. The currents are notoriously irregular, and you should judge your leeway by watching Virgin Gorda behind you. Chances are you will be set well to the west. Once you can see the island, you may be able to spot the buoys marking the channel into the anchorage on the south side of the island. Stay in deep water until you are sure of your course. Several buoys should lead you on a course of about 60° or 70° True towards the wharf and hotels on shore. Jost Van Dyke should be on your stern when you are headed towards the hotel. If in doubt, call the Anegada Reef Hotel on VHF channel 16, or one of the boats in the anchorage. The controlling depth is about 7 feet to the hotel, then 6 feet in the anchorage area west of the hotel.

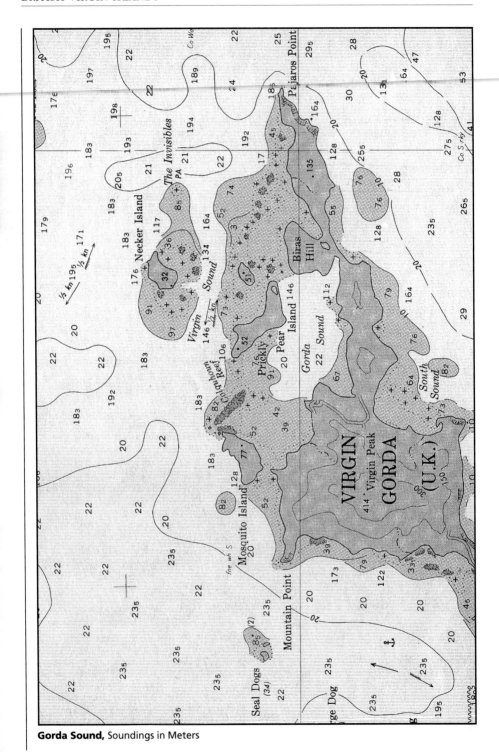

Gorda Sound, Soundings in Meters

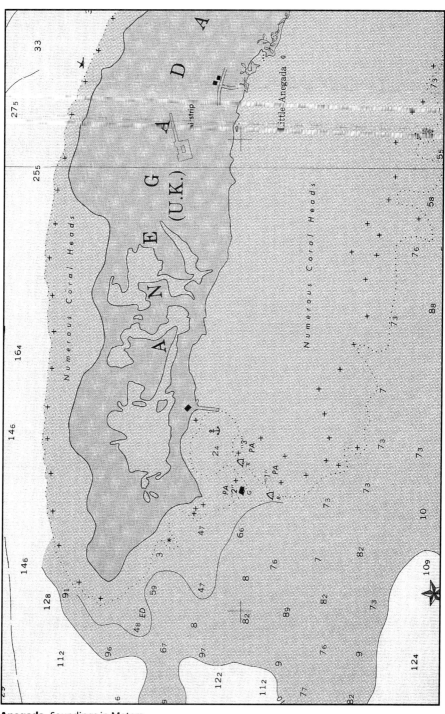

Anegada, Soundings in Meters

Anchorage: Anchor in the cove west of the hotel, watching for coral heads. This area is surprisingly sheltered, even in high winds. Boats sometimes anchor west of the restaurant on Pomato Point. Enter when the restaurant bears approximately 90°. Call Pomato Point on VHF channel 16 for directions.

Services: Neptune's Treasure rents tents and has a restaurant. Call them on VHF channel 16, or at (809) 495-9439. The Anegada Reef Hotel has rooms and meals. They also monitor channel 16 and can be called at (809) 495-8002. The Pomato Point Restaurant monitors VHF channel 16, and has an interesting museum of local artifacts. Call ahead for reservations at these establishments.

Anegada's fringing reefs have always been a treacherous trap for passing ships. This has created a diving and treasure hunter's paradise. Most bareboat charterer's won't be allowed to visit here, so you can get away from some of the crowds. Note that anchoring and fishing on Horseshoe Reef have been prohibited while fish stocks are restored.

SOMBRERO, UNITED KINGDOM

18 36N, 63 25W

SOMBRERO LIGHT, SE side, 18 35.8N, 63 23.0W, Fl W 10s, 157ft., 23M. Red iron framework tower.

This small island lies about 30 miles northwest of Anguilla. Its lighthouse is the only mark in the Anegada Passage. It lies on a small circular bank with depths of 10 to 30 fathoms. The island has precipitous sides, and rises in sharp jagged points. Vegetation is sparse, but there is abundant bird life on the island.

A light is exhibited from a square metal frame work tower on a white concrete base, situated near the center of the island. The keeper's dwellings and a flag staff stand north of the light-tower. A 20 foot high circular concrete base of a former light-tower stands east of the light. A ruined chimney about 33 feet high is about 175 yards southwest of the light.

You can anchor off the west side of the island in depths of about 12 fathoms.

ANGUILLA

CAUTION: Our information on aids to navigation comes from official government sources. The latitudes and longitudes of these marks may not correspond to the readings from GPS receivers. Some aids have been reported as unreliable, missing, off position or showing incorrect characteristics. No single aid to navigation, or waypoint, should be relied upon as a sole means of fixing your position.

ENTRY PROCEDURES

Anguilla is a British dependency, though it is basically self governing.

Ports of Entry are Road Bay, on the north coast, and Blowing Point, on the south coast. Road Bay is the preferred place of entry for pleasure vessels. Customs and Immigration are open from 0830 to 1200 and from 1300 to 1600, Monday through Friday. Saturday hours are 1300 to 1600, and the office is closed on Sundays and holidays.

Vessels over 20 tons must pay port and lighthouse dues. The charge is $20.00 for vessels from 20 to 50 tons, $60.00 for vessels from 50 to 100 tons and $150.00 for vessels from 100 to 250 tons. Charter boats must purchase a cruising permit for the duration of their stay. For vessels up to 5 tons the charge is $25.00 per day, or $150.00 per week. For vessels from 5 to 20 tons the charge is $100.00 per day, or $600.00 per week. For vessels over 20 tons the charge is $150.00 per day, or $900.00 per week.

All charges are in Eastern Caribbean, or EC, dollars. The exchange rate, when converting EC dollars to U.S. dollars, is about .40. In other words, $100 EC = $40 U.S. Registered tonnage is the basis for all charges.

Privately owned boats are not currently subject to charges in Anguilla. Spear fishing, and commercial fishing are prohibited aboard foreign boats. Check with Customs for certain areas where anchoring is prohibited.

For further information contact Customs in Road Bay at (809) 497-5461. The language spoken is English, and the official currency is the Eastern Caribbean dollar.

ANGUILLA APPROACHES

ANGUILLITA ISLAND LIGHT, 18 09.4N, 63 10.6W, Fl (2) W 15s, 48ft., 5M, Aluminum skeleton tower, R top.

ANGUILLA ISLAND LIGHT, Road Point,
18 12.2N, 63 05.7W, Fl (3) W R 20s, 59ft., 10M
white, 6M red, White concrete triangular
structure, W 070° to 089°, R 089° to 116°,
W 116° to 218°.
WINDWARD POINT LIGHT, 18 16.8N,
62 58.1W, Fl (3) W 14.5s, 72ft.

ROAD BAY

18 12N, 63 06W

Emergencies: Call Saba Radio on VHF channel 16.
Pilotage: Anguilla is quite low, with no conspicuous hills. The approach should be made in good light. Hazards include Dog Island, located about 10 miles northwest of Road Bay, and Prickly Pear Cays, located 5 miles north of the harbor. Seal Island reefs extend about 5 miles in an easterly direction from Prickly Pear Cays. The water is quite deep right up to the edge of the reefs. Dowling Shoals and Sandy Island lie about 2 miles northwest of the harbor. The white and red sectored light shown from Road Point helps direct you around the hazards. Boats are warned to watch for anchored vessels not showing anchor lights in the bay.

Port of Entry: The offices are located near the main commercial wharf. Contact Customs at (809) 497-5461.
Anchorage: There is good anchorage in depths of 7 to 20 feet. Keep the channel to the commercial wharf clear. The area immediately inside the hook of Road Point has a coral reef, and shallows extending towards town. You can dinghy in to the dock in the north part of the bay. There is a wide variety of uncrowded anchorages on other parts of the island, or on nearby cays.
Services: There are few services oriented directly towards yachts, but there are sources for fuel, water, ice and groceries ashore. You'll have to ferry supplies to your boat via dinghy. There is a good variety of restaurants, bars and shops. Tamarian Watersports is a full service scuba center. They can be reached at (809) 497-2020, or on VHF channel 16.

Being somewhat off the beaten track, and having a charter boat fee, Anguilla is less visited than most islands in this area. There are few yacht oriented services, but there are interesting anchorages, abundant dive sites and pleasant eateries.

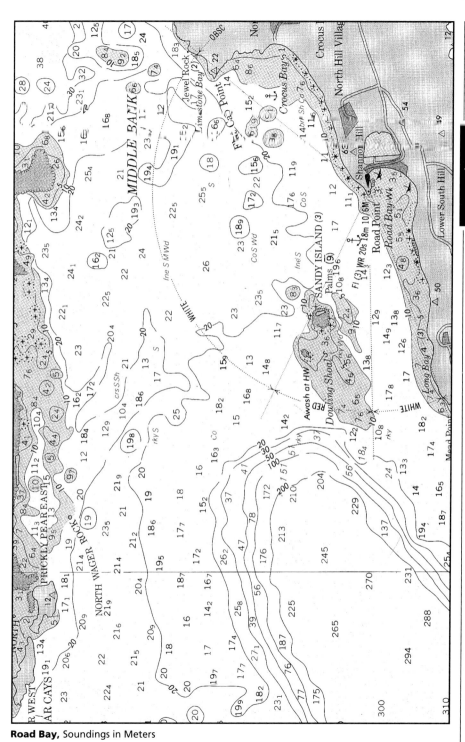

Road Bay, Soundings in Meters

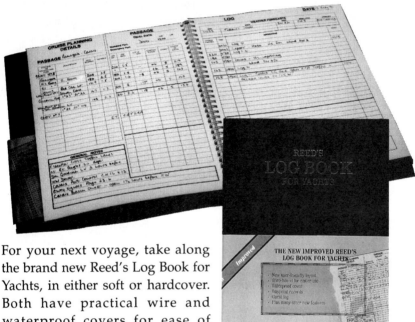

ST. MARTIN

CAUTION: Our information on aids to navigation comes from official government sources. The latitudes and longitudes of these marks may not correspond to the readings from GPS receivers. Some aids have been reported as unreliable, missing, off position or showing incorrect characteristics. No single aid to navigation, or waypoint, should be relied upon as a sole means of fixing your position.

ENTRY PROCEDURES

St. Martin and St. Barthelemy (St. Barts) are part of the French overseas department of Guadeloupe. You should fly the French courtesy flag here. The Dutch portion of the island, known as Sint Marrten, is discussed later in this chapter. The procedures for arriving yachts are handled informally, but you should check in with the officials when arriving from another country, or when leaving. You should clear in and out, when passing from French St. Martin to Dutch Sint Maarten, and back.

Clear with the officials in Marigot or Anse Marcel. Officials in the harbors are located in the port authority offices. In Marigot the office is near the ferry wharf. St. Martin has no duty on imports, so this is a good place to do some shopping, or have parts shipped to your boat.

The country code for calling French St. Martin from the United States is 590. When calling within French St. Martin, or to St. Barts, you only need the last six digits. When calling Dutch Sint Maarten you must dial the International Access Code of 19, then the country code of 599, then the city code of 5 and then your 5 digit Dutch number. The calls are routed through Guadeloupe.

The official currency is the French franc, which is currently trading at about 5.47 to the dollar. U.S. dollars are widely accepted. The language spoken is French.

ST. MARTIN APPROACHES

BREAKWATER LIGHT, N end, Head of breakwater, 18 06.9N, 63 03.0W, Fl R 2.5s, 10ft., 5M, W framework tower, R top.
SPUR LIGHT, 18 06.9N, 63 03.0W, Fl G 2.5s, 10ft., 5M, W framework tower, G top.
BAIE DU MARIGOT LIGHT, 18 04.1N, 63 05.7W, Fl W R G 4s, 66ft., 8M, W tower w/R top, R 104° to 120°, W 120° to 132°, G 132° to 185°, Obscured 185° to 104°.

MARIGOT

18 04N, 63 05W
Emergencies: Contact Saba Radio on VHF channel 16.
Pilotage: A flashing white, red and green light is shown from the 200 foot high hill topped by the ruins of Fort de Marigot. You can approach the commercial pier, below the light, on a bearing of 143° T. Anchor away from the approaches to the pier.
Port of Entry: The port authority office is near the ferry and commercial wharf.
Bridge to Simpson Bay Lagoon: The bridge normally opens at 0830 and 1730, but at this writing (June 1993) it is closed for repairs, and there is no access to the Lagoon from the French side. It will probably be out of operation until some time in 1994. The bridge at the Simpson Bay end opens at 0600, 1100, 1600 and 1800. The Simpson Bay bridge operator monitors VHF channels 12 and 16.
Dockage: Most of the marinas are on the Dutch side of Simpson Bay Lagoon. In Marigot try the Marina Port La Royal at (590) 87 20 43, or Caraibes Sport Boats at (590) 87 89 38. They are located in the eastern end of the bay, off Marigot. There is a dinghy dock here.
Anchorage: Marigot Bay is a good anchorage, though it can be subject to swells from the north. Simpson Bay Lagoon is very sheltered, but be careful of your depths. This is a possible hurricane hole, being very sheltered from wave action, yet open to the breeze.
Services: There is an extensive variety of yacht services here, and more in Sint Maarten

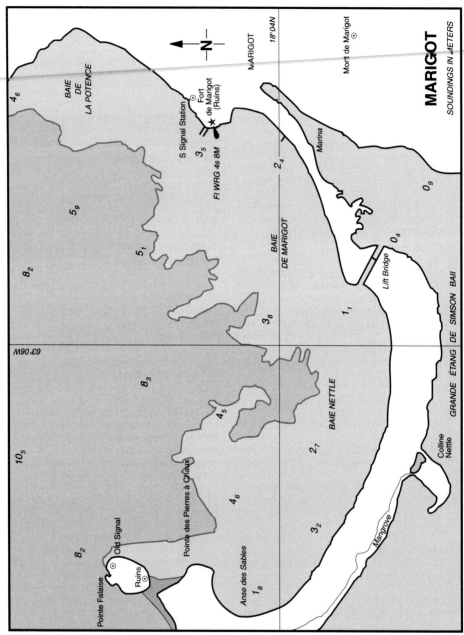

Marigot, Soundings in Meters

if you can't find what you want. Egreteau Marine Services is an inflatable and liferaft specialist. Contact them at (590) 87 23 92, or on VHF channel 77. Boat rentals are available from Caraibes Sport Boats, mentioned above. The St. Martin Marine Center is a Mercury engine dealer and service center. They are near the bridge, and can be reached at (590) 87 86 32 or on VHF channel 72. There are excellent grocery, liquor and gourmet shops, as befits a French island. There are offices of UPS and Federal Express if you need something in a hurry from the United States.

Being only 74 miles from Virgin Gorda, St. Martin is often the first port of call in the Leeward Islands. Marigot is the capital of the French half of the island, and has a good harbor where you may clear with the authorities quite easily. Ashore are many fine restaurants and shops, stocking a wide variety of items at duty-free prices. With the sheltered waters of Simpson Bay Lagoon nearby, and a continental atmosphere, Marigot is a favorite long term stop for many.

GRANDE CASE

18 06N, 63 03W

Emergencies: Contact Saba Radio on VHF channel 16. You may not be able to call very far on the VHF due to the high hills.

Pilotage: There is a shoal area north of the point forming the south end of Baie Grande Case. It is reported to be as shallow as 5 feet.

Anchorage: Anchor well in towards shore in the southeast part of the bay, to avoid any swells rolling around Roche Crole off Bell Point. Depths are 15 to 20 feet, shoaling to 6 to 8 feet close to the beach. There is a dinghy dock on the beach.

Services: The main thing to do here is enjoy some of the dozens of fine restaurants lined up along the main street. Provisions can be purchased, and there are general shops for browsing.

ANSE MARCEL

18 07N, 63 02W

Emergencies: Contact Saba Radio on VHF channel 16. You may not be able to call very far on the VHF due to the high hills.

Pilotage: This small bay is located west of the

northernmost part of the island. It is the only major indentation on the northern part of the island. Marcel Rock is located in the mouth of the bay. Do not pass between the rock and the mainland to the southwest, as the waters are quite shoal.

Port of Entry: Check in at the port authority office.

Dockage: Port Lonvilliers is entered via a narrow channel that begins in the southeast corner of the bay. Contact the marina at (590) 87 31 94, or on VHF channels 11 and 16. This is a very protected spot.

Anchorage: There is sheltered anchorage in the bay, north of town. Depths run from 8 to 15 feet.

Services: The marina has fuel, water and ice. For repairs and marine supplies contact St. Martin Yachting Services and Lonvilliers Yachting at (590) 87 38 78. There is a small grocery store and several shops. Several restaurants are nearby.

OYSTER POND

18 03N, 63 01W

Emergencies: Contact Saba Radio on VHF channel 16. You may not be able to call very far on the VHF due to the high hills.

Pilotage: The small pond is located near the middle of the east coast of the island. With its east facing entrance surrounded by reefs, this is no place to enter after dark, or in rough conditions. The entrance channel is privately marked by Captain Oliver's Marina. Controlling depth is reported to be about 10 feet as far as the fuel dock. If in any doubt as to your navigation, or the conditions, call the marina on VHF channels 16 and 67.

Dockage: Captain Oliver's Marina can be reached at (590) 87 30 00, or at 87 40 26, or on VHF channels 16 and 67. The Moorings charter fleet is also located here—call them at (590) 87 32 55.

Anchorage: The harbor is quite shoal, except for the area near the docks. There is a shoal in the middle of the harbor, with depths of 5 to 6 feet around most of the perimeter. Captain Oliver's Dinghy Dock is north of the marina.

Services: The Moorings has their own ship's store and grocery, which visitors are welcome to use. Captain Oliver's has a gourmet restaurant, and there are others nearby. Fuel, water and ice are available at the marina.

WE STOCK WHAT SAILORS WANT !

Before Budget Marine, cruising sailors found it difficult to find yachting parts in the Caribbean.

Robbie Ferron, a cruising yachtsmen, set out to fill that need over a decade ago.

Today, Budget Marine in St. Maarten stocks a huge inventory of marine products from the U.S., England, France, Germany, Italy and Venezuela. Thanks to Sint Maarten's truly duty-free status, you get what you want at the best prices.

Budget Marine's staff are all experienced sailors with the technical knowledge that is often hard to find in the Caribbean

Each member of the Budget team has their own area of specialized knowledge in electronics, rigging, marine coatings, pumps, propulsion and steering systems.

In fact, our staff's knowledge is world-wide and chances are that the Budget team speaks your language, be it French, German, Dutch, Spanish, Swedish or English.

If you are looking for pump parts or a new inflatable, or a source for a complete refit, you can rely on Budget Marine to have in stock what you want.

TECHNICALLY THE BEST CHANDLERY IN THE CARIBBEAN

BUDGET MARINE

ST. MAARTEN OPPOSITE BOBBYS MARINA TEL.: 22068 · FAX 23804

SINT MAARTEN

ENTRY PROCEDURES

Dutch Sint Maarten lies on the southern side of the same island as French St. Martin, and is part of the Netherlands Antilles. You should fly the Dutch courtesy flag while in these waters. It is a duty-free port and has no customs as such, but you should clear with the Immigration officials in the police station near the ferry dock in Philipsburg. Contact Immigration at (599 5) 22740. You should check in when traveling back and forth to the French side of the island. Formalities are swift and simple.

You can reach the Philipsburg police at (599 5) 22222. The country code is 599, and the city code 5, when calling from the United States, or from French St. Martin. When calling from the French side of the island, begin with the International Access Code of 19. The calls must be routed through Guadeloupe. When calling the French side from the Dutch side, use the code 06 before the 6 digit number.

The official language is Dutch, but English is widely spoken. Dutch Guilders currently trade at 1.79 to the U.S. dollar, but again, U.S. currency is widely accepted.

SINT MAARTEN APPROACHES

SIMSON BAAI AVIATION LIGHT, 18 02.4N, 63 06.7W, Al Fl W G 6s, 52ft., 13M, On station building.
GROOT BAAI, On side of old Fort Amsterdam, 18 00.8N, 63 03.6W, Fl (2) W 10s, 120ft., 15M, Wooden post, Visible 300° to 096°.

PHILIPSBURG

18 01N, 63 03W

Emergencies: Contact Saba Radio on VHF channel 16.
Pilotage: Groot Baai (Grand Bay) is the main port, and the location of the capital of Dutch Sint Maarten, Philipsburg. A light is shown from old Fort Amsterdam on the western point of land at the mouth of the bay. There is a stranded wreck about 200 yards south of Fort Amsterdam. There is a 300 yard long, L-shaped, cruise ship pier at the south end of the eastern part of the bay. The bay is generally free of obstructions, except for some shoaling in the northwest portion.
Port of Entry: Contact the Immigration officials in the police station. You can call them at (599 5) 22740.
Dockage: Bobby's Marina and Great Bay Marina are on the eastern side of Groot Baai. Contact Bobby's at (599 5) 22366, or on VHF channel 16. Contact Great Bay at (599 5) 22167, or on VHF channel 69.
Anchorage: There is good anchorage in the bay, with depths from about 6 to 20 feet.
Services: Almost anything is available here, and at very good prices for the Caribbean. We will be able to mention just a few of the more useful businesses oriented toward yachtsmen. Fuel, water and ice are available at the marinas, and Bobby's can haul boats to 70 tons. Dockside Management is your telephone, fax, information, message and shipping center. The people are very helpful and speak English. Contact them at (599 5) 24096, or FAX 22858. They will also hold your mail for you—P.O. Box 999, Philipsburg, Sint Maarten, Netherlands Antilles. Necol is an electronics specialist at (599 5) 23571, and the Trade Winds Dive Center can handle your tanks at (599 5) 54387. Robbie Ferron's Budget Marine, (599 5) 22068 and VHF channel 68, has most equipment and can get anything you need. The Nautical Instrument and Navigation Center at (599 5) 23605 specializes in navigation equipment, books, charts and general marine gear. They are stockists of Reed's products. There are Federal Express and UPS offices on the island, so it is easy to get equipment quickly from the United States. There are several good grocery stores.

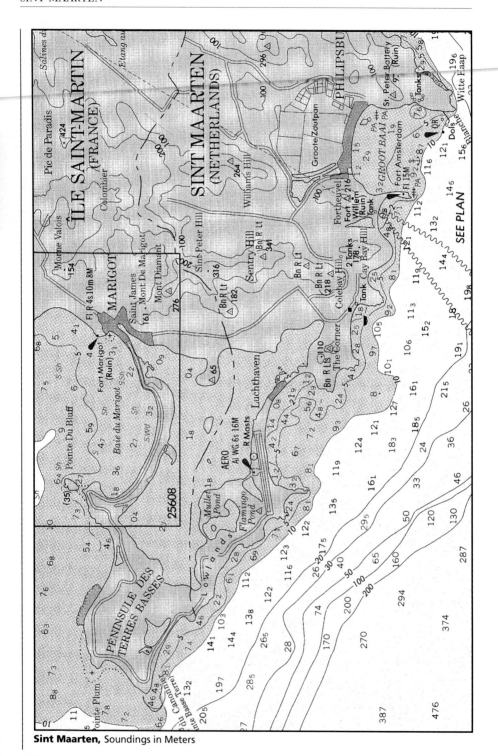

Sint Maarten, Soundings in Meters

Philipsburg is a favorite stop for cruising yachtsmen, and one of the best places for repairs or stocking up in the Caribbean. The harbor is sometimes rolly, but is generally a good anchorage. Nearby Simpson Bay Lagoon provides better shelter, and more marine services.

SIMSON BAAI

18 02N, 63 00W

Emergencies: Contact Saba Radio on VHF channel 16.

Pilotage: Simson Baai, or Simpson Bay, is about 3 miles to the northwest of Groot Baai and Philipsburg. Prinses Juliana Airport lies along the north side of the bay, and there is an aviation light shown from just north of the runway. The entrance to the Lagoon is on the eastern side of the bay.

Bridge to Simpson Bay Lagoon: The bridge at the Simpson Bay end opens at 0600, 1100, 1600 and 1800. The Simpson Bay bridge operator monitors VHF channels 12 and 16. The bridge at the Marigot end normally opens at 0830 and 1730, but at this writing (June 1993) it is closed for repairs, and there is no access to the Lagoon from the French side. It will probably be out of operation until some time in 1994.

Dockage: There are several marinas in the Lagoon. Contact the Simpson Bay Yacht Club at (599 5) 43378 or on VHF channel 16. The Port Plaisance Marina has luxurious services (599 5) 45222. Island Water World has dockage and can be reached at (599 5) 43310, or on VHF channel 74. Lagoon Marina is for shoal draft boats at (599 5) 45210.

Anchorage: The various anchorages in the Lagoon are some of the most protected around. This is considered a hurricane hole.

Services: Extensive marine services are available here, in Philipsburg and in Marigot on the French side. Fuel, water and ice are available at the marinas. Tropicold specializes in refrigeration and air conditioning at (599 5) 42648. Island Water World, (599 5) 43299, or on VHF channel 74, is an Evinrude dealer and

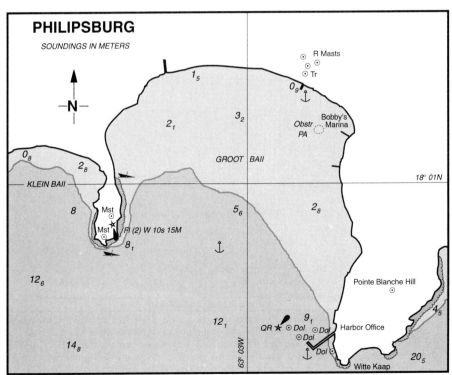

Philipsburg, Soundings in Meters

chandler. FKG Yacht Rigging and Marine Fabricating can handle your rigging needs, and many repairs, at (599 5) 42171, or on VHF channel 70 (call "Squarerigger"). There are good grocery stores and restaurants nearby. There are many other fine services we have not mentioned.

Simson Baai Lagoon is one of the best places in the Caribbean for restocking and repairs. It is also a sheltered place to stay while enjoying the continental atmosphere ashore. If you tire of being in Dutch waters, simply cross the Lagoon to the French side!

ST. BARTHELEMY

CAUTION: Our information on aids to navigation comes from official government sources. The latitudes and longitudes of these marks may not correspond to the readings from GPS receivers. Some aids have been reported as unreliable, missing, off position or showing incorrect characteristics. No single aid to navigation, or waypoint, should be relied upon as a sole means of fixing your position.

ENTRY PROCEDURES

St. Martin and St. Barthelemy (St. Barts) are part of the French overseas department of Guadeloupe. You should fly the French courtesy flag here. The procedures for arriving yachts are handled informally, but you should check in with the officials when arriving from another country, or when leaving.

Clear in at the Port Captain's office on the east side of Gustavia harbor. They monitor VHF channel 16.

The country code for calling St. Barts from the United States is 590. Local phone numbers will be six digits, which is all you need when on the island, or when calling from St. Martin.

The official currency is the French franc, which is currently trading at about 5.47 to the dollar. U.S. dollars are widely accepted. The language spoken is French.

GUSTAVIA

17 54N, 62 51W

FORT GUSTAVIA LIGHT, 17 54.3N, 62 51.2W, Fl (3) W R G 12s, 210ft., 10M white, 7M red, 6M green, White truncated tower, Red top, White 054° to 071°, Green 071° to 095°, White 095° to 111°, Green 111° to 160°, Obscured 160° to 340°, Red 340° to 054°.

Emergencies: Call Saba Radio on VHF channel 16.

Pilotage: The port lies on the west coast of the island. The light is shown from Fort Gustavia, which is north of the inner harbor. The safest approaches are made by coming in on the white sectors of the light. Depths in the inner harbor The Port Captain monitors VHF channel 16.

Port of Entry: Check in with the Port Captain, on the east side of the inner harbor.

Dockage: It may be possible to tie up stern to one of the quays (Mediterranean style) in the inner harbor. Check with the Port Captain for the daily charge.

Anchorage: You can anchor in the inner harbor if there is room, or outside the marked channel into the inner harbor. Daily charges will be collected by a patrol boat, or at the Port Captain's office.

Services: Fuel is available at the commercial wharf north of Fort Gustave. Contact St. Barth Marine at (590) 27 60 38. Loulou's Marine is a well known chandler and source of information or assistance to boaters. Contact them at (590) 27 62 74. Le Shipchandler is another source of boat gear at (590) 27 85 73, or on VHF channel 16. The AMC supermarket will supply your groceries. Contact them at (590) 27 60 09. There's a good selection of French restaurants. Being a duty free port, there is a wide variety of stores of all types. Prices are very good, for the Caribbean.

Gustavia is a popular harbor, but can get very crowded in season. There may be some difficulty finding a secure spot for your boat. Once ashore, you'll find a good variety of services and supplies, though not as extensive as St. Martin and Sint Maarten. Being French, the dining can be particularly enjoyable here.

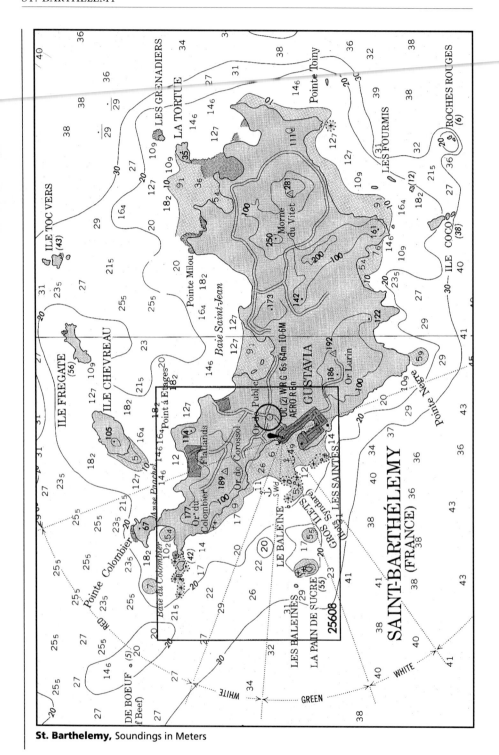

St. Barthelemy, Soundings in Meters

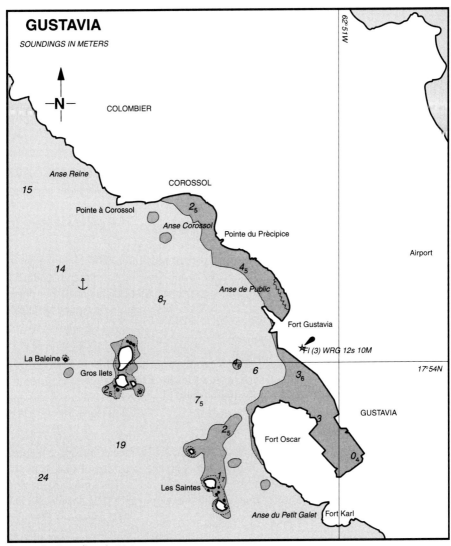

GUSTAVIA

SOUNDINGS IN METERS

—N—

COLOMBIER

62°51W

Anse Reine

15

COROSSOL

Pointe à Corossol

2_5

Anse Corossol

Pointe du Prècipice

Airport

14

⚓

8_7

4_5

Anse de Public

Fort Gustavia

☆Fl (3) WRG 12s 10M

La Baleine ⬤

Gros llets ⬤

2_5

4_6

6

3_6

17°54N

7_5

3

GUSTAVIA

19

2_5

Fort Oscar

0_4

24

1_7

Les Saintes

Anse du Petit Galet Fort Karl

Gustavia, Soundings in Meters

REED'S
NAUTICAL ALMANACS & COMPANIONS

1994

CARIBBEAN

The only almanac which covers the entire Caribbean basin including Bermuda, the Bahamas, Caribbean islands, the north coast of South America, Central America, Panama and Mexico. Contains 200 harbor chartlets, complete tide and celestial tables, coast pilot with aids to navigation, weather and communication information.   800 pages $29.95(US) Retail

NORTH AMERICAN: EAST COAST

Now in its 21st year of publication, it includes over 200 harbor chartlets, tide and current tables from Nova Scotia to the Bahamas, light and buoy lists, waypoints, radio and communication information, a complete nautical ephemeris and lots more.
900 pages $29.95(US) Retail

NORTH AMERICAN: PACIFIC NORTHWEST

The only almanac to include US and Canadian Hydrographic information in a single volume, and covers from the head of the Columbia River to the Gulf of Alaska and Kodiak Island, including Puget Sound and the British Columbia coastline. More than 170 harbor charts, tide and current tables, nautical ephemeris, aids to navigation, communication and weather information.   900 pages $29.95(US) Retail

NORTHERN EUROPEAN

Our flagship almanac, now enjoying its 63rd year of publication. Its coverage ranges from Skagen, on the northern coast of Denmark, to the French-Spanish border and Biarritz. This extensive European coverage includes 450 chartlets and illustrations, 2000 ports and complete tidal information for each area.   1,200 pages $45.00(US) Retail

SOUTHERN EUROPEAN

A completely reorganized and updated version of our Mediterranean almanac, featuring the Atlantic-European coast and islands, as well as the complete coastline of one of the world's most popular cruising areas, the Mediterranean sea. This edition is an excellent reference book for those planning a transatlantic voyage including stopovers in the Azores and entry via Gibraltar to the Mediterranean.   800 pages $45.00(US) Retail

NAUTICAL COMPANION

The COMPANION is designed to complement the Caribbean, North American East Coast and Pacific Northwest REED'S ALMANACS, and is full of practical information for the cruising boater. It includes extensive chapters on seamanship, rules of the road, coastal passage making, signaling, first aid and more.   444 pages $19.95(US) Retail

NAUTICAL COMPANION (European edition)

An outstanding nautical reference with essential information on subjects similar to those included in our US COMPANION. Designed to complement our European editions.
450 pages $24.95(US) Retail

Call 1-800-995-4995 for your nearest dealer!

SABA

CAUTION: Our information on aids to navigation comes from official government sources. The latitudes and longitudes of these marks may not correspond to the readings from GPS receivers. Some aids have been reported as unreliable, missing, off position or showing incorrect characteristics. No single aid to navigation, or waypoint, should be relied upon as a sole means of fixing your position.

ENTRY PROCEDURES

Saba lies about 26 miles southwest of St. Barthelemy and is part of the Netherlands Antilles. You should fly the Dutch courtesy flag while in these waters. It is a duty-free port and has no customs as such, but you should clear with the Harbormaster in Fort Baai. You can contact the Harbormaster at (599 46) 3294, or on VHF channels 11 and 16. If you can't locate the Harbormaster check in with the Saba Marine Park office at (599 46) 3295. You must check in with the Saba Marine Park before proceeding to the mooring area in the Ladder Baai/Weels Baai area. Formalities are swift and simple.

The country code is 599, and the city code 46, when calling from the United States. Local numbers are 4 digits long. When calling Dutch Sint Maarten you should dial the prefix 05, then the 5 digit local number.

English is widely spoken, but you may encounter Dutch as well. Dutch Guilders currently trade at 1.79 to the U.S. dollar, but again, U.S. currency is widely accepted.

SABA

17 38N, 63 14W

ST. JOHN'S LIGHT, 17 37.1N, 63 14.6W, Fl (2) W 10s, 15M.

Emergencies: Contact Saba Radio on VHF channel 16.
Pilotage: The coast of the island rises nearly perpendicular from the sea, with the 2,853 foot summit of the island usually enveloped in clouds. The island is a mass of rugged mountains, with deep precipitous ravines. Two conspicuous radio masts stand on the island. St. Johns Light is exhibited about 1/2 mile ENE of Fort Baai. The Saba Bank, located south and west of the island, is deep enough to sail over, but should be avoided in heavy weather.
Port of Entry: Check with the harbor officials in Fort Baai. They monitor VHF channels 11 and 16.
Saba Radio, Call Sign PJS: This is the main communications service in this part of the Caribbean, with a 200 mile range on VHF (with its antenna at 3083 feet above sea level). This area extends from the British Virgin Islands to Antigua. For emergencies they are in contact with the U.S. Coast Guard and other rescue agencies. During hurricane season they broadcast reports as received. You can contact them on VHF channels 16, 26 and 84, seven days a week from 0600 to 2400. They will accept phone credit cards, or place collect calls for you. To make calls from a landline to a boat, call them at (599 46) 3402. For more information on Saba Radio's services call (599 46) 3211.
Dockage: You may be able to tie inside the 100 yard long jetty at Fort Baai. Check with the harbormaster.
Anchorage and Moorings: Much of the coastline is part of the Saba Marine Park, and no anchoring is allowed. You must check in with the Saba Marine Park office in Fort Baai before proceeding to the mooring area. At this time you can anchor outside of Fort Baai, and from Ladder Baai to the southern part of Wells Baai. The center of Wells Baai offers excellent holding in clear sand with plenty of swinging room. Ladder Baai offers good holding in depths of about 20 feet. There are rocks close in to shore, and the swirling winds require a stern anchor if you are leaving the boat unattended. There are two orange moorings outside Fort Baai. Five yellow moorings, with blue stripes have been reported available in the Wells Baai/Ladder Baai area. These moorings are for boats under 60 feet long, and consist of two one ton blocks chained together. The orange and white buoys, with blue stripes, are for both commercial and private dive boats.

Chapter 2

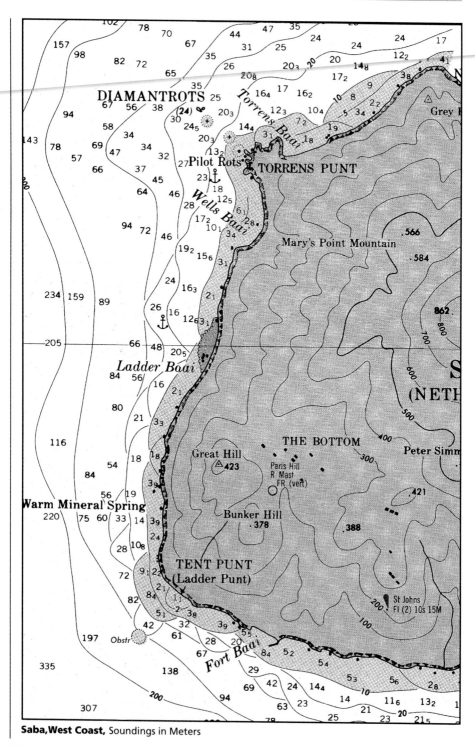

Saba, West Coast, Soundings in Meters

White buoys are for boats less than 60 feet long. There is a fee of $2.00 per person, per week, for boats under 30 meters, and a fee of $0.10 per registered ton, per week, for boats over 30 meters in length. When diving or snorkeling you should display the dive flag, and you should stay 150 yards seaward of any dive operations when underway. There is a fee of $2.00 per dive (snorkeling is included in the boat fee). No fishing or collecting of any marine life, dead or alive, is allowed in the park. For the latest regulations check with the Marine Park office in Fort Baai at (599 46) 3295.

Services: You may be able to get some fuel via jug, or some limited provisions. There are several interesting restaurants and shops. Take a taxi tour of the island via the famous road which winds among the mountains. There are two dive shops in Fort Baai. Contact Saba Deep at (599 46) 3347. Contact Wilson's Dive Shop at (599 46) 3410. Sea Saba is in Windwardside at (599 46) 2246. You can get information on some of the great diving opportunities from the Saba Tourist Bureau, P.O. Box 527, Windwardside, Saba, Netherlands Antilles, (599 46) 2231.

SINT EUSTATIUS

ENTRY PROCEDURES

Sint Eustatius, known as Statia, is located about 30 miles south of Sint Maarten, and is part of the Netherlands Antilles. You should fly the Dutch courtesy flag while in these waters. It is a duty-free port and has no customs as such, but you should clear with the Harbormaster in Oranjestad. Contact them at (599 3) 82205. Formalities are swift and simple.

The country code is 599, and the city code 3, when calling from the United States. Local numbers are 5 digits long. When calling Dutch Sint Maarten you should dial the prefix 05, then the 5 digit local number.

English is widely spoken, but you may encounter Dutch as well. Dutch Guilders currently trade at 1.79 to the U.S. dollar, but again, U.S. currency is widely accepted.

ORANJESTAD

17 29N, 62 59W

TUMBLEDOWN DICK BAY LIGHT, Head of oil pier, 17 29.4N, 63 00.1W, Fl W 5s, 10M.
ORANJESTAD LIGHT, 17 28.8N, 62 59.2W, Fl (3) W 15s, 131 ft., 17M.

Emergencies: Contact Saba Radio on VHF channel 16.

Pilotage: The island is dominated by an extinct 1900 foot high volcano near its southeast extremity. Except for the slopes of the volcano, the island is devoid of trees. A group of rugged hills is located on the northwest portion of the island. Fish pots may be encountered up to 3 miles off the west coast. Tumbledown Dick Light is located at the end of a 1/2 mile long jetty located about 1 mile northwest of Oranjestad. The oil terminal at the jetty stands by on the VHF radio.

Port of Entry: Contact the Harbormaster near the foot of the large dock. You may call them at (599 3) 82205.

Anchorage: The anchorage off town is reported to be rolly. You may want to try a stern anchor to hold your boat into the swells.

Services: You can jug water and fuel to your boat, and there are good markets ashore. Contact Dive Statia at (599 3) 82435, or on VHF channel 16. There are many historic buildings to see, and several good restaurants, though the tourist industry is quite small. This is a great place to "get away from it all".

Chapter 2

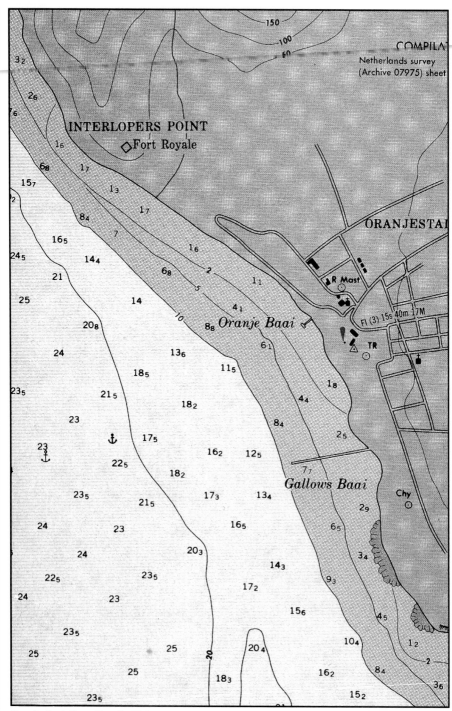

Oranjestad, Soundings in Meters

ST. CHRISTOPHER AND NEVIS

ENTRY PROCEDURES

St. Christopher, known as St. Kitts, and Nevis are located about 40 miles west of Antigua. They are separate islands, but one country, sharing a British heritage.

The Port of Entry on St. Kitts is Basseterre, and on Nevis it is Charlestown. A Cruising Permit must be obtained to visit anchorages other than the Ports of Entry. The cost is $10.00 U.S. for boats under 20 tons, and is good on both islands. Port Authority charges apply to vessels over 20 tons. Charter boats must pay $3.00 per passenger. When traveling between the islands you must obtain a Boat Pass, then check in with the authorities when you arrive.

In Basseterre the Customs and Immigration offices are in the Port Authority building, and normal hours are 0800 to 1600, Monday through Friday. If you arrive on a weekend or after hours, contact one of the guards at the Port Authority who will summon the officials. Contact Basseterre Customs at (809) 465-2521, extensions 1076 and 1077.

In Charlestown normal hours are 0800 to 1600, with a lunch break from 1200 to 1300. Contact Customs at (809) 469-9343.

You should have your passports, clearance from last port of call, ship's papers and two crew lists. Firearms must be secured under lock and key, while in port.

The area code for the islands is 809 followed by a prefix of 465 for phones on St. Kitts, and 469 for phones on Nevis, then a 4 digit number.

The official currency is the Eastern Caribbean, or EC, dollar, though U.S. dollars are widely accepted. The exchange rate, when converting EC dollars to U.S. dollars, is about .40 In other words, $100 EC = $40 U.S. Registered tonnage is the basis for all charges.

HALF MOON POINT LIGHT, 17 19.1N, 62 42.2W, Oc R 2s, F R, Tower.

BASSETERRE

17 18N, 62 43W

FORT THOMAS LIGHT, West side of harbor, 17 17.3N, 62 44.2W, F R, 67 ft., Metal mast, Aero Al Fl W G (occasional) 1.6M to the northeast.

TREASURY BUILDINGS LIGHT, F R, 46 ft., 10M.

FORT SMITH LIGHT, E side of harbor, 17 17.3N, 62 42.6W, F G, 35 ft., 2M, Concrete block, Fl W 2s 2M on dolphin 300 meters to the northwest.

Emergencies: Contact Saba Radio on VHF channel 16.

Pilotage: The north end of the island rises to the 3798 foot high Mount Misery. The summit is usually covered with clouds. The southeast end of the island is only connected by a narrow neck of sand. Caution is advised as the hydrography is incomplete around St. Kitts and Nevis. The port is situated on the southwest side of the island. A 283 foot high white chimney is located about 1/2 mile NNE of the east end of town. Contact the Port Authority on VHF channels 6 and 16.

Port of Entry: Check with Customs and Immigration in the Port Authority building. You can contact them at (809) 465-2521, extensions 1076 and 1077.

Anchorage: The anchorage area is subject to swells when the wind shifts to the south. You might want to try the area off the Salt Ponds about a mile southeast of Basseterre.

Services: You can jug water and fuel to your boat. Brooks Boat Company is located on the waterfront and does repairs. They can haul catamarans up to 14 tons. Contact them on VHF channel 16, or at (809) 465-8411. There is a good variety of restaurants, grocery stores and general shops. The Tourist Office can be reached at (809) 465-4040.

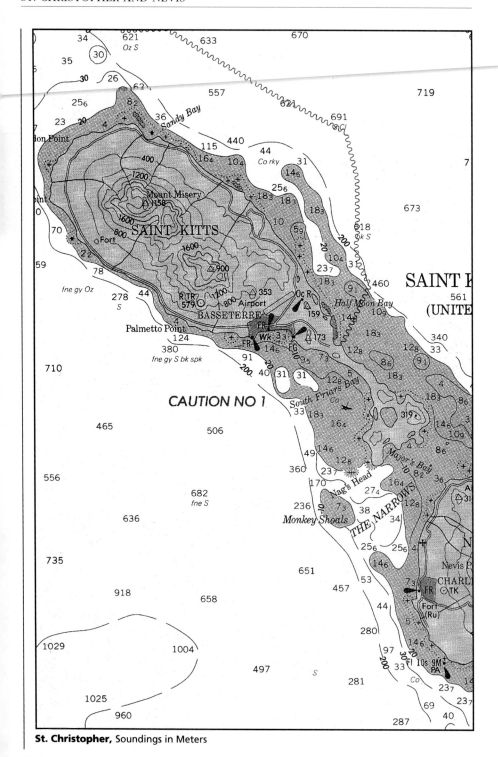

St. Christopher, Soundings in Meters

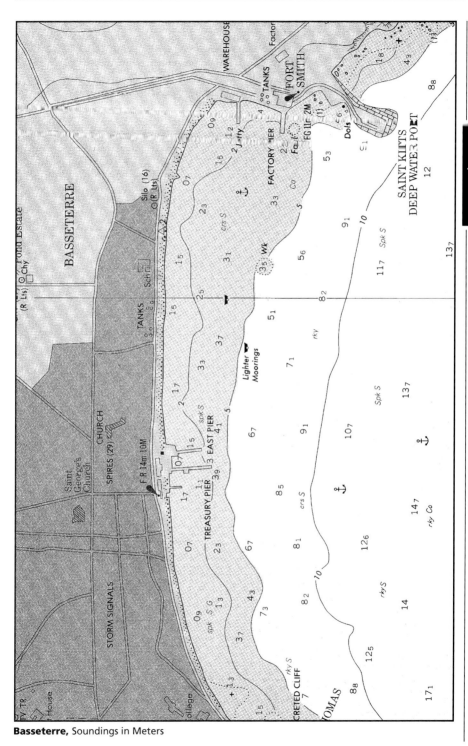

Basseterre, Soundings in Meters

CHARLESTOWN

17 08N, 62 28W

CHARLESTOWN LIGHT, Root of pier,
17 08.2N, 62 36.9W, F R, 15 ft , Post, Iso R light
on radio mast 0.7M SSE.
DOGWOOD POINT LIGHT, South end of island,
17 05.7N, 62 36.4W, Fl W 10s, 29 ft.

Emergencies: Contact Saba Radio on VHF
channel 16.
Pilotage: See the information on Basseterre.
Charlestown is located on the west coast of
Nevis, and is the capital of the island. Nevis
peak rises to 3230 feet in the center of the
island, and is usually hidden in the clouds. A
concrete pier with depths from 11 to 15 feet
alongside projects from the town waterfront.
A prominent radio mast stands near the root
of the pier.

Port of Entry: Contact Customs at (809)
469-9343.

Anchorage: Anchor right off the town waterfront. There is a ladder on the pier, where you
can land your dinghy.

Services: Fuel and water are available by jug,
or at the wharf if getting large quantities.
There is a good variety of shops, restaurants
and grocery stores. Contact the Tourist Office
at (809) 469-5521.

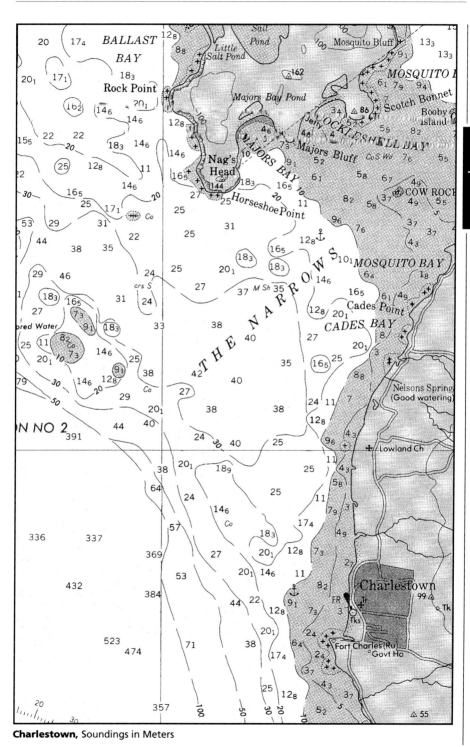

Charlestown, Soundings in Meters

MONTSERRAT

CAUTION: Our information on aids to navigation comes from official government sources. The latitudes and longitudes of these marks may not correspond to the readings from GPS receivers. Some aids have been reported as unreliable, missing, off position or showing incorrect characteristics. No single aid to navigation, or waypoint, should be relied upon as a sole means of fixing your position.

ENTRY PROCEDURES

Montserrat lies about 25 miles southwest of Antigua, and is a British Crown Colony.

The Port of Entry is Plymouth, on the southwest side of the island. You should check in with Customs and Immigration in the Port Authority office near the main wharf. Their hours are 0800 to 1600 Monday, Tuesday, Thursday and Friday. On Wednesdays and Saturdays they are open from 0800 to 1130. Overtime charges apply for checking in outside of normal working hours.

You should apply for a coastwise clearance if planning a visit to harbors other than Plymouth. Firearms must be locked on board, or held at the police station for stays longer than a couple of days. There is a $5.00 EC charge upon departure.

Contact Customs and Immigration at (809) 491-2436, or the Comptroller at (809) 491-3211, for the latest information.

The area code for the island is 809, and the island code 491. The last four digits are the local number, and are all you need for telephone calls within the colony.

The official currency is the Eastern Caribbean, or EC, dollar, though U.S. dollars are widely accepted. The exchange rate, when converting EC dollars to U.S. dollars, is about .40. In other words, $100 EC = $40 U.S.

MONTSERRAT APPROACHES

AVIATION LIGHT, 16 45.9N, 62 09.9W, Oc R 1.5s, 197 ft., Occasional.
BLACKBURNE AIRPORT LIGHT, 16 45.5N, 62 09.5W, Aero Al Fl W G 6s, 33 ft., Occasional.
CASTLE PEAK LIGHT, 16 42.5N, 62 10.9W, Aero Fl R 1.5s, 3179 ft., 6M, Mast, Obstruction light.
AVIATION LIGHT, 16 40.7N, 62 11.7W, Oc R 2s, 341 ft., 22M, Radio Tower.

PLYMOUTH

16 43N, 62 13W

PLYMOUTH LIGHT, Jetty root, 16 42.3N, 62 13.3W, F R, Terminal building.

Emergencies: Call Saba Radio on VHF channel 16.
Pilotage: The island presents a rugged and uneven appearance from seaward. The Soufriere Hills on the south end of the island rise to a height of almost 3000 feet. The hills are wooded, and may rise into the clouds. The coasts tend to be bold and steep to. An L-shaped jetty projects 100 yards seaward at Plymouth. The ruins of an old dolphin near the end of the wharf have been reported to be a hazard. Another obstruction is marked by a buoy located about 115 feet northwest of the jetty head. The Yacht Club is situated south of the jetty. Anchorage is prohibited in much of the area off the town — see the chartlet for details.
Port of Entry: Contact Customs and Immigration in the Port Authority building near the main wharf. You can call them at (809) 491-2436.
Radio Antilles: Called the "Big RA", by many boaters. 930kHz 20kw, Marine weather forecasts at 1335 and 2225 UTC. Radio Antilles is a good source of weather information for the Eastern Caribbean.
Dockage: You may be able to get permission from the Port Authority to tie alongside the wharf while taking on fuel or supplies. Be careful if a swell is running.

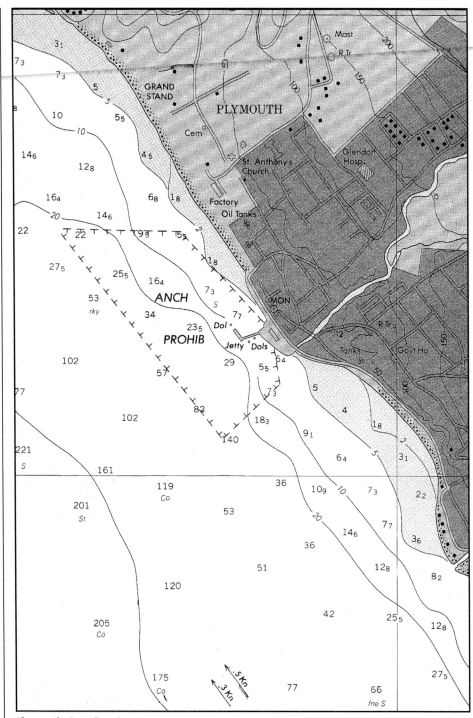

Plymouth, Soundings in Meters.

Anchorage: Anchorage is prohibited in much of the area directly off Plymouth. You might want to try directly off the Yacht Club, south of the main wharf. This area is reported to be very rolly. Old Road Bay, north of town, is reported to be a better anchorage, but you still may need a stern anchor to hold your boat into the swells. You can dinghy in to the Vue Pointe Hotel dock in Old Road Bay.

Services: Large quantities of fuel and water can be obtained at the wharf via truck, but you'll have to jug smaller amounts. The Sea Wolf Diving School can be reached at (809) 491-7807. The tourist office can be very helpful at (809) 491-2230. There is a good variety of supermarkets, restaurants and general shops. The Vue Pointe Hotel, located near the north end of Old Road Bay, is reported to be very friendly to yachtsmen. They have a landing, water showers, a telephone, garbage facilities, ice and a bus into town. They may be able to hold mail for you. Contact them at (809) 491-5210, or 5211.

Chapter 2

REED'S NAUTICAL COMPANION

Table of Contents

To get your **REED'S NAUTICAL COMPANION,** call 1-800-995-4995 and ask for the **REED'S** dealer nearest you!

ANTIGUA AND BARBUDA

CAUTION: Our Information on aids to navigation comes from official government sources. The latitudes and longitudes of these marks may not correspond to the readings from GPS receivers. Some aids have been reported as unreliable, missing, off position or showing incorrect characteristics. No single aid to navigation, or waypoint, should be relied upon as a sole means of fixing your position.

ENTRY PROCEDURES

Antigua and Barbuda form an independent country, having formerly been British colonies. The small island of Redonda is also part of the country.

Ports of Entry are English Harbour, Crabb's Marina in Parham and St. John's. There is a customs station near the boat harbor south of Codrington on Barbuda. You can only clear out at the customs station. To obtain a Cruising Permit you must go to one of the Ports of Entry on Antigua.

At English Harbour hours of operation are about 0600 to 1700 daily. Port entry fees range from $10.00 EC to $20.00 EC. There is a fee of $5.00 EC per person to enter the Dockyard. You must obtain a Cruising Permit to visit other places in the country. For boats in the 30 to 40 foot range the fee is $20.00 EC per month. The fee for tying up stern-to in the Dockyard is $0.25 per foot, per day. The fee for anchoring is $.03 per foot, per day. Contact the officials at (809) 460-1397 for the latest information on procedures.

When clearing in English Harbour you may anchor in Freeman Bay flying the Q flag. If the Customs and Immigration officials do not come in a reasonable amount of time, you can proceed to their office in the Dockyard, on the western side of the channel leading in to the harbor.

St. John's is primarily a commercial port, but vessels can clear with the officials at the wharf on the north side of the harbor. Hours of operation are 0800 to 1600 most days. The

local phone number for the boarding officer is 462-0814.

Crabb's Marina is located on the northeast part of the island. Hours of operation are 0830 to 1630, Monday through Friday. The local phone number for the officials is 463-2372.

Contact the Customs and Immigration authorities in the small boat harbor located on the west side of Barbuda. They are reported to monitor VHF channel 16. You must have obtained a Cruising Permit in Antigua to be able to cruise Barbuda. You can get an outward clearance here.

The area code for the island is 809, and the island numbers are seven digits, as in the U.S. On the island you only need dial the last seven digits. Many phone numbers are restricted to local calls only, which means you may not be able to reach every number from overseas.

The official currency is the Eastern Caribbean, or EC, dollar, though U.S. dollars are widely accepted. The exchange rate, when converting EC dollars to U.S. dollars, is about .40. In other words, $100 EC = $40 U.S.

BARBUDA
17 36N, 61 50W
Emergencies: Call the Antigua Coast Guard on VHF channels 16 and 68, or contact Saba Radio on VHF channel 16.
Pilotage: The small boat landing on Barbuda lies about 28 miles north of St. John's, Antigua. A hotel, partly obscured by tall shrubs, is prominent on Cocoa Point, the southern point of the island. A Martello tower, partly ruined, is visible about 2 miles east of Palmetto Point. The boat harbor is located about 3/4 mile east of the Martello tower. Sand piles, from a sand mining operation, indicate the location of the harbor. There are numerous reefs around the island, including ones along the shore near the boat harbor. The channel into the dock is locally marked. Many coral heads are found up to 2 1/2 miles off the northwestern part of the island.
Customs Station: You can clear out of the country from here, but you should have a

Chapter 2

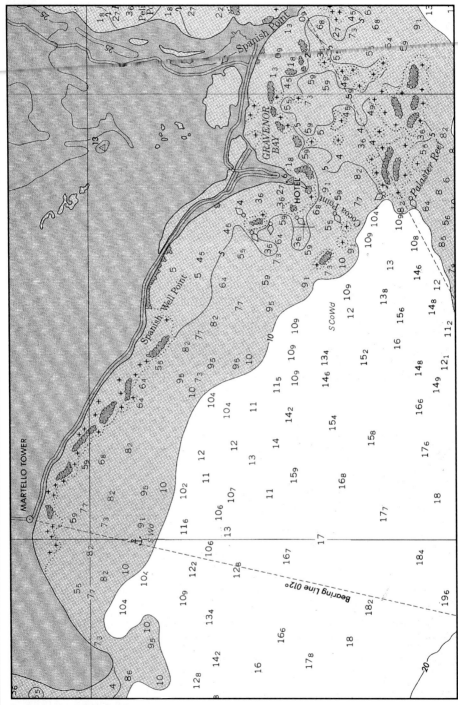

Barbuda, Soundings in Meters

Cruising Permit from Antigua before visiting. The station is located near the boat harbor.

Anchorages: You can anchor in the small basin at the boat harbor , in depths reported to be 5 to 9 feet. The town of Codrington is almost 3 miles north of the harbor via road. Most boats will want to anchor north of Palmetto Point, or among the reefs along the south coast. This is an area where "eyeball navigation" is critical. You should never be underway around Barbuda at night, or in poor visibility.

Services: A couple of hotels and restaurants are all that might interest boaters. There are some small stores and a telephone in Codrington. This is a place for "getting away from it all".

Palaster Reef, off the south coast of Barbuda, is a national park, where no fishing is permitted. This a wonderful place for snorkeling and diving on the coral reefs and coral heads. These both add to the beauty and add to the difficulties. Be sure of your navigation, your charts and your guides before heading to Barbuda.

NORTH ANTIGUA

PRICKLY PEAR ISLAND LIGHT, 17 10.5N, 68 48.9W, Q W, 26 ft., Black round metal structure.

SANDY ISLAND LIGHT, Near center of island, 17 08.1N, 61 55.4W, Fl W 15s, 53 ft., 13M, White iron framework structure, Reported irregular April 1985.

PARHAM

17 08N, 61 45W

Emergencies: Call the Antigua Coast Guard on VHF channels 16 and 68, or contact Saba Radio on VHF channel 16.

Pilotage: Approach the harbors on the north coast of Antigua via the Boon Channel starting north of St. John's. The major hazards are the reefs surrounding Prickly Pear Island, which is marked by a light. After passing Prickly Pear you can head to the southeast. You'll see some buoys which lead toward the vicinity of Crabb's Marina on North Sound Point. Parham harbor is south of the west side of the point. Due to the many shoals and reefs, you should only travel the north shore in good light.

Port of Entry: Clear in at Crabb's Marina. Contact the officials at their local number 463-2372.

Dockage: Contact Crabb's Marina at (809) 463-2113. They have some dockage, fuel, water, but no electricity at the docks.

Anchorage: You can anchor off of Crabb's, or further south near town. This area is well protected in most conditions.

Services: Crabb's can do repairs and hauls boats. Parham Marine is located near the commercial wharf. They handle repairs of all kinds, and have a chandlery. Contact them at 463-2148. There is a supermarket and a restaurant ashore.

ST. JOHN'S
17 08N, 61 52W

PILLAR ROCK LIGHT, South side of entrance to harbor, 17 07.8N, 61 52.6W, Fl G 4s, 106 ft., 5M, White house, Worded PILLAR ROCK in black, Visible 067° to 093°, Obscured 093° to 108°, Visible thence to shore southeast of light.

RANGE (Front Light), 17 07.1N, 61 50.5W, Iso R 6s, 62 ft., 6M, Metal framework tower. **(Rear Light),** 440 meters, 113° from front light, Iso R 6s, 92 ft., 6M, Metal framework tower.

FORT JAMES LIGHT, North side of entrance to harbor, 17 07.9N, 61 51.7W, Fl R 4s, 48 ft., 5M, White pillar, Visible between Ledwell Point and center of Week Bay.

RANGE (Front Light), 17 01.4N, 61 46.3W, Q G, 35 ft., Wooden pile. **(Rear Light),** 290 meters, 029° from front light, Iso G 2s, 75 ft., Wooden pile.

Emergencies: Call the Antigua Coast Guard on VHF channels 16 and 68, or contact Saba Radio on VHF channel 16.

Pilotage: If approaching from the north, be careful to stay west of the reefs and Diamond Bank. Sandy Island, marked by a light, lies in the western approaches. When coming from the northwest Fort James Light in alignment with the cathedral spires bearing 110° should keep you clear of dangers. When you get closer there is a charted range on a bearing of 113°. Warrington Bank, north of the channel, is less than 3 feet deep. The harbor pilot and harbor authorities monitor VHF channel 16, and the latter 2182kHz. The oil terminal call sign is "Marine Center", and they monitor 2182kHz and VHF channel 16.

Port of Entry: St. John's is primarily a commercial port, but vessels can clear with the officials at the wharf on the north side of the harbor. Hours of operation are 0800 to 1600 most days. The local phone number for the boarding officer is 462-0814.

Dockage: A marina is under development in the Redcliffe Quay area, south of the cruise

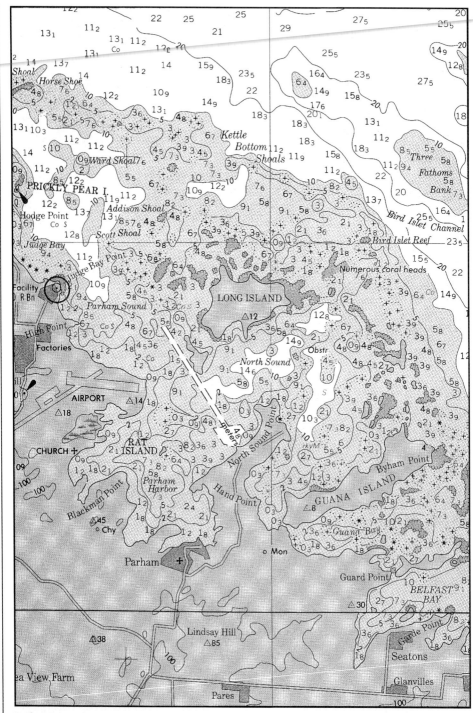

Parham, Soundings in Meters

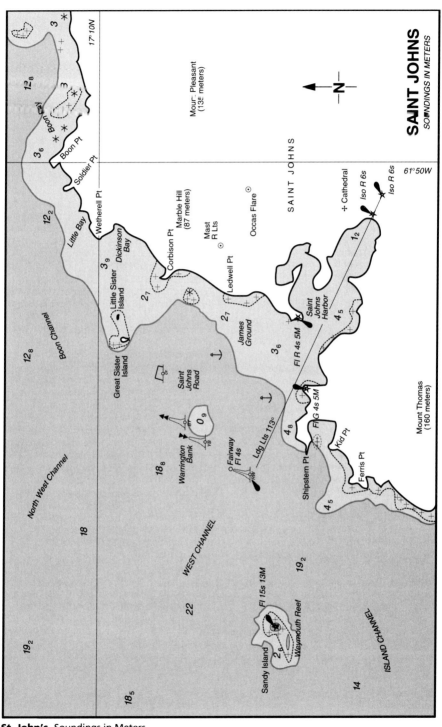

SAINT JOHNS
SOUNDINGS IN METERS

Chapter 2

17° 10N

3

12₈

3

Boon I.

3₆

Boon Pt

Soldier Pt

Mount Pleasant
(135 meters)

12₂

Little Bay

Wetherell Pt

N

Marble Hill
(87 meters)

Corbison Pt

Mast
R Lts

Ledwell Pt

Occas Flare

SAINT JOHNS

61° 50W

Iso R 6s

Iso R 6s

+ Cathedral

3₉

Dickinson
Bay

Little Sister
Island

2₁

2₁

James
Ground

3₆

1₂

Saint
Johns
Harbor

Fl R 4s 5M

4₅

Boon Channel

Great Sister
Island

12₈

Saint
Johns
Road

0₆

0₉

Warrington
Bank

Fairway
Fl 4s

Ldg Lts 113°

Fl G 4s 5M

4₈

Shipstem Pt

Kid Pt

Mount Thomas
(160 meters)

North West Channel

18₈

Ferris Pt

4₅

18

22

WEST CHANNEL

Fl 15s 13M

19₂

19₂

Sandy Island

Weymouth Reef

2₆

ISLAND CHANNEL

14

18₅

ship dock. Call Redcliffe Quay at (809) 462-1847 to see if it is open.

Anchorage: Anchor either north or south of the main ship channel. At times, you may encounter a swell from the north.

Services: There is good general shopping in St. John's. The Redcliffe Quay area is oriented toward cruise ship passengers. Island Motors Limited is a Yamaha motor dealer at (809) 462-2138, or on VHF channel 82. The Epicurean is a gourmet provisioning stop at (809) 462-2565 or 1546. The Joseph Dew Supermarket and Liquor Stores are here at (809) 462-1210. Govee's Marine Supplies is the local chandler at (809) 462-2975. There is a Radio Shack at (809) 462-2685. There are many bars, restaurants and hotels here, or nearby.

St. John's is the capital and major port of Antigua. The harbor is not yet geared for pleasure boaters, but a marina is under development near the cruise ship dock. There is an excellent variety of shops and restaurants, so you may want to visit here even if based in English Harbour.

FALMOUTH HARBOUR
17 01N, 61 47W

Emergencies: Call the Antigua Coast Guard on VHF channels 16 and 68, or contact Saba Radio on VHF channel 16.

Pilotage: Falmouth is located one mile west of English Harbour, on the south coast of Antigua. There may be a lighted range of 029° leading into the harbor. Several private buoys indicate shoal areas in the harbor, but some of the shallow patches are not marked. There is a prominent shoal extending west from Blacks Point, at the mouth of the harbor.

English Harbour Radio V2MA2: Nicholson Yacht Charters provides the local communications link for many boaters. Contact them on VHF channel 68 or on 8294.0kHz, Monday through Friday from 8:30AM to 4:30PM, and on Saturdays from 8:30AM until noon.

Dockage: The Catamaran Club is at the head of the bay, and offers stern-to dockage. Contact the club at (809) 460-1503, or on VHF channel 68. The Antigua Yacht Club Marina is in the eastern portion of the bay. Call them at (809) 460-1444, or on VHF channel 68.

Anchorage: There is good anchorage in the southeast portion of the bay. Be careful to observe the many shoal areas when searching for an anchoring spot. There is a fee of $0.03 per foot, per night, if anchored in Falmouth or English Harbour.

Services: There is a fuel dock at the Catamaran Club. For other services see the listings under English Harbour, which is located right next door. Every type of boating service is available in this area.

Falmouth and English Harbour are "sister cities", sharing many of the same shops and facilities. Falmouth may offer more room for those who want to anchor out. This harbor is the center of many activities during the famous Antigua Race Week.

ENGLISH HARBOUR
17 00N, 61 45W

RANGE (Front Light), 17 00.4N, 61 45.4W, Q R, 35 ft., Wooden pile, Reported extinguished 1985. **(Rear Light),** 100 meters, 055° from front light, Iso R 2s, 85 ft., Wooden pile, Reported extinguished 1985.
CAPE SHIRLEY LIGHT, 17 00.1N, 61 44.7W, Fl (4) W 20s, 494ft., 20M, Metal mast, Visible 264° to 084°, Reported extinguished February 1987.

Emergencies: Call the Antigua Coast Guard on VHF channels 16 and 68, or contact Saba Radio on VHF channel 16.

Pilotage: The approaches to the south coast of Antigua are generally clear, except for the reefs extending east and south from Johnston Point. The harbor is entered between Charlotte Point and Barclay Point, where a range leads you in on a bearing of 055° T. The front light is near a large anchor on the beach. Contact the port authorities on VHF channel 16.

Communications: Many businesses and services stand by on VHF channel 68 in this area.

English Harbour Radio V2MA2: Nicholson Yacht Charters provides the local communications link for many boaters. Contact them on VHF channel 68 or on 8294.0kHz, Monday through Friday from 8:30AM to 4:30PM, and on Saturdays from 8:30AM until noon.

Port of Entry: When clearing with the officials in English Harbour you may anchor in Freeman Bay flying the Q flag. If the Customs and Immigration officials do not come in a reasonable amount of time, you can proceed to their office in the Dockyard, on the western side of the channel leading in to the inner harbor. Contact the officials at (809) 460-1397 for the latest information.

Dockage: Contact Antigua Slipway at (809) 463-1056, or on VHF channels 12 and 68. They are located on the eastern side of the inner harbor mouth. You can tie up stern-to in the

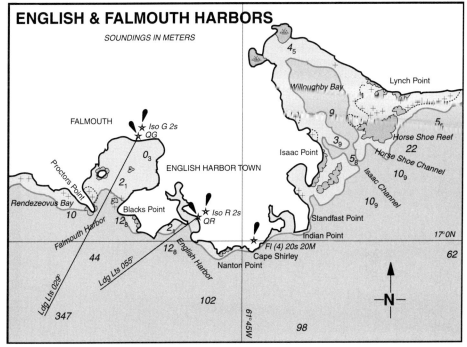

Falmouth and English Harbour, Soundings in Meters

Dockyard area for $0.25 per foot, per night. There are longer term rates available. The Dockyard has public toilets and showers.

Anchoring: There is some room to anchor in Freeman Bay, outside the channel, or in the inner harbor. This can be a good hurricane hole, if you can get in before the crowd. There is a fee of $0.03 per foot, per night, if anchored in Falmouth or English Harbour.

Services: All services are available here, or in Falmouth. Antigua Slipway can haul your boat up to 120 feet long, 125 tons in displacement and 13 foot draft. They have full repair facilities, and a fuel dock. Contact them at (809) 463-1056, or on VHF channels 12 and 68. Pumps and Power, at (809) 463-1242, or on VHF channel 68, can repair engines, fill propane and handle electrical and plumbing repairs. Bailey's Supermarket is opposite the Catamaran Marina in Falmouth. The Chandlery is a real chandler at (809) 460-1225. A&F Sails and Antigua Sails are at (809) 460-1522 and (809) 460-1527 respectively. They both

monitor VHF channel 68. Nicholson Yacht Charters provides message, and mail services of all types. See English Harbour Radio above. Carib Marine is a combination grocery and hardware store at (809) 460-1521. They can handle major provisioning for your charter yacht. Seagull Services is a complete engine and general repair facility at (809) 460-3050. They do dinghy repairs and liferaft servicing. This is just a sample of some of the many fine services oriented toward boaters. There are many interesting bars and restaurants to entertain your crew.

This is the location of the famous shipyard that serviced the great British sailing fleets, and now services some of the premier charter yachts in the Caribbean. There is limited anchoring and docking room, which may be jammed with luxury charter boats. Many formal, and informal, regattas originate here, and this is a favorite watering hole for Caribbean "yachties".

REED'S NEEDS YOU!

It is difficult to obtain accurate and up-to-date information on many areas in the Caribbean. To provide the mariner with the best possible product we utilize many sources. *Reed's* welcomes your contributions, suggestions and updates. Please be as specific as possible, and include your address and phone number.
Thank you!

GUADELOUPE

CAUTION: Our information on aids to navigation comes from official government sources. The latitudes and longitudes of these marks may not correspond to the readings from GPS receivers. Some aids have been reported as unreliable, missing, off position or showing incorrect characteristics. No single aid to navigation, or waypoint, should be relied upon as a sole means of fixing your position.

To make phone calls you will need to purchase a phone card at the post office, or in many shops. To make credit card calls, or collect calls, dial 10 for an operator.

The official currency is the French franc, which is currently trading at about 5.47 to the dollar. The language spoken is French, and some proficiency in the language is recommended.

ENTRY PROCEDURES

Guadeloupe is located about 40 miles south of English Harbour, Antigua. It consists of two large islands, Basse-Terre and Grande-Terre, and the off-lying islands of Iles des Saintes, Marie-Galante and La Désirade. It is an Overseas Department of France, and is allied with St. Barts, St. Martin, La Désirade, Marie Galante and Iles des Saintes. You should fly the French courtesy flag here.

Ports of Entry are Deshayes, Basse-Terre, Pointe-à-Pitre and Grand-Bourg on Marie-Galante. There is a customs office (Bureau de Douane) near the marina complex in Pointe-à-Pitre. Call (590) 83 96 07 in Pointe-à-Pitre for the latest information on procedures.

There is no charge for entering the country. The officials may not allow the entry of boats from the U.S. that have only a state registration, so you should have federal documentation for your vessel. No chartering is allowed by foreign yachts, though charter boats may pass through with non-French passengers.

You should check in with the local police (les gendarmes), when visiting Iles des Saintes before clearing in officially in Guadeloupe.

When calling Guadeloupe from the U.S., use the area code 590, followed by a six digit local number. On the island you only need the six digits. You can call St. Barts, St. Martin, La Désirade, Marie Galante and Iles des Saintes directly using the six digit local numbers.

BASSE-TERRE

ANSE A LA BARQUE, Head of cove, 16 05.4N, 61 46.1W, Fl (2) W R G 6s, 36ft., 8M white, 5M red, 5M green, W tower, G top, R 050° to 064°, W 064° to 081°, G 081° to 115°.
NORTH SIDE OF ENTRANCE LIGHT, 16 05.4N, 61 46.4W, Q (9) W 15s, 91ft., 9M, West CARDINAL YB.
BASSE TERRE LIGHT, On quay near customs house, 15 59.8N, 61 43.8W, Fl W G 4s, 46ft., 10M white, 7M green, W metal pylon, R lantern, W 325° – 110°, G 110° – 135°.

BASSE-TERRE
15 59N, 61 44W

Pilotage: Between Guadeloupe and Antigua the current is basically west-going, and off the southwest point of the island of Basse-Terre the current reaches speeds of 2 knots. The southwest part of the island is dark rock, and quite steep-to. The three peaks of Soufrière may be visible if they are not obscured by clouds. A tower on a church and the steeple of the cathedral are prominent. A statue and a cross are on the church tower. The port authority monitors VHF channel 16.
Port of Entry: Officials are in the Marina de Rivière Sens, or in town.
Dockage: Marina de Rivière Sens is located in a protected basin about 1 1/4 miles southeast of the commercial wharf. Contact them at (590) 81 88 71. They have all services.
Anchorage: Anchor north or south of the town wharf, or off the entrance to the marina. There is no shelter in south or west winds.

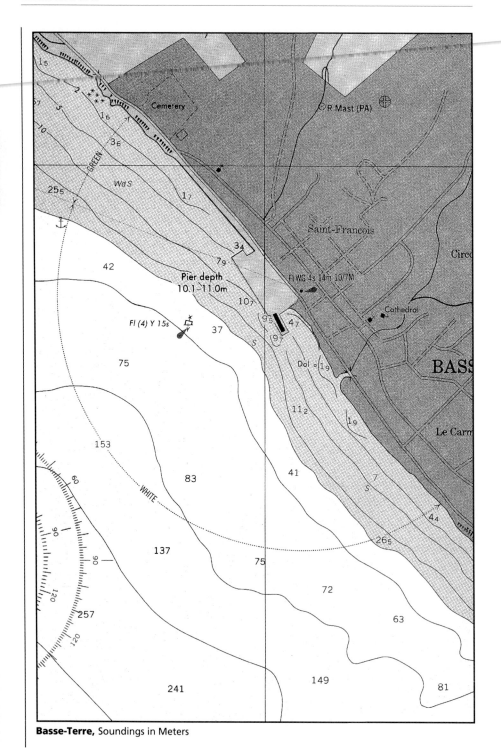

Basse-Terre, Soundings in Meters

Services: There are good yacht services in the area around the marina. The town has good general shopping and groceries.

Basse-Terre, the capital of Guadeloupe, was founded in 1643. The historic city rests in a dramatic setting below towering volcanic peaks. There are good markets and supplies for those who can find room in the marina.

POINTE DU VIEUX FORT, 15 56.9N, 61 42.6W, Fl (2+1) W 15s, 85ft., 22M, W tower, Gray top, Obscured 297° – 331° by Les Saintes, Reserve light F W.
TROIS RIVIERES LIGHT, On the point, 15 58.1N, 61 38.8W, Iso W R G 4s, 82ft., 10M white, 7M red, 7M green, W tower, R top, R 275° to 349°, W 349° to 054°,G 054° to 068°.
Passe de la Baleine, West Pass Buoy BA, 15 52.8N, 61 35.5W, Fl (2) G 6s, Green pillar, Can topmark, Radar reflector.
SAINTE MARIE LIGHT, Root of E pier, 16 06.1N, 61 33.9W, Fl G 4s, 36ft., 6M, W square tower, G top.
PETIT BOURG LIGHT, on jetty, 16 11.5N, 61 35.1W,Fl (2) G 6s, 4M, White tripod, Green top.

POINTE-A-PITRE APPROACHES

ENTRANCE RANGE, (Front Light) S end Monroux peninsula, 16 13.3N, 61 31.6W, Dir. Q W, 49ft., 13M, W pylon, W rectangular topmark, Intensified 4° either side of range. **(Rear Light)** Pointe Fouillole 640 meters 348° from front, Q W, 69ft., 13M, W mast, Topmark W slats.
AVIATION LIGHT, 16 15.8N, 61 31.7W, Mo (P) W 30s, Aero Radiobeacon, Occasional.

POINTE-À-PITRE
16 14N, 61 32W

Pilotage: The approaches to the commercial port of Pointe-à-Pitre are well marked by buoys, lights and ranges. The buoyage is laid out on the "red-right-returning" scheme. Beware the coral reefs extending from the shore of Basse-Terre in the approaches. The west side of the inner harbor is commercial in nature, while the pleasure boat facilities are concentrated to the east. The Captain of the Port monitors VHF channel 16.
Port of Entry: There is an office in the marina, and one in town. Contact them at (590) 83 96 07.

Dockage: Marina Bas du Fort is located in the first bay to the east as you enter the harbor. This area is known as Port du Plaisance. Contact them at (590) 90 84 85.
Anchorage: There are various places to anchor, tucked just outside of the marked channels near shore. Most boats try to be near the shipyard and marina complexes on the east side of the harbor
Services: Extensive services are available here, including several places for haulouts. There are many marine businesses in the Port du Plaisance area, rivaling the facilities available in Antigua. Karukera Marine (590) 90 90 96, Electro Nautique (590) 82 18 35 and SCAM (590) 90 80 40, are chandlers. The North Sails loft can be reached at (590) 90 80 44. Sorema is a diesel engine, electrics and general engineering service at (590) 90 88 77. LGEM Electronic Marine repairs electronics at (590) 90 89 19. There are supermarkets, restaurants and shops in the area around the marina, or in town.

This is a well sheltered harbor, offering some of the best facilities and services for boaters available in the Caribbean. It is also a busy commercial port, and center of commerce for Guadeloupe.

GRANDE-TERRE

PORT LOUIS LIGHT, On the beach, 16 25.1N, 61 32.2W, Q (9) W 15s, 33ft., 9M, West CARDINAL YBY, Beacon, Visible 252° to 162°.
ANSE BERTRAND LIGHT, 16 28.4N, 61 30.7W, Fl (2) W R G 6s, 46ft., 9M white, 6M red, 6M green, W concrete tower, R 120 to 163, W 163° to 170°, G 170° to 200°.
PORT DU MOULE LIGHT, W side of entrance, 16 20.0N, 61 20.8W, Fl W R 4s, 39ft., 9M white, 6M red, W concrete pylon, G lantern, R 110° to 202°, W 202° to 312°, R 312° to 340°.
EAST SIDE OF ENTRANCE LIGHT, Fl (2) W R G 6s, 23ft., 7M white, 5M red, 5M green, W pillar, R top, R 353° to 133°, W 133° to 138°, G 138° to 165°, W on Hastings Pass.
PORT DE SAINT FRANCOIS LIGHT, Directional light, 16 15.1N, 61 16.7W, Dir Q W R G, 33ft., 9M white, 7M red, 7M green, W tower, R 345° to 358°, W 358° to 002°, G 002° to 015°.
PORT DE SAINT FRANCOIS, On wharf, 16 15.1N, 61 16.6W, Fl G 4s, 30ft., 6M, W metal post, G top.
ILET A GOZIER, 16 12.0N, 61 29.2W, Fl (2) R 10s, 79ft., 26M, W cylindrical masonry tower, Visible 259° to 115°, Obscured on certain bearings toward Pointe Caraibe.

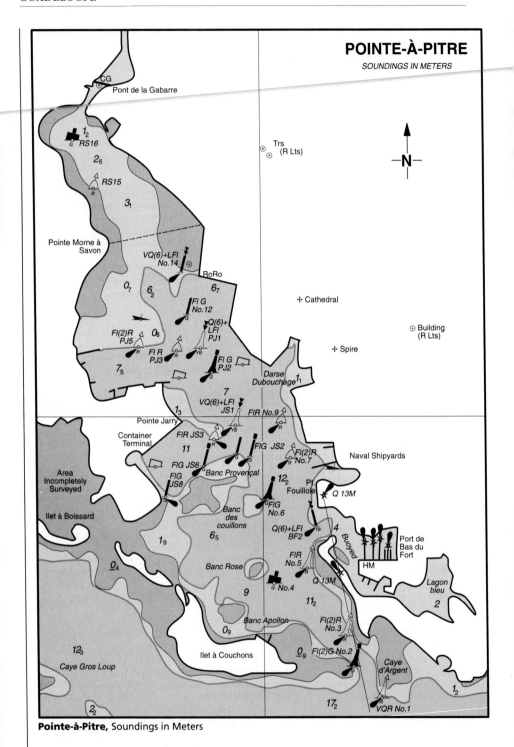

POINTE-À-PITRE
SOUNDINGS IN METERS

—N—

CG
Pont de la Gabarre

1₂
RS16
G

2₆

RS15
R

3₁

Pointe Morne à Savon

Trs
(R Lts)

VQ(6)+LFl
No.14

RoRo

0₇   6₂   6₇

✛ Cathedral

⊙ Building
(R Lts)

Fl G
No.12
G

Q(6)+LFl
PJ1

Fl(2)R
PJ5

0₈

✛ Spire

Fl R
PJ3
R

YB

Fl G
PJ2
G

7₅

Darse
Dubouchage   1₁

7

1₃   VQ(6)+LFl
JS1

Pointe Jarry

Fl R No.9
R
YB

Container
Terminal

Fl R JS3

Fl G JS2

Fl(2)R
No.7
R

Naval Shipyards

11

Fl G JS6
G

Banc Provençal

Fl G
JS8
G

12₂

Pt
Fouillole
★ Q 13M

Area
Incompletely
Surveyed

G Fl G
No.6

Q(6)+LFl
BF2
YB

Ilet à Boissard

Banc
des
couillons

4

Buoyed

Port de
Bas du
Fort

1₉   6₅

0₄

Banc Rose

Fl R
No.5
R

Q 13M
★

HM

Lagon
bleu

2

9

G No.4

11₂

Banc Apollon

Fl(2)R
No.3
R

0₉

12₃
Caye Gros Loup

Ilet à Couchons

0₉   Fl(2)G No.2

Caye
d'Argent

1₂

2₂

17₂   VQR No.1

Pointe-à-Pitre, Soundings in Meters

ISLANDS OF GUADELOUPE

LA DESIRADE LIGHT, Near SE point of island, 16 19.6N, 61 00.7W, Fl (2) W 10s, 165ft., 20M, W framework tower, R top, Upper part enclosed, Dwelling.
BAIE MAHAULT RANGE, (Front Light) 16 19.7N, 61 01.1W, Fl R 2s, 16ft., 1M, W pylon, R top. **(Rear Light)** 35 meters 327° from front, Fl R 2s, 23ft., 4M, W pylon, R top, Synchronized with front.
GRANDE ANSE LIGHT, Head of pier, 16 18.2N, 61 04.8W, Fl G 2.5s, 23ft., 1M, W mast.
LEADING LIGHT, Dir. Oc (2) W R G 6s, 23ft., 8M white, 6M red, 6M green, W stone structure, R top, R from 250° to 335°, W from 335° to 339°, G from 339° to 056°.
ILES DE PETITE TERRE, E extremity of Ilot Terre d'en Bas, 16 10.3N, 61 06.8W, Fl (3) W 12s, 108ft., 15M, Gray cylindrical tower, Square stone base, Obscured by Ile La Desinade 185° to 213°.

LES SAINTES

BOURG DES SAINTES LIGHT, Terre d'en Haut, Root of wharf, 15 52.1N, 61 35.2W, Fl W R G 4s, 30ft., 10M white, 7M red, 7M green, W metal framework tower, R 075° to 142°, W 142° to 154°, G 154° to 160°, Obstruction light on aerial.

BOURG DES SAINTES
15 52N, 61 35W

Pilotage: The town is located on the western side of Terre d'en Haut, near the middle of the island. A large conspicuous cross is illuminated at night, and stands south of the church. Note the shoal patch, halfway to Ilet à Cabrit, marked by a buoy. There is a 100 foot long pier projecting from the waterfront. There is a light shown from near the root of the pier.

Vessel Clearance: Check with the gendarmes if arriving here from another country, before clearing with the authorities on Guadeloupe.
Anchorage: Anchor away from the ferry dock and ferry channels.
Services: There is little in the way of marine services, but there is a good selection of boutiques, restaurants and general stores.

MARIE-GALANTE

GRAND-BOURG LIGHT, On wharf, 15 52.9N, 61 19.2W, Fl (2) G 6s, 30ft., 6M, W metal post, G top.

GRAND BOURG
15 53N, 61 19W

Pilotage: This town lies on the southwest side of Marie Galante. The fort and the hospital on the northwest side of the town, and the church with its belfry on its northeast side, are all prominent landmarks. A conspicuous lighted TV tower stands about 1 mile north of the town. Lighted buoys mark the edge of the reefs in the approach to the pier from the west.
Port of Entry: You can clear in here, but you must get your outward clearance on Guadeloupe.
Anchorage: Anchor in, or near, the small basin near the ferry dock.
Services: General supplies are available.

ST. LOUIS LIGHT, W of church, 15 57.4N, 61 19.3W, Fl G 4s, 36ft., 6M, W square tower, G top.
CAPESTERRE RANGE, (Front Light) 15 53.9N, 61 13.2W, Q R, 39ft., 6M, Square tower, R+W bands, Visible 246.5° to 051.5°. **(Rear Light)** 100 meters 313° from front, Q R, 52ft., 6M, Square tower, R + W bands, Visible 246.5° to 051.5°.

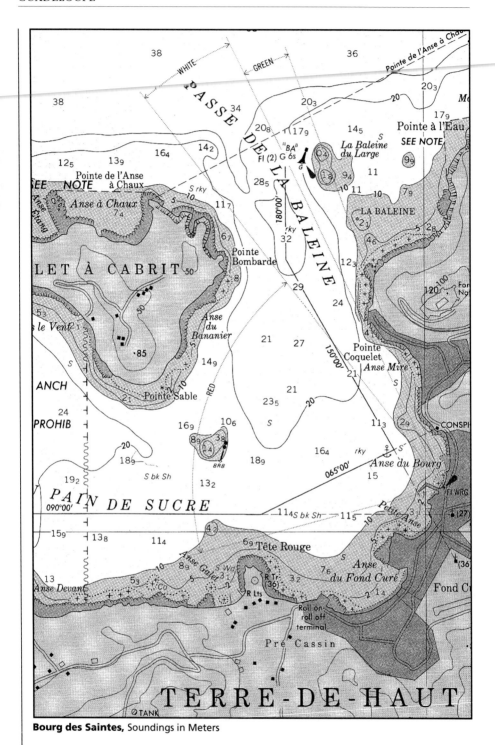

Bourg des Saintes, Soundings in Meters

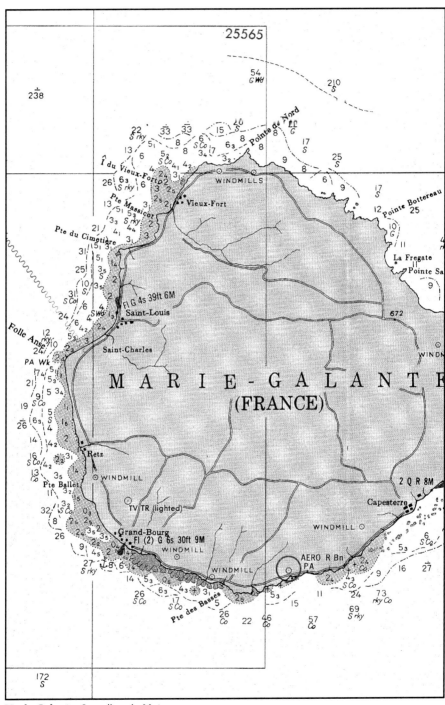

Marie-Galante, Soundings in Meters

ISLA AVES, VENEZUELA

CAUTION: It has been reported that much of this island was washed away in a 1979 hurricane, leaving two sand cays bordered by coral reefs, with a pool between. The latitude and longitude of this island has been reported to be inaccurate by some yachtsmen. All of the following information should, therefore, be used with great caution.

15 40N, 63 37W

Venezuelan Coast Guard: Call sign "Simon Bolivar Coast Guard Station".

ISLA AVES LIGHT, 15 40.1N, 63 37.0W, FL W 5s, 49ft., 13M, RACON: A (–).

This is a Venezuelan possession with a latitude slightly north of the northern tip of Dominica, but 128 miles to the west. It is nearly 600 yards long in a north–south direction, and 100 yards wide. The maximum elevation of about 10 feet is near the northern end of the island, and the sea breaks across the center in anything more than a moderate swell. The island is formed of coral, overlaid with sand which supports some vegetation. Birds abound and the island is a protected nature sanctuary.

An oil-rig style Texas tower, with a radar reflector, stands on the island. The structure on top of the tower is the size of an average house. The platform is approximately 60 feet high. This is a manned Venezuelan Coast Guard Station, call sign "Simon Bolivar Coast Guard Station". The island has been reported as a good radar target up to 30 miles distant. There is also a transmitting radar beacon (RACON).

A jetty, with a depth of about 9 feet alongside its head, projects about 88 yards west of the island. It is located about 100 yards from the south end of the island. Less than five foot depths are found on several shoal patches in the western approaches to the jetty.

In moderate weather you may be able to land near the center of the western side of the island. A narrow sandy beach extends down to the low water line here.

Vessels without local knowledge are advised to give the islands a berth of at least 1 1/2 miles. If you wish to anchor, the best approach is from the south–southwest. Keep a good lookout for coral heads. The recommended anchorage is with the mast bearing 077°, distant 600 yards. Depths should be about 17 feet in this area, though there is a 9 foot patch reported about 100 yards east-northeast of this position.

Chapter 2

DOMINICA

CAUTION: Our information on aids to navigation comes from official government sources. The latitudes and longitudes of these marks may not correspond to the readings from GPS receivers. Some aids have been reported as unreliable, missing, off position or showing incorrect characteristics. No single aid to navigation, or waypoint, should be relied upon as a sole means of fixing your position.

ENTRY PROCEDURES

The northern tip of Dominica is located about 38 miles south of Pointe-à-Pitre, Guadeloupe. Though the island has most recently been a British possession, a strong French influence seeps in from the neighboring islands. The

Commonwealth of Dominica is now an independent country.

Ports of entry are Portsmouth in Prince Rupert Bay, and Roseau, the capital of the country. Both are on the west coast of the island. Contact Customs in Portsmouth at (809) 44-55340, and in Roseau at (809) 44-82222. Immigration in Portsmouth can be reached at (809) 44-55222.

In Roseau you might want to call the Anchorage Hotel on VHF channel 16 to see if you can contact the officials from their anchorage. In Portsmouth try calling the Portsmouth Beach Hotel (on VHF channel 16) for the same reason. These facilities are owned by the same family, and specialize in making yachtsmen feel welcome. They can assist with most of your needs while on the island. Contact the

Anchorage Hotel at (809) 44-82638, or the Portsmouth Beach Hotel at (809) 44-55142.

In Roseau call the Port Manager on VHF channel 16 to obtain permission to anchor off the commercial wharves, which are north of town. You can then dinghy in to clear with the officials. The area north of the mouth of the Roseau River, including the commercial wharves, is a Restricted Anchorage. In Portsmouth you should visit the officials near the commercial wharf south of town.

A cruising permit should be obtained for your itinerary on the island. There is a departure charge of $5.00 EC dollars per boat.

Normal working hours for the officials are about 0800 to 1200, then 1300 to 1600, Monday through Friday. Overtime charges apply outside of these hours.

The telephone area code for Dominica is 809, followed by the island code of 44, if calling from outside the country. On the island you only need the 5 digit local number.

All charges are in Eastern Caribbean, or EC, dollars. The exchange rate, when converting EC dollars to U.S. dollars, is about .40. In other words, $100 EC = $40 U.S. You will probably find many people accepting U.S. dollars, especially in tourist areas.

The official language is English, but you will also encounter French Creole, due to the proximity of French territories.

PORTSMOUTH
15 34N, 61 29W

Pilotage: Prince Rupert Bay is a well sheltered bay near the north end of the west coast of the island. There are no dangers in the approach to this steep-to coast. The gray spire and red roof of the Catholic Church in town are conspicuous. The white Methodist Chapel, east of the Catholic Church, is prominent from offshore. There are two jetties and a prominent warehouse 1 mile south of Portsmouth.
Port of Entry: Contact Customs at (809) 44-55340, and Immigration at (809) 44-55222.
Dockage: The Portsmouth Beach Hotel may have some dockage, either bow or stern-to, at their facility about 1 mile south of town. They

also have rental moorings. Contact them on VHF channel 16, or at (809) 44-55142.
Anchorage: Anchor near the Portsmouth Beach Hotel, and you can dinghy in to their dock. Other boats anchor north of town near the Purple Turtle or Mamie's on the Beach. You can probably dinghy in to one of these restaurants.
Services: Contact the Portsmouth Beach Hotel to obtain fuel or water at their wharf. They also offer a mail drop, showers, a restaurant, telephones and assistance with most projects on the island. Ask for recommendations on guides, or taxis. Basic supplies and groceries are available in town. Mamie's (809) 44-55997, and The Purple Turtle (809) 44-55296, will assist yachtsmen. The "boat boys" will offer you their services here.

BARROUI LIGHT, 15 26.0N, 61 26.8W, 2 F R (vertical).

ROSEAU
15 18N, 61 24W

ROSEAU LIGHT, On Fort Young, 15 17.4N, 61 23.7W, Oc R 3s, 80ft., 8M, White concrete structure, Partially obscured from 117° to 125°, Obscured from 125° to shore. *Temporarily extinguished 1983.*

Pilotage: The port of Roseau comprises Woodbridge Bay and Roseau Roads. A deepwater wharf is situated 1600 yards north of the mouth of the Roseau River. This area is a Restricted Anchorage, and boaters should contact the Port Manager on VHF channel 16 for permission to drop the hook. Morne Bruce is a tableland rising to a height of 475 feet east of town. There are several old military buildings on its summit. There is a prominent flagstaff on the west corner of Fort Young at the south end of town. The Catholic Church and Wesleyan Church spires are also prominent. The red bridge crossing the mouth of the Roseau River is a good landmark.
Port of Entry: Contact Customs at (809) 44-82222.
Anchorage: Anchor near the Anchorage Hotel, located about 1 mile south of town. They have moorings, a dinghy dock, showers, water, telephones and a mail drop. Contact them on VHF channel 16, or at (809) 44-82638. They can also assist in obtaining fuel, or finding anything you might need.

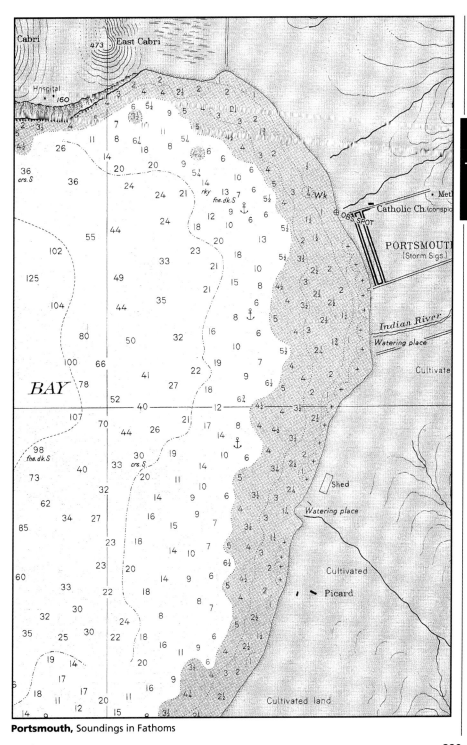

Portsmouth, Soundings in Fathoms

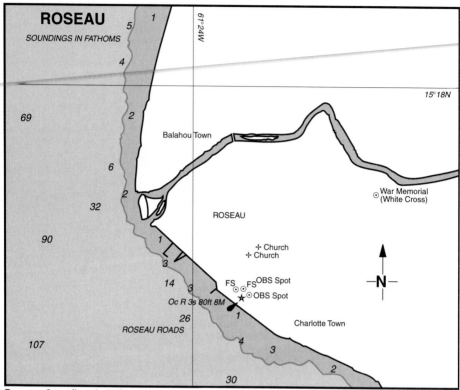

Roseau, Soundings in Fathoms

Services: There are few yachting services here, but you can obtain most general supplies and groceries. Contact the Division of Tourism at (809) 44-82351 for information on visiting the "Nature Island of the Caribbean". The Castaways Beach Hotel, located about 7 miles north of town, is a dive and watersports center. Contact them at (809) 44-96244, or on VHF channel 16 (call sign "Castaways"). There are also dive facilities at the Anchorage Hotel. The "boat boys" will offer you their services here.

SEND FOR YOUR FREE 1994 SUPPLEMENT

Just return the post-paid reply card and questionnaire to receive your free list of navigation updates, changes and special notices. Publishing date — Spring 1994.

330   REED'S NAUTICAL ALMANAC

MARTINIQUE

ENTRY PROCEDURES

This island country is a department of France, and with its population of over 350,000 people, it is one of the commercial centers of the Antilles. You should fly the French courtesy flag here.

The main port of entry is Fort-de-France, but you can also check in at St. Pierre or Marin. Hours are about 0800 to 1100 and 1500 to 1730. The main Customs office can be reached at (596) 63 04 82, or fax (596) 63 61 80, and the main Immigration office at (596) 51 48 85.

You will need a clearance from your last port of call, several crew lists, your boat documents and your passports. Check on the latest regulations if you plan on staying in the country, or leaving your boat, for more than six months. You may be liable for duty after this period.

The telephone code for the island is 596, followed by a six digit local number. When on the island you only need dial the local number.

To make phone calls you will need to purchase a phone card at the post office, or in many shops. To make credit card calls, or collect calls, dial 10 for an operator.

The official currency is the French franc, which is currently trading at about 5.47 to the dollar. The language spoken is French, and some proficiency in the language is recommended.

MARTINIQUE, WEST COAST

PRECHEUR POINT LIGHT, 14 48.0N, 61 13.8W, Fl R 1s, 72ft., 14M, Iron tower, Stone base, Visible 338° to 162°.

POINTE DES NEGRES LIGHT, 14 35.9N, 61 05.6W, Fl W 5s, 118ft., 25M, W metal framework tower, Gray lantern, Visible 276° to 126°, Aero Radiobeacon.

Banc Mitan Buoy, W side of shoal, 14 35.0N, 61 05.0W, Q W, R+B horizontally banded buoy, Black ball topmark, Radar reflector.

FORT-DE-FRANCE

FORT ST. LOUIS LIGHT, In SW part of fortress, 14 35.9N, 61 04.4W, Fl (4) W R G, 102ft., 17M white, 10M red, W iron framework structure, R 320° to 057°, W 057° to 087°, G 087° to 140°, Obscured 140° to 320°.

BAIE DU CARENAGE RANGE, (Front Light) 14 36.3N, 61 03.7W, Iso G 4s, 138ft., 14M, Yellow rectangle, W metal framework tower, Black bands, Intensified 001° to 007°. **(Rear Light)** 145 meters 004° from front, Iso G 4s, 164ft., 14M, Yellow rectangle, W metal framework tower, Black bands, Synchronized with front, Intensified 001° to 007°.

OIL PIER LIGHT, SW corner, 14 35.9N, 61 04.1W, F R, 3ft., 6M, R pedestal.

BEACON, 14 36.0N, 61 03.0W, 2 F R, 3 F R vertical 20 feet below and 20 feet apart, R + W banded radio mast, Obstruction light.

BEACON, 2 F R, 3 F R vertical 20 feet below and 20 feet apart, R + W banded radio mast, Obstruction light.

BEACON, 2 F R, 3 F R vertical 20 feet below and 20 feet apart, R + W banded radio mast, Obstruction light.

LE LAMENTIN AVIATION LIGHT, 14 35.7N, 61 00.0W, Fl (3 + 1) W 12s, 105ft., 20M, Occasional.

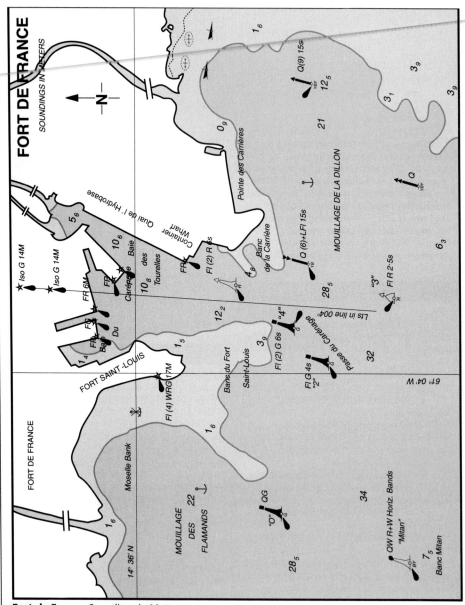

Fort-de-France, Soundings in Meters

FORT-DE-FRANCE
14 36N, 61 04W

Pilotage: The island is very mountainous, and it easily identified by three outstanding peaks towering above the main mountain chain that traverses it in a northwest to southeast direction. There are shoals, banks and other dangers marked by buoys in the approaches to the city. Note the 004° range leading into the main harbor. Local port authorities and pilots may be contacted on VHF channels 13 and 16. This city of 100,000 inhabitants has a very busy port.

Port of Entry: The officials are located near the Abri Cotier dock, on the western portion of the waterfront.

Dockage: There may be some stern-to dockage on the wharf east of Fort Saint-Louis, but most boats anchor out. There should be some dockage available across the way on the Pointe du Bout at Anse Mitan.

Anchorage: Most boast anchor in the western part of Baie des Flamands, near the Abri Cotier dock. Customs is near the dock, and you can dinghy in there. For a more peaceful anchorage try one of the nearby bays, or the area around Anse Mitan.

Ferry: Several ferries run across the bay to Anse Mitan. Service is frequent.

Services: Every type of marine service is here, or nearby. Fuel and water are available at the Abri Cotier dock — contact Philippe Vatier Distribution at (596) 70 11 39. Sea Services (596) 70 26 69, Littoral (596) 70 28 70, Martinique Ship Chandler (596) 60 49 01 and the Ship Shop (596) 71 43 40 are all chandlers. Puces Nautiques (596) 60 58 48 describe themselves as a "nautical fleamarket". Sailmakers include North Sails (596) 63 58 09, R. Helenon (596) 60 22 05 and West Indies Sails (596) 70 35 44. The repair yards are Martinique Drydock (596) 72 69 40, and the Ship Shop, who have a Travelift. Engine repairs are done by Madia Boat (596) 63 48 70, metalwork by Chalemessin Enterprise (596) 60 03 79 and woodwork or fiberglass (and supplies) by Polymar (596) 70 62 88. There are large first class supermarkets and general stores of all types.

Fort-de-France is the busy, and very European, capital of Martinique. It is also the largest city in the Antilles and a great place to find things a modern city can provide. Nearby are peaceful anchorages when you tire of all the hustle-bustle.

POINT DU BOUT

POINTE DU BOUT LIGHT, Marina E jetty head, 14 33.4N, 61 03.5W, Fl G 2.5s, 13ft., 2M, G post.
POINTE DU BOUT LIGHT, Marina W jetty head, Fl R 2.5s, 13ft., 2M, R post.

ANSE MITAN
14 34N, 61 03W

Pilotage: There is a buoyed reef, Caye de l'Anse Mitan, west of Pointe du Bout where Anse Mitan is located. There are also some reefs close to shore around Pointe du Bout. A ferry runs from the marina basin to Fort-de-France, and one from a dock in the big bay on the southern end of the western side of the peninsula.

Dockage: The Ponton du Bakoua has some dockage about halfway down the peninsula on the western side. Contact them at (596) 66 05 45, or on VHF channel 68. The Somatras Marina is in the square dredged basin. Contact them at (596) 66 07 74.

Anchorage: Anchor along the western shore of the peninsula, taking care to avoid the small reef marked by a buoy. The reef is located west of the Ponton du Bakoua dock.

Ferry: Frequent ferries run to Fort-de-France from the marina basin, and from the dock at the southwestern end of Pointe du Bout.

Services: Fuel and water are available at the Ponton du Bakoua. Mecanique Plaisance is located in the marina and does inboard engine repairs. Contact them at (596) 66 05 40. The Captain's Shop is a chandlery and repair shop. Call them at (596) 66 06 77. The local sail shop is Voilerie Caraibe Martinique at (596) 66 07 24, or on VHF channel 16. There are nearby supermarkets and general shops. For anything you can't find, take the ferry across to Fort-de-France.

Anse Mitan is a convenient anchorage, and less commercial, than Fort-de-France. There are good facilities in a less hectic atmosphere than in the big city across the way.

MARTINIQUE, SOUTH COAST

POINT DU MARIN, On W side of point, 14 26.9N, 60 53.2W, Dir Q W R G, 23ft., 9M white, 6M red, 6M green, W structure, G top, R 015° to 071°, W 071° to 075°, G 075° to 080°.

Chapter 2

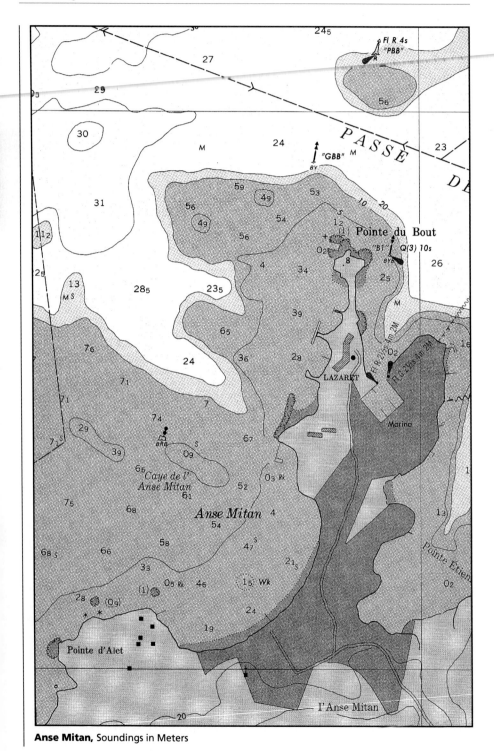

Anse Mitan, Soundings in Meters

NORTH HEAD LIGHT, 14 27.1N, 60 53.1W,
Fl R 2.5s, 16ft., 2M, STARBOARD, R, Beacon,
Topmark.
BANC MAJOR LIGHT, 14 27.7N, 60 52.6W,
Fl G 2.5s, 7M, 2M, PORT, G, Beacon, Topmark.
BANC DU MILIEU LIGHT, 14 27.7N, 60 52.5W,
Fl R 2.5s, 7ft., 2M, STARBOARD, R, Beacon,
Topmark.
BANC DE LA DOUANE LIGHT, S side,
14 28.0N, 60 52.2W, V Q (3) G 5s, 7ft., 2M,
PORT, G, Beacon, Topmark.
E SIDE LIGHT, 14 28.1N, 60 52.2W, Q (3) G 10s,
7ft., 2M, PORT, G, Beacon, Topmark.

LE MARIN

14 28N, 60 52W

Pilotage: There are quite a few reefs in Cul-
de-Sac Marin, but the clear water and good
aids to navigation should make the approach
easy. There are three conspicuous chimneys
west of town, and a light is shown from Pointe
du Marin. Due to the shoals, an approach in
good light is recommended.
Port of Entry: The official's hours vary — clear
in Fort-de-France if in a hurry.
Dockage: The SAEPP marina is located in the
lagoon at the eastern end of the waterfront.
Contact them at (596) 74 85 33. Space is apt to
be tight due to the many charter operations in
this area.
Anchorage: Anchor directly south of the
waterfront, keeping the designated channels
clear.
Services: Get fuel and water in the marina.
Carene Antilles is a large repair yard located
west of the main docks. There is also a large
chandlery here. Contact them at (596) 74 77 70.

Nearby is the Marine Paint Factory at (596) 74
84 14. La Voilerie du Marin is the sailmaker at
(596) 74 73 10. They also do laundry. There is a
good selection of supermarkets and general
shops ashore.

Le Marin has become the charter boat center
of Martinique, bringing many marine services
to this small city. The harbor is well sheltered,
and a good alternative to busy Fort-de-France.

MARTINIQUE, EAST COAST

BAIE TRINITE RANGE, (Front Light)
14 45.2N, 60 58.2W, Iso W 4s, 20ft., 8M, W
structure. **(Rear Light)** 284.2° from front,
Iso W 4s, 23ft., 8M, W structure.
LA CARAVELLE LIGHT, 14 46.2N, 60 53.1W,
Fl (3) W 15s, 423ft., 10M, Yellow square tower,
W lantern, Visible 113° to 345°.
BAIE DU FRANCOIS DIRECTIONAL LIGHT,
14 38.0N, 60 53.7W, Dir Q W R G, 108ft., 8M
white, 6M red, 6M green, W tower, G top,
R 200° to 245°, W 245° to 248°, G 248° to 280°,
W sector indicates preferred channel.
PORT VAUCLIN LIGHT, N point, 14 33.0N,
60 50.4W, Q W R G, 46ft., 11M white, 9M red,
9M green, R 220° to 230°, W 230° to 232°,
G 232° to 250°.
DIQUE EST LIGHT, Head, 14 32.7N, 60 50.1W,
Fl G 2.5s, 13ft., 2M, W tower, G top.
EPI OUEST LIGHT, Head, 14 32.8N, 60 50.1W,
Fl R 2.5s, 10ft., 2M, W tower, R top.
ILET CABRIT LIGHT, N part, 14 23.4N,
60 52.3W, Fl R 5s, 138ft., 16M, R pylon, Hex-
agonal base, Visible 235° to 106° and 107° to
108°.

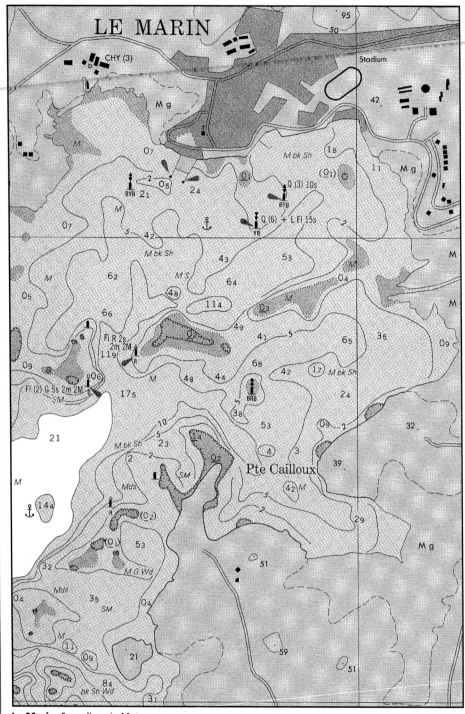

Le Marin, Soundings in Meters

FORT-DE-FRANCE, MARTINIQUE

HIGH & LOW WATER 1994 14°35'N 61°03'W

ATLANTIC STANDARD TIME (GMT -4H)

JANUARY

Day	Time	ft	Time	ft	Time	ft	Time	ft
1 Sa	0736	1.7	1012	1.6	1638	2.0		
16 Su	0020	1.2	0700	1.7	1224	1.6	1736	1.8
2 Su	0032	1.1	0747	1.7	1146	1.6	1736	1.9
17 M	0042	1.3	0755	1.8	1357	1.5	1829	1.6
3 M	0104	1.2	0808	1.8	1323	1.5	1845	1.8
18 Tu	0058	1.3	0822	1.8	1535	1.5	1942	1.5
4 Tu	0136	1.3	0836	1.8	1501	1.5	2012	1.6
19 W	0103	1.4	0850	1.9	1704	1.4	2152 ◑	1.5
5 W	0204	1.4	0910	1.9	1632	1.3	2208 ◑	1.6
20 Th	0043	1.4	0921	1.9	1809	1.3		
6 Th	0227	1.5	0949	2.0	1749	1.2		
21 F	0954	2.0	1855	1.2				
7 F	0032	1.5	0237	1.5	1032	2.0	1853	1.1
22 Sa	1029	2.0	1933	1.2				
8 Sa	1118	2.1	1949	1.0				
23 Su	1108	2.0	2007	1.1				
9 Su	1206	2.2	2039	1.0				
24 M	1149	2.1	2040	1.1				
10 M	1254	2.2	2124	0.9				
25 Tu	1233	2.1	2113	1.0				
11 Tu ●	1343	2.2	2206	0.9				
26 W	1319	2.1	2146	1.0				
12 W	1430	2.1	2245	1.0				
27 Th ○	1407	2.1	2218	1.1				
13 Th	0639	1.6	0812	1.6	1517	2.1	2321	1.0
28 F	0546	1.6	0807	1.6	1548	2.0	2251	1.1
14 F	0649	1.7	0938	1.6	1602	2.0	2352	1.1
29 Sa	0550	1.7	0931	1.6	1552	2.0	2323	1.2
15 Sa	0707	1.7	1059	1.6	1648	1.9		
30 Su	0606	1.7	1049	1.5	1650	1.9	2353	1.3
31 M	0629	1.8	1207	1.5	1755	1.8		

FEBRUARY

Day	Time	ft	Time	ft	Time	ft	Time	ft
1 Tu	0021	1.3	0735	1.9	1325	1.1	1911	1.7
16 W	0705	1.9	1452	1.4	2028	1.0	2340	1.0
2 W	0046	1.4	0735	1.9	1452	1.3	2047	1.6
17 Th	0736	2.0	1602	1.4				
3 Th	0105	1.5	0816	2.0	1613	1.2	2255 ◑	1.6
18 F	0810	2.0	1702	1.3				
4 F	0112	1.5	0903	2.1	1727	1.2		
19 Sa	0849	2.0	1753	1.3				
5 Sa	0955	2.1	1830	1.1				
20 Su	0933	2.1	1837	1.2				
6 Su	1049	2.1	1926	1.1				
21 M	1023	2.1	1917	1.2				
7 M	1144	2.1	2015	1.0				
22 Tu	1117	2.1	1955	1.2				
8 Tu	1240	2.1	2058	1.1				
23 W	1213	2.1	2031	1.2				
9 W	0450	1.6	0610	1.6	1333	2.1	2138	1.1
24 Th	0405	1.7	0609	1.7	1311	2.1	2106	1.2
10 Th ●	0452	1.7	0744	1.6	1426	2.0	2212	1.2
25 F	0359	1.7	0739	1.6	1410	2.0	2139	1.3
11 F	0507	1.7	0900	1.6	1517	2.0	2243	1.2
26 Sa ○	0410	1.8	0852	1.6	1510	2.0	2211	1.3
12 Sa	0526	1.7	1010	1.6	1607	1.9	2309	1.3
27 Su	0429	1.8	1000	1.5	1611	1.9	2240	1.4
13 Su	0548	1.8	1119	1.5	1658	1.8	2329	1.4
28 M	0454	1.9	1106	1.4	1716	1.9	2307	1.5
14 M	0612	1.8	1228	1.5	1752	1.7	2344	1.4
15 Tu	0638	1.9	1340	1.6	1857	1.6	2350	1.5

MARCH

Day	Time	ft	Time	ft	Time	ft	Time	ft
1 Tu	0501	2.0	1214	1.4	1828	1.8	2231	1.0
16 W	0525	2.0	1311	1.1	1951	1.7	2226	1.7
2 W	0600	2.0	1323	1.3	1950	1.7	2351	1.6
17 Th	0553	2.1	1405	1.4				
3 Th	0641	2.1	1435	1.3	2135	1.7		
18 F	0624	2.1	1459	1.4				
4 F	0001	1.6	0728	2.1	1546	1.2		
19 Sa	0701	2.1	1552	1.3				
5 Sa	0821	2.2	1654	1.2				
20 Su	0745	2.1	1643	1.3				
6 Su	0919	2.2	1755	1.2				
21 M	0838	2.1	1732	1.3				
7 M	1022	2.1	1850	1.2				
22 Tu	0941	2.1	1817	1.3				
8 Tu	1126	2.1	1938	1.2				
23 W	1052	2.0	1900	1.3				
9 W	0259	1.7	0545	1.7	1231	2.1	2020	1.3
24 Th	0213	1.8	0543	1.7	1205	2.0	1939	1.4
10 Th	0311	1.8	0713	1.7	1333	2.0	2056	1.3
25 F	0219	1.8	0706	1.7	1317	2.0	2015	1.4
11 F	0329	1.8	0825	1.6	1432	2.0	2126	1.4
26 Sa	0235	1.9	0814	1.6	1426	2.0	2049	1.5
12 Sa ●	0350	1.8	0929	1.6	1530	1.9	2152	1.5
27 Su ○	0257	1.9	0915	1.5	1534	1.9	2119	1.6
13 Su	0412	1.9	1027	1.5	1626	1.8	2212	1.6
28 M	0324	2.0	1014	1.4	1643	1.9	2146	1.6
14 M	0435	1.9	1123	1.5	1725	1.8	2226	1.6
29 Tu	0356	2.1	1112	1.3	1754	1.8	2211	1.7
15 Tu	0459	2.0	1830	1.7	2232	1.6		
30 W	0431	2.1	1910	1.8	2231	1.7		
31 Th	0512	2.2	1311	1.2	2040	1.8	2245	1.8

APRIL

Day	Time	ft	Time	ft	Time	ft	Time	ft
1 F	0556	2.2	1412	1.2				
16 Sa	0525	2.2	1406	1.3				
2 Sa	0018	2.2	1513	1.2				
17 Su	0604	2.2	1451	1.0				
3 Su	0741	2.2	1613	1.3				
18 M	0652	2.1	1538	1.3				
4 M	0844	2.1	1709	1.3				
19 Tu	0752	2.1	1625	1.4				
5 Tu	0112	1.8	0306	1.8	0955	2.1	1800	1.4
20 W	0040	1.8	0253	1.8	0908	2.0	1711	1.4
6 W	0119	1.8	0507	1.8	1112	2.0	1845	1.4
21 Th	0032	1.9	0459	1.8	1038	2.0	1755	1.5
7 Th	0137	1.9	0638	1.7	1230	2.0	1923	1.5
22 F	0045	1.9	0625	1.7	1210	1.9	1835	1.5
8 F	0157	1.9	0750	1.6	1344	1.9	1955	1.6
23 Sa	0105	2.0	0732	1.5	1336	1.9	1911	1.6
9 Sa	0219	2.0	0850	1.5	1453	1.9	2021	1.7
24 Su	0131	2.0	0831	1.5	1456	1.9	1944	1.7
10 Su	0242	2.0	0943	1.5	1600	1.8	2041	1.7
25 M	0201	2.1	0925	1.3	1612	1.9	2013	1.7
11 M ●	0306	2.1	1031	1.4	1706	1.8	2053	1.7
26 Tu	0235	2.2	1018	1.2	1726	1.8	2038	1.8
12 Tu	0330	2.2	1115	1.4	1818	1.8	2057	1.7
27 W ○	0312	2.2	1110	1.2	1842	1.8	2059	1.8
13 W	0355	2.3	1158	1.3				
28 Th	0352	2.3	1202	1.2	2010	1.8	2110	1.8
14 Th	0422	2.2	1240	1.3				
29 F	0435	2.3	1254	1.2				
15 F	0451	2.2	1322	1.3				
30 Sa	0521	2.3	1345	1.2				

TIME MERIDIAN 60°W

Heights in feet are referred to the chart datum of sounding.

0000h is midnight, 1200h is noon.

Chapter 2

FORT-DE-FRANCE, MARTINIQUE

HIGH & LOW WATER 1994   14°35'N 61°03'W

ATLANTIC STANDARD TIME (GMT -4H)

MAY

Time	ft		Time	ft
1 Su	0610 2.2 1436 1.2	**16** M	0526 2.2 1402 1.3	
2 M ☽	0706 2.1 1526 1.3 2328 1.9	**17** Tu	0617 2.1 1442 1.4 2250 1.9	
3 Tu	0205 1.8 0810 2.0 1612 1.4 2345 1.9	**18** W ☽	0144 1.9 0723 2.0 1523 1.4 2256 1.9	
4 W	0412 1.8 0930 1.9 1655 1.5	**19** Th	0352 1.8 0852 1.9 1604 1.5 2314 2.0	
5 Th	0006 1.9 0555 1.7 1104 1.9 1733 1.6	**20** F	0529 1.7 1041 1.9 1643 1.6 2339 2.1	
6 F	0030 2.0 0712 1.6 1243 1.8 1804 1.6	**21** Sa	0642 1.6 1232 1.8 1719 1.7	
7 Sa	0054 2.0 0811 1.5 1415 1.8 1828 1.7	**22** Su	0009 2.1 0741 1.4 1414 1.8 1752 1.7	
8 Su	0119 2.1 0900 1.4 1542 1.8 1843 1.7	**23** M	0043 2.2 0835 1.3 1545 1.8 1819 1.8	
9 M	0145 2.1 0943 1.4 1712 1.8 1843 1.8	**24** Tu	0120 2.3 0925 1.2 1712 1.8 1840 1.8	
10 Tu ●	0210 2.2 1022 1.3	**25** W ○	0200 2.4 1014 1.2	
11 W	0236 2.2 1058 1.3	**26** Th	0241 2.4 1101 1.1	
12 Th	0304 2.2 1134 1.3	**27** F	0325 2.4 1147 1.1	
13 F	0333 2.3 1209 1.2	**28** Sa	0409 2.4 1232 1.2	
14 Sa	0406 2.2 1245 1.2	**29** Su	0456 2.3 1315 1.2 2136 1.9 2256 1.9	
15 Su	0443 2.2 1323 1.3	**30** M	0544 2.2 1356 1.3 2150 1.9	
		31 Tu	0051 1.9 0638 2.1 1434 1.4 2212 2.0	

JUNE

Time	ft		Time	ft
1 W ☽	0253 1.9 0742 2.0 1509 1.5 2237 2.0	**16** Th ☽	0221 1.9 0720 2.0 1427 1.6 2142 2.1	
2 Th	0451 1.8 0911 1.9 1537 1.6 2303 2.1	**17** F	0406 1.8 0859 1.9 1458 1.7 2211 2.2	
3 F	0622 1.7 1111 1.8 1558 1.7 2331 2.1	**18** Sa	0532 1.7 1105 1.8 1526 1.7 2246 2.3	
4 Sa	0726 1.6 1330 1.8 1605 1.7 2359 2.2	**19** Su	0640 1.5 1318 1.8 1547 1.8 2325 2.3	
5 Su	0814 1.5	**20** M	0737 1.4	
6 M	0027 2.2 0854 1.4	**21** Tu	0007 2.4 0829 1.3	
7 Tu	0055 2.3 0930 1.3	**22** W	0051 2.5 0917 1.2	
8 W	0124 2.3 1003 1.3	**23** Th ○	0136 2.5 1002 1.2	
9 Th ●	0154 2.3 1034 1.3	**24** F	0222 2.5 1045 1.2	
10 F	0226 2.4 1106 1.3	**25** Sa	0308 2.5 1127 1.3 1948 2.0	
11 Sa	0301 2.3 1138 1.3	**26** Su	0355 2.4 1205 1.3 1951 2.0 2209 2.0	
12 Su	0339 2.3 1211 1.3	**27** M	0442 2.3 1241 1.4 2011 2.0 2341 2.0	
13 M	0421 2.3 1245 1.3 2113 1.9 2224 1.9	**28** Tu	0531 2.2 1313 1.5 2035 2.1	
14 Tu	0509 2.2 1319 1.4 2104 2.0	**29** W	0121 1.9 0624 2.1 1340 1.6 2102 2.1	
15 W	0028 1.9 0606 2.1 1353 1.5 2118 2.0	**30** Th ☽	0311 1.9 0731 2.0 1400 1.7 2131 2.2	

JULY

Time	ft		Time	ft
1 F	0458 1.8 0911 1.9 1410 1.8 2202 2.3	**16** Sa ☽	0357 1.8 0929 2.0 1354 1.9 2117 2.4	
2 Sa	0618 1.7 1206 1.8 1341 1.8 2234 2.3	**17** Su	0517 1.7 1153 1.9 1401 1.9 2201 2.5	
3 Su	0713 1.6 2306 2.4	**18** M	0624 1.6 2249 2.5	
4 M	0756 1.5 2338 2.4	**19** Tu	0721 1.5 2339 2.6	
5 Tu	0831 1.5	**20** W	0812 1.4	
6 W	0012 2.4 0904 1.4	**21** Th	0030 2.6 0859 1.4	
7 Th	0047 2.5 0934 1.4	**22** F ○	0121 2.6 0942 1.4	
8 F ●	0123 2.5 1005 1.4	**23** Sa	0212 2.6 1022 1.5 2005 2.1	
9 Sa	0202 2.5 1035 1.4	**24** Su	0302 2.5 1059 1.5 1809 2.1 2126 2.1	
10 Su	0244 2.5 1106 1.4	**25** M	0351 2.5 1132 1.6 1830 2.2 2244 2.0	
11 M	0329 2.4 1137 1.5 1911 2.1 2154 2.0	**26** Tu	0441 2.4 1200 1.7 1854 2.2	
12 Tu	0418 2.4 1208 1.5 1919 2.1 2324 2.0	**27** W	0004 2.0 0534 2.2 1224 1.8 1921 2.3	
13 W	0514 2.3 1238 1.6 1938 2.2	**28** Th	0129 2.0 0632 2.1 1241 1.9 1951 2.3	
14 Th	0054 2.0 0619 2.2 1307 1.7 2005 2.2	**29** F	0300 2.0 0748 2.0 1248 2.0 2023 2.4	
15 F	0227 1.9 0741 2.1 1333 1.8 2038 2.3	**30** Sa ☽	0427 1.9 0953 2.0 1227 2.0 2056 2.4	
		31 Su	0539 1.8 2132 2.5	

AUGUST

Time	ft		Time	ft
1 M	0633 1.7 2210 2.5	**16** Tu	0556 1.7 2217 2.7	
2 Tu	0716 1.7 2250 2.5	**17** W	0654 1.6 2316 2.7	
3 W	0752 1.6 2332 2.6	**18** Th	0745 1.6	
4 Th	0825 1.6	**19** F	0015 2.7 0831 1.6 1604 2.2 1803 2.2	
5 F	0016 2.6 0857 1.6	**20** Sa	0113 2.6 0912 1.7 1613 2.2 1933 2.1	
6 Sa	0102 2.6 0928 1.6	**21** Su ○	0210 2.6 0949 1.7 1630 2.2 2048 2.1	
7 Su ●	0151 2.6 0959 1.6 1721 2.1 1958 2.1	**22** M	0306 2.5 1021 1.8 1652 2.3 2157 2.1	
8 M	0241 2.5 1029 1.7 1723 2.2 2118 2.1	**23** Tu	0400 2.4 1048 1.9 1715 2.3 2304 2.0	
9 Tu	0335 2.5 1059 1.7 1737 2.2 2231 2.0	**24** W	0456 2.3 1111 2.0 1741 2.4	
10 W	0432 2.4 1127 1.8 1759 2.3 2344 2.0	**25** Th	0011 2.0 0555 2.3 1127 2.0 1809 2.5	
11 Th	0535 2.3 1154 1.9 1827 2.4	**26** F	0118 2.0 0703 2.2 1134 2.1 1839 2.5	
12 F	0059 1.9 0648 2.2 1218 2.0 1901 2.5	**27** Sa	0227 1.9 0837 2.1 1123 2.1 1911 2.5	
13 Sa	0218 1.9 0818 2.1 1237 2.0 1942 2.5	**28** Su	0334 1.9 1946 2.5	
14 Su	0336 1.8 1017 2.1 1246 2.1 2029 2.6	**29** M ☽	0436 1.8 2025 2.6	
15 M	0450 1.7 2121 2.6	**30** Tu	0529 1.8 2109 2.6	
		31 W	0615 1.8 2159 2.6	

TIME MERIDIAN 60°W   0000h is midnight, 1200h is noon.
Heights in feet are referred to the chart datum of sounding.

FORT-DE-FRANCE, MARTINIQUE

HIGH & LOW WATER 1994 14°35'N 61°03'W

ATLANTIC STANDARD TIME (GMT -4H)

SEPTEMBER

Day	Time	ft	Time	ft	Time	ft	Time	ft
1 Th	0056	1.8	2254	2.6				
2 F	0733	1.8	2352	2.6				
3 Sa	0808	1.8	1539	2.2	1806	2.2		
4 Su	0052	2.5	0842	1.8	1533	2.3	1932	2.2
5 M	0152	2.5	0914	1.8	1542	2.3	● 2041	2.1
6 Tu	0253	2.5	0944	1.9	1600	2.3	2145	2.0
7 W	0355	2.4	1013	2.0	1624	2.4	2247	1.9
8 Th	0500	2.4	1039	2.0	1653	2.5	2350	1.9
9 F	0610	2.3	1103	2.1	1728	2.5		
10 Sa	0054	1.8	0729	2.2	1123	2.1	1808	2.6
11 Su	0201	1.8	0906	2.2	1136	2.2	1853	2.6
12 M ○	0309	1.7	1945	2.7				
13 Tu	0415	1.7	2044	2.7				
14 W	0518	1.7	2149	2.6				
15 Th	0615	1.7	1421	2.2	1529	2.2	2257	2.6
16 F	0706	1.7	1419	2.2	1731	2.2		
17 Sa	0007	2.5	0750	1.8	1435	2.3	1859	2.1
18 Su	0115	2.5	0828	1.8	1455	2.3	2012	2.1
19 M ○	0220	2.4	0901	1.9	1518	2.3	2116	2.0
20 Tu	0323	2.4	0929	2.0	1542	2.4	2215	1.9
21 W	0424	2.3	0950	2.0	1608	2.4	2310	1.9
22 Th	0527	2.2	1006	2.1	1634	2.5		
23 F	0003	1.8	0636	2.2	1013	2.1	1702	2.5
24 Sa	0056	1.8	0804	2.1	1003	2.1	1731	2.5
25 Su	0147	1.8	1801	2.5				
26 M	0238	1.8	1836	2.5				
27 Tu	0328	1.8	1917	2.5				
28 W	0417	1.8	2007	2.5				
29 Th	0504	1.8	2108	2.4				
30 F	0548	1.8	1429	2.2	2221	2.4		

OCTOBER

Day	Time	ft	Time	ft	Time	ft	Time	ft
1 Sa	0630	1.8	1349	2.2	1739	2.1	2339	2.4
2 Su	0703	1.8	1353	2.2	1859	2.1		
3 M	0055	2.3	0744	1.9	1408	2.3	2003	2.0
4 Tu	0208	2.3	0817	1.9	1429	2.3	2101	1.8
5 W	0319	2.3	0847	2.0	1455	2.4	● 2157	1.7
6 Th	0428	2.2	0915	2.0	1526	2.5	2252	1.7
7 F	0539	2.2	0939	2.1	1602	2.5	2347	1.6
8 Sa	0654	2.2	1000	2.1	1641	2.6		
9 Su	0043	1.6	0819	2.1	1016	2.1	1725	2.6
10 M	0141	1.5	1813	2.6				
11 Tu ○	0239	1.5	1908	2.5				
12 W	0337	1.6	2010	2.5				
13 Th ○	0432	1.6	1226	2.1	1447	2.1	2122	2.4
14 F	0524	1.7	1241	2.2	1646	2.1	2243	2.3
15 Sa	0611	1.7	1302	2.2	1820	2.0		
16 Su	0007	2.2	0652	1.8	1329	2.0	1934	1.9
17 M	0129	2.2	0726	1.9	1350	2.3	2036	1.8
18 Tu	0245	2.1	0754	1.9	1416	2.3	2130	1.7
19 W	0358	2.1	0815	2.0	1442	2.4	2219	1.6
20 Th	0510	2.1	0829	2.1	1509	2.4	● 2304	1.6
21 F	0628	2.0	0830	2.0	1536	2.4	2347	1.5
22 Sa	1603	2.4						
23 Su	0028	1.5	1632	2.4				
24 M	0108	1.5	1703	2.4				
25 Tu	0148	1.5	1739	2.4				
26 W	0229	1.5	1821	2.3				
27 Th	0311	1.6	1915	2.3				
28 F	0353	1.6	1219	2.1	1441	2.0	2027	2.2
29 Sa	0436	1.6	1209	2.1	1651	2.0	2200	2.1
30 Su	0518	1.7	1220	2.1	1816	1.9	2340	2.1
31 M	0557	1.7	1239	2.2	1921	1.7		

NOVEMBER

Day	Time	ft	Time	ft	Time	ft	Time	ft
1 Tu	0115	2.0	0633	1.8	1304	2.2	2017	1.6
2 W	0240	2.0	0700	1.9	1334	2.3	2109	1.5
3 Th ●	0359	2.0	0735	1.9	1407	2.4	2159	1.4
4 F	0515	2.0	0800	1.9	1445	2.4	2249	1.3
5 Sa	0631	2.0	0821	2.0	1525	2.4	2338	1.3
6 Su	1608	2.4						
7 M	0028	1.3	1654	2.4				
8 Tu	0117	1.3	1743	2.4				
9 W	0206	1.3	1037	2.0	1838	2.3		
10 Th ○	0254	1.4	1047	2.0	1340	1.9	1941	2.2
11 F	0340	1.5	1108	2.0	1543	1.9	2059	2.0
12 Sa	0422	1.6	1132	2.0	1730	1.8	2236	1.9
13 Su	0500	1.6	1159	2.1	1851	1.7		
14 M	0022	1.9	0532	1.7	1226	2.1	1954	1.6
15 Tu	0204	1.8	0556	1.8	1255	2.2	2046	1.5
16 W	0342	1.8	0611	1.8	2101	1.4		
17 Th	1352	2.3	2211	1.3				
18 F	1420	2.3	2248	1.3				
19 Sa	1449	2.3	2323	1.2				
20 Su	1518	2.3	2357	1.2				
21 M	1549	2.2						
22 Tu	0031	1.2	1623	2.2				
23 W	0104	1.3	1702	2.1				
24 Th	0139	1.3	1747	2.1				
25 F	0215	1.3	1028	1.9	1324	1.8	1846	2.0
26 Sa	0251	1.4	1032	1.9	1534	1.8	2008	1.9
27 Su	0328	1.5	1048	1.9	1714	1.7	2159	1.8
28 M	0403	1.5	1112	2.0	1827	1.5		
29 Tu	0002	1.7	0436	1.6	1142	2.1	1925	1.4
30 W	0155	1.7	0506	1.7	1216	2.2	2017	1.3

DECEMBER

Day	Time	ft	Time	ft	Time	ft	Time	ft
1 Th	0337	1.7	0530	1.7	2106	1.1		
2 F ●	1334	2.3	2153	1.1				
3 Sa	1416	2.3	2239	1.0				
4 Su	1501	2.3	2324	1.0				
5 M	1546	2.3						
6 Tu	0008	1.0	1634	2.2				
7 W	0050	1.1	0851	1.8	1043	1.8	1724	2.1
8 Th	0131	1.2	0910	1.8	1227	1.7	1818	2.0
9 F ◑	0208	1.3	0934	1.8	1419	1.7	1922	1.8
10 Sa	0242	1.4	1002	1.9	1614	1.6	2047	1.7
11 Su	0311	1.4	1032	1.9	1751	1.5	2245	1.6
12 M	0332	1.5	1103	2.0	1902	1.4		
13 Tu	0112	1.6	0335	1.6	1135	2.0	1955	1.3
14 W	1207	2.1	2039	1.2				
15 Th	1238	2.1	2117	1.1				
16 F	1310	2.1	2152	1.1				
17 Sa	1341	2.1	2224	1.1				
18 Su	1413	2.1	2255	1.1				
19 M	1447	2.1	2325	1.1				
20 Tu	1523	2.1	2355	1.1				
21 W	1602	2.0						
22 Th	0025	1.1	0847	1.7	1013	1.7	1647	2.0
23 F	0056	1.2	0839	1.7	1208	1.7	1740	1.9
24 Sa	0126	1.2	0852	1.8	1356	1.7	1847	1.7
25 Su	0156	1.3	0913	1.8	1540	1.5	2019	1.6
26 M	0224	1.4	0942	1.9	1708	1.4	2224	1.4
27 Tu	0247	1.5	1017	2.0	1817	1.3		
28 W	0050	1.5	0300	1.5	1056	2.0	1915	1.1
29 Th	1139	2.1	2006	1.0				
30 F	1224	2.2	2054	1.0				
31 Sa	1311	2.2	2139	0.9				

Chapter 2

TIME MERIDIAN 60°W
Heights in feet are referred to the chart datum of sounding.

0000h is midnight, 1200h is noon.

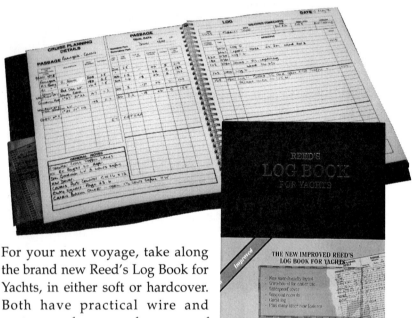

ST. LUCIA

CAUTION: Our information on aids to navigation comes from official government sources. The latitudes and longitudes of these marks may not correspond to the readings from GPS receivers. Some aids have been reported as unreliable, missing, off position or showing incorrect characteristics. No single aid to navigation, or waypoint, should be relied upon as a sole means of fixing your position.

FC dollars to U.S. dollars, is about .40. In other words, $100 EC = $40 U.S. You will probably find many people accepting U.S. dollars, especially in tourist areas.

The official language is English, but you will also encounter a French patois, due to the proximity of French territories and the island's tumultuous history.

ENTRY PROCEDURES

With France, England and the Caribs battling for control of the island for three hundred years St. Lucia has a dramatic history. The island was an English colony until gaining independence in 1979. It remains a member nation of the British Commonwealth. See *Reed's Nautical Companion* for an example of the country flag.

Ports of Entry are Rodney Bay, Castries, Marigot and Vieux Fort. Port dues are charged in Castries and Vieux Fort.

In Rodney Bay the officials are located right in the marina, and can be contacted at (809) 452-0235. They are open from 0800 to 1800 every day, but there is a $15.00 EC fee for clearing on weekends or a $10.00 fee after normal working hours during the week.

In Castries call (809) 452-3487 to contact Customs. They are located on the north wharf. In Marigot contact Customs at (809) 451-4257. In Vieux Fort call (809) 454-6074 or 6526. On weekends, you will have to clear in at the airport. Hours of operation are usually 0800 to 1800.

You should have a clearance from your last port of call, ship's papers and passports. A cruising permit is needed if you are planning on visiting any other harbors on St. Lucia.

The telephone area code for St. Lucia is 809, followed by the seven digit local number.

All charges are in Eastern Caribbean, or EC, dollars. The exchange rate, when converting

ST. LUCIA, WEST COAST

MARINA LIGHT, N entrance, 14 04.6N, 60 57.3W, Q G, 3ft., 2M.
MARINA LIGHT, S entrance, 14 04.6N, 60 57.2W, Q R, 3ft., 2M.
MARINA RANGE, (Front Light) 14 04.6N, 60 57.0W, Fl W 15ft., 2M. **(Rear Light)** 251 meters 098.6° from front, Fl W 31ft., 2M.

RODNEY BAY
14 05N, 60 57W

Pilotage: Rodney Bay is a dredged basin off of Gros Islet Bay on the northwest coast of the island. A light is shown from Foureur Islet in the approaches. There are lights at the entrance, and a range of 098.6° leads into the marina. Approach depths are reported to be about 10 feet, with 6 to 12 feet in the lagoon. The tidal range averages about .8 foot to 1.2 feet. Call Rodney Bay Marina if in need of assistance getting in.
Port of Entry: The Customs office is located in Rodney Bay Marina. They can be called at (809) 452-0235.
Dockage: Rodney Bay Marina has over 230 berths and all facilities. Contact them at (809) 452-0324, or on VHF channel 16.
Anchorage: You can anchor in Rodney Bay, or outside along the beach south of the channel.
Services: All marine services are available here. The marina has fuel, water, dry storage, haulouts, repairs, banking, car hire and provisioning — all on site. Rodney Bay Ship Services Ltd. is a major chandler at (809) 452-9973, or on VHF channels 16 and 71. Their call sign is "RBSS". Cay Electronics (809) 452-9922 services and sells all sorts of electric and electronic

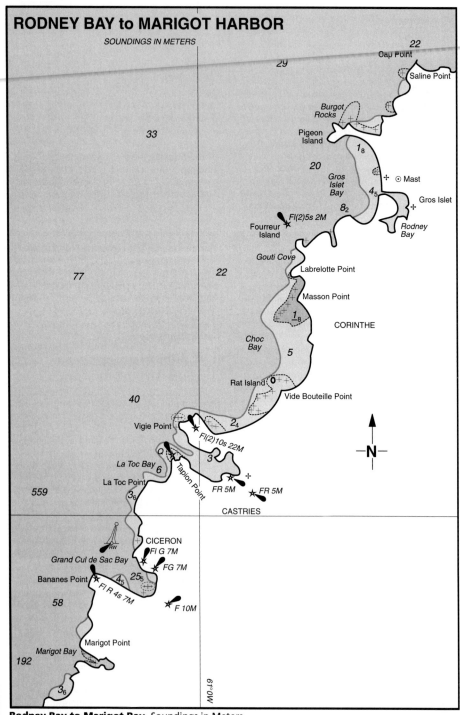

RODNEY BAY to MARIGOT HARBOR

SOUNDINGS IN METERS

22

29

Oap Point

Saline Point

Burgot
Rocks

33

Pigeon
Island

1_8

20

Gros
Islet
Bay

+ ⊙ Mast

4_5

Gros Islet

8_2

Fl(2)5s 2M

Fourreur
Island

Rodney
Bay

Gouti Cove

77

22

Labrelotte Point

Masson Point

$\underline{1}_8$

CORINTHE

Choc
Bay

5

Rat Island O

Vide Bouteille Point

40

2_4

Vigie Point

Fl(2)10s 22M

Q

3

La Toc Bay 6

Tapion Point

559

La Toc Point

3_6

FR 5M

+

FR 5M

CASTRIES

—N—

CICERON

Fl G 7M

Grand Cul de Sac Bay

FG 7M

Bananes Point

4_5

25_5

Fl R 4s 7M

58

F 10M

Marigot Point

Marigot Bay

192

3_6

61°0'W

Rodney Bay to Marigot Bay, Soundings in Meters

devices. Sunsail specializes in servicing charter yachts, but can do repairs for anyone. Call them at (809) 452-8648. There are many other services on the island that can travel to Rodney Bay. There are good supermarkets and general shops nearby.

Rodney Bay is a favorite place to leave your boat while making an extended trip back home. There are good in-the-water and dry storage facilities, and the island is south of the most frequented hurricane tracks. A large charter industry has spawned an excellent variety of marine services.

FOURREUR ROCK LIGHT, 14 04.2N, 60 58.7W, Fl (2) W 5s, 23ft., 2M.

PORT OF CASTRIES

VIGIE LIGHT, Summit N side of entrance to Castries, 14 01.2N, 61 00.0W, Fl (2) W 10s, 320ft., 22M, W circular masonry tower, R roof, Visible 039° to 212°, Partially obscured by Pigeon Island 206° to 209°.
TAPION ROCK LIGHT, S side of entrance to Castries, 14 00.9N, 61 00.4W, Q W, 50ft., 8M, Old battery, Visible outside harbor from 046° to 192·, Inside harbor from 192° to 287°.
AIRFIELD EXTENSION LIGHT, 14 00.9N, 61 00.1W, Q G, 14ft., 2M, On sunken barge.
WEST WHARF, (Front Light) 14 00.5N, 60 59.5W, F R, 43ft., 5M, W triangle, Orange stripe, On metal skeleton tower. **(Rear Light)** 740 meters 121° from front, F R, 110ft., 5M, W triangle, Orange stripe, On metal skeleton tower.
NORTH WHARF LIGHT, Corner of Berth No. 4 and 5, 14 00.6N, 60 59.6W, F Y, 1M.

CASTRIES
14 01N, 61 00W

Pilotage: This is the principal commercial port on St. Lucia. Vigie Point, with Vigie Light on its summit, rises to a height of about 295 feet. To the south, Morne Fortune rises to 852 feet, with Fort Charlotte on its summit. The range of 121° should guide you in safely to the main wharf area. The pilots and port authorities, call sign "Castries Lighthouse", stand by on VHF channel 16 and 2182kHz.
Port of Entry: Proceed to the Custom's wharf on North Wharf, or anchor off and dinghy in. They may be contacted at (809) 452-3487. There is a charge for port dues.
Dockage: St. Lucia Yacht Services is located in

the Vigie Yacht Harbour — contact them at (809) 452-5057.
Anchorage: The yacht anchorage is in Vigie Yacht Harbour, or west of the area. Many of the boating services are concentrated in the Vigie area.
Services: The marina has fuel and water. Nearby are several yacht services including: International Diesel and Marine Services Ltd. (809) 453-1311, A.F. Valmont Yamana Outboards (809) 452-3817, Johnsons Hardware (809) 452-6026, B&L Upholstery Clinic (809) 452-7644 or "Bounding Home" on VHF channel 16, Andrew Tyson Cabinet Maker and Joiner (809) 452-5794, Richard Cox Fiberglass Repair Specialist (809) 453-2361 and the Castries Yacht Center for haulouts and repairs (809) 542-6234 or on VHF channel 16. There are good supermarkets and general shops, and the airport is right next to the Yacht Harbour.

GRAND CUL DE SAC BAY

CICERON POINT LIGHT, 14 00.0N, 61 01.0W, Fl G 6s, 39ft., 7M, G square on tower.
BANANES POINT LIGHT, 13 59.0N, 61 02.0W, Fl R 4s, 85ft., 7M, R triangle on tower.
DIRECTIONAL LIGHT, 13 59.0N, 61 01.0W, F W, 115ft., 10M.

MARIGOT
13 58N, 61 02W

Pilotage: The entrance to this bay is located about a mile south of the Hess oil terminal in Grande Cul de Sac Bay.
Port of Entry: Customs is located on the south shore of the harbor, west of the docks. Contact them at (809) 451-4257.
Dockage: The Moorings Marina is in the inner harbor. Contact them at (809) 451-4357, or on VHF channels 16 and 85.
Anchorage: Anchor anywhere, avoiding the Cable Crossing at the narrow point in the harbor. The shelter is excellent, and some consider this a hurricane hole.
Services: The Moorings complex features all the amenities of a modern resort including hotels, swimming pools, restaurants and a dive center. They have fuel, gasoline, propane, a commissary and laundry at the docks.

VIEUX FORT BAY

MATHURIN POINT LIGHT, 13 42.6N, 60 57.5W, Fl (2) W 5s, 16ft., 2M, R skeleton tower, Concrete base.

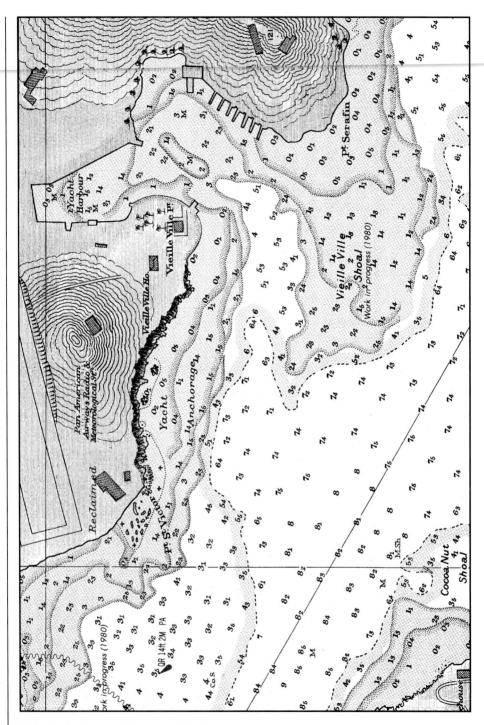

Vigie Yacht Harbour, Soundings in Fathoms

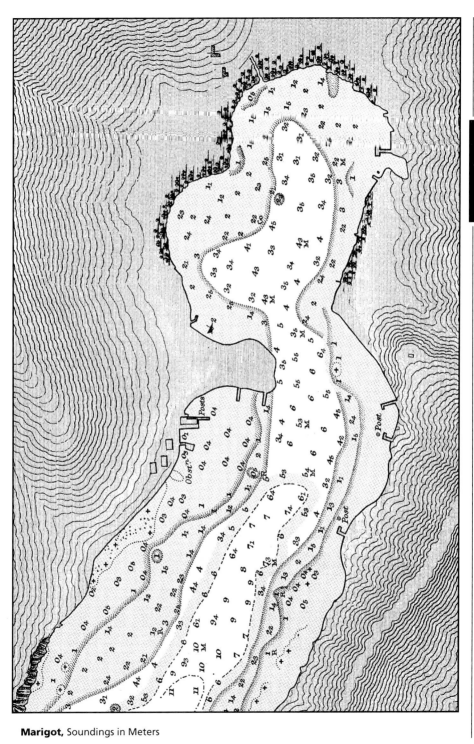

Marigot, Soundings in Meters

VIEUX FORT BAY RANGE, (Front Light)
Head of wharf, 13 43.1N, 60 57.2W, F R, 16ft.,
2M, Orange rectangle on building. **(Rear
Light)** 500 meters 059.9° from front, F R, 65ft.,
R metal framework tower, W bands.
NO. 1. 13 43.3N, 60 57.5W, Q G, 15ft, 5M, Port,
Green beacon.
NO. 2, 13 43.1N, 60 57.2W, Q R, 15ft, 5M, Star-
board, Red beacon.
NO. 3, 13 43.3N, 60 57.3W, Fl Y, 15ft, 5M, Yel-
low beacon.
NO. 4, 13 43.1N, 60 57.2W, Fl Y, 15ft, 5M, Yel-
low beacon.
CAPE MOULE A CHIQUE LIGHT, Brandon
Point, 13 42.6N, 60 56.5W, Fl W 5s, 745ft.,
19M, Masonry tower, Visible 197° to 123°.

VIEUX FORT

13 43N, 60 57W

Pilotage: The town is located on the south tip
of St. Lucia. Several obstructions in the bay are
marked by buoys, and a range of 059.9° leads
you in safely. The charted dome of the Custom
House is prominent. The pilots and port officials (call sign "Vieux Fort Lighthouse") monitor VHF channel 16 and 2182kHz.

Port of Entry: Contact the officials near the
commercial wharf. You can call them at (809)
454-6074, or 6526. There is a port fee for
entering boats, and on weekends you may
have to clear at the airport.
Anchorage: The recommended area is in the
southeast portion of the bay, under the lee of
Moule a Chique. This is south of the commercial wharf. Anchoring is prohibited in an area
north of the wharf, as there are pipelines and
commercial moorings in the area.
Services: There are few yacht services in Vieux
Fort, but there are several restaurants and most
general supplies are available. The Il Pirata
Restaurant has a dock northwest of town
where they offer some moorings and showers
for yachtsmen. Call them at (809) 454-6610.

ST. LUCIA, EAST COAST

CAPE MARQUIS LIGHT, 14 03.3N, 60 53.6W,
Fl (2) W 20s, 197ft., W square support.
MOUNT TOURNEY AVIATION LIGHT,
13 44.4N, 60 57.9W, Iso R 485ft., R skeleton
tower, W bands.
MOUNT BELLEVUE AVIATION LIGHT,
13 44.4N, 60 56.7W, Al Fl W G 5s, 351ft.,
Beacon.

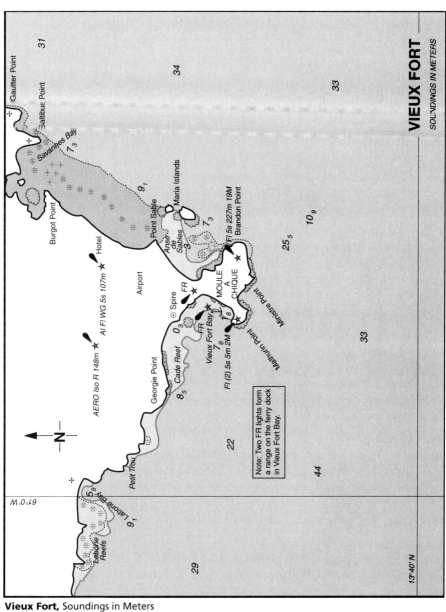

Vieux Fort, Soundings in Meters

VIEUX FORT

SOUNDINGS IN METERS

Chapter 2

Note: Two FR lights form a range on the ferry dock in Vieux Fort Bay.

61°0′W

13°40′N

REED'S
NAUTICAL ALMANACS & COMPANIONS

1994

CARIBBEAN
The only almanac which covers the entire Caribbean basin including Bermuda, the Bahamas, Caribbean islands, the north coast of South America, Central America, Panama and Mexico. Contains 200 harbor chartlets, complete tide and celestial tables, coast pilot with aids to navigation, weather and communication information.   800 pages $29.95(US) Retail

NORTH AMERICAN: EAST COAST
Now in its 21st year of publication, it includes over 200 harbor chartlets, tide and current tables from Nova Scotia to the Bahamas, light and buoy lists, waypoints, radio and communication information, a complete nautical ephemeris and lots more
                                                              900 pages $29.95(US) Retail

NORTH AMERICAN: PACIFIC NORTHWEST
The only almanac to include US and Canadian Hydrographic information in a single volume, and covers from the head of the Columbia River to the Gulf of Alaska and Kodiak Island, including Puget Sound and the British Columbia coastline. More than 170 harbor charts, tide and current tables, nautical ephemeris, aids to navigation, communication and weather information.   900 pages $29.95(US) Retail

NORTHERN EUROPEAN
Our flagship almanac, now enjoying its 63rd year of publication. Its coverage ranges from Skagen, on the northern coast of Denmark, to the French-Spanish border and Biarritz. This extensive European coverage includes 450 chartlets and illustrations, 2000 ports and complete tidal information for each area.   1,200 pages $45.00(US) Retail

SOUTHERN EUROPEAN
A completely reorganized and updated version of our Mediterranean almanac, featuring the Atlantic-European coast and islands, as well as the complete coastline of one of the world's most popular cruising areas, the Mediterranean sea. This edition is an excellent reference book for those planning a transatlantic voyage including stopovers in the Azores and entry via Gibraltar to the Mediterranean.   800 pages $45.00(US) Retail

NAUTICAL COMPANION
The COMPANION is designed to complement the Caribbean, North American East Coast and Pacific Northwest REED'S ALMANACS, and is full of practical information for the cruising boater. It includes extensive chapters on seamanship, rules of the road, coastal passage making, signaling, first aid and more.   444 pages $19.95(US) Retail

NAUTICAL COMPANION (European edition)
An outstanding nautical reference with essential information on subjects similar to those included in our US COMPANION. Designed to complement our European editions.
                                                              450 pages $24.95(US) Retail

Call 1-800-995-4995 for your nearest dealer!

St. Vincent and the Grenadines

ENTRY PROCEDURES

This nation includes the islands of St. Vincent, Bequia, Mustique, Canouan, the Tobago Cays, Union Island and Petit St. Vincent (PSV). They were a British colony until gaining independence in 1979. The islands of Carriacou and Petit Martinique belong to Grenada. All told, there are over 100 islands, islets and rocks, extending for a distance of 52 miles between St. Vincent and Grenada. See *Reed's Nautical Companion* for an example of the country flag.

Ports of Entry on St. Vincent are Wallilabou Bay and Kingstown. On Bequia the station is in Port Elizabeth, and on Union it is in Clifton. It may be possible to clear on Mustique and Canouan by finding the officials at the airports. Yachtsmen often recommend Wallilabou Bay, Port Elizabeth and Clifton as the most convenient places to handle this process.

You can contact Customs in Kingstown at (809) 456-1083, in Port Elizabeth at (809) 457-3044 and in Clifton at (809) 458-8360. Generally, hours are about 0800 to 1600 or 1800, with a break for lunch.

You should have a clearance from your last port of call, ship's papers and passports. A cruising permit is required for further exploration within the country. There is a fee for charter boats, but no charge for pleasure vessels. There is a charge of $10.00 EC per person on board. The telephone area code for all of the islands is 809, followed by the seven digit local number.

All charges are in Eastern Caribbean, or EC, dollars. The exchange rate, when converting EC dollars to U.S. dollars, is about .40. In other words, $100 EC = $40 U.S. You will probably find many people accepting U.S. dollars, especially in tourist areas.

The official language is English.

ST. VINCENT

OWIA LIGHT(Cow and Calves), 13 22.3N, 61 09.0W, Fl W 10s, 118ft., 8M, White metal framework tower, Visible 101° to 307°.
DARK HEAD LIGHT, 13 16.8N, 61 16.0W, Fl W 5s, 338 ft., 12M, Metal framework tower, Visible 020° to 211°.

WALLILABOU BAY, ST. VINCENT
13 15N, 61 17W

Pilotage: There is a radio tower near the point of land forming the southern entrance to the bay.
Port of Entry: Customs officials here are geared to clearing in pleasure boats.
Moorings: Contact the Wallilabou Anchorage Restaurant at (809) 458-7270, or on VHF channel 68.
Anchorage: Due to the depths of 35 to 50 feet right off the beach you might want to hire a boat boy to take a stern line ashore. Contact the restaurant if you are in doubt as to a good location.
Services: The major facilities here are the aforementioned Wallilabou Anchorage Restaurant and Ashton's Country Style Restaurant. Call the latter at (809) 458-7989. Both businesses may be able to assist with phone calls and tours of the island.

KINGSTOWN, ST. VINCENT
13 09N, 61 14W

FORT CHARLOTTE LIGHT, 13 09.4N, 61 15.0W, Fl (3) W 20s, 640 ft., 16M, Octagonal structure, Visible from shore to 143°, Aero Oc R (occasional) 1.5M southeast of light.

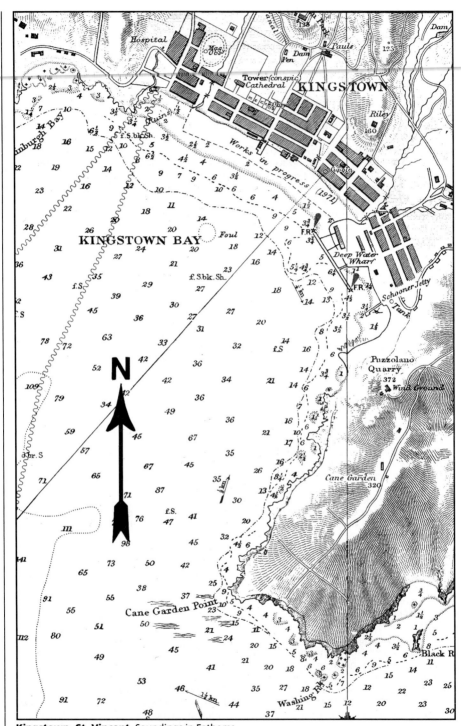

Kingstown, St. Vincent, Soundings in Fathoms

KINGSTOWN WHARF LIGHT, Northwest end of wharf, 13 09.1N, 61 14.1W, F R, Column.
KINGSTOWN WHARF LIGHT, Southeast end of wharf, 13 08.9N, 61 14.0W, F R, Column.

Pilotage: This is the capital of St. Vincent, and its major port. The cathedral with its square white tower in the northwestern part of town is conspicuous. The clock on the tower is lighted at night. The Police Station has a conspicuous red cupola located north of the main wharf. The pilots and port authorities use call sign ZQS, and monitor VHF channel 16 and 2182kHz.
Port of Entry: Contact the officials in their office near the main wharf. You can call them at (809) 456-1083. Many yachtsmen prefer to clear in Wallilabou or Bequia, where the formalities are more geared to pleasure boaters.
Dockage: Proceed to the Lagoon marina for dockage on the south coast of the island. They are located in the Blue Lagoon about 2 miles southeast of Kingstown. You can contact them at (809) 458-4308, or on VHF channel 68.
Anchorage: Anchor north or south of the main commercial wharf. During the day strong gusts of wind may blow down through the valleys with great violence. At night the breeze will usually be light.
Services: In Kingstown you may be able to get fuel at the fish boat dock, but it is easier down in the Blue Lagoon at the marina. The Lagoon also has laundry showers, ice, water, a scuba shop and a hotel. St. Vincent Sales and Service (809) 457-1820 is a Yamaha dealer, and general chandler. They are located in Kingstown. Nichols Marine repairs starters and alternators. They also handle welding and can be contacted at (809) 456-4118, or on VHF channel 68. There is a good selection of supermarkets and general provisioning stores in Kingstown.

Though the harbor of Kingstown offers few amenities for yachtsmen, the nearby Young Island , Calliaqua and Blue Lagoon areas feature a good variety. Many boaters visit Kingstown by road, or ferry, as it is more pleasant to clear customs elsewhere. The wild interior of the island is well worth a sightseeing tour, or hiking trip. Contact the Tourist Office in Kingstown at (809) 457-1502.

CALLIAQUA

YOUNG ISLAND CARENAGE LIGHT, 13 07.7N, 61 12.6W, Fl G 4s, Port, Green, Pillar with topmark.

ROOKES POINT SHOAL LIGHT, 13 07.7N, 61 12.5W, V Q (6) and L Fl W 10s, South cardinal, Yellow and black, Pillar with topmark.
DUVERNETTE ISLAND LIGHT, 13 07.5N, 61 12.8W, V Q (2) W 2s, 229 ft., 6M, White metal framework tower.
CALLIAQUA BAY LIGHT, 13 07.5N, 61 12.3W, Fl R 4s, Starboard, Red, Pillar with topmark.
BRIGHTON LIGHT, 13 07.3N, 61 10.6W, Fl W 4s, 118 ft., 8M, White metal framework tower, visible 217° to 077°.

ADMIRALTY BAY, BEQUIA

DEVIL'S TABLE LIGHT, 13 00.7N, 61 15.6W, V Q (9) W 10s, West cardinal, Yellow black yellow, Pillar with topmark.
ADMIRALTY BAY LIGHT, Root of jetty, 13 00.5N, 61 14.7W, Fl W R G 4s, 19 ft., 5M, White metal framework tower, Red shore to 048°, White 048° to 058°, Green 058° to shore.
WEST CAY LIGHT, 12 59.3N, 61 18.0W, Fl W 10s, 42ft., 8M, White metal framework tower.

PORT ELIZABETH, BEQUIA
13 00N, 61 15W

Pilotage: The town of Port Elizabeth is situated near the head of Admiralty Bay, on the west coast of Bequia. A conspicuous radio mast stands south-southeast of the town. A reef, charted as Belmont Shoal, extends from the eastern shore of the bay south of the main wharf. A light is shown from the commercial wharf.
Port of Entry: The office is located near the commercial wharf, and can be contacted at (809) 457-3044.
Dockage: You may be able to tie up temporarily at the Bequia Marina, north of the main wharf. Contact them at (809) 458-3272.
Moorings: Contact Handy Andy's at (809) 458-3722 or 3370.
Anchorage: You can anchor west of the marina or south of the commercial wharf. Check your charts carefully for the shoal areas extending out from shore.
Services: You can get diesel and water at the marina, or by calling Daffodil's Marine Service. The latter offers a mobile service station, and can be reached at (809) 458-3942, or on VHF channel 68. They also do mechanical and dinghy repairs, laundry and organize snorkeling trips. Sunsports is another dive agency at (809) 458-3577, or on VHF channel 68. Dive Bequia can be called at (809) 458-3504, or on

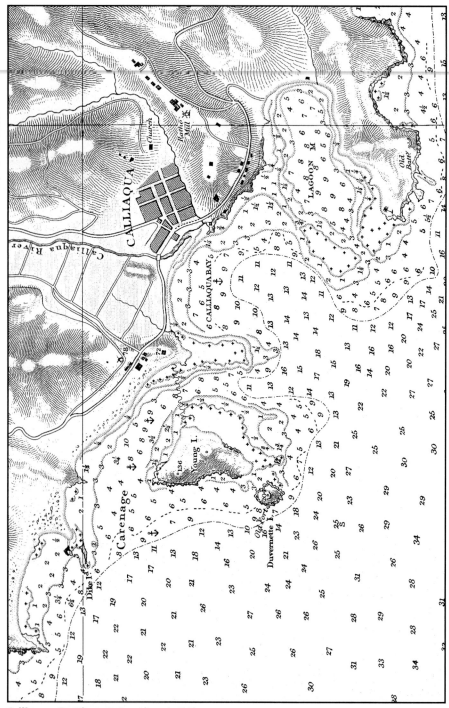

Calliaqua, St. Vincent, Soundings in Fathoms

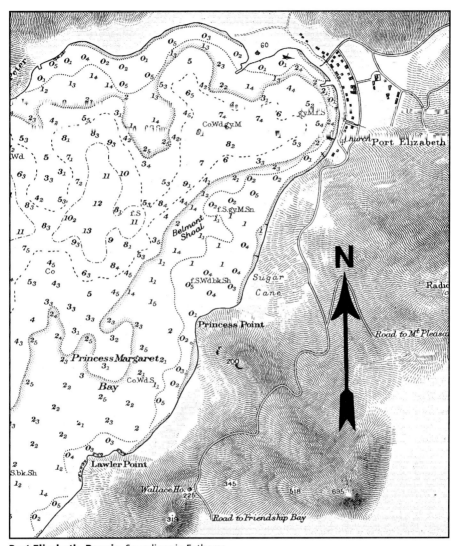

Port Elizabeth, Bequia, Soundings in Fathoms

Chapter 2

VHF channel 68. Fishing and diving gear is available from Lulley's Tackle Shop at (809) 458-3420 or 3088. Grenadines Yacht Equipment is an Evinrude dealer and supplier of plumbing supplies, hardware and lumber. They sell West system epoxy and can be reached at (809) 458-3347, or on VHF channels 16 and 68. Bo'sun's Locker is a complete chandler at (809) 458-3246 or 3634. Handy Andy's at (809) 458-3722 or 3370 have bike rentals, showers, moorings, laundry and they do boat repairs! The Bequia Bookshop (809) 458-3905 stocks charts courtesy flags and cruising guides. There is a good variety of boutiques, restaurants and supermarkets.

Bequia is a favorite of sailors. The waters around here are often windy and boisterous, with gusts over 30 knots a matter of course. The gaps between some of the islands tend to funnel the wind into pockets of higher intensity. On Bequia you may be able find traditional West Indian boats being built under the trees on the beach.

BATTOWIA TO PETIT CANOUAN

BATTOWIA ISLAND LIGHT, 12 57.7N, 61 08.3W, Fl (2) W 20s, 708 ft., 8M, White metal framework tower.
MUSTIQUE LIGHT, Montezuma Shoal, 12 52.7N, 61 12.5W, Fl (2) W, Isolated danger, Black red black, Pillar with topmark.
PETIT CANOUAN ISLAND LIGHT, 12 47.5N, 61 17.0W, Fl (4) W 40s, 252ft., 8M, White metal framework tower.

CANOUAN

CHARLESTOWN BAY RANGE (Front Light), Canouan Island, 12 42.1N, 61 19.9W, F W, 18ft., Beacon. **(Rear Light),** 500 meters, 158° 32' from front light, F W, 165ft., Beacon.
RANGE (Front Light), Marks the approach to the pier in Charlestown Bay, 12 42.7N, 61 19.5W, Iso W 4s, 46ft., 5M, Black and white square on white framework tower, Visible on rangeline only. **(Rear Light),** 60 meters, 060° from front light, Fl W 5s, 91., 5M, Black and white square on white framework tower, Visible on rangeline only.
CHARLESTOWN BAY PIER HEAD LIGHT, 12 42.2N, 61 19.8W, F W.

CATHOLIC ISLAND TO UNION

CATHOLIC ISLAND, 12 39.6N, 61 24.1W, Fl (2) W 20s, 144ft., 8M, White metal framework tower.
CLIFTON HARBOR RANGE (Front Light), 12 35.8N, 61 25.0W, F W, 13ft., White concrete tower, Lighted beacons mark reef and shoal. **(Rear Light),** 555 meters, 327.5° from front light, F W, 125ft., White concrete tower.
MISS IRENE POINT LIGHT, 12 35.5N, 61 27.8W, Fl (2) W 20s, 410ft., 8M, Metal framework tower.
RED ISLAND LIGHT, 12 36.1N, 61 24.5W, Fl R 10s, 128ft., 6M, White metal framework tower.
GRAND DE COI LIGHT, 12 35.1N, 61 24.9W, V Q (9) W 10s, West cardinal, Yellow black yellow, Pillar with topmark.

CLIFTON, UNION

12 36N, 61 25W

Pilotage: Clifton lies in a bay on the southeast end of Union Island. It is protected to the east by Thompson Reef. The new buoyage leading in to the harbor should be on the IALA B system, indicating you should follow the "red-right-returning" rule. This may vary with what your charts show. Copper Reef, with a ruined concrete structure on its southwest end, lies in the middle of the harbor. There may be a range of 327.5° leading safely into the harbor.
Port of Entry: This is the southern check in point for boats headed north through the Grenadines towards St. Vincent. Contact the officials at (809) 458-8360.
Dockage: The Anchorage Yacht Club can be contacted at (809) 458-8221, or on VHF channels 16 and 68.
Anchorage: There is good anchorage in most of the harbor, taking care to avoid the various reefs. Depths are from 16 to 40 feet, with a sand bottom.
Services: You can jug fuel, but water and ice is available at the marina. The marina also has a mechanic, a sailmaker and a marine railway. There is a good selection of small shops, restaurants and supermarkets.

PETIT ST. VINCENT (PSV)

12 32N, 61 23W

Pilotage: Extensive reefs lie east, north and northwest of the island. The anchorage is near

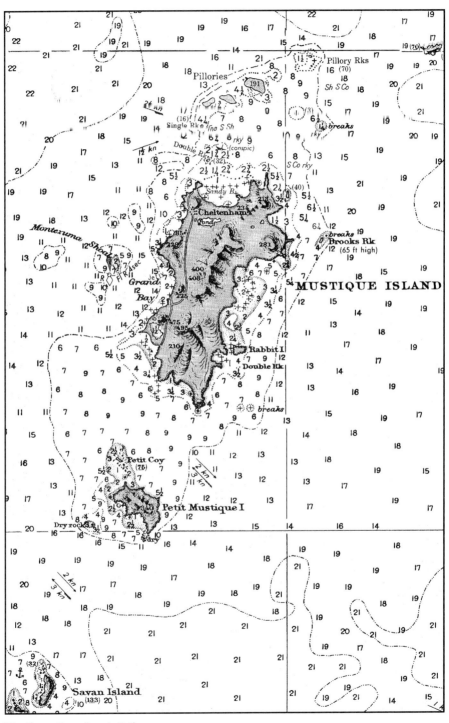

Mustique, Soundings in Fathoms

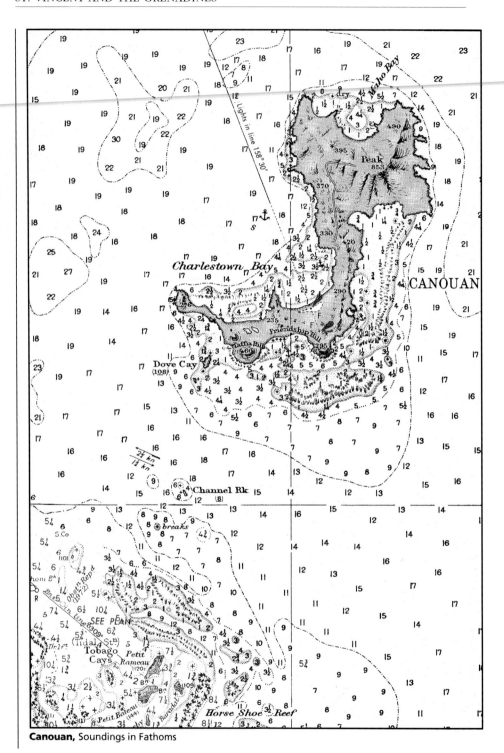

Canouan, Soundings in Fathoms

the east end of the south coast of the island. Though this is a private island, yachtsmen are invited to visit. You can contact the island on VHF channel 16.

Services: You may be able to purchase fuel from the resort in an emergency. Ice, bread and phones are available during office hours. You can visit the bar, restaurant and boutique, or ask about joining one of their barbecues on the beach. Cottage rentals are available. Contact Petit St. Vincent Resort at (809) 458-8801, or on VHF channel 16.

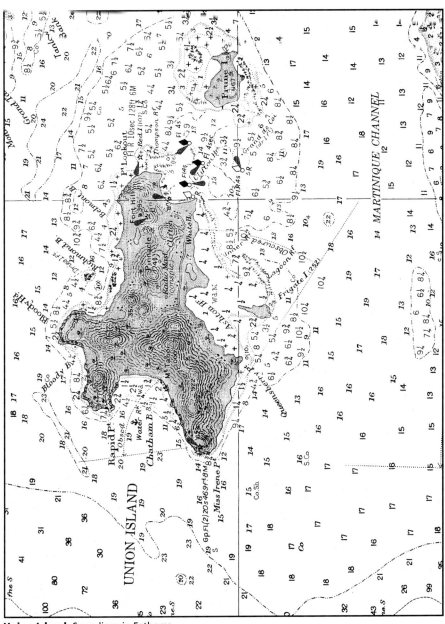

Union Island, Soundings in Fathoms

KEEP YOUR ALMANAC UP-TO-DATE

Return the post-paid reply card to receive your free *1994 Supplement,* and always use Notices To Mariners and Local Notices to Mariners. To obtain these notices contact the Coast Guard District Commanders for the areas where you travel. See *Reed's Nautical Companion* for more information

GRENADA

CAUTION. Our information on aids to navigation comes from official government sources. The latitudes and longitudes of these marks may not correspond to the readings from GPS receivers. Some aids have been reported as unreliable, missing, off position or showing incorrect characteristics. No single aid to navigation, or waypoint, should be relied upon as a sole means of fixing your position.

ENTRY PROCEDURES

This country includes the islands of Grenada, Petit Martinique, Carriacou, Ronde Island, Isle de Caille, The Sisters and a handful of smaller islets. Carriacou and Petit Martinique are part of the Grenadines, though the rest of the island group is allied with St. Vincent. Grenada was a British colony until gaining independence in 1974. In 1979 a "People's" government took over, gradually extending ties to Cuba, and attracting the notice of the U.S. Government with it's Communist leanings. In 1983 the U.S. invaded the island after rival factions began shooting each other in their bids to gain power. Today the government is stable and the island is an independent nation member of the British Commonwealth. See *Reed's Nautical Companion* for an example of the country flag.

The Port of Entry on Carriacou is Hillsborough. Unfortunately, you cannot clear Customs on Petit Martinique. On Grenada clear in St. George's or Prickly Bay, and Grenville on the east coast.

Generally, hours are about 0800 to 1600, with a break for lunch from 1200 to 1300. Contact Customs at (809) 440-3270, 2239 or 2240 in St. George's. In Prickly Bay they can be reached at (809) 444-4549

You should have a clearance from your last port of call, ship's papers, crew lists and passports. A coastwise clearance should be granted allowing you to visit other ports in the country. There is a fee for charter boats, but no charge for pleasure vessels. Charter boats

should contact the Port Authority in St. George's at (809) 440-3013 or 3015 for the latest information.

For general information call the Tourism office at (809) 440-2872. This office specializes in cruise ship information, but they can answer many questions for yachtsmen.

The telephone area code for all of the islands is 809, followed by the seven digit local number.

All charges are in Eastern Caribbean, or EC, dollars. The exchange rate, when converting EC dollars to U.S. dollars, is about .40. In other words, $100 EC = $40 U.S. You will probably find many people accepting U.S. dollars, especially in tourist areas.

The official language is English.

CARRIACOU

JACK A DAN LIGHT, 12 29.7N, 61 28.3W, Q G, 14ft., 3M, Visible 243° to 182°.
SANDY ISLAND LIGHT, 12 29.2N, 61 28.9W, Q R.

HILLSBOROUGH, CARRIACOU
12 29N, 61 28W

Pilotage: Hillsborough Bay is entered between Jack a Dan and Sandy Island, both of which have lights on them. The town has a 210 foot long jetty, with a depth of about 8 feet alongside its head. A church and tower stands at the southwest end of the village.
Port of Entry: You can clear here if headed south to Grenada, or if you want to visit Petit Martinique. Obtain your coastwise clearance for proceeding south.
Moorings: The Silver Beach Resort has free moorings and a dinghy dock. Contact them at (809) 443-7337, or on VHF channel 16.
Anchorage: Good anchorage along the waterfront beach in depths of ten to 20 feet.
Services: The Silver Beach Resort, mentioned above, provides showers, laundry, a boutique, a small market, a bar and restaurant and a

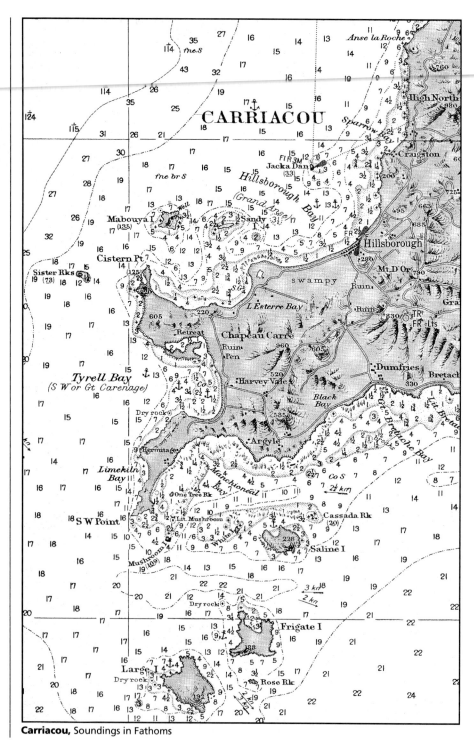

Carriacou, Soundings in Fathoms

liquor store. Silver Beach Diving, on VHF channel 16, can take you on a dive tour. There is a good selection of small markets and restaurants.

CARRIACOU TO GRENADA

RONDE ISLAND
12 18N, 61 35W

This small islet lies about 5 miles northeast of the north coast of Grenada. Reefs fringe the shores in places and extend across the bays on its north and east sides. Yachts may be able to anchor off the northwest side of the island, north of a shoal which extends along the western coast.

ISLE DE CAILLE
12 17N, 61 35W

This small islet lies south of Ronde Island. The narrow channel between the two islands has depths of 12 to 30 feet. During strong winds the sea breaks in this channel. You may be able to anchor under the lee of the island in an emergency.

THE SISTERS
12 18N, 61 36W

The Sisters is two groups of small islets just west of Ronde Island. *CAUTION: Volcanic activity has been reported in an area about 1 3/4 miles west of The Sisters. Eruptions have been reported as recently as 1986, 1988 and 1989.*

ST. GEORGE'S APPROACHES

West Buoy, 750 meters, 251.5° from St. George's Harbor Light, 12 03N, 61 46W, Q R, Starboard, Red.
East Buoy, 530 meters, 238° from St. George's Harbor Light, 12 03N, 61 46W, Q G, Port, Green.
ST. GEORGE'S HARBOR LIGHT, Extremity of north bastion of Fort George Point, 12 03.0N, 61 45.3W, F R, 188ft 15M, Brick building, Visible 056.5° to 151° (a faint light is visible inshore of these bearings), Two pair of F R range lights lead into the harbor, The first pair bears 132°, The second pair bears 068°, *Reported extinguished 1985.*

ST. GEORGE'S, GRENADA
12 03N, 61 45W

Pilotage: This is the capital of Grenada and its most important harbor. The inner part of the harbor has two basins, with the small craft facilities being in the southern one known as the Lagoon. Two pairs of range lights are shown. The first pair, bearing 132°, lead you from the north into Martins Bay. The second pair, bearing 068°, lead from Martins Bay into the inner harbor. Be careful not to cut the corner too close when turning into the channel leading to the Lagoon — Harbor Reef is located there. You can contact Port Control, call sign J3YA, on VHF channel 16.

Port of Entry: Yachts should proceed to the Grenada Yacht Services docks in the Lagoon. Contact the officials at (809) 440-3270. The main Customs office can be reached at (809) 440-2239 or 2240.

Dockage: Try Grenada Yacht Services, located in the Lagoon. You can call them at (809) 440-2508.

Anchorage: The best shelter is in the Lagoon, but you can try in the Carenage. The Carenage area is very busy with commercial traffic.

Services: Grenada Yacht Services has haulout facilities, water, fuel and some repair shops. Lagoon Marine specializes in refrigeration at (809) 440-3381. There is a Neil Pryde sail loft at (809) 440-2249. Mc Intyre Brothers Ltd. is a Yamaha dealer, and engine repair shop. There are other marine services here, and in nearby Prickly Bay. Ashore you'll find a good variety of general shops, supermarkets and restaurants.

St. George's is well sheltered and south of most hurricane tracks. The island may once again become a favorite of yachtsmen now that the political situation seems to have stabilized.

ST. GEORGE'S TO PRICKLY BAY

PETIT CABRITS LIGHT, 12 01.0N, 61 46.4W, Fl (2+1) W 20s, 354ft 18M, Red framework tower.
POINT SALINE LIGHT, 12 00.2N, 61 47.8W, Q (9) W 15s, 7M, West cardinal.
GLOVER ISLAND LIGHT, 11 59.2N, 61 47.2W, Q (6) and L Fl W 15s, 7M, South cardinal.

Chapter 2

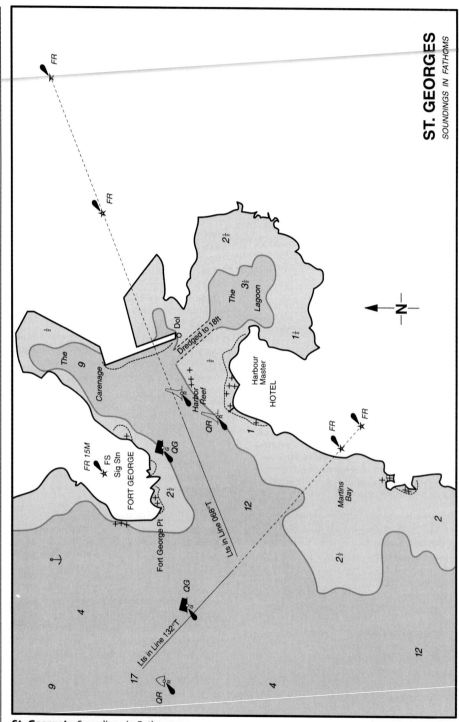

ST. GEORGES
SOUNDINGS IN FATHOMS

FR

FR

2½

The
Lagoon
3½

1½

N

½
The
9
Carenage

Dol

Dredged to 18ft

½

Harbour
Master
HOTEL

Harbor
Reef

QR

FR

FR

QR

1

FR 15M
FS
Sig Stn
FORT GEORGE

G
QG

2½

Lts in Line 068°T

12

Martins
Bay

2

Fort George Pt

2½

QG
G

17

Lts in Line 132°T

4

9

2½

12

QR
QR

4

St. George's, Soundings in Fathoms

Chapter 2

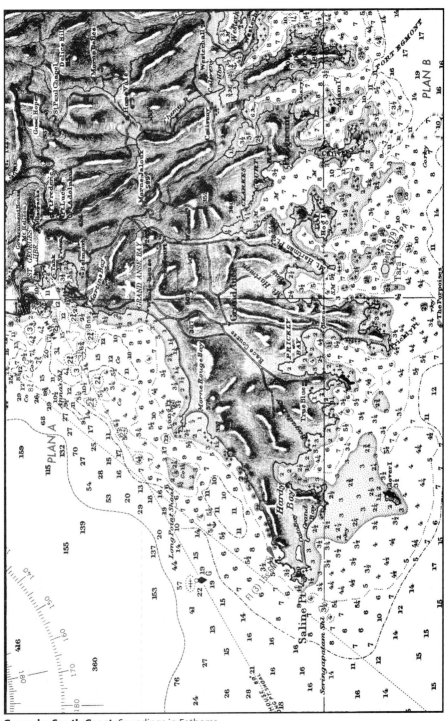

Grenada, South Coast, Soundings in Fathoms

PRICKLY BAY, GRENADA

12 00N, 61 46W

Pilotage: The bay is located on the south coast of Grenada, about 2 1/2 miles east of Saline Point. When traveling from St. George's to Prickly Bay be sure to stay well outside Long Point Shoal. A course of 240° T, with Ft. George point in line with Government House (in St. George's), is reported to keep you clear of the shoal. There is a shoal spot in the bay, due west of the boatyard.

Port of Entry: You can contact the officials at (809) 444-4549. They are located in the boatyard.

Dockage: Spice Island Marine Services is located on the eastern side of the bay. Contact them at (809) 444-4257 or 4342. They monitor VHF channels 16 and 68, or SSB 4125kHz. There is also some dockage at the True Blue Inn, in the small bay west of Prickly Bay. Contact the inn at (809) 444-2000, or on VHF channel 68. The Moorings Secret Harbour Marina is located in the next cove to the east, known as Hartmann Bay. Contact them at (809) 444-4549, or on VHF channels 16, 66 and 71.

Anchorage: There is good anchorage in both True Blue and Prickly Bay.

Services: Fuel, water, ice, showers, haulouts, repairs, a chandlery, sail repairs, a canvas shop, and a telephone are all available at Spice Island Marine Services. The Hard specializes in message services, boat watching, dive work, personalized dinghies and customs clearance for parts. Call them at (809) 444-4638, or on VHF channels 16 and 70. The Moorings operation also has fuel laundry, showers and a commissary. There are markets and restaurants nearby.

The south coast of Grenada has several good anchorages, with convenient yachting services nearby. You are a short taxi or bus ride from St. George's, but in a much more natural setting. These harbors are also convenient to the airport near Saline Point.

GRENVILLE BAY

12 07N, 61 37W

Pilotage: This harbor, about midway up the east coast of the island, is protected by coral reefs to the east. The entrance channel is difficult to negotiate, and should only be attempted in good weather, good light and with local knowledge. During strong winds the sea breaks right across the entrance. There are reported to be two white beacons, on a bearing of 291°, that lead through the outer reef. The channel through the inner reef, called Luffing Channel, leads in a northerly direction. There may be some buoys marking these channels. The town pier is reported to have depths of 10 feet alongside its head.

Port of Entry: This is the only Port of Entry on the east coast of the island. The officials are located near the pier.

Anchorage: Anchor in the area clear of reefs off the town pier.

Services: This is not a yachting area, but there are good markets and general shops.

This harbor is not visited by many yachtsmen, due to its position on the east coast, and its tricky reef entrance. It is a Port of Entry, and might be worth visiting for those who want to get off the "beaten track".

BARBADOS

Chapter 2

CAUTION: Our information on aids to navigation comes from official government sources. The latitudes and longitudes of these marks may not correspond to the readings from GPS receivers. Some aids have been reported as unreliable, missing, off position or showing incorrect characteristics. No single aid to navigation, or waypoint, should be relied upon as a sole means of fixing your position.

ENTRY PROCEDURES

Barbados is the easternmost of the Windward Islands, lying about 89 miles to windward of St. Vincent. It is a former British colony, having gained independence in 1966. See *Reed's Nautical Companion* for an example of the country flag.

The Port of Entry is Bridgetown, located on the southwest part of the island. You should contact the Port Control Station (call sign 8PA) for permission to enter the Deepwater Harbour east of the breakwater where the station is located. They monitor VHF channels 12, 16 and 2182kHz. Customs officials are on duty from 0600 to 2200, seven days a week, and you can call them at (809) 427-5940.

You should have a clearance from your last port of call, ship's papers, crew lists and passports. A coastwise clearance should be requested if you want to anchor on another part of the island.

The telephone area code for all of the islands is 809, followed by the seven digit local number.

The official currency is the Barbados dollar. One U.S. dollar is equal to 1.98 Barbados dollars. You may be able to use U.S. money, especially in tourist areas.

For general information call the Tourist Office at (809) 427-2623.

The official language is English.

BARBADOS, WEST COAST

HARRISON POINT LIGHT, NW side of island, 13 18.3N, 59 39.0W, Fl (2) W 15s, 193ft., 22M, W stone tower.
MAYCOCKS BAY LIGHT, Jetty N end, 13 16.8N, 59 39.3W, Q R, 3M.
MAYCOCKS BAY LIGHT, Jetty S end, 13 16.9N, 59 39.3W, Q G, 3M.

APPROACHES TO BRIDGETOWN

BULK FACILITY LIGHT, 13 06.5N, 59 37.8W, Fl G 5s, 29ft., R metal mast.
CONTAINER BERTH LIGHT, 13 06.2N, 59 37.9W, Q G, 26ft., 6M.
BRIDGETOWN BREAKWATER LIGHT, 13 06.3N, 59 38.0W, Q (3) R 10s, 49ft., 12M, F W shown when required, On flagstaff at shore end of pipeline at Spring Garden anchorage, 1.15M north.
OIL PIER LIGHT, SE end, 13 05.9N, 59 37.8W, Q R, 16ft., 5M, Silver metal mast.
OIL PIER LIGHT, Center, F R, 39ft., 5M, Silver metal mast.
OIL PIER LIGHT, NW end, Q R, 16ft., 5M, Silver metal mast.
FISHING HARBOR ENTRANCE LIGHT, S side, 13 05.7N, 59 37.2W, F G.
FISHING HARBOR ENTRANCE LIGHT, N side, 13 05.7N, 59 37.2W, F R.
BRIDGETOWN CAREENAGE LIGHT, S side of entrance, 13 05.6N, 59 37.1W, Fl (2) G 10s, 26ft., 2M, Silver metal framework structure.

BRIDGETOWN

13 06N, 59 38W

Pilotage: The approaches to Bridgetown are generally free of hazards. Due to the area known as The Shallows, and the reef along the east coast of the island, there can be very heavy seas when rounding South Point. Overfalls have been reported near the point. Contact the Port Control Station in Bridgetown (call sign 8PA) on VHF channels 12, 16 and 2182kHz

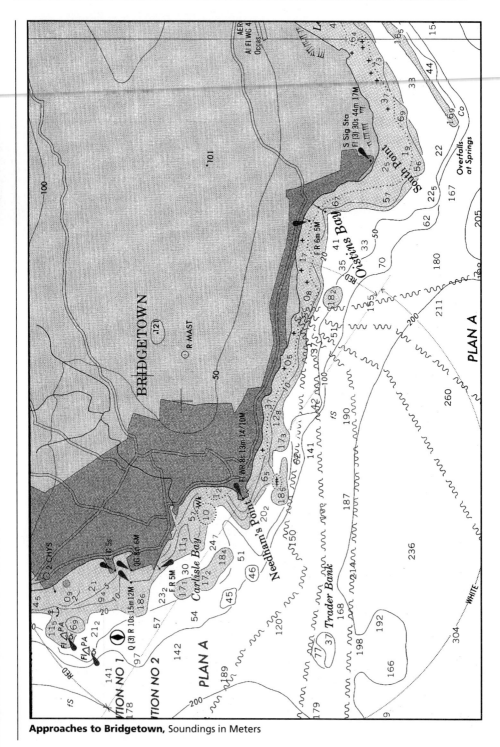

Approaches to Bridgetown, Soundings in Meters

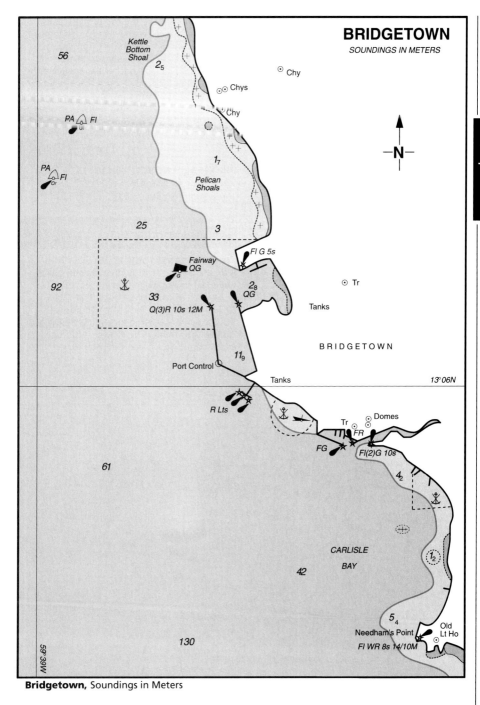

BRIDGETOWN

SOUNDINGS IN METERS

56

Kettle
Bottom
Shoal
2₅

⊙ Chy

⊙⊙ Chys

⊙ Chy

PA ◬ Fl
lit

–N–

PA
◬ Fl
Or

1₇

Pelican
Shoals

25

3

92

Fl G 5s

Fairway
QG
G

⚓

33
Q(3)R 10s 12M ⚓

2₈
QG ⚓

⊙ Tr

Tanks

BRIDGETOWN

11₉

Port Control ⚓

Tanks

13°06N

R Lts ⚓

⚓

Tr ⊙ ⊙ Domes

FR

FG

Fl(2)G 10s

61

4₂

⚓

CARLISLE

42

BAY

1₂

5₄

Needham's Point

Old
Lt Ho
⊙

Fl WR 8s 14/10M

130

59°39W

Bridgetown, Soundings in Meters

Chapter 2

for permission to enter the Deepwater Harbour for Customs clearance.

Port of Entry: See above. Customs can be reached at (809) 427-5940.

Public Correspondence: Call Barbados Radio, call sign 8PO, on 2182kHz or VHF channel 16.

Dockage: It may be possible to tie up in the Carenage, which has a flashing green light at the entrance. Call the Port Authority at (809) 436-6883, for information on tying up.

Anchorage: Most yachts anchor in Carlisle Bay, north of Needham Point. You can land your dinghy at the Boatyard, the Yacht Club, Bay Boat Supplies, the Cruising Club or in the Carenage.

Services: The Boatyard can assist yachtsmen with many services. Contact them at (809) 436-9060. They have a dinghy landing pier in the northern part of Carlisle Bay. You might want to contact the Barbados Yacht Club at (809) 427-1125, or the Barbados Cruising Club for assistance. They are located near a pier at the south end of Carlisle Bay, and both have bars overlooking the anchorage. Fuel should be available at a jetty near the mouth of the Carenage, or in the Deepwater Harbour. Shallow draft boats can be hauled in the Carenage. There are good supermarkets and general stores.

Few sailors will make the rough trip against the trade winds to reach Barbados from the rest of the Antilles, but this is often the first stop for those making the big crossing from the Canaries. The approaches are easy, and if you miss the island, you'll get another chance to make a landfall the next day!

NEEDHAM POINT LIGHT, 13 04.5N, 59 36.9W, Fl W R 8s, 43ft., 14M white, 10M red, R metal mast, R from 274° to 304°, W from 304° to 124°, R from 124° to 154°.

OISTINS FISHING JETTY LIGHT, 13 03.6N, 59 32.8W, F R, 20ft., 5M.

BARBADOS, EAST COAST

RAGGED POINT LIGHT, 13 09.6N, 59 26.1W, Fl W 15s, 213ft., 21M, W circular coral stone tower, Obscured when bearing less than 135°.

SEAWALL AVIATION LIGHT, 13 04.5N, 59 29.7W, Al Fl W G 4s, 210ft., Occasional.

SOUTH POINT LIGHT, 13 02.8N, 59 31.8W, Fl (3) W 30s, 145ft., 17M, Tower, Alternate R + W bands, Storm signal station.

TRINIDAD AND TOBAGO

ENTRY PROCEDURES

The islands of Trinidad and Tobago lie east of the Venezuelan coast. They form an independent country, with ties to the British Commonwealth. See *Reed's Nautical Companion* for an example of the country flag.

The Port of Entry for Tobago is Scarborough, located on the southwest end of the island. In Trinidad most yachtsmen will clear in Port of Spain, or the new Customs station in Chaguaramas. When approaching Chaguaramas, call the Customs office on VHF channel 16 to alert them of your arrival, and to check on the latest procedures. The Immigration officers must be summoned from Port of Spain, invoking a traveling fee of $25.00 TT. Working hours are 0800 to 1600, Monday through Friday, with an hour off for lunch. Clearing outside of these hours invokes a charge.

You should have a clearance from your last port of call, ship's papers, crew lists and passports. Any guns and ammunition (including flare guns) must be declared and turned over to the officials for the duration of your stay. When moving your boat anywhere on the islands, be sure to call Customs. When arriving on either island, having cleared already on the other, call Immigration to alert them of your presence. Check with the officials for the latest rules on boats passing between the two islands.

To contact Customs in Scarborough call (809) 639-3075 or 2415. Immigration is located at (809) 639-2931 or 8236. In Port of Spain call

Customs at (809) 632-3425, 3426, 3308 or 3309. Contact Immigration at (809) 623-8147.

The telephone area code for both islands is 809, followed by the seven digit local number.

The official currency is the Trinidad and Tobago (TT) dollar. One U.S. dollar is equal to 4.65 TT dollars. The use of U.S. dollars is not legal, though you may be approached by money-changers on the streets. You may be required to produce exchange receipts (from official exchange offices) upon your departure.

For general information call the Tourist Office at (809) 623-1932, 1933 or 1934.

The official language is English, though you may hear many other languages, reflecting the varied origins of its inhabitants.

TOBAGO, NORTH COAST

ST. GILES ISLAND LIGHT, E end, 11 21.2N, 60 31.1W, Fl W 7.5s, 16M.
LITTLE TOBAGO LIGHT, 11 17.5N, 60 29.5W, Fl (3) W 10s, 59ft., 5M.
MAN OF WAR BAY LIGHT, 11 19.1N, 60 32.8W, Q W R G, 82ft., 5M white, 4M red, 4M green, R from 098° to 108°, W from 108° to 131°, G from 131° to 141°.
THE SISTERS LIGHT, 11 19.7N, 60 38.7W, Fl (2) W 10s, 8M.
COURTLAND POINT LIGHT, 11 13.2N, 60 46.8W, L Fl W 10s, 8M.
BOOBY POINT LIGHT, 11 10.9N, 60 48.8W, Fl Y 3s, 4M.
MILFORD BAY LIGHT, 11 09.4N, 60 50.4W, Q W R G, 23ft., 5M white, 4M red, 4M green, R 073° to 083°, W 083° to 128°, G 128° to 138°.
CROWN POINT LIGHT, SW extremity of island, 11 08.7N, 60 50.7W, Fl (4) W 20s, 115ft., 11M, Steel lattice tower painted aluminum.

TOBAGO, SOUTH COAST

SMITHS ISLAND LIGHT, 11 11.0N, 60 39.1W, Fl W R 5s, 59ft., 7M white, 5M red, R from 068° to 276°, W from 276° to 068°.

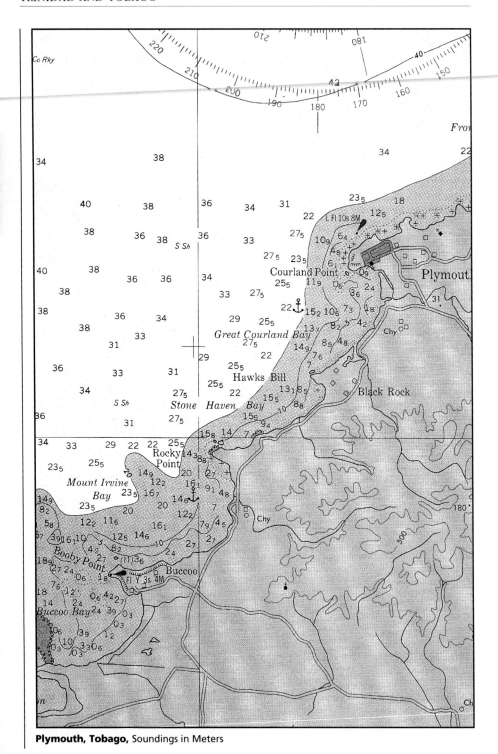

Plymouth, Tobago, Soundings in Meters

SCARBOROUGH LIGHT, On Fort George Point, 11 10.4N, 60 43.7W, Fl (2) W 20s, 462ft., 30M, W rectangular building with tower, Visible 258° to 090°.

SCARBOROUGH HARBOR LIGHT, East Beacon, 11 10.6N, 60 44.2W, Q R, 18ft., 2M, W steel structure on piles.

RANGE, (Front Light) 11 11.0N, 60 44.5W, V Q G, 11ft 5M, Pile. **(Rear Light),** 115 meters 329.5° from front, Iso W R G 2s, 49ft., 7M white, 5M red, 5M green, R 313.5° to 323.5°, W 323.5° to 335.5°, G 335.5° to 345.5°.

LOWER TOWN LIGHT, 11 11.1N, 60 44.5W, Oc W 5s, 66ft., 11M, W triangular daymark, Point down, On beacon.

ROCKLY BAY LIGHT, 11 10.9N, 60 44.4W, Oc W 5s, 33ft., 11M.

SCARBOROUGH, TOBAGO

11 11N, 60 44W

Pilotage: Tobago lies about 19 miles north-northeast of Trinidad and 78 miles southeast of Grenada. The equatorial current runs in a northwesterly direction between Tobago and Grenada at speeds around 3 knots. Near the northeast end of Tobago currents may run up to 4 knots. Take careful note of the charted, and buoyed, shoals to the east and west of the entrance to Rockly Bay. Fort George, and several nearby radio towers, are conspicuous. A lighted range of 329.5° should lead you in safely. When sailing to Trinidad avoid Wasp Shoal and Drew Bank located about 3 miles off the southwestern tip of the island.

Port of Entry: This is the only Port of Entry on Tobago. Customs is located near the docks. You can contact Customs at (809) 639-3075 or 2415, and Immigration at (809) 639-2931 or 8236. If arriving from Trinidad, you should call Immigration upon your arrival.

Coast Station: Call sign 9YL, North Post. They monitor VHF channel 16 and 2182kHz. For the daily weather schedule see Communications and Weather Services.

Dockage: You may be able to tie up Mediterranean style (stern-to) behind the breakwater.

Anchorage: Anchor outside the jetty in depths of around 10 to 12 feet. This area is reported to suffer from surge.

Services: You can get water and jug your fuel. There are few yacht oriented services of any kind, but there are good general stores, markets and restaurants. There are several dive shops on the island. Contact the Tobago Division of Tourism at (809) 639-2125 for general information on the area.

TRINIDAD SOUTH COAST

SOLDADO ROCK, 10 04.2N, 62 00.9W, Fl W 10s, 8M.

WOLF ROCK, 10 03.0N, 61 56.1W, Q (6) + L Fl W 15s, 13ft., 5M, Temporarily extinguished (1988).

PUNTA DEL ARENAL, 10 02.8N, 61 55.7W, Fl W 7.5s, 72ft., 16M, White steel structure, Obscured when bearing less than 301°.

CHATHAM JETTY HEAD, 10 04.8N, 61 44.1W, F R, 3M.

TAPARO POINT, 10 03.4N, 61 37.7W, Fl (3) W 15s, 226ft., 14M.

LA LUNE POINT, 10 04.5N, 61 18.9W, Fl (4) W 20s, 148ft., 14M.

GALEOTA POINT, 10 08.5N, 60 59.7W, Fl W 5s, 285ft., 16M, White steel framework tower.

TRINIDAD EAST COAST

BRIGAND HILL, 10 29.4N, 61 04.2W, Fl (2 + 1) W 30s, 712ft., 20M, White steel framework tower.

GALERA POINT, 10 50.0N, 60 54.3W, Oc W 10s, 141ft., 16M, White concrete tower.

TRINIDAD, NORTH COAST

PETITE MATELOT POINT, 10 49.2N, 61 07.7W, Fl (3) W 15s, 7M.

CHUPARA POINT, 10 48.2N, 61 22.0W, Fl (2) W 10s, 325ft., 12M, White metal framework tower and hut.

SAUT D'EAU ISLAND, 10 46.2N, 61 30.7W, Q W, 7M.

NORTH POST, POINT A DIABLE, 10 44.7N, 61 33.8W, Fl W 5s, 747ft., 14M, Beacon, Visible 087°– 252°.

NOTE: The current between Trinidad and Tobago sets to the northwest, usually with sufficient strength to prevent a sailing vessel from working through against it. The strength of the current is somewhat lessened by the ebb tidal stream. Current runs to the westward along the north shore of Trinidad.

GULF OF PARIA

CHACACHACARE, 10 41.7N, 61 45.2W, Fl W 10s, 825ft., 26M, White concrete tower. Beacon, about 640 meters 216° from main

Chapter 2

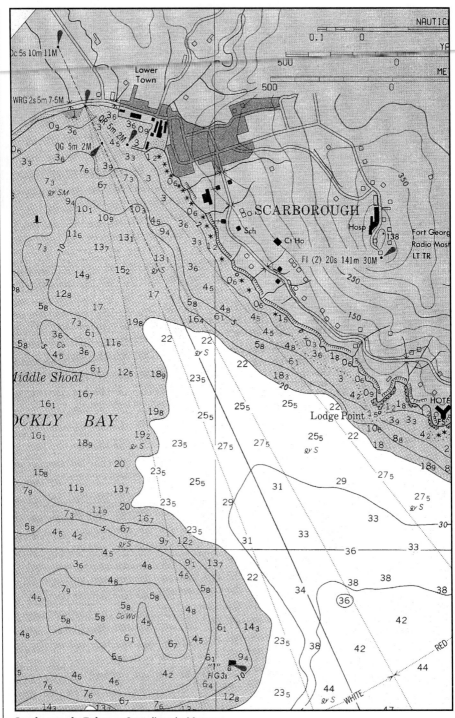

Oc 5s 10m 11M

Lower
Town

WRG 2s 5m 7-5M

QR 5m 2M

QG 5m 2M

SCARBOROUGH

Sch

Ct Ho

Hosp

Fort George
Radio Mast
LT TR

138

Fl (2) 20s 141m 30M

Middle Shoal

COCKLY BAY

Lodge Point

HOTE

NAUTIC

0.1   0

YA

500   0

ME

500   0

Scarborough, Tobago, Soundings in Meters

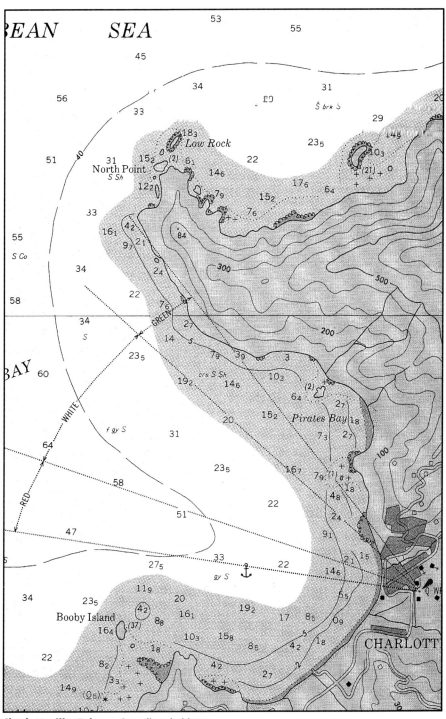

Charlotteville, Tobago, Soundings in Meters

light, 10 41.4N, 61 45.4W, Fl W 2s, 503ft., 11M, White square on white metal framework tower, In line 036° with Chacachacare.

POINT DE CABRAS, S end of Huevos, 10 40.9N, 61 43.2W, V Q (6) + L Fl W 10s, 40ft., 5M.

LE CHAPEAU ROCK, 10 42.3N, 61 40.6W, Fl (3) W 10s.

TETERON ROCK, 10 40.8N, 61 40.1W, Fl G 4s, 24ft., 4M, White metal structure on concrete base, Reported extinguished.

LA RETRAITE COAST GUARD STATION, 10 40.7N, 61 39.5W, 2 F R.

GASPARILLO ISLAND, W end, 10 40.4N, 61 39.4W, Q W, 36ft., White mast.

ESPOLON POINT, SW point of Gaspar Grande Island, 10 39.8N, 61 40.1W, Fl W 4s, 42ft., 12M, White framework tower, Reported extinguished Dec 1981.

CRONSTADT ISLAND, W end, 10 39.4N, 61 37.9W, Q R, 4M.

REYNA POINT, 10 40.0N, 61 38.8W, Q G, 33ft., 4M.

ESCONDIDA COVE, off N point, 10 40.3N, 61 38.3W, Q R, 17ft., White tripodal beacon, Unrealiable.

FURNESS SMITH FLOATING DOCK, 10 40.7N, 61 38.9W, 2 F R.

ON S END OF ALUMINUM COMPANY PIER, W side of Point Gourde, Chaguaramas Bay, 10 40.5N, 61 38.1W, F G, 13ft., Unreliable.

CHAGUARAMAS, TRINIDAD

10 41N, 61 39W

Pilotage: Off the north coast of Trinidad the north and northwest going tidal streams attain velocities of 2 to 3 knots. Between July and October the influence may be felt 15 to 20 miles offshore. The Dragons Mouth has several channels leading south into the Gulf of Paria. In Boca de Monos (the easternmonst channel) there is no south current during the flood, but the north running ebb has speeds of 2 to 3 knots. The tidal currents create eddies around piers 4 and 5 in Chaguaramas. A tidal surge, known locally as the Re-Mou, is strongest in July and August. It may appear as a clear line moving through the channel north of Gaspar Grande, achieving speeds of 1 to 5 knots. The Customs office and the yacht facilities are located in the northeast portion of the bay.

Port of Entry: Call Chaguaramas Customs on VHF channel 16 to announce your arrival. There is a Customs dock near the aluminum plant. If arriving from Tobago, you should call Immigration in Port of Spain at (809) 623-8147.

Coast Station: Call sign 9YL, North Post. They monitor VHF channel 16 and 2182kHz. For the daily weather schedule see Communications and Weather Services.

Dockage: Contact Trinity Yacht Facilities at (809) 634-4303, or on VHF channel 72. They are primarily a repair yard.

Anchorage: Anchor near the Trinity Yacht Facility.

Services: The Trinity Yacht Facility is the main boat hauling operation in Trinidad. They also have fuel, ice, water and showers. Repair services are available.

Chaguaramas has become a popular place to clear Customs and Immigration for those arriving from abroad. This is also the best place to accomplish major repairs or maintenance.

NELSON, E end, 10 39.4N, 61 36.0W, Fl W 2.5s, 61ft., 5M White pole beacon.

POINT SINET RANGE (Front Light) 10 40.9N, 61 36.0W, Oc W 2.5s, 98ft., 14M, White square daymark, black stripe, 5M, Visible 038°– 046°, Reduced visibility due to dust (occas), Unreliable. **(Rear Light)** 180 meters 042°14′ from front, Oc W 5s, 102ft., 14M, White square daymark, black stripe, Visible 038°– 046°, Unreliable.

PIER 2 RANGE, (Front Light) 10 41.0N, 61 36.5W, F R, 23ft. **(Rear Light)** about 290 meters 346°30′ from front, F R, 39ft.

PORT OF SPAIN

GRIER CHANNEL RANGE (Front Light) 10 39.2N, 61 31.4W, Oc W 4s, 135ft., 10M, F G 6M, White and orange checkered rectangular daymark on white framework tower. **(Rear Light)** 181 meters 061°32′ from front, Iso W 2s, 157ft., 11M, F R 6M, Orange rectangular daymark on white framework tower, Visible 058°24′– 064°24′.

DREDGED CHANNEL ENTRANCE, 10 37.8N, 61 33.9W, Iso Y 10s, 20ft., 8M, Concrete platform on pilings.

GRIER CHANNEL NO "1", entrance, N side, 10 38.2N, 61 33.2W, Fl G 3s, Concrete platform on pilings.

NO "2", entrance S side, 10 38.1N, 61 33.2W, Fl R 3s, Concrete platform on pilings.

NO "3", 10 38.4N, 61 32.9W, Q G, Concrete platform on pilings.

NO "4", 10 38.3N, 61 32.8W, Q R, Concrete platform on pilings.

NO "5", 10 38.7N, 61 32.3W, Q G, Concrete platform on pilings.

NO "6", 10 38.6N, 61 32.3W, Q R, Concrete platform on pilings.

Chapter 2

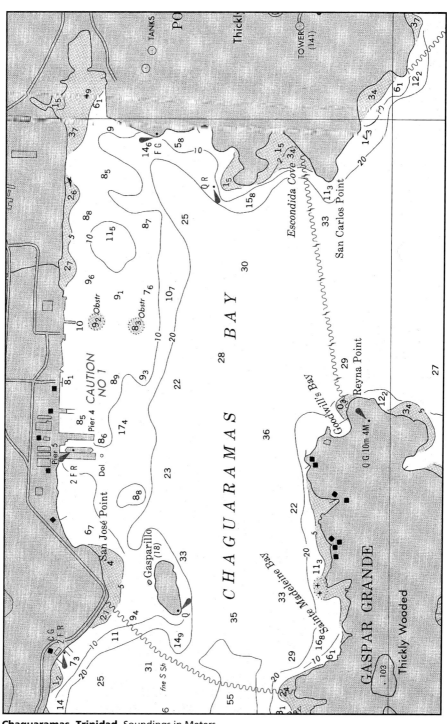

Chaguaramas, Trinidad, Soundings in Meters

NO "7", 10 38.9N, 61 31.9W, Fl G 5s, Concrete platform on pilings.
NO "8", 10 38.8N, 61 31.9W, Fl R 5s, Concrete platform on pilings.
NO "9", 10 39.1N, 61 31.9W, Q G, Concrete platform on pilings.
NO "10", 10 38.9N, 61 31.5W, Q R, Concrete platform on pilings.
NO "12", 10 38.8N, 61 31.3W, Q R, Concrete platform on pilings.
NO "14", 10 38.7N, 61 31.1W, Q R, Concrete platform on pilings.
HEAD OF ST VINCENT JETTY, 10 38.6N, 61 30.9W, F R, 23ft., 4M, Wooden post.
SEA LOTS CHANNEL NO "1", entrance, N side, 10 37.6N, 61 32.0W, Fl (2) G 7.5s, Pile.
NO "2", entrance S side, 10 37.6N, 61 31.9W, V Q (9) W 10s, Pile.
NO "3", 10 37.7N, 61 31.6W, Q G, Pile.
NO "4", 10 37.7N, 61 31.6W, Q R, Pile.
NO "5", 10 37.9N, 61 31.1W, V Q G, Pile.
NO "6", 10 37.9N, 61 31.1W, V Q R, Pile.
NO "7", 10 38.1N, 61 30.6W, Q G, Pile.
NO "8", 10 38.1N, 61 30.6W, Q R, Pile.
NO "9", 10 38.3N, 61 30.3W, L Fl G 5s, Pile.
NO "10", 10 38.2N, 61 30.3W, L Fl R 5s, Pile.
NO "12", 10 38.2N, 61 30.1W, Q R, Pile.
NO "13", 10 38.0N, 61 29.9W, Q G, Pile.
NO "14", 10 38.1N, 61 30.0W, Q R, Pile.
SEA LOTS CHANNEL RANGE (Front Light) 10 38.4N, 61 29.8W, Oc W 10s, 85ft., 6M, F R, Orange rectangular daymark on white framework tower. **(Rear Light)** 640 meters 069°10′ from front, Fl W 2s, 128 ft., 6M, F R, Orange rectangular daymark on white framework tower.

PORT OF SPAIN, TRINIDAD
10 39N, 61 31W

Pilotage: This is the principal port in Trinidad, and one of the most important ports in the West Indies. The Grier Channel range lights are often obscured by smoke, and there are several submerged obstructions outside the marked channels. Tidal currents set southeast at about 1/2 knot on the flood, and 1 1/2 knots on the ebb. The Harbour Master monitors VHF channels 10 and 16 — call sign "Maritime Services".
Coast Station: Call sign 9YL, North Post. They monitor VHF channel 16 and 2182kHz. For the daily weather schedule see Communications and Weather Services.
Port of Entry: The Customs dock is located inshore of the dredged area at the southeast end of the Grier Channel. Call Customs at

(809) 632-3425, 3426, 3308 or 3309. Contact Immigration at (809) 623-8147. You must check with Immigration if arriving from Tobago.
Dockage: You may be able to tie up right in Port of Spain. For information contact the Harbour Master at (809) 625-3858, or on VHF channels 10 and 16. Many boaters prefer to dock at the Trinidad and Tobago Yacht Club in Cumana Bay, 4 miles northwest of town. Contact the club at (809) 637-4260. During Carnival, the docks are likely to be very crowded, if not totally full.
Anchorage: Anchor off the Trinidad and Tobago Yachting Association docks in the northwest part of Carenage Bay, or off the Yacht Club docks. You can contact the Yachting Association at (809) 634-4376, or on VHF channel 68. Both clubs offer the use of their facilities to visitors who purchase temporary memberships.
Services: Most services are available. Fuel, water and showers are available at the Yacht Club, while the Yachting Association offers haulouts, water and showers but no fuel. Either place would be a good place to start if searching for a particular marine service.
Venezuelan Embassy: Contact them at (809) 627-9821 or 9823. Visitors to Venezuela must have a visa before entering the country.

Port of Spain, with a population of over 300,000, is a bustling commercial place. In the weeks following Christmas it is the location for the world famous Carnival, or "Mas". For this reason alone yachtsmen have begun to flock to the area in increasing numbers, but they also enjoy the advantage of being south of the hurricane belt. For those heading to Venezuela, this is a good place to obtain your visas.

POINT LISAS

RANGE (Front Light) No 13, 10 22.7N, 61 29.0W, Q W, 30ft., 8M, F R, 30ft., 4M, Visible 083°48′– 098°48′. **(Rear Light)** No 14, 530 meters 091°20′ from front, Oc W 5s, 52ft., 8M, F R, 56ft., 4M, Visible 087°18′– 095°18′.
MARINE TERMINAL RANGE (Front Light) 10 20.9N, 61 27.9W, Q Y, 69ft., 10M, Building. **(Rear Light)** 260 meters 081°25′ from front, Oc Y 3s, 82ft., 10M, Silo.
CHANNEL ENTRANCE, N side, No 1, 10 22.7N, 61 31.0W, Fl (2) G 5s, 26ft., 8M, White beacon.
CHANNEL ENTRANCE, S side, No 2, 10 22.6N, 61 31.0W, Fl W 3s, 26ft., 8M, White beacon.

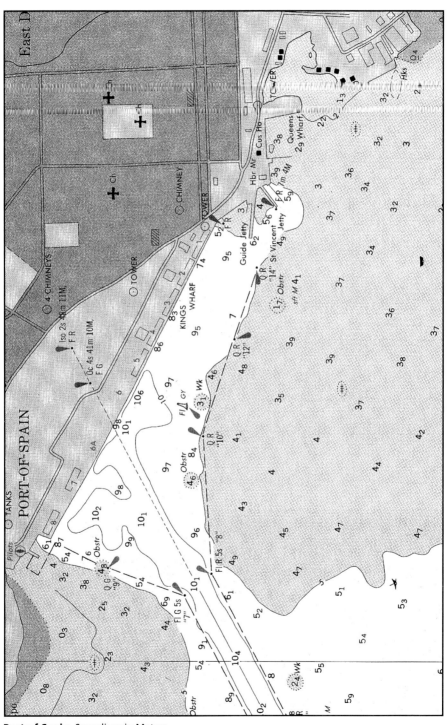

Port of Spain, Soundings in Meters

SAVONNETA RANGE (Front Light) 10 24.2N, 61 29.5W, Fl W 2s, 98ft., 8M, Orange rectangle stripe, Visible 049°18'– 055°18', Identification light Fl R 4s. **(Rear Light)** 700 meters 052°16' from front, Fl W 2s, 135ft., 8M, Orange rectangle, white stripe, Synchronized with front, Identification light Fl R 4s.

POINTE-A-PIERRE

LA CARRIERE, 10 19.3N, 61 27.6W, Fl W 2.5s, 233ft., 23M, White water tower, Emergency light range 18M.
HEAD OF PIPELINE VIADUCT, 10 18.8N, 61 28.8W, Fl (4) W 10s, 98ft., 14M, White metal tower.
TURNING BASIN, 10 18.8N, 61 28.7W, Fl R, Wood pile.
OROPUCHE BANK BEACON, 10 16.8N, 61 33.9W, V Q W, 4M, Steel caisson.

BRIGHTON (Front Light) head of pier, 10 14.9N, 61 38.1W, Fl (3) W 10s, 52ft., 15M, White metal tower, Visible 134°12'– 144°12', Berthing signals. **(Rear Light)** 852 meters 139°15' from front, Fl W 5s, 100ft., 8M, Visible 134°12'– 144°12'.
LA BREA, head of Pitch Point pier, 10 15.2N, 61 37.1W, Iso W 2s, 26ft., 10M, White framework tower.

POINT FORTIN

HEAD OF PIPELINE PIER, 10 12.6N, 61 42.2W, Fl (2) W 10s, 98ft., 14M, Aluminum framework tower.
N BREAKWATER, 10 11.3N, 61 41.6W, Fl G 3s.
S BREAKWATER, head, 10 11.2N, 61 41.6W, Fl R 3s.

PORT OF SPAIN, TRINIDAD

HIGH & LOW WATER 1994 10°39'N 61°31'W

ATLANTIC STANDARD TIME (GMT -4H)

JANUARY

Day	Time	ft	Time	ft	Time	ft	Time	ft
1 Sa	0016	0.7	0642	3.5	1219	1.3	1827	3.8
16 Su	0033	0.9	0649	3.3	1246	1.3	1844	3.3
2 Su	0056	0.8	0724	3.5	1309	1.3	1917	0.0
17 M	0107	1.1	0724	3.2	1329	1.4	1858	3.1
3 M	0139	1.0	0810	3.6	1405	1.3	2012	3.4
18 Tu	0139	1.3	0801	3.2	1418	1.5	2013	2.8
4 Tu	0225	1.2	0859	3.6	1508	1.3	2113	3.2
19 W	0213	1.4	0842	3.1	1518	1.5	2109	2.6
5 W	0317	1.4	0953	3.6	1617	1.3	2224	3.0
20 Th	0251	1.6	0929	3.1	1630	1.5	2220	2.4
6 Th	0415	1.5	1051	3.6	1729	1.2	2343	2.9
21 F	0342	1.8	1025	3.0	1746	1.4	2350	2.3
7 F	0519	1.7	1152	3.6	1839	1.0		
22 Sa	0453	1.9	1128	3.1	1854	1.3		
8 Sa	0103	2.9	0624	1.7	1253	3.7	1942	0.9
23 Su	0118	2.4	0610	1.9	1233	3.2	1950	1.1
9 Su	0210	3.0	0726	1.7	1350	3.8	2037	0.7
24 M	0216	2.6	0715	1.8	1332	3.3	2035	0.8
10 M	0304	3.1	0822	1.6	1443	3.8	2124	0.6
25 Tu	0300	2.8	0809	1.6	1545	3.5	2116	0.7
11 Tu	0349	3.1	0912	1.5	1530	3.9	2207	0.5
26 W	0340	3.0	0858	1.4	1512	3.7	2155	0.5
12 W	0429	3.2	0958	1.4	1612	3.9	2246	0.6
27 Th	0417	3.2	0943	1.2	1557	3.8	2232	0.4
13 Th	0506	3.3	1041	1.3	1651	3.8	2323	0.6
28 F	0454	3.4	1029	1.0	1642	3.9	2310	0.4
14 F	0541	3.3	1123	1.3	1729	3.7	2359	0.7
29 Sa	0532	3.6	1115	0.9	1630	3.9	2349	0.5
15 Sa	0615	3.3	1204	1.3	1806	3.5		
30 Su	0611	3.7	1202	0.8	1812	3.7		
31 M	0028	0.6	0652	3.7	1253	0.8	1901	3.5

FEBRUARY

Day	Time	ft	Time	ft	Time	ft	Time	ft
1 Tu	0110	0.8	0735	3.7	1347	0.8	1955	3.2
16 W	0052	1.2	0708	3.2	1334	1.1	1939	2.7
2 W	0153	1.0	0823	3.6	1447	0.9		
17 Th	0122	1.3	0743	3.1	1423	1.2		
3 Th	0245	1.3	0917	3.5	1554	1.0	2206	2.7
18 F	0155	1.5	0826	3.0	1526	1.3	2137	2.3
4 F	0344	1.5	1018	3.4	1707	1.0	2330	2.6
19 Sa	0242	1.7	0922	2.9	1644	1.3	2301	2.3
5 Sa	0454	1.7	1127	3.3	1822	1.0		
20 Su	0356	1.8	1031	2.9	1803	1.2		
6 Su	0055	2.6	0608	1.7	1238	3.4	1930	0.9
21 M	0034	2.4	0528	1.8	1148	3.0	1908	1.1
7 M	0202	2.7	0716	1.6	1342	3.4	2026	0.8
22 Tu	0140	2.6	0644	1.7	1300	3.2	2000	0.9
8 Tu	0251	2.9	0813	1.5	1435	3.5	2109	0.7
23 W	0226	2.8	0744	1.5	1401	3.4	2043	0.7
9 W	0331	3.0	0901	1.3	1520	3.6	2146	0.7
24 Th	0306	3.1	0836	1.2	1453	3.6	2123	0.5
10 Th	0405	3.2	0943	1.2	1559	3.6	2221	0.7
25 F	0344	3.4	0924	0.9	1540	3.8	2202	0.5
11 F	0437	3.3	1022	1.1	1634	3.6	2253	0.7
26 Sa	0421	3.6	1011	0.7	1626	3.8	2241	0.4
12 Sa	0507	3.3	1100	1.0	1707	3.5	2325	0.8
27 Su	0459	3.8	1058	0.5	1712	3.8	2320	0.5
13 Su	0537	3.4	1138	1.0	2355	0.9		
28 M	0538	0.4	1146	0.4	1759	3.6		
14 M	0606	3.4	1215	1.0	1817	3.2		
15 Tu	0024	1.0	0636	3.3	1253	1.0	1855	3.0

MARCH

Day	Time	ft	Time	ft	Time	ft	Time	ft
1 Tu	0001	0.6	0619	3.9	1236	0.4	1849	3.4
16 W	0555	3.4	1225	0.8	1836	2.9		
2 W	0043	0.8	0702	3.8	1329	0.5	1940	3.1
17 Th	0018	1.2	0625	3.3	1303	0.9	1910	0.7
3 Th	0129	1.1	0750	3.6	1427	0.6	2043	2.8
18 F	0048	1.4	0658	3.2	1346	1.0	2009	2.6
4 F	0222	1.3	0845	3.4	1531	0.8	2154	2.6
19 Sa	0124	1.6	0739	3.0	1440	1.2	2111	2.4
5 Sa	0325	1.6	0951	3.2	1644	1.0	2318	2.5
20 Su	0215	1.7	0836	2.9	1549	1.3	2225	2.4
6 Su	0441	1.7	1109	3.1	1801	1.0		
21 M	0333	1.9	0952	2.9	1708	1.3	2346	2.5
7 M	0044	2.6	0601	1.7	1229	3.1	1913	1.0
22 Tu	0502	1.8	1115	2.9	1820	1.2		
8 Tu	0146	2.8	0713	1.6	1335	3.2	2006	1.0
23 W	0054	2.8	0619	1.7	1233	3.1	1918	1.0
9 W	0229	2.9	0808	1.4	1427	3.3	2046	0.9
24 Th	0144	3.0	0722	1.4	1339	3.3	2005	0.9
10 Th	0304	3.1	0852	1.2	1509	3.4	2120	0.9
25 F	0227	3.4	0817	1.0	1434	3.5	2049	0.8
11 F	0335	3.3	0930	1.0	1545	3.4	2152	0.9
26 Sa	0307	3.6	0906	0.7	1525	3.7	2130	0.7
12 Sa	0405	3.4	1006	0.9	1618	3.4	2223	0.9
27 Su	0346	3.9	0954	0.4	1613	3.7	2211	0.7
13 Su	0433	3.4	1041	0.8	1650	3.4	2253	0.9
28 M	0426	4.0	1042	0.2	1701	3.7	2253	0.7
14 M	0500	3.5	1115	0.8	1722	3.3	2322	1.0
29 Tu	0506	4.0	1130	0.1	1749	3.6	2336	0.8
15 Tu	0527	3.4	1150	0.8	1758	3.1	2350	1.1
30 W	0548	4.0	1219	0.1	1839	3.3		
31 Th	0021	1.0	0633	3.8	1311	0.3	1932	3.1

APRIL

Day	Time	ft	Time	ft	Time	ft	Time	ft
1 F	0110	1.3	0722	3.6	1406	0.5	2031	2.9
16 Sa	0030	1.6	0629	3.2	1322	1.0	1955	2.7
2 Sa	0208	1.3	0818	3.3	1507	0.8	2130	2.7
17 Su	0112	1.7	0712	3.1	1410	1.1	2051	0.7
3 Su	0313	1.7	0928	3.1	1616	1.0	2258	2.7
18 M	0209	1.8	0810	3.0	1509	1.2	2154	2.7
4 M	0431	1.8	1052	2.9	1731	1.2		
19 Tu	0321	1.9	0928	2.9	1619	1.3	2302	2.8
5 Tu	0018	2.7	0555	1.7	1217	2.9	1840	1.3
20 W	0440	1.8	1050	3.0	1730	1.3		
6 W	0114	2.9	0709	1.5	1324	3.0	1934	1.3
21 Th	0005	3.0	0555	1.6	1208	3.1	1832	1.3
7 Th	0156	3.1	0801	1.3	1415	3.1	2014	1.3
22 F	0059	3.3	0701	1.2	1318	3.3	1926	1.2
8 F	0231	3.2	0841	1.1	1456	3.2	2049	1.2
23 Sa	0146	3.6	0758	0.9	1418	3.4	2014	1.1
9 Sa	0302	3.4	0916	1.0	1532	3.2	2122	1.2
24 Su	0230	3.8	0850	0.5	1512	3.6	2100	1.0
10 Su	0332	3.4	0949	0.8	1604	3.3	2153	1.2
25 M	0313	4.0	0938	0.2	1602	3.6	2145	1.0
11 M	0400	3.5	1022	0.7	1636	3.2	2224	1.2
26 Tu	0356	4.1	1026	0.1	1650	3.6	2230	1.0
12 Tu	0427	3.5	1056	0.7	1710	3.2	2254	1.2
27 W	0439	4.1	1114	0.0	1739	3.5	2316	1.1
13 W	0455	3.5	1130	0.7	1746	3.1	2324	1.3
28 Th	0523	4.0	1202	0.1	1828	3.3		
14 Th	0524	3.4	1205	0.7	1825	2.9	2355	1.4
29 F	0004	1.2	0609	3.8	1252	0.3	1919	3.1
15 F	0554	3.3	1241	0.8	1908	2.8		
30 Sa	0055	1.4	0659	3.5	1344	0.5	2014	3.0

TIME MERIDIAN 60°W

Heights in feet are referred to the chart datum of sounding.

0000h is midnight, 1200h is noon.

PORT OF SPAIN, TRINIDAD

HIGH & LOW WATER 1994

10°39'N 61°31'W

ATLANTIC STANDARD TIME (GMT -4H)

MAY

Day	Time	ft	Time	ft		Day	Time	ft	Time	ft
1 Su	0152	1.6			16 M	0107	1.7		
	0756	3.3				0702	3.2		
	1440	0.9				1349	1.1		
	2114	2.9				2031	2.9		
2 M	0257	1.7			17 Tu	0202	1.8		
	0904	3.0				0801	3.1		
	1543	1.2				1441	1.2		
☽	2223	2.8				2125	3.0		
3 Tu	0412	1.8			18 W	0306	1.8		
	1025	2.9				0911	3.0		
	1649	1.4				1540	1.4		
	2332	2.9			☾	2223	3.1		
4 W	0535	1.7			19 Th	0419	1.7		
	1151	2.8				1027	3.0		
	1753	1.5				1645	1.5		
						2322	3.3		
5 Th	0029	3.0			20 F	0533	1.5		
	0651	1.5				1145	3.0		
	1303	2.9				1749	1.5		
	1849	1.6							
6 F	0114	3.1			21 Sa	0018	3.5		
	0743	1.3				0641	1.2		
	1357	2.9				1300	3.1		
	1935	1.6				1848	1.5		
7 Sa	0153	3.3			22 Su	0110	3.7		
	0823	1.2				0741	0.8		
	1440	3.0				1405	3.3		
	2015	1.6				1942	1.4		
8 Su	0227	3.4			23 M	0159	3.9		
	0858	1.0				0834	0.5		
	1518	3.1				1501	3.4		
	2051	1.5				2033	1.3		
9 M	0300	3.5			24 Tu	0247	4.1		
	0932	0.8				0924	0.3		
	1553	3.1				1552	3.4		
	2126	1.5				2122	1.3		
10 Tu	0330	3.5			25 W	0333	4.1		
	1006	0.7				1012	0.1		
	1626	3.1				1640	3.5		
●	2159	1.5			○	2211	1.3		
11 W	0401	3.5			26 Th	0419	4.1		
	1040	0.7				1059	0.1		
	1701	3.1				1727	3.4		
	2232	1.5				2259	1.3		
12 Th	0431	3.5			27 F	0505	4.0		
	1115	0.6				1146	0.2		
	1738	3.1				1813	3.4		
	2306	1.5				2347	1.4		
13 F	0503	3.5			28 Sa	0552	3.8		
	1150	0.7				1232	0.4		
	1817	3.0				1900	3.3		
	2341	1.5							
14 Sa	0537	3.4			29 Su	0038	1.5		
	1226	0.8				0640	3.6		
	1858	3.0				1320	0.7		
						1948	3.2		
15 Su	0021	1.7			30 M	0131	1.6		
	0615	3.3				0733	3.3		
	1306	0.9				1409	1.0		
	1942	2.9				2039	3.1		
					31 Tu	0231	1.7		
						0831	3.1		
						1501	1.3		
						2134	3.0		

JUNE

Day	Time	ft		Day	Time	ft
1 W	0339	1.7		16 Th	0251	1.6
	0939	2.8			0856	3.2
	1557	1.6			1509	1.4
☽	2232	3.0		☾	2150	3.4
2 Th	0456	1.7		17 F	0401	1.5
	1101	2.7			1007	3.0
	1657	1.7			1608	1.6
	2331	3.1			2247	3.5
3 F	0612	1.6		18 Sa	0514	1.4
	1226	2.7			1125	3.0
	1755	1.8			1712	1.7
					2345	3.7
4 Sa	0023	3.2		19 Su	0624	1.1
	0713	1.4			1245	3.0
	1331	2.8			1816	1.7
	1849	1.8				
5 Su	0110	3.3		20 M	0042	3.8
	0759	1.2			0727	0.9
	1420	2.8			1355	3.1
	1938	1.8			1917	1.7
6 M	0151	3.4		21 Tu	0137	3.9
	0838	1.1			0822	0.6
	1501	2.9			1452	3.3
	2021	1.7			2014	1.6
7 Tu	0229	3.5		22 W	0230	4.1
	0914	0.9			0912	0.4
	1538	3.0			1542	3.4
	2100	1.7			2106	1.5
8 W	0305	3.5		23 Th	0319	4.1
	0949	0.8			0959	0.3
	1614	3.1			1628	3.4
	2137	1.6		○	2155	1.5
9 Th	0340	3.6		24 F	0407	4.1
	1025	0.7			1044	0.4
	1650	3.1			1712	3.5
●	2213	1.6			2243	1.4
10 F	0415	3.6		25 Sa	0452	4.0
	1100	0.7			1128	0.5
	1727	3.2			1753	3.5
	2250	1.6			2329	1.4
11 Sa	0451	3.6		26 Su	0536	3.9
	1136	0.7			1210	0.6
	1804	3.2			1834	3.4
	2329	1.6				
12 Su	0530	3.6		27 M	0016	1.5
	1213	0.8			0620	3.7
	1843	3.2			1252	0.9
					1915	3.4
13 M	0011	1.6		28 Tu	0105	1.5
	0611	3.5			0705	3.4
	1251	0.9			1333	1.1
	1924	3.3			1956	3.3
14 Tu	0058	1.6		29 W	0157	1.6
	0659	3.4			0753	3.2
	1332	1.1			1416	1.4
	2008	3.3			2041	3.3
15 W	0150	1.6		30 Th	0257	1.7
	0753	3.3			0848	2.9
	1417	1.2			1501	1.6
	2056	3.3		☽	2129	3.2

JULY

Day	Time	ft		Day	Time	ft
1 F	0406	1.7		16 Sa	0345	1.4
	0955	2.7			0953	3.1
	1552	1.8			1540	1.7
	2223	3.2		☾	2218	3.7
2 Sa	0521	1.7		17 Su	0457	1.3
	1124	2.6			1113	3.0
	1653	2.0			1646	1.8
	2321	3.2			2320	3.8
3 Su	0631	1.5		18 M	0609	1.2
	1254	2.6			1237	3.0
	1757	2.0			1756	1.9
4 M	0019	3.3		19 Tu	0024	3.8
	0728	1.4			0715	1.0
	1356	2.7			1347	3.1
	1858	2.0			1903	1.9
5 Tu	0113	3.4		20 W	0125	3.9
	0814	1.2			0812	0.8
	1442	2.9			1443	3.3
	1950	1.9			2002	1.8
6 W	0200	3.5		21 Th	0221	4.1
	0854	1.0			0902	0.7
	1521	3.0			1530	3.4
	2034	1.9			2054	1.7
7 Th	0243	3.6		22 F	0311	4.1
	0931	1.0			0946	0.7
	1557	3.1			1612	3.6
	2115	1.8		○	2142	1.5
8 F	0323	3.7		23 Sa	0357	4.0
	1007	0.9			1027	0.7
	1632	3.3			1650	3.6
●	2154	1.7			2227	1.5
9 Sa	0402	3.8		24 Su	0439	4.0
	1043	0.7			1106	0.8
	1708	3.4			1726	3.7
	2233	1.6			2310	1.4
10 Su	0442	3.9		25 M	0519	4.0
	1119	0.7			1143	0.9
	1743	3.5			1801	3.7
	2314	1.5			2353	1.4
11 M	0522	3.9		26 Tu	0558	3.8
	1155	0.8			1220	1.1
	1821	3.6			1836	3.7
	2358	1.4				
12 Tu	0605	3.8		27 W	0037	1.5
	1232	0.9			0637	3.6
	1900	3.6			1255	1.3
					1912	3.6
13 W	0045	1.4		28 Th	0123	1.5
	0651	3.7			0719	3.3
	1311	1.1			1330	1.5
	1942	3.7			1950	3.5
14 Th	0138	1.4		29 F	0215	1.6
	0743	3.5			0807	3.1
	1354	1.3			1406	1.7
	2028	3.7			2032	3.4
15 F	0237	1.4		30 Sa	0316	1.7
	0843	3.3			0906	2.8
	1443	1.5			1447	1.9
	2120	3.7		☽	2121	3.3
				31 Su	0427	1.7
					1023	2.7
					1544	2.1
					2220	3.3

AUGUST

Day	Time	ft		Day	Time	ft
1 M	0542	1.7		16 Tu	0554	1.3
	1205	2.6			1230	3.1
	1703	2.2			1748	2.1
	2326	3.3				
2 Tu	0649	1.5		17 W	0014	3.9
	1326	2.8			0704	1.2
	1819	2.2			1338	3.3
					1857	2.0
3 W	0033	3.4		18 Th	0119	4.0
	0744	1.4			0801	1.1
	1417	3.0			1430	3.5
	1919	2.1			1956	1.9
4 Th	0131	3.6		19 F	0215	4.1
	0827	1.2			0848	1.1
	1456	3.2			1512	3.6
	2009	2.0			2046	1.7
5 F	0220	3.7		20 Sa	0304	4.1
	0906	1.0			0928	1.0
	1531	3.4			1549	3.8
	2052	1.8			2130	1.6
6 Sa	0304	3.9		21 Su	0346	4.2
	0942	0.9			1004	1.1
	1605	3.6			1623	3.9
	2133	1.6		○	2211	1.5
7 Su	0346	4.1		22 M	0425	4.1
	1018	0.9			1039	1.1
	1639	3.8			1655	3.9
●	2215	1.4			2251	1.4
8 M	0428	4.1		23 Tu	0501	4.0
	1054	0.9			1113	1.2
	1715	3.9			1726	3.9
	2258	1.3			2330	1.4
9 Tu	0510	4.1		24 W	0536	3.9
	1130	0.9			1147	1.4
	1752	4.0			1758	3.9
	2344	1.1				
10 W	0555	4.0		25 Th	0010	1.4
	1208	1.0			0613	3.7
	1831	4.1			1219	1.5
					1830	3.8
11 Th	0032	1.2		26 F	0052	1.5
	0642	3.9			0653	3.4
	1248	1.2			1251	1.7
	1913	4.1			1905	3.7
12 F	0125	1.2		27 Sa	0138	1.6
	0735	3.6			0740	3.2
	1332	1.4			1324	1.9
	2001	4.0			1944	3.6
13 Sa	0224	1.3		28 Su	0231	1.7
	0835	3.4			0836	3.0
	1423	1.7			1402	2.1
	2054	3.9			2030	3.5
14 Su	0329	1.3		29 M	0336	1.8
	0946	3.2			0946	2.8
	1523	1.9			1456	2.3
☽	2155	3.9			2128	3.4
15 M	0441	1.3		30 Tu	0451	1.8
	1107	3.1			1115	2.8
	1633	2.0			1618	2.4
	2303	3.8			2239	3.4
				31 W	0604	1.7
					1245	3.0
					1742	2.4
					2354	3.5

TIME MERIDIAN 60°W

Heights in feet are referred to the chart datum of sounding.

0000h is midnight, 1200h is noon.

REED'S NAUTICAL ALMANAC

PORT OF SPAIN, TRINIDAD

HIGH & LOW WATER 1994 10°39'N 61°31'W

ATLANTIC STANDARD TIME (GMT -4H)

Chapter 2

SEPTEMBER

Day	Time	ft	Time	ft	Day	Time	ft	Time	ft
1 Th	0704	1.6	1340	3.2	16 F	0112	3.9	0742	1.4
	1849	2.2				1407	3.7	1951	1.9
2 F	0100	0.7	0752	1.4	17 Sa	0200	4.0	0826	1.4
	1419	3.4	1942	2.0		1445	3.8	2030	1.7
3 Sa	0154	3.9	0832	1.3	18 Su	0253	4.1	0903	1.4
	1454	3.7	2028	1.8		1519	4.0	2118	1.6
4 Su	0242	4.1	0910	1.2	19 M ○	0333	4.1	0937	1.5
	1529	3.9	2112	1.5		1551	4.1	2155	1.4
5 M ●	0327	4.2	0947	1.1	20 Tu	0410	4.1	1010	1.5
	1605	4.1	2156	1.3		1622	4.1	2232	1.4
6 Tu	0412	4.3	1024	1.1	21 W	0444	4.0	1043	1.5
	1641	4.4	2241	1.1		1652	4.1	2309	1.3
7 W	0457	4.3	1102	1.1	22 Th	0518	3.9	1116	1.6
	1720	4.4	2328	1.0		1722	4.1	2346	1.3
8 Th	0543	4.2	1143	1.2	23 F	0555	3.7	1147	1.8
	1801	4.4				1753	4.0		
9 F	0018	0.9	0633	4.0	24 Sa	0026	1.4	0635	3.5
	1226	1.4	1845	4.4		1219	1.9	1827	3.8
10 Sa	0111	1.0	0728	3.7	25 Su	0108	1.5	0721	3.3
	1313	1.6	1935	4.2		1253	2.1	1904	3.7
11 Su	0209	1.1	0829	3.5	26 M	0156	1.6	0815	3.2
	1408	1.9	2031	4.1		1334	2.2	1949	3.6
12 M ◑	0313	1.3	0939	3.2	27 Tu	0253	1.8	0918	3.1
	1512	2.1	2137	3.9		1430	2.4	2048	3.5
13 Tu	0423	1.4	1058	3.3	28 W ◑	0401	1.8	1032	3.1
	1626	2.2	2251	3.8		1546	2.5	2200	3.4
14 W	0537	1.4	1217	3.4	29 Th	0512	1.8	1149	3.2
	1743	2.2				1706	2.4	2316	3.5
15 Th	0006	3.8	0646	1.5	30 F	0616	1.8	1248	3.4
	1320	3.5	1854	2.1		1815	2.3		

OCTOBER

Day	Time	ft	Time	ft	Day	Time	ft	Time	ft
1 Sa	0026	3.7	0707	1.7	16 Su	0152	3.8	0754	1.7
	1332	3.7	1912	2.0		1412	3.9	2025	1.7
2 Su	0120	3.9	0751	1.6	17 M	0238	3.9	0832	1.8
	1411	3.9	2000	1.7		1447	4.0	2100	1.5
3 M	0219	4.1	0832	1.5	18 Tu	0318	3.9	0906	1.8
	1449	4.2	2050	1.4		1519	4.1	2138	1.4
4 Tu	0308	4.2	0912	1.4	19 W ○	0354	3.8	0941	1.8
	1528	4.4	2136	1.1		1550	4.1	2213	1.3
5 W ●	0355	4.3	0953	1.3	20 Th	0429	3.8	1014	1.8
	1607	4.6	2224	0.9		1620	4.1	2249	1.2
6 Th	0443	4.2	1034	1.4	21 F	0504	3.7	1048	1.8
	1649	4.6	2312	0.7		1651	4.0	2326	1.2
7 F	0532	4.1	1118	1.5	22 Sa	0541	3.6	1121	1.9
	1732	4.6				1723	4.0		
8 Sa	0002	0.7	0624	4.0	23 Su	0004	1.3	0622	3.5
	1205	1.6	1820	4.5		1155	2.0	1757	3.9
9 Su	0055	0.8	0719	3.8	24 M	0044	1.4	0706	3.3
	1257	1.8	1912	4.3		1232	2.1	1835	3.7
10 M	0151	1.0	0818	3.6	25 Tu	0128	1.5	0755	3.3
	1355	2.0	2011	4.1		1315	2.3	1920	3.6
11 Tu ◑	0253	1.2	0925	3.3	26 W	0217	1.7	0850	3.2
	1501	2.1	2119	3.9		1409	2.4	2017	3.5
12 W	0400	1.4	1038	3.2	27 Th ◑	0314	1.8	0950	3.2
	1615	2.2	2235	3.8		1515	2.4	2125	3.5
13 Th	0510	1.6	1150	3.5	28 F	0417	1.8	1052	3.3
	1732	2.2	2350	3.7		1627	2.3	2237	3.5
14 F	0615	1.7	1249	3.6	29 Sa	0519	1.7	1149	3.5
	1844	2.0				1738	2.1	2348	3.6
15 Sa	0057	3.8	0710	1.7	30 Su	0614	1.7	1239	3.8
	1334	3.8	1940	1.8		1841	1.9		
					31 M	0054	3.7	0704	1.7
						1325	4.0	1937	1.5

NOVEMBER

Day	Time	ft	Time	ft	Day	Time	ft	Time	ft
1 Tu	0154	3.8	0751	1.6	16 W	0301	3.5	0834	1.9
	1409	4.3	2028	1.2		1446	3.9	2120	1.3
2 W	0248	4.0	0837	1.6	17 Th	0339	3.5	0911	1.9
	1452	4.5	2110	0.8		1520	3.9	2156	1.2
3 Th ●	0340	4.0	0922	1.5	18 F ○	0415	3.5	0948	1.8
	1536	4.6	2206	0.6		1554	3.9	2231	1.1
4 F	0430	4.0	1009	1.5	19 Sa	0451	3.4	1023	1.8
	1621	4.6	2256	0.5		1627	3.9	2308	1.1
5 Sa	0520	3.9	1057	1.6	20 Su	0529	3.4	1059	1.6
	1708	4.6	2346	0.6		1701	3.9	2346	1.1
6 Su	0611	3.8	1147	1.7	21 M	0608	3.4	1135	1.9
	1758	4.4				1737	3.8		
7 M	0037	0.7	0704	3.7	22 Tu	0024	1.2	0649	3.3
	1240	1.8	1851	4.2		1213	2.0	1816	3.7
8 Tu	0131	0.9	0800	3.6	23 W	0104	1.3	0733	3.3
	1337	1.9	1950	4.0		1256	2.1	1900	3.6
9 W	0228	1.2	0859	3.5	24 Th	0146	1.4	0819	3.3
	1441	2.0	2054	3.7		1346	2.1	1952	3.5
10 Th ◑	0328	1.4	1003	3.5	25 F	0232	1.6	0909	3.3
	1551	2.1	2206	3.6		1444	2.1	2052	3.4
11 F	0430	1.6	1107	3.5	26 Sa ◑	0324	1.7	1001	3.4
	1707	2.0	2321	3.5		1550	2.0	2158	3.4
12 Sa	0530	1.8	1204	3.6	27 Su	0420	1.7	1055	3.6
	1819	1.9				1701	1.9	2309	3.3
13 Su	0031	3.4	0625	1.9	28 M	0518	1.8	1149	3.7
	1252	3.7	1918	1.7		1809	1.6		
14 M	0130	3.4	0713	1.9	29 Tu	0022	3.4	0616	1.8
	1334	3.8	2005	1.6		1241	4.0	1911	1.3
15 Tu	0219	3.5	0755	1.9	30 W	0130	3.5	0711	1.7
	1411	3.8	2044	1.4		1332	4.2	2008	1.0

DECEMBER

Day	Time	ft	Time	ft	Day	Time	ft	Time	ft
1 Th	0231	3.6	0804	1.6	16 F	0323	3.1	0843	1.8
	1422	4.3	2100	0.7		1454	3.7	2138	1.0
2 F ●	0326	3.6	0856	1.6	17 Sa	0400	3.1	0923	1.8
	1511	4.4	2150	0.5		1531	3.7	2215	0.9
3 Sa	0417	3.7	0947	1.5	18 Su	0437	3.2	1001	1.7
	1600	4.5	2240	0.4		1608	3.7	2251	0.9
4 Su	0506	3.7	1037	1.5	19 M	0513	3.2	1037	1.7
	1649	4.4	2328	0.4		1644	3.8	2327	0.9
5 M	0555	3.6	1128	1.5	20 Tu	0549	3.3	1115	1.7
	1739	4.3				1721	3.7		
6 Tu	0017	0.6	0643	3.6	21 W	0003	0.9	0627	3.3
	1219	1.6	1830	4.1		1154	1.7	1800	3.7
7 W	0105	0.8	0731	3.5	22 Th	0039	1.0	0705	3.3
	1313	1.7	1923	3.8		1236	1.7	1842	3.6
8 Th	0155	1.0	0821	3.4	23 F	0116	1.1	0745	3.4
	1410	1.7	2018	3.5		1323	1.7	1928	3.5
9 F	0246	1.3	0913	3.4	24 Sa ◑	0155	1.2	0829	3.4
	1514	1.8	2119	3.3		1417	1.7	2022	3.3
10 Sa	0338	1.6	1008	3.4	25 Su	0239	1.4	0916	3.4
	1624	1.8	2229	3.1		1520	1.6	2120	3.2
11 Su	0432	1.8	1103	3.4	26 M	0330	1.5	1009	3.5
	1737	1.8	2346	3.0		1630	1.5	2235	3.0
12 M	0528	1.9	1157	3.4	27 Tu	0429	1.6	1106	3.6
	1843	1.6				1742	1.3	2354	3.0
13 Tu	0057	2.9	0622	1.9	28 W	0533	1.7	1204	3.8
	1247	3.5	1938	1.5		1849	1.0		
14 W	0155	2.9	0713	1.9	29 Th	0112	3.0	0638	1.7
	1333	3.5	2022	1.3		1303	3.9	1950	0.8
15 Th	0242	3.0	0800	1.9	30 F	0218	3.1	0739	1.6
	1414	3.6	2101	1.1		1400	4.0	2045	0.6
					31 Sa	0314	3.3	0836	1.5
						1454	4.1	2136	0.4

TIME MERIDIAN 60°W

0000h is midnight, 1200h is noon.

Heights in feet are referred to the chart datum of sounding.

1994 CARIBBEAN

VENEZUELA

<CAUTION: Our information on aids to navigation comes from official government sources. The latitudes and longitudes of these marks may not correspond to the readings from GPS receivers. Some aids have been reported as unreliable, missing, off position or showing incorrect characteristics. No single aid to navigation, or waypoint, should be relied upon as a sole means of fixing your position.>

ENTRY PROCEDURES

As the crow flies, it is almost 600 nautical miles from the Gulf of Paria to the Colombian border. The entire Caribbean coast of Venezuela measures about 1,700 miles. This area has become a popular cruising ground, especially during the hurricane season. See *Reed's Nautical Companion* for the country flag.

Before sailing to Venezuela you must obtain visas for everyone on board. This should be done at a Venezuelan embassy, such as the one in Port of Spain, on Bonaire, or the one on Grenada. In Port of Spain call (809) 627-9821 or 9823. You will need several passport photos to submit with your application. Generally, a visa is good for a two month stay initially, with extensions available for 1000 Bs (about $11.00 U.S.). Check on this when you arrive in the country. It is wise to request clearance for a stay longer than you intend, as the best laid plans tend to change. Your stay is timed from the day you enter the country, not from when you receive your visa.

For more information on visas contact the Venezuelan Embassy, 1099 30th Street NW, Washington, DC, 20007, (202) 342-2214. In the U.S. there are embassies in Miami, Chicago, New York and San Juan, Puerto Rico.

Ports of Entry include Güiria (10° 34'N, 62° 18'W), Carúpano (10° 40'N, 63° 15'W), Pampatar (10° 59'N, 63° 48'W), Cumaná (10° 28'N, 64° 11'W), Puerto La Cruz (10° 14'N, 64° 38'W), La Guaira (10° 37'N, 66° 56'W), Puerto Cabello (10° 29'N, 68° 00'W), Le Vela (11° 28'N, 69° 35'W), Las Piedras (11° 43'N, 70° 13'W) and Maracaibo (10° 38'N, 71° 36'W).

A pilot must be used when entering Maracaibo. The Islas Los Testigos do not have an official Port of Entry, but you can try reporting to the local officials. You should present your clearances in every harbor with a port captain or customs office. Business hours are general 0830 to 1600, with a break for lunch.

Upon arrival in port you should proceed to Customs (aduana), the National Guard, Immigration then the port officer. Any weapons must be declared to the National Guard, and will be sealed on board. Upon arrival in any port, you should repeat this process, showing your clearance, or "zarpe", from the last port. When requesting clearance to your next port, ask for permission to stop at any intermediate harbor along the way. To speed and simplify this process you might want to hire one of the commercial agents found in many ports.

Certain areas of the Orinoco basin suffer from malaria, and there is some cholera.

There are U.S. Consulates in Caracas and Maracaibo. In Caracas call (58 2) 285-3111, 2222 or 2475. In Maracaibo call (58 61) 84 25 3, or 84 25 4.

The monetary unit is the Bolivar (Bs). There are 100 centimos in 1 Bolivar. The current exchange rate (mid 1993) is about 90 Bolivars to one U.S. dollar.

The telephone country code for Venezuela is 58, followed by a one or two digit city code, then a local number.

The language spoken is Spanish.

REED'S NEEDS YOU!

It is difficult to obtain accurate and up-to-date information on many areas in the Caribbean. To provide the mariner with the best possible product we utilize many sources. *Reed's* welcomes your contributions, suggestions and updates. Please be as specific as possible, and include your address and phone number.
Thank you!

<Chapter 2>

RÍO ORINOCO

Orinoco Entrance Buoy EO, 9 00.0N, 60 18.0W, Fl W 6s, Black buoy marked "EO", Radar reflector.

Río Orinoco Approach Lighted Buoy "0.1.", 8 56.1N, 60 11.0W, Fl W 10s, 4M, SAFE WATER RW, pillar, Radar reflector 14M, RACON O(– – –).

GULF OF PARIA

PUNTA GORDA, 10 09.8N, 62 37.8W, Fl R 5s, 19ft., 3M, Aluminum and white column.

RÍO SAN JUAN

Buoy "E-1.", 10 19.0N, 62 28.0W, Fl W 5s, 11ft., Black buoy.
LIGHT 1, 10 18.5N, 62 29.2W, Q W, 13ft., 6M.
LIGHT 1-B, 10 18.4N, 62 31.0W, Q W, 14ft., 6M.
Güiria Approach Lighted Buoy, 10 34.0N, 62 15.0W, Fl W 3s, White buoy.
GÜIRIA EAST BREAKWATER, S extremity, 10 33.7N, 62 17.3W, Fl R 4.3s, 30ft., 8M, Gray round concrete tower, F R lights on radio tower 0.9 mile N.
SOUTH BREAKWATER, E extremity, 10 33.8N, 62 17.5W, Fl G 9s, 16ft., 4M, Gray round concrete tower.

GÜIRIA
10 34N, 62 18W

Pilotage: This is a small harbor located in the northwestern portion of the Gulf of Paria. It is about 30 miles west of the tip of the peninsula. The port may be identified by the red-roofed towers of a church, the radio towers north of the harbor and the white tank on the high cliffs north of town. Several lights mark the entrance to the harbor. The pilot station for the Río San Juan and the Orinoco area is located here.
Port of Entry: This is the closest port to Trinidad for those headed west. The customs house is inshore of the western docks.
Dockage: You may be able to tie up along the breakwater in the western part of the harbor.
Anchorage: The best shelter would be inside the breakwaters, if there is room. Depths are reported to be better than fifteen feet.
Services: Limited supplies are available, including fuel.

PUERTO DE HIERRO, 10 38.2N, 62 05.6W, Fl W 6s, 262ft., 12M, White metal framework tower, red bands, Fl R on dolphin 789 meters ESE, Reported extinguished (1989).
ISLA DE PATOS, 10 38.1N, 61 52.1W, Fl W 6s, 374ft., 16M, White metal framework tower, black bands, Q R marks platform 15 miles S.
ENSENADA MACURO, E head of pier, 10 39.0N, 61 56.6W, Fl W 2s, 52ft., 9M, Metal tower.

NORTH COAST

ISLA TESTIGO GRANDE, 11 22.8N, 63 07.1W, Fl W 4.5s, 814ft., 10M, Tower, black and white bands.

LOS TESTIGOS
11 23N, 63 07W

Pilotage: This is a group of several islets and above-water rocks located about 48 miles northeast of Isla de Margarita, on the direct route from Grenada. Isla Testigo Grande, the largest island, rises to a height of over 800 feet on its northwest part. A light stands near the summit, but it has been reported as not visible from a distance of 5 miles. The island has been reported to be a good radar target at distances up to 22 miles.

The channels between some of the islands are deep and clear. The north islands are mostly unlighted, and surrounded by deep water. They should be given a wide berth at night, keeping in mind the constant northwestward-going current. This current varies in intensity and set. In August the rate may be as much as 1 1/2 knots. In February the set is more north-northwest, at a rate of 2 knots. In July, it may attain a speed of up to 3 knots.

There are several potential anchorages on the lee side of Isla Testigo Grande during periods of settled weather. Vessels should report to the authorities ashore, but this is not a Port of Entry.

CARÚPANO, Cerro Miranda SW exremity of Hernan Vasquez Bay, 10 40.5N, 63 14.6W, Fl W 9s, 190ft., 24M, Black metal framework tower.
HERNAN VASQUEZ, head of breakwater, 10 40.7N, 63 14.8W, Fl G 3.5s, 10ft., 3M, White metal tower black bands.

COAST PILOT

CARÚPANO

10 40N, 63 15W

Pilotage: This harbor lies near the western end of the Peninsula de Paria. It is about 40 miles southeast of Isla de Margarita. Depths of less than 36 feet can be found up to a mile off-shore in this area. Boats should stay in depths of over 36 feet until directly off the port, due to the shoals and foul areas on either side of the harbor. Vessels should stay at least 1 1/2 miles off the coast from here to Morro de Chacopata, 33 miles to the west. A strong westward setting current will be found all along this coast. Some radio masts 3/4 mile south of the the break-water, a cathedral, and a white church with twin spires are prominent landmarks. The port has a pier protected by a breakwater on its northeast side.

Port of Entry: This is the first port of entry west of Trinidad, and north of the Peninsula de Paria.

Dockage: You may be able to tie up stern-to on one of the wharves.

Anchorage: Anchor off the docks. Reports of swells and rough conditions are frequent.

Services: Most basic supplies are available.

MORRO DE CHACOPATA, 10 42.5N, 63 48.8W, Fl W 15s, 164ft., 16M, White metal framework tower, black bands, Reported extinguished (1990).
Isla Coche Buoy, 10 50.0N, 64 01.0W, Fl W 4s, Black buoy.

ISLA CUBAGUA

PUNTA CHARAGATO, NE extremity, 10 50.5N, 64 09.4W, Fl W 3s, 20ft., 10M, White concrete hexagonal tower with black bands.
PUNTA PALANQUETE, NW side of island, 10 49.8N, 64 12.6W, Fl W 8s, 42ft., 10M, Fiberglass tower.

LOS FRAILES

11 12N, 63 44W

Pilotage: This is a group of rocky islets, locat-ed about 7 to 9 miles east-northeast of Cabo de La Isla on Isla de Margarita. The islets have sparse vegetation, and are steep-to. The south islet is the largest, rising to a height of 300 feet. The group has been reported to be a good radar target at distances up to 24 miles. Roca del Norte (11° 16'N, 63° 45'W) is a small rock about 10 feet high, located about 3 miles

north of Los Frailes. La Sola is a small rock about 25 feet high, located about 10 3/4 miles east-northeast of Roca del Norte.

ISLA DE MARGARITA

CABO DE LA ISLA (Cabo Negro), on summit of hill at point, 11 10.5N, 63 53.1W, Fl W 10s, 1360., 12M, White fiberglass tower, Orange boards.
AVIATION LIGHT 10 55.0N, 63 58.2W, Al Fl W G 10s, On roof of control tower.
PUNTA MOSQUITO, 10 54.0N, 63 53.7W, Fl W 5.5s, 95ft., 12M, White fiberglass tower, orange bands, R lights mark mast 7 miles NNW.

PAMPATAR

10 59N, 63 48W

Pilotage: The harbor is located on the eastern end of Isla de Margarita, and is convenient for those voyaging from the Lesser Antilles via the Islas Los Testigos. The bay is generally clear of dangers. A fort with two towers stands on the shore and is a good landmark. The bay is very exposed to the prevailing easterly winds, but there is a new breakwater providing some protection. You can land at the public pier.

Port of Entry: Cruisers report favorably on the agents known as Shore Base — they moni-tor VHF channel 68.

Dockage: There are a couple of small marinas in Porlamar.

Anchorage: The anchorage area has some protection from the east, but is wide open to the southeast.

Services: Limited supplies are available. For help with marine problems contact Shore Base. You can take a bus to Porlamar for the supermarkets and open-air market.

MORRO DEL ROBLEDAR, 11 02.8N, 64 22.4W, Fl W 5s, 262ft., 16M, White fiberglass tower, orange bands.
Araya Bank Lighted Buoy, outer end of bank, 10 39.0N, 64 19.0W, Fl W 3s, Red buoy.
CUMANA, Puerto Sucre, SE corner of pier, 10 27.6N, 64 11.7W, Fl W 4.4s, 33ft., 6M, Concrete hexagonal pyramid black and white bands.

CUMANÁ

10 28N, 64 11W

Pilotage: The harbor is located on Punta Caranero at the entrance to the Golfo de Cari-aco. There is a light at the airport reported on

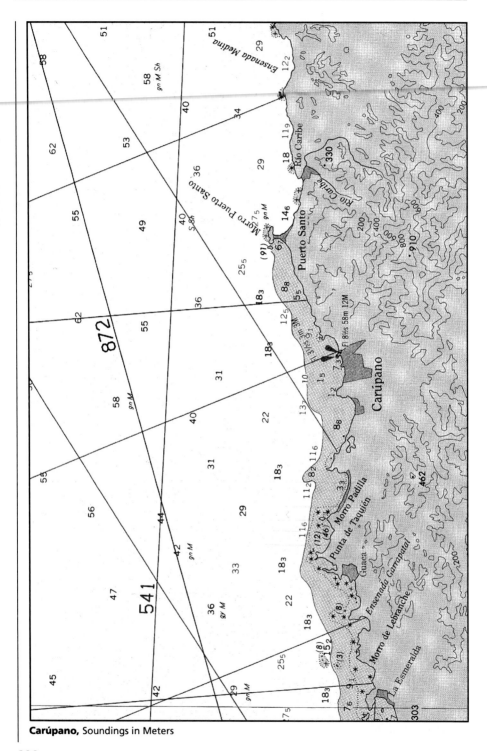

Carúpano, Soundings in Meters

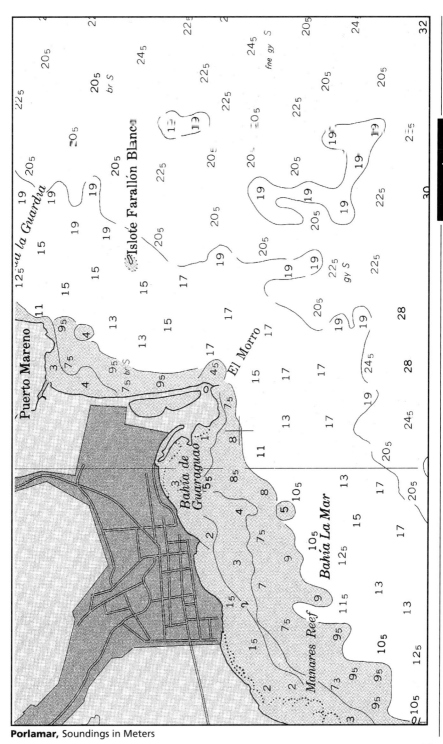

Porlamar, Soundings in Meters

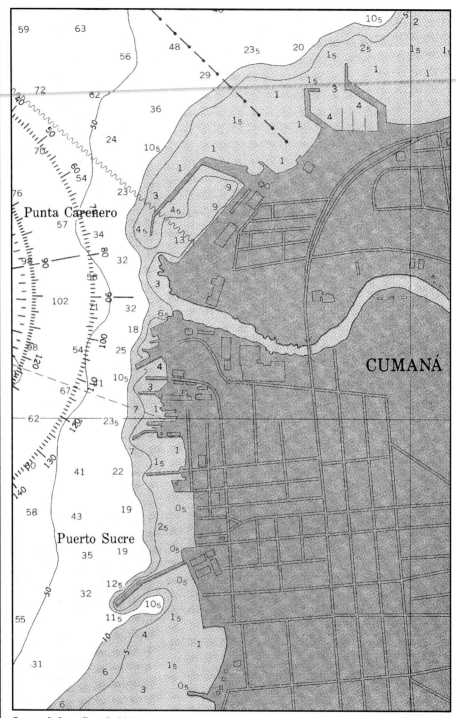

Cumaná, Soundings in Meters

the chart to be Al Fl W G. This is located south, and inland of the commercial port known as Puerto Sucre. The main pier projects southwest from the coast for 400 yards. The Customs office is near the root of the pier. The yacht marina is located on the north side of the point, a bit northeast of the fishing harbor. There are reported to be red and green private marks indicating the dredged channel into the marina.

Port of Entry

Anchorage: You can anchor off of town, near the commercial pier.

Services: Fuel and water are available in the marina. There are haulout facilities and workboat oriented repair shops. There are several good chandleries.

BAHÍA GUANTA

PUNTA QUEQUE, 10 15.1N, 64 35.6W, Fl G 6s, 30ft., 5M, Black metal framework tower.
ISLA REDONDA, 10 15.4N, 64 35.6W, Fl G 6s, 27ft., 5M, Concrete hexagonal pyramid tower, red and white bands.
MORRO DE PITAHAYA, 10 15.4N, 64 35.7W, Fl R 3.5s, 65ft., 6M, Concrete hexagonal pyramid tower, red and white bands.

PUERTO LA CRUZ
10 14N, 64 38W

Pilotage: This is a major commercial and oil port, as well as a growing recreational boating center. The adjacent islands are relatively high and rocky with sparse vegetation. The radio towers 4 miles southwest and 3 miles south of the town are prominent. There is a major light on the summit of Morro Pelotas 2 miles east of town.

Port of Entry: Call Zip Express on VHF channel 68 for assistance with the formalities.

Dockage: There are several marinas in this area including Paseo Colón, El Morro and Americo Vespucio .

Anchorage: Many boats anchor off the beach. Dinghy theft has been reported in this area. This is a favorite area for those waiting out the hurricane season.

Services: Fuel is available in the marinas. Most marine services are available, including haulouts. There are good supermarkets and general stores of all types.

ISLA CHIMANA SEGUNDA, W end, 10 17.8N, 64 36.4W, Fl W 10s, 157ft., 10M, White fiberglass tower, orange bands.

ISLA LA BLANQUILLA, S end, 11 49.7N, 64 36.1W, L Fl W 10s, 66ft., 12M, Cylindrical, fiberglass tower with white and orange bands, Visible 090°-260°.

LA BLANQUILLA
11 52N, 64 36W

Pilotage: This roundish island is about 5 miles in diameter, rising to a height of about 60 feet. It is located about 50 miles north-northwest of the western end of Isla de Margarita. The island is reported to be a good radar target at distances of up to 13 miles. The radar image is better when approaching from the west. There is a light on the south side.

There are several possible anchorages on the southeastern side of the island.

LOS HERMANOS
11 47N, 64 25W

Pilotage: This chain of 7 barren, rocky islets lie about 45 miles north of the west end of Isla de Margarita. All of the islets are steep-to, and have clear deep passages between them. Isla Grueso, the largest, rises to a height of 650 feet, and is reported to be a good radar target at distances up to 25 miles. Isla Chiquito is the smallest islet, and is at the southern end of the group.

BAHÍA BERGANTIN

Entrance Buoy, 10 15.0N, 64 39.0W, Fl W 3s.
ISLA BURRO LIGHT "3", 10 14.7N, 64 38.2W, Fl R 3s, 13ft., 2M, Yellow hut on concrete platform.
LIGHT "4", 10 14.6N, 64 38.1W, Fl R 3s, 13ft., 2M, Yellow hut on concrete platform.
LIGHT "5", 10 14.7N, 64 37.9W, Fl R 3s, 13ft., 2M, Yellow hut on concrete platform. F R on radio mast 1 mile ESE.
LIGHT "6", 10 14.8N, 64 37.8W, Fl W 3s, 13ft., 2M, Yellow hut on concrete platform.
LIGHT "7", 10 14.8N, 64 37.9W, Fl R 3s, 13ft., 2M, Yellow hut on concrete platform.
CARGO DOCK, W end, 10 14.4N, 64 38.1W, Q R, 3M.
BARCELONA AVIATION LIGHT, 10 07.2N, 64 41.0W, Al Fl W G 20s, FL R on radio tower 4 miles N, 5 F R on radio tower 1 mile NW, F R on radio towers 5 miles NE, F W and F R on radio towers 9 miles NE.
Punta Puinare Buoy, about 274 meters S of point on Chimana del Oeste, 10 17.0N, 64 41.0W, Fl W 3s, Black buoy.

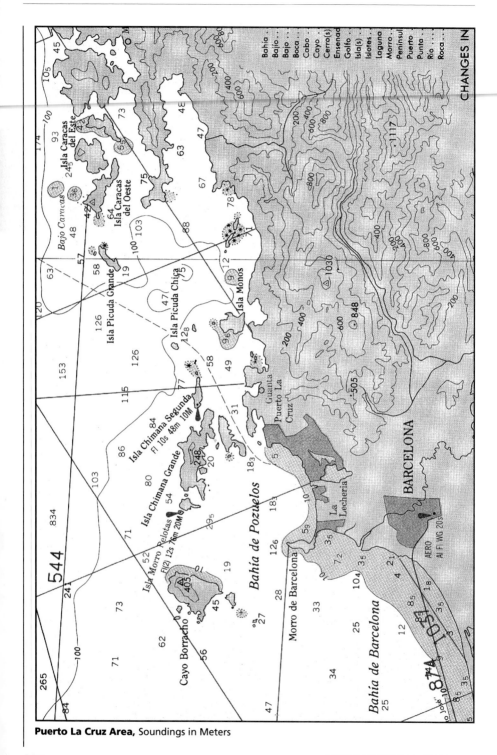

Puerto La Cruz Area, Soundings in Meters

MORRO PELOTA, summit, 10 18.3N, 64 41.1W, Fl (2) W 12s, 250ft., 15M, White framework tower, Visible 320°– 056°, 101°– 180°, Irregular (1979).

CAYO BARRACHO, 10 18.2N, 64 44.1W, 30M, RACON B(– · · ·).

ISLAS PIRITU, W end of W island, 10 10.1N, 64 58.7W, Fl W 10s, 36ft., 11M, Cylindrical fiberglass tower and white and orange bands.

ISLA LA TORTUGA

PUNTA ORIENTAL, 10 53.9N, 65 12.1W, Fl W 7s, 56ft., 14M, White metal framework tower, black bands, F R on radio towers 3.7 miles W, 8 miles WNW and 4.1 miles NW.

CAYO HERRADURA, 10 59.5N, 65 23.7W, Fl W 12s, 59ft., 9M, Black metal framework tower.

ISLA LA TORTUGA

10 56N, 65 18W

Pilotage: This barren island is about 12 miles long (east to west) and 6 miles wide. It rises to a height of over 130 feet. The island is located about 46 miles west of Isla de Margarita.

The south coast of the island is bold and steep-to, but the west and northwest sides are fringed by a sand and coral shoal that extends up to 2 miles offshore. Las Tortuguillas (2 small islets) and Cayo Herradura lie near the outer edge of this shoal area. Several lighted radio towers stand in various locations on the island, and there are lights on Punta Oriental and Cayo Herradura. The island has been reported to be a good radar target at distances up to 24 miles.

There are several possible anchorages along the west and north coasts.

ISLA FARALLIN, "El Centinela", 10 48.9N, 66 05.5W, Fl (2) W 15s, 125ft., 15M, White fiberglass tower, with orange bands.

FARALLON CENTINELA

10 49N, 66 05W

Pilotage: This prominent, light colored rock, from which a light is shown, rises to an elevation of about 90 feet. It lies about 14 miles north of Cabo Codera on the Venezuelan coast. The northeast side is steep, but the southwest side slopes gradually to the sea. A rock, which breaks, lies 1/4 mile to the north-west. Farallon Centinella has been reported to be a poor radar target at a distance of 7 miles.

HIGUEROTE, E breakwater, head, 10 29.7N, 66 05.7W, Fl R.

PUERTO CARENERO, 10 32.3N, 66 06.8W, Fl W 9s, 138ft., 10M, Skeleton tower building.

CABO CODERA, 10 34.7N, 66 02.9W, Fl W 6s, 876ft., 25M, Black skeleton tower.

PUNTA CAMURI-GRANDE, 10 37.7N, 66 43.0W, Fl W R 3s, 43ft., 7M, Yellow masonry tower, black bands, W 029 – 063°, R 029°.

NAIGUATA, 10 36.9N, 66 45.0W, Iso W R G 2s, 52ft., 8M, White concrete tower, black bands.

PUERTO DEL GUAICAMACUTO HOTEL, W head, main breakwater, 10 37.6N, 66 50.7W, Fl W 5s, 22ft., 8M, White concrete tower, red bands, F R on hotel 5.55 miles 204°, Extinguished (1984).

LA GÜAIRA

AVIATION LIGHT, 10 36.4N, 66 59.5W, Al Fl W G 10s, 465ft., 15M, Metal framework tower.

LA GÜAIRA, 10 35.1N, 66 56.7W, L Fl W 15.5s, 1,394ft., 25M, Orange barrel, Visible 291°– 028°.

N BREAKWATER, 10 36.6N, 66 56.9W, Fl G 3.7s, 33ft., 6M, Green metal tower, Extinguished (1984).

S BREAKWATER, 10 36.1N, 66 57.3W, Fl R 3s, 29ft., 5M, Pyramid tower, red and white bands.

BREAKWATER, head, 10 36.3N, 66 56.6W, Fl R 2.5s, 23ft., 5M, Concrete pyramid tower, red and white bands.

LA GÜAIRA

10 37N, 66 56W

Pilotage: This is an artificial harbor created by breakwaters to serve the city of Caracas. The north breakwater is 1500 meters long. There can be considerable scend in the harbor. This harbor is very commercial and is generally avoided by pleasure boats except those wishing to clear in to the country. The nearby marinas offer better shelter to yachtsmen.

Port of Entry

Dockage: There are marinas in Catia La Mar, 4 miles to the west, and at Caraballeda, 6 miles to the east. There is another marina at Punta Naiguata, a further 6 miles east of Caraballeda. Most yachtsmen will want to berth at one of these locations if visiting Caracas or La Güaira. You may be able to tie up at the main docks in La Güaira while clearing with the officials.

Chapter 2

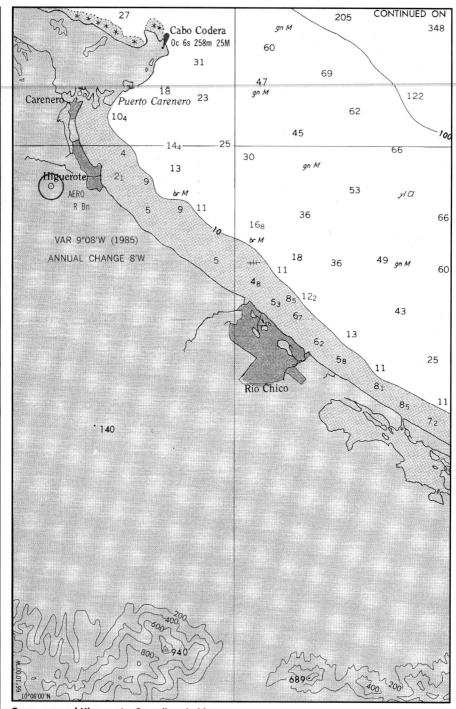

Caranero and Higuerote, Soundings in Meters

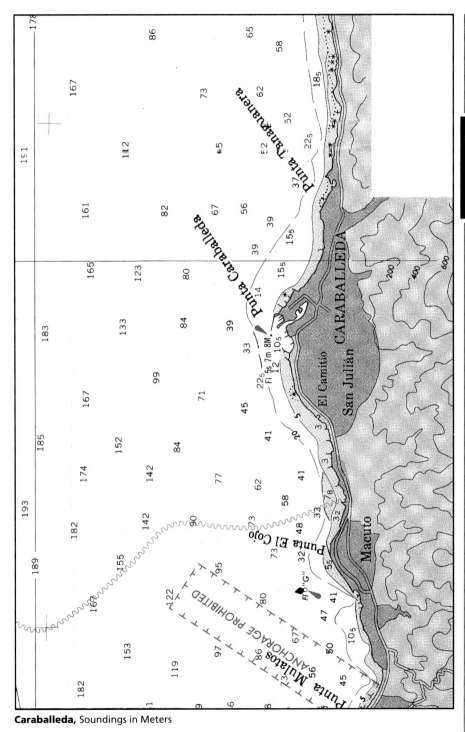

Caraballeda, Soundings in Meters

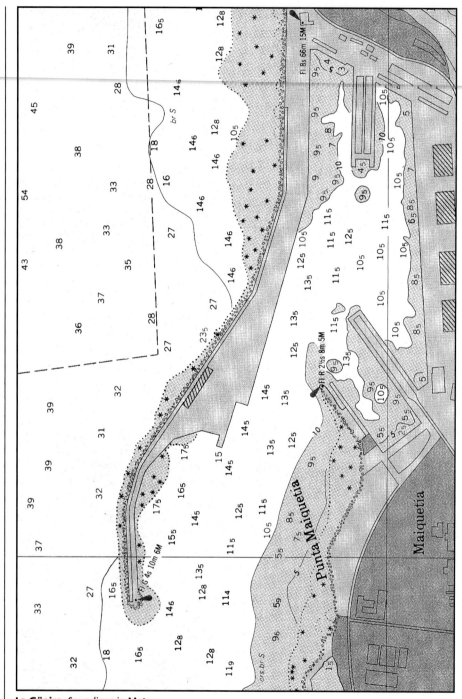

La Güaira, Soundings in Meters

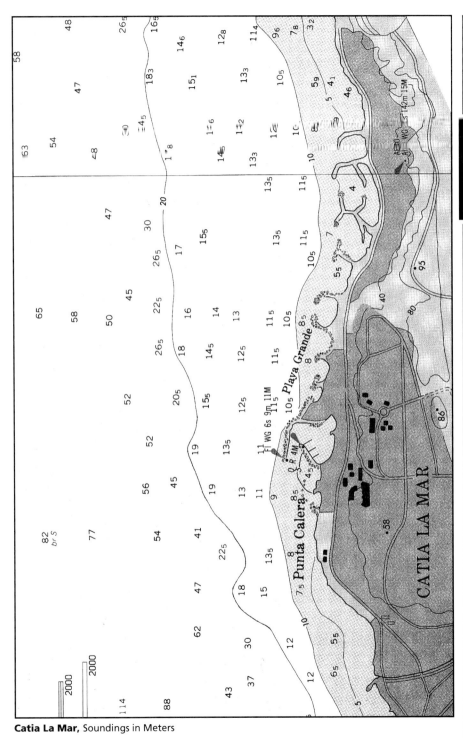

Catia La Mar, Soundings in Meters

Anchorage: This would be an emergency anchorage only. You can anchor near one of the marinas mentioned above.
Services: There are no yacht oriented facilities in La Guaira, but you can find most services at the marinas.

PLAYA GRANDE YACHT BASIN WESTERN LIGHT, 10 37.2N, 67 00.9W, Fl G 6s, 30ft., 11M, Truncated tower, red bands.
EASTERN LIGHT, Q R, 16ft., 4M, Metal tower.
CATIA LA MAR, outer end of pier, 10 36.4N, 67 02.4W, Fl R 2s, 20ft., 9M, Triangular daymark point upward.
TACOA, 10 35.5N, 67 04.9W, Fl R.

LA ORCHILLA

CERRO WALKER, 11 49.1N, 66 11.0W, Fl W 11.5s, 449ft., 15M, Black metal structure.
LA ORCHILLA, head of pier, 11 48.6N, 66 11.9W, Fl W 4s, 19ft., 5M, Concrete pyramid tower, orange and white bands.

LA ORCHILLA
11 48N, 66 08W

Pilotage: This small (6 miles long) island is generally low and flat, but has seven distinct hills on its north side. These hills are visible from 15 miles, and when first sighted from the north or south, appear as separate islands. A 262 foot high hill stands on the west end of the island, and Cerro Walker, the summit of the island, rises to 457 feet about 1 mile east of this hill. The island is reported to be a good radar target at distances up to 16 miles.

Cayo Nordeste (11° 52'N, 66° 06'W) is the largest of a series of small cays lying on a bank extending north-northeast from the northeast end of La Orchilla. Some ruined buildings can be seen on the north end of Cayo Nordeste.

CAUTION: Due to a naval base, the area around La Orchilla is restricted and closed to general navigation.

ISLAS LOS ROQUES

CAYO GRANDE, Sebastopol, 11 46.8N, 66 34.9W, Fl W 6s, 26ft., 12M, Cylindrical, fiberglass tower with white and orange bands.
CAYO DE AGUA, 11 50.3N, 66 57.2W, Fl W 9s, 49ft., 10M, Cylindrical, fiberglass tower with white and orange bands.

EL GRAN ROQUE, 11 57.5N, 66 41.1W, Fl W 10s, 220ft., 10M, Black framework tower.

ISLAS LOS ROQUES
11 50N, 66 43W

Pilotage: This group of many cays, and an extensive and dangerous coral reef, lie 22 miles west of La Orchilla and about 70 miles north of La Guaira. The cays tend to be covered with scrub and they are all lower than 25 feet except for El Roque, which rises to 380 feet. El Roque lies on the northern extremity of the reef. The north extremity of the cay is in position 11° 58'N, 66° 41'W. A light is shown from this cay, and there is a prominent disused lighthouse nearby. It has been reported as a good radar target at distances up to 23 miles.

A light is also shown from the southeast point of Cayo Grande, at the southeast end of the island group. There is a light at the western end of the group in position 11° 50'N, 66° 57'W.

The south side of the group is steep-to, but be careful when approaching the eastern side as the strong west-northwest-going current and easterly winds can make this a dangerous lee shore.

Puerto El Roque (11° 57'N, 66° 39'W) is an anchorage area near the north part of Los Roques. Vessels should obtain local knowledge before entering.

ISLAS DE AVES

AVES DE BARLOVENTO, on S island of group, 11 56.6N, 67 26.6W, Fl W 8.5s, 72ft., 12M, Black metal framework tower.
AVE DE SOTAVENTO, on N island of group, 12 03.6N, 67 41.0W, Fl W 15s, 75ft., 14M, Black metal framework tower.
MORRO CHORONI, 10 30.6N, 67 36.1W, Fl W 5s, 246ft., 10M, White metal framework tower.
ISLA TURIAMO, 10 29.0N, 67 50.4W, Fl W 9s, 66ft., 10M, White framework tower.
BAHÍA DE TURIAMO, pier head, 10 27.5N, 67 50.7W, Fl W 3.3s, 17ft., 6M, Black metal structure.
ISLA ALCATRAZ, 10 30.5N, 67 58.6W, Fl W 6s, 69ft., 10M, Black metal framework tower, black stripes.

ISLA DE AVES
12 00N, 67 24W

Pilotage: Another island with this name, also a Venezuelan possession, lies in position 15° 40'N, 63° 37'W (128 miles west of Dominica). This group of cays lies about 28 1/2 miles west of Islas Los Roques. There are two groups of low cays, about 8 1/2 miles apart lying on dangerous coral reefs.

The eastern group (11° 58'N, 67° 26'W) is called Ave de Barlovento. It is an area of small cays and shoals forming a circle about 5 miles in diameter. The east and north sides of the group form an almost continuous drying reef. Heavy breakers occur along this reef. The group is reported to be a good radar target at distances up to 15 miles. There are possible local-knowledge-only anchorages on the north sides of the cays.

Ave de Sotavento (12° 00'N, 67° 40'W) is the western group, and is only about 33 miles east of Bonaire. A large cay on its southern side is mostly covered with mangroves. An unbroken drying reef extends from this cay along the east and north sides of the group. Heavy surf breaks along the entire reef, and there is foul ground up to 1/2 mile from it. The cay is reported to be a good radar target at distances up to 14 miles. There are possible anchorages within the reefs, for those with local knowledge.

PUERTO CABELLO

PUNTA BRAVA, 10 29.4N, 68 00.6W, Fl W 8s, 95ft., 18M, White metal framework tower on white square tower, red bands, Visible 105°– 255°, F R lights on radio mast 0.6 mile S, Reported Fl W 6s (1987).
ISLA GUAIGUAZA, 10 29.6N, 68 02.6W, Fl W 7.5s, 34ft., 8M, Black metal framework tower.
FORT LIBERTADOR, on pier, 10 29.0N, 68 00.7W, Fl G 7s, 6ft., 1M, Black concrete tower, white bands.
NAVAL QUAY SW END, 10 29.1N, 68 00.2W, Fl G, 20ft., 4M, Black framework tower.
PIER P.I., 10 29.0N, 68 00.5W, Oc R, Red mast.
Buoy, S side of channel entrance, 10 29.0N, 68 01.0W, Fl R 7s, 7ft., 1M, Red buoy.
PIER HEAD, 10 29.3N, 68 00.0W, F G, 20ft., White concrete pyramid tower, green bands.
FORTIN SOLANO, 10 27.8N, 68 01.2W, Fl (3) W 15.5s, 525ft., 18M, Metal framework tower.

PUERTO CABELLO
10 29N, 68 00W

Pilotage: This is the third ranking port in Venezuela. Bajo Larne is a 19 to 20 foot deep shoal located about 1/4 mile northeast of Isla Goaigoaza. The shoal breaks when any sea is raised. There is a prominent power plant located about 2 miles west of town. The marina is located in the outer harbor, south of the main ship channel. The northern part of the inner harbor is a prohibited naval area. The port authority and customs house is located on the wharves to the south, near the entrance.
Port of Entry
Dockage: Tie up in the Marina Puerto Cabello, located west of the charted steeple.
Anchorage: Anchor near the marina.
Services: Most services are available. Some marine supplies There are good supermarkets and general shops in town.

PIERHEAD, 10 29.4N, 68 02.1W, Fl R, Reported Fl Y (Dec 1985).
PUERTO CABELLO AVIATION LIGHT, 10 28.6N, 68 04.5W, Al Fl W G 4s, 73ft., 14M, On airport control tower.
PUNTA CHAVEZ, NW head of pier, 10 29.6N, 68 07.4W, Oc R 3s, 80ft., 10M, Aluminum tower, Reported extinguished (1980).
PUNTA CHAVEZ, SE head of pier, Fl G 3s, 80ft., 10M, Aluminum tower, Reported extingusihed (1980).
MORON OIL TERMINAL, 10 31.1N, 68 11.3W, Fl W 3s, 10M, Red post, white bands.
CAYO BORRACHO, 10 59.0N, 68 14.9W, Fl W 8s, 46ft., 12M, Black metal tower.
CAYO NOROESTE, N side, 11 13.2N, 68 26.9W, Fl W 5.3s, 33ft., 10M, Black skeleton tower.
PUNTA AGUIDE, 11 21.0N, 68 41.1W, L Fl W R 15s, 190ft., W 18M R 7M, White metal framework tower, black bands, W shore 198°, R 218°, W shore.
PUNTA ZAMURO, 11 26.6N, 68 50.0W, Fl W 10s, 36ft., 12M, White metal and concrete framework tower, black top.
PUNTA MANZANILLO, 11 32.0N, 69 16.2W, Fl W 6s, 150ft., 15M, White metal framework tower, black bands.
PUEBLO CUMAREBO, 11 29.0N, 69 21.2W, F R, 57ft., 9M, White masonry tower.
PUNTA TAIMA TAIMA, 11 30.2N, 69 30.0W, Fl W 7s, 191ft., 12M, White metal framework tower, black bands.
LA VELA, 11 27.7N, 69 34.1W, Fl W, 65ft., 6M.

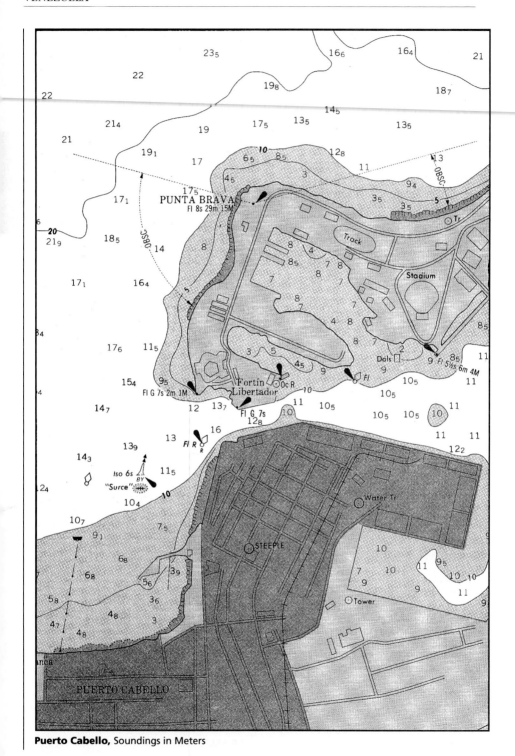

Puerto Cabello, Soundings in Meters

LA VELA

11 28N, 69 35W

Pilotage: The harbor is located in the southeast portion of Bahía Vela de Coro. It is the last harbor before rounding the Peninsula de Paraguaná. There is a pier located about 1 3/4 miles northeast of the town. The customhouse is a conspicuous white building with a red roof and the word "Aduana" painted on top.

Caution: An abnormal magnetic disturbance has been observed between Puerto Cumarebo and La Vela.

Port of Entry

Anchorage: Punta Taimataima is reported to provide little shelter to the east. This harbor can be rough to untenable in strong winds. This is the last shelter for many miles if headed west in Venezuela.

Services: General supplies are available.

PUNTA ADICORA, 11 56.7N, 69 48.2W, Fl W 16s, 66ft., 16M, Black metal framework tower.

PENINSULA DE PARAGUANA

CABO SAN ROMAN, N side of peninsula, 12 11.3N, 70 00.1W, Fl W 6s, 79ft., 16M, Black metal framework tower.

MACOLLA, NW side of peninsula, 12 05.7N, 70 12.5W, Fl (2) W 15s, 131ft., 25M, Black metal tower, concrete base.

BAHÍA DE AMUAY, (Front Light) 11 45.1N, 70 12.4W, F G, 122ft., 5M, Orange diamond daymark on aluminum tank, Oc R 2s and 2 F R on each of 2 towers, 0.93 and 1.2 miles ESE. **(Rear Light)** 365 meters 074°45′ from front, F G, 156ft., 5M, Orange diamond daymark on aluminum tank.

LAS PIEDRAS, head of Naval Pier, 11 42.2N, 70 13.2W, Fl G 3s, 24ft., 8M, Concrete pyramid tower, white and green bands.

LAS PIEDRAS

11 43N, 70 13W

Pilotage: This village is located on the west side of the Peninsula de Paraguaná. There is a dangerous wreck located about 1 mile westsouthwest of Punta Piedras. Conspicuous water tanks stand on the eastern shore of Bahía Boca de Las Piedras. There are several commercial piers projecting from the town.

Port of Entry: Customs is located about 2 miles south of ß Boca de Las Piedras in Caleta Guaranao.

Anchorage: Strong northeast trade winds have been reported here, but you should have good shelter with the land to the east.

PUNTA GORDA, 11 38.1N, 70 13.9W, Fl W R 10s, 204ft., 21M, Radio tower, R 340°– 009°, W 202°, Reported extinguished (1992).

PUNTA BOTIJA

PIER NO 3, 11 37.1N, 70 14.0W, F W, 7ft., 5M, Concrete structure, Chimneys marked by red lights 0.6 mile and 1.5 miles NE.
PIER NO 1, (Front Light) 11 37.3N, 70 14.0W, F G, 13ft., 5M, Concrete structure. **(Rear Light)** 160 meters 061° from front, F G, 43ft., 5M, Metal structure.
PIER NO 2, (Front Light) 11 37.5N, 70 14.2W, F R, 13ft., 5M, Concrete structure. **(Rear Light)** 160 meters 061° from front, F R, 43ft., 5M, Metal structure.
PIER NO 4, 11 37.7N, 70 14.3W, F Blue, 13ft., 5M, Concrete structure.

PUERTO DE GUARANAO

GUARANAO PIER, S side, 11 40.3N, 70 13.0W, F R, 16ft., 3M.
N SIDE, 11 40.3N, 70 13.0W, F G, 16ft., 3M.

LAGO DE MARACAIBO ENTRANCE

MALECON DEL ESTE, E breakwater head, 11 01.4N, 71 34.9W, Fl Y 4s, 51ft., 10M, Fiberglass tower, white and orange bands. *Approach Whistle Buoy EM,* 11 13.6N, 71 33.5W, Fl (2) W 10s, SAFE WATER RW, pillar, topmark, Radar reflector, Whistle.

MARACAIBO

10 38N, 71 36W

Pilotage: This very commercial city is one of the busiest ports in Venezuela, and a major oil industry center. Be wary of large commercial ships inthe marked channels. When within ten miles of "EM" buoy you should establish contact with the pilot station (call San Carlos Pilot) on VHF channel 16. You may be required to carry a pilot to Maracaibo. In any case, it is wise to monitor the VHF while in this area. Squalls, known locally as chubascos, occur frequently from May to August, usually between the hours

Chapter 2

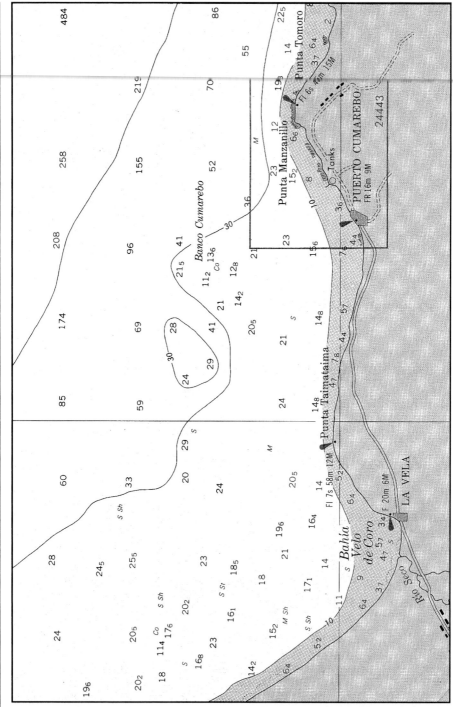

La Vela, Soundings in Meters

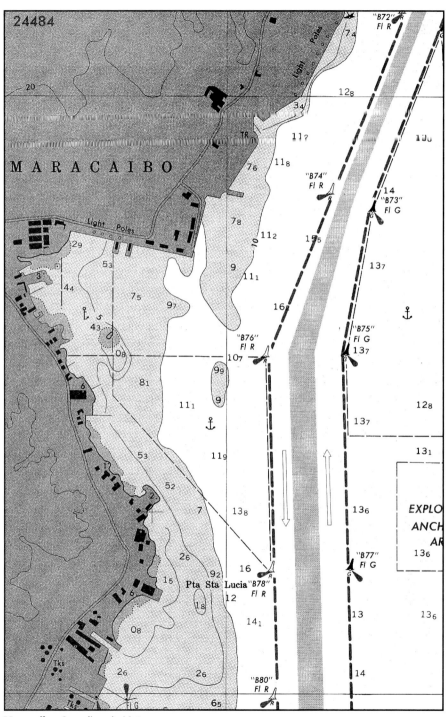

Maracaibo, Soundings in Meters

of 1400 and 1900. Winds are generally south to southeast with velocities of up to 50 knots. They may last for 1/2 to 1 hour. A heavy rain usually follows these squalls. In general, the waters of the Golfo de Venezuela are reported to be very rough with frequent high winds.

Port of Entry

Dockage: Contact the Club Nautico de Maracaibo or the Los Andes Yacht Club.

Anchorage: You might be able to anchor near the clubs, but the water is reported to be less than 6 feet deep.

Services: There is fuel, water and a haulout facility at Club Nautico. The city has good supermarkets, general stores and restaurants.

PUNTA PERRET, 11 47.7N, 71 20.3W,.Fl W 15s, 43ft., 15M, Black framework tower.
MONJES DEL SUR, 12 21.3N, 70 54.1W, Fl W 10.6s, 253ft., 10M, Conical stone tower, white and orange

PUNTA GORDA, VENEZUELA

HIGH & LOW WATER 1994 10°10'N 62°38'W

ATLANTIC STANDARD TIME (GMT -4H)

JANUARY

Day				
1 Sa	0134 -0.7	0721 6.5	1352 0.2	1926 6.8
2 Su	0215 -0.5	0803 6.5	1440 0.2	2013 6.5
3 M	0302 -0.2	0850 6.4	1536 0.3	2106 6.1
4 Tu	0356 0.2	0943 6.2	1640 0.4	2208 5.6
5 W	0500 0.6	1044 6.0	1749 0.3	◗ 2320 5.2
6 Th	0610 0.8	1154 5.9	1859 0.1	
7 F	0042 5.1	0721 0.8	1308 5.9	2005 -0.3
8 Sa	0202 5.2	0826 0.7	1418 6.1	2106 -0.7
9 Su	0312 5.4	0925 0.4	1520 6.4	2200 -1.1
10 M	0409 5.8	1018 0.1	1613 6.6	2249 -1.3
11 Tu	0456 6.0	1106 -0.1	1659 6.8	● 2334 -1.5
12 W	0537 6.1	1150 -0.2	1741 6.8	
13 Th	0017 -1.4	0614 6.2	1232 -0.3	1819 6.7
14 F	0057 -1.2	0649 6.2	1313 -0.2	1856 6.6
15 Sa	0136 -0.9	0722 6.1	1353 -0.1	1931 6.3
16 Su	0215 -0.6	0755 6.0	1433 0.1	2008 6.0
17 M	0254 -0.2	0830 5.8	1517 0.3	2048 5.6
18 Tu	0337 0.3	0908 5.6	1605 0.6	2132 5.2
19 W	0425 0.7	0952 5.4	1701 0.7	◗ 2225 4.8
20 Th	0521 1.1	1043 5.2	1804 0.8	2329 4.5
21 F	0624 1.3	1144 5.1	1908 0.7	
22 Sa	0043 4.4	0727 1.3	1251 5.1	2009 0.4
23 Su	0156 4.5	0826 1.1	1356 5.3	2104 0.1
24 M	0257 4.8	0919 0.8	1453 5.6	2153 -0.4
25 Tu	0347 5.1	1006 0.4	1546 5.9	2237 -0.7
26 W	0429 5.5	1050 0.1	1627 6.3	2318 -1.0
27 Th	0508 5.9	1130 -0.6	1709 6.6	O 2357 -1.2
28 F	0545 6.2	1212 -0.6	1750 6.8	
29 Sa	0036 -1.3	0623 6.5	1253 -0.7	1832 6.8
30 Su	0115 -1.2	0702 6.6	1336 -0.8	1915 6.7
31 M	0156 -0.9	0743 6.6	1423 -0.8	2001 6.4

FEBRUARY

Day				
1 Tu	0241 -0.6	0828 6.5	1516 -0.6	2052 5.9
2 W	0333 -0.1	0918 6.2	1616 -0.3	2150 5.4
3 Th	0435 0.4	1016 5.8	1724 -0.2	◖ 2300 4.9
4 F	0547 0.8	1126 5.5	1836 -0.1	
5 Sa	0023 4.6	0701 0.8	1247 5.4	1945 -0.3
6 Su	0150 4.7	0810 0.7	1405 5.6	2048 -0.6
7 M	0303 5.0	0910 0.3	1510 5.8	2143 -1.0
8 Tu	0358 5.4	1003 -0.1	1604 6.1	2232 -1.2
9 W	0442 5.7	1050 -0.4	1648 6.3	2315 -1.4
10 Th	0519 5.9	1132 -0.6	1727 6.4	● 2355 -1.3
11 F	0551 6.0	1211 -0.7	1802 6.4	
12 Sa	0032 -1.2	0621 6.1	1249 -0.7	1835 6.3
13 Su	0108 -1.0	0650 6.1	1325 -0.6	1906 6.1
14 M	0143 -0.6	0719 6.0	1401 -0.5	1939 5.9
15 Tu	0218 -0.3	0750 5.9	1438 -0.2	2014 5.6
16 W	0255 0.2	0825 5.8	1519 0.1	2053 5.3
17 Th	0336 0.0	0904 5.5	1608 0.4	2139 4.9
18 F	0428 1.0	0951 5.2	1710 0.6	◖ 2236 4.5
19 Sa	0534 1.3	1048 5.0	1821 0.7	2348 4.3
20 Su	0645 1.4	1158 4.9	1929 0.5	
21 M	0108 4.3	0752 1.1	1314 5.0	2030 0.2
22 Tu	0218 4.6	0849 0.7	1421 5.3	2122 -0.3
23 W	0314 5.1	0940 0.2	1518 5.8	2209 -0.7
24 Th	0401 5.6	1026 -0.3	1608 6.2	2252 -1.0
25 F	0442 6.1	1110 -0.8	1653 6.6	2333 -1.3
26 Sa	0522 6.5	1152 -1.2	1736 6.8	O
27 Su	0013 -1.3	0601 6.8	1235 -1.5	1819 6.9
28 M	0054 -1.2	0640 7.0	1319 -1.5	1903 6.7

MARCH

Day				
1 Tu	0137 -0.9	0722 6.9	1406 -1.4	1949 6.4
2 W	0220 -0.5	0806 6.6	1457 -1.1	2039 5.9
3 Th	0315 0.0	0855 6.2	1555 -0.7	2136 5.4
4 F	0417 0.5	0953 5.7	1701 -0.3	◖ 2244 4.9
5 Sa	0528 0.9	1103 5.3	1813 -0.1	◗ 2304 4.6
6 Su	0006 4.6	0642 0.9	1227 5.1	1922 -0.2
7 M	0133 4.7	0752 0.7	1350 5.2	2026 -0.4
8 Tu	0245 5.0	0852 0.3	1457 5.5	2120 -0.6
9 W	0337 5.3	0944 -0.1	1550 5.8	2208 -0.8
10 Th	0418 5.7	1029 -0.5	1632 6.0	2250 -0.9
11 F	0452 5.9	1110 -0.7	1709 6.2	2329 -0.9
12 Sa	0522 6.1	1148 -0.9	1741 6.2	●
13 Su	0005 -0.8	0550 6.2	1223 -0.9	1812 6.2
14 M	0040 -0.6	0617 6.2	1257 -0.8	1842 6.1
15 Tu	0113 -0.3	0645 6.2	1331 -0.7	1913 5.9
16 W	0146 0.0	0715 6.1	1405 -0.4	1946 5.7
17 Th	0220 0.4	0748 6.0	1441 -0.1	2011 5.1
18 F	0257 0.8	0826 5.8	1524 0.2	2106 5.1
19 Sa	0343 1.1	0911 5.5	1621 0.5	2158 4.8
20 Su	0448 1.4	1006 5.2	1733 0.7	◗ 2304 4.6
21 M	0605 1.5	1115 5.0	1846 0.7	
22 Tu	0022 4.6	0717 1.2	1233 5.0	1951 0.4
23 W	0136 4.9	0818 0.7	1348 5.3	2047 0.0
24 Th	0237 5.4	0912 0.1	1452 5.7	2137 -0.4
25 F	0327 6.0	1001 -0.6	1546 6.2	2223 -0.7
26 Sa	0412 6.5	1047 -1.1	1635 6.6	2307 -0.9
27 Su	0455 6.9	1132 -1.6	1721 6.8	O 2350 -1.0
28 M	0537 7.2	1216 -1.8	1806 6.9	
29 Tu	0034 -0.9	0618 7.3	1301 -1.8	1851 6.8
30 W	0119 -0.6	0701 7.1	1349 -1.6	1938 6.5
31 Th	0207 -0.2	0747 6.8	1440 -1.2	2028 6.0

APRIL

Day				
1 F	0300 0.3	0836 6.3	1536 -0.8	2123 5.5
2 Sa	0401 0.7	0934 5.8	1639 -0.3	2132 5.2
3 Su	0509 1.0	1043 5.3	1747 0.0	◖ 2344 4.9
4 M	0621 1.0	1204 5.0	1854 0.1	
5 Tu	0103 4.9	0728 0.8	1326 5.1	1956 0.1
6 W	0211 5.2	0828 0.4	1434 5.3	2050 -0.1
7 Th	0302 5.5	0919 -0.0	1527 5.6	2138 -0.2
8 F	0343 5.8	1004 -0.4	1609 5.8	2221 -0.3
9 Sa	0417 6.0	1044 -0.7	1645 6.0	2300 -0.3
10 Su	0448 6.2	1122 -0.8	1718 6.1	2337 -0.2
11 M	0517 6.3	1157 -0.9	1749 6.1	●
12 Tu	0012 -0.1	0545 6.4	1232 -0.8	1819 6.1
13 W	0046 0.2	0614 6.4	1305 -0.7	1850 6.0
14 Th	0119 0.4	0645 6.3	1339 -0.4	1923 5.9
15 F	0153 0.7	0719 6.2	1414 -0.2	1959 5.7
16 Sa	0229 1.0	0757 6.0	1454 0.1	2041 5.5
17 Su	0314 1.3	0842 5.8	1545 0.4	2132 5.2
18 M	0416 1.4	0936 5.5	1650 0.6	2232 5.1
19 Tu	0530 1.4	1042 5.2	1802 0.7	◗ 2342 5.1
20 W	0642 1.2	1158 5.0	1909 0.6	
21 Th	0053 5.4	0746 0.6	1315 5.4	2010 0.3
22 F	0157 5.8	0843 -0.0	1424 5.7	2104 0.0
23 Sa	0252 6.4	0935 -0.7	1523 6.1	2154 -0.3
24 Su	0342 6.8	1024 -1.3	1616 6.5	2242 -0.4
25 M	0429 7.2	1112 -1.7	1705 6.8	O 2329 -0.5
26 Tu	0514 7.4	1158 -1.9	1753 6.8	
27 W	0015 -0.4	0558 7.4	1245 -1.9	1840 6.7
28 Th	0103 -0.2	0643 7.2	1333 -1.6	1927 6.5
29 F	0152 0.1	0730 6.9	1423 -1.2	2016 6.2
30 Sa	0245 0.5	0820 6.4	1517 -0.7	2109 5.8

TIME MERIDIAN 60°W 0000h is midnight, 1200h is noon.
Heights in feet are referred to the chart datum of sounding.

PUNTA GORDA, VENEZUELA

HIGH & LOW WATER 1994 10°10'N 62°38'W

ATLANTIC STANDARD TIME (GMT -4H)

MAY

Day	Time	ft	Day	Time	ft
1	0344	0.8	16	0256	1.2
	0915	5.9		0821	6.1
Su	1615	-0.3	M	1519	0.2
	2208	5.5		2110	5.7
2	0447	1.0	17	0353	1.3
	1019	5.4		0914	5.8
M	1716	0.1	Tu	1615	0.5
☾	2312	5.3		2205	5.7
3	0553	1.0	18	0500	1.2
	1132	5.1		1016	5.5
Tu	1818	0.4	W	1721	0.7
			☽	2308	5.7
4	0020	5.3	19	0610	1.0
	0657	0.9		1128	5.4
W	1248	5.0	Th	1829	0.7
	1918	0.5			
5	0122	5.4	20	0014	5.9
	0755	0.5		0715	0.5
Th	1357	5.1	F	1245	5.4
	2013	0.5		1933	0.6
6	0215	5.6	21	0119	6.2
	0847	0.2		0816	-0.1
F	1453	5.3	Sa	1358	5.6
	2102	0.4		2033	0.4
7	0259	5.9	22	0219	6.6
	0933	-0.2		0911	-0.7
Sa	1539	5.6	Su	1502	6.0
	2147	0.3		2128	0.2
8	0337	6.1	23	0315	7.0
	1016	-0.5		1004	-1.2
Su	1618	5.7	M	1600	6.3
	2229	0.3		2220	0.1
9	0412	6.2	24	0406	7.2
	1055	-0.6		1054	-1.6
M	1654	5.9	Tu	1652	6.5
	2308	0.4		2310	-0.0
10	0445	6.4	25	0455	7.4
	1133	-0.7		1142	-1.8
Tu	1727	5.9	W	1741	6.7
●	2345	0.8	○	2359	-0.0
11	0516	6.4	26	0542	7.4
	1209	-0.7		1230	-1.8
W	1759	6.0	Th	1829	6.6
12	0021	0.6	27	0048	0.1
	0547	6.5		0628	7.2
Th	1244	-0.6	F	1317	-1.5
	1831	6.0		1915	6.5
13	0056	0.8	28	0137	0.3
	0620	6.5		0715	6.9
F	1318	-0.4	Sa	1405	-1.2
	1904	5.9		2001	6.3
14	0132	0.9	29	0228	0.5
	0655	6.4		0803	6.5
Sa	1354	-0.3	Su	1455	-0.7
	1941	5.9		2049	6.1
15	0211	1.1	30	0321	0.7
	0735	6.3		0853	6.0
Su	1433	-0.2	M	1546	-0.2
	2023	5.8		2138	5.8
			31	0418	0.9
				0949	5.6
			Tu	1641	0.2
				2231	5.6

JUNE

Day	Time	ft	Day	Time	ft
1	0518	1.0	16	0433	0.8
	1051	5.2		0954	5.7
W	1737	0.6	Th	1646	0.6
	2327	5.5		2236	6.2
2	0618	0.9	17	0540	0.7
	1159	5.0		1102	5.5
Th	1834	0.8	F	1753	0.8
				2340	6.3
3	0025	5.6	18	0647	0.3
	0716	0.7		1218	5.3
F	1307	4.9	Sa	1901	0.9
	1930	0.9			
4	0120	5.6	19	0047	6.4
	0811	0.4		0751	-0.1
Sa	1409	5.0	Su	1335	5.4
	2023	0.9		2007	0.8
5	0211	5.8	20	0152	6.6
	0900	0.1		0851	-0.6
Su	1503	5.2	M	1446	5.7
	2112	0.9		2107	0.7
6	0256	6.0	21	0253	6.8
	0946	-0.2		0946	-1.1
M	1548	5.4	Tu	1547	6.0
	2158	0.8		2203	0.5
7	0337	6.2	22	0350	7.1
	1029	-0.4		1038	-1.4
Tu	1628	5.6	W	1642	6.3
	2241	0.8		2255	0.3
8	0415	6.3	23	0441	7.2
	1109	-0.5		1127	-1.6
W	1705	5.8	Th	1731	6.5
	2321	0.8	○	2345	0.2
9	0450	6.4	24	0529	7.2
	1147	-0.6		1214	-1.6
Th	1739	5.9	F	1816	6.6
●	2359	0.8			
10	0525	6.5	25	0032	0.2
	1224	-0.6		0615	7.1
F	1813	6.0	Sa	1259	-1.4
				1859	6.6
11	0037	0.8	26	0119	0.2
	0601	6.6		0659	6.9
Sa	1300	-0.5	Su	1344	-1.1
	1847	6.1		1939	6.5
12	0114	0.9	27	0206	0.4
	0638	6.6		0743	6.5
Su	1336	-0.4	M	1428	-0.7
	1924	6.2		2020	6.3
13	0154	0.9	28	0254	0.5
	0719	6.5		0827	6.1
M	1414	-0.2	Tu	1514	-0.2
	2004	6.2		2101	6.1
14	0239	0.9	29	0344	0.7
	0804	6.3		0914	5.7
Tu	1456	0.0	W	1601	0.3
	2049	6.2		2145	6.0
15	0332	0.9	30	0437	0.8
	0855	6.0		1006	5.3
W	1546	0.3	Th	1653	0.8
	2139	6.2	☽	2232	5.8

JULY

Day	Time	ft	Day	Time	ft
1	0534	0.9	16	0514	0.4
	1100	5.0		1049	5.5
F	1748	1.1	Sa	1725	1.0
	2325	5.7		2310	6.4
2	0633	0.9	17	0623	0.3
	1211	4.8		1157	5.3
Sa	1846	1.3	Su	1838	1.2
3	0022	5.6	18	0021	6.4
	0731	0.7		0730	0.2
Su	1319	4.8	M	1319	5.3
	1943	1.4		1947	1.2
4	0120	5.7	19	0133	6.5
	0826	0.4		0833	-0.4
M	1423	5.0	Tu	1435	5.5
	2038	1.3		2051	1.0
5	0214	5.9	20	0240	6.7
	0916	0.1		0931	-0.8
Tu	1517	5.2	W	1539	5.9
	2128	1.2		2149	0.7
6	0304	6.1	21	0339	6.9
	1003	-0.1		1023	-1.1
W	1602	5.5	Th	1632	6.3
	2214	1.0		2241	0.4
7	0348	6.3	22	0431	7.1
	1045	-0.4		1111	-1.3
Th	1642	5.7	F	1718	6.5
	2257	0.7	○	2329	0.2
8	0428	6.5	23	0518	7.2
	1125	-0.5		1155	-1.3
F	1718	6.0	Sa	1758	6.7
●	2337	0.4			
9	0506	6.7	24	0014	0.1
	1202	-0.6		0600	7.1
Sa	1753	6.2	Su	1238	-1.1
				1836	6.7
10	0016	0.6	25	0057	0.1
	0544	6.8		0640	6.9
Su	1239	-0.6	M	1318	-0.8
	1828	6.4		1911	6.7
11	0055	0.5	26	0140	0.2
	0623	6.8		0718	6.7
M	1315	-0.5	Tu	1358	-0.4
	1904	6.6		1945	6.6
12	0136	0.5	27	0222	0.4
	0704	6.8		0757	6.3
Tu	1353	-0.3	W	1438	0.1
	1943	6.7		2020	6.5
13	0220	0.4	28	0306	0.6
	0749	6.6		0837	6.0
W	1433	-0.1	Th	1520	0.5
	2025	6.8		2057	6.3
14	0310	0.4	29	0354	0.8
	0839	6.3		0921	5.6
Th	1521	0.3	F	1607	1.0
	2113	6.7		2139	6.1
15	0408	0.5	30	0448	1.0
	0935	5.9		1012	5.2
F	1617	0.7	Sa	1700	1.4
	2208	6.6	☽	2228	5.9
			31	0547	1.1
				1114	4.9
			Su	1800	1.7
				2325	5.7

AUGUST

Day	Time	ft	Day	Time	ft
1	0650	1.1	16	0001	6.3
	1226	4.8		0712	0.3
M	1904	1.8	Tu	1309	5.3
				1933	1.5
2	0029	5.7	17	0121	6.3
	0750	0.9		0817	0.0
Tu	1339	4.9	W	1427	5.6
	2004	1.7		2039	1.3
3	0133	5.8	18	0232	6.6
	0845	0.6		0914	-0.3
W	1442	5.2	Th	1529	6.1
	2059	1.5		2135	0.9
4	0232	6.0	19	0331	6.8
	0934	0.2		1005	-0.6
Th	1533	5.5	F	1618	6.5
	2148	1.2		2226	0.5
5	0322	6.3	20	0421	7.1
	1019	-0.1		1051	-0.8
F	1615	5.9	Sa	1659	6.8
	2233	0.9		2311	0.2
6	0407	6.7	21	0504	7.2
	1059	-0.4		1133	-0.8
Sa	1653	6.3	Su	1735	6.9
	2314	0.6	○	2353	0.1
7	0448	6.9	22	0543	7.2
	1138	-0.5		1213	-0.6
Su	1728	6.7	M	1807	7.0
●	2354	0.3			
8	0528	7.1	23	0033	0.1
	1215	-0.5		0618	7.1
M	1804	7.0	Tu	1250	-0.3
				1838	7.0
9	0034	0.1	24	0111	0.2
	0608	7.2		0652	6.9
Tu	1252	-0.5	W	1326	0.0
	1840	7.2		1908	7.0
10	0115	-0.0	25	0149	0.3
	0650	7.1		0726	6.6
W	1330	-0.3	Th	1402	0.5
	1919	7.3		1939	6.9
11	0200	-0.0	26	0228	0.6
	0734	6.9		0802	6.3
Th	1411	0.1	F	1440	0.9
	2001	7.3		2013	6.7
12	0249	0.1	27	0311	0.9
	0823	6.6		0841	5.9
F	1459	0.7	Sa	1522	1.4
	2048	7.1		2052	6.5
13	0346	0.3	28	0401	1.2
	0918	6.1		0927	5.6
Sa	1556	1.0	Su	1612	1.8
	2142	6.8		2137	6.2
14	0451	0.4	29	0500	1.4
	1023	5.6		1023	5.2
Su	1705	1.4	M	1715	2.1
☽	2246	6.5	☽	2233	5.9
15	0602	0.5	30	0606	1.5
	1142	5.3		1134	5.0
M	1821	1.6	Tu	1824	2.3
				2339	5.8
			31	0712	1.3
				1253	5.1
			W	1930	2.1

TIME MERIDIAN 60°W

0000h is midnight, 1200h is noon.

Heights in feet are referred to the chart datum of sounding.

REED'S NAUTICAL ALMANAC

PUNTA GORDA, VENEZUELA

ATLANTIC STANDARD TIME (GMT -4H)

Chapter 2

SEPTEMBER

Day	Time	ft	Day	Time	ft
1 Th	0052	5.9	16 F	0222	6.5
	0811	1.0		0854	0.2
	1403	5.4		1512	6.4
	2029	1.8		2119	1.0
2 F	0159	6.1	17 Sa	0320	6.8
	0903	0.6		0943	-0.0
	1458	5.8		1556	6.7
	2120	1.3		2207	0.8
3 Sa	0255	6.5	18 Su	0407	7.0
	0949	0.3		1028	-0.1
	1543	6.3		1633	7.0
	2206	0.9		2250	0.3
4 Su	0344	6.9	19 M	0447	7.2
	1031	-0.0		1108	-0.1
	1622	6.8		1706	7.2
	2249	0.4		2330 ○	0.1
5 M ●	0428	7.2	20 Tu	0523	7.2
	1110	-0.2		1145	0.0
	1700	7.3		1736	7.3
	2331	0.0			
6 Tu	0511	7.5	21 W	0007	0.1
	1149	-0.3		0555	7.1
	1737	7.6		1221	0.2
				1804	7.3
7 W	0012	-0.3	22 Th	0043	0.2
	0553	7.6		0627	7.0
	1228	-0.2		1256	0.6
	1815	7.9		1833	7.3
8 Th	0055	-0.4	23 F	0118	0.4
	0635	7.5		0658	6.8
	1308	0.0		1330	0.9
	1855	7.9		1902	7.2
9 F	0140	-0.3	24 Sa	0155	0.6
	0720	7.2		0731	6.5
	1352	0.4		1404	1.3
	1938	7.8		1935	7.0
10 Sa	0230	-0.1	25 Su	0233	0.9
	0809	6.8		0808	6.3
	1441	0.9		1442	1.7
	2026	7.5		2012	6.8
11 Su	0326	0.2	26 M	0318	1.2
	0904	6.8		0850	5.9
	1540	1.4		1528	2.1
	2120	7.0		2056	6.5
12 M ◑	0431	0.7	27 Tu	0414	1.5
	1010	5.9		0943	5.6
	1651	1.8		1631	2.4
	2227	6.6		2149	6.2
13 Tu	0542	0.7	28 W	0521	1.7
	1129	5.6		1048	5.4
	1807	2.0		1744	2.5
	2347	6.3		2255 ◑	6.0
14 W	0652	0.7	29 Th	0629	1.6
	1257	5.6		1205	5.4
	1919	1.8		1855	2.3
15 Th	0110	6.3	30 F	0010	6.0
	0757	0.5		0732	1.4
	1414	5.9		1317	5.7
	2023	1.4		1956	1.9

OCTOBER

Day	Time	ft	Day	Time	ft
1 Sa	0123	6.2	16 Su	0301	6.6
	0826	1.0		0916	0.5
	1417	6.2		1526	6.8
	2050	1.3		2143	0.6
2 Su	0226	6.6	17 M	0347	6.8
	0915	0.7		1000	0.4
	1506	6.8		1602	7.1
	2133	0.7		2226	0.3
3 M	0319	7.0	18 Tu	0426	6.9
	1000	0.4		1040	0.4
	1549	7.3		1634	7.2
	2224	0.2		2305	0.1
4 Tu	0407	7.4	19 W	0501	7.0
	1042	0.1		1118	0.5
	1631	7.8		1704	7.3
	2308	-0.3		2342 ○	0.1
5 W ●	0453	7.6	20 Th	0533	7.0
	1124	0.1		1154	0.7
	1711	8.1		1733	7.4
	2351	-0.4			
6 Th	0537	7.6	21 F	0018	0.2
	1206	0.1		0603	6.9
	1752	8.3		1228	0.9
				1802	7.4
7 F	0036	-0.7	22 Sa	0052	0.3
	0622	7.6		0634	6.8
	1249	0.4		1302	1.2
	1834	8.3		1832	7.3
8 Sa	0123	-0.6	23 Su	0127	0.5
	0708	7.4		0706	6.6
	1335	0.7		1336	1.5
	1919	8.0		1905	7.2
9 Su	0213	-0.3	24 M	0204	0.8
	0757	7.0		0742	6.4
	1427	1.1		1412	1.8
	2008	7.4		1942	7.0
10 M	0309	0.1	25 Tu	0245	1.1
	0852	6.5		0823	6.2
	1527	1.6		1455	2.1
	2103	7.1		2025	6.7
11 Tu ◑	0411	0.5	26 W	0334	1.3
	0957	6.1		0911	5.9
	1635	1.9		1552	2.3
	2210	6.6		2115	6.4
12 W	0519	0.8	27 Th ◑	0434	1.6
	1112	5.8		1009	5.8
	1748	2.0		1704	2.4
	2329	6.3		2217	6.2
13 Th	0627	0.9	28 F	0542	1.6
	1234	5.9		1118	5.8
	1859	1.8		1816	2.2
				2329	6.0
14 F	0051	6.2	29 Sa	0647	1.5
	0730	0.8		1228	6.0
	1355	6.1		1921	1.8
	2001	1.5			
15 Sa	0204	6.4	30 Su	0045	6.1
	0826	0.9		0747	1.3
	1442	6.5		1332	6.4
	2056	1.0		2019	1.2
			31 M	0154	6.4
				0840	1.0
				1428	6.9
				2111	0.5

NOVEMBER

Day	Time	ft	Day	Time	ft
1 Tu	0254	6.8	16 W	0402	6.4
	0929	0.7		1012	0.8
	1517	7.5		1603	6.9
	2200	-0.1		2240	0.1
2 W	0347	7.1	17 Th	0439	6.5
	1016	0.4		1052	0.8
	1604	7.9		1636	7.0
	2247	0.0		2310	0.0
3 Th ●	0436	7.4	18 F	0512	6.5
	1102	0.3		1130	0.8
	1648	8.2		1707	7.1
	2333	-0.9		2356 ○	-0.0
4 F	0524	7.5	19 Sa	0544	6.5
	1147	0.3		1206	1.0
	1733	8.3		1738	7.1
5 Sa	0020	-1.0	20 Su	0031	0.0
	0610	7.5		0615	6.5
	1234	0.4		1241	1.1
	1818	8.2		1809	7.1
6 Su	0108	-0.9	21 M	0106	0.2
	0658	7.3		0648	6.4
	1322	0.7		1315	1.3
	1904	8.0		1843	7.1
7 M	0158	-0.6	22 Tu	0142	0.4
	0747	7.0		0722	6.3
	1414	1.0		1351	1.5
	1953	7.5		1919	6.9
8 Tu	0251	-0.2	23 W	0219	0.6
	0840	6.6		0801	6.2
	1512	1.4		1432	1.6
	2048	7.0		2001	6.7
9 W	0349	0.3	24 Th	0301	0.8
	0938	6.2		0845	6.1
	1615	1.6		1522	1.8
	2150	6.5		2049	6.4
10 Th ◑	0450	0.7	25 F	0352	1.1
	1044	6.0		0936	6.0
	1723	1.7		1625	1.8
	2301	6.1		2146	6.1
11 F	0554	0.9	26 Sa ◑	0453	1.2
	1154	5.9		1035	6.0
	1829	1.6		1736	1.7
				2253	5.9
12 Sa	0019	5.9	27 Su	0600	1.3
	0655	1.0		1141	6.1
	1302	6.0		1844	1.3
	1931	1.3			
13 Su	0131	5.9	28 M	0008	5.8
	0752	1.0		0705	1.2
	1359	6.3		1248	6.4
	2026	0.9		1947	0.8
14 M	0232	6.0	29 Tu	0122	5.9
	0843	0.9		0806	1.0
	1447	6.5		1351	6.7
	2115	0.4		2045	0.1
15 Tu	0321	6.2	30 W	0230	6.2
	0930	0.8		0902	0.8
	1527	6.7		1448	7.2
	2200	0.3		2138	-0.5

DECEMBER

Day	Time	ft	Day	Time	ft
1 Th	0329	6.5	16 F	0417	5.8
	0954	0.5		1027	0.8
	1541	7.5		1610	6.5
	2229	-0.9		2257	-0.3
2 F ●	0423	6.8	17 Sa	0453	5.9
	1044	0.3		1108	0.7
	1631	7.8		1645	6.6
	2314	-1.0		2323	-0.1
3 Sa	0513	7.0	18 Su ○	0527	6.0
	1133	0.2		1145	0.7
	1719	7.9		1719	6.7
4 Su	0006	-1.4	19 M	0012	-0.4
	0601	7.0		0559	6.1
	1221	0.2		1222	0.7
	1806	7.9		1752	6.8
5 M	0053	-1.3	20 Tu	0047	-0.3
	0648	7.0		0631	6.1
	1309	0.3		1257	0.7
	1853	7.6		1826	6.8
6 Tu	0142	-1.0	21 W	0122	-0.2
	0734	6.8		0704	6.2
	1359	0.5		1333	0.8
	1940	7.2		1903	6.7
7 W	0231	-0.6	22 Th	0157	-0.1
	0822	6.5		0740	6.2
	1452	0.8		1412	0.8
	2030	6.7		1943	6.6
8 Th	0322	-0.2	23 F	0234	0.1
	0911	6.2		0820	6.2
	1548	1.0		1457	0.9
	2124	6.2		2028	6.3
9 F ◑	0417	0.3	24 Sa	0317	0.4
	1005	5.9		0906	6.2
	1649	1.2		1552	0.9
	2224	5.7		2121	6.0
10 Sa	0514	0.7	25 Su ◑	0410	0.7
	1103	5.7		0958	6.1
	1751	1.2		1658	0.9
	2332	5.4		2222	5.6
11 Su	0613	1.0	26 M	0516	0.9
	1204	5.7		1059	6.0
	1853	1.1		1809	0.7
				2334	5.4
12 M	0044	5.2	27 Tu	0627	1.1
	0712	1.1		1208	6.1
	1305	5.7		1918	0.3
	1951	0.8			
13 Tu	0151	5.3	28 W	0053	5.3
	0807	1.1		0736	1.0
	1401	5.9		1319	6.2
	2044	0.5		2021	-0.2
14 W	0248	5.4	29 Th	0209	5.5
	0858	1.0		0840	0.7
	1449	6.1		1425	6.5
	2132	0.2		2120	-0.7
15 Th	0336	5.6	30 F	0316	5.8
	0944	0.9		0937	0.4
	1532	6.3		1525	6.9
	2216	-0.1		2214	-1.2
			31 Sa	0413	6.2
				1031	0.1
				1620	7.2
				2304	-1.5

TIME MERIDIAN 60°W

Heights in feet are referred to the chart datum of sounding.

0000h is midnight, 1200h is noon.

AMUAY, VENEZUELA

HIGH & LOW WATER 1994   11°45'N 70°13'W

ATLANTIC STANDARD TIME (GMT -4H)

JANUARY

Day	Time	ft	Time	ft	Time	ft	Time	ft
1 Sa	0041	-0.4	0853	0.8	1239	0.6	1717	0.9
2 Su	0123	-0.3	0917	0.9	1359	0.4	1840	0.8
3 M	0207	-0.2	0943	1.0	1517	0.2	2056	0.6
4 Tu	0253	-0.1	1014	1.1	1629	0.0	2256	0.5
5 W ☽	0340	0.0	1049	1.2	1734	-0.2		
6 Th	0023	0.5	0430	0.2	1129	1.2	1833	-0.4
7 F	0136	0.6	0520	0.2	1212	1.4	1928	-0.6
8 Sa	0241	0.6	0611	0.4	1256	1.4	2020	-0.7
9 Su	0341	0.6	0702	0.4	1342	1.4	2110	-0.7
10 M	0438	0.6	0754	0.4	1427	1.3	2157	-0.7
11 Tu ●	0532	0.7	0846	0.4	1512	1.3	2243	-0.6
12 W	0624	0.7	0941	0.5	1557	1.1	2326	-0.5
13 Th	0713	0.7	1040	0.5	1643	1.0		
14 F	0007	-0.4	0759	0.7	1145	0.5	1733	0.8
15 Sa	0045	-0.3	0842	0.7	1256	0.4	1846	0.6
16 Su	0121	-0.2	0921	0.8	1413	0.3	2027	0.5
17 M	0157	-0.1	0956	0.8	1533	0.2	2201	0.4
18 Tu	0234	0.1	1029	0.8	1643	0.1	2322	0.4
19 W ☽	0313	0.1	1059	0.9	1736	-0.0		
20 Th	0031	0.4	0354	0.2	1125	0.9	1818	-0.2
21 F	0133	0.4	0435	0.3	1148	0.9	1857	-0.3
22 Sa	0228	0.4	0517	0.3	1208	1.0	1935	-0.4
23 Su	0318	0.4	0558	0.3	1228	1.0	2012	-0.5
24 M	0404	0.5	0640	0.4	1255	1.1	2050	-0.5
25 Tu	0446	0.6	0725	0.4	1327	1.1	2127	-0.6
26 W	0523	0.5	0814	0.3	1406	1.1	2205	-0.6
27 Th ○	0556	0.5	0909	0.3	1450	1.0	2244	-0.5
28 F	0626	0.5	1011	0.3	1541	0.9	2324	-0.5
29 Sa	0654	0.6	1118	0.2	1643	0.8		
30 Su	0006	-0.4	0725	0.7	1231	0.1	1805	0.6
31 M	0051	-0.3	0800	0.8	1346	-0.0	2002	0.5

FEBRUARY

Day	Time	ft	Time	ft	Time	ft	Time	ft
1 Tu	0138	-0.1	0842	0.9	1500	-0.2	2150	0.5
2 W	0230	-0.0	0929	1.0	1612	-0.4	2316	0.5
3 Th ○	0324	0.1	1019	1.1	1717	-0.5		
4 F	0028	0.5	0419	0.2	1110	1.1	1817	-0.6
5 Sa	0130	0.5	0515	0.2	1202	1.2	1912	-0.7
6 Su	0226	0.6	0609	0.2	1253	1.2	2003	-0.7
7 M	0317	0.6	0701	0.2	1343	1.2	2050	-0.7
8 Tu	0406	0.6	0752	0.2	1432	1.1	2134	-0.6
9 W	0452	0.6	0843	0.2	1520	1.0	2214	-0.6
10 Th ●	0536	0.6	0934	0.2	1608	0.8	2251	-0.4
11 F	0618	0.6	1028	0.2	1701	0.7	2325	-0.2
12 Sa	0658	0.6	1124	0.2	1803	0.6	2358	-0.1
13 Su	0736	0.6	1224	0.1	1923	0.5		
14 M	0031	0.0	0812	0.6	1328	0.1	2050	0.4
15 Tu	0108	0.1	0846	0.6	1434	0.0	2211	0.4
16 W	0148	0.2	0918	0.6	1537	-0.1	2321	0.4
17 Th	0232	0.2	0947	0.7	1633	-0.2		
18 F ○	0020	0.4	0320	0.3	1015	0.7	1721	-0.3
19 Sa	0109	0.4	0409	0.3	1045	0.8	1805	-0.3
20 Su	0152	0.4	0457	0.3	1118	0.9	1846	-0.4
21 M	0229	0.5	0544	0.3	1155	0.9	1926	-0.5
22 Tu	0302	0.5	0632	0.2	1237	1.0	2005	-0.5
23 W	0331	0.5	0722	0.2	1322	1.0	2043	-0.5
24 Th	0356	0.5	0815	0.1	1412	1.0	2123	-0.4
25 F	0420	0.6	0911	0.0	1509	0.9	2203	-0.4
26 Sa ○	0447	0.6	1010	-0.1	1615	0.8	2246	-0.2
27 Su	0519	0.7	1113	-0.2	1736	0.7	2331	-0.1
28 M	0558	0.8	1220	-0.2	1912	0.6		

MARCH

Day	Time	ft	Time	ft	Time	ft	Time	ft
1 Tu	0021	0.0	0647	0.9	1330	-0.3	2045	0.6
2 W	0115	0.1	0744	0.9	1440	-0.4	2207	0.6
3 Th	0215	0.2	0848	1.0	1548	-0.5	2316	0.6
4 F ○	0317	0.3	0952	1.0	1653	-0.6		
5 Sa	0016	0.7	0419	0.3	1055	1.1	1752	-0.6
6 Su	0109	0.7	0519	0.3	1155	1.1	1846	-0.6
7 M	0157	0.7	0615	0.2	1252	1.1	1934	-0.5
8 Tu	0241	0.7	0708	0.2	1347	1.0	2018	-0.4
9 W	0323	0.7	0757	0.2	1441	0.9	2057	-0.2
10 Th	0401	0.7	0845	0.1	1535	0.8	2132	-0.1
11 F	0436	0.7	0932	0.1	1631	0.7	2204	0.0
12 Sa ●	0507	0.6	1019	0.0	1733	0.6	2234	0.1
13 Su	0533	0.6	1107	0.0	1843	0.6	2305	0.2
14 M	0544	0.6	1157	-0.0	1959	0.5	2339	0.3
15 Tu	0456	0.6	1250	-0.0	2114	0.5		
16 W	0018	0.4	0503	0.7	1345	-0.1	2222	0.5
17 Th	0104	0.5	0542	0.7	1441	-0.1	2318	0.6
18 F	0157	0.5	0638	0.8	1534	-0.2		
19 Sa ○	0003	0.6	0254	0.6	0750	0.8	1624	-0.2
20 Su	0039	0.6	0350	0.6	0909	0.8	1710	-0.3
21 M	0109	0.6	0444	0.5	1021	0.9	1753	-0.3
22 Tu	0134	0.7	0528	0.3	1124	0.9	1834	-0.3
23 W	0155	0.7	0628	0.2	1224	0.9	1915	-0.3
24 Th	0214	0.8	0720	0.1	1324	0.9	1955	-0.2
25 F	0234	0.8	0813	-0.0	1429	0.9	2037	-0.1
26 Sa	0259	0.9	0909	-0.2	1539	0.8	2120	0.0
27 Su ○	0330	0.9	1006	-0.3	1657	0.8	2206	0.1
28 M	0408	1.1	1106	-0.4	1819	0.8	2257	0.3
29 Tu	0453	1.1	1208	-0.5	1941	0.8	2353	0.4
30 W	0547	1.1	1312	-0.5	2057	0.8		
31 Th	0056	0.5	0653	1.1	1417	-0.5	2204	0.9

APRIL

Day	Time	ft	Time	ft	Time	ft	Time	ft
1 F	0204	0.5	0809	1.1	1521	-0.5	2302	0.9
2 Sa	0315	0.5	0927	1.1	1621	-0.5	2353	1.0
3 Su ○	0424	0.5	1040	1.0	1718	-0.4		
4 M	0040	1.0	0527	0.4	1147	1.0	1808	-0.3
5 Tu	0122	1.0	0624	0.3	1250	1.0	1853	-0.1
6 W	0200	1.0	0716	0.2	1351	0.9	1933	-0.0
7 Th	0235	1.0	0803	0.1	1451	0.9	2008	0.1
8 F	0306	0.9	0848	0.1	1551	0.8	2039	0.3
9 Sa	0330	0.9	0930	0.0	1654	0.8	2109	0.4
10 Su	0342	0.9	1010	-0.0	1801	0.7	2138	0.5
11 M ●	0314	0.9	1052	-0.1	1913	0.7	2208	0.6
12 Tu	0254	0.9	1134	-0.1	2025	0.7	2242	0.7
13 W	0311	1.0	1220	-0.1	2134	0.8	2324	0.7
14 Th	0344	1.0	1307	-0.1	2228	0.8		
15 F	0019	0.8	0427	1.0	1356	-0.1	2308	0.8
16 Sa	0134	0.8	0521	1.0	1444	-0.1	2338	0.9
17 Su	0232	0.8	0628	0.9	1531	-0.2		
18 M	0001	0.9	0336	0.7	0751	0.9	1617	-0.1
19 Tu ○	0020	0.8	0435	0.6	0927	0.9	1700	-0.1
20 W	0036	1.0	0531	0.4	1101	0.9	1742	-0.1
21 Th	0051	1.0	0625	0.2	1224	0.9	1824	
22 F	0109	1.1	0718	0.1	1341	0.9	1907	0.1
23 Sa	0133	1.2	0811	-0.2	1455	0.9	1952	0.3
24 Su	0203	1.3	0905	-0.3	1610	0.9	2038	0.4
25 M ○	0240	1.4	0959	-0.4	1725	0.9	2129	0.5
26 Tu	0322	1.4	1056	-0.5	1838	0.9	2224	0.6
27 W	0410	1.4	1154	-0.6	1948	1.0	2327	0.7
28 Th	0505	1.3	1253	-0.5	2052	1.0		
29 F	0037	0.7	0612	1.2	1352	-0.5	2148	1.1
30 Sa	0153	0.7	0734	1.1	1450	-0.4	2239	1.2

TIME MERIDIAN 60°W
Heights in feet are referred to the chart datum of sounding.

0000h is midnight, 1200h is noon.

REED'S NAUTICAL ALMANAC

AMUAY, VENEZUELA

HIGH & LOW WATER 1994

ATLANTIC STANDARD TIME (GMT -4H)

MAY

Day	Time	ft	Time	ft	Time	ft	Time	ft
1 Su	0311	0.7	0901	1.1	1545	-0.3	2325	1.2
2 M ☽	0427	0.6	1023	1.0	1635	-0.2		
3 Tu	0006	1.2	0534	0.4	1138	0.9	1721	-0.0
4 W	0044	1.2	0632	0.3	1247	0.9	1802	0.1
5 Th	0117	1.2	0722	0.1	1354	0.9	1838	0.3
6 F	0147	1.2	0805	0.1	1459	0.8	1911	0.6
7 Sa	0211	1.2	0845	0.0	1604	0.8	1941	0.6
8 Su	0224	1.2	0922	-0.1	1710	0.8	2011	0.7
9 M	0213	1.1	0958	-0.1	1818	0.8	2039	0.8
10 Tu ●	0155	1.2	1035	-0.1	1930	0.9	2108	0.9
11 W	0206	1.2	1113	-0.2	2043	0.9		
12 Th	0232	1.2	1154	-0.2	2145	1.0		
13 F	0307	1.2	1235	-0.2	2217	1.0	2335	1.0
14 Sa	0350	1.2	1318	-0.2	2240	1.0		
15 Su	0055	1.0	0441	1.1	1402	-0.1	2259	1.0
16 M	0212	0.9	0544	1.0	1445	-0.1	2314	1.1
17 Tu	0001	0.0	0705	0.9	1528	-0.0	2327	1.1
18 W ◑	0428	0.6	0856	0.8	1611	0.0	2339	1.2
19 Th	0527	0.4	1109	0.8	1654	0.1	2356	1.3
20 F	0621	0.3	1246	0.8	1738	0.3		
21 Sa	0020	1.4	0714	-0.1	1406	0.8	1824	0.4
22 Su	0051	1.5	0806	-0.3	1519	0.8	1912	0.5
23 M	0128	1.6	0858	-0.5	1628	0.9	2003	0.6
24 Tu	0209	1.6	0951	-0.6	1735	1.0	2057	0.7
25 W	0254	1.6	1044	-0.6	1839	1.0	2157	0.8
26 Th	0343	1.5	1137	-0.6	1938	1.1	2303	0.8
27 F	0437	1.4	1231	-0.5	2033	1.1		
28 Sa	0016	0.8	0540	1.3	1324	-0.4	2123	1.2
29 Su	0137	0.8	0701	1.1	1415	-0.3	2209	1.3
30 M	0302	0.7	0836	1.0	1503	-0.1	2251	1.3
31 Tu	0425	0.6	1007	0.9	1548	0.0	2328	1.3

JUNE

Day	Time	ft	Time	ft	Time	ft	Time	ft
1 W ○	0537	0.4	1129	0.8	1629	0.2		
2 Th	0003	1.3	0633	0.3	1244	0.8	1707	0.4
3 F	0034	1.3	0718	0.1	1354	0.8	1742	0.5
4 Sa	0100	1.3	0756	0.0	1501	0.8	1815	0.6
5 Su	0120	1.3	0831	-0.1	1605	0.8	1848	0.7
6 M	0129	1.3	0905	-0.1	1710	0.9	1920	0.8
7 Tu	0122	1.3	0939	-0.2	1815	0.9	1951	0.9
8 W	0125	1.3	1014	-0.2	1922	0.9		
9 Th ●	0145	1.3	1050	-0.2	2027	1.0		
10 F	0215	1.3	1127	-0.2	2105	1.0		
11 Sa	0252	1.3	1205	-0.2	2128	1.0	2314	1.0
12 Su	0334	1.3	1243	-0.2	2146	1.0		
13 M	0035	0.9	0425	1.1	1323	-0.1	2202	1.1
14 Tu	0155	0.8	0527	1.0	1403	-0.0	2215	1.1
15 W	0310	0.7	0653	0.8	1445	0.1	2229	1.2
16 Th ◑	0418	0.4	0930	0.7	1529	0.2	2247	1.3
17 F	0510	0.0	1145	0.7	1614	0.3	2313	1.5
18 Sa	0615	-0.1	1311	0.7	1702	0.4	2347	1.6
19 Su	0707	-0.3	1424	0.8	1752	0.5		
20 M	0025	1.7	0759	-0.4	1528	0.9	1844	0.6
21 Tu	0108	1.7	0849	-0.6	1629	0.9	1939	0.7
22 W	0153	1.7	0944	-0.6	1726	1.0	2036	0.8
23 Th ○	0240	1.6	1029	-0.6	1821	1.0	2137	0.8
24 F	0329	1.5	1118	-0.5	1913	1.1	2244	0.8
25 Sa	0422	1.4	1205	-0.4	2003	1.1	2356	0.8
26 Su	0521	1.2	1251	-0.3	2048	1.2		
27 M	0115	0.8	0640	1.0	1335	-0.1	2131	1.2
28 Tu	0242	0.7	0821	0.9	1417	0.1	2210	1.3
29 W	0411	0.5	0958	0.8	1457	0.2	2246	1.3
30 Th ◑	0526	0.4	1124	0.7	1536	0.4	2320	1.3

JULY

Day	Time	ft	Time	ft	Time	ft	Time	ft
1 F	0617	0.2	1240	0.7	1614	0.5	2349	1.3
2 Sa	0007	0.1	1349	0.7	1652	0.6		
3 Su	0015	1.3	0731	-0.0	1451	0.8	1730	0.7
4 M	0035	1.4	0804	-0.1	1549	0.8	1809	0.8
5 Tu	0047	1.4	0836	-0.2	1644	0.9	1847	0.8
6 W	0055	1.4	0910	-0.2	1737	0.9	1926	0.9
7 Th	0112	1.4	0944	-0.3	1826	0.9	2009	0.9
8 F ●	0138	1.4	1019	-0.3	1908	0.9	2059	0.9
9 Sa	0212	1.4	1055	-0.2	1942	1.0	2159	0.9
10 Su	0251	1.3	1130	-0.2	2007	1.0	2307	0.9
11 M	0337	1.2	1207	-0.1	2028	1.0		
12 Tu	0022	0.8	0432	1.1	1246	-0.0	2045	1.1
13 W	0138	0.6	0545	0.9	1327	0.1	2105	1.2
14 Th	0253	0.5	0805	0.7	1410	0.2	2130	1.3
15 F	0403	0.2	1040	0.7	1457	0.4	2202	1.4
16 Sa ○	0505	0.0	1210	0.7	1548	0.5	2242	1.6
17 Su	0603	-0.2	1321	0.8	1642	0.6		
18 M	0656	-0.3	1423	0.9	1737	0.7		
19 Tu	0013	1.7	0747	-0.5	1518	0.8	1833	0.7
20 W	0101	1.7	0836	-0.5	1610	1.0	1930	0.7
21 Th	0150	1.7	0923	-0.5	1700	1.0	2028	0.8
22 F ○	0239	1.6	1009	-0.4	1748	1.1	2127	0.8
23 Sa	0329	1.4	1052	-0.3	1834	1.1	2230	0.7
24 Su	0422	1.3	1134	-0.2	1919	1.1	2337	0.7
25 M	0525	1.1	1213	0.0	2001	1.2		
26 Tu	0050	0.7	0648	0.9	1251	0.2	2042	1.2
27 W	0209	0.6	0827	0.8	1328	0.3	2120	1.2
28 Th	0331	0.5	1000	0.7	1406	0.5	2156	1.3
29 F	0441	0.3	1123	0.7	1447	0.6	2230	1.3
30 Sa ○	0532	0.2	1233	0.8	1529	0.7	2300	1.3
31 Su	0612	0.1	1333	0.8	1614	0.7	2327	1.3

AUGUST

Day	Time	ft	Time	ft	Time	ft	Time	ft
1 M	0648	0.0	1426	0.9	1700	0.8	2350	1.4
2 Tu	0122	-0.0	1513	0.9	1746	0.8		
3 W	0010	1.4	0757	-0.1	1556	0.9	1831	0.8
4 Th	0033	1.4	0831	-0.1	1635	0.9	1917	0.8
5 F	0102	1.4	0906	-0.1	1711	1.0	2006	0.8
6 Sa	0137	1.4	0941	-0.1	1741	1.0	2100	0.8
7 Su ●	0218	1.4	1016	-0.1	1806	1.0	2158	0.8
8 M	0305	1.3	1052	0.0	1828	1.1	2302	0.7
9 Tu	0402	1.1	1130	0.1	1849	1.1		
10 W	0010	0.6	0519	1.0	1211	0.3	1915	1.2
11 Th	0122	0.4	0728	0.8	1255	0.4	1950	1.4
12 F	0233	0.3	0932	0.8	1344	0.5	2035	1.5
13 Sa	0342	0.1	1102	0.9	1439	0.6	2125	1.5
14 Su ◐	0445	-0.1	1213	0.9	1538	0.7	2220	1.6
15 M	0544	-0.2	1312	1.0	1638	0.8	2315	1.7
16 Tu	0638	-0.3	1404	1.1	1738	0.8		
17 W	0010	1.7	0728	-0.3	1452	1.1	2000	0.8
18 Th	0104	1.7	0815	-0.3	1538	1.1	1933	0.8
19 F	0157	1.6	0859	-0.1	1621	1.2	2029	0.7
20 Sa	0250	1.5	0940	-0.1	1703	1.2	2125	0.7
21 Su ○	0344	1.3	1018	0.1	1743	1.2	2222	0.7
22 M	0445	1.2	1054	0.3	1822	1.2	2322	0.6
23 Tu	0556	1.1	1128	0.4	1859	1.2		
24 W	0024	0.6	0720	1.0	1202	0.6	1935	1.2
25 Th	0129	0.6	0848	0.9	1237	0.8	2009	1.2
26 F	0235	0.5	1011	0.9	1317	0.8	2043	1.3
27 Sa	0336	0.4	1123	0.9	1402	0.8	2115	1.3
28 Su	0428	0.3	1222	1.0	1454	0.9	2147	1.3
29 M ◐	0513	0.2	1309	1.0	1548	0.9	2220	1.4
30 Tu	0553	0.2	1350	1.1	1641	0.9	2253	1.4
31 W	0631	0.1	1426	1.1	1732	0.9	2330	1.4

TIME MERIDIAN 60°W

0000h is midnight, 1200h is noon.

Heights in feet are referred to the chart datum of sounding.

Chapter 2

AMUAY, VENEZUELA

HIGH & LOW WATER 1994 **11°45'N 70°13'W**

ATLANTIC STANDARD TIME (GMT -4H)

SEPTEMBER

Day	Time ft	Time ft	Time ft	Time ft
1 Th	0708 0.1	1457 1.1	1822 0.9	
2 F	0010 1.5	0744 0.1	1525 1.1	1912 0.8
3 Sa	0054 1.4	0819 0.1	1548 1.1	2004 0.8
4 Su	0142 1.4	0855 0.2	1607 1.2	2058 0.7
5 M ●	0236 1.3	0932 0.2	1625 1.3	2155 0.6
6 Tu	0341 1.2	1010 0.4	1647 1.3	2255 0.5
7 W	0504 1.1	1052 0.5	1717 1.4	2358 0.3
8 Th	0646 1.1	1137 0.6	1757 1.5	
9 F	0104 0.2	0826 1.1	1228 0.8	1847 1.6
10 Sa	0212 0.1	0950 1.1	1327 0.9	1948 1.6
11 Su	0317 0.0	1100 1.1	1431 0.9	2055 1.6
12 M ◐	0420 -0.1	1158 1.2	1538 0.9	2203 1.7
13 Tu	0518 -0.1	1249 1.3	1644 0.9	2308 1.7
14 W	0611 -0.1	1335 1.3	1747 0.9	
15 Th	0010 1.6	0700 0.0	1418 1.4	1846 0.8
16 F	0110 1.6	0745 0.1	1458 1.4	1941 0.8
17 Sa	0208 1.5	0825 0.2	1536 1.4	2035 0.7
18 Su	0308 1.4	0901 0.4	1611 1.4	2127 0.6
19 M O	0410 1.3	0935 0.5	1642 1.4	2218 0.6
20 Tu	0517 1.2	1006 0.7	1710 1.3	2308 0.5
21 W	0632 1.1	1036 0.8	1729 1.3	
22 Th	0000 0.5	0752 1.1	1107 0.9	1723 1.3
23 F	0052 0.5	0912 1.1	1141 1.0	1705 1.4
24 Sa	0145 0.4	1025 1.1	1224 1.1	1728 1.4
25 Su	0238 0.4	1122 1.2	1320 1.1	1812 1.4
26 M	0327 0.3	1205 1.2	1424 1.1	1911 1.4
27 Tu	0413 0.3	1239 1.2	1527 1.1	2023 1.4
28 W ◐	0456 0.3	1308 1.3	1627 1.1	2137 1.4
29 Th	0536 0.3	1333 1.3	1722 1.0	2245 1.4
30 F	0614 0.3	1354 1.3	1815 0.9	2348 1.4

OCTOBER

Day	Time ft	Time ft	Time ft	Time ft
1 Sa	0651 0.3	1411 1.3	1907 0.8	
2 Su	0051 1.4	0729 0.4	1425 1.4	1959 0.6
3 M	0157 1.3	0807 0.4	1442 1.5	2053 0.5
4 Tu	0309 1.3	0846 0.6	1506 1.6	2148 0.3
5 W ●	0429 1.2	0928 0.7	1538 1.7	2246 0.2
6 Th	0554 1.2	1014 0.8	1617 1.7	2345 0.1
7 F	0719 1.2	1106 0.9	1705 1.8	
8 Sa	0047 0.6	0837 1.3	1206 1.0	1802 1.7
9 Su	0150 -0.1	0945 1.3	1314 1.1	1911 1.7
10 M	0252 -0.1	1043 1.4	1427 1.1	2029 1.7
11 Tu ◑	0351 -0.1	1134 1.5	1542 1.1	2148 1.6
12 W	0447 0.0	1219 1.5	1653 0.9	2302 1.5
13 Th	0537 0.1	1301 1.5	1758 0.9	
14 F	0011 1.5	0623 0.2	1340 1.6	1857 0.7
15 Sa	0116 1.4	0704 0.4	1416 1.6	1951 0.6
16 Su	0221 1.3	0741 0.5	1448 1.5	2041 0.5
17 M	0326 1.3	0814 0.7	1517 1.5	2128 0.5
18 Tu	0433 1.2	0843 0.8	1538 1.5	2212 0.4
19 W	0544 1.1	0911 0.9	1543 1.5	2255 0.4
20 Th	0659 1.1	0937 1.0	1519 1.5	2337 0.3
21 F	0819 1.1	1004 1.1	1517 1.5	
22 Sa	0021 0.3	0940 1.2	1541 1.5	
23 Su	0106 0.3	1045 1.2	1616 1.5	
24 M	0151 0.3	1116 1.3	1701 1.5	
25 Tu	0236 0.3	1141 1.3	1756 1.4	
26 W	0319 0.3	1203 1.3	1508 1.2	1905 1.4
27 Th ◐	0401 0.3	1222 1.3	1614 1.1	2028 1.3
28 F	0441 0.3	1237 1.4	1713 0.9	2204 1.2
29 Sa	0520 0.3	1249 1.4	1808 0.7	2339 1.2
30 Su	0559 0.4	1301 1.5	1901 0.5	
31 M	0104 1.2	0639 0.5	1319 1.6	1953 0.3

NOVEMBER

Day	Time ft	Time ft	Time ft	Time ft
1 Tu	0223 1.1	0720 0.6	1344 1.7	2046 0.2
2 W	0340 1.1	0803 0.7	1417 1.8	2140 -0.0
3 Th ●	0457 1.1	0850 0.8	1457 1.8	2235 -0.1
4 F	0612 1.2	0942 0.9	1542 1.9	2331 -0.2
5 Sa	0723 1.2	1040 1.0	1633 1.8	
6 Su	0029 -0.2	0828 1.3	1147 1.1	1732 1.7
7 M	0127 -0.2	0926 1.4	1301 1.1	1843 1.6
8 Tu	0224 -0.2	1017 1.4	1421 1.0	2007 1.5
9 W	0319 -0.1	1103 1.5	1542 0.9	2134 1.4
10 Th ◑	0410 0.0	1146 1.5	1659 0.8	2255 1.3
11 F	0457 0.2	1225 1.6	1807 0.7	
12 Sa	0010 1.2	0540 0.3	1301 1.6	1906 0.5
13 Su	0121 1.1	0618 0.5	1334 1.6	1957 0.4
14 M	0230 1.1	0652 0.6	1403 1.5	2042 0.3
15 Tu	0338 1.0	0723 0.8	1427 1.5	2123 0.2
16 W	0447 1.0	0751 0.9	1439 1.5	2201 0.1
17 Th	0557 1.0	0817 1.0	1429 1.5	2238 0.1
18 F O	0713 1.0	0840 1.0	1421 1.5	2315 0.1
19 Sa	1436 1.5	2353 0.1		
20 Su	1505 1.5			
21 M	0032 0.1	1541 1.4		
22 Tu	0112 0.0	1049 1.1	1200 1.1	1624 1.4
23 W	0152 0.1	1102 1.2	1329 1.1	1717 1.3
24 Th	0231 0.1	1116 1.2	1449 1.0	1822 1.2
25 F ◐	0311 0.1	1127 1.2	1600 0.8	1948 1.0
26 Sa	0350 0.2	1137 1.3	1702 0.6	2152 0.9
27 Su	0430 0.3	1148 1.4	1759 0.4	2359 0.8
28 M	0512 0.3	1206 1.5	1853 0.2	
29 Tu	0129 0.8	0555 0.4	1233 1.6	1945 -0.1
30 W	0245 0.9	0640 0.5	1308 1.7	2037 -0.3

DECEMBER

Day	Time ft	Time ft	Time ft	Time ft
1 Th	0355 0.9	0728 0.6	1349 1.8	2129 -0.4
2 F ●	0502 0.9	0820 0.7	1434 1.8	2222 -0.5
3 Sa	0606 1.0	0917 0.8	1523 1.7	2315 -0.5
4 Su	0707 1.0	1019 0.8	1616 1.6	
5 M	0009 -0.5	0804 1.1	1129 0.9	1715 1.5
6 Tu	0102 -0.4	0856 1.2	1246 0.8	1826 1.3
7 W	0153 -0.3	0944 1.2	1409 0.8	1951 1.1
8 Th	0243 -0.2	1028 1.3	1534 0.7	2123 1.0
9 F ◑	0330 -0.0	1109 1.3	1656 0.5	2250 0.9
10 Sa	0414 0.1	1147 1.4	1807 0.3	
11 Su	0009 0.8	0454 0.3	1222 1.4	1903 0.2
12 M	0122 0.8	0531 0.4	1254 1.4	1949 0.1
13 Tu	0231 0.8	0605 0.5	1323 1.3	2029 -0.1
14 W	0336 0.8	0637 0.6	1345 1.3	2105 -0.1
15 Th	0440 0.8	0708 0.7	1357 1.3	2140 -0.2
16 F	0545 0.8	0737 0.7	1356 1.3	2214 -0.2
17 Sa	0653 0.8	0804 0.8	1400 1.3	2248 -0.2
18 Su	1420 1.3	2323 -0.2		
19 M	1450 1.3	2358 -0.2		
20 Tu	0929 0.8	1526 1.2		
21 W	0034 -0.2	0945 0.9	1146 0.8	1610 1.1
22 Th	0111 -0.2	1000 0.9	1309 0.8	1702 1.0
23 F	0148 -0.1	1012 0.9	1428 0.6	1810 0.8
24 Sa	0227 -0.0	1022 1.0	1542 0.4	1953 0.6
25 Su ◐	0307 0.1	1034 1.1	1647 0.2	2250 0.5
26 M	0350 0.1	1055 1.2	1746 -0.0	
27 Tu	0030 0.5	0436 0.2	1126 1.4	1840 -0.3
28 W	0145 0.3	0524 0.3	1205 1.5	1933 -0.5
29 Th	0250 0.4	0615 0.4	1248 1.5	2024 -0.6
30 F	0350 0.6	0708 0.4	1335 1.6	2115 -0.7
31 Sa	0447 0.7	0804 0.5	1424 1.5	2205 -0.7

TIME MERIDIAN 60°W   0000h is midnight, 1200h is noon.

Heights in feet are referred to the chart datum of sounding.

MALECON · ZAPARA, VENEZUELA

HIGH & LOW WATER 1994 11°00'N 71°35'W

ATLANTIC STANDARD TIME (GMT -4H)

JANUARY

Day	Time	ft	Time	ft	Day	Time	ft	Time	ft
1 Sa	0113	0.9	0753	4.1	16 Su	0259	1.4	0924	3.9
	1340	1.9	1945	4.3		1542	1.7	2120	3.8
2 Su	0204	1.0	0843	4.2	17 M	0351	1.6	1009	3.9
	1442	1.7	2045	4.3		1654	1.6	2214	3.7
3 M	0258	1.1	0935	4.3	18 Tu	0439	1.7	1050	3.9
	1545	1.4	2148	4.2		1720	1.5	2304	3.7
4 Tu	0354	1.2	1027	4.4	19 W	0521	1.8	1129	3.9
	1646	1.2	2252	4.2		1801	1.4	2351 ◗	3.7
5 W	0451	1.2	1119	4.6	20 Th	0558	1.8	1206	4.0
	1746	0.9	2355 ◗	4.2		1837	1.3		
6 Th	0550	1.3	1212	4.7	21 F	0035	3.7	0630	1.9
	1843	0.6				1242	4.1	1910	1.1
7 F	0057	4.2	0648	1.4	22 Sa	0117	3.7	0701	1.8
	1305	4.8	1940	0.4		1319	4.2	1943	1.0
8 Sa	0157	4.2	0747	1.4	23 Su	0158	3.7	0734	1.8
	1358	4.8	2035	0.3		1356	4.3	2018	0.8
9 Su	0255	4.2	0845	1.5	24 M	0238	3.8	0811	1.7
	1452	4.8	2130	0.2		1434	4.4	2055	0.7
10 M	0353	4.2	0943	1.6	25 Tu	0319	3.9	0851	1.7
	1545	4.8	2225	0.3		1514	4.5	2135	0.7
11 Tu	0450	4.1	1042	1.6	26 W	0401	3.9	0936	1.6
	1639	4.7	2320 ●	0.5		1556	4.5	2217	0.6
12 W	0547	4.1	1142	1.7	27 Th	0445	4.0	1025	1.6
	1734	4.5				O 2303	0.7		
13 Th	0015	0.7	0644	4.0	28 F	0530	4.0	1118	1.5
	1243	1.8	1830	4.4		1732	4.5	2351	0.7
14 F	0110	0.9	0740	4.0	29 Sa	0619	4.1	1217	1.4
	1344	1.8	1927	4.2		1828	4.4		
15 Sa	0205	1.2	0834	3.9	30 Su	0044	0.8	0711	4.1
	1445	1.8	2024	4.0		1319	1.3	1929	4.3
					31 M	0140	1.0	0807	4.2
						1423	1.1	2034	4.2

FEBRUARY

Day	Time	ft	Time	ft	Day	Time	ft	Time	ft
1 Tu	0240	1.1	0906	4.2	16 W	0407	1.9	1002	3.5
	1528	0.9	2142	4.1		1632	1.4	2233	3.5
2 W	0343	1.2	1006	4.3	17 Th	0448	1.9	1044	3.6
	1632	0.6	2249	4.1		1710	1.2	2319	3.5
3 Th	0447	1.2	1106	4.4	18 F	0526	1.8	1124	3.7
	1734	0.4	2355 ◗	4.1		1746	1.1		
4 F	0550	1.3	1204	4.5	19 Sa	0001	3.6	0553	1.8
	1833	0.3				1203	3.8	1820	1.0
5 Sa	0056	4.1	0650	1.3	20 Su	0041	3.6	0626	1.7
	1300	4.6	1930	0.2		1241	3.9	1855	0.8
6 Su	0154	4.1	0748	1.3	21 M	0120	3.7	0701	1.6
	1354	4.6	2024	0.2		1320	4.1	1933	0.7
7 M	0249	4.1	0844	1.3	22 Tu	0159	3.8	0741	1.4
	1446	4.6	2118	0.3		1400	4.3	2013	0.6
8 Tu	0341	4.1	0939	1.3	23 W	0237	3.9	0824	1.3
	1538	4.5	2210	0.5		1442	4.4	2055	0.5
9 W	0432	4.0	1033	1.4	24 Th	0318	4.0	0911	1.1
	1629	4.4	2301	0.7		1528	4.5	2141	0.5
10 Th	0522	3.9	1128	1.5	25 F	0401	4.1	1002	1.0
	1719	4.2	2353 ●	0.9		1619	4.5	2229	0.6
11 F	0610	3.8	1222	1.5	26 Sa	0447	4.2	1057	0.8
	1811	4.0				1713	4.4	2322 O	0.7
12 Sa	0044	1.2	0659	3.7	27 Su	0537	4.2	1157	0.7
	1316	1.5	1904	3.8		1813	4.3		
13 Su	0136	1.5	0746	3.6	28 M	0018	0.9	0633	4.2
	1410	1.5	1958	3.7		1259	0.6	1918	4.2
14 M	0229	1.7	0833	3.5					
	1502	1.5	2051	3.6					
15 Tu	0320	1.8	0919	3.5					
	1549	1.4	2144	3.5					

MARCH

Day	Time	ft	Time	ft	Day	Time	ft	Time	ft
1 Tu	0120	1.1	0735	4.2	16 W	0246	2.0	0825	3.3
	1405	0.4	2027	4.1		1457	1.2	2116	3.4
2 W	0227	1.2	0840	4.2	17 Th	0333	2.0	0912	3.3
	1511	0.3	2137	4.1		1536	1.1	2204	3.4
3 Th	0335	1.2	0947	4.2	18 F	0413	2.0	0957	3.3
	1616	0.2	2246	4.1		1614	1.1	2248	3.5
4 F	0445	1.2	1052	4.2	19 Sa	0447	1.9	1040	3.4
	1718	0.1	2350 ◗	4.1		1651	1.0	2328	3.6
5 Sa	0550	1.2	1154	4.3	20 Su	0519	1.8	1122	3.6
	1818	0.1				1729 ◗	0.8		
6 Su	0049	4.2	0650	1.1	21 M	0006	3.7	0555	1.6
	1251	4.4	1915	0.2		1203	3.8	1808	0.7
7 M	0144	4.2	0747	1.0	22 Tu	0043	3.8	0633	1.4
	1346	4.4	2008	0.3		1245	4.0	1849	0.6
8 Tu	0234	4.1	0840	1.0	23 W	0119	4.0	0716	1.2
	1438	4.3	2100	0.5		1329	4.1	1932	0.6
9 W	0321	4.0	0931	1.0	24 Th	0157	4.1	0802	0.9
	1528	4.2	2150	0.8		1415	4.3	2018	0.6
10 Th	0405	3.9	1021	1.1	25 F	0237	4.3	0851	0.7
	1617	4.1	2238	1.1		1506	4.3	2107	0.6
11 F	0447	3.8	1109	1.1	26 Sa	0321	4.4	0944	0.4
	1705	3.9	2326	1.3		1600	4.3	2159	0.8
12 Sa	0528	3.6	1157	1.2	27 Su	0409	4.4	1040	0.2
	1754	3.7				1659	4.3	2255 ●	0.9
13 Su	0015	1.6	0609	3.5	28 M	0503	4.3	1140	0.1
	1244	1.2	1843	3.6		1803	4.2	2357	1.1
14 M	0104	1.8	0652	3.4	29 Tu	0602	4.3	1242	-0.0
	1330	1.2	1934	3.5		1910	4.2		
15 Tu	0155	1.9	0738	3.3	30 W	0105	1.2	0708	4.2
	1414	1.2	2026	3.4		1347	-0.1	2021	4.2
					31 Th	0218	1.3	0817	4.1
						1452	-0.1	2131	4.2

APRIL

Day	Time	ft	Time	ft	Day	Time	ft	Time	ft
1 F	0331	1.3	0927	4.1	16 Sa	0331	2.2	0907	3.3
	1557	-0.1	2237	4.2		1521	0.9	2217	3.7
2 Sa	0441	1.2	1035	4.1	17 Su	0409	2.1	0954	3.4
	1659	0.0	2339	4.3		1601	0.9	2255	3.8
3 Su	0545	1.1	1139	4.2	18 M	0447	1.9	1040	3.5
	1758 ◗	0.2				1643	0.8	2331	3.9
4 M	0034	4.3	0644	1.0	19 Tu	0528	1.6	1126	3.7
	1238	4.2	1854	0.4		1725 ◗	0.8		
5 Tu	0125	4.3	0738	0.9	20 W	0006	4.1	0610	1.3
	1333	4.1	1947	0.6		1213	3.8	1810	0.7
6 W	0210	4.2	0829	0.8	21 Th	0042	4.3	0656	1.0
	1425	4.1	2036	0.9		1302	4.0	1856	0.8
7 Th	0252	4.1	0917	0.8	22 F	0121	4.4	0744	0.6
	1515	3.9	2123	1.2		1354	4.1	1945	0.8
8 F	0330	4.0	1002	0.8	23 Sa	0203	4.6	0835	0.3
	1602	3.8	2209	1.5		1449	4.2	2038	0.9
9 Sa	0406	3.8	1046	0.9	24 Su	0250	4.6	0929	0.0
	1648	3.7	2253	1.7		1548	4.2	2134	1.1
10 Su	0443	3.7	1127	0.9	25 M	0341	4.6	1025	-0.0
	1735	3.6	2338	1.9		1649	4.2	2234 O	1.2
11 M	0520	3.5	1207	0.9	26 Tu	0437	4.6	1124	-0.3
	1823	3.5				1754	4.2	2341	1.4
12 Tu	0024	2.1	0601	3.4	27 W	0538	4.4	1226	-0.3
	1246	1.0	1911	3.4		1903	4.2		
13 W	0113	2.2	0645	3.3	28 Th	0052	1.5	0645	4.3
	1325	1.0	2001	3.4		1329	-0.3	2012	4.3
14 Th	0202	2.2	0732	3.2	29 F	0208	1.5	0755	4.2
	1403	1.0	2049	3.5		1433	-0.2	2120	4.4
15 F	0249	2.2	0820	3.2	30 Sa	0321	1.4	0906	4.1
	1442	1.0	2135	3.6		1536	0.0	2223	4.4

TIME MERIDIAN 60°W
Heights in feet are referred to the chart datum of sounding.

0000h is midnight, 1200h is noon.

Chapter 2

MALECON · ZAPARA, VENEZUELA

HIGH & LOW WATER 1994
11°00'N 71°35'W

ATLANTIC STANDARD TIME (GMT -4H)

MAY

Day	Time ft	Time ft	Time ft	Time ft
1 Su	0431 1.3	1014 4.1	1637 0.2	2321 4.5
2 M	0534 1.1	1119 4.0	1734 0.5	
3 Tu	0013 4.5	0631 1.0	1220 4.0	1829 0.7
4 W	0059 4.5	0724 0.9	1316 3.9	1920 1.0
5 Th	0140 4.4	0812 0.8	1408 3.8	2007 1.3
6 F	0217 4.3	0857 0.7	1456 3.7	2051 1.6
7 Sa	0252 4.2	0939 0.7	1542 3.7	2133 1.8
8 Su	0326 4.0	1017 0.7	1627 3.6	2213 2.0
9 M	0400 3.9	1054 0.7	1711 3.5	2252 2.2
10 Tu	0437 3.8	1128 0.7	1757 3.5	2333 2.3
11 W	0517 3.6	1203 0.8	1844 3.6	
12 Th	0018 2.4	0559 3.6	1239 0.8	1932 3.6
13 F	0106 2.4	0644 3.5	1316 0.8	2018 3.7
14 Sa	0156 2.4	0731 3.4	1355 0.8	2103 3.8
15 Su	0244 2.3	0819 3.5	1436 0.9	2143 3.9
16 M	0331 2.2	0910 3.5	1519 0.9	2221 4.0
17 Tu	0417 2.0	1001 3.6	1603 0.9	2257 4.2
18 W	0504 1.6	1054 3.7	1649 0.9	2333 4.4
19 Th	0552 1.3	1148 3.8	1737 1.0	
20 F	0011 4.6	0641 0.9	1243 3.9	1827 1.0
21 Sa	0053 4.7	0731 0.5	1340 4.0	1920 1.1
22 Su	0138 4.8	0823 0.1	1439 4.1	2016 1.3
23 M	0227 4.9	0917 -0.2	1539 4.2	2115 1.4
24 Tu	0321 4.9	1013 -0.3	1642 4.2	2219 1.6
25 W	0418 4.8	1110 -0.4	1746 4.3	2328 1.7
26 Th	0519 4.6	1210 -0.3	1853 4.3	
27 F	0040 1.8	0625 4.5	1310 -0.2	1959 4.4
28 Sa	0155 1.7	0733 4.3	1412 0.1	2103 4.5
29 Su	0307 1.6	0842 4.1	1512 0.3	2203 4.6
30 M	0415 1.3	0950 4.0	1611 0.6	2257 4.6
31 Tu	0517 1.3	1056 3.9	1707 0.9	2345 4.6

JUNE

Day	Time ft	Time ft	Time ft	Time ft
1 W	0613 1.1	1157 3.8	1800 1.2	
2 Th	0028 4.5	0703 1.0	1253 3.8	1849 1.5
3 F	0106 4.5	0749 0.8	1344 3.7	1933 1.7
4 Sa	0141 4.4	0831 0.8	1431 3.6	2014 1.9
5 Su	0214 4.3	0908 0.7	1515 3.6	2051 2.1
6 M	0248 4.2	0943 0.7	1558 3.6	2126 2.2
7 Tu	0323 4.2	1016 0.7	1641 3.6	2202 2.3
8 W	0400 4.1	1048 0.7	1725 3.7	2241 2.4
9 Th	0439 4.0	1122 0.7	1810 3.7	2325 2.5
10 F	0519 3.9	1157 0.7	1856 3.8	
11 Sa	0014 2.5	0602 3.8	1235 0.7	1941 3.9
12 Su	0106 2.5	0649 3.8	1316 0.8	2024 4.0
13 M	0201 2.4	0739 3.7	1358 0.9	2105 4.1
14 Tu	0256 2.2	0834 3.7	1444 0.9	2145 4.3
15 W	0350 1.9	0932 3.7	1531 1.0	2224 4.4
16 Th	0443 1.5	1032 3.7	1621 1.1	2305 4.6
17 F	0536 1.1	1229 3.8	1714 1.2	2348 4.8
18 Sa	0628 0.7	1233 3.9	1808 1.3	
19 Su	0034 4.9	0720 0.3	1333 4.0	1905 1.5
20 M	0123 5.0	0813 0.0	1433 4.1	2004 1.6
21 Tu	0214 5.0	0907 -0.2	1534 4.1	2106 1.7
22 W	0309 5.0	1002 -0.3	1635 4.2	2210 1.8
23 Th	0405 4.9	1057 -0.2	1737 4.3	2318 1.9
24 F	0505 4.7	1154 -0.1	1839 4.4	
25 Sa	0028 1.9	0607 4.5	1251 0.2	1941 4.4
26 Su	0139 1.9	0711 4.3	1349 0.4	2041 4.5
27 M	0248 1.8	0818 4.1	1447 0.8	2136 4.5
28 Tu	0354 1.6	0924 3.9	1544 1.1	2227 4.5
29 W	0454 1.4	1029 3.8	1639 1.3	2312 4.5
30 Th	0548 1.5	1130 3.7	1729 1.6	2352 4.5

JULY

Day	Time ft	Time ft	Time ft	Time ft
1 F	0636 1.1	1225 3.6	1916 1.8	
2 Sa	0029 4.5	0719 1.0	1314 3.6	1857 2.0
3 Su	0104 4.4	0757 0.9	1358 3.6	1933 2.1
4 M	0138 4.4	0831 0.8	1440 3.6	2007 2.2
5 Tu	0213 4.4	0903 0.7	1522 3.7	2040 2.3
6 W	0249 4.4	0934 0.7	1603 3.7	2117 2.3
7 Th	0326 4.4	1006 0.6	1645 3.8	2157 2.3
8 F	0404 4.4	1041 0.6	1728 3.9	2242 2.4
9 Sa	0445 4.3	1118 0.6	1812 4.0	2333 2.3
10 Su	0529 4.2	1158 0.7	1856 4.1	
11 M	0027 2.3	0617 4.1	1241 0.8	1939 4.2
12 Tu	0125 2.1	0711 4.0	1327 0.9	2024 4.3
13 W	0225 1.9	0811 3.9	1416 1.1	2109 4.4
14 Th	0326 1.6	0915 3.8	1508 1.2	2155 4.6
15 F	0424 1.3	1020 3.8	1604 1.4	2243 4.7
16 Sa	0521 0.9	1126 3.8	1702 1.5	2333 4.9
17 Su	0616 0.5	1229 3.8	1801 1.6	
18 M	0024 5.0	0710 0.2	1331 4.0	1901 1.6
19 Tu	0115 5.0	0804 0.0	1430 4.1	2002 1.7
20 W	0208 5.1	0857 -0.1	1528 4.2	2103 1.8
21 Th	0302 5.0	0950 -0.1	1625 4.3	2205 1.8
22 F	0356 4.8	1043 0.1	1722 4.3	2309 1.9
23 Sa	0453 4.7	1137 0.3	1820 4.3	
24 Su	0014 1.9	0551 4.4	1231 0.6	1916 4.4
25 M	0120 1.9	0651 4.2	1326 0.9	2011 4.4
26 Tu	0225 1.8	0754 3.9	1422 1.2	2103 4.3
27 W	0328 1.7	0858 3.7	1516 1.5	2150 4.3
28 Th	0425 1.5	1001 3.6	1609 1.7	2234 4.3
29 F	0517 1.4	1100 3.5	1658 1.9	2313 4.3
30 Sa	0602 1.3	1152 3.5	1742 2.0	2350 4.3
31 Su	0641 1.1	1239 3.5	1819 2.1	

AUGUST

Day	Time ft	Time ft	Time ft	Time ft
1 M	0026 4.4	0716 1.0	1321 3.6	1852 2.2
2 Tu	0102 4.4	0747 0.9	1402 3.7	1925 2.2
3 W	0138 4.5	0818 0.8	1441 3.8	2000 2.2
4 Th	0215 4.5	0850 0.7	1521 3.9	2038 2.1
5 F	0253 4.6	0924 0.6	1601 4.0	2121 2.1
6 Sa	0332 4.6	1000 0.6	1641 4.1	2209 2.0
7 Su	0415 4.5	1040 0.7	1723 4.2	2300 2.0
8 M	0502 4.4	1123 0.7	1807 4.3	2357 1.8
9 Tu	0554 4.3	1210 0.9	1853 4.4	
10 W	0057 1.7	0652 4.1	1300 1.0	1943 4.4
11 Th	0159 1.4	0756 4.0	1355 1.2	2035 4.5
12 F	0303 1.2	0905 3.9	1454 1.4	2130 4.6
13 Sa	0405 0.9	1015 3.9	1557 1.5	2226 4.8
14 Su	0506 0.6	1123 3.9	1700 1.6	2322 4.9
15 M	0604 0.3	1227 4.0	1803 1.6	
16 Tu	0017 4.9	0659 0.2	1327 4.1	1904 1.7
17 W	0111 5.0	0753 0.1	1424 4.2	2004 1.7
18 Th	0204 5.0	0845 0.1	1518 4.3	2102 1.7
19 F	0257 4.9	0937 0.3	1611 4.3	2200 1.7
20 Sa	0349 4.7	1028 0.5	1702 4.3	2259 1.8
21 Su	0442 4.5	1119 0.8	1753 4.3	2358 1.8
22 M	0537 4.2	1210 1.1	1843 4.2	
23 Tu	0058 1.8	0634 4.0	1302 1.4	1932 4.2
24 W	0158 1.7	0733 3.8	1355 1.7	2020 4.1
25 Th	0255 1.6	0833 3.6	1449 1.9	2106 4.1
26 F	0349 1.5	0932 3.5	1540 2.0	2150 4.1
27 Sa	0437 1.4	1028 3.5	1626 2.1	2231 4.1
28 Su	0518 1.3	1117 3.5	1706 2.2	2310 4.2
29 M	0555 1.2	1202 3.6	1741 2.2	2348 4.2
30 Tu	0627 1.1	1242 3.7	1813 2.2	
31 W	0025 4.4	0658 1.0	1321 3.8	1847 2.1

TIME MERIDIAN 60°W
Heights in feet are referred to the chart datum of sounding.

0000h is midnight, 1200h is noon.

MALECON - ZAPARA, VENEZUELA

HIGH & LOW WATER 1994 **11°00'N 71°35'W**

ATLANTIC STANDARD TIME (GMT -4H)

Chapter 2

SEPTEMBER

Day	DOW	Time ft	Time ft	Time ft	Time ft
1	Th	0102 4.5	0730 0.9	1359 3.9	1925 2.0
16	F	0159 4.8	0831 0.5	1502 4.4	2058 1.5
2	F	0140 4.6	0804 0.8	1436 4.0	2007 1.9
17	Sa	0251 4.7	0901 0.7	1549 4.4	2153 1.5
3	Sa	0220 4.8	0841 0.7	1514 4.2	2052 1.8
18	Su	0342 4.5	1010 1.0	1635 4.3	2246 1.5
4	Su	0303 4.7	0921 0.7	1553 4.3	2141 1.6
19		0433 4.3	1058 1.3	1719 4.2	O 2340 1.6
5	M	0349 4.6	1004 0.8	1635 4.4	● 2235 1.4
20	Tu	0524 4.0	1147 1.6	1803 4.1	
6	Tu	0440 4.5	1051 0.9	1721 4.5	2332 1.3
21	W	0033 1.6	0617 3.8	1236 1.8	1848 4.0
7	W	0537 4.4	1142 1.0	1811 4.5	
22	Th	0125 1.6	0712 3.6	1327 2.0	1932 3.9
8	Th	0033 1.1	0639 4.2	1238 1.2	1907 4.6
23	F	0216 1.6	0808 3.5	1418 2.2	2018 3.9
9	F	0137 0.9	0747 4.1	1339 1.4	2006 4.6
24	Sa	0304 1.5	0903 3.5	1507 2.3	2102 3.9
10	Sa	0242 0.7	0858 4.1	1446 1.5	2109 4.7
25	Su	0347 1.5	0955 3.5	1550 2.3	2146 3.9
11	Su	0347 0.5	1010 4.1	1554 1.6	2211 4.8
26	M	0426 1.4	1042 3.6	1628 2.3	2227 4.0
12	M	0449 0.4	1118 4.1	1701 1.6	◑ 2312 4.8
27	Tu	0500 1.3	1125 3.7	1702 2.3	2307 4.1
13	Tu	0548 0.3	1220 4.2	1805 1.6	
28	W	0533 1.2	1204 3.8	1737 2.2	◑ 2346 4.3
14	W	0010 4.9	0645 0.3	1318 4.3	1905 1.6
29	Th	0607 1.1	1240 3.9	1814 2.1	
15	Th	0106 4.9	0739 0.3	1411 4.4	2003 1.5
30	F	0026 4.4	0642 1.0	1316 4.1	1855 1.9

OCTOBER

Day	DOW	Time ft	Time ft	Time ft	Time ft
1	Sa	0107 4.5	0720 0.9	1352 4.3	1940 1.6
16	Su	0242 4.5	0901 1.2	1522 4.5	2140 1.3
2	Su	0150 4.6	0800 0.9	1429 4.4	2028 1.4
17	M	0332 4.3	0945 1.7	1602 4.4	2229 1.3
3	M	0237 4.6	0844 0.9	1509 4.6	2119 1.2
18	Tu	0421 4.1	1035 1.7	1642 4.2	2316 1.4
4	Tu	0328 4.6	0931 1.0	1554 4.7	2213 0.9
19	W	0510 3.9	1120 2.0	1721 4.1	O
5	W	0423 4.5	1022 1.1	1643 4.7	● 2311 0.7
20	Th	0002 1.4	0559 3.7	1205 2.2	1802 4.0
6	Th	0523 4.4	1118 1.3	1737 4.8	
21	F	0047 1.4	0650 3.6	1251 2.3	1845 3.9
7	F	0013 0.6	0628 4.3	1220 1.4	1838 4.8
22	Sa	0131 1.5	0741 3.6	1338 2.4	1929 3.9
8	Sa	0117 0.5	0738 4.3	1327 1.6	1942 4.8
23	Su	0213 1.5	0832 3.6	1423 2.5	2014 3.9
9	Su	0222 0.4	0850 4.2	1438 1.7	2049 4.8
24	M	0252 1.4	0921 3.6	1505 2.5	2059 3.9
10	M	0327 0.3	1000 4.3	1550 1.7	2155 4.8
25	Tu	0329 1.4	1007 3.7	1544 2.5	2142 4.0
11	Tu	0430 0.3	1106 4.4	1658 1.6	◑ 2259 4.8
26	W	0405 1.3	1047 3.8	1623 2.4	2225 4.1
12	W	0530 0.4	1207 4.5	1801 1.5	2359 4.8
27	Th	0441 1.3	1125 4.0	1703 2.2	2308 4.2
13	Th	0627 0.5	1302 4.6	1900 1.4	
28	F	0518 1.2	1200 4.1	1745 2.0	2351 4.3
14	F	0056 4.8	0721 0.7	1352 4.6	1956 1.4
29	Sa	0558 1.1	1234 4.3	1830 1.7	
15	Sa	0150 4.6	0812 0.9	1438 4.5	2049 1.3
30	Su	0037 4.4	0640 1.1	1310 4.5	1917 1.4
31	M	0125 4.5	0725 1.1	1350 4.7	2007 1.1

NOVEMBER

Day	DOW	Time ft	Time ft	Time ft	Time ft
1	Tu	0216 4.5	0813 1.1	1433 4.8	2100 0.8
16	W	0403 3.9	1006 2.0	1604 4.3	2247 1.2
2	W	0311 4.5	0901 1.0	1521 4.9	2156 0.5
17	Th	0448 3.8	1045 2.2	1641 4.2	2327 1.3
3	Th	0409 4.5	0959 1.3	1614 5.0	● 2254 0.3
18	F	0534 3.7	1126 2.3	1720 4.1	O
4	F	0511 4.4	1059 1.5	1712 5.0	2355 0.3
19	Sa	0005 1.3	0620 3.7	1205 2.4	1801 4.0
5	Sa	0617 4.4	1205 1.6	1815 4.9	
20	Su	0043 1.3	0708 3.7	1246 2.5	1844 4.0
6	Su	0058 0.2	0727 4.4	1315 1.7	1921 4.9
21	M	0121 1.4	0757 3.7	1329 2.6	1929 4.0
7	M	0202 0.3	0837 4.4	1428 1.7	2029 4.8
22	Tu	0158 1.4	0844 3.8	1414 2.6	2014 4.0
8	Tu	0306 0.3	0945 4.5	1540 1.7	2137 4.8
23	W	0236 1.4	0928 3.8	1459 2.5	2059 4.0
9	W	0409 0.4	1049 4.6	1648 1.6	2242 4.7
24	Th	0315 1.4	1008 4.0	1545 2.4	2145 4.1
10	Th	0509 0.6	1147 4.7	1750 1.5	◑ 2344 4.7
25	F	0355 1.3	1045 4.1	1632 2.1	2233 4.1
11	F	0606 0.8	1240 4.7	1849 1.3	
26	Sa	0437 1.3	1120 4.3	1720 1.8	◑ 2322 4.2
12	Sa	0042 4.6	0700 1.0	1327 4.7	1943 1.2
27	Su	0521 1.3	1157 4.5	1808 1.5	
13	Su	0137 4.4	0751 1.3	1410 4.6	2033 1.2
28	M	0013 4.3	0608 1.3	1236 4.7	1859 1.1
14	M	0228 4.3	0839 1.6	1450 4.5	2120 1.2
29	Tu	0106 4.3	0657 1.3	1320 4.8	1951 0.7
15	Tu	0317 4.1	0924 1.8	1527 4.4	2205 1.2
30	W	0201 4.2	0749 1.3	1407 5.0	2045 0.4

DECEMBER

Day	DOW	Time ft	Time ft	Time ft	Time ft
1	Th	0258 4.4	0844 1.4	1459 5.1	2140 0.2
16	F	0417 3.8	1006 2.2	1605 4.3	2246 1.1
2	F	0357 4.4	0942 1.5	1554 5.1	● 2238 0.1
17	Sa	0459 3.7	1040 2.3	1643 4.2	2320 1.2
3	Sa	0459 4.4	1045 1.6	1654 5.1	2338 0.1
18	Su	0543 3.7	1116 2.3	1723 4.2	2356 1.2
4	Su	0604 4.4	1152 1.7	1756 5.0	
19	M	0629 3.7	1155 2.4	1805 4.1	
5	M	0039 0.2	0712 4.4	1303 1.7	1902 4.9
20	Tu	0032 1.2	0715 3.8	1240 2.4	1848 4.1
6	Tu	0142 0.3	0819 4.5	1415 1.7	2009 4.8
21	W	0110 1.3	0800 3.8	1328 2.4	1934 4.0
7	W	0245 0.5	0925 4.6	1525 1.7	2117 4.7
22	Th	0151 1.3	0843 3.9	1420 2.3	2022 4.0
8	Th	0347 0.7	1026 4.6	1632 1.5	2223 4.5
23	F	0233 1.3	0924 4.0	1512 2.1	2114 4.0
9	F	0447 0.9	1122 4.6	1734 1.4	◑ 2326 4.4
24	Sa	0318 1.4	1004 4.1	1605 1.8	2207 4.0
10	Sa	0544 1.1	1212 4.6	1830 1.3	
25	Su	0405 1.4	1044 4.3	1657 1.5	● 2302 4.1
11	Su	0025 4.3	0638 1.4	1257 4.6	1922 1.2
26	M	0455 1.4	1127 4.5	1750 1.1	2358 4.1
12	M	0119 4.2	0727 1.6	1338 4.5	2010 1.1
27	Tu	0546 1.4	1212 4.6	1843 0.8	
13	Tu	0208 4.0	0813 1.8	1416 4.5	2053 1.1
28	W	0054 4.2	0640 1.4	1300 4.8	1937 0.5
14	W	0253 3.9	0854 1.9	1452 4.4	2133 1.1
29	Th	0150 4.2	0735 1.4	1352 5.0	2031 0.2
15	Th	0335 3.8	0931 2.1	1528 4.3	2211 1.1
30	F	0248 4.3	0833 1.4	1445 5.1	2127 0.1
31	Sa	0346 4.3	0933 1.5	1542 5.1	2223 0.1

TIME MERIDIAN 60°W
Heights in feet are referred to the chart datum of sounding.

0000h is midnight, 1200h is noon.

BONAIRE

ENTRY PROCEDURES

The Dutch ABC islands are actually the ACB group, if you read left to right. Bonaire is the furthest to the east, making a good first stop for boaters headed from Venezuela to Panama. The island is one of the Netherlands Antilles along with Curaçao. Aruba has separated from the group, and is scheduled to become an independent nation in 1996.

The Port of Entry is Kralendijk, located midway up the western side of the island. Yachts can enter the marina north of town to clear in. Customs and Immigration are open 24 hours a day, seven days a week. You should contact the officials from the marina, and await their arrival from town. You can tie up to the Customs wharf at the commercial pier, but this area is quite rough. Boaters have reported no problem in traveling to town to visit the offices in person.

Firearms and spearguns will be held during your stay. There are strict rules preventing the taking of marine life, as most of the islands reefs are part of Bonaire Marine Park.

Formalities are reported to be simple and swift, once you get in touch with the officials.

The telephone area code for the island is 599 7, followed by a four digit local number. On the island you only need the last four digits.

The official currency is the Netherlands Antilles florin, but U.S. currency is widely accepted. The exchange rate is 1.79 florins to 1 U.S. dollar.

Dutch is the official language, but you will find many people who speak English. The local dialect, known as Papiamento, will be heard.

For those planning a visit to Venezuela, there is a consulate where visa applications may be submitted.

BONAIRE

BOCA SPELONK, NE side of island, 12 13.0N, 68 11.7W, Fl W 5s, 100ft., 15M, white circular stone structure, Visible 127°– 002°, Visibility variable on account of salt deposits which constantly form on the lenses.

LACRE PUNT, S point of island, 12 01.9N, 68 14.1W, Fl W 9s, 75ft., 13M, White circular stone tower, Visible 203°– 147°, Visibility variable on account of salt deposits which constantly form on the lenses.

PUNT VIERKANT, 12 07.0N, 68 17.6W, Fl (3) W 22s, 30ft., 5M, Gray square tower, red lantern.

KRALENDIJK, W side of island opposite Klein Bonaire, 12 09.1N, 68 16.5W, Fl W 2s, 44ft., 5M, White square stone structure, Visible 027°– 150°.

KLEIN BONAIRE, SW point, 12 09.4N, 68 19.8W, Fl (2) W 20s, 19ft., 9M, White round tower, Visible 278°– 143°, obscured elsewhere.

KRALENDIJK

12 09N, 68 17W

Pilotage: The island is high at the north end, but low and sandy to the south. The highest peak, Brandaris, is about 787 feet high, and is located on the northwest part of the island. The coast is all steep to with no offlying hazards. However, the east coast of the island was where Peter Tangvald put his boat on the reefs, and lost his life. There have been many reports of confusion in identifying the lights of the island when approaching from offshore. The lights have been reported to be unreliable. Contact the harbor master on VHF channel 16.

Port of Entry: Most boats will want to dock in the marina 1 mile north of the commercial wharves.

Communications: See Communications and Weather Services for information on Trans

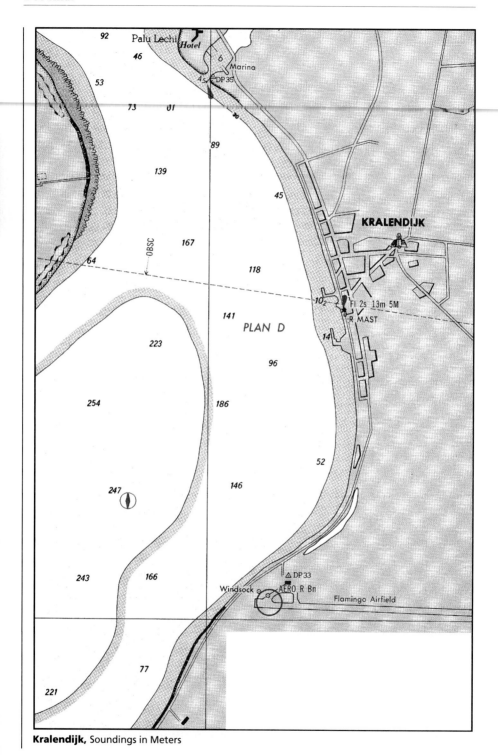

92 Palu Lechi *Hotel*
46   6
        Marina
53   4.5 DP 35
73   01   20
             89
    139
             45
                    KRALENDIJK
        167
OBSC
64   118
        102 Fl 2s 13m 5M
        141   R MAST
    PLAN D   14
    223
        96
254   186
        52
247   146
243 166
    Windsock △ DP 33
        AERO R Bn
        Flamingo Airfield
77
221

Kralendijk, Soundings in Meters

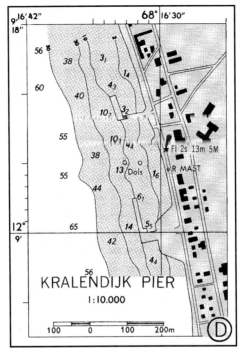

Kralendijk Pier Area, Soundings in Meters

World Radio. Yachts use VHF channel 77 for calling, switching to channel 71 to talk.

Dockage: Contact the Harbour Village Marina at (599 7) 8384, or on VHF channel 17. It is located in a small basin about 1 mile north of the commercial docks. Boaters report this is a safe place to leave your boat for extended periods.

Anchorage: Most boats anchor on the narrow shelf of shallow water between the marina and the commercial docks. You should check your anchor set carefully, and use two anchors if in doubt. The holding has been reported to be poor, and you don't have much dragging room before you're off the shelf. Strong southwest winds can make the anchorage unsafe. These are usually experienced from September through early November. If you anchor out, dinghy in to the main wharf area or the dinghy dock at the Zee Zicht restaurant. The latter is located just north of the commercial wharves.

Services: Fuel and water (desalinized and expensive) is available in the marina. There is a

bank, some restaurants, markets, and most general supplies. The island is a world famous diving center, so those services are excellent. Contact the Tourist Bureau at (599 7) 8322 or 8649, for information on the islands parks and recreation opportunities. The flocks of pink flamingoes are well worth seeing. There may be more than 10,000 of these amazing birds.

GOTO, 12 13.5N, 68 23.8W, Q W 6ft., 5M,

RANGE, No 1, (Front), 12 13.3N, 68 23.0W, F G, 46ft., 9M. **(Rear),** 197 meters, 067°47' from front, F R, 82ft., 9M.

GOTO RANGE No 2, (Front). 12 13.4N, 68 21.4W, Q R, 26ft., 8M. **(Rear),** 126 meters 081°04' from front, Q G, 33ft., 6M.

PUNT WEKOEWA, 12 14.0N, 68 25.0W, Fl (3) W 20s, 49ft., 12M, Visible 285° – 155°, obscured elsewhere.

CERU BENTANA, 12 18.2N, 68 22.8w, Fl (4) W 22s, 144ft., 17M, Square building, yellow tower. Visible 069°30'– 073° and 074°– 303°, obscured elsewhere.

REED'S NAUTICAL COMPANION

Table of Contents

To get your **REED'S NAUTICAL COMPANION,** call 1-800-995-4995 and ask for the **REED'S** dealer nearest you!

CURAÇAO

CAUTION: Our information on aids to navigation comes from official government sources. The latitudes and longitudes of these marks may not correspond to the readings from GPS receivers. Some aids have been reported as unreliable, missing, off position or showing incorrect characteristics. No single aid to navigation, or waypoint, should be relied upon as a sole means of fixing your position.

ENTRY PROCEDURES

Curaçao is the middle island of the ABC group. It is located about 35 miles north of the Venezuela coast and 30 miles west of Bonaire. Bonaire and Curaçao are part of the Netherlands Antilles. Aruba has separated from the group, and is scheduled to become an independent nation in 1996.

Ports of Entry are Spaansche (Spanish) Water and Willemstad. Yachtsmen prefer to clear customs in Spaansche Water, due to the commercial nature of Willemstad harbor. You still must voyage overland to Willemstad to clear with Immigration.

The entrance channel at Willemstad is called Sint Anna Baai, and is crossed by two bridges. The port officials are near the fuel dock, after the high-level bridge on the starboard side of the channel. Call "Fort Nassau" on VHF channel 12 for information and berthing instructions. In Spaansche Water, contact the officials from Sarifundy's Marina.

Immigration will generally grant you three months in the country. Firearms will be held during your stay.

Formalities are reported to be simple and swift, once you get in touch with the officials.

The telephone area code for the island is 599 9, followed by a five or six digit local number. On the island you only need the local number.

The official currency is the Netherlands Antilles florin, but U.S. currency is widely accepted. The exchange rate is about 1.79 florins to 1 U.S. dollar.

Dutch is the official language, but you will find many people who speak English. The local dialect, known as Papiamento, will be heard.

CURAÇAO

KLEIN CURAÇAO, near center of island. 11 59.5N, 68 39.0W, Fl (2) W 15s, 82ft., 15M, white circular stone tower, lower part red.

PUNT KANON, SE point of island, 12 02.5N, 68 44.5W, Fl W 4s, 39ft, 8M, Red-white banded round stone tower.

FUIK BAAI, Range, (Front). 12 03.2N, 68 49.7W, F G, 32ft., 2M, Red and white beacon with cross topmark. **(Rear),** 50 meters, 027°30' from front, F R, 42ft., 4M, Red and white beacon with triangular topmark.

SPAANSCHE WATER
12 04N, 68 51W

Pilotage: Spaanse Haven, the narrow channel leading into Spaansche (Spanish) Water, is reported to be hard to spot from offshore. The obscure entrance is identified by a cluster of oil storage tanks standing on top, and fringing, the side of the hill forming the left bank of the entrance. The channel is 1 1/2 miles northwest of the marked entrance to Fuikbaai, and 1 1/4 miles southeast of Lijhoek Light in Caracasbaai. The channel is reported to be privately marked and flanked by several shallow spots and reefs. An approach in good light is recommended.

Port of Entry: Contact the officials from Sarifundy's Marina. You will have to travel to Willemstad to visit the Immigration office.

Dockage: Sarifundy's Marina is located in the northwest arm of Spaansche Water. Call the marina at (599 9) 677643 or 674672. The Curaçao Yacht Club is located nearby, as is the Shell Yacht Club. They may be able to provide some dockage.

Anchorage: Anchor near the marina where you can dinghy in and use their services for a fee.

Services: Sarifundy's has water, ice, laundry, showers, a dinghy dock, telephones, message

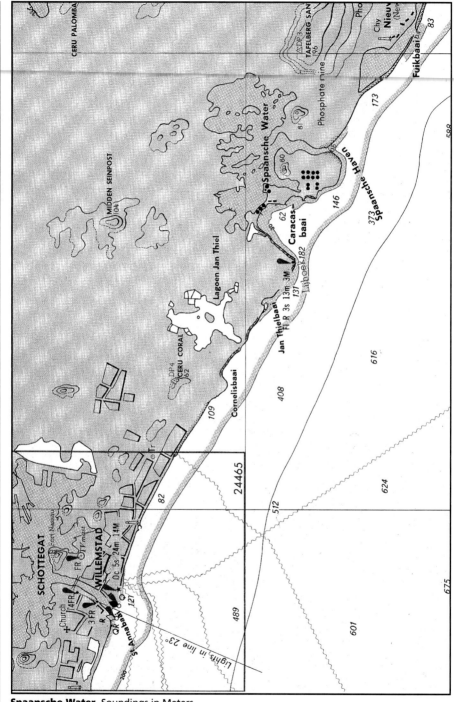

Spaansche Water, Soundings in Meters

services, rental cars and some groceries. They can help you find what you need on the island. There are several chandlers in nearby Willemstad, and frequent buses run into town. All general supplies are available.

CARACAS BAAI ON LIJ HOEK, W point of bay, Fl R 3s, 42ft., 4M, Red and white metal framework tower, red lantern,
Range, (Front), 12 04.8N, 68 51.8W, F R, Beacon with cross topmark. **(Rear),** 90 meters, 043°30′ from front, F G, Beacon with triangular topmark, point down.
DR. ALBERT PLESMAN FIELD, Aviation Light, 12 11.0N, 68 57.1W, Al Fl W G, 10s, 148ft., White, 26M, Green 21M, Iron skeleton tower, Occasional.
Buoy, E side entrance to St. Anna Baai, 12 06.0N, 68 56.0W, Q W, 5M, Black buoy.
Buoy, W side entrance to harbor, 12 06.0N, 68 56.0W, Q R, 5M, Red buoy.
WILLEMSTAD, about 247 meters, 263° from Riffort Light, 12 06.2N, 68 56.3W, Fl G 4s, 6ft., 1M, Black pole.
RIFFORT, SINT ANNA (WILLEMSTAD), E side of entrance, 12 06.4N, 68 55.9W, Oc W 5s, 83ft., 14M, Gray structure on battery wall.
RANGE,(Front), 12 06.8N, 68 55.7W, F R, Orange diamond daymark. **(Rear),** 580 meters, 042° from front, F R, Orange diamond daymark.
W SIDE OF ENTRANCE, F R, 23ft., Red iron structure.
E SIDE OF ENTRANCE, F G., 26ft., Green wooden pile against battery wall.
RANGE, (Front), 12 06.6N, 68 56.0W, 3 F R, 54ft., Black metal mast, yellow bands, orange square, rectangular shape. **(Rear),** 480 meters, 023°30′ from front, 4 F R, 108ft., Steel mast, yellow circular shape, Lights arranged in diamond shape.
W SIDE, NEAR W WHARF, SINT ANNA BAY, F R, 23ft., Iron post.
E SIDE OF ENTRANCE TO SCHOTTEGAT, F G, 67ft., Aluminium painted structure, Visible only when entering or leaving Shottegat.
N SIDE, 12 07.5N, 68 55.1W, F G.
BAAI MACOLA, 12 07.1N, 68 55.1W, Q W.

WILLEMSTAD

12 07N, 68 56W

Pilotage: The well marked entrance to the harbor is called Sint Anna Baai. Approaching vessels should contact the harbor control office on VHF channel 12 — call sign "Fort Nassau". The first bridge is a floating pontoon structure and can be opened by calling "Fort

Nassau". The second bridge has a vertical clearance of 180 feet. The pontoon bridge will show a blue flag during the day, and a blue light at night, when it is about to open within 5 minutes. One long blast on the siren means it will open within 1 minute. Four long blasts on the siren indicate the bridge will not, or cannot, open. The correct signal to request an opening is 3 long blasts of the boat's horn,
Storm Signals: The following signals are shown from the light at Riffort: A red flag with white background indicates a storm is expected over Curaçao. Two red flags with black backgrounds indicate a hurricane is expected over Curaçao (at night this is 1 white light between 2 red lights vertically). A green pennant below the hurricane signal indicates the storm is expected between longitudes 60° and 65°. A black pennant below the hurricane signal indicates the storm is expected between 65° and 70° longitude.
Port of Entry: Tie up to the fueling wharf along the starboard side of Sint Anna Baai north of the high-level bridge. The harbor official's office is nearby.
Dockage: Contact the harbor officials about the possibility of mooring to the bulkhead between the bridges, on the starboard side of the channel. The wharves are named Kleine Wharf, Groote Wharf and Salazar Wharf, proceeding from seaward. The wharves on the west side of the channel are for larger ships.
Anchorage: Anchor in nearby Spaansche Water (see previous description).
Services: This is the commercial center of Curaçao, and a major port. Most services are available, including haulouts and repairs. There are several chandlers.

BULLENBAAI

BULLENBAAI, 12 10.9N, 69 00.9W, Fl W 2s, Square iron tower.
FIRST RANGE, (Front), 12 12.1N, 69 02.1W, F R, Red daymark. **(Rear),** 251 meters, 043° from front, 12 12.2N 69 01.9W, F G, Red daymark.
SECOND RANGE, (Front), 12 11.7N, 69 01.2W, Q R, On tank. **(Rear),** 640 meters 095° from front, Q R, On tank.
THIRD RANGE, (Front), 12 11.2N, 69 00.9W, F G, **(Rear),** 200 meters, 123° from front, F R.
KAAP ST. MARIE, 12 11.4N, 69 03.4W, Fl (2) W 9s, 41ft., 9M, Red rectangular iron tower.
NOORDPUNT, 12 23.2N, 69 09.5W, Fl (3) W 15s, 138ft., 12M, White masonry structure, Visible 006°– 271°, also on certain bearings N of 271°.

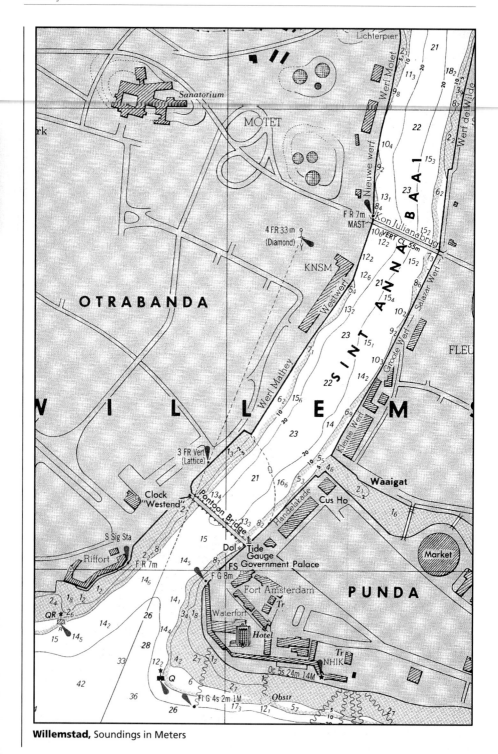

Willemstad, Soundings in Meters

ARUBA

CAUTION: Our information was aids for navigation comes from official government sources. The latitudes and longitudes of these marks may not correspond to the readings from GPS receivers. Some aids have been reported as unreliable, missing, off position or showing incorrect characteristics. No single aid to navigation, or waypoint, should be relied upon as a sole means of fixing your position.

ENTRY PROCEDURES

Aruba is the western island of the ABC group. It is located about 15 miles north of the Peninsula de Paraguaná, on the Venezuelan coast. It is about 60 miles west-northwest of the Willemstad area on Curaçao. This is frequently the last stop for cruisers headed to Panama. Aruba has separated from the Netherlands Antilles, and is scheduled to become an independent nation in 1996.

The Port of Entry is Oranjestad, which is about 12 miles northwest of the southern tip of the island. Tie up to the southern end of the main commercial wharves. The officials are located nearby. Call Oranjestad port radio on VHF channel 16 for instructions. Firearms will be held until your departure.

The telephone area code for the island is 297 8, followed by a five digit local number. On the island you only need the local number.

The official currency is the Aruban florin, but U.S. currency is widely accepted. The exchange rate is about 1.77 florins to 1 U.S. dollar.

Dutch is the official language, but you will find many people who speak English. The local dialect, known as Papiamento, will be heard.

ARUBA

PUNT BASORA (COLORADO POINT), SE extremity of island, 12 25.3N, 69 52.1W, Fl W 6s,

14Tft., 31m, Gray square stone tower, visible 160°– 109°. *Reported extinguished (1992).*
INDIAANSKOP, No 10, 12 25.1N, 69 53.6W, Q G, 10 ft., Steel trellis mast.

ST NICHOLAS BAAI

East Channel Entrance Buoy, 12 25.0N, 69 54.0W, Fl W 3s, 10ft., Red buoy.
Buoy Janet, East side of entrance, 12 25.0N, 69 54.0W, Fl R 4s, 10 ft., Red buoy.
BEACON NO. 6, W side of entrance, E channel, 12 25.7N, 69 54.1W, Fl R 2s, 11ft., Beacon.
BEACON NO. 5, W side of Entrance E channel, 12 25.6N, 69 54.2W, Q G, 11ft., Dolphin. F R and F G lights are shwon from heads of laker piers.
West Channel Entrance Buoy, 12 26.0N, 69 55.0W, Fl W 3s, Black buoy.
W ENTRANCE RANGE, near marine railway, **(Front),** 12 26.0N, 69 54.3W, 4 F R, 102ft., Occasional, Lights arranged in diamond shape. **(Rear),** 240 meters, 083°14′ from front, 4 F R, 134ft., Occasional, Lights arranged in diamond shape, N side of channel marked by Fl R light on dolphin and two F R lights on dock, F G and F R lights are shown from outer corners of finger piers.
ENTRANCE, N SIDE, NO. 2, 12 26.1N, 69 54.9W, Fl R 2s, 23ft., 7M.

COMMANDEURS BAAI

RANGE, (Front), 12 27.1N, 69 56.8W, 2 F G (vert), 19ft., 1M, Pole, **(Rear),** 34 meters, 059° from front, 2 F R (vert), 23ft., 1M, Pole.

BACADERA

N Entrance Buoy, 12 29.0N, 70 00.0W, Fl R 5s, Red buoy.

PAARDEN BAAI

S Entrance Buoy, 12 29.0N, 70 00.0W, Fl W 5s, Red buoy.
ORANJESTAD, PRINSES BEATRIX AVIATION LIGHT, 12 31.0N, 70 00.0W, F R, 669ft., Tower.

SOUTH ENTRANCE, 12 30.5N, 70 02.1W, Q W, Concrete column.
SOUTH ENTRANCE LIGHT "1", 12 30.7N, 70 02.1W, Fl (2) R 4s, Concrete column.
SOUTH ENTRANCE LIGHT "4", 12 30.8N, 70 02.2w, Fl G 2s, Concrete column.
SOUTH ENTRANCE LIGHT "5", 12 30.9N, 70 02.2W, Fl (2) G 4s, 10ft., Concrete column.
SOUTH ENTRANCE LIGHT "2", 12 31.0N, 70 02.1W, Fl (3) R 5s, 10ft., Concrete column.
SOUTH ENTRANCE LIGHT "6", 12 31.0N, 70 02.3W, Fl (3) G 5s, Concrete column.
WEST ENTRANCE, N side of channel, 12 31.8N, 70 03.3W, Fl R 2s, Concrete column.
WEST ENTRANCE, 12 31.7N, 70 03.1W, Fl (2) R 4s.
West Entrance Buoy, S side of channel, 12 32.0N, 70 03.0W, Fl W 3s, Yellow buoy.
WEST ENTRANCE LIGHT "3", N side of channel, 12 31.7N, 70 00.0W, Fl R 2s, Concrete column.
WEST ENTRANCE LIGHT "7", S side of entrance, 12 31.5N, 70 02.9W, Fl (2) G 4s, Concrete column.
WESTERN ENTRANCE RANGE, (Front), 12 31.5N, 70 02.6W, 3 F G (vert), Triangle on black mast with orange bands on N side of building. **(Rear),** 430 meters, 110° from front, 5 F G, orange diamond on black mast, orange bands, F R lights are shown from NW and SW corners of Oosthaven.

ORANJESTAD
12 31N, 70 02W

Pilotage: The harbor is located in Paarden Baai, and is protected by a barrier reef on its west side. This is the capital of Aruba. There is a westward flowing current in this area of 2 to 3 knots. Prominent landmarks are the white circular water tower, and the Roman Catholic church standing close northwest of the tower. Contact Oranjestad port radio on VHF channel 16 for information on entering the harbor.

Port of Entry: Tie up at the southern end of the main piers.

Dockage: Harbour Town Marina is opposite the commercial wharves. There are two yacht clubs located to the southeast inside the reefs. Inquire locally for directions to these areas.

Anchorage: You can anchor southeast of the harbor area, in the patch of deeper water extending east from marker 1. There are reports boats anchor close in to the beach, avoiding the shallow spots on the way in. The depths in this area may be poorly charted.

Services: There are good supermarkets and general supplies. Air connections are excellent. Marine supplies are rather limited. Fuel and water are available at the marina.

Chapter 2

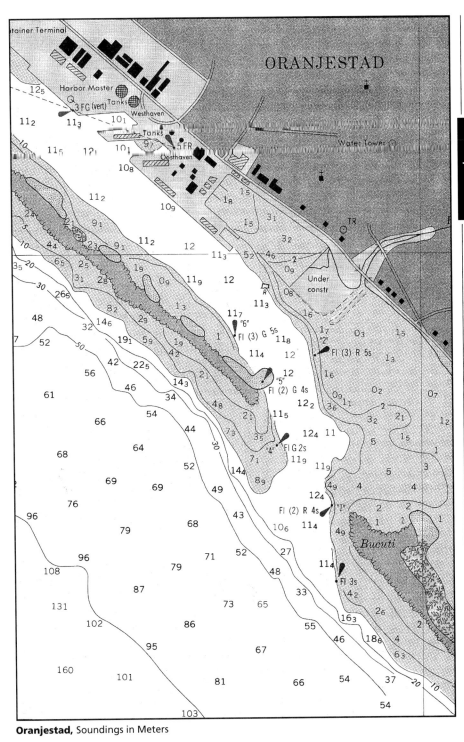

Oranjestad, Soundings in Meters

REED'S
NAUTICAL ALMANACS & COMPANIONS

1994

CARIBBEAN

The only almanac which covers the entire Caribbean basin including Bermuda, the Bahamas, Caribbean islands, the north coast of South America, Central America, Panama and Mexico. Contains 200 harbor chartlets, complete tide and celestial tables, coast pilot with aids to navigation, weather and communication information.   800 pages $29.95(US) Retail

NORTH AMERICAN: EAST COAST

Now in its 21st year of publication, it includes over 200 harbor chartlets, tide and current tables from Nova Scotia to the Bahamas, light and buoy lists, waypoints, radio and communication information, a complete nautical ephemeris and lots more.

900 pages $29.95(US) Retail

NORTH AMERICAN: PACIFIC NORTHWEST

The only almanac to include US and Canadian Hydrographic information in a single volume, and covers from the head of the Columbia River to the Gulf of Alaska and Kodiak Island, including Puget Sound and the British Columbia coastline. More than 170 harbor charts, tide and current tables, nautical ephemeris, aids to navigation, communication and weather information.   900 pages $29.95(US) Retail

NORTHERN EUROPEAN

Our flagship almanac, now enjoying its 63rd year of publication. Its coverage ranges from Skagen, on the northern coast of Denmark, to the French-Spanish border and Biarritz. This extensive European coverage includes 450 chartlets and illustrations, 2000 ports and complete tidal information for each area.   1,200 pages $45.00(US) Retail

SOUTHERN EUROPEAN

A completely reorganized and updated version of our Mediterranean almanac, featuring the Atlantic-European coast and islands, as well as the complete coastline of one of the world's most popular cruising areas, the Mediterranean sea. This edition is an excellent reference book for those planning a transatlantic voyage including stopovers in the Azores and entry via Gibraltar to the Mediterranean.   800 pages $45.00(US) Retail

NAUTICAL COMPANION

The **COMPANION** is designed to complement the Caribbean, North American East Coast and Pacific Northwest **REED'S ALMANACS**, and is full of practical information for the cruising boater. It includes extensive chapters on seamanship, rules of the road, coastal passage making, signaling, first aid and more.   444 pages $19.95(US) Retail

NAUTICAL COMPANION (European edition)

An outstanding nautical reference with essential information on subjects similar to those included in our US **COMPANION**. Designed to complement our European editions.

450 pages $24.95(US) Retail

Call 1-800-995-4995 for your nearest dealer!

COLOMBIA

CAUTION: Our information on aids to navigation comes from official government sources. The latitudes and longitudes of these marks may not correspond to the readings from GPS receivers. Some aids have been reported as unreliable, missing, off position or showing incorrect characteristics. No single aid to navigation, or waypoint, should be relied upon as a sole means of fixing your position.

ENTRY PROCEDURES

From Punta Gallinas to the Panama Canal is about 530 miles. From Aruba to the Canal is about 630 miles. More and more yachtsmen are breaking up this long run with a cruise along the Colombian coast, or at least a stop in Cartagena and the Islas del Rosario. It is about 324 miles from Cartagena to the Canal. The country's ancient Spanish heritage, and beautiful scenery are an interesting contrast to some of the Caribbean countries to the east. See *Reed's Nautical Companion* for an example of the country flag.

Ports of Entry on the Caribbean include Riohacha, Santa Marta, Barranquilla, Cartagena, Turbo, Zapzurro and the island of San Andrés, which is discussed later in this book in the section *Western Caribbean — Offshore Islands*.

Some nationalities are required to have a visa upon arrival, but citizens of the U.S., Germany, the Netherlands, the United Kingdom and many others are granted 90 days when they clear in. Those traveling on business should check the latest visa requirements. For more information contact the Colombian Embassy at 2118 Leroy Place NW, Washington, DC, 20008, (202) 387-8338. There are also Colombian Consulates in Miami, Chicago, New York and San Juan.

The importation of firearms into the country is strictly forbidden, and all weapons must be declared.

Yachts are generally required to use the services of an agent to handle this paperwork. A cruising permit, or "zarpe", will be issued, and should be presented in every port visited.

WARNING: The U.S. State Department is advising U.S. citizens not to visit Colombia, due to the prevalence of violence and theft, particularly in the Bogotá and Medellín areas. The activities of drug smugglers present a particular hazard to boaters. The cities of Cartagena and Barranquilla are considered relatively safe, but even there visitors should be extremely vigilant. For the current status of these warnings call the State Department Travel Advisory Service at (202) 647-5225.

Some boaters advise staying well offshore when underway, and all boats should avoid anchoring in remote areas.

U.S. citizens can seek advice and assistance at the U.S. consulate in Bogotá by calling (57 1) 320 1300, or in Barranquilla at (57 58) 457 088.

Malaria, cholera and other diseases may be encountered. For the latest information contact the Center for Disease Control at (404) 332-4559 in Atlanta, Georgia.

The telephone area code for the country is 57, followed by a one or two digit city code and a local number. The city code for Cartagena is 59, for Bogotá 1, for Cali 23, for Medellín 4 and for Palmira 31.

The currency is the Peso, divided into 100 centavos. The exchange rate in mid 1993 was about 669 Pesos per U.S. dollar.

The language spoken is Spanish.

REED'S NEEDS YOU!

It is difficult to obtain accurate and up-to-date information on many areas in the Caribbean. To provide the mariner with the best possible product we utilize many sources. *Reed's* welcomes your contributions, suggestions and updates. Please be as specific as possible, and include your address and phone number. *Thank you!*

PENINSULA DE LA GUAJIRA

CASTILLETES, 11 51.4N, 71 19.5W, Fl W 9s, 72ft., 15M, Metal structure, black and white bands.
PUNTA ESPADA, 12 05.5N, 71 06.8W, Fl W 8s, 105ft., 18M, White metal tower.
CHICHIBACOA, 12 17.7N, 71 13.1W, Fl W 10s, 89ft., 20M, Black and white tower.
CHIMARE, 12 23.2N, 71 26.5W, Fl W 12s, 82ft., 20M, Orange tower.
PUNTA GALLINAS, 12 28.0N, 71 40.0W, Fl W 10s, 110ft., 16M, Aluminum square tower.
Puerto Bolivar, Buoy No 1, 12 17.5N, 71 58.4W, Fl G 2s, Green buoy, RACON M(– –).
PUERTO BOLIVAR, on pier, 12 15.5N, 71 57.7W, Fl W 2s, 115ft., 19M, Coal loading gantry.
PUERTO BOLIVAR, harbor approach light, 12 15.6N, 71 57.9W, Fl W 2s, 148ft., 16M, Atop coal pier.
PUNTA LATATA, Fl W 3s, 5M.
CABO DE LA VELA, 12 13.1N, 72 10.5W, Fl W 10s, 302ft., 16M, White round masonry tower, red band.

CABO DE LA VELA
12 13N, 72 11W

Pilotage: The cape is reported to give a good radar return up to a distance of 21 miles. There is a light on the point. This is a possible anchorage for coasting vessels.

PUNTA MANAURE TO POZOS COLORADO

PUNTA MANAURE, 11 45.2N, 72 33.2W, Fl (2) W 15s, 74ft., 14M, Aluminum framework tower, black bands.
PIPELINE BEACON 1, 11 44.4N, 72 44.1W, Fl (2) Y 10s, 16ft., 3M.
BEACON 2, L Fl Y 10s, 16ft., 3M.
RIOHACHA, 11 33.7N, 72 54.3W, Fl W 10s, 82ft., 14M, White metal tower, Aero Radio-beacon about 1 mile NE.

RIOHACHA
11 34N, 72 55W

Pilotage: The town lies about 60 miles south-west of Cabo de la Vela. The river is reported to have a navigable depth of about 12 feet, but cargo is lightered out to the anchorage to be loaded. Only small coasters frequent this port. There is a small pier off of town.
Port of Entry: This is reported to be the first Port of Entry west of the Venezuelan border.

Anchorage: Basically an open roadstead, the harbor can be rolly.
Services: Some supplies are available.

MORRO GRANDE, summit N side of bay, 11 15.1N, 74 13.8W, Fl (3) W 15s, 269ft., 20M, Tower on white square building, Obscured E of 203° by the high land of Aguja Island, Visible over a small arc between the island and the mainland at 212°.

SANTA MARTA
11 15N, 74 13W

Pilotage: The harbor is located about 40 miles east-northeast of the entrance to Barranquilla. It is a commercially important port. Isla El Morro is a steep-sided islet about 1/2 mile west of the harbor. A light marks the island, and there are the ruins of a fort on it. A small rock, Morro Chico, lies just west of Punta Morrito at the harbor entrance. The northeast trades are reported to be gusty here. Between the months of March and December a local wind blows from the southwest between the hours of 1000 and 1300. A cathedral with two domes and a radio tower are conspicuous. A white stone monument stands on the summit of a hill about 3/4 mile north-northwest of the cathedral. There are also several tanks in the vicinity of the monument.
Port of Entry: The Customs house is near the wharves on the eastern side of the harbor.
Anchorage: Drop the hook south of the wharf area.
Services: Basic supplies are available.

POZOS COLORADOS, (Front Light) 11 09.3N, 74 12.8W, Q R, 5M, White, orange and red rectangular daymark on metal tower. **(Rear Light)** 395 meters 085°30' from front, Iso R 6s, 5M, White, orange and red rectangular daymark on metal tower.
SIMON BOLIVAR AVIATION LIGHT, 11 07.0N, 74 14.0W, Al Fl W G 10s, Airport control tower.

RÍO MAGDALENA

F-2, head of W breakwater, 11 06.5N, 74 51.3W, Fl R 5s, 72ft., 12M, White metal tower.
F-1, head of E breakwater, 11 06.6N, 74 51.3W, Fl G W 5s, 72ft., 12M, White metal tower.
Z-3 RANGE, (Front Light) on E breakwater, 11 06.4N, 74 50.9W, Fl G 5s, 27ft., 6M, White metal tower, red bands. **(Rear Light)** Z-5, 310 meters 135° from front, Fl G 5s, 59ft., 7M, White metal tower.

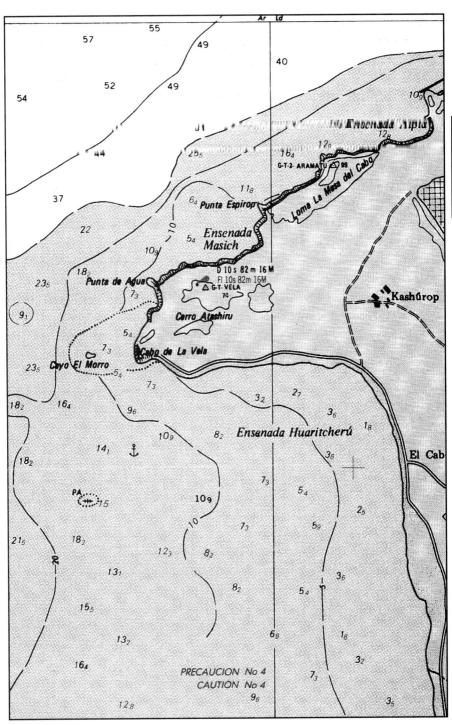

Cabo de la Vela, Soundings in Meters

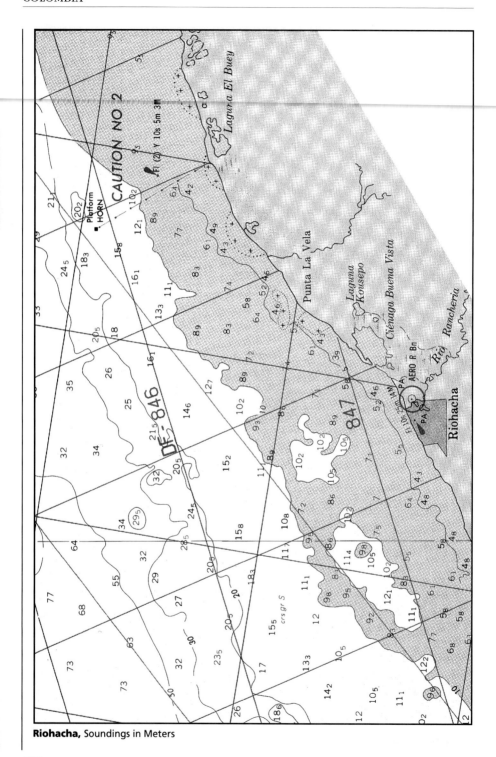

Riohacha, Soundings in Meters

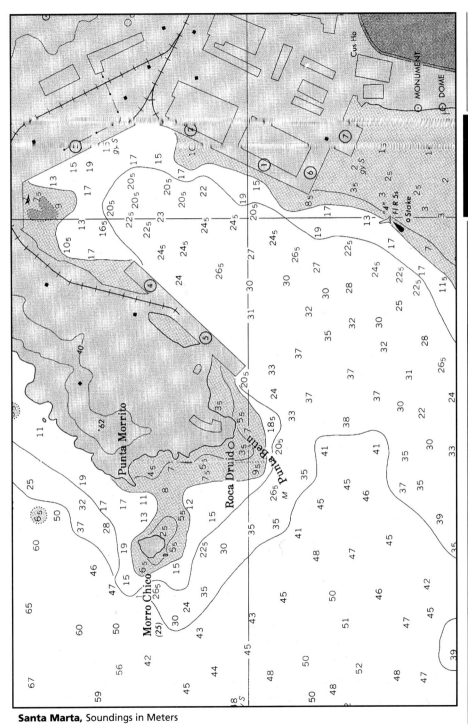

Santa Marta, Soundings in Meters

X-2, W side of river, 11 05.6N, 74 51.1W, Fl R 5s, 26ft., 9M, R and W bands on white metal tower.

X-4, W side of river, 11 04.9N, 74 51.0W, Fl R 5s, 23ft., 6M, Red and white bands on metal tower.

LAS FLORES RANGE, (Front Light) (down river, on W breakwater, 11 04.2N, 74 50.8W, Q G, 21ft., 7M, White circle on red metal mast, white bands, white square concrete base. **(Rear Light)** 393 meters 322°54′ from front, Iso G 6s, 33ft., 7M, Red and white square on square metal tower.

X-6, W side of river, 11 04.1N, 74 50.6W, Fl R 5s, 23ft., 6M, White metal tower, red bands.

ENTRANGE RANGE, (Front Light) spur of W jetty, 11 03.9N, 74 50.7W, Fl W 5s, 40ft., 6M, White metal tower. **(Rear Light)** 697 meters 168° from front, Fl W 5s, 66ft., 6M, White metal tower.

X-8, W side of river, 11 03.5N, 74 50.4W, Fl R 5s, 23ft., 6M, Red and white bands on metal tower.

X-10, W side of river below Las Flores, 11 03.1N, 74 49.9W, Fl R 5s, 23ft., 6M, White metal tower, red bands.

LAS FLORES RANGE (Front Light) (up river), W side of river, 11 02.6N, 74 49.6W, Fl G, 18ft., 7M, White square on metal mast white square concrete base. **(Rear Light)** 500 meters 142°54′ from front, Iso G 6s, 36ft., 7M, Red and white square on square metal tower.

X-1, 11 01.9N, 74 47.9W, Fl G 5s, 23ft., 6M, White metal tower, red bands..

LAS FLORES, on pier, 11 02.5N, 74 49.2W, 2 F R (vert), 30ft., 3M, Tower.

A-1 RANGE, (Front Light) 11 01.0N, 71 46.5W, Fl W 5s, 23ft., 5M, White metal tower, red bands. **(Rear Light)** A-2, 118° from front, Fl W 5s, 36ft., 5M, White metal tower, red bands.

X-3, 11 00.6N, 74 45.0W, Fl G 5s, 23ft., 6M, White metal tower, red bands.

X-5, E side of river below new canal to Cienaga, 10 59.9N, 74 45.8W, Fl G 5s, 23ft., 6M, White metal tower, red bands.

X-7, E side of river below Isla de Trupillo, 10 58.6N, 74 45.3W, Fl G 5s, 23ft., 6M, White metal tower, red bands, Mark the Eastern limit turning basin off Isla de Trupillo.

BARRANQUILLA
11 00N, 74 48W

Pilotage: The port is in the outer 10 miles of the Río Magdalena, which is the main artery of commercial traffic in Colombia. The river is navigable for 800 miles inland. Being in an area of strong northeast trades, it is sometimes not possible to enter the river safely. The waves at the entrance can be very short and steep. Generally, the winds and seas moderate at night.

When the water level is low in the river from February to April and August to October, the current does not exceed 2 knots. When the water level is high in July and November the current can reach 6 knots, and floating debris can be a problem.

The coast east of the river entrance is backed by low flat sand dunes. West of the entrance the water is very shoal in places, causing areas of breakers. The breakwater heads are reported to give good radar returns up to 10 miles off.

Port of Entry: Proceed 10 miles upstream to the city of Barranquilla.
Dockage: There may be some room at the yacht clubs.
U.S. Consulate: Call (57 58) 457 088.
Services: This is a large city and has good stocks of general supplies. Repairs and parts should be more available here than in the ports further east.

PUNTA HERMOSA TO CARTAGENA

PUNTA HERMOSA, 10 57.8N, 75 01.0W, Fl (3) W 20s, 440ft., 22M, White square concrete tower, black stripe.

ISLA VERDE
11 02N, 75 00W

Pilotage: This is actually a sandspit covered at all stages of the tide. This coast has many shoal areas within a distance of 3 miles from shore. Boaters should plot their courses carefully until past the shoals along the coast for the thirteen miles between the Río Magdalena and Punta Hermosa. Generally, sailing beyond the 10 fathom line is safe. There is a light on Punta Hermosa and one on Punta de La Garita, as well as one on Punta Canoas.

PUNTA GALERA, 10 48.4N, 75 19.8W, Fl W 7s, 60ft., 13M, White metal framework tower.
PUNTA CANOAS, N side of point, 10 34.5N, 75 30.0W, Fl W 10s, 289ft., 24M, White cylindrical tower, black bands.

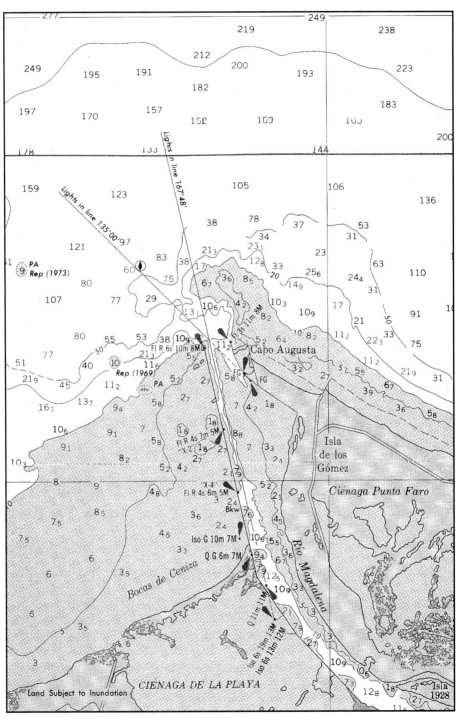

Approaches to Barranquilla, Soundings in Meters

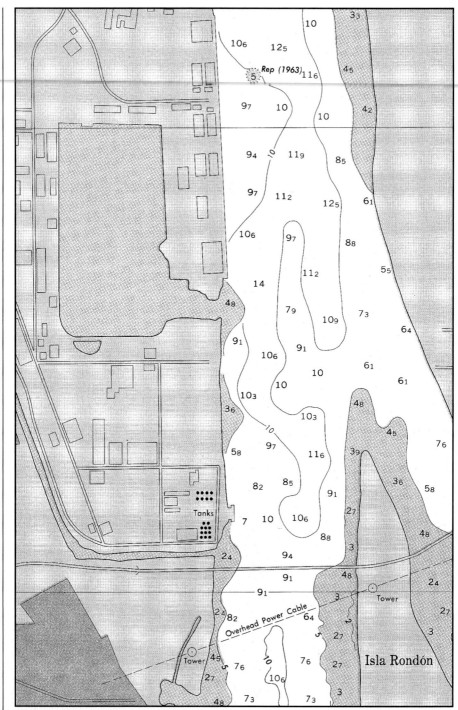

Barranquilla, Soundings in Meters

CRESPO AVIATION LIGHT, 10 27.2N,
75 31.0W, Al FL W G 10s, 20M.
BANCO SALMEDINA, 10 22.8N, 75 38.8W,
Fl W 10s, 46ft., 10M, White concrete tower.

BANCOS DE SALMEDINA
10 23N, 75 40W

Pilotage: Two detached shoal areas of sand
and coral lie about 5 miles northwest of the
Boca Chica entrance buoy to Cartagena
Breakers have been reported on the western
shoals, which have a least depth of about 15
feet. There is a light on the eastern bank.

CARTAGENA

ISLA TIERRA BOMBA, 10 20.6N, 75 35.1W,
Fl (2) W 20s, 259ft., 23M, White metal frame-
work tower, red bands, Radiobeacon.
BOYA DE MAR, 10 19.1N, 75 36.2W, Fl W 8s,
Red and white sripes, Radar reflector,
Reported extinguished 1991.
Buoy 1, W end of Boca Chica entrance,
10 19.2N, 75 35.5W, Fl G 3s, Green buoy.
Buoy 2, S side of W entrance to dredged
channel, Fl R 3s, Red buoy.
ISLA BRUJAS, NO 2, 10 20.0N, 75 31.1W,
Fl W 3s, 65ft., 10M, White metal tower, F W on
water tower 0.48 mile ENE.
CANAL DEL DIQUE, E side of canal, 10 17.8N,
75 31.6W, Fl W 10s, 59ft., 10M, White tower.
CASTILLO GRANDE, 10 23.6N, 75 32.9W,
Fl W 4s, 79ft., 14M, Stone tower.

CARTAGENA
10 25N, 75 32W

Pilotage: This is the largest and most secure
port on the north coast of Colombia. It is
located about 324 miles east-northeast of the
Panama Canal. The main entrance to the bay
is Boca Chica, lying between two islands about
6 3/4 miles south-southwest of the city. The
northern entrance, known as Boca Grande,
has a submerged rock barrier across its entire
width. The small boat passages through the
barrier should be attempted only with local
knowledge.

In the season of strong winds, January to June,
the sea breeze sets in from the west and then
veers northwest. At about noon it blows parallel to the coast. During the wet season, April
to October, the climate is hot and early morning land breezes are usually preceded by rain

squalls of short duration. During the dry season from November to March the winds are
stronger.

The maximum tide range is about 2.6 feet,
and the mean range about one foot. The tidal
current off the entrance to the inner harbor
sets east-southeast on the flood at a velocity
of 1/2 knot, and west at the same speed during the maximum ebb.

There are several Restricted Areas in the harbor, and vessels should not travel or anchor in
these areas. One of them fills most of the
western harbor off Boca Grande and Castillo
Grande, extending almost all the way east to
Manga island.
Port of Entry: Many cruisers dock or anchor
at the Club Nautico, where you can contact an
agent.
Dockage: Cruisers recommend Club Nautico
located on the west coast of Manga island.
Depths are reported to be less than 7 feet at
the docks. The Club de Pesca is nearby on the
north end of the island. Be prepared if strong
winds come in from the south.
Anchorage: Yachts anchor off Club Nautico,
or north of the northeast corner of Manga
island. Be prepared if strong winds come in
from the south.
Services: Fuel is available at the Club de Pesca,
and you can get water, ice and showers at
Club Nautico. Repair facilities, or assistance in
finding services, are all found at Club Nautico.
Haulouts can be arranged at several shipyards.
There are good supermarkets and general supplies of all types.

This city has a five hundred year history and
has done a good job of preserving memories
of it. The old walled city is a short walk from
the marinas, and is reported to be fascinating.
The strategic location that so attracted the
Spanish galleons still brings in the cruisers.

ISLAS DEL ROSARIO

ISLA DEL TESORO, 10 14.2N, 75 44.4W,
Fl (3) W 12s, 75ft., 15M, White metal frame-
work tower, RACON C(– · – ·).
ROSARIO LIGHTHOUSE, 10 09.7N, 75 48.6W,
Fl W 6s, 39ft., 10M, White tower.
ISLA DEL ROSARIO, 10 10.1N, 75 48.2W,
Fl R 5s, 16ft., 5M, Tower.
ISLA ARENAS, 10 08.8N, 75 43.7W, Fl W 8s,
39ft., 10M, White metal framework tower.

Chapter 2

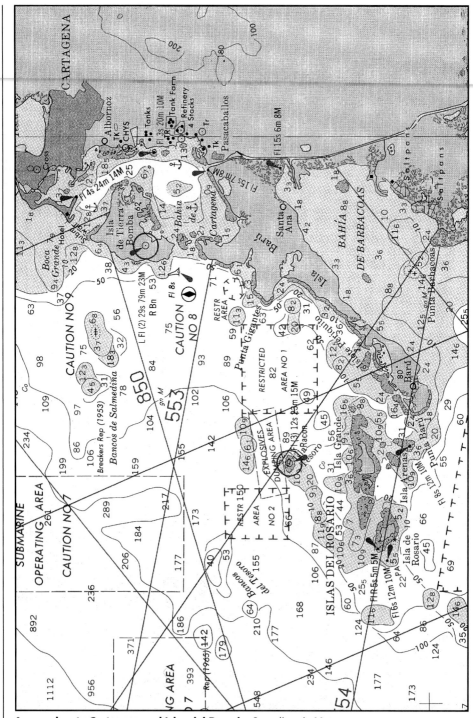

Approaches to Cartagena and Islas del Rosario, Soundings in Meters

Chapter 2

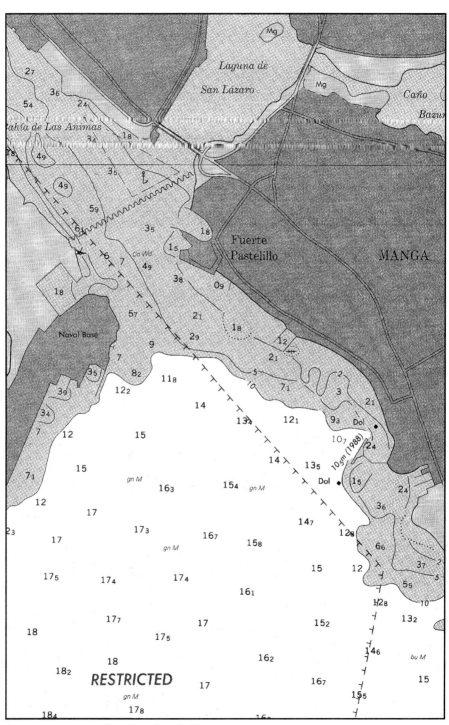

Cartagena Inner Harbor, Soundings in Meters

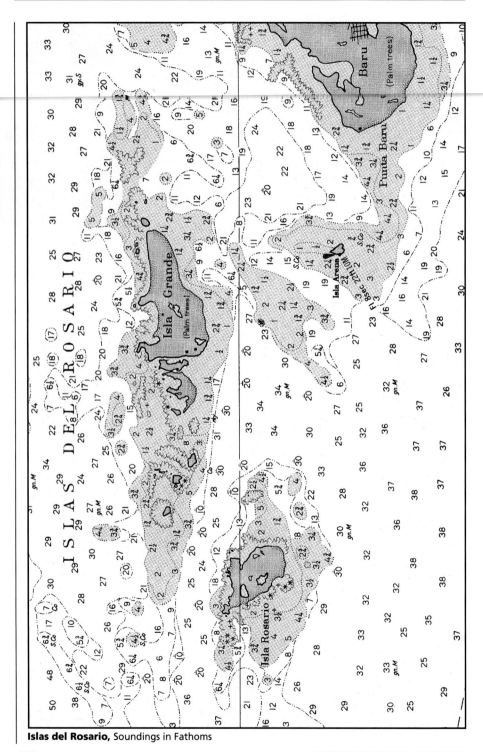

Islas del Rosario, Soundings in Fathoms

ISLAS DEL ROSARIO
10 11N, 75 45W

Pilotage: This group of small islands is located about 12 miles southwest of the Boca Chica entrance to Cartagena. They are surrounded by banks and shoals, making the area a danger to those approaching Cartagena from the southwest. This area is a popular cruising ground for local boaters.

The north island of the group, Isla Tesoro, is marked by a light. There are two lights on the west end of the group and one on Isla Arenas. Note the charted Restricted Areas north and south of the islands.

Isla del Rosario lies about 5 miles west of Punta Baru and is covered by palm trees. Isla Grande is the largest of the group and lies about 2 1/4 miles east-northeast of Isla del Rosario. There are several good anchorages within the group, but bear in mind the depths between the islands are very irregular, and there are many rocks and reefs.

BAHÍA DE BARBACOAS, head of the bay, 10 14.5N, 75 31.4W, Fl W 15s, 19ft., 8M, Beacon.
ISLA MUCURA, 9 47.1N, 75 52.3W, Fl (2) W 10s, 79ft., 10M, White square metal tower.
ISLA CEYCEN, 9 41.8N, 75 51.3W, L Fl W 10s, 78ft., 15M, White metal tower.

ISLAS SAN BERNARDO
9 45N, 75 50W

Pilotage: This group of low rocks, wooded cays and shoals lies about 20 miles south of Islas del Rosario. They extend for about 13 1/2 miles west of Punta San Bernardo. Note the Target and Restricted Areas in the vicinity of the group. There are lights on Isla Mucura and Isla Ceycen.

There is a small village, Islote, on a tiny island south of Isla Tintipan. There are several possible anchorages in this vicinity, but the many shoals and reefs must be avoided. An approach in good light is recommended.

There are several deepwater channels between the group and the mainland.

COVENAS, 9 24.5N, 75 41.3W, Fl W 5s, 100ft., 14M, Top of cooling plant, F R on water tank 0.1 mile SW.

PIER HEAD, 9 25.0N, 75 41.2W, 2 F R (vert), 50ft., 2M.
Covenas Buoy, 9 26.0N, 75 42.0W, Fl W 3s, Red buoy.
Roca Morrosquillo Buoy, 9 35.6N, 75 59.6W, Fl (2) W 14s, 30ft., 15M, ISOLATED DANGER BRB, topmark, RACON Q(– – · –).

ROCA MORROSQUILLO
9 36N, 76 00W

Pilotage: This is a coral shoal consisting of two major heads. One has a depth of about 30 feet over it, and the other about 69 feet. The group is marked by a lighted buoy. This would make a good position indicator if approaching the Islas San Bernardo from the south.

ISLA FUERTE, 9 23.6N, 76 10.6W, Fl W 10s, 135ft., 18M, Metal framework tower.

ISLA FUERTE
9 23N, 76 11W

Pilotage: This is a low wooded islet. It lies about 6 1/2 miles west-northwest of Punta Piedras, and is surrounded by foul ground that extends up to 2 1/2 miles from the south side, and nearly 1 1/2 miles from its west side. The islet is difficult to distinguish when approaching from the west, but there is a light on its eastern side.

There is a small village on the south side of the islet, and an area suitable for anchoring on the east side.

ISLA TORTUGUILLA, 9 01.9N, 76 20.6W, Fl W 10s, 59ft., 15M, White metal tower.

ISLA TORTUGUILLA
9 02N, 76 20W

Pilotage: This tiny wooded islet lies about 5 miles west of Colina Tortugon. There is a navigation light shown from its northwest extremity. Depths of less than 30 feet lie within 3/4 miles of its shores. It may be possible to anchor here.

GOLFO DE URABÁ

PUNTA CARIBANA, 8 37.5N, 76 53.1W, Fl W 12s, 275ft., 20M, White square concrete tower.

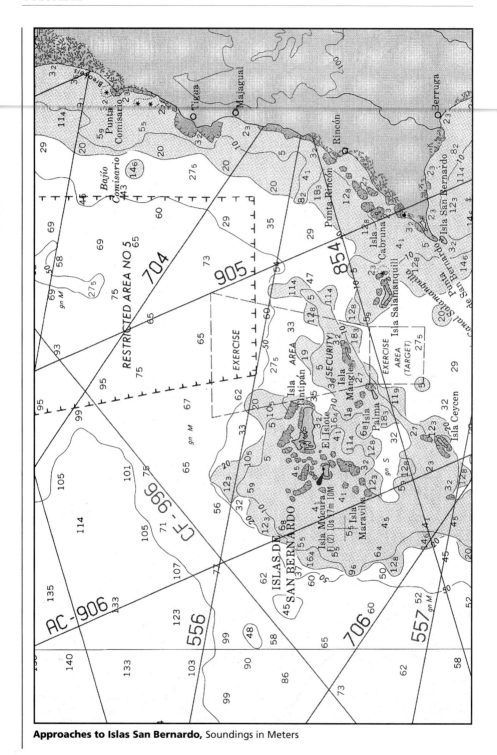

Approaches to Islas San Bernardo, Soundings in Meters

Chapter 2

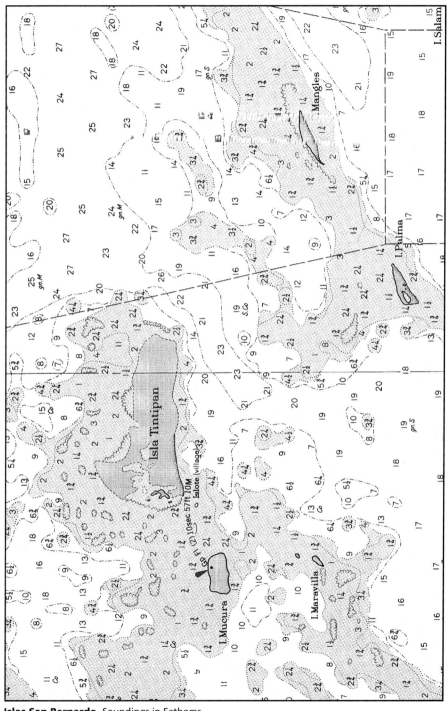

Islas San Bernardo, Soundings in Fathoms

PUNTA CARIBANA
8 37N, 76 53W

Pilotage: This is the eastern point of the entrance to the Golfo de Urabá. It is low, wooded and marked by a light. Cerro Aguilla, at over 1100 feet high, makes an excellent landmark. Foul ground, with some rocks awash, extends about 3 3/4 miles north-northwest from the point. This reef can be dangerous for coasting vessels, and a good offing is recommended.

The Golfo de Urubá experiences a northward flowing current of up to 2 knots at times. This area experiences a severe local storm in the months from June to October. It is called Chocosanas, and occurs most frequently between 2200 and 2400. It is preceded by light north winds and general lightning around the horizon. The wind gradually shifts from the north to the south, and increases to near hurricane force in some instances. The storms last about 1/2 hour, and are accompanied by heavy rain and lightning. As much as 4 inches of rain may fall in one storm.

PUNTA ARENAS, 8 32.5N, 76 56.1W, Fl W 9s, 44ft., 11M, White metal tower.
PUNTA CAIMAN, 8 16.5N, 76 46.4W, Fl W 7.5s, 59ft., 12M, White tower, black bands.
PUNTA DE LAS VACAS, 8 04.2N, 76 44.6W, Fl W 6s, 59ft., 12M, White metal framework tower.
TURBO AIRFIELD TOWER, 8 04.5N, 76 44.1W, F R, 40M, Tower, Obstruction light, Radiobeacon.

TURBO
8 06N, 76 43W

Pilotage: The harbor is located about 30 miles south of Punta Arenas del Norte. This coast is reported to be gradually creeping to the west. Vessels should keep a good offing to avoid shoal areas. There is a light shown from Punta Las Vacas at the entrance to Bahía Turbo. The bay is quite shallow. Check with the port officials for the latest depths in the channel. Officials board commercial vessels west of Punta Las Vacas, so you could anchor in this area to wait for clearance.

Port of Entry
Services: Basic supplies and fuel are reported to be available.

BOCAS RÍO LEON, 7 55.9N, 76 45.0W, Fl W 8s, 59ft., 12M, White metal framework tower.
PUNTA YARUMAL, 8 07.0N, 76 45.1W, Fl W 5s, 65ft., 15M, White metal tower, black bands.
MATUTUNGO, 8 07.6N, 76 50.6W, Fl W 10s, 52ft., 12M, White tower.
ISLA DE LOS MUERTOS, E end, 8 07.9N, 76 49.3W, Fl R 6s, 72ft., 6M, White metal framework tower.

ISLA NAPU
8 25N, 77 07W

Pilotage: This is a steep rocky island lying about 2 3/4 miles east-southeast of Punta de La Goleta. It is covered with brush and small trees.

ACANDI
8 31N, 77 16W

Pilotage: This town lies at the mouth of the Río Acandi about 11 miles southeast of Cabo Tiburón. An excellent landmark between Cabo Tiburón and Acandi is Terron de Azucar, a precipitous dark rock lying about 1 1/4 miles offshore midway between the two positions. A rocky ridge, upon which the sea breaks, connects the rock with the coast. South of Acandi is a sandy beach broken by hills 2 miles southeast of town.

CABO TIBURON, 8 40.5N, 77 21.6W, Fl (2) W 15s, 275ft., 15M, White square concrete tower.

CABO TIBURÓN
8 41N, 77 22W

Pilotage: This bold promontory marks the border between Colombia and Panama. It rises to a height of about 405 feet, and there are two concrete beacons on its northwest extremity marking the border. The seaward beacon stands on a pinnacle rock.

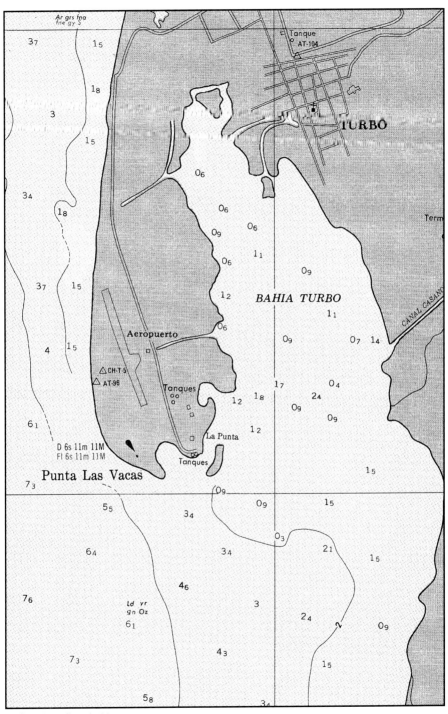

Turbo, Soundings in Meters

USE NOTICES TO MARINERS!

Your 1994 almanac is up-to-date at the time of publication, but prudent mariners will always use Notices to Mariners and Local Notices to Mariners to keep abreast of the latest navigational changes. To obtain these notices contact the Coast Guard District Commanders for the areas where you travel. See *Reed's Nautical Companion* for more information, and send in the post-paid reply card to receive your *FREE 1994 Supplement* for this almanac.

PANAMA

CAUTION: Our information on aids to navigation comes from official government sources. The latitudes and longitudes of these marks may not correspond to the readings from GPS receivers. Some aids have been reported as unreliable, missing, off position or showing incorrect characteristics. No single aid to navigation, or waypoint, should be relied upon as a sole means of fixing your position.

ENTRY PROCEDURES

The Panama Canal is a natural crossroads for many Caribbean cruisers. Some are headed across the Pacific, or around the world. Others will attempt the hard slog north up the west coast of North America. Some are headed to Hawaii, and others are just arriving in the Caribbean from the Pacific side. The Canal is about 1072 miles from Charlotte Amalie, 1202 from Martinique, 1202 from Trinidad, 661 from Aruba, 324 from Cartagena and 594 from Jamaica. See *Reed's Nautical Companion* for distance tables and an example of the country flag.

The Port of Entry in the San Blas Islands is Porvenir. On the Panamanian mainland clear at either end of the Canal — Colón on the Caribbean side, or Balboa on the Pacific. The town of Colón is located in Puerto Cristóbal on a peninsula of land jutting northward into the eastern part of the bay.

Most nationals will need visas, but these can be purchased in Colón if you do not have one on arrival. The cost is $10.00 per passport. Generally, you will be given permission for a three month stay, with extensions possible. For more information and visa applications contact the Panama Consulate at 2862 McDill Terrace NW, Washington, DC, 20008, (202) 483-1407. The Immigration office is next to the Panama Canal Yacht Club in Colón, and should be your first stop in the clearance procedure. You will also pay $10.00 for quarantine inspection.

You will be given a map showing you where to proceed for Customs and the Port Authority.

You must purchase a Cruising Permit from the Port Authority, which costs about $40.00. You need this permit to visit the San Blas Islands, Firearms will be held until your departure.

The international phone code for Panama is 507, followed by a 6 digit local number. The currency used is the U.S. dollar.

Cholera is present in the country. To obtain the latest health information contact the Center for Disease Control at (404) 332-4559 in Atlanta Georgia.

The U.S. Southern Command Network broadcasts on both television and radio. There is a U.S. Consulate in Panama City at (507) 27 17 77, and one in Cristóbal at (507) 41 24 40 or 24 78.

Spanish is the main language of Panama, but English is widely spoken. Canal operations are conducted in English.

WARNING: The U.S. State Department warns of high rates of crime in Panama. The streets of Colón and Panama City are not considered safe after dark, and many visitors prefer to take taxis even during the day. Cruisers report many crimes in these areas. The Darien peninsula area is reported to be frequented by Colombian criminals, and is not considered safe. For the latest advisory contact the State Department at (202) 647-5225.

THE PANAMA CANAL

After you have cleared into the country you can proceed to the Panama Canal Commission Admeasurers Office, phone (507) 43 72 93. You make an appointment to have your boat measured, which is usually a quick process. These measurements determine the fee you will pay for the transit.

Now you can proceed to Canal Operations Captain's Office, phone (507) 52 42 11, or 52 42 15. You will be informed of the equipment requirements for passage, given a schedule of passage and notified of other safety informa-

tion. Yachts are currently being allowed to transit every day, but there is a limit of 4 pleasure boats per day. You will usually be able to make your transit within 2 days of making your application.

You should have four lines (the Operations Office recommends 7/8" nylon) over 100 feet long, and four line handlers. The captain of the boat is not counted as a line handler. Line handlers are often crews from other boats who wish to get a preview of the trip. There are paid line handlers available for about $50.00 per day. They must also be housed, fed and returned (via public transport) to Colón.

On the day before (preferably 24 hours prior to) your transit you must contact the Marine Traffic Control Office at (507) 52 42 02, or the Cristóbal Signal Station on VHF channels 12 and 16. They will confirm your transit and schedule the arrival of your pilot. You should be ready to go on time, as there are stiff fines for delays, or cancellation.

There are basically three ways to negotiate the locks: Sidewall tie up, center tie up, or rafted to a tug. Yachts report a preference for one of the first two options, as there seems to be less chance of damage. However, some people report being alongside a tug as the easiest method, as you don't need to constantly handle your lines. Don't let the tug pull away from the lock wall with your boat tied alongside! Sometimes a group of yachts will be rafted together in the center of the lock. You will be given a choice of these methods at the Operations Office, but be prepared to change to one of the other methods along the way.

You are required to maintain a speed of at least 5 knots. Slower boats will probably have to anchor overnight in Gatún Lake at Gamboa. If you are planning on stopping at the Pedro Miguel Yacht Club, you must make arrangements in advance, and be able to show written confirmation of your reservations to your pilot. The club is located in Miraflores Lake near the Pedro Miguel Locks. Contact them at (507) 32 45 09, or by fax at (507) 52 81 05. Call the Canal Operations office when you are ready to resume your passage through the Canal.

There are three up-locks on the Caribbean side, and three down-locks on the Pacific side. They lift you 85 feet from sea level to Gatún Lake, then lower you into the Pacific Ocean on the other side. The lock chambers measure 1000 feet long by 110 feet wide. The entire trip is about 50 miles in length.

The system of lighting and buoyage in the Canal utilizes range lights, generally green, in the longest reaches and light buoys and beacons along the sides. In general, there are red lights on one side and white lights on the other. The IALA (Region B) Maritime Buoyage System is used. The direction of buoyage changes at Puedro Miguel Locks (9° 01'N, 79° 37'W).

The Panama Canal Commission rigidly controls all radio communications in this area. All radio communications between vessels in the Panama Canal operating area, or calls to stations outside the area must be forwarded through the Canal Radio Station (call sign HPN) located in Balboa. Except for emergency traffic and routine bridge to bridge VHF communications, no vessel in transit through the canal shall communicate with any other station.

The Canal is currently controlled jointly by the United States and Panama, but will become the sole responsibility of Panama on January 1, 2000.

REED'S NEEDS YOU!

It is difficult to obtain accurate and up-to-date information on many areas in the Caribbean. To provide the mariner with the best possible product we utilize many sources. Reed's welcomes your contributions, suggestions and updates. Please be as specific as possible, and include your address and phone number. Thank you!

NORTHEAST COAST

PUERTO OBALDIA, 8 40.0N, 77 25.0W, L Fl W 10s, 39ft., 8M, White framework tower.

PUERTO OBALDIA
8 40N, 77 26W

Pilotage: This is a small cove located about 4 miles west of Cabo Tiburon, and the Colombian border. There is a small village in the cove. The coast between here and the cape is steep-to and rocky, with heavily wooded hills rising inland. A prominent rock lies about 1 mile north of the east entrance point to the cove.

PUERTO PERME

8 45N, 77 32W

Pilotage: This is a narrow cove about 8 miles northwest of Puerto Obaldia. A village is located about 1 mile south-southwest of Puerto Perme. The port is abandoned but anchorage can be taken.

PUERTO CARRETO

Pilotage: This small cove is just west of Punta Carreto. Two steep-to rocky patches lie about 2 1/2 miles north of Punta Carreto, and seas break here in fresh breezes. The cove has depths of 18 to 54 feet. There is a small village near the mouth of a river on the west side of the cove.

Between Punta Carreto and Punta Brava located 39 1/2 miles to the northwest the coast is fronted by many dangers extending up to 5 miles offshore. A prominent headland in this area is Punta Escoces, rising to a height of 580 feet, about 5 1/2 miles northwest of Puerto Carreto.

There are several roadstead anchorages along this coast. Isla de Pinos is prominent at 400 feet high. It stands about 1/4 mile offshore, about 2 1/2 miles northwest of Punta Sasardi. Isla Pajaros, a low islet surrounded by reefs, lies about 2 1/2 miles farther northwest. This island has been reported as a good landmark, as it is covered with tall palm trees.

PUNTA BRAVA

9 15N, 78 03W

Pilotage: Between here and Punta Mandinga, 56 1/2 miles to the west-northwest, the coast is fronted by the Archipielago De Las Mulatas. This is a group of small cays, reefs and banks, lying within 10 miles of the coast. There are a number of navigable channels in the group. Many vessels with local knowledge navigate this area.

RÍO DIABLO

9 26N, 78 29W

Pilotage: This village stands on two small islands near shore. They are located about 34 miles west-northwest of Punta Brava. Depths in this area are reported to be less than charted.

GOLFO DE SAN BLAS

9 30N, 79 00W

Pilotage: This area lies between Punta San Blas and Punta Mandinga. It can be entered from the north via Canal De San Blas, located about 2 1/2 miles east of Punta San Blas. There are numerous detached dangers in the south and west parts of the gulf. Numerous creeks and rivers discharge into the gulf, but their entrances are obstructed by bars. The north shore of the gulf is swampy and fringed with mangroves. The south shore is low, but east of Punta Mandinga the high land approaches the coast. This area has been reported to be poorly charted.

PUNTA SAN BLAS

9 34N, 78 58W

Pilotage: This point has a low extremity, but a 150 foot high hill stands about 1/2 mile to the northwest. A 200 foot high hill, the highest of a group of four, stands about 1 1/2 miles west-southwest of the end of the point. A conspicuous tower stands about 3/4 mile southwest of the end.

Between Punta San Blas and Punta Macolla, 28 miles to the west, the coast is low and wooded.

PORVENIR

9 33.5N, 78 57W

Pilotage: Isla Porvenir lies about 1 mile east of Punta San Blas, and 1/4 mile north-northwest of Sail Rock. A government compound with two conspicuous, buff-colored buildings and several lesser structures stands on the west side of the islet. All vessels in the Golfo De San Blas must clear in and out of this station. *CAUTION: The charts in this area are reported to be inaccurate. Passages should be made in good light.*
Port of Entry: You should check in at this station, whether or not you have obtained a cruising permit in Colón. This is the administrative center for the San Blas area.

PUNTA MACOLLA

9 36N, 79 26W

Pilotage: This point is bold, high and easily identified. Near the point the mountains begin to approach the coast — two of which have conspicuous high peaks. From the west it appear as a dark bluff.

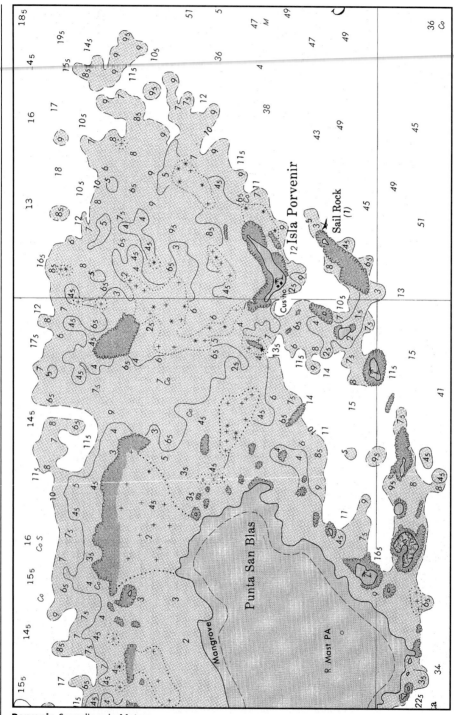

Porvenir, Soundings in Meters

PUNTA PESCADOR
9 36N, 79 28W

Pilotage: This point is located a bit west of Punta Macolla. It is fringed by reefs.

PUNTA MANZANILLA
9 38N, 79 33W

Pilotage: This is the northernmost point in Panama. It is a high, precipitous projection, with two conical hillocks resembling a saddle. This is the termination of a mountain ridge that extends along the coast to the mouth of the Río Piedras.

Several offlying rocks and islets are northeast and northwest of the point, including Islas Los Magotes and Isla Tambor, which is connected to Isla Grande by reefs.

ISLA GRANDE
9 38N, 79 34W

Pilotage: This high, palm tree covered island, lies about 1 mile west of Punta Manzanilla, and is reported to give a good radar return up to a distance of 20 miles. There is a light on the northeast part of the island. A confused sea and tide rips are found in the vicinity.

Isla Tambor is connected to the island by reefs. The coast of the island is foul ground except for the northeast part, but a deep channel runs between the island and Punta Manzanilla.

PUERTO GAROTE
9 36N, 79 35W

Pilotage: This small harbor is entered about 1/2 mile west of Isla Grande. It is formed by the coast and several offlying islands. The narrow entrance has depths of 36 to 72 feet, while the inlet leading into the harbor has a depth of 34 feet. The center of the harbor is about 20 feet deep. There is a small pier and room for vessels to anchor.

ISLA GRANDE, off Punta Manzanillo, 9 38.0N, 79 34.0W, Fl W 5s, 305ft., 12M. White metal tower, stone base.
FARALLON SUCIO ROCK, summit, 9 39.0N, 79 38.0W, Fl R, 5s, 107ft., 12M, White concrete pyramidal tower; Reported at reduced intensity (1984).

LOS FARALLONES
9 39N, 79 38W

Pilotage: This group of rocks lies about 2 miles offshore to the north-northwest of Punta Cacique. They're about 4 miles west of Isla Tambor. There is a light on the westernmost rock.

PORTOBELO
9 33N, 79 40W

Pilotage: This good harbor of refuge lies about 18 miles northeast of the entrance to Puerto Cristóbal and 11 miles southwest of Isla Grande. Bajo Salmedina, a coral reef upon which the sea breaks, is located about 3/4 mile west of Punta Mantilla. Depths in the harbor may be less than charted due to silting. A church with a large red roof and small white tower is conspicuous. This is reported to be a good anchorage, with some supplies available in town. Without local knowledge, vessels should stay at least 3 miles offshore from here to the entrance to Puerto Cristóbal.

BAHÍA LAS MINAS
RANGE, (Front). 9 23.9N, 79 49.5W, F G, Orange diamond daymark on beacon. **(Rear),** 80 meters 170° from front, F G, Orange diamond daymark on beacon.
RANGE, (Front), 9 23.4N, 79 48.8W, F G. Orange diamond daymark on beacon. **(Rear),** 160 meters, 148°45' from front. F G, Orange diamond daymark on beacon.
NW PIER, N end, 9 23.8N, 79 49.1W, F R.
TANKER JETTY, N end. 9 23.6N, 79 49.1W, F R.

PUERTO DE BAHÍA DE LAS MINAS
9 24N, 79 49W

Pilotage: This commercial port is entered via a well marked channel located about 6 miles northeast of the entrance to Puerto Cristóbal. There is a large refinery located in the bay. Without local knowledge, vessels should stay at least 3 miles offshore from here to the entrance to Puerto Cristóbal.

COLÓN — CRISTÓBAL
TORO POINT, W. side of entrance to Limón Bay, 9 22.4N, 79 57.1W, L Fl W, 30s, 108ft., 16M, White metal tower, stone base.

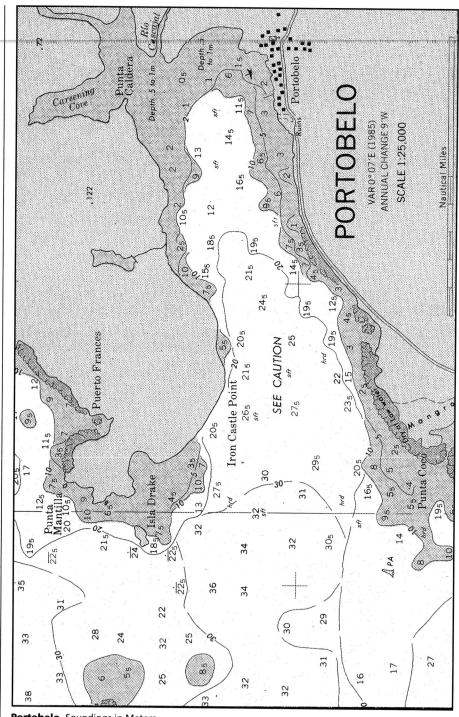

Portobelo, Soundings in Meters

**Cristóbal Approach, Lighted Whistle
Buoy A,** 9 26.3N, 79 55.1W, Iso W 6s, Red and
white stripes. Reported Missing (1989).
W BREAKWATER, head, 9 23.4N, 79 55.5W V
Q (2) R 2s 100ft., 16M, Red square on metal
tower, Radar reflector.
E BREAKWATER, head, 9 23.3N, 79 54.9W,
Mo (U) G 20s, 100ft., 16M, Green triangle on
green metal tower, F R on chimney 5.9M E, F R
on signal station 1.7M, E, Q R and 3 F R (vert) on
mast 1.9M, SSE, 4 F R on each of 2 water tanks,
3.5M, SSE, F R 2.1M SSE – Racon **C (– · – ·)**
EXPLOSIVE ANCHORAGE, near W limit,
9 22.4N, 79 56.7W, Fl Y 2s, 15ft., Special Yellow.
CRISTÓBAL HARBOR, BEACON NO 2,
9 20.9,N, 79 54.4W, Q R, Starboard Red.
BEACON NO 3, 9 20.8N, 79 54.4W, Oc G 5s,
Port Green.
BEACON NO 4, 9 20.8N, 79 54.3W, Oc R 5s,
Starboard Red.
BEACON NO 5, 9 20.8N, 79 54.2W, Oc G 5s,
Port Green.
BEACON NO 6, 9 20.8N, 79 54.3W, Oc R 5s,
Starboard Red.
BEACON NO 8, 9 20.7N, 79 54.3W, Oc R 5s,
Starboard, Red.
BEACON NO 7, 9 20.6N, 79 54.2W, Oc G 5s,
Port, Green.
BEACON NO 9, Q G, Port Green.
BEACON NO 10, 9 20.6N, 79 54.3W, Oc R 5s,
Starboard, Red.
BEACON E OF TORO POINT LIGHT, 9 22.3N,
79 56.3W, Fl Y 2s, 15ft., Yellow beacon.
**PANAMA CANAL, ATLANTIC ENTRANCE
RANGE (Front),** 9 17.7N, 79 55.4W, F G, Red
lights shown on W side and Green lights
shown on E side of dredged channel and in
Limón Bay. The canal is marked by lights, and
leading lights mark the center of the channel.
**PANAMA CANAL, ENTRANCE RANGE,
(Middle),** 1037 meters, 180° 15′ from front,
F G, 98ft., 15M, Concrete conical tower, Visible
on range line only. **(Rear),** 2278 meters, 180° 15′
from front, Oc G, 158ft., 15M, Concrete conical
tower, Visible on range line only, F R lights
shown on each of 2 radio towers 1.1 miles NE.

PUERTO CRISTÓBAL
9 21N, 79 55W

Pilotage: This is the entrance to the Panama
Canal. Entrance to the harbor is made between
tow breakwaters about 1/4 mile apart. There
are lights at the end of both breakwaters, and
an offshore approach buoy. All vessels must
contact the Cristóbal Signal Station on VHF
channels 12 or 16, before entering the harbor.

The station is located on the western end of
the Muelle Cristóbal, which extends westward
into the harbor from Colón. Vessels should
maintain a continuous watch on channel 12
while in the harbor.
Dockage: The Panama Canal Yacht Club is
located on the east side of Canal French,
northeast of Anchorage Area F. This is where
you can begin your trek to the various port
offices. Check with the club for their advice on
street crime before heading out. If planning a
stop at the Pedro Miguel Boat Club you must
obtain written permission in advance, or your
Canal pilot will not let you stop. Contact them
at (507) 32 45 09, or by fax at (507) 52 81 05.
They reserve a certain number of slips for transients. Club Nautico is located on the eastern
shore of Colón.
Anchorage: Yachts should anchor in Anchorage Area F, located south of the Muelle
Cristóbal. This area is marked by flashing yellow buoys and is known as "The Flats".
Services: Fuel, water, showers, laundry, haulout facilities, a bar and restaurant can all be
found at the yacht club. This is also the place
to get advice on locating something you might
need, or to get advice on the Canal passage.
The Pedro Miguel Boat Club is set up for those
who want "do-it-yourself" type repairs, including haulouts. This is reported to be a good
place to store your boat while traveling ashore.
The Panama Canal: See the information at
the beginning of the Panama section.

LAGUNA DE CHIRIQUÍ

ESCUDO DE VERAGUAS, 9 05.3N, 81 32.2,
Fl W 7s, 120ft., 6M, White square framework
tower
CHIRIQUÍ RANGE, (Front), 8 56.5N, 82 06.8W,
Q W, White cylindrical tower with black stripe.
F R obstruction lights on tower 1.4M, W, F Y
on oil tanks 1.5 miles W, Visible 202°– 222°.
(Rear), 60m, 212° from front, Fl W 4s, White
cylindrical tower with black stripe, Visible
202°– 222°

LAGUNA DE BLUEFIELD
9 09N, 81 54W

Pilotage: Located south of Punta Valiente, in
the entrance to Laguna Chiriquí, this is a possible anchorage. The ground is foul west of
Punta Valiente, and along the shores in the
Laguna. The bottom is reported to be mud.

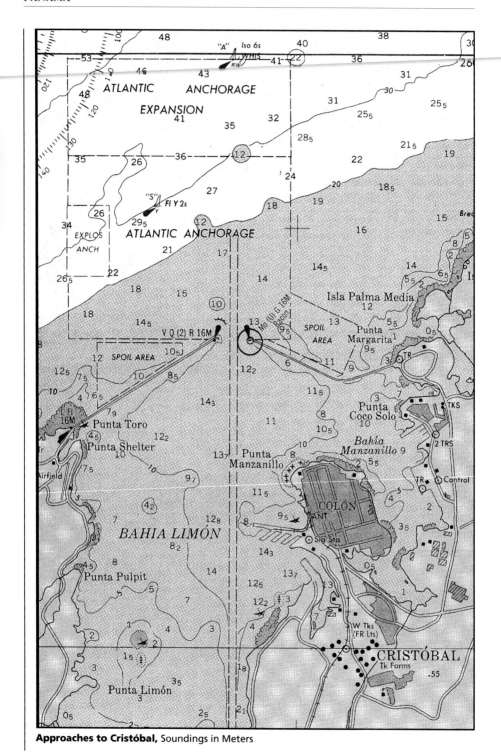

Approaches to Cristóbal, Soundings in Meters

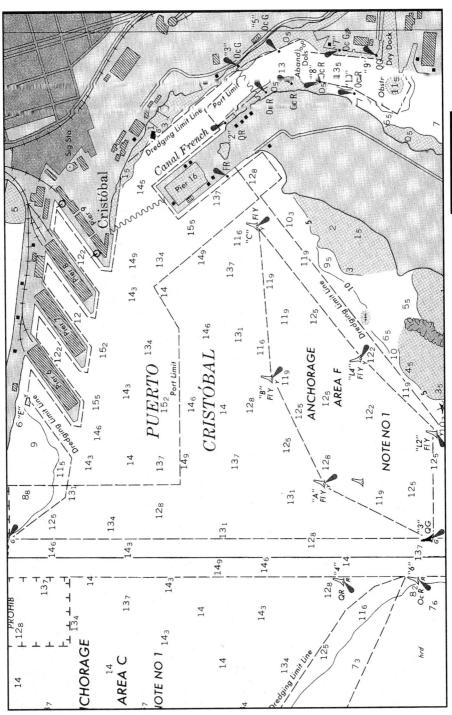

Cristóbal, Soundings in Meters

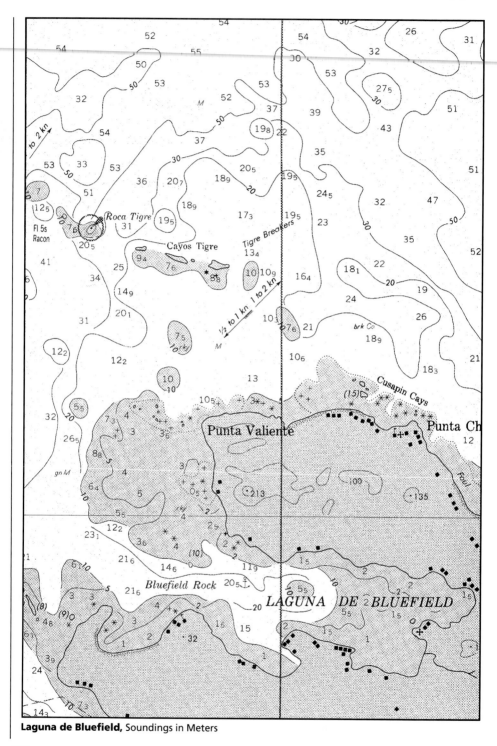

Laguna de Bluefield, Soundings in Meters

LAGUNA DE CHIRIQUÍ

8 56N, 82 07W

Pilotage: There are many anchoring possibilities in the Laguna De Chiriquí. The entrance, through Canal Del Tigre, is well marked because of the oil terminal at Chiriquí Grande. Currents in the inlet are generally weaker than 1 knot. The Chiriquí Grande pilots stand by on VHF channel 14, and the terminal can be contacted by calling "Rambala Control" on VHF channel 16. The terminal is located on the south side of the bay. There are several lit moorings, and a range of 212° for the terminal.

PUNTA VALIENTE

9 11N, 81 55W

Pilotage: This is the eastern point at the entrance to Laguna De Chiriquí. It is about 120 miles west of the entrance to the Canal. There is foul ground west of the point, extending south to the entrance to Laguna De Bluefield. Valiente Peak, a conspicuous 758 foot high peak, stands about 1 mile south of Punta Valiente.

ROCA TIGRE, 9 13.0N, 81 56.5W, Fl W 5s, 50ft., Metal tower. – Racon **P** (· – – ·)

BAHÍA DE ALMIRANTE

HOSPITAL POINT, 9 19.9N, 82 13.2W, Fl (2) W 10s, 36ft., 13M, Metal pedestal, F R

lights on radio masts 1.2M, 1.9M and 2.2M WNW.
BEACON 8, 9 20.4N, 82 13.6W, Q R, 15ft.
BEACON 9, 9 19.9N, 82 13.5W, Q G.
BOCAS DEL TORO, pier NE corner, 9 20.0N, 82 14.4W, Fl G, 27ft., White pedestal
PIER, SW corner, Fl R.

BOCAS DEL TORO

9 21N, 82 14W

Pilotage: The harbor is entered via Canal De Bocas Del Toro, which begins west of Cabo Toro (9° 22'N, 82° 12'W). There is a breaking reef around the shores of Cabo Toro, and Toro lies awash about 350 yards northeast of the cape. Heavy seas break on the shoals extending up to a mile off Long Bay Point to the north. The channel to town is marked with lighted aids to navigation. The pilot boat can be called on VHF channel 12.

Anchorage: Anchor off of town as depths permit. Some general supplies may be available. This is the last good anchorage before reaching the border of Costa Rica.

JUAN POINT, 9 18.2N, 82 17.8W, Fl G 4s, 15ft., 5M, Green tower.
PONDSOCK REEF, 9 17.3N, 82 19.8W, Fl W 6s, 15ft., 5M, Black tower, red bands.
ALMIRANTE, pier, 9 17.3N, 82 23.5W, Fl R, Post, Occasional.
ISLA PASTORES, NW end, 9 14.7N, 82 21.2W, Fl W 10s, 60ft., 9M, metal windmill tower.

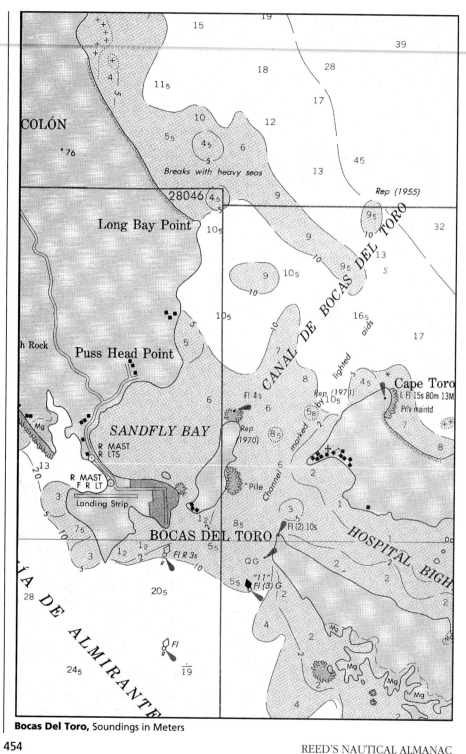

15
19
39
18
28
17
COLÓN
11₅
10
12
5₅
4₅
6
5
• 76
Breaks with heavy seas
13
45
Rep (1955)
28046 4₅
9
9₅
5
Long Bay Point
10₅
10
32
9
9
10
13
9₅
S
9
10₅
10
16₅
aids
17
10₅
h Rock
Puss Head Point
5₅
5
7
lighted
5
4₅
*
Cape Toro
6
Fl 4s
6
8
Rep (197)
by 10₅
L Fl 15s 80m 13M
Priv maintd
SANDFLY BAY
Rep
(1970)
5₈
8₅
marked
Channel
2
7
8
R MAST
R LTS
R MAST
F R LT
Pile
6
2
Landing Strip
1₂
5₅
3
1
13
20
3
7₅
8₅
Fl (2) 10s
3₅
HOSPITAL BIGH
1
10
1₂
2
Fl R 3s
R
2
QG
2
2
Oc
5
BOCAS DEL TORO
28
20₅
"11"
Fl (3) G
5₅
2
Mg
2
DE
4
ALMIRANTE
Fl
R
Mg
24₅
19
2
Mg
Mg
4

Bocas Del Toro, Soundings in Meters

CRISTÓBAL-COLÓN, PANAMA

HIGH & LOW WATER 1994 **9°21'N 79°55'W**

EASTERN STANDARD TIME (GMT -5H)

JANUARY

Day	Time ft	Time ft	Time ft	Time ft
1 Sa	0504 0.5	0800 0.4	1442 1.0	2222 -0.2
16 Su	0532 0.7	1047 0.3	1602 0.7	2256 -0.1
2 Su	0519 0.6	0954 0.4	1536 0.8	2247 -0.2
17 M	0602 0.8	1201 0.3	1651 0.5	2320 -0.1
3 M	0548 0.8	1126 0.3	1634 0.7	2315 -0.2
18 Tu	0630 0.9	1304 0.2	1739 0.4	2341 -0.1
4 Tu	0622 1.0	1246 0.2	1733 0.6	2345 -0.2
19 W	0659 0.9	1400 0.1	1826 0.3	
5 W	0701 1.2	1356 0.2	1835 0.4	
20 Th	0000 -0.1	0728 1.0	1451 0.1	1911 0.3
6 Th	0018 -0.2	0744 1.3	1502 -0.0	1938 0.3
21 F	0020 -0.0	0759 1.1	1542 0.0	1957 0.1
7 F	0054 -0.2	0828 1.4	1605 -0.1	2045 0.2
22 Sa	0039 -0.0	0831 1.1	1632 -0.0	2045 0.1
8 Sa	0131 -0.1	0915 1.5	1707 -0.2	2156 0.2
23 Su	0058 -0.0	0905 1.2	1723 -0.1	2138 0.1
9 Su	0211 -0.1	1004 1.4	1806 -0.2	2315 0.1
24 M	0119 -0.0	0942 1.2	1811 -0.1	2241 0.1
10 M	0253 -0.0	1053 1.4	1903 -0.3	
25 Tu	0144 0.0	1021 1.2	1854 -0.1	2358 0.1
11 Tu	0043 0.2	0340 0.1	1144 1.3	1956 -0.3
26 W	0218 0.0	1104 1.1	1931 -0.1	
12 W	0212 0.2	0438 0.2	1236 1.2	2043 -0.2
27 Th	0117 0.1	0316 0.1	1150 1.1	2003 -0.2
13 Th	0326 0.3	0600 0.3	1328 1.1	2124 -0.2
28 F	0216 0.2	0456 0.2	1241 1.0	2032 -0.2
14 F	0418 0.4	0741 0.4	1420 0.9	2200 -0.2
29 Sa	0300 0.4	0656 0.3	1338 0.9	2102 -0.2
15 Sa	0458 0.6	0920 0.4	1511 0.8	2230 -0.2
30 Su	0341 0.6	0847 0.2	1439 0.7	2133 -0.2
31 M	0422 0.7	1021 0.2	1544 0.6	2206 -0.2

FEBRUARY

Day	Time ft	Time ft	Time ft	Time ft
1 Tu	0505 0.9	1138 0.1	1647 0.5	2210 0.0
16 W	0333 0.0	1239 0.0	1745 0.3	2251 0.0
2 W	0549 1.1	1245 -0.1	1750 0.4	2321 -0.2
17 Th	0605 0.9	1323 -0.0	1826 0.3	2318 0.0
3 Th	0634 1.2	1346 -0.2	1850 0.3	
18 F	0637 0.9	1404 -0.1	1904 0.2	2343 -0.0
4 F	0001 -0.2	0720 1.3	1443 -0.2	1948 0.3
19 Sa	0710 1.0	1446 -0.1	1940 0.2	
5 Sa	0043 -0.2	0807 1.3	1540 -0.2	2047 0.2
20 Su	0010 -0.0	0745 1.0	1526 -0.1	2018 0.2
6 Su	0127 -0.1	0856 1.3	1635 -0.2	2148 0.2
21 M	0042 -0.0	0822 1.1	1607 -0.1	2059 0.2
7 M	0212 -0.1	0945 1.2	1730 -0.2	2253 0.2
22 Tu	0121 -0.0	0901 1.0	1646 -0.1	2147 0.2
8 Tu	0300 -0.0	1035 1.1	1824 -0.2	2242 0.2
23 W	0208 -0.0	0944 1.0	1723 -0.1	2242 0.2
9 W	0004 0.2	0355 0.1	1146 1.0	1915 -0.2
24 Th	0310 0.1	1032 0.9	1800 -0.1	2343 0.3
10 Th	0118 0.3	0504 0.2	1219 0.9	2001 -0.1
25 F	0429 0.1	1126 0.8	1837 -0.1	
11 F	0225 0.4	0633 0.2	1315 0.7	2041 -0.1
26 Sa	0044 0.4	0605 0.1	1229 0.7	1915 -0.1
12 Sa	0318 0.5	0811 0.2	1413 0.6	2115 -0.0
27 Su	0143 0.6	0744 0.1	1339 0.6	1956 -0.1
13 Su	0359 0.5	0940 0.2	1512 0.5	2144 -0.0
28 M	0239 0.8	0913 -0.0	1452 0.5	2040 -0.1
14 M	0434 0.6	1052 0.2	1608 0.4	2209 0.0
15 Tu	0505 0.7	1150 0.1	1659 0.4	2232 0.0

MARCH

Day	Time ft	Time ft	Time ft	Time ft
1 Tu	0808 0.0	1028 -0.1	1602 0.4	2126 -0.1
16 W	0057 0.7	1131 -0.1	1730 0.3	2126 0.2
2 W	0423 1.1	1131 -0.2	1707 0.4	2213 -0.1
17 Th	0431 0.8	1209 -0.1	1806 0.3	2156 0.1
3 Th	0514 1.2	1229 -0.3	1805 0.3	2302 -0.1
18 F	0506 0.9	1244 -0.2	1835 0.2	2229 0.1
4 F	0604 1.2	1322 -0.3	1900 0.3	2351 -0.1
19 Sa	0541 0.9	1318 -0.2	1902 0.2	2305 0.1
5 Sa	0653 1.2	1413 -0.3	1952 0.3	
20 Su	0617 0.9	1350 -0.2	1930 0.2	2346 0.1
6 Su	0041 -0.1	0743 1.2	1503 -0.3	2044 0.3
21 M	0655 1.0	1422 -0.2	2001 0.3	
7 M	0131 -0.1	0833 1.1	1552 -0.3	2136 0.3
22 Tu	0033 0.0	0736 0.9	1453 -0.2	2037 0.3
8 Tu	0225 -0.0	0923 1.0	1640 -0.2	2230 0.3
23 W	0128 0.0	0819 0.9	1525 -0.1	2119 0.4
9 W	0324 0.0	1014 0.8	1726 -0.1	2326 0.4
24 Th	0233 0.0	0907 0.8	1557 -0.1	2207 0.5
10 Th	0432 0.1	1109 0.7	1810 -0.0	
25 F	0349 0.0	1002 0.7	1633 -0.1	2300 0.6
11 F	0023 0.4	0553 0.1	1211 0.6	1852 0.0
26 Sa	0515 0.0	1108 0.5	1712 -0.1	2356 0.8
12 Sa	0116 0.5	0722 0.0	1321 0.5	1929 0.1
27 Su	0644 -0.1	1225 0.4	1757 -0.0	
13 Su	0204 0.6	0847 0.0	1436 0.4	2001 0.1
28 M	0054 0.9	0807 -0.2	1350 0.3	1848 -0.0
14 M	0245 0.6	0955 0.0	1547 0.3	2031 0.2
29 Tu	0152 1.0	0919 -0.3	1510 0.3	1945 0.0
15 Tu	0322 0.7	1047 -0.0	1645 0.3	2059 0.2
30 W	0249 1.1	1020 -0.4	1619 0.3	2045 0.2
31 Th	0345 1.2	1115 -0.4	1719 0.3	2146 0.0

APRIL

Day	Time ft	Time ft	Time ft	Time ft
1 F	0439 1.2	1205 -0.5	1812 0.4	2245 0.0
16 Sa	0407 0.9	1208 -0.3	1852 0.3	2129 0.3
2 Sa	0532 1.2	1253 -0.5	1901 0.4	2344 0.0
17 Su	0445 0.9	1234 -0.3	1903 0.3	2230 0.2
3 Su	0624 1.1	1338 -0.4	1949 0.5	
18 M	0525 0.9	1259 -0.3	1921 0.4	2332 0.2
4 M	0043 0.0	0714 1.0	1421 -0.3	2036 0.5
19 Tu	0606 0.9	1324 -0.2	1947 0.5	
5 Tu	0143 0.1	0804 0.9	1502 -0.2	2121 0.5
20 W	0037 0.1	0650 0.8	1350 -0.2	2020 0.6
6 W	0247 0.1	0856 0.7	1539 -0.1	2207 0.6
21 Th	0147 0.1	0738 0.7	1417 -0.2	2059 0.7
7 Th	0357 0.1	0950 0.6	1613 -0.1	2251 0.6
22 F	0303 0.1	0833 0.5	1447 -0.1	2143 0.9
8 F	0516 0.1	1054 0.4	1643 0.1	2334 0.7
23 Sa	0424 0.0	0938 0.4	1521 -0.1	2232 1.0
9 Sa	0639 0.0	1214 0.3	1707 0.1	
24 Su	0547 -0.1	1056 0.3	1601 -0.1	2325 1.1
10 Su	0015 0.7	0758 -0.0	1359 0.2	1723 0.2
25 M	0704 -0.2	1227 0.2	1647 -0.0	
11 M	0055 0.7	0902 -0.1	1606 0.2	1721 0.2
26 Tu	0020 1.2	0812 -0.3	1400 0.2	1744 0.0
12 Tu	0134 0.8	0952 -0.2		
27 W	0117 1.2	0912 -0.4	1521 0.2	1852 0.1
13 W	0212 0.8	1033 -0.2		
28 Th	0215 1.3	1005 -0.5	1627 0.3	2005 0.1
14 Th	0250 0.8	1108 -0.2		
29 F	0311 1.2	1054 -0.5	1722 0.4	2119 0.1
15 F	0328 0.9	1139 -0.3	1852 0.3	2023 0.2
30 Sa	0406 1.2	1140 -0.5	1810 0.4	2230 0.2

TIME MERIDIAN 75°W
Heights in feet are referred to the chart datum of sounding.

0000h is midnight, 1200h is noon.

Chapter 2

CRISTÓBAL-COLÓN, PANAMA

HIGH & LOW WATER 1994 9°21'N 79°55'W

EASTERN STANDARD TIME (GMT -5H)

MAY

Day	Time	ft	Day	Time	ft
1 Su	0500 / 1222 / 1856 / 2340	1.1 / -0.5 / 0.5 / 0.2	16 M	0357 / 1153 / 1852 / 2215	0.9 / -0.3 / 0.4 / 0.3
2 M ◐	0551 / 1302 / 1939	1.0 / -0.4 / 0.6	17 Tu	0440 / 1213 / 1905 / 2338	0.9 / -0.3 / 0.5 / 0.3
3 Tu	0048 / 0642 / 1338 / 2021	0.2 / 0.8 / -0.3 / 0.7	18 W ○	0525 / 1234 / 1929	0.8 / -0.3 / 0.7
4 W	0158 / 0732 / 1410 / 2101	0.1 / 0.7 / -0.2 / 0.8	19 Th	0057 / 0614 / 1258 / 2001	0.2 / 0.6 / -0.3 / 0.8
5 Th	0311 / 0824 / 1437 / 2140	0.1 / 0.5 / -0.1 / 0.8	20 F	0215 / 0708 / 1325 / 2039	0.1 / 0.5 / -0.3 / 1.0
6 F	0427 / 0922 / 1458 / 2216	0.1 / 0.3 / -0.0 / 0.8	21 Sa	0332 / 0810 / 1355 / 2123	0.0 / 0.3 / -0.2 / 1.2
7 Sa	0545 / 1036 / 1510 / 2252	0.0 / 0.2 / 0.1 / 0.9	22 Su	0448 / 0922 / 1430 / 2210	-0.1 / 0.2 / -0.2 / 1.3
8 Su	0700 / 1224 / 1500 / 2326	-0.1 / 0.1 / 0.1 / 0.9	23 M	0559 / 1048 / 1509 / 2301	-0.2 / 0.1 / -0.1 / 1.3
9 M	0804	-0.1	24 Tu	0705 / 1224 / 1555 / 2355	-0.3 / 0.1 / -0.1 / 1.4
10 Tu ●	0002 / 0855	0.9 / -0.2	25 W ○	0804 / 1400 / 1652	-0.4 / 0.1 / 0.0
11 W	0038 / 0938	0.9 / -0.3	26 Th	0050 / 0857 / 1521 / 1806	1.4 / -0.5 / 0.2 / 0.1
12 Th	0116 / 1013	1.0 / -0.3	27 F	0146 / 0946 / 1624 / 1931	1.3 / -0.5 / 0.3 / 0.2
13 F	0155 / 1043	1.0 / -0.3	28 Sa	0242 / 1031 / 1715 / 2057	1.2 / -0.5 / 0.4 / 0.2
14 Sa	0235 / 1109	1.0 / -0.3	29 Su	0336 / 1112 / 1800 / 2221	1.1 / -0.5 / 0.5 / 0.3
15 Su	0316 / 1132 / 1909 / 2031	1.0 / -0.3 / 0.3 / 0.3	30 M	0429 / 1150 / 1842 / 2340	1.0 / -0.4 / 0.6 / 0.3
			31 Tu	0520 / 1224 / 1921	0.8 / -0.4 / 0.8

JUNE

Day	Time	ft	Day	Time	ft
1 W ◐	0056 / 0610 / 1254 / 1958	0.2 / 0.7 / -0.3 / 0.8	16 Th ◐	0002 / 0502 / 1152 / 1904	0.3 / 0.6 / -0.3 / 0.9
2 Th	0210 / 0700 / 1320 / 2034	0.2 / 0.5 / -0.2 / 0.9	17 F	0121 / 0557 / 1218 / 1939	0.2 / 0.5 / -0.1 / 1.1
3 F	0322 / 0753 / 1340 / 2107	0.1 / 0.3 / -0.1 / 1.0	18 Sa	0234 / 0657 / 1248 / 2020	0.1 / 0.3 / -0.3 / 1.2
4 Sa	0434 / 0851 / 1355 / 2140	0.1 / 0.2 / -0.1 / 1.0	19 Su	0343 / 0803 / 1321 / 2104	-0.1 / 0.2 / -0.2 / 1.3
5 Su	0543 / 1004 / 1359 / 2213	-0.0 / 0.1 / 0.0 / 1.0	20 M	0449 / 0916 / 1359 / 2151	-0.2 / 0.1 / -0.2 / 1.4
6 M	0647 / 1157 / 1333 / 2246	-0.1 / 0.1 / 0.0 / 1.1	21 Tu	0551 / 1038 / 1440 / 2242	-0.3 / 0.1 / -0.1 / 1.4
7 Tu	0744 / 2321	-0.2 / 1.1	22 W	0651 / 1208 / 1527 / 2334	-0.3 / 0.1 / -0.1 / 1.4
8 W	0832 / 2357	-0.2 / 1.1	23 Th ○	0746 / 1341 / 1625	-0.4 / 0.1 / 0.0
9 Th ●	0912	-0.3	24 F	0028 / 0836 / 1503 / 1740	1.3 / -0.4 / 0.2 / 0.2
10 F	0035 / 0945	1.1 / -0.3	25 Sa	0123 / 0923 / 1605 / 1913	1.2 / -0.4 / 0.3 / 0.2
11 Sa	0114 / 1012	1.1 / -0.3	26 Su	0217 / 1004 / 1655 / 2049	1.1 / -0.4 / 0.5 / 0.3
12 Su	0155 / 1033	1.0 / -0.3	27 M	0311 / 1042 / 1738 / 2221	1.0 / -0.4 / 0.6 / 0.3
13 M	0238 / 1052 / 1822 / 2041	1.0 / -0.3 / 0.4 / 0.4	28 Tu	0404 / 1116 / 1816 / 2344	0.8 / -0.3 / 0.7 / 0.3
14 Tu	0323 / 1110 / 1817 / 2233	0.9 / -0.3 / 0.5 / 0.4	29 W	0456 / 1145 / 1852	0.7 / -0.3 / 0.8
15 W	0411 / 1130 / 1835	0.8 / -0.3 / 0.7	30 Th ◐	0058 / 0547 / 1212 / 1925	0.2 / 0.5 / -0.2 / 0.9

JULY

Day	Time	ft	Day	Time	ft
1 F	0206 / 0637 / 1235 / 1958	0.2 / 0.4 / -0.1 / 1.0	16 Sa ◑	0128 / 0605 / 1149 / 1915	0.1 / 0.4 / -0.2 / 1.2
2 Sa	0309 / 0728 / 1254 / 2030	0.1 / 0.3 / -0.1 / 1.1	17 Su	0231 / 0706 / 1225 / 1958	-0.1 / 0.3 / -0.1 / 1.3
3 Su	0409 / 0821 / 1310 / 2102	0.0 / 0.2 / -0.1 / 1.1	18 M	0331 / 0808 / 1304 / 2045	-0.1 / 0.2 / -0.1 / 1.4
4 M	0507 / 0920 / 1320 / 2135	-0.0 / 0.1 / -0.0 / 1.1	19 Tu	0429 / 0914 / 1347 / 2133	-0.2 / 0.1 / -0.2 / 1.4
5 Tu	0605 / 1033 / 1321 / 2208	-0.1 / 0.0 / 0.0 / 1.1	20 W	0527 / 1025 / 1433 / 2223	-0.2 / 0.1 / -0.1 / 1.4
6 W	0659 / 2244	-0.1 / 1.1	21 Th	0623 / 1143 / 1524 / 2315	-0.3 / 0.1 / 0.0 / 1.3
7 Th	0748 / 2321	-0.2 / 1.1	22 F ○	0716 / 1305 / 1627	-0.3 / 0.2 / 0.1
8 F ●	0828	-0.2	23 Sa	0009 / 0806 / 1422 / 1747	1.2 / -0.2 / 0.3 / 0.2
9 Sa	0001 / 0859	1.1 / -0.2	24 Su	0104 / 0851 / 1526 / 1923	1.1 / -0.2 / 0.4 / 0.3
10 Su	0043 / 0923	1.0 / -0.2	25 M	0201 / 0930 / 1616 / 2101	0.9 / -0.2 / 0.6 / 0.3
11 M	0128 / 0944 / 1703 / 1917	1.0 / -0.2 / 0.4 / 0.4	26 Tu	0258 / 1006 / 1658 / 2229	0.8 / -0.2 / 0.7 / 0.3
12 Tu	0217 / 1003 / 1704 / 2126	0.9 / -0.2 / 0.5 / 0.4	27 W	0354 / 1037 / 1735 / 2344	0.7 / -0.1 / 0.8 / 0.2
13 W	0310 / 1024 / 1726 / 2301	0.7 / -0.2 / 0.7 / 0.3	28 Th	0449 / 1105 / 1809	0.5 / -0.1 / 0.9
14 Th	0407 / 1049 / 1757	0.6 / -0.2 / 0.9	29 F	0047 / 0540 / 1130 / 1842	0.2 / 0.4 / -0.1 / 1.0
15 F	0020 / 0505 / 1117 / 1834	0.2 / 0.5 / -0.1 / 1.1	30 Sa	0142 / 0628 / 1153 / 1913	0.1 / 0.4 / -0.0 / 1.0
			31 Su	0232 / 0713 / 1215 / 1946	0.1 / 0.3 / 0.0 / 1.1

AUGUST

Day	Time	ft	Day	Time	ft
1 M	0321 / 0757 / 1236 / 2019	0.0 / 0.2 / 0.0 / 1.1	16 Tu	0303 / 0814 / 1301 / 2024	-0.2 / 0.3 / -0.1 / 1.4
2 Tu	0409 / 0842 / 1257 / 2053	-0.0 / 0.1 / 0.0 / 1.1	17 W	0356 / 0911 / 1350 / 2114	-0.2 / 0.3 / -0.0 / 1.3
3 W	0458 / 0930 / 1318 / 2128	-0.0 / 0.1 / 0.0 / 1.1	18 Th	0448 / 1011 / 1443 / 2205	-0.2 / 0.3 / 0.0 / 1.2
4 Th	0546 / 1026 / 1342 / 2206	-0.0 / 0.1 / 0.1 / 1.1	19 F	0540 / 1116 / 1543 / 2259	-0.1 / 0.3 / 0.1 / 1.1
5 F	0631 / 1133 / 1412 / 2246	-0.1 / 0.1 / 0.1 / 1.1	20 Sa	0631 / 1224 / 1655 / 2355	-0.1 / 0.4 / 0.2 / 1.0
6 Sa	0709 / 1248 / 1502 / 2330	-0.1 / 0.2 / 0.2 / 1.0	21 Su ○	0719 / 1331 / 1822	-0.0 / 0.5 / 0.3
7 Su ●	0741 / 1349 / 1632	-0.1 / 0.3 / 0.2	22 M	0056 / 0803 / 1430 / 1957	0.8 / 0.0 / 0.6 / 0.3
8 M	0019 / 0809 / 1433 / 1830	0.9 / -0.0 / 0.4 / 0.3	23 Tu	0200 / 0842 / 1519 / 2124	0.7 / 0.1 / 0.7 / 0.2
9 Tu	0115 / 0836 / 1513 / 2023	0.8 / -0.0 / 0.6 / 0.3	24 W	0306 / 0918 / 1602 / 2236	0.6 / 0.1 / 0.8 / 0.2
10 W	0216 / 0905 / 1553 / 2157	0.7 / -0.0 / 0.7 / 0.2	25 Th	0408 / 0949 / 1639 / 2334	0.5 / 0.1 / 0.9 / 0.1
11 Th	0320 / 0936 / 1634 / 2313	0.6 / -0.1 / 0.9 / 0.1	26 F	0502 / 1017 / 1714	0.5 / 0.2 / 0.9
12 F	0424 / 1011 / 1717	0.5 / -0.1 / 1.1	27 Sa	0022 / 0549 / 1044 / 1748	0.1 / 0.4 / 0.2 / 1.0
13 Sa	0017 / 0525 / 1049 / 1802	0.0 / 0.4 / -0.1 / 1.2	28 Su	0105 / 0629 / 1111 / 1821	0.0 / 0.4 / 0.2 / 1.0
14 Su	0115 / 0623 / 1131 / 1848	-0.0 / 0.4 / -0.1 / 1.3	29 M ◐	0146 / 0706 / 1138 / 1855	0.0 / 0.3 / 0.1 / 1.1
15 M	0210 / 0719 / 1215 / 1935	-0.2 / 0.3 / -0.1 / 1.4	30 Tu	0225 / 0741 / 1207 / 1930	0.0 / 0.3 / 0.1 / 1.1
			31 W	0304 / 0816 / 1239 / 2006	0.0 / 0.3 / 0.1 / 1.1

TIME MERIDIAN 75°W

0000h is midnight, 1200h is noon.

Heights in feet are referred to the chart datum of sounding.

CRISTÓBAL-COLÓN, PANAMA

HIGH & LOW WATER 1994 **9°21′N 79°55′W**

EASTERN STANDARD TIME (GMT -5H)

Chapter 2

SEPTEMBER

Day	Time	ft	Day	Time	ft
1 Th	0342 0853 1316 [illegible]	0.0 0.3 0.1 [illegible]	16 F	0400 0958 1508 [illegible]	-0.1 0.6 0.2 [illegible]
2 F	0420 0935 1401 2125	0.0 0.3 0.2 1.0	17 Sa	0444 1051 1619 2243	0.0 0.6 0.2 0.9
3 Sa	0455 1023 1459 2210	0.1 0.4 0.2 1.0	18 Su	0527 1146 1741 2349	0.1 0.7 0.2 0.7
4 Su	0529 1116 1615 2302	0.1 0.5 0.2 0.9	19 M ○	0608 1238 1909	0.2 0.7 0.2
5 M ●	0603 1212 1747	0.1 0.6 0.2	20 Tu	0105 0648 1328 2032	0.6 0.3 0.8 0.2
6 Tu	0003 0638 1308 1924	0.7 0.1 0.7 0.2	21 W	0228 0725 1414 2139	0.5 0.3 0.9 0.1
7 W	0114 0717 1403 2052	0.6 0.1 0.9 0.1	22 Th	0346 0800 1456 2233	0.5 0.4 0.9 0.1
8 Th	0230 0800 1456 2204	0.5 0.1 1.0 0.0	23 F	0449 0835 1534 2316	0.5 0.4 1.0 0.0
9 F	0341 0846 1548 2306	0.5 0.1 1.2 -0.1	24 Sa	0536 0909 1611 2354	0.5 0.4 1.0 -0.0
10 Sa	0445 0936 1639	0.5 0.1 1.3	25 Su	0611 0944 1647	0.5 0.4 1.0
11 Su	0000 0543 1027 1729	-0.2 0.5 0.1 1.3	26 M	0028 0639 1019 1723	-0.0 0.4 0.3 1.1
12 M ◑	0051 0635 1119 1820	-0.2 0.5 0.1 1.4	27 Tu	0101 0705 1058 1759	-0.0 0.4 0.3 1.1
13 Tu	0140 0726 1212 1910	-0.2 0.5 0.1 1.3	28 W ◐	0132 0731 1139 1836	-0.0 0.5 0.3 1.1
14 W	0228 0816 1307 2001	-0.2 0.5 0.1 1.3	29 Th	0202 0759 1226 1915	-0.0 0.5 0.3 1.0
15 Th	0315 0906 1405 2052	-0.1 0.5 0.1 1.1	30 F	0230 0830 1320 1956	0.0 0.6 0.3 1.0

OCTOBER

Day	Time	ft	Day	Time	ft
1 Sa	0258 0906 1423 [illegible]	0.1 0.6 0.3 [illegible]	16 Su	0341 1026 1702 [illegible]	0.1 0.9 0.2 [illegible]
2 Su	0327 0948 1536 2134	0.1 0.7 0.3 0.8	17 M	0410 1110 1824 2353	0.2 1.0 0.2 0.5
3 M	0357 1034 1700 2238	0.1 0.9 0.2 0.6	18 Tu	0434 1152 1942	0.3 1.0 0.1
4 Tu	0431 1125 1826 2355	0.2 1.0 0.1 0.5	19 W ○	0142 0448 1233 2047	0.4 0.4 1.0 0.1
5 W ●	0510 1220 1947	0.2 1.1 0.0	20 Th	1313 2138	1.0 0.0
6 Th	0122 0558 1316 2056	0.5 0.2 1.2 -0.1	21 F	1352 2220	1.1 -0.0
7 F	0246 0655 1413 2156	0.4 0.2 1.3 -0.2	22 Sa	1431 2255	1.1 -0.1
8 Sa	0358 0758 1509 2249	0.4 0.2 1.4 -0.3	23 Su	1509 2326	1.1 -0.1
9 Su	0457 0903 1604 2338	0.5 0.2 1.4 -0.3	24 M	1547 2354	1.1 -0.1
10 M	0550 1008 1658	0.5 0.2 1.4	25 Tu	0705 0909 1625	0.5 0.5 1.1
11 Tu ◑	0024 0638 1112 1750	-0.3 0.6 0.2 1.3	26 W	0019 0708 1016 1704	-0.1 0.5 0.5 1.1
12 W	0108 0725 1215 1842	-0.3 0.7 0.2 1.2	27 Th ◐	0043 0721 1120 1743	-0.1 0.6 0.4 1.0
13 Th	0150 0811 1320 1934	-0.2 0.7 0.3 1.1	28 F	0105 0742 1226 1825	-0.1 0.7 0.4 0.9
14 F	0230 0857 1429 2028	-0.1 0.8 0.3 0.9	29 Sa	0127 0809 1335 1910	-0.0 0.8 0.4 0.8
15 Sa	0307 0942 1542 2125	-0.0 0.9 0.3 0.8	30 Su	0151 0842 1450 2002	0.0 0.9 0.3 0.7
			31 M	0217 0922 1609 2103	0.0 1.1 0.2 0.5

NOVEMBER

Day	Time	ft	Day	Time	ft
1 Tu	0240 1006 1728 [illegible]	0.1 1.2 0.1 [illegible]	16 W	0232 1112 1947	0.3 1.2 0.0
2 W	0320 1055 1842 2348	0.1 1.3 0.0 0.3	17 Th	1148 2040	1.2 -0.0
3 Th ●	0401 1148 1949	0.1 1.4 -0.1	18 F ○	1224 2125	1.2 -0.1
4 F	0125 0452 1243 2047	0.3 0.2 1.5 -0.2	19 Sa	1301 2201	1.2 -0.1
5 Sa	0252 0558 1340 2139	0.3 0.3 1.5 -0.3	20 Su	1338 2232	1.2 -0.1
6 Su	0401 0715 1437 2228	0.4 0.3 1.5 -0.4	21 M	1417 2258	1.1 -0.2
7 M	0457 0835 1533 2313	0.5 0.3 1.4 -0.4	22 Tu	1456 2320	1.1 -0.1
8 Tu	0546 0954 1628 2355	0.6 0.4 1.3 -0.3	23 W	1535 2339	1.1 -0.1
9 W	0632 1109 1721	0.7 0.4 1.2	24 Th	0658 0954 1616 2357	0.6 0.5 1.0 -0.1
10 Th ◑	0035 0716 1223 1814	-0.3 0.8 0.4 1.0	25 F	0701 1122 1659	0.7 0.5 0.9
11 F	0111 0758 1337 1907	-0.2 0.9 0.3 0.9	26 Sa ◐	0015 0718 1242 1745	-0.1 0.8 0.4 0.8
12 Sa	0145 0840 1453 2002	-0.1 1.0 0.3 0.7	27 Su	0035 0745 1358 1837	-0.1 1.0 0.4 0.6
13 Su	0214 0920 1610 2103	0.0 1.1 0.2 0.5	28 M	0059 0819 1513 1935	-0.1 1.2 0.2 0.5
14 M	0238 0958 1727 2216	0.1 1.1 0.2 0.4	29 Tu	0126 0858 1625 2043	-0.1 1.3 0.1 0.3
15 Tu	0254 1035 1841 2357	0.2 1.1 0.1 0.3	30 W	0158 0943 1734 2203	-0.1 1.4 -0.0 0.2

DECEMBER

Day	Time	ft	Day	Time	ft
1 Th	0234 1032 1837 [illegible]	-0.0 1.5 -0.1 [illegible]	16 F	1109 2016	1.2 -0.1
2 F ●	0317 1123 1936	0.1 1.6 -0.2	17 Sa	1144 2059	1.2 -0.1
3 Sa	0112 0411 1218 2029	0.2 0.1 1.6 -0.3	18 Su ○	1221 2134	1.2 -0.2
4 Su	0239 0520 1314 2118	0.3 0.2 1.5 -0.4	19 M	1258 2201	1.1 -0.2
5 M	0348 0646 1410 2203	0.4 0.3 1.4 -0.4	20 Tu	1337 2223	1.1 -0.2
6 Tu	0443 0818 1507 2245	0.5 0.4 1.3 -0.4	21 W	1418 2240	1.0 -0.2
7 W	0531 0948 1602 2324	0.7 0.4 1.2 -0.3	22 Th	0640 0800 1501 2255	0.5 0.5 0.9 -0.1
8 Th	0615 1113 1656	0.8 0.4 1.0	23 F	0612 1012 1547 2311	0.6 0.5 0.8 -0.1
9 F ◑	0000 0657 1233 1750	-0.3 0.9 0.3 0.8	24 Sa	0622 1144 1636 2330	0.8 0.4 0.7 -0.1
10 Sa	0033 0736 1349 1844	-0.2 1.0 0.3 0.6	25 Su ◐	0645 1301 1729 2353	0.9 0.3 0.6 -0.2
11 Su	0102 0814 1502 1940	-0.1 1.1 0.2 0.5	26 M	0717 1411 1826	1.1 0.2 0.4
12 M	0127 0851 1613 2040	-0.0 1.2 0.1 0.4	27 Tu	0021 0754 1517 1928	-0.2 1.3 0.1 0.3
13 Tu	0145 0926 1721 2150	0.1 1.2 0.1 0.2	28 W	0054 0836 1619 2036	-0.2 1.4 -0.0 0.2
14 W	0155 1000 1826 2324	0.1 1.2 0.0 0.2	29 Th	0131 0922 1719 2151	-0.1 1.5 -0.1 0.1
15 Th	0146 1035 1924	0.2 1.2 -0.1	30 F	0212 1011 1817 2314	-0.1 1.5 -0.2 0.1
			31 Sa	0300 1103 1911	-0.0 1.5 -0.3

TIME MERIDIAN 75°W

0000h is midnight, 1200h is noon.

Heights in feet are referred to the chart datum of sounding.

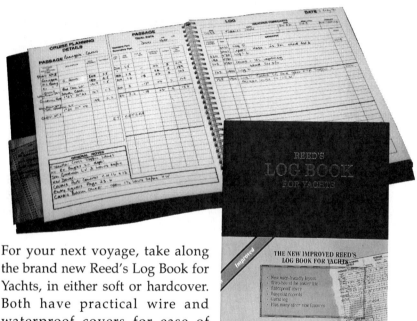

COSTA RICA

ENTRY PROCEDURES

The only harbor of interest on the Caribbean coast of Costa Rica is Puerto Limón. This is the Port of Entry, and a major shipping center for the country. Bananas and cocoa are the principal exports, but a considerable amount of general cargo is handled. See *Reed's Nautical Companion* for an example of the country flag.

Visitors should have the usual papers — passports, ship's documents, clearance from your last port and crew lists. You can get a visa upon arrival in the country. For more information on entry requirements contact the Embassy of Costa Rica at 1825 Connecticut Avenue NW, Suite 211, Washington, DC, 20009, (202) 328-6628.

For assistance within the country, U.S. citizens might want to call the United States Consulate in San José at (506) 20 39 39, or 20 31 27 after hours.

Cases of malaria have been reported from the Puerto Limón area. Travelers should contact the Center for Disease Control's travel advisory line at (404) 332-4559.

The telephone country code is 506, followed by a 6 digit local number.

The currency is the Colon, divided into 100 centimos. Currently (mid 1993) the exchange rate is about .008164 to 1 U.S. dollar. In other words, 123 Colons equals $1.00 U.S.

The language spoken is Spanish, but English is frequently heard, especially in tourist areas and cities.

COSTA RICA

SIXAOLA, 9 34.1N, 82 33.6W, Fl W 10s, 46 ft., 11M, White skeleton steel tower, Visible 114°– 315°

LIMÓN, ISLA UVITA, summit, 9 59.6N, 83 00.7W, Fl W 10s, 134 ft., 5M, White metal framework tower, Fl R 2s and F R on radio tower 0.9M WNW, Aero Al Fl W G 10s, 2M SW, R lights on radio tower 1.5M SW.

CONTAINER PIER, S end. 9 59.0N, 83 01.0W, F R, 49 ft., 10M.

BAHÍA MOÍN, ISLA PAJAROS, 10 01.0N, 83 04.6W, Fl W 2.5s, Tower.

PUERTO MOÍN RANGE, (Front), 10 00.2N, 83 04.6W, F W, Tower. **(Rear),** 130 meters, 151° from front, F W, Tower.

PUERTO LIMÓN
10 00N, 83 01W

Pilotage: This open coastal harbor is about 234 miles west-northwest of the entrance to the Panama Canal. The approaches are safe and easy of access. At night the loom of the bright pier lights is seen well out to sea. Two radio masts on Punta Blanca are reported to be prominent. A south setting current is generally experienced between Isla Uvita and Puerto Limón. During the dry season it attains a velocity of less than 1 knot, but during the rainy season may run at 3/4 to 1 1/4 knots. In general, the current sets southeast along this stretch of coast. There is a strong discharge from the rivers during the rainy season. A continual swell from the northeast breaks along the beaches of this entire coast.

Volcan Turrialba (10° 01′N, 83° 45′W) is an 11,349 foot high inactive volcano located about 43 miles west of Puerto Limón. When seen from the east, the peak and crater appear clearly defined, with the hollow of the crater being on the north side. The peak is generally hidden by clouds.

Monte Irazu, an 11,897 foot high mountain, stands close south of the volcano. On a clear day, these conspicuous peaks can be seen for a considerable distance.

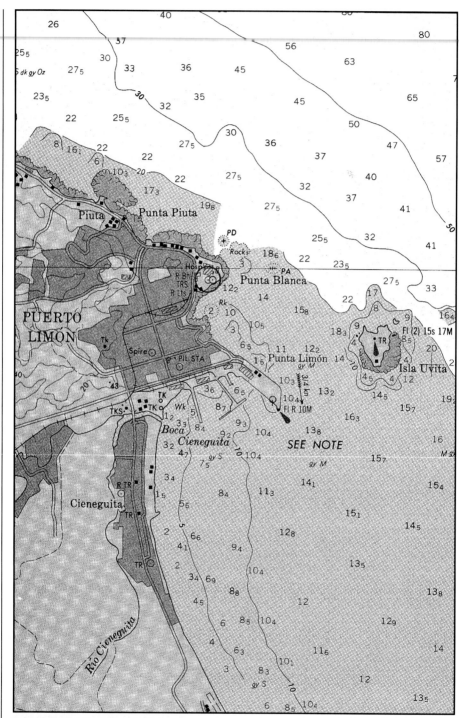

Puerto Limón, Soundings in Meters

You can contact Puerto Limón on VHF channel 16, or 2182kHz.

Port of Entry: The Customs office is across the street from the gates of the port area.

Radio Communications: Call sign TIM, Public Correspondence on VHF channel 16 and 2182kHz.

Anchorage: The anchorage is rather exposed, and open to swells. There is some shelter from Isla Uvita. There is reported to be a strong surge along the docks here. Be prepared to leave quickly if bad weather threatens.

Services: There are good markets and general stores. You can make rail connections to San José, and other parts of the country. Many people speak English here.

BAHÍA MOÍN

10 00N, 83 05W

Pilotage: This bay is the location of the commercial port facility Puerto Moín. It is located on the western side of the same peninsula as Puerto Limón. It is primarily a banana exporting and oil importing terminal. There is a light on Isla Pájaros, and a rock close to the northwest. The tanker moorings in the bay are subject to frequent changes of positions, colors and characteristics. There is a continual surge in this harbor, and this entire coast has a continual swell breaking on the beach.

Chapter 2

REED'S NEEDS YOU!

It is difficult to obtain accurate and up-to-date information on many areas in the Caribbean. To provide the mariner with the best possible product we utilize many sources. *Reed's* welcomes your contributions, suggestions and updates. Please be as specific as possible, and include your address and phone number.
Thank you!

NICARAGUA

CAUTION: Mariners are advised to avoid both the Caribbean and Pacific ports and waters of Nicaragua until further notice. There have been several cases of foreign flag vessels seized off the Nicaraguan coast by Nicaraguan authorities. While in all cases the ships, passengers and crews have been released within a short period of time, prompt U.S. Embassy consular access to detained U.S. citizens may not be possible due to non-notification of the Embassy by the Nicaraguan government. It should also be noted that there have been recent incidents of piracy in the Caribbean waters off the coast of Nicaragua.

Inland travelers should be aware of occasional flare-ups of armed violence, especially in the northern part of the country. The roads connecting Nicaragua and Honduras may be dangerous. All roads are considered dangerous at night.

ENTRY PROCEDURES

The Port of Entry on the Caribbean coast is Bluefields. This harbor is located about 275 miles northwest of the Panama Canal, and 120 miles north of Puerto Limón, Costa Rica. You can probably check in with the. For an example of the country flag see *Reed's Nautical Companion*.

Your passports should be at least six months from their expiration date, and you may be asked to prove you have financial resources of about $200 U.S. You should also have the usual papers — clearance from your last port, ship's documents and crew lists. Many nationals can get a tourist card upon entering the country. For visa information contact the Nicaraguan Embassy at 1627 New Hampshire Avenue NW, Washington, DC, 20009, (202) 387-4371.

For information, or assistance, while within the country, U.S. citizens might want to contact the United States Embassy in Managua at (505 2) 666 010, 666 026 or 666 027.

Credit cards and traveler's checks are not widely accepted, even in the larger cities. The biggest hotels in Managua may be able to accept credit cards, or change your traveler's checks. Traveler's checks may be changed at banks, or other official exchange stations. The currency is the Cordoba, divided into 100 centavos. In mid 1993 the exchange rate was approximately .16. In other words, 6.2 Cordobas equal $1.00 U.S.

Cases of malaria have been reported. For more information travelers should contact the Center for Disease Control's travel advisory line at (404) 332-4559.

The telephone calling code for Nicaragua is 505, followed by a one, two or three digit city code, then the local number. The city code for Leone is 311, for Managua 2, for San Juan Del Sur 466 and for San Marcos 43.

The main language spoken is Spanish, but English is heard in some Caribbean coastal areas.

CAUTION: Our information on aids to navigation comes from official government sources. The latitudes and longitudes of these marks may not correspond to the readings from GPS receivers. Some aids have been reported as unreliable, missing, off position or showing incorrect characteristics. No single aid to navigation, or waypoint, should be relied upon as a sole means of fixing your position.

CURRENTS

Between Punta Mico and Punta Gorda the currents on the edge of the 200 meter depth curve are affected by the equatorial current. Generally, part of the current recurves to the southwest in the vicinity of Isla de Providencia, while the main flow continues northwest across Miskito Bank.

The currents along the coast are variable and subject to great and sudden change. They are

influenced to a large extent by the wind, but they do tend to run south at a velocity varying from 1/2 to 3 knots. This southerly set sometimes reverses its direction for several days before resuming its normal flow.

The current is stronger in the vicinity of Punta Mico, where it sometimes sets east, then between Cayos de Perlas and Puerto Cabezas. Between Puerto Cabezas and Punta Gorda the current is variable, but tends to set north. However, this current may be completely reversed by a norther. A countercurrent setting south may be experienced close inshore.

PUNTA CASTILLO
10 56N, 83 40W

Pilotage: This low point marked by breakers is about 10 miles north-northwest of the Río Colorado. The entrance to San Juan del Norte is located about 2 3/4 miles west of the point. Morris shoal, about 4 miles long and 1 mile wide, lies about 10 miles east of the point. Depths over the shoal range from 60 feet to about 72 feet.

SAN JUAN DEL NORTE
10 56N, 83 42W

Pilotage: This harbor was once the proposed terminus of the Nicaraguan ship canal. The project was abandoned in 1893, and the harbor is now closed to ocean-shipping because of silting, but it is still possible for small craft to enter. The village and equipment are reported to be obscured by trees.

North of the harbor the coast is low and sandy for about 29 miles, until a bold rocky point is reached. A small wooded island lies near the point. The surf breaks constantly along these sandy beaches. The twin peaks of Round Hill rise to about 617 feet about 20 miles northwest of Punta Castillo. The coast then becomes higher and extends irregularly northeast to Punta Gorda.

PUNTA GORDA
11 26N, 83 48W

Pilotage: This is a prominent rocky point, with several steep-to islets lying close offshore. Río de Punta Gorda discharges into the sea about 4 1/2 miles northeast of the point. There are several settlements at the river mouth. From the

point the coast extends irregularly for 12 1/2 miles northeast to Punta Mico.

ISLA DEL PAJARO BOBO
11 30N, 83 43W

Pilotage: This 154 foot high wooded islet lies about 5 3/4 miles southwest of Punta Mico and 3 miles offshore. When seen from the east it appears as a small green conical hill, but from the south it appears wedge-shaped, with the higher end to the west.

PUNTA MICO
11 36N, 83 40W

Pilotage: This is the south extremity of a bold rocky peninsula, which extends about 1 1/2 miles southeast and is about 2 miles wide. In the middle of the promontory stands Red Hill, about 100 feet high and red in color. Red cliffs extend about 1 mile northwest from Black Bluff on the northeast end of the promontory. Shoal water and several cays lie within 1 mile of Punta Mico.

From the point the low coast extends about 45 miles north to Punta Mosquito at the entrance to Laguna de Perlas. El Bluff, a bold promontory, stands about midway along this stretch of coast.

FRENCH CAY
11 44N, 83 37W

Pilotage: This small, flat, wooded islet rises to a height of 90 feet. It stands about 7 1/2 miles north-northeast of Black Bluff, on the north part of a narrow reef about 1 1/4 miles long. Sister cays, three small islets, stand 8 1/2 miles north of Black Bluff. Two breaking reefs lie about 3 miles southeast and 2 1/2 miles east of Green Point. Cayo de la Paloma is a 108 foot high cay with a saddle-shaped summit lying about 1 1/2 miles east-northeast of Green Point. It is the largest cay in this area. Other hazards in the area include White Rock and Guano Cay — caution should be used in this area due to the many reefs and dangers.

EL BLUFF
12 00N, 83 41W

EL BLUFF SUMMIT LIGHT, Bluefields, 12 00N, 83 41W, Fl W 3.8s, 163ft., 14M, Red metal framework tower.

Pilotage: This bold promontory is over 137 feet high and wooded. It stands on the east side of the entrance to Laguna De Bluefields, but looks like an island from seaward. Red cliffs stand on the east side of the promontory.

BLUEFIELDS
12 01N, 83 43W

Pilotage: Cayo Casaba, a low wooded islet with a smaller islet to the west of it, lies in the middle of the entrance to Laguna De Blue-fields. The navigable channel between this islet and El Bluff is about 200 to 400 yards wide. The town of Bluefields is located on the west side of the lagoon about 3 1/2 miles inside the entrance. The port for the town is on the west and northwest sides of El Bluff. This is where all cargo is handled. The entrance bar has a minimum depth of about 9 feet, and the harbor has depths of less than 18 feet. Currents off the entrance generally set south at about 1 1/2 to 2 knots, but can reverse for a day for no apparent reason. A conspicuous white house on the northwest side of El Bluff and the radio towers in town are conspicuous. The pilots monitor VHF channel 16.

Port of Entry: Check in at the office on the El Bluff docks.

THE MISKITO BANK

Pilotage: From a position about 25 miles south of Punta Mico the 200 meter depth curve extends north-northeast to a position 28 miles east of the point, and then extends north-northeast to a position about 72 miles east of Punta Gorda. The Miskito Bank lies within this 200 meter depth curve.

The depths within the curve are irregular and numerous cays, islands and other dangers exist in the area. There are numerous detached shallow patches — some with depths of less than 6 feet. Most of the bank has depths of around 78 to 108 feet.

The turtle fishermen in this area are reported to know where most of the rocks are, and are adept at estimating depths. This is an area for "eyeball navigation" during the day. You should travel when the sun is high, and preferably behind you.

Coral reefs grow about two tenths of a foot annually, and depths may be less than charted in some areas.

CAUTION: Great care is required in navigating this area due to the unreliability and/or age of the chart surveys, the growth of reefs and reports of new shoals.

BLOWING ROCK
12 02N, 83 02W

Pilotage: This rock is about four feet high and has a hole through the center from which water is occasionally forced like the spouting of a whale. It lies about 38 miles east of El Bluff.

ISLA DEL MAIZ GRANDE
12 10N, 83 03W

Pilotage: This island is about 2 1/2 miles long by 2 miles wide, and lies about 38 miles east-northeast of El Bluff. Mount Pleasant rises to a 371 foot wooded peak in the middle of the north part of the island. A 98 foot high rocky bluff stands at the south end of the island. The island is fringed by foul ground extending about 1/4 to 1 1/2 miles offshore. There is a stranded wreck located about 1 1/4 miles north-northeast of Mount Pleasant which is reported to give a good radar return.

Anchorage: There is an anchorage in Southwest Bay on the southwest side of the island. Depths run about 27 to 30 feet. There are also anchorages in Brig Bay on the island's west side and in Long Bay on the southeast side. Care must be taken to avoid the reefs and shoal patches in or near these anchorages.

A 321 foot long pier extends from the shore near a shrimp processing plant in the head of Southwest Bay. Depths range from 6 to 13 feet alongside. There is a conspicuous building that is lighted at night. A similar building stands at the head of Brig Bay.

ISLA DEL MAIZ PEQUENA
12 18N, 82 59W

Pilotage: This 125 foot high island is about 1/2 mile long and 1/2 mile wide. It lies about 7 1/2 miles north-northeast of Isla del Maiz Grande. The north and northeast sides of the island are fringed by reefs extending about 1/2 to 1 mile offshore. The west side of the island is fairly steep-to seaward of the 10 meter curve, which lies between 1/4 and 1/2 mile offshore.

Anchorage: There is an anchorage in Pelican Bay on the southwest side of the island. Depths are reported to be about 36 feet with the west tangent of the island bearing 342° and the south tangent of the island bearing 106°.

SEAL CAY
12 25N, 83 17W

Pilotage: This is the most southeastern of the Cayos de Perlas. It is a small coral ridge about 3 feet high, lying about 12 1/2 miles east of Punta de Perlas. Foul ground extends about 1/2 mile northwest and about 1 mile south-southwest from the cay, but the southeast side is steep-to.

The south limits of Cayos de Perlas are marked by Columbilla Cay, a steep-to reef-fringed islet, 110 feet high to the tops of the trees, located about 6 1/2 miles southwest of Seal Cay. Maroon Cay, a similar islet on the edge of a reef extending about 2 miles east from Punta de Perlas, marks the southwest extremity of the area.

CAYOS DE PERLAS
12 29N, 83 19W

Pilotage: These cays and reefs lie between Punta de Perlas and a position about 13 1/2 miles east. They extend about 12 miles to the north within the 20 meter depth curve, which runs about 8 to 17 miles offshore.

Although there are depths of 36 to 60 feet in this area, navigation is very hazardous because of the numerous charted and uncharted reefs and shoals. Some of these may not be visible because of the turbid waters. A mud bottom may be only a thin covering over coral, and you should anchor with care.

BODEN REEF
12 30N, 83 19W

Pilotage: This area is about 3/4 mile long, with a least depth of 14 feet. It lies along the eastern edge of the Cayos de Perlas about midway between Seal Cay and the Northeast Cays located 8 miles northwest of Seal Cay. The Northeast Cays are a small group of reef-fringed islets with several rocks awash about 1 mile to the northwest. They mark the northeastern extremity of the Cayos de Perlas. Numerous rocks awash and 9 to 18 foot patches lie up to about 5 miles west-southwest of

these cays. Within this area lie the Crawl Cays and the Tungawarra Cays, as well as numerous small cays and shoals.

Anchorage: Good anchorage can be taken about 1/4 mile southwest of a mooring buoy lying 1/4 mile west of Little Tungawarra Cay. This anchorage should be approached from the south. Other anchorages may be found in the lee of the larger cays.

GREAT KING CAY
12 45N, 83 21W

Pilotage: This 70 foot high cay is the largest of a group of islets lying about 12 miles north of the Cayos de Perlas, and about 9 to 13 miles off the mainland. Little King Cay is about 32 feet high and stands about 3/4 of a mile east of Great King. The two Rocky Cays lie about 1 mile to the northwest, and 8 foot high Little Tyra Cay lies about 2 to 3 miles west-southwest of Great King.

GREAT TYRA CAY
12 52N, 83 23W

Pilotage: This cay is about 60 feet high to the tops of the trees. There is foul ground extending about 1/2 mile north from it. It is the largest of a group of islets and shoals lying about 8 miles north of Great King Cay. Seal Cay, two barren rocks about 10 feet high, lie about 3/4 of a mile south of Great Tyra, and a dangerous shoal patch lies about 1 mile east of Seal Cay. Several detached reefs lie between 1 and 3 miles southwest of Great Tyra Cay. There are two shoals located about 1 mile and 5 miles northwest of Great Tyra.

Tyra Rock is about 8 feet high and located about 4 1/2 miles northeast of Great Tyra Cay. Numerous detached reefs and shoals, over which the sea breaks, lie up to 3 1/2 miles west and 1 mile north of Tyra Rock.

RÍO GRANDE
12 54N, 83 32W

Pilotage: This river is navigable by barges for 106 miles upstream. The bar entrance has a depth of about 5 feet. Río Grande village stands on the north bank of the river near the entrance. A fruit station and a wharf are on the south bank, and two radio towers to the south are conspicuous. Sandy bay village is 3 1/2 miles north of the river.

CAYOS MAN O WAR

13 01N, 83 23W

Pilotage: This cluster of islets stands about 11 miles offshore and 6 3/4 miles northwest of Tyra Rock. The largest rises to a height of about 50 feet. An old oil barge, formerly used as a storage tank, stands on the west cay. A sheltered bight on the west side of this cay has pilings where vessels formerly moored to load lightered cargo. Depths alongside range from 13 feet to 22 feet.

Numerous detached reefs and shoals lie up to about 3 miles south-southwest and west-northwest of Cayos Man O War.

CAUTION: Many vessels have reported striking coral heads inside the 20 meter curve in the vicinity of Cayos Man O War, and between the cay and Puerto Cabezas.

EGG ROCK

13 02N, 83 22W

Pilotage: This 6 foot high steep-to rock is located about 1 1/3 miles northeast of Cayos Man O War. A dangerous shoal lies about 13 miles north-northwest of Cayos Man O War.

PUERTO ISABEL

13 22N, 83 34W

PUERTO ISABEL RANGE (Front Light), 13 21N, 83 33W, F R, Roof of shed. **(Rear Light),** 90 meters, 276° from front light, FW. **Pilotage:** This open roadstead is a privately owned port. There is a 1/2 mile long pier extending east from shore. From March to April currents run north, and from May to February south, at a velocity from 1 to 2 knots.

RÍO PRINZAPOLCA

13 25N, 83 34W

Pilotage: There is a small village on the south bank of the river. Shoal water, with depths of less than 6 feet, extends 1 mile east from the river.

RÍO WALPASIXA

13 29N, 83 33W

Pilotage: The sea breaks heavily on the bar at the entrance to this river, which is located about 4 miles north of the Río Prinzapolca. There is a

village at the river mouth and one called Wounta on the south side of a small lagoon about 4 miles north of the river. Foul ground extends about 3 miles east from just north of the lagoon entrance.

Several prominent mounds, each about 80 feet high, stand near the coast about 14 miles north of Wounta. From east of the mounds, south to 11 miles north of the Río Grande, the area within the 20 meter curve is restricted by numerous dangers. From the mounds, north to Puerto Cabezas, there are few dangers within the 10 meter curve, which lies within 2 to 4 miles from the coast.

RÍO HUAHUA

13 53N, 83 27W

Pilotage: This river is about 21 miles north of Wounta. After heavy rains, muddy river water discolors the sea for some distance offshore. From the river the coast extends about 10 miles north to Bragman Bluff, a bold headland about 98 feet high with red cliffs extending about 1/2 mile along its east edge.

PUERTO CABEZAS

14 01N, 83 23W

BRAGMAN BLUFF LIGHT, 14 02N, 83 25W, Mo (B) W 10.6s, 168ft., 14M, Southern square water tower, Visible 201° 30' to 021° 30', Private light. **Pilotage:** This harbor is an open roadstead with a government wharf extending about 1/2 mile southeast from Bragman Bluff. It is a banana and lumber exporting port. Some water towers, the radio towers on the east side of town and several chimneys in its southeast part are prominent landmarks. At night, the loom of the town's lights may be seen long before the navigational light can be spotted. The beach shows poorly on radar, although the railroad cars on the siding are reported to make an excellent return. The pier is reported to have a good radar return up to 14 miles. The current in the vicinity of the pier sets south or south-southwest at a velocity of about 1 1/4 knots. This is a possible Port of Entry, though the harbor is not sheltered, and makes a poor anchorage.

NED THOMAS CAY

14 10N, 82 48W

Pilotage: This cay and The Witties lie about in the center of a group of reefs. The group is about 8 miles in diameter, and lie about 11 1/2 miles

south of Cayos Miskitos. Sea Devil Reef and Franklin Reef lie on the south limits of the Cayos Miskitos group. They have depths of at least 15 feet over them.

SOUTHEAST ROCK
14 10N, 82 29W

Pilotage: This rock lies within 9 feet of the surface, and is on the southeast extremity of the Cayos Miskitos.

TSIANKUALAIA ROCK
14 20N, 83 04W

Pilotage: This rock, with a depth of about 9 feet over it, lies on the southwest side of the Cayos Miskito group about 7 3/4 miles east of Punta Gorda. Several rocks within 6 feet of the surface lie within 1/2 mile south and southeast of this rock. Waham Cay, 3 feet high, stands about 3 1/2 miles north-northeast of the rock. Toro Cay and Kisura Cay, two similar islets, stand about 2 miles north-northwest and 2 miles north, respectively, of Waham Cay.

Alice Agnes Rocks consist of several awash rocks, and lie on the southwest limits of the Cayos Miskitos group. They are about 13 miles west-southwest of Cayos Miskitos, and about the same distance southeast of Punta Gorda.

PUNTA GORDA
14 21N, 83 12W

Pilotage: This mainland point is low, wooded and has almost no identifying features. The Cayos Miskitos group lie about 7 1/2 miles to the east.

CAYOS MISKITOS
14 23N, 82 46W

Pilotage: This is the center of a group of cays and reefs with a diameter of about 19 miles. Approaches to this area are dangerous due to the many detached reefs and shoals, and the lack of any navigational aids. Cayos Miskitos is the largest of the group, being about 2 1/2 miles in diameter. Several smaller islands and islets lie adjacent to it. This are is part of a reef which extends 19 miles north-northeast from a position about 21 miles east of Punta Gorda. Currents in this vicinity generally run north to northwest at speeds of 1/4 to 1 knot. Inside the 20 meter curve close to the coast there

may be a southerly countercurrent. These currents are variable, and may even reverse, especially with a norther.

Porgee Channel (14° 26'N, 82° 41'W) is a narrow and intricate route bisecting the reef from east to west about 1/2 mile northeast of the northeasternmost island.

BLUE CHANNEL
14 25N, 82 50W

Pilotage: This channel is about 1 1/2 to 3 miles wide and runs parallel to the west side of Miskito Reef. Depths range from 30 to 84 feet. The Morrison Dennis Cays and the Valpatara Reefs (14° 27'N, 82° 58'W) extend about 12 miles north.

HANNIBAL SHOALS
14 26N, 82 31W

Pilotage: This 25 foot deep shoal marks the eastern side of the Cayos Miskitos.

AUIAPUNI REEF
14 31N, 83 05W

Pilotage: This is a group of shoal patches about 1 1/2 miles in extent, which lie about 7 1/2 miles southwest of Outer Mohegan. They are at the west extremity of the Cayos Miskitos group.

HAMKERA
14 34N, 82 58W

Pilotage: This small group of islets and reefs lies about 15 miles north-northwest of Cayos Miskitos. From Outer Mohegan, the largest of the Hamkera group, numerous detached reefs extend about 3 1/2 miles north to several rocks awash. This group is the most northwestern portion of the Cayos Miskitos.

EDINBURGH REEF
14 50N, 82 39W

Pilotage: This 4 mile long reef lies awash about 8 1/4 miles north of the northern limits of the Cayos Miskitos group. Edinburgh Cay is about 1 1/2 miles west-northwest of the southwest end of the reef. Edinburgh Channel is a clear passage between this reef and the ones to the south.

Cock Rocks are a series of drying rocks about 1/2 mile in extent that lie about 4 1/2 miles north of Edinburgh Reef.

CABO GRACIAS A DIOS
15 00N, 83 10W

Pilotage: This is a small town on the south side of the cape, at the mouth of the Río Coco. The river is obstructed by several cays at its mouth. The depth over the bar is about 6 feet, but is subject to change because of silting This is the seat of the governor, and a timber and banana exporting port. Except for some radio masts, the town cannot be seen from the south due to heavy foliage.

Chapter 2

WESTERN CARIBBEAN: OFFSHORE ISLANDS AND BANKS

CAUTION: Our information on aids to navigation comes from official government sources. The latitudes and longitudes of these marks may not correspond to the readings from GPS receivers. Some aids have been reported as unreliable, missing, off position or showing incorrect characteristics. No single aid to navigation, or waypoint, should be relied upon as a sole means of fixing your position.

ENTRY PROCEDURES

For information on entry procedures to the various countries that own these islands you should refer to the separate section on that country. The Cayos de Albuquerque, Cayos del Este Sudeste, Isla de San Andrés and Isla de Providencia are all part of Colombia. Only San Andrés Island and Isla de Providencia have settlements with customs stations where formalities may be complicated, but you should be prepared to check in with any officials found on the smaller cays. The Swan Islands are part of Honduras.

CAYOS DE ALBUQUERQUE (COLOMBIA)

12 10N, 81 51W

CAYOS DE ALBUQUERQUE LIGHT, On Cayo del Norte, 12 10.2N, 81 50.0W. Fl (2) W 20s, 59ft., 14M, Black and white banded tower.

Pilotage: These small cays lie about 111 miles east-northeast of Punta Mico on the Nicaraguan coast. This is about 204 miles northwest of the Panama Canal. They lie on a bank about 5 miles in extent, with steep-to sides. Numerous rocky heads and drying reefs exist, particularly near the east and south sides of the bank.

Cayo del Norte and Cayo del Sur are near the east side of the bank. They stand about 6 feet high and 4 feet high respectively, and are reported to give a good radar return at distances

of up to 12 miles. Both cays are heavily wooded with palm trees about 60 feet high. A light is shown from Cayo del Norte.

CAYOS DEL ESTE SUDESTE (COLOMBIA)

12 24N, 81 28W

CAYOS DEL ESTE SUDESTE LIGHT, Courtown Cays, Cayo Bolivar, 12 24.0N, 81 27.9W, Fl W 15s, 107ft., 17M, Metal tower, Radar reflector.

Pilotage: These cays lie on a 7 mile long (north-south), 2 mile wide, coral bank about 24 miles northeast of Cayos de Albuquerque. A reef extends across the northern portion of the bank, and a broken reef extends along the eastern side of the bank. The middle and western parts of the bank have numerous shoal patches. There is a stranded wreck about 3 1/4 miles northwest of Cayo Bolivar light.

Cayo del Este is on the southeast portion of the bank and is thickly wooded with palm trees. Cayo Bolivar is about 1 1/4 miles west of Cayo del Este. It is about 6 feet high with several palm trees on it. West Cay is a small low cay about 800 yards west-northwest of Cayo del Este. Cayo Arena is a small dry sandbank about 1 1/4 miles northwest of Cayo del Este. It is reported to give a good radar return at 14 miles. Fishermen's huts may be seen on these cays. You can anchor, with care, on the western part of the banks.

ISLA DE SAN ANDRÉS (COLOMBIA)

12 33N, 81 43W

PUNTA SUR LIGHT, 12 28.9N, 81 43.8W, Fl W 10s, 82ft., 14M, White tower.
COVE LIGHT, 12 31.0N, 81 43.8W, Fl R 3s, 65ft., 8M, Red tower.
PUNTA EVANS LIGHT, 12 31.9N, 81 44.1W, Fl G 5s, 65ft., 8M, Green tower.
AVIATION LIGHT, 12 35.1N, 81 41.7W, Al Fl W G 10s, 16M, Radio mast.

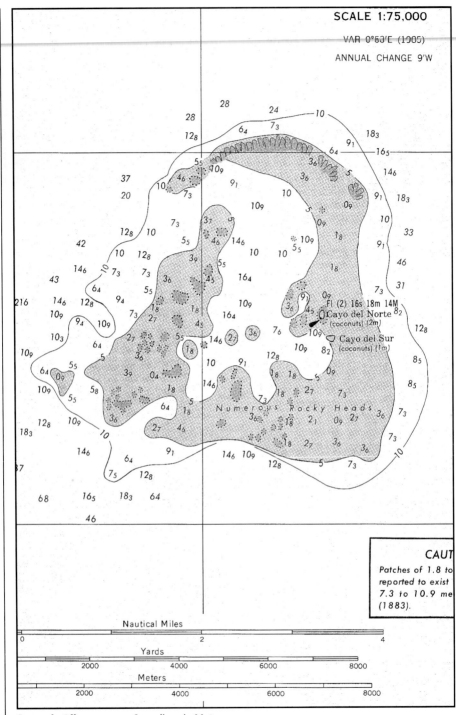

Cayos de Albuquerque, Soundings in Meters

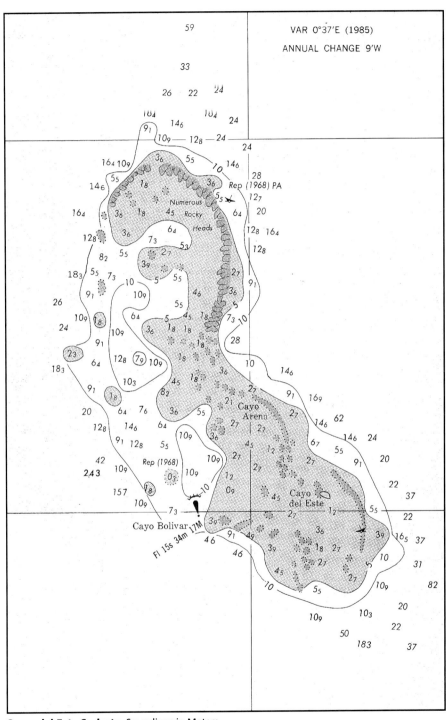

Cayos del Este Sudeste, Soundings in Meters

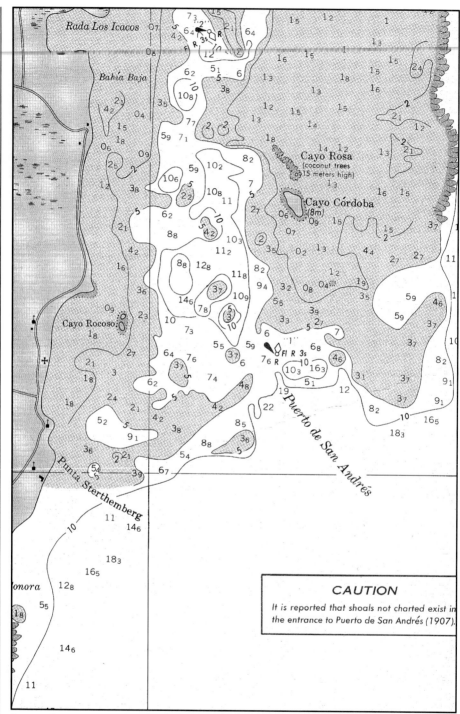

Approaches to San Andrés, Soundings in Meters

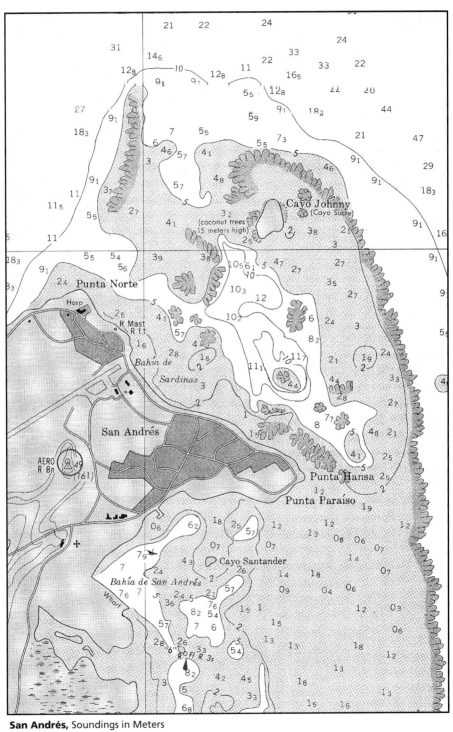

San Andrés, Soundings in Meters

Chapter 2

RADIOBEACON, 12 35.1N, 81 42.3W, SPP (··· ·——· ·——·), 387kHz NON, A2A, 192M.
CAYO CORDOBA LIGHT, Southeast end, 12 33.1N, 81 41.3W, Fl W 5s, 72ft , 10M, White tower.

Pilotage: The island lies about 16 miles west-northwest of Cayos del Este Sudest, or about 218 miles northwest of the Panama Canal. It is about 7 miles long (north-south) and 1 1/2 miles wide. A ridge of hills extends most of the length of the island. Three flat-topped summits rise above the ridge, but they appear as only two hills when viewed from north or south. A cliff at the north end of the ridge is distinctive. The island is reported to give a good radar return at up to 23 miles.

PUNTA NORTE
12 36N, 81 42W

Pilotage: This is the northern extremity of the island. It is fringed by foul ground up to 1 mile north of the point. Blowing Rocks are located about 3/4 mile north of the point, and the sea breaks heavily here during north winds.

Cayo Johnny (Cayo Sucre) is low and covered by palm trees. It stands on the the northwest end of a detached reef about 1 mile east-northeast of Punta Norte. The coastal reef extends about 1/2 mile north and east of Cayo Johnny, then about 4 miles south to a position about 1 3/4 miles east-northeast of Punta Sterthemberg. The south side of this reef is indented by a narrow, irregular channel which leads north to Bahía de San Andrés. South of Punta Sterthemberg the reef lies within 1/4 mile of the eastern coastline of the island. The west side of the island is steep-to and free of dangers.

PUNTA SUR
12 29N, 81 44W

Pilotage: This south extremity of the island is wooded. The western side of the island is mainly rocky cliffs. It is indented about 2 1/2 miles north of Punta Sur by Rada El Cove. Temporary anchorage may be found off the mouth of the cove, or inside for small craft.

BAHÍA DE SAN ANDRÉS
12 35N, 81 42W

Pilotage: This bay is formed by the reef to the east mentioned above, and the east side of Isla de San Andrés. A 300 meter long wharf

lies parallel to the shore in the southwest part of the bay. You should proceed with caution when entering the channel and when maneuvering within the harbor — the charted depths and shoals may be inaccurate.
Port of Entry: Fees were reported to be about $12.00 U.S., plus a $35.00 agent fee. An agent is required.
Dockage: Several marinas are located here.
Anchorage: Yachts can anchor on either side of Cayo Santander, but should pass around the south side of the cay, as a shallow bar connects to the mainland on the north side. Yachts report anchoring off Club Nautico in the deep water east of the cay. Dinghies can be landed at the marina east of Club Nautico. Proceed cautiously in this area, as depths and shoals may not be accurately charted. The anchorage is reported to be cool and comfortable, with clean water.
Services: This is a duty-free port and a tourist center for Colombians. There is very good shopping, good supermarkets and fine restaurants.

With its good anchorage and fine shopping, Isla de San Andrés makes a good stopping point if making the run from Honduras to Panama, or vice versa.

ISLA DE PROVIDENCIA (COLOMBIA)
13 21N, 81 22W

PROVIDENCE ISLAND LIGHT, 13 19.3N, 81 23.5W, Fl (2) W 14s, 180ft., 15M, White metal tower, Visible 318° to 157°, Reported at reduced intensity (August 1986).
LOW CAY LIGHT, 13 31.6N, 81 20.6W, Fl W 10s, 23ft., 10M, Reported extinguished (August 1986).

Pilotage: The island lies about 50 miles northeast of Isla de San Andrés. Together with Isla Santa Catalina, nearby to the north, these islands extend about 4 1/2 miles in a north-south direction. The mountainous center rises to three peaks of about the same elevation, with the highest being over 1190 feet. The north extremity of Isla de Providencia is Jones Point. On a spur extending south from this point stands 551 foot high Spit Hill. From the northwest or southeast a rocky chasm is prominent on Spit Hill.

The island is reported to give a good radar return up to 37 miles. A reef lies within about

2 miles of the east and south sides of the island, and up to 8 miles north from its north end. The west side of the island is foul except for an area about 1 1/2 miles in extent west of Catalina Harbor. Strong and irregular currents exist in the vicinity of Isla de Providencia.

CATALINA HARBOR

13 23N, 81 23W

Pilotage: This harbor is located on the west side of the northern part of Isla de Providencia. Morgan Head, the west extremity of the island, is a prominent 40 foot high rock. Isla Santa Catalina forms the northern side of the harbor area. Basalt Cay and Palm Cay are located about 1/4 mile north of Isla Santa Catalina. The suggested approach from the northwest is with Morgan Head in line with Fairway Hill bearing 143°. The approach from the southwest may be marked by some buoys, and runs very close to shore. Any approach should be made in good light, with the sun behind you, as there are many shoal patches and reefs.

Port of Entry: Check with the government officials in Isabel Village, located in the northeastern part of Catalina Harbor.

Anchorage: The harbor is reported to be well sheltered, with good holding in sand. Depths off of Isabel Village range from 6 to 9 feet over most of the anchorage area.

Services: This is a quiet little island settlement. There are telephones, general stores, a post office and a government office.

LOW CAY
13 32N, 81 21W

Pilotage: This cay is located on the northwest extremity of the reef, about 8 1/2 miles north of Jones Point on Isla de Providencia. A reef, that dries in places, extends about 1/2 mile south. There is a light on the cay.

Anchorage: The area 1 mile south of the cay is reported to be a good anchorage. There are shoal patches in this area.

RONCADOR BANK

13 34N, 80 04W

RONCADOR BANK LIGHT, On Roncador Cay, North end of bank, 13 34.9N, 80 05.3W, Fl W 11s, 79ft., 15M, Red metal tower.

Pilotage: The bank lies about 75 miles east-northeast of Isla de Providencia. It is very steep-to, and is about 7 miles long (north-south) with a maximum width of about 3 1/2 miles. Roncador Cay, composed of sand and blocks of coral, lies on the north part of the bank and is 13 feet high. A light is shown from the cay. The bank is mostly covered by reefs, drying sandbanks and coral heads. A conspicuous stranded wreck lies on the south end of the bank. A strong northwest current usually sets over the bank. **CAUTION: In 1980, the wreck and the south end of the bank were reported to be 1 1/2 miles southeast of their charted positions.**

Anchorage: Good anchorage can be taken on the west edge of the bank, but care should be taken to avoid the coral heads, which can be easily seen.

SERRANA BANK

14 24N, 80 16W

SERRANA BANK LIGHT, Southwest Cay, 14 16.3N, 80 23.5W, Fl W 10s, 82ft., 15M, White metal tower, Black band.

Pilotage: This extensive dangerous shoal area lies with its southwest end about 44 miles north-northwest of Roncador Cay. The bank is steep-to and about 20 miles long (NE to SW), and about 6 miles wide. All sides, except the west and southwest edges, are fringed by a nearly unbroken reef. The sea breaking over the reef on the east side of the bank is visible for several miles farther than the cays which stand on it. Mariners are advised to use extreme caution when in the vicinity of Serrana Bank because of the strong currents. On the west and southwest side of the bank are numerous live coral heads with less than a meter of water over them. **CAUTION: Serrana Bank has been reported (1989) to lie about 5 miles east of its charted position.**

SOUTHWEST CAY
14 16N, 80 24W

Pilotage: This small cay is composed of sand covered with grass and stunted brushwood. It is about 32 feet high, and the largest cay of the few on Serrana Bank. It is reported to be a good radar target at distances up to 10 miles. A steep-to reef extends about 9 miles northeast from the cay, but it is not always visible. A ledge on the edge of the reef 6 miles northeast of Southwest Cay is about 2 feet high. A drying sandbank stands about 1 1/2 miles farther northeast.

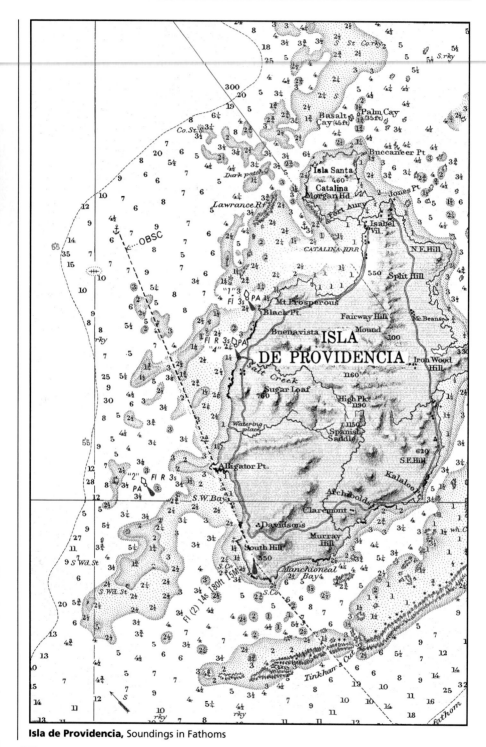

Isla de Providencia, Soundings in Fathoms

SOUTH CAY CHANNEL
14 21N, 80 15W

Pilotage: This 1/4 mile wide channel is located about midway along the southeast side of Serrana Bank. Depths in the fairway range from 24 feet to 42 feet. The currents in the channel run from 1 1/2 to 2 knots.

Anchorage: Temporary anchorage can be found with a depth of about 27 feet, in a position 1 mile northeast of the channel entrance. You can anchor in depths of about 42 feet midway between the cays at the channel entrance.

EAST CAY CHANNEL
14 21N, 80 11W

Pilotage: This channel is located about 4 miles east of South Cay Channel. It is about 1/2 mile wide, with depths of 60 to 84 feet in the fairway. East Cay lies on the west side of the entrance and a spur of the reef extends about 2 miles north from it.

NORTH CAY
14 28N, 80 17W

Pilotage: This cay is about 13 1/2 miles northeast of Southwest Cay on the north end of the reef. It is small and low, with a reef extending about 3 miles from the cay to the southwest. A stranded wreck was reported (1971) to lie about 1 mile southwest of North Cay. Northwest Rocks and the border of the bank are visible by radar from distances of less than 10 miles. Turtle fishermen visit this area from March to August. On occasion, the masts of their vessels and their temporary huts may be sighted before the reefs themselves. Currents run at 1 1/2 to 2 knots.

QUITA SUENO BANK

14 15N, 81 15W

QUITA SUENO BANK LIGHT, North end, 14 29.2N, 81 08.2W, Fl W 9s, 75ft., 15M, White metal tower.

Pilotage: The bank's south end is about 39 miles north-northeast of Isla de Providencia. It is very steep-to and dangerous. A 22 mile long reef lies along its east side. *CAUTION: Take great care when passing east of the bank as the current here sets strongly to the west.* Two wrecks stranded on the reef are reported to give a good radar return. There are

reported to be other wrecks on the reef. A detached shoal with depths of 17 to 22 feet lies about 14 miles west-northwest of the north edge of the reef. A vessel struck a coral head about 14 miles southwest, and a dangerous sunken rock is charted about 19 miles south-southwest of the north edge of the reef. It seems probable that another unsurveyed reef exists west of Quita Sueno Bank. A depth of 60 feet was reported (1964) to lie 38 miles west-northwest of Quita Sueno Light.

Anchorage: Good anchorage can be taken in about 60 feet, clear sand and coral, west of the rocky ground that lies near the middle of the reef.

SERRANILLA BANK

15 55N, 79 54W

SERRANILLA BANK LIGHT, 15 47.7N, 79 50.7W, Fl (2) W 20s, 65ft., 15M, White metal tower.

Pilotage: The bank lies about 78 miles north-northeast of Serrana Bank. It is very steep-to, with depths of 30 feet to 120 feet over most of it. There are shoal areas in the vicinity of the cays on the east and south parts of the bank. There is no perceptible current on the bank, but the current runs west-northwest at 1/4 to 1 knot in the vicinity.

BEACON CAY
15 47N, 79 50W

Pilotage: This is the largest of the three cays on Serranilla Bank. It lies about 7 1/2 miles southwest of East Cay. It is about 8 feet high, covered by grass and marked with a coral stone beacon on its west end. A light is shown from this cay. There is a 7 foot deep shoal located about 5 miles south of the light. There are numerous obstructions north of Beacon and East Cays for a distance of about 4 1/2 miles.

Anchorage: Good anchorage is reported in depths of 36 feet about 1 mile northwest of Beacon Cay. Take care to avoid the coral heads on the bank.

WEST BREAKER
15 48N, 79 59W

Pilotage: This is a dangerous breaking ledge about 2 feet high. It lies almost 8 miles west of Beacon Cay, and is the westernmost danger on the bank.

EAST CAY
15 52N, 79 44W

Pilotage. This is the easternmost above-water feature on Serranilla Bank. It is small, covered by bushes and about 7 feet high. It lies about 3 miles west of the east edge of the bank. Foul ground extends about 2 1/2 miles north and northeast from the cay. Three miles northeast of East Cay lies Northeast Breaker. This is a coral ledge with a rock awash on its south side.

BAJO NUEVO (HONDURAS)

15 53N, 78 33W (East End)

BAJO NUEVO LIGHT, Located on Low Cay, 15 51.2N, 78 38.0W, Fl (2) W 15s, 69ft., 15M, White tower, Black stripes.

Pilotage: This bank has not been well surveyed. It has been reported (1967) to extend west to about 15° 48'N, 78° 55'W. Its southwest end is not well defined, but the northwest side of the bank is reported to be clear of known dangers. Depths of 12 feet are reported to extend up to 10 miles west of Bajo Nuevo. Seals gather on the reefs here, and are hunted in March and April.

East Reef and West Reef, separated by a 1/2 mile wide opening, extend along the southeast side of the bank. They are over 2 1/2 miles wide and steep-to on the southeast and north sides. Sand accumulates on the reefs, forming low ridges, sometimes barely awash. A stranded wreck at the northeast end of East Reef is reported to be visible on radar. Another stranded wreck lies on the west end of West Reef.

Currents in the vicinity of the bank set west and southwest at speeds of up to 2 knots.

LOW CAY
15 52N, 78 39W

Pilotage: This cay, which lies at the north end of West Reef, is about 5 feet high and barren. It is composed of broken coral, driftwood and sand.
Anchorage: In moderate weather exposed anchorage can be taken in depths of 42 to 48 feet. This sand and coral bottom can be found about 1 1/2 miles west of Low Cay. Approach the anchorage from the west, taking care to avoid coral heads.

ROSALIND BANK

16 26N, 80 31W

Pilotage: The south extremity of the bank is located about 167 miles east-northeast of Cabo Gracias a Dios. As defined by the 200 meter depth curve the bank is about 63 miles long and 35 miles wide. General depths range from 60 feet to 121 feet over coarse sand and coral. The shallowest spots are about 35 feet deep.

The current generally sets northwest at a velocity of 1 1/2 knots over the bank. On striking the ledge near the southeast edge, the current causes a race which has the appearance of breakers.

An extensive bank, about 41 miles long and 10 miles wide, lies about 11 miles west of Rosalind Bank. Depths range from 24 feet to 216 feet. The shallowest detached patches are found along the east edge of the bank. A detached 36 foot patch lies on the north part of the bank.

THUNDER KNOLL

16 27N, 81 20W

Pilotage: This bank is about 11 miles in extent and composed of coral sand. It lies about 4 miles west of the "extensive bank" mentioned in the section on Rosalind Bank. Depths range from 79 feet to 230 feet. Two detached shoals with depths of 42 feet to 51 feet and 115 feet to 121 feet lie between 4 1/2 and 8 1/2 miles west of Thunder Knoll. A detached 36 foot patch was reported to lie about 4 miles southwest of the southwest part of Thunder Knoll.

SWAN ISLANDS (HONDURAS)

17 25N, 83 56W

ISLAS DE EL CISNE, Aviation light, Near the west end of the largest island, 17 24.5N, 83 56.5W, Fl W 5s, 70ft., 28M, 3 Fl R 1.5s (vertical) on tower 1 mile east, Occasional.

Pilotage: The Swan Islands (Islas Santanilla) are located about 150 miles north-northwest of Cabo Gracias a Dios. There are two small islands lying close together near the west part of a narrow bank about 18 miles long. The east island is 1 1/2 miles long, 60 feet high and has a bold rocky shore. The island is densely covered by trees and bushes. The west island is

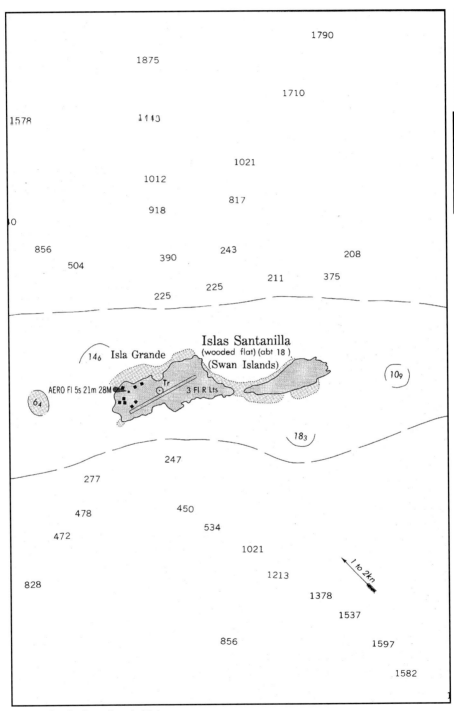

Swan Islands, Soundings in Meters

flat, about 1 3/4 miles long and covered by trees about 60 feet high. A Honduran navy post and a cattle farm exist on the southwest end of the west island. The passage separating the islands is foul. The islands have been reported to be good radar targets at distances up to 25 miles. The light with an aero light stands on the northwest side of the west island.

Anchorage: When the wind is in the northeast or east, anchor off the sandy bay at the west end of the west island. During north winds anchor south of the west end of the island. During south and southwest gales anchorage can be taken north of the islands, nearer the east than the west end.

This island was formerly a U.S. weather station, but has been given to Honduras to operate. Presumably, the Honduran government will continue to man the island's facilities.

MISTERIOSA BANK

18 51N, 83 50W

Pilotage: This bank is about 24 miles long and from 2 to 7 miles wide. It is centered about 87 miles north of the Swan Islands. Depths over the reddish coral bank range from 42 feet to 161 feet. There are other shallow banks in the vicinity. A detached 24 foot patch was reported to lie about 6 miles east of the east side of Rosario Bank.

ROSARIO BANK

18 30N, 84 04W

Pilotage: This bank is about 10 miles in extent and lies about 62 miles north of the Swan Islands. Depths range from 60 feet to 210 feet. There are other shallow banks in the vicinity.

HONDURAS

CAUTION: Our information on aids to navigation comes from official government sources. The latitudes and longitudes of these marks may not correspond to the readings from GPS receivers. Some aids have been reported as unreliable, missing, off position or showing incorrect characteristics. No single aid to navigation, or waypoint, should be relied upon as a sole means of fixing your position.

ENTRY PROCEDURES

Ports of Entry in the Bay Islands include Guanaja and Coxen's Hole on Roatán. On the mainland, clear at Puerto Castilla, La Ceiba and Puerto Cortés. See *Reed's Nautical Companion* for an example of the country flag.

You should have passports, your clearance from the last port of call, ship's papers and the proper courtesy flag. Fly the yellow Q flag upon arrival. Obtain a "zarpe", or cruising permit, from the officials, and be sure to list any place you are planning on visiting. You will have to clear in and out of each port as you cruise through Honduras.

Visas are usually issued for stays of 30 days, with renewals possible. For the latest information on entry requirements contact the Honduras Embassy, 3007 Tilden Street NW, Washington, DC, 20008, (202) 966-7702.

The border areas between Nicaragua or El Salvador and Honduras are considered quite dangerous and should be avoided. There are mine fields in some of these areas. You should check with the U.S. Embassy if planning an overland trip across these borders.

Contact the U.S. Embassy in Tegucigalpa at (504) 32 31 20.

The telephone code for Honduras is 504, followed by a 6 digit local number. The currency is the lempira which is currently trading at about 5.7 to 1 U.S. dollar. The main language is Spanish, but English is widely spoken in the Bay Islands area.

CABO GRACIÁS A DÍOS

15 00N, 83 09W

Pilotage: This point marks the border between Nicaragua and Honduras. It is low, swampy and covered with trees which attain a height of about 79 feet. The 151 foot high radio masts standing close west of the disused lighthouse are the best landmarks during the day.

CAUTION: The cape was reported in 1969 and 1973 to lie about 2 miles east of its charted position. Less depths than charted have been reported to lie 4 miles southeast and from 4 to 10 miles east of the cape. Vessels should give the cape a berth of at least 10 miles, and in thick weather, should keep in depths of over 60 feet.

ARRECIFE DE LA MEDIA LUNA (HALF MOON REEF)
15 13N, 82 38W

Pilotage: This group of reefs and cays has its north extremity located about 34 miles east-northeast of Cabo Graciás a Dios. This area is about 11 miles wide by 20 miles high (north-south), as defined by the 20 meter curve. The southern extremity is marked by Cock Rocks. Logwood Cay (Cayo Modera) stands on the west side of the bank.

Cayo Media Luna (Half Moon Cay) lies about 2 1/2 miles south of Logwood Cay, and a crescent shaped reef extends about 1/2 mile east, then 3/4 mile north from it.

Bobel Cay stands about 4 miles south-southeast of Cayo Media Luna. Two cays stand close together between 6 1/4 and 7 miles east-southeast of Cayo Media Luna. Several rocky heads lie in the vicinity of these cays.

Savanna Cut is a narrow passage with depths of 36 to 60 feet. It lies between Arrecife de Media Luna and **Savanna Reefs** (15° 10'N, 82° 25'W), which are located about 5 miles to the east.

Arrecife Alagardo (Alargate Reefs) are the easternmost visible danger on the Miskito bank. They lay about 5 miles east of the Savanna Reefs, where they are marked by heavy breakers. During periods of fresh northeast winds there is often a strong set toward the east side of the reef. *NOTE: It has been reported that Arrecife Alagardo lies 2 miles east of its charted position.*

BANCO DEL CABO
(MAIN CAPE SHOAL)
15 16N, 82 57W

Pilotage: This nearly awash shoal lies about 17 miles northeast of Cabo Graciás a Dios. It is about 4 miles long. The sea seldom breaks over it, but it may be spotted by the discoloration of the water in the area.

Main Cape Channel is the passage between Banco del Cabo and Arrecife de La Media Luna. It is clear of known dangers, and has depths ranging from 60 feet to 95 feet.

GORDA BANK
15 36N, 82 13W

Pilotage: This bank, with depths of less than 66 feet, extends for about 52 miles northwest of a position about 18 miles east-northeast of the northeast extremity of Arrecife Alagardo. Shallower depths than those charted may exist on the bank. The bottom is clearly visible, and on the north side there are a number of patches of flat coral, covered with dark weed.

CAYO GORDA
15 52N, 82 24W

Pilotage: This barren cay stands on the north edge of Gorda Bank. It is about 12 feet high, and is composed of sand, broken coral and large stones. A reef extends about 1 3/4 miles northwest from it, but its east and south sides are steep-to.

CAUTION: An obstruction was reported to lie about 4 1/2 miles southwest of Cayo Gorda.

Farral Rock, located 5 miles east of Cayo Gorda, breaks in heavy weather, and can be identified by its dark appearance, in contrast to the white sandy bank on which it lies. The two parts of the stranded wreck near the rock were reported to be good radar targets up to 10 miles distant.

BANCOS DEL CABO FALSO
(FALSE CAPE BANK)
15 32N, 83 03W

Pilotage: This is a dangerous, steep-to, breaking bank, lying about 32 miles north-northeast of Cabo Graciás a Dios.

CAYOS COCOROCUMA
15 43N, 83 00W

Pilotage: This reef lies about 44 miles north-northeast of Cabo Graciás a Dios. It is about 5 miles long, but a detached coral patch, on which the sea breaks, lies about 3/4 mile west of its north end. A group of seven small cays, not over 2 feet high and 1 mile in extent, lie on the south end of the reef. The southernmost, and largest, cay, is covered with bushes and some coconut trees on its east end. Another cay, about 1 mile to the north, has a square clump of brushwood about 15 feet high on it. This clump resembles an isolated rock when seen from a distance.

CAYOS PICHONES
(PIGEON CAYS)
15 45N, 82 56W

Pilotage: These two cays lie 3 miles east of Cayos Cocorocuma. The westernmost is a small islet at the south end of a dangerous, steep-to, half-moon shaped reef. The reef is about 3/4 mile in extent, and the sea breaks heavily here in stormy weather. A steep-to reef lies about 2 3/4 miles southeast of this islet.

BANCO VIVORILLO (VIVARIO BANK)
15 54N, 83 22W

Pilotage: This 10 mile long coral bank lies with its northwest extremity about 59 miles north of Cabo Graciás a Dios. Depths over the bank range from about 9 feet to 33 feet.

CAYOS VIVORILLO
(VIVARIO CAYS)
15 50N, 83 18W

CAYOS VIVORILLO LIGHT, 15 50.0N, 83 17.7W, Fl W 10s, 13M.
Pilotage: These cays lie on a coral reef at the southeast end of Banco Vivorillo. They are covered with trees and bushes. A continuous line of breakers front the steep-to east side of the reef. Practically all of this reef is usually dry or awash.

CAYOS BECERRO

15 55N, 83 16W

Pilotage: This group of 8 small cays lie about 5 1/2 miles northeast of Cayos Vivorillo. They lie on a coral ledge about 3 1/2 miles long by 1 mile wide. The sea always breaks along the east and north sides of the reef.

Grand Becerro is the largest cay, consisting of two parts. It stands near the south part of the ledge, and is marked by mangroves and a conspicuous palm tree on its west side.

El Becerro, a rock over which the sea usually breaks, stands 1 1/4 miles southeast of Grand Becerro. It is surrounded by a coral reef with depths of 12 to 30 feet. Rocky pinnacles, with depths of about 30 feet, lie about 5 1/2 miles north-northeast of El Becerro.

Hannibal Banks consists of two small shoals about 3/4 mile apart, lying in the southeast part of the passage between Cayos Vivorillo and Cayos Becerro. The north shoal has a least depth of 34 feet and the south shoal a least depth of 42 feet.

CAYOS CARATASCA

16 02N, 83 20W

Pilotage: This group of seven small cays lies about in the middle of a shoal bank located about 9 miles northwest of Cayos Becerro. The southernmost cay has some vegetation, but the others are barren.

CAYOS CAJONES (HOBBIES)

16 06N, 83 13W

Pilotage: This steep-to reef, about 13 miles long in an east-west direction, lies centered about 11 miles north of El Becerro. The narrow west part nearly always dries, but it does not always break. A small cay with bushes and coconut trees, stands about 3 miles west of the east end of the reef. A 23 foot patch is reported to lie (1970) about 5 1/2 miles northwest of the middle part of Cayos Cajones. Another 30 foot patch lies about 6 miles south of the middle of the reef.

CAUTION: Exercise great caution when approaching this reef. A vessel approaching from the north, at night or in hazy weather, should not come within depths of less than 180 feet, which lie up to 11 miles north of the reef. Depths of 121 feet will be found about 4 miles off. Within that depth the bottom is coral and sand, and outside it is mud.

During periods of strong northeast winds there is often a strong current set toward the north side of Cayos Cajones, which adds considerably to their danger.

CABO FALSO

15 12N, 83 20W

CABO FALSO LIGHT, 15 15.2N, 83 23.7W, Fl W 5s, 75ft., 19M.

Pilotage: This low point is about 21 1/2 miles northwest of Cabo Graciás a Dios. It is backed by several isolated trees and brushwood. It should be approached with caution, as a hard sandbank, with depths of less than 18 feet, lies about 3 miles northeast of it. The sea usually breaks over this bank and the inner part dries in places. The 36 foot line lies about 6 1/2 miles northeast of the cape.

CAUTION: Cabo Falso has been reported to lie about 3 miles west of its charted position. The area in the vicinity of the cape has not been thoroughly examined and passing vessels should give it a wide berth.

The Río Cruta lies about 3 1/2 miles northwest of Cabo Falso. Its shallow mouth is marked by high trees, which have the appearance of a bluff. When viewed from the west, they may be mistaken for Cabo Falso. In 1973 the mouth of the river was easily identified by radar. A light is shown from the mouth of the river.

PUNTA PATUCA

15 49N, 84 17W

PUNTA PATUCA LIGHT, 15 49.0N, 84 18.2W, Fl W 10s, 73ft., 19M.

Pilotage: This low, but prominent, point lies about 64 miles northwest of Río Cruta. The coast presents the same generally low aspect as the coast southeast of Río Cruta.

The entrance to the **Laguna Caratasca** lies about 27 miles west-northwest of the Río

Cruta, and can be identified by a large group of 89 foot high trees on either side. This large freshwater lagoon parallels the coast for about 35 miles, and is separated from the sea by a low, narrow, thinly-wooded ridge of sand. In 1973, the prominent point on the east side of the entrance was reported to be a good radar target.

Estero Tabacunta, the west outlet for the Laguna Caratasca, lies about 28 miles north-west of the above entrance. Both entrances are fronted by shallow bars, but the latter entrance has a channel with a depth of about 6 feet. Low white sand cliffs serve to identify the coast in the vicinity of Estero Tabacunta.

Río Patuca lies about 9 miles north-northwest of Estero Tabacunta. Punta Patuca is the west entrance point to the river, which at 150 miles long, is one of the largest in Honduras. The mouth is about 225 yards wide, but is difficult to make out unless a vessel is close-in. A light stands at the mouth. The controlling depth over the bar is about 6 feet during the dry season, and from 8 to 10 feet in the wet season. The outgoing current, even in the dry season, attains a rate of 1 1/2 knots. The only landmarks are a series of light colored bluffs, which stand south-east of the river mouth, and a low rounded hill in the which the land to the east seems to end. The east entrance point of the river is low and sandy.

LAGUNA DE BRUS

Pilotage: The entrance to this lagoon is at its western end, which is about 22 miles west of Punta Patuca. The entrance is marked on its west side by a clump of trees, higher than those elsewhere in the vicinity. This entrance is hard to spot from seaward. The bar across the entrance has depths of 6 to 7 feet in the dry season, and is usually fronted by heavy break-ers. There are depths of 10 to 11 feet within the lagoon, but there are many shoals and shallow areas.

RÍO SICO

Pilotage: The river entrance is about 16 miles west-northwest of the entrance to the Laguna de Brus, or about 38 miles from Punta Patuca. This is about where 3,700 foot high Cerro Payas (15° 45'N, 84° 56'W) rises abruptly from the low land along the coast. This mountain forms the eastern end of the Sierras La Cruz, an irregular mountain chain. The peak is fre-quently obscured by clouds, but Pico Panoche,

2,050 feet high, about 5 miles to the north, is usually visible. A vessel proceeding west will sight these peaks soon after passing Punta Patuca.

The bar at the river entrance has a least depth of about 5 feet in the dry season, and as much as 9 feet in the rainy season. It is only passable by boats in moderate weather.

The land rises abruptly on both sides of the river, and the mountains approach fairly close to the coast. The flat, swampy part of Hon-duras ends here, and the land to the west is traversed by numerous ridges, which reach the coast in places.

CABO CAMARÓN

16 00N, 85 00W

CABO CAMARÓN LIGHT, 15 59.2N, 85 01.9W, Fl W 5s, 73ft., 19M.

Pilotage: This point is located about 5 miles west-northwest of the Río Sico. It is low, rounded and topped by trees 79 feet high. The land is flat for some distance inland. A light is shown from the cape.

The coast between Cabo Camarón and the Río Aquan, 42 miles to the west, is indented by a bight extending about 6 miles to the south. The east part of the bight is low and sandy, and the west part is a low, thinly-wooded beach topped by some sand hills, 40 to 60 feet high.

From Cabo Camarón the coast trends about 15 miles west-southwest to Piedracito, a small distinctive rocky bluff. Cabeza Piedra Grande (15° 54'N, 85° 29'W), a rocky bluff about 400 feet high, is located a further 11 miles to the west. Cerro Sangrelaya (15° 52'N, 85° 09'W) rises to 6,150 feet high in a position about 5 miles southeast of Piedracito. A conical peak rises to 3,149 feet, 7 miles south of the same point. A saddle shaped summit stands about 5 miles southwest of the latter peak.

Iriona is a small settlement located 8 miles southwest of Cabo Camarón. This is the seat of government for the territory east to the Nicaraguan border.

A lower ridge of mountains rises south of Iriona and extends west to a position close

south of Cabeza Piedra Grande. From a position about midway between Cabo Camarón and Piedracito, as far west as Cabeza Piedra Grande, the lower slopes of the mountains nearly reach the coast.

RÍO AQUAN

Pilotage: This river enters the sea via two mouths located about 2 1/2 miles apart. The river extends 120 miles inland. The east mouth is located 16 miles west-northwest of Cabeza Piedra Grande, and is shallow. The east side of this entrance forms a distinctive point, and about 3 miles southeast of it is a 79 foot high hill close to the coast. The hill appears round when seen from the east or west, but from the north its west end appears as a flattened summit and its east end as a sugar-loaf hill. The two ends are separated by a chasm.

The settlement of Santa Rosa de Aquan stands on the east bank of the river, about 1 mile within the east entrance.

Vessels bound for the Río Aquan should call at Trujillo for clearance in entering and departing.

PUNTA CAXINAS

16 02N, 86 01W

Pilotage: This point is located at the west extremity of **Cabo de Honduras**, which is a narrow neck of low land about 5 miles in length. The cape is bordered by a scantily wooded beach with some scattered 40 to 60 foot sand hills. A light is shown from here.

Depths are about 60 feet, 3 miles offshore, and less than 240 feet up to 17 miles out. Within 17 miles of Cabo de Honduras the depths become irregular, with shoals of between 30 and 60 feet to the northeast, 57 feet to the north and 30 to 56 feet to the northwest.

The mountain range south of Cabeza Piedra Grande extends west for about 14 miles and then appears to terminate rather abruptly in a saddle-shaped summit, 2499 feet high. This summit is about 8 miles south of the mouth of the Río Aquan. A sugar-loaf peak of much less elevation stands west of the summit. A wide valley lies between this peak and Montanas de Trujillo.

ISLA DE LA BAHÍA (THE BAY ISLANDS)

Pilotage: This group of islands fronts the coast for a distance of about 75 miles in a west-southwest direction from a position about 30 miles north-northeast of Punta Castilla. The group consists of Isla Guanaja, Isla Roatán, Isla Utila and three small islands.

Currents: The currents in and around the islands are extremely uncertain, particularly during the summer. The Equatorial current north of the islands sets west, but when the northers have ceased, its surface influence is felt on the islands. The countercurrent generally sets in the opposite direction south of the islands.

The currents in the area may be greatly altered, or even reversed, by winds and tides. The range of the tropic tide at Isla Roatán is greater than anywhere else in the area. The current sets west and north with a rising tide, and with a falling tide, south and east. A counterclockwise eddy is observed north of Isla Utila.

Winds: The prevailing winds on the sheltered south sides of the islands are from the southeast, and at times attain a maximum velocity of 45 knots. During the winter months the winds may come from any direction.

ISLA DE GUANAJA (BONACCA ISLAND)

16 28N, 85 54W

BLACK ROCK POINT LIGHT, 16 29.9N, 85 49.0W, Fl W 10s, 200ft., 25M.
POND CAY LIGHT, Isla de Guanaja, 16 26.3N, 85 52.8W, Q G, 2M, Gray concrete column.

Pilotage: This is the easternmost of the Bay Islands group. It is about 8 1/4 miles long and 2 1/2 miles wide, at its widest part. The island is composed of densely-wooded hills that rise to a height of 1200 feet near its center. The northeast extremity is a bold peninsula terminating in 102 foot high **East Cliff**, which is ochre in color. **Ochre Bluff**, at the southwest end of the island is of the same height and color. Several anchorages are available within the coastal reefs, especially on the southeast side of the island. Numerous reefs, shoals and small cays fringe the island, especially on its southeast side.

GUANAJA SETTLEMENT
16 26N, 85 54W

Pilotage: This small town is located on Sheen Cays, about 1/4 mile off the southeast side of the island. Some of the buildings stand on piles around the cays. The approach depths are reported to be around 30 feet, with depths of 9 to 18 feet alongside the piers. You should be able to contact the port captain by VHF radio.
Port of Entry
Anchorage: Anchor west of the main cay, in depths of 8 to 30 feet.
Services: Fuel, water, groceries and basic supplies should be available. There are restaurants, a post office and communication facilities.

ISLA DE ROATÁN
16 25N, 86 23W

Pilotage: This is the largest island of the Bay Islands group. It lies about 15 miles west of Isla Guanaja, and is about 28 miles long and 2 miles wide. Isla Santo Elena, Isla Morat and Isla Barbareta stand close off its east end.

The island is densely-wooded and hilly, with general heights of 298 to 499 feet. A 735 foot high peak rises about 7 miles from the east end, and an 800 foot peak rises about 6 miles from the west end.

Punta Oueste is the southwest extremity of the island. A light is shown from the point. A conspicuous white church, with a red roof and a square bell tower, stands about 2 miles east-northeast of Punta Oueste.

The south shore of the island is indented with bays and coves suitable for small craft. The west and southwest parts of the island are steep-to, but elsewhere the island is fringed by a steep-to reef that extends up to about 1 mile offshore. Isla Barbareta, off the east end, is fronted by a reef that lies up to about 2 miles off its east and south sides.

By keeping the west extremity of Isla de Roatán bearing 272°, a vessel will pass south of all off-lying dangers when approaching from the east.

PUERTO REAL
16 25N, 86 19W

Pilotage: This harbor is located on the south side of the island, near the eastern end. Shelter is provided from the south by George Reef, George Cay and Long Reef. George Reef extends about 1 mile west from the east side of the harbor entrance. George Cay, low and wooded with the ruins of a fort at its west end, stands about 250 yards from the west end of the reef. Long reef is separated from George Reef by a channel 200 yards wide. Long Reef is a nearly dry ledge, 3/4 mile long, that protects the west side of the harbor. Enter the harbor via the channel between the reefs, which has reported depths of 18 to 27 feet. The reefs are steep-to and easily seen. A good landmark is the 735 foot peak that stands about 3/4 mile west of the harbor.
Anchorage: Anchor in the eastern part of the protected water north of the reefs.

OAK RIDGE HARBOR

Pilotage: This anchorage is located about 4 miles west of Puerto Real. It is entered through a narrow channel with a least depth of 20 feet, which leads north to the town. Depths off town are about 20 feet. A conspicuous stranded wreck lies close west of the entrance to the channel, and is a good mark in the approach. A pier extends from the shore of the harbor.
Services: Fuel and water should be available at the fish docks.

FRENCH HARBOUR
FRENCH HARBOUR LIGHT, 16 23.5N, 86 23.0W, Q W, 15M, Mast.

Pilotage: This harbor is about 10 miles west of Puerto Real. The town is almost surrounded by water, as extensive lagoons back it.
Dockage: Contact the French Harbor Yacht Club.
Anchorage: Anchor off the French Harbor Yacht Club in the lagoon east of town.
Services: Fuel, water, ice, groceries and general supplies are available.

COXEN HOLE
16 18N, 86 35W

COXEN HOLE REEF LIGHT, Southwest extremity of reef at entrance, 16 18.6N, 86 32.3W, F W, 25ft., *Reported extinguished 1989.*

Pilotage: This is the principal town on the island, and the seat of government for the Bay Islands. It occupies the east part of a bight on the south shore of the island, about 3 3/4 miles east-northeast of Punta Oueste. Its west side is bordered by dark 20 foot high cliffs, and its east and south sides by the reef upon which Coxen Cay stands. Carib Point, about in the middle of

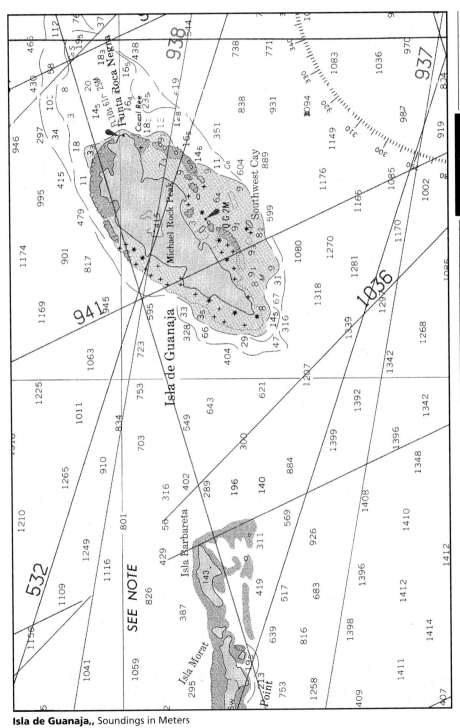

Isla de Guanaja,, Soundings in Meters

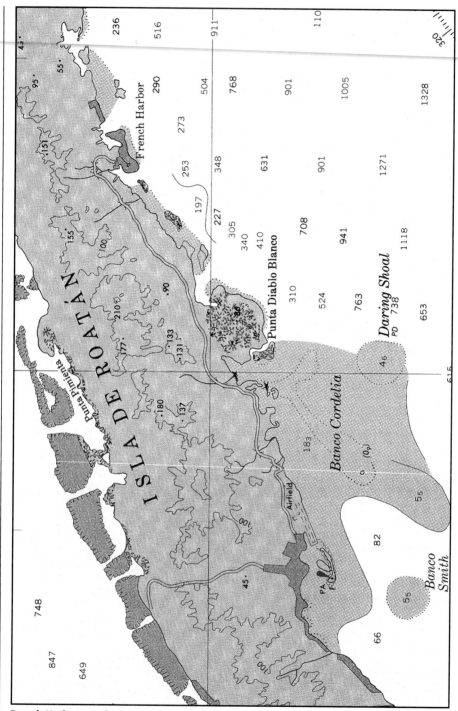

French Harbour and Coxen Hole, Soundings in Meters

the bight, has high coconut trees on it. Hendricks Hill rises to 298 feet about 1/2 mile north of the point. An 899 foot peak rises about 3/4 mile northeast of Hendricks Hill. When Hendricks Hill bears 020° a vessel will be in the fairway of the west channel and may steer in on this bearing until abeam of Coxen Cay. Care should be taken to clear the reef off the west side of the cay. The settlement is on the north shore of the bight, north of the cay.

Banco Becerro (Seal Bank) lies nearly awash about 1/3 mile southwest of Coxen Cay. The channel between this reef and the reef southwest of Coxen Cay is about 300 yards wide.

Banco Smith (16° 17'N, 86° 35'W) lies about 1 mile south-southwest of Coxen Cay. It has a least depth of about 21 feet.

Banco Cordelia, which dries, lies about 1 mile east-southeast of Banco Smith. A bank, about 1 mile in extent, with depths of 18 to 72 feet, lies 1 1/2 miles southeast of Coxen Cay.

Daring Shoal is a detached 15 foot patch about 2 1/2 miles east of Coxen Cay. It is reported joined to Banco Cordelia by a narrow ridge, with depths of less than 60 feet.

Port of Entry: This is the administrative center for the Bay Islands.
Dockage: The town wharf is reported to have depths of 6 to 10 feet alongside.
Anchorage: Anchor either northwest or northeast of Coxen Cay. The airport runway partially extends along the reef toward Coxen Cay in the eastern part of the harbor. The bottom is reported to be sand and coral heads.
Services: Fuel, water, ice, groceries and general supplies should be available. There are banks, a post office and communication facilities.

PUNTA OUESTE LIGHT, 16 16.1N, 86 36.1W, Fl W 5s, 74ft., 19M, *Reported extinguished 1989.*
ISLA DE ROATÁN WEST END LIGHT, 16 18.0N, 86 35.3W, Fl W 20s, 10M, Red framework tower, Visible 320° to 190°, *Reported extinguished 1989.*

ISLA DE UTILA

16 06N, 86 56W

UTILA PEAK LIGHT, Northeast end of island on summit, 16 07N, 86 53W, Fl W 10s, 325ft., 20M, Red metal framework tower.

Pilotage: This is the westernmost island of the Bay Islands group. It lies about 18 miles southwest of Isla de Roatán. The island is about 7 1/2 miles long and varies from 1 1/4 to 2 3/4 miles wide. It is generally, low, swampy and thickly wooded. A range of 60 to 70 feet high hills is located near its east end. Pumpkin Hill, 289 feet high and conical, stands near the northeast extremity of the island. A disused, black framework light structure, 102 feet high, stands near the west extremity of the island.

NOTE: In 1962, Isla de Utila and Isla de Roatán were reported to lie 2 to 4 miles farther apart than charted.

The island is steep to, except for its southwest side. The north side of the island is indented by several shallow bays. An area of foul ground extends about 4 3/4 miles southwest from the southwest side of the island, and is about 3 to 4 miles wide. Several good anchorages lie within this area, for those with local knowledge.

PUERTO ESTE

16 06N, 86 54W

PUERTO ESTE LIGHT, East Reef, 16 05N, 86 55W, F W, 4M, Wooden building.

Pilotage: This harbor lies about 1 mile west of the 20 foot black and red cliffs that form the southeast extremity of Isla de Utila. The harbor is about 3/4 mile in extent and provides anchorage in depths of 12 to 40 feet, with a clay bottom over coral.

Reefs narrow the entrance to about 300 yards, but depths run 30 to 36 feet. Two small coral heads lie about 1/4 mile from the east shore of the harbor. A church steeple in range 020° with a prominent tree is the leading mark used by local pilots.

It has been reported that entering vessels should steer 040°, passing about 200 yards off a stake on the coral reef to the east.

PUNTA CAXINAS

16 02N, 86 01W

PUNTA CAXINAS LIGHT, 16 01.5N, 86 00.6W, Fl W 7s, 75ft., 19M.

Pilotage: This point is located at the west extremity of **Cabo de Honduras** on the main-

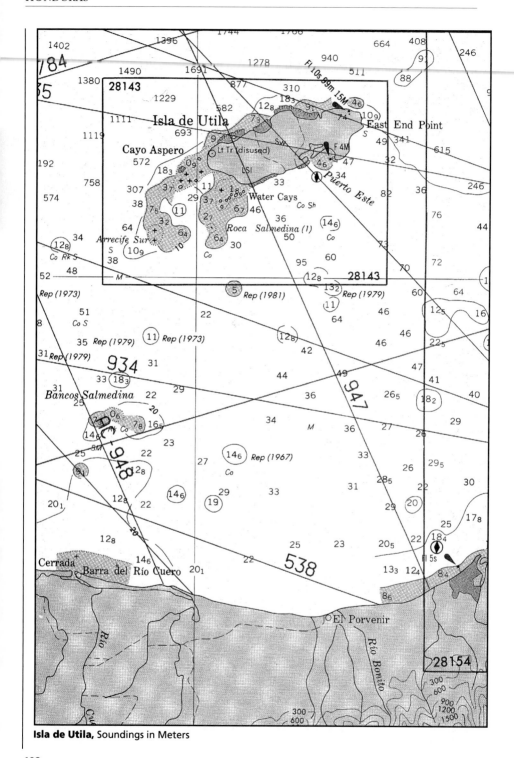

Isla de Utila, Soundings in Meters

Chapter 2

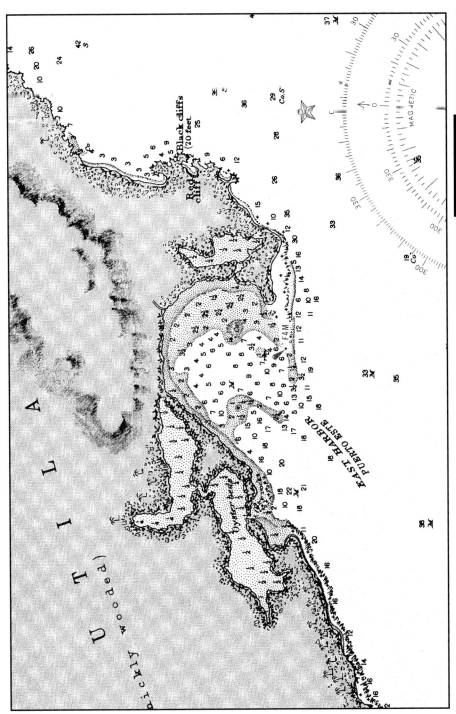

Puerto Este, Soundings in Fathoms

land, which is a narrow neck of low land about 5 miles in length. This is about 24 miles south of Isla de Guanaja. The cape is bordered by a scantily wooded beach with some scattered 40 to 60 foot sand hills. A light is shown from here.

Depths are about 60 feet 3 miles offshore and less than 240 feet up to 17 miles out. Within 17 miles of Cabo de Honduras the depths become irregular, with shoals of between 30 and 60 feet to the northeast, 57 feet to the north and 30 to 56 feet to the northwest.

The mountain range south of Cabeza Piedra Grande extends west for about 14 miles and then appears to terminate rather abruptly in a saddle-shaped summit, 2499 feet high. This summit is about 8 miles south of the mouth of the Río Aquan. A sugar-loaf peak of much less elevation stands west of the summit. A wide valley lies between this peak and Montanas de Trujillo.

BAHÍA DE TRUJILLO

15 58N, 86 00W

Pilotage: This bay is about 7 miles wide between Punta Caxinas and the coast to the south. The coast from the south entrance point to the bay extends west for about 115 miles to Punta Caballos. The shore is generally low, wooded and bordered by sandy beaches. Mountain ranges reach the shore in places, but are 10 miles inland in others. The mountains extend west to Tela, about 85 miles away. South of Tela the ranges curve inland and extend to the southwest. An extensive low, densely-wooded plain lies between the base of the ranges and Montanas de Omoa, about 30 miles to the west.

The mountain ranges rise to high prominent peaks south and southwest of Bahía de Trujillo, and south and southeast of Punta Congrejal. These peaks are good landmarks from offshore, particularly Cerro Congrejal, an 8,049 foot high mountain that is located about 10 miles southwest of Punta Congrejal.
There are few navigational aids along this coast. Puerto Castilla is on the north side of the bay, and Trujillo on the southeast side. A shallow channel at the eastern end o f the bay leads into a spacious lagoon. Depths in the central part of the bay average 39 to 184 feet. When approaching from the north give Punta Caxi-

nas a berth of 1 to 1 1/2 miles. The tank in Puerto Castilla is higher than the surrounding vegetation and can be seen from about 12 miles to the north.

The north and east shores of the bay are low, swampy and wooded, with no prominent landmarks. The south shore is backed by a high mountain chain which extends almost to the shore at Trujillo. Pico Colentura, a 3,198 foot peak, rises 3 miles south of the town. A vigia, or lookout hill, 2,499 feet high, stands at the northeast end of the mountain chain. These mountains are sometimes referred to as Montanas de Trujillo.

Callo Blanco is a dangerous reef located about 5 miles south of Punta Caxinas.

Currents: The usual set of the current off this coast is east within the 100 fathom curve. This current is uncertain due to the influence of the tides and winds. Within Bahía de Trujillo there is very little current during calms, or east winds. With west winds the current sets east and counter-clockwise around the bay at rates up to 2 knots.

Winds: The winds along the coast of Honduras are easterly for most of the year, with a pronounced diurnal variation. Calms and light offshore winds are frequent during the late night and early morning. Strong winds seldom blow in the early morning, except during the months of November and December. During these months there are several days with northerly winds that attain gale force. During periods of strong northwest to northeast winds a heavy swell enters Bahía de Trujillo.

PUERTO CASTILLA

16 00N, 85 58W

Pilotage: This port is located on the south side of Cabo de Honduras, about 2 miles southeast of Punta Caxinas, on the north side of Bahía de Trujillo. There are several piers on the waterfront, and others under construction.
Port of Entry
Anchorage: Anchor east of the commercial port area. Check locally for the latest depths over the bar at the entrance to the lagoon in the eastern part of the bay.
Services: Fuel, water and general supplies should be available.

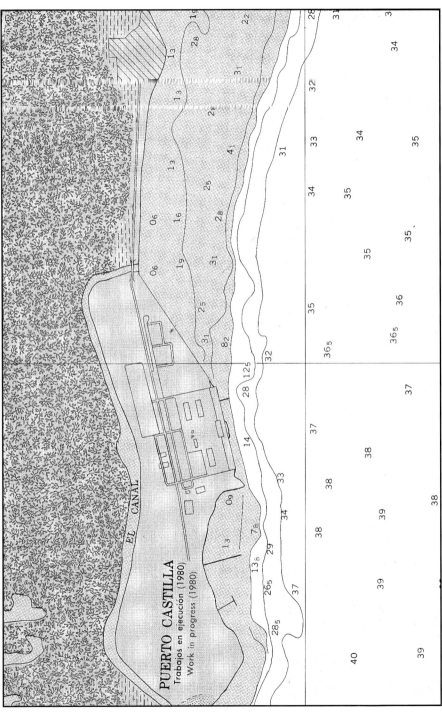

Puerto Castilla, Soundings in Meters

Chapter 2

TRUJILLO

15 55N, 85 57W

Pilotage: The port is located on the southeast shore of Bahía de Trujillo. The twin spires of the church in town are conspicuous when making your approach. A small fort looks out over the bay. The town pier is about 200 feet long and has a least depth of 16 feet along its south side.

Port of Entry

Anchorage: In calm weather you can anchor here, but you should move north in the bay when swells invade.

Services: Fuel, water and general supplies should be available.

CAYOS COCHINOS

15 58N, 86 34W

COCHINO GRANDE LIGHT, 15 58.6N, 86 28.5W, Fl W 7s, 516ft., 40M.

Pilotage: This group of cays lies about 27 miles west of Punta Caxinas and 9 miles north of Punta Catchabutan. The island furthest to the east is densely wooded and rises to a height of 430 feet. The north side of the island is steep-to, but a coral spit with depths of 24 to 36 feet extends 1 1/4 miles from the east side. A group of cays and rocks lie a short distance off the south side. A light stands on the east side of the island.

A wooded island about 1 mile farther southwest rises to a height of 499 feet. A steep-to coral ledge, with numerous cays and sandbanks, extends about 3 miles southwest from the islands. The channel between the islands has depths of 85 to 95 feet. Depths of 25 to 37 feet lie off the northwest side of these two islands.

BANCO PROVIDENCIA

15 55N, 86 38W

Pilotage: This dangerous bank lies 9 miles northwest of Punta Catchabutan.

CAUTION: Dangerous uncharted shoals are likely to be encountered anywhere within the 200 meter contour in this area.

BANCO SALMEDINA

15 55N, 87 05W

Pilotage: This bank lies 25 miles west of Banco Providencia and about 10 miles offshore. It is a

dangerous steep-to patch of coral, with a least depth of 2 feet near its east end. This reef breaks when there is any swell. A detached 24 foot patch lies 1 mile south-southeast of the bank and a 15 foot patch lies 6 miles northeast of it. Banco Salmedina should be given a berth of at least 2 miles.

PUNTA CONGREJAL

15 47N, 86 51W

Pilotage: This low sandy point is marked by the trunks of trees, and the discolored water from the Río Congrejal, which extends some distance out to sea. Depths of less than 36 feet extend up to 1 1/2 miles off the point. A tall tree, prominent from the east, stands about 3/4 mile west of the point.

The mountain chain that backs this part of the coast rises to Cerro Nana Cruz, a 6,098 foot peak, located 9 miles southeast of the point. Cerro Congrejal (Bonito Peak) is 8,049 feet high, and lies about 10 miles southwest of the point. This peak appears as a well defined, sharp cone, when seen from the northeast, but when seen from the northwest has a small, flat shoulder projecting east from just below the summit.

PUERTO LA CEIBA

15 46N, 86 48W

LA CEIBA LIGHT, Head of pier, 15 47.5N, 86 47.8W, Fl W 5s, 16ft., Wooden tower.

Pilotage: This open roadstead harbor is located about 1 mile southwest of Punta Congrejal. It is one of the principal ports of Honduras. A 1,423 foot long wooden pier projects from the town.

Currents: The current in the area has been reported to be westward, attaining a velocity of 2 knots at times. During northers the current sets south.

Winds: The prevailing winds during the day are northeast, and at night southwest. Normally the weather is calm with gentle breezes, except during the season of the northers (November and December) when winds of gale force occur.

Port of Entry

Anchorage: Anchorage is prohibited east of the pier. On the approach of a norther vessels are advised to proceed to sea. Swells are likely to be felt in this anchorage.

Chapter 2

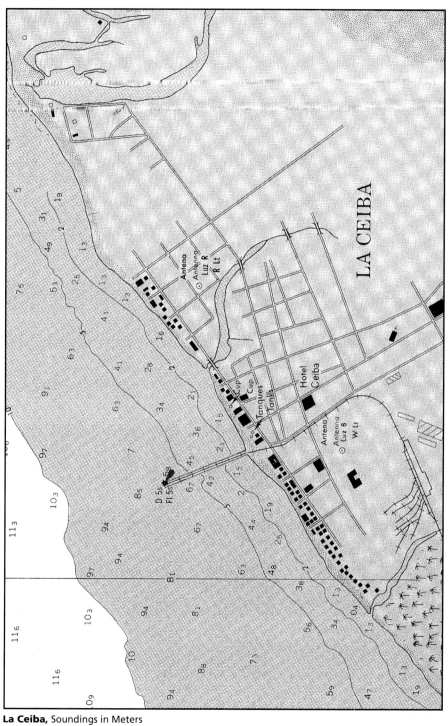

La Ceiba, Soundings in Meters

PUNTA OBISPO

15 51N, 87 23W

PUNTA OBISPO LIGHT, 15 50.9N, 87 22.5W, Fl W 5s, 132ft., 20M, White framework tower.

Pilotage: Punta Obispo is about 34 miles west of Punta Congrejal. The flat coastal plain along this coast gradually widens as the mountains become more sloping and recede inland. There are swamps and marshes a short distance inland, and numerous streams discharge into the sea. The shore is covered with trees and thick vegetation that almost reach the water's edge.

The point is a bluff, rocky, tree-covered headland. It is the termination of a conspicuous, conical, grassy hill. **The Clerks,** a group of 20 foot high rocks, lie close off the point. Depths of 121 feet lie within 1/2 mile of the rocks.

The entire area northeast to northwest of the point has depths of as little as 21 feet in places.

Cabo Triunfo, a bold rocky projection, stands about 4 miles southwest of Punta Obispo.

BAHÍA DE TELA

15 47N, 87 27W

Pilotage: This bay is entered between Cabo Triunfo and Punta Sal, about 12 1/2 miles to the northwest. It is bordered by a low sandy coast, but is backed by a high mountain ridge about 8 miles south of Punta Obispo. A range of mountains 2000 to 3000 feet high backs the coast in the vicinity of Tela, but just west of the town it veers inland and extends south.

Laguna de los Micos, a large, shallow, body of water, backs the bay, and is entered about 6 miles northwest of Tela.

TELA

15 47N, 87 27W

TELA LIGHT, Head of pier, 15 47.2N, 87 27.6W, Fl W 10s, 45ft., 6M, Red metal tower.
Pilotage: This open roadstead harbor is located in the southeast part of Bahía de Tela, near the eastern entrance point. This is the second ranking port in Honduras. The prevailing winds are east and northeast, but strong northers

may be experienced in the winter months. The average tidal range is about 1 foot, but the water level is also raised or lowered by the wind. The current off the pier has been reported to set west in the morning and east in the afternoon. A pier about 2000 feet long extends north from shore in front of the town. During north winds it is impossible to remain at the dock.
Anchorage: You are probably best off anchored west of the pier, but a swell is likely here. Be prepared to put to sea if a norther threatens.

PUNTA SAL

15 55N, 87 36W

PUNTA SAL LIGHT, 15 55.5N, 87 36.1W, Fl (4) W 30s, 275ft., 15M, White framework tower.
Pilotage: This bold, rocky promontory is the western boundary of Bahía de Tela. It projects 2 miles northeast from the coast, rising to wooded, irregular hills. It appears as an island when viewed against the low land to the south. A light is shown from the north end of the point. Three or four rocks, similar to The Clerks but much higher, lie about 1/2 mile off the east extremity of the point.

The coast between Punta Sal and Punta Caballos, about 22 miles to the west-southwest, is low, sandy and densely-wooded. Montanas de Omoa back the western part of this coast.

Puerto Escondido lies 2 miles southwest of Punta Sal. This small cove is a good anchorage for small craft.

Laguna Tinto lies 1 mile southwest of Puerto Escondido. This small bay should be approached with local knowledge. There is reported to be good anchorage for small craft.

Río Ulua is entered about 4 miles west of the entrance to Laguna Tinto. Punta Ulua, at the river entrance, is low and well defined. This large river is navigable by small river steamers for about 139 miles. The muddy discharge from the river discolors the sea for some distance offshore. A dangerous rock lies about 8 miles south-southwest of Punta Ulua. It lies within the 10 meter curve, about 1 mile offshore.

Río Chamelecon is located about 6 miles west-southwest of the Río Ulua. An isolated 636 foot conical hill is nearby. This is about 9 miles east-northeast of Punta Caballos.

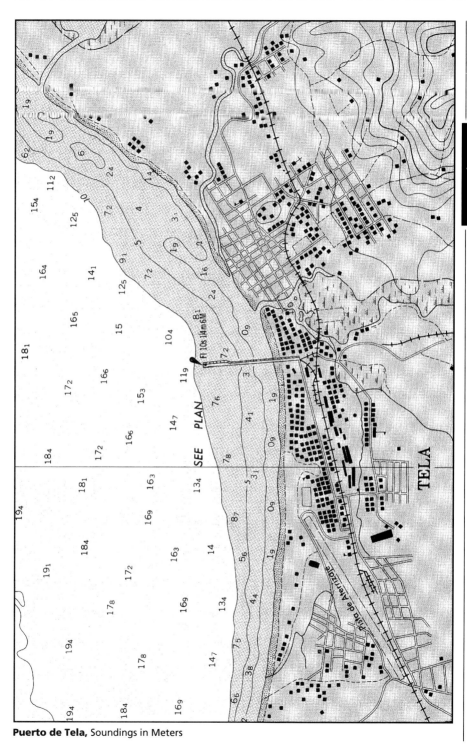

Puerto de Tela, Soundings in Meters

PUNTA CABALLOS

15 50N, 87 58W

PUNTA CABALLOS LIGHT, 15 51.0N, 87 57.7W, Fl W 5s, 190ft., 20M, Tower, FR lights 0.22, 0.25 and 3 miles east-southeast, Fl R on tank 2.34 miles southeast, *Reported destroyed 1989.*
NO. 1 LIGHT, 15 51.2N, 87 57.8W, Q (3) G, Green articulated light, *Missing March 1986.*
NO. 2 LIGHT, 15 51.0N, 87 58.2W, Q (3) R, Red articulated light, *Reported extinguished April 1985.*
NO. 3 LIGHT, 15 51.2N, 87 57.7W, Q (3) G, Articulated light, *Radar reflector reported 1985.*
NO. 4 LIGHT, 15 50.5N, 87 58.3W, Q (3) R, Articulated light,

Pilotage: This is the west extremity of a low, wooded peninsula that forms the north side of the harbor of Puerto Cortés. The radio masts on the point are good landmarks, as are the towers of a refinery located about 1/4 mile east of the light. Caution is necessary when navigating in this area as it has not been completely examined. A dangerous below water rock lies 1 1/2 miles northwest of Cerro Cardona (15° 53'N, 87° 51'W), an isolated conical 518 foot high hill situated 7 1/2 miles east-northeast of Punta Caballos.

The coast from Punta Caballos to Cabo Tres Puntas, about 39 miles west-northwest, forms a bight that indents the coast about 11 miles to the south. Puerto Cortés occupies the east part of this bight and Ensenada de Omoa occupies the south part. The Río Montagua enters the sea near the west part of Ensenada de Omoa and forms the boundary between Honduras and Guatemala. The east side of the bight is bounded by the base of the Montanas de Omoa, which rise to several prominent peaks. This range extends inland to the southwest from the head of the bight, and the land to the west becomes low and swampy.

PUERTO CORTÉS

15 50N, 87 57W

Pilotage: This is the major port of Honduras. It is situated on the north side of Bahía de

Cortés. The red roof of a hotel, and the water tank 2 1/4 miles southeast of Punta Caballos are good landmarks. The pilots monitor VHF channels 6 and 16.
Port of Entry
Anchorage: The best anchorage is reported to be off the Naval Base southeast of town. This area is near the charted "Coast Guard Pier".
Services: There is reported to be fuel, water, provisions and some repairs available. There are banks, a post office, restaurants and communication facilities. The Naval Base may be able to haul your vessel, and assist with repairs. Contact the base on VHF channel 21.

PUNTA DE OMOA

15 47N, 88 03W

Pilotage: This low but prominent point is about 6 1/4 miles southwest of Punta Caballos. Red cliffs stand on the coast about 3 miles east of the point. The coast is low, sandy and backed by high, wooded ground and mountains. A disused lighthouse stands on Punta de Omoa.

Omoa is a small sheltered port, which stands close south of Punta de Omoa. A small wharf extends from the town.

Ensenada de Omoa is a bight which lies between Punta de Omoa and the mouth of the Río Montagua, about 10 1/2 miles to the west-southwest. A heavy swell rolls in during northers.

Montanas de Omoa backs this section of coast. Pico de Montagua, a 7,308 foot peak, lies about 9 miles southwest of the head of Ensenada de Omoa. This is the termination of the mountain chain. The other prominent peaks in this range are usually obscured.

RÍO MONTAGUA

15 44N, 88 13W

Pilotage: This river marks the boundary between Honduras and Guatemala. It is a fairly large, shallow river, navigable by river boats up to about 35 miles above its mouth.

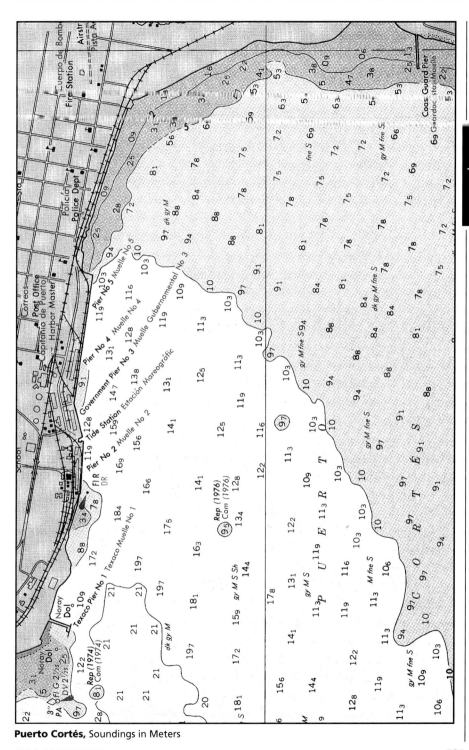

Puerto Cortés, Soundings in Meters

REED'S NAUTICAL COMPANION
Table of Contents

To get your **REED'S NAUTICAL COMPANION,** call 1-800-995-4995 and ask for the **REED'S** dealer nearest you!

GUATEMALA

CAUTION: Our information on aids to navigation comes from official government sources. The latitudes and longitudes of these marks may not correspond to the readings from GPS receivers. Some aids have been reported as unreliable, missing, off position or showing incorrect characteristics. No single aid to navigation, or waypoint, should be relied upon as a sole means of fixing your position.

ENTRY PROCEDURES

Guatemala has a democratic government, which was temporarily suspended in May of 1993, but now appears restored. Clashes between guerilla and government forces occur periodically, and much of the countryside is currently considered unsafe for travel. In addition, theft, robbery and violent attacks by criminals are frequent. Visitors should contact the U.S. State Department hotline at (202) 647-5225, for the latest travel advisory. When in the country, contact the Consular Section of the United States Embassy in Guatemala City. They may be reached at (502 2) 31 15 41.

In general, travel outside of major cities is considered very dangerous. Reports of car-jackings, hold-ups, rapes and murders are frequent. You should not travel at night, and even during the day, buses are stopped by armed robbers. Cholera is present and other tropical diseases can be encountered. Contact the Center for Disease Control at (404) 332-4559 for the latest travel advisory.

Cruising visitors seem to be able to avoid some of the problems on land — many report pleasant visits to Guatemala and the Río Dulce. Ports of Entry include Puerto Barrios, Santo Tomas de Castilla and Livingston. For an example of the country flag see *Reed's Nautical Companion.* Port officials are reported to be strict about showing the proper flags.

You should have passports, a clearance from your last port, ship's papers, a visa or tourist card, and you must declare your firearms, which will be held by the port captain. Tourist cards can be purchased upon your arrival, and are usually good for a maximum of 30 days. You should request a cruisng permit, or "zarpe", stating where you intend to visit. Permits are usually good for 90 days. You should carry some form of identification with you, other than your passport, in case of robbery or theft.

U.S. citizens must have a passport to <u>depart</u> Guatemala. If your passport is stolen you must immediately contact the U.S. Embassy in Guatemala City and the local police. You will need to show your passport application, and the police report, before you will be allowed to depart.

For the latest regulations contact the Guatemalan Embassy at 2220 R Street NW, Washington, DC, 20008, (202) 745-4952.

All payments should be in quetzals, the local currency. At this writing, in mid-1993, one quetzal is equal to about .211 U.S. dollars. In other words, 4.7 quetzals equal $1.00 U.S. Currency values are subject to change.

The telephone code for the country is 502, followed by a 2 if calling Guatemala City, or a 9 for all other locations in the country. Local numbers are six digits.

RÍO MONTAGUA

15 44N, 88 13W

Pilotage: This river marks the boundary between Honduras and Guatemala. It is a fairly large, shallow river, navigable by river boats up to about 35 miles above its mouth.

Between the Río Montagua and Cabo Tres Puntas, about 27 miles to the northwest, the low, swampy coast is bordered by a dark sandy beach, backed by trees.

Río San Francisco del Mar discharges about 14 miles northwest of the Río Montagua, and a branch of the river leads to Bahía La Graciosa. A conspicuous 600 foot high tableland stands about 8 miles southwest of the mouth of this river.

CABO TRES PUNTAS (CAPE THREE POINTS)

15 58N, 88 37W

CABO TRES PUNTAS LIGHT, 15 57.4N, 88 36.2W, Fl W 10s, 132ft., 17M, White framework tower.
Pilotage: This is a prominent, well-wooded point, which is the northwest extremity of a low, wooded peninsula about 11 miles long that borders the northeast side of Bahía de Amatique. A conspicuous tower stands on the cape. Steep-to foul ground, which usually breaks, extends about 1/2 mile west from the cape.

BAHÍA DE AMATIQUE (HONDURAS BAY)

15 56N, 88 44W

Pilotage: The bay is entered between Cabo Tres Puntas and Punta Gorda, about 13 1/2 miles to the northwest in Belize. It has general depths of 30 feet to 102 feet over its central portion, with gradual shoaling toward the eastern shore. The east side of the bay recedes about 13 miles south to the narrow entrance of Bahía de Santo Tomas de Castilla, which recedes an additional 2 1/2 miles south to its head. The land on the east side of the bay is generally flat, swampy and densely wooded. From the entrance to Bahía de Santo Tomas de Castilla the west side of the bay extends about 23 miles northwest, and then about 10 miles northeast to Punta Gorda. The land on the west side of the bay is higher, densely wooded, and backed by mountain ranges.

From Cabo Tres Puntas the east side of the bay extends about 1 1/2 miles south-southeast to **Punta Manabique**, and then about 5 3/4 miles southeast to **Firewood Point**.

Bahía La Graciosa (Hospital Bight) is a shallow bight that recedes about 4 miles to the southeast and is entered between Firewood Point and **Punta Manglar**. A sand bar, with a depth of 14 feet, extends across the entrance. From Punta Manglar, the coast which is low and swampy, extends about 7 1/2 miles south-southwest to the east entrance point of Bahía de Santo Tomas de Castilla.

OX TONGUE SHOAL
15 53N, 88 38W

OX TONGUE SHOAL LIGHT, 15 53.9N, 88 41.1W, Fl W 3s, 13ft., 12M, White and orange framework structure, Radar reflector.

Pilotage: This narrow shoal has depths of 18 feet, and less, over it. It extends about 7 1/2 miles west-northwest from Punta Manglar. A light stands on the west extremity of the shoal. It has been reported, in 1984, that due to reef buildup, this light should be kept at least 1 1/4 miles to the east when entering or leaving port.

HEREDIA SHOAL LIGHT, 15 50.8N, 88 40.4W, Fl R 6s, 20ft., White and orange framework structure, *Reported extinguished 1989.*

Heredia Shoal, with a least depth of 18 feet, lies about 3 miles south-southeast of the light on Ox Tongue Shoal. A light is on the west side of the shoal.

A shoal with depths of 28 feet lies about 3 1/4 miles southeast of Heredia Shoal, and another with depths of 23 feet lies a further 1 1/2 miles southeast.

BAJO VILLEDO
15 45N, 88 37W

BAJO VILLEDO LIGHT, 15 44.7N, 88 36.9W, Fl W 2s, 17ft., Aluminum framework tower, Radar reflector.

Pilotage: This reef has a least charted depth of about 15 feet. It is marked by a light, and lies west of the range lights leading to Puerto Barrios.

BAHÍA SANTO TOMAS DE CASTILLA

Pilotage: The bay is entered between Punta Manglar and **Punta Palma** about 1 1/2 miles west-northwest. Its densely wooded shores are bordered by a mud flat, leaving a navigable basin about 2 miles in extent within the 5 meter depth curve.

PUERTO BARRIOS
15 44N, 88 36W

PUERTO BARRIOS LIGHT, 15 43.8N, 88 35.8W, Fl W 8s, 25M.

HEAD OF PIER LIGHT, 15 44.5N, 88 36.6W, Oc W 4s, 5M, **3 F R mark jetty ruins (1982).**
Pilotage: This port, formerly the busiest in Guatemala, is located on the east side of Bahía de Santo Tomas de Castilla. A dredged channel leads south from a position 2 miles north-north-east of Bajo Villado. Lights at Santo Tomas de Castilla lead through this channel, bearing 109° 30'. A 1000 foot long pier extends west from the shore. Ruins, marked by lights, extend 1100 feet further to the west-northwest. There is a minimum depth of about 24 feet at the pier.
Winds: Land and sea breezes are the predominating winds at Puerto Barrios. The sea breeze blows from the north during the day, gradually diminishing toward evening. The land breeze blows from the south from about midnight to sunrise. This regular cycle is altered by northers during the winter months.
Currents: The current off the pier is reported to be diurnal in nature. During the morning the current sets northwest at a rate of 0.4 knots, and occasionally at 2.3 knots. The velocity increases after a strong norther has abated, and during periods of heavy rain. In the afternoon the current reverses and sets southeast at a rate of 0.2 to 0.6 knots. The mean rise and fall of the tide is less than 1 foot.
Port of Entry
Anchorage: Anchorage is prohibited north of the pier, due to incoming traffic — anchor south of the pier.
Services: Fuel, water, groceries and general supplies should be available.

PUERTO SANTO TOMAS DE CASTILLA
15 42N, 88 37W

MATIAS DE GALVEZ RANGE (Front),
15 41.6N, 88 37.2W, Q Y, 35ft., Metal framework tower, Red triangular-shaped daymark, Point up, Visible on rangeline only.
(Rear), South, About 347 meters 189° 30' from front, 15 41.4N, 88 37.3W, Oc Y 4s, 80ft., Metal framework tower, Red triangular-shaped daymark, Point up, Visible on rangeline only.

Pilotage: This is the main commercial port facility for Guatemala. It is located on the south shore of Bahía de Santo Tomas de Castilla. There is a single 3000 foot long wharf with a depth of about 33 feet alongside. Commercial vessels often moor stern-to this wharf. The wharf may be extended beyond this length.
Winds: Sea breezes predominate between 1100 and sunset, reaching force 4, or occasionally force 6, at about 1500. At other times it is calm, or there are light southerly breezes. This pattern is disturbed by the passage of a depression to the north, when squalls and southwest winds may be expected.
Currents: A weak current, seldom exceeding 1/2 knot, sets southwest across the turning basin.
Port of Entry: This is the primary commercial port of entry for Guatemala, but cruisers report that pleasure boats are discouraged from entering here. You can enter at nearby Puerto Barrios.

PUNTA HERRERIA
15 49N, 88 44W

Pilotage: This point is located about 7 miles northwest of Punta Palma, which is the western point at the entrance to Bahía de Santo Tomas de Castilla. The south shore of Bahía de Amatique is backed by high ground that reaches an elevation of 1118 feet about 3 miles south of Livingston Bay.

LIVINGSTON BAY

Pilotage: The bay is entered between Punta Herreria and a point 1 1/4 miles northwest. The Río Dulce enters the head of the bay. The 6 foot depth contour extends across the entrance to the bay, and about 1/2 mile farther seaward. Depths reach about 18 feet a further 1/2 mile offshore.

LIVINGSTON
15 50N, 88 45W
Pilotage: This is an important city for the transit of goods on the Río Dulce, and a port of entry. A marked 6 foot deep channel leads across the entrance bar, and to the custom house wharf in Livingston. A refinery with four conspicuous chimneys is situated 1 mile NW of Livingston.
Winds: The winds in this area are mostly northeast, with the strongest breezes being from May to September, with frequent heavy thunder squalls at night. The air is moist in all seasons, but May to October is the wettest.
Port of Entry

Chapter 2

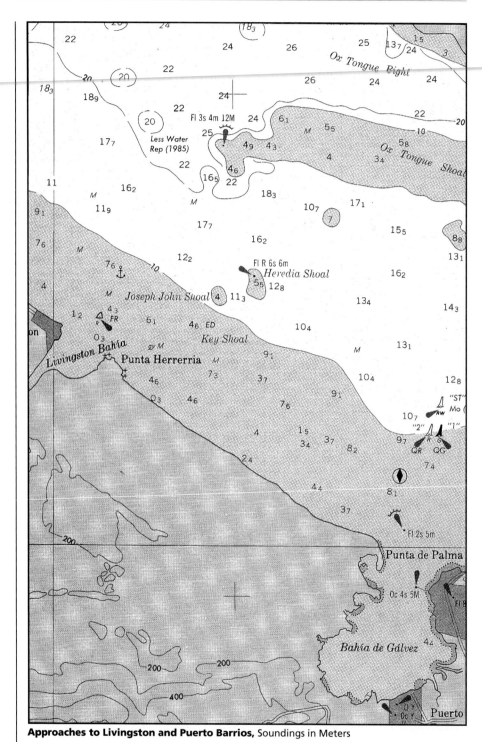

Approaches to Livingston and Puerto Barrios, Soundings in Meters

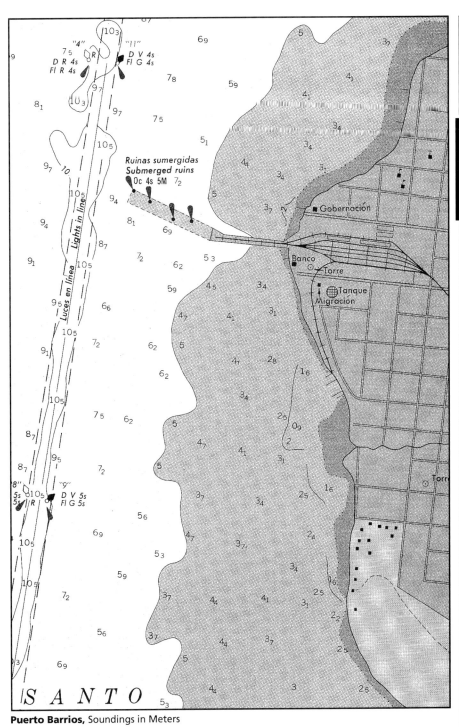

Puerto Barrios, Soundings in Meters

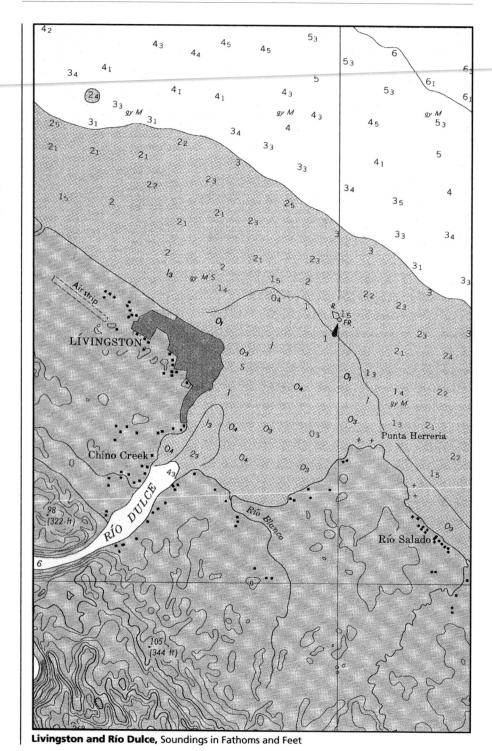

Livingston and Río Dulce, Soundings in Fathoms and Feet

Anchorage: Cruisers generally anchor near the Texaco fuel dock, which is located a bit southwest of the town dock.
Services: Fuel, water, groceries and general supplies are available.

RIO QUEHUECHE
15 51N, 88 46W

Pilotage: This river discharges into the sea about 1 1/4 miles northwest of Livingston. It may be identified by a waterfall located 1 mile northwest of it, and by the refinery with four conspicuous chimneys located about 1/4 mile to the southeast.

PUNTA COCOLI
15 53N, 88 49W

Pilotage: This prominent round bluff is located about 3 3/4 miles northwest of the entrance to Río Quehueche. Río Cocoli flows into the sea about 3/4 of a mile southwest of the bluff.

From Punta Cocoli the coast trends 2 1/2 miles west-southwest to Punta San Martin, and then about 3 miles north-northwest to the mouth of the Sarstoon River. The coast is low, but about 2 miles inland it is backed by heavily wooded mountains, which rise to a height of 1394 feet. These mountains are about 2 3/4 miles south-southwest of the mouth of the Sarstoon River. They extend about 6 miles to the west at the same height.

SARSTOON RIVER

Pilotage: This river forms the boundary between Guatemala and Belize. The river's banks are low, swampy and covered with mangroves. The entrance is about 1/2 mile wide, with a bar across the mouth. The bar has a depth of about 6 feet, and generally breaks heavily. Depths of less than 18 feet lie about 1 mile east-northeast of the river's mouth.

Chapter 2

BELIZE

CAUTION: Our information on aids to navigation comes from official government sources. The latitudes and longitudes of these marks may not correspond to the readings from GPS receivers. Some aids have been reported as unreliable, missing, off position or showing incorrect characteristics. No single aid to navigation, or waypoint, should be relied upon as a sole means of fixing your position.

ENTRY PROCEDURES

Belize was formerly a British Crown Colony, but gained independence in 1981. For an example of the country flag see *Reed's Nautical Companion.*

Ports of entry include Punta Gorda, Dangriga (formerly Stann Creek) and Belize City. In addition, there are reports you can have the officials flown out to San Pedro on Ambergris Cay. This would be an advantage if you are coming from the north into Belize, as it would save a trip to Belize City before you can begin exploring. The charges for this process are reported to be about $50 to $60 U.S. When coming from the south, vessels check in at Punta Gorda, or Dangriga, where the formalities are easier than in Belize City, which is geared for big commercial traffic.

You should have passports, your clearance from the last port of call, crew lists, stores lists and the ship's papers. Most nationalities will be granted a 30 day stay, but a permit is needed for longer visits. U.S. citizens do not need a visa for stays of less than 3 months. You may be requested to prove you have sufficient funds for your planned visit.

For the latest information on entry procedures contact the Belize Embassy, 2535 Massachusetts Avenue, Washington, DC 20008, (202) 332-9636. The Belize Government Tourism Office can be contacted at (800) 624-0686.

Tropical diseases may be encountered in Belize. Contact the Center for Disease Control at (404) 332-4559 for the latest travel advisory.

U.S. citizens may have need to contact the Consular Section of the United States Embassy in Belize City. Their phone number is (501 2) 77 16 1.

The telephone code for the country is 501, followed by a city code and the local number. The city code for Punta Gorda is 7, for Dangriga 5, for Placentia 6, for Belize City 2, for San Pedro 026, for Corozal 04, and for San Ignacio 92.

The currency is the Belize dollar, which is currently (mid-1993) trading at about .577 to one U.S. dollar. In other words, 1.7 Belize dollars equal 1 U.S. dollar. Exchange rates are subject to change.

SARSTOON RIVER

Pilotage: This river forms the boundary between Guatemala and Belize. The river's banks are low, swampy and covered with mangroves. The entrance is about 1/2 mile wide, with a bar across the mouth. The bar has a depth of about 6 feet, and generally breaks heavily. Depths of less than 18 feet lie about 1 mile east-northeast of the river's mouth.

From the mouth of the river the coast trends about 5 miles north-northwest to the mouth of the **Temash River.** The sea breaks heavily on the bar at the mouth of this river. Its banks are swampy and fringed with impenetrable mangroves for about 40 or 50 miles inland; then the banks become firm and covered with mahogany trees. The current in the river runs about 1 knot.

The coast then trends about 5 miles northeast to **Mother Point,** a prominent high bluff. About 9 miles north-northwest of the Sarstoon River, a small isolated hill rises to a height of 400 feet. There are red cliffs between the Temash River and Mother Point.

River Moho enters the sea about 1 1/2 miles north-northeast of Mother Point, and about 2 3/4 miles southwest of **Orange Point.** Like the Temash River, the bar breaks heavily here

and the banks of the river have similar vegetation. The current in the river runs about 1 knot.

ORANGE POINT

16 05N, 88 49W

Pilotage: This point is located about 12 miles north-northeast of the Sarstoon River and the Guatemala border. This is about 2 3/4 miles northeast of the River Moho, and just south of **Punta Gorda**. The point is readily identified, as the land is about 30 feet high, dropping abruptly to the coast. The coast and the land are flat and densely wooded for a considerable distance inland. Some of the trees reach a height of around 200 feet.

PUNTA GORDA

16 06N, 88 48W

PUNTA GORDA LIGHT, At Carib Settlement, 16 06.3N, 88 47.9W, F W, 56ft., 9M, White mast, Red lights on radio tower 0.6 mile southwest.

Pilotage: The town is located just north of Orange Point. **Gorda Hill** is a conspicuous saddle-shaped hill located about 2 3/4 miles north-northwest of Punta Gorda. A mountain range rises to an elevation of 1000 feet, about 6 miles west of Gorda Hill. This range forms part of a chain of mountains that parallels the coast, from 10 to 20 miles inland, to within 13 miles southwest of Belize City. A light is shown from Punta Gorda.

Port of Entry: Formalities are reported to be easier here than in Belize City. This is a good place to clear in if coming north from Guatemala or Honduras.

Anchorage: Anchor off the town dock, where you can dinghy in. The dock is reported to have less than 6 feet of water alongside. This is an open roadstead, and is subject to swells. Be prepared to get under way, if things get too rough.

Services: Groceries, communications and general supplies are available.

PORK AND DOUGHBOY POINT

16 11N, 88 44W

Pilotage: This point lies about 6 miles northeast of Punta Gorda on the mainland. The **Río Grande** flows into the sea about 2 1/4 miles south-southwest of the point.

Between Pork and Doughboy Point and **Punta Ycacos** (Icacos Point), 9 1/2 miles northeast, is

Port Honduras. This extensive bay is fouled with many dangers.

Deep River, or Río Hondo, flows into the north part of Port Honduras, about 4 1/2 miles northwest of Punta Ycacos. Depths over the bar are about 2 feet, and inside depths run about 12 to 18 feet.

PUNTA YCACOS

16 15N, 88 35W

Pilotage: This is the southern extremity of a small cay situated close south of a tongue of land, which extends 1 mile south. The cay is covered with pine trees.

Wilson Cay is located about 3/4 mile south of Punta Ycacos, and about 1 1/2 miles west of the point are the **Bedford Cays.** There are numerous other cays in Port Honduras.

SNAKE CAYS

16 12N, 88 32W

EAST SNAKE CAY LIGHT, 16 12.5N, 88 30.4W, Fl W 3s, 65ft., 13M, Concrete framework tower.

Pilotage: These cays lie just outside the 20 meter depth curve, about 30 miles northeast of Punta Gorda, and 4 miles southeast of Punta Ycacos. They cover an area about 8 miles long from southwest to northeast, and about 4 miles from southeast to northwest. There are four densely-wooded cays and numerous shoal patches with depths of 6 to 30 feet. **East Snake Cay** is the farthest northeast, and is marked by a light. Trees on the cay grow to heights of 89 feet.

PUNTA NEGRA

16 16N, 88 33W

Pilotage: This is a conspicuous bluff, which stands about 2 3/4 miles northeast of Punta Ycacos. Between Punta Negra and **Monkey River**, 6 1/2 miles to the north-northeast, the coast is more elevated and is bordered by a sandy beach.

MONKEY RIVER

MONKEY RIVER LIGHT, North side of entrance, 16 22.0N, 88 29.1W, F W, 52ft., 8M, White mast, *Reported extinguished 1985.*

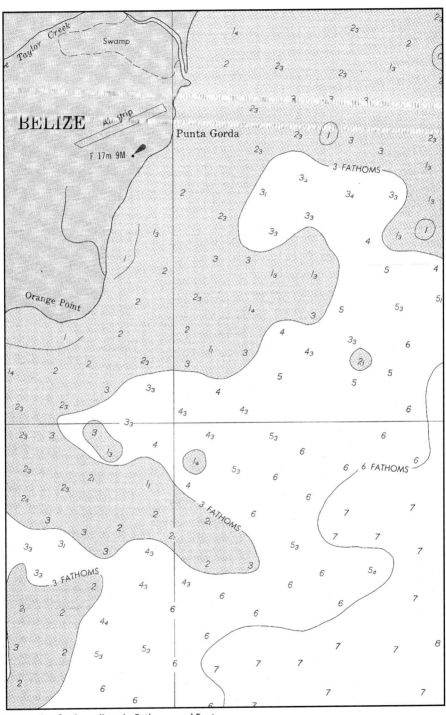

Punta Gorda, Soundings in Fathoms and Feet

Chapter 2

Pilotage: This area may be identified by some of the prominent houses in the town, centered principally on the south bank of the river. A light is also on the south bank of the river, at its entrance.

The 10 meter depth curve is well defined, and lies 1 mile east of the mouth of the river. Numerous dangers lie within the 10 meter curve, along this coast.

From Monkey River the coast extends in a north-northeast direction about 11 miles to **Placentia Point**, then continues north-northeast another 19 miles to **Sittee Point**. This coast is low, swampy and wooded. The shore is fringed by low, wooded cays and intersected by numerous small creeks and streams.

MONKEY SHOAL
16 23N, 88 25W

Pilotage: A light buoy is moored 1 mile east of Monkey Shoal, which has general depths over 13 feet.

Penguin Shoals has a least depth of about 1 0 feet, and lies about 3 miles north-northeast of Monkey Shoal.

Middle Shoal is about 1/2 mile north-northeast of Penguin Shoal, with a least depth of about 13 feet. A light buoy is moored 1 mile north-east of Middle Shoal.

Potts Shoal, with a least depth of 12 feet, lies about 1 1/2 miles north of Middle Shoal.

BUGLE CAYS
16 29N, 88 19W

BUGLE CAYS LIGHT, Southwest cay, East side of the Narrows, 16 29.4N, 88 19.2W, Fl (2) W 10s, 61ft., 10M, White framework tower.

Pilotage: These two cays lie about 3 miles southeast of **Placentia Point**, on the east side of the channel. Without local knowledge, these cays will not be distinguished from a distance of more than 4 miles.

Shoals with depths of 6 feet to 18 feet extend about 4 3/4 miles south of Bugle Cays. **The Narrows** lie between these dangers, **Potts Shoal** and the other dangers on the west side

of the passage. The Narrows are about 1 1/2 miles wide, with general depths of 33 to 85 feet.

HARVEST CAY
Pilotage: This cay is about 2 miles south of the entrance to **Placentia Lagoon,** and has a conspicuous 79 foot high, table hill on it. This is just south of the buoyed channel leading into **Big Creek.**

BIG CREEK
16 30N, 88 25W

Pilotage: This narrow river lies about 2 1/2 miles west of Placentia Point. It is approached by a buoyed channel, dredged to a depth of 22 feet, entered east of **Harvest Cay**. A small 34 foot long pier, with depths of 18 feet alongside, extends from the right bank of the creek. Vessels up to 230 feet long berth port side-to, heading downstream. Pilots from Belize City operate here, and you may be able to contact one on VHF channel 16. This is primarily a commercial port.

PLACENTIA POINT
16 31N, 88 22W

PLACENTIA LAGOON AVIATION LIGHT, 16 32.0N, 88 25.2W, F R, 315ft., 35M, Mast.

Pilotage: This is the southern point on the narrow ridge of low land that protects the east side of **Placentia Lagoon**. This shallow lagoon parallels the coast for about 10 miles to the north.

Placentia Cay stands close east of the point, and the bight thus formed is a good anchorage for small craft. There is a small settlement on Placentia Point with some groceries, a post office, a hotel and some restaurants.

FALSE CAY
16 36N, 88 20W

Pilotage: This cay is about 3/4 mile offshore and about 5 miles north-northeast of Placentia Point. The cay is low, narrow and covered with bushes and palms. Foul ground extends about 1/4 mile from it to the northeast through east, to its southwest side. The west and northwest sides are steep-to, with depths up to 34 feet between the cay and shore.

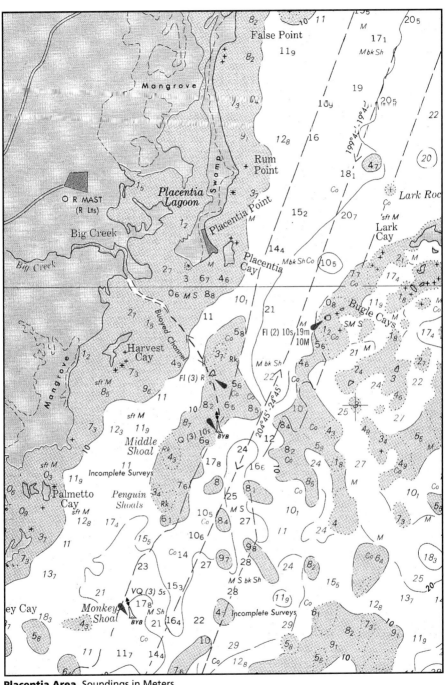

Placentia Area, Soundings in Meters

Anchorage: There is reported to be good anchorage between the cay and shore, in depths of about 34 feet.

From Placentia Point the coast runs about 8 3/4 miles north-northeast to **Jonathan Point**. A series of small bays are formed on this coast by **Rum Point, False Point and Rocky Point.** They lie 1 3/4 miles, 4 1/4 miles and 5 1/4 miles north of Placentia Point, respectively. A pier extends about 499 feet from shore at the village of **Riverdale,** about 2 3/4 miles north of Jonathan Point. A fixed white light is shown from the pier head.

From Jonathan Point the coast trends about 4 miles north to the mouth of **South Stann Creek,** then about 3 miles north to the entrance to **Sapodilla Lagoon.** The coast between Placentia Point and the mouth of South Stann Creek is backed by an extensive plain of ridges from 49 to 98 feet high. About 10 miles inland is a ridge of mountains rising to a height of 3680 feet about 18 miles west of Sapodilla Lagoon. Two peaks of 2034 feet and 1679 feet rise, respectively, about 11 1/4 miles northwest and 9 1/2 miles west-south-west of the entrance to Sapodilla Lagoon. A fixed white light is shown in Sapodilla Lagoon.

South Stann Creek flows into the sea across a shallow bar about 2 miles north-northeast of Riverdale.

SITTEE POINT

16 48N, 88 15W

SITTEE POINT LIGHT, 16 48.4N, 88 14.8W, Fl W 5s, 30ft., 8M, White metal framework tower, F W shown at all times in Sapodilla Lagoon 3 miles west-southwest and on pier head at Riverdale 7.8 miles south-southwest.

Pilotage: This is a well defined, wooded point that extends about 3/4 mile from the coast. It forms the south entrance point to the **Sittee River**.

The river has a depth of about 3 feet over the bar at its entrance. Dead tree stumps rise from the bottom. Depths of less than 18 feet extend about 1/2 mile east from the river.

Some ledges situated 3 3/4 miles southeast, and 4 miles northeast, have depths over them of 13 and 15 feet respectively. The ledges restrict the fairway of the **Inner Channel** to 3 miles in width.

False Sittee Point is a narrow projection of land located about 2 miles north-northwest of Sittee Point. Shoal ground extends about 3/4 mile east and northeast from the point.

Commerce Bight is entered north of False Sittee Point, and extends about 3 miles to the west. The depths within the bight decrease gradually from 36 feet in the entrance to 18 feet about 1/4 mile to 1/2 mile offshore. A conspicuous white building is close to the coast, about 2 miles north-northwest of False Sittee Point.

A pier, with depths of 5 feet alongside the west and south sides, lies 1/2 mile east of the mouth of **Yemeri Creek**. This is about 5 1/4 miles north-northeast of False Sittee Point. A road connects the pier with **Stann Creek** 2 1/4 miles to the northeast. A light stands on the pier.

STANN CREEK
16 58N, 88 13W

Pilotage: The town, known as Dangriga, is located on **North Stann Creek,** just north of **Commerce Bight**. The village is on both shores of the creek, and fronts the coast for about 1 mile. This is the seat of government for the district of Stann Creek. There is a 400 foot pier, with shallow depths alongside, located about 1/4 mile north-northwest of the mouth of the creek. There are many prominent buildings between the jetty and the creek. A private 600 foot jetty is located about 1/2 mile south of the creek.

In 1972 it was reported that a church with a white tower, and a conspicuous square tank on a metal framework tower, stood in the town. A conspicuous radio mast stands close west of the tank, and a second conspicuous radio mast was reported to stand about 3/4 mile west of town.

Port of Entry: Formalities are reported to be easier here than in Belize City.
Anchorage: Anchor off the town docks north of the river mouth.
Services: Groceries, fuel (by jug), a post office, telephones and general supplies are available.

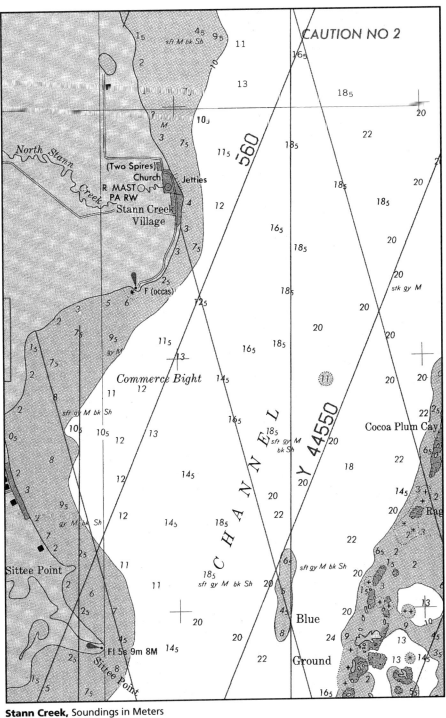

Stann Creek, Soundings in Meters

COLSON POINT

17 04N, 88 15W

COLSON POINT LIGHT, 17 04.4N, 88 14.2W, Fl W 10s, 39ft., 9M, White metal framework tower.

Pilotage: The point is located about 6 1/4 miles north-northwest of North Stann Creek. The 10 meter depth curve lies about 2 1/4 miles off the point. There is a light marking the point.

A rock, with a depth of 6 1/2 feet over it, lies 1/4 mile north-northwest of Colson Point light structure.

From Colson Point the coast trends about 1 1/4 miles west, then turns north-northwest. **Mullins River** flows into the sea 2 3/4 miles northwest of Colson Point. The town of Mullins River is located on the north shore of the river near the mouth. The bar at the mouth of this river shifts frequently, and is considered dangerous.

MANATEE RIVER

17 13N, 88 18W

MANATEE RIVER LIGHT, 17 13.8N, 88 18.2W, F W, 33ft., 2M.

Pilotage: This river discharges about 7 3/4 miles north of Mullins River. It leads to a shallow lagoon, and the shifting bar at the mouth is considered dangerous. A light is occasionally exhibited from a post on the south side of the river mouth.

Dolphin Head is a 400 foot high hill located about 5 miles northwest of the Manatee River light structure. **The Paps** is a 351 foot high hill, and **Saddle Hill** is 298 feet high — these two hummocks are situated about 2 and 5 1/4 miles north-northwest of Dolphin Head respectively. These hills are the terminus of the mountain range that backs the coast of Belize. The coast to the north, and the terrain well into the interior, is low and swampy in places.

There are several shoals with depths of around 20 feet located west of the Manatee River. The **Río Sibun** flows into the sea about 12 miles north-northeast of Manatee River.

TRIANGLES LIGHT, 17 21.5N, 88 12.3W, Fl G 5s, 16ft., 5M, Black concrete pile.

ROBINSON POINT LIGHT, West point of island, 17 22.0N, 88 11.7W, Q W, 38ft., 8M, White framework tower.
FRANK KNOLL LIGHT, 17 23.8N, 88 11.7W, Q W, 16ft., 5M, Concrete pile.
SUGAR BERTH B LIGHT, 17 23.5N, 88 10.6W, Fl R 2.5s, 16ft., 5M, Black concrete pile.
SUGAR BERTH A LIGHT, 17 25.5N, 88 08.9W, Fl G 2.5s, 16ft., 5M, Black concrete pile.
WESTWARD PATCH LIGHT, 17 25.5N, 88 11.3W, Q R, 16ft., 5M, Red concrete pile.
MIDDLE GROUND LIGHT, 17 28.0N, 88 10.5W, Fl R 2.5s, 16ft., 5M, Red concrete pile.

BELIZE CITY

17 30N, 88 11W

FORT GEORGE LIGHT, 17 29.6N, 88 10.7W, Fl R 5s, 52ft., 8M, White concrete pillar, Red band on base, F R lights on radio mast 670 meters west-northwest, F R and FL R lights on radio mast 1.3 miles northwest.
BELIZE CITY AVIATION LIGHT, 17 32.5N, 88 18.5W, Q W, 30M, Radio mast.

Pilotage: The city is located on the south branch of the **Belize River,** about 17 miles north-northeast of the Manatee River. The harbor is an open roadstead, with limited docking facilities for large vessels. It is approached from inside the reef via **Inner or Main Channel,** and from outside the reef via **Eastern Channel** (See the description later in this section).

The city is situated on both sides of **Haulover Creek,** which is the southern part of the Belize River.
Winds: Easterly and southeast winds prevail from the middle of February to the end of September, with the greatest period of calm occurring at the end of February. Northeast through northwest winds prevail during the rest of the year. The average wind velocity is about 10 knots. Northers are most likely to occur in November and December, but they rarely exceed force 4 or 5.
Currents: The current generally sets south through the harbor at a rate of 1 1/2 knots, but during the season of the northers this rate may increase to 3 knots. North currents, which attain a velocity of 1 1/2 to 2 knots may be experienced during the rainy season. The mean range of the tide is negligible; however, east winds raise the water level and north winds lower it. During northers the fall may be as much as 2 to 2 1/2 feet.

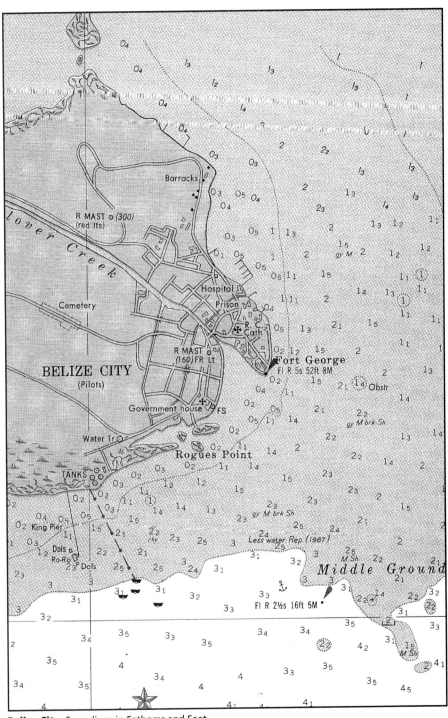

Belize City, Soundings in Fathoms and Feet

Port of Entry: This harbor is geared to the needs of commercial ships, and the formalities for yachts may be less convenient than at some other ports. Customs is near the pier at Ft. George Point.

Dockage: The 1500 foot wharf at Ft. George Point is reported to have depths of 1 to 6 feet alongside. Cruisers dinghy in here, but report there is a problem with petty theft. There is reported to be a shallow-draft marina near the Ramada Inn.

Anchorage: Cruisers usually anchor off the pier at Fort George Point. This area is open to the wind and swells.

Services: Fuel and water are available at the pier on Fort George Point. There are good grocery stores, general supplies, communication links, banks, a post office and a U.S. Embassy. There are hardware stores and there is a marine railway in Haulover Creek.

BELIZE CITY TO AMBERGRIS CAY

Pilotage: From **Saint George's Cay** the reef trends about 19 miles north to abreast the south end of **Ambergris Cay.** The reef's eastern edge is steep-to. The area west of the barrier reef is shoal, with general depths of 4 to 15 feet. The route between Belize City and Ambergris Cay, inside the reef, is shoal, and should only be attempted by those with less than 6 or 7 foot draft. Numerous cays are located in this shoal area.

ROCK POINT
17 40N, 88 15W

Pilotage: This point is about 12 miles north-northwest of Fort George in Belize City. Between Belize City and here lie **Peter's Bluff,** a low cay covered with trees about 2 1/2 miles north of Fort George, and **Riders Cay,** a small islet north of the former cay. There are depths of about 6 to 7 feet in the area east of the cays.

Hicks Cays lie east of Rock Point and about mid-way between the coast and the barrier reef. Depths in the area run 6 to 10 feet.

CAY CORKER (CAY CAULKER)
17 47N, 88 01W

Pilotage: This cay is about 5 miles south of the south end of Ambergris Cay. There is a small town and an anchorage in the bight on the southwest part of the island.

CANGREJO CAY
17 32N, 88 02W

Pilotage: This cay is located about 2 1/2 miles out on the reef extending southwest from the southern end of Ambergris Cay. The description of Ambergris Cay follows, under the heading **Barrier Reef.**

CHETUMAL BAY

BULKHEAD LIGHT, 17 56N, 88 08W, Fl W 1.5s, 30ft., 10M, Red metal framework tower.

Pilotage: This area is entered via an intricate channel located between **Cangrejo Cay** and **Northern River,** 10 miles away on the mainland to the west. It is about 22 miles from Belize to the Northern River, as the crow flies. The coast is low and covered with mangroves, which extend to the shore. The water is shoal.

The channel leading north into Chetumal Bay has a least charted depth of about 6 feet. This channel takes you to the mouth of the **Hondo River,** which forms part of the boundary with Mexico. Parts of the channel are marked with stake beacons, but its use is recommended only to those with local knowledge.

COROZAL
18 22N, 88 24W

COROZAL LIGHT, 18 22N, 88 27W, F R, 5M.

Pilotage: This small town stands near the west head of Chetumal Bay, and is fronted by a small pier with a depth of 4 feet alongside. Anchorage can be taken about 300 yards to the southeast of the pier.

HONDO RIVER (RÍO HONDO)
CONSEJO POINT LIGHT, 18 27N, 88 20W, F W, 50ft., 5M, Mast.

Pilotage: Consejo Point, about 8 miles northeast of Corozal, is the south entrance point to the Hondo River, which forms part of the border with Mexico. The Mexican settlement of **Payo Obispo** is located about 2 1/2

miles north of Consejo Point. The river is navigable by small craft drawing less than 4 feet for about 70 miles. A bar, with a depth of about 5 feet, fronts the river mouth.

THF RARRIER REEF

Pilotage: This reef fronts the coast of Belize, and lies from 10 to 22 miles east of the coast. It extends from the **Sapodilla Cays,** which lie about 31 miles east of Punta Gorda, north for 118 miles to **Ambergris Cay.** Abreast of Belize City the reef lies about 8 miles offshore. There are general depths of 6 to 18 feet on the reef, but numerous small cays, rocks and coral banks are interspersed along its entire length.

The seaward side is extremely steep-to with depths over 656 feet close off the outer edge. A heavy sea usually breaks along the entire seaward extremity.

In the area west of the reef between Sapodilla Cays and **Blue Ground Range**, about 44 miles to the north-northeast, foul ground with numerous cays and shoals extends west to the fairway of the **Inner or Main Channel.** In the vicinity of Blue Ground Range the west side of the reef becomes regular and fairly steep-to as it extends north to the dangers on the south side of Belize City.

NOTE: Navigation through the various intricate openings in the barrier reef should not be attempted without local knowledge, or the assistance of a pilot.

Many of the cays have been planted with coconut palms and some have houses on them. Hurricanes periodically devastate the area, or some part of it, and the descriptions of the cays which follow may be out of date. Though the vegetation usually recovers quickly, the shape of individual cays may be permanently altered and some may disappear completely.

SAPODILLA CAYS
16 07N, 88 16W

HUNTING CAY LIGHT, 16 06.6N, 88 15.8W, L Fl W 10s, 57ft., 13M, White metal framework tower.

Pilotage: This group of small cays is located about 20 miles southeast of Punta Ycacos. This group is the farthest south on the great barrier reef. They extend about 3 3/4 miles northeast from Sapodilla Cay to **Grassy Cay.** The reef extends about 32 miles north-northeast from here to **Gladden Spit.** Between Sapodilla Cays and Gladden Spit the barrier reef is generally broken and there are numerous cays, rocks and openings along its entire length.

Sapodilla Cay (16° 05'N, 88° 17'W) has a conspicuous clump of coconut trees on it. **Hunting and Nicolas Cays,** the middle cays of the group, are densely wooded with coconut trees. They are inhabited.

There are numerous dangerous heads and irregular depths in the area.

SEAL CAY
16 10N, 88 20W

Pilotage: This islet has a few trees on it. It is situated on the northeast part of a small circular reef enclosing a lagoon. The former Seal Cays, 2 1/2 miles south, are reported to have been destroyed by a hurricane in 1945, and in 1972 only a sand bore remained. Shoal patches are in the area.

LAWRENCE ROCK
16 10N, 88 20W

Pilotage: This rock lies about 3 1/4 miles west of Seal Cay, and has a least depth of under four feet. This rock is dangerous because the water over it is not sufficiently discolored to indicate its position. The ground is foul between the rock and Seal Cay.

RANGUANA CAY
16 20N, 88 10W

Pilotage: This cay lies about midway along the section of reef between Sapodilla Cay and Gladden Spit, and about 1 1/4 miles from the seaward side. Trees up to 50 feet high cover the cay. **Ranguana Entrance,** an opening through the reef about 1/4 mile wide, lies about 1 1/2 miles southeast of the cays. There are depths of 20 to 24 feet in this passage.

POMPION CAY
16 24N, 88 06W

Pilotage: This is actually a group of wooded islands that lie about 4 3/4 miles northeast of Ranguana Cay. They are reported to be inhabited.

Little Water Cay and **Hatchet Cay** are two wooded cays lying about 3 miles north and 4 1/4 miles north-northeast of Pompion Cay, respectively. The two cays have been reported to be good radar targets.

GLADDEN SPIT

16 31N, 87 59W

Pilotage: This is the easternmost projection of the barrier reef.

CAUTION: This spit has been reported to lie about 2 miles east of its charted position.

Gladden and **Queen Cay Entrances** lie about 1 1/2 and 4 1/2 miles southwest of Gladden Spit. They have least charted depths of about 8 feet, and 13 feet, respectively. These openings lead to the Inner or Main Channel through narrow intricate passages. They should not be attempted without local knowledge or the services of a pilot.

Victoria Channel is the navigable passage which lies between the dangers extending east from **Bugle Cays**, and those extending west from Gladden Spit. Victoria channel may be used as an alternate route to Inner or Main Channel. **Laughing Bird Cay** (16° 26'N, 88° 12'W), **Moho Cay** (16° 30'N, 88° 10'W), **Bakers Rendezvous** and **Crawl Cay** are all on the western side of Victoria Channel. **Quamino Cay** (16° 39'N, 88° 13'W) is located on the north side of the northwest end of the Victoria Channel.

For about 14 miles to **South Cut**, the barrier reef extends north-northwest in a solid coral barrier, with no cays. Then for about 6 miles farther north-northwest to **Water Cay,** it is broken with numerous drying sandbanks and some above-water rocky heads. There are several cuts along this part of the barrier reef, which are usable by small vessels with local knowledge. The west side of the reef is irregular and the area west to Inner or Main Channel is interspersed with numerous cays and shoals.

WATER CAY
16 49N, 88 05W

Pilotage: This is a fairly large, wooded cay, with trees about 59 feet high.

BLUE GROUND RANGE
16 48N, 88 09W

Pilotage: This group of cays is located on the west side of the reef opposite **South Water Cay,** and about 5 1/2 miles east of Sittee Point. They are about 2 1/2 miles in extent in a north/south direction.

TOBACCO CAY
16 54N, 88 09W

Pilotage: This small wooded cay has trees on it which reach a height of 69 feet. The cay lies on the north side of **Tobacco Cay Entrance,** 5 miles north of Water Cay.

Tobacco Cay Entrance is a 13 foot deep passage that leads west toward **Tobacco Range,** 1 mile west of the entrance. The passage leads to the Inner or Main Channel, where it joins about 2 1/2 miles north of **Cocoa Plum Cay** (16° 53'N, 88° 07'W).

Tobacco Reef, which is nearly dry in many places, lies between Water Cay and Tobacco Cay Entrance.

From Tobacco Cay to **Glory Cay**, about 12 1/2 miles to the north, the reef is almost continuous and practically dry. This section of the reef is known as **Columbus Reef**.

Cross Cay, with trees 59 feet high, and **Columbus Cay**, with trees 49 feet high, lie close west of the barrier reef. They lie 5 miles and 6 1/2 miles north-northeast of Tobacco Cay, respectively. Several cays lie west of Cross and Columbus Cays.

GLORY CAY
17 06N, 88 01W

Pilotage: This small, sandy cay is located 3/4 mile northwest of Columbus Reef. **Southern Long Cay** is a wooded cay located inside the barrier reef 1 mile southwest of Glory Cay.

From Glory Cay the barrier reef, which is broken in many places, trends north-northwest about 28 miles to **Saint George's Cay,** which is north of Eastern Channel. The cays west of the barrier reef, and those northwest to north-northwest of Glory Cay, are wooded.

SKIFF SAND
17 13N, 88 03W

Pilotage: Skiff Sand is about 1 meter high. It is located 7 1/4 miles north-northwest of Glory Cay

Rendezvous Cay stands about 1 1/2 miles north of Skiff Sand in the middle of a break in the barrier reef. It is covered with bushes and coconut trees 45 feet high. A clump of palm trees, 46 feet high, also stands on the cay.

Bluefield Range, a group of mangrove covered cays, stand near the west side of the barrier reef west-northwest of Skiff Sand.

The barrier reef between Rendezvous Cay and **English Cay**, about 5 miles to the north, is broken and marked by numerous banks, cays and coral reefs. Immediately north of English Cay is Eastern Channel. **Goffs Cay** is located about 1 1/4 miles north of English Cay, and north of the entrance to Eastern Channel. This cay is small and sandy, and a drying coral head lies about 1/2 mile southeast of it.

EASTERN CHANNEL

17 20N, 88 02W (ENGLISH CAY)

EASTERN CHANNEL RANGE (Front),
17 19.7N, 88 02.6W, Q W, 23ft., 9M, Concrete pillar. **(Rear),** On English Cay, 300 meters 300° from front, Fl W 2.5s, 62ft., 11M, White tower.
GOFFS CAY SANDBORE LIGHT, 17 20.4N, 88 02.0W, Fl R 5s, 16ft., 3M, Red concrete pile.
WATER CAY SPIT LIGHT, 17 21.4N, 88 04.4W, Q R, 16ft., 5M, Red concrete pile.
NORTHEAST SPIT LIGHT, 17 23.0N, 88 05.3W, Q G, 16ft., Black concrete pile.
WHITE GROUNDS SPIT LIGHT, 17 22.8N, 88 06.8W, Fl W 2.5s, 16ft., 5M, Red concrete pile.
SPANISH CAY SPIT LIGHT, 17 22.7N, 88 08.2W, Q G, 16ft., 5M, Black concrete pile.
HALFWAY LIGHT, Marks One Man Cay Channel, 17 22.2N, 88 09.5W, Q R, 16ft., 5M, Red concrete pile.
SOUTHWEST SIDE LIGHT, Marks One Man Cay Channel, 17 22.0N, 88 09.7W, Q G, 16ft., 5M, Black concrete pile.

Pilotage: When approaching Eastern Channel from the north, steer for a position about 7 1/2 miles west of **Mauger Cay** (17° 36'N, 87° 46'W),

which is the northernmost of the Turneffe Islands. Steer a south-southwest course to pass near mid-channel between **Turneffe Islands** and the barrier reef, until the lights on **English Cay** are in line on a bearing of 300°.

When approaching Eastern Channel from the south, steer for a position 2 3/4 miles south of **Cay Bokel** (17° 10'N, 87° 54'W), at the southern end of the Turneffe Islands. Then steer a mid-channel course between the Turneffe Islands Reef and Rendezvous Cay until the lights on English Cay are in line on a bearing of 300°.

To enter Eastern Channel steer for the lights on English Cay bearing 300°, until the east side of **Water Cay** (17° 23'N, 88° 04'W) bears 340°. Alter course to 340° and maintain it until Eastern Channel opens to the west-northwest. Then proceed through the sinuous passage, maintaining a mid-channel course until **One Man Cay Channel** is reached.

The east entrance to One Man Cay Channel is about 400 yards wide between the reefs, each of which is marked by a light. Steer a northwest course through the channel until **Robinson Point** (17° 22'N, 88° 12'W), marked by a light, bears 233°. Then steer as required to the anchorage off Belize City.

PAUNCH CAY
17 24N, 88 02W

Pilotage: This barren cay lies close to the edge of the reef about 3 miles north of Goffs Cay.

From Paunch Cay the steep-to reef extends about 9 1/2 miles north to **Saint George's Cay.** This low sandy cay is easily identified by the houses and coconut palms on it. From Saint George's Cay the reef trends about 19 miles north to abreast the south end of Ambergris Cay.

Drowned Cays are located about 1 to 2 miles west of the barrier reef.

AMBERGRIS CAY
18 02N, 87 55W

Pilotage: This cay's northern end is separated from Mexico, and the mainland, by **Boca Bacalar Chico**, a narrow boat channel with

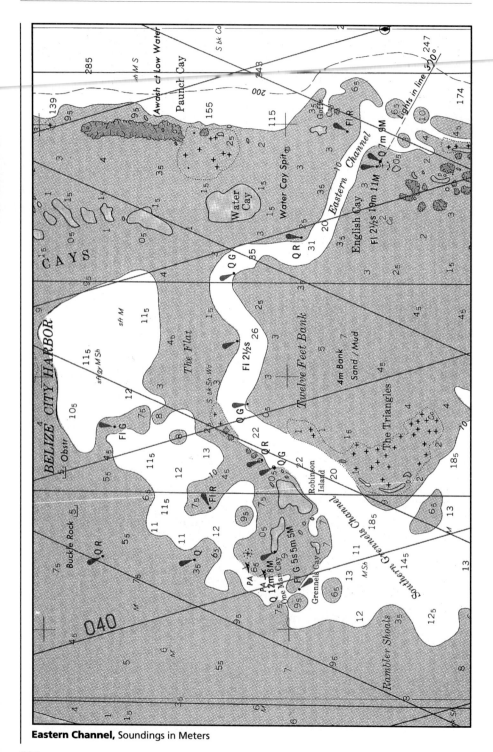

Eastern Channel, Soundings in Meters

very shallow depths. The island appears to be part of the coast from offshore. The east extremity of the island, known as **Reef Point**, is about 1/2 to 1 1/2 miles inside the reefline. The reefs gradually approach the coast of the mainland about 9 miles north of Reef Point.

CAUTION: The current generally sets strongly west toward the barrier reef, accompanied by a heavy swell, so that every possible caution should be observed here.

San Pedro: This settlement is on the east side of Ambergris Cay, toward the south end. This is inside the barrier reef, and the only approaches from the sea are via reef channels. This is reported to be a dangerous entrance with a sea running, and should not be attempted without local knowledge. A shallow channel leads south from here, inside the reefs to Belize City. It is reported that you can fly government officials to here from Belize City, to complete your entrance clearance.

OFFSHORE REEFS

Pilotage: The dangers offshore consist of Glover Reef, Lighthouse Reef and the Turneffe Islands. They are all located east of the barrier reef described previously. There are deep passages between all three reefs and the barrier reef. **Currents:** In the vicinity of the reefs, currents in November, December and January depend on the winds. A north setting current is experienced during west winds and a south setting current with north winds. During February and March the currents usually sets north at a rate of about 1 1/2 knots. In April and May they usually set south at a rate of 1 1/2 knots. In June, July and August the current usually sets north at a rate of 1 1/2 knots. In September and October the north-setting current increases to 2 knots.

GLOVER REEF

16 50N, 87 47W

SOUTHWEST CAYS LIGHT, 16 42.9N, 87 50.6W, Fl (2) W 5s, 9M, White metal framework tower.
NORTHEAST SIDE OF REEF LIGHT, 16 54.6N, 87 42.0W, Fl W 5s, 9M, White metal framework tower.

Pilotage: The south extremity of this reef is located about 13 miles north-northeast of

Gladden Spit, on the barrier reef. It is about 14 miles long and 6 miles wide. There is a barrier reef around the perimeter, which is impassable except for a small opening at its southern extremity, west of **Southwest Cays**, and one north of **Long Cay** on the southeastern side. The latter entrance is dangerous due to its location on the windward side of the reef.

CAUTION: Glover Reef must be approached with great care, especially from the north, as the reef is low and not always visible from a distance. The reef is steep-to, and soundings give little warning. A strong west-going current has been experienced on several occasions between Glover Reef and Lighthouse Reef.

The north point of the reef is known as **Amounme Point**. A light is exhibited on the northeast edge of the reef, 4 miles southeast of Amounme Point.

Southwest Cays (16° 43'N, 87° 51'W) are the farthest south of the five cays situated on the south extremity of Glover Reef. The opening in the reef west of Southwest Cays will accommodate vessels up to 12 foot draft, with local knowledge.

LIGHTHOUSE REEF

17 16N, 87 32W

HALF MOON CAY LIGHT, East end, 17 12.3N, 87 31.6W, Fl (4) W 15s, 80ft., 14M, White metal framework tower.
SANDBORE CAY LIGHT, North end of reef, 17 28.1N, 87 29.2W, Fl W 10s, 83ft., 17M, Red metal framework tower.

Pilotage: This reef is the danger farthest to the east of Belize's barrier reef. It lies about 13 1/2 miles north-northeast of the northeast extremity of Glover Reef. The reef is steep-to and unbroken except in the vicinity of **Half Moon Cay**, where there is a passage. There is reported to be a pass at the northwest tip of the reef.

CAUTION: Lighthouse Reef should be approached with great care as there is considerable doubt about the exact position of the edges of the reef. The western edge, and the southern part of the reef, are reported to lie up to 1 mile west of their charted positions.

Chapter 2

Half Moon Cay (17° 12'N, 87° 32'W) is marked by a light. It lies within the southeast part of the reef. Numerous coral heads surround the islet, but there is a shallow opening about 1/2 mile to the west. The islet has been reported to give a good radar return at distances up to 20 miles.

Sandbore Cay (17° 28'N, 87° 30'W) lies near the north extremity of the reef. It is a small, tree covered islet. Four small white buildings and a wooden jetty stand close to the lighthouse on the north side of the cay. **Northern Cay,** about 3/4 mile southwest of Sandbore Cay, is wooded.

TURNEFFE ISLANDS
17 22N, 87 51W

CAY BOKEL LIGHT, Southern extremity of Turneffe Islands, 17 09.8N, 87 54.4W, Fl (3) W 15s, 33ft., 8M, White metal framework tower.
MAUGER CAY LIGHT, 17 36.5N, 87 46.2W, Fl (2) W 10s, 61ft., 13M, White metal framework tower.

Pilotage: This extensive group of mangrove covered islands and cays, on a coral and sand reef, lie about 12 miles west of Lighthouse Reef. The barrier reef surrounding these islands is about 30 miles long and up to 10 miles wide. These islands are so closely grouped that from

a distance they appear as one large flat island. It was reported in 1964 that radar returns from **Grand Point**, the south end of the islands, may be easily mistaken for **Cay Bokel.**

CAUTION: The east side of the Turneffe Islands is charted from old surveys and should be approached with caution.

The reef that fringes this group lies at an average distance of 1/2 mile off the east side, and 1 mile off the west side. The reef on the west side is awash in many places, but the seaward edge on all sides is steep-to. There are several shallow openings and numerous lagoons between the various islands, which are used by small craft with local knowledge.

Cay Bokel (17° 10'N, 87° 54'W) is a small patch of sand that lies at the south extremity of the reef extending south from Grand Point. There are several detached cays near the south extremity of the reef, but from a distance, they appear as part of the main group of islands. On one of these, **Big Cay Bokel**, there are several fishing lodges.

Several detached cays stand on the reef north of the main group of islands. **Mauger Cay** (17° 36'N, 87° 46'W) is the northernmost cay in the Turneffe group. The lighthouse on the cay is prominent, and is a good landmark if heading toward Eastern Channel from the north.

MEXICO

Hydrographic and cartographic information in this section has been supplied, in part, courtesy of the Secretaría de Marina, Dirección de Oceanografía Naval of Mexico.

CAUTION: Our information on aids to navigation comes from official government sources. The latitudes and longitudes of these marks may not correspond to the readings from GPS receivers. Some aids have been reported as unreliable, missing, off position or showing incorrect characteristics. No single aid to navigation, or waypoint, should be relied upon as a sole means of fixing your position.

NOTE: The lights of Mexico are characterized by the number of flashes — the periods being subject to fluctuation.

ENTRY PROCEDURES

The Yucatan coast of Mexico is becoming a more popular cruising destination, as it is located only about 340 miles southwest of Key West, Florida. Some cruisers slog out against the current from Florida, while others visit the Yucatan as part of a clockwise circuit of the Caribbean basin. The area west of the Yucatan Peninsula is still seldom visited by pleasure boaters. See *Reed's Nautical Companion* for an example of the country flag.

Ports of Entry include Xcalak, San Miguel on Cozumel, Puerto Morelos and Isla Mujeres on the Yucatan coast. On the north side of the Yucatan, and in the Gulf of Mexico, you should clear at Progreso, Campeche, Frontera, Coatzacoalcos, Veracruz and Tampico. When you check in you will be issued a coastwise clearance, or "zarpe", on which you should have listed all of the ports you are planning to visit while in Mexico. You should have the officials grant permission to visit intermediate ports, if possible. You will have to check in with the port officials in any port you stop at along the way.

Mexican paperwork is reported to be time consuming and exacting. You should have multiple copies of your crew list typed in *Spanish*, which you will probably have to give to the officials in each port. You should have a tourist card or visa for each crew member. If coming from Belize, these are available from the Mexican Consulate in Belize City. Generally a tourist card will be good for 30 to 90 days. Citizens of the U.S., the United Kingdom, Canada, and most West European countries do not need a visa for entry. Many nationalities can obtain tourist cards when they enter the country. You must turn in your tourist card when leaving the country.

You should have passports, ship's papers and a clearance from your last port of call outside the country. U.S. citizens can get by with just a driver's license, or other positive identification, but having a passport is always best. All firearms must be declared, and have proper permits. Your guns will be held for the duration of your stay, unless you have a Mexican hunting license for them, which should be applied for in advance of your arrival. For more information on hunting licenses write to Direccion General de Caza, Serdan 27, Mexico, D.F.

Fishing licenses must be purchased for each crew member and the boat, if you have any fishing gear onboard. Again, this is best applied for before arriving in the country. For more information on fishing write to General de Pesca, Av. Alvaro Obregón 269, Mexico 7, D.F.

To obtain information on the latest entry requirements contact the Mexican Embassy at 1911 Pennsylvania Avenue NW, Washington, DC 20006, (202) 728-1600. When in Mexico, U.S. citizens might want to contact the United States Embassy in Mexico City at (52 5) 211 0042.

Tropical diseases may be encountered in Mexico, and visitors should contact the Center for Disease Control at (404) 332-4559 for the latest travel advisory. Care should be taken to drink only sterile water, well cooked vegetables and well cooked shellfish.

The telephone code for Mexico is 52, followed by a city code, then the local number. The city code for Cancún is 988, for Veracruz 29, and for Mexico City 5.

Mexican currency is the peso, currently worth about 0.325 U.S. dollars (mid–1993). In other words, about 3 pesos equal 1 U.S. dollar. Exchange rates are subject to change.

The main language is Spanish, but many people speak some English in tourist areas.

BAHÍA DE CHETUMAL

CIUDAD CHETUMAL (Payo Obispo),
18 30.0N, 88 20.0W, Fl W 6s, 59ft., 17M, White cylindrical concrete tower, Visible 115°– 064°.
HEAD OF FISCAL MOLE, Q W, 23ft., Wooden post.
AVIATION LIGHT, 18 30.0N, 88 22.0W, Al Fl W G 10s, 57ft., Tower, Radiobeacon.

PAYO OBISPO (CIUDAD CHETUMAL)
18 30N, 88 17W

Pilotage: This settlement is in **Chetumal** on the north side of the **Río Hondo**, which forms the border with Belize. It is the site of a Mexican Naval Base, which maintains the radio station in the town. A T-Head pier, about 130 feet long and 80 feet across the face, with a depth of 6 feet alongside the face, and 3 feet alongside its west side, extends from the shore in front of town. Lighters and tugs are used to unload cargo from freighters anchored off the west side of Cay Corker, in Belize.

Chetumal Bay extends about 26 miles north-northeast from the Río Hondo. It narrows in its northern part where the **Río Kik** flows into it.

LA AGUADA, 18 14.0N, 87.55.0W, Fl (2) W 10s, 40ft., 11M, Concrete cylindrical tower.
XCALAK, 18 16.0N, 87 50.0W, Fl (3) W 12s, 43ft., 17M, Cylindrical concrete tower; Visible 214°– 360°. A Fl W light shows close by.

BOCA BACALAR CHICO
18 11N, 87 52W

Pilotage: This narrow boat passage separates the north end of **Ambergris Cay**, in Belize, from the Mexican mainland to the north. **Xcalak** is a small coastal port of entry located about 6 miles north of Boca Bacalar Chico. Vessels drawing less than 15 feet can enter and anchor inside the reef — local knowledge is recommended. The bottom is reported to be mud and rock, with patches of white sand, providing good holding.

From Xcalak the coast trends about 65 miles north-northeast to **Punta Herrero**. It is low,

flat and wooded, with the tops of the trees being about 60 to 80 feet high. Nearly all of this stretch of coast is fronted by a reef which lies from 1 to 1 1/2 miles offshore. There are several channels through the reef, but they should not be attempted without local knowledge.

CAYO LOBOS, center of cay, 18 23.0N, 87 23.0W, Fl (3) W 12s, 50ft., 11M, Square galvanized tower.
PUNTA GAVILAN, 18 25.0N, 87 45.0W, Fl W 6s, 36ft., 11M, White cylindrical concrete tower.
CAYO CENTRO, 18 36.0N, 87 20.0W, Fl (2) W 10s, 50ft., 11M, Square galvanized tower.
EL MAJAHUAL, 18 43.0N, 87 41.0W, Fl (4) W 16s, 33ft., 11M, Square galvanized tower.
BANCO CHINCHORRO, N of the two islets which form Cayo Norte, 18 46.0N, 87 19.0W, Fl W 6s, 52ft., 11M, Cylindrical concrete tower.

BANCO CHINCHORRO
18 35N, 87 27W

Pilotage: This dangerous steep-to shoal lies about 28 miles northeast of Ambergris Cay in Belize. It is about 14 to 16 miles offshore. The greater part of the shoal has depths ranging from 6 to 24 feet, but there are numerous rocky heads and sandbanks. The stranded wrecks which lie along the east side of the shoal have been reported to be conspicuous visually and on radar. It has been reported that Banco Chinchorro is a good radar target for southbound vessels.

Cayo Lobos is a small cay near the south extremity of the bank. There are several openings through the reef to the west and northwest of the cay — local knowledge is recommended.

Cayo Centro (18° 36'N, 87° 20'W) lies in the middle of the bank, about 1 1/2 miles from its east side. This low cay lies about 2 1/2 miles long. It is composed of sand with a covering of bushes and coconut trees. A 1 mile long salt water lagoon lies in the middle of the cay. A dangerous strong current sets into **Firefly Bight**, about 2 miles southeast of Cayo Centro.

Cayo Norte (18° 45'N, 87° 19'W) lies about 1 1/2 miles south of the northern extremity of the bank. It actually consists of two cays, cov-

ered with dense vegetation and trees about 40 to 50 feet high. A disused lighthouse and building stand close south of the current lighthouse.

CAUTION: in the vicinity of Banco Chinchorro there is usually a very strong current setting toward its east side.

The passage between the bank and the coast of the mainland to the west is clear of dangers and deep.

EL UVERO, 19 04.0N, 87 33.0W, Fl (3) W 12s, 33ft., 11M, Square aluminum tower.
PUNTA HERRERO, S side of entrance to Bahía del Espiritu Santo, 19 18.0N, 87 27.0W, Fl (2) W 10s, 75ft., 15M, White metal framework tower, Visible 090°– 022°.

PUNTA HERRERO

19 18N, 87 26W

Pilotage: This is the southern entrance point to **Bahía del Espiritu Santo**. It is fronted by foul ground extending about 1 mile offshore. The entrance to the bay to the north is also generally foul.

The coast extends about 53 miles north from here to **Salta Iman**. The southern part of this coast is indented by Bahía del Espiritu Santo, about 10 miles wide, and by **Bahía de La Ascension**, about 10 miles farther north.

The coast between Bahía de La Ascension and Salta Iman is quite regular, low and densely wooded. **Punta Yaan** is a group of conspicuous cliffs, which stand on an otherwise flat section of the coast.

The coast from Punta Yaan extends northeast for about 50 miles to **Puerto Morelos**. Moderately elevated land extends about 6 miles north from Punta Yaan, then becomes low and flat. **Isla Cozumel** lies about 17 miles south of Puerto Morelos, and 9 miles offshore. The coast about 5 miles southwest of Puerto Morelos is fringed by a steep-to reef which extends up to 1 1/4 miles offshore.

The coast from Puerto Morelos extends north-northeast about 14 miles, then gradually curves north-northwest for about 36 miles to **Cabo Catoche**. Numerous islands, cays and other dangers lie within 1 to 15 miles offshore in this area.

BAHÍA DEL ESPIRITU SANTO

19 22N, 87 28W

Pilotage: The bay is entered between Punta Herrero and **Punta Fupar**, about 11 miles to the north. It recedes about 16 miles to the southwest and is about 7 to 10 miles wide. The depths in the entrance and for a short distance within the bay range from 20 to 30 feet, but in 1943, it was reported the actual depths in this area were 45 to 48 feet. The general depths within the bay range from 8 to 15 feet, about 2 3/4 miles northwest of Punta Herrero.

From Punta Fupar the coast, which is bordered by a rocky ledge, trends about 7 3/4 miles north-northeast to **Punta Pájaros** (19° 34'N, 87° 25'W). A drying reef extends about 1/2 mile east from Punta Pájaros.

PUNTA OWEN, 19 20.0N, 87 27.0W, Fl (3) W 12s, 39ft., 11M, White cylindrical concrete tower.
PUNTA PÁJAROS, 19 34.0N, 87 25.0W, Fl W 6s, 36ft., 10M, Aluminum tower.
PUNTA NOHKU, 19 38.0N, 87 27.0W, Fl (2) W 10s, 39ft., 11M, White cylindrical concrete tower.
CAYO CULEBRAS, 19 42.0N, 87 28.0W, Fl (3) W 12s, 46ft., 11M, White cylindrical concrete tower.
PUNTA VIGIA CHICO, 19 48.0N, 87 30.0W, Fl (4) W 16s, 39ft., 11M, White cylindrical concrete tower.
PUNTA ALLEN, Bahía de la Ascension, 19 47.0N, 87 28.0W, Fl (4) W 16s, 72ft., 16M, White concrete tower, Visible 200°– 070°.

BAHÍA DE LA ASCENSION

19 41N, 87 30W

Pilotage: This bay is entered between **Punta Nohku** (19° 37'N, 87° 28'W), about 3 1/4 miles northwest of Punta Pájaros, and **Punta Allen**, about 8 miles north. The bay recedes about 16 miles southwest and is from 5 to 11 miles wide.

The opening through the reef stretching across the entrance is about 2 miles wide. Depths are reported to be 18 to 22 feet through this opening, and as far west as the seaward side of the bar blocking the entrance to the bay itself.

The opening north of **Cayos Culebra** is about 3 3/4 miles wide, but the entrance to the bay is obstructed by a bar with a depth of under 8 feet. Cayos Culebra are a group of mangrove cays, which stand in the middle of the entrance just within the bar. Two yellow range beacons stand on these cays. There are depths of 10 to 18 feet within the bar, but the inner reaches of the bay have not been examined.

The opening south of Cayos Culebra, between them and Punta Nohku, is shallow and should not be attempted.

The coast between Punta Allen and Punta Yaan, about 23 miles to the north, is low, flat and densely wooded.

TULUM, Salta Iman, 20 13.0N, 87 25.0W, Fl W 6s, 79ft., 15M, White square concrete tower.

PUNTA YAAN

20 11N, 87 27W

Pilotage: Punta Yaan is conspicuous, with the only cliffs along this coast. They are about 79 feet high and front the coast for about 3 miles. The ruins of a large, square watchtower stand at their north end.

Tulum is a small settlement fronted by a white beach located about 4 miles north-northeast of Punta Yaan. A small pier extends from the shore abreast of the settlement. A conspicuous, small stone temple on a truncated pyramid stands about 1/2 mile inland. It is overgrown with vegetation. There is a lighthouse at Tulum, and some cruisers report anchoring inside the reef here.

The coast between Tulum and **Puerto Morelos** extends about 45 miles northeast, and again becomes low and flat. The trees along this part of the coast are about 50 feet high.

The only known off-lying dangers are **Isla de Cozumel** and **Cozumel Bank**, which together front the coast for almost 30 miles, and lie from 9 to 13 miles offshore. The passage between the island and the mainland is deep and clear of any known dangers.

Puerto Aventura is a marina located on the mainland about 11 1/2 miles southwest of **Playa del Carmen** (20° 37'N, 87° 04'W). Cruisers report anchoring off the latter town, inside the barrier reef. Ferries run from here to San Miguel, on Isla de Cozumel, so there are good navigational aids in the approach to the pier.

ISLA DE COZUMEL

20 26N, 86 53W

Pilotage: The south extremity of the island lies about 25 miles east-northeast of Punta Yaan on the mainland. The island is generally low and densely wooded, and extends for 24 miles along the coast. The average width is about 9 miles. The passage between the island and the mainland to the west is deep and clear of dangers.

Punta Celerain (South Point) is low but well defined. It is fringed by a steep-to reef, which extends about 1/2 mile offshore.

The east side of the island is composed of sandy beaches separated by rocky points. The coast extends about 24 miles northeast to **Punta Molas**.

The west side of the island extends about 8 miles north-northwest, and then about 13 miles north-northeast to its northwest extremity. The shore is bordered by a narrow coral beach, with vegetation extending down almost to the water's edge.

Caleta Bay is a small body of water, lying about 8 miles south-southwest of the northwest extremity of the island. The entrance channel is narrow and shoal. A wharf, some buildings and some fuel tanks stand on the shores of the bay, and a conspicuous hotel lies close southwest of it. It may be possible to anchor inside the small bay, but check locally for the latest information on the rocks and depths inside. The controlling depth is reported to be less than 6 feet.

The town of **San Miguel** lies about 3 miles north-northeast of Caleta Bay.

Punta Norte is the northwest extremity of Isla de Cozumel lies about 3 1/4 miles northeast of the entrance to Banco Playa Yacht Harbor. The shore between is lined with numerous hotels, one of which, a white building, is conspicuous and can be seen from a considerable distance seaward. A conspicuous clump of trees stands about 2 1/2 miles east of the northwest extremity of the island. A reef extends up to

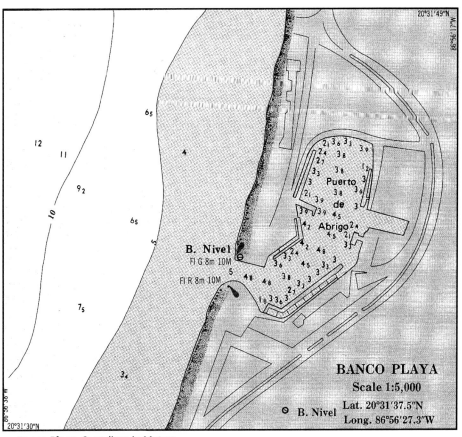

Banco Playa, Soundings in Meters

Within the image:
- 20°31′49″N
- 86°56′17.7″W
- Chapter 2
- 6₅
- 12
- 11
- 4
- 9₂
- 10
- 6₅
- 5
- B. Nivel
- Fl G 8m 10M
- Fl R 8m 10M
- 5
- 7₅
- 3₄
- 2₁ 3₆ 3₃
- 2₄ 3₈ 3₉
- 2₇
- 3₃ 3₈
- 3 Puerto 3 1₂
- 2₁ 3₈ 3₆
- 3₉ 3 de
- 3₉ 3₉ 3
- 4₂ Abrigo 2₄
- 4₅
- 3₃ 2₄ 4₂ 4₈ 2₁ 3₃
- 3₆ 4₅ 3₃ 3
- 5 4₈ 4₈ 3₈ 3 3
- 2₇ 3
- 1₆ 3 3₆ 3
- BANCO PLAYA
- Scale 1:5,000
- B. Nivel Lat. 20°31′37.5″N
- Long. 86°56′27.3″W
- 86°56′30″W
- 20°31′30″N

1 3/4 miles offshore. Some coral heads lie within the 10 meter depth curve, which lies up to 2 3/4 miles offshore.

La Laguna is an almost landlocked body of water lying across the northern part of the island.

The north side of the island extends about 10 miles east-northeast from its northwest extremity to **Punta Molas** (20° 35′N, 86° 44′W), the northeastern extremity of the island. It may be identified by a tall isolated tree and some huts. The point is marked by a light.

Cozumel Bank extends north from the north side of the island and lies up to 6 miles north of Punta Molas. The bank has been reported to extend up to 14 miles north-northeast and 4 miles east from Punta Molas. General depths on the bank range from 30 to 132 feet. Ripples, which at times have the appearance of breakers, mark the east edge of this bank.

PUNTA CELARAIN, S point of island, 20 16.3N, 86 59.3W, Fl W 5s, 87ft., 20M, White masonry tower, white house, Visible 240°– 155°.
BANCO PLAYA, entrance N side, 20 32.0N, 86 58.0W, Fl G 5s, 30ft., 6M, Metal tower. S side, Fl R 5s, 28ft., 6M, Metal tower.
GOVERNMENT WHARF, 20 30.7N, 86 57.1W, Iso R 2s, 20ft., 6M.
SAN MIGUEL DE COZUMEL, 20 30.2N, 86 57.0W, Fl (2) W 5s, 56ft., 15M, White concrete tower, Visible 031°-182°.
AVIATION LIGHT, 20 30.6N, 86 56.6W, Al Fl W G 10s, 82ft., 14M, Skeleton tower, Aero Radiobeacon.

SAN MIGUEL DE COZUMEL
20 30N, 86 58W

Pilotage: The town lies about 3 miles north-northeast of Caleta Bay. It is the principal settlement on the island, and a popular tourist destination. The International Pier, known as Mulle del Transbordador, is located about 1 mile northeast of Caleta Bay. This is the primary cruise ship dock. A radiobeacon is located close southeast of the International Pier. A light is shown from the 43 foot high lighthouse located 2 miles northeast of the International Pier. There is a dolphin berth for small tankers near the lighthouse. An aeronautical lightbeacon is shown from a 72 foot high tower standing about 1 1/2 miles east of the lighthouse.

An aeronautical radiobeacon is near the aeronautical lightbeacon. A pier extends northwest from the shore adjacent to town about 1 mile northeast of the lighthouse. It is 180 feet long, with a depth of about 11 feet at its head. Ferries run from here to Playa del Carmen and Puerto Morelos.
Landmarks: A conspicuous hotel stands close east of the International Pier. A conspicuous clock tower, painted white and dimly illuminated at night, stands near the root of the town pier at San Miguel. A blue-domed water tower and a framework radio tower, both conspicuous, stand close northeast and 1/2 mile southwest respectively, of the clock tower. A prominent airport control tower stands about 1 1/2 miles northeast of the town.
Port of Entry: Cruisers report that formalities can be difficult here. Some people report good success using the services of an agent, available to those docked in the marina. Charges are reported to be around $40.00 U.S. for this service. Other agents are available to those anchored out.
Dockage: The Club Nautico marina is entered about 1 mile northeast of the town dock in San Miguel. This basin is charted as the Banco Playa Yacht Harbor — see the detailed chart. The marina is reported to respond to "Puerto Abbrigo", when calling on the VHF radio. The docks are likely to be crowded with sportfishing boats.
Anchorage: Cruisers usually anchor north of the town dock. Be prepared to get out of here if the wind is shifting to the north or northwest.
Services: Fuel and water are available in the marina. There are boutiques, restaurants and tourist shops of all sorts ashore. Most types of groceries and general supplies are available.

PUNTA MOLAS, N point of island, 20 35.2N, 86 44.6W, Fl (3) W 8s, 72ft., 20M, Red masonry tower, house; 66. Visible 070°– 337°.
CALETA DE XEL-HA, 20 28.0N, 87 16.0W, Fl W 6s, 39ft., 11M, Aluminum tower.
CALETA DE CHACHALET, 20 34.0N, 87 09.0W, Fl (2) W 10s, 36ft., 11M, Square aluminum tower.
PLAYA DEL CARMEN, 20 37.2N, 87 04.5W, Fl (3) W 12s, 40ft., 11m, Silver metal framwork tower.
PUNTA MAROMA, 20 43.7N, 86 52.8W, Fl (2) W 10s, 36ft., 11M, Silver metal framework tower.
PUNTA BRAVA, 20 48.4N, 86 56.3W, Fl (4) W 16s, 35ft., 11M, Silver metal framework tower.

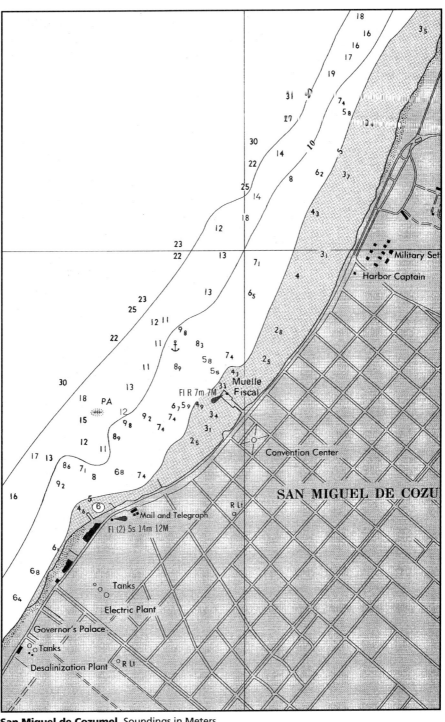

San Miguel de Cozumel, Soundings in Meters

PUERTO MORELOS, near wharf, 20 50.0N, 86 53.0W, Fl W 6s, 56ft., 18M, White concrete tower, visible 205°– 035°.

PUERTO MORELOS
20 51N, 86 54W

Pilotage: This is a small fishing and ferry port, with depths of 22 to 33 feet. Ferries run from here out to San Miguel de Cozumel. The village is on the mainland about 1 1/2 miles north of the reef entrance. The reefs lie about 1/4 mile offshore from the village, and up to 1 mile offshore abreast the south part of the harbor. Some of these reefs are 2 to 3 feet high in places. A small pier, with depths of 16 feet at its head, extends from the shore north of the village.

The coast should be approached from the east to a position about 1 3/4 miles south of the light, which stands north of the village. When this light bears 024° a vessel should steer for it on that bearing.

The coast between Puerto Morelos and **Cabo Catoche** extends about 14 miles northeast and then curves north-northwest for 36 miles. The terrain is generally low and wooded. Sand hills stand along some parts of the coast. The terrain in the north part of this area becomes more elevated with trees about 121 to 131 feet high.
Port of Entry
Anchorage: Anchor north of the town pier, where the ferries come in from Isla de Cozumel. The offlying reef provides adequate shelter.
Services: Water, fuel and some basic supplies of groceries and general stores are available.

DUQUE DE ALBA, 20 50.4N, 86 52.7W, Iso R 2s, 17ft., 11M, Metal framework tower.
PUNTA NIZUK, 21 02.1N, 86 46.7W, Fl (4) W 16s, 36ft., 11M, Silver metal framework tower.
CANCÚN, 21 08.3N, 86 44.5W, Fl (3) W 12s, 49ft., 11M, White cylindrical concrete tower.

ISLA CANCÚN
21 05N, 86 47W

Pilotage: This island lies about 14 miles north-northeast of Puerto Morelos. It is composed of 40 to 60 foot high sand hills. The north and south extremities of the island curve to the west and almost reach the mainland. There are two bridges connecting the island with the mainland. A 1970 report stated that the south end of the island appeared to be connected to the mainland when viewed by radar.

A conspicuous tower, marked by a fixed red obstruction light, and a structure in the shape of a truncated pyramid, stand near **Punta Cancún.** Another tower, marked by a fixed red obstruction light stands 2 3/4 miles south-southwest of the point.

Isla Cancún encloses a series of interconnected lagoons having shallow channels to the sea. A natural harbor for small craft is located south of **Punta Nizuk,** the south extremity of the island, and is protected by a reef. Local knowledge is required to enter this harbor. Club Med has a facility located on Punta Nizuk. The harbors on Isla Cancún are only suitable for shallow draft craft that can clear the low bridges to the mainland. This is a major international tourist destination.

ARROWSMITH BANK
21 05N, 86 25W

Pilotage: This bank lies about 16 miles east of Isla Cancún. The bank is about 20 miles long and from 1 1/2 to 5 miles wide. There are depths of 54 to 150 feet over it, with the shoalest part lying on the center of its west part.

CAUTION: The east edge of this bank lies about 2 miles farther east than charted.

A north-northeast setting current crosses Arrowsmith Bank, attaining a rate of from 2 to 3 knots. The south end of the bank is marked by strong rips.

In 1980 an area of heavily breaking seas was reported centered in position 20° 50'N, 86° 35'W. This is south of the bank, and there was a moderate southeast breeze at the time of the observation.

A shoal with a depth of 27 feet over it was reported to lie near the northeast extremity of Arrowsmith Bank.

EL MECO, 7.4 kilometers N of ruins, 21 13.0N, 86 49.0W, Fl W 6s, 26ft., 11M, Square white tower.

ROCA DE LA BANDERA (Becket Rock), 21 10.0N, 86 44.5W, Fl (2) W 10s, 13ft., 11M, Tower, black and white bands, Visible 306°– 077°.

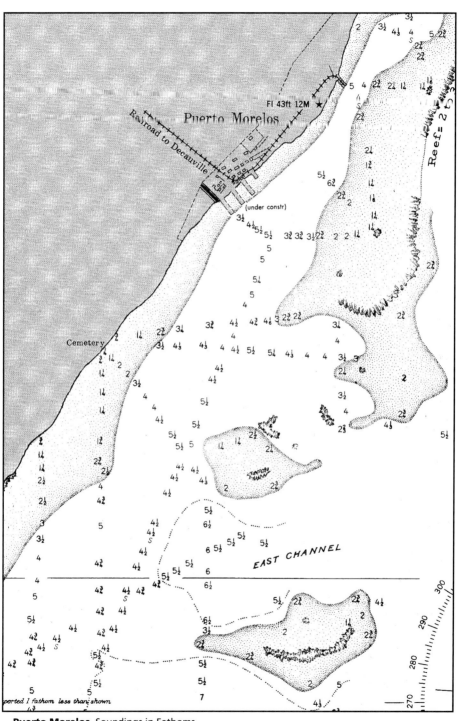

Puerto Morelos, Soundings in Fathoms

ROCA YUNKE, N point of island, 21 16.0N, 86 45.0W, Fl G 5s, 16ft., 6M, Red tower.
PIEDRA LA CARBONERA RANGE, (Front Light) 21 14.8N,k 86 45.4W, Fl R 3s, 20ft., 6M, Masonry tower. **(Rear Light),** 980 meters 000° from front, 21 15.3N, 86 45.4W, Fl (2) W 10s, 62ft., 20M, White masonry tower, red stripes.
ISLA MUJERES, S extremity, 21 12.0N, 86 43.0W, Fl (4) W 16s, 75ft., 14M, White masonry tower; 39, Visible 150°– 131°.

BAHÍA MUJERES

21 13N, 86 46W

Pilotage: This bay lies between **Isla Mujeres** and the mainland. It is entered between the northeast extremity of Isla Cancún and the south extremity of Isla Mujeres. A sandbank extends about 2 miles west from the south extremity of Isla Mujeres, then trends north about 2 miles toward the island. The 5 meter depth curve marks this sandbank. There are many coral heads on this bank, and some of them near the south end nearly dry. The southwest edge of the bank is marked by a light buoy.

A passage between this bank and the shoals to the west is about 1/4 mile wide and leads north past **Puerto Mujeres** where it joins **Canal las Pailas**. This passage rounds the north end of Isla Mujeres, and turns back towards the sea about 1/2 mile north of El Yunque.

The general depths in this bay are from 6 1/2 feet to 26 feet.

Puerto Juarez is located in the southwest part of Bahía Mujeres, on the mainland about 5 1/2 miles west-southwest of the lighthouse on the south end of Isla Mujeres. The town serves as a terminal for ferries servicing Isla Mujeres. An 800 foot long pier has depths of about 6 feet alongside.

Punta Sam is located 3 miles north of Puerto Juarez, and is also a ferry terminal.

ISLA MUJERES

21 14N, 86 45W

Pilotage: This island lies about 4 1/2 miles north-northeast of Isla Cancún. Its location is strategic for cruisers arriving from, or departing to, the United States via the Yucatan Channel. See the section on Cuba for more information on the Yucatan Channel.

The island is about 4 miles long, low, narrow and wooded. The south part is slightly elevated and has trees about 89 feet above sea level. The ruins of a square watch tower stand near the south part of the island. The east side of the island is composed of fairly steep-to rocky shelves. They terminate at the north end in **El Yunque** (Anvil Rock), which is square, black and about 6 feet high. Some white cliffs stand about midway along the east side of the island. A large, square, white hotel stands on the north extremity of the island, and has been reported to be a good radar target.

The channel leads along the western shore of the island into the harbor. There is a shoal area north of the light on **Roca La Carbonera.**
Port of Entry: Enter at **Puerto Mujeres** (21° 16′N, 86° 45′W), located at the north end of the island, on its west side.
Dockage: Marina Paraiso is located in the southern part of the harbor, with reported dockside depths of about 9 feet. They have showers and laundry.
Anchorage: Anchor south of the main commercial piers.
Services: The fuel dock is located just southeast of the light in the harbor. There is reported to be good supplies of groceries and general stores. You can take a ferry across to the tourist pleasures of Cancún.

ISLA BLANCA
21 22N, 86 49W

Pilotage: This is a narrow ridge of sand, about 7 feet high, which is a continuation of the ridge extending south into Bahía Mujeres. From the south end of the ridge of sand a reef fringes the coast extending past Isla Blanca to **Isla Contoy**, about 4 miles farther north. This reef begins about 3 miles north-northwest of the northern extremity of Isla Mujeres. There are one or two openings for boats in this reef.

ISLA CONTOY, near N point, 21 32.2N, 86 49.4W, Fl W 7s, 105ft., 21M, White masonry tower, white house, Visible 010°– 350°, RACON T (–).

ISLA CONTOY
21 30N, 86 49W

Pilotage: This island lies about 4 miles north-northeast of Isla Blanca and 6 1/2 miles offshore. Its east side is composed of a narrow ridge of

Chapter 2

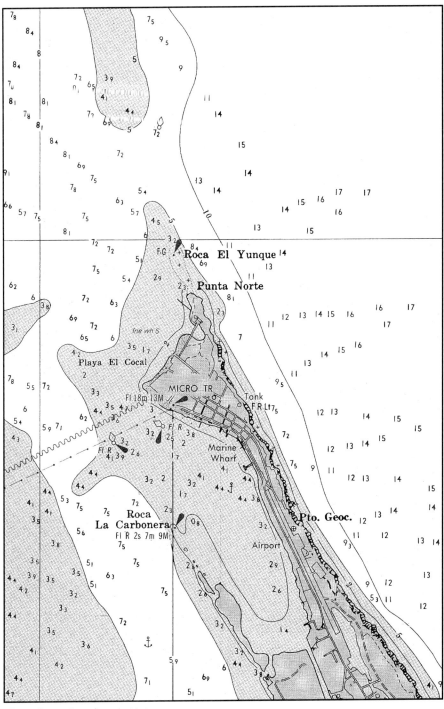

Isla Mujeres, Soundings in Meters

sandhills covered with bushes and trees to within 1 1/2 miles of its northwest extremity. A narrow ridge of coral with depths of 18 feet, extends about 3 miles north-northwest from two rocks close off the northwest extremity of the island. The greater part of the west side of the island is intersected by numerous small lagoons. This island is a bird and wildlife sanctuary. **Anchorage:** Cruisers take temporary anchorage off the west side of the island. You may be checked by the Mexican navy, or other government officials, if anchored here.

CABO CATOCHE, 21 36.0N, 87 04.0W, Fl (4) W 20s, 49ft., 25M, White concrete tower, masonry dwelling, Visible 080°– 285°.

CAYO SUCIO
21 25N, 86 53W

Pilotage: This cay is close to the coast, about 3 miles northwest of Isla Blanca. The coast trends about 8 miles to the northwest from here, and is more elevated with dense woods ashore. Some trees stand up to 131 feet above sea level. The conspicuous ruins of a church stand at the north end of this coast.

From the ruins of the church the coast extends about 6 miles west-northwest to abreast of **Cabo Catoche**, which is on the north side of **Isla Holbox**.

CABO CATOCHE
21 36N, 87 04W

Pilotage: This is a sand projection on the northern side of Isla Holbox. Depths of 18 to 30 feet extend 10 miles to the north and east.

The coast extends from here about 85 miles west to **Punta Yalkubul**, and then about 105 miles west-southwest to **Punta Boxcohuo**. This north coast of the Peninsula de Yucatan is low and arid, with few conspicuous landmarks. The coast is fringed with many detached shoals and coral patches. **Lagartos Lagoon** lies parallel to almost all of this section of coast.

A shallow coastal bank, as defined by the 5 meter depth curve, lies between 1 and 5 miles from this shore.

Tides and Currents: Between Cabo Catoche and Punta Boxcohuo the current sets west at a rate of 1/2 to 1 knot, following the trend of the coast about 30 miles offshore.

The mean rise at springs ranges from about 1.3 to 2.3 feet. The water on the off-lying banks is influenced by the winds as well as the tides. The wind may offset the normal tides for several days.

CHIQUILA, 21 26.0N, 87 15.0W, Fl W, 29ft., 9M, Red iron column, hut, Marks outer limit of anchorage.
CHIQUILA RANGE, (Front Light) 21 26.0N, 87 17.0W, Fl W 3s, 15ft., 11M, Aluminum tower. **(Rear Light)** Iso W 2s, 46ft., 11M, Aluminum tower.
ISLA HOLBOX, W end 21 32.8N, 87 18.0W, Fl W 6s, 26ft., 14M, White concrete tower.
HOLBOX RANGE, (Front Light) 21 33.0N, 87 18.0W, Fl W 3s, 44ft., 12M, Metal tower. **(Rear Light)** Iso W 2s, 61ft., 12M, Metal tower.
PUNTA FRANCISCA, (Mosquito), 21 33.0N, 87 18.5W, Fl (2) W 10s, 39ft., 14M, Red skeleton tower.

ISLA HOLBOX
21 33N, 87 14W

Pilotage: This is one of a chain of low, narrow islands which front the coast between Cabo Catoche and **Boca de Conil** to the west. **Punta Francisca** is the northwest extremity of the island.

A chain of cays, fronted by numerous sand ridges, with depths of 8 to 30 feet, extends 8 miles northeast from Cabo Catoche and 9 miles northwest from Punta Francisca. **Bajo Corsario**, with a least depth of 15 feet, lies 8 miles north of Punta Francisca.

CAMPECHE BANK

Pilotage: This bank extends about 155 miles north from the north coast of the Yucatan Peninsula, and about 120 miles west from the peninsula's west side. The limits of the bank can best be seen on the appropriate chart, such as NOAA 411.

This steep-to bank has very irregular depths and is marked on its east and north edges by heavy ripples and a confused sea. Some of the dangers on the banks are marked by discolored water. Many cays, shoals and reefs are found within its limits. Small vessels have reported encountering very heavy seas on parts of the bank during periods of stormy weather.

CAUTION: Banco de Campeche has not been surveyed for many years, and as reports of new shoals are constantly received, it is reasonable to assume that many more dangers exist than are shown on the charts. Many isolated shallow patches, with depths of as little as 18 feet, have been reported north of the Yucatan Peninsula.

BOCA DE CONIL
21 29N, 87 35W

Pilotage: This is the 3 mile-wide west entrance to **Laguna de Yalahua**, which is a shallow body of water lying between Isla Holbox and the mainland. Foul ground extends about 7 miles northwest from Boca de Conil.

The low, sandy coast between Boca de Conil and **Cuyo**, about 16 miles to the west, is marked by conspicuous groves of trees near its east end.

MONTE DE CUYO, summit, 21 31.0N, 87 43.0W, Fl (3) W 12s, 86ft., 14M, Red concrete tower, Visible 100°– 273°.
PIER, W side, 21 30.0N, 87 12.0W, Fl R 5s, 39ft., 7M, Metal tower.
PIER, E side, 21 30.0N, 87 12.0W, Fl G 5s, 39ft., 7M, Metal tower.
EL CUYO RANGE, (Front Light) 21 30.9N, 87 41.9W, Fl W 3s, 51ft., 11M, Metal tower. **(Rear Light)** Iso W 2s, 64ft., 11M, Metal tower.

CUYO
21 32N, 87 41W

Pilotage: This town has a wharf over 350 feet long, with a depth of almost 7 feet at its outer end. The town stands on the narrow strip of land between the sea and the lagoon which parallels this coast. **El Cuyo**, a 40 foot high hill, stands close to the town. A 12 foot shoal lies about 5 miles north of town.

COLORADAS, 21 36.0N, 87 59.0W, Fl (2) W 10s, 43ft., 11M, Metal tower.
RÍO LAGARTOS, 21 36.0N, 88 12.0W, Fl (3) W 12s, 59ft., 11M, Red metal tower.
BREAKWATER, W side, 21 40.0N, 88 12.0W, Fl R 3s, 33ft., 6M, Tubular tower.
BREAKWATER, E side, 21 40.0N, 88 12.0W, Fl G 3s, 33ft., 6M, Tubular tower.
PIER, W side, 21 36.0N, 88 12.0W, Fl R 5s, 40ft., 7M, Aluminum tower.

PIER, E side, 21 36.0N, 88 12.0W, Fl W 5s, 40ft., 7M, Aluminum tower.

LAS COLORADOS
21 37N, 88 01W

Pilotage: This open roadstead harbor has two small piers. The principal export is salt, which is barged out to the anchorage. From the north, depths in the approach range from 24 to 30 feet, and are quite regular. The two piers form good radar targets from a distance of about 17 miles.

The coast between Cuyo and the **Río Lagartos**, 30 miles to the west, is fronted by a low, sandy beach. The Río Lagartos is the outlet of the narrow lagoon that parallels this coast.

Bajo Antonieta is a shoal which uncovers to a height of 2 feet. It is located about 4 miles west-northwest of the Río Lagartos.

Between the Río Lagartos and **Punta Yalkubul**, about 22 miles to the west, the coast is more elevated. It is 170 feet higher, about 6 miles east of the point.

YALKUBUL, 21 32.0N, 88 37.0W, Fl (4) W 16s, 69ft., 14M, concrete tower, red and white bands, dwelling, visible 057°– 251°.
DZILAM DE BRAVO, 21 22.0N, 88 54.0W, Fl W 6s, 59ft., 14M, White concrete tower.
BREAKWATER, W side, 21 22.2N, 88 53.6W, Fl R 5s, 40ft., 7M, Aluminum tower.
BREAKWATER, E side, 21 22.2N, 88 53.3W, Fl G 5s, 40ft., 7M, Aluminum tower.
DZILAM DE BRAVO RANGE, (Front Light) 21 21.9N, 88 53.6W, Fl W 3s, 46ft., 11M, Aluminum tower. **(Rear Light)** Iso W 2s, 59ft., 11M, Metal tower.

PUNTA YALKUBUL
21 32N, 88 37W

Pilotage: This point is low and marked by trees. **Bajo Carmelita**, a shoal with depths of less than 15 feet, lies 11 miles northwest of the point. **Bajo Pawashick**, a shoal with a least depth of 9 feet lies 9 miles west of the point.

The coast between Punta Yalkubul and **Punta Arenas**, 13 miles to the southwest remains low. A shallow lagoon entrance lies close east of the latter point.

Dzilam (Silan) is a small town fronted by a pier located 6 miles west of Punta Arenas.

Between Punta Arenas and **Progreso**, about 48 miles to the west, the coast consists of low sandy beach, slightly wooded, and backed by swampy ground. Several villages lie along this section of coast.

Chicxulub is a small village fronted by a pier located about 2 miles east of Progreso.

TELCHAC, 21 20.0N, 89 14.0W, Fl (3) W 8s, 72ft., 14M, White tower.
BREAKWATER, W side, 21 20.0N, 89 16.0W, Fl R 5s, 40ft., 7M, Aluminum tower.
BREAKWATER, E side, 21 20.0N, 89 16.0W, Fl G 5s, 40ft., 7M, Metal tower.
TELCHAC RANGE, (Front Light) 21 20.0N, 89 16.0W, Fl W 3s, 46ft., 11M, Metal tower.
(Rear Light) Iso W 2s, 59ft., 11M, Metal tower.

PROGRESO

PROGRESO, near pier, 21 17.2N, 89 40.1W, Fl W 6s, 108ft., 16M, Gray concrete tower, Visible 066°– 250°.
HEAD OF PIER, W side, 21 17.0N, 89 40.0W, Iso R 2s, 33ft., 6M, Concrete tower.
HEAD OF PIER, E side, 21 17.0N, 89 40.0W, Iso G 2s, 33ft., 6M, Concrete tower.
PIER LIGHT, 21 18.9N, 89 40.04W, Fl (2) R 10s, 16ft., 7M, Iron tower.
HEAD OF PIER, W side, 21 20.7N, 89 40.5W, Fl (2) W 10s, 26ft., 9M, Metal tower.
HEAD OF PIER, E side, 21 20.7N, 89 40.8W, Fl (2) W 10s, 26ft., 9M, Metal tower.
TERMINAL REMOTA, NW corner, 21 20.7N, 89 40.9W, Iso R 2s, 79ft., 6M, On corner of warehouse.
NE CORNER, 21 20.7N, 89 40.6W, Iso R 2s, 79ft., 6M, On corner of warehouse.

PROGRESO
21 17N, 89 40W

Pilotage: This is the most important port on the Yucatan Peninsula. The harbor is an open roadstead, with a long pier fronting the town. Sisal is the principal export.

The major danger to small craft is a wreck lying 1 1/2 miles north of **New Pier**. When approaching the port, the lighthouse is usually the first object sighted. A square gray tower,

about 60 feet high, stands close west of the lighthouse. East of the town, and somewhat detached from it, is a large square building close to the coast and partly surrounded by trees. The town itself appears as a group of low gray or white buildings. The piers, together with the warehouses on them, are prominent from a distance of 4 miles.

Terminal Remota has two berths (for commercial vessels) protected by an artificial island. It is situated at the north end of a long causeway and pier, about 1/4 mile in length, with its root near Progreso Light. **Muelle Fiscal** also has two berths located on the same causeway about 5,970 feet from shore. **Pino Suárez Pier** is located close to the west of the other two piers. It is about 200 yards long with depths of 8 to 9 feet alongside.

Winds: The prevailing winds are from the northeast to southeast. Northers occur between October and March. Storm signals are displayed from a flagstaff near the lighthouse.
Currents: The current along this coast sets to the west.
Port of Entry

Puerto de Yucalpeten Approach Buoy No 1, 21 18.0N, 89 43.0W, Fl (2) W 10s, Black and red banded buoy.
PUERTO DE YUCALPETEN RANGE, (Front Light) 21 16.0N, 89 42.0W, Fl W 3s, 45ft., 5M, Red metal tower. **(Rear Light)** 169° from front, Iso W 2s, 58ft., 5M, Red metal tower.
HEAD OF JETTY, E side, 21 16.1N, 89 42.1W, Fl G 5s, 38ft., 7M, Red metal tower.
W side, 21 16.1N, 89 41.1W, Fl R 5s, 38ft., 7M, Red metal tower.

PUERTO DE YUKALPETÉN
21 17N, 89 43W

Pilotage: This new "Free Port" is located about 3 miles west of Progreso. The east breakwater extends approximately 600 feet from the shore, while the west breakwater is less prominent. The least depth between the breakwaters is just under 8 feet. Inside the harbor, alongside the two piers, there is a least depth of under 7 feet.

The coast between Puerto de Yukalpetén and **Sisal**, about 20 miles to the west-southwest, is marked by several villages and is more wooded than elsewhere in the vicinity. Sisal is now nearly abandoned.

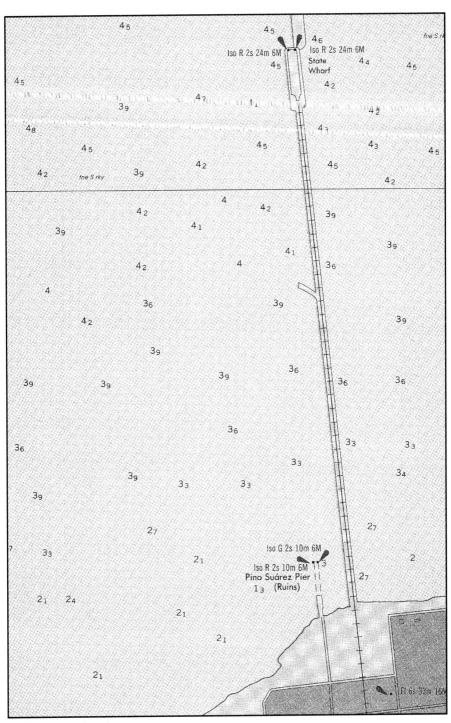

Progreso, Soundings in Meters

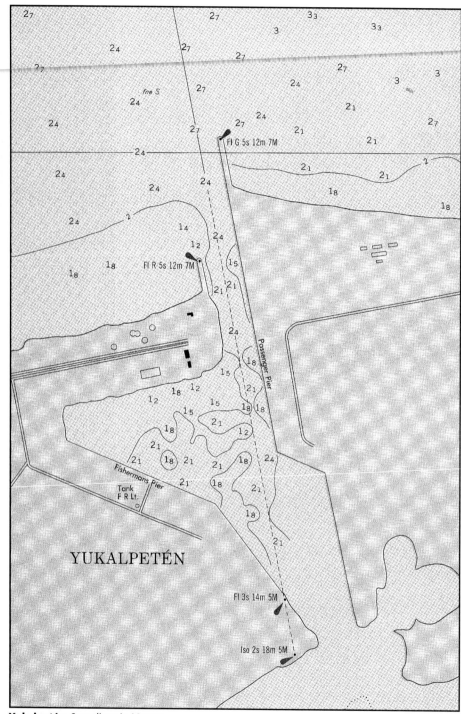

Yukalpetén, Soundings in Meters

ARRECIFE SISAL
21 21N, 90 09W

Pilotage: This is a coral reef with an obstruction on it located about 12 miles north-northwest of Sisal. It may be marked by discolored water under certain weather conditions. A 21 foot deep coral shoal lies about 6 1/2 miles west-northwest of Sisal

The coast between Sisal and **Punta Boxcohuo**, about 17 miles southwest, is low and sandy. A building in ruins, about 5 miles southwest of Sisal, is the only conspicuous landmark. The coast between Sisal and a position about 5 miles south of **Celestun**, is radar conspicuous.

SISAL, on old white fort, 21 10.0N, 90 01.09W, Fl (3) W 12s, 72ft., 12M, circular concrete tower, red and white bands, Visible 055°– 260°.
HEAD OF PIER, W side, 21 10.0N, 90 02.0W, Iso R 2s, 33ft., 9M, Fiberglass post.
HEAD OF PIER, E side, Iso G 2s, 33ft., 9M, Fiberglass post.
ISLA PEREZ, on S part of Alacrán Reef, 22 23.5N, 89 41.5W, Fl (2) W 8s, 69ft., 13M, Red concrete tower, RACON **Z** (– – · ·).
ISLA DESTERREDA, on N part of Alacrán Reef, 22 31.7N, 89 47.4W, Fl (4) W 16s, 46ft., 10M, Tubular metal tower.

ARRECIFE ALACRÁN
22 29N, 89 42W

Pilotage: This steep-to half-moon shaped reef lies about 34 miles northwest of **Granville Shoal**. This is about 68 miles north-northwest of Progreso, on the Campeche Bank. The main part of the reef consists of a compact mass of coral heads about 14 miles long and 8 miles wide. The entire northeast side of the reef is awash. **Isla Chica** and **Isla Pájaros**, two small low cays about 1/4 mile apart, stand near the south end of the reef. **Isla Desterrada** is a small 10 foot high cay located on the northwest end of Arrecife Alacrán.

Isla Perez is a narrow cay, about 14 feet high. It lies near the south end of the reef. The light structure on this cay has been reported to be a good radar target at distances up to 18 miles. The light is shown from a round red masonry tower with a parapet. A gray masonry tower stands adjacent to the light. The lighthouse and tower are fully visible when approaching

from the west. A stranded wreck close east of the light structure was reported to be a good radar target at distances up to 13 miles.
Anchorage: Small vessels anchor in depths of 36 to 60 feet over fine sand, mud and coral, about 1/4 mile east of Isla Perez. The anchorage is approached from the south through an unmarked channel with a depth of about 24 feet. This channel should not be attempted without local knowledge.

Isla Desertora (not to be confused with Isla Desterrada farther to the north-northwest) is a small 12 foot high cay located about 3 miles northwest of Isla Perez.

Currents: The current usually sets west at about 1 knot in the vicinity of these reefs, but may set north or south, depending upon the wind.

ARRECIFE MADAGASCAR
21 26N, 90 18W

Pilotage: This narrow coral ledge, with a least depth of under 9 feet, lies about 69 miles south-southwest of Arrecife Alacrán. The sea does not break on this ledge, which is covered with weed that appears the same color as the water.

Breakers were reported about 6 miles north-northeast of the ledge in 1909.

Arrecife de La Serpiente, with a least depth of 27 feet, lies about 11 1/2 miles west of Arrecife Madagascar.

PUNTA PALMAS, 21 02.0N, 90 18.0W, Fl (2) W 10s, 138ft., 12M, White concrete tower, on white house, Visible 048°– 236°.
CELESTUN, center of town, near shore, 20 51.0N, 90 24.0W, Fl (3) W 12s, 69ft., 10M, White round concrete tower, Visible 002°– 188°.
NORTH BREAKWATER, 20 51.0N, 90 53.0W, Fl G 5s, 33ft., 7M, White tubular tower.
SOUTH BREAKWATER, 20 51.0N, 90 53.0W, Fl R 5s, 33ft., 7M, White tubular tower.
CELESTUN RANGE, (Front Light) 20 51.0N, 90 23.0W, Fl W 3s, 46ft., 9M, Aluminum tower.
(Rear Light) Iso W 2s, 59ft., 9M, Aluminum tower.
ISLA ARENA, 20 36.0N, 90 28.0W, Fl W 6s, 46ft., 10M, White round concrete tower.
CAYO ARENAS, 22 08.0N, 91 24.0W, L Fl W 12s, 79ft., 12M, White concrete tower, RACON **X** (– · · –).

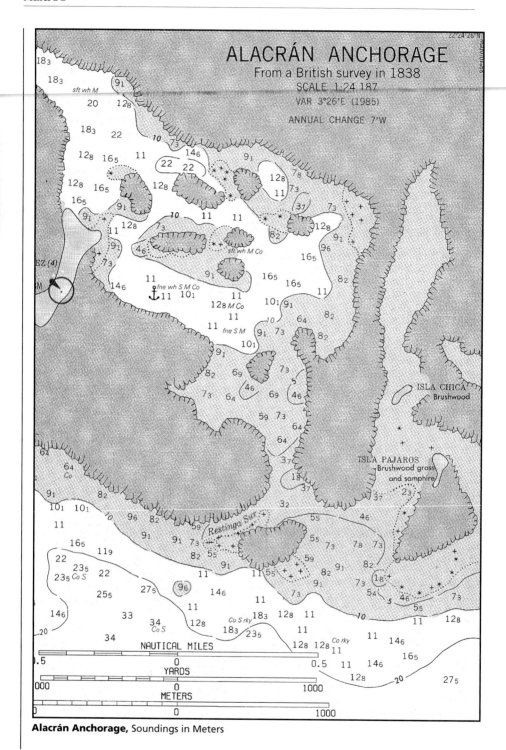

ALACRÁN ANCHORAGE

From a British survey in 1838

SCALE 1:24 187

VAR 3°26'E (1985)

ANNUAL CHANGE 7'W

Alacrán Anchorage, Soundings in Meters

NAUTICAL MILES

YARDS

METERS

ISLA CHICA
Brushwood

ISLA PAJAROS
Brushwood grass
and samphire

Restinga Sur

CAYO ARENAS
22 07N, 91 24W

Pilotage: This guano covered cay is about 20 feet high, and is located on the southeast edge of a detached reef 3/4 of a mile long. The cay lies about 93 miles west-southwest of Arrecife Alacran. The horns of the reef extend 1/2 mile northwest and 1/4 mile west from the cay. A small wharf stands on the northwest side of the cay.

A detached reef, 1 1/4 miles long with a rocky patch 7 feet high on its south end and a small coral patch 2 feet high off its northwest end, lies 1 mile east of Cayo Arenas. The intervening channel is about 1/2 mile wide at its north entrance. At its south end are three coral patches, with depths of 14 to 19 feet. These patches are about 3/4 mile southeast of Cayo Arenas.
Anchorage: Vessels can anchor in this channel in depths of 60 to 72 feet, about 1/2 mile east of the cay. Depths of 24 to 36 feet can be found between the horns of the reef 1/4 mile northwest of the cay.

BAJO NUEVO
21 50N, 92 05W

Pilotage: This reef has depths of less than 6 feet. It lies about 40 miles west-southwest of Cayo Arenas, and is marked by breakers.

BANCOS INGLESES
21 49N, 91 56W

Pilotage: These two banks lie with their shoalest part about 8 miles southeast of Bajo Nuevo. They have least depths of 30 to 113 feet.

ISLA TRIANGULOS OESTE, 20 59.0N, 92 18.0W, Fl (3) W 20s, 70ft., 12M, Red rectangular concrete tower.

ARRECIFES TRIÁNGULOS
20 57N, 92 14W

Pilotage: This group of two reefs lie about 82 miles southwest of Cayos Arenas. The two groups are about 6 miles apart.

Triángulo Oest is a 3/4 mile long reef with an eleven foot high cay on its southwest end. A disused lighthouse stands near the lighthouse on the cay near the southwest end.

CAUTION: A dangerous wreck lies about 22 miles northeast of the lighthouse on Triángulo Oest. An awash rock was reported to lie about 18 miles north-northeast of Triángulo Oest.

Triángulo Este (20° 55'N, 92° 13'W) and **Triángulo Sur** (20° 54'N, 92° 14'W), which nearly dry, are separated by a channel 1/4 mile wide with depths of 42 to 60 feet. A 24 foot high cay stands on the south end of Triángulo Este. A reef extends about 1 mile northeast from the cay and a coral ledge extends about 1 mile farther northeast. Triángulo Sur has a ledge extending about 1 mile southwest from the southwesternmost cay of several which stand on it.
Anchorage: Vessels can anchor off the southwestern end of Triángulo Sur.

OBISPO NORTE
AND OBISPO SUR
20 29N, 92 12W

Pilotage: These shoals lie about 25 miles south of Triángulo Oest. They have depths of 24 to 60 feet. They are marked by discolored water. Obispo Norte has a depth of 15 feet near its north end. A dangerous wreck lies between the two shoals.

BANCO PERA
20 42N, 91 56W

Pilotage: This shoal bank has depths of 54 feet, and is located about 28 miles southeast of Triángulo Oest. **Banco Nuevo** has a depth of 48 feet in a position about 38 miles southeast of Triángulo Oest.

CAYOS ARCAS RANGE, (Front Light) W side of Cay del Centro, 20 12.7N, 91 58.2W, Fl W 3s, 42ft., 10M, Metal Tower.
(Rear Light) 80 meters 107° from front, Fl (2) W 15s, 72ft., 13M, White round concrete tower and house, Radar reflector.

CAYOS ARCAS
20 13N, 91 58W

Pilotage: This is the southernmost group of dangers on the Banco de Campeche. It consists of a group of three islets, with surrounding reefs. They lie about 44 miles south-southeast of Triángulo Este.

Cayo del Centro is the northernmost and largest. It is composed of sand and rises, at its south end, to a height of 21 feet. It lies on the southeast end of a reef which extends about 1 mile northwest and about 1/2 mile west from it. This reef is always visible. The islet is scantily covered with grass, some bushes and several clumps of palm trees. A pair of lighted beacons in range 107° stand on the cay. A stranded wreck stands on the reef about 800 yards northwest of the north extremity of Cayo del Centro. **Anchorage:** Vessels use the range to work into the anchorage west-northwest of the cay.

Cayo del Este is a small 10 foot high cay on a detached reef about 1/4 mile southeast of Cayo del Centro. The intervening channel has depths of 36 to 84 feet. A stranded wreck stands on the edge of the reef about 300 yards northeast of the islet.

Cayo del Oeste is a small 6 foot high cay lying on a small detached reef about 3/4 mile west of the south end of Cayo del Centro. The narrow intervening passage has depths of 24 to 27 feet.

PLATFORM PR-1 REBOMBEO, 18 56.7N, 92 37.2W, Q W, 56ft., 10M, 4 lights, one installed on each corner of platform.
PLATFORM POOL-C, 19 13.4N, 92 15.8W, Q W, 56ft., 10M, 4 lights, one installed on each corner of platform.
PLATFORM CAAN-A, 19 13.3N, 92 05.4W, Q W, 56ft., 10M, 4 lights, one installed on each corner of platform.
PLATFORM ECO-1, 19 01.8N, 92 01.1W, Q W, 56ft., 10M, 4 lights, one installed on each corner of platform.
PLATFORM CHUC-1, 19 10.3N, 92 17.1W, Q W, 56ft., 10M, 4 lights, one installed on each corner of platform.
PLATFORM POOL-D, 19 14.5N, 92 17.3W, Q W, 56ft., 10M, 4 lights, one installed on each corner of platform.
PLATFORM POOL-B, 19 14.2N, 92 16.6W, Q W, 56ft., 10M, 4 lights, one installed on each corner of platform.
PLATFORM ABKATUM-D, 19 17.9N, 92 12.1W, Q W, 56ft., 10M, 4 lights, one installed on each corner of platform.
PLATFORM ABKATUM-C, 19 19.7N, 92 11.3W, Q W, 56ft., 10M, 4 lights, one installed on each corner of platform.
PLATFORM ABKATUM-F, 19 16.7N, 92 09.5W, Q W, 56ft., 10M, 4 lights, one installed on each corner of platform.

PLATFORM ABKATUM-G, 19 18.0N, 92 08.4W, Q W, 56ft., 10M, 4 lights, one installed on each corner of platform.
PLATFORM ABKATUM-J, 19 16.4N, 92 07.9W, Q W, 56ft., 10M, 4 lights, one installed on each corner of platform.
PLATFORM AKAL-F, 19 23.9N, 92 03.7W, Q W, 56ft., 10M, 4 lights, one installed on each corner of platform.
PLATFORM ABKATUM-H, 19 20.5N, 92 13.2W, Q W, 56ft., 10M, 4 lights, one installed on each corner of platform.
PLATFORM ABKATUM-93, 19 18.0N, 92 10.9W, Q W, 56ft., 10M, 4 lights, one installed on each corner of platform.
PLATFORM ABKATUM-E, 19 16.4N, 92 11.1W, Q W, 56ft., 10M, 4 lights, one installed on each corner of platform.
PLATFORM ABKATUM-A, 19 17.7N, 92 10.2W, Q W, 56ft., 10M, 4 lights, one installed on each corner of platform.
PLATFORM NOHOCH-A, 19 22.0N, 92 00.3W, Q W, 56ft., 10M, 4 lights, one installed on each corner of platform.
PLATFORM ABKATUM-I, 19 15.3N, 92 10.0W, Q W, 56ft., 10M, 4 lights, one installed on each corner of platform.
PLATFORM AKAL-J, 19 25.5N, 92 04.6W, Q W, 56ft., 10M, 4 lights, one installed on each corner of platform.
PLATFORM AKAL-G, 19 22.8N, 92 03.0W, Q W, 56ft., 10M, 4 lights, one installed on each corner of platform.
PLATFORM KU-1, 19 29.9N, 92 08.3W, Q W, 56ft., 10M, 4 lights, one installed on each corner of platform.
PLATFORM AKAL-L, 19 23.9N, 92 00.9W, Q W, 56ft., 10M, 4 lights, one installed on each corner of platform.
PLATFORM AKAL-M, 19 27.7N, 92 03.7W, Q W, 56ft., 10M, 4 lights, one installed on each corner of platform.
PLATFORM IXTOC-1, 19 24.4N, 92 12.7W, Q W, 56ft., 10M, 4 lights, one installed on each corner of platform.
PLATFORM AKAL-E, 19 25.1N, 92 03.0W, Q W, 56ft., 10M, 4 lights, one installed on each corner of platform.
PLATFORM AKAL-N, 19 26.2N, 92 03.7W, Q W, 56ft., 10M, 4 lights, one installed on each corner of platform.
PLATFORM AKAL-O, 19 24.4N, 92 04.9W, Q W, 56ft., 10M, 4 lights, one installed on each corner of platform.
PLATFORM AKAL-D, 19 25.0N, 92 01.6W, Q W, 56ft., 10M, 4 lights, one installed on each corner of platform.

PLATFORM AKAL-C, 19 25.9N, 92 02.4W, RACON Z (– – · ·).
PLATFORM POOL-A, 19 14.3N, 92 15.2W, Q W, 56ft., 10M, 4 lights, one installed on each corner of platform.
PLATFORM AKAL-R, 19 20.9N, 92 02.9W, Q W, 56ft., 10M, 4 lights, one installed on each corner of platform.
PLATFORM NOHO CH-B, 19 20.6N, 92 00.3W, Q W, 56ft., 10M, 4 lights, one installed on each corner of platform.
PLATFORM KU-A, 19 31.2N, 92 11.3W, Q W, 56ft., 10M, 4 lights, one installed on each corner of platform.
PLATFORM AKAL-C, 19 23.9N, 92 02.3W, Q W, 56ft., 10M, 4 lights, one installed on each corner of platform, RACON Y (– · – –).
PLATFORM KU-H, 19 35.3N, 92 12.0W, Q W, 56ft., 10M, 4 lights, one installed on each corner of platform.
PLATFORM KU-F, 19 29.7N, 92 10.4W, Q W, 56ft., 10M, 4 lights, one installed on each corner of platform.
PLATFORM KU-G, 19 30.8N, 92 09.3W, Q W, 56ft., 10M, 4 lights, one installed on each corner of platform.
PLATFORM KU-M, 19 33.8N, 92 11.0W, Q W, 56ft., 10M, 4 lights, one installed on each corner of platform.
PLATFORM ECO-1, 19 01.8N, 92 01.1W, Q W, 56ft., 10M, 4 lights, one installed on each corner of platform, RACON Q (– – · –).
PLATFORM AKAL-P, 19 22.8N, 92 04.4W, Q W, 56ft., 10M, 4 lights, one installed on each corner of platform.
PLATFORM CHUC-A, 19 10.8N, 92 17.2W, Q W, 56ft., 10M, 4 lights, one installed on each corner of platform.
PLATFORM CHUC-B, 19 08.7N, 92 18.3W, Q W, 56ft., 10M, 4 lights, one installed on each corner of platform.
TOWER B-3, 20 11.5N, 91 59.4W, Q W, 56ft., 10M, 4 Lights, one installed on each corner of platform.
CAYO ARCAS OIL TERMINAL, 20 09.6N, 91 57.8W, Q W, 56ft., 10M, 4 lights, one installed on each corner of platform.

CAYO ARCAS TERMINAL

20 10N, 91 59W

Pilotage: This oil production and export facility lies about 1 to 3 miles south of Cayos Arcas. The distribution platform is the north end of a pipeline carrying oil from a marine oil field 45 miles to the south. A racon on the platform is a prominent radar target at 26 miles. Pipelines are laid from this platform to two tanker moorings, known as SBMs. The terminal monitors VHF channel 9.

CAUTION: A major offshore oilfield is located between 40 and 58 miles southsouthwest of Cayos Arcas. A number of production platforms, interconnected by submarine pipelines are located throughout this area. Mobile drilling rigs, platforms and associated structures, sometimes unlit, may be encountered anywhere in the area. Numerous pipelines, many uncharted, exist within the oilfields, and between them and shore.

An oil platform is located at 19° 24'N, 92° 02'W.

Akbatum A Oil/Gas Platform is located in position 19° 17.9'N, 92° 10.3'W. Contact "Marine Control" on VHF channels 9 and 16.

PLATFORM ABKATUM-O, 19 16.9N, 92 13.7W, Q W, 56ft., 10M, 4 lights, one installed on each corner of platform.
PLATFORM AKAL-H, 19 22.4N, 92 01.9W, Q W, 56ft., 10M, 4 lights, one installed on each corner of platform.
PLATFORM AKAL-L, 19 26.9N, 92 05.0W, Q W, 56ft., 10M, 4 lights, one installed on each corner of platform.
PLATFORM AKAL-S, 19 21.7N, 92 04.2W, Q W, 56ft., 10M, 4 lights, one installed on each corner of platform.
PLATFORM BATAB-1A, 19 17.6N, 92 18.6W, Q W, 56ft., 10M, 4 lights, one installed on each corner of platform.
PLATFORM BATAB-A, 19 17.8N, 92 19.0W, Q W, 56ft., 10M, 4 lights, one installed on each corner of platform.
PLATFORM CAAN-1, 19 12.2N, 92 05.1W, Q W, 56ft., 10M, 4 lights, one installed on each corner of platform.
PLATFORM VECH-A, 19 05.8N, 92 31.9W, Q W, 56ft., 10M, 4 lights, one installed on each corner of platform.
PLATFORM YUM-1, 18 46.9N, 92 34.1W, Q W, 56ft., 10M, 4 lights, one installed on each corner of platform.
BAY OF CAMPECHE RADAR STATION PR-1, 18 56.6N, 92 37.3W, Q W, 56ft., 10M, 4 lights, one installed on each corner of platform. RACON O (– – –).

PUNTA BOXCOHUO

21 02N, 90 18W

Pilotage: This is the northwest extremity of the Yucatan Peninsula. It is a low and sandy projection. Several shoals are reported to lie near the 10 meter depth curve, about 9 miles seaward of the point. A 9 foot shoal lies 3 miles north of the point. A shoal, with depth unknown, is reported to lie 20 miles west-northwest of the lighthouse on the point.

The section of coast forming the west side of the Yucatan Peninsula, and the east side of the **Bay of Campeche**, extends 13 miles south-southwest from Punta Boxcohua to Celeston, then 60 miles farther south to the town of **Campeche**. A wide and shallow bank fronts this portion of the coast.

Between Campeche and **Punta Morro**, about 13 miles to the southwest, and **Champoton**, 20 miles farther south, the coast is bolder and backed by prominent ridges of hills.

Between Champoton and **Punta Xicalango**, about 80 miles to the southwest, the coast is low, wooded and fronted by a continuous sandy beach. **Laguna de Terminos** indents the south part of the coast. For a distance of 30 miles southwest of Champoton numerous sand and shell patches, with depths of 14 to 30 feet, extend as far as 12 miles offshore.

From Punta Xicalango the coast extends to the west for about 45 miles to **Punta Buey**, and is low and free of dangers. There are no ports of importance along this section of coast.

Winds: During the rainy season, from June to September, squalls blow at times with considerable force. The prevailing winds are from northeast to southeast.
Currents: There is seldom any current off the west coast of the Yucatan Peninsula.

REAL DE LAS SALINAS
20 45N, 90 26W

Pilotage: This is the west entrance to the lagoon, which parallels the north coast of the Yucatan Peninsula. It lies about 6 miles south of Celestun.

Between Real Salinas and **Campeche**, about 55 miles to the south, the low coast is bordered by swampy ground for about 25 miles and then becomes more elevated, rising to heights of 100 to 280 feet north of Campeche.

Isla de Piedras is about 30 feet high, and located close offshore about 23 miles north of Campeche.

SAN BARTOLO HILL, Campeche, 19 48.9N, 90 35.0W, Fl (2) W 12s, 256ft., 26M, Square white concrete tower, A F W light is shown from the mole.
LERMA RANGE, (Front Light) 19 48.3N, 90 36.0W, Fl W 3s, 85ft., 8M, Metal framework tower. **(Rear Light)** 178 meters 139° from front, Iso W 2s, 245ft., 9M, Metal framework tower.
WHARF, at head, 19 49.0N, 90 35.7W, Iso W 2s, 30ft., 9M, Column.
PIER, Lerma No 2, 19 48.8N, 90 35.9W, Iso R 2s, 21ft., 6M, Concrete tower.
PIER, Lerma No 1, 19 48.8N, 90 35.9W, Iso R 2s, 21ft., 6M, concrete tower.
PIER, Breton No 3, 19 49.1N, 90 35.6W, Iso R 2s, 30ft., 6M, Green pipe.
PIER, Breton No 2, 19 49.1N, 90 35.7W, Iso R 2s, 30ft., 6M, Red pipe.

CAMPECHE

19 51N, 90 33W

Pilotage: This is the capital of the state of Campeche, and a major sisal exporting port. It stands on a plain bordered on three sides by a small amphitheater of hills. Two forts stand 1 1/4 miles northeast, and two similar forts stand 1 3/4 miles southwest of the city.

A signal station is located atop an old fort near the waterfront. A blue flag indicates bad weather and a red flag indicates that the port is closed.

A pier, extending from the shore abreast of the city, was reported to have a dredged channel with a depth of 18 feet leading up to it.
Port of Entry

Muelle Castillo Breton, a new 550 yard long pier, with a depth of 12 feet alongside, stands at the village of **Lerma,** about 3 1/2 miles southwest of Campeche.

Puerto de Abrigo is situated about 1/4 mile southeast of Muelle Castillo Breton, and there is a small pier 1/4 mile northeast of the same jetty.

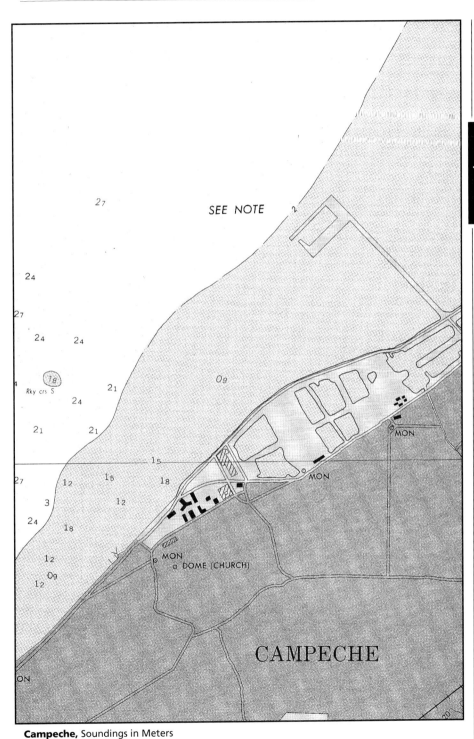

Campeche, Soundings in Meters

Chapter 2

Between Campeche and **Punta Mastun Grande**, a wooded 423 foot high headland about 9 miles southwest, and **Punta Morro**, about 5 miles farther south-southwest, the coast is bold and backed by ridges of hills.

CAUTION: Dangerous wrecks lie 10 miles northwest and 18 miles west of Punta Mastun.

Between Punta Morro and the **Río Champoton**, about 20 miles to the south, the coast is backed by a ridge of hills that are more broken than those to the north. The ridge terminates in a prominent 360 foot high hill about 8 miles south of the river.

PUNTA MORRO, 19 41.4N, 90 42.1W, Fl (3) W 6s, 177ft., 27M, White octagonal masonry tower, white dwelling, Visible 000°–197°.

RÍO CHAMPOTON, S side of entrance, 19 20.8N, 90 43.2W, Fl W 5s, 82ft., 25M, White square concrete tower, Visible 045°–180°.

CHAMPOTON
19 22N, 90 43W

Pilotage: This is a small village on the south side of the entrance to the Río Champoton. An old fort and two churches stand in the town. **Observation Cay**, 5 feet high, stands close off the river entrance.

Between the Río Champoton and **Barra de Puerto Real**, about 55 miles to the southwest, the low, wooded coast is fronted by a continuous stretch of sandy beach. Numerous sand and shell patches, with depths of 8 to 18 feet, lie up to 5 miles off this section of coast.

BANCOS CHAMPOTON
19 23N, 90 50W

Pilotage: This is a group of detached patches with depths of 14 to 27 feet extending 10 to 15 miles west from Champoton.

BANCOS DE SABUNCUY
19 10N, 91 16W

Pilotage: This is a group of patches with depths of 14 to 30 feet lying about 32 miles southwest of Champoton. They extend up to 12 miles offshore.

SABANCUY, 19 00.0N, 91 11.0W, Fl (3) W 12s, 42ft., 11M, White concrete tower.

LAGUNA DE TERMINOS

ISLA AGUADA RANGE, (Front Light) on Punta del Tigre entrance, 18 47.8N, 91 30.2W, Fl W 3s, 33ft., 11M, White concrete tower.
(Rear Light) 400 meters 151° from front, Fl (4) W 12s, 66ft., 9M, White concrete tower, Radar reflector.
BOCA DE LOS PARGOS, 18 37.0N, 91 16.0W, Fl W 6s, 36ft., 11M, Masonry tower.
LAGUNA DE TERMINOS, Tio Campo, S end, 18 31.5N, 91 47.7W, Fl W 6s, 30ft., 11M, Round masonry tower.
PUNTA DEL ZACATAL, 18 37.3N, 91 51.9W, Fl W 5s, 49ft., 17M, Aluminum tower with concrete base.
PUNTA ATALAYA, W end of Isla del Carmen, 18 39.4N, 91 51.2W, Fl (3) W R 12s, 69ft., 21M, White masonry tower, red cupola, R 086°–113°, W–086°.

BARRA DE PUERTO REAL
18 47N, 91 30W

Pilotage: This is the east entrance to **Laguna de Terminos**. It is 2 miles wide and has depths ranging from 6 to 12 feet. A pair of lighted beacons in range 152° stand on **Punta del Tigre** on the north side of the entrance. A shallow, breaking spit extends 2 1/2 miles west-northwest from the point. A channel for vessels drawing less than 10 feet leads to an anchorage off Punta del Tigre, but should not be attempted without local knowledge.

Isla del Carmen, low and sparsely wooded, fronts Laguna de Terminos between Barra de Puerto Real and **Barra Principal**, the west entrance of the lagoon, which is located about 20 miles west-southwest.

CARMEN
18 39N, 91 50W

Pilotage: Barra Principal is about 6 miles wide between **Punta Atalaya**, 1/2 mile southeast of the southwest end of Isla del Carmen, and **Punta Xicalango** to the northwest. A breaking spit extends 4 1/2 miles northwest from Punta Atalaya, and depths of 6 to 12 feet extend 3 miles north from Punta Xicalango. A buoyed channel, with depths of 12 to 14 feet, leads through these shoals to the town of Car-

men on the southeast side of Punta Atalaya. Two lighted beacons in range 180° stand on the west side of the entrance and indicate the fairway of this channel.

CAUTION: Considerable changes to depths, navigation aids and the coastline have taken place in the approaches to Carmen. The most recent editions of appropriate charts should be consulted.

The wharves which front the town have a depth of 11 feet alongside. A pier, with a depth of 18 feet alongside, extends from the shore at the naval base near the southeast end of the town. In 1979 an artificial harbor was under construction in the area north of Punta Atalaya.

Between Barra Principal and the **Río Grijalva,** about 46 miles to the west, the coast is low and has no prominent features.

Entrance Buoy, 18 41.0N, 92 42.0W, Fl W 2s, Black buoy.
XICALANGO RANGE, (Front Light) 18 38.5N, 91 54.5W, Fl W 3s, 42ft., 11M, Metal frame-work tower. **(Rear Light)** 330 meters 180° from front, Fl W 6s, 104ft., 20M, Red concrete tower.
GOVERNMENT PIER, at head, N side, 18 38.9N, 91 50.7W, Iso G 2s, 26ft., 4M, Cylindrical concrete tower.
S Side, 18 38.9N, 91 50.7W, Iso G 2s, 26ft., 4M, Cylindrical concrete tower.
FRONTERA, 18 36.8N, 92 41.5W, Fl W 6s, 98ft., 14M, White skeleton iron tower with 8 columns, Visible 045°– 245°, Two F W range lights mark entrance to Grijalva Canal, Radar reflector.
E BREAKWATER, 18 37.1N, 92 41.2W, Fl G 5s, 25ft., 6M, White concrete tower.
FRONTERA RANGE, (Front Light) 18 37.0N, 92 41.0W, Fl W 3s, 38ft., 10M, White tower. **(Rear Light)** Iso W 2s, 55ft., 10M, White tower.

PUNTA BUEY

18 39N, 92 43W

Pilotage: This low point has been reported to be extending north and northwest. Depths of 18 to 24 feet extend about 1 1/2 miles north and northwest from the point.

The coast recedes about 8 miles southwest from Punta Buey, then extends in a general west-southwest direction for about 95 miles to **Coatzacoalcos,** then west for 10 miles, then north-northwest for an additional 25 miles to **Punta Zapotitlan.** This low, marshy coast is indented by several lagoons and is covered with very heavy vegetation except in the tidal marshes. Several rivers discharge into the gulf, and hills stand 3 to 8 miles inland on the west part of this coast.

Winds: The winds tend to blow from the north. Northers occur at about 8 day intervals between October and March.
Current: From October to March the current near the shore sets east at a rate of 1 to 1 1/2 knots.

FRONTERA (ALVARO OBREGÓN)

18 35N, 92 39W

Pilotage: Puerto Frontera stands on the east bank of the Río Grijalva about 5 miles south of the entrance. The port is used mainly by small coast vessels.

Depths of less than 18 feet extend about 3/4 mile north and 1 mile northwest from the east entrance point, and similar depths extend about 1 1/2 miles north and 1/2 mile west from Punta Buey. The bar lying north of the entrance points has been reported to be dredged to a depth of 20 feet. The buoyed channel within the river has a navigable width of about 250 yards with depths ranging from 32 to 40 feet. The preferred channel passes east of **Isla Buey** about 3 miles south of the entrance.

Grijalva Canal, which crosses the peninsula about 1 1/2 miles south of Punta Buey, was formerly used to enter the river. In 1974 this canal was reported no longer in use.

When the river is at its highest level the bar has the least depth over it, and when the river is at its lowest the channel is scoured out, so the depths are better. At the end of the rainy season in December, the least depths may be expected, but the first norther will increase the depth by about 3 feet. A freshet can reduce the depth by as much as 3 feet.

There is only one tidal rise every 24 hours, and the rise at springs is only about 2 feet. An overhead cable north of Frontera has a clearance of about 118 feet.

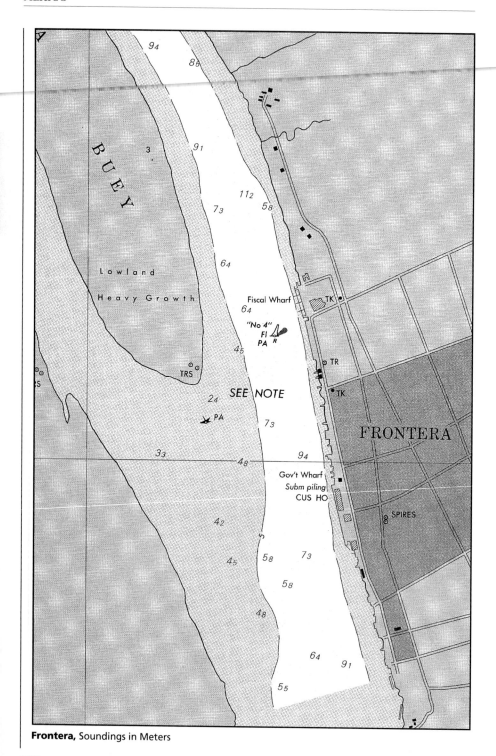

Frontera, Soundings in Meters

Fiscal Wharf parallels the shore abreast town, with depths of 18 to 20 feet alongside. Anchorage can be taken in the river off the town, according to the direction of the port authority.

Port of Entry

Between Punta Buey and Coatzacoalcos, about 100 miles to the west southwest the coast is low, fairly steep-to and bordered by mangroves and palm trees.

CHILTEPEC, at river entrance, 18 26.5N, 93 05.0W, Fl (3) W 12s, 49ft., 14M, White cylindrical tower, Radar reflector.

DOS BOCAS, 18 26.1N, 93 11.5W, RACON **B** (– · · ·).

RÍO GONZALEZ
18 26N, 93 04W

Pilotage: This river is located about 23 miles southwest of Punta Buey. It is shallow, but is navigated by small draft craft up to 90 miles inland. **Barra de Chiltepec** is the east entrance of this river and has the village of Chiltepec on its west entrance point. Small coastal vessels frequent this port.

Barra de dos Bocas is the entrance to a lagoon about 3 1/2 miles west of the Río Gonzalez. A dangerous wreck lies about 9 miles northeast of Barra de dos Bocas.

Dos Bocas Terminal, 5 miles west of the Chiltepec lighthouse, lies at the end of the pipeline from the marine oil field to the north. See the previous section on the Cayo Arcas Terminal. The terminal here has a 3600 foot long berth and three moorings for large tankers located 11 miles to the north. Pipelines connect the tanker moorings to shore. Anchoring is prohibited within an area shown on the chart enclosing the moorings and pipelines.

TUPILCO, 18 25.0N, 93 25.0W, Fl (4) W 16s, 79ft., 14M, Cylindrical concrete tower.

BARRA DE TUPILCO
18 26N, 93 25W

Pilotage: This is a shallow entrance to a lagoon. It is located about 16 miles west of Barra de dos Bocas. A tower stands on the west side of the entrance.

Laguna del Carmen is located about 26 miles west of Barra de Tupilco. In 1976 an awash rock was reported to lie 17 miles north-northwest of Laguna del Carmen.

TONALA, W side of entrance to Río Tonala, 18 13.0N, 94 07.3W, Fl (3) W 12s, 75ft., 16M, Concrete tower and dwelling, red and white bands, Visible 081°– 246°, Two F W range lights mark entrance to Tonala River.

RÍO TONALA
18 13N, 94 08W

Pilotage: This river has a bar with depths of under 8 feet at its entrance. It lies about 16 miles west of Laguna del Carmen. Each entrance point is marked by a conspicuous sand hill. Local knowledge is needed to enter the river. Vessels anchor here to load mahogany.

COATZACOALCOS

CERRO DEL GAVILAN, 18 08.9N, 94 24.0W, Fl (2) W 18s, 177ft., 20M, White octagonal tower with dwelling, Radar reflector, Iso R 2s marks top of mast.
RANGE, (Front Light) E side of river, 18 08.1N, 94 24.2W, Fl W 3s, 147ft., 9M, White skeleton iron tower, orange bands, Radar reflector. **(Rear Light)** 310 meters 162° from front, Iso W 2s, 168ft., 9M, White skeleton iron tower, orange bands, Radar reflector.
PIEDRA NANCHITAL, 18 06.0N, 94 25.0W, Fl (2) W 10s, 33ft., 10M, White framework tower.
E BREAKWATER HEAD, 18 09.9N, 94 24.8W, Fl G 5s, 59ft., 7M, White column on concrete base.
W BREAKWATER HEAD, 18 09.9N, 94 24.7W, Fl R 5s, 46ft., 7M, White column on concrete base.
DARSENA DE PAJARITOS RANGE, (Front Light) 18 07.0N, 94 24.0W, Fl W 3s, 61ft., 10M, White framework tower. **(Rear Light)** 300 meters 180° from front, Iso W 2s, 85ft., 10M, White framework tower.
BERTH 6 RANGE, (Front Light) 18 07.5N, 94 24.4W, Q Y, White metal column, red bands. **(Rear Light)** 100 meters 270° from front, Fl (3) Y 10s, White metal column, red bands.
BASIN LIGHT E, 18 07.9N, 94 24.2W, Fl G 3s, Metal column.
BASIN LIGHT W, 18 07.9N, 94 24.3W, Fl R 3s, metal column.

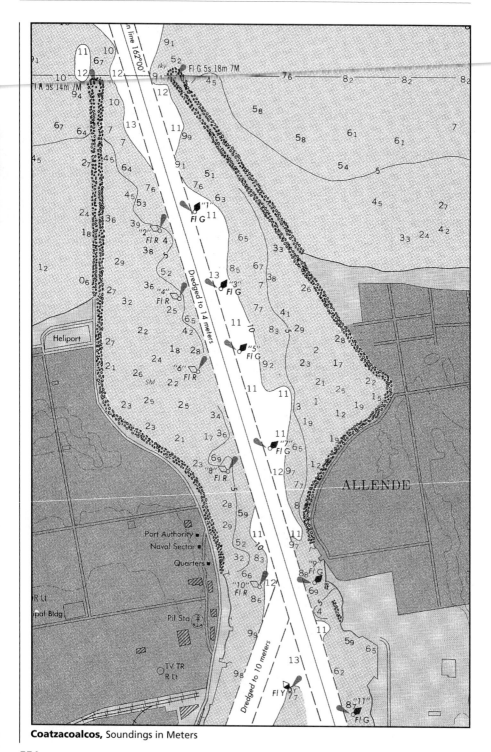

Coatzacoalcos, Soundings in Meters

COATZACOALCOS
18 08N, 94 25W

Pilotage: This port was formerly known as **Puerto Mexico**. It lies on the west bank of the Río Coatzacoalcos, close within the entrance. There is a free port on the same side of the river, south of town. The town, with its buildings and radio towers, is prominent from seaward, and can be identified during the day by smoke, or at night by the loom of its lights. Approaching from seaward several high dark green hills will be observed east of the entrance. On the east side of the entrance is a round hill. Westward of the entrance will appear some low sandhills, the tops of which are covered with green vegetation. Low land fronts the hills on either side. The water is muddy for about 1 1/2 miles outside the heads of the breakwater. The breakwaters are conspicuous, and the east side of the river mouth is a radar target at 40 miles. The range leads up the main channel bearing 162°.

This port is occasionally closed for up to several days during strong northers, which generally occur from November to March. These storms can raise the water level considerably in the port.

Maximum draft crossing the bar is 37 feet, but it has been reported that the depths over the bar are liable to decrease considerably because of unusually strong currents setting to the west. When the river is flooding from June to October, depths are liable to decrease even more.

The wharf along the west side of the river is over 6200 feet long, with depths of over 28 feet alongside. There are strong currents in the vicinity of the wharves in the river. The inner harbor basin on the east side of the river is called Darsena de Pajaritos. Several oil loading facilities lie upriver.

Between Coatzacoalcos and the **Río Barilla**, about 12 miles to the west, the coast is low and unvaried. The Río Barilla is the entrance to a lagoon, which is connected to Coatzacoalcos by a river south of the city.
Port of Entry

Tides and Currents: Offshore the current sets northwest, but near the breakwaters it sets east. The current in the river varies with the stage of the tide, attaining its maximum rate of 5 to 5 1/2 knots about 2 hours after high water. During the first 3 hours of the flood the rate ranges from 2 1/2 to 3 knots. The rise of the tide is about 2 feet.

PUNTA SAN JUAN
18 17N, 94 37W

Pilotage: This point is located about 5 miles north of the Río Barilla, and has a small islet lying close off it.

Between Punta San Juan and **Punta Zapotitlan**, about 20 miles north-northwest, the coast is backed by mountain ranges about 3 to 8 miles inland. Cerro San Martin, conspicuous from seaward, stands about 8 miles inland west of Punta San Juan.

PUNTA ZAPOTITLAN, 18 31.2N, 94 48.0W, Fl W 6s, 98ft., 20M, White round masonry tower, Visible 116°– 324°.

PUNTA ZAPOTITLAN
18 33N, 94 48W

Pilotage: This prominent point is bordered by a reef which extends 1/2 mile offshore. Depths of greater than 60 feet lie about 1 1/2 miles off the point. An old disused lighthouse stands near the lighthouse on the point.

The coast between Punta Zapotitlan and **Cabo Rojo** extends in a general northwest direction for about 230 miles. Mountain ranges with some conspicuous peaks back the coastal plain. The more prominent coastal features and dangers are lighted. Numerous islets, shoals and other dangers lie off this section of the coast.

Between Punta Zapotitlan and **Alvarado**, about 56 miles west-northwest, the first 33 miles of coast is backed by ranges of hills about 3 to 8 miles inland. The remaining part of the coast is lower, being composed of sand hills 50 to 200 feet high.

Barra Zontecomapan obstructs the entrance to the **Laguna Coxcoapan**, about 10 miles west of Punta Zapotitlan. This bar has a depth of about 6 feet over it. The entrance may be identified by a conspicuous umbrella-shaped tree which stands on a bluff a little to the west of it.

Chapter 2

Punta Morrillo is a bold, rounded bluff standing about 15 miles west-northwest of Punta Zapotitlan.

Punta Roca Partida (18° 42'N, 95° 11'W) is a group of perpendicular cliffs which stand about 8 miles west-northwest of Punta Morrillo. A rocky islet stands close off the point.

Volcan San Martin Tuxtla (18° 33'N, 95° 12'W) is a 4600 foot high volcano about 10 miles south of Punta Roca Partida. This can be seen from a great distance in clear weather. When active, the column of smoke by day, and the flames at night, make this volcano an excellent landmark.

Currents: The currents off this coast are variable and uncertain. They are usually dependent on the force and direction of the wind. The coastal current usually sets south in the winter and north in the summer.

Winds: The trade winds blow from northeast to east-northeast. After the season of the northers, from October to March, there are light north breezes, calms, squally rains and thick weather up to the middle of August, when the trades resume again.

ROCA PARTIDA, 18 42.0N, 94 11.0W, Fl (4) W 16s, 318ft., 22M, White masonry tower, house, Visible 112°-294°, Radar reflector.
ALVARADO, GASODUCTO DE PEMEX, 18 47.0N, 94 45.0W, Fl Y 2s, 29ft., 11M, Yellow round tower.
E FORTIN (Punta Alvarado), on point SE of town, 18 46.3N, 95 45.9W, Fl W 6s, 30ft., 13M, White square concrete tower, Visible 005°30'–021°30'.
ALVARADO, on E entrance point of Río Papaloapan, 18 47.2N, 95 45.3W, Fl (3) W 12s, 125ft., 21M, Square concrete tower and dwelling, Visible 136°-274°, Radar reflector.
ALVARADO, E BREAKWATER, 18 47.4N, 95 44.5W, Fl G 5s, 29ft., 11M, Green aluminum tower.
W BREAKWATER, 18 47.7N, 95 45.0W, Fl R 5s, 29ft., 11M, Red aluminum tower.

ALVARADO
18 47N, 95 46W

Pilotage: This is primarily a fishing port. It lies within the entrance to a lagoon of the same name located about 32 miles west-northwest of Punta Roca Partida. A 14 foot deep shoal lies

1 3/4 miles north of the east entrance point. Two patches, with depths of 8 and 7 feet lie in mid-channel about 1/4 mile northwest and 3/4 mile south-southwest of the east entrance point. Depths of less than 36 feet extend 1 mile north of the east entrance point.

The bar is situated about 1/2 mile outside the entrance points. It is constantly shifting and the sea nearly always breaks on it. In 1985 a depth of 26 feet was reported over the bar.

A conspicuous sandy bluff and a beacon stand on the east entrance point. A beacon stands on the west entrance point.

The coast between Alvarado and **Punta Coyal**, about 20 miles northwest, is bordered by two large lagoons along its southern half, and by low land along its northwest half.

ANEGADA DE AFUERA, on NW point of reef, 19 10.3N, 95 52.2W, Fl (4) W 16s, 36ft., 11M, metal structure, red and black bands.
ARRECIFE SANTIAGUILLO, center of island, 19 08.6N, 95 48.4W, Fl (2) W R 10s, 118ft., 22M, Red concrete cylindrical tower, R 002°-056°, W 084°, R 126°, W 002°, RACON **S** (· · ·).
ARRECIFE DE CABEZO, N end, 19 05.6N, 95 51.9W, Fl (2) W 10s, 30ft., 11M, Square concrete tower, Reported extinguished (1989).
S END, 19 03.1N, 95 49.7W, Fl R 6s, 26ft., 8M, Square concrete tower.
ARRECIFE EL RIZO, S end, 19 03.2N, 95 55.4W, Fl (3) W 12s, 39ft., 11M, Rectangular concrete tower.

PUNTA COYAL
19 03N, 95 58W

Pilotage: This blunt point is composed of low sand hills. A 262 foot high sand hill stands about 3 miles west of the point. The village of **Anton Lizardo** stands on the north side of this point. **Arrecife El Giote** extends 3/4 mile from the coast close west of Anton Lizardo.

Anton Lizardo Anchorage (19° 04'N, 95° 59'W) lies between Arrecife Chopas and Punta Coyal. This anchorage is used by commercial vessels sheltering from northers.

Between Punta Coyal and **Punta Mocambo**, about 9 miles to the northwest, the coast recedes about 2 miles to form a sandy bay bordered by low sand hills. A reef lies about 3/4 mile southeast of Punta Mocambo. The **Río Jamapa**, with

depths of 3 to 6 feet over the bar, discharges into the gulf about 2 1/2 miles south of Punta Mocambo.

The coast between Punta Mocambo and **Puerto Veracruz**, 4 miles to the northwest, is low and sandy.

ARRECIFE SANTIAGUILLO
19 09N, 95 48W

Pilotage: This reef stands at the northeast end of a group of reefs located 11 miles east-northeast of **Punta Coyal**. It stands about 8 feet high.

Arrecife Anegadilla is the outermost reef of the group off Punta Coyal. It lies 1/2 mile east-southeast of Arrecife Santiaguillo.

ARRECIFE ANEGADA DE AFUERA
19 09N, 95 51W

Pilotage: This reef is about 2 1/2 miles long, and it lies about 1 1/2 miles west-northwest of Arrecife Santiaguillo. There is a cay on a small reef close off its south end.

Arrecife Cabeza is about 3 1/2 miles long and 1 1/2 miles wide. It lies about 4 miles south-southwest of Arrecife Santiaguillo.

Arrecife de Enmedio, with shoal patches close off its west side and a small reef and another patch close off its north end, lies about 3 1/2 miles northeast of Punta Coyal. A small cay stands on the south end of the reef.

Arrecife Rizo, about 1 1/2 miles long, lies 1 1/2 miles south of Arrecife de Enmedio. A spit with a depth of 10 feet over its outer end, extends a little more than 1/2 mile north from the north extremity of Arrecife Rizo.

ANTON LIZARDO ANCHORAGE

BLANCA REEF, 19 05.0N, 96 00.0W, Fl (2) W 10s, 35ft., 11M, Concrete pyramidal tower.
EL GIOTE REEF, 19 04.0N, 96 00.0W, Fl R 6s, 30ft., 8M, Square concrete tower.
ISLA SALMEDINA, S part, 19 04.1N, 95 57.2W, Fl W 1.5s, 23ft., 3M, Metal mast, black and red bands.
ISLA DE ENMEDIO, 19 06.0N, 95 56.3W, Fl (3) W R G, 46ft., W13M R8M G7M, White

cylindrical concrete tower, with dwelling, W 147°– 220°, R 260°, W 268°, G 299°, W 327°, R 032°, W 057°, R 147°.

ARRECIFE CHOPAS
19 05N, 95 58W

Pilotage: This reef is about 3 1/4 miles long and lies about 2 miles north of Punta Coyal. A small reef lies close south of a grass-covered cay on the south end of the reef. Several small reefs lie close off the north and northwest ends.

Arrecife Blanca is about 1/4 mile in extent with a small cay on it. It lies about 1 mile west of Arrecife Chopas.

NOTE: Vessels without local knowledge should not attempt the passages between Arrecife Rizo, Arrecife de Enmedio and Arrecife Chopas. Foul ground lies in the passage between Arrecife Chopas and Arrecife Blanca — this passage should not be used.

ARRECIFE ANEGADA DE LA ADENTRO
19 14N, 96 04W

Pilotage: This is the outermost reef in the approaches to Veracruz. These reefs all break and are easily identified in clear weather. This one is located 4 miles east-northeast of the harbor entrance.

Isla Verde is a low white cay, standing on the south end of a reef about 1 1/2 miles south-southwest of Arrecife Anegada de La Adentro. The intervening channel is about 1 mile wide and deep.

Bajo Paducah (19° 12'N, 96° 05'W) is a shoal with a least depth of almost 15 feet. It lies about 1/4 mile west of the north end of the reef on which Isla Verde stands.

Arrecife de Pájaros is about 1 mile long and lies about 1 1/4 mile west-southwest of Isla Verde.

Isla de Sacrificios is a small cay on the south end of a reef close south of Arrecife de Pájaros. The passage between here and Arrecife de Pájaros is narrow and foul.

Bajo Mersey (19° 11'N, 96° 06'W) has a least depth of 15 feet.

Arrecife Blanquilla lies about 1 3/4 miles west of Arrecife Anegada de La Adentro. The channel between the two reefs is 1 1/2 miles wide and deep. The channel west of Arrecife Blanquilla has depths of 60 feet and is 3/4 mile wide.

Arrecife de La Gallega extends 1 1/4 miles north from the north side of the harbor entrance, and **Arreciffe Galleguilla** lies close northeast of its north end.

Arrecife Hornos extends about 1/4 mile east from the root of the southeast breakwater.

RÍO JAMAPA, N breakwater, 19 06.2N, 96 05.8W, Fl R 5s, 29ft., 7M, Red metal tower. **S BREAKWATER,** 19 06.0N, 96 05.9W, Fl G 5s, 23ft., 7M, Green metal tower.

VERACRUZ

LA GALLEGUILLA, on E side of reef, 19 13.8N, 96 07.3W, Fl (2) 10s, 36ft., 15M, White cylindrical concrete tower.
ARRECIFE BLANQUILLA, 19 13.6N, 96 06.1W, Fl (4) R 16s, 52ft., 9M, Red concrete tower with white bands.
ARRECIFE LA BLANQUILLA, S side of reef, 19 13.4N, 96 05.8W, Fl (2) R 10s, 49ft., 9M, Red cylindrical concrete tower, Occasional, RACON B (– · · ·).
ANEGADA DE ADENTRO, NW extremity, 19 13.7N, 96 03.7W, Fl (3) G 12s, 36ft., 9M, Green cylindrical concrete tower.
ISLA VERDE, on bands S of island, 19 11.9N, 96 04.9W, Fl (4) W 16s, 26ft., 15M, Red concrete tower.
ARRECIFE PAJAROS, NW end, 19 11.6N, 96 05.7W, Fl W 6s, 23ft., 15M, White concrete tower.
ISLA DE SACRIFICIOS, 19 10.4N, 96 05.5W, Fl W 6s, 127ft., 22M, Cylindrical concrete tower, black and white bands, R 134°-157°, W 163°, G 187°, W 195°, R 238°, W 334°, obsc 134°, RACON V (· · · –), 25M.
ARRECIFE HORNOS, 19 11.5N, 96 07.3W, Fl (2) W 10s, 10ft., 7M, Black framework tower with 2 red bands.
EL MAREGRAPO, 19 11.4N, 96 07.4W, Fl G 2s, 19ft., 6M, Green square concrete tower.
HEAD OF NE BREAKWATER, 19 12.2N, 96 07.2W, Fl R 5s, 39ft., 10M, Red pyramidal tower, concrete base.
HEAD OF SE BREAKWATER, 19 12.0N, 96 07.3W, Fl G 5s, 33ft., 10M, Green pyramidal tower, concrete base.

HEAD OF INNER BREAKWATER NO 3, 19 12.1N, 96 07.6W, Iso W 2s, 49ft., 11M, White concrete tower with small house.
PILOT PIER, N side, 19 12.0N, 96 08.0W, Iso G 2s, 16ft., 7M, White concrete tower. S side, 19 12.0N, 96 08.0W, Iso G 2s, 16ft., 7M, White concrete tower.
MUELLE DE PEMEX, E HEAD, 19 12.2N, 96 07.4W, Iso R 2s, 13ft., 7M, Red tower.
MUELLE DE PEMEX, W side, 19 12.2N, 96 07.4W, Iso R 2s, 13ft., 7M, Red tower.
HOTEL PUERTO BELLO RANGE, (Front Light) 19 11.0N, 96 08.0W, Fl W 3s, 81ft., 20M. **(Rear Light)** Iso W 2s, 102ft., 25M, On hotel.

PUERTO VERACRUZ
19 12N, 96 08W

Pilotage: This is one of the principal ports of Mexico. The harbor is an artificial basin protected by breakwaters on three sides.

Volcan Citaletepet (Pico de Orizaba) is a 17,392 foot high volcano located 63 miles west of the city. The volcano is inactive, but its 3 1/2 mile diameter crater can easily be distinguished from a considerable distance on a clear day. **Cerro Nauhcampatepetl** (19° 29'N, 97° 08'W) is a 14,040 foot high mountain with a peculiar shape. It stands about 25 miles north-northeast of the above volcano. Snow falls on isolated spots at higher elevations.

A prominent high radio tower stands about 3/4 mile south of the root of the southeast breakwater. To enter the harbor steer for the cathedral dome about 1/3 mile west-southwest of Benito Juarez tower on a heading of 261°. At night steer for the light on Muro de Pescadores on a heading of 270° until the light structure on the east corner of Muelle de La Terminal bears 290°, which will lead through the entrance in mid-channel between the breakwater heads.

Storm signals are displayed from a red and white banded flagstaff on Benito Juarez tower. **Port of Entry**

Winds: With the exception of land breezes at night, the winds usually blow from seaward and are heavily saturated with moisture. March and April are the least humid months. Offshore the trade winds blow from northeast to eastsoutheast. During the season of the northers, from October to March, winds of up to 50 knots

Chapter 2

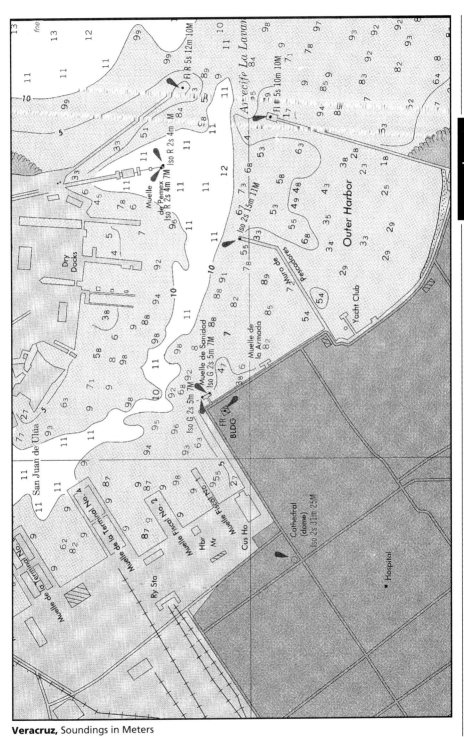

Veracruz, Soundings in Meters

occur making it impossible for vessels to enter the harbor. After April, there are light north winds, calms, squally rains and unsettled weather, until about the middle of August when the trade winds resume. Land and sea breezes alternate regularly, even in the intervals between northers. The former begin shortly after sunset and the latter at about 0900.

Tides and Currents: The diurnal range of the tide is about 1.6 feet, but the water level is influenced by the force and direction of the winds. The tidal currents are weak and are overcome by the coastal currents, which are also affected by the winds. During the winter, the current usually sets south, and in the summer it sets north.

VERACRUZ TO RÍO TUXPAN

Pilotage: Between Arrecife de La Gallega, which extends north from Puerto Veracruz, and **Punta Gorda** about 3 miles northwest, the coast recedes about 2 miles forming **Bahía de Veragua**.

From Punta Gorda the coast extends about 6 3/4 miles west-northwest to **Punta Antigua**, on the south side of the entrance to the **Río de La Antigua**. It then extends about 9 1/2 miles to **Punta Zempoala**. Punta Antigua has been reported to be a good radar target at distances up to 29 miles and is reported to be identifiable with charted features by radar at distances up to 19 miles.

Bajo Zempoala has depths of 16 to 26 feet about 4 miles north of **Punta Zempoala**, and two miles offshore.

Between Punta Zempoala and **Punta del Morro**, about 25 miles north-northwest, the coast has several reef-fringed points and is marked by several conspicuous peaks.

Pico Zempoala (19° 33'N, 96° 27'W) is the southernmost peak. It is 2299 feet high, and stands about 10 miles northwest of Punta Zempoala. **Los Dos Antriscos**, a peak 2620 feet high, stands 5 miles southwest of Punta del Morro. A bare chimney rock, 875 feet high and prominent, stands 2 miles west-northwest of **Punta Penon**, which lies about 9 miles north-northwest of Punta Zempoala.

Isla Bernal Chico (19° 40'N, 96° 23'W) is a 144 foot high island lying close offshore about

12 miles north-northwest of Punta Zempoala. A prominent bare rocky hill, over 300 feet high, stands on the coast 1 3/4 miles west-southwest of this island.

The coast between Punta Gorda and the **Río Nautla**, about 30 miles to the northwest, and the **Río Tecolutla** 18 miles farther northwest, is fronted by a narrow, thickly-wooded strip of land paralleled by a narrow lagoon. A range of hills stands about 5 miles inland.

Dos Hermanos (20° 06'N, 96° 52'W) is a conspicuous peak rising to an elevation of 1169 feet about 9 miles south-southwest of the Río Nautla. **Cerro Burras** stands about 9 miles southwest of the Río Tecolutla. A dangerous wreck lies 4 miles east of the north side of the mouth of Río Tecolutla.

Between the Río Tecolutla and Punta de Piedras, a reef-fringed point about 25 miles northwest, several rivers discharge into the gulf from the lagoon which backs the coast.

Between Punta Piedras and the **Río de Tuxpan**, about 9 miles northwest, the coast is about 100 feet high.

CHACHALACAS, 19 24.8N, 96 19.3W, Fl W 6s, 30ft., 15M, White framework tower.
PUNTA DELGADA, located on Punta del Morro, 19 51.0N, 96 28.0W, Fl (3) W 12s, 151ft., 19M, White cylindrical concrete tower.
RÍO NAUTLA, S bank, 20 14.0N, 96 47.0W, Fl W 6s, 98ft., 25M, White concrete cylindrical tower, Visible 150°– 300°, Radiobeacon (about 5 miles SSE).
TECOLUTLA, N side of Río Tecolutla, 20 29.0N, 97 00.0W, Fl (2) W 10s, 82ft., 25M, White round concrete tower, Visible 149°– 301°, Radar reflector.

BAJO BLAKE
20 45N, 96 58W

Pilotage: This shoal has a depth of 26 feet in a location about 13 miles southeast of **Punta de Piedras**.

S BREAKWATER, Fl G 5s, 27ft., 8M, Silver metal tower.
N BREAKWATER, Fl R 5s, 27ft., 8M, Silver metal tower.
ESCUALO, 20 41.5N, 97 56.5W, Q W, 84ft., 10M, Yellow rectangular metal tower.
MORSA, 20 46.2N, 97 58.2W, Q W, 84ft., 10M, Yellow rectangular metal platform.

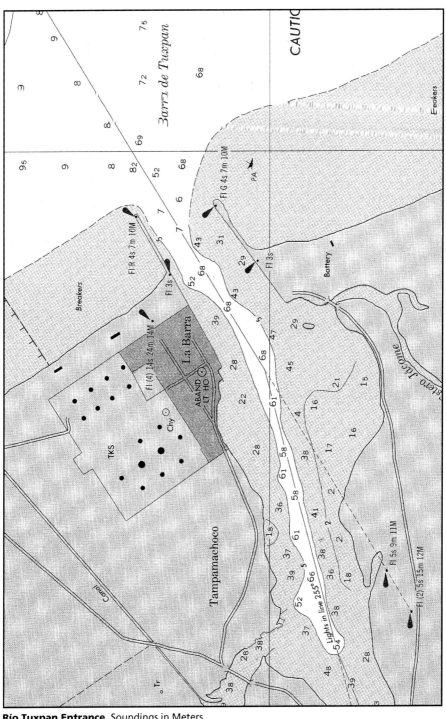

Río Tuxpan Entrance, Soundings in Meters

ATUM "C", 20 53.6N, 97 01.0W, Q W, 84ft., 10M, Yellow rectangular metal tower.
ATUM "B", 20 52.6N, 97 00.9W, Q W, 84ft., 10M, Yellow rectangular metal platform.
ATUM "A", 20 51.6N, 97 00.1W, Q W, 84ft., 10M, Yellow rectangular metal platform.
BARGE "B", 20 57.9N, 97 02.3W, Q W, 84ft., 10M, Yellow rectangular metal platform.
BARGE "A", 20 56.6N, 97 02.3W, Q W, 84ft., 10M, Yellow rectangular metal platform.
MARSOPA, 21 03.5N, 97 02.5W, Q W, 84ft., 10M, Yellow rectangular metal platform.
TIBURON, 21 24.1N, 97 08.0W, Q W, 84ft., 10M, Yellow rectangular metal platform.
ARENQUE "B", 22 16.7N, 97 31.0W, Q W, 84ft., 10M, Yellow rectangular metal platform.
ARENQUE "A", 22 14.0N, 97 30.1W, Q W, 84ft., 10M, Yellow rectangular metal platform.
BARRA DE CAZONES, 20 45.0N, 97 12.0W, Fl W 5s, 86ft., 14M, Concrete tower.
PUNTA CAZONES, 20 46.0N, 97 12.0W, Fl (2) 10s, 49ft., 9M, Metal framework tower.

TUXPAN

N BREAKWATER, 20 58.4N, 97 18.2W, Fl R 5s, 27ft., 8M, Metal column.
S BREAKWATER, 20 58.1N, 97 18.1W, Fl G 5s, 27ft., 8M, Metal column.
N SIDE, mouth of river, 20 58.0N, 97 19.0W, Fl (4) W 7s, 79ft., 14M, White truncated conical masonry tower and hut.
RANGE, (Front Light) 20 57.3N, 97 20.6W, Fl W 3s, 38ft., 16M, White metal tower. **(Rear Light)** 95 meters 248° from front, Iso W 2s, 55ft., 16M, White metal tower.
S SIDE RANGE, (Front Light) 20 57.6N, 97 19.2W, Fl W 3s, 30ft., 20M, Metal framework tower. **(Rear Light)** 270 meters 238° from front, Iso W 2s, 75ft., 20M, Metal framework tower.
N SIDE RANGE 1, (Front Light) 20 57.5N, 97 20.1W, Fl W 3s, 30ft., 20M, Metal framework tower. **(Rear Light)** 250 meters 255° from front, Iso W 2s, 56ft., 16M, Metal framework tower.

RÍO TUXPAN

20 58N, 97 19W

Pilotage: The entrance has a maximum depth of 16 feet over the bar, and is fronted by breakwaters which extend 1/4 mile offshore from the entrance points. It was reported in 1991 the breakwaters were being lengthened, and the harbor was to be dredged to 36 feet to

accommodate a new container terminal. Within the bar depths increase considerably. The least depth, as far as the town of Tuxpan, is under 9 feet. Vessels drawing under 7 feet can proceed up to 36 miles above the entrance.

From seaward several tall stacks and oil tanks on the banks of the river are conspicuous. The navigation lights at the river entrance are hard to identify, and are often confused with the numerous fishing vessels found in the vicinity.

Tuxpan is located about 5 miles above the entrance to the river, and is a **Port of Entry.**

Between the Río Tuxpan and **Cabo Rojo** the low coast extends northwest for about 19 miles, then north-northeast an additional 18 miles forming a bight called **Puerto Lobos**. This bight provides some protection from the northers which blow with considerable strength during the winter.

ARRECIFE TUXPAN, BAJO CENTRO, 21 01.1N, 97 12.6W, Fl (2) W 10s, 36ft., 11M, Truncated pyramidal concrete tower, Reported to lie 1.1 miles further NE (1981), RACON X (– · · –).
ARRECIFE TANGUIJO, 21 07.0N, 97 17.0W, Fl (3) W 12s, 36ft., 11M, Concrete truncated pyramidal tower.

BAJO DE TUXPAN
21 01N, 97 12W

Pilotage: This small steep-to reef has a low cay on it, in a position about 6 miles east-northeast of the Río de Tuxpan.

Bajo de Enmedio is a small reef lying about 3 miles northwest of Bajo de Tuxpan.

Bajo de Tanguijo lies about 7 miles northwest of Bajo de Tuxpan. It is a small, steep-to drying reef.

ARRECIFE MEDIO, 21 31.0N, 97 14.0W, Fl R 3s, 33ft., 8M, Silver metal tower.
ARRECIFE LA BLANQUILLA, 21 32.3N, 97 16.5W, Fl W 6s, 33ft., 11M, Concrete tower.
ISLA DE LOBOS, 21 27.2N, 97 13.7W, Fl W 5s, 105ft., 20M, Cylindrical concrete tower, RACON O (– – –), 25M.
LOBOS OUTER LIGHT OFF SW SHORE OF ISLA DE LOBOS, 21 27.2N, 97 13.5W, Fl R 3s, 13ft., 8M, Cylindrical concrete tower, Visible 250°– 090°.

ISLA LOBOS
21 28N, 97 13W

Pilotage: This small islet is about 30 feet high to the tops of the trees. It lies 9 miles southeast of **Cabo Rojo**. A reef extends about 1 mile north from the islet.

Arrecife Medio is a small steep-to breaking reef, lying about 2 1/2 miles north-northwest of Isla Lobos.

BAJO DE LA BLANQUILLA
21 32N, 97 16W

Pilotage: This is a breaking reef with a drying sandbank on it. It lies 6 miles northwest of Isla Lobos. A disused light structure stands on the reef. The passage between here and Cabo Rojo is of doubtful safety as the soundings are irregular.

CABO ROJO

21 33N, 97 20W

Pilotage: This blunt headland is composed of sand hills about 35 feet high. It is bordered by a reef which extends about 1 3/4 miles east from it.

The coast trends northwest for 49 miles to the **Río Panuco**, then about 160 miles north and an additional 67 miles north-northeast to the **Río Grande.** In general, the coast is composed of sand dunes and wooded hummocks. Mountain ranges with conspicuous peaks lie farther inland along the south part of this coast. Several extensive lagoons, separated from the coast by narrow strips of land, lie along this section. Several rivers discharge into the gulf.

Between Cabo Rojo and the Río Panuco the coast is bordered by a narrow strip of land, a few hundred feet to 5 miles wide, fronting the **Laguna de Tamiahua**. **Canal del Chijol** crosses this lagoon and is frequented by small craft going from Tuxpan to Tampico. The sand hills backing the coast about 4 miles north of Cabo Rojo are 70 feet high, and rise to heights of 348 feet about 18 miles farther north. The coast then becomes very low as far north as the Río Panuco.

An 8 foot shoal lies 5 miles south-southeast of the entrance to **Tampico**.

Winds: The winds are east-southeast from August to April, and east from April to June. During the summer the land breezes blow from midnight to 0900, and then yield to the sea breezes as far north as 26°, where the mountain ranges terminate.

Currents: During the winter the current sets north and in the opposite direction during the summer. About 15 to 20 miles offshore the current generally sets north at a rate of about 1 knot.

BAJOS DE BURROS, 21 42.5N, 97 36.2W, Fl (2) W 10s, 19ft., 5M, Fiberglass tower, white and orange bands.
LA LAJA, 21 42.1N, 97 41.4W, Fl R 6s, 19ft., 8M, White metal tower.
MOCTEZUMA, 21 44.2N, 97 45.5W, Fl R 5s, 19ft., 11M, White concrete tower.
PUNTA MORALES, 21 46.5N, 97 37.2W, Fl W 5s, 19ft., 11M, White concrete tower.
PUNTA MANGLES, 21 54.6N, 97 41.7W, Fl W 5s, 19ft., 11M, White concrete tower.

TAMPICO

TAMPICO, N point of river entrance, 21 15.8N, 97 47.7W, Fl (3) W 6s, 141ft., 24 Aluminum colored tower, Fl R and Fl G lights mark the bridge at Tamos, above Tampico.
ENTRANGE RANGE, (Front Light) N bank of river, 22 15.5N, 97 48.0W, Fl W 3s, 69ft., 24M, Iron framework tower, red and white square daymark. **(Rear Light)** 420 yards 256°30' from front, Iso W 2s, 119ft., 24M, Iron framework tower, red and white square daymark, 92.
HEAD OF N BREAKWATER, ESCOLLERA NORTE, 22 16.1N, 97 46.3W, Fl R 5s, 39ft., 9M, White square tower, Visible 188°– 322°.
HEAD OF S BREAKWATER, ESCOLLERA SUR, 22 15.7N, 97 46.3W, Fl G 5s, 33ft., 9M, Concrete tower, Visible 188°– 322°.
ROOT OF S BREAKWATER DIRECTIONAL LIGHT, 22 15.6n, 97 47.2W, Dir Fl W 3s, 33ft., 11M, White concrete tower.
CANAL DE CHIJOL, on W bank, 22 14.8N, 97 49.0W, Fl W 3s, 29ft., 10M, Concrete tower.
ARBOL GRANDE, on E bank, 22 14.0N, 97 50.0W, Fl W 3s, 23ft., 10M, Concrete tower.
COLONIA DEL GOLFO, on E bank, 22 13.8N, 97 50.2W, Fl W 3s, 33ft., 10M, Concrete tower.
COLONIA DE LA ISLETA, on E bank, 22 12.9N, 97 50.0W, Fl W 3s, 23ft., 10M, Concrete tower.
ISLA PEREZ, on E bank, 22 12.5N, 97 50.2W, Fl W 3s, 30ft., 10M, Concrete tower.
CANAL DE PUEBLO VIEJO RANGE, (Front Light) 22 12.5N, 07 50.7W, Fl W 3s, 22ft., 11M,

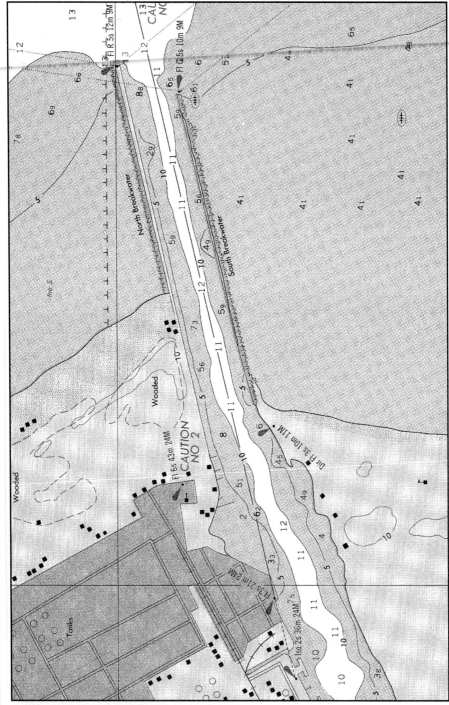

13

13

13

13 Fl R 5s 12m 9M

CAL
NO

Fl R 5s 12m 9M

3

12

13

12

Fl G 5s 10m 9M

65

12

66

11

65

6

5

5

4

41

88

65

6

6

69

59

41

78

41

41

5

29

41

41

North Breakwater

10

6

41

41

5

59

11

10

59

49

South Breakwater

12

10

59

me S

73

59

11

10

56

5

Wooded

11

Wooded

8

6

Dir Fl 3s 10m 11M

10

Fl 6s 13m 24M

CAUTION
NO 2

5

45

51

Wooded

2

62

49

12

4

10

Tanks

33

11

5

5

Iso 2s 36m 24M

75

11

Fl 3s 21m 24M

11

10

10

10

38

5

Tampico Entrance Channel, Soundings in Meters

White concrete tower. **(Rear Light)** 660 meters 110°30′ from front, Fl W 4s, 69ft., 13M, Concrete tower.
RIHL FIELD AVIATION LIGHT, 22 12.0N, 97 49.0W, Al Fl W G 5s, 78ft., Beacon.

TAMPICO

22 16N, 97 50W

Pilotage: Tampico is on the lower reaches of the **Río Panuco.** This is an important petroleum port. A 100 yard wide channel leads across the bar and mid-way between the breakwaters. The bar has a least depth of about 30 feet. During the rainy season, depths decrease due to heavy silting. The harbor can be identified from offshore by the numerous chimneys and tanks of the oil refineries. The hills to the south of the river are grass covered and higher than those to the north, which are composed of whitish-gray sand. On closer approach Tampico lighthouse, on the north side of the river entrance, and the light structures on the breakwater heads, will be sighted.

CAUTION: The smoke from the refineries may make Tampico light appear red when the wind is from the southwest and the humidity is high.

The entrance range is on a bearing of 257°. The current sets north across the entrance at times, and vessels usually enter at a good speed to offset its effect.

Several offshore oil platforms lie about 18 miles in a generally easterly direction from the harbor. Submarine pipelines run from these platforms to the shore. Anchorage in the vicinity of these platforms and pipelines is prohibited.

Winds: Hot southwest winds blow in the months of March and April from about 1100, sometimes lasting until 1500 or 1600, before switching back to the east-southeast. Northers are frequent during the winter season, and usually last from 8 to 24 hours. At such times the port is closed.
Tides and Currents: The tides are irregular, and in the vicinity of the bar are greatly affected by the prevailing winds and the rate of discharge of the Río Panuco. The maximum rise above MLW is about 2 feet. When the river is in flood currents attain a velocity of 8 1/2 knots between the seawalls, and a velocity of 6 knots in the upper reaches. Normally the current in the river flows at a rate of 3 knots.

ALTAMIRA

ALTAMIRA, 22 29.5N, 97 51.7W, Fl W 6s, 138ft., 14M, Concrete octagonal tower.
ESCOLLERA SUR, 22 28.9N, 97 50.9W, Fl G 5s, 36ft., 9M, Silver truncated tower.
ESCOLLERA NORTE, 22 29.5N, 97 51.2W, Fl R 5s, 42ft., 9M, Truncated tower.
RANGE, (Front Light) 22 29.2N, 97 55.5W, Fl W 3s, 39ft., 11M, White framework. **(Rear Light)** 229 meters 270° from front, Fl W 3r, 59ft., 11M, White framework tower.
ESPIGON SUR, 22 29.1N, 97 51.4W, Fl G 5s, 36ft., 9M, Silver truncated tower.
ESPIGON NORTE, 22 29.3N, 97 51.4W, Fl R 5s, 36ft., 9M, Silver truncated tower.
CANAL DE NAVIGATION, NO 3, 22 28.7N, 97 53.1W, Fl G 3s, 42ft., 7M, Aluminum tower.
NO 1, 22 29.7N, 97 52.7W, Fl G 3s, 33ft., 7M, Aluminum tower.
NO 6, 22 28.7N, 97 53.4W, Fl R 3s, 41ft., 7M, Aluminum tower.
NO 4, 22 29.4N, 97 52.8W, Fl R 3s, 28ft., 7M, Metal tower.
NO 2, 22 29.5N, 97 52.1W, Fl R 3s, 33ft., 7M, Metal tower.

ALTAMIRA

22 25N, 97 55W

Pilotage: This port was reported to be under construction in 1985. It will be a general cargo terminal when complete.

TAMPICO TO RÍO SAN FERNANDO

Pilotage: Between Tampico and **Barra de Chavarria** and **Barra de La Trinidad,** two shallow lagoon entrances about 23 and 30 miles north, the coast is backed by wooded hills about 200 feet high. Shallow water lies up to 1 1/2 miles offshore between the entrances to the lagoons.

An eighteen foot patch was reported to lie about 9 miles north of Tampico entrance in 1912. An obstruction was reported in 1928 about 17 miles north of Tampico entrance.

Cerro Metate (22° 47′N, 97° 58′W) is a flat topped hill 866 feet high, located about 32 miles north-northwest of Tampico.

Between Barra de La Trinidad and **Barra del Torda,** a shallow lagoon entrance about 18

Chapter 2

miles north, the coast is low and sandy. Some rocks lie up to 2 miles offshore in places.

Between Barra del Torda and **Río Indios Morales** (23° 24'N, 97° 46'W), about 28 miles to the north, the coast is backed by wooded hummocks 70 feet high. From abreast **Punta Jerez** a range of hills, **Sierra de San Jose de Las Rusias**, extends about 52 miles north at a distance of from 7 to 12 miles inland. A conspicuous sugarloaf peak stands about 18 miles southwest of the Río Indios Morales.

The coast between the Río Indios Morales and the **Río Soto La Marina**, about 21 miles to the north, is bordered by a narrow strip of land that fronts a lagoon.

Between the Río Soto La Marina and **Boquillas Ceradas** (25° 02'N, 97° 30'W), about 77 miles to the north, and the **Río Fernando**, about 25 miles farther north-northeast, the coast is bordered by a strip of land 1 to 5 miles wide fronting **Laguna de La Madre**. The high hills in the inteRíor terminate about 24 miles north of the Río Soto de La Marina.

A shoal, about 3 miles in extent with a least depth of 15 feet, lies about 25 miles north of the Río Soto La Marina and 2 miles offshore.

Boquillas Ceradas are four nearly closed entrances to Laguna de La Madre.

The Río Fernando (25° 58'N, 97° 09'W), with a depth of 3 feet over the bar, drains a lagoon in the interior.

A shoal, 3 miles long with a least depth of 10 feet, lies with its south end 5 miles north of the Río San Fernando and about 3 miles offshore.

PUNTA JEREZ, on low sandy beach, 22 53.5N, 97 46.1W, Fl W 6s, 78ft., 24M, Concrete tower, white dwelling, Visible 176°– 014°.

BARRA CARRIZO, 23 21.5N, 97 46.0W, Fl (2) W 10s, 30ft., 11M, Metal tower.

LA PESA RANGE, (Front Light) 23 46.7N, 97 45.1W, Fl W 3s, 28ft., 11M, Aluminum colored metal tower. **(Rear Light)** Iso W 2s, 56ft., 11M, Aluminum colored metal tower.

LA CARBONERA, 23 37.6N, 97 43.0W, Fl W 6s, 38ft., 14M, concrete tower, red and white stripes.

N BREAKWATER, 23 46.2N, 97 43.9W, Fl R 5s, 22ft., 9M, Tubular metal tower.

S BREAKWATER, 23 46.0N, 97 44.1W, Fl G 5s, 25ft., 9M, Metal tower.

LA PESCA, 23 46.5N, 97 44.2W, Fl (4) W 16s, 60ft., 24M, Concrete tower.

SOTO LA MARINA, 23 46.5N, 97 47.5W, Fl W 2s, 52ft., 13M, Metal tower, Radar reflector.

CANAL DE CHAVEZ, 25 52.0N, 97 10.1W, Fl W 6s, 38ft., 14M, Concrete tower.

EL MEZQUITAL, 25 17.0N, 97 23.0W, Fl (3) W 10s, 89ft., 24M, White concrete tower and hut.

RÍO BRAVO, 25 57.1N, 97 09.0W, Fl W 5.5s, 59ft., 24M, Concrete tower and hut.

RÍO GRANDE

25 58N, 97 09W

Pilotage: This river is located about 36 miles north of the Río San Fernando. It forms the boundary with the United States. By international agreement the river is closed to navigation.

TAMPICO, MEXICO

HIGH & LOW WATER 1994 22°13'N 97°51'W

CENTRAL STANDARD TIME (GMT - 6H)

JANUARY

Day	Time	ft	Day	Time	ft
1 Sa	0203 / 1029 / 1830	0.8 / -0.4 / 1.0	16 Su	0429 / 1107 / 1801	0.6 / 0.1 / 0.7
2 Su	0028 / 0656 / 1112 / 1841	0.6 / 0.7 / -0.1 / 0.9	17 M	0027 / 0606 / 1132 / 1800	0.2 / 0.5 / 0.3 / 0.7
3 M	0108 / 0600 / 1159 / 1849	0.3 / 0.6 / 0.2 / 0.8	18 Tu	0117 / 0826 / 1140 / 1754	0.1 / 0.5 / 0.5 / 0.7
4 Tu	0154 / 0838 / 1251 / 1851	0.1 / 0.6 / 0.5 / 0.8	19 W	0209 / 1744	0.1 / 0.8
5 W	0245 / 1128 / 1408 / 1845	-0.2 / 0.8 / 0.7 / 0.9	20 Th	0303 / 1723	-0.2 / 0.8
6 Th	0338 / 1318 / 1706	-0.4 / 1.0 / 0.9	21 F	0355 / 1532	-0.3 / 0.9
7 F	0433 / 1417	-0.6 / 1.1	22 Sa	0444 / 1507	-0.4 / 1.0
8 Sa	0527 / 1504	-0.8 / 1.2	23 Su	0530 / 1518	-0.5 / 1.0
9 Su	0619 / 1545	-0.9 / 1.3	24 M	0613 / 1535	-0.6 / 1.1
10 M	0709 / 1621	-0.9 / 1.2	25 Tu	0655 / 1555	-0.6 / 1.1
11 Tu	0757 / 1652 / 2142 / 2324	-0.8 / 1.1 / 0.9 / 1.0	26 W	0736 / 1615 / 2108 / 2332	-0.7 / 1.1 / 0.8 / 0.9
12 W	0841 / 1717 / 2157	-0.7 / 1.0 / 0.8	27 Th	0817 / 1633 / 2127	-0.6 / 1.0 / 0.7
13 Th	0046 / 0923 / 1736 / 2225	0.9 / -0.6 / 0.9 / 0.7	28 F	0054 / 0858 / 1648 / 2156	0.9 / -0.5 / 1.0 / 0.6
14 F	0158 / 1001 / 1750 / 2301	0.8 / -0.4 / 0.8 / 0.5	29 Sa	0213 / 0941 / 1700 / 2231	0.8 / -0.4 / 0.9 / 0.4
15 Sa	0310 / 1036 / 1758 / 2342	0.7 / -0.2 / 0.8 / 0.4	30 Su	0337 / 1024 / 1708 / 2314	0.8 / -0.1 / 0.8 / 0.2
			31 M	0512 / 1108 / 1713	0.7 / 0.2 / 0.8

FEBRUARY

Day	Time	ft	Day	Time	ft
1 Tu	0003 / 0706 / 1154 / 1741	-0.1 / 0.7 / 0.5 / 0.8	16 W	0814 / 1104 / 1613	0.7 / 0.7 / 0.8
2 W	0059 / 0934 / 1245 / 1708	-0.3 / 0.8 / 0.8 / 0.9	17 Th	0050 / 1607	-0.0 / 0.9
3 Th	0202 / 1220 / 1435 / 1631	-0.4 / 1.0 / 1.0 / 1.0	18 F	0150 / 1548	-0.1 / 0.9
4 F	0308 / 1334	-0.5 / 1.1	19 Sa	0255 / 1430	-0.2 / 1.0
5 Sa	0414 / 1416	-0.6 / 1.2	20 Su	0357 / 1414	-0.2 / 1.0
6 Su	0516 / 1451	-0.7 / 1.2	21 M	0454 / 1422	-0.3 / 1.1
7 M	0613 / 1519 / 2025	-0.7 / 1.1 / 1.0	22 Tu	0545 / 1436 / 1939 / 2133	-0.4 / 1.1 / 0.9 / 0.9
8 Tu	0705 / 1542 / 2013 / 2319	-0.6 / 1.1 / 0.9 / 0.8	23 W	0633 / 1451 / 1939 / 2318	-0.4 / 1.1 / 0.8 / 0.9
9 W	0751 / 1600 / 2031	-0.5 / 1.0 / 0.7	24 Th	0720 / 1505 / 2000	-0.4 / 1.0 / 0.7
10 Th	0037 / 0833 / 1613 / 2057	0.9 / -0.4 / 0.9 / 0.6	25 F	0040 / 0807 / 1517 / 2028	1.0 / -0.2 / 0.9 / 0.5
11 F	0145 / 0911 / 1621 / 2126	0.9 / -0.2 / 0.8 / 0.5	26 Sa	0157 / 0853 / 1526 / 2102	1.0 / -0.1 / 0.9 / 0.3
12 Sa	0248 / 0946 / 1625 / 2159	0.8 / 0.0 / 0.7 / 0.3	27 Su	0312 / 0940 / 1532 / 2142	1.0 / 0.2 / 0.8 / 0.1
13 Su	0351 / 1017 / 1625 / 2234	0.8 / 0.2 / 0.7 / 0.2	28 M	0432 / 1028 / 1536 / 2228	1.0 / 0.4 / 0.8 / -0.1
14 M	0459 / 1044 / 1622 / 2312	0.7 / 0.4 / 0.7 / 0.1			
15 Tu	0619 / 1103 / 1618 / 2357	0.7 / 0.5 / 0.8 / 0.0			

MARCH

Day	Time	ft	Day	Time	ft
1 Tu	0600 / 1118 / 1536 / 2320	1.1 / 0.7 / 0.9 / -0.3	16 W	0627 / 1100 / 1433 / 2257	1.0 / 0.8 / 0.9 / 0.0
2 W	0744 / 1215 / 1531	1.1 / 0.9 / 1.0	17 Th	0757 / 1118 / 1430 / 2346	1.0 / 0.9 / 1.0 / -0.0
3 Th	0019 / 0952	-0.4 / 1.1	18 F	1413	1.0
4 F	0126 / 1150	-0.4 / 1.2	19 Sa	0044 / 1215	-0.0 / 1.1
5 Sa	0240 / 1253	-0.4 / 1.2	20 Su	0151 / 1225	-0.1 / 1.1
6 Su	0354 / 1331	-0.4 / 1.2	21 M	0302 / 1242	-0.1 / 1.1
7 M	0503 / 1357 / 1906 / 2105	-0.3 / 1.1 / 1.0 / 1.0	22 Tu	0410 / 1258 / 1849 / 2021	-0.1 / 1.1 / 0.9 / 0.9
8 Tu	0603 / 1416 / 1904 / 2303	-0.3 / 1.1 / 0.8 / 1.0	23 W	0512 / 1313 / 1831 / 2241	-0.1 / 1.1 / 0.8 / 1.0
9 W	0656 / 1431 / 1923	-0.1 / 1.0 / 0.7	24 Th	0610 / 1326 / 1848	-0.0 / 1.0 / 0.6
10 Th	0025 / 0743 / 1440 / 1948	1.0 / 0.0 / 0.9 / 0.5	25 F	0012 / 0706 / 1336 / 1915	1.0 / 0.1 / 1.0 / 0.4
11 F	0131 / 0825 / 1446 / 2014	1.0 / 0.2 / 0.8 / 0.4	26 Sa	0130 / 0801 / 1344 / 1948	1.1 / 0.3 / 0.9 / 0.1
12 Sa	0231 / 0904 / 1447 / 2042	1.0 / 0.3 / 0.8 / 0.3	27 Su	0243 / 0855 / 1349 / 2027	1.2 / 0.5 / 0.9 / -0.1
13 Su	0327 / 0938 / 1445 / 2111	1.0 / 0.5 / 0.8 / 0.2	28 M	0355 / 0951 / 1352 / 2110	1.3 / 0.7 / 0.9 / -0.3
14 M	0422 / 1010 / 1441 / 2142	1.0 / 0.6 / 0.8 / 0.1	29 Tu	0509 / 1049 / 1353 / 2157	1.4 / 0.9 / 1.0 / -0.4
15 Tu	0520 / 1037 / 1436 / 2217	1.0 / 0.7 / 0.9 / 0.0	30 W	0629 / 1158 / 1344 / 2250	1.4 / 1.1 / 1.1 / -0.5
			31 Th	0758 / 2349	1.4 / -0.4

APRIL

Day	Time	ft	Day	Time	ft
1 F	0933	1.3	16 Sa	0857 / 2355	1.2 / -0.1
2 Sa	0056 / 1052	-0.3 / 1.3	17 Su	0957	1.2
3 Su	0209 / 1142	-0.2 / 1.2	18 M	0056 / 1036	-0.1 / 1.2
4 M	0326 / 1213 / 1810 / 2002	-0.1 / 1.1 / 0.9 / 0.9	19 Tu	0205 / 1103	-0.0 / 1.1
5 Tu	0440 / 1234 / 1803 / 2231	0.0 / 1.0 / 0.7 / 0.9	20 W	0321 / 1731 / 2143	0.1 / 0.7 / 0.8
6 W	0545 / 1248 / 1822	0.2 / 1.0 / 0.6	21 Th	0436 / 1136 / 1742 / 2335	0.2 / 1.0 / 0.4 / 0.9
7 Th	0004 / 0643 / 1257 / 1847	1.0 / 0.3 / 0.9 / 0.4	22 F	0548 / 1147 / 1808	0.4 / 0.9 / 0.2
8 F	0115 / 0735 / 1301 / 1914	1.0 / 0.4 / 0.8 / 0.2	23 Sa	0100 / 0658 / 1154 / 1842	1.1 / 0.5 / 0.9 / -0.1
9 Sa	0215 / 0823 / 1301 / 1941	1.1 / 0.6 / 0.8 / 0.1	24 Su	0213 / 0806 / 1158 / 1920	1.3 / 0.7 / 0.9 / -0.3
10 Su	0308 / 0907 / 1257 / 2008	1.1 / 0.7 / 0.8 / 0.0	25 M	0320 / 0914 / 1200 / 2003	1.4 / 0.9 / 0.9 / -0.5
11 M	0358 / 0947 / 1250 / 2036	1.2 / 0.8 / 0.9 / -0.1	26 Tu	0426 / 1028 / 1153 / 2049	1.5 / 1.0 / 1.0 / -0.7
12 Tu	0447 / 1026 / 1242 / 2106	1.2 / 0.9 / 0.9 / -0.1	27 W	0533 / 2138	1.5 / -0.7
13 W	0537 / 1106 / 1231 / 2140	1.2 / 1.0 / 1.0 / -0.1	28 Th	0641 / 2230	1.5 / -0.6
14 Th	0635 / 2218	1.2 / -0.2	29 F	0750 / 2326	1.4 / -0.5
15 F	0743 / 2303	1.2 / -0.1	30 Sa	0853	1.3

TIME MERIDIAN 90°W

0000h is midnight, 1200h is noon.

Heights in feet are referred to the chart datum of sounding.

TAMPICO, MEXICO

HIGH & LOW WATER 1994 22°13′N 97°51′W

CENTRAL STANDARD TIME (GMT - 6H)

MAY

Day	Time	ft	Time	ft	Time	ft	Time	ft
1 Su	0000	0.5	0942	1.2				
2 M	0132	-0.1	1017	1.1				
3 Tu	0244	0.1	1039	1.0	1657	0.6	2126	0.7
4 W	0401	0.3	1054	0.9	1719	0.4	2328	0.8
5 Th	0517	0.5	1103	0.8	1747	0.2		
6 F	0053	0.9	0628	0.6	1107	0.8	1815	0.0
7 Sa	0158	1.0	0735	0.7	1104	0.8	1844	-0.1
8 Su	0252	1.1	0841	0.8	1052	0.8	1913	-0.2
9 M	0339	1.2	1942	-0.3				
10 Tu	0423	1.2	2012	-0.3				
11 W	0506	1.2	2044	-0.4				
12 Th	0549	1.2	2117	-0.4				
13 F	0635	1.2	2155	-0.4				
14 Sa	0720	1.2	2235	-0.3				
15 Su	0803	1.2	2321	-0.3				
16 M	0839	1.1						
17 Tu	0014	-0.1	0907	1.1				
18 W	0116	0.0	0928	1.0	1623	0.5	2010	0.6
19 Th	0231	0.2	0942	0.9	1633	0.3	2247	0.7
20 F	0400	0.5	0952	0.9	1701	0.0		
21 Sa	0029	0.9	0534	0.7	0957	0.9	1737	-0.3
22 Su	0145	1.2	0708	0.8	0957	0.9	1818	-0.5
23 M	0251	1.3	0855	1.0	1902	-0.7		
24 Tu	0351	1.5	1948	-0.9				
25 W	0448	1.5	2036	-0.9				
26 Th	0543	1.5	2125	-0.8				
27 F	0635	1.4	2215	-0.7				
28 Sa	0720	1.3	2305	-0.5				
29 Su	0758	1.2	2355	-0.2				
30 M	0826	1.0	1507	0.7	1616	0.7		
31 Tu	0048	0.0	0846	0.9	1526	0.5	1926	0.6

JUNE

Day	Time	ft	Time	ft	Time	ft	Time	ft
1 W	0147	0.3	0859	0.9	1600	0.3	2217	0.6
2 Th	0259	0.5	0905	0.8	1635	0.1		
3 F	0021	0.8	0432	0.7	0904	0.8	1710	-0.1
4 Sa	0140	0.9	0621	0.8	0851	0.8	1744	-0.2
5 Su	0236	1.0	1817	-0.3				
6 M	0321	1.1	1850	-0.4				
7 Tu	0401	1.2	1923	-0.4				
8 W	0437	1.2	1955	-0.5				
9 Th	0511	1.2	2029	-0.5				
10 F	0543	1.2	2103	-0.5				
11 Sa	0614	1.2	2139	-0.5				
12 Su	0642	1.2	2218	-0.4				
13 M	0707	1.2	2259	-0.2				
14 Tu	0728	1.1	2345	-0.0				
15 W	0744	1.0	1436	0.5	1828	0.6		
16 Th	0038	0.3	0754	1.0	1505	0.3	2130	0.7
17 F	0146	0.5	0800	0.9	1543	-0.0	2353	0.9
18 Sa	0329	0.8	0800	1.0	1627	-0.3		
19 Su	0123	1.1	0552	1.0	0743	1.0	1714	-0.5
20 M	0226	1.3	1802	-0.7				
21 Tu	0320	1.5	1851	-0.8				
22 W	0408	1.5	1940	-0.8				
23 Th	0453	1.5	2029	-0.8				
24 F	0532	1.4	2116	-0.7				
25 Sa	0605	1.3	1108	1.1	1252	1.1	2201	-0.5
26 Su	0630	1.2	1140	0.9	1416	1.0	2244	-0.2
27 M	0650	1.1	1224	0.8	1546	0.9	2325	0.0
28 Tu	0704	1.0	1314	0.6	1734	0.7		
29 W	0005	0.3	0712	1.0	1405	0.4	1959	0.7
30 Th	0042	0.6	0715	0.8	1455	0.3	2311	0.8

JULY

Day	Time	ft	Time	ft	Time	ft	Time	ft
1 F	0115	0.8	0710	1.0	1543	0.1		
2 Sa	0649	1.0	1628	-0.0				
3 Su	0236	1.1	1711	-0.1				
4 M	0307	1.2	1751	-0.2				
5 Tu	0336	1.3	1829	-0.3				
6 W	0402	1.3	1905	-0.3				
7 Th	0426	1.3	1941	-0.4				
8 F	0448	1.4	2016	-0.4				
9 Sa	0509	1.4	2051	-0.3				
10 Su	0528	1.3	1049	1.1	1238	1.1	2128	-0.2
11 M	0545	1.3	1113	1.0	1402	1.0	2206	-0.1
12 Tu	0559	1.2	1146	0.8	1536	1.0	2247	0.2
13 W	0610	1.2	1227	0.6	1727	0.9	2329	0.5
14 Th	0616	1.1	1313	0.4	1947	0.9		
15 F	0016	0.8	0619	1.1	1405	0.2	2241	1.1
16 Sa	0113	1.0	0614	1.2	1501	-0.1		
17 Su	0100	1.3	0336	1.3	0544	1.3	1559	-0.2
18 M	0200	1.5	1657	-0.4				
19 Tu	0246	1.6	1752	-0.5				
20 W	0325	1.6	1845	-0.5				
21 Th	0400	1.6	1936	-0.4				
22 F	0428	1.6	0905	1.4	1122	1.4	2022	-0.3
23 Sa	0451	1.5	0922	1.3	1246	1.4	2106	-0.1
24 Su	0509	1.4	0952	1.1	1401	1.3	2147	0.1
25 M	0521	1.3	1029	1.0	1514	1.2	2225	0.3
26 Tu	0530	1.2	1110	0.8	1632	1.1	2300	0.6
27 W	0534	1.2	1155	0.7	1803	1.1	2330	0.8
28 Th	0534	1.2	1245	0.6	2007	1.1	2347	1.0
29 F	0529	1.2	1340	0.5				
30 Sa	0517	1.3	1438	0.4				
31 Su	0446	1.4	1537	0.3				

AUGUST

Day	Time	ft	Time	ft	Time	ft	Time	ft
1 M	0318	1.4	1631	0.2				
2 Tu	0306	1.5	1720	0.2				
3 W	0315	1.5	1804	0.1				
4 Th	0327	1.6	1844	0.1				
5 F	0340	1.6	0835	1.4	1005	1.4	1923	0.1
6 Sa	0354	1.6	0838	1.4	1136	1.4	2002	0.1
7 Su	0407	1.6	0859	1.3	1251	1.4	2041	0.2
8 M	0419	1.5	0927	1.2	1405	1.4	2121	0.4
9 Tu	0430	1.5	1000	1.0	1522	1.4	2203	0.6
10 W	0437	1.4	1040	0.8	1648	1.4	2246	0.9
11 Th	0442	1.4	1126	0.6	1829	1.4	2331	1.1
12 F	0442	1.4	1219	0.4	2039	1.5		
13 Sa	0020	1.4	0437	1.5	1320	0.3	2323	1.6
14 Su	0144	1.6	0408	1.6	1427	0.2		
15 M	0103	1.8	1536	0.1				
16 Tu	0150	1.9	1643	0.1				
17 W	0225	1.9	1744	0.1				
18 Th	0252	1.8	0800	1.7	0901	1.7	1840	0.1
19 F	0314	1.8	0745	1.6	1108	1.7	1930	0.2
20 Sa	0330	1.7	1232	1.7	2016	0.4		
21	0342	1.6	0832	1.3	1343	1.6	2058	0.6
22 M	0350	1.5	0903	1.1	1449	1.6	2136	0.8
23 Tu	0356	1.5	0936	1.0	1553	1.6	2212	1.0
24 W	0357	1.5	1012	0.9	1700	1.6	2244	1.2
25 Th	0356	1.5	1051	0.8	1817	1.5	2311	1.4
26 F	0351	1.5	1135	0.7	2000	1.5	2323	1.5
27 Sa	0343	1.6	1226	0.7				
28 Su	0331	1.6	1326	0.6				
29 M	0304	1.7	1433	0.7				
30 Tu	0213	1.8	1539	0.6				
31 W	0202	1.8	1638	0.6				

TIME MERIDIAN 90°W
Heights in feet are referred to the chart datum of sounding.

0000h is midnight, 1200h is noon.

TAMPICO, MEXICO

HIGH & LOW WATER 1994 **22°13'N 97°51'W**

CENTRAL STANDARD TIME (GMT - 6H)

SEPTEMBER

Day	Time	ft		Day	Time	ft
1 Th	0206 / 1730	1.8 / 0.5		16 F	0142 / 0641 / 1046 / 1831	1.9 / 1.6 / 1.8 / 0.7
2 F	0214 / 0716 / 0935 / 1010	1.8 / 1.6 / 1.7 / 0.5		17 Sa	0156 / 0700 / 1215 / 1923	1.8 / 1.4 / 1.8 / 0.9
3 Sa	0224 / 0718 / 1116 / 1903	1.8 / 1.6 / 1.7 / 0.6		18 Su	0206 / 0727 / 1326 / 2010	1.7 / 1.3 / 1.8 / 1.0
4 Su	0235 / 0738 / 1235 / 1948	1.8 / 1.4 / 1.7 / 0.7		19 M	0213 / 0755 / 1429 / 2054	1.6 / 1.1 / 1.9 / 1.2
5 M	0245 / 0805 / 1348 / 2034	1.7 / 1.2 / 1.8 / 0.8		20 Tu	0216 / 0825 / 1527 / 2134	1.6 / 1.0 / 1.9 / 1.3
6 Tu	0254 / 0837 / 1459 / 2121	1.7 / 1.0 / 1.8 / 1.0		21 W	0215 / 0855 / 1623 / 2212	1.6 / 0.9 / 1.9 / 1.5
7 W	0300 / 0915 / 1613 / 2210	1.6 / 0.8 / 1.9 / 1.3		22 Th	0211 / 0927 / 1721 / 2247	1.6 / 0.8 / 1.9 / 1.6
8 Th	0303 / 0957 / 1734 / 2301	1.6 / 0.7 / 1.9 / 1.5		23 F	0204 / 1002 / 1825 / 2318	1.7 / 0.8 / 1.8 / 1.7
9 F	0303 / 1046 / 1907	1.7 / 0.5 / 1.9		24 Sa	0156 / 1041 / 1947 / 2348	1.7 / 0.7 / 1.8 / 1.8
10 Sa	0000 / 0257 / 1142 / 2100	1.7 / 1.6 / 0.4 / 2.0		25 Su	0144 / 1126 / 2149	1.8 / 0.8 / 1.8
11 Su	1246 / 2258	0.4 / 2.0		26 M	1220 / 2334	0.8 / 1.9
12 M	1357	0.4		27 Tu	1324 / 2358	0.8 / 1.9
13 Tu	0013 / 1513	2.1 / 0.4		28 W	1434	0.8
14 W	0056 / 1626	2.0 / 0.5		29 Th	0013 / 1543	1.9 / 0.8
15 Th	0123 / 0653 / 0827 / 1732	2.0 / 1.8 / 1.8 / 0.6		30 F	0027 / 0638 / 0808 / 1647	1.9 / 1.6 / 1.6 / 0.8

OCTOBER

Day	Time	ft		Day	Time	ft
1 Sa	0040 / 0614 / 1034 / 1747	1.8 / 1.5 / 1.7 / 0.9		16 Su	0020 / 0628 / 1308 / 1917	1.6 / 1.0 / 1.7 / 1.2
2 Su	0051 / 0629 / 1205 / 1811	1.8 / 1.3 / 1.8 / 1.0		17 M	0026 / 0657 / 1412 / 2012	1.5 / 0.8 / 1.8 / 1.5
3 M	0101 / 0655 / 1321 / 1940	1.7 / 1.1 / 1.9 / 1.1		18 Tu	0027 / 0726 / 1507 / 2104	1.5 / 0.7 / 1.9 / 1.4
4 Tu	0109 / 0727 / 1430 / 2036	1.7 / 0.9 / 2.0 / 1.3		19 W	0024 / 0755 / 1558 / 2156	1.5 / 0.6 / 1.9 / 1.5
5 W	0115 / 0803 / 1539 / 2134	1.6 / 0.6 / 2.1 / 1.5		20 Th	0013 / 0825 / 1648 / 2256	1.5 / 0.5 / 1.9 / 1.6
6 Th	0118 / 0844 / 1649 / 2236	1.7 / 0.4 / 2.1 / 1.7		21 F	0856 / 1738	0.5 / 1.8
7 F	0116 / 0930 / 1803 / 2355	1.7 / 0.3 / 2.2 / 1.8		22 Sa	0929 / 1832	0.5 / 1.8
8 Sa	0059 / 1021 / 1925	1.8 / 0.2 / 2.1		23 Su	1005 / 1932	0.5 / 1.8
9 Su	1117 / 2051	0.2 / 2.1		24 M	1046 / 2034	0.5 / 1.8
10 M	1219 / 2208	0.3 / 2.1		25 Tu	1132 / 2126	0.5 / 1.7
11 Tu	1329 / 2301	0.4 / 2.0		26 W	1226 / 2201	0.6 / 1.7
12 W	1444 / 2334	0.6 / 1.9		27 Th	1329 / 2225	0.6 / 1.7
13 Th	0607 / 1600 / 2356	1.6 / 0.7 / 1.8		28 F	1441 / 2244	0.7 / 1.6
14 F	0541 / 1007 / 1712	1.4 / 1.6 / 0.9		29 Sa	0515 / 0924 / 1558 / 2258	1.2 / 1.3 / 0.9 / 1.5
15 Sa	0010 / 0601 / 1151 / 1817	1.6 / 1.2 / 1.6 / 1.0		30 Su	0524 / 1123 / 1715 / 2309	1.0 / 1.4 / 1.0 / 1.5
				31 M	0548 / 1249 / 1831 / 2317	0.7 / 1.6 / 1.1 / 1.4

NOVEMBER

Day	Time	ft		Day	Time	ft
1 Tu	0621 / 1400 / 1944 / 2321	0.4 / 1.8 / 1.3 / 1.4		16 W	0702 / 1539	0.1 / 1.6
2 W	0630 / 1506 / 2058 / 2201	0.2 / 1.9 / 1.5 / 1.5		17 Th	0733 / 1624	0.0 / 1.6
3 Th	0740 / 1609	-0.0 / 2.0		18 F	0804 / 1706	0.0 / 1.6
4 F	0825 / 1713	-0.2 / 2.0		19 Sa	0836 / 1748	-0.0 / 1.6
5 Sa	0914 / 1817	-0.2 / 2.0		20 Su	0908 / 1828	-0.0 / 1.5
6 Su	1005 / 1921	-0.2 / 1.9		21 M	0943 / 1905	-0.0 / 1.5
7 M	1059 / 2019	-0.1 / 1.8		22 Tu	1019 / 1939	0.0 / 1.5
8 Tu	1156 / 2105	0.1 / 1.7		23 W	1059 / 2007	0.1 / 1.4
9 W	1257 / 2138	0.3 / 1.6		24 Th	1144 / 2031	0.2 / 1.4
10 Th	1405 / 2201	0.5 / 1.4		25 F	1237 / 2049	0.3 / 1.3
11 F	0429 / 0851 / 1520 / 2216	1.0 / 1.1 / 0.7 / 1.2		26 Sa	0401 / 0728 / 1343 / 2104	0.8 / 0.8 / 0.5 / 1.2
12 Sa	0455 / 1110 / 1641 / 2226	0.8 / 1.2 / 0.9 / 1.3		27 Su	0410 / 1023 / 2113	0.5 / 0.9 / 1.1
13 Su	0526 / 1201 / 1803 / 2230	0.6 / 1.3 / 1.1 / 1.2		28 M	0438 / 1214 / 1651 / 2118	0.3 / 1.1 / 1.0 / 1.1
14 M	0558 / 1354 / 1923 / 2227	0.4 / 1.5 / 1.2 / 1.2		29 Tu	0514 / 1332 / 1838 / 2116	-0.0 / 1.4 / 1.1 / 1.2
15 Tu	0630 / 1450 / 2048 / 2208	0.2 / 1.5 / 1.2 / 1.3		30 W	0555 / 1436	-0.3 / 1.5

DECEMBER

Day	Time	ft		Day	Time	ft
1 Th	0639 / 1534	-0.5 / 1.7		16 F	0717 / 1636	-0.4 / 1.2
2 F	0728 / 1630	-0.7 / 1.7		17 Sa	0750 / 1708	-0.4 / 1.2
3 Sa	0814 / 1723	-0.7 / 1.7		18 Su	0822 / 1736	-0.4 / 1.2
4 Su	0904 / 1811	-0.7 / 1.6		19 M	0854 / 1800	-0.4 / 1.2
5 M	0953 / 1854	-0.6 / 1.5		20 Tu	0926 / 1821	-0.4 / 1.1
6 Tu	1043 / 1927	-0.4 / 1.3		21 W	1000 / 1839	-0.3 / 1.1
7 W	1132 / 1953	-0.2 / 1.2		22 Th	1037 / 1856	-0.2 / 1.0
8 Th	0202 / 0419 / 1223 / 2011	0.9 / 0.9 / 0.1 / 1.1		23 F	0136 / 0312 / 1214 / 1909	0.7 / 0.7 / -0.0 / 1.0
9 F	0243 / 0655 / 1317 / 2024	0.6 / 0.7 / 0.4 / 1.0		24 Sa	0156 / 0548 / 1203 / 1919	0.5 / 0.6 / 0.2 / 0.9
10 Sa	0327 / 0945 / 1422 / 2031	0.4 / 0.8 / 0.6 / 1.0		25 Su	0231 / 0842 / 1258 / 1925	0.2 / 0.6 / 0.5 / 0.9
11 Su	0409 / 1206 / 1555 / 2031	0.2 / 0.9 / 0.8 / 0.9		26 M	0312 / 1127 / 1425 / 1924	-0.0 / 0.7 / 0.7 / 0.9
12 M	0449 / 1334 / 1802 / 2014	-0.0 / 1.0 / 0.9 / 0.9		27 Tu	0357 / 1308 / 1657 / 1906	-0.3 / 1.0 / 0.9 / 0.9
13 Tu	0528 / 1432	-0.2 / 1.1		28 W	0446 / 1410	-0.6 / 1.2
14 W	0606 / 1519	-0.3 / 1.2		29 Th	0536 / 1502	-0.8 / 1.3
15 Th	0642 / 1559	-0.4 / 1.2		30 F	0627 / 1549	-0.9 / 1.4
				31 Sa	0718 / 1632	-1.0 / 1.4

TIME MERIDIAN 90°W

0000h is midnight, 1200h is noon.

Heights in feet are referred to the chart datum of sounding.

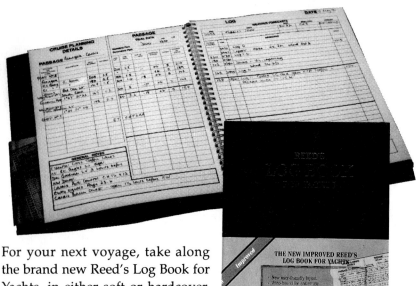

TIDE AND CURRENT DIFFERENCES

3

Chapter 3

TIDE DIFFERENCES

For more information on tides and currents in the Caribbean see the introduction to Chapter 2, and *Reed's Nautical Companion*.

The following list of tide differences for the Caribbean has been created exclusively for Reed's, to provide the best, and easiest to use tide information available. Reed's has made every effort to create the most complete and accurate tables possible. Unfortunately, hydrographic data for the Caribbean is sparse, and less accurate than information available in the United States or Europe; however, we feel this table represents the best tidal information ever printed for the Caribbean.

INSTRUCTIONS

The following table of tide differences is organized geographically. It begins with Bermuda, moves south to Florida and the Bahamas, then circles the entire Caribbean basin in a clockwise direction.

First, locate the harbor, or location, in the table you are interested in. Note the bold heading, centered on the page, referring you to the appropriate *tide reference station*. The main reference tables are located in Chapter 2, at the end of the various country sections. These thirteen tidal reference tables are included in Chapter 2: St. George's, Bermuda; Miami, Florida; Key West, Florida; Nassau, Bahamas; San Juan, Puerto Rico; Charlotte Amalie, U.S. Virgin Islands; Fort-de-France, Martinique; Port of Spain, Trinidad; Punta Gorda, Venezuela; Amuay, Venezuela; Malecon-Zapara, Venezuela; Cristóbal-Colón, Panama; and Tampico, Mexico.

The first two columns to the right of the harbor names list the approximate latitude and longitude of the location.

The next two columns give the *time differences* to be added, or subtracted, to the times taken from the reference table for the day of the year you are interested in. You'll note the first column gives the time difference for *high tide*, and the second column gives the difference for *low tide*. A + sign indicates you should add the time to the reference time. A - sign indicates you should subtract the time from the reference time. The time differences are given in *hours and minutes*.

The next two columns to the right give the *height differences* that should be applied to the *tide heights* taken from the reference table. **Note: These height differences are generally not simple additions or subtractions.** If the figures are in parentheses you must multiply the first value, with the asterisk (*) next to it, by the tide height from the reference table. Then take the second value in the parentheses, and add, or subtract it, to the first value derived.

If there are no parentheses around the entries, simply multiply when you see an asterisk (*), add when there is a plus sign, or subtract when there is a minus sign. The first difference applies to the high tide height from the reference table, and the second number applies to the low tide value from the reference table.

The heights derived using these tables must be applied to *chart soundings* to obtain *water depths*. In all cases, this tidal data is based on the *chart datum of soundings*, whatever it may be. In general, chart datums tend to be similar to the U.S. standard, which is Mean Lower Low Water. In other words, charted depths are usually near the lowest average depth to be expected, when meteorological conditions are normal. It should always be born in mind that local phenomena can greatly alter water depths. In some places, strong winds alter water depths — by as much as 3 feet along parts of the Mexican coast. Hurricanes may push storm surges of over 10 feet ahead of them. Harbors at the mouths of rivers often experience seasonal fluctuations in depths, based upon rainfall on the river's watershed. Unusual astronomical situations often create unusual tides — similar to the familiar effects of a full moon, or a new moon.

The last column gives the *spring tide range* in feet for the tide difference station. Keep in mind these values are averages, and the actual range may be strongly influenced by local winds, rainfall or other factors.

EXAMPLE

Let's put it all together with a real example. Look up the tide difference information for Grand Turk, in the Turks and Caicos (it's located after the Bahamas differences). Note these differences should be applied to the reference table for Nassau, Bahamas (found in Chapter 2).

The latitude and longitude of this tide position is 21° 26'N, 71° 09'W. The time difference for high tide is 15 minutes, which should be subtracted. The time difference for low tide happens to be the same — subtract 15 minutes from the reference time.

On March 1, 1994, in Nassau, the tide will be low at 0405, high at 1008, low at 1618 and high again at 2242. So, at Grand Turk the times will be: low 0350, high 0953, low at 1603 and high at 2228.

The height differences for Grand Turk are in parenthesis, so we must multiply the first

number by the height from the reference table, and subtract the second number in parenthesis from the result of the first multiplication. On March 1, 1994 we will get the following heights at Grand Turk: low about 0.44 feet, high about 2.48 feet, low about .31 feet and high about 2.68 feet.

You can see the tides are running a bit higher and a bit lower than average on March 1, 1994, by comparing the calculated tide range (2 to 2.3 feet) with the average tide range of 1.9 feet given in the last column of the tide difference table for Grand Turk.

TIDE DIFFERENCES

PLACE	POSITION		DIFFERENCES				RANGE
			Time		Height*		
	Latitude	Longitude	High	Low	High	Low	Spring
	North	West	h m	h m	ft	ft	ft

FLORIDA

Eastern Standard Time (GMT –5h)   Add one hour Daylight Saving April 3 – October 29

ON MIAMI, FLORIDA

PLACE	Latitude	Longitude	High	Low	High	Low	Spring
Ponce de Leon Inlet	29° 04'	80° 55'	+0 04	+0 21	*0.92	*0.94	2.7
Cape Canaveral	28° 26'	80° 34'	−0 43	−0 40	*1.39	*1.38	4.1
Indian River							
Palm Bay	28° 02'	80° 35'	+3 38	+4 20	*0.10	*0.10	0.2
Wabasso	27° 45'	80° 26'	+2 46	+3 20	*0.15	*0.19	0.5
Vero Beach	27° 38'	80° 22'	+3 19	+3 51	*0.34	*0.31	1.0
Fort Pierce	27° 27'	80° 19'	+1 06	+1 02	*0.48	*0.50	1.4
Jensen Beach	27° 14'	80° 13'	+2 38	+3 07	*0.41	*0.38	1.2
Sebastian Inlet	27° 52'	80° 27'	−0 26	−0 19	*0.81	*0.81	2.5
Vero Beach (ocean)	27° 40'	80° 22'	−0 33	−0 24	*1.35	*1.38	4.0
Fort Pierce Inlet, south jetty	27° 28'	80° 17'	−0 11	−0 13	*1.03	*1.06	3.1
St. Lucie River							
North Fork, St. Lucie River	27° 15'	80° 19'	+2 48	+3 30	*0.41	*0.38	1.2
Stuart, St. Lucie River	27° 12'	80° 16'	+2 35	+3 34	*0.37	*0.38	1.1
South Fork, St. Lucie River	27° 10'	80° 15'	+2 52	+3 35	*0.37	*0.38	1.1
Sewall Point, St. Lucie Ri	27° 10'	80° 11'	+1 33	+2 12	*0.37	*0.38	1.1
Seminole Shores	27° 11'	80° 10'	−0 32	−0 13	*1.19	*1.19	3.6
Great Pocket	27° 09'	80° 10'	+1 16	+1 52	*0.44	*0.44	1.3
Gomez, South Jupiter Narrows	27° 06'	80° 08'	+1 54	+2 42	*0.52	*0.50	1.6
Hobe Sound – State Park	27° 02'	80° 06'	+1 44	+2 23	*0.63	*0.63	1.9
Conch Bar, Jupiter Sound	26° 59'	80° 06'	+1 17	+1 39	*0.67	*0.63	2.0
Jupiter Sound, south end	26° 57'	80° 05'	+0 44	+0 50	*0.78	*0.75	2.4
Jupiter Inlet	26° 57'	80° 04'	+0 13	+0 02	*1.00	*1.00	3.0
Loxahatchee River							
Tequesta	26° 57'	80° 06'	+1 16	+2 03	*0.71	*0.69	2.2
North Fork	26° 58'	80° 07'	+1 25	+2 00	*0.74	*0.75	2.3
Southwest Fork (spillway)	26° 56'	80° 09'	+1 13	+1 50	*0.79	*0.81	2.4
Northwest Fork	26° 59'	80° 08'	+1 32	+2 11	*0.78	*0.81	2.4
Southwest Fork	26° 57'	80° 07'	+1 13	+1 48	*0.74	*0.75	2.3
Jupiter, Lake Worth Creek	26° 56'	80° 05'	+0 55	+1 17	*0.81	*0.81	2.5
Donald Ross Bridge	26° 53'	80° 04'	+0 41	+0 55	*0.92	*0.94	2.8
North Palm Beach, Lake Worth	26° 50'	80° 03'	+0 03	+0 18	*1.15	*1.19	3.4
Port of Palm Beach, Lake Worth	26° 46'	80° 03'	−0 02	+0 13	*1.04	*1.00	3.1
Palm Beach (ocean)	26° 43'	80° 02'	−0 23	−0 17	*1.11	*1.12	3.3
West Palm Beach Canal	26° 39'	80° 03'	+1 06	+1 37	*1.00	*1.00	2.8
Lake Worth Pier (ocean)	26° 37'	80° 02'	−0 21	−0 16	*1.11	*1.12	3.3
Boynton Beach	26° 33'	80° 03'	+1 24	+2 10	*1.00	*1.00	2.8
Delray Beach	26° 28'	80° 04'	+1 43	+2 10	*1.00	*1.00	2.9
Yamato	26° 24'	80° 04'	+1 41	+2 00	*0.97	*0.94	2.8
Boca Raton	26° 21'	80° 05'	+0 45	+1 14	*0.85	*0.88	2.5
Deerfield Beach	26° 19'	80° 05'	+0 49	+1 08	*0.96	*0.94	2.9
Hillsboro Beach, Intracoastal	26° 16'	80° 05'	+0 24	+0 39	*1.11	*1.12	3.2
Hillsboro Inlet (inside)	26° 16'	80° 05'	+0 06	+0 07	*1.00	*1.00	2.9
Lauderdale–by–the–sea	26° 11'	80° 06'	−0 10	−0 07	*1.04	*1.06	3.1

*Heights of tides are found by multiplying heights from the Tide Tables by the *Ratio listed here. When parenthesis are used, multiply heights by the *Ratio and then add or subtract the second number as indicated.

PLACE	POSITION		DIFFERENCES				RANGE
			Time		Height*		
	Latitude	Longitude	High	Low	High	Low	Spring
	North	West	h m	h m	ft	ft	ft

FLORIDA (Continued)

Eastern Standard Time (GMT –5h)   Add one hour Daylight Saving April 3 – October 29

ON **MIAMI** , FLORIDA

Fort Lauderdale

Bahia Mar Yacht Club	26° 07'	80° 06'	+0 17	+0 39	*0.94	*0.94	2.8
Andrews Ave bridge, New Ri	26° 07'	80° 09'	+0 37	+0 57	*0.79	*0.81	2.4
Port Everglades	26° 06'	80° 07'	−0 08	−0 05	*1.05	*1.06	3.1
South Port Everglades	26° 05'	80° 07'	−0 02	+0 02	*1.00	*1.00	2.9
Hollywood Beach	26° 02'	80° 07'	+0 58	+1 09	*0.81	*0.81	2.4
Golden Beach	25° 58'	80° 08'	+1 34	+2 05	*0.81	*0.81	2.4
Sunny Isles, Biscayne Creek	25° 56'	80° 08'	+2 21	+2 28	*0.71	*0.69	2.2
North Miami Beach	25° 56'	80° 07'	−0 06	+0 01	*1.00	*1.00	3.0
Bakers Haulover Inlet (inside)	25° 54'	80° 08'	+1 15	+1 36	*0.78	*0.81	2.4
Indian Creek	25° 52'	80° 09'	+1 34	+1 51	*0.81	*0.81	2.5
Miami Beach	25° 46'	80° 08'	−0 02	+0 01	*1.00	*1.00	3.0
MIAMI HARBOR ENTRANCE	25° 46'	80° 08'	**Daily Predictions**				3.0

Biscayne Bay

Miami, 79th St. Causeway	25° 51'	80° 10'	+1 43	+2 14	*0.78	*0.75	2.4
Miami, Marina	25° 47'	80° 11'	+0 54	+1 18	*0.81	*0.81	2.4
Miami, Causeway (east end)	25° 46'	80° 09'	+1 17	+1 11	*0.78	*0.81	2.4
Dinner Key Marina	25° 44'	80° 14'	+1 17	+1 51	*0.74	*0.75	2.3

Florida Keys

Cape Florida (west),Key Biscayne	25° 40'	80° 10'	+0 47	+1 03	*0.67	*0.69	2.0
Cutler, Biscayne Bay	25° 37'	80° 18'	+1 23	+2 02	*0.78	*0.81	2.3
Soldier Key	25° 35'	80° 10'	+0 53	+1 20	*0.74	*0.75	2.3
Fowey Rocks	25° 35'	80° 06'	+0 01	+0 03	*0.97	*0.94	2.9
Ragged Keys, Biscayne Bay	25° 32'	80° 10'	+1 13	+1 45	*0.64	*0.64	1.9
Elliot Key (outside)	25° 29'	80° 11'	−0 04	+0 00	*0.93	*0.94	2.8
Elliot Key Harbor	25° 27'	80° 12'	+2 26	+3 25	*0.56	*0.56	1.6
Adams Key, Biscayne Bay	25° 24'	80° 14'	+2 48	+2 34	*0.52	*0.50	1.6
Christmas Point, Elliot Key	25° 24'	80° 14'	+0 35	+0 39	*0.72	*0.72	2.1
Turkey Point, Biscayne Bay	25° 26'	80° 20'	+2 33	+3 26	*0.60	*0.63	1.8
Totten Key	25° 23'	80° 15'	+2 48	+3 45	*0.49	*0.50	1.4
Ocean Reef Club, Key Largo	25° 18'	80° 17'	+0 11	+0 20	*0.93	*0.94	2.8
Garden Cove, Key Largo	25° 10'	80° 22'	+0 34	+1 10	*0.85	*0.88	2.6
Mosquito Bank	25° 04'	80° 24'	+0 22	+0 31	*0.85	*0.88	2.6
Molasses Reef	25° 01'	80° 23'	+0 14	+0 12	*0.88	*0.88	2.6
Pumpkin Key, Card Sound	25° 20'	80° 18'	+3 10	+3 16	*0.28	*0.28	0.8
Tavernier, Hawk Channel	25° 00'	80° 31'	+0 29	+0 28	*0.86	*0.50	2.6
Alligator Reef Light	24° 51'	80° 37'	+0 40	+0 34	*0.76	*0.76	2.3

ON **KEY WEST**, FLORIDA

Florida Bay

Channel Five, east	24° 50'	80° 46'	−0 55	−0 42	*0.81	*0.84	1.4
Channel Five, west	24° 50'	80° 47'	−0 59	−0 40	*0.90	*0.17	1.5
Long Key Channel, east	24° 48'	80° 51'	−1 10	−1 07	*0.84	*0.42	1.5
Long Key Channel, west	24° 48'	80° 53'	+5 58	+5 40	*0.79	*0.38	1.4

*Heights of tides are found by multiplying heights from the Tide Tables by the *Ratio listed here. When parenthesis are used, multiply heights by the *Ratio and then add or subtract the second number as indicated.

Chapter 3

TIDE DIFFERENCES

PLACE	POSITION		DIFFERENCES				RANGE
			Time		Height*		
	Latitude	Longitude	High	Low	High	Low	Spring
	North	West	h m	h m	ft	ft	ft

FLORIDA (Continued)

Eastern Standard Time (GMT −5h)   Add one hour Daylight Saving April 3 − October 29

ON KEY WEST, FLORIDA

PLACE	Latitude	Longitude	High	Low	High	Low	Spring
Duck Key	24° 46'	80° 55'	−1 11	−0 40	*0.96	*0.54	1.7
Grassy Key, north side	24° 46'	80° 56'	+5 38	+6 47	*0.72	*0.88	1.3
Grassy Key, south side	24° 45'	80° 58'	−1 07	−0 40	*1.20	*0.54	2.1
Flamingo	25° 09'	80° 56'	+5 35	+7 28	*1.48	*1.25	2.5
Fat Deer Key	24° 44'	81° 01'	+5 09	+6 26	*0.85	*0.79	1.5
Boot Key Harbor, Vaca Key	24° 42'	81° 06'	−1 04	−0 37	*1.12	*0.75	2.0
Sombrero Key	24° 38'	81° 07'	−1 01	−0 38	*1.17	*0.79	2.0
Knight Key Channel	24° 42'	81° 08'	+0 17	−0 18	*0.53	*0.53	1.0
Pigeon Key, south side	24° 42'	81° 09'	−1 09	−0 39	*0.81	*0.46	1.5
Pigeon Key, inside	24° 42'	81° 09'	−0 17	+0 18	*0.48	*0.58	1.0
Molasses Key	24° 41'	81° 12'	−0 50	−0 11	*0.77	*0.50	1.4
Money Key	24° 41'	81° 13'	+0 56	+1 42	*0.56	*0.46	1.1
West Bahía Honda Key	24° 47'	81° 16'	+3 59	+4 01	*0.97	*1.00	1.59
Horseshoe Keys, south end	24° 46'	81° 17'	+3 54	+3 09	*0.86	*1.00	1.36
Johnson Keys, south end	24° 45'	81° 18'	+3 36	+2 33	*0.72	*0.96	1.10
Johnson Keys, north end	24° 46'	81° 19'	+3 35	+4 22	*1.31	*1.38	2.12
Bahía Honda Key, Bahía Honda Ch	24° 39'	81° 17'	−0 45	−0 27	*0.86	*0.62	1.49
Spanish Harbor, Big Pine Key	24° 39'	81° 20'	−0 44	−0 03	*0.75	*0.42	1.34
Doctors Arm, Bogie Channel	24° 41'	81° 21'	+0 41	+1 47	*0.63	*0.71	1.00
Bogie Channel Bridge	24° 42'	81° 21'	+2 10	+2 11	*0.65	*0.83	1.00
No Name Key, E side, Bahía Hon.	24° 42'	81° 19'	+1 35	+1 33	*0.58	*0.83	0.88
Little Pine Key, South End	24° 43'	81° 18'	+1 07	+1 07	*0.56	*0.79	0.85
Porpoise Key, Big Spanish Chnl	24° 43'	81° 21'	+3 23	+2 29	*0.72	*1.00	1.10
Water Key, West End Big Spanish	24° 44'	81° 21'	+3 23	+2 37	*0.81	*1.04	1.25
Mayo Key, Big Spanish Channel	24° 44'	81° 22'	+3 35	+3 01	*0.92	*1.08	1.46
Little Pine Key, North End	24° 45'	81° 20'	+3 38	+3 28	*1.05	*1.21	1.66
Big Pine Key, Northeast Shore	24° 44'	81° 23'	+3 19	+2 30	*0.86	*1.08	1.35
Crawl Key, Big Spanish Channel	24° 45'	81° 22'	+3 34	+4 13	*1.33	*1.33	2.18
Big Pine Key, North End	24° 45'	81° 24'	+4 24	+5 56	*0.96	*0.83	1.61
Annette Key, North End, Big Span	24° 46'	81° 23'	+3 30	+4 33	*1.44	*1.29	2.40
Little Spanish Key, Spanish Bnks	24° 47'	81° 22'	+3 25	+4 30	*1.74	*1.62	2.88
Big Spanish Key	24° 47'	81° 25'	+3 19	+4 29	*1.97	*1.50	3.36
Munson Island, Newfound Hbr Ch	24° 37'	81° 24'	−0 40	−0 12	*0.98	*0.67	1.70
Ramrod Key, Newfound Harbor	24° 39'	81° 24'	−0 41	+0 05	*0.90	*0.50	1.60
Middle Torch Ky, Torch Ramrod C	24° 40'	81° 24'	−0 16	+1 29	*0.69	*0.38	1.22
Little Torch Key, Torch Channel	24° 40'	81° 24'	+0 11	+1 45	*0.57	*0.33	1.00
Big Pine Key, Newfound Harbor Ch	24° 39'	81° 23'	−0 09	+0 44	*0.82	*0.46	1.45
Big Pine Key, Coupon Bight	24° 39'	81° 21'	−0 20	+0 49	*0.87	*0.54	1.52
Little Torch Key, Pine Chnl Br S	24° 40'	81° 23'	−0 15	+0 57	*0.68	*0.33	1.21
Little Torch Key, Pine Chnl Br N	24° 40'	81° 23'	−0 13	+0 54	*0.69	*0.38	1.22
Big Pine Key, Pine Chnl Br, S	24° 40'	81° 22'	−0 13	+1 03	*0.67	*0.33	1.20
Big Pine Key, Pine Chnl Br, N	24° 40'	81° 22'	+0 03	+1 44	*0.57	*0.33	1.01
Big Pine Key, west side, Pine Ch	24° 41'	81° 23'	+0 21	+1 52	*0.52	*0.42	0.89
Howe Key, south end, Harbor Ch	24° 44'	81° 24'	+4 43	+4 49	*0.72	*0.62	1.20
Big Torch Key, Harbor Channel	24° 44'	81° 27'	+3 47	+5 51	*1.58	*1.29	2.68

*Heights of tides are found by multiplying heights from the Tide Tables by the *Ratio listed here. When parenthesis are used, multiply heights by the *Ratio and then add or subtract the second number as indicated.

PLACE	POSITION		DIFFERENCES				RANGE
			Time		Height*		
	Latitude	Longitude	High	Low	High	Low	Spring
	North	West	h m	h m	ft	ft	ft

FLORIDA (Continued)

Eastern Standard Time (GMT –5h)   Add one hour Daylight Saving April 3 – October 29

ON **KEY WEST, FLORIDA**

PLACE	Latitude	Longitude	High	Low	High	Low	Spring
Water Keys, south end, Harbor Ch	24° 45'	81° 27'	+3 42	+5 41	*1.50	*1 00	2.64
Howe Key, northwest end	24° 46'	81° 26'	+3 29	+5 22	*1.68	*1.33	2.85
Summerland Key, Niles Channel S	24° 39'	81° 26'	–0 36	+0 11	*0.95	*0 71	1.42
Summerland Key, Niles Channel Br	24° 40'	81° 26'	–0 10	+0 56	*0.67	*0.58	1.12
Ramrod Key, Niles Channel Bridge	24° 40'	81° 25'	–0 13	+1 12	*0.67	*0.46	1.16
Big Torch Key, Niles Channel	24° 42'	81° 26'	+3 15	+2 05	*0.61	*0.71	0.96
Knockemdown Key, north end	24° 43'	81° 29'	+3 30	+4 54	*1.35	*1.21	2.25
Raccoon Key, east side	24° 45'	81° 29'	+3 20	+5 09	*1.50	*1.21	2.55
Content Key, Content Passage	24° 47'	81° 29'	+2 47	+3 50	*2.13	*1.83	3.58
Key Lois, southest end	24° 36'	81° 28'	–1 15	–0 45	*1.06	*0.75	1.82
Sugarloaf Key, east side, Tarpon ..	24° 38'	81° 31'	–0 41	+0 15	*0.89	*0.58	1.55
Gopher Key, Cudjoe Bay	24° 39'	81° 29'	–0 46	+0 17	*0.90	*0.71	1.52
Sugarloaf Key, Pirates Cove	24° 39'	81° 31'	–0 48	+1 41	*0.59	*0.75	0.92
Cudjoe Key, Cudjoe Bay	24° 40'	81° 30'	–0 38	+0 41	*0.87	*0.71	1.48
Summerland Key, SW, Kemp Chnl	24° 39'	81° 27'	–0 26	+0 50	*0.81	*0.54	1.40
Cudjoe Key, north end, Kemp Chnl	24° 42'	81° 31'	+3 32	+4 40	*1.63	*1.46	2.71
Sugarloaf Key, NE side, Bow Chnl	24° 40'	81° 32'	+3 47	+3 24	*1.01	*0.71	1.75
Cudjoe Key, Pirates Cove	24° 40'	81° 31'	+3 50	+2 55	*0.77	*0.79	1.26
Sugarloaf Key, north end, Bow Ch	24° 42'	81° 33'	+3 37	+5 20	*1.29	*0.75	2.28
Pumpkin Key, Bow Chnl	24° 43'	81° 34'	+3 17	+4 39	*1.56	*1.17	2.68
Sawyer Key, outside, Cudjoe Chnl	24° 46'	81° 34'	+2 45	+5 24	*1.57	*0.50	2.90
Sawyer Key, inside, Cudjoe Chnl ..	24° 46'	81° 34'	+2 37	+5 19	*1.43	*0.50	2.62
Johnston Key, SW end, Turkey Bsn	24° 43'	81° 36'	+3 26	+5 38	*1.10	*0.50	1.99
Upper Sugarloaf Sound							
Perky	24° 39'	81° 34'	+5 37	+8 25	*0.28	*0.08	0.52
Park Channel Bridge	24° 39'	81° 32'	+5 47	+8 33	*0.26	*0.29	0.42
North Harris Channel	24° 39'	81° 33'	+5 32	+8 04	*0.25	*0.25	0.41
Tarpon Creek	24° 38'	81° 31'	–0 29	+0 17	*0.35	*0.38	0.58
Snipe Keys							
Snipe Keys, SE, Inner Nrws	24° 40'	81° 37'	+3 25	+5 39	*1.28	*0.83	2.24
Snipe Keys, Middle Narrows	24° 40'	81° 38'	+3 44	+5 54	*1.02	*0.67	1.78
Snipe Keys, Snipe Pt	24° 42'	81° 40'	+2 15	+3 33	*1.69	*1.29	2.89
Waltz Key Basin							
Waltz Key, Waltz Key Basin	24° 39'	81° 39'	+3 53	+5 33	*1.03	*0.96	1.70
Duck Key Pt, Duck Key	24° 37'	81° 41'	+3 27	+4 57	*1.19	*0.96	2.01
O'Hara Key, North End	24° 37'	81° 39'	+3 53	+5 39	*1.03	*0.83	1.75
Saddlebunch Keys							
Saddlebunch Keys, Chnl # 5	24° 37'	81° 38'	+4 32	+6 58	*0.66	*1.12	0.95
Saddlebunch Keys, Chnl # 4	24° 37'	81° 37'	+4 35	+5 36	*0.54	*0.29	0.95
Saddlebunch Keys, Chnl # 3	24° 37'	81° 36'	+1 44	–0 10	*0.43	*0.21	0.78
Similar Sound							
Bird Key, Similar Snd	24° 35'	81° 38'	–0 21	+1 03	*0.59	*0.42	1.02
Shark Key, SE, Similar Snd	24° 36'	81° 39'	+0 18	+1 51	*0.52	*0.46	0.88
Saddlebunch Keys, Similar Snd	24° 36'	81° 37'	+0 39	+2 41	*0.37	*0.21	0.65
Big Coppitt Key, NE side, Waltz	24° 36'	81° 39'	+4 21	+6 54	*0.84	*0.33	1.52

Chapter 3

*Heights of tides are found by multiplying heights from the Tide Tables by the *Ratio listed here. When parenthesis are used, multiply heights by the *Ratio and then add or subtract the second number as indicated.

PLACE	POSITION		DIFFERENCES				RANGE
			Time		Height*		
	Latitude	Longitude	High	Low	High	Low	Spring
	North	West	h m	h m	ft	ft	ft

FLORIDA (Continued)

Eastern Standard Time (GMT –5h)   Add one hour Daylight Saving April 3 – October 29

ON **KEY WEST, Florida**

PLACE	Latitude	Longitude	High	Low	High	Low	Spring
Rockland Key, Rockland Chnl Br ..	24° 36'	81° 40'	+5 02	+6 06	*0.76	*0.88	1.21
Boca Chica Key, Long Pt	24° 36'	81° 42'	+3 54	+5 22	*0.94	*0.71	1.60
Channel Key, West Side	24° 36'	81° 44'	+3 09	+3 07	*0.70	*0.71	1.14
Boca Chica Channel Bridge	24° 35'	81° 43'	+1 23	+1 29	*0.57	*0.67	0.90
Key Haven – Stock Island Chnl	24° 35'	81° 44'	+2 25	+2 57	*0.73	*0.79	1.18
Sigsbee Park, Garrison Bight Ch ...	24° 35'	81° 47'	+1 59	+2 06	*0.81	*0.88	1.30
Key West, south side, Hawk Chnl ..	24° 33'	81° 47'	–0 52	–0 30	*1.07	*0.92	1.80
KEY WEST	24° 33'	81° 49'	**Daily Predictions**				1.64
Sand Key Lighthouse, Sand K. Ch	24° 27'	81° 53'	–1 03	–0 39	*0.94	*0.79	1.58
Garden Key, Dry Tortugas	24° 38'	82° 52'	+0 29	+0 33	*0.94	*1.33	1.42
Cape Sable, East Cape	25° 07'	81° 05'	+3 56	+4 43	*2.26	*2.20	3.8
Shark River entrance	25° 21'	81° 08'	+3 20	+4 38	*2.71	*2.50	4.5
Lostmans River entrance	25° 33'	81° 13'	+3 22	+4 42	*2.31	*2.31	3.9
Onion Key, Lostmans River	25° 37'	81° 08'	+5 32	+7 46	*0.46	*0.46	0.9
Chatham River entrance	25° 41'	81° 17'	+3 22	+4 46	*2.82	*2.50	4.2

BERMUDA

Atlantic Standard Time (GMT –4h)   Add one hour Daylight Saving April 3 – October 29

ON **ST GEORGE, BERMUDA**

PLACE	Latitude	Longitude	High	Low	Height		Spring
ST GEORGE'S ISLAND	32° 23'	64° 42'	**Daily Predictions**				3.0
St David's Island	32° 22'	64° 39'	–0 07	–0 07	(*0.96+0.23)		2.6
Great Sound	32° 19'	64° 50'	+0 15	+0 15	(*1.08–0.14)		3.2

BAHAMA ISLANDS

Eastern Standard Time (GMT –5h)   Add one hour Daylight Saving April 3 – October 29

ON **NASSAU, BAHAMAS**

PLACE	Latitude	Longitude	High	Low	Height		Spring
Grand Bahama							
Freeport Harbour	26° 31'	78° 46'	+0 00	+0 00	(*1.13–1.15)		3.3
Little Bahama Bank							
Memory Rock	26° 57'	79° 07'	+0 24	+0 29	*0.88	*0.88	2.7
Walker Cay	27° 16'	78° 24'	+1 25	+1 25	(*0.95–0.64)		2.9
The Abacos							
Allans–Pensacola Cay....................	26° 59'	77° 40'	+0 35	+0 45	(*0.95–0.64)		2.9
Green Turtle Cay	26° 46'	77° 18'	+0 05	+0 05	(*1.00–0.95)		3.0
Pelican Harbour.............................	26° 23'	76° 58'	+0 25	+0 25	(*0.95–0.64)		2.9
Great Bahama Bank							
North Bimini..................................	25° 44'	79° 18'	+0 13	+0 25	*0.92	*0.92	2.9
Cat Cay...	25° 33'	79° 17'	+0 23	+0 23	(*0.88–0.47)		2.6
South Riding Rock.........................	25° 14'	79° 10'	+0 40	+0 40	(*0.88–0.48)		2.6
Guinchos Cay	22° 45'	78° 07'	+0 14	+0 19	*0.81	*0.81	2.6
Cay Sal Bank							
Elbow Cay, Cay Sal Bank...............	23° 57'	80° 28'	+1 26	+1 31	*0.81	*0.81	2.6

*Heights of tides are found by multiplying heights from the Tide Tables by the *Ratio listed here. When parenthesis are used, multiply heights by the *Ratio and then add or subtract the second number as indicated.

PLACE	POSITION		DIFFERENCES				RANGE
			Time		Height*		
	Latitude	Longitude	High	Low	High	Low	Spring
	North	West	h m	h m	ft	ft	ft

BAHAMA ISLANDS (Continued)

Eastern Standard Time (GMT –5h)   Add one hour Daylight Saving April 3 – October 29
ON **NASSAU,** BAHAMAS

The Berry Islands							
Great Stirrup Cay............................	24° 49'	77° 55'	+0 25	+0 25	(*0.88–0.48)		2.6
Andros Island							
Mastic Point....................................	25° 03'	77° 58'	+0 05	+0 05	(*0.97–0.73)		2.6
Fresh Creek....................................	24° 42'	77° 46'	+0 05	+0 05	(*1.08–0.77)		3.2
New Providence							
NASSAU, BAHAMAS	25° 05'	77° 21'	**Daily Predictions**				3.0
Eleuthera							
Royal Island Harbour......................	25° 31'	76° 51'	+0 05	+0 05	(*0.88–0.48)		2.6
Wide Opening..................................	25° 25'	76° 41'	+0 25	+0 25	(*0.95–0.64)		2.9
Tracking Station..............................	25° 15'	76° 19'	+2 17	+2 36	*0.92	*0.92	2.9
Eleuthera Island East Coast...........	24° 56'	76° 09'	+0 15	+0 18	(*0.88–0.47)		2.6
The Exumas							
Ship Channel..................................	24° 52'	76° 48'	–0 15	–0 15	(*0.95–0.64)		2.9
Steventon	23° 40'	75° 58'	–0 05	–0 05	(*0.88–0.48)		2.6
George Town...................................	23° 32'	75° 49'	–0 20	–0 20	(*0.83–0.30)		2.6
Long Island							
Clarence Harbor	23° 06'	74° 59'	+0 49	+0 54	*1.00	*1.00	3.1
Hard Bargain	23° 00'	74° 57'	+0 40	+0 40	(*0.76–0.15)		2.3
Jumentos Cays							
Nurse Channel................................	22° 31'	75° 51'	+0 15	+0 10	(*0.92–0.46)		2.9
Cat Island							
The Bight..	24° 19'	75° 26'	–0 35	–0 35	(*0.92–0.46)		2.9
San Salvador..................................	24° 06'	74° 26'	–0 35	–0 35	(*0.92–0.46)		2.9
Acklin Island							
Datum Bay.......................................	22° 10'	74° 18'	–0 15	–0 15	(*0.80–0.17)		2.6
Mayaguana							
Abraham Bay...................................	22° 22'	73° 00'	+0 10	+0 13	*0.77	*0.77	2.5
Start Point......................................	22° 20'	73° 03'	+0 25	+0 25	(*0.51+0.32)		1.6
Little Inagua	21° 27'	73° 01'	+0 10	+0 10	(*0.88–0.46)		2.6
Great Inagua							
Mathew Town	20° 57'	73° 41'	+0 15	+0 15	(*0.52+0.38)		1.6

TURKS & CAICOS

Eastern Standard Time (GMT –5h)   Add one hour Daylight Saving April 3 – October 29
ON **NASSAU,** BAHAMAS

Turks Islands							
Grand Turk	21° 26'	71° 09'	–0 15	–0 15	(*0.64–0.14)		1.9
Hawks Nest Anchorage	21° 26'	71° 07'	–0 19	–0 14	*0.81	*0.81	2.6
North Caicos Island							
Sandy Point	21° 56'	72° 03'	+0 38	+0 38	(*0.56–0.00)		1.6

*Heights of tides are found by multiplying heights from the Tide Tables by the *Ratio listed here. When parenthesis are used, multiply heights by the *Ratio and then add or subtract the second number as indicated.

Chapter 3

PLACE	POSITION		DIFFERENCES				RANGE
			Time		Height*		
	Latitude	Longitude	High	Low	High	Low	Spring
	North	West	h m	h m	ft	ft	ft

CUBA

Eastern Standard Time (GMT –5h)Add one hour Daylight Saving March 20 – October 15

ON PORT OF SPAIN, TRINIDAD

North Coast Cuba

Los Arroyos	22° 22'	84° 23'	+4 55	+6 05	(*0.31+0.18)		1.0

ON SAN JUAN, PUERTO RICO

La Coloma.	22° 14'	83° 34'	+2 04	+ 2 23	*0.54	*0.54	0.9

ON KEY WEST, FLORIDA

Cabo San Antonio	21° 52'	84° 58'	–0 50	– 0 07	*0.92	*0.92	1.5
Bahía Honda...................................	22° 58'	83° 13'	–1 04	– 0 23	*0.76	*0.76	1.4
Havana	23° 09'	82° 20'	–0 48	– 0 40	*0.76	*0.76	1.5
Matanzas	23° 04'	81° 32'	–0 59	– 0 59	*0.92	*0.92	1.5
Cardenas	23° 04'	81° 12'	–0 11	+ 0 34	*1.08	*1.08	1.8

ON NASSAU, BAHAMAS

La Isabela	22° 56'	80° 00'	+1 41	+1 42	*0.62	*0.62	2.0
Cayo Paredon Grande....................	22° 29'	78° 09'	+0 15	+0 05	(*0.79–0.99)		2.6
Bahía Nuevitas							
Entrance	21° 38'	77° 07'	+1 15	+1 05	(*0.44–0.51)		1.3
Nuevitas...	21° 35'	77° 15'	+2 55	+2 55	(*0.51–0.67)		1.6
North Coast Cuba							
Puerto Padre	21° 12'	76° 36'	+1 25	+1 15	(*0.76–1.02)		2.3
Puerto Gibara	21° 06'	76° 08'	+0 25	+0 20	(*0.64–0.80)		2.0
Bahía Nipe							
Punta Caranero	20° 47'	75° 34'	+0 30	+0 25	(*0.76–1.02)		2.3
Antilla...	20° 50'	75° 44'	+0 50	+0 50	(*0.76–1.02)		2.3
North Coast Cuba							
Bahía de Levisa entrance..............	20° 45'	75° 28'	+0 18	+0 19	*0.74	*0.74	2.2
Puerto Tanamo..............................	20° 43'	75° 19'	+0 20	+0 20	(*0.64–0.80)		2.0
Baracoa	20° 21'	74° 30'	+0 10	+0 10	(*0.60–0.91)		1.9
Puerto Maysi..................................	20° 15'	74° 08'	+0 05	+0 05	(*0.79–0.99)		2.6

ON SAN JUAN, PUERTO RICO

South Coast Cuba							
Guantanamo Bay...........................	19° 54'	75° 09'	–0 27	–0 23	*0.89	*0.89	1.3
Puerto de Santiago de Cuba	19° 59'	75° 52'	+0 30	+0 17	*0.89	*0.89	1.2
Manzanillo	20° 21'	77° 07'	+1 41	+1 38	*1.39	*1.39	2.1
Ensenada de Mora							
Puerto de Pilon..............................	19° 54'	77° 19'	+0 11	+0 13	*0.72	*0.72	1.0
South Coast Cuba							
Casilda..	21° 45'	79° 59'	+1 04	+0 52	*0.65	*0.65	0.9
Bahía de Cienfuegos							
Punta Pasacaballos........................	22° 04'	80° 27'	+0 49	+0 58	*0.80	*0.80	1.3
Cienfuegos	22° 08'	80° 27'	+0 51	+0 58	*0.81	*0.81	1.3

*Heights of tides are found by multiplying heights from the Tide Tables by the *Ratio listed here. When parenthesis are used, multiply heights by the *Ratio and then add or subtract the second number as indicated.

REED'S NAUTICAL ALMANAC

PLACE	POSITION		DIFFERENCES				RANGE
			Time		Height*		
	Latitude	Longitude	High	Low	High	Low	Spring
	North	West	h m	h m	ft	ft	ft

CUBA (Continued)

Eastern Standard Time (GMT –5h)Add one hour Daylight Saving March 20 – October 15

ON **SAN JUAN, PUERTO RICO**

South Coast Cuba

Carapachibey, Isla de Pinos	21° 27'	82° 00'	+0 43	+0 52	*0.54	*0.54	0.9

ON **KEY WEST, FLORIDA**

Cabo San Antonio	21° 52'	84° 58'	–0 50	– 0 07	*0.92	*0.92	1.5

CAYMAN ISLANDS

Eastern Standard Time (GMT –5h)   *Daylight Saving Time Not Observed*

ON **CHARLOTTE AMALIE, USVI**

Grand Cayman	19° 20'	81° 20'	+0 11	+0 15	*1.63	*1.63	1.3

JAMAICA

Eastern Standard Time (GMT –5h)   *Daylight Saving Time Not Observed*

ON **CHARLOTTE AMALIE, USVI**

North Coast

South Negril Point	18° 18'	78° 24'	+5 25	+5 29	*3.88	*2.12	1.7
Montego Bay	18° 28'	77° 55'	+1 28	+1 36	*1.25	*1.25	1.0
St Anns Bay	18° 25'	77° 14'	+0 55	+0 59	*1.00	*1.00	0.8

ON **CRISTÓBAL, PANAMA**

Port Antonio	18° 11'	76°27°	–2 45	–3 00	(*0.89+0.26)		0.9
South Coast							
Port Morant	17° 53'	76°19°	–1 55	–2 15	(*0.90+0.63)		0.9
Port Royal	17° 57'	76°50°	–1 25	–1 40	(*0.60+0.87)		0.6
Port Esquivel	17° 53'	77° 08'	–1 22	–1 45	(*0.70+0.24)		0.6
Black River	18° 01'	77° 51'	–1 38	–2 15	(*0.58+0.69)		0.6
Savanna la Mar	18° 12'	78° 08'	–1 53	–2 30	(*1.00+0.67)		0.9

HAITI

Eastern Standard Time (GMT –5h)   *Add one hour Daylight Saving April 3 – October 29*

ON **SAN JUAN, PUERTO RICO**

Massacre, Riviere du entrance	19° 43'	71° 46'	–1 01	–1 01	*1.45	*1.45	2.3
Port–au–Prince	18° 33'	72° 21'	–0 32	–0 32	+0.1	+0.1	.6

ON **CHARLOTTE AMALIE, USVI**

Jacmel	18° 13'	72° 34'	–1 48	–1 44	(*2.68–0.31)		1.3

*Heights of tides are found by multiplying heights from the Tide Tables by the *Ratio listed here. When parenthesis are used, multiply heights by the *Ratio and then add or subtract the second number as indicated.

Chapter 3

PLACE	POSITION		DIFFERENCES				RANGE
			Time		Height*		
	Latitude	Longitude	High	Low	High	Low	Spring
	North	West	h m	h m	ft	ft	ft

DOMINICAN REPUBLIC

Eastern Standard Time (GMT –5h)   Add one hour Daylight Saving April 3 – October 29

ON SAN JUAN, PUERTO RICO

Puerto Plata........................	19° 49'	70° 42'	−1 09	−1 14	*1.45	*1.45	2.3
Sanchez..............................	19° 13'	69° 36'	−0 37	−0 37	*2.05	*2.05	3.3
Santa Barbara de Samana	19° 12'	69° 20'	−0 51	−0 47	*1.25	*1.25	2.0

ON CHARLOTTE AMALIE, USVI

Santo Domingo..........................	18° 27'	69° 53'	+1 44	−2 45	*1.00	*1.00	0.8

PUERTO RICO

Atlantic Standard Time (GMT –4h)   *Daylight Saving Time Not Observed*

ON SAN JUAN, PUERTO RICO

West Coast – Puerto Rico

Puerto Real............................	18° 05'	67° 11'	−0 33	−0 26	*0.72	*0.72	1.2
Mayaguez..............................	18° 13'	67° 09'	−0 30	−0 21	*0.99	*0.99	1.6

North Coast – Puerto Rico

SAN JUAN....................................	18° 28'	66° 01'	**Daily Predictions**				1.6

East Coast – Puerto Rico

Playa de Fajardo	18° 20'	65° 38'	−0 10	−0 13	*1.00	*1.00	1.6
Roosevelt Roads	18° 14'	65° 37'	+0 02	+0 20	*0.63	*0.63	1.0

Culebra

Ensenada Honda......................	18° 18'	65° 17'	−0 34	−0 15	*0.99	*0.99	1.0

ON CHARLOTTE AMALIE, USVI

Culebrita, Isla....................	18° 19'	65° 14'	−0 57	+0 24	*1.39	*1.39	1.1

ON SAN JUAN, PUERTO RICO

Isla de Vieques

Punta Mulas........................	18° 09'	65° 26'	−0 14	−0 17	*0.72	*0.72	1.2

ON CHARLOTTE AMALIE, USVI

Puerto Ferro	18° 06'	65° 26'	−0 49	+0 45	*1.00	*1.00	0.8

South Coast – Puerto Rico

Puerto Maunabo	18° 00'	65° 53'	+0 41	−1 03	*0.88	*0.88	0.7
Arroyo.	17° 58'	66° 04'	+2 29	−2 03	*1.00	*1.00	0.8
Playa Cortada.......................	17° 59'	66° 27'	+1 15	−2 53	*1.00	*1.00	0.8
Playa de Ponce	17° 58'	66° 37'	+0 58	−2 29	*1.00	*1.00	0.8
Guanica	17° 58'	66° 55'	+0 15	−1 58	*0.88	*0.88	0.7
Magueyes Island	17° 58'	67° 03'	+1 35	−2 08	*0.88	*0.88	0.7

U.S. VIRGIN ISLANDS

Atlantic Standard Time (GMT –4h)   *Daylight Saving Time Not Observed*

ON SAN JUAN, PUERTO RICO

Magens Bay, St Thomas	18° 22'	64° 55'	−0 16	−0 01	*0.91	*0.91	1.4

*Heights of tides are found by multiplying heights from the Tide Tables by the *Ratio listed here. When parenthesis are used, multiply heights by the *Ratio and then add or subtract the second number as indicated.

PLACE	POSITION		DIFFERENCES				RANGE
			Time		Height*		
	Latitude	Longitude	High	Low	High	Low	Spring
	North	West	h m	h m	ft	ft	ft

U.S. VIRGIN ISLANDS (Continued)

Atlantic Standard Time (GMT –4h)   *Daily Saving Time Not Observed*
ON **CHARLOTTE AMALIE, USVI**

CHARLOTTE AMALIE	18° 20'	64° 56'	**Daily Predictions**				0.9
St Johns..........................	18° 20'	64° 40'	+1 12	+1 16	(*0.82+0.31)		1.3
Christiansted, St Croix..........	17° 45'	64° 42'	–1 05	–1 07	*1.00	1.00	0.9

BRITISH VIRGIN ISLANDS

Atlantic Standard Time (GMT –4h)   *Daylight Saving Time Not Observed*
ON **CHARLOTTE AMALIE, USVI**

Tortola	18° 26'	64° 37'	+0 07	+0 11	(*0.82+1.01)		1.0
Anegada	18° 44'	64° 23'	–0 58	–0 04	(*2.33–0.48)		1.9

ANGUILLA

Atlantic Standard Time (GMT –4h)   *Daylight Saving Time Not Observed*
ON **CHARLOTTE AMALIE, USVI**

Road Bay	18° 12'	63° 06'	–0 18	–0 14	(*0.84+0.66)		1.3

ST. BARTHELEMY

Atlantic Standard Time (GMT –4h)   *Daylight Saving Time Not Observed*
ON **CHARLOTTE AMALIE, USVI**

St. Barthelemy	17° 54'	62° 51'	–1 48	–1 02	*1.75	*1.75	1.4

ANTIGUA

Atlantic Standard Time (GMT –4h)   *Daylight Saving Time Not Observed*
ON **CHARLOTTE AMALIE, USVI**

St. Johns..........................	17° 08'	61° 52'	+0 12	+0 12	(*0.81+0.62)		1.3

GUADELOUPE

Atlantic Standard Time (GMT –4h)   *Daylight Saving Time Not Observed*
ON **CHARLOTTE AMALIE, USVI**

Sainte Rose	16° 20'	61° 42'	–2 28	–2 24	(*1.28+0.67)		0.9
Pointe–a–Pitre	16° 14'	61° 32'	–1 58	–1 54	(*1.05+1.59)		0.9
Iles des Saintes	15° 52'	61° 36'	–3 33	–3 34	(*0.84+1.12)		0.6

DOMINICA

Atlantic Standard Time (GMT –4h)   *Daylight Saving Time Not Observed*
ON **CHARLOTTE AMALIE, USVI**

Portsmouth	15° 34'	61° 28'	+0 08	+0 06	(*1.09+1.33)		1.0
Woodbridge Bay	15° 19'	61° 24'	+0 12	+0 16	(*1.47+0.69)		1.3

*Heights of tides are found by multiplying heights from the Tide Tables by the *Ratio listed here. When parenthesis are used, multiply heights by the *Ratio and then add or subtract the second number as indicated.

Chapter 3

PLACE	POSITION		DIFFERENCES				RANGE
			Time		Height*		
	Latitude	Longitude	High	Low	High	Low	Spring
	North	West	h m	h m	ft	ft	ft

DOMINICA

Atlantic Standard Time (GMT –4h)   *Daylight Saving Time Not Observed*

ON **FORT–DE–FRANCE**, MARTINIQUE

Roseau	15° 18'	61° 24'	+0 26	+0 13	*1.71	*1.71	1.2

MARTINIQUE

Atlantic Standard Time (GMT –4h)   *Daylight Saving Time Not Observed*

ON **FORT–DE–FRANCE**, MARTINIQUE

Fort–de–France, Martinique	14° 35'	61° 03'	**Daily Predictions**				0.5

SAINT LUCIA

Atlantic Standard Time (GMT –4h)   *Daylight Saving Time Not Observed*

ON **FORT–DE–FRANCE**, MARTINIQUE

Castries	14° 01'	61° 00'	–0 10	–0 52	(*1.14–0.65)		1.0
Vieux Fort Bay, St Lucia	13° 44'	60° 58'	+0 53	+0 40	*1.82	*1.82	1.0

ST. VINCENT & THE GRENADINES

Atlantic Standard Time (GMT –4h)   *Daylight Saving Time Not Observed*

ON **FORT–DE–FRANCE**, MARTINIQUE

Kingstown, St Vincent.....................	13° 10'	61° 13'	–0 10	–1 12	(*0.35+1.12)		1.0
Mustique	12° 51'	61° 11'	+0 55	+0 23	(*1.50–1.88)		1.2
Charlestown Bay, Canouan.............	12° 42'	61° 20'	+0 17	–0 32	(*1.50–1.23)		1.3
Tobago Cays	12° 38'	61° 21'	+0 30	–0 22	(*1.49–1.37)		1.3
Clifton Harbour, Union	12° 36'	61° 25'	+0 40	–0 44	(*1.14+0.01)		0.9

GRENADA

Atlantic Standard Time (GMT –4h)   *Daylight Saving Time Not Observed*

ON **FORT–DE–FRANCE**, MARTINIQUE

Hillsborough Bay, Carriacou...........	12° 29'	61° 27'	+0 10	–0 15	(*1.14–0.99)		0.9
St George's Harbour.......................	12° 03'	61° 45'	–0 10	–0 22	(*0.66+0.41)		0.7
Prickly Bay.....................................	12° 00'	61° 45'	+0 35	–0 34	(*1.60–1.36)		1.3

BARBADOS

Atlantic Standard Time (GMT –4h)   *Daylight Saving Time Not Observed*

ON **PORT OF SPAIN**, Trinidad

Carlisle Bay, Bridgetown	13° 06'	59° 37'	–0 35	–0 36	(*0.89–0.48)		1.9

*Heights of tides are found by multiplying heights from the Tide Tables by the *Ratio listed here. When parenthesis are used, multiply heights by the *Ratio and then add or subtract the second number as indicated.

PLACE	POSITION		DIFFERENCES				RANGE
			Time		Height*		
	Latitude	Longitude	High	Low	High	Low	Spring
	North	West	h m	h m	ft	ft	ft

TOBAGO

Atlantic Standard Time (GMT –4h)   *Daylight Saving Time Not Observed*
on PORT OF SPAIN, Trinidad

Plymouth	11° 13'	60° 47'	–1 05	–1 05	(*0.87+0.00)		2.0
Man of War Bay	11° 19'	60° 32'	–0 05	–0 35	(*0.98–1.12)		2.3
Scarborough	11° 11'	60° 44'	–0 14	–0 13	(*0.98–0.12)		2.3

TRINIDAD

Atlantic Standard Time (GMT –4h)   *Daylight Saving Time Not Observed*
ON PORT OF SPAIN, Trinidad

North Coast – Trinidad

Las Cuevas Bay	10° 47'	61° 24'	–1 01	–0 58	(*0.82–0.20)		1.9
Toco	10° 50'	60° 56'	–1 10	–1 10	(*1.32–0.61)		2.9

East Coast – Trinidad

Guayamare Point	10° 45'	60° 58'	–1 00	–1 00	(*1.39–0.52)		3.0

ON PUNTA GORDA, Venezuela

Nariva River	10° 24'	61° 02'	–1 06	–2 16	(*0.41 +1.3)		3.1

South Coast – Trinidad

Erin Bay	10° 04'	61° 39'	–0 50	–1 41	–0.3	+1.2	5.6
Guayaguayare Bay	10° 09'	61° 01'	–1 32	–2 09	(*0.53 +1.3)		3.8

West Coast – Trinidad

Bonasse pier	10° 05'	61° 52'	–0 43	–1 15	–1.0	+1.4	4.4
Point Fortin	10° 11'	61° 42'	–0 54	–1 27	(*0.47 1.26)		3.6

ON PORT OF SPAIN, Trinidad

Lisas Point	10° 23'	61° 29'	–0 09	–0 08	(*1.42–0.87)		3.2
PORT OF SPAIN	10° 39'	61° 31'	**Daily Predictions**				2.3
Carenage Bay	10° 41'	61° 36'	–0 58	–1 40	(*0.34 +1.6)		2.6
Staubles Bay	10° 41'	61° 39'	–1 07	–2 02	(*0.33 +1.7)		2.5

VENEZUELA

Atlantic Standard Time (GMT –4h)   *Daylight Saving Time Not Observed*
ON PUNTA GORDA, Venezuela

Río Orinoco

Isla Ramon Isidro	8° 39'	60° 35'	+0 07	–0 12	+0.2	+1.0	6.7

Gulf of Paria

PUNTA GORDA, Río San Juan	10° 10'	62° 38'	**Daily Predictions**				7.1
Barra de Maturin, chan. entr.	10° 18'	62° 31'	–0 22	–0 45	–1.0	+0.2	5.7
Boca Pedernales entrance	10° 01'	62° 12'	–0 03	–0 34	–1.3	+0.2	5.4
Puerto de Hierro	10° 37'	62° 05'	–0 46	–1 19	*0.59	*0.59	4.2
Macuro	10° 39'	61° 56'	–1 15	–2 05	*0.38	*0.38	2.7

ON AMUAY, Venezuela

Punta Penas to Amuay

Carúpano	10° 40'	63° 15'	–1 17	–0 42	+0.2	0.0	1.4

*Heights of tides are found by multiplying heights from the Tide Tables by the *Ratio listed here. When parenthesis are used, multiply heights by the *Ratio and then add or subtract the second number as indicated.*

PLACE	POSITION		DIFFERENCES				RANGE
			Time		Height*		
	Latitude	Longitude	High	Low	High	Low	Spring
	North	West	h m	h m	ft	ft	ft

VENEZUELA (CONTINUED)

Atlantic Standard Time (GMT –4h)   *Daylight Saving Time Not Observed*

ON **AMUAY**, Venezuela

Porlamar, Isla de Margarita	10° 57'	63° 51'	−1 19	−0 59	+0.6	0.0	1.8
Cumaná..	10° 28'	64° 11'	−2 37	−1 02	−0.1	0.0	1.1
Carenero......................................	10° 32'	66° 07'	−1 51	−1 59	+0.8	+1.0	1.0
La Güaira.....................................	10° 36'	66° 56'	−2 29	−1 59	+0.8	+1.0	1.0
AMUAY...	11° 45'	70° 13'	**Daily Predictions**				1.2

ON **MALECON**, Venezuela

Maracaibo

MALECON–ISLA ZAPARA.............	11° 00'	71° 35'	**Daily Predictions**				3.6
Bahía de Tablazos........................	10° 53'	71° 35'	+0 30	+0 11	*0.61	*0.31	2.3
Punta de Palmas	10° 48'	71° 37'	+0 35	+0 16	*0.49	*0.31	1.8

BONAIRE

Atlantic Standard Time (GMT –4h)   *Daylight Saving Time Not Observed*

ON **CRISTÓBAL**, Panama

Kralendijk.......................................	12° 09'	68° 17'	+0 35	+1 42	(*0.65+0.98)	1.0

CURAÇAO

Atlantic Standard Time (GMT –4h)   *Daylight Saving Time Not Observed*

ON **CRISTÓBAL**, Panama

Schottegat, Curaçao......................	12° 07'	68° 56'	+0 25	+1 09	*0.82 *0.82	0.9
Willemstad	12° 06'	68° 56'	+0 42	+1 38	(*0.65+0.98)	1.0

ARUBA

Atlantic Standard Time (GMT –4h)   *Daylight Saving Time Not Observed*

ON **CRISTÓBAL**, Panama

Oranjestad	12° 31'	70° 03'	+0 21	+1 16	(*0.65+0.98)	1.0
Malmok Bay....................................	12° 36'	70° 03'	+0 33	+1 36	(*0.65+0.98)	1.0

COLOMBIA

Eastern Standard Time (GMT –5h)   *Daylight Saving Time Not Observed*

ON **CRISTOBAL**, Panama

Río Hacha.......................................	11° 33'	72° 55'	−0 35	−0 35	(*1.01−0.18)	1.0
Santa Marta...................................	11° 15'	74° 13'	−1 19	−1 08	(*0.99−0.06)	1.0
Puerto Colombia............................	11° 00'	74° 58'	−0 52	−1 08	(*1.29−0.16)	1.3
Cartagena......................................	10° 26'	75° 34'	−1 16	−0 48	(*0.90−0.05)	1.0
Puerto Covenas.............................	9° 20'	75° 40'	−1 06	−0 46	(*0.99−0.06)	1.0
Turbo	8° 10'	76° 45'	−0 49	−0 30	*1.43 *1.43	1.4
Punta Yarumal...............................	8° 07'	76° 45'	−0 49	−0 30	(*1.62−0.16)	1.6

*Heights of tides are found by multiplying heights from the Tide Tables by the *Ratio listed here. When parenthesis are used, multiply heights by the *Ratio and then add or subtract the second number as indicated.

PLACE	POSITION		DIFFERENCES				RANGE
			Time		Height*		
	Latitude	Longitude	High	Low	High	Low	Spring
	North	West	h m	h m	ft	ft	ft

PANAMA

Eastern Standard Time (GMT –5h)   *Daylight Saving Time Not Observed*
ON **CRISTÓBAL**, PANAMA

Puerto Caledonia.........	8° 54'	77° 41'	+0 12	0 00	(*1.01+0.04)		1.0
Puerto Mandinga	9° 30	78° 00'	+0 08	–0 05	(*1.01+0.04)		1.0
CRISTÓBAL–COLÓN	9° 21'	79° 55'	**Daily Predictions**				1.1
Escudo de Veragua	9° 07'	81° 34'	+0 30	+0 15	(*0.89–0.07)		1.0
Boca del Toro	9° 21'	82° 15'	+0 20	+0 25	(*0.99–0.06)		1.0

COSTA RICA

Central Standard Time (GMT –6h)   *Daylight Saving Time Not Observed*
ON **CRISTÓBAL**, PANAMA

Puerto Limon	10° 00'	83° 02'	–0 39	–0 37	(*0.90–0.02)		1.0

NICARAGUA

Central Standard Time (GMT –6h)   *Daylight Saving Time Not Observed*
ON **PORT OF SPAIN**, TRINIDAD

Greytown (San Juan del Norte)	10° 55'	83° 42'	–2 30	–1 50	(*0.50–0.58)		1.3
Bluefields Bluff...............................	12° 00'	83° 40'	–2 35	–1 55	(*0.33–0.40)		1.0
Isla del Maiz Grande (Great Corn) .	12° 10'	83° 03'	–1 55	–1 40	(*0.49–0.36)		1.3
Cayos del Perlas (Pearl Cays)	12° 25'	83° 25'	–1 40	–1 20	(*0.49–0.36)		1.3
			ON **NASSAU**, BAHAMAS				
Puerto Cabezas.............................	14° 01'	83° 23'	+4 26	+4 37	*0.54	*0.54	1.9
Cabo Gracias a Dios	15° 00'	83° 10'	+1 44	+0 54	*0.54	*0.54	1.6

HONDURAS

Central Standard Time (GMT –6h)   *Daylight Saving Time Not Observed*
ON **KEY WEST**, FLORIDA

Swan Island, Harbor Bay	17° 24'	83° 42'	–1 18	–0 33	*0.51	*0.51	0.9
Isla de Guanaja (Bonacca)	16° 29'	85° 54'	–1 26	–1 42	*0.72	*0.72	1.3
Puerto Castilla	16° 00'	85° 54'	–0 48	–0 13	*0.46	*0.46	0.8
Isla de Roatán, Port Royal..............	16° 24'	86° 20'	–2 41	–2 35	*0.92	*0.92	1.4
Puerto Cortés	15° 50'	87° 57'	–0 43	–0 02	*0.38	*0.38	0.6

GUATEMALA

Central Standard Time (GMT –6h)   *Daylight Saving Time Not Observed*
ON **KEY WEST**, FLORIDA

Río Dulce entrance.........................	15° 50'	88° 49'	–1 25	–1 35	*0.92	*0.92	1.5

Chapter 3

*Heights of tides are found by multiplying heights from the Tide Tables by the *Ratio listed here. When parenthesis are used, multiply heights by the *Ratio and then add or subtract the second number as indicated.*

PLACE	POSITION		DIFFERENCES				RANGE
			Time		Height*		
	Latitude	Longitude	High	Low	High	Low	Spring
	North	West	h m	h m	ft	ft	ft

BELIZE

Central Standard Time (GMT –6h)   *Daylight Saving Time Not Observed*
                                                  ON **KEY WEST, FLORIDA**

Place	Latitude	Longitude	High	Low	High	Low	Spring
Punta Gorda	16° 06'	88° 49'	−0 27	+0 30	*0.46	*0.46	0.8
Belize City	17° 30'	88° 11'	+0 14	+0 47	*0.46	*0.46	0.7

MEXICO

Central Standard Time (GMT –6h)   *Daylight Saving Time Not Observed*
                                                  ON **TAMPICO, MEXICO**

Place	Latitude	Longitude	High	Low	Height		Spring
Progreso	21° 18'	89° 40'	+1 19	+0 23	*1.29	*1.29	1.8
Campeche	19° 51'	90° 32'	−0 15	+0 50	(*2.14−0.60)		2.0
Cuidad del Carmen	18° 40'	91° 51'	−0 40	+0 30	(*1.00+0.70)		1.4
Frontera (Alvaro Mexico)	18° 32'	92° 39'	−0 18	−0 27	*1.14	*1.14	1.6
Coatzacoalcos (Puerto Mexico)	18° 09'	94° 25'	−0 40	+0 05	*1.07	*1.07	1.5
Alvarado	18° 46'	95° 46'	+0 51	+0 27	*0.93	*0.93	1.3
Veracruz	19° 12'	96° 08'	−0 19	−0 12	*1.21	*1.21	1.7
Tuxpan	21° 00'	97° 20'	+0 02	+0 04	*1.21	*1.21	1.7
TAMPICO HARBOR (Madero)	22° 13'	97° 51'	**Daily Predictions**				1.4
Matamoros	25° 53'	97° 31'	+0 55	+0 40	*1.00	*1.00	1.4

*Heights of tides are found by multiplying heights from the Tide Tables by the *Ratio listed here. When parenthesis are used, multiply heights by the *Ratio and then add or subtract the second number as indicated.

CURRENT DIFFERENCES

For more information on tides and currents in the Caribbean see the introduction to Chapter 2, and *Reed's Nautical Companion*.

The following list of current differences must be applied to one of the current reference tables found at the end of the Florida and Puerto Rico sections of Chapter 2. The main tidal current reference tables included in this almanac are Miami Harbor Entrance, Florida; Key West, Florida; and Vieques Passage, Puerto Rico.

Unfortunately, tidal current data is extremely limited for most of the Caribbean. The introduction to Chapter 2 includes two general current charts illustrating the trend of the average currents to be found in the Caribbean. Local currents are discussed in the appropriate country section of Chapter 2.

Mariners should bear in mind the effects of local winds and weather conditions. For instance, the currents off the Yucatan coast of Mexico can be reversed by a strong norther. Rivers often create local currents near their mouths, that may reinforce the coastal currents, or may flow in opposition to local currents.

INSTRUCTIONS

The following table is organized geographically beginning with Florida, then heading south into the Caribbean. Locate the place in the left hand column of the difference table you are interested in. The main bold heading will indicate which *current reference table* you must apply these differences to. The columns to the right of the place names give the *latitude and longitude* of the current difference location.

The third set of columns list *time differences*, which must be applied to the times derived from the reference table. The headings are Slack Before Flood, Max. Flood, Slack Before Ebb and Max. Ebb. The term "Slack" refers to the moment when the current is at a minimum, before turning to flood or ebb.

The time differences for Slack Before Flood and Slack Before Ebb should be added, or subtracted to the times from the column labeled Slack Time on the reference table. When

trying to find Slack Before Flood, use the entry under Slack Time that has a current speed (in knots) under the Flood column, to the right of the Max. time column. When trying to find the Slack Before Ebb, use the entry under Slack Time that has a current speed (in knots) under the Ebb column, to the right of the Max time column.

The last two columns in the current difference tables give ratios to multiply by the speeds given in the reference table. Multiply the ratio under the heading Flood by the speed (in knots) under the heading Fld on the reference table. Multiply the ratio under the heading Ebb by the speed (in knots) under the heading Ebb on the reference table. The resulting figures are the approximate maximum current speeds to be expected.

EXAMPLE

Look up the current differences for Fajardo Harbor channel, listed near the end of the current differences list. The reference station to be used with these differences is Vieques Passage.

The approximate position these current differences relate to is 18° 20'N, 65° 37'W.

Turn to the listing for March 27, 1994 in the Vieques Passage, Puerto Rico current table. This table is located at the end of the section on Puerto Rico in Chapter 2. On this date the current is slack at 0129, at maximum ebb (0.9 knots) at 0447, slack at 0810, at maximum flood (0.7 knots) at 1101, slack at 1356, at maximum ebb (0.7 knots) at 1658, slack at 1955, and at maximum flood (0.9 knots) at 2311.

The tide current difference of 1 hour and 13 minutes for Fajardo under Slack Before Flood should be subtracted from the slack times, before the floods. Minimum currents before floods will occur at 0657 and 1842.

The tide current difference of 1 hour and 52 minutes under Max. Flood should be subtracted from the flood Max. times. Maximum floods will occur at 0909 and 2119.

The tide current difference of 2 hours and 27 minutes under Slack Before Ebb should be subtracted from the slack times, before the

ebbs. Minimum currents before ebbs will occur at 2302 on March 26th (the previous day) and 1129 on March 27th.

The tide current difference of 1 hour and 45 minutes under Max. Ebb should be subtracted from the ebb Max. times. Maximum ebbs will occur at 0302 and 1513.

The speed ratios given in the final column of the difference tables are 0.5 for the maximum flood currents and 1.6 for the maximum ebb currents. The maximum floods at 0909 and 2119 will have speeds of .35 knots and .45 knots, respectively. The maximum ebbs at 0302 and 1513 will have speeds of 1.44 knots and 1.12 knots.

Current Differences

	POSITION		TIME DIFFERENCES				SPEED RATIOS		CURRENT DIRECTION & MAX SPEED			
	North Latitude	West Longitude	Slack before Flood	Max Flood	Slack before Ebb	Max Ebb	Flood	Ebb	Flood	Ebb	Flood	Ebb
			h m	h m	h m	h m			Dir	Dir	knots	knots
FLORIDA	*Eastern Standard Time (GMT −5h)*		**ON MIAMI HARBOR ENT.**					*Add one hour Daylight Saving April 3—October 29*				
Ft Pierce Inlet	27°28.30'	80°17.50'	+1:19	+0:39	+0:48	+0:35	1.5	2.0	250°	072°	2.6	3.1
Lake Worth Inlet (btwn jetties)...	26°46.33'	80°02.13'	+0:13	−0:07	−0:01	0:00	1.3	2.3	273°	054°	2.4	3.6
Fort Lauderdale, New River.......	26°06.73'	80°07.18'	−0:43	−0:39	−0:06	−0:16	0.4	0.3	005°	130°	0.8	0.5
PORT EVERGLADES												
Entrance (between jetties).........	26°05.58'	80°06.32'	−0:08	−0:49	−0:43	−0:34	0.3	0.4	275°	035°	0.6	0.7
Entrance from southward (canal)	26°05.20'	80°06.90'	+0:40	+0:07	+0:31	−0:09	0.7	1.1	167°	358°	1.3	1.7
Turning Basin	26°05.70'	80°07.05'	−1:01	−1:07	−1:02	−1:11	0.1	0.3	320°	155°	0.2	0.5
Turning Basin, 300 yards N of ...	26°05.80'	80°07.10'	−0:20	−1:09	−0:27	−0:14	0.5	1.1	349°	160°	0.9	1.8
17th Street Bridge	26°06.02'	80°07.13'	−0:38	−0:53	−0:28	−0:55	1.1	1.2	350°	170°	1.9	1.9
MIAMI HARBOR												
Bakers Haulover Cut	25°54.00'	80°07.40'	−0:01	+0:07	+0:14	−0:17	1.6	1.6	270°	090°	2.9	2.5
Government Cut												
East entrance, off N jetty	25°45.59'	80°07.35'	−0:02	−0:19	−0:08	−0:26	0.4	0.9	236°	092°	0.6	1.5
East entrance, inside S jetty	25°45.61'	80°07.66'	−0:07	−0:06	−0:04	0:00	1.2	1.1	343°	116°	2.1	1.8
Midway, N side	25°45.84'	80°07.96'	−0:12	−0:03	−0:07	−0:08	0.7	0.5	292°	108°	1.2	0.7
MIAMI HARBOR ENTRANCE..	25°45.90'	80°08.17'	**Daily Predictions**						293°	112°	1.8	1.6
West entrance, S side	25°45.85'	80°08.25'	+0:09	+0:10	−0:04	+0:01	0.9	1.6	288°	100°	1.6	2.5
Main Channel												
Causeway I, 0.2 nm SE of	25°46.06'	80°08.58'	+0:01	+0:23	−0:01	−0:14	0.8	0.4	306°	131°	1.4	0.7
Lummus I, NE corner	25°46.02'	80°08.70'	−0:07	−0:02	+0:06	−0:04	0.1	0.4	265°	104°	0.2	0.7
Lummus I..18 nm off NW corner	25°46.32'	80°09.45'	−0:05	+0:50	+0:28	−0:08	0.3	0.3	285°	102°	0.5	0.5
Dodge I, 0.1 nm off NW corner.	25°46.89'	80°10.90'	+0:17	−0:14	+0:01	+0:04	0.2	0.3	277°	093°	0.4	0.4
Fishermans Channel												
Lummus I, SE corner	25°45.95'	80°08.71'	+0:08	+0:06	+0:19	−0:20	0.5	0.2	208°	086°	0.9	0.4
Fisher I, 0.2 nm NW of	25°45.87'	80°09.08'	+0:14	+0:38	+0:17	+0:39	0.6	0.7	280°	090°	1.0	1.1
Lummus I,.15 nm off SW corner	25°45.45'	80°09.69'	+0:20	−0:20	+0:10	+0:22	0.3	0.6	271°	095°	0.6	0.9
West end, SW of Dodge I	25°46.36'	80°10.74'	−0:05	−0:32	−0:15	−0:21	0.1	0.2	277°	085°	0.2	0.3
Miami River entrance	25°46.21'	80°11.23'	+0:15	−0:02	−0:01	+0:46	0.1	0.4	261°	07-°	0.2	0.6

Chapter 3

Current Differences

Current Differences	North Latitude	West Longitude	Slack before Flood h m	Max Flood h m	Slack before Ebb h m	Max Ebb h m	Flood	Ebb	Flood Dir	Ebb Dir	Flood knots	Ebb knots
FLORIDA REEFS				ON KEY WEST								
Caesar Creek, Biscayne Bay	25°23.20'	80°13.60'	+0:07	−0:08	−0:14	−0:05	1.2	1.0	316°	123°	1.2	1.8
Long Key, drawbridge E of	24°50.40'	80°46.20'	+0:58	+1:27	+2:21	+1:33	1.1	0.7	000°	202°	.1	1.2
Long Key Viaduct	24°48.10'	80°51.90'	+1:34	+1:28	+2:02	+1:57	0.9	0.7	349°	170°	0.9	1.2
Moser Channel, swingbridge	24°42.00'	81°10.20'	+1:07	+1:30	+1:50	+1:47	1.4	1.0	339°	166°	1.4	1.8
Bahia Honda Harbor, bridge	24°39.40'	81°17.30'	+1:01	+0:39	+1:53	+1:05	1.4	1.2	004°	182°	1.4	2.1
No Name Key, NE of	24°42.30'	81°18.80'	+0:55	+1:24	+1:20	+0:53	0.7	0.5	312°	142°	0.7	0.9
Key West												
Main Ship Channel entrance	24°28.40'	81°48.10'	−0:44	−0:12	+0:10	+0:10	0.2	0.3	040°	178°	0.2	0.4
Main Ship Channel	24°30.50'	81°48.30'	0:30	0:30	0:30	+0:30	0.1	0.2	064°	133°	−|−	0.4
KEY WEST, 0.3 nm W Ft Taylor	24°32.90'	81°49.00'		Daily Predictions					022°	194°	1.0	1.7
Ft Taylor, 0.6 nm N of	24°33.50'	81°48.60'	+0:20	+0:13	−0:11	+0:13	0.6	0.7	042°	202°	0.5	1.2
Turning Basin	24°34.00'	81°48.25'	+0:43	+0:44	+0:29	+1:06	0.8	0.6	048°	216°	0.3	1.1
Northwest Channel	24°35.00'	81°50.90'	−0:08	−0:03	−0:09	−0:07	1.2	0.8	353°	162°	1.2	1.4
Northwest Channel	24°37.30'	81°52.80'	−0:28	−0:19	−0:20	−0:20	0.6	0.4	346°	168°	0.6	0.6
Boca Grande Channel	24°34.00'	82°04.00'	−0:40	−0:45	−0:01	−0:06	1.1	0.8	353°	194°	1.1	1.2
New Ground	24°39.00'	82°25.00'	+1:36	+1:55	+1:28	+1:18	0.7	0.4	068°	244°	0.2	0.7
Isaac Shoal	24°33.50'	82°32.20'	+1:00	+0:54	+1:52	+1:55	1.0	0.5	002°	181°	1.0	0.8
Southeast Channel	24°37.62'	82°51.07'	−0:27	−0:06	+0:37	+0:36	0.6	0.4	004°	172°	0.6	0.6
Southwest Channel	24°36.92'	82°54.70'	+0:45	+0:59	+1:25	+2:04	0.4	0.4	001°	209°	0.4	0.6
Atlantic Standard Time (GMT −4h) Daylight Saving Time Not Observed												
PUERTO RICO				ON VIEQUES PASSAGE								
Punta Ostiones, 1.5 nm W of	18°05.20'	67°13.60'	−0:26	−0:52	−0:04	−0:35	1.7	1.3	187°	001°	1.0	0.9
VIEQUES PASSAGE	18°11.30'	65°37.10'		Daily Predictions					250°	057°	0.6	0.7
Vieques Sound	18°15.87'	65°34.20'	−0:44	−1:16	−1:28	−1:05	0.7	0.9	180°	355°	0.4	0.6
Largo Shoals, W of	18°19.00'	65°35.00'	−0:52	−1:28	−1:33	−1:08	0.7	1.0	186°	330°	0.4	0.7
Ramos Cay, 0.3 nm SE of	18°18.60'	65°36.40'	−0:40	−0:42	−0:40	−0:44	0.3	0.1	120°	284°	0.2	0.1
Palominos I, 0.9 nm SW of	18°20.10'	65°34.80'	−0:40	−0:48	−0:40	−0:48	0.1	0.7		307°	−|−	0.5
Fajardo Harbor (channel)	18°20.00'	65°37.38'	−1:13	−1:52	−2:27	−1:45	0.5	1.6	162°	339°	0.3	1.1
Isla Marina, 0.2 nm W of	18°20.50'	65°37.30'	−2:00	−2:00	−2:00	−2:06	0.1	1.0	−°	335°	−|−	0.7
Coronala Laja, 0.4 nm NW of	18°21.60'	65°37.30'	−1:30	−1:30	−1:30	−1:33	0.0	0.4	−°	000°	−|−	0.3
Pasaje de San Juan	18°23.90'	65°36.90'	−1:10	−1:15	−1:10	−1:15	0.0	1.7	−°	310°	−|−	1.2

ELECTRONIC NAVIGATION AIDS

4

Chapter 4

RADIOBEACON REFERENCE MAP

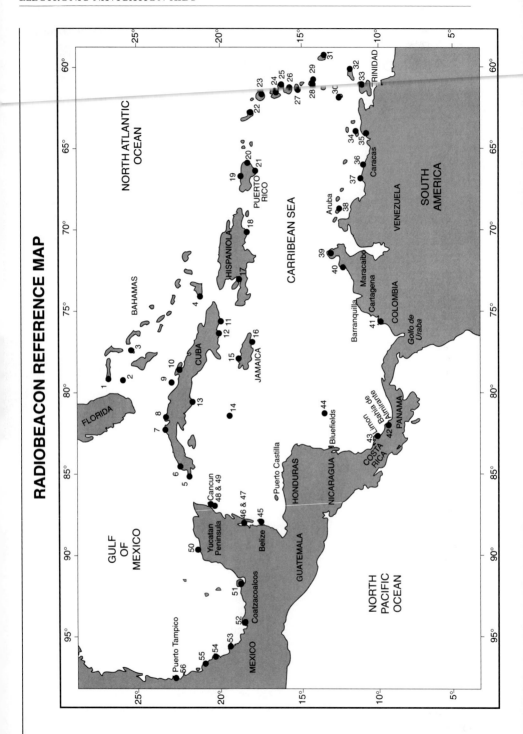

Radiobeacon Reference Map

MORSE CODE FOR IDENTIFICATION OF RADIOBEACONS

A ·–	I ··	Q ––·–	Y –·––	1 ·––––	9 ––––·
B –···	J ·–––	R ·–·	Z ––··	2 ··–––	0 –––––
C –·–·	K –·–	S ···	3 ···––		
D –··	L ·–··	T –	4 ····–		
E ·	M ––	U ··–	5 ·····		
F ··–·	N –·	V ···–	6 –····		
G ––·	O –––	W ·––	7 ––···		
H ····	P ·––·	X –··–	8 –––··		

RADIOBEACONS

The radiobeacon numbers refer to the map on the preceding page.

Most radiobeacons in the Caribbean are Aero beacons. These are located to best serve the needs of aircraft, and should be used with caution. All radiobeacons are subject to interference and refraction errors. As with all aids to navigation in the Caribbean, users are cautioned that radiobeacons have been reported as unreliable.

When the distance to a radiobeacon is greater than 50 miles, a correction is usually applied to the bearing before plotting on a mercator chart. Refer to the *Companion* for more information on radiobeacons.

BERMUDA

NOTE: Bermuda radiobeacons are not shown on the radiobeacon reference map.

St. Davids Head, 32 22.0N, 64 38.9W, BSD (–··· ··· –··), 323kHz A2A, 150M.

Gibbs Hill Light Station, 32 15.1N, 64 50.0W, BDA (–··· –·· ·–), 295kHz A2A, 130M.

BAHAMA ISLANDS

1) West End International Airport Aero, 26 41N, 78 59W, ZWE (––·· ·–– ·), 317kHz A2A, 100M.

2) Bimini Islands Aero, 25 42.5N, 79 16.3W, ZBB (––·· –··· –···), 396kHz A2A, 300M.

3) Nassau International Airport Aero, 25 02N, 77 28W, ZQA (––·· ––·– ·–), 251kHz A1A, 240M.

4) Great Inagua Aero, 20 57.6N, 73 40.5W, ZIN (––·· ·· –··), 376kHz A2A, 50M.

CUBA

5) Cabo San Antonio Light Station, 21 52N, 84 57W, AB (·– –···) period 360s, transmit 60s, silent 300s, 301kHz A2A, 155M, Temporarily inoperative (Oct. 1986).

6) San Julian Aero, 22 05N, 84 13W, USJ (··– ··· ·–––), 402kHz, 155M.

7) Havana Aero, 22 58N, 82 26W, A (·–), 339kHz, 256M.

8) Varder Aero, 23 05N, 81 22W, UVR (··– ···– ·–·), 272kHz A2A, 216M.

9) Cayo Caiman Grande, 22 41.1N, 78 53W, CCG (–·–· –·–· ––·), 290kHz NON, A2A, 155M.

10) Punta Alegre, 22 22.5N, 78 47.3W, UPA (··– ·––· ·–), 382kHz A2A, 70M.

11) Guantanamo Bay Aero, 19 54N, 75 10W, NBW (–· –··· ·––), 276.2kHz.

12) Santiago de Cuba Aero, 19 58N, 75 50W, UCU (··– –·–· ··–), 339kHz A2A, 70M.

13) Los Colorados Light Station, 22 02.1N, 80 26.5W, WY (·–– –·––) 298.8kHz NON, A2A, Transmits upon request through Central Territorial Hydrographic office (COX41) on 6818kHz during day or 3904kHz at night.

Chapter 4

CAYMAN ISLANDS

14) Grand Cayman Aero, 19 17N, 81 23W, ZIY (−−·· ·· −·−−·), 344kHz NON, A2A, 240M.

JAMAICA

15) Montego Bay Aero, 18 30N, 77 55W, MBJ (−− −··· ·−−−) 248kHz NON, A2A, 150M.

16) Kingston Aero, 17 58N, 76 53W, KIN (−·− ·· −·), 360kHz NON, A2A, 250M.

HAITI

17) Port-au-Prince Aero, 18 35N, 72 17W, HHP (···· ···· ·−−·), 270kHz A2A, 240M.

DOMINICAN REPUBLIC

18) Punta Caucedo Aero, 18 27N, 69 40W, HIV (···· ·· ····−), 400kHz A2A, 240M.

PUERTO RICO

19) Dorado Aero (16 miles west of San Juan), 18 28N, 66 25 W, DDP (−·· −·· ·−−·), 391kHz NON, A2A, 365M.

20) Roosevelt Roads Aero, 18 14N, 65 37W, NRR (−· ·−· ·−·), 264kHz NON, A2A, 115M.

21) Punta Tuna Light Station, 17 59.4N, 65 53.1W, X (−··−), period 60s, transmit 50s, long tone for 10s, 288kHz A2A, 55M, Antenna Lead-In: 40 yards 345 degrees from light tower. Carrier Signal.

LEEWARD ISLANDS

22) Saint Barthelemy Aero, 17 54N, 62 51W, BY (−··· ·−−−), 338kHz A1A, 50M.

23) Antigua (Coolidge) Aero, 17 07.5N, 61 47.6, ZDX (−−·· −·· −··−) 369kHz NON, A2A, 256M.

24) Guadeloupe (Point-a Pitre) Aero, 16 16N, 61 32W, FXG (··−· −··− −−·), 300kHz NON, A2A, 250M.

25) Guadeloupe (Marie-Galante/Grand Bourg) Aero, 15 52N, 61 16W, MG (−− −−·), 376kHz A2A, 50M.

26) Dominica Aero, 15 32.8N, 61 18.4W, DOM (−·· −−− −−), 273kHz, 100M.

WINDWARD ISLANDS

27) Martinique (Fort de France) Aero, 14 36N, 61 06N, FXF (··−· −··− ··−·) 314kHz A2A, 100M.

28) Saint Lucia (Hewanorra) Aero, 13 44N, 60 59W, BNE (−··· −· ·), 305kHz, 100M.

29) Saint Vincent (Arnos Vale) Aero, 13 09N, 61 13W, SV (··· ···−), 403kHz, 143M.

30) Grenada Aero, 12 00.5N, 61 46.8W, GND (−−· −· −··), 362kHz NON, A2A, 115M.

BARBADOS

31) Barbados (Seawell Aerodome) Aero, 13 04N, 59 30W, BGI (−··· −−· ··), 345kHz NON, A2A, 256M.

TOBAGO

32) Tobago (Crown Point) Aero, 11 09N, 60 51N, TAB (− ·− −···), 323kHz A2A, 100M.

TRINIDAD

33) Trinidad (Piarco) Aero, 10 36N, 61 26W, POS (·−−· −−− ···), 382kHz NON A2A, 256M.

VENEZUELA

34) Margarita Aero, 10 55.3N, 63 57.6W, MTA (−− − ·−), 206kHz A2A, 100M.

35) Higuerote Aero, 10 28N, 64 05.7W, HOT (···· −−− −), 353kHz A2A, 240M.

36) La Orchilla, 11 48N, 66 07W, ORC (−−− ·−· −·−·) 320kHZ A2A, 180M.

37) Maiquetia Aero, 10 37N, 66 59N, MIQ (−− ·· −−·−), 292kHz A2A, 130M.

NETHERLANDS ANTILLES

38) Curacao Aero, 12 13N, 69 04W, PJG (·−−· ·−−− −−·), 343kHz NON, A2A, 150M.

COLOMBIA — ATLANTIC COAST

39) Puerto Bolivar Aero, 12 14.2N, 71 59.7W, 415kHz.

40) Riohacha Aero, 11 33N, 72 54W, RHC (·−· ···· −·−·), 295kHz NON, A2A, 75M.

41) Isla Tierra Bomba Light Station, 10 20.6N, 75 34.8W, CG (−·−· −−·) period 540s, transmits 60s, silent 120s, repeats (2)

360s, 280kHz A2A, 100M, Transmits at 00 and 30 minutes past each hour.

PANAMA — ATLANTIC COAST

42) Almirante, 9 17.4N, 82 23.6W, B (–···), 290kHz A2A, Transmits continuously between 0500 and1300.

COSTA RICA

43) Limon (TIM), 10 00.1N, 83 01.6W, M (––), period 600s, 290kHz A2A, 50M, Transmits upon request through Limon (TIM) at 00 and 30 minutes past the hour requested.

SAN ANDRES ISLAND — COLUMBIA

44) Isla San Andres, 12 35.1N, 81 42.3W, SPP (··· ·––· ·––·), 387kHz NON, A2A, 40M.

BELIZE

45) Belize Aero, 17 32N, 88 18W, BZE (–··· ––·· ·), 392kHz NON, A2A, 192M.

MEXICO

46) Chetumal Aero, 18 30N, 88 19W, CTM (–·–· – ––), 262.5kHz A2A, 256M.

47) Chetumal, 18 30N, 88 24N, XFP (–··– ···– ·––·), 293kHz A2A, 100M.

48) Cozumel, 20 28N, 86 59W, XFC (–··– ···– –·–·), 319kHz A2A, 100M.

49) Cozumel Aero, 20 30.6N, 86 56.6W, CZM (–·–· ––·· ––), 330kHz A2A, 240M.

50) Progreso, 21 16N, 89 43W, XFN (–··– ···– –·), 306kHz A2A, 100M.

51) Ciudad del Carmen Aero, 18 39.8N, 91 48.6N, CME (–·–· –– ·), 288kHz A2A, 256M.

52) Coatzacoalcos, 18 09.4N, 94 24.3, XFF (–··– ···– ···–·), 319kHz A2A, 100M.

53) Vera Cruz, 19 09.3N, 96 08.6W, XFU (–··– ···– ···–), 296kHz A2A, 100M.

54) Nautla Aero, 20 12N, 96 46W, NAU (–· ·– ··–), 392kHz A2A, 256M.

55) Tuxpan Aero, 20 57N, 97 22W, TUX (– ··– –··–), 262.5kHz A2A, 256M.

56) Tampico, 22 13.9N, 97 50.8W, XFS (–··– ···– ···), 287kHz A2A.

LORAN STATUS

LORAN-C is of some use in the northern regions of the Caribbean. Groundwave coverage extends from the northern Bahamas to Cuba, to the Gulf of Honduras and into the Gulf of Mexico along the Mexican coast.

Many users have reported good success in returning to positions where a LORAN reading was previously recorded. Even though the latitude/longitude readouts may be inaccurate, the readings received at a particular location have proven to be repeatable. The best results will be obtained by recording (or storing in the units memory) on-site Time Difference readings.

Keep in mind the possible differences between the NAD-83 Coordinate System and the NAD-27 System used on some Caribbean charts. Differences of over a mile have been reported when comparing latitude/longitude positions in the two systems. Government charts will list the coordinate system used.

Skywave coverage is much less accurate, and is subject to false readings. Skywave fixes must be used with great caution and should be confirmed with other navigational means. Skywaves may be useable as far to the southeast as the Virgin Islands; as far to the south as Maracaibo, Venezuela; and into Columbia, Panama and Costa Rica. Reed's has received reports of useable signals being picked up throughout the Caribbean.

The Southeast U.S. 7980 Chain is in use in this area. It consists of the following broadcast sites:

    Malone, FL, 31 00N, 85 10W, 7980 Master.
    Grangeville, LA, 30 44N, 90 50W, 7980-W.
    Raymondville, TX, 26 32N, 97 50W, 7980-X.
    Jupiter, FL, 27 02N, 80 07W, 7980-Y.
    Carolina Beach, NC, 34 04N, 77 55W, 7980-Z.

For best use of LORAN-C in the Caribbean you should obtain charts with a LORAN grid overlay. Increased position accuracy is possible by plotting LORAN Time Differences on these charts. The latitude/longitude conversion programs on many LORAN sets have been found to be much less accurate in these waters than in the continental U.S.

Chapter 4

GPS STATUS

As of March 1993 users of the Global Positioning System (GPS) are warned the system is not yet fully operational. Signal availability and accuracy are subject to change due to an incomplete constellation and operational test activities.

The GPS constellation consists of 22 satellites, 21 of which are operational. Selective avail-ability (SA) is on, offering approximately 100 meter accuracy.

Keep in mind the possible differences between the NAD-83 Coordinate System and the NAD-27 System used on some Caribbean charts. Differences of over a mile have been reported when comparing latitude/longitude positions in the two systems. Government charts will list the coordinate system used, and your GPS unit should be adjusted accordingly.

Differential GPS users are advised that the exper-imental DGPS reference stations are located in the NAD-83 Coordinate System. All users must use charts updated to NAD-83/WGS-84 to receive acceptable position results from DGPS.

For more information on GPS, and the latest system status, contact the U.S. Coast Guard's Global Positioning Information Center (GPSIC). A 24 hour recording may be heard at (703) 313-5907. A 24 hour computer bulletin board (300 to 14,400 baud) is at (703) 313-5910. The fax number is (703) 313-5920.

GPSIC watchstanders can answer your questions 24 hours-a-day at (703) 313-5900.

The U.S. Coast Guard broadcasts warnings and information on GPS in their regular Marine Information Broadcasts. These may be heard by listening on VHF channel 16 (switching 22A) and on medium frequency 2182 (switching 2670). Messages are also broadcast on NAVTEX. Those with a modem link to NAVINFONET can access GPS information - call GPSIC for more information.

Radio station WWV also broadcasts GPS status reports at 14 and 15 minutes past the hour on 2.5, 5, 10, 15 and 20 MHz. WWVH broadcasts these reports at 43 and 44 minutes past the hour on 2.5, 5, 10 and 15 MHz. For more information on the WWV and WWVH time and weather broadcasts see the Communi-cations and Weather Services chapter of this almanac.

GPS and Omega publications are available from:

Commanding Officer
Omega NAVSYSCEN/GPSIC
7323 Telegraph Road
Alexandria, VA 22310-3998

COMMUNICATION & WEATHER SERVICES

Chapter 5

CONTACTING THE U.S. COAST GUARD

Channel	Transmit	Receive
424	4134kHz	4426kHz
601	6200kHz	6501kHz
816	8240kHz	8764kHz
1205	12242kHz	13089kHz
1625	16432kHz	17314kHz

In coastal waters of the United States, Puerto Rico and the Virgin Islands vessels may often contact the Coast Guard on VHF channel 16. Channel 16 may only be used for Distress and Calling. Routine radio checks on this frequency are prohibited.

After initial contact on channel 16 you will usually be asked to switch to channel 22A or channel 12.

The international hailing and distress frequency is 2182kHz in the medium frequency band. This frequency is monitored by all Coast Guard stations, any vessel equipped with the proper equipment while underway, and many Coast Stations. After initial contact on 2182kHz you will usually be asked to switch to 2670kHz, which is the U.S. Coast Guard working frequency for weather broadcasts, Notices to Mariners and marine safety broadcasts.

Starting August 1, 1993 the U.S. Coast Guard will no longer monitor 500kHz, and will cease all morse code services in the medium frequency band. It is felt there are more efficient communication systems in place.

EMERGENCY MEDICAL ADVICE

Contact the U.S. Coast Guard on 2182kHz, or via one of the high frequency channels listed at the end of this section. In addition, High Seas Radiotelephone and Coastal Marine Operators can transfer emergency calls to the nearest Coast Guard station. No charge is made for such calls when the ship states it is an emergency involving the safety of life or property at sea.

CONTACT AND LONG RANGE LIASON

The U.S. Coast Guard monitors the following frequencies as part of the CALL (Contact and Long Range Liason) system. Allow at least one minute for a response before switching channels. These frequencies are also used for voice weather broadcasts, navigation warnings and medical communications. The Coast Guard is monitoring many channels at once, and may not be able to respond immediately.

VOICE RADIO BROADCASTS

NOTE: Most times in this section are in UTC (Universal Coordinated Time), which is the same as Greenwich Mean Time.

NOAA Weather Radio operates VHF-FM radio stations on frequencies of 162.55, 162.40 and 162.475 MHz. These stations provide continuous weather broadcasts, including both regional and local weather. Broadcast tapes are generally updated every three hours during the day, and at least every six hours.

Broadcasts vary, but generally include the following information:
1) Marine forecasts and warnings for coastal waters out to 60 miles.
2) Offshore waters forecast for waters 60 to 250 miles from land.
3) State forecasts and local forecasts.
4) Selected weather observations from the Coast Guard, buoys and other stations.

Whenever severe weather warnings are necessary, the tape will be updated and the transmission devoted to "up-to-the-minute" information on storm dangers.

Outside the continental United States NOAA weather broadcasts are transmitted from Puerto Rico and the U.S. Virgin Islands. Bermuda, the Bahamas and the British Virgin Islands have local VHF broadcasts as well.

WX-1: 162.55MHz
WX-2: 162.40MHz
WX-3: 162.475MHz

The United States Coast Guard also transmits navigation information on medium frequency (usually 2670.0kHz). The broadcast will be announced on 2182kHz and VHF channel 16 before commencing.

Coast Guard broadcasts will usually include Notices to Mariners, marine warnings, hurricane information and weather.

The Coast Guard's high seas weather information is transmitted from Portsmouth, Virginia via station NMN. For many mariners in the Caribbean, this is the best source of complete weather data.

Coast Stations should respond to calls on the International Hailing and Distress Frequencys; VHF channel 16 or 2182kHz. These stations include pilots, port authorities and public correspondence stations. The latter can be used for making telephone calls. Most stations monitoring 2182kHz will also respond to calls on VHF channel 16. This is a partial list — Reed's welcomes any additions to this material.

Commercial Broadcast Stations are listed after weather broadcasts and Coast Stations. Whenever possible, we have listed English language stations in countries where the predominant language is not English. Schedules and frequencies are subject to frequent change.

*Stations of particular interest to boaters are preceded by a *.

WWV

*MARINE STORM WARNINGS for the North Atlantic Ocean are broadcast by station WWV. They follow the regular Time Announcements at 8 and 9 minutes after the hour. Frequencies are 2500, 5000, 10000, 15000, and 20000 kHz. See the section on Time Signals for more information on station WWV.

The National Weather Service issues warning updates at 0500, 1100, 1700 and 2300 UTC. The updates are announced at the next broadcast following time of issue. Topics include locations of storm centers, low pressure systems and hurricanes, and their predicted positions for the next 12 to 24 hours.

PORTSMOUTH, VA

*Call sign NMN, U.S. Coast Guard. NMN provides the most complete offshore weather information available in this region. Broadcasts include forecasts and a synopsis for New England, the West Central North Atlantic, the Southwest North Atlantic (including the Bahamas), the Gulf of Mexico and the Caribbean.

0400, 0530, 1000 UTC on 4426.0, 6501.0 and 8764.0 kHz.

1130, 1600 UTC on 6501.0, 8764.0 and 13089.0 kHz.
1730 UTC on 8764.0, 13089.0 and 17314.0 kHz.
2200 and 2330 UTC on 6501.0, 8764.0 and 13089.0 kHz.

VOICE OF AMERICA

Voice of America
Washington, DC 20547
(202) 619-2538.

Directed to the Caribbean:
0000 to 0030 UTC on 930, 6130, 9455 and 11695 kHz.
0030 to 0100 UTC on 6130, 9455 and 11695 kHz.
0100 to 0200 UTC on 930, 5995, 6130, 7405, 9455, 9775, 11580, 15120 and 15205 kHz.
0200 to 0300 UTC on 930kHz.
1000 to 1100 UTC on 9590, 11915 and 15120 kHz.
1100 to 1200 UTC on 930, 9590, 11915 and 15120 kHz.
1200 to 1230 UTC on 930kHz.
1700 to 1730 UTC on 930kHz.
2100 to 2200 UTC on 930kHz.

Directed to the American Republics:
0000 to 0030 UTC on 5995, 7405, 9775, 11580, 15120 and 15205 kHz.
0030 to 0100 UTC on 5995, 7405, 9775, 11580, 15120 and 15205 kHz.
0100 to 0200 UTC on 930, 5995, 6130, 7405, 9455, 9775, 11580, 15120 and 15205 kHz.
Ends at 0200 UTC Saturday and Sunday.
0200 to 0230 UTC on 5995, 7405, 9775, 11580, 15120 and 15205 kHz.

Directed to northern Central America:
0030 to 0100 UTC on 1530 and 1580 kHz.
0100 to 0200 UTC on 930, 5995, 6130, 7405, 9455, 9775, 11580, 15120 and 15205 kHz.
0200 to 0230 UTC on 5995, 7405, 9775, 11580, 15120 and 15205 kHz.
0400 to 0500 UTC on 1530 and 1580 kHz.
Monday through Friday.

BBC WORLD SERVICE

British Broadcasting Corporation
World Service
Bush House
London, WC2B 4PH
England
71-257-2875

Chapter 5

Directed to the Caribbean:
0000 to 0430 UTC on 5975, 7325 and 9915 kHz.
0300 to 0330 UTC on 930kHz.
1100 to 1400 UTC on 15220kHz.
1100 to 1430 UTC on 6195kHz.
1100 to 1200 UTC on 930kHz.
1400 to 1615 UTC on 17840kHz.
1600 to 1615 UTC on 930kHz.
1800 to 1830 UTC on 930kHz.
2000 to 2400 UTC on 5975kHz.
2200 to 2400 UTC on 7325kHz.
2200 to 2400 UTC on 9915kHz.
2230 to 2400 UTC on 930kHz.

Directed to Central America and Mexico:
0000 to 0630 UTC on 5975kHz.
0000 to 0430 UTC on 7325 and 9915 kHz.
0030 to 0230 UTC on 9590kHz.
0500 to 0630 UTC on 9640kHz.
1100 to 1400 UTC on 15220kHz.
1400 to 1615 UTC on 17840kHz.
2300 to 2400 UTC on 5975, 7325 and 9915 kHz.

BERMUDA
WEATHER
*Call sign ZBM,** Bermuda Harbour Radio, St. Georges. VHF channel 07 at 0900 Local Time. VHF channel 27 at 1235 and 2035 UTC. 1235 and 2035 UTC on 2582kHz.

COAST STATIONS
Call sign ZBM, Bermuda Harbour Radio, St. Georges. Stands by on VHF channel 16 and 2182kHz.
Call sign VRT, Bermuda Radio, Public Correspondence. VHF channels 26 and 28.

GENERAL BROADCAST STATIONS
ZBM, 1340kHz 1kW, FM 89.1MHz.
ZFB, 1230kHz 1kW, FM 94.9MHz.
VSB, 1160kHz, 1280kHz, 1450kHz 1kW, FM 106.2MHz.

NORTHERN FLORIDA
WEATHER
Call sign NMA-10, Mayport, U.S. Coast Guard. 0015 and 1215 UTC on VHF channel 22A. 0620 and 1820 UTC on 2670.0kHz.
Call sign KHB-39, Jacksonville, WX-1.
Call sign WXJ-60, Gainesville, WX-3.
Call sign KIH-26, Daytona Beach, WX-2.
Call sign KIH-63, Orlando, WX-3.
Call sign WXJ-70, Melbourne, WX-1.
Call sign KEC-50, West Palm Beach, WX-3.

FT. LAUDERDALE, FL
WEATHER
*Call sign WOM,** AT&T Coast Station. 1300 and 2300 UTC on 4363.0, 8722.0, 13092.0, 17242.0 and 22738.0 kHz.

MIAMI, FL
WEATHER
Call sign KHB-34, Miami, WX-1.
Call sign NCF, U.S. Coast Guard. 1230 and 2230 UTC on VHF channel 22A. 0350 and 1550 UTC on 2670.0kHz.

KEY WEST, FL
WEATHER
Call sign WXJ-95, Key West, WX-2.
Call sign NOK, U.S. Coast Guard. 1200 and 2200 UTC on VHF channel 22A.

ST. PETERSBURG, FL
WEATHER
Call sign NMA-21, U.S. Coast Guard. 1300 and 2300 UTC on VHF channel 22A. 0320 and 1420 UTC on 2670.0kHz.

PANAMA CITY, FL
WEATHER
Call sign NOQ-7, U.S. Coast Guard. 1035, 1635, 2235 UTC on VHF channel 22A. 1005, 1205, 1605 and 2205 UTC on 2670.0kHz.

MOBILE, AL
WEATHER
Call sign NOQ, U.S. Coast Guard. 1020, 1220, 1620, and 2220 UTC on VHF channel 22A. 1020, 1220, 1620 and 2220 UTC on 2670.0kHz.
Call sign WLO, Mobile Coast Station. 0000, 0600, 1200 and 1800 UTC on 4369.0, 8788.0, 13152.0 17362.0 and 22804.0kHz.

NEW ORLEANS, LA
WEATHER
Call sign NMG-2, U.S. Coast Guard. 0100 and 1550 UTC on 432kHz. 1035, 1235, 1635 and 2235 UTC on VHF channel 22A and 2670.0kHz.

GALVESTON, TX
WEATHER
Call sign NOY, U.S. Coast Guard. 1045, 1245, 1645 and 2245 UTC on VHF channel 22A. 1050, 1250, 1650 and 2250 UTC on 2670.0kHz.

CORPUS CHRISTI, TX
WEATHER
Call sign NOY-8, U.S. Coast Guard. 1040, 1240, 1640 and 2240 UTC on VHF channel 22A and 2670.0kHz.

BAHAMAS

WEATHER
Call sign C6N, Nassau.
VHF channel 27 every even hour.
*Radio Bahamas, 810 kHz 1kW, 1240kHz
1kW, 1540kHz 20kW, FM 107.1MHz,
FM 107.9MHz. Weather at 1230 and 2330 UTC
and with the news on the hour.

COAST STATIONS
There are numerous coast stations monitoring
VHF channel 16 in the Bahamas. Most marinas
will be standing by, and there is always a boater
willing to assist within radio range. This is only
a partial listing of some widely used stations.

*Call sign "BASRA", Bahamas Air Sea Rescue
Association. Contact on VHF channel 16 or
2182kHz.
Call sign "Jack Tar", West End Marina. Con-
tact on VHF channel 16.
Call sign "Walker's Cay", Walker's Cay
Marina. Contact on VHF channel 16.
Call sign C6X2, Marsh Harbor Public Corre-
spondence. Stands by on 2182kHz.
Call sign "Treasure Cay", Treasure Cay
Marina. Contact on VHF channel 16.
Call sign ZFP-81, Freeport Harbor Control.
VHF channel 16 or 2182kHz.
Call sign "Bortow Pilots", Freeport pilots.
Contact on VHF channels 6, 10, 13, 14 and 16.
Call sign "Borco Marine", The Bahamas Oil
Refining Company, Freeport. Contact on VHF
channel 16.
Call sign "Cat Cay Club", Cat Cay, Bahamas.
Contact on VHF channel 16.
Call sign "Chub Cay", Chub Cay Marina.
Contact on VHF channel 16.
Call sign "Great Harbour Cay Marina",
Great Harbour, Berry Islands. Contact on VHF
channel 16.
Call sign "Nassau Harbor Control", Con-
tact on VHF channels 6, 10, 13, 14 and 16.
Stands by on 2182kHz.
Call sign C6N3, Nassau Public Correspon-
dence. VHF channel 27.
Call sign C6N2, Nassau Public Correspon-
dence. Stands by on 2182kHz.
Call sign "Wee Watin", Highborne Cay, Exu-
mas. Contact on VHF channel 16.
Call sign "Sampson", Sampson Cay, Exumas.
Contact on VHF channel 16.
Call sign "Stella Maris", Stella Maris Mari-
na, Long Island. Contact on VHF channel 16.
Call sign "Morton Salt", Commercial wharf
on Great Inagua. Contact on VHF channel 16
or 2182kHz.

TURKS AND CAICOS
Caicos Pilots, Contact on VHF channel 16.
Call sign VSI, Grand Turk Public Correspon-
dence. VHF channel 16 or 2182kHz.
Cockburn Town Pilots, Grand Turk. Contact
on VHF channel 16.
Radio Turks and Caicos, 1460kHz 2.5kW.
Atlantic Beacon 1570kHz 50kW.
Coral Radio, 89.3MHz, 89.9MHz, 90.5MHz
FM 92.5MHz
WPRT Radio, FM 88.7MHz.

CUBA
WEATHER
Call signs CLT, CLA, Habana. 0105, 1305,
2005 and 2205 UTC on 476kHz and 500kHz.
Broadcasts in Spanish.
Call sign CLX, Casa Blanca. 0145 UTC on
3560kHz. 1345, 1700, 1900, 1945 and 2200 on
6995kHz. Broadcasts in Spanish.

COAST STATIONS
Call sign "Mariel Practice", Mariel Pilots.
Contact on VHF channel 16.
Call signs CLT, CLA, Habana, Public Corre-
spondence. Stands by on 2182kHz.
Call sign "Habana Practicos", Habana
Pilots. Contact on VHF channels 13 and 16.
Call sign "Morro Habana", Habana port sig-
nal station. Contact on VHF channels 13, 16
and 68.
Call sign "Habana Capitonia", Habana Port
Captain. Contact on channels 16 and 68.
Call sign "Terminales Contenedores",
Container terminal. Contact on VHF channels
16 and 74.
Call sign CLX, Casa Blanca. Stands by on
2182kHz.
Call sign CLW, Cardenas, Public Correspon-
dence. Stands by on 2182kHz.
Call sign CLC2, Isabela de Sagua, Public Cor-
respondence. Stands by on 2182kHz.
Isabela de Sagua Pilots, Contact on VHF
channel 16.
Call sign CLG-50 Caiman, Old Bahama Chan-
nel Traffic Control. Contact on VHF channel 13.
Call sign CLG-60 Confites, Old Bahama
Channel Traffic Control. Contact on VHF channel 13.
Call sign CLC3, Caibarien, Public Correspondence. Stands by on 2182kHz.
Call sign CLK, Nuevitas, Public Correspondence. Stands by on 2182kHz.
Call sign CLM4, Guardalabarca, Public Correspondence. Stands by on 2182kHz.

Chapter 5

Call sign CLM3, Baracoa, Public Correspondence. Stands by on 2182kHz.
Call sign "Guantanamo Port Control", Contact on VHF channel 12.
Guantanamo Bay Pilots, Contact on VHF channel 74.
Call sign CLM, Santiago de Cuba. Stands by on 2182kHz.
Call sign "Santiago Practicos", Santiago de Cuba pilots. Contact on VHF channels 13 and 16.
Call sign "Castilda Practicos", Golfo De Guancanayabo pilots. Contact on VHF channels 13 and 16.
Call sign CLK2, Santa Cruz del Sur, Public Correspondence. Stands by on 2182kHz.
Call sign CLC, Cienfuegos, Public Correspondence. Stands by on 2182kHz.
Call sign CLT2, Batabano, Public Correspondence. Stands by on 2182kHz.
Call sign CLT3, Nueva Gerona, Public Correspondence. Stands by on 2182kHz.
Call sign CLF3, El Morrillo, Public Correspondence. Stands by on 2182kHz.
Call sign CLF-2, Arroyos de Mantua. Stands by on 2182kHz.

GENERAL BROADCASTS
There are dozens of Spanish language broadcast stations, on all segments of the dial.
Radio Taíno, 830kHz 300kW, 1160kHz 300kW. English language from 0100 to 0200, from 0300 to 0430 and from 2000 to 2200 UTC.
Radio Habana, Shortwave. English 0000 to 0600 UTC on 11950kHz, 0200 to 0430 UTC on 5965kHz, and 0400 to 0600 UTC on 6180kHz and 11760kHz.
AFRTS, Armed Forces Radio, Guantánamo Bay, 1340kHz 0.25kW, FM 102MHz, FM 103MHz.

CAYMAN ISLANDS
Call sign "Cayman Harbor", Cayman Brac Agent. Contact on VHF channel 16.
Call sign "Cayman Energy", Cayman Brac operations control. Contact on VHF channel 16.
Call sign "Bonito", Cayman Brac pilots. Contact on VHF channel 16.
Radio Cayman, 1205kHz 1kW, 1555kHz 10kW, FM 89.9MHz, FM 91.9MHz, FM 105.3MHz.

JAMAICA
WEATHER
*Call sign 6YX, Jamaica Coast Guard. 0130, 1330, 1430, 1830 and 1900 UTC on VHF channel 13. 1330 and 1830 UTC on 2738kHz.

COAST STATIONS
Call sign 6YX, Kingston, Jamaica Coast Guard. Stands by on 2182kHz.

Call sign 6YI, Kingston, Public Correspondence. Stands by on 2182kHz.
Kingston Pilots, Contact on VHF channels 11 and 16.
Call sign "Silver Spray", Port Esquivel pilots. Contact on VHF channel 16.
Port Antonio Pilots, Contact on VHF channel 16.
Discovery Bay Pilots, Contact on VHF channel 16.
Montego Bay Pilots, Contact on VHF channel 16.

GENERAL BROADCASTS
Jamaica Broadcasting Corporation, 560kHz 5kW, 620kHz 5kW, 700kHz 10kW, 750kHz 10kW, 850kHz 10kW, 1090kHz 1kW, FM 91.1MHz, FM 92.1MHz, FM 93.3MHz, FM 97.1MHz, FM 97.3MHz, FM 98.7MHz, FM 99.7MHz, FM 100.3MHz, FM 103.9MHz, FM 105.7MHz. Weather and fishermen's forecast weekdays at 2248 UTC.

Radio Jamaica, 550kHz 5kW, 580kHz 10kW, 720kHz 10kW, 770kHz 5kW, FM 90.5MHz, FM 91.5MHz, FM 92.7MHz, FM 92.9MHz, FM 94.5MHz, FM 95.7MHz, FM 98.1MHz, FM 101.3MHz, FM 104.5MHz.

Island Broadcasting Services, KLAS, FM 89.3MHz.

HAITI
COAST STATIONS
Call sign MF, Port-au-Prince, Public Correspondence. Stands by on VHF channel 16 and 2182kHz.
Port-au-Prince Pilots, Contact on VHF channel 16.
Cap Haitién Pilots, Stands by on VHF channel 16.

GENERAL BROADCASTS
There are dozens of French and Creole language stations in Haiti. This is a listing of English language broadcasts.

*Radio 4VEH, 1030kHz 10kW. Cap-Haitién. News and Weather at 1200 UTC. English from 1100 to 1400, and from 2300 to 2400 UTC.

DOMINICAN REPUBLIC
Call sign HIA, Santo Domingo Piloto, Public Correspondence. Stands by on VHF channel 16 or on 2182kHz.
Call sign HIW 19, San Pedro de Macoris Pilots. Stands by on VHF channel 16 and 2182kHz.

Call sign HIW 20, Puerto de Haina Pilots. Stands by on VHF channel 16 or on 2182kHz.
Call sign HIW 9, Romano Pilots. Stands by on VHF channel 16.
Call sign HIW 8, Puerto Plata Pilots. Stands by on VHF channel 16.

There are dozens of Spanish language broadcast stations, on all segments of the dial.

PUERTO RICO
WEATHER
*Call sign WXJ-69, Maricao, WX-1.
*Call sign WXJ-68, San Juan, WX-2.
*Call sign NMR-1, U.S. Coast Guard, San Juan. 1210 and 2210 UTC on VHF channel 22A. 0305 and 1505 UTC on 2670.0kHz.
*WOSO, San Juan, 1030kHz 10kW, All English news and talk.

COAST STATIONS
Call sign KRV, Public Correspondence, Ponce Playa. VHF channel 28.
Call sign WHU 645, Public Correspondence, Luquillo. VHF channel 86.
Call sign WCU 243, Public Correspondence, Maricao. VHF channel 27.
Call sign WCT, Public Correspondence, Santurce. VHF channel 26.
Call sign KMD 214, Public Correspondence, San Juan. VHF channel 28.

GENERAL BROADCASTS
There are dozens of Spanish language broadcast stations in Puerto Rico, on all segments of the dial. This is a partial list of English broadcasts:

*WOSO, San Juan, 1030kHz 10kW, All English news and talk.
WBMJ, San Juan, 1190kHz, 10kW, 0930 to 0300 UTC, English and Spanish religious.
WIVV, Vieques, 1370kHz, 5kW, 0925 to 0230 UTC, English and Spanish religious.
AFRTS, Armed Forces Radio, U.S. Air Force, 780kHz 0.05kW Aguadilla, 1040kHz 0.05kW San Juan, 1200kHz 0.05kW Roosevelt Roads, 1460kHz.

U.S. VIRGIN ISLANDS
WEATHER
*Call sign WXM-96, St. Thomas, WX-3.
*Call sign WAH, Virgin Islands Radio, St. Thomas. VHF channels 28 and 85 at 0000, 0200, 1000, 1200 and 1800 UTC. 0200, 1000, and 1800 UTC on 2506.0, 4357.0, 4381.0, 6510.0 and 13077.0 kHz.

COAST STATIONS
*Call sign WAH, Virgin Islands Radio, Public Correspondence, St. Thomas. VHF channels 24, 25, 28, 84, 85, 87 and 88. Stands by on 2182kHz. See High Seas Radiotelephone Service for more information.

GENERAL BROADCASTS
WSTX, 970kHz 5kW, FM 100.3MHz.
WVWI, 1000kHz 5kW.
WGOD, 1090kHz 0.25kW, FM 97.9MHz.
WRRA, 1290kHz 0.5kW.
WSTA, 1340kHz 1kW.
WIUJ, FM 88.9MHz.
WDCM, FM 92.3MHz.
WAVI, FM 93.5MHz.

BRITISH VIRGIN ISLANDS
WEATHER
Call sign Tortola Radio, VHF channel 27 at 1300 and 1600 UTC.

COAST STATIONS
Call sign Tortola Radio, Contact on VHF channel 16.
Tortola Pilots, Contact on VHF channel 16.

GENERAL BROADCASTS
ZBVI, 780kHz 10kW. Tortola.
Caribbean Broadcasting System, FM 91.7MHz (Z Gold), FM 94.3MHz (The Heat), FM 103.7 (ZROD).

ANGUILLA
Radio Anguilla, 1505kHz 1kW.
ZJF-FM, 105MHz.
The Caribbean Beacon, 690kHz 15kW, 1610kHz 50kW, FM 100.1MHz.

ST. MARTIN
Radiodiffusion Francaise D'Outre-Mer (RFO), FM 99.2MHz. Broadcasts in French.
Radio Caraibes International, FM 104.7MHz. Broadcasts in French.
Radio St. Martin, FM 95.3MHz. Broadcasts in French and English.
Radio Voix Chretiennes de St. Martin, FM 106MHz. Broadcasts in French and English.

ST. MAARTEN
Philipsburg Harbor Master, Contact on VHF channel 16.

SABA
* Call sign PJS, "Saba Radio", Public Correspondence. This is the main communications service in the Leeward Islands, with a 200 mile range on VHF (with its antenna at 3083 feet

Chapter 5

above sea level). This area extends from the British Virgin Islands to Antigua. For emergencies they are in contact with the U.S. Coast Guard and other rescue agencies. During hurricane season they broadcast reports as received. You can contact them on VHF channels 16, 26 and 84, seven days a week from 0600 to 2400. They will accept phone credit cards, or place collect calls for you. To make calls from a landline to a boat, call them at (599 46) 3402. For more information on Saba Radio's services call (599 46) 3211.

ST. EUSTATIUS

Oranjestad Pilots, Call on VHF channel 16.

ST. CHRISTOPHER AND NEVIS

Basseterre Pilots and Port Authorities, Contact on VHF channel 16.
Radio ZIZ, 555kHz 20kW, FM 90MHz.
Radio Paradise, 825kHz 50kW.
Voice of Nevis, 895kHz 10kW.

MONTSERRAT

*Radio Antilles, 930kHz 20kw, Marine weather forecasts at 1335 and 2225 UTC. Radio Antilles is a good source of weather information for the Eastern Caribbean.

ANTIGUA

COAST STATIONS
*English Harbour Radio V2MA2, Nicholson Yacht Charters. Contact on VHF channel 68 or on 8294.0kHz. Monday through Friday from 8:30AM to 4:30PM Local Time. Saturdays 8:30AM until noon.
English Harbour Port Authority, Contact on VHF channel 16.
Saint John's Harbour Authorities, Contact on VHF channel 16 or 2182kHz.
Call sign "Marine Center", Saint John's oil terminal. Contact on VHF channel 16 or 2182kHz.

GENERAL BROADCASTS
Antigua and Barbuda Broadcast Service, 620kHz 10Kw.
Radio ZDK, 1100kHz 10kW, FM 99.0MHz.
Caribbean Radio Lighthouse, 1165kHz 10kW, FM 90.0MHz.
BBC Relay Station, 5975 kHz, 6110kHz, 6195kHz, 9640kHz, 15205kHz, 15220kHz.
VOA Relay Station, 1580kHz 50kW.

GUADELOUPE

Pointe-a-Pitre Pilots, Contact on VHF channel 16.

Basse-Terre Port Authority, Contact on VHF channel 16.
Radiodiffusion Francaise D'Outre-Mer (RFO), 640kHz 40kW, 1420kHz 3kW, FM 97.0MHz, Broadcasts in French.

DOMINICA

Roseau Pilots, Contact on VHF channel 16.
Dominica Broadcasting Corporation, 595kHz 10kW, FM 88.1MHz.
Gospel Broadcasting Corporation, ZGBC, 740kHz 10kW, FM 102.1MHz.

MARTINIQUE

WEATHER
Call sign FFP, Fort de France. Every odd hour on the half-hour on VHF channels 26 and 27. Every hour, 1218 and 2018 UTC on 435kHz. Every odd hour plus 33 minutes on 2545kHz. Broadcasts in French.

COAST STATIONS
Call sign FFP, Fort de France, Public Correspondence. Stands by on 2182kHz.
Fort de France Port Authorities, Contact on VHF channels 13 and 16.

GENERAL BROADCASTS
Société Nationale de Radio-Télévision Française d'Outre Mer, 1310kHz 20kW, FM 92MHz, FM 95MHz. Broadcasts in French.
Radio Caraibes International, 1090kHz 20kW, FM 89.9MHz, FM 92.5MHz, FM 98.7MHz, FM 106.1MHz. Broadcasts in French.

ST. LUCIA

COAST STATIONS
Call sign "Vieux Fort Lighthouse", Vieux Fort Port Officials. Contact them on VHF channel 16 or 2182kHz.
Call sign "Hess St. Lucia", Oil terminal in Grande Cul de Sac Bay. Contact on VHF channel 16.
Call sign "Castries Lighthouse", Port Castries port authorities. Contact on VHF channel 16 or 2182kHz.

GENERAL BROADCASTS
Radio St. Lucia, 660kHz 10kW, FM 97.3MHz, 99.5MHz, 107.3MHz. In English and Creole.
Radio Caribbean International, 840kHz 20kW, FM 95.5MHz, FM 99.1MHz, FM 101.1MHz. In English and Creole.

ST. VINCENT AND THE GRENADINES

Call sign ZQS, Kingstown port authorities. Contact on VHF channel 16 and 2182kHz.

St. Vincent and the Grenadines National Broadcasting Corporation, 705kHz 10kW.

GRENADA

Call sign J3YA, Saint George Port Control. Contact on VHF channel 16.
Call sign J3YB, Joint George Pilots, Contact on VHF channel 16.
Radio Grenada, 535kHz 20kW.

BARBADOS

COAST STATIONS

Call sign 8PA, Bridgetown, Port Signal Station. Stands by on VHF channels 12 and 16. Monitors 2182kHz.
Call sign 8PO, Public Correspondence. Stands by on 2182kHz.

GENERAL BROADCASTS

Caribbean Broadcasting, 900kHz 10kW, FM 98.1MHz.
Radio Liberty, FM 98.1MHz.
Barbados Rediffusion, 790kHz 20kW, FM 104.1MHz.
Voice of Barbados, 790kHz.
Yess Ten Four, FM 104.1MHz.
Barbados Broadcasting, FM 90.7MHz, FM 102.1MHz.

TRINIDAD AND TOBAGO

WEATHER

Call sign 9YL, North Post. 1340 and 2040 UTC on VHF channels 24, 25, 26 and 27. 1250 and 1850 UTC on 3165kHz. 2300 UTC on 6470.5kHz. 0100, 0600, 0900, 1300, 1500, 1730 and 2130 on 8441kHz. 1330 and 2050 on 12885kHz. 1200 and 1530 UTC on 17184.8kHz.

COAST STATION

Call sign 9YL, North Post, Public Correspondence. Stands by on 2182kHz.

GENERAL BROADCASTS

National Broadcasting Service, 610kHz 50kW, FM 98.9MHz, 100.0MHz,
Trinidad Broadcasting Company, 730kHz 20kW, FM 91.1MHz, FM 95.1MHz, FM 105.1MHz.

VENEZUELA

Call sign YVG, La Guaira, Public Correspondence. Stands by on 2182kHz.
Puerto Cabello Pilots, Monitor VHF channel 16.
Puerto El Guamache, Isla de Margarita. Contact on VHF channel 16.
Call sign "Meneven Puerto La Cruz", Puerto La Cruz pilots. Contact on VHF channel 16.

Call sign "San Carlos Pilot", Pilots for Lago De Maracaibo. Contact on VHF channel 16.
Puerto Cabello Pilots, Contact on VHF channel 16.
There are hundreds of Spanish language general broadcast stations, on all segments of the dial.

BONAIRE

WEATHER

*Trans World Radio PJB, 800kHz 500kW. News and weather in English 1230 UTC Weekdays, 1300 UTC Saturday and Sunday, and 0300 UTC.

COAST STATIONS

Pilots, Contact Curacao Coast Radio PJC.
Goto Oil Terminal, Contact on VHF channel 16.

GENERAL BROADCASTS

Trans World Radio PJB, See above.
Trans World Radio, Shortwave. English 0255 to 0430 UTC on 11930kHz, 0300 to 0430 UTC on 9535 kHz, and 1055 to 1330 UTC on 11815kHz and 15345kHz.

CURACAO

Call sign "Fort Nassau", Port Operations, VHF channels 12 and 16.
Call sign PJC, Curacao Coast Radio, Public Correspondence. Stands by on 2182kHz.
PJC-9, 1500kHz 3kW, FM 105.1MHz. Dutch and some English.
PJL-3, 1100kHz 0.25kW. Voice of America News at 1800 UTC. Sunday religious broadcast in English from 1200 to 1400 and 2200 to 2300 UTC.
Radio Korsou, FM 93.9MHz, FM 101.1MHz. English Tuesdays at 0000 UTC.

ARUBA

Sint Nicolaas Baai Pilots, Contact on VHF channels 14 and 16.
Oranjestad Port Radio, Contact on VHF channel 16.
Radio Victoria, 960kHz 10kW, FM 93.1MHz. Dutch.
Radio 1270, 1270kHz 1.5kW. Dutch.
Voice of Aruba, 1320kHz 1kW, FM 89.9MHz. Dutch.
Radio Kelkboom, 1440kHz 1kW, FM 106.7MHz. Dutch.
Radio Caruso Booy, FM 97.9MHz. Dutch.
Radio Carina, FM 103.5MHz. Dutch.

COLOMBIA

Call sign HKB, Barranquilla, Public Correspondence. Stands by on 2182kHz.

Chapter 5

COMMUNICATION AND WEATHER SERVICES

Call sign "Puerto Bolivar", Port authorities. Contact on VHF channels 6 and 16.
Cartagena Pilots, Contact on VHF channels 11 and 16.
There are hundreds of Spanish language general broadcast stations, on all segments of the dial.

PANAMA

Puerto De Bahia De Las Minas Pilots, Contact on VHF channel 16.
Puerto Cristobal Signal Station, Contact on VHF channel 12.
Call sign HPN, Canal Radio Station, Balboa. All vessels must communicate with the Port Captain through HPN. Other than emergency traffic and routine bridge to bridge VHF communications, no vessels in transit through the Canal shall communicate with any other station, local or distant. Contact on VHF channel 16 or 2182kHz.
Call sign HPP, Public Correspondence. Stands by on 2182kHz.
There are dozens of Spanish language general broadcast stations, on all segments of the dial.
Call sign "Rambala Control", Oil terminal in Laguna de Chiriqui. Contact on VHF channel 16.
Call sign "Chiriqui Grande Pilots", Laguna de Chiriqui. Contact on VHF channel 16.
ACA20, 790kHz 10kW. AFRTS Armed Forces Radio, Southern Command Network, Ft. Clayton, Canal Zone.

COSTA RICA

Call sign TIM, Limon, Public Correspondence. Stands by on 2182kHz.
Limon Pilots, Contact on VHF channel 16.
There are dozens of Spanish language general broadcast stations, on all segments of the dial.
AWR, Shortwave 5030kHz, 5970kHz, 6150kHz, 9725kHz, 11870kHz, 13750kHz and 15460kHz 50kW. English from 1100 to 1300 UTC, and from 2300 to 0100 UTC. Saturdays at 1230 UTC.

NICARAGUA

Bluefields Pilots, Contact on VHF channel 16.
There are dozens of Spanish language general broadcast stations, on all segments of the dial.

HONDURAS

Puerto Cortes Pilots, Contact on VHF channels 6 and 16.
There are dozens of Spanish language general broadcast stations, on all segments of the dial.
La Voz Evangélica, 810kHz 1kW, 1310kHz 1kW, 1390kHz 10kW. Shortwave 4820.2kHz. English from 0300 to 0500 Mondays. Religious.

GUATEMALA

GENERAL BROADCASTS
There are dozens of Spanish language general broadcast stations, on all segments of the dial.
Radio Cultural, 730kHz 10kW. English from 0300 to 0430 UTC and Sundays from 2345 to 0430 UTC.
Unión Radio, 1330kHz 10 kW. English from 0200 to 0400 UTC.

BELIZE

WEATHER
*Radio Belize, 830kHz 10kW, 910kHz 1kW, 930kHz 1kW, 940kHz 1kW, FM 88.9MHz, FM 91.1MHz. News and weather in English at 0100, 0300, 1300, 1500, 1700, 1830, 2100 and 2300 UTC.

COAST STATIONS
Belize Pilot Station, Stands by on 2182kHz.
Belize Customs Control, Stands by on 2750kHz.
Belize City Pilots, Contact on VHF channel 16.

GENERAL BROADCASTS
Radio Belize, See above.
British Forces Broadcast Service, FM 93.1MHz, FM 99.1MHz.
VOA Relay Station, 1530kHz 50kW, 1580kHz 50kW.

MEXICO

WEATHER
Call sign XFU, Veracruz. 0400, 1600 and 2100 UTC on 451kHz and 8656kHz.

COAST STATIONS
Call sign XFP, Chetumal, Public Correspondence. Stands by on 2182kHz.
San Miguel de Cozumel Pilot, Contact on VHF channel 16.
Call sign XFC, Cozumel, Public Correspondence. Stands by on 2182kHz.
Cayo Arcas Terminal, Contact on VHF channel 09.
Call sign XFN, Progreso, Public Correspondence. Stands by on 2182kHz.
Call sign XFF, Coatzacoalcos, Public Correspondence. Stands by on 2182kHz.
Call sign XFU, Puerto Veracruz, Public Correspondence. Stands by on 2182kHz.
Call sign XFS, Tampico, Public Correspondence. Stands by on 2182kHz.

There are hundreds of Spanish language general broadcast stations on all segments of the dial.

608   REED'S NAUTICAL ALMANAC

NAVTEX

To receive these broadcasts of Notices to Mariners and marine weather you need a special NAVTEX receiver. All broadcasts are on 518kHz.

Bermuda Harbor Radio ZBM, Identifier B. 0100, 0500, 0900, 1300, 1700 and 2100 UTC.
Portsmouth, VA, NMN, Identifier N. 0130, 0530, 0930, 1330, 1730 and 2130 UTC.
Miami, FL, NMA, Identifier A. 0000, 0400, 0800, 1200, 1600 and 2000 UTC.
New Orleans, LA, NMG, Identifier G. 0300, 0900, 1500 and 2100 UTC.
San Juan, PR, NMR, Identifier R. 0200, 0600, 1000, 1400, 1800 and 2200 UTC.

WEATHER FACSIMILE

For best reception subtract 1.9kHz from the assigned frequencies. See your weather facsimile instructions for more information.

NORFOLK, VA

Call sign NAM.
Continuous on 3357.0kHz.
On Call on 8080.0kHz.
Continuous on 10865.0kHz.
0900 to 2100 UTC on 15959.0kHz.
1200 to 2100 UTC on 20015.0kHz.

Time	UTC	Subject
0001		Schedule
0015,	1215	850mb Height, Temp., Wind 36 Hour
0030,	1230	500mb Height, Temp., Wind 36 Hour
0045,	1245	500mb Height, Temp., Wind 48 Hour
0100,	1300	Surface Pressure, 36 Hour Prognosis (S. Atl.)
0115,	1315	Surface Pressure, 48 Hour Prognosis (S. Atl.)
0130,	1330	500mb Height, Wind 36 Hour Prognosis (S. Atl.)
0145,	1345	500mb Height, Wind 48 Hour Prognosis (S. Atl.)
0200,	1400	Goes Satellite CH2 (Full Disk)
0215		NMC Extended Surface U/A Prognosis
	1415	NMC 200mb Tropical Analysis
0230,	1430	Open Period

Time	UTC	Subject
0240,	1440	RAFC Significant Weather 12 Hour Prognosis.
0250,	1450	NMC 36 Hour 500mb Height/Isotach Prognosis
0300		NEOC Gulf Stream Analysis
	1500	FNOC SST Analysis
0315,	1515	NEOC 36 Hour Prognosis Blend
0330,	1530	NWS Radar Summary
0345,	1545	Open Period
0400,	1600	500mb Pressure Analysis (S. Atl.)
0415,	1615	FNOC Preliminary AFC Analysis (N. Atl.)
0430,	1630	SFC Tropical Pressure, wind Analysis
0445,	1645	Surface Pressure Analysis (S. Atl.)
0500,	1700	NMC NGM 24 Hour Prognosis
0515,	1715	Goes Satellite CH14 (GOMEX)
0530,	1730	Bracknell 24 Hour Surface Prognosis
0545,	1745	Goes Satellite CH15 (N. Atl.)
0600,	1800	NMC NGM 48 Hour Prognosis
0615		NMC Radar Summary
	1815	NEOC Sea Height Analysis
0630,	1830	850mb Height, Temperature, Wind Analysis
0645,	1845	700mb Height, Temperature, Wind Analysis
0700,	1900	500mb Height, Temperature, Wind Analysis
0715,	1915	300mb Height, Temperature, Wind Analysis
0730,	1930	Surface Pressure, Wind 12 Hour Prognosis
0745,	1945	Goes Satellite CH14 (GOMEX)
0800,	2000	Surface Pressure, Wind 24 Hour Prognosis
0815,	2015	Surface Pressure, Wind 48 Hour Prognosis
0830,	2030	NMC 24 Hour Significant Wave
0840,	2040	NMC 36/48 Hour Significant Wave
0850,	2050	200mb Height, Temperature, Wind 24 Hour Prognosis
0905,	2105	Significant Wave Height 24 Hour Prognosis

Chapter 5

Time UTC	Subject
0920, 2120	Surface Pressure Analysis Preliminary
0935, 2135	Open Period (Tropical Warnings)
0945	Bracknell 48 Hour Significant Wave
2145	NEOC 84 Hour Prognosis Blend
1000, 2200	NEOC 12 Hour High Wind, Sea Warnings
1015, 2215	850mb Height, Temperature, Wind 24 Hour
1030, 2230	700mb Height, Temperature, Wind 24 Hour
1045, 2245	500mb Height, Temperature, Wind 24 Hour
1100, 2300	400mb Height, Temperature, Wind 24 Hour
1115, 2315	Goes Satellite CH15 (N. Atl.)
1130, 2330	300mb Height, Temperature, Wind 24 Hour
1145, 2345	Freezing Level 24 Hour Prognosis
1200	NMC Boundary Layer Analysis

MOBILE, AL

Call sign WLO.
All charts are broadcast simultaneously on 6852.0 and 9157.0 kHz.

Time UTC	Subject
0250, 0900, 1450, 2030	Gulf of Mexico Surface Analysis
0300, 1500	North American Surface Analysis
0310, 1510	Gulf Offshore Marine Forecast
0910, 2050	Gulf Surface Prognosis
0920, 2100	Gulf Coastal Marine Forecast
1100, 1900	North Gulf Aviation Forecast
1440	Radio Fax Schedule on Monday
2040	Gulf Sea Surface Temperature Analysis (Mon., Wed., Fri.)
2040	Gulf Stream Flow Analysis (Tue., Thu., Sat.)

MARTINIQUE

Call sign FFP.
1200 and 2230 UTC on 5013kHz and 14515kHz.

HIGH SEAS RADIO-TELEPHONE SERVICE

AT&T COAST STATION WOO

P.O. Box 550
End of Beach Avenue
Manahawkin, NJ 08050
Technical information: (609) 597-2201

DSC-ID: 00-366-0002

Shore to Ship Calls: (800) SEA-CALL
Individual registration: (800) SEA-CALL
Ship registration: (800) 752-0279 or
(407) 850-4895 (collect)

Cost — $14.98 for the first three minutes, $4.98 for each additional minute or fraction thereof. There is a three minute minimum charge per call. You are not charged until the actual phone call begins.

Channel	Coast Station Transmit	Ship Station Transmit
232	2558.0 kHz	2166.0 kHz
242	2450.0	2366.0
410	4384.0	4092.0
411	4387.0	4095.0
416	4402.0	4110.0
422	4420.0	4128.0
808	8740.0	8216.0
811	8749.0	8225.0
815	8761.0	8237.0
826	8794.0	8270.0
1203	13083.0	12236.0
1210	13104.0	12257.0
1211	13107.0	12260.0
1228	13158.0	12311.0
1605	17254.0	16372.0
1620	17299.0	16417.0
1626	17317.0	16435.0
1631	17332.0	16450.0
2201	22696.0	22000.0
2205	22708.0	22012.0
2210	22723.0	22027.0
2236	22801.0	22105.0

Voice Broadcasts
Channels 411 and 811

Traffic Lists: 0000, 0200, 0400, 0600, 0800, 1000, 1200, 1400, 1600, 1800, 2000, 2200 UTC.

Weather from the National Weather Service: 1200, 2200 UTC.

SITOR/DSC Data Broadcasts
Frequency (center): 8051.5 kHz

Traffic Lists continuously
Weather at 20 past every even hour UTC.

Morse Data Broadcasts
Frequencies (carrier): 8749.0 and 13083 kHz.
Traffic Lists Continuously

AT&T COAST STATION WOM

1340 N.W. 40th Avenue
Fort Lauderdale, FL 33313
Technical Information: (305) 587-0910 (collect)

DSC – ID: 00-366-0001

Shore to Ship Calls: (800) SEA-CALL
Individual registration: (800) SEA-CALL
Ship registration: (800) 752-0279 or
(407) 850-4895 (collect)

Cost — $14.98 for the first three minutes,
$4.98 for each additional minute or fraction
thereof. There is a three minute minimum
charge per call. You are not charged until the
actual phone call begins.

Channel	Coast Station Transmit	Ship Station Transmit
209	2490.0 kHz	2031.5 kHz
221	2514.0	2118.0
245	2566.0	2390.0
247	2442.0	2406.0
403	4363.0	4071.0
412	4390.0	4098.0
417	4405.0	4113.0
423	4423.0	4131.0
802	8722.0	8198.0
805	8731.0	8207.0
810	8746.0	8222.0
814	8758.0	8234.0
825	8791.0	8267.0
831	8809.0	8285.0
1206	13092.0	12245.0
1208	13098.0	12251.0
1209	13101.0	12254.0
1215	13119.0	12272.0
1223	13143.0	12296.0
1230	13164.0	12317.0
1601	17242.0	16360.0
1609	17266.0	16384.0
1610	17269.0	16387.0
1611	17272.0	16390.0
1616	17287.0	16405.0
2215	22738.0	22042.0
2216	22741.0	22045.0
2222	22759.0	22063.0

Voice Broadcasts
Channels: 403, 802, 1206, 1601 and 2215

Traffic Lists: 0100, 0300, 0500, 0700, 0900,
1100, 1300, 1500, 1700, 1900, 2100, 2300 UTC.
**Weather from the National Weather
Service:** 1300, 2300 UTC.

No Sitor/dsc broadcasts

Morse Data Broadcasts
Frequencies (carrier):
4423.0 and 8746.0 kHz.
Traffic Lists Continuously

AT&T COAST STATION KMI

P.O. Box 9
Inverness, CA 94937
Technical information: (415) 669-1055 (collect)

DSC -ID: 00-366-000

Shore to Ship Calls: (800) SEA-CALL
Individual registration: (800) SEA-CALL
Ship registration: (800) 752-0279 or
(407) 850-4895 (collect)

Cost — $14.98 for the first three minutes,
$4.98 for each additional minute or fraction
thereof. There is a three minute minimum
charge per call. You are not charged until the
actual phone call begins.

Channel	Coast Station Transmit	Ship Station Transmit
242	2450.0 kHz	2003.0 kHz
248	2506.0	2406.0
401	4357.0	4065.0
416	4402.0	4110.0
417	4405.0	4113.0
804	8728.0	18204.0
809	8743.0	8219.0
822	8782.0	8258.0
1201	13077.0	12230.0
1202	13080.0	12233.0
1203	13083.0	12236.0
1229	13161.0	12314.0
1602	17245.0	16363.0
1603	17248.0	16366.0
1624	17311.0	16429.0
2214	22735.0	22039.0
2223	22762.0	22066.0
2228	22777.0	22081.0
2236	22801.0	22105.0

Voice Broadcasts
Channels 416 and 1203

Traffic Lists: 0000, 0400, 0800, 1200, 1600,
2000 UTC.

Chapter 5

Weather from the National Weather Service:
0000, 1200 UTC

SITOR/DSC Data Broadcasts
Frequency (center): 0007.0 kHz
Traffic Lists Continuously
Weather at 20 past every odd hour UTC.

Morse Data Broadcasts
Frequencies (carrier): 4402.0, 8728.0, 13161.0 and 17245.0 kHz. Traffic Lists continuously.

COAST STATION WLO

Coast Station WLO
Mobile Marine Radio Inc.
7700 Rinla Avenue
Mobile, AL 36619

Technical information: (800) 633-1312 or (205) 666-5110
Shore to ship calls may be made by dialling "O" and asking for the Mobile Alabama Marine Operator. You may also call WLO direct at (800) 633-1634, (205) 666-2998 or (205) 666-3555.

Channel	Coast Station Transmit	Ship Station Transmit
205	2572.0 kHz	2430.0 kHz
405	4369.0	4077.0
414	4396.0	4104.0
419	4411.0	4119.0
607	6519.0	6218.0
824	8788.0	8264.0
830	8806.0	8282.0
836	8713.0	8113.0
1212	13110.0	12263.0
1226	13152.0	12305.0
1233	13173.0	12326.0
1607	17260.0	16378.0
1641	17362.0	16480.0
1647	17380.0	16438.0
1807	19773.0	18798.0
2237	22804.0	22108.0
2503	26151.0	25076.0

Voice Broadcasts
Channels: 405, 824, 1212, 1641 and 2237
Traffic Lists: Every hour on the hour.
Weather Broadcasts: 0000, 0600, 1200 and 1800 UTC.

COAST STATION WAH

Virgin Islands Radio
Global Communication Corp.
P.O. Box 7009
St. Thomas, VI 00801
Telex: 3470021, GLOCOM

For shore to ship calls and information dial (809) 776-8282 or (800) LEEWARD. Forms of payment include: Visa, Master Card, American Express, telephone credit cards, collect calls, third numbers and Marine Identification Numbers. Other services include Telex, Cable and FAX. VI Radio offers a full answering and message service.

Channel	Coast Station Transmit	Ship Station Transmit
Calling	2182.0 kHz	2182.0 kHz
Coastal	2506.0	2009.0
Coastal	2585.0	2086.0
401	4357.0	4065.0
409	4381.0	4089.0
604	6510.0	6209.0
605	6513.0	6212.0
804	8728.0	8204.0
809	8743.0	8219.0
1201	13077.0	12230.0
1202	13080.0	12233.0
1602	17245.0	16363.0
1603	17248.0	16366.0
2223	22762.0	22066.0

Voice Broadcasts
Traffic Lists are broadcast hourly on the hour.
Even hours: 409, 604, 1201 and coastal 2506 kHz.
Odd hours: 401 and 1201.

Weather Broadcasts: 0200, 1000, 1800 UTC. Channels: 401, 409, 604, 1201 and coastal 2506 kHz.

TIME SIGNALS

The U.S. Naval Observatory (USNO) provides recorded time announcements via telephone. Call (900) 410-8463 or (202) 653-1800.

Station WWV from Fort Collins, Colorado and station WWVH from Kekaha, Kauai, Hawaii broadcast continuous time announcements. WWV transmits on 2500, 5000, 10000, 15000 and 20000 kHz. WWVH transmits on 2500, 5000, 10000 and 15000 kHz. These broadcasts

are prepared by the National Institute of Standards and Technology, Time and Frequency Division, Boulder, CO, 80303.

Time announcements are made every minute, commencing at 15 seconds before the minute on WWVH and 7 1/2 seconds before the minute on WWV. The time given is Coordinated Universal Time (UTC) - this is essentially the same as Greenwich Mean Time. This refers to the time at the Prime Meridian, 0 longitude, Greenwich, England.

UTC is used by Reed's whenever possible in listing radio broadcast times. See the Nautical Almanac and Ephemeris for a listing of local, or zone times, for the world.

WWV and WWVH also broadcast Storm Warnings, which are explained in the section on Voice Radio Broadcasts.

Station CHU broadcasts Canada's official time from a station near Ottawa, Ontario, Canada. This station can be heard in the North Atlantic. Frequencies are 3330, 7335 and 14670 kHz, and the time is announced in both French and English. This broadcast is the responsibility of the Physics Division, National Research Council, Ottawa, Ontario, Canada.

AMATEUR RADIO

Many boaters are "hams", or amateur radio operators. This is a list of some popular nets of interest to mariners. Some of these are informal nets and may have changed times, frequencies and nature of traffic. It is up to the individual radio operator to determine if a particular net exists and will handle his traffic.

Many of these nets carry local weather reports and sea conditions. The East Coast Waterway Net is particularly popular among boaters. All times and frequencies are subject to change.

The editors welcome current information on nets for our list.

UTC	Frequency MHz	Net Name, Area, Type of Information
0030	3.923	Tar Heel Emergency (NC, WX/TFC)
0100	3.935	Gulf Coast Hurricane (Gulf, WX/TFC)
0200	14.334	Brazil, East U.S. TFC (WX/TFC)

UTC	Frequency MHz	Net Name, Area, Type of Information
0330	14.040	E. Coast Maritime CW (East Coast U.S.)
0400	14.310	Maritime Emergency (NE Canada, TFC)
0630	14.313	International Maritime Mobile (TFC)
1030	3.815	Caribbean Weather (Carib, WX/TFC)
1100	3.750	Maritime Weather (NE Canada, WX/TFC)
1100	7.237	Caribbean Maritime (TFC)
1100	14.283	Caribus Traffic (E. Coast, Carib, TFC)
1110	3.930	Puerto Rico Weather (PR, VI, WX/TFC)
1145	14.121	Mississauga (E. Canada, Atl, Carib, TFC)
1145	7.268	E. Coast Waterway (E. Coast, Carib, TFC)
1200	14.040	E. Coast Maritime CW (East Coast U.S.)
1230	7.185	Barbados Info. (Carib, TFC)
1245	7.268	E. Coast Waterway (E. Coast, Carib, TFC)
1300	21.400	Trans Atlantic (Atl, Med, Carib, TFC)
1345	3.968	E Coast Waterway (E. Coast, Carib, TFC)
1400	7.085	Bluewater (E. Atlantic, U.S., TFC)
1400	7.292	Florida Coast (Florida, TFC)
1600	14.300	Maritime Mobile Service
	14.313	(Atl, Carib, TFC)
1700	14.313	Intercontinental (Atl, Med, Carib, TFC)
1800	14.303	UK Maritime (Atl, Med, Carib, TFC)
1800	14.313	Maritime Mobile Service (Worldwide, TFC)
2130	14.290	E. coast Waterway (E. Coast, Carib, TFC)
2200	3.930	West Indies SSB (PR, VI, TFC)
2230	3.815	Caribbean Weather (Carib, WX/TFC)
2230	3.958	Massachusetts, Rhode Island (TFC)
2310	3.930	Puerto Rico Weather (PR, VI, WX/TFC)
2400	14.313	Maritime Mobile service (Worldwide, TFC)
2400	14.325	Hurricane (Atl, Carib, Pac, Emerg, WX)

WX = Weather information
TFC = Traffic

Chapter 5

OTHER SOURCES OF WEATHER INFORMATION

National Hurricane Center
Florida
(305) 661-0738 FAX
(305) 661-4707
Use the FAX number to receive current Gulf Stream information from south of Cape Hatteras to the Straits of Florida and the Gulf of Mexico. Current speeds, water temperature and the locations of the eddies are included.

National Climatic Data Center
Federal Building
Asheville, NC 28801
(704) 259-0619
Detailed Gulf Stream charts and information, from Nova Scotia to the Bahamas, is available. You can receive data via mail or FAX machine. A charge applies.

NOAA Information Hotline
(800) 662-6622 Information

(900) 884-6622 Weather Reports
Call the 900 number to receive hurricane reports, NOAA weather reports from around the country, or the WWV Time Signal. Have the telephone area code ready for the region you're interested in. The charge is $0.98 per minute.

Naval Oceanography Command Facility
U.S. Naval Air Station
Bermuda
(809) 293-5339
Departure weather packages are available with 24 hours notice. You may call from the Bermuda Yacht Reporting Office on Ordnance Island. Packages include satellite photos, weather FAX charts and detailed Gulf Stream information.

Nassau Meteorological Service
Nassau, Bahamas
Telephone 915, when in Nassau, for local area weather.

NAUTICAL EPHEMERIS

6

Chapter 6

AN INTRODUCTION TO CELESTIAL NAVIGATION

The ephemeris section of *Reed's Nautical Almanac* continues to carry all the information necessary to calculate the position of a boat by celestial navigation. This introduction is intended as an aide-memoire for the principles involved as well as a guide to the tables that follow, on pages 630 – 744.

Fig 1 shows that by measuring the angle between a heavenly body and the horizon, it is possible to find the angular distance, or **zenith distance**, between your position and the spot on the Earth's surface at which the body is directly overhead (its **geographical position**). This gives a position line, just as the range of a terrestrial landmark can be used to derive a position line in coastal navigation.

For this to be of any practical value, we must:

(a) be able to see a suitable heavenly body;

(b) know the body's geographical position;

(c) be able to correct the **sextant altitude** for errors such as those caused by atmospheric refraction; and

(d) be able to plot the position line on the chart.

FINDING THE POSITION OF A HEAVENLY BODY

By convention, celestial navigation assumes that the Sun, Moon, planets and stars are located on the inner surface of a **celestial sphere**, whose center is at the center of the Earth, and whose Poles, Equator, and Prime Meridian are precisely aligned with their terrestrial counterparts. Latitude and longitude, however, are not used.

Declination is the celestial equivalent of latitude: it is measured in degrees, north or south of the celestial equator.

Greenwich Hour Angle is equivalent to longitude, except that it is always measured in a westerly direction. So a star whose Declination is N39° and whose GHA is 40° would appear overhead to an observer at 39°N 40°W, while one whose Declination is S17° and whose GHA is 219° would be overhead when seen from 17°S 141°E.

The Sun, planets, stars and Moon are not fixed, but their positions at any given time can be found from the ephemerides. In *Reed's*, the ephemerides are divided into twelve sections, each covering one month, with six pages in each section.

CORRECTING THE SEXTANT ALTITUDE

The sextant altitude is subject to a number of errors:

Index error is caused by imperfect adjustment of the sextant. A quick check of index error can be achieved by moving the index arm until the horizon — seen through the sextant — appears as an unbroken line. The sex-

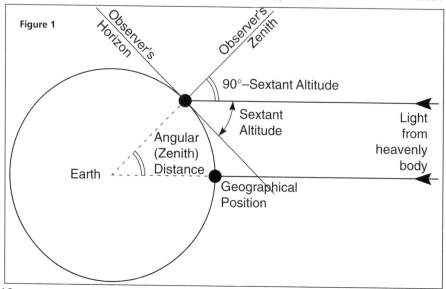

Figure 1

Observer's Horizon

Observer's Zenith

90°–Sextant Altitude

Sextant Altitude

Angular (Zenith) Distance

Earth

Geographical Position

Light from heavenly body

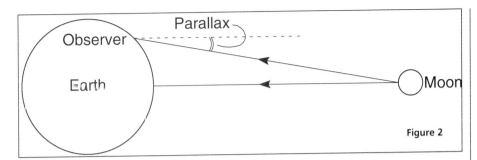

Figure 2

tant should then read 0, but there is often a small discrepancy. Note the size of this discrepancy, and whether it is "on the arc" (i.e. the index arm is to the left of 0) or "off the arc" (i.e. the index arm is to the right of 0).

To apply index error to the sextant altitude, the simple rule is that "If it's on the arc, take it off, if it's off the arc add it on" — i.e. an index error "on the arc" should be subtracted from the sextant altitude. This correction will give the **observed altitude,** which then needs to be converted to a **true altitude** by applying another four corrections.

Dip arises from the fact that the horizon is slightly below an observer above sea level, and varies with the observer's **height of eye**.

Refraction is caused by the atmosphere distorting the light from heavenly bodies. It is greatest for bodies near the horizon, so it is best to avoid taking sights giving an altitude of less than about 10°.

Parallax is caused by the size of the Earth (Fig 2). For most practical purposes, it is only significant in the case of the Moon.

Semi-diameter arises from the physical size of the body being observed, and the fact that tabulated values refer to the center of the body concerned. In the case of the Sun and Moon, this is about 15' higher than the lower edge of the visible disc.

PLOTTING A POSITION LINE

Although the zenith distance gives the diameter of a circular position line centered on the body's geographical position, in practice this is usually far too large to be plotted on a chart. So in most cases, the results of sights have to be reduced to more manageable dimensions. Two special cases, however — a 'noon sight' of the Sun, and the Pole Star — are of great practical value.

SUN SIGHTS

Finding the Sun's position

The Declination and GHA of the Sun are given on the third and fourth pages of each monthly section, tabulated at two-hourly intervals for each day.

The Sun's declination changes so slowly that the necessary accuracy can be achieved by mental interpolation.

Its GHA increases at a rate of 15° per hour, but to simplify the job of interpolating accurately, a **Sun's GHA correction table** appears on page 706.

Note that the GHA correction must always be added because GHA is always measured to the west of Greenwich, but the Declination correction may be positive or negative. Its sign can be found by looking at the preceding entry, to see whether the declination is increasing (+) or decreasing (–).

Sun Altitude Corrections

Refraction, dip, and parallax tables are on page 704, and the Sun's semi-diameter is given on the first page of each monthly section, but for convenience, all four corrections have been combined in the **Sun Altitude Total Correction Table** on page 705. For greater accuracy, another small correction will be found at the foot of this table, to account for the Sun's apparently changing diameter.

Note that the Sun Altitude Total Correction Table relates only to sights of the Sun's **lower limb**: sights of the upper limb must be corrected using the separate tables. In this case, parallax should be added to the observed altitude, while dip, refraction, and semi-diameter should be subtracted.

STAR SIGHTS

Finding the time of twilight

Star sights can only be taken when the star and the horizon are both visible — i.e. at **twilight**. Strictly speaking, Civil Twilight occurs

Chapter 6

when the Sun is 6° below the horizon, and Nautical Twilight when it is 12° below the horizon. Civil twilight is the best time to take star sights, so this is the twilight listed in *Reed's Almanac*, on the first page of each monthly section.

The times given for twilight, sunrise and sunset are correct for 52°N 0°W. They must therefore be corrected to take account of your own latitude and longitude.

The **twilight latitude correction** is given in the subsidiary table on the right hand side of the same page. The **longitude correction** is found by adding 4 minutes for every degree of westerly longitude, or subtracting 4 minutes for every degree of easterly longitude.

Finding the position of a star

The essential information for sixty stars which are bright enough to be visible at twilight is given in the star list, on the second page of each monthly section.

This lists the GHA of each star at 0000 on the first day of the month (from the monthly list of stars). The tables on page 706 can be used to correct this for date and time.

An alternative method is to use the star's **Right Ascension** or **Sidereal Hour Angle**, which gives its position relative to a point on the celestial equator called the **First Point of Aries**.

Right Ascension refers to the star's position measured eastward from the First Point of Aries, and is usually given in terms of time (1 hour = 15°).

Sidereal Hour Angle (SHA) refers to the star's position measured westwards from the First Point of Aries, expressed as an angle.

To find the GHA of a star, first find the GHA of Aries. This is tabulated at two-hourly intervals on the third and fourth pages of each monthly section. The correction tables on page 706 simplify the job of interpolation.

Then add the SHA, from the star list. If the result is more than 360°, subtract 360°.

The Declinations of stars change so slowly that for navigational purposes they can be regarded as being fixed throughout a month, and can be taken directly from the monthly star list.

Star Altitude Corrections

It is possible to allow for each error individually, using the refraction and dip tables on page 708. Both should be subtracted from the observed altitude. The semi-diameter and parallax are negligible.

For convenience, refraction and dip have been combined into the **Star or Planet Altitude Total Correction Table** on page 708.

PLANET SIGHTS

To determine which planets will be visible

Only Venus, Jupiter, Mars, and Saturn are of navigational significance. Their ephemerides are on the fifth page of each monthly section, with a note under each describing it as a morning or an evening star. As the words suggest, 'morning stars' are only visible in the morning, in the eastern sky; while 'evening stars' are visible in the evening, in the western sky.

Finding the position of a planet

The **Declination** and **GHA of the navigational planets** are tabulated at midnight (00h00m) for each day, on the fifth page of each monthly section.

The GHAs of planets increase at about 15° per hour: the rate of change on any particular day is given more accurately in the column headed **Mean Var**. To save space, only the minutes are shown: so a Mean Var of 3.2 means an hourly increase of 15°03.2′, while a Mean Var of 59.4 means an hourly increase of 14°59.4′.

Knowing the Mean Var, the Planets GHA Correction Tables on pages 713 – 714 will interpolate to the nearest hour, while the table on page 715 interpolates to minutes and seconds.

The Declination is also shown for midnight on each day, with the mean hourly variation: its interpolation table is on page 716. As with the Sun, it is important to note whether the declination of a planet is increasing or decreasing.

Planet Altitude Corrections

Corrections for planet sights are exactly the same as those for stars.

MOON SIGHTS

Finding the position of the Moon

The Moon is so much closer than any other heavenly body, and moves so much faster, that finding its position and correcting its observed altitude are much more complicated and error-prone. The layout of the tables, and the processes involved, however, are similar to those for the planets.

The **Moon's Declination** and **GHA** are given on the sixth page of each monthly section, tabulated at six-hourly intervals for each day.

Its GHA increases at just under 15° per hour. The precise rate of increase is given in the col-

umn headed **Mean Var**, but to save space only the minutes are shown. So a Mean Var of 27.7 means an hourly increase of 14°27.7'.

Knowing the Mean Var, the **Moon GHA Correction Table** on page 708 can be used to interpolate to the nearest hour, while the table on pages 709 – 710 interpolates to minutes and seconds.

Similarly, the Declination is shown along with its mean hourly variation: mental arithmetic is used to interpolate to the nearest hour, while the Moon Declination Correction Table on page 711 interpolates for minutes.

Moon Altitude Corrections
The corrections to be applied to Moon sights can be found from the Moon Altitude Total Correction Table on page 707.

First, however, you need to know the **horizontal parallax** (the parallax error that would occur if the observed altitude were 0°), which can be obtained from the first page of the monthly sections.

Taking care to choose the correct part of the table — depending on whether the sight was of the upper or lower limb — find the column in the table corresponding to the value of horizontal parallax, and the row corresponding to the observed altitude. The correction obtained must be added, unless it is for an observation of the upper limb in excess of 64°, in which case it must be subtracted.

Finally, add the correction for **height of eye**, found from the subsidiary table on the same page.

Note: do not use the standard Dip tables in conjunction with the Moon Altitude Total Correction Table.

PLOTTING SIGHTS

THE NOON SIGHT
The so-called 'noon sight' — taken at approximately noon (local time) — gives the simplest of all astro position lines. It is more correctly called a **Meridian Passage** sight, because it is taken at the moment when the Sun crosses the observer's meridian — i.e. when it is at its highest, and directly south or north of the observer.

So the first step in taking a noon sight is to determine when meridian passage will occur. This can be found from the column headed **Transit** in the top half of the first page in the appropriate monthly section. This gives the time (GMT) at which the Sun crosses the Greenwich Meridian.

As the Sun moves westward at the rate of 15° per hour, or one degree every four minutes, it is easy to calculate the time at which it will cross your own meridian. An approximation is all that is required, because in practice it is usual to measure the Sun's altitude a few minutes before the expected time, and to repeat the observation at intervals until the Sun stops rising in the sky, and starts to descend.

Having corrected the sextant altitude in the usual way, subtracting the observed altitude from 90° gives the **zenith distance.**

Latitude is then equal to either the sum or the difference of the Declination and the Zenith Distance. It is usually obvious whether declination should be added or subtracted, but if there is any ambiguity, note whether the Sun is north or south of you, and give the Zenith Distance the opposite name. If the Zenith Distance and Declination have the same name they should be added together. If they have different names, take the smaller from the larger, and name the latitude after the larger.

LATITUDE BY POLARIS

If **Polaris** were perfectly aligned with the pole, as its alternative name of Pole Star suggests, its altitude (after correction for the usual errors) would be exactly the same as the observer's latitude. Fig 3 illustrates the principle. It is not, in fact, in perfect alignment, but is sufficiently close that only minor arithmetical adjustments are required.

Figure 3

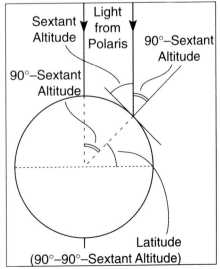

Sextant Altitude
Light from Polaris
90°–Sextant Altitude
90°–Sextant Altitude
Latitude
(90°–90°–Sextant Altitude)

Polaris is not a particularly bright star, but it can usually be found at twilight by setting the sextant index arm to the approximate latitude, and scanning the northern sky with the sextant.

A table giving the correction to be applied to the observed altitude is on page 702. It is first necessary to find the **Local Hour Angle of Aries**. This is done by finding the GHA of Aries and subtracting your longitude if you are west of Greenwich, or adding your longitude if east of Greenwich.

THE INTERCEPT METHOD

All other astro position lines are most easily plotted using the Marc St. Hilaire or Intercept method.

This involves calculating what the altitude of a heavenly body would be, as seen from some convenient chosen position, and comparing this with its **observed altitude**. If the observed altitude (Ho) is greater than the **calculated altitude** (Hc), the true position must be closer to the heavenly body than the chosen position, and vice versa. The size of the discrepancy shows how much closer, and is called the **intercept**.

If a position line could be plotted directly from the zenith distance, it would form a circle centered on the heavenly body's geographical position. In most cases, this circle is so big that

a section up to about sixty miles in length can be regarded as a straight line, at right angles to the intercept (Fig 4).

It is obvious from Fig 4 that in order to plot the position line, you need to know not just how long the intercept should be, but also its direction. This will be the same as the bearing of the heavenly body, but it is more accurate to calculate it than to measure it.

The intercept and bearing can both be found from pre-computed tables such as the *Sight Reduction Tables for Air Navigation* (H.O. 249); or by the more compact **Versine** and **Log Cosine tables** on pages 725 – 744, and the **ABC tables** on pages 719 – 724; or with an electronic calculator.

Whichever method is chosen, the calculations require the Declination of the body; the latitude of a **chosen position** (it will be found most convenient to take your own EP, correct to the nearest whole degree); and the **Local Hour Angle** (LHA).

The LHA is the difference in longitude between your chosen position and the geographical position of the heavenly body. So it is found by subtracting westerly longitude from the GHA (+360° if necessary) or by adding easterly longitude (–360° if necessary). It will be found most convenient to make CP such that LHA becomes a whole number of

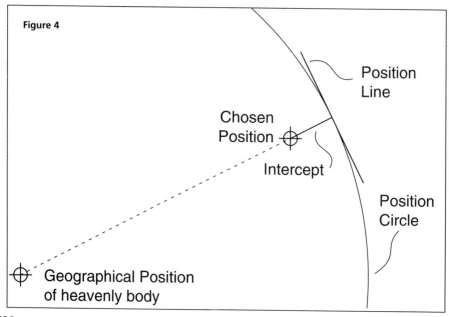

Figure 4

Position Line

Chosen Position

Intercept

Position Circle

Geographical Position of heavenly body

degrees. If the EP is 34°50'N 36°40'W, for instance, and the GHA of the body is 110°35.4', a suitable CP would be 35°N 36°35.4'W.

The answer will eventually emerge as a **calculated altitude** (Hc) (which should be within 43' of HO), and an azimuth. The azimuth will always be less than 90°, and can be regarded as giving the bearing relative to the North or South Pole, measuring east or west. An azimuth of 70°, for instance, could correspond to a bearing of 070° (N70°E), 110° (S70°E), 250° (S70°W) or 290° (N70°W). The easiest way to decide which of the four is correct is to note the approximate bearing of the heavenly body at the time of the sight. Alternatively, it can be found from the rules at the foot of the ABC tables (see pages 723 – 724).

ELECTRONIC SIGHT REDUCTION
For electronic sight reduction a calculator capable of handling trigonometric functions is essential, and at least one memory is useful, but be prepared to have to store data on a separate notepad as well.

The first task is to convert the declination into degrees and decimals, and to select a suitable chosen position that gives a latitude and an LHA in whole degrees.

Then the **Calculated Altitude** (Hc) is given by the formula:

Sin Hc = Cos LHA x Cos Lat x Cos Dec ± Sin Lat x Sin Dec

(Note that if Lat and Dec have the same name they should be **added**, and if they have opposite names they should be **subtracted**.)

The **Azimuth** is given by using the formula:

$$Sin\ Az = \frac{(Sin\ LHA \times Cos\ Dec)}{Cos\ Hc}$$

The exact process required to carry out these calculations depends on the calculator being used. The example on page 622 was worked using a standard scientific calculator (a Texas TI31).

SIGHT REDUCTION BY TABLES
The same formulae could be used in conjunction with a set of mathematical tables instead of a pocket calculator, but the calculations can be made simpler by applying the **versine formula** (the versine of an angle is equal to 1 minus its cosine):

Vers Zenith Distance = Vers LHA x Cos Lat x Cos Dec + Vers (Lat ± Dec)

(Note that if Lat and Dec have the same name they should be **subtracted**, and if they have opposite names they should be **added**.).

Hc is then found by subtracting the Zenith Distance from 90°.

To simplify the multiplication process, *Reed's* **Versine Tables** (pages 725 – 738) include logarithms of versines in bold type, and the tables on pages 739 – 743 are log cosines.

The **Azimuth** is most easily found from the **ABC Tables** on pages 719 – 724. These are so named because A+B=C.

A is found from the A table, using LHA to find the correct column and Declination to find the row. If the LHA is between 90° and 270° A will be negative.

B is found from the B table, again with LHA determining the correct column, but this time with Declination determining the row. B is negative if the latitude and declination have the same name (i.e. are both South or both North).

The C table is used to convert the sum of A and B into the azimuth. If C is positive, the azimuth is the same name (north or south) as your latitude, and if the LHA is less than 180° the azimuth is westerly.

WORKED EXAMPLES

Noon Sight
Mer Pass September 10 EP 35°00'N, 35°40'W
Sext Alt of Sun Lower Limb (LL) 59°38.2'
Index Error (IE) 0, Height of Eye (HE) 10ft

1. Find the time of Meridian Passage on September 10. The time of transit given in the monthly ephemeris is 1157, so the calculation will be as follows:

	1157
Add for 30°W	0200
Add for 5°W	0020
Add for 40'W	0003
	1420 GMT

2. Calculate Declination of Sun. From the monthly ephemeris:

Dec at 1400 GMT	N 4°53.2'
Correct for 20min by interpolation	– 0.3'
Dec at 1420 GMT	N 4°52.9'

3. Calculate True Altitude

Observed Altitude	59°38.2'
Total correction (from p 705)	+ 12.4'
Monthly correction (from p 705)	– 0.1'
True Altitude	59°50.5'

Chapter 6

4. Calculate Latitude

Adjustment to True Altitude	– 90°00.0′
Zenith Distance	(N) 30°09.5′
Declination	N 4°52.9′
Latitude	35°02.4 N

Morning/Afternoon Sun Sight

15h35m42s GMT Sep 10, EP 34°55′N 35°50′W
Sext Alt of Sun LL 54°58.8′
IE O, HE 10ft

1. Find the position of the Sun at 15h35m42s GMT on September 10 from the monthly ephemeris:

GHA at 1400	GHA 30°45.0′
Correct for 1h35m (from p 706)	23°45.0′
Correct for 42s (from p 706)	10.5′
GHA at 15h35m42s	54°40.5′

Dec at 1400	N 4°53.2′
Correct for 1h35m by interpolation	– 1.5′
Dec at 15h35m42s	N 4°51.7′

2. Correct the sextant altitude:

Sextant Altitude	54°58.8′
Sun Total Corr (from p 705)	+ 12.3′
Monthly correction (from p 705)	– 0.1′
Observed Altitude	55°11.0′

3. Reduce the sight. If using an electronic calculator:

Find the LHA from the chosen position:

GHA	54°40.5′
Chosen Position	35°N 35°40.5′W
Local Hour Angle	19°00.0′

Convert declination to degrees and decimals:

4 degrees	4.000°
46.2 minutes ÷ 60	0.770°
	4.770°

Find the intercept. If you have a scientific calculator with Store and Recall functions the sequence will be:

LHA COS STO Lat COS × RCL = STO Dec
COS × RCL =

19 COS STO 35 COS × RCL = STO 4.77
COS × RCL =

In this case the answer will be 0.7718. Write down this interim answer for use in the next calculation (the + is because Lat and Dec are both N):

Lat SIN STO Dec SIN × RCL = +
0.7718 = INV SIN

35 SIN STO 4.77 SIN × RCL = +
0.7718 = INV SIN

In this case the answer will be 55.0344. This is the Calculated Altitude. Write it down, and then, with the answer still on the display, convert the figure to degrees and minutes:

– 55 = × 60 = 2.3

Calculated Altitude (Hc) =	55°02.1′
Observed Altitude (Ho) =	55°11.0′
Intercept	8.9′

Find the Azimuth/Bearing:

LHA SIN STO Dec COS × RCL = STO Hc
COS 1/x × RCL = INV SIN

19 SIN STO 4.77 COS × RCL = STO
55.0344 COS 1/x × RCL = INV SIN

In this case the answer is 34.4808, so the Azimuth is 34° — actually S34°W, or 214°.

Evening Stars/Planet Sight

2110 GMT Sep 10, EP 34°30′N 36°40′W
Sext Alt Jupiter 21°32.9′ at 21h07m26s GMT
Sext Alt Arcturus 37°44.0′ at 21h11m19s GMT
IE 0, HE 10ft

1. Find the time of evening twilight at 35°N, 36°W on September 10:

Twilight (from p 678)	1902 GMT
Latitude correction (from p 678)	– 0017
	1845 GMT
Longitude corr (36°at 4min/°)	+ 0224
Corrected time of Twilight	2109 GMT

2. Find the position of Jupiter at 21h07m26s GMT on September 10:

GHA at 0000	129°41.5′
Mean Var per hour 15°02.1′	
Correction for 21h (from p 714)	315°44.1′
Correction for 07m (from p 715)	1°45.2′
Correction for 26s (from p 715)	6.5′
	447°17.3′
This is over 360°, so subtract	360°00.0′
GHA at 21h07m26s	87°17.3′

Dec at 0000	S 14°19.8′
Mean Var per hour	+ 0.1′
Correction for 21h07m (from p 717)	+ 2.1′
Dec at 21h07m26s	S 14°21.9′

3. Correct the sextant altitude:

Sextant altitude	21°32.9′
Planet total corr (from p 708)	– 5.7′
Observed Altitude	21°27.2′

4. Reduce the sight. Using versine tables:

Find the LHA from the chosen position:

GHA	87°17.3′
Chosen Position	35°N 36°17.3′W
Local Hour Angle	51°00.0′

Find the intercept:

Log versine LHA	9.5690
Log cos Lat	9.9134
Log cos Dec	9.9862
Total	29.4686
Delete tens digit	9.4686
Convert Log to Nat	0.2941

Add Lat and Dec (because opposite names):

Dec	S 11°21.9'
Lat	N 35°00.0'
	49°21.9'

Nat versine of 49°21.9'	0.3488
Add previous answer	0.2941
Nat versine Zenith Distance	0.6429
Zenith Distance	69°04.0'
Subtract 90°	90°00.0'
Hc	20°56.0'
Ho	21°27.0'
Intercept	31.0'

5. Find the Bearing:

A (from p 721)	+ 0.568
B (from p 721)	+ 0.337
A + B	0.905
C (from p 723)	S54°W
Bearing	234°

6. Find the position of Arcturus at 21h11m19s GMT on Sep 10:

GHA Aries at 2000	289°37.3'
Correction for 1h11m (from p 706)	17°48.0'
Correction for 19s (from p 706)	4.8'
GHA Aries at 21h11m19s	307°30.1'
SHA Arcturus (from p 679)	146°08.8'
GHA Arcturus	453°38.9'
Dec Arcturus	N 45°15.8'
CP	35°N 36°38.9'W

Calculate intercept by electronic or tabular methods:

Intercept 4.1' towards, bearing 268°.

Latitude by Polaris

2113 GMT Sep 10, EP 34°40'N 36°50'W
Sext Alt Polaris 34°09.1'
IE 0, HE 10ft

GHA Aries at 2000	289°37.3'
Correction for 1h13m (from p 706)	18°18.0'
GHA Aries at 2113	307°55.3'
Longitude	36°50.0'
LHA Aries	271°05.3'
Sextant Altitude	34°09.1'
Star Altitude correction (from p 708)	– 4.4'
Observed Altitude	34°04.7'
Polaris Correction (from p 702)	+ 27.0
Latitude	34°31.7'

Moon

21h15m07s GMT Sep 10, EP 34°40'N 36°40'W
Sext Alt Moon LL 67°30.6'
IE 0, HE 10ft

To find the position of the Moon at 21h15m07s GMT on September 10:

GHA at 1800	26°42.2'
Mean Var per hour 14°25.0'	
Correction for 3h (from p 708)	43°15.0'
Correction for 15m (from p 709)	3°36.2'
Correction for 07s (from p 709)	1.7'
GHA at 21h15m07s	73°35.1'
Dec at 1800	N 18°16.8'
Mean Var per hour +5.1'	
Correction for 3h (mental arithmetic)	+ 15.3'
Correction for 15m (from p 711)	+ 1.3'
Dec at 07h44m27s	S 18°33.4'

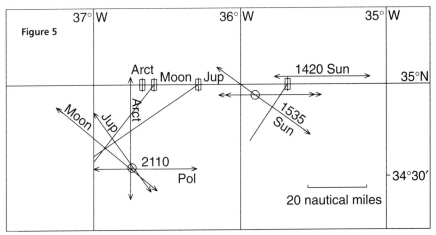

Figure 5

20 nautical miles

Chapter 6

TIME

Standard Times and Summer Time

Standard Time is the same as Zone Time. In Britain the standard is Greenwich Mean Time, (GMT), also known as Universal Coordinated Time (UTC). All the tables in this section are based on GMT, and all the tide tables in Chapter 2 on the appropriate Standard Time. Some countries keep Daylight Saving Time during the summer months. When Daylight Saving Time is in effect, clocks are advanced one hour over Standard Time.

Some countries that have close links with another country in a different time zone adopt the time of that country for convenience. This is known as Clock Time. In the following tables, where the Clock Time of a country differs from its Zone Time, Clock Time is given.

MEASUREMENT OF TIME

Definitions

Mean Time. The Earth does not orbit uniformly round the Sun, but for the purposes of celestial navigation it is assumed that it does.
1 Mean Solar Day = 24 Mean Solar Hours. The average time taken for the Sun to make two successive transits of the same meridian. This represents slightly more than a 360° rotation of the Earth, because the Earth is constantly moving on in its orbit and will therefore have to revolve a little further in order to present the same face to the Sun once more.
1 Sidereal Day = 23h 56m 04.1s of Mean Solar Time. The time taken for the Earth to complete a 360° rotation. Because the stars are so distant, Earth's progress along its orbit is relatively insignificant. The Sidereal Day can therefore be treated as the time taken for a star to make two successive transits of the same meridian.
1 Lunar Day = approx 24h 50m of Mean Solar Time (average).
1 Calendar Month = 28, 29, 30 or 31 days, depending on the month.
1 Lunar Month (or **Lunation**, or **Synodical Month**). The time interval between successive New Moons — about 29½ Mean Solar Days. As with the Mean Solar Day, this represents slightly more than a 360° rotation.

Common and Leap Years

Under the Gregorian calendar, a common year consists of 365 calendar days, a leap year of 366 calendar days. This would suggest that with leap years every four years, the average year works out at 365.25 days. In fact, this is close, but not close enough, to the length of the Mean Solar Year, so leap years are defined as those years which are divisible by 4 (as 1988, 1992, etc), excluding century years unless they are divisible by 400: thus the year 2000 will be a leap year, but 2100 a common year. One complete cycle of the Gregorian calendar takes 400 years, in which there will be:

97 (leap) years of 366 days each	=	35,502
and 303 years of 365 days each	=	110,595
Therefore the total number of days	=	146,097

The mean length of year over the whole cycle will thus be 146,097/400 days, or 365.425 days. This is known as the Civil Year.

Time zones

ZONE **0**		0° Greenwich Meridian
ZONE **+1**		7°30'W
ZONE **+2**		22°30'W
ZONE **+3**		37°30'W
ZONE **+4**		52°30'W
ZONE **+5**		67°30'W
ZONE **+6**		82°30'W
ZONE **+7**		97°30'W
ZONE **+8**		112°30'W
ZONE **+9**		127°30'W
ZONE **+10**		142°30'W
ZONE **+11**		157°30'W
ZONE **+12**		172°30'W
ZONE **–12**		180°00' Intl Date Line
ZONE **–11**		172°30'E
ZONE **–10**		157°30'E
ZONE **–9**		142°30'E
ZONE **–8**		127°30'E
ZONE **–7**		112°30'E
ZONE **–6**		97°30'E
ZONE **–5**		82°30'E
ZONE **–4**		67°30'E
ZONE **–3**		52°30'E
ZONE **–2**		37°30'E
ZONE **–1**		22°30'E
ZONE **0**		7°30'E
		0°Greenwich Meridian

Note that the International Date Line does not follow the 180° meridian throughout its length, but deviates in order to avoid populated areas and land masses.

CLOCK TIME

Countries normally keeping GMT

Ascension Island
Burkina-Faso
* Canary Islands
† Channel Islands
* Faeroes
Gambia
Ghana
† Great Britain
Guinea-Bissau
Guinea Republic
Iceland
† Ireland, Northern
† Irish Republic
Ivory Coast
Liberia
* Madeira
Mali
Mauritania
Morocco
* Portugal
Principe
St Helena
São Tomé
Senegal
Sierra Leone
Togo Republic
Tristan da Cunha

* May keep Summer
Time or Daylight
Saving Time.
† British Summer Time,
one hour in advance of
GMT, is kept from
March 27 0100h to Oct
23 0100h GMT.

Countries keeping times fast on GMT

Add to GMT to find
Standard Time;
subtract from Standard
Time to find GMT.

* Albania 1h
Algeria 1h
Andaman Is 5½h
* Angola 1h
Australia:
* Victoria 10h
* NSW 10h
* Tasmania 10h
* Queensland 10h

* South 9½h
  N Territory 9½h
* West 8h
* Austria 1h
Bahrain 3h
* Balearic Is 1h
Bangladesh 6h
* Belgium 1h
* Bulgaria 2h
Burma 6½h
Cameroon 1h
* China 8h
Congo 1h
* Corsica 1h
* Crete 2h
* Cyprus 2h
* Czechoslovakia 1h
* Denmark 1h
* Egypt 2h
* Estonia 2h
Ethiopia 3h
Fiji 12h
* Finland 2h
* France 1h
* Germany 1h
* Gibraltar 1h
* Greece 2h
* Holland 1h
Hong Kong 8h
* Hungary 1h
India 5½h
* Iran 3½h
* Iraq 3h
* Israel 2h
* Italy 1h
Japan 9h
* Jordan 2h
Kenya 3h
Korea 9h
Laos 7h
* Latvia 2h
* Lebanon 2h
Libya 2h
* Liechtenstein 1h
* Lithuania 2h
* Luxembourg 1h
Madagascar 3h
Malawi 2h
Malaysia 8h
* Malta 1h
Marshall Is 12h
Mauritius 4h
* Monaco 1h
Mozambique 2h
* New Zealand 12h

Nigeria 1h
* Norway 1h
Pakistan 5h
Philippines 8h
* Poland 1h
* Romania 2h
Russia 3-12h
Seychelles 4h
* Sicily 1h
Singapore 8h
Solomon Is 11h
Somalia 3h
South Africa 2h
* Spain 1h
Sri Lanka 5½h
* Sweden 1h
* Switzerland 1h
* Syria 2h
Taiwan 8h
Tanzania 3h
Thailand 7h
Tunisia 1h
* Turkey 2h
Uganda 3h
Vietnam 7h
* Yugoslavia 1h
Zambia 2h
Zimbabwe 2h

* May keep Summer
Time or Daylight
Saving Time.

Countries keeping times slow on GMT

Subtract from GMT to
find Standard Time;
add to Standard Time
to find GMT.

* Argentina 3h
* Azores 1h
* Bahamas 5h
Barbados 4h
Belize 6h
* Bermuda 4h
Brazil E 3h
Brazil W 4h
Canada:
* Alberta 7h
* Brit Columbia 8h
* Labrador 4h
* Manitoba 6h
* Newfndland 3½h
* Nova Scotia 4h
* Ontario 5h

* Quebec 5h
* Saskatchewan 6h
* Yukon 8h
Cape Verde Is 1h
* Chile 4h
Colombia 5h
* Cook Is 10h
* Costa Rica 6h
* Cuba 5h
Dominican Rep 4h
Ecuador 5h
* Easter Island 6h
El Salvador 6h
* Falkland Is 4h
French Guiana 3h
* Greenland 1-4h
Grenada 4h
Guadeloupe 4h
* Guatemala 6h
Guyana 3h
* Haiti 5h
Honduras 6h
Jamaica 5h
Leeward Is 4h
Mexico 6-8h
Midway Is 11h
Nicaragua 6h
Niue Is 11h
Panama 5h
* Paraguay 4h
Peru 5h
Puerto Rico 4h
* St Pierre and
  Miquelon 3h
Samoa 11h
South Georgia 2h
Trinidad and
Tobago 4h
* Turks & Caicos Is
  5h
United States:
* Eastern Zone 5h
* Central Zone 6h
* Pacific Zone 8h
* Mountain Zn 7h
* Alaska Zone 9hr
Hawaiian Is 10h
* Uruguay 3h
Venezuela 4h
Virgin Is 4h
Windward Is 4h

* May keep Summer
Time or Daylight
Saving Time.

Chapter 6

USING A CALCULATOR TO FIND GHA AND DECLINATION OF THE SUN

Greenwich Hour Angle (GHA) and Declination (Dec) of the Sun for 1994 can be calculated using an electronic calculator and the following sets of monthly polynomial coefficients.

The date and time In GMT are used to form the interpolation factor p. This can be expressed as $p = d/32$ where d is the sum of the month and decimal of a day. Then GHA – GMT in hours and Dec in degrees are calculated from polynomial expressions of the form:

$$a_0 + a_1 p + a_2 p^2 + a_3 p^3 + a_4 p^4$$

where p is the interpolating factor. The simplest way of evaluating this is to use the nested form:

$$(((a_4 p + a_3) p + a_2) p + a_1) p + a_0$$

Example. Calculate GHA and Dec of Sun on July 23 1994, at 17h 02m 15s GMT

$$GMT = 17h.0375 \text{ and the interpolation factor is}$$
$$p = (23 + 17.0375/24) / 32 = 0.740934$$
$$GHA - GMT = 11h.94213 - 0h.10568p + 0h.02442p^2 + 0h.04883p^3 - 0h.01515p^4$$
$$= 11h.89253$$

Hence, $\quad$ GHA $= 11h.89253 + GMT = 11h.89253 + 17h.0375$

Remove multiples of 24h from GHA and multiply by 15 to convert from hours to degrees.

Then, $\qquad$ GHA $= 73°.9505 = 73°.57.0'$

$$Dec = 23°.1972 - 1°.8341p - 3°.4977p^2 + 0°.2063p^3 + 0°.0569p^4$$
$$= 20°.0191 = N20°.01.1'$$

Semi-diameter of the Sun (in critical cases, use the higher value)

Jan 1– Feb 4	16.3'	Apr 20–May 14	1.9'	Oct 12–Nov 3	16.1'
Feb 5–Mar 5	16.2'	May 15–Aug 25	15.8'	Nov 4–Dec 2	16.2'
Mar 6–Mar 28	16.1'	Aug 26–Sep 19	15.9'	Dec 3–Dec 31	16.3'
Mar 29–Apr 19	16.0'	Sep 20–Oct 11	16.0'		

To correct for the effect of parallax of the Sun it is normally sufficient to add 0.1' to all observed altitudes less than 70°. If greater accuracy is required, the correction is 0.15' x cos altitude.

Monthly polynomial coefficients for the Sun, 1994

		JANUARY GHA–GMT h	Dec °	FEBRUARY GHA–GMT h	Dec °	MARCH GHA–GMT h	Dec °	APRIL GHA–GMT h	Dec °
Sun	a_0	11.95282	–23.1113	11.77709	–17.5031	11.78879	–8.1330	11.92714	3.9793
	a_1	–0.25369	2.2768	–0.08114	8.8624	0.09805	12.0629	0.16133	12.4042
	a_2	0.02948	3.9917	0.11048	2.6962	0.06996	1.0510	–0.01778	-0.5963
	a_3	0.06358	–0.2890	–0.00789	–0.7005	–0.02073	–0.6583	–0.02117	-0.5802
	a_4	–0.01751	–0.0919	–0.01223	–0.0350	0.00390	–0.0437	0.00009	0.0341
check sum		11.77468	–17.2237	11.80209	–6.6100	11.93217	4.3663	12.04961	15.2411

		MAY GHA–GMT h	Dec °	JUNE GHA–GMT h	Dec °	JULY GHA–GMT h	Dec °	AUGUST GHA–GMT h	Dec °
Sun	a_0	12.04537	14.6325	12.04126	21.8486	11.94213	23.1972	11.89372	18.3756
	a_1	0.07294	9.8672	–0.07460	4.6410	–0.10568	–1.8341	0.02414	–7.8228
	a_2	–0.08208	–2.0334	–0.06941	–3.2401	0.02442	–3.4977	0.08281	–2.5896
	a_3	–0.00154	–0.5403	0.04224	–0.2928	0.04883	0.2063	–0.00806	0.4925
	a_4	0.00416	0.0645	0.00386	0.1122	–0.01515	0.0569	–0.01195	0.0130
check sum		12.03885	219905	11.93563	23.0689	11.89455	18.1286	11.99678	8.4427

		SEPTEMBER GHA–GMT h	Dec °	OCTOBER GHA–GMT h	Dec °	NOVEMBER GHA–GMT h	Dec °	DECEMBER GHA–GMT h	Dec °
Sun	a_0	11.99164	8.8033	12.16327	–2.6227	12.27228	–13.9590	12.19268	–21.5671
	a_1	0.16393	–11.5014	0.17481	–12.4401	0.02359	–10.4279	–0.19117	–5.2963
	a_2	0.04432	–1.2025	–0.03713	0.2204	–0.10943	1.8866	–0.09757	3.4906
	a_3	–0.02016	0.5089	–0.02796	0.5494	–0.01602	0.6619	0.04030	0.4860
	a_4	–0.00570	0.0076	0.00008	0.0100	0.00992	–0.0460	0.00260	–0.1672
check sum		12.17403	–3.3993	12.27291	–14.2830	12.18034	–21.8844	11.94684	–23.0540

Prepared by HM Nautical Almanac Office, Royal Greenwich Observatory, reproduced with permission from data supplied by the Science and Engineering Research Council.

ALPHABETICAL INDEX OF PRINCIPAL STARS

With their approximate places, 1994

Proper Name	Constellation Name	Mag	RA	Dec	SHA	No
Acamar	Eridani	3.1	2 58	S 40	315	8
Achernar	Eridani	0.6	1 37	S 57	336	5
Acrux	Crucis	1.1	12 26	S 63	173	32
Adhara	Canis Majoris	1.6	6 58	S 28	255	20
Aldebaran	Tauri	1.1	4 36	N 16	291	11
Alioth	Ursae Majoris	1.7	12 54	N 56	167	35
Alkaid	Ursae Majoris	1.9	13 47	N 49	153	37
Al Na'ir	Gruis	2.2	22 08	S 47	28	58
Alnilam	Orionis	1.8	5 36	S 1	276	16
Alphard	Hydrae	2.2	9 27	S 9	218	27
Alphecca	Coronae Bor	2.3	15 34	N 27	126	44
Alpheratz	Andromedae	2.2	0 08	N 29	358	1
Altair	Aquilae	0.9	19 50	N 9	62	54
Ankaa	Phoenicis	2.4	0 26	S 42	354	2
Antares	Scorpii	1.2	16 29	S 26	113	45
Arcturus	Bootis	0.2	14 15	N 19	146	40
Atria	Triang Aust	1.9	16 48	S 69	108	46
Avior	Carinae	1.7	8 22	S 59	234	24
Bellatrix	Orionis	1.7	5 25	N 6	279	14
Betelgeuse	Orionis	0.1-1.2	5 55	N 7	271	17
Canopus	Carinae	−0.9	6 24	S 53	264	18
Capella	Aurigae	0.2	5 16	N 46	281	13
Castor	Geminorum	1.6	7 34	N 32	246	21
Deneb	Cygni	1.3	20 41	N 45	50	56
Denebola	Leonis	2.2	11 49	N 15	183	30
Diphda	Ceti	2.2	0 43	S 18	349	4
Dubhe	Ursae Majoris	2.0	11 03	N 62	194	29
Elnath	Tauri	1.8	5 26	N 29	279	15
Eltanin	Draconis	2.4	17 56	N 51	91	50
Enif	Pegasi	2.5	21 44	N 10	34	57
Fomalhaut	Piscis Aust	1.3	22 57	S 30	16	59
Gacrux	Crucis	1.6	12 31	S 57	172	33
Gienah	Corvi	2.8	12 16	S 18	176	31
Hadar	Centauri	0.9	14 03	S 60	149	38
Hamal	Arietis	2.2	2 07	N 23	328	7
Kaus Aust	Sagittarii	2.0	18 24	S 34	84	51
Kochab	Ursae Minoris	2.2	14 51	N 74	137	43
Markab	Pegasi	2.6	23 04	N 15	14	60
Menkar	Ceti	2.8	3 02	N 4	315	9
Menkent	Centauri	2.3	14 06	S 36	148	39
Miaplacidus	Carinae	1.8	9 13	S 70	222	26
Mimosa	Crucis	1.5	12 47	S 60	168	34
Mirfak	Persei	1.9	3 24	N 50	309	10
Nunki	Sagittarii	2.1	18 55	S 26	76	53
Peacock	Pavonis	2.1	20 25	S 57	54	55
POLARIS	Ursae Minoris	2.1	2 26	N 89	323	6
Pollux	Geminorum	1.2	7 45	N 28	244	23
Procyon	Canis Minoris	0.5	7 39	N 5	245	22
Rasalhague	Ophiuchi	2.1	17 35	N 13	96	49
Regulus	Leonis	1.3	10 08	N 12	208	28
Rigel	Orionis	0.3	5 14	S 8	281	12
Rigil Kent	Centauri	0.1	14 39	S 61	140	41
Sabik	Ophiuchi	2.6	17 10	S 16	102	47
Schedar	Cassiopeiae	2.5	0 40	N 56	350	3
Shaula	Scorpii	1.7	17 33	S 37	97	48
Sirius	Canis Majoris	−1.6	6 45	S 17	259	19
Spica	Virginis	1.2	13 25	S 11	159	36
Suhail	Velorum	2.2	9 08	S 43	223	25
Vega	Lyrae	0.1	18 37	N 39	81	52
Zuben'ubi	Librae	2.9	14 51	S 16	137	42

The last column refers to the number given to the Star in this Almanac. The Star's exact position may be found according to this number on the monthly pages.

Chapter 6

Action

Features

Heritage

History

MQ

GUIDE TO THE EPHEMERIS

CELESTIAL PHENOMENA 1994

SEASONS 1994

Vernal Equinox. Spring begins when Sun enters Aries, 20h28 March 20.

Summer Solstice. Summer begins when Sun enters Cancer, 14h48 June 21.

Autumn Equinox. Autumn begins when Sun enters Libra, 06h19 September 23.

Winter Solstice. Winter begins when Sun enters Capricorn, 02h23 December 22.

Earth is at Perihelion (closest to the Sun) 06h January 2, at Aphelion (furthest from the Sun) 19h July 5.

ECLIPSES 1994

There are two eclipses of the Sun and two of the Moon in 1994:

May 10. Annular eclipse of the Sun, begins 14h12, ends 20h10. Visible in North America, NW Europe and part of W Africa.

May 25. Partial eclipse of the Moon, begins 01h17, ends 05h42, visible in Africa, most of Europe and North America.

November 3. Total eclipse of the Sun, begins 11h05, ends 16h13, visible in Central and South America and South Africa.

November 18. Penumbral eclipse of the Moon, begins 04h25, ends 09h02, visible North, Central and South America, Eastern Pacific, Europe and West Africa.

Further celestial phenomena including phases of the moon can be found in the Diary section on the second of each set of monthly pages. Festivals, anniversaries etc based on celestial events are listed in the General Information section at the front of the Almanac.

1995 DATA

If the 1995 Almanac is not available at the start of the year, it will be possible to use the data given in these tables for Sun and star sights. The details will be approximate but of quite sufficient accuracy for navigational purposes, as any error would be unlikely to exceed 0.4'.

It is not possible to use the 1994 data for 1995 observations of the Moon or planets.

Chapter 6

JANUARY 1994   SUN & MOON   GMT

SUN

Day of			Equation of Time		Transit	Semi-diam	Lat 52°N				Lat Corr to Sunrise, Sunset etc				
Yr	Mth	Week	0h	12h			Twilight	Sunrise	Sunset	Twilight	Lat	Twilight	Sunrise	Sunset	Twilight
			m s	m s	h m	′	h m	h m	h m	h m	°	h m	h m	h m	h m
1	1	Sat	+03 18	+03 32	12 04	16.3	07 28	08 08	15 59	16 40	N70	+1 57	SBH	SBH	−1 56
2	2	Sun	+03 46	+04 00	12 04	16.3	07 28	08 08	16 00	16 41	68	+1 32	+2 34	−2 33	−1 32
3	3	Mon	+04 14	+04 28	12 04	16.3	07 27	08 08	16 01	16 42	66	+1 13	+1 53	−1 53	−1 13
4	4	Tue	+04 42	+04 56	12 05	16.3	07 27	08 08	16 02	16 43	64	+0 57	+1 25	−1 25	−0 57
5	5	Wed	+05 09	+05 23	12 05	16.3	07 27	08 07	16 04	16 44	62	+0 44	+1 04	−1 04	−0 44
6	6	Thu	+05 36	+05 49	12 06	16.3	07 27	08 07	16 05	16 45	N60	+0 32	+0 47	−0 47	−0 33
7	7	Fri	+06 02	+06 15	12 06	16.3	07 27	08 07	16 06	16 46	58	+0 22	+0 33	−0 32	−0 23
8	8	Sat	+06 28	+06 41	12 07	16.3	07 26	08 06	16 08	16 47	56	+0 14	+0 21	−0 20	−0 14
9	9	Sun	+06 54	+07 06	12 07	16.3	07 26	08 06	16 09	16 49	54	+0 07	+0 10	−0 09	−0 07
10	10	Mon	+07 19	+07 31	12 08	16.3	07 25	08 05	16 10	16 50	50	−0 06	−0 08	+0 09	+0 06
11	11	Tue	+07 43	+07 55	12 08	16.3	07 25	08 04	16 12	16 51	N45	−0 20	−0 26	+0 27	+0 20
12	12	Wed	+08 07	+08 18	12 08	16.3	07 24	08 04	16 13	16 53	40	−0 33	−0 41	+0 42	+0 32
13	13	Thu	+08 30	+08 41	12 09	16.3	07 24	08 03	16 15	16 54	35	−0 43	−0 54	+0 54	+0 42
14	14	Fri	+08 52	+09 03	12 09	16.3	07 23	08 02	16 16	16 56	30	−0 52	−1 05	+1 05	+0 52
15	15	Sat	+09 14	+09 25	12 09	16.3	07 22	08 01	16 18	16 57	20	−1 08	−1 24	+1 24	+1 08
16	16	Sun	+09 35	+09 46	12 10	16.3	07 22	08 01	16 19	16 58	N10	−1 24	−1 41	+1 41	+1 24
17	17	Mon	+09 56	+10 06	12 10	16.3	07 21	08 00	16 21	17 00	0	−1 39	−1 56	+1 56	+1 39
18	18	Tue	+10 16	+10 25	12 10	16.3	07 20	07 59	16 23	17 01	S10	−1 55	−2 13	+2 11	+1 55
19	19	Wed	+10 35	+10 44	12 11	16.3	07 19	07 58	16 24	17 03	20	−2 14	−2 30	+2 28	+2 14
20	20	Thu	+10 53	+11 02	12 11	16.3	07 18	07 56	16 26	17 04	30	−2 36	−2 49	+2 48	+2 36
21	21	Fri	+11 11	+11 19	12 11	16.3	07 17	07 55	16 28	17 06	S35	−2 49	−3 01	+3 00	+2 49
22	22	Sat	+11 27	+11 35	12 12	16.3	07 16	07 54	16 29	17 08	40	−3 06	−3 15	+3 13	+3 06
23	23	Sun	+11 43	+11 51	12 12	16.3	07 15	07 53	16 31	17 09	45	−3 26	−3 31	+3 29	+3 26
24	24	Mon	+11 58	+12 06	12 12	16.3	07 14	07 52	16 33	17 11	S50	−3 51	−3 51	+3 49	+3 52
25	25	Tue	+12 13	+12 20	12 12	16.3	07 13	07 50	16 35	17 12					
26	26	Wed	+12 26	+12 33	12 13	16.3	07 12	07 49	16 37	17 14					
27	27	Thu	+12 39	+12 45	12 13	16.3	07 10	07 48	16 38	17 16					
28	28	Fri	+12 51	+12 57	12 13	16.3	07 09	07 46	16 40	17 17					
29	29	Sat	+13 03	+13 08	12 13	16.3	07 08	07 45	16 42	17 19					
30	30	Sun	+13 13	+13 18	12 13	16.3	07 06	07 43	16 44	17 21					
31	31	Mon	+13 23	+13 27	12 13	16.3	07 05	07 42	16 46	17 22					

NOTES

Lat corrections are for Jan 15.
SBH = Sun is below the horizon.
Equation of Time is the excess of Mean Time over Apparent Time.

MOON

Day of			Age	Transit Diff (Upper)		Semi-diam	Hor Par	Lat 52°N		Phases of the Moon
Yr	Mth	Week						Moonrise	Moonset	
			days	h m	m	′	′	h m	h m	
1	1	Sat	19	02 40	51	15.9	58.5	20 44	09 39	
2	2	Sun	20	03 31	50	16.0	58.8	22 03	10 02	☽ Last Quarter 5 00 00
3	3	Mon	21	04 21	50	16.1	59.0	23 21	10 25	● New Moon 11 23 10
4	4	Tue	22	05 11	51	16.1	59.2	– –	10 47	☾ First Quarter 19 20 27
5	5	Wed	23	06 02	54	16.1	59.2	00 41	11 12	○ Full Moon 27 13 23
6	6	Thu	24	06 56	55	16.1	59.2	02 00	11 42	
7	7	Fri	25	07 51	57	16.1	59.2	03 18	12 17	
8	8	Sat	26	08 48	59	16.1	59.0	04 33	13 01	Perigee 6 01
9	9	Sun	27	09 47	58	16.0	58.7	05 39	13 54	Apogee 19 05
10	10	Mon	28	10 45	56	15.9	58.3	06 35	14 57	Perigee 31 04
11	11	Tue	29	11 41	53	15.7	57.8	07 20	16 07	
12	12	Wed	01	12 34	49	15.6	57.2	07 56	17 19	
13	13	Thu	02	13 23	47	15.4	56.5	08 24	18 32	
14	14	Fri	03	14 10	45	15.2	55.9	08 48	19 43	
15	15	Sat	04	14 55	43	15.1	55.3	09 09	20 52	
16	16	Sun	05	15 38	42	14.9	54.8	09 28	21 59	
17	17	Mon	06	16 20	42	14.8	54.5	09 47	23 05	
18	18	Tue	07	17 02	43	14.8	54.3	10 06	– –	
19	19	Wed	08	17 45	45	14.8	54.2	10 28	00 10	
20	20	Thu	09	18 30	47	14.8	54.4	10 52	01 15	
21	21	Fri	10	19 17	49	14.9	54.7	11 21	02 19	
22	22	Sat	11	20 06	52	15.0	55.2	11 57	03 22	
23	23	Sun	12	20 58	53	15.2	55.8	12 41	04 21	
24	24	Mon	13	21 51	54	15.4	56.5	13 35	05 15	
25	25	Tue	14	22 45	53	15.6	57.2	14 39	06 01	
26	26	Wed	15	23 38	54	15.8	57.9	15 50	06 41	
27	27	Thu	16	24 32	_	16.0	58.6	17 06	07 14	
28	28	Fri	17	00 32	52	16.1	59.1	18 26	07 42	
29	29	Sat	18	01 24	52	16.2	59.5	19 46	08 07	
30	30	Sun	19	02 16	51	16.3	59.6	21 07	08 30	
31	31	Mon	20	03 07	52	16.3	59.7	22 28	08 54	

Phases of the Moon:

		d	h	m
☽	Last Quarter	5	00	00
●	New Moon	11	23	10
☾	First Quarter	19	20	27
○	Full Moon	27	13	23

	d	h
Perigee	6	01
Apogee	19	05
Perigee	31	04

NOTES

For Latitude corrections to Moonrise and Moonset see page 706.

JANUARY 1994   STARS   0h GMT January 1

No	Name	Mag	Transit h m	Dec ° ′	GHA ° ′	RA h m	SHA ° ′
	ARIES...............		17 15		100 25.1		
1	Alpheratz 2.2		17 24	N 29 03.7	98 23.8	0 08	357 58.7
2	Ankaa............... 2.4		17 41	S 42 20.5	93 55.2	0 26	353 30.1
3	Schedar............ 2.5		17 56	N 56 30.6	90 22.3	0 40	349 57.2
4	Diphda 2.2		17 55	S 10 01.0	89 35.6	0 43	349 10.5
5	Achernar 0.6		18 53	S 57 16.3	76 02.6	1 38	335 37.5
6	POLARIS 2.1		19 41	N 89 14.6	63 49.2	2 26	323 24.1
7	Hamal.............. 2.2		19 22	N 23 26.2	68 42.2	2 07	318 17.1
8	Acamar 3.1		20 13	S 40 19.9	55 54.3	2 58	315 29.2
9	Menkar............ 2.8		20 17	N 4 04.0	54 55.2	3 02	314 30.1
10	Mirfak 1.9		20 39	N 49 50.6	49 26.0	3 24	309 00.9
11	Aldebaran 1.1		21 50	N 16 29.8	31 30.9	4 36	291 05.8
12	Rigel 0.3		22 29	S 8 12.6	21 50.8	5 14	281 25.7
13	Capella 0.2		22 31	N 45 59.6	21 20.6	5 16	280 55.5
14	Bellatrix........... 1.7		22 39	N 6 20.6	19 12.4	5 25	278 47.3
15	Elnath 1.8		22 41	N 28 36.1	18 55.7	5 26	278 30.6
16	Alnilam 1.8		22 51	S 1 12.5	16 25.9	5 36	276 00.8
17	Betelgeuse 0.1-1.2		23 09	N 7 24.3	11 41.8	5 55	271 16.7
18	Canopus .... −0.9		23 38	S 52 41.7	4 27.1	6 24	264 02.0
19	Sirius .... −1.6		0 03	S 16 42.6	359 11.2	6 45	258 46.1
20	Adhara 1.6		0 17	S 28 58.0	355 48.6	6 58	255 23.5
21	Castor 1.6		0 52	N 31 53.9	346 51.1	7 34	246 26.0
22	Procyon 0.5		0 57	N 5 14.3	345 39.6	7 39	245 14.5
23	Pollux 1.2		1 03	N 28 02.3	344 10.2	7 45	243 45.1
24	Avior 1.7		1 40	S 59 29.5	334 48.4	8 22	234 23.3
25	Suhail 2.2		2 26	S 43 24.6	323 27.8	9 08	223 02.7
26	Miaplacidus 1.8		2 31	S 69 41.6	322 06.9	9 13	221 41.8
27	Alphard 2.2		2 45	S 8 38.1	318 35.1	9 27	218 10.0
28	Regulus........... 1.3		3 26	N 11 59.6	308 23.8	10 08	207 58.7
29	Dubhe 2.0		4 21	N 61 46.6	294 34.1	11 03	194 09.0
30	Denebola........ 2.2		5 06	N 14 36.1	283 13.4	11 49	182 48.3
31	Gienah 2.8		5 33	S 17 30.6	276 32.2	12 16	176 07.1
32	Acrux............... 1.1		5 44	S 63 03.8	273 50.4	12 26	173 25.3
33	Gacrux 1.6		5 48	S 57 04.6	272 42.1	12 31	172 17.0
34	Mimosa............ 1.5		6 05	S 59 39.2	268 34.0	12 47	168 08.9
35	Alioth.............. 1.7		6 11	N 55 59.1	266 58.4	12 54	166 33.3
36	Spica................ 1.2		6 42	S 11 07.9	259 11.6	13 25	158 46.5
37	Alkaid 1.9		7 04	N 49 20.2	253 35.4	13 47	153 10.3
38	Hadar 0.9		7 21	S 60 20.5	249 33.7	14 03	149 08.6
39	Menkent.......... 2.3		7 23	S 36 20.4	248 49.9	14 06	148 24.8
40	Arcturus.......... 0.2		7 32	N 19 12.6	246 34.1	14 15	146 09.0
41	Rigil Kent........ 0.1		7 56	S 60 48.4	240 36.8	14 39	140 11.7
42	Zuben'ubi....... 2.9		8 08	S 16 01.0	237 46.7	14 51	137 21.6
43	Kochab............ 2.2		8 08	N 74 10.4	237 45.0	14 51	137 19.9
44	Alphecca......... 2.3		8 51	N 26 43.9	226 48.6	15 34	126 23.5
45	Antares............ 1.2		9 46	S 26 25.1	213 09.4	16 29	112 44.3
46	Atria 1.9		10 05	S 69 00.8	208 24.8	16 48	107 59.7
47	Sabik 2.6		10 27	S 15 43.0	202 54.6	17 10	102 29.5
48	Shaula............. 1.7		10 50	S 37 05.9	197 07.1	17 33	96 42.0
49	Rasalhague 2.1		10 51	N 12 33.8	196 45.3	17 35	96 20.2
50	Eltanin 2.4		11 13	N 51 29.3	191 18.5	17 56	90 53.4
51	Kaus Aust........ 2.0		11 40	S 34 23.2	184 28.5	18 24	84 03.4
52	Vega 0.1		11 53	N 38 46.7	181 14.3	18 37	80 49.2
53	Nunki 2.1		12 11	S 26 18.2	176 41.7	18 55	76 16.6
54	Altair............... 0.9		13 07	N 8 51.2	162 47.8	19 50	62 22.7
55	Peacock........... 2.1		13 41	S 56 45.2	154 07.7	20 25	53 42.6
56	Deneb 1.3		13 57	N 45 15.7	150 06.9	20 41	49 41.8
57	Enif 2.5		15 00	N 9 51.0	134 26.7	21 44	34 01.6
58	Al Na'ir 2.2		15 24	S 46 59.5	128 27.4	22 08	28 02.3
59	Fomalhaut 1.3		16 13	S 29 39.3	116 05.3	22 57	15 40.2
60	Markab 2.6		16 20	N 15 10.5	114 18.1	23 04	13 53.0

Stars Transit Corr Table

Date	Corr	Date	Corr
	h m		h m
1	−0 00	17	−1 03
2	−0 04	18	−1 07
3	−0 08	19	−1 11
4	−0 12	20	−1 15
5	−0 16	21	−1 19
6	−0 20	22	−1 23
7	−0 24	23	−1 27
8	−0 28	24	−1 30
9	−0 31	25	−1 34
10	−0 35	26	−1 38
11	−0 39	27	−1 42
12	−0 43	28	−1 46
13	−0 47	29	−1 50
14	−0 51	30	−1 54
15	−0 55	31	−1 58
16	−0 59		

STAR'S TRANSIT

To find the approx time of transit of a star for any day of the month use above table. All corrections are subtractive. If the quantity taken from the table is greater than the time of transit for the first of the month, add 23h 56min to the time of transit before subtracting the correction.

Example: What time will Adhara (No 20) be on the Meridian on January 30?

	h min
Transit on Jan 1	00 17
	+23 56
	24 13
Corr for Jan 30	−01 54
Transit on Jan 30	22 19

JANUARY DIARY

2 06   Earth at perihelion
3 20   Mercury in superior conjunction
5 00   Last Quarter
6 01   Moon at perigee
6 22   Jupiter 3°N of Moon
11 08   Neptune in conjunction with Sun
11 23   New Moon
12 17   Uranus in conjunction with Sun
15 00   Saturn 7°S of Moon
17 02   Venus in superior conjunction
19 05   Moon at apogee
19 20   First Quarter
27 13   Full Moon
31 04   Moon at perigee

Chapter 6

JANUARY 1994 — SUN & ARIES — GMT

Saturday, January 1 | Thursday, January 6 | Tuesday, January 11

Time	SUN GHA	Dec	ARIES GHA	Time	SUN GHA	Dec	ARIES GHA	Time	SUN GHA	Dec	ARIES GHA	Time
00	179 10.3	S23 02.2	100 36.1	00	178 35.9	S22 32.7	105 20.8	00	178 04.2	S21 52.2	110 16.5	00
02	209 09.7	23 01.8	130 30.0	02	208 35.3	22 32.2	135 25.7	02	208 03.7	21 51.4	140 21.4	02
04	239 09.1	23 01.4	160 35.0	04	238 34.8	22 31.6	165 30.7	04	238 03.2	21 50.7	170 26.3	04
06	269 08.5	23 01.0	190 39.9	06	268 34.2	22 31.0	195 35.6	06	268 02.7	21 49.9	200 31.3	06
08	299 07.9	23 00.6	220 44.8	08	298 33.7	22 30.4	225 40.5	08	298 02.2	21 49.1	230 36.2	08
10	329 07.4	23 00.2	250 49.7	10	328 33.1	22 29.8	255 45.4	10	328 01.7	21 48.3	260 41.1	10
12	359 06.8	22 59.7	280 54.7	12	358 32.6	22 29.2	285 50.4	12	358 01.2	21 47.5	290 46.1	12
14	29 06.2	22 59.3	310 59.6	14	28 32.0	22 28.6	315 55.3	14	28 00.7	21 46.8	320 51.0	14
16	59 05.6	22 58.9	341 04.5	16	58 31.5	22 28.0	346 00.2	16	58 00.2	21 46.0	350 55.9	16
18	89 05.0	22 58.5	11 09.5	18	88 30.9	22 27.4	16 05.2	18	87 59.7	21 45.2	21 00.8	18
20	119 04.4	22 58.1	41 14.4	20	118 30.4	22 26.7	46 10.1	20	117 59.2	21 44.4	51 05.8	20
22	149 03.8	S22 57.6	71 19.3	22	148 29.8	S22 26.1	76 15.0	22	147 58.7	S21 43.6	81 10.7	22

Sunday, January 2 | Friday, January 7 | Wednesday, January 12

Time	SUN GHA	Dec	ARIES GHA	Time	SUN GHA	Dec	ARIES GHA	Time	SUN GHA	Dec	ARIES GHA	Time
00	179 03.2	S22 57.2	101 24.2	00	178 29.3	S22 25.5	106 19.9	00	177 58.2	S21 42.8	111 15.6	00
02	209 02.7	22 56.8	131 29.2	02	208 28.7	22 24.9	136 24.9	02	207 57.7	21 42.0	141 20.6	02
04	239 02.1	22 56.3	161 34.1	04	238 28.2	22 24.3	166 29.8	04	237 57.2	21 41.2	171 25.5	04
06	269 01.5	22 55.9	191 39.0	06	268 27.7	22 23.6	196 34.7	06	267 56.8	21 40.4	201 30.4	06
08	299 00.9	22 55.4	221 44.0	08	298 27.1	22 23.0	226 39.7	08	297 56.3	21 39.6	231 35.3	08
10	329 00.3	22 55.0	251 48.9	10	328 26.6	22 22.4	256 44.6	10	327 55.8	21 38.7	261 40.3	10
12	358 59.7	22 54.5	281 53.8	12	358 26.0	22 21.7	286 49.5	12	357 55.3	21 37.9	291 45.2	12
14	28 59.2	22 54.1	311 58.7	14	28 25.5	22 21.1	316 54.4	14	27 54.8	21 37.1	321 50.1	14
16	58 58.6	22 53.6	342 03.7	16	58 25.0	22 20.4	346 59.4	16	57 54.3	21 36.3	351 55.1	16
18	88 58.0	22 53.2	12 08.6	18	88 24.4	22 19.8	17 04.3	18	87 53.9	21 35.5	22 00.0	18
20	118 57.4	22 52.7	42 13.5	20	118 23.9	22 19.1	47 09.2	20	117 53.4	21 34.6	52 04.9	20
22	148 56.8	S22 52.2	72 18.5	22	148 23.4	S22 18.5	77 14.1	22	147 52.9	S21 33.8	82 09.8	22

Monday, January 3 | Saturday, January 8 | Thursday, January 13

Time	SUN GHA	Dec	ARIES GHA	Time	SUN GHA	Dec	ARIES GHA	Time	SUN GHA	Dec	ARIES GHA	Time
00	178 56.3	S22 51.8	102 23.4	00	178 22.8	S22 17.8	107 19.1	00	177 52.4	S21 33.0	112 14.8	00
02	208 55.7	22 51.3	132 28.3	02	208 22.3	22 17.2	137 24.0	02	207 52.0	21 32.1	142 19.7	02
04	238 55.1	22 50.8	162 33.2	04	238 21.7	22 16.5	167 28.9	04	237 51.5	21 31.3	172 24.6	04
06	268 54.5	22 50.3	192 38.2	06	268 21.2	22 15.8	197 33.9	06	267 51.0	21 30.4	202 29.6	06
08	298 54.0	22 49.9	222 43.1	08	298 20.7	22 15.2	227 38.8	08	297 50.5	21 29.6	232 34.5	08
10	328 53.4	22 49.4	252 48.0	10	328 20.2	22 14.5	257 43.7	10	327 50.1	21 28.7	262 39.4	10
12	358 52.8	22 48.9	282 53.0	12	358 19.6	22 13.8	287 48.6	12	357 49.6	21 27.9	292 44.3	12
14	28 52.2	22 48.4	312 57.9	14	28 19.1	22 13.2	317 53.6	14	27 49.1	21 27.0	322 49.3	14
16	58 51.7	22 47.9	343 02.8	16	58 18.6	22 12.5	347 58.5	16	57 48.7	21 26.2	352 54.2	16
18	88 51.1	22 47.4	13 07.7	18	88 18.0	22 11.8	18 03.4	18	87 48.2	21 25.3	22 59.1	18
20	118 50.5	22 46.9	43 12.7	20	118 17.5	22 11.1	48 08.4	20	117 47.7	21 24.5	53 04.1	20
22	148 50.0	S22 46.4	73 17.6	22	148 17.0	S22 10.4	78 13.3	22	147 47.3	S21 23.6	83 09.0	22

Tuesday, January 4 | Sunday, January 9 | Friday, January 14

Time	SUN GHA	Dec	ARIES GHA	Time	SUN GHA	Dec	ARIES GHA	Time	SUN GHA	Dec	ARIES GHA	Time
00	178 49.4	S22 45.9	103 22.5	00	178 16.5	S22 09.7	108 18.2	00	177 46.8	S21 22.7	113 13.9	00
02	208 48.8	22 45.4	133 27.4	02	208 15.9	22 09.0	138 23.1	02	207 46.3	21 21.8	143 18.8	02
04	238 48.2	22 44.9	163 32.4	04	238 15.4	22 08.3	168 28.1	04	237 45.9	21 21.0	173 23.8	04
06	268 47.7	22 44.3	193 37.3	06	268 14.9	22 07.6	198 33.0	06	267 45.4	21 20.1	203 28.7	06
08	298 47.1	22 43.8	223 42.2	08	298 14.4	22 06.9	228 37.9	08	297 45.0	21 19.2	233 33.6	08
10	328 46.5	22 43.3	253 47.2	10	328 13.9	22 06.2	258 42.9	10	327 44.5	21 18.3	263 38.6	10
12	358 46.0	22 42.8	283 52.1	12	358 13.3	22 05.5	288 47.8	12	357 44.1	21 17.4	293 43.5	12
14	28 45.4	22 42.2	313 57.0	14	28 12.8	22 04.8	318 52.7	14	27 43.6	21 16.6	323 48.4	14
16	58 44.8	22 41.7	344 01.9	16	58 12.3	22 04.1	348 57.6	16	57 43.1	21 15.7	353 53.3	16
18	88 44.3	22 41.2	14 06.9	18	88 11.8	22 03.3	19 02.6	18	87 42.7	21 14.8	23 58.3	18
20	118 43.7	22 40.6	44 11.8	20	118 11.3	22 02.6	49 07.5	20	117 42.2	21 13.9	54 03.2	20
22	148 43.1	S22 40.1	74 16.7	22	148 10.8	S22 01.9	79 12.4	22	147 41.8	S21 13.0	84 08.1	22

Wednesday, January 5 | Monday, January 10 | Saturday, January 15

Time	SUN GHA	Dec	ARIES GHA	Time	SUN GHA	Dec	ARIES GHA	Time	SUN GHA	Dec	ARIES GHA	Time
00	178 42.6	S22 39.5	104 21.7	00	178 10.2	S22 01.2	109 17.4	00	177 41.3	S21 12.1	114 13.0	00
02	208 42.0	22 39.0	134 26.6	02	208 09.7	22 00.4	139 22.3	02	207 40.9	21 11.2	144 18.0	02
04	238 41.5	22 38.4	164 31.5	04	238 09.2	21 59.7	169 27.2	04	237 40.4	21 10.3	174 22.9	04
06	268 40.9	22 37.9	194 36.4	06	268 08.7	21 59.0	199 32.1	06	267 40.0	21 09.3	204 27.8	06
08	298 40.3	22 37.3	224 41.4	08	298 08.2	21 58.2	229 37.1	08	297 39.6	21 08.4	234 32.8	08
10	328 39.8	22 36.8	254 46.3	10	328 07.7	21 57.5	259 42.0	10	327 39.1	21 07.5	264 37.7	10
12	358 39.2	22 36.2	284 51.2	12	358 07.2	21 56.7	289 46.9	12	357 38.7	21 06.6	294 42.6	12
14	28 38.7	22 35.6	314 56.2	14	28 06.7	21 56.0	319 51.9	14	27 38.2	21 05.7	324 47.5	14
16	58 38.1	22 35.1	345 01.1	16	58 06.2	21 55.2	349 56.8	16	57 37.8	21 04.7	354 52.5	16
18	88 37.5	22 34.5	15 06.0	18	88 05.7	21 54.5	20 01.7	18	87 37.4	21 03.8	24 57.4	18
20	118 37.0	22 33.9	45 10.9	20	118 05.2	21 53.7	50 06.6	20	117 36.9	21 02.9	55 02.3	20
22	148 36.4	S22 33.3	75 15.9	22	148 04.7	S21 53.0	80 11.6	22	147 36.5	S21 01.9	85 07.3	22

JANUARY 1994 — SUN & ARIES — GMT

Sunday, January 16

Time	SUN GHA	Dec	ARIES GHA
00	177 36.0	S21 01.0	115 12.2
02	207 35.6	21 00.1	145 17.1
04	237 35.2	20 59.1	175 22.0
06	267 34.8	20 58.1	205 27.0
08	297 34.3	20 57.2	235 31.9
10	327 33.9	20 56.3	265 36.8
12	357 33.5	20 55.3	295 41.0
14	27 33.0	20 54.4	325 46.7
16	57 32.6	20 53.4	355 51.6
18	87 32.2	20 52.5	25 56.5
20	117 31.8	20 51.5	56 01.5
22	147 31.3	S20 50.5	86 06.4

Monday, January 17

Time	SUN GHA	Dec	ARIES GHA
00	177 30.9	S20 49.6	116 11.3
02	207 30.5	20 48.6	146 16.3
04	237 30.1	20 47.6	176 21.2
06	267 29.7	20 46.6	206 26.1
08	297 29.3	20 45.6	236 31.0
10	327 28.8	20 44.7	266 36.0
12	357 28.4	20 43.7	296 40.9
14	27 28.0	20 42.7	326 45.8
16	57 27.6	20 41.7	356 50.8
18	87 27.2	20 40.7	26 55.7
20	117 26.8	20 39.7	57 00.6
22	147 26.4	S20 38.7	87 05.5

Tuesday, January 18

Time	SUN GHA	Dec	ARIES GHA
00	177 26.0	S20 37.7	117 10.5
02	207 25.6	20 36.7	147 15.4
04	237 25.2	20 35.7	177 20.3
06	267 24.8	20 34.7	207 25.2
08	297 24.4	20 33.7	237 30.2
10	327 24.0	20 32.6	267 35.1
12	357 23.6	20 31.6	297 40.0
14	27 23.2	20 30.6	327 45.0
16	57 22.8	20 29.6	357 49.9
18	87 22.4	20 28.6	27 54.8
20	117 22.0	20 27.5	57 59.7
22	147 21.6	S20 26.5	88 04.7

Wednesday, January 19

Time	SUN GHA	Dec	ARIES GHA
00	177 21.2	S20 25.5	118 09.6
02	207 20.8	20 24.4	148 14.5
04	237 20.5	20 23.4	178 19.5
06	267 20.1	20 22.3	208 24.4
08	297 19.7	20 21.3	238 29.3
10	327 19.3	20 20.2	268 34.2
12	357 18.9	20 19.2	298 39.2
14	27 18.5	20 18.1	328 44.1
16	57 18.2	20 17.1	358 49.0
18	87 17.8	20 16.0	28 54.0
20	117 17.4	20 15.0	58 58.9
22	147 17.0	S20 13.9	89 03.8

Thursday, January 20

Time	SUN GHA	Dec	ARIES GHA
00	177 16.7	S20 12.8	119 08.7
02	207 16.3	20 11.8	149 13.7
04	237 15.9	20 10.7	179 18.6
06	267 15.5	20 09.6	209 23.5
08	297 15.2	20 08.5	239 28.5
10	327 14.8	20 07.5	269 33.4
12	357 14.4	20 06.4	299 38.3
14	27 14.1	20 05.3	329 43.2
16	57 13.7	20 04.2	359 48.2
18	87 13.4	20 03.1	29 53.1
20	117 13.0	20 02.0	59 58.0
22	147 12.6	S20 00.9	90 03.0

Friday, January 21

Time	SUN GHA	Dec	ARIES GHA
00	177 12.3	S19 59.8	120 07.9
02	207 11.9	19 58.7	150 12.8
04	237 11.6	19 57.6	180 17.7
06	267 11.2	19 56.5	210 22.7
08	297 10.9	19 55.4	240 27.6
10	327 10.5	19 54.3	270 32.5
12	357 10.2	19 53.2	300 37.5
14	27 09.8	19 52.1	330 42.4
16	57 09.5	19 50.9	0 47.3
18	87 09.1	19 49.8	30 52.2
20	117 08.8	19 48.7	60 57.2
22	147 08.4	S19 47.6	91 02.1

Saturday, January 22

Time	SUN GHA	Dec	ARIES GHA
00	177 08.1	S19 46.4	121 07.0
02	207 07.8	19 45.3	151 11.9
04	237 07.4	19 44.2	181 16.9
06	267 07.1	19 43.0	211 21.8
08	297 06.7	19 41.9	241 26.7
10	327 06.4	19 40.8	271 31.7
12	357 06.1	19 39.6	301 36.6
14	27 05.7	19 38.5	331 41.5
16	57 05.4	19 37.3	1 46.4
18	87 05.1	19 36.2	31 51.4
20	117 04.8	19 35.0	61 56.3
22	147 04.4	S19 33.8	92 01.2

Sunday, January 23

Time	SUN GHA	Dec	ARIES GHA
00	177 04.1	S19 32.7	122 06.2
02	207 03.8	19 31.5	152 11.1
04	237 03.5	19 30.4	182 16.0
06	267 03.1	19 29.2	212 20.9
08	297 02.8	19 28.0	242 25.9
10	327 02.5	19 26.9	272 30.8
12	357 02.1	19 25.7	302 35.7
14	27 01.9	19 24.5	332 40.7
16	57 01.6	19 23.3	2 45.6
18	87 01.2	19 22.1	32 50.5
20	117 00.9	19 21.0	62 55.4
22	147 00.6	S19 19.8	93 00.4

Monday, January 24

Time	SUN GHA	Dec	ARIES GHA
00	177 00.3	S19 18.6	123 05.3
02	207 00.0	19 17.4	153 10.2
04	236 59.7	19 16.2	183 15.2
06	266 59.4	19 15.0	213 20.1
08	296 59.1	19 13.8	243 25.0
10	326 58.8	19 12.6	273 29.9
12	356 58.5	19 11.4	303 34.9
14	26 58.2	19 10.2	333 39.8
16	56 57.9	19 09.0	3 44.7
18	86 57.6	19 07.8	33 49.7
20	116 57.3	19 06.5	63 54.6
22	146 57.0	S19 05.3	93 59.5

Tuesday, January 25

Time	SUN GHA	Dec	ARIES GHA
00	176 56.7	S19 04.1	124 04.4
02	206 56.4	19 02.9	154 09.4
04	236 56.1	19 01.7	184 14.3
06	266 55.8	19 00.4	214 19.2
08	296 55.6	18 59.2	244 24.1
10	326 55.3	18 58.0	274 29.1
12	356 55.0	18 56.7	304 34.0
14	26 54.7	18 55.5	334 38.9
16	56 54.4	18 54.3	4 43.9
18	86 54.1	18 53.0	34 48.8
20	116 53.9	18 51.8	64 53.7
22	146 53.6	S18 50.5	94 58.6

Wednesday, January 26

Time	SUN GHA	Dec	ARIES GHA
00	176 53.3	S18 49.3	125 03.6
02	206 53.0	18 48.0	155 08.5
04	236 52.8	18 46.8	185 13.4
06	266 52.5	18 45.5	215 18.4
08	296 52.2	18 44.3	245 23.3
10	326 52.0	18 43.0	275 28.2
12	356 51.7	18 41.8	305 33.1
14	26 51.4	18 40.5	335 38.1
16	56 51.2	18 39.2	5 43.0
18	86 50.9	18 38.0	35 47.9
20	116 50.6	18 36.7	65 52.9
22	146 50.4	S18 35.4	95 57.8

Thursday, January 27

Time	SUN GHA	Dec	ARIES GHA
00	176 50.1	S18 34.1	126 02.7
02	206 49.9	18 32.8	156 07.6
04	236 49.6	18 31.6	186 12.6
06	266 49.3	18 30.3	216 17.5
08	296 49.1	18 29.0	246 22.4
10	326 48.8	18 27.7	276 27.4
12	356 48.6	18 26.4	306 32.3
14	26 48.3	18 25.1	336 37.2
16	56 48.1	18 23.8	6 42.1
18	86 47.8	18 22.5	36 47.1
20	116 47.6	18 21.2	66 52.0
22	146 47.4	S18 19.9	96 56.9

Friday, January 28

Time	SUN GHA	Dec	ARIES GHA
00	176 47.1	S18 18.6	127 01.9
02	206 46.9	18 17.3	157 06.8
04	236 46.6	18 16.0	187 11.7
06	266 46.4	18 14.7	217 16.6
08	296 46.2	18 13.4	247 21.6
10	326 45.9	18 12.1	277 26.5
12	356 45.7	18 10.8	307 31.4
14	26 45.5	18 09.4	337 36.3
16	56 45.2	18 08.1	7 41.3
18	86 45.0	18 06.8	37 46.2
20	116 44.8	18 05.5	67 51.1
22	146 44.5	S18 04.1	97 56.1

Saturday, January 29

Time	SUN GHA	Dec	ARIES GHA
00	176 44.3	S18 02.8	128 01.0
02	206 44.1	18 01.5	158 05.9
04	236 43.9	18 00.1	188 10.8
06	266 43.6	17 58.8	218 15.8
08	296 43.4	17 57.5	248 20.7
10	326 43.2	17 56.1	278 25.6
12	356 43.0	17 54.8	308 30.6
14	26 42.8	17 53.4	338 35.5
16	56 42.6	17 52.1	8 40.4
18	86 42.4	17 50.7	38 45.3
20	116 42.1	17 49.4	68 50.3
22	146 41.9	S17 48.0	98 55.2

Sunday, January 30

Time	SUN GHA	Dec	ARIES GHA
00	176 41.7	S17 46.6	129 00.1
02	206 41.5	17 45.3	159 05.1
04	236 41.3	17 43.9	189 10.0
06	266 41.1	17 42.6	219 14.9
08	296 40.9	17 41.2	249 19.8
10	326 40.7	17 39.8	279 24.8
12	356 40.5	17 38.4	309 29.7
14	26 40.3	17 37.1	339 34.6
16	56 40.1	17 35.7	9 39.6
18	86 39.9	17 34.3	39 44.5
20	116 39.7	17 32.9	69 49.4
22	146 39.5	S17 31.6	99 54.3

Monday, January 31

Time	SUN GHA	Dec	ARIES GHA
00	176 39.3	S17 30.2	129 59.3
02	206 39.1	17 28.8	160 04.2
04	236 38.9	17 27.4	190 09.1
06	266 38.8	S17 26.0	220 14.1
08	296 38.6	S17 24.6	250 19.0
10	326 38.4	17 23.2	280 23.9
12	356 38.2	17 21.8	310 28.8
14	26 38.0	S17 20.4	340 33.8
16	56 37.8	S17 19.0	10 38.7
18	86 37.7	17 17.6	40 43.6
20	116 37.5	17 16.2	70 48.6
22	146 37.3	S17 14.8	100 53.5

Chapter 6

JANUARY 1994   PLANETS   0h GMT

VENUS   JUPITER

Mer Pass h m	GHA ° ′	Mean Var/hr 14°+	Dec ° ′	Mean Var/hr ′			GHA ° ′	Mean Var/hr 15°+	Dec ° ′	Mean Var/hr ′	Mer Pass h m
11 47	183 19.6	59.0	S23 00.0	0.1	1	Sat	242 41.6	2.1	S13 39.5	0.1	07 48
11 49	182 56.4	59.0	S23 37.0	0.1	2	SUN	243 31.7	2.1	S13 42.3	0.1	07 45
11 51	182 33.1	59.0	S23 34.5	0.1	3	Mon	244 22.0	2.1	S13 45.0	0.1	07 41
11 52	182 09.9	59.0	S23 31.3	0.2	4	Tue	245 12.3	2.1	S13 47.7	0.1	07 38
11 54	181 46.8	59.0	S23 27.3	0.2	5	Wed	246 02.8	2.1	S13 50.3	0.1	07 35
11 55	181 23.8	59.0	S23 22.6	0.2	6	Thu	246 53.4	2.1	S13 52.9	0.1	07 31
11 57	181 00.9	59.0	S23 17.2	0.3	7	Fri	247 44.1	2.1	S13 55.4	0.1	07 28
11 58	180 38.1	59.1	S23 11.1	0.3	8	Sat	248 34.9	2.1	S13 57.9	0.1	07 25
12 00	180 15.5	59.1	S23 04.3	0.3	9	SUN	249 25.8	2.1	S14 00.4	0.1	07 21
12 01	179 53.0	59.1	S22 56.7	0.3	10	Mon	250 16.8	2.1	S14 02.8	0.1	07 18
12 03	179 30.7	59.1	S22 48.4	0.4	11	Tue	251 08.0	2.1	S14 05.1	0.1	07 14
12 04	179 08.5	59.1	S22 39.5	0.4	12	Wed	251 59.3	2.1	S14 07.4	0.1	07 11
12 06	178 46.6	59.1	S22 29.8	0.4	13	Thu	252 50.7	2.1	S14 09.7	0.1	07 08
12 07	178 24.8	59.1	S22 19.5	0.5	14	Fri	253 42.2	2.2	S14 11.9	0.1	07 04
12 09	178 03.3	59.1	S22 08.5	0.5	15	Sat	254 33.9	2.2	S14 14.1	0.1	07 01
12 10	177 42.0	59.1	S21 56.8	0.5	16	SUN	255 25.7	2.2	S14 16.2	0.1	06 57
12 11	177 20.9	59.1	S21 44.5	0.5	17	Mon	256 17.6	2.2	S14 18.3	0.1	06 54
12 13	177 00.1	59.1	S21 31.4	0.6	18	Tue	257 09.6	2.2	S14 20.3	0.1	06 50
12 14	176 39.5	59.2	S21 17.8	0.6	19	Wed	258 01.8	2.2	S14 22.3	0.1	06 47
12 15	176 19.2	59.2	S21 03.5	0.6	20	Thu	258 54.2	2.2	S14 24.2	0.1	06 43
12 17	175 59.2	59.2	S20 48.6	0.6	21	Fri	259 46.6	2.2	S14 26.1	0.1	06 40
12 18	175 39.5	59.2	S20 33.1	0.7	22	Sat	260 39.2	2.2	S14 28.0	0.1	06 36
12 19	175 20.0	59.2	S20 16.9	0.7	23	SUN	261 32.0	2.2	S14 29.7	0.1	06 33
12 21	175 00.8	59.2	S20 00.2	0.7	24	Mon	262 24.9	2.2	S14 31.5	0.1	06 29
12 22	174 42.0	59.2	S19 42.9	0.7	25	Tue	263 17.9	2.2	S14 33.2	0.1	06 26
12 23	174 23.4	59.2	S19 25.0	0.8	26	Wed	264 11.1	2.2	S14 34.8	0.1	06 22
12 24	174 05.2	59.2	S19 06.5	0.8	27	Thu	265 04.5	2.2	S14 36.4	0.1	06 19
12 25	173 47.2	59.3	S18 47.5	0.8	28	Fri	265 58.0	2.2	S14 37.9	0.1	06 15
12 27	173 29.6	59.3	S18 28.0	0.8	29	Sat	266 51.6	2.2	S14 39.4	0.1	06 12
12 28	173 12.2	59.3	S18 07.9	0.9	30	SUN	267 45.4	2.3	S14 40.9	0.1	06 08
12 29	172 55.2	59.3	S17 47.3	0.9	31	Mon	268 39.4	2.3	S14 42.2	0.1	06 04

VENUS, Av Mag –3.9
SHA January
5 77; 10 71; 15 64; 20 57; 25 51; 30 44.

JUPITER, Av Mag –1.9
SHA January
5 142; 10 141; 15 140; 20 140; 25 139; 30 139.

MARS   SATURN

Mer Pass h m	GHA ° ′	Mean Var/hr 15°+	Dec ° ′	Mean Var/hr ′			GHA ° ′	Mean Var/hr 15°+	Dec ° ′	Mean Var/hr ′	Mer Pass h m
11 58	180 29.2	0.4	S23 57.1	0.1	1	Sat	130 42.3	2.2	S13 50.9	0.1	15 15
11 57	180 38.4	0.4	S23 54.3	0.1	2	SUN	131 35.8	2.2	S13 48.9	0.1	15 11
11 57	180 47.6	0.4	S23 51.2	0.1	3	Mon	132 29.3	2.2	S13 46.9	0.1	15 08
11 56	180 56.8	0.4	S23 47.8	0.2	4	Tue	133 22.8	2.2	S13 44.8	0.1	15 04
11 55	181 06.0	0.4	S23 44.2	0.2	5	Wed	134 16.2	2.2	S13 42.7	0.1	15 01
11 55	181 15.2	0.4	S23 40.3	0.2	6	Thu	135 09.6	2.2	S13 40.6	0.1	14 57
11 54	181 24.4	0.4	S23 36.1	0.2	7	Fri	136 02.9	2.2	S13 38.5	0.1	14 54
11 53	181 33.6	0.4	S23 31.7	0.2	8	Sat	136 56.1	2.2	S13 36.4	0.1	14 50
11 53	181 42.8	0.4	S23 27.0	0.2	9	SUN	137 49.4	2.2	S13 34.2	0.1	14 47
11 52	181 52.1	0.4	S23 22.0	0.2	10	Mon	138 42.5	2.2	S13 32.0	0.1	14 43
11 52	182 01.4	0.4	S23 16.8	0.2	11	Tue	139 35.6	2.2	S13 29.9	0.1	14 39
11 51	182 10.7	0.4	S23 11.3	0.2	12	Wed	140 28.7	2.2	S13 27.6	0.1	14 36
11 50	182 20.0	0.4	S23 05.5	0.3	13	Thu	141 21.7	2.2	S13 25.4	0.1	14 32
11 50	182 29.3	0.4	S22 59.5	0.3	14	Fri	142 14.7	2.2	S13 23.2	0.1	14 29
11 49	182 38.7	0.4	S22 53.3	0.3	15	Sat	143 07.6	2.2	S13 20.9	0.1	14 25
11 48	182 48.2	0.4	S22 46.7	0.3	16	SUN	144 00.5	2.2	S13 18.6	0.1	14 22
11 48	182 57.7	0.4	S22 40.0	0.3	17	Mon	144 53.4	2.2	S13 16.3	0.1	14 18
11 47	183 07.2	0.4	S22 32.9	0.3	18	Tue	145 46.2	2.2	S13 14.0	0.1	14 15
11 47	183 16.8	0.4	S22 25.6	0.3	19	Wed	146 39.0	2.2	S13 11.7	0.1	14 11
11 46	183 26.4	0.4	S22 18.1	0.3	20	Thu	147 31.7	2.2	S13 09.4	0.1	14 08
11 45	183 36.1	0.4	S22 10.3	0.3	21	Fri	148 24.4	2.2	S13 07.0	0.1	14 04
11 45	183 45.9	0.4	S22 02.2	0.3	22	Sat	149 17.1	2.2	S13 04.7	0.1	14 01
11 44	183 55.7	0.4	S21 54.0	0.4	23	SUN	150 09.7	2.2	S13 02.3	0.1	13 57
11 43	184 05.6	0.4	S21 45.4	0.4	24	Mon	151 02.3	2.2	S12 59.9	0.1	13 54
11 43	184 15.5	0.4	S21 36.6	0.4	25	Tue	151 54.9	2.2	S12 57.5	0.1	13 50
11 42	184 25.5	0.4	S21 27.6	0.4	26	Wed	152 47.5	2.2	S12 55.1	0.1	13 47
11 41	184 35.6	0.4	S21 18.4	0.4	27	Thu	153 40.0	2.2	S12 52.7	0.1	13 43
11 41	184 45.8	0.4	S21 08.9	0.4	28	Fri	154 32.5	2.2	S12 50.2	0.1	13 40
11 40	184 56.0	0.4	S20 59.2	0.4	29	Sat	155 24.9	2.2	S12 47.8	0.1	13 36
11 39	185 06.3	0.4	S20 49.2	0.4	30	SUN	156 17.4	2.2	S12 45.3	0.1	13 33
11 39	185 16.7	0.4	S20 39.0	0.4	31	Mon	157 09.8	2.2	S12 42.9	0.1	13 29

MARS, Av Mag +1.2
SHA January
5 77; 10 73; 15 68; 20 64; 25 60; 30 56.

SATURN, Av Mag +0.9
SHA January
5 30; 10 29; 15 29; 20 28; 25 28; 30 27.

JANUARY 1994   MOON

Day	GMT hr	GHA ° ′	Mean Var/hr 14°+	Dec ° ′	Mean Var/hr ′	Day	GMT hr	GHA ° ′	Mean Var/hr 14°+	Dec ° ′	Mean Var/hr ′
1 Sat	0	321 16.2	29.4	N10 34.4	11.3	17 Mon	0	122 02.4	34.4	N 2 32.2	10.9
	6	48 12.4	29.6	N 9 26.5	11.6		6	209 28.8	34.5	N 3 37.5	10.8
	12	135 09.5	29.6	N 8 16.7	11.9		12	296 55.5	34.4	N 4 42.0	10.6
	18	222 07.2	29.8	N 7 03.0	12.2		18	24 22.1	34.4	N 5 45.6	10.4
2 Sun	0	309 05.6	29.8	N 5 51.9	12.4	18 Tue	0	111 48.5	34.4	N 6 48.2	10.2
	6	36 04.4	29.9	N 4 37.4	12.6		6	199 14.6	34.3	N 7 49.8	10.0
	12	123 03.5	29.8	N 3 22.0	12.7		12	286 40.2	34.2	N 8 50.0	9.8
	18	210 02.8	29.9	N 2 05.7	12.8		18	14 05.2	34.0	N 9 49.0	9.6
3 Mon	0	297 02.1	29.9	N 0 48.9	12.8	19 Wed	0	101 29.3	33.8	N10 46.4	9.3
	6	24 01.3	29.8	S 0 28.1	12.9		6	188 52.4	33.7	N11 42.2	9.0
	12	111 00.1	29.7	S 1 45.1	12.8		12	276 14.4	33.4	N12 36.4	8.6
	18	197 58.4	29.5	S 3 01.9	12.7		18	3 35.1	33.2	N13 28.7	8.3
4 Tue	0	284 56.0	29.5	S 4 18.2	12.6	20 Thu	0	90 54.4	33.0	N14 19.0	8.1
	6	11 52.7	29.3	S 5 33.7	12.4		6	178 12.2	32.7	N15 07.2	7.6
	12	98 48.4	29.1	S 6 48.2	12.1		12	265 28.4	32.4	N15 53.2	7.2
	18	185 42.9	28.8	S 8 01.4	11.9		18	352 42.8	32.1	N16 36.8	6.8
5 Wed	0	272 36.1	28.6	S 9 13.0	11.6	21 Fri	0	79 55.5	31.7	N17 17.9	6.3
	6	359 27.8	28.3	S 10 22.7	11.3		6	167 06.2	31.4	N17 56.4	5.9
	12	86 17.8	28.1	S 11 30.4	10.9		12	254 15.0	31.1	N18 32.1	5.4
	18	173 06.2	27.8	S 12 35.7	10.4		18	341 21.8	30.8	N19 04.8	4.9
6 Thu	0	259 52.8	27.4	S 13 38.3	9.9	22 Sat	0	68 26.7	30.4	N19 34.5	4.3
	6	346 37.5	27.1	S 14 38.1	9.4		6	155 29.5	30.1	N20 01.0	3.8
	12	73 20.3	26.8	S 15 34.7	8.9		12	242 30.3	29.8	N20 24.1	3.2
	18	160 01.2	26.5	S 16 27.9	8.2		18	329 29.2	29.5	N20 43.8	2.6
7 Fri	0	246 40.3	26.2	S 17 17.4	7.5	23 Sun	0	56 26.2	29.2	N20 59.8	2.0
	6	333 17.6	25.9	S 18 03.1	6.9		6	143 21.4	28.9	N21 12.1	1.3
	12	59 53.2	25.6	S 18 44.7	6.2		12	230 14.8	28.6	N21 20.5	0.7
	18	146 27.2	25.4	S 19 21.9	5.4		18	317 06.7	28.4	N21 24.9	0.0
8 Sat	0	232 59.8	25.2	S 19 54.7	4.6	24 Mon	0	43 57.2	28.2	N21 25.3	0.7
	6	319 31.3	25.1	S 20 22.8	3.8		6	130 46.3	28.0	N21 21.5	1.4
	12	46 01.7	25.0	S 20 46.2	3.0		12	217 34.3	27.8	N21 13.5	2.1
	18	132 31.5	24.9	S 21 04.6	2.2		18	304 21.4	27.7	N21 01.2	2.8
9 Sun	0	219 00.9	24.9	S 21 18.1	1.3	25 Tue	0	31 07.7	27.6	N20 44.6	3.6
	6	305 30.2	25.0	S 21 26.6	0.6		6	117 53.4	27.5	N20 23.7	4.3
	12	31 59.7	25.0	S 21 30.0	0.4		12	204 38.7	27.5	N19 58.4	5.0
	18	118 29.8	25.2	S 21 28.5	1.1		18	291 23.7	27.5	N19 28.9	5.7
10 Mon	0	205 00.7	25.4	S 21 21.9	1.9	26 Wed	0	18 08.7	27.6	N18 55.2	6.4
	6	291 32.7	25.6	S 21 10.5	2.7		6	104 53.8	27.5	N18 17.3	7.1
	12	18 06.2	25.8	S 20 54.3	3.5		12	191 39.2	27.6	N17 35.4	7.7
	18	104 41.4	26.2	S 20 33.5	4.2		18	278 24.9	27.7	N16 49.6	8.3
11 Tue	0	191 18.5	26.6	S 20 08.2	5.0	27 Thu	0	5 11.2	27.8	N16 00.0	8.9
	6	277 57.9	27.0	S 19 38.7	5.7		6	91 58.0	27.9	N15 06.7	9.5
	12	4 39.6	27.4	S 19 05.0	6.3		12	178 45.5	28.1	N14 10.0	10.1
	18	91 23.8	27.8	S 18 27.6	6.9		18	265 33.7	28.2	N13 10.1	10.5
12 Wed	0	178 10.6	28.3	S 17 46.4	7.4	28 Fri	0	352 22.7	28.3	N12 07.2	10.9
	6	265 00.1	28.7	S 17 02.0	7.9		6	79 12.4	28.4	N11 01.4	11.4
	12	351 52.4	29.3	S 16 14.4	8.5		12	166 02.8	28.5	N 9 53.2	11.8
	18	78 47.5	29.7	S 15 23.9	8.9		18	252 53.9	28.6	N 8 42.6	12.1
13 Thu	0	165 45.4	30.1	S 14 30.8	9.3	29 Sat	0	339 45.6	28.8	N 7 30.1	12.4
	6	252 45.9	30.6	S 13 35.3	9.6		6	66 38.0	28.8	N 6 15.8	12.6
	12	339 49.1	31.0	S 12 37.7	10.0		12	153 30.7	28.8	N 5 00.0	12.9
	18	66 54.9	31.4	S 11 38.2	10.2		18	240 23.9	28.9	N 3 43.1	13.0
14 Fri	0	154 03.2	31.9	S 10 37.1	10.4	30 Sun	0	327 17.3	28.9	N 2 25.3	13.0
	6	241 13.9	32.2	S 9 34.5	10.6		6	54 10.9	28.9	N 1 06.9	13.1
	12	328 26.7	32.5	S 8 30.7	10.8		12	141 04.5	28.9	S 0 11.8	13.1
	18	55 41.6	32.9	S 7 25.9	10.9		18	227 57.9	28.9	S 1 30.4	13.1
15 Sat	0	142 58.5	33.1	S 6 20.3	11.0	31 Mon	0	314 51.1	28.8	S 2 48.8	13.0
	6	230 17.1	33.4	S 5 14.1	11.1		6	41 43.9	28.7	S 4 06.5	12.8
	12	317 37.3	33.6	S 4 07.5	11.2		12	128 36.1	28.6	S 5 23.3	12.6
	18	44 59.0	33.8	S 3 00.6	11.1		18	215 27.7	28.4	S 6 38.9	12.3
16 Sun	0	132 21.9	34.1	S 1 53.6	11.2						
	6	219 45.8	34.1	S 0 46.7	11.1						
	12	307 10.7	34.3	N 0 20.0	11.1						
	18	34 36.3	34.3	N 1 26.4	10.9						

Chapter 6

FEBRUARY 1994   SUN & MOON   GMT

SUN

Yr	Mth	Week	Eq of Time 0h	12h	Transit	Semi-diam	Lat 52°N Twilight	Sunrise	Sunset	Twilight	Lat	Twilight	Sunrise	Sunset	Twilight
			m s	m s	h m	′	h m	h m	h m	h m	°	h m	h m	h m	h m
32	1	Tue	+13 31	+13 35	12 14	16.3	07 04	07 40	16 47	17 24	N70	+0 48	+1 23	−1 22	−0 49
33	2	Wed	+13 39	+13 43	12 14	16.3	07 02	07 39	16 49	17 26	68	+0 39	+1 06	−1 06	−0 40
34	3	Thu	+13 46	+13 50	12 14	16.3	07 01	07 37	16 51	17 28	66	+0 32	+0 53	−0 53	−0 32
35	4	Fri	+13 53	+13 56	12 14	16.3	06 59	07 36	16 53	17 29	64	+0 26	+0 42	−0 41	−0 26
36	5	Sat	+13 58	+14 01	12 14	16.2	06 58	07 34	16 55	17 31	62	+0 20	+0 32	−0 32	−0 20
37	6	Sun	+14 03	+14 05	12 14	16.2	06 56	07 32	16 57	17 33	N60	+0 15	+0 25	−0 25	−0 16
38	7	Mon	+14 07	+14 09	12 14	16.2	06 55	07 30	16 59	17 35	58	+0 10	+0 17	−0 17	−0 11
39	8	Tue	+14 10	+14 12	12 14	16.2	06 53	07 29	17 00	17 36	56	+0 06	+0 11	−0 11	−0 07
40	9	Wed	+14 13	+14 14	12 14	16.2	06 51	07 27	17 02	17 38	54	+0 03	+0 05	−0 05	−0 04
41	10	Thu	+14 15	+14 15	12 14	16.2	06 50	07 25	17 04	17 40	50	−0 03	−0 05	+0 04	+0 03
42	11	Fri	+14 15	+14 16	12 14	16.2	06 48	07 23	17 06	17 42	N45	−0 10	−0 15	+0 15	+0 10
43	12	Sat	+14 15	+14 15	12 14	16.2	06 46	07 21	17 08	17 43	40	−0 16	−0 23	+0 23	+0 16
44	13	Sun	+14 15	+14 14	12 14	16.2	06 44	07 19	17 10	17 45	35	−0 22	−0 30	+0 31	+0 21
45	14	Mon	+14 13	+14 12	12 14	16.2	06 42	07 18	17 12	17 47	30	−0 27	−0 37	+0 37	+0 26
46	15	Tue	+14 11	+14 10	12 14	16.2	06 41	07 16	17 14	17 49	20	−0 36	−0 48	+0 48	+0 35
47	16	Wed	+14 08	+14 07	12 14	16.2	06 39	07 14	17 15	17 50	N10	−0 45	−0 59	+0 58	+0 44
48	17	Thu	+14 05	+14 03	12 14	16.2	06 37	07 12	17 17	17 52	0	−0 55	−1 08	+1 07	+0 54
49	18	Fri	+14 00	+13 58	12 14	16.2	06 35	07 10	17 19	17 54	S10	−1 05	−1 18	+1 16	+1 04
50	19	Sat	+13 55	+13 52	12 14	16.2	06 33	07 08	17 21	17 56	20	−1 16	−1 28	+1 26	+1 15
51	20	Sun	+13 49	+13 46	12 14	16.2	06 31	07 06	17 23	17 57	30	−1 31	−1 40	+1 38	+1 30
52	21	Mon	+13 43	+13 40	12 14	16.2	06 29	07 04	17 25	17 59	S35	−1 40	−1 48	+1 45	+1 49
53	22	Tue	+13 36	+13 32	12 14	16.2	06 27	07 01	17 26	18 01	40	−1 50	−1 55	+1 53	+1 49
54	23	Wed	+13 28	+13 24	12 13	16.2	06 25	06 59	17 28	18 03	45	−2 02	−2 05	+2 02	+2 00
55	24	Thu	+13 20	+13 15	12 13	16.2	06 23	06 57	17 30	18 04	S50	−2 17	−2 16	+2 13	+2 16
56	25	Fri	+13 11	+13 06	12 13	16.2	06 21	06 55	17 32	18 06					
57	26	Sat	+13 01	+12 56	12 13	16.2	06 19	06 53	17 34	18 08					
58	27	Sun	+12 51	+12 46	12 13	16.2	06 17	06 51	17 36	18 10					
59	28	Mon	+12 40	+12 35	12 13	16.2	06 15	06 49	17 37	18 11					

NOTES

Lat corrections are for Feb 15.
Equation of Time is the excess of Mean Time over Apparent Time.

MOON

Yr	Mth	Week	Age	Transit Diff (Upper)	Semi-diam	Hor Par	Lat 52°N Moonrise	Moonset
			days	h m m	′		h m	h m
32	1	Tue	21	03 59 53	16.2	59.6	23 48	09 19
33	2	Wed	22	04 52 55	16.2	59.3	− −	09 47
34	3	Thu	23	05 47 56	16.1	59.0	01 07	10 20
35	4	Fri	24	06 43 57	16.0	58.6	02 22	11 00
36	5	Sat	25	07 40 57	15.9	58.2	03 30	11 49
37	6	Sun	26	08 37 55	15.8	57.8	04 28	12 48
38	7	Mon	27	09 32 53	15.6	57.4	05 16	13 53
39	8	Tue	28	10 25 51	15.5	56.9	05 55	15 03
40	9	Wed	29	11 16 47	15.4	56.4	06 26	16 14
41	10	Thu	30	12 03 46	15.2	55.9	06 51	17 25
42	11	Fri	01	12 49 43	15.1	55.4	07 13	18 35
43	12	Sat	02	13 32 43	15.0	55.0	07 33	19 43
44	13	Sun	03	14 15 42	14.9	54.6	07 53	20 49
45	14	Mon	04	14 57 43	14.8	54.3	08 12	21 55
46	15	Tue	05	15 40 44	14.8	54.2	08 33	23 00
47	16	Wed	06	16 24 46	14.8	54.2	08 56	− −
48	17	Thu	07	17 10 47	14.8	54.3	09 23	00 04
49	18	Fri	08	17 57 50	14.9	54.6	09 55	01 07
50	19	Sat	09	18 47 51	15.0	55.1	10 35	02 07
51	20	Sun	10	19 38 53	15.2	55.8	11 23	03 02
52	21	Mon	11	20 31 53	15.4	56.6	12 20	03 51
53	22	Tue	12	21 24 53	15.6	57.4	13 27	04 33
54	23	Wed	13	22 17 53	15.9	58.3	14 40	05 09
55	24	Thu	14	23 10 53	16.1	59.1	15 58	05 40
56	25	Fri	15	24 03 _	16.3	59.8	17 19	06 07
57	26	Sat	16	00 03 53	16.4	60.3	18 42	06 32
58	27	Sun	17	00 56 54	16.5	60.6	20 05	06 56
59	28	Mon	18	01 50 55	16.5	60.6	21 29	07 22

Phases of the Moon

	d	h	m
◑ Last Quarter	3	08	06
● New Moon	10	14	30
◐ First Quarter	18	17	47
○ Full Moon	26	01	15
Apogee	16	02	
Perigee	27	22	

NOTES

For Latitude corrections to Moonrise and Moonset see page 706.

FEBRUARY 1994 — STARS — 0h GMT February 1

No	Name	Mag	Transit h m	Dec ° '	GHA ° '	RA h m	SHA ° '
	ARIES.................		15 14		130 58.4		
1	Alpheratz 2.2		15 22	N 29 03.6	128 57.2	0 08	357 58.8
2	Ankaa............. 2.4		15 40	S 42 20.4	124 28.6	0 26	353 30.2
3	Schedar 2.5		15 54	N 56 30.5	120 55.8	0 40	349 57.4
4	Diphda 2.2		15 57	S 18 01.2	120 09.0	0 43	349 10.6
5	Achernar 0.6		16 51	S 57 16.2	106 36.1	1 37	335 37.7
6	POLARIS 2.1		17 30	N 89 14.6	94 33.8	2 26	323 35.4
7	Hamal............ 2.2		17 20	N 23 26.2	99 15.6	2 07	320 17.2
8	Acamar 3.1		18 11	S 40 20.0	86 27.7	2 58	315 29.3
9	Menkar 2.8		18 15	N 4 03.9	85 28.6	3 02	314 30.2
10	Mirfak 1.9		18 37	N 49 50.6	79 59.5	3 24	309 01.1
11	Aldebaran 1.1		19 48	N 16 29.8	62 04.3	4 36	291 05.9
12	Rigel 0.3		20 27	S 8 12.7	52 24.2	5 14	281 25.8
13	Capella 0.2		20 29	N 45 59.6	51 54.0	5 16	280 55.6
14	Bellatrix.......... 1.7		20 38	N 6 20.5	49 45.8	5 25	278 47.4
15	Elnath 1.8		20 39	N 28 36.2	49 29.1	5 26	278 30.7
16	Alnilam 1.8		20 49	S 1 12.5	46 59.3	5 36	276 00.9
17	Betelgeuse 0.1-1.2		21 08	N 7 24.2	42 15.1	5 55	271 16.7
18	Canopus .... –0.9		21 36	S 52 41.9	35 00.6	6 24	264 02.2
19	Sirius .... –1.6		21 57	S 16 42.7	29 44.6	6 45	258 46.2
20	Adhara 1.6		22 11	S 28 58.1	26 22.0	6 58	255 23.6
21	Castor 1.6		22 47	N 31 54.0	17 24.4	7 34	246 26.0
22	Procyon 0.5		22 51	N 5 14.2	16 12.9	7 39	245 14.5
23	Pollux 1.2		22 57	N 28 02.3	14 43.4	7 45	243 45.0
24	Avior 1.7		23 35	S 59 29.7	5 21.7	8 22	234 23.3
25	Suhail 2.2		0 24	S 43 24.7	354 01.0	9 08	223 02.6
26	Miaplacidus 1.8		0 29	S 69 41.8	352 40.2	9 13	221 41.8
27	Alphard 2.2		0 43	S 8 38.2	349 08.3	9 27	218 09.9
28	Regulus.......... 1.3		1 24	N 11 59.5	338 56.9	10 08	207 58.5
29	Dubhe 2.0		2 19	N 61 46.7	325 07.1	11 03	194 08.7
30	Denebola........ 2.2		3 04	N 14 36.0	313 46.5	11 49	182 48.1
31	Gienah 2.8		3 31	S 17 30.7	307 05.3	12 16	176 06.9
32	Acrux............. 1.1		3 42	S 63 03.9	304 23.4	12 26	173 25.0
33	Gacrux 1.6		3 46	S 57 04.8	303 15.0	12 31	172 16.6
34	Mimosa.......... 1.5		4 03	S 59 39.3	299 06.9	12 47	168 08.5
35	Alioth............. 1.7		4 09	N 55 59.1	297 31.4	12 54	166 33.0
36	Spica............... 1.2		4 40	S 11 08.0	289 44.7	13 25	158 46.3
37	Alkaid 1.9		5 03	N 49 20.2	284 08.4	13 47	153 10.0
38	Hadar 0.9		5 19	S 60 20.5	280 06.6	14 03	149 08.2
39	Menkent......... 2.3		5 22	S 36 20.4	279 22.9	14 06	148 24.5
40	Arcturus......... 0.2		5 31	N 19 12.5	277 07.2	14 15	146 08.8
41	Rigil Kent........ 0.1		5 54	S 60 48.4	271 09.7	14 39	140 11.3
42	Zuben'ubi....... 2.9		6 06	S 16 01.1	268 19.8	14 51	137 21.4
43	Kochab........... 2.2		6 06	N 74 10.4	268 17.6	14 51	137 19.2
44	Alphecca......... 2.3		6 49	N 26 43.8	257 21.6	15 34	126 23.2
45	Antares........... 1.2		7 44	S 26 25.1	243 42.5	16 29	112 44.1
46	Atria 1.9		8 03	S 69 00.8	238 57.5	16 48	107 59.1
47	Sabik 2.6		8 25	S 15 43.1	233 27.7	17 10	102 29.3
48	Shaula 1.7		8 48	S 37 05.9	227 40.1	17 33	96 41.7
49	Rasalhague 2.1		8 49	N 12 33.7	227 18.4	17 35	96 20.0
50	Eltanin 2.4		9 11	N 51 29.2	221 51.6	17 56	90 53.2
51	Kaus Aust........ 2.0		9 38	S 34 23.1	215 01.6	18 24	84 03.2
52	Vega 0.1		9 51	N 38 46.5	211 47.4	18 37	80 49.0
53	Nunki 2.1		10 09	S 26 18.2	207 14.9	18 55	76 16.5
54	Altair.............. 0.9		11 05	N 8 51.1	193 21.0	19 50	62 22.6
55	Peacock........... 2.1		11 39	S 56 45.1	184 40.9	20 25	53 42.5
56	Deneb 1.3		11 55	N 45 15.6	180 40.2	20 41	49 41.8
57	Enif 2.5		12 58	N 9 50.9	165 00.0	21 44	34 01.6
58	Al Na'ir 2.2		13 22	S 46 59.4	159 00.7	22 08	28 02.3
59	Fomalhaut 1.3		14 11	S 29 39.2	146 38.6	22 57	15 40.2
60	Markab 2.6		14 18	N 15 10.5	144 51.4	23 04	13 53.0

Stars Transit Corr Table

Date	Corr h m	Date	Corr h m
1	–0 00	17	–1 03
2	–0 04	18	–1 07
3	–0 08	19	–1 11
4	–0 12	20	–1 15
5	–0 16	21	–1 19
6	–0 20	22	–1 23
7	–0 24	23	–1 27
8	–0 28	24	–1 30
9	–0 31	25	–1 34
10	–0 35	26	–1 38
11	–0 39	27	–1 42
12	–0 43	28	–1 46
13	–0 47		
14	–0 51		
15	–0 55		
16	–0 59		

STAR'S TRANSIT

To find the approx time of transit of a star for any day of the month use above table. All corrections are subtractive. If the quantity taken from the table is greater than the time of transit for the first of the month, add 23h 56min to the time of transit before subtracting the correction.

Example: Will Rigel (No 12) be on the meridian between 1700h and 1900h on Feb 28?

	h min
Transit on Feb 1	20 27
Corr for 28	–01 46
Transit on Feb 28	18 41

FEBRUARY DIARY

2 04 Mercury 1.3°N of Saturn
3 08 Jupiter 3°N of Moon
3 08 Last Quarter
4 21 Mercury greatest elongation E(18°)
8 08 Neptune 3°S of Moon
8 12 Uranus 5°S of Moon
10 14 New Moon
10 18 Mercury stationary
16 02 Moon at apogee
18 18 First Quarter
20 08 Mercury in inferior conjunction
21 17 Saturn in conjunction with Sun
23 14 Juno stationary
26 01 Full Moon
27 01 Mercury 4°N of Mars
27 22 Moon at perigee
28 21 Jupiter stationary

Chapter 6

FEBRUARY 1994 — SUN & ARIES — GMT

Column headings for each group: **Time | SUN GHA | Dec | ARIES GHA**

Tuesday, February 1

Time	SUN GHA	Dec	ARIES GHA
00	176 37.1	S17 13.4	130 58.4
02	206 37.0	17 12.0	161 03.3
04	236 36.8	17 10.6	191 08.3
06	266 36.6	17 09.1	221 13.2
08	296 36.4	17 07.7	251 18.1
10	326 36.3	17 06.3	281 23.0
12	356 36.1	17 04.9	311 28.0
14	26 35.9	17 03.5	341 32.9
16	56 35.8	17 02.0	11 37.8
18	86 35.6	17 00.6	41 42.8
20	116 35.5	16 59.2	71 47.7
22	146 35.3	S16 57.7	101 52.6

Wednesday, February 2

Time	SUN GHA	Dec	ARIES GHA
00	176 35.1	S16 56.3	131 57.5
02	206 35.0	16 54.9	162 02.5
04	236 34.8	16 53.4	192 07.4
06	266 34.7	16 52.0	222 12.3
08	296 34.5	16 50.5	252 17.3
10	326 34.4	16 49.1	282 22.2
12	356 34.2	16 47.6	312 27.1
14	26 34.1	16 46.2	342 32.0
16	56 33.9	16 44.7	12 37.0
18	86 33.8	16 43.3	42 41.9
20	116 33.6	16 41.8	72 46.8
22	146 33.5	S16 40.4	102 51.8

Thursday, February 3

Time	SUN GHA	Dec	ARIES GHA
00	176 33.3	S16 38.9	132 56.7
02	206 33.2	16 37.5	163 01.6
04	236 33.1	16 36.0	193 06.5
06	266 32.9	16 34.5	223 11.5
08	296 32.8	16 33.1	253 16.4
10	326 32.7	16 31.6	283 21.3
12	356 32.5	16 30.1	313 26.3
14	26 32.4	16 28.6	343 31.2
16	56 32.3	16 27.2	13 36.1
18	86 32.1	16 25.7	43 41.0
20	116 32.0	16 24.2	73 46.0
22	146 31.9	S16 22.7	103 50.9

Friday, February 4

Time	SUN GHA	Dec	ARIES GHA
00	176 31.8	S16 21.2	133 55.8
02	206 31.6	16 19.8	164 00.8
04	236 31.5	16 18.3	194 05.7
06	266 31.4	16 16.8	224 10.6
08	296 31.3	16 15.3	254 15.5
10	326 31.1	16 13.8	284 20.5
12	356 31.0	16 12.3	314 25.4
14	26 30.9	16 10.8	344 30.3
16	56 30.8	16 09.3	14 35.2
18	86 30.7	16 07.8	44 40.2
20	116 30.6	16 06.3	74 45.1
22	146 30.5	S16 04.8	104 50.0

Saturday, February 5

Time	SUN GHA	Dec	ARIES GHA
00	176 30.4	S16 03.3	134 55.0
02	206 30.3	16 01.8	164 59.9
04	236 30.1	16 00.3	195 04.8
06	266 30.0	15 58.8	225 09.7
08	296 29.9	15 57.2	255 14.7
10	326 29.8	15 55.7	285 19.6
12	356 29.7	15 54.2	315 24.5
14	26 29.6	15 52.7	345 29.5
16	56 29.5	15 51.2	15 34.4
18	86 29.4	15 49.6	45 39.3
20	116 29.4	15 48.1	75 44.2
22	146 29.3	S15 46.6	105 49.2

Sunday, February 6

Time	SUN GHA	Dec	ARIES GHA
00	176 29.2	S15 45.1	135 54.1
02	206 29.1	15 43.5	165 59.0
04	236 29.0	15 42.0	196 04.0
06	266 28.9	15 40.4	226 08.9
08	296 28.8	15 38.9	256 13.8
10	326 28.7	15 37.4	286 18.7
12	356 28.6	15 35.8	316 23.7
14	26 28.6	15 34.3	346 28.6
16	56 28.5	15 32.7	16 33.5
18	86 28.4	15 31.2	46 38.5
20	116 28.3	15 29.6	76 43.4
22	146 28.2	S15 28.1	106 48.3

Monday, February 7

Time	SUN GHA	Dec	ARIES GHA
00	176 28.2	S15 26.5	136 53.2
02	206 28.1	15 25.0	166 58.2
04	236 28.0	15 23.4	197 03.1
06	266 28.0	15 21.9	227 08.0
08	296 27.9	15 20.3	257 13.0
10	326 27.8	15 18.8	287 17.9
12	356 27.8	15 17.2	317 22.8
14	26 27.7	15 15.6	347 27.7
16	56 27.6	15 14.1	17 32.7
18	86 27.6	15 12.5	47 37.6
20	116 27.5	15 10.9	77 42.5
22	146 27.4	S15 09.4	107 47.5

Tuesday, February 8

Time	SUN GHA	Dec	ARIES GHA
00	176 27.4	S15 07.8	137 52.4
02	206 27.3	15 06.2	167 57.3
04	236 27.3	15 04.6	198 02.2
06	266 27.2	15 03.0	228 07.2
08	296 27.2	15 01.5	258 12.1
10	326 27.1	14 59.9	288 17.0
12	356 27.1	14 58.3	318 21.9
14	26 27.0	14 56.7	348 26.9
16	56 27.0	14 55.1	18 31.8
18	86 26.9	14 53.5	48 36.7
20	116 26.9	14 51.9	78 41.7
22	146 26.8	S14 50.3	108 46.6

Wednesday, February 9

Time	SUN GHA	Dec	ARIES GHA
00	176 26.8	S14 48.8	138 51.5
02	206 26.7	14 47.2	168 56.4
04	236 26.7	14 45.6	199 01.4
06	266 26.7	14 44.0	229 06.3
08	296 26.6	14 42.4	259 11.2
10	326 26.6	14 40.8	289 16.2
12	356 26.5	14 39.1	319 21.1
14	26 26.5	14 37.5	349 26.0
16	56 26.5	14 35.9	19 30.9
18	86 26.5	14 34.3	49 35.9
20	116 26.4	14 32.7	79 40.8
22	146 26.4	S14 31.1	109 45.7

Thursday, February 10

Time	SUN GHA	Dec	ARIES GHA
00	176 26.4	S14 29.5	139 50.7
02	206 26.3	14 27.9	169 55.6
04	236 26.3	14 26.2	200 00.5
06	266 26.3	14 24.6	230 05.4
08	296 26.3	14 23.0	260 10.4
10	326 26.3	14 21.4	290 15.3
12	356 26.2	14 19.8	320 20.2
14	26 26.2	14 18.1	350 25.2
16	56 26.2	14 16.5	20 30.1
18	86 26.2	14 14.9	50 35.0
20	116 26.2	14 13.2	80 39.9
22	146 26.2	S14 11.6	110 44.9

Friday, February 11

Time	SUN GHA	Dec	ARIES GHA
00	176 26.2	S14 10.0	140 49.8
02	206 26.1	14 08.3	170 54.7
04	236 26.1	14 06.7	200 59.7
06	266 26.1	14 05.0	231 04.6
08	296 26.1	14 03.4	261 09.5
10	326 26.1	14 01.8	291 14.4
12	356 26.1	14 00.1	321 19.4
14	26 26.1	13 58.5	351 24.3
16	56 26.1	13 56.8	21 29.2
18	86 26.1	13 55.2	51 34.1
20	116 26.1	13 53.5	81 39.1
22	146 26.1	S13 51.9	111 44.0

Saturday, February 12

Time	SUN GHA	Dec	ARIES GHA
00	176 26.1	S13 50.2	141 48.9
02	206 26.1	13 48.6	171 53.9
04	236 26.2	13 46.9	201 58.8
06	266 26.2	13 45.2	232 03.7
08	296 26.2	13 43.6	262 08.6
10	326 26.2	13 41.9	292 13.6
12	356 26.2	13 40.3	322 18.5
14	26 26.2	13 38.6	352 23.4
16	56 26.2	13 36.9	22 28.4
18	86 26.2	13 35.3	52 33.3
20	116 26.3	13 33.6	82 38.2
22	146 26.3	S13 31.9	112 43.1

Sunday, February 13

Time	SUN GHA	Dec	ARIES GHA
00	176 26.3	S13 30.2	142 48.1
02	206 26.3	13 28.6	172 53.0
04	236 26.4	13 26.9	202 57.9
06	266 26.4	13 25.2	233 02.9
08	296 26.4	13 23.5	263 07.8
10	326 26.4	13 21.8	293 12.7
12	356 26.5	13 20.2	323 17.6
14	26 26.5	13 18.5	353 22.6
16	56 26.5	13 16.8	23 27.5
18	86 26.6	13 15.1	53 32.4
20	116 26.6	13 13.4	83 37.4
22	146 26.6	S13 11.7	113 42.3

Monday, February 14

Time	SUN GHA	Dec	ARIES GHA
00	176 26.7	S13 10.0	143 47.2
02	206 26.7	13 08.3	173 52.1
04	236 26.7	13 06.7	203 57.1
06	266 26.8	13 05.0	234 02.0
08	296 26.8	13 03.3	264 06.9
10	326 26.9	13 01.6	294 11.9
12	356 26.9	12 59.9	324 16.8
14	26 27.0	12 58.2	354 21.7
16	56 27.0	12 56.5	24 26.6
18	86 27.1	12 54.7	54 31.6
20	116 27.1	12 53.0	84 36.5
22	146 27.2	S12 51.3	114 41.4

Tuesday, February 15

Time	SUN GHA	Dec	ARIES GHA
00	176 27.2	S12 49.6	144 46.3
02	206 27.3	12 47.9	174 51.3
04	236 27.3	12 46.2	204 56.2
06	266 27.4	12 44.5	235 01.1
08	296 27.4	12 42.8	265 06.1
10	326 27.5	12 41.1	295 11.0
12	356 27.6	12 39.3	325 15.9
14	26 27.6	12 37.6	355 20.8
16	56 27.7	12 35.9	25 25.8
18	86 27.7	12 34.2	55 30.7
20	116 27.8	12 32.5	85 35.6
22	146 27.9	S12 30.7	115 40.6

FEBRUARY 1994 — SUN & ARIES — GMT

Wednesday, February 16

Time	SUN GHA	Dec	ARIES GHA	Time
00	176 27.9	S12 29.0	145 45.5	00
02	206 28.0	12 27.3	175 50.4	02
04	236 28.1	12 25.6	205 55.2	04
06	265 28.2	12 23.8	236 00.3	06
08	296 28.2	12 22.1	266 05.2	08
10	326 28.3	12 20.4	296 10.1	10
12	356 28.4	12 18.6	326 15.1	12
14	26 28.5	12 16.9	356 20.0	14
16	56 28.5	12 15.2	26 24.9	16
18	86 28.6	12 13.4	56 29.8	18
20	116 28.7	12 11.7	86 34.8	20
22	146 28.8	S12 09.9	116 39.7	22

Thursday, February 17

Time	SUN GHA	Dec	ARIES GHA	Time
00	176 28.9	S12 08.2	146 44.6	00
02	206 28.9	12 06.4	176 49.6	02
04	236 29.0	12 04.7	206 54.5	04
06	266 29.1	12 03.0	236 59.4	06
08	296 29.2	12 01.2	267 04.3	08
10	326 29.3	11 59.5	297 09.3	10
12	356 29.4	11 57.7	327 14.2	12
14	26 29.5	11 56.0	357 19.1	14
16	56 29.6	11 54.2	27 24.1	16
18	86 29.7	11 52.5	57 29.0	18
20	116 29.8	11 50.7	87 33.9	20
22	146 29.9	S11 48.9	117 38.8	22

Friday, February 18

Time	SUN GHA	Dec	ARIES GHA	Time
00	176 30.0	S11 47.2	147 43.8	00
02	206 30.1	11 45.4	177 48.7	02
04	236 30.2	11 43.7	207 53.6	04
06	266 30.3	11 41.9	237 58.6	06
08	296 30.4	11 40.1	268 03.5	08
10	326 30.5	11 38.4	298 08.4	10
12	356 30.6	11 36.6	328 13.3	12
14	26 30.7	11 34.8	358 18.3	14
16	56 30.8	11 33.1	28 23.2	16
18	86 30.9	11 31.3	58 28.1	18
20	116 31.0	11 29.5	88 33.0	20
22	146 31.1	S11 27.8	118 38.0	22

Saturday, February 19

Time	SUN GHA	Dec	ARIES GHA	Time
00	176 31.2	S11 26.0	148 42.9	00
02	206 31.3	11 24.2	178 47.8	02
04	236 31.5	11 22.4	208 52.8	04
06	266 31.6	11 20.7	238 57.7	06
08	296 31.7	11 18.9	269 02.6	08
10	326 31.8	11 17.1	299 07.5	10
12	356 31.9	11 15.3	329 12.5	12
14	26 32.0	11 13.5	359 17.4	14
16	56 32.2	11 11.8	29 22.3	16
18	86 32.3	11 10.0	59 27.3	18
20	116 32.4	11 08.2	89 32.2	20
22	146 32.5	S11 06.4	119 37.1	22

Sunday, February 20

Time	SUN GHA	Dec	ARIES GHA	Time
00	176 32.7	S11 04.6	149 42.0	00
02	206 32.8	11 02.8	179 47.0	02
04	236 32.9	11 01.0	209 51.9	04
06	266 33.1	10 59.2	239 56.8	06
08	296 33.2	10 57.4	270 01.8	08
10	326 33.3	10 55.7	300 06.7	10
12	356 33.5	10 53.9	330 11.6	12
14	26 33.6	10 52.1	0 16.5	14
16	56 33.7	10 50.3	30 21.5	16
18	86 33.9	10 48.5	60 26.4	18
20	116 34.0	10 46.7	90 31.3	20
22	146 34.1	S10 44.9	120 36.3	22

Monday, February 21

Time	SUN GHA	Dec	ARIES GHA	Time
00	176 34.3	S10 43.1	150 41.2	00
02	206 34.4	10 41.3	180 46.1	02
04	236 34.6	10 39.5	210 51.0	04
06	266 34.7	10 37.8	240 56.0	06
08	296 34.9	10 35.8	271 00.9	08
10	326 35.0	10 34.0	301 05.8	10
12	356 35.2	10 32.2	331 10.9	12
14	26 35.3	10 30.4	1 15.7	14
16	56 35.5	10 28.6	31 20.6	16
18	86 35.6	10 26.8	61 25.5	18
20	116 35.8	10 25.0	91 30.5	20
22	146 35.9	S10 23.2	121 35.4	22

Tuesday, February 22

Time	SUN GHA	Dec	ARIES GHA	Time
00	176 36.1	S10 21.3	151 40.3	00
02	206 36.2	10 19.5	181 45.2	02
04	236 36.4	10 17.7	211 50.2	04
06	266 36.5	10 15.9	241 55.1	06
08	296 36.7	10 14.1	272 00.0	08
10	326 36.9	10 12.3	302 05.0	10
12	356 37.0	10 10.4	332 09.9	12
14	26 37.2	10 08.6	2 14.8	14
16	56 37.3	10 06.8	32 19.7	16
18	86 37.5	10 05.0	62 24.7	18
20	116 37.7	10 03.1	92 29.6	20
22	146 37.8	S10 01.3	122 34.5	22

Wednesday, February 23

Time	SUN GHA	Dec	ARIES GHA	Time
00	176 38.0	S9 59.5	152 39.5	00
02	206 38.2	9 57.6	182 44.4	02
04	236 38.3	9 55.8	212 49.3	04
06	266 38.5	9 54.0	242 54.2	06
08	296 38.7	9 52.2	272 59.2	08
10	326 38.9	9 50.3	303 04.1	10
12	356 39.0	9 48.5	333 09.0	12
14	26 39.2	9 46.6	3 14.0	14
16	56 39.4	9 44.8	33 18.9	16
18	86 39.6	9 43.0	63 23.8	18
20	116 39.7	9 41.1	93 28.7	20
22	146 39.9	S9 39.3	123 33.7	22

Thursday, February 24

Time	SUN GHA	Dec	ARIES GHA	Time
00	176 40.1	S9 37.5	153 38.6	00
02	206 40.3	9 35.6	183 43.5	02
04	236 40.5	9 33.8	213 48.5	04
06	266 40.6	9 31.9	243 53.4	06
08	296 40.8	9 30.1	273 58.3	08
10	326 41.0	9 28.2	304 03.2	10
12	356 41.2	9 26.4	334 08.2	12
14	26 41.4	9 24.5	4 13.1	14
16	56 41.6	9 22.7	34 18.0	16
18	86 41.8	9 20.8	64 23.0	18
20	116 42.0	9 19.0	94 27.9	20
22	146 42.2	S9 17.1	124 32.8	22

Friday, February 25

Time	SUN GHA	Dec	ARIES GHA	Time
00	176 42.3	S9 15.3	154 37.7	00
02	206 42.5	9 13.4	184 42.7	02
04	236 42.7	9 11.6	214 47.6	04
06	266 42.9	9 09.7	244 52.5	06
08	296 43.1	9 07.9	274 57.4	08
10	326 43.3	9 06.0	305 02.4	10
12	356 43.5	9 04.1	335 07.3	12
14	26 43.7	9 02.3	5 12.2	14
16	56 43.9	9 00.4	35 17.2	16
18	86 44.1	8 58.6	65 22.1	18
20	116 44.3	8 56.7	95 27.0	20
22	146 44.5	S8 54.8	125 31.9	22

Saturday, February 26

Time	SUN GHA	Dec	ARIES GHA	Time
00	176 44.7	S8 53.0	155 36.9	00
02	206 44.9	8 51.1	185 41.8	02
04	236 45.2	8 49.2	215 46.7	04
06	266 45.4	8 47.4	245 51.7	06
08	296 45.6	8 45.5	275 56.6	08
10	326 45.8	8 43.6	306 01.5	10
12	356 46.0	8 41.8	336 06.4	12
14	26 46.2	8 39.9	6 11.4	14
16	56 46.4	8 38.0	36 16.3	16
18	86 46.6	8 36.2	66 21.2	18
20	116 46.8	8 34.3	96 26.2	20
22	146 47.1	S8 32.4	126 31.1	22

Sunday, February 27

Time	SUN GHA	Dec	ARIES GHA	Time
00	176 47.3	S8 30.5	156 36.0	00
02	206 47.5	8 28.7	186 40.9	02
04	236 47.7	8 26.8	216 45.9	04
06	266 47.9	8 24.9	246 50.8	06
08	296 48.2	8 23.0	276 55.7	08
10	326 48.4	8 21.1	307 00.7	10
12	356 48.6	8 19.3	337 05.6	12
14	26 48.8	8 17.4	7 10.5	14
16	56 49.0	8 15.5	37 15.4	16
18	86 49.3	8 13.6	67 20.4	18
20	116 49.5	8 11.7	97 25.3	20
22	146 49.7	S8 09.9	127 30.2	22

Monday, February 28

Time	SUN GHA	Dec	ARIES GHA	Time
00	176 50.0	S8 08.0	157 35.2	00
02	206 50.2	8 06.1	187 40.1	02
04	236 50.4	8 04.2	217 45.0	04
06	266 50.6	8 02.3	247 49.9	06
08	296 50.9	8 00.4	277 54.9	08
10	326 51.1	7 58.5	307 59.8	10
12	356 51.3	7 56.6	338 04.7	12
14	26 51.6	7 54.8	8 09.7	14
16	56 51.8	7 52.9	38 14.6	16
18	86 52.1	7 51.0	68 19.5	18
20	116 52.3	7 49.1	98 24.4	20
22	146 52.5	S7 47.2	128 29.4	22

Chapter 6

FEBRUARY 1994 — PLANETS — 0h GMT

VENUS / JUPITER

Mer Pass h m	GHA ° '	Mean Var/hr 14°+	Dec ° '	Mean Var/hr			GHA ° '	Mean Var/hr 15°+	Dec ° '	Mean Var/hr	Mer Pass h m
12 30	172 00.3	59.3	S17 26.2	0.9	1	Tue	269 33.5	2.3	S14 43.6	0.1	06 01
12 31	172 22.1	59.3	S17 04.6	0.9	2	Wed	270 27.8	2.3	S14 44.9	0.0	05 57
12 32	172 06.0	59.3	S16 42.5	0.9	3	Thu	271 22.2	2.3	S14 46.1	0.1	05 54
12 33	171 50.3	59.4	S16 20.0	1.0	4	Fri	272 16.8	2.3	S14 47.3	0.0	05 50
12 34	171 34.8	59.4	S15 57.0	1.0	5	Sat	273 11.6	2.3	S14 48.4	0.0	05 46
12 35	171 19.6	59.4	S15 33.6	1.0	6	SUN	274 06.5	2.3	S14 49.5	0.0	05 43
12 36	171 04.8	59.4	S15 09.7	1.0	7	Mon	275 01.6	2.3	S14 50.5	0.0	05 39
12 37	170 50.2	59.4	S14 45.4	1.0	8	Tue	275 56.9	2.3	S14 51.4	0.0	05 35
12 38	170 35.9	59.4	S14 20.7	1.0	9	Wed	276 52.4	2.3	S14 52.4	0.0	05 32
12 39	170 22.0	59.4	S13 55.7	1.1	10	Thu	277 48.0	2.3	S14 53.2	0.0	05 28
12 40	170 08.3	59.4	S13 30.2	1.1	11	Fri	278 43.8	2.3	S14 54.0	0.0	05 24
12 41	169 54.9	59.5	S13 04.4	1.1	12	Sat	279 39.7	2.3	S14 54.8	0.0	05 21
12 42	169 41.8	59.5	S12 38.2	1.1	13	SUN	280 35.9	2.3	S14 55.5	0.0	05 17
12 43	169 28.9	59.5	S12 11.7	1.1	14	Mon	281 32.2	2.4	S14 56.1	0.0	05 13
12 43	169 16.3	59.5	S11 44.9	1.1	15	Tue	282 28.7	2.4	S14 56.7	0.0	05 09
12 44	169 04.0	59.5	S11 17.7	1.1	16	Wed	283 25.4	2.4	S14 57.2	0.0	05 06
12 45	168 51.9	59.5	S10 50.3	1.2	17	Thu	284 22.2	2.4	S14 57.7	0.0	05 02
12 46	168 40.1	59.5	S10 22.6	1.2	18	Fri	285 19.2	2.4	S14 58.1	0.0	04 58
12 47	168 28.5	59.5	S 9 54.6	1.2	19	Sat	286 16.5	2.4	S14 58.5	0.0	04 54
12 47	168 17.1	59.5	S 9 26.3	1.2	20	SUN	287 13.9	2.4	S14 58.8	0.0	04 50
12 48	168 05.9	59.5	S 8 57.8	1.2	21	Mon	288 11.4	2.4	S14 59.1	0.0	04 46
12 49	167 55.0	59.6	S 8 29.0	1.2	22	Tue	289 09.2	2.4	S14 59.3	0.0	04 43
12 49	167 44.3	59.6	S 8 00.1	1.2	23	Wed	290 07.2	2.4	S14 59.5	0.0	04 39
12 50	167 33.7	59.6	S 7 30.9	1.2	24	Thu	291 05.3	2.4	S14 59.6	0.0	04 35
12 51	167 23.4	59.6	S 7 01.5	1.2	25	Fri	292 03.6	2.4	S14 59.6	0.0	04 31
12 51	167 13.2	59.6	S 6 31.9	1.2	26	Sat	293 02.1	2.4	S14 59.6	0.0	04 27
12 52	167 03.2	59.6	S 6 02.2	1.2	27	SUN	294 00.8	2.5	S14 59.5	0.0	04 23
12 53	166 53.3	59.6	S 5 32.3	1.3	28	Mon	294 59.7	2.5	S14 59.4	0.0	04 19

VENUS, Av Mag –3.9
SHA February
5 37; 10 31; 15 24; 20 19; 25 13; 28 9.

JUPITER, Av Mag –2.1
SHA February
5 138; 10 138; 15 138; 20 138; 25 137; 28 137.

MARS / SATURN

Mer Pass h m	GHA ° '	Mean Var/hr 15°+	Dec ° '	Mean Var/hr			GHA ° '	Mean Var/hr 15°+	Dec ° '	Mean Var/hr	Mer Pass h m
11 38	185 27.2	0.4	S20 28.6	0.4	1	Tue	158 02.2	2.2	S12 40.4	0.1	13 26
11 37	185 37.8	0.4	S20 17.9	0.5	2	Wed	158 54.5	2.2	S12 37.9	0.1	13 22
11 36	185 48.4	0.4	S20 07.1	0.5	3	Thu	159 46.9	2.2	S12 35.4	0.1	13 19
11 36	185 59.2	0.4	S19 56.0	0.5	4	Fri	160 39.2	2.2	S12 32.9	0.1	13 15
11 35	186 10.0	0.5	S19 44.7	0.5	5	Sat	161 31.5	2.2	S12 30.4	0.1	13 12
11 34	186 20.9	0.5	S19 33.2	0.5	6	SUN	162 23.8	2.2	S12 27.9	0.1	13 09
11 34	186 31.9	0.5	S19 21.4	0.5	7	Mon	163 16.1	2.2	S12 25.3	0.1	13 05
11 33	186 43.0	0.5	S19 09.5	0.5	8	Tue	164 08.4	2.2	S12 22.8	0.1	13 02
11 32	186 54.2	0.5	S18 57.3	0.5	9	Wed	165 00.6	2.2	S12 20.3	0.1	12 58
11 31	187 05.5	0.5	S18 45.0	0.5	10	Thu	165 52.9	2.2	S12 17.7	0.1	12 55
11 31	187 16.9	0.5	S18 32.4	0.5	11	Fri	166 45.1	2.2	S12 15.2	0.1	12 51
11 30	187 28.3	0.5	S18 19.7	0.5	12	Sat	167 37.3	2.2	S12 12.6	0.1	12 48
11 29	187 39.9	0.5	S18 06.7	0.5	13	SUN	168 29.5	2.2	S12 10.1	0.1	12 44
11 28	187 51.6	0.5	S17 53.6	0.6	14	Mon	169 21.7	2.2	S12 07.5	0.1	12 41
11 27	188 03.4	0.5	S17 40.2	0.6	15	Tue	170 13.9	2.2	S12 04.9	0.1	12 37
11 27	188 15.3	0.5	S17 26.7	0.6	16	Wed	171 06.1	2.2	S12 02.3	0.1	12 34
11 26	188 27.3	0.5	S17 13.0	0.6	17	Thu	171 58.2	2.2	S11 59.8	0.1	12 30
11 25	188 39.3	0.5	S16 59.1	0.6	18	Fri	172 50.4	2.2	S11 57.2	0.1	12 27
11 24	188 51.5	0.5	S16 45.0	0.6	19	Sat	173 42.6	2.2	S11 54.6	0.1	12 23
11 23	189 03.8	0.5	S16 30.8	0.6	20	SUN	174 34.7	2.2	S11 52.0	0.1	12 20
11 23	189 16.2	0.5	S16 16.4	0.6	21	Mon	175 26.9	2.2	S11 49.4	0.1	12 16
11 22	189 28.7	0.5	S16 01.8	0.6	22	Tue	176 19.1	2.2	S11 46.9	0.1	12 13
11 21	189 41.3	0.5	S15 47.0	0.6	23	Wed	177 11.3	2.2	S11 44.3	0.1	12 09
11 20	189 54.1	0.5	S15 32.1	0.6	24	Thu	178 03.4	2.2	S11 41.7	0.1	12 06
11 19	190 06.9	0.5	S15 17.0	0.6	25	Fri	178 55.6	2.2	S11 39.1	0.1	12 03
11 18	190 19.8	0.5	S15 01.8	0.6	26	Sat	179 47.8	2.2	S11 36.5	0.1	11 59
11 17	190 32.8	0.5	S14 46.4	0.6	27	SUN	180 40.0	2.2	S11 33.9	0.1	11 56
11 17	190 45.9	0.6	S14 30.9	0.7	28	Mon	181 32.2	2.2	S11 31.4	0.1	11 52

MARS, Av Mag +1.2
SHA February
5 51; 10 47; 15 43; 20 39; 25 35; 28 33.

SATURN, Av Mag +0.9
SHA February
5 27; 10 26; 15 25; 20 25; 25 24; 28 24.

FEBRUARY 1994   MOON

Day	GMT hr	GHA ° '	Mean Var/hr 14°+	Dec ° '	Mean Var/hr '	Day	GMT hr	GHA ° '	Mean Var/hr 14°+	Dec ° '	Mean Var/hr '
1 Tue	0	302 18.4	28.3	S 7 53.0	12.0	17 Thu	0	110 30.6	32.4	N 16 06.9	6.9
	6	29 08.3	28.1	S 9 05.4	11.7		6	197 45.4	32.1	N 16 48.5	6.4
	12	115 57.1	27.9	S 10 15.8	11.3		12	284 58.6	31.9	N 17 27.4	6.0
	18	202 44.8	27.7	S 11 25.8	10.8		18	12 10.1	31.7	N 18 03.7	5.5
2 Wed	0	289 31.3	27.6	S 12 29.2	10.4	18 Fri	0	99 20.1	31.4	N 18 37.2	5.0
	6	10 16.5	27.2	S 13 31.9	9.9		6	186 28.3	31.1	N 19 07.7	4.5
	12	103 00.4	27.1	S 14 31.4	9.3		12	273 34.9	30.8	N 19 35.1	4.0
	18	189 43.0	26.9	S 15 27.7	8.7		18	0 39.7	30.5	N 19 59.4	3.5
3 Thu	0	276 24.3	26.6	S 16 20.4	8.1	19 Sat	0	87 42.8	30.3	N 20 20.3	2.9
	6	3 04.4	26.5	S 17 09.4	7.5		6	174 44.3	29.9	N 20 37.8	2.3
	12	89 43.2	26.3	S 17 54.4	6.8		12	261 44.1	29.7	N 20 51.8	1.7
	18	176 20.8	26.1	S 18 35.4	6.1		18	348 42.3	29.5	N 21 02.1	1.0
4 Fri	0	262 57.5	25.9	S 19 12.0	5.3	20 Sun	0	75 39.0	29.2	N 21 08.7	0.4
	6	349 33.3	25.8	S 19 44.3	4.6		6	162 34.3	29.0	N 21 11.5	0.3
	12	76 08.4	25.7	S 20 12.0	3.8		12	249 28.3	28.8	N 21 10.3	0.9
	18	162 42.9	25.7	S 20 35.1	3.0		18	336 21.0	28.6	N 21 05.2	1.6
5 Sat	0	249 17.1	25.7	S 20 53.4	2.2	21 Mon	0	63 12.6	28.4	N 20 56.0	2.2
	6	335 51.3	25.7	S 21 07.0	1.4		6	150 03.3	28.3	N 20 42.7	3.0
	12	62 25.6	25.8	S 21 15.9	0.6		12	236 53.0	28.2	N 20 25.2	3.7
	18	149 00.2	25.9	S 21 19.9	0.1		18	323 42.1	28.0	N 20 03.6	4.4
6 Sun	0	235 35.5	26.0	S 21 19.2	1.0	22 Tue	0	50 30.5	28.0	N 19 37.9	5.1
	6	322 11.7	26.2	S 21 13.8	1.7		6	137 18.5	27.9	N 19 08.0	5.7
	12	48 49.0	26.4	S 21 03.7	2.5		12	224 06.1	27.9	N 18 34.0	6.4
	18	135 27.6	26.7	S 20 49.1	3.3		18	310 53.4	27.9	N 17 55.9	7.0
7 Mon	0	222 07.7	27.0	S 20 30.1	3.9	23 Wed	0	37 40.6	27.9	N 17 13.9	7.7
	6	308 49.5	27.4	S 20 06.8	4.6		6	124 27.8	27.9	N 16 28.0	8.3
	12	35 33.3	27.6	S 19 39.4	5.2		12	211 15.0	27.8	N 15 38.3	8.9
	18	122 19.0	28.0	S 19 08.1	5.9		18	298 02.3	27.9	N 14 44.9	9.5
8 Tue	0	209 06.9	28.4	S 18 33.0	6.5	24 Thu	0	24 49.8	27.9	N 13 48.1	10.1
	6	295 57.1	28.7	S 17 54.3	7.0		6	111 37.4	28.0	N 12 47.9	10.6
	12	22 49.6	29.2	S 17 12.3	7.6		12	198 25.2	28.0	N 11 44.6	11.1
	18	109 44.4	29.6	S 16 27.1	8.0		18	285 13.2	28.0	N 10 38.4	11.5
9 Wed	0	196 41.6	30.0	S 15 39.0	8.5	25 Fri	0	12 01.4	28.1	N 9 29.6	11.9
	6	283 41.2	30.4	S 14 48.3	8.9		6	98 49.7	28.1	N 8 18.3	12.3
	12	10 43.2	30.7	S 13 55.0	9.3		12	185 38.1	28.0	N 7 04.8	12.5
	18	97 47.4	31.1	S 12 59.5	9.7		18	272 26.6	28.1	N 5 49.5	12.9
10 Thu	0	184 53.8	31.4	S 12 02.0	9.9	26 Sat	0	359 15.0	28.0	N 4 32.5	13.0
	6	272 02.4	31.8	S 11 02.6	10.2		6	86 03.3	28.0	N 3 14.3	13.2
	12	359 13.1	32.1	S 10 01.6	10.4		12	172 51.4	28.0	N 1 55.1	13.4
	18	86 25.8	32.4	S 8 59.3	10.6		18	259 39.2	27.9	N 0 35.3	13.3
11 Fri	0	173 40.2	32.7	S 7 55.8	10.7	27 Sun	0	346 26.5	27.8	S 0 44.8	13.4
	6	260 56.4	33.0	S 6 51.3	10.9		6	73 13.4	27.7	S 2 04.9	13.3
	12	348 14.2	33.2	S 5 46.0	11.0		12	159 59.6	27.5	S 3 24.7	13.1
	18	75 33.4	33.4	S 4 40.1	11.1		18	246 45.1	27.4	S 4 43.7	13.0
12 Sat	0	162 53.9	33.6	S 3 33.8	11.1	28 Mon	0	333 29.9	27.3	S 6 01.6	12.7
	6	250 15.6	33.8	S 2 27.2	11.1		6	60 13.7	27.2	S 7 18.2	12.5
	12	337 38.2	33.9	S 1 20.6	11.1		12	146 56.5	26.9	S 8 33.0	12.0
	18	65 01.8	34.1	S 0 14.1	11.1		18	233 38.3	26.8	S 9 45.8	11.7
13 Sun	0	152 26.0	34.1	N 0 52.2	11.0						
	6	239 50.8	34.2	N 1 58.1	10.9						
	12	327 16.0	34.2	N 3 03.5	10.8						
	18	54 41.4	34.3	N 4 08.2	10.6						
14 Mon	0	142 07.0	34.3	N 5 12.0	10.4						
	6	229 32.5	34.3	N 6 14.9	10.3						
	12	316 57.8	34.1	N 7 16.7	10.1						
	18	44 22.7	34.1	N 8 17.3	9.9						
15 Tue	0	131 47.2	34.0	N 9 16.5	9.6						
	6	219 11.0	33.9	N 10 14.2	9.3						
	12	306 34.2	33.7	N 11 10.4	9.1						
	18	33 56.4	33.5	N 12 04.8	8.8						
16 Wed	0	121 17.7	33.3	N 12 57.4	8.4						
	6	208 37.8	33.1	N 13 48.0	8.0						
	12	295 56.8	33.0	N 14 36.6	7.7						
	18	23 14.4	32.7	N 15 22.9	7.3						

Chapter 6

MARCH 1994 — SUN & MOON — GMT

SUN

Day of Yr Mth Week	Equation of Time 0h	12h	Transit	Semi-diam	Lat 52°N Twilight	Sun-rise	Sun-set	Twi-light	Lat	Twi-light	Sun-rise	Sun-set	Twi-light
	m s	m s	h m	′	h m	h m	h m	h m	°	h m	h m	h m	h m
60 1 Tue	+12 29	+12 23	12 12	16.2	06 13	06 46	17 39	18 13	N70	−0 18	+0 08	−0 06	+0 19
61 2 Wed	+12 17	+12 11	12 12	16.2	06 10	06 44	17 41	18 15	68	−0 15	+0 06	−0 05	+0 15
62 3 Thu	+12 05	+11 59	12 12	16.2	06 08	06 42	17 43	18 17	66	−0 12	+0 05	−0 04	+0 13
63 4 Fri	+11 53	+11 46	12 12	16.2	06 06	06 40	17 45	18 18	64	−0 09	+0 04	−0 03	+0 10
64 5 Sat	+11 39	+11 33	12 12	16.2	06 04	06 38	17 46	18 20	62	−0 06	+0 03	−0 02	+0 07
65 6 Sun	+11 26	+11 19	12 11	16.1	06 02	06 35	17 48	18 22	N60	−0 04	+0 03	−0 02	+0 05
66 7 Mon	+11 12	+11 05	12 11	16.1	06 00	06 33	17 50	18 24	58	−0 03	+0 02	−0 02	+0 04
67 8 Tue	+10 58	+10 50	12 11	16.1	05 57	06 31	17 52	18 25	56	−0 01	+0 01	−0 01	+0 02
68 9 Wed	+10 43	+10 35	12 11	16.1	05 55	06 29	17 53	18 27	54	−0 01	+0 01	−0 01	+0 01
69 10 Thu	+10 28	+10 20	12 10	16.1	05 53	06 26	17 55	18 29	50	+0 01	0 00	0 00	−0 01
70 11 Fri	+10 12	+10 05	12 10	16.1	05 51	06 24	17 57	18 31	N45	+0 03	−0 01	+0 02	−0 02
71 12 Sat	+09 57	+09 49	12 10	16.1	05 48	06 22	17 59	18 32	40	+0 05	−0 02	+0 02	−0 04
72 13 Sun	+09 41	+09 33	12 10	16.1	05 46	06 20	18 01	18 34	35	+0 06	−0 03	+0 03	−0 05
73 14 Mon	+09 24	+09 16	12 09	16.1	05 44	06 17	18 02	18 36	30	+0 07	−0 04	+0 04	−0 06
74 15 Tue	+09 08	+09 00	12 09	16.1	05 41	06 15	18 04	18 38	20	+0 07	−0 05	+0 05	−0 06
75 16 Wed	+08 51	+08 43	12 09	16.1	05 39	06 13	18 06	18 39	N10	+0 07	−0 07	+0 06	−0 06
76 17 Thu	+08 34	+08 25	12 08	16.1	05 37	06 10	18 07	18 41	0	+0 06	−0 08	+0 07	−0 05
77 18 Fri	+08 17	+08 08	12 08	16.1	05 34	06 08	18 09	18 43	S10	+0 04	−0 09	+0 09	−0 03
78 19 Sat	+07 59	+07 51	12 08	16.1	05 32	06 06	18 11	18 45	20	+0 01	−0 11	+0 10	0 00
79 20 Sun	+07 42	+07 33	12 08	16.1	05 30	06 03	18 13	18 46	30	−0 03	−0 14	+0 12	+0 04
80 21 Mon	+07 24	+07 15	12 07	16.1	05 27	06 01	18 14	18 48	S35	−0 06	−0 15	+0 14	+0 07
81 22 Tue	+07 06	+06 57	12 07	16.1	05 25	05 59	18 16	18 50	40	−0 10	−0 17	+0 15	+0 11
82 23 Wed	+06 48	+06 39	12 07	16.1	05 23	05 56	18 18	18 52	45	−0 13	−0 18	+0 17	+0 14
83 24 Thu	+06 30	+06 21	12 06	16.1	05 20	05 54	18 20	18 53	S50	−0 18	−0 20	+0 19	+0 20
84 25 Fri	+06 12	+06 03	12 06	16.1	05 18	05 52	18 21	18 55					
85 26 Sat	+05 53	+05 44	12 06	16.1	05 16	05 50	18 23	18 57					
86 27 Sun	+05 35	+05 26	12 05	16.1	05 13	05 47	18 25	18 59					
87 28 Mon	+05 17	+05 08	12 05	16.0	05 11	05 45	18 26	19 01					
88 29 Tue	+04 58	+04 49	12 05	16.0	05 09	05 43	18 28	19 02					
89 30 Wed	+04 40	+04 31	12 05	16.0	05 06	05 40	18 30	19 04					
90 31 Thu	+04 22	+04 13	12 04	16.0	05 04	05 38	18 32	19 06					

NOTES
Lat corrections are for the middle of March. **Equation of Time** is the excess of Mean Time over Apparent Time.

MOON

Day of Yr Mth Week	Age	Transit Diff (Upper)	Semi-diam	Hor Par	Moon-rise	Moon-set
	days	h m m	′	′	h m	h m
60 1 Tue	19	02 45 56	16.4	60.3	22 51	07 50
61 2 Wed	20	03 41 57	16.3	59.8	– –	08 22
62 3 Thu	21	04 38 58	16.1	59.3	00 10	09 01
63 4 Fri	22	05 36 57	16.0	58.6	01 21	09 48
64 5 Sat	23	06 33 56	15.8	58.0	02 23	10 44
65 6 Sun	24	07 29 53	15.6	57.3	03 14	11 47
66 7 Mon	25	08 22 50	15.5	56.7	03 55	12 54
67 8 Tue	26	09 12 48	15.3	56.2	04 28	14 04
68 9 Wed	27	10 00 45	15.2	55.7	04 55	15 14
69 10 Thu	28	10 45 44	15.1	55.3	05 18	16 22
70 11 Fri	29	11 29 42	15.0	54.9	05 39	17 30
71 12 Sat	00	12 11 43	14.9	54.5	05 58	18 37
72 13 Sun	01	12 54 43	14.8	54.3	06 18	19 43
73 14 Mon	02	13 37 43	14.7	54.1	06 38	20 48
74 15 Tue	03	14 20 45	14.7	54.0	07 00	21 52
75 16 Wed	04	15 05 47	14.7	54.1	07 26	22 55
76 17 Thu	05	15 52 48	14.8	54.2	07 56	23 55
77 18 Fri	06	16 40 49	14.9	54.5	08 33	– –
78 19 Sat	07	17 29 51	15.0	55.0	09 16	00 51
79 20 Sun	08	18 20 51	15.2	55.7	10 09	01 42
80 21 Mon	09	19 11 52	15.4	56.4	11 09	02 26
81 22 Tue	10	20 03 52	15.6	57.3	12 17	03 03
82 23 Wed	11	20 55 52	15.9	58.3	13 31	03 36
83 24 Thu	12	21 47 53	16.1	59.2	14 49	04 04
84 25 Fri	13	22 40 54	16.4	60.1	16 10	04 30
85 26 Sat	14	23 34 55	16.6	60.8	17 33	04 55
86 27 Sun	15	24 29 _	16.7	61.2	18 58	05 20
87 28 Mon	16	00 29 58	16.7	61.2	20 24	05 48
88 29 Tue	17	01 27 59	16.6	61.0	21 47	06 19
89 30 Wed	18	02 26 60	16.5	60.5	23 05	06 57
90 31 Thu	19	03 26 59	16.3	59.8	– –	07 43

Phases of the Moon

		d	h	m
◑	Last Quarter	4	16	53
●	New Moon	12	07	05
◐	First Quarter	20	12	14
○	Full Moon	27	11	09

Apogee	15	17
Perigee	28	06

NOTES
For Latitude corrections to Moonrise and Moonset see page 706.

MARCH 1994   STARS   0h GMT March 1

No	Name	Mag	Transit h m	Dec ° '	GHA ° '	RA h m	SHA ° '
	ARIES		13 24		158 34.3		
1	Alpheratz	2.2	13 32	N29 03.5	156 33.1	0 08	357 58.8
2	Ankaa	2.4	13 49	S 42 20.3	152 04.6	0 26	353 30.3
3	Schedar	2.5	14 04	N56 30.4	148 31.8	0 40	349 57.5
4	Diphda	2.2	14 07	S 18 01.2	147 44.9	0 43	349 10.6
5	Achernar	0.6	15 01	S 57 16.1	134 12.2	1 37	335 37.9
6	POLARIS	2.1	16 19	N89 14.5	122 18.9	2 25	323 44.6
7	Hamal	2.2	15 30	N23 26.1	126 51.6	2 07	328 17.3
8	Acamar	3.1	16 21	S 40 19.9	114 03.8	2 58	315 29.5
9	Menkar	2.8	16 25	N 4 03.9	113 04.6	3 02	314 30.3
10	Mirfak	1.9	16 47	N49 50.6	107 35.6	3 24	309 01.3
11	Aldebaran	1.1	17 58	N16 29.8	89 40.3	4 36	291 06.0
12	Rigel	0.3	18 37	S 8 12.7	80 00.2	5 14	281 25.9
13	Capella	0.2	18 39	N45 59.6	79 30.1	5 16	280 55.8
14	Bellatrix	1.7	18 47	N 6 20.5	77 21.8	5 25	278 47.5
15	Elnath	1.8	18 49	N28 36.2	77 05.1	5 26	278 30.8
16	Alnilam	1.8	18 59	S 1 12.5	74 35.3	5 36	276 01.0
17	Betelgeuse	0.1-1.2	19 17	N 7 24.2	69 51.2	5 55	271 16.9
18	Canopus	-0.9	19 46	S 52 41.9	62 36.7	6 24	264 02.4
19	Sirius	-1.6	20 07	S 16 42.8	57 20.6	6 45	258 46.3
20	Adhara	1.6	20 21	S 28 58.2	53 58.0	6 58	255 23.7
21	Castor	1.6	20 57	N31 54.0	45 00.4	7 34	246 26.1
22	Procyon	0.5	21 01	N 5 14.2	43 48.9	7 39	245 14.6
23	Pollux	1.2	21 07	N28 02.3	42 19.4	7 45	243 45.1
24	Avior	1.7	21 45	S 59 29.8	32 57.8	8 22	234 23.5
25	Suhail	2.2	22 30	S 43 24.9	21 37.0	9 08	223 02.7
26	Miaplacidus	1.8	22 35	S 69 41.9	20 16.2	9 13	221 41.9
27	Alphard	2.2	22 49	S 8 38.3	16 44.3	9 27	218 10.0
28	Regulus	1.3	23 30	N11 59.5	6 32.8	10 08	207 58.5
29	Dubhe	2.0	0 29	N61 46.8	352 42.9	11 03	194 08.6
30	Denebola	2.2	1 14	N 14 36.0	341 22.3	11 49	182 48.0
31	Gienah	2.8	1 41	S 17 30.8	334 41.1	12 16	176 06.8
32	Acrux	1.1	1 52	S 63 04.1	331 59.1	12 26	173 24.8
33	Gacrux	1.6	1 56	S 57 04.9	330 50.8	12 31	172 16.5
34	Mimosa	1.5	2 13	S 59 39.5	326 42.6	12 47	168 08.3
35	Alioth	1.7	2 19	N55 59.2	325 07.1	12 54	166 32.8
36	Spica	1.2	2 50	S 11 08.0	317 20.5	13 25	158 46.2
37	Alkaid	1.9	3 13	N49 20.3	311 44.1	13 47	153 09.8
38	Hadar	0.9	3 29	S 60 20.7	307 42.2	14 03	149 07.9
39	Men kent	2.3	3 32	S 36 20.5	306 58.6	14 06	148 24.3
40	Arcturus	0.2	3 41	N19 12.5	304 42.9	14 15	146 08.6
41	Rigil Kent.	0.1	4 04	S 60 48.6	298 45.2	14 39	140 10.9
42	Zuben'ubi	2.9	4 16	S 16 01.2	295 55.5	14 51	137 21.2
43	Kochab	2.2	4 16	N74 10.5	295 53.0	14 51	137 18.7
44	Alphecca	2.3	4 59	N26 43.8	284 57.3	15 34	126 23.0
45	Antares	1.2	5 54	S 26 25.1	271 18.2	16 29	112 43.9
46	Atria	1.9	6 13	S 69 00.8	266 32.9	16 48	107 58.6
47	Sabik	2.6	6 35	S 15 43.1	261 03.3	17 10	102 29.0
48	Shaula	1.7	6 58	S 37 05.9	255 15.8	17 33	96 41.5
49	Rasalhague	2.1	6 59	N12 33.7	254 54.1	17 35	96 19.8
50	Eltanin	2.4	7 21	N51 29.1	249 27.2	17 56	90 52.9
51	Kaus Aust.	2.0	7 48	S 34 23.1	242 37.3	18 24	84 03.0
52	Vega	0.1	8 01	N38 46.5	239 23.1	18 37	80 48.8
53	Nunki	2.1	8 19	S 26 18.2	234 50.6	18 55	76 16.3
54	Altair	0.9	9 15	N 8 51.1	220 56.8	19 51	62 22.5
55	Peacock	2.1	9 49	S 56 45.0	212 16.5	20 25	53 42.2
56	Deneb	1.3	10 05	N45 15.4	208 15.9	20 41	49 41.6
57	Enif	2.5	11 08	N 9 50.9	192 35.8	21 44	34 01.5
58	Al Na'ir	2.2	11 32	S 46 59.2	186 36.5	22 08	28 02.2
59	Fomalhaut	1.3	12 21	S 29 39.2	174 14.5	22 57	15 40.2
60	Markab	2.6	12 28	N15 10.4	172 27.3	23 04	13 53.0

Stars Transit Corr Table

Date	Corr h m	Date	Corr h m
1	-0 00	17	-1 03
2	-0 04	18	-1 07
3	-0 08	19	-1 11
4	-0 12	20	-1 15
5	-0 16	21	-1 19
6	-0 20	22	-1 23
7	-0 24	23	-1 27
8	-0 28	24	-1 30
9	-0 31	25	-1 34
10	-0 35	26	-1 38
11	-0 39	27	-1 42
12	-0 43	28	-1 46
13	-0 47	29	-1 50
14	-0 51	30	-1 54
15	-0 55	31	-1 58
16	-0 59		

STAR'S TRANSIT

To find the approx time of transit of a star for any day of the month use above table. All corrections are subtractive. If the quantity taken from the table is greater than the time of transit for the first of the month, add 23h 56min to the time of transit before subtracting the correction.

Example: A bright star in the southern hemisphere is observed on the meridian at 19h 26min on March 6. What is it?

	h min
Transit on March 6	19 25
Corr for the 6th	+00 20
Transit on March 1	19 45

Answer: Canopus (No 18)

MARCH DIARY

d h	
2 16	Jupiter 2°N of Moon
4 01	Pluto stationary
4 12	Mercury stationary
4 17	Last Quarter
7 16	Neptune 4°S of Moon
7 21	Uranus 5°S of Moon
10 04	Mercury 5°S of Moon
10 23	Mars 7°S of Moon
11 04	Saturn 7°S of Moon
12 07	New Moon
13 17	Venus 5°S of Moon
14 10	Mars 0.4°N of Saturn
15 17	Moon at apogee
19 02	Mercury greatest elongation W(28°)
20 03	Pallas in conjunction with Sun
20 12	First Quarter
20 20	Equinox
24 08	Mercury 0.3°S of Saturn
27 11	Full Moon
28 06	Moon at perigee
29 23	Jupiter 2°N of Moon

Chapter 6

MARCH 1994 — SUN & ARIES — GMT

Tuesday, March 1

Time	SUN GHA ° ′	Dec ° ′	ARIES GHA ° ′
00	176 52.8	S7 45.3	150 34.3
02	206 53.0	7 43.4	188 39.2
04	236 53.2	7 41.5	218 44.1
06	266 53.5	7 39.6	248 49.1
08	296 53.7	7 37.7	278 54.0
10	326 54.0	7 35.8	308 58.9
12	356 54.2	7 33.9	339 03.9
14	26 54.5	7 32.0	9 08.8
16	56 54.7	7 30.1	39 13.7
18	86 55.0	7 28.2	69 18.6
20	116 55.2	7 26.3	99 23.6
22	146 55.5	S7 24.4	129 28.5

Wednesday, March 2

Time	SUN GHA ° ′	Dec ° ′	ARIES GHA ° ′
00	176 55.7	S7 22.5	159 33.4
02	206 55.9	7 20.6	189 38.4
04	236 56.2	7 18.7	219 43.3
06	266 56.5	7 16.8	249 48.2
08	296 56.7	7 14.9	279 53.1
10	326 57.0	7 13.0	309 58.1
12	356 57.2	7 11.0	340 03.0
14	26 57.5	7 09.1	10 07.9
16	56 57.7	7 07.2	40 12.9
18	86 58.0	7 05.3	70 17.8
20	116 58.2	7 03.4	100 22.7
22	146 58.5	S7 01.5	130 27.6

Thursday, March 3

Time	SUN GHA ° ′	Dec ° ′	ARIES GHA ° ′
00	176 58.8	S6 59.6	160 32.6
02	206 59.0	6 57.7	190 37.5
04	236 59.3	6 55.8	220 42.4
06	266 59.5	6 53.8	250 47.4
08	296 59.8	6 51.9	280 52.3
10	327 00.1	6 50.0	310 57.2
12	357 00.3	6 48.1	341 02.1
14	27 00.6	6 46.2	11 07.1
16	57 00.9	6 44.3	41 12.0
18	87 01.1	6 42.3	71 16.9
20	117 01.4	6 40.4	101 21.9
22	147 01.7	S6 38.5	131 26.8

Friday, March 4

Time	SUN GHA ° ′	Dec ° ′	ARIES GHA ° ′
00	177 01.9	S6 36.6	161 31.7
02	207 02.2	6 34.7	191 36.6
04	237 02.5	6 32.7	221 41.6
06	267 02.7	6 30.8	251 46.5
08	297 03.0	6 28.9	281 51.4
10	327 03.3	6 27.0	311 56.3
12	357 03.6	6 25.0	342 01.3
14	27 03.8	6 23.1	12 06.2
16	57 04.1	6 21.2	42 11.1
18	87 04.4	6 19.3	72 16.1
20	117 04.7	6 17.3	102 21.0
22	147 04.9	S6 15.4	132 25.9

Saturday, March 5

Time	SUN GHA ° ′	Dec ° ′	ARIES GHA ° ′
00	177 05.2	S6 13.5	162 30.8
02	207 05.5	6 11.6	192 35.8
04	237 05.8	6 09.6	222 40.7
06	267 06.1	6 07.7	252 45.6
08	297 06.3	6 05.8	282 50.6
10	327 06.6	6 03.8	312 55.5
12	357 06.9	6 01.9	343 00.4
14	27 07.2	6 00.0	13 05.3
16	57 07.5	5 58.0	43 10.3
18	87 07.7	5 56.1	73 15.2
20	117 08.0	5 54.2	103 20.1
22	147 08.3	S5 52.2	133 25.1

Sunday, March 6

Time	SUN GHA ° ′	Dec ° ′	ARIES GHA ° ′
00	177 08.6	S5 50.3	163 30.0
02	207 08.9	5 48.4	193 34.9
04	237 09.2	5 46.4	223 39.8
06	267 09.5	5 44.5	253 44.8
08	297 09.8	5 42.6	283 49.7
10	327 10.0	5 40.6	313 54.6
12	357 10.3	5 38.7	343 59.6
14	27 10.6	5 36.7	14 04.5
16	57 10.9	5 34.8	44 09.4
18	87 11.2	5 32.9	74 14.3
20	117 11.5	5 30.9	104 19.3
22	147 11.8	S5 29.0	134 24.2

Monday, March 7

Time	SUN GHA ° ′	Dec ° ′	ARIES GHA ° ′
00	177 12.1	S5 27.0	164 29.1
02	207 12.4	5 25.1	194 34.1
04	237 12.7	5 23.2	224 39.0
06	267 13.0	5 21.2	254 43.9
08	297 13.3	5 19.3	284 48.8
10	327 13.6	5 17.3	314 53.8
12	357 13.9	5 15.4	344 58.7
14	27 14.2	5 13.4	15 03.6
16	57 14.5	5 11.5	45 08.5
18	87 14.8	5 09.5	75 13.5
20	117 15.1	5 07.6	105 18.4
22	147 15.4	S5 05.6	135 23.3

Tuesday, March 8

Time	SUN GHA ° ′	Dec ° ′	ARIES GHA ° ′
00	177 15.7	S5 03.7	165 28.3
02	207 16.0	5 01.8	195 33.2
04	237 16.3	4 59.8	225 38.1
06	267 16.6	4 57.9	255 43.0
08	297 16.9	4 55.9	285 48.0
10	327 17.2	4 54.0	315 52.9
12	357 17.5	4 52.0	345 57.8
14	27 17.8	4 50.1	16 02.8
16	57 18.1	4 48.1	46 07.7
18	87 18.4	4 46.2	76 12.6
20	117 18.7	4 44.2	106 17.5
22	147 19.1	S4 42.2	136 22.5

Wednesday, March 9

Time	SUN GHA ° ′	Dec ° ′	ARIES GHA ° ′
00	177 19.4	S4 40.3	166 27.4
02	207 19.7	4 38.3	196 32.3
04	237 20.0	4 36.4	226 37.3
06	267 20.3	4 34.4	256 42.2
08	297 20.6	4 32.5	286 47.1
10	327 20.9	4 30.5	316 52.0
12	357 21.2	4 28.6	346 56.9
14	27 21.6	4 26.6	17 01.9
16	57 21.9	4 24.7	47 06.8
18	87 22.2	4 22.7	77 11.8
20	117 22.5	4 20.7	107 16.7
22	147 22.8	S4 18.8	137 21.6

Thursday, March 10

Time	SUN GHA ° ′	Dec ° ′	ARIES GHA ° ′
00	177 23.1	S4 16.8	167 26.5
02	207 23.4	4 14.9	197 31.5
04	237 23.8	4 12.9	227 36.4
06	267 24.1	4 11.0	257 41.3
08	297 24.4	4 09.0	287 46.3
10	327 24.7	4 07.0	317 51.2
12	357 25.0	4 05.1	347 56.1
14	27 25.4	4 03.1	18 01.0
16	57 25.7	4 01.2	48 06.0
18	87 26.0	3 59.2	78 10.9
20	117 26.3	3 57.2	108 15.8
22	147 26.7	S3 55.3	138 20.8

Friday, March 11

Time	SUN GHA ° ′	Dec ° ′	ARIES GHA ° ′
00	177 27.0	S3 53.3	168 25.7
02	207 27.3	3 51.3	198 30.6
04	237 27.6	3 49.4	228 35.5
06	267 28.0	3 47.4	258 40.5
08	297 28.3	3 45.5	288 45.4
10	327 28.6	3 43.5	318 50.3
12	357 28.9	3 41.5	348 55.2
14	27 29.3	3 39.6	19 00.2
16	57 29.6	3 37.6	49 05.1
18	87 29.9	3 35.6	79 10.0
20	117 30.2	3 33.7	109 15.0
22	147 30.6	S3 31.7	139 19.9

Saturday, March 12

Time	SUN GHA ° ′	Dec ° ′	ARIES GHA ° ′
00	177 30.9	S3 29.7	169 24.8
02	207 31.2	3 27.8	199 29.7
04	237 31.6	3 25.8	229 34.7
06	267 31.9	3 23.8	259 39.6
08	297 32.2	3 21.9	289 44.5
10	327 32.6	3 19.9	319 49.5
12	357 32.9	3 17.9	349 54.4
14	27 33.2	3 16.0	19 59.3
16	57 33.6	3 14.0	50 04.2
18	87 33.9	3 12.0	80 09.2
20	117 34.2	3 10.1	110 14.1
22	147 34.6	S3 08.1	140 19.0

Sunday, March 13

Time	SUN GHA ° ′	Dec ° ′	ARIES GHA ° ′
00	177 34.9	S3 06.1	170 24.0
02	207 35.2	3 04.2	200 28.9
04	237 35.6	3 02.2	230 33.8
06	267 35.9	3 00.2	260 38.7
08	297 36.3	2 58.2	290 43.7
10	327 36.6	2 56.3	320 48.6
12	357 36.9	2 54.3	350 53.5
14	27 37.3	2 52.3	20 58.5
16	57 37.6	2 50.4	51 03.4
18	87 38.0	2 48.4	81 08.3
20	117 38.3	2 46.4	111 13.2
22	147 38.6	S2 44.5	141 18.2

Monday, March 14

Time	SUN GHA ° ′	Dec ° ′	ARIES GHA ° ′
00	177 38.9	S2 42.5	171 23.1
02	207 39.3	2 40.5	201 28.0
04	237 39.7	2 38.5	231 33.0
06	267 40.0	2 36.6	261 37.9
08	297 40.4	2 34.6	291 42.8
10	327 40.7	2 32.6	321 47.7
12	357 41.0	2 30.6	351 52.7
14	27 41.4	2 28.7	21 57.6
16	57 41.7	2 26.7	52 02.5
18	87 42.1	2 24.7	82 07.4
20	117 42.4	2 22.8	112 12.4
22	147 42.8	S2 20.8	142 17.3

Tuesday, March 15

Time	SUN GHA ° ′	Dec ° ′	ARIES GHA ° ′
00	177 43.1	S2 18.8	172 22.2
02	207 43.5	2 16.8	202 27.2
04	237 43.8	2 14.9	232 32.1
06	267 44.2	2 12.9	262 37.0
08	297 44.5	2 10.9	292 41.9
10	327 44.9	2 08.9	322 46.9
12	357 45.2	2 07.0	352 51.8
14	27 45.6	2 05.0	22 56.7
16	57 45.9	2 03.0	53 01.7
18	87 46.3	2 01.0	83 06.6
20	117 46.6	1 59.1	113 11.5
22	147 47.0	S1 57.1	143 16.4

MARCH 1994 — SUN & ARIES — GMT

Wednesday, March 16

Time	SUN GHA	Dec	ARIES GHA
00	177 47.3	S1 55.1	173 21.4
02	207 47.7	1 53.1	203 26.3
04	237 48.0	1 51.2	233 31.3
06	267 48.4	1 49.2	263 36.2
08	297 48.7	1 47.2	293 41.1
10	327 49.1	1 45.2	323 46.0
12	357 49.4	1 43.3	353 50.9
14	27 49.8	1 41.3	23 55.9
16	57 50.1	1 39.3	54 00.8
18	87 50.5	1 37.3	84 05.7
20	117 50.9	1 35.3	114 10.7
22	147 51.2	S1 33.4	144 15.6

Thursday, March 17

Time	SUN GHA	Dec	ARIES GHA
00	177 51.6	S1 31.4	174 20.5
02	207 51.9	1 29.4	204 25.4
04	237 52.3	1 27.4	234 30.4
06	267 52.6	1 25.5	264 35.3
08	297 53.0	1 23.5	294 40.2
10	327 53.4	1 21.5	324 45.2
12	357 53.7	1 19.5	354 50.1
14	27 54.1	1 17.6	24 55.0
16	57 54.4	1 15.6	54 59.9
18	87 54.8	1 13.6	85 04.9
20	117 55.2	1 11.6	115 09.8
22	147 55.5	S1 09.7	145 14.7

Friday, March 18

Time	SUN GHA	Dec	ARIES GHA
00	177 55.9	S1 07.7	175 19.6
02	207 56.2	1 05.7	205 24.6
04	237 56.6	1 03.7	235 29.5
06	267 57.0	1 01.7	265 34.4
08	297 57.3	0 59.8	295 39.4
10	327 57.7	0 57.8	325 44.3
12	357 58.1	0 55.8	355 49.2
14	27 58.4	0 53.8	25 54.1
16	57 58.8	0 51.9	55 59.1
18	87 59.2	0 49.9	86 04.0
20	117 59.5	0 47.9	116 08.9
22	147 59.9	S0 45.9	146 13.9

Saturday, March 19

Time	SUN GHA	Dec	ARIES GHA
00	178 00.2	S0 43.9	176 18.8
02	208 00.6	0 42.0	206 23.7
04	238 01.0	0 40.0	236 28.6
06	268 01.3	0 38.0	266 33.6
08	298 01.7	0 36.0	296 38.5
10	328 02.1	0 34.1	326 43.4
12	358 02.4	0 32.1	356 48.4
14	28 02.8	0 30.1	26 53.3
16	58 03.2	0 28.1	56 58.2
18	88 03.5	0 26.2	87 03.1
20	118 03.9	0 24.2	117 08.1
22	148 04.3	S0 22.2	147 13.0

Sunday, March 20

Time	SUN GHA	Dec	ARIES GHA
00	178 04.7	S0 20.2	177 17.9
02	208 05.0	0 18.3	207 22.9
04	238 05.4	0 16.3	237 27.8
06	268 05.8	0 14.3	267 32.7
08	298 06.1	0 12.3	297 37.6
10	328 06.5	0 10.3	327 42.6
12	358 06.9	0 08.4	357 47.5
14	28 07.2	0 06.4	27 52.4
16	58 07.6	0 04.4	57 57.4
18	88 08.0	0 02.4	88 02.3
20	118 08.4	0 00.5	118 07.2
22	148 08.7	N0 01.5	148 12.1

Monday, March 21

Time	SUN GHA	Dec	ARIES GHA
00	178 09.1	N0 03.5	178 17.1
02	208 09.5	0 05.5	208 22.0
04	238 09.8	0 07.4	238 26.9
06	268 10.2	0 09.4	268 31.8
08	298 10.6	0 11.4	298 36.8
10	328 11.0	0 13.4	328 41.7
12	358 11.3	0 15.3	358 46.6
14	28 11.7	0 17.3	28 51.6
16	58 12.1	0 19.3	58 56.5
18	88 12.5	0 21.3	89 01.4
20	118 12.8	0 23.2	119 06.3
22	148 13.2	N0 25.2	149 11.3

Tuesday, March 22

Time	SUN GHA	Dec	ARIES GHA
00	178 13.6	N0 27.2	179 16.2
02	208 14.0	0 29.2	209 21.1
04	238 14.3	0 31.1	239 26.1
06	268 14.7	0 33.1	269 31.0
08	298 15.1	0 35.1	299 35.9
10	328 15.5	0 37.0	329 40.8
12	358 15.8	0 39.0	359 45.8
14	28 16.2	0 41.0	29 50.7
16	58 16.6	0 43.0	59 55.6
18	88 17.0	0 44.9	90 00.6
20	118 17.3	0 46.9	120 05.5
22	148 17.7	N0 48.9	150 10.4

Wednesday, March 23

Time	SUN GHA	Dec	ARIES GHA
00	178 18.1	N0 50.9	180 15.3
02	208 18.5	0 52.8	210 20.3
04	238 18.8	0 54.8	240 25.2
06	268 19.2	0 56.8	270 30.1
08	298 19.6	0 58.7	300 35.1
10	328 20.0	1 00.7	330 40.0
12	358 20.4	1 02.7	0 44.9
14	28 20.7	1 04.6	30 49.8
16	58 21.1	1 06.6	60 54.8
18	88 21.5	1 08.6	90 59.7
20	118 21.9	1 10.6	121 04.6
22	148 22.3	N1 12.5	151 09.6

Thursday, March 24

Time	SUN GHA	Dec	ARIES GHA
00	178 22.6	N1 14.5	181 14.5
02	208 23.0	1 16.5	211 19.4
04	238 23.4	1 18.4	241 24.3
06	268 23.8	1 20.4	271 29.3
08	298 24.1	1 22.4	301 34.2
10	328 24.5	1 24.3	331 39.1
12	358 24.9	1 26.3	1 44.1
14	28 25.3	1 28.3	31 49.0
16	58 25.7	1 30.2	61 53.9
18	88 26.0	1 32.2	91 58.8
20	118 26.4	1 34.2	122 03.8
22	148 26.8	N1 36.1	152 08.7

Friday, March 25

Time	SUN GHA	Dec	ARIES GHA
00	178 27.2	N1 38.1	182 13.6
02	208 27.6	1 40.1	212 18.5
04	238 27.9	1 42.0	242 23.5
06	268 28.3	1 44.0	272 28.4
08	298 28.7	1 46.0	302 33.3
10	328 29.1	1 47.9	332 38.3
12	358 29.5	1 49.9	2 43.2
14	28 29.8	1 51.9	32 48.1
16	58 30.2	1 53.8	62 53.0
18	88 30.6	1 55.8	92 58.0
20	118 31.0	1 57.7	123 02.9
22	148 31.4	N1 59.7	153 07.8

Saturday, March 26

Time	SUN GHA	Dec	ARIES GHA
00	178 31.8	N2 01.7	183 12.8
02	208 32.1	2 03.6	213 17.7
04	238 32.5	2 05.6	243 22.6
06	268 32.9	2 07.6	273 27.5
08	298 33.3	2 09.5	303 32.5
10	328 33.7	2 11.5	333 37.4
12	358 34.0	2 13.4	3 42.3
14	28 34.4	2 15.4	33 47.2
16	58 34.8	2 17.4	63 52.2
18	88 35.2	2 19.3	93 57.1
20	118 35.6	2 21.3	124 02.0
22	148 35.9	N2 23.2	154 07.0

Sunday, March 27

Time	SUN GHA	Dec	ARIES GHA
00	178 36.3	N2 25.2	184 11.9
02	208 36.7	2 27.2	214 16.8
04	238 37.1	2 29.1	244 21.8
06	268 37.5	2 31.1	274 26.7
08	298 37.8	2 33.0	304 31.6
10	328 38.2	2 35.0	334 36.5
12	358 38.6	2 36.9	4 41.5
14	28 39.0	2 38.9	34 46.4
16	58 39.4	2 40.9	64 51.3
18	88 39.8	2 42.8	94 56.3
20	118 40.1	2 44.8	125 01.2
22	148 40.5	N2 46.7	155 06.1

Monday, March 28

Time	SUN GHA	Dec	ARIES GHA
00	178 40.9	N2 48.7	185 11.0
02	208 41.3	2 50.6	215 16.0
04	238 41.7	2 52.6	245 20.9
06	268 42.0	2 54.5	275 25.8
08	298 42.4	2 56.5	305 30.7
10	328 42.8	2 58.4	335 35.7
12	358 43.2	3 00.4	5 40.6
14	28 43.6	3 02.3	35 45.5
16	58 43.9	3 04.3	65 50.5
18	88 44.3	3 06.2	95 55.4
20	118 44.7	3 08.2	126 00.3
22	148 45.1	N3 10.1	156 05.2

Tuesday, March 29

Time	SUN GHA	Dec	ARIES GHA
00	178 45.5	N3 12.1	186 10.2
02	208 45.9	3 14.0	216 15.1
04	238 46.2	3 16.0	246 20.0
06	268 46.6	3 17.9	276 25.0
08	298 47.0	3 19.9	306 29.9
10	328 47.4	3 21.8	336 34.8
12	358 47.7	3 23.8	6 39.7
14	28 48.1	3 25.7	36 44.7
16	58 48.5	3 27.7	66 49.6
18	88 48.9	3 29.6	96 54.5
20	118 49.2	3 31.6	126 59.5
22	148 49.6	N3 33.5	157 04.4

Wednesday, March 30

Time	SUN GHA	Dec	ARIES GHA
00	178 50.0	N3 35.5	187 09.3
02	208 50.4	3 37.4	217 14.2
04	238 50.8	3 39.3	247 19.2
06	268 51.1	3 41.3	277 24.1
08	298 51.5	3 43.2	307 29.0
10	328 51.9	3 45.2	337 34.0
12	358 52.3	3 47.1	7 38.9
14	28 52.6	3 49.1	37 43.8
16	58 53.0	3 51.0	67 48.7
18	88 53.4	3 52.9	97 53.7
20	118 53.8	3 54.9	127 58.6
22	148 54.1	N3 56.8	158 03.5

Thursday, March 31

Time	SUN GHA	Dec	ARIES GHA
00	178 54.5	N3 58.8	188 08.5
02	208 54.9	4 00.7	218 13.4
04	238 55.3	4 02.6	248 18.3
06	268 55.7	N4 04.6	278 23.2
08	298 56.0	N4 06.5	308 28.2
10	328 56.4	4 08.4	338 33.1
12	358 56.8	4 10.4	8 38.0
14	28 57.2	N4 12.3	38 42.9
16	58 57.5	N4 14.2	68 47.9
18	88 57.9	4 16.2	98 52.8
20	118 58.3	4 18.1	128 57.7
22	148 58.7	N4 20.0	159 02.7

Chapter 6

MARCH 1994 — PLANETS — 0h GMT

VENUS / JUPITER

Mer Pass h m	GHA ° '	Mean Var/hr 14°+	Dec ° '	Mean Var/hr '			GHA ° '	Mean Var/hr 15°+	Dec ° '	Mean Var/hr '	Mer Pass h m
12 53	166 43.0	59.6	S 5 02.3	1.3	1	Tue	295 58.8	2.5	S14 59.2	0.0	04 15
12 54	166 34.0	59.6	S 4 32.1	1.3	2	Wed	296 58.1	2.5	S14 59.0	0.0	04 11
12 55	166 24.6	59.6	S 4 01.8	1.3	3	Thu	297 57.5	2.5	S14 58.7	0.0	04 07
12 55	166 15.2	59.6	S 3 31.4	1.3	4	Fri	298 57.1	2.5	S14 58.4	0.0	04 04
12 56	166 06.0	59.6	S 3 00.9	1.3	5	Sat	299 56.9	2.5	S14 58.0	0.0	04 00
12 57	165 56.8	59.6	S 2 30.3	1.3	6	SUN	300 57.0	2.5	S14 57.6	0.0	03 56
12 57	165 47.8	59.6	S 1 59.6	1.3	7	Mon	301 57.1	2.5	S14 57.1	0.0	03 52
12 58	165 38.8	59.6	S 1 28.9	1.3	8	Tue	302 57.5	2.5	S14 56.5	0.0	03 48
12 58	165 29.8	59.6	S 0 58.1	1.3	9	Wed	303 58.1	2.5	S14 55.9	0.0	03 43
12 59	165 21.0	59.6	S 0 27.3	1.3	10	Thu	304 58.8	2.5	S14 55.2	0.0	03 39
13 00	165 12.1	59.6	N 0 03.5	1.3	11	Fri	305 59.8	2.5	S14 54.5	0.0	03 35
13 00	165 03.3	59.6	N 0 34.3	1.3	12	Sat	307 00.9	2.6	S14 53.8	0.0	03 31
13 01	164 54.5	59.6	N 1 05.2	1.3	13	SUN	308 02.2	2.6	S14 53.0	0.0	03 27
13 01	164 45.7	59.6	N 1 36.0	1.3	14	Mon	309 03.7	2.6	S14 52.1	0.0	03 23
13 02	164 36.9	59.6	N 2 06.8	1.3	15	Tue	310 05.3	2.6	S14 51.2	0.0	03 19
13 02	164 28.1	59.6	N 2 37.6	1.3	16	Wed	311 07.1	2.6	S14 50.2	0.0	03 15
13 03	164 19.2	59.6	N 3 08.3	1.3	17	Thu	312 09.2	2.6	S14 49.2	0.0	03 11
13 04	164 10.4	59.6	N 3 39.0	1.3	18	Fri	313 11.4	2.6	S14 48.1	0.0	03 07
13 04	164 01.4	59.6	N 4 09.5	1.3	19	Sat	314 13.7	2.6	S14 47.0	0.1	03 03
13 05	163 52.5	59.6	N 4 40.0	1.3	20	SUN	315 16.2	2.6	S14 45.8	0.1	02 58
13 05	163 43.5	59.6	N 5 10.4	1.3	21	Mon	316 19.0	2.6	S14 44.6	0.1	02 54
13 06	163 34.4	59.6	N 5 40.7	1.3	22	Tue	317 21.8	2.6	S14 43.4	0.1	02 50
13 07	163 25.2	59.6	N 6 10.9	1.3	23	Wed	318 24.9	2.6	S14 42.0	0.1	02 46
13 07	163 15.9	59.6	N 6 40.9	1.2	24	Thu	319 28.1	2.6	S14 40.7	0.1	02 42
13 08	163 06.6	59.6	N 7 10.7	1.2	25	Fri	320 31.4	2.6	S14 39.3	0.1	02 37
13 09	162 57.1	59.6	N 7 40.4	1.2	26	Sat	321 34.9	2.7	S14 37.8	0.1	02 33
13 09	162 47.5	59.6	N 8 10.0	1.2	27	SUN	322 38.6	2.7	S14 36.3	0.1	02 29
13 10	162 37.7	59.6	N 8 39.3	1.2	28	Mon	323 42.4	2.7	S14 34.8	0.1	02 25
13 11	162 27.9	59.6	N 9 08.4	1.2	29	Tue	324 46.4	2.7	S14 33.2	0.1	02 20
13 11	162 17.8	59.6	N 9 37.4	1.2	30	Wed	325 50.5	2.7	S14 31.6	0.1	02 16
13 12	162 07.6	59.6	N10 06.1	1.2	31	Thu	326 54.7	2.7	S14 29.9	0.1	02 12

VENUS, Av Mag –3.9
SHA March
5 4; 10 358; 15 352; 20 347; 25 341; 30 335.

JUPITER, Av Mag –2.3
SHA March
5 137; 10 138; 15 138; 20 138; 25 138; 30 139.

MARS / SATURN

Mer Pass h m	GHA ° '	Mean Var/hr 15°+	Dec ° '	Mean Var/hr '			GHA ° '	Mean Var/hr 15°+	Dec ° '	Mean Var/hr '	Mer Pass h m
11 16	190 59.2	0.6	S14 15.2	0.7	1	Tue	182 24.4	2.2	S11 28.8	0.1	11 49
11 15	191 12.5	0.6	S13 59.4	0.7	2	Wed	183 16.6	2.2	S11 26.2	0.1	11 45
11 14	191 25.9	0.6	S13 43.5	0.7	3	Thu	184 08.8	2.2	S11 23.6	0.1	11 42
11 13	191 39.4	0.6	S13 27.4	0.7	4	Fri	185 01.0	2.2	S11 21.0	0.1	11 38
11 12	191 53.0	0.6	S13 11.1	0.7	5	Sat	185 53.3	2.2	S11 18.5	0.1	11 35
11 11	192 06.8	0.6	S12 54.8	0.7	6	SUN	186 45.5	2.2	S11 15.9	0.1	11 31
11 10	192 20.6	0.6	S12 38.3	0.7	7	Mon	187 37.8	2.2	S11 13.4	0.1	11 28
11 09	192 34.5	0.6	S12 21.7	0.7	8	Tue	188 30.1	2.2	S11 10.8	0.1	11 24
11 08	192 48.5	0.6	S12 05.0	0.7	9	Wed	189 22.4	2.2	S11 08.3	0.1	11 21
11 07	193 02.5	0.6	S11 48.1	0.7	10	Thu	190 14.7	2.2	S11 05.7	0.1	11 17
11 06	193 16.7	0.6	S11 31.2	0.7	11	Fri	191 07.0	2.2	S11 03.2	0.1	11 14
11 05	193 31.0	0.6	S11 14.1	0.7	12	Sat	191 59.4	2.2	S11 00.7	0.1	11 10
11 05	193 45.3	0.6	S10 57.0	0.7	13	SUN	192 51.8	2.2	S10 58.1	0.1	11 07
11 04	193 59.8	0.6	S10 39.7	0.7	14	Mon	193 44.2	2.2	S10 55.6	0.1	11 03
11 03	194 14.3	0.6	S10 22.3	0.7	15	Tue	194 36.6	2.2	S10 53.1	0.1	11 00
11 02	194 28.9	0.6	S10 04.9	0.7	16	Wed	195 29.1	2.2	S10 50.6	0.1	10 56
11 01	194 43.6	0.6	S 9 47.3	0.7	17	Thu	196 21.5	2.2	S10 48.1	0.1	10 53
11 00	194 58.4	0.6	S 9 29.7	0.7	18	Fri	197 14.0	2.2	S10 45.6	0.1	10 49
10 59	195 13.3	0.6	S 9 12.0	0.7	19	Sat	198 06.5	2.2	S10 43.2	0.1	10 46
10 58	195 28.2	0.6	S 8 54.2	0.7	20	SUN	198 59.1	2.2	S10 40.7	0.1	10 42
10 57	195 43.3	0.6	S 8 36.3	0.8	21	Mon	199 51.7	2.2	S10 38.3	0.1	10 39
10 56	195 58.4	0.6	S 8 18.3	0.8	22	Tue	200 44.3	2.2	S10 35.8	0.1	10 35
10 55	196 13.6	0.6	S 8 00.3	0.8	23	Wed	201 36.9	2.2	S10 33.4	0.1	10 32
10 54	196 28.9	0.6	S 7 42.2	0.8	24	Thu	202 29.6	2.2	S10 31.0	0.1	10 28
10 53	196 44.2	0.6	S 7 24.0	0.8	25	Fri	203 22.3	2.2	S10 28.6	0.1	10 25
10 52	196 59.6	0.6	S 7 05.8	0.8	26	Sat	204 15.0	2.2	S10 26.2	0.1	10 21
10 51	197 15.1	0.7	S 6 47.5	0.8	27	SUN	205 07.8	2.2	S10 23.8	0.1	10 18
10 49	197 30.7	0.7	S 6 29.2	0.8	28	Mon	206 00.6	2.2	S10 21.5	0.1	10 14
10 48	197 46.3	0.7	S 6 10.8	0.8	29	Tue	206 53.5	2.2	S10 19.1	0.1	10 11
10 47	198 01.9	0.7	S 5 52.4	0.8	30	Wed	207 46.3	2.2	S10 16.8	0.1	10 07
10 46	198 17.7	0.7	S 5 33.9	0.8	31	Thu	208 39.2	2.2	S10 14.5	0.1	10 04

MARS, Av Mag +1.2
SHA March
5 29; 10 26; 15 22; 20 18; 25 15; 30 11.

SATURN, Av Mag +1.0
SHA March
5 23; 10 23; 15 22; 20 22; 25 21; 30 21.

MARCH 1994 — MOON

Day	GMT hr	GHA ° '	Mean Var/hr 14°+	Dec ° '	Mean Var/hr '	Day	GMT hr	GHA ° '	Mean Var/hr 14°+	Dec ° '	Mean Var/hr '
1 Tue	0	320 19.1	26.6	S 10 56.1	11.3	17 Thu	0	129 34.1	31.9	N 17 43.0	5.5
	6	46 58.7	26.4	S 12 03.8	10.7		6	216 45.5	31.6	N 18 16.5	5.1
	12	133 37.2	26.2	S 13 08.5	10.2		12	303 55.5	31.4	N 18 47.1	4.5
	18	220 14.6	26.0	S 14 10.0	9.6		18	31 04.2	31.1	N 19 14.7	4.0
2 Wed	0	306 50.9	25.9	S 15 07.9	9.0	18 Fri	0	118 11.4	31.0	N 19 39.2	3.5
	6	33 26.2	25.7	S 16 02.1	8.3		6	205 17.3	30.8	N 20 00.4	3.0
	12	120 00.5	25.6	S 16 52.3	7.6		12	292 21.9	30.5	N 20 18.4	2.4
	18	206 34.1	25.5	S 17 38.3	6.9		18	19 25.1	30.3	N 20 32.5	1.8
3 Thu	0	293 06.9	25.4	S 18 20.0	6.1	19 Sat	0	106 27.2	30.2	N 20 44.0	1.2
	6	19 39.2	25.3	S 18 57.2	5.3		6	193 28.0	30.0	N 20 51.5	0.6
	12	106 11.1	25.3	S 19 29.8	4.5		12	280 27.8	29.8	N 20 55.4	0.0
	18	192 42.9	25.3	S 19 57.6	3.8		18	7 26.5	29.6	N 20 55.5	0.6
4 Fri	0	279 14.7	25.3	S 20 20.7	2.9	20 Sun	0	94 24.2	29.4	N 20 51.9	1.3
	6	5 46.7	25.5	S 20 38.9	2.2		6	181 21.1	29.4	N 20 44.5	1.9
	12	92 19.3	25.6	S 20 52.3	1.3		12	268 17.2	29.2	N 20 33.3	2.6
	18	178 52.5	25.7	S 21 00.8	0.6		18	355 12.6	29.1	N 20 18.2	3.2
5 Sat	0	265 26.8	25.9	S 21 04.6	0.2	21 Mon	0	82 07.4	29.0	N 19 59.2	3.9
	6	352 02.1	26.1	S 21 03.6	1.0		6	169 01.7	29.0	N 19 36.3	4.5
	12	78 38.9	26.4	S 20 58.0	1.7		12	255 55.5	28.9	N 19 09.5	5.1
	18	165 17.2	26.7	S 20 47.9	2.5		18	342 49.0	28.8	N 18 38.8	5.8
6 Sun	0	251 57.2	27.1	S 20 33.3	3.2	22 Tue	0	69 42.1	28.8	N 18 04.3	6.5
	6	338 39.2	27.4	S 20 14.5	3.9		6	156 35.0	28.7	N 17 26.1	7.0
	12	65 23.2	27.7	S 19 51.5	4.5		12	243 27.7	28.7	N 16 44.1	7.6
	18	152 09.4	28.1	S 19 24.6	5.2		18	330 20.2	28.7	N 15 58.4	8.3
7 Mon	0	238 57.8	28.5	S 18 53.9	5.8	23 Wed	0	57 12.6	28.7	N 15 09.3	8.9
	6	325 48.5	28.8	S 18 19.6	6.3		6	144 04.8	28.7	N 14 16.6	9.3
	12	52 41.6	29.3	S 17 41.9	6.8		12	230 56.9	28.7	N 13 20.7	9.9
	18	139 37.1	29.7	S 17 01.0	7.3		18	317 48.8	28.7	N 12 21.5	10.4
8 Tue	0	226 34.9	30.1	S 16 17.1	7.8	24 Thu	0	44 40.5	28.6	N 11 19.4	10.9
	6	313 35.1	30.5	S 15 30.5	8.3		6	131 31.9	28.5	N 10 14.4	11.4
	12	40 37.6	30.8	S 14 41.2	8.7		12	218 23.1	28.4	N 9 06.7	11.7
	18	127 42.4	31.2	S 13 49.6	9.0		18	305 13.9	28.3	N 7 56.6	12.1
9 Wed	0	214 49.4	31.6	S 12 55.7	9.4	25 Fri	0	32 04.3	28.3	N 6 44.3	12.4
	6	301 58.4	31.9	S 11 59.9	9.6		6	118 54.1	28.2	N 5 30.0	12.7
	12	29 09.5	32.2	S 11 02.3	9.9		12	205 43.3	28.1	N 4 14.0	13.0
	18	116 22.4	32.5	S 10 03.1	10.2		18	292 31.8	27.9	N 2 56.6	13.1
10 Thu	0	203 37.1	32.7	S 9 02.5	10.3	26 Sat	0	19 19.4	27.8	N 1 38.1	13.2
	6	290 53.4	33.0	S 8 00.7	10.4		6	106 06.1	27.5	N 0 18.7	13.3
	12	18 11.3	33.2	S 6 57.8	10.6		12	192 51.7	27.4	S 1 01.1	13.4
	18	105 30.6	33.4	S 5 54.1	10.7		18	279 36.2	27.2	S 2 21.0	13.3
11 Fri	0	192 51.1	33.7	S 4 49.7	10.9	27 Sun	0	6 19.4	27.0	S 3 40.7	13.2
	6	280 12.7	33.7	S 3 44.7	10.8		6	93 01.3	26.7	S 4 59.9	13.0
	12	7 35.3	33.9	S 2 39.5	10.9		12	179 41.7	26.5	S 6 18.1	12.8
	18	94 58.7	34.0	S 1 34.0	10.9		18	266 20.6	26.2	S 7 35.0	12.5
12 Sat	0	182 22.8	34.1	S 0 28.6	10.9	28 Mon	0	352 57.9	26.0	S 8 50.1	12.1
	6	269 47.4	34.2	N 0 36.8	10.9		6	79 33.7	25.6	S 10 03.2	11.7
	12	357 12.5	34.3	N 1 41.8	10.7		12	166 07.8	25.4	S 11 13.9	11.3
	18	84 37.8	34.3	N 2 46.4	10.7		18	252 40.4	25.1	S 12 21.8	10.7
13 Sun	0	172 03.3	34.3	N 3 50.4	10.5	29 Tue	0	339 11.4	25.0	S 13 26.5	10.2
	6	259 28.7	34.3	N 4 53.7	10.4		6	65 40.9	24.7	S 14 27.8	9.6
	12	346 54.1	34.1	N 5 56.1	10.2		12	152 09.1	24.5	S 15 25.3	8.9
	18	74 19.2	34.1	N 6 57.5	10.0		18	238 36.0	24.3	S 16 18.7	8.1
14 Mon	0	161 43.9	34.1	N 7 57.8	9.8	30 Wed	0	325 01.9	24.2	S 17 07.9	7.3
	6	249 08.1	33.9	N 8 56.7	9.5		6	51 26.9	24.0	S 17 52.5	6.6
	12	336 31.7	33.8	N 9 54.2	9.3		12	137 51.3	24.0	S 18 32.4	5.7
	18	63 54.6	33.7	N 10 50.2	9.0		18	224 15.2	24.0	S 19 07.4	4.9
15 Tue	0	151 16.6	33.6	N 11 44.5	8.7	31 Thu	0	310 39.1	24.0	S 19 37.4	4.0
	6	238 37.8	33.4	N 12 37.0	8.4		6	37 03.0	24.1	S 20 02.3	3.2
	12	325 58.0	33.1	N 13 27.5	8.1		12	123 27.5	24.2	S 20 22.1	2.4
	18	53 17.1	33.0	N 14 16.0	7.7		18	209 52.7	24.4	S 20 36.7	1.5
16 Wed	0	140 35.0	32.8	N 15 02.2	7.3						
	6	227 51.7	32.6	N 15 46.2	6.9						
	12	315 07.2	32.3	N 16 27.7	6.5						
	18	42 21.3	32.1	N 17 06.7	6.0						

Chapter 6

APRIL 1994 — SUN & MOON — GMT

SUN

Yr	Mth	Week	Equation of Time 0h (m s)	Equation of Time 12h (m s)	Transit (h m)	Semi-diam (')	Lat 52°N Twilight (h m)	Sunrise (h m)	Sunset (h m)	Twilight (h m)	Lat	Lat Corr Twilight	Sunrise	Sunset	Twilight
91	1	Fri	+04 04	+03 55	12 04	16.0	05 01	05 36	18 33	19 08	N70	-1 50	-1 05	+1 09	+1 50
92	2	Sat	+03 46	+03 37	12 04	16.0	04 59	05 33	18 35	19 09	68	-1 26	-0 53	+0 55	+1 27
93	3	Sun	+03 28	+03 20	12 03	16.0	04 57	05 31	18 37	19 11	66	-1 07	-0 42	+0 44	+1 08
94	4	Mon	+03 11	+03 02	12 03	16.0	04 54	05 29	18 38	19 13	64	-0 52	-0 33	+0 35	+0 53
95	5	Tue	+02 53	+02 45	12 03	16.0	04 52	05 26	18 40	19 15	62	-0 40	-0 26	+0 27	+0 41
96	6	Wed	+02 36	+02 27	12 02	16.0	04 49	05 24	18 42	19 17	N60	-0 30	-0 19	+0 20	+0 30
97	7	Thu	+02 19	+02 11	12 02	16.0	04 47	05 22	18 44	19 19	58	-0 21	-0 13	+0 14	+0 21
98	8	Fri	+02 02	+01 54	12 02	16.0	04 45	05 20	18 45	19 20	56	-0 13	-0 08	+0 09	+0 13
99	9	Sat	+01 46	+01 37	12 02	16.0	04 42	05 17	18 47	19 22	54	-0 06	-0 04	+0 04	+0 06
100	10	Sun	+01 29	+01 21	12 01	16.0	04 40	05 15	18 49	19 24	50	+0 05	+0 04	-0 04	-0 05
101	11	Mon	+01 13	+01 05	12 01	16.0	04 38	05 13	18 50	19 26	N45	+0 17	+0 12	-0 11	-0 17
102	12	Tue	+00 57	+00 50	12 01	16.0	04 35	05 11	18 52	19 28	40	+0 26	+0 19	-0 18	-0 25
103	13	Wed	+00 42	+00 34	12 01	16.0	04 33	05 08	18 54	19 30	35	+0 33	+0 25	-0 24	-0 33
104	14	Thu	+00 27	+00 19	12 00	16.0	04 31	05 06	18 56	19 31	30	+0 40	+0 30	-0 29	-0 40
105	15	Fri	+00 12	+00 05	12 00	16.0	04 28	05 04	18 57	19 33	20	+0 51	+0 38	-0 38	-0 50
106	16	Sat	-00 03	-00 10	12 00	16.0	04 26	05 02	18 59	19 35	N10	+0 59	+0 45	-0 42	-0 59
107	17	Sun	-00 17	-00 24	12 00	16.0	04 24	05 00	19 01	19 37	0	+1 07	+0 52	-0 53	-1 07
108	18	Mon	-00 31	-00 37	11 59	16.0	04 21	04 58	19 02	19 39	S10	+1 12	+0 59	-0 59	-1 13
109	19	Tue	-00 44	-00 51	11 59	15.9	04 19	04 55	19 04	19 41	20	+1 18	+1 05	-1 06	-1 18
110	20	Wed	-00 57	-01 04	11 59	15.9	04 17	04 53	19 06	19 43	30	+1 24	+1 13	-1 15	-1 24
111	21	Thu	-01 10	-01 16	11 59	15.9	04 14	04 51	19 07	19 44	S35	+1 27	+1 17	-1 19	-1 27
112	22	Fri	-01 22	-01 28	11 59	15.9	04 12	04 49	19 09	19 46	40	+1 30	+1 22	-1 24	-1 30
113	23	Sat	-01 34	-01 40	11 58	15.9	04 10	04 47	19 11	19 48	45	+1 34	+1 28	-1 30	-1 34
114	24	Sun	-01 45	-01 51	11 58	15.9	04 08	04 45	19 13	19 50	S50	+1 38	+1 35	-1 36	-1 38
115	25	Mon	-01 56	-02 02	11 58	15.9	04 05	04 43	19 14	19 52					
116	26	Tue	-02 07	-02 12	11 58	15.9	04 03	04 41	19 16	19 54					
117	27	Wed	-02 17	-02 22	11 58	15.9	04 01	04 39	19 18	19 56					
118	28	Thu	-02 26	-02 31	11 57	15.9	03 59	04 37	19 19	19 58					
119	29	Fri	-02 35	-02 39	11 57	15.9	03 57	04 35	19 21	20 00					
120	30	Sat	-02 43	-02 47	11 57	15.9	03 54	04 33	19 23	20 01					

NOTES

Equation of time changes its sign on the 16th. Lat corrections are for the middle of April. **Equation of Time** is the excess of Mean Time over Apparent Time.

MOON

Yr	Mth	Week	Age (days)	Transit Diff (Upper) (h m m)	Semi-diam (')	Hor Par (')	Lat 52°N Moonrise (h m)	Moonset (h m)
91	1	Fri	20	04 25 58	16.1	59.0	00 13	08 37
92	2	Sat	21	05 23 55	15.8	58.1	01 09	09 39
93	3	Sun	22	06 18 51	15.6	57.3	01 54	10 47
94	4	Mon	23	07 09 49	15.4	56.5	02 30	11 56
95	5	Tue	24	07 58 46	15.2	55.8	02 59	13 06
96	6	Wed	25	08 44 43	15.1	55.3	03 23	14 14
97	7	Thu	26	09 27 43	14.9	54.8	03 44	15 22
98	8	Fri	27	10 10 42	14.8	54.5	04 04	16 28
99	9	Sat	28	10 52 43	14.8	54.2	04 24	17 33
100	10	Sun	29	11 35 43	14.7	54.0	04 44	18 38
101	11	Mon	00	12 18 44	14.7	54.0	05 05	19 43
102	12	Tue	01	13 02 46	14.7	54.0	05 30	20 46
103	13	Wed	02	13 48 48	14.7	54.1	05 59	21 47
104	14	Thu	03	14 36 49	14.8	54.3	06 33	22 44
105	15	Fri	04	15 25 49	14.9	54.6	07 14	23 36
106	16	Sat	05	16 14 50	15.0	55.0	08 03	- -
107	17	Sun	06	17 04 50	15.1	55.6	09 00	00 22
108	18	Mon	07	17 54 50	15.3	56.3	10 03	01 01
109	19	Tue	08	18 44 51	15.6	57.1	11 12	01 34
110	20	Wed	09	19 35 50	15.8	58.0	12 26	02 03
111	21	Thu	10	20 25 52	16.1	59.0	13 43	02 29
112	22	Fri	11	21 17 54	16.3	59.9	15 02	02 54
113	23	Sat	12	22 11 56	16.5	60.6	16 25	03 18
114	24	Sun	13	23 07 59	16.7	61.2	17 49	03 44
115	25	Mon	14	24 06 _	16.7	61.4	19 15	04 14
116	26	Tue	15	00 06 61	16.7	61.3	20 37	04 48
117	27	Wed	16	01 07 62	16.6	60.9	21 53	05 31
118	28	Thu	17	02 09 61	16.4	60.2	22 57	06 23
119	29	Fri	18	03 10 58	16.2	59.4	23 48	07 24
120	30	Sat	19	04 08 55	15.9	58.4	- -	08 33

Phases of the Moon

	d	h	m
◑ Last Quarter	3	02	55
● New Moon	11	00	17
◐ First Quarter	19	02	34
○ Full Moon	25	19	45
Apogee	12	00	
Perigee	25	17	

NOTES

For Latitude corrections to Moonrise and Moonset see page 706.

APRIL 1994   STARS   0h GMT April 1

No	Name	Mag	Transit h m	Dec ° '	GHA ° '	RA h m	SHA ° '
	ARIES...............		11 22		189 07.6		
1	Alpheratz 2.2		11 30	N 29 03.5	187 06.3	0 08	357 58.7
2	Ankaa 2.4		11 48	S 42 20.2	182 37.8	0 26	353 30.2
3	Schedar........... 2.5		12 02	N 56 20.3	179 05.1	0 40	349 57.5
4	Diphda 2.2		12 05	S 18 01.1	178 18.2	0 43	349 10.6
5	Achernar 0.6		12 59	S 57 15.9	164 45.6	1 37	335 38.0
6	POLARIS 2.1		13 46	N 89 14.4	152 37.8	2 25	323 49.4
7	Hamal.............. 2.2		13 28	N 23 26.1	157 24.9	2 07	328 17.3
8	Acamar 3.1		14 19	S 40 19.8	144 37.2	2 58	315 29.6
9	Menkar 2.8		14 23	N 4 03.9	143 38.0	3 02	314 30.4
10	Mirfak 1.9		14 45	N 49 50.5	138 09.0	3 24	309 01.4
11	Aldebaran 1.1		15 56	N 16 29.8	120 13.7	4 36	291 06.1
12	Rigel 0.3		16 35	S 8 12.7	110 33.7	5 14	281 26.1
13	Capella.............. 0.2		16 37	N 45 59.6	110 05.3	5 16	280 56.0
14	Bellatrix........... 1.7		16 46	N 6 20.5	107 55.2	5 25	278 47.6
15	Elnath 1.8		16 47	N 28 36.1	107 38.6	5 26	278 31.0
16	Alnilam 1.8		16 57	S 1 12.5	105 08.7	5 36	276 01.1
17	Betelgeuse 0.1-1.2		17 16	N 7 24.2	100 24.6	5 55	271 17.0
18	Canopus ....–0.9		17 44	S 52 41.9	93 10.3	6 24	264 02.7
19	Sirius ....–1.6		18 05	S 16 42.8	87 54.0	6 45	258 46.4
20	Adhara 1.6		18 19	S 28 58.2	84 31.5	6 58	255 23.9
21	Castor 1.6		18 55	N 31 54.0	75 33.8	7 34	246 26.2
22	Procyon 0.5		18 59	N 5 14.2	74 22.4	7 39	245 14.8
23	Pollux............... 1.2		19 05	N 28 02.3	72 52.9	7 45	243 45.3
24	Avior 1.7		19 43	S 59 29.9	63 31.4	8 22	234 23.8
25	Suhail 2.2		20 28	S 43 25.0	52 10.5	9 08	223 02.9
26	Miaplacidus.... 1.8		20 33	S 69 42.1	50 49.9	9 13	221 42.3
27	Alphard 2.2		20 47	S 8 38.3	47 17.7	9 27	218 10.1
28	Regulus 1.3		21 28	N 11 59.5	37 06.2	10 08	207 58.6
29	Dubhe 2.0		22 23	N 61 46.9	23 16.3	11 03	194 08.7
30	Denebola......... 2.2		23 08	N 14 36.1	11 55.6	11 49	182 48.0
31	Gienah 2.8		23 35	S 17 30.9	5 14.4	12 16	176 06.8
32	Acrux................ 1.1		23 46	S 63 04.3	2 32.3	12 26	173 24.7
33	Gacrux 1.6		23 50	S 57 05.1	1 24.0	12 31	172 16.4
34	Mimosa............ 1.5		0 11	S 59 39.7	357 15.8	12 47	168 08.2
35	Alioth............... 1.7		0 17	N 55 59.4	355 40.3	12 54	166 32.7
36	Spica................. 1.2		0 48	S 11 08.1	347 53.7	13 25	158 46.1
37	Alkaid 1.9		1 11	N 49 20.4	342 17.3	13 47	153 09.7
38	Hadar 0.9		1 27	S 60 20.8	338 15.3	14 03	149 07.7
39	Menkent......... 2.3		1 30	S 36 20.6	337 31.7	14 06	148 24.1
40	Arcturus........... 0.2		1 39	N 19 12.6	335 16.1	14 15	146 08.5
41	Rigil Kent. 0.1		2 02	S 60 48.7	329 18.3	14 39	140 10.7
42	Zuben'ubi....... 2.9		2 14	S 16 01.2	326 28.6	14 51	137 21.0
43	Kochab............ 2.2		2 14	N 74 10.6	326 25.9	14 51	137 18.3
44	Alphecca.......... 2.3		2 57	N 26 43.9	315 30.5	15 34	126 22.9
45	Antares............ 1.2		3 52	S 26 25.2	301 51.2	16 29	112 43.6
46	Atria 1.9		4 11	S 69 00.9	297 05.6	16 48	107 58.0
47	Sabik 2.6		4 33	S 15 43.1	291 36.4	17 10	102 28.8
48	Shaula.............. 1.7		4 56	S 37 05.9	285 48.8	17 33	96 41.2
49	Rasalhague 2.1		4 57	N 12 33.7	285 27.2	17 35	96 19.6
50	Eltanin............. 2.4		5 19	N 51 29.1	280 00.2	17 56	90 52.6
51	Kaus Aust........ 2.0		5 46	S 34 23.1	273 10.3	18 24	84 02.7
52	Vega 0.1		5 59	N 38 46.5	269 56.2	18 37	80 48.6
53	Nunki 2.1		6 17	S 26 18.1	265 23.6	18 55	76 16.0
54	Altair................ 0.9		7 13	N 8 51.1	251 29.8	19 51	62 22.2
55	Peacock............ 2.1		7 47	S 56 44.9	242 49.5	20 25	53 41.9
56	Deneb 1.3		8 03	N 45 15.4	238 49.0	20 41	49 41.4
57	Enif 2.5		9 06	N 9 50.9	223 09.0	21 44	34 01.4
58	Al Na'ir 2.2		9 30	S 46 59.1	217 09.6	22 08	28 02.0
59	Fomalhaut 1.3		10 19	S 29 39.1	204 47.6	22 57	15 40.0
60	Markab 2.6		10 26	N 15 10.4	203 00.5	23 04	13 52.9

Stars Transit Corr Table

Date	Corr h m	Date	Corr h m
1	–0 00	17	–1 03
2	–0 04	18	–1 07
3	–0 08	19	–1 11
4	–0 12	20	–1 15
5	–0 16	21	–1 19
6	–0 20	22	–1 23
7	–0 24	23	–1 27
8	–0 28	24	–1 30
9	–0 31	25	–1 34
10	–0 35	26	–1 38
11	–0 39	27	–1 42
12	–0 43	28	–1 46
13	–0 47	29	–1 50
14	–0 51	30	–1 54
15	–0 55		
16	–0 59		

STAR'S TRANSIT

To find the approx time of transit of a star for any day of the month use above table. All corrections are subtractive. If the quantity taken from the table is greater than the time of transit for the first of the month, add 23h 56min to the time of transit before subtracting the correction.

Example: What is the time of transit of Hamal (No 7) on April 8?

	h min
Transit on April 1	13 28
Corr for April 8	–00 28
Transit on April 8	13 00

APRIL DIARY

3 03 Last Quarter
3 22 Neptune 4°S of Moon
4 02 Mercury 1.5°S of Mars
4 04 Uranus 5°S of Moon
7 16 Saturn 7°S of Moon
9 02 Mars 6°S of Moon
9 11 Mercury 7°S of Moon
11 00 New Moon
12 00 Moon at apogee
12 23 Venus 1.0°S of Moon
15 01 Juno at opposition
19 03 First Quarter
25 09 Neptune stationary
25 17 Moon at perigee
25 20 Full Moon
26 05 Jupiter 3°N of Moon
28 05 Vesta in conjunction with Sun
30 09 Jupiter at opposition
30 10 Mercury in superior conjunction

Chapter 6

APRIL 1994 — SUN & ARIES — GMT

Friday, April 1

Time	SUN GHA	Dec	ARIES GHA
00	178 50.0	N4 22.0	189 07.6
02	208 59.4	4 23.9	219 12.5
04	238 59.8	4 25.8	249 17.4
06	269 00.2	4 27.8	279 22.4
08	299 00.5	4 29.7	309 27.3
10	329 00.9	4 31.6	339 32.2
12	359 01.3	4 33.6	9 37.2
14	29 01.7	4 35.5	39 42.1
16	59 02.0	4 37.4	69 47.0
18	89 02.4	4 39.4	99 51.9
20	119 02.8	4 41.3	129 56.9
22	149 03.2	N4 43.2	160 01.8

Saturday, April 2

Time	SUN GHA	Dec	ARIES GHA
00	179 03.5	N4 45.1	190 06.7
02	209 03.9	4 47.1	220 11.7
04	239 04.3	4 49.0	250 16.6
06	269 04.6	4 50.9	280 21.5
08	299 05.0	4 52.8	310 26.4
10	329 05.4	4 54.8	340 31.4
12	359 05.8	4 56.7	10 36.3
14	29 06.1	4 58.6	40 41.2
16	59 06.5	5 00.5	70 46.2
18	89 06.9	5 02.4	100 51.1
20	119 07.2	5 04.4	130 56.0
22	149 07.6	N5 06.3	161 00.9

Sunday, April 3

Time	SUN GHA	Dec	ARIES GHA
00	179 08.0	N5 08.2	191 05.9
02	209 08.4	5 10.1	221 10.8
04	239 08.7	5 12.0	251 15.7
06	269 09.1	5 13.9	281 20.7
08	299 09.5	5 15.9	311 25.6
10	329 09.8	5 17.8	341 30.5
12	359 10.2	5 19.7	11 35.4
14	29 10.6	5 21.6	41 40.4
16	59 10.9	5 23.5	71 45.3
18	89 11.3	5 25.4	101 50.2
20	119 11.7	5 27.3	131 55.1
22	149 12.0	N5 29.3	162 00.1

Monday, April 4

Time	SUN GHA	Dec	ARIES GHA
00	179 12.4	N5 31.2	192 05.0
02	209 12.8	5 33.1	222 09.9
04	239 13.1	5 35.0	252 14.9
06	269 13.5	5 36.9	282 19.8
08	299 13.9	5 38.8	312 24.7
10	329 14.2	5 40.7	342 29.6
12	359 14.6	5 42.6	12 34.6
14	29 15.0	5 44.5	42 39.5
16	59 15.3	5 46.4	72 44.4
18	89 15.7	5 48.3	102 49.4
20	119 16.0	5 50.2	132 54.3
22	149 16.4	N5 52.1	162 59.2

Tuesday, April 5

Time	SUN GHA	Dec	ARIES GHA
00	179 16.8	N5 54.1	193 04.1
02	209 17.1	5 56.0	223 09.1
04	239 17.5	5 57.9	253 14.0
06	269 17.9	5 59.8	283 18.9
08	299 18.2	6 01.7	313 23.9
10	329 18.6	6 03.6	343 28.8
12	359 18.9	6 05.5	13 33.7
14	29 19.3	6 07.4	43 38.6
16	59 19.7	6 09.2	73 43.6
18	89 20.0	6 11.1	103 48.5
20	119 20.4	6 13.0	133 53.4
22	149 20.7	N6 14.9	163 58.4

Wednesday, April 6

Time	SUN GHA	Dec	ARIES GHA
00	179 21.1	N6 16.8	194 03.3
02	209 21.4	6 18.7	224 08.2
04	239 21.8	6 20.6	254 13.1
06	269 22.2	6 22.5	284 18.1
08	299 22.5	6 24.4	314 23.0
10	329 22.9	6 26.3	344 27.9
12	359 23.2	6 28.2	14 32.9
14	29 23.6	6 30.1	44 37.8
16	59 23.9	6 32.0	74 42.7
18	89 24.3	6 33.8	104 47.6
20	119 24.6	6 35.7	134 52.6
22	149 25.0	N6 37.6	164 57.5

Thursday, April 7

Time	SUN GHA	Dec	ARIES GHA
00	179 25.3	N6 39.5	195 02.4
02	209 25.7	6 41.4	225 07.4
04	239 26.0	6 43.3	255 12.3
06	269 26.4	6 45.1	285 17.2
08	299 26.8	6 47.0	315 22.1
10	329 27.1	6 48.9	345 27.1
12	359 27.5	6 50.8	15 32.0
14	29 27.8	6 52.7	45 36.9
16	59 28.2	6 54.5	75 41.8
18	89 28.5	6 56.4	105 46.8
20	119 28.8	6 58.3	135 51.7
22	149 29.2	N7 00.2	165 56.6

Friday, April 8

Time	SUN GHA	Dec	ARIES GHA
00	179 29.5	N7 02.1	196 01.6
02	209 29.9	7 03.9	226 06.5
04	239 30.2	7 05.8	256 11.4
06	269 30.6	7 07.7	286 16.3
08	299 30.9	7 09.5	316 21.3
10	329 31.3	7 11.4	346 26.2
12	359 31.6	7 13.3	16 31.1
14	29 32.0	7 15.2	46 36.1
16	59 32.3	7 17.0	76 41.0
18	89 32.7	7 18.9	106 45.9
20	119 33.0	7 20.8	136 50.8
22	149 33.3	N7 22.6	166 55.8

Saturday, April 9

Time	SUN GHA	Dec	ARIES GHA
00	179 33.7	N7 24.5	197 00.7
02	209 34.0	7 26.4	227 05.6
04	239 34.4	7 28.2	257 10.6
06	269 34.7	7 30.1	287 15.5
08	299 35.1	7 31.9	317 20.4
10	329 35.4	7 33.8	347 25.3
12	359 35.7	7 35.7	17 30.3
14	29 36.1	7 37.5	47 35.2
16	59 36.4	7 39.4	77 40.1
18	89 36.7	7 41.2	107 45.1
20	119 37.1	7 43.1	137 50.0
22	149 37.4	N7 44.9	167 54.9

Sunday, April 10

Time	SUN GHA	Dec	ARIES GHA
00	179 37.8	N7 46.8	197 59.8
02	209 38.1	7 48.7	228 04.8
04	239 38.4	7 50.5	258 09.7
06	269 38.8	7 52.4	288 14.6
08	299 39.1	7 54.2	318 19.6
10	329 39.4	7 56.1	348 24.5
12	359 39.8	7 57.9	18 29.4
14	29 40.1	7 59.8	48 34.3
16	59 40.4	8 01.6	78 39.3
18	89 40.8	8 03.4	108 44.2
20	119 41.1	8 05.3	138 49.1
22	149 41.4	N8 07.1	168 54.0

Monday, April 11

Time	SUN GHA	Dec	ARIES GHA
00	179 41.8	N8 09.0	198 59.0
02	209 42.1	8 10.8	229 03.9
04	239 42.4	8 12.7	259 08.8
06	269 42.8	8 14.5	289 13.8
08	299 43.1	8 16.3	319 18.7
10	329 43.4	8 18.2	349 23.6
12	359 43.7	8 20.0	19 28.5
14	29 44.1	8 21.9	49 33.5
16	59 44.4	8 23.7	79 38.4
18	89 44.7	8 25.5	109 43.3
20	119 45.1	8 27.4	139 48.3
22	149 45.4	N8 29.2	169 53.2

Tuesday, April 12

Time	SUN GHA	Dec	ARIES GHA
00	179 45.7	N8 31.0	199 58.1
02	209 46.0	8 32.9	230 03.0
04	239 46.4	8 34.7	260 08.0
06	269 46.7	8 36.5	290 12.9
08	299 47.0	8 38.3	320 17.8
10	329 47.3	8 40.2	350 22.8
12	359 47.7	8 42.0	20 27.7
14	29 48.0	8 43.8	50 32.6
16	59 48.3	8 45.6	80 37.5
18	89 48.6	8 47.5	110 42.5
20	119 48.9	8 49.3	140 47.4
22	149 49.3	N8 51.1	170 52.3

Wednesday, April 13

Time	SUN GHA	Dec	ARIES GHA
00	179 49.6	N8 52.9	200 57.3
02	209 49.9	8 54.7	231 02.2
04	239 50.2	8 56.6	261 07.1
06	269 50.5	8 58.4	291 12.0
08	299 50.9	9 00.2	321 17.0
10	329 51.2	9 02.0	351 21.9
12	359 51.5	9 03.8	21 26.8
14	29 51.8	9 05.6	51 31.8
16	59 52.1	9 07.4	81 36.7
18	89 52.4	9 09.3	111 41.6
20	119 52.7	9 11.1	141 46.5
22	149 53.1	N9 12.9	171 51.5

Thursday, April 14

Time	SUN GHA	Dec	ARIES GHA
00	179 53.4	N9 14.7	201 56.4
02	209 53.7	9 16.5	232 01.3
04	239 54.0	9 18.3	262 06.2
06	269 54.3	9 20.1	292 11.2
08	299 54.6	9 21.9	322 16.1
10	329 54.9	9 23.7	352 21.0
12	359 55.2	9 25.5	22 26.0
14	29 55.5	9 27.3	52 30.9
16	59 55.9	9 29.1	82 35.8
18	89 56.2	9 30.9	112 40.7
20	119 56.5	9 32.7	142 45.7
22	149 56.8	N9 34.5	172 50.6

Friday, April 15

Time	SUN GHA	Dec	ARIES GHA
00	179 57.1	N9 36.3	202 55.5
02	209 57.4	9 38.1	233 00.5
04	239 57.7	9 39.9	263 05.4
06	269 58.0	9 41.6	293 10.3
08	299 58.3	9 43.4	323 15.2
10	329 58.6	9 45.2	353 20.2
12	359 58.9	9 47.0	23 25.1
14	29 59.2	9 48.8	53 30.0
16	59 59.5	9 50.6	83 35.0
18	89 59.8	9 52.4	113 39.9
20	120 00.1	9 54.1	143 44.8
22	150 00.4	N9 55.9	173 49.7

APRIL 1994 — SUN & ARIES — GMT

Saturday, April 16

Time	SUN GHA	Dec	ARIES GHA
00	180 00.7	N9 57.7	203 54.7
02	210 01.0	9 55.5	233 59.6
04	240 01.3	10 01.3	264 04.5
06	270 01.6	10 03.0	294 09.5
08	300 01.9	10 04.8	324 14.4
10	330 02.2	10 06.6	354 19.3
12	0 02.5	10 08.4	24 24.2
14	30 02.8	10 10.1	54 29.2
16	60 03.1	10 11.9	84 34.1
18	90 03.4	10 13.7	114 39.0
20	120 03.7	10 15.4	144 44.0
22	150 04.0	N10 17.2	174 48.9

Sunday, April 17

Time	SUN GHA	Dec	ARIES GHA
00	180 04.3	N10 19.0	204 53.8
02	210 04.6	10 20.7	234 58.7
04	240 04.9	10 22.5	265 03.7
06	270 05.1	10 24.3	295 08.6
08	300 05.4	10 26.0	325 13.5
10	330 05.7	10 27.8	355 18.4
12	0 06.0	10 29.6	25 23.4
14	30 06.3	10 31.3	55 28.3
16	60 06.6	10 33.1	85 33.2
18	90 06.9	10 34.8	115 38.2
20	120 07.2	10 36.6	145 43.1
22	150 07.5	N10 38.3	175 48.0

Monday, April 18

Time	SUN GHA	Dec	ARIES GHA
0	180 07.7	N10 40.1	205 52.9
02	210 08.0	10 41.8	235 57.9
04	240 08.3	10 43.6	266 02.8
06	270 08.6	10 45.3	296 07.7
08	300 08.9	10 47.1	326 12.7
10	330 09.2	10 48.8	356 17.6
12	0 09.4	10 50.6	26 22.5
14	30 09.7	10 52.3	56 27.4
16	60 10.0	10 54.0	86 32.4
18	90 10.3	10 55.8	116 37.3
20	120 10.6	10 57.5	146 42.2
22	150 10.8	N10 59.3	176 47.2

Tuesday, April 19

Time	SUN GHA	Dec	ARIES GHA
00	180 11.1	N11 01.0	206 52.1
02	210 11.4	11 02.7	236 57.0
04	240 11.7	11 04.5	267 01.9
06	270 11.9	11 06.2	297 06.9
08	300 12.2	11 07.9	327 11.8
10	330 12.5	11 09.7	357 16.7
12	0 12.8	11 11.4	27 21.7
14	30 13.0	11 13.1	57 26.6
16	60 13.3	11 14.9	87 31.5
18	90 13.6	11 16.6	117 36.4
20	120 13.8	11 18.3	147 41.4
22	150 14.1	N11 20.0	177 46.3

Wednesday, April 20

Time	SUN GHA	Dec	ARIES GHA
00	180 14.4	N11 21.7	207 51.2
02	210 14.6	11 23.5	237 56.2
04	240 14.9	11 25.2	268 01.1
06	270 15.2	11 26.9	298 06.0
08	300 15.4	11 28.6	328 10.9
10	330 15.7	11 30.3	358 15.9
12	0 16.0	11 32.0	28 20.8
14	30 16.2	11 33.8	58 25.7
16	60 16.5	11 35.5	88 30.6
18	90 16.8	11 37.2	118 35.6
20	120 17.0	11 38.9	148 40.5
22	150 17.3	N11 40.6	178 45.4

Thursday, April 21

Time	SUN GHA	Dec	ARIES GHA
00	180 17.5	N11 42.3	208 50.4
02	210 17.8	11 44.0	238 55.3
04	240 18.1	11 45.7	269 00.2
06	270 18.3	11 47.4	299 05.1
08	300 18.6	11 49.1	329 10.1
10	330 18.8	11 50.8	359 15.0
12	0 19.1	11 52.5	29 19.9
14	30 19.4	11 54.2	59 24.9
16	60 19.6	11 55.9	89 29.8
18	90 19.9	11 57.6	119 34.7
20	120 20.1	11 59.3	149 39.6
22	150 20.4	N12 01.0	179 44.6

Friday, April 22

Time	SUN GHA	Dec	ARIES GHA
00	180 20.6	N12 02.7	209 49.5
02	210 20.9	12 04.4	239 54.4
04	240 21.1	12 06.0	269 59.4
06	270 21.4	12 07.7	300 04.3
08	300 21.6	12 09.4	330 09.2
10	330 21.9	12 11.1	0 14.1
12	0 22.1	12 12.8	30 19.1
14	30 22.4	12 14.4	60 24.0
16	60 22.6	12 16.1	90 28.9
18	90 22.8	12 17.8	120 33.9
20	120 23.1	12 19.5	150 38.8
22	150 23.3	N12 21.2	180 43.7

Saturday, April 23

Time	SUN GHA	Dec	ARIES GHA
00	180 23.6	N12 22.8	210 48.6
02	210 23.8	12 24.5	240 53.6
04	240 24.1	12 26.2	270 58.5
06	270 24.3	12 27.8	301 03.4
08	300 24.5	12 29.5	331 08.4
10	330 24.8	12 31.2	1 13.3
12	0 25.0	12 32.8	31 18.2
14	30 25.2	12 34.5	61 23.1
16	60 25.5	12 36.2	91 28.1
18	90 25.7	12 37.8	121 33.0
20	120 26.0	12 39.5	151 37.9
22	150 26.2	N12 41.1	181 42.9

Sunday, April 24

Time	SUN GHA	Dec	ARIES GHA
00	180 26.4	N12 42.8	211 47.8
02	210 26.6	12 44.4	241 52.7
04	240 26.9	12 46.1	271 57.6
06	270 27.1	12 47.7	302 02.6
08	300 27.3	12 49.4	332 07.5
10	330 27.6	12 51.0	2 12.4
12	0 27.8	12 52.7	32 17.3
14	30 28.0	12 54.3	62 22.3
16	60 28.2	12 56.0	92 27.2
18	90 28.5	12 57.6	122 32.1
20	120 28.7	12 59.3	152 37.1
22	150 28.9	N13 00.9	182 42.0

Monday, April 25

Time	SUN GHA	Dec	ARIES GHA
00	180 29.1	N13 02.5	212 46.9
02	210 29.4	13 04.2	242 51.8
04	240 29.6	13 05.8	272 56.8
06	270 29.8	13 07.4	303 01.7
08	300 30.0	13 09.1	333 06.6
10	330 30.2	13 10.7	3 11.6
12	0 30.5	13 12.3	33 16.5
14	30 30.7	13 14.0	63 21.4
16	60 30.9	13 15.6	93 26.3
18	90 31.1	13 17.2	123 31.3
20	120 31.3	13 18.8	153 36.2
22	150 31.5	N13 20.5	183 41.1

Tuesday, April 26

Time	SUN GHA	Dec	ARIES GHA
00	180 31.8	N13 22.1	213 46.1
02	210 32.0	13 23.7	243 51.0
04	240 32.2	13 25.3	273 55.9
06	270 32.4	13 26.9	304 00.8
08	300 32.6	13 28.5	334 05.8
10	330 32.8	13 30.1	4 10.7
12	0 33.0	13 31.8	34 15.6
14	30 33.2	13 33.4	64 20.6
16	60 33.4	13 35.0	94 25.5
18	90 33.6	13 36.6	124 30.4
20	120 33.8	13 38.2	154 35.3
22	150 34.0	N13 39.8	184 40.3

Wednesday, April 27

Time	SUN GHA	Dec	ARIES GHA
00	180 34.2	N13 41.4	214 45.2
02	210 34.4	13 43.0	244 50.1
04	240 34.6	13 44.6	274 55.1
06	270 34.8	13 46.2	305 00.0
08	300 35.0	13 47.8	335 04.9
10	330 35.2	13 49.4	5 09.8
12	0 35.4	13 51.0	35 14.8
14	30 35.6	13 52.6	65 19.7
16	60 35.8	13 54.1	95 24.6
18	90 36.0	13 55.7	125 29.5
20	120 36.2	13 57.3	155 34.5
22	150 36.4	N13 58.9	185 39.4

Thursday, April 28

Time	SUN GHA	Dec	ARIES GHA
00	180 36.6	N14 00.5	215 44.3
02	210 36.8	14 02.1	245 49.3
04	240 37.0	14 03.6	275 54.2
06	270 37.2	14 05.2	305 59.1
08	300 37.3	14 06.8	336 04.0
10	330 37.5	14 08.4	6 09.0
12	0 37.7	14 09.9	36 13.9
14	30 37.9	14 11.5	66 18.8
16	60 38.1	14 13.1	96 23.8
18	90 38.3	14 14.6	126 28.7
20	120 38.5	14 16.2	156 33.6
22	150 38.6	N14 17.8	186 38.5

Friday, April 29

Time	SUN GHA	Dec	ARIES GHA
00	180 38.8	N14 19.3	216 43.5
02	210 39.0	14 20.9	246 48.4
04	240 39.2	14 22.5	276 53.3
06	270 39.4	14 24.0	306 58.3
08	300 39.5	14 25.6	337 03.2
10	330 39.7	14 27.1	7 08.1
12	0 39.9	14 28.7	37 13.0
14	30 40.1	14 30.2	67 18.0
16	60 40.2	14 31.8	97 22.9
18	90 40.4	14 33.3	127 27.8
20	120 40.6	14 34.9	157 32.8
22	150 40.7	N14 36.4	187 37.7

Saturday, April 30

Time	SUN GHA	Dec	ARIES GHA
00	180 40.9	N14 38.0	217 42.6
02	210 41.1	14 39.5	247 47.5
04	240 41.2	14 41.0	277 52.5
06	270 41.4	14 42.6	307 57.4
08	300 41.6	14 44.1	338 02.3
10	330 41.7	14 45.7	8 07.3
12	0 41.9	14 47.2	38 12.2
14	30 42.1	14 48.7	68 17.1
16	60 42.2	14 50.3	98 22.0
18	90 42.4	14 51.8	128 27.0
20	120 42.5	14 53.3	158 31.9
22	150 42.7	N14 54.8	188 36.8

Chapter 6

APRIL 1994 — PLANETS — 0h GMT

VENUS / JUPITER

Mer Pass h m	GHA ° '	Mean Var/hr 14°+	Dec ° '	Mean Var/hr			GHA ° '	Mean Var/hr 15°+	Dec ° '	Mean Var/hr	Mer Pass h m
13 13	161 57.3	59.6	N10 34.6	1.2	1	Fri	327 59.1	2.7	S14 28.2	0.1	02 08
13 13	161 46.7	59.6	N11 02.9	1.2	2	Sat	329 03.7	2.7	S14 26.4	0.1	02 03
13 14	161 36.0	59.5	N11 30.8	1.2	3	SUN	330 08.3	2.7	S14 24.6	0.1	01 59
13 15	161 25.1	59.5	N11 58.5	1.1	4	Mon	331 13.2	2.7	S14 22.8	0.1	01 55
13 15	161 13.9	59.5	N12 26.0	1.1	5	Tue	332 18.1	2.7	S14 21.0	0.1	01 50
13 16	161 02.6	59.5	N12 53.1	1.1	6	Wed	333 23.1	2.7	S14 19.1	0.1	01 46
13 17	160 51.0	59.5	N13 19.9	1.1	7	Thu	334 28.3	2.7	S14 17.1	0.1	01 42
13 18	160 39.2	59.5	N13 46.4	1.1	8	Fri	335 33.6	2.7	S14 15.2	0.1	01 37
13 19	160 27.2	59.5	N14 12.5	1.1	9	Sat	336 39.0	2.7	S14 13.2	0.1	01 33
13 19	160 14.9	59.5	N14 38.3	1.1	10	SUN	337 44.5	2.7	S14 11.1	0.1	01 29
13 20	160 02.4	59.5	N15 03.8	1.0	11	Mon	338 50.1	2.7	S14 09.1	0.1	01 24
13 21	159 49.7	59.5	N15 28.9	1.0	12	Tue	339 55.8	2.7	S14 07.0	0.1	01 20
13 22	159 36.7	59.4	N15 53.6	1.0	13	Wed	341 01.6	2.7	S14 04.9	0.1	01 16
13 23	159 23.4	59.4	N16 17.9	1.0	14	Thu	342 07.5	2.8	S14 02.7	0.1	01 11
13 24	159 09.9	59.4	N16 41.8	1.0	15	Fri	343 13.5	2.8	S14 00.6	0.1	01 07
13 25	158 56.2	59.4	N17 05.2	1.0	16	Sat	344 19.5	2.8	S13 58.4	0.1	01 03
13 26	158 42.2	59.4	N17 28.3	0.9	17	SUN	345 25.6	2.8	S13 56.2	0.1	00 58
13 27	158 27.9	59.4	N17 50.9	0.9	18	Mon	346 31.8	2.8	S13 53.9	0.1	00 54
13 28	158 13.3	59.4	N18 13.0	0.9	19	Tue	347 38.1	2.8	S13 51.7	0.1	00 49
13 29	157 58.5	59.4	N18 34.7	0.9	20	Wed	348 44.4	2.8	S13 49.4	0.1	00 45
13 30	157 43.4	59.4	N18 55.8	0.9	21	Thu	349 50.8	2.8	S13 47.1	0.1	00 40
13 31	157 28.1	59.4	N19 16.5	0.8	22	Fri	350 57.2	2.8	S13 44.9	0.1	00 36
13 32	157 12.5	59.3	N19 36.7	0.8	23	Sat	352 03.6	2.8	S13 42.5	0.1	00 32
13 33	156 56.6	59.3	N19 56.4	0.8	24	SUN	353 10.1	2.8	S13 40.2	0.1	00 27
13 34	156 40.5	59.3	N20 15.5	0.8	25	Mon	354 16.7	2.8	S13 37.9	0.1	00 23
13 35	156 24.1	59.3	N20 34.1	0.8	26	Tue	355 23.2	2.8	S13 35.6	0.1	00 18
13 36	156 07.4	59.3	N20 52.2	0.7	27	Wed	356 29.8	2.8	S13 33.2	0.1	00 14
13 37	155 50.5	59.3	N21 09.7	0.7	28	Thu	357 36.4	2.8	S13 30.9	0.1	00 10
13 38	155 33.3	59.3	N21 26.6	0.7	29	Fri	358 43.0	2.8	S13 28.5	0.1	00 05
13 40	155 15.9	59.3	N21 42.9	0.7	30	Sat	359 49.7	2.8	S13 26.2	0.1	00 01

VENUS, Av Mag –3.9
SHA April
5 328; 10 322; 15 316; 20 310; 25 304; 30 298.

JUPITER, Av Mag -2.5
SHA April
5 139; 10 140; 15 140; 20 141; 25 141; 30 142.

MARS / SATURN

Mer Pass h m	GHA ° '	Mean Var/hr 15°+	Dec ° '	Mean Var/hr			GHA ° '	Mean Var/hr 15°+	Dec ° '	Mean Var/hr	Mer Pass h m
10 45	198 33.5	0.7	S 5 15.4	0.8	1	Fri	209 32.2	2.2	S10 12.2	0.1	10 00
10 44	198 49.3	0.7	S 4 56.6	0.8	2	Sat	210 25.2	2.2	S10 09.9	0.1	09 57
10 43	199 05.2	0.7	S 4 38.2	0.8	3	SUN	211 18.2	2.2	S10 07.6	0.1	09 53
10 42	199 21.2	0.7	S 4 19.6	0.8	4	Mon	212 11.3	2.2	S10 05.4	0.1	09 50
10 41	199 37.2	0.7	S 4 00.9	0.8	5	Tue	213 04.4	2.2	S10 03.1	0.1	09 46
10 40	199 53.2	0.7	S 3 42.2	0.8	6	Wed	213 57.6	2.2	S10 00.9	0.1	09 43
10 39	200 09.3	0.7	S 3 23.5	0.8	7	Thu	214 50.8	2.2	S 9 58.7	0.1	09 39
10 38	200 25.5	0.7	S 3 04.8	0.8	8	Fri	215 44.1	2.2	S 9 56.5	0.1	09 36
10 37	200 41.7	0.7	S 2 46.0	0.8	9	Sat	216 37.4	2.2	S 9 54.4	0.1	09 32
10 36	200 57.9	0.7	S 2 27.3	0.8	10	SUN	217 30.7	2.2	S 9 52.2	0.1	09 29
10 35	201 14.2	0.7	S 2 08.5	0.8	11	Mon	218 24.1	2.2	S 9 50.1	0.1	09 25
10 33	201 30.5	0.7	S 1 49.8	0.8	12	Tue	219 17.6	2.2	S 9 48.0	0.1	09 21
10 32	201 46.9	0.7	S 1 31.0	0.8	13	Wed	220 11.1	2.2	S 9 45.9	0.1	09 18
10 31	202 03.3	0.7	S 1 12.2	0.8	14	Thu	221 04.6	2.2	S 9 43.9	0.1	09 14
10 30	202 19.7	0.7	S 0 53.5	0.8	15	Fri	221 58.2	2.2	S 9 41.8	0.1	09 11
10 29	202 36.2	0.7	S 0 34.7	0.8	16	Sat	222 51.9	2.2	S 9 39.8	0.1	09 07
10 28	202 52.7	0.7	S 0 16.0	0.8	17	SUN	223 45.6	2.2	S 9 37.8	0.1	09 04
10 27	203 09.2	0.7	N 0 02.8	0.8	18	Mon	224 39.4	2.2	S 9 35.8	0.1	09 00
10 26	203 25.7	0.7	N 0 21.5	0.8	19	Tue	225 33.2	2.2	S 9 33.9	0.1	08 56
10 25	203 42.3	0.7	N 0 40.2	0.8	20	Wed	226 27.1	2.2	S 9 32.0	0.1	08 53
10 24	203 58.9	0.7	N 0 58.9	0.8	21	Thu	227 21.0	2.3	S 9 30.1	0.1	08 49
10 22	204 15.5	0.7	N 1 17.5	0.8	22	Fri	228 15.0	2.3	S 9 28.2	0.1	08 46
10 21	204 32.2	0.7	N 1 36.1	0.8	23	Sat	229 09.1	2.3	S 9 26.3	0.1	08 42
10 20	204 48.8	0.7	N 1 54.7	0.8	24	SUN	230 03.2	2.3	S 9 24.5	0.1	08 38
10 19	205 05.5	0.7	N 2 13.3	0.8	25	Mon	230 57.4	2.3	S 9 22.7	0.1	08 35
10 18	205 22.1	0.7	N 2 31.8	0.8	26	Tue	231 51.6	2.3	S 9 20.9	0.1	08 31
10 17	205 38.8	0.7	N 2 50.3	0.8	27	Wed	232 45.9	2.3	S 9 19.2	0.1	08 28
10 16	205 55.5	0.7	N 3 08.7	0.8	28	Thu	233 40.3	2.3	S 9 17.4	0.1	08 24
10 15	206 12.2	0.7	N 3 27.1	0.8	29	Fri	234 34.7	2.3	S 9 15.7	0.1	08 20
10 14	206 28.9	0.7	N 3 45.4	0.8	30	Sat	235 29.2	2.3	S 9 14.1	0.1	08 17

MARS, Av Mag +1.2
SHA April
5 7; 10 3; 15 359; 20 356; 25 352; 30 349.

SATURN, Av Mag +1.0
SHA April
5 20; 10 20; 15 19; 20 19; 25 18; 30 18.

APRIL 1994   MOON

Day	GMT hr	GHA ° '	Mean Var/hr 14°+	Dec ° '	Mean Var/hr '	Day	GMT hr	GHA ° '	Mean Var/hr 14°+	Dec ° '	Mean Var/hr '
1 Fri	0	296 18.9	24.6	S 20 46.2	0.6	17 Sun	0	112 32.8	29.7	N 20 10.1	3.0
	6	22 46.4	24.8	S 20 50.7	0.2		6	199 31.5	29.8	N 19 51.9	3.7
	12	109 15.3	25.0	S 20 50.1	0.9		12	286 29.9	29.7	N 19 30.1	4.3
	18	195 46.5	25.5	S 20 44.7	1.7		18	13 28.3	29.7	N 19 04.6	4.9
2 Sat	0	282 19.6	25.9	S 20 34.6	2.5	18 Mon	0	100 26.3	29.7	N 18 35.5	5.5
	6	8 54.9	26.5	S 20 19.9	3.2		6	187 24.8	29.8	N 18 02.8	6.1
	12	95 32.7	26.8	S 20 00.8	3.9		12	274 23.1	29.7	N 17 26.5	6.6
	18	182 13.1	27.2	S 19 37.6	4.6		18	1 21.4	29.7	N 16 46.8	7.2
3 Sun	0	268 56.1	27.6	S 19 10.3	5.2	19 Tue	0	88 19.8	29.7	N 16 03.8	7.8
	6	355 41.9	28.1	S 18 39.3	5.8		6	175 18.2	29.8	N 15 17.4	8.3
	12	82 30.6	28.7	S 18 04.6	6.4		12	262 16.7	29.7	N 14 27.7	8.9
	18	169 22.0	29.1	S 17 26.7	6.9		18	349 15.1	29.7	N 13 35.0	9.3
4 Mon	0	256 16.3	29.5	S 16 45.6	7.4	20 Wed	0	76 13.5	29.7	N 12 39.3	9.8
	6	343 13.4	30.0	S 16 01.6	7.8		6	163 11.7	29.7	N 11 40.8	10.2
	12	70 13.2	30.5	S 15 15.0	8.2		12	250 09.8	29.6	N 10 39.5	10.7
	18	157 15.6	30.8	S 14 25.8	8.6		18	337 07.5	29.5	N 9 35.6	11.1
5 Tue	0	244 20.6	31.3	S 13 34.4	8.9	21 Thu	0	64 04.9	29.4	N 8 29.4	11.5
	6	331 28.0	31.6	S 12 41.0	9.2		6	151 01.7	29.4	N 7 20.9	11.8
	12	58 37.7	32.1	S 11 45.6	9.5		12	237 58.0	29.2	N 6 10.4	12.1
	18	145 49.7	32.4	S 10 48.6	9.7		18	324 53.4	29.1	N 4 58.0	12.4
6 Wed	0	233 03.6	32.7	S 9 50.1	9.9	22 Fri	0	51 48.0	28.9	N 3 44.1	12.5
	6	320 19.5	32.9	S 8 50.3	10.2		6	138 41.5	28.7	N 2 28.8	12.8
	12	47 37.1	33.2	S 7 49.4	10.3		12	225 33.8	28.5	N 1 12.5	12.8
	18	134 56.2	33.4	S 6 47.4	10.5		18	312 24.8	28.3	S 0 04.7	12.9
7 Thu	0	222 16.8	33.7	S 5 44.7	10.5	23 Sat	0	39 14.3	28.0	S 1 22.5	13.0
	6	309 38.7	33.8	S 4 41.4	10.6		6	126 02.2	27.7	S 2 40.5	13.0
	12	37 01.7	34.0	S 3 37.6	10.7		12	212 48.3	27.4	S 3 58.3	12.9
	18	124 25.6	34.2	S 2 33.4	10.8		18	299 32.5	27.0	S 5 15.8	12.8
8 Fri	0	211 50.3	34.2	S 1 29.1	10.7	24 Sun	0	26 14.7	26.6	S 6 32.4	12.5
	6	299 15.6	34.3	S 0 24.7	10.7		6	112 54.7	26.3	S 7 48.0	12.3
	12	26 41.4	34.4	N 0 39.5	10.6		12	199 32.6	26.0	S 9 02.0	12.0
	18	114 07.5	34.4	N 1 43.5	10.6		18	286 08.3	25.5	S 10 14.1	11.6
9 Sat	0	201 33.8	34.4	N 2 47.1	10.5	25 Mon	0	12 41.7	25.1	S 11 23.9	11.2
	6	289 00.1	34.3	N 3 50.2	10.4		6	99 12.8	24.8	S 12 31.1	10.7
	12	16 26.4	34.3	N 4 52.6	10.2		12	185 41.6	24.4	S 13 35.3	10.1
	18	103 52.4	34.3	N 5 54.2	10.1		18	272 08.4	24.1	S 14 36.1	9.5
10 Sun	0	191 18.0	34.2	N 6 54.8	9.9	26 Tue	0	358 33.1	23.8	S 15 33.2	8.8
	6	278 43.1	34.1	N 7 54.3	9.7		6	84 55.9	23.5	S 16 26.2	8.0
	12	6 07.7	34.0	N 8 52.6	9.5		12	171 17.1	23.3	S 17 14.8	7.3
	18	93 31.5	33.9	N 9 49.6	9.2		18	257 36.8	23.1	S 17 58.8	6.5
11 Mon	0	180 54.5	33.7	N 10 45.0	9.0	27 Wed	0	343 55.4	22.9	S 18 38.0	5.6
	6	268 16.7	33.6	N 11 38.8	8.6		6	70 13.2	22.9	S 19 12.0	4.8
	12	355 37.8	33.3	N 12 30.9	8.3		12	156 30.4	22.9	S 19 40.9	3.9
	18	82 57.8	33.1	N 13 21.0	8.0		18	242 47.6	22.9	S 20 04.4	3.0
12 Tue	0	170 16.8	32.9	N 14 09.1	7.6	28 Thu	0	329 05.0	23.1	S 20 22.5	2.0
	6	257 34.5	32.8	N 14 55.1	7.2		6	55 23.1	23.2	S 20 35.2	1.1
	12	344 51.0	32.5	N 15 38.7	6.8		12	141 42.2	23.5	S 20 42.4	0.3
	18	72 06.3	32.3	N 16 20.0	6.4		18	228 02.7	23.7	S 20 44.3	0.6
13 Wed	0	159 20.2	32.1	N 16 58.7	6.0	29 Fri	0	314 24.9	24.1	S 20 41.0	1.5
	6	246 32.9	31.8	N 17 34.7	5.5		6	40 49.3	24.5	S 20 32.5	2.3
	12	333 44.3	31.6	N 18 07.9	5.0		12	127 16.0	24.9	S 20 19.2	3.1
	18	60 54.4	31.5	N 18 38.3	4.6		18	213 45.3	25.4	S 20 01.0	3.9
14 Thu	0	148 03.2	31.3	N 19 05.6	3.9	30 Sat	0	300 17.5	25.9	S 19 38.4	4.5
	6	235 10.8	31.1	N 19 29.9	3.5		6	26 52.7	26.4	S 19 11.4	5.2
	12	322 17.2	30.8	N 19 50.9	2.9		12	113 31.0	27.0	S 18 40.4	5.9
	18	49 22.5	30.7	N 20 08.7	2.4		18	200 12.6	27.5	S 18 05.6	6.4
15 Fri	0	136 26.7	30.5	N 20 23.1	1.8						
	6	223 30.0	30.3	N 20 34.1	1.2						
	12	310 32.3	30.3	N 20 41.5	0.6						
	18	37 33.9	30.1	N 20 45.4	0.0						
16 Sat	0	124 34.8	30.1	N 20 45.5	0.6						
	6	211 35.0	29.9	N 20 42.3	1.2						
	12	298 34.7	29.9	N 20 35.2	1.8						
	18	25 33.9	29.8	N 20 24.5	2.4						

Chapter 6

MAY 1994   SUN & MOON   GMT

SUN

Day of Yr Mth Week	Equation of Time 0h	Equation of Time 12h	Transit	Semi-diam	Lat 52°N Twi-light	Lat 52°N Sun-rise	Lat 52°N Sun-set	Lat 52°N Twi-light	Lat	Lat Corr to Sunrise, Sunset etc Twi-light	Sun-rise	Sun-set	Twi-light
	m s	m s	h m	′	h m	h m	h m	h m	°	h m	h m	h m	h m
121 1 Sun	−02 51	−02 55	11 57	15.9	03 52	04 31	19 24	20 03	N70	TAN	−3 17	+3 32	TAN
122 2 Mon	−02 59	−03 02	11 57	15.9	03 50	04 29	19 26	20 05	68	TAN	−2 16	+2 20	TAN
123 3 Tue	−03 05	−03 08	11 57	15.9	03 48	04 27	19 28	20 07	66	TAN	−1 42	+1 45	TAN
124 4 Wed	−03 12	−03 14	11 57	15.9	03 46	04 25	19 29	20 09	64	−2 12	−1 17	+1 20	+2 13
125 5 Thu	−03 17	−03 20	11 57	15.9	03 44	04 23	19 31	20 11	62	−1 31	−0 58	+1 01	+1 31
126 6 Fri	−03 22	−03 24	11 57	15.9	03 42	04 22	19 33	20 13	N60	−1 04	−0 43	+0 44	+1 03
127 7 Sat	−03 27	−03 29	11 57	15.9	03 40	04 20	19 34	20 15	58	−0 42	−0 30	+0 30	+0 45
128 8 Sun	−03 31	−03 32	11 56	15.9	03 38	04 18	19 36	20 16	56	−0 27	−0 18	+0 19	+0 27
129 9 Mon	−03 34	−03 35	11 56	15.9	03 36	04 16	19 38	20 18	54	−0 12	−0 08	+0 09	+0 12
130 10 Tue	−03 37	−03 38	11 56	15.9	03 34	04 15	19 39	20 20	50	+0 11	+0 08	−0 08	−0 11
131 11 Wed	−03 39	−03 40	11 56	15.9	03 32	04 13	19 41	20 22	N45	+0 33	+0 25	−0 24	−0 32
132 12 Thu	−03 40	−03 41	11 56	15.9	03 30	04 11	19 42	20 24	40	+0 50	+0 39	−0 38	−0 49
133 13 Fri	−03 41	−03 42	11 56	15.9	03 28	04 10	19 44	20 26	35	+1 04	+0 50	−0 50	−1 03
134 14 Sat	−03 42	−03 42	11 56	15.8	03 26	04 08	19 45	20 28	30	+1 17	+1 00	−1 00	−1 16
135 15 Sun	−03 42	−03 42	11 56	15.8	03 25	04 07	19 47	20 29	20	+1 35	+1 17	−1 17	−1 35
136 16 Mon	−03 41	−03 41	11 56	15.8	03 23	04 05	19 49	20 31	N10	+1 51	+1 32	−1 32	−1 51
137 17 Tue	−03 40	−03 39	11 56	15.8	03 21	04 04	19 50	20 33	0	+2 06	+1 46	−1 46	−2 06
138 18 Wed	−03 38	−03 37	11 56	15.8	03 19	04 02	19 52	20 35	S10	+2 19	+1 59	−2 00	−2 19
139 19 Thu	−03 36	−03 35	11 56	15.8	03 18	04 01	19 53	20 36	20	+2 32	+2 13	−2 15	−2 32
140 20 Fri	−03 33	−03 32	11 56	15.8	03 16	03 59	19 54	20 38	30	+2 46	+2 30	−2 31	−2 47
141 21 Sat	−03 30	−03 28	11 57	15.8	03 14	03 58	19 56	20 40	S35	+2 54	+2 39	−2 41	−2 54
142 22 Sun	−03 26	−03 24	11 57	15.8	03 13	03 57	19 57	20 41	40	+3 03	+2 50	−2 52	−3 03
143 23 Mon	−03 21	−03 19	11 57	15.8	03 11	03 56	19 59	20 43	45	+3 13	+3 03	−3 04	−3 13
144 24 Tue	−03 17	−03 14	11 57	15.8	03 10	03 54	20 00	20 45	S50	+3 24	+3 18	−3 20	−3 24
145 25 Wed	−03 11	−03 08	11 57	15.8	03 08	03 53	20 01	20 46					
146 26 Thu	−03 05	−03 02	11 57	15.8	03 07	03 52	20 03	20 48					
147 27 Fri	−02 59	−02 55	11 57	15.8	03 06	03 51	20 04	20 51			NOTES		
148 28 Sat	−02 52	−02 48	11 57	15.8	03 04	03 50	20 05	20 51					
149 29 Sun	−02 45	−02 41	11 57	15.8	03 03	03 49	20 07	20 52					
150 30 Mon	−02 37	−02 33	11 57	15.8	03 02	03 48	20 08	20 54					
151 31 Tue	−02 29	−02 24	11 58	15.8	03 01	03 47	20 09	20 55					

NOTES

Lat corrections are for the middle of May. TAN = Twilight all night. **Equation of Time** is the excess of Mean Time over Apparent Time.

MOON

Day of Yr Mth Week	Age	Transit Diff (Upper)	Semi-diam	Hor Par	Lat 52°N Moon-rise	Lat 52°N Moon-set	Phases of the Moon
	days	h m m	′	′	h m	h m	
121 1 Sun	20	05 03 51	15.7	57.5	00 29	09 44	
122 2 Mon	21	05 54 47	15.4	56.6	01 01	10 55	◗ Last Quarter d 2 h 14 m 32
123 3 Tue	22	06 41 45	15.2	55.8	01 27	12 05	● New Moon 10 17 07
124 4 Wed	23	07 26 43	15.0	55.2	01 50	13 13	◖ First Quarter 18 12 50
125 5 Thu	24	08 09 42	14.9	54.7	02 10	14 20	○ Full Moon 25 03 39
126 6 Fri	25	08 51 43	14.8	54.3	02 30	15 25	
127 7 Sat	26	09 34 42	14.7	54.1	02 49	16 30	
128 8 Sun	27	10 16 44	14.7	54.0	03 10	17 34	Apogee 9 02
129 9 Mon	28	11 00 46	14.7	54.0	03 34	18 38	Perigee 24 03
130 10 Tue	29	11 46 47	14.7	54.0	04 01	19 40	
131 11 Wed	01	12 33 49	14.8	54.2	04 34	20 39	
132 12 Thu	02	13 22 49	14.8	54.5	05 13	21 33	
133 13 Fri	03	14 11 50	14.9	54.8	06 00	22 20	
134 14 Sat	04	15 01 50	15.0	55.2	06 54	23 01	
135 15 Sun	05	15 51 49	15.2	55.7	07 55	23 36	
136 16 Mon	06	16 40 49	15.4	56.4	09 02	− −	
137 17 Tue	07	17 29 49	15.5	57.1	10 12	00 06	
138 18 Wed	08	18 18 49	15.8	57.8	11 25	00 32	
139 19 Thu	09	19 07 51	16.0	58.6	12 41	00 56	
140 20 Fri	10	19 58 53	16.2	59.4	13 59	01 20	
141 21 Sat	11	20 51 56	16.4	60.2	15 20	01 44	
142 22 Sun	12	21 47 59	16.5	60.7	16 43	02 10	
143 23 Mon	13	22 46 62	16.6	61.1	18 06	02 41	
144 24 Tue	14	23 48 62	16.6	61.1	19 26	03 19	
145 25 Wed	15	24 50 _	16.6	60.8	20 37	04 06	
146 26 Thu	16	00 50 62	16.4	60.3	21 36	05 04	
147 27 Fri	17	01 52 58	16.2	59.5	22 23	06 10	NOTES
148 28 Sat	18	02 50 54	16.0	58.6	23 00	07 23	
149 29 Sun	19	03 44 51	15.7	57.7	23 29	08 37	For Latitude corrections to
150 30 Mon	20	04 35 47	15.5	56.7	23 54	09 50	Moonrise and Moonset see
151 31 Tue	21	05 22 44	15.2	55.9	− −	11 00	page 706.

MAY 1994   STARS   0h GMT May 1

No	Name	Mag	Transit h m	Dec ° ′	GHA ° ′	RA h m	SHA ° ′
	ARIES................		9 24		218 41.7		
1	Alpheratz	2.2	9 32	N 29 03.4	216 40.2	0 08	357 58.5
2	Ankaa	2.4	9 50	S 42 20.0	212 11.8	0 26	353 30.1
3	Schedar............	2.5	10 04	N 56 30.2	208 39.0	0 40	349 57.3
4	Diphda	2.2	10 07	S 18 01.0	207 52.2	0 43	349 10.5
5	Achernar	0.6	11 01	S 57 15.8	194 19.6	1 37	335 37.9
6	POLARIS..........	2.1	11 48	N 89 14.3	182 10.6	2 25	323 46.8
7	Hamal..............	2.2	11 30	N 23 26.1	186 59.0	2 07	328 17.3
8	Acamar	3.1	12 21	S 40 19.7	174 11.3	2 58	315 29.6
9	Menkar	2.8	12 25	N 4 04.0	173 12.0	3 02	314 30.3
10	Mirfak	1.9	12 47	N 49 50.4	167 43.1	3 24	309 01.4
11	Aldebaran	1.1	13 59	N 16 29.8	149 47.8	4 36	291 06.1
12	Rigel	0.3	14 37	S 8 12.6	140 07.8	5 14	281 26.1
13	Capella............	0.2	14 39	N 45 59.5	139 37.7	5 16	280 56.0
14	Bellatrix..........	1.7	14 48	N 6 20.6	137 29.4	5 25	278 47.7
15	Elnath	1.8	14 49	N 28 36.1	137 12.8	5 26	278 31.1
16	Alnilam............	1.8	14 59	S 1 12.5	134 42.9	5 36	276 01.2
17	Betelgeuse........	0.1-1.2	15 18	N 7 24.2	129 58.8	5 55	271 17.1
18	Canopus	-0.9	15 46	S 52 41.9	122 44.6	6 24	264 02.9
19	Sirius	-1.6	16 07	S 16 42.7	117 28.2	6 45	258 46.5
20	Adhara............	1.6	16 21	S 28 58.2	114 05.7	6 58	255 24.0
21	Castor	1.6	16 57	N 31 54.0	105 08.1	7 34	246 26.4
22	Procyon	0.5	17 01	N 5 14.2	103 56.6	7 39	245 14.9
23	Pollux	1.2	17 07	N 28 02.4	102 27.1	7 45	243 45.4
24	Avior	1.7	17 45	S 59 29.9	93 05.8	8 22	234 24.1
25	Suhail	2.2	18 30	S 43 25.0	81 44.7	9 08	223 03.0
26	Miaplacidus	1.8	18 35	S 69 42.1	80 24.4	9 13	221 42.7
27	Alphard	2.2	18 49	S 8 38.3	76 51.9	9 27	218 10.2
28	Regulus..........	1.3	19 30	N 11 59.6	66 40.4	10 08	207 58.7
29	Dubhe	2.0	20 25	N 61 47.0	52 50.6	11 03	194 08.9
30	Denebola..........	2.2	21 11	N 14 36.1	41 29.8	11 49	182 48.1
31	Gienah	2.8	21 37	S 17 30.9	34 48.5	12 16	176 06.8
32	Acrux	1.1	21 48	S 63 04.4	32 06.5	12 26	173 24.8
33	Gacrux	1.6	21 53	S 57 05.2	30 58.2	12 31	172 16.5
34	Mimosa............	1.5	22 09	S 59 39.8	26 50.0	12 47	168 08.3
35	Alioth	1.7	22 15	N 55 59.5	25 14.5	12 54	166 32.8
36	Spica................	1.2	22 46	S 11 08.1	17 27.8	13 25	158 46.1
37	Alkaid	1.9	23 09	N 49 20.5	11 51.4	13 47	153 09.7
38	Hadar	0.9	23 25	S 60 20.9	7 49.3	14 03	149 07.6
39	Menkent..........	2.3	23 28	S 36 20.7	7 05.8	14 06	148 24.1
40	Arcturus	0.2	23 37	N 19 12.6	4 50.2	14 15	146 08.5
41	Rigil Kent.	0.1	0 04	S 60 48.8	358 52.3	14 39	140 10.6
42	Zuben'ubi........	2.9	0 16	S 16 01.2	356 02.6	14 51	137 20.9
43	Kochab............	2.2	0 16	N 74 10.8	356 00.0	14 51	137 18.3
44	Alphecca..........	2.3	1 00	N 26 44.0	345 04.5	15 34	126 22.8
45	Antares............	1.2	1 54	S 26 25.2	331 25.2	16 29	112 43.5
46	Atria	1.9	2 13	S 69 01.0	326 39.3	16 48	107 57.6
47	Sabik	2.6	2 35	S 15 43.1	321 10.3	17 10	102 28.6
48	Shaula..............	1.7	2 58	S 37 05.9	315 22.7	17 33	96 41.0
49	Rasalhague	2.1	2 59	N 12 33.8	315 01.1	17 35	96 19.4
50	Eltanin	2.4	3 21	N 51 29.3	309 34.0	17 57	90 52.3
51	Kaus Aust........	2.0	3 48	S 34 23.1	302 44.2	18 24	84 02.5
52	Vega................	0.1	4 01	N 38 46.6	299 30.0	18 37	80 48.3
53	Nunki	2.1	4 19	S 26 18.1	294 57.5	18 55	76 15.8
54	Altair................	0.9	5 15	N 8 51.2	281 03.7	19 51	62 22.0
55	Peacock............	2.1	5 49	S 56 44.9	272 23.2	20 25	53 41.5
56	Deneb	1.3	6 05	N 45 15.4	268 22.8	20 41	49 41.1
57	Enif	2.5	7 08	N 9 50.9	252 42.9	21 44	34 01.2
58	Al Na'ir	2.2	7 32	S 46 59.0	246 43.4	22 08	28 01.7
59	Fomalhaut	1.3	8 21	S 29 38.9	234 21.5	22 57	15 39.8
60	Markab	2.6	8 28	N 15 10.4	232 34.4	23 04	13 52.7

Stars Transit Corr Table

Date	Corr h m	Date	Corr h m
1	−0 00	17	−1 03
2	−0 04	18	−1 07
3	−0 08	19	−1 11
4	−0 12	20	−1 15
5	−0 16	21	−1 19
6	−0 20	22	−1 23
7	−0 24	23	−1 27
8	−0 28	24	−1 30
9	−0 31	25	−1 34
10	−0 35	26	−1 38
11	−0 39	27	−1 42
12	−0 43	28	−1 46
13	−0 47	29	−1 50
14	−0 51	30	−1 54
15	−0 55	31	−1 58
16	−0 59		

STAR'S TRANSIT

To find the approx time of transit of a star for any day of the month use above table. All corrections are subtractive. If the quantity taken from the table is greater than the time of transit for the first of the month, add 23h 56min to the time of transit before subtracting the correction.

Example: The time is 1900h on May 12. What stars would be suitable for a meridian altitude sight within the next hour, latitude 40°N?

	h min
Present time	19 00
Corr for 13th	−00 43
Transit on May 1	19 43

Star needs to be Dec N, transit between 1943h and

MAY DIARY

1 01 Uranus stationary
1 06 Neptune 4°S of Moon
1 12 Uranus 5°S of Moon
2 15 Last Quarter
5 00 Venus 6°N of Aldebaran
5 03 Saturn 7°S of Moon
8 04 Mars 4°S of Moon
9 02 Moon at apogee
10 17 New Moon (Eclipse)
13 06 Venus 4°N of Moon
15 11 Mercury 8°N of Aldebaran
17 20 Pluto at opposition
18 13 First Quarter
23 11 Jupiter 3°N of Moon
24 03 Moon at perigee
25 04 Full Moon
28 14 Neptune 4°S of Moon
28 20 Uranus 5°S of Moon
30 07 Mercury greatest elongation E(23°)

Chapter 6

MAY 1994 — SUN & ARIES — GMT

Sunday, May 1

Time	SUN GHA	Dec	ARIES GHA
00	180 42.9	N14 50.4	218 41.7
02	210 43.0	14 57.9	248 46.7
04	240 43.2	14 59.4	278 51.6
06	270 43.3	15 00.9	308 56.5
08	300 43.5	15 02.4	339 01.5
10	330 43.6	15 03.9	9 06.4
12	0 43.8	15 05.5	39 11.3
14	30 43.9	15 07.0	69 16.2
16	60 44.1	15 08.5	99 21.2
18	90 44.2	15 10.0	129 26.1
20	120 44.4	15 11.5	159 31.0
22	150 44.5	N15 13.0	189 36.0

Monday, May 2

Time	SUN GHA	Dec	ARIES GHA
00	180 44.7	N15 14.5	219 40.9
02	210 44.8	15 16.0	249 45.8
04	240 45.0	15 17.5	279 50.7
06	270 45.1	15 19.0	309 55.7
08	300 45.3	15 20.5	340 00.6
10	330 45.4	15 22.0	10 05.5
12	0 45.6	15 23.5	40 10.5
14	30 45.7	15 25.0	70 15.4
16	60 45.8	15 26.4	100 20.3
18	90 46.0	15 27.9	130 25.2
20	120 46.1	15 29.4	160 30.2
22	150 46.2	N15 30.9	190 35.1

Tuesday, May 3

Time	SUN GHA	Dec	ARIES GHA
00	180 46.4	N15 32.4	220 40.0
02	210 46.5	15 33.9	250 45.0
04	240 46.6	15 35.3	280 49.9
06	270 46.8	15 36.8	310 54.8
08	300 46.9	15 38.3	340 59.7
10	330 47.0	15 39.7	11 04.7
12	0 47.2	15 41.2	41 09.6
14	30 47.3	15 42.7	71 14.5
16	60 47.4	15 44.2	101 19.5
18	90 47.5	15 45.6	131 24.4
20	120 47.7	15 47.1	161 29.3
22	150 47.8	N15 48.5	191 34.2

Wednesday, May 4

Time	SUN GHA	Dec	ARIES GHA
00	180 47.9	N15 50.0	221 39.2
02	210 48.0	15 51.5	251 44.1
04	240 48.2	15 52.9	281 49.0
06	270 48.3	15 54.4	311 53.9
08	300 48.4	15 55.8	341 58.9
10	330 48.5	15 57.3	12 03.8
12	0 48.6	15 58.7	42 08.7
14	30 48.7	16 00.2	72 13.7
16	60 48.9	16 01.6	102 18.6
18	90 49.0	16 03.1	132 23.5
20	120 49.1	16 04.5	162 28.4
22	150 49.2	N16 05.9	192 33.4

Thursday, May 5

Time	SUN GHA	Dec	ARIES GHA
00	180 49.3	N16 07.4	222 38.3
02	210 49.4	16 08.8	252 43.2
04	240 49.5	16 10.2	282 48.2
06	270 49.6	16 11.7	312 53.1
08	300 49.7	16 13.1	342 58.0
10	330 49.8	16 14.5	13 02.9
12	0 50.0	16 16.0	43 07.9
14	30 50.1	16 17.4	73 12.8
16	60 50.2	16 18.8	103 17.7
18	90 50.3	16 20.2	133 22.7
20	120 50.4	16 21.6	163 27.6
22	150 50.5	N16 23.1	193 32.5

Friday, May 6

Time	SUN GHA	Dec	ARIES GHA
00	180 50.6	N16 24.5	223 37.4
02	210 50.7	16 25.9	253 42.4
04	240 50.8	16 27.3	283 47.3
06	270 50.9	16 28.7	313 52.2
08	300 51.0	16 30.1	343 57.2
10	330 51.0	16 31.5	14 02.1
12	0 51.1	16 32.9	44 07.0
14	30 51.2	16 34.3	74 11.9
16	60 51.3	16 35.7	104 16.9
18	90 51.4	16 37.1	134 21.8
20	120 51.5	16 38.5	164 26.7
22	150 51.6	N16 39.9	194 31.7

Saturday, May 7

Time	SUN GHA	Dec	ARIES GHA
00	180 51.7	N16 41.3	224 36.6
02	210 51.8	16 42.7	254 41.5
04	240 51.9	16 44.1	284 46.4
06	270 51.9	16 45.5	314 51.4
08	300 52.0	16 46.8	344 56.3
10	330 52.1	16 48.2	15 01.2
12	0 52.2	16 49.6	45 06.1
14	30 52.3	16 51.0	75 11.1
16	60 52.3	16 52.4	105 16.0
18	90 52.4	16 53.8	135 20.9
20	120 52.5	16 55.1	165 25.9
22	150 52.6	N16 56.5	195 30.8

Sunday, May 8

Time	SUN GHA	Dec	ARIES GHA
00	180 52.7	N16 57.8	225 35.7
02	210 52.7	16 59.2	255 40.6
04	240 52.8	17 00.6	285 45.6
06	270 52.9	17 01.9	315 50.5
08	300 52.9	17 03.3	345 55.4
10	330 53.0	17 04.7	16 00.4
12	0 53.1	17 06.0	46 05.3
14	30 53.2	17 07.4	76 10.2
16	60 53.2	17 08.7	106 15.1
18	90 53.3	17 10.1	136 20.1
20	120 53.4	17 11.4	166 25.0
22	150 53.4	N17 12.8	196 29.9

Monday, May 9

Time	SUN GHA	Dec	ARIES GHA
00	180 53.5	N17 14.1	226 34.9
02	210 53.5	17 15.4	256 39.8
04	240 53.6	17 16.8	286 44.7
06	270 53.7	17 18.1	316 49.6
08	300 53.7	17 19.5	346 54.6
10	330 53.8	17 20.8	16 59.5
12	0 53.8	17 22.1	47 04.4
14	30 53.9	17 23.5	77 09.4
16	60 54.0	17 24.8	107 14.3
18	90 54.0	17 26.1	137 19.2
20	120 54.1	17 27.4	167 24.1
22	150 54.1	N17 28.8	197 29.1

Tuesday, May 10

Time	SUN GHA	Dec	ARIES GHA
00	180 54.2	N17 30.1	227 34.0
02	210 54.2	17 31.4	257 38.9
04	240 54.3	17 32.7	287 43.9
06	270 54.3	17 34.0	317 48.8
08	300 54.4	17 35.3	347 53.7
10	330 54.4	17 36.7	17 58.6
12	0 54.5	17 38.0	48 03.6
14	30 54.5	17 39.3	78 08.5
16	60 54.6	17 40.6	108 13.4
18	90 54.6	17 41.9	138 18.3
20	120 54.6	17 43.2	168 23.3
22	150 54.7	N17 44.5	198 28.2

Wednesday, May 11

Time	SUN GHA	Dec	ARIES GHA
00	180 54.7	N17 45.8	228 33.1
02	210 54.7	17 47.1	258 38.1
04	240 54.8	17 48.4	288 43.0
06	270 54.8	17 49.6	318 47.9
08	300 54.9	17 50.9	348 52.8
10	330 54.9	17 52.2	18 57.8
12	0 54.9	17 53.5	49 02.7
14	30 55.0	17 54.8	79 07.6
16	60 55.0	17 56.1	109 12.6
18	90 55.0	17 57.3	139 17.5
20	120 55.0	17 58.6	169 22.4
22	150 55.1	N17 59.9	199 27.3

Thursday, May 12

Time	SUN GHA	Dec	ARIES GHA
00	180 55.1	N18 01.2	229 32.3
02	210 55.1	18 02.4	259 37.2
04	240 55.2	18 03.7	289 42.1
06	270 55.2	18 05.0	319 47.1
08	300 55.2	18 06.2	349 52.0
10	330 55.2	18 07.5	19 56.9
12	0 55.3	18 08.7	50 01.8
14	30 55.3	18 10.0	80 06.8
16	60 55.3	18 11.3	110 11.7
18	90 55.3	18 12.5	140 16.6
20	120 55.3	18 13.8	170 21.6
22	150 55.3	N18 15.0	200 26.5

Friday, May 13

Time	SUN GHA	Dec	ARIES GHA
00	180 55.4	N18 16.2	230 31.4
02	210 55.4	18 17.5	260 36.3
04	240 55.4	18 18.7	290 41.3
06	270 55.4	18 20.0	320 46.2
08	300 55.4	18 21.2	350 51.1
10	330 55.4	18 22.4	20 56.1
12	0 55.4	18 23.7	51 01.0
14	30 55.5	18 24.9	81 05.9
16	60 55.5	18 26.1	111 10.8
18	90 55.5	18 27.4	141 15.8
20	120 55.5	18 28.6	171 20.7
22	150 55.5	N18 29.8	201 25.6

Saturday, May 14

Time	SUN GHA	Dec	ARIES GHA
00	180 55.5	N18 31.0	231 30.6
02	210 55.5	18 32.2	261 35.5
04	240 55.5	18 33.5	291 40.4
06	270 55.5	18 34.7	321 45.3
08	300 55.5	18 35.9	351 50.3
10	330 55.5	18 37.1	21 55.2
12	0 55.5	18 38.3	52 00.1
14	30 55.5	18 39.5	82 05.0
16	60 55.5	18 40.7	112 10.0
18	90 55.5	18 41.9	142 14.9
20	120 55.5	18 43.1	172 19.8
22	150 55.5	N18 44.3	202 24.8

Sunday, May 15

Time	SUN GHA	Dec	ARIES GHA
00	180 55.5	N18 45.5	232 29.7
02	210 55.4	18 46.7	262 34.6
04	240 55.4	18 47.9	292 39.5
06	270 55.4	18 49.1	322 44.5
08	300 55.4	18 50.2	352 49.4
10	330 55.4	18 51.4	22 54.3
12	0 55.4	18 52.6	52 59.3
14	30 55.4	18 53.8	83 04.2
16	60 55.4	18 55.0	113 09.1
18	90 55.3	18 56.1	143 14.0
20	120 55.3	18 57.3	173 19.0
22	150 55.3	N18 58.5	203 23.9

MAY 1994 SUN & ARIES GMT

Time	SUN GHA ° ′	Dec ° ′	ARIES GHA ° ′	Time	SUN GHA ° ′	Dec ° ′	ARIES GHA ° ′	Time	SUN GHA ° ′	Dec ° ′	ARIES GHA ° ′	Time
	Monday, May 16				**Saturday, May 21**				**Thursday, May 26**			
00	180 55.3	N18 59.6	233 28.8	00	180 52.4	N20 05.5	238 24.5	00	180 46.3	N21 02.7	243 20.2	00
02	210 55.3	19 00.8	263 33.8	02	210 52.4	20 06.5	268 29.4	02	210 46.1	21 03.6	273 25.1	02
04	240 55.3	19 02.0	293 38.7	04	240 52.3	20 07.5	298 34.4	04	240 46.0	21 04.5	303 30.1	04
06	270 55.2	19 03.1	323 43.6	06	270 52.2	20 08.5	328 39.3	06	270 45.9	21 05.4	333 35.0	06
08	300 55.2	19 04.3	353 48.5	08	300 52.1	20 09.6	358 44.2	08	300 45.8	21 06.2	3 39.9	08
10	330 55.2	19 05.4	23 53.5	10	330 52.0	20 10.6	28 49.2	10	330 45.6	21 07.1	33 44.9	10
12	0 55.2	19 06.6	53 58.4	12	0 52.0	20 11.6	58 54.1	12	0 45.5	21 08.0	63 49.8	12
14	30 55.1	19 07.7	84 03.3	14	30 51.9	20 12.6	88 59.0	14	30 45.4	21 08.8	93 54.7	14
16	60 55.1	19 08.9	114 08.3	16	60 51.8	20 13.6	119 03.9	16	60 45.2	21 09.7	123 59.6	16
18	90 55.1	19 10.0	144 13.2	18	90 51.7	20 14.6	149 08.9	18	90 45.1	21 10.6	154 04.6	18
20	120 55.0	19 11.2	174 18.1	20	120 51.6	20 15.6	179 13.8	20	120 45.0	21 11.4	184 09.5	20
22	150 55.0	N19 12.3	204 23.0	22	150 51.5	N20 16.6	209 18.7	22	150 44.8	N21 12.3	214 14.4	22
	Tuesday, May 17				**Sunday, May 22**				**Friday, May 27**			
00	180 55.0	N19 13.5	234 28.0	00	180 51.5	N20 17.6	239 23.7	00	180 44.7	N21 13.1	244 19.4	00
02	210 55.0	19 14.6	264 32.9	02	210 51.4	20 18.6	269 28.6	02	210 44.5	21 14.0	274 24.3	02
04	240 54.9	19 15.7	294 37.8	04	240 51.3	20 19.6	299 33.5	04	240 44.4	21 14.8	304 29.2	04
06	270 54.9	19 16.9	324 42.8	06	270 51.2	20 20.6	329 38.4	06	270 44.3	21 15.7	334 34.1	06
08	300 54.9	19 18.0	354 47.7	08	300 51.1	20 21.6	359 43.4	08	300 44.1	21 16.5	4 39.1	08
10	330 54.8	19 19.1	24 52.6	10	330 51.0	20 22.6	29 48.3	10	330 44.0	21 17.3	34 44.0	10
12	0 54.8	19 20.3	54 57.5	12	0 50.9	20 23.6	59 53.2	12	0 43.8	21 18.2	64 48.9	12
14	30 54.8	19 21.4	85 02.5	14	30 50.8	20 24.6	89 58.2	14	30 43.7	21 19.0	94 53.8	14
16	60 54.7	19 22.5	115 07.4	16	60 50.7	20 25.5	120 03.1	16	60 43.5	21 19.8	124 58.8	16
18	90 54.7	19 23.6	145 12.3	18	90 50.6	20 26.5	150 08.0	18	90 43.4	21 20.7	155 03.7	18
20	120 54.6	19 24.7	175 17.2	20	120 50.5	20 27.5	180 12.9	20	120 43.2	21 21.5	185 08.6	20
22	150 54.6	N19 25.9	205 22.2	22	150 50.4	N20 28.5	210 17.9	22	150 43.1	N21 22.3	215 13.6	22
	Wednesday, May 18				**Monday, May 23**				**Saturday, May 28**			
00	180 54.6	N19 27.0	235 27.1	00	180 50.3	N20 29.4	240 22.8	00	180 43.0	N21 23.1	245 18.5	00
02	210 54.5	19 28.1	265 32.0	02	210 50.3	20 30.4	270 27.7	02	210 42.8	21 23.9	275 23.4	02
04	240 54.5	19 29.2	295 37.0	04	240 50.2	20 31.4	300 32.7	04	240 42.7	21 24.8	305 28.3	04
06	270 54.4	19 30.3	325 41.9	06	270 50.1	20 32.3	330 37.6	06	270 42.5	21 25.6	335 33.3	06
08	300 54.4	19 31.4	355 46.8	08	300 50.0	20 33.3	0 42.5	08	300 42.4	21 26.4	5 38.2	08
10	330 54.3	19 32.5	25 51.7	10	330 49.9	20 34.3	30 47.4	10	330 42.2	21 27.2	35 43.1	10
12	0 54.3	19 33.6	55 56.7	12	0 49.8	20 35.2	60 52.4	12	0 42.0	21 28.0	65 48.1	12
14	30 54.2	19 34.7	86 01.6	14	30 49.6	20 36.2	90 57.3	14	30 41.9	21 28.8	95 53.0	14
16	60 54.2	19 35.8	116 06.5	16	60 49.5	20 37.1	121 02.2	16	60 41.7	21 29.6	125 57.9	16
18	90 54.1	19 36.9	146 11.5	18	90 49.4	20 38.1	151 07.2	18	90 41.6	21 30.4	156 02.8	18
20	120 54.1	19 38.0	176 16.4	20	120 49.3	20 39.0	181 12.1	20	120 41.4	21 31.2	186 07.8	20
22	150 54.0	N19 39.1	206 21.3	22	150 49.2	N20 40.0	211 17.0	22	150 41.3	N21 32.0	216 12.7	22
	Thursday, May 19				**Tuesday, May 24**				**Sunday, May 29**			
00	180 54.0	N19 40.1	236 26.2	00	180 49.1	N20 40.9	241 21.9	00	180 41.1	N21 32.8	246 17.6	00
02	210 53.9	19 41.2	266 31.2	02	210 49.0	20 41.8	271 26.9	02	210 41.0	21 33.6	276 22.6	02
04	240 53.9	19 42.3	296 36.1	04	240 48.9	20 42.8	301 31.8	04	240 40.8	21 34.3	306 27.5	04
06	270 53.8	19 43.4	326 41.0	06	270 48.8	20 43.7	331 36.7	06	270 40.6	21 35.1	336 32.4	06
08	300 53.8	19 44.5	356 46.0	08	300 48.7	20 44.6	1 41.6	08	300 40.5	21 35.9	6 37.3	08
10	330 53.7	19 45.5	26 50.9	10	330 48.6	20 45.6	31 46.6	10	330 40.3	21 36.7	36 42.3	10
12	0 53.6	19 46.6	56 55.8	12	0 48.5	20 46.5	61 51.5	12	0 40.1	21 37.4	66 47.2	12
14	30 53.6	19 47.7	87 00.7	14	30 48.3	20 47.4	91 56.4	14	30 40.0	21 38.2	96 52.1	14
16	60 53.5	19 48.7	117 05.7	16	60 48.2	20 48.3	122 01.4	16	60 39.8	21 39.0	126 57.1	16
18	90 53.5	19 49.8	147 10.6	18	90 48.1	20 49.3	152 06.3	18	90 39.7	21 39.8	157 02.0	18
20	120 53.4	19 50.9	177 15.5	20	120 48.0	20 50.2	182 11.2	20	120 39.5	21 40.5	187 06.9	20
22	150 53.3	N19 51.9	207 20.5	22	150 47.9	N20 51.1	212 16.1	22	150 39.3	N21 41.3	217 11.8	22
	Friday, May 20				**Wednesday, May 25**				**Monday, May 30**			
00	180 53.3	N19 53.0	237 25.4	00	180 47.8	N20 52.0	242 21.1	00	180 39.2	N21 42.0	247 16.8	00
02	210 53.2	19 54.0	267 30.3	02	210 47.6	20 52.9	272 26.0	02	210 39.0	21 42.8	277 21.7	02
04	240 53.1	19 55.1	297 35.2	04	240 47.5	20 53.8	302 30.9	04	240 38.8	21 43.5	307 26.6	04
06	270 53.1	19 56.1	327 40.2	06	270 47.4	20 54.7	332 35.9	06	270 38.6	21 44.3	337 31.6	06
08	300 53.0	19 57.2	357 45.1	08	300 47.3	20 55.6	2 40.8	08	300 38.5	21 45.0	7 36.5	08
10	330 52.9	19 58.2	27 50.0	10	330 47.2	20 56.5	32 45.7	10	330 38.3	21 45.8	37 41.4	10
12	0 52.9	19 59.3	57 55.0	12	0 47.0	20 57.4	62 50.6	12	0 38.1	21 46.5	67 46.3	12
14	30 52.8	20 00.3	87 59.9	14	30 46.9	20 58.3	92 55.6	14	30 38.0	21 47.3	97 51.3	14
16	60 52.7	20 01.3	118 04.8	16	60 46.8	20 59.2	123 00.5	16	60 37.8	21 48.0	127 56.2	16
18	90 52.6	20 02.4	148 09.7	18	90 46.7	21 00.1	153 05.4	18	90 37.6	21 48.7	158 01.1	18
20	120 52.6	20 03.4	178 14.7	20	120 46.5	21 01.0	183 10.4	20	120 37.4	21 49.5	188 06.0	20
22	150 52.5	N20 04.4	208 19.6	22	150 46.4	N21 01.9	213 15.3	22	150 37.3	N21 50.2	218 11.0	22
					Tuesday, May 31							
00	180 37.1	N21 50.9	248 15.9	08	300 36.4	N21 53.8	8 35.6	16	60 35.7	N21 56.6	128 55.3	16
02	210 36.9	21 51.7	278 20.8	10	330 36.2	21 54.5	38 40.5	18	90 35.5	21 57.3	159 00.3	18
04	240 36.7	21 52.4	308 25.8	12	0 36.0	21 55.2	68 45.5	20	120 35.3	21 58.0	189 05.2	20
06	270 36.6	N21 53.1	338 30.7	14	30 35.8	N21 55.9	98 50.4	22	150 35.1	N21 58.7	219 10.1	22

Chapter 6

MAY 1994   PLANETS   0h GMT

VENUS / JUPITER

Mer Pass h m	GHA ° ′	Mean Var/hr 14°+	Dec ° ′	Mean Var/hr ′			GHA ° ′	Mean Var/hr 15°+	Dec ° ′	Mean Var/hr ′	Mer Pass h m
13 41	154 58.3	59.3	N21 58.6	0.6	1	SUN	0 56.3	2.8	S13 23.8	0.1	23 52
13 42	154 40.4	59.2	N22 13.8	0.6	2	Mon	2 02.9	2.8	S13 21.4	0.1	23 47
13 43	154 22.3	59.2	N22 28.3	0.6	3	Tue	3 09.6	2.8	S13 19.1	0.1	23 43
13 44	154 03.9	59.2	N22 42.2	0.6	4	Wed	4 16.2	2.8	S13 16.8	0.1	23 39
13 46	153 45.4	59.2	N22 55.5	0.5	5	Thu	5 22.7	2.8	S13 14.4	0.1	23 34
13 47	153 26.6	59.2	N23 08.1	0.5	6	Fri	6 29.3	2.8	S13 12.1	0.1	23 30
13 48	153 07.7	59.2	N23 20.1	0.5	7	Sat	7 35.9	2.8	S13 09.8	0.1	23 25
13 50	152 48.6	59.2	N23 31.4	0.4	8	SUN	8 42.4	2.8	S13 07.5	0.1	23 21
13 51	152 29.3	59.2	N23 42.1	0.4	9	Mon	9 48.8	2.8	S13 05.2	0.1	23 16
13 52	152 09.8	59.2	N23 52.1	0.4	10	Tue	10 55.2	2.8	S13 02.9	0.1	23 12
13 53	151 50.2	59.2	N24 01.4	0.4	11	Wed	12 01.6	2.8	S13 00.7	0.1	23 08
13 55	151 30.5	59.2	N24 10.1	0.3	12	Thu	13 07.9	2.8	S12 58.4	0.1	23 03
13 56	151 10.7	59.2	N24 18.1	0.3	13	Fri	14 14.2	2.8	S12 56.2	0.1	22 59
13 57	150 50.7	59.2	N24 25.3	0.3	14	Sat	15 20.4	2.8	S12 54.0	0.1	22 54
13 59	150 30.7	59.2	N24 31.9	0.2	15	SUN	16 26.5	2.8	S12 51.9	0.1	22 50
14 00	150 10.5	59.2	N24 37.8	0.2	16	Mon	17 32.6	2.8	S12 49.7	0.1	22 46
14 01	149 50.3	59.2	N24 43.0	0.2	17	Tue	18 38.6	2.7	S12 47.6	0.1	22 41
14 03	149 30.1	59.2	N24 47.5	0.2	18	Wed	19 44.5	2.7	S12 45.5	0.1	22 37
14 04	149 09.9	59.2	N24 51.2	0.1	19	Thu	20 50.3	2.7	S12 43.5	0.1	22 33
14 05	148 49.6	59.2	N24 54.3	0.1	20	Fri	21 56.0	2.7	S12 41.4	0.1	22 28
14 07	148 29.3	59.2	N24 56.6	0.1	21	Sat	23 01.6	2.7	S12 39.4	0.1	22 24
14 08	148 09.1	59.2	N24 58.3	0.0	22	SUN	24 07.2	2.7	S12 37.5	0.1	22 19
14 10	147 48.8	59.2	N24 59.2	0.0	23	Mon	25 12.6	2.7	S12 35.6	0.1	22 15
14 11	147 28.7	59.2	N24 59.4	0.0	24	Tue	26 17.9	2.7	S12 33.7	0.1	22 11
14 12	147 08.6	59.2	N24 58.9	0.1	25	Wed	27 23.2	2.7	S12 31.8	0.1	22 06
14 14	146 48.6	59.2	N24 57.6	0.1	26	Thu	28 28.3	2.7	S12 30.0	0.1	22 02
14 15	146 28.6	59.2	N24 55.7	0.1	27	Fri	29 33.3	2.7	S12 28.2	0.1	21 58
14 16	146 08.8	59.2	N24 53.0	0.1	28	Sat	30 38.1	2.7	S12 26.5	0.1	21 54
14 18	145 49.2	59.2	N24 49.7	0.2	29	SUN	31 42.9	2.7	S12 24.8	0.1	21 49
14 19	145 29.6	59.2	N24 45.6	0.2	30	Mon	32 47.5	2.7	S12 23.2	0.1	21 45
14 20	145 10.3	59.2	N24 40.9	0.2	31	Tue	33 52.0	2.7	S12 21.6	0.1	21 41

VENUS, Av Mag –3.9
SHA May
5 291; 10 285; 15 278; 20 271; 25 265; 30 258.

JUPITER, Av Mag –2.5
SHA May
5 143; 10 143; 15 144; 20 145; 25 145; 30 146.

MARS / SATURN

Mer Pass h m	GHA ° ′	Mean Var/hr 15°+	Dec ° ′	Mean Var/hr ′			GHA ° ′	Mean Var/hr 15°+	Dec ° ′	Mean Var/hr ′	Mer Pass h m
10 12	206 45.6	0.7	N 4 03.7	0.8	1	SUN	236 23.7	2.3	S 9 12.4	0.1	08 13
10 11	207 02.4	0.7	N 4 22.0	0.8	2	Mon	237 18.4	2.3	S 9 10.8	0.1	08 10
10 10	207 19.1	0.7	N 4 40.1	0.8	3	Tue	238 13.1	2.3	S 9 09.2	0.1	08 06
10 09	207 35.8	0.7	N 4 58.2	0.8	4	Wed	239 07.8	2.3	S 9 07.6	0.1	08 02
10 08	207 52.5	0.7	N 5 16.3	0.8	5	Thu	240 02.7	2.3	S 9 06.1	0.1	07 59
10 07	208 09.2	0.7	N 5 34.3	0.7	6	Fri	240 57.6	2.3	S 9 04.6	0.1	07 55
10 06	208 25.8	0.7	N 5 52.2	0.7	7	Sat	241 52.5	2.3	S 9 03.1	0.1	07 51
10 05	208 42.5	0.7	N 6 10.0	0.7	8	SUN	242 47.6	2.3	S 9 01.7	0.1	07 48
10 04	208 59.2	0.7	N 6 27.8	0.7	9	Mon	243 42.7	2.3	S 9 00.3	0.1	07 44
10 02	209 15.9	0.7	N 6 45.5	0.7	10	Tue	244 37.9	2.3	S 8 58.9	0.1	07 40
10 01	209 32.5	0.7	N 7 03.1	0.7	11	Wed	245 33.2	2.3	S 8 57.6	0.1	07 37
10 00	209 49.1	0.7	N 7 20.6	0.7	12	Thu	246 28.5	2.3	S 8 56.2	0.1	07 33
09 59	210 05.8	0.7	N 7 38.1	0.7	13	Fri	247 23.9	2.3	S 8 54.9	0.1	07 29
09 58	210 22.4	0.7	N 7 55.4	0.7	14	Sat	248 19.4	2.3	S 8 53.7	0.1	07 26
09 57	210 39.0	0.7	N 8 12.7	0.7	15	SUN	249 15.0	2.3	S 8 52.5	0.1	07 22
09 56	210 55.5	0.7	N 8 29.8	0.7	16	Mon	250 10.7	2.3	S 8 51.3	0.1	07 18
09 55	211 12.1	0.7	N 8 46.9	0.7	17	Tue	251 06.4	2.3	S 8 50.1	0.1	07 14
09 54	211 28.6	0.7	N 9 03.9	0.7	18	Wed	252 02.2	2.3	S 8 49.0	0.0	07 11
09 53	211 45.1	0.7	N 9 20.7	0.7	19	Thu	252 58.1	2.3	S 8 47.9	0.0	07 07
09 51	212 01.6	0.7	N 9 37.5	0.7	20	Fri	253 54.0	2.3	S 8 46.8	0.0	07 03
09 50	212 18.1	0.7	N 9 54.1	0.7	21	Sat	254 50.1	2.3	S 8 45.8	0.0	07 00
09 49	212 34.5	0.7	N10 10.7	0.7	22	SUN	255 46.2	2.3	S 8 44.8	0.0	06 56
09 48	212 50.9	0.7	N10 27.1	0.7	23	Mon	256 42.4	2.3	S 8 43.9	0.0	06 52
09 47	213 07.3	0.7	N10 43.4	0.7	24	Tue	257 38.7	2.3	S 8 43.0	0.0	06 48
09 46	213 23.6	0.7	N10 59.6	0.7	25	Wed	258 35.1	2.4	S 8 42.1	0.0	06 45
09 45	213 40.0	0.7	N11 15.7	0.7	26	Thu	259 31.6	2.4	S 8 41.2	0.0	06 41
09 44	213 56.3	0.7	N11 31.7	0.7	27	Fri	260 28.1	2.4	S 8 40.4	0.0	06 37
09 43	214 12.5	0.7	N11 47.5	0.7	28	Sat	261 24.8	2.4	S 8 39.6	0.0	06 33
09 42	214 28.7	0.7	N12 03.2	0.6	29	SUN	262 21.5	2.4	S 8 38.9	0.0	06 30
09 41	214 44.9	0.7	N12 18.8	0.6	30	Mon	263 18.3	2.4	S 8 38.2	0.0	06 26
09 39	215 01.1	0.7	N12 34.2	0.6	31	Tue	264 15.2	2.4	S 8 37.5	0.0	06 22

MARS, Av Mag +1.2
SHA May
5 345; 10 342; 15 338; 20 335; 25 331; 30 327.

SATURN, Av Mag +1.0
SHA May
5 17; 10 17; 15 17; 20 16; 25 16; 30 16.

MAY 1994 — MOON

Day	GMT hr	GHA ° ′	Mean Var/hr 14°+	Dec ° ′	Mean Var/hr ′	Day	GMT hr	GHA ° ′	Mean Var/hr 14°+	Dec ° ′	Mean Var/hr ′
1 Sun	0	286 57.4	28.0	S 17 27.3	7.0	17 Tue	0	106 22.6	30.5	N 13 36.4	9.0
	6	13 15.6	28.6	S 16 45.7	7.5		6	193 25.2	30.4	N 12 42.2	9.5
	12	100 37.0	29.1	S 16 01.1	0.0		12	280 28.0	30.5	N 11 45.3	10.0
	18	187 31.6	29.6	S 15 13.7	8.3		18	7 31.0	30.5	N 10 46.0	10.3
2 Mon	0	274 29.3	30.2	S 14 23.9	8.7	18 Wed	0	94 34.0	30.4	N 9 44.3	10.7
	6	1 30.1	30.6	S 13 31.7	9.0		6	181 36.9	30.5	N 8 40.4	11.0
	12	88 33.8	31.1	S 12 37.5	9.4		12	268 39.7	30.4	N 7 34.4	11.3
	18	175 40.2	31.6	S 11 41.4	9.6		18	355 42.1	30.3	N 6 26.6	11.6
3 Tue	0	262 49.2	31.9	S 10 43.8	9.8	19 Thu	0	82 44.0	30.2	N 5 17.1	11.9
	6	350 00.7	32.4	S 9 44.7	10.0		6	169 45.3	30.1	N 4 06.1	12.1
	12	77 14.5	32.6	S 8 44.4	10.3		12	256 45.8	29.9	N 2 53.8	12.3
	18	164 30.3	33.0	S 7 43.1	10.4		18	343 45.3	29.7	N 1 40.5	12.3
4 Wed	0	251 48.1	33.3	S 6 40.9	10.5	20 Fri	0	70 43.6	29.5	N 0 26.2	12.5
	6	339 07.6	33.5	S 5 38.0	10.5		6	157 40.7	29.3	S 0 48.6	12.6
	12	66 28.6	33.7	S 4 34.6	10.6		12	244 36.2	29.0	S 2 03.8	12.6
	18	153 50.9	33.9	S 3 30.7	10.6		18	331 30.0	28.6	S 3 19.0	12.5
5 Thu	0	241 14.4	34.1	S 2 26.7	10.7	21 Sat	0	58 22.0	28.3	S 4 34.1	12.5
	6	328 38.9	34.2	S 1 22.5	10.7		6	145 12.0	28.0	S 5 48.8	12.3
	12	56 04.1	34.3	S 0 18.4	10.6		12	231 59.8	27.5	S 7 02.6	12.1
	18	143 30.0	34.4	N 0 45.5	10.6		18	318 45.2	27.1	S 8 15.3	11.8
6 Fri	0	230 56.4	34.5	N 1 49.2	10.5	22 Sun	0	45 28.3	26.7	S 9 26.6	11.6
	6	318 23.0	34.5	N 2 52.3	10.5		6	132 08.8	26.3	S 10 36.1	11.2
	12	45 49.7	34.4	N 3 55.0	10.3		12	218 46.7	25.9	S 11 43.5	10.8
	18	133 16.3	34.4	N 4 56.9	10.1		18	305 21.9	25.4	S 12 48.5	10.3
7 Sat	0	220 42.8	34.3	N 5 58.0	10.0	23 Mon	0	31 54.5	25.0	S 13 50.5	9.8
	6	308 08.9	34.3	N 6 58.1	9.8		6	118 24.5	24.5	S 14 49.4	9.2
	12	35 34.5	34.1	N 7 57.2	9.6		12	204 51.9	24.1	S 15 44.8	8.6
	18	122 59.5	34.0	N 8 55.1	9.4		18	291 16.9	23.7	S 16 36.3	7.8
8 Sun	0	210 23.7	33.9	N 9 51.6	9.1	24 Tue	0	17 39.7	23.4	S 17 23.6	7.0
	6	297 47.1	33.7	N 10 46.6	8.8		6	104 00.4	23.1	S 18 06.4	6.2
	12	25 09.5	33.5	N 11 40.1	8.5		12	190 19.4	22.9	S 18 44.5	5.4
	18	112 30.8	33.3	N 12 31.8	8.2		18	276 36.9	22.7	S 19 17.6	4.6
9 Mon	0	199 51.0	33.1	N 13 21.6	8.0	25 Wed	0	2 53.2	22.6	S 19 45.5	3.7
	6	287 10.0	32.9	N 14 09.5	7.6		6	89 08.9	22.5	S 20 08.1	2.8
	12	14 27.7	32.7	N 14 55.2	7.2		12	175 24.2	22.5	S 20 25.3	1.9
	18	101 44.0	32.5	N 15 38.7	6.8		18	261 39.6	22.7	S 20 36.9	0.9
10 Tue	0	188 59.0	32.2	N 16 19.7	6.4	26 Thu	0	347 55.6	22.8	S 20 43.1	0.0
	6	276 12.6	32.0	N 16 58.3	5.9		6	74 12.5	23.1	S 20 43.7	0.8
	12	Eclipse of the sun					12	160 30.7	23.3	S 20 39.0	1.7
	18	90 35.6	31.6	N 18 07.3	5.0		18	246 50.7	23.7	S 20 29.0	2.6
11 Wed	0	177 45.1	31.3	N 18 37.6	4.5	27 Fri	0	333 12.9	24.2	S 20 13.8	3.4
	6	264 53.2	31.1	N 19 04.8	3.9		6	59 37.4	24.6	S 19 53.8	4.2
	12	352 00.0	30.9	N 19 28.9	3.4		12	146 04.7	25.1	S 19 29.0	5.0
	18	79 05.6	30.8	N 19 49.8	2.8		18	232 35.0	25.6	S 18 59.7	5.6
12 Thu	0	166 10.1	30.5	N 20 07.4	2.3	28 Sat	0	319 08.4	26.2	S 18 26.3	6.3
	6	253 13.6	30.4	N 20 21.7	1.7		6	45 45.1	26.7	S 17 48.9	6.9
	12	340 16.1	30.3	N 20 32.4	1.1		12	132 25.1	27.3	S 17 07.8	7.5
	18	67 17.8	30.2	N 20 39.6	0.6		18	219 08.6	27.9	S 16 23.5	7.9
13 Fri	0	154 18.7	30.0	N 20 43.3	0.0	29 Sun	0	305 55.5	28.5	S 15 36.0	8.4
	6	241 19.1	29.9	N 20 43.3	0.6		6	32 45.8	29.0	S 14 45.8	8.8
	12	328 19.0	29.9	N 20 39.7	1.3		12	119 39.5	29.6	S 13 53.1	9.2
	18	55 18.5	29.8	N 20 32.4	1.8		18	206 36.4	30.1	S 12 58.1	9.5
14 Sat	0	142 17.8	29.8	N 20 21.4	2.5	30 Mon	0	293 36.4	30.5	S 12 01.2	9.8
	6	229 16.9	29.9	N 20 06.7	3.1		6	20 39.5	31.1	S 11 02.5	10.0
	12	316 16.1	29.9	N 19 48.4	3.7		12	107 45.3	31.4	S 10 02.4	10.3
	18	43 15.4	29.9	N 19 26.5	4.3		18	194 53.9	31.9	S 9 00.9	10.4
15 Sun	0	130 14.8	29.9	N 19 01.0	4.9	31 Tue	0	282 04.9	32.2	S 7 58.4	10.6
	6	217 14.5	30.0	N 18 32.0	5.5		6	9 18.2	32.6	S 6 55.1	10.7
	12	304 14.5	30.1	N 17 59.5	6.0		12	96 33.7	32.9	S 5 51.1	10.8
	18	31 14.8	30.2	N 17 23.6	6.6		18	183 51.0	33.2	S 4 46.6	10.9
16 Mon	0	118 15.6	30.2	N 16 44.4	7.2						
	6	205 16.7	30.2	N 16 01.9	7.7						
	12	292 18.3	30.4	N 15 16.4	8.1						
	18	19 20.3	30.4	N 14 27.9	8.6						

Chapter 6

JUNE 1994 — SUN & MOON — GMT

SUN

Yr	Mth	Week	0h m s	12h m s	Transit h m	Semi-diam '	Twi-light h m	Sun-rise h m	Sun-set h m	Twi-light h m	Lat °	Twi-light h m	Sun-rise h m	Sun-set h m	Twi-light h m
152	1	Wed	−02 20	−02 15	11 58	15.8	03 00	03 46	20 10	20 57	N70	SAH	SAH	SAH	SAH
153	2	Thu	−02 11	−02 06	11 58	15.8	02 59	03 45	20 11	20 58	68	SAH	SAH	SAH	SAH
154	3	Fri	−02 01	−01 56	11 58	15.8	02 58	03 45	20 12	20 59	66	SAH	SAH	SAH	SAH
155	4	Sat	−01 51	−01 46	11 58	15.8	02 57	03 44	20 13	21 00	64	TAN	−2 06	+2 07	TAN
156	5	Sun	−01 41	−01 36	11 58	15.8	02 56	03 43	20 14	21 02	62	TAN	−1 29	+1 30	TAN
157	6	Mon	−01 30	−01 25	11 59	15.8	02 55	03 43	20 15	21 03	N60	−1 57	−1 03	+1 04	+1 58
158	7	Tue	−01 19	−01 14	11 59	15.8	02 54	03 42	20 16	21 04	58	−1 09	−0 43	+0 43	+1 11
159	8	Wed	−01 08	−01 03	11 59	15.8	02 54	03 42	20 17	21 05	56	−0 39	−0 26	+0 26	+0 40
160	9	Thu	−00 57	−00 51	11 59	15.8	02 53	03 41	20 18	21 06	54	−0 17	−0 12	+0 12	+0 18
161	10	Fri	−00 45	−00 39	11 59	15.8	02 53	03 41	20 18	21 07	50	+0 16	+0 11	−0 11	−0 15
162	11	Sat	−00 33	−00 27	12 00	15.8	02 52	03 40	20 19	21 07	N45	+0 45	+0 33	−0 34	−0 46
163	12	Sun	−00 21	−00 14	12 00	15.8	02 52	03 40	20 20	21 08	40	+1 07	+0 51	−0 51	−1 07
164	13	Mon	−00 08	−00 02	12 00	15.8	02 51	03 40	20 20	21 09	35	+1 25	+1 06	−1 06	−1 25
165	14	Tue	+00 04	+00 11	12 00	15.8	02 51	03 40	20 21	21 10	30	+1 40	+1 19	−1 20	−1 40
166	15	Wed	+00 17	+00 24	12 00	15.8	02 51	03 39	20 22	21 10	20	+2 05	+1 41	−1 41	−2 05
167	16	Thu	+00 30	+00 37	12 01	15.8	02 51	03 39	20 22	21 11	N10	+2 26	+2 00	−2 00	−2 26
168	17	Fri	+00 43	+00 49	12 01	15.8	02 50	03 39	20 23	21 11	0	+2 44	+2 18	−2 18	−2 44
169	18	Sat	+00 56	+01 02	12 01	15.8	02 50	03 39	20 23	21 12	S10	+3 01	+2 35	−2 36	−3 01
170	19	Sun	+01 09	+01 15	12 01	15.8	02 50	03 39	20 23	21 12	20	+3 18	+2 54	−2 54	−3 18
171	20	Mon	+01 22	+01 29	12 01	15.8	02 51	03 39	20 24	21 12	30	+3 37	+3 15	−3 15	−3 37
172	21	Tue	+01 35	+01 42	12 02	15.8	02 51	03 40	20 24	21 13	S35	+3 48	+3 27	−3 28	−3 48
173	22	Wed	+01 48	+01 54	12 02	15.8	02 51	03 40	20 24	21 13	40	+4 00	+3 41	−3 42	−3 59
174	23	Thu	+02 01	+02 07	12 02	15.8	02 51	03 40	20 24	21 13	45	+4 13	+3 58	−3 58	−4 13
175	24	Fri	+02 14	+02 20	12 02	15.8	02 52	03 40	20 24	21 13	S50	+4 29	+4 19	−4 19	−4 29
176	25	Sat	+02 26	+02 33	12 03	15.8	02 52	03 41	20 24	21 13					
177	26	Sun	+02 39	+02 45	12 03	15.8	02 52	03 41	20 24	21 13					
178	27	Mon	+02 52	+02 58	12 03	15.8	02 53	03 42	20 24	21 13					
179	28	Tue	+03 04	+03 10	12 03	15.8	02 54	03 42	20 24	21 12					
180	29	Wed	+03 16	+03 22	12 03	15.8	02 54	03 43	20 24	21 12					
181	30	Thu	+03 28	+03 34	12 04	15.8	02 55	03 43	20 23	21 12					

Day of / Equation of Time (0h, 12h) / Transit / Semi-diam / Lat 52°N: Twi-light, Sun-rise, Sun-set, Twi-light / Lat Corr to Sunrise, Sunset etc: Lat, Twi-light, Sun-rise, Sun-set, Twi-light

NOTES

Equation of Time changes its sign on the 14th. Lat corrections are for the middle of June. SAH = Sun above horizon. TAN = Twilight all night. Equation of Time is the excess of Mean Time over Apparent Time.

MOON

Yr	Mth	Week	Age days	Transit Diff (Upper) h m m	Semi-diam '	Hor Par '	Moon-rise h m	Moon-set h m
152	1	Wed	22	06 06 43	15.1	55.2	00 15	12 08
153	2	Thu	23	06 49 43	14.9	54.7	00 35	13 15
154	3	Fri	24	07 32 42	14.8	54.3	00 55	14 20
155	4	Sat	25	08 14 44	14.7	54.1	01 16	15 25
156	5	Sun	26	08 58 45	14.7	54.0	01 38	16 29
157	6	Mon	27	09 43 46	14.7	54.1	02 04	17 32
158	7	Tue	28	10 29 49	14.8	54.3	02 35	18 32
159	8	Wed	29	11 18 49	14.9	54.5	03 12	19 28
160	9	Thu	00	12 07 51	14.9	54.9	03 56	20 18
161	10	Fri	01	12 58 50	15.1	55.3	04 48	21 02
162	11	Sat	02	13 48 50	15.2	55.7	05 48	21 39
163	12	Sun	03	14 38 49	15.3	56.2	06 53	22 10
164	13	Mon	04	15 27 48	15.5	56.7	08 03	22 38
165	14	Tue	05	16 15 49	15.6	57.3	09 15	23 02
166	15	Wed	06	17 04 49	15.8	57.9	10 29	23 25
167	16	Thu	07	17 53 50	15.9	58.5	11 44	23 48
168	17	Fri	08	18 43 53	16.1	59.1	13 02	− −
169	18	Sat	09	19 36 56	16.2	59.6	14 21	00 13
170	19	Sun	10	20 32 58	16.4	60.1	15 42	00 40
171	20	Mon	11	21 30 61	16.4	60.3	17 01	01 13
172	21	Tue	12	22 31 62	16.5	60.4	18 15	01 55
173	22	Wed	13	23 33 60	16.4	60.2	19 20	02 46
174	23	Thu	14	24 33 _	16.3	59.8	20 13	03 47
175	24	Fri	15	00 33 57	16.1	59.2	20 55	04 58
176	25	Sat	16	01 30 53	15.9	58.4	21 28	06 12
177	26	Sun	17	02 23 50	15.7	57.6	21 56	07 27
178	27	Mon	18	03 13 47	15.5	56.8	22 19	08 41
179	28	Tue	19	04 00 44	15.3	56.0	22 40	09 52
180	29	Wed	20	04 44 44	15.1	55.3	23 00	11 00
181	30	Thu	21	05 28 42	14.9	54.8	23 21	12 07

Phases of the Moon

	d	h	m
☽ Last Quarter	1	04	02
● New Moon	9	08	26
☾ First Quarter	16	19	56
○ Full Moon	23	11	33
☽ Last Quarter	30	19	31
Apogee	5	13	
Perigee	21	07	

NOTES

For Latitude corrections to Moonrise and Moonset see page 706.

JUNE 1994 STARS 0h GMT June 1

No	Name	Mag	Transit h m	Dec ° ′	GHA ° ′	RA h m	SHA ° ′
	ARIES...............		7 22		249 15.0		
1	Alpheratz	2.2	7 30	N 29 03.5	247 13.3	0 08	357 58.3
2	Ankaa..............	2.4	7 48	S 42 19.9	242 44.8	0 26	353 29.8
3	Schedar...........	2.5	8 03	N 56 30.2	239 11.9	0 40	349 56.9
4	Diphda	2.2	8 05	S 18 00.9	238 25.3	0 43	349 10.3
5	Achernar	0.6	8 59	S 57 15.6	224 52.7	1 37	335 37.7
6	POLARIS..........	2.1	9 47	N 89 14.1	210 52.8	2 25	323 38.8
7	Hamal..............	2.2	9 28	N 23 26.1	217 32.1	2 07	328 17.1
8	Acamar	3.1	10 19	S 40 19.5	204 44.5	2 58	315 29.5
9	Menkar	2.8	10 23	N 4 04.1	203 45.2	3 02	314 30.2
10	Mirfak	1.9	10 45	N 49 50.3	198 16.2	3 24	309 01.2
11	Aldebaran	1.1	11 57	N 16 29.8	180 21.1	4 36	291 06.1
12	Rigel	0.3	12 35	S 8 12.6	170 41.1	5 14	281 26.1
13	Capella............	0.2	12 37	N 45 59.5	170 11.0	5 16	280 56.0
14	Bellatrix..........	1.7	12 46	N 6 20.6	168 02.6	5 25	278 47.6
15	Elnath	1.8	12 47	N 28 36.1	167 46.0	5 26	278 31.0
16	Alnilam	1.8	12 57	S 1 12.4	165 16.2	5 36	276 01.2
17	Betelgeuse......0.1-1.2		13 16	N 7 24.3	160 32.0	5 55	271 17.0
18	Canopus ....−0.9		13 45	S 52 41.7	153 18.0	6 24	264 03.0
19	Sirius ....−1.6		14 06	S 16 42.6	148 01.6	6 45	258 46.6
20	Adhara............	1.6	14 19	S 28 58.0	144 39.1	6 58	255 24.1
21	Castor	1.6	14 55	N 31 54.0	135 41.4	7 34	246 26.4
22	Procyon	0.5	15 00	N 5 14.2	134 29.9	7 39	245 14.9
23	Pollux	1.2	15 05	N 28 02.3	133 00.4	7 45	243 45.4
24	Avior	1.7	15 43	S 59 29.8	123 39.3	8 22	234 24.3
25	Suhail	2.2	16 28	S 43 24.9	112 18.2	9 08	223 03.2
26	Miaplacidus....	1.8	16 33	S 69 42.1	110 58.2	9 13	221 43.2
27	Alphard	2.2	16 48	S 8 38.3	107 25.2	9 27	218 10.2
28	Regulus...........	1.3	17 28	N 11 59.6	97 13.8	10 08	207 58.8
29	Dubhe	2.0	18 23	N 61 47.0	83 24.2	11 03	194 09.2
30	Denebola.........	2.2	19 09	N 14 36.2	72 03.1	11 49	182 48.1
31	Gienah	2.8	19 35	S 17 30.9	65 21.9	12 16	176 06.9
32	Acrux..............	1.1	19 46	S 63 04.5	62 40.0	12 26	173 25.0
33	Gacrux	1.6	19 51	S 57 05.3	61 31.6	12 31	172 16.6
34	Mimosa...........	1.5	20 07	S 59 39.9	57 23.5	12 47	168 08.5
35	Alioth	1.7	20 13	N 55 59.6	55 48.0	12 54	166 33.0
36	Spica................	1.2	20 45	S 11 08.1	48 01.1	13 25	158 46.1
37	Alkaid	1.9	21 07	N 49 20.6	42 24.8	13 47	153 09.8
38	Hadar	0.9	21 23	S 60 21.1	38 22.7	14 03	149 07.7
39	Menkent	2.3	21 26	S 36 20.8	37 39.1	14 06	148 24.1
40	Arcturus	0.2	21 35	N 19 12.7	35 23.5	14 15	146 08.5
41	Rigil Kent.	0.1	21 59	S 60 48.9	29 25.6	14 39	140 10.6
42	Zuben'ubi.......	2.9	22 10	S 16 01.2	26 35.9	14 51	137 20.9
43	Kochab............	2.2	22 10	N 74 10.9	26 33.6	14 51	137 18.6
44	Alphecca	2.3	22 54	N 26 44.1	15 37.7	15 34	126 22.7
45	Antares...........	1.2	23 48	S 26 25.2	1 58.4	16 29	112 43.4
46	Atria	1.9	0 11	S 69 01.1	357 12.4	16 48	107 57.4
47	Sabik	2.6	0 33	S 15 43.0	351 43.5	17 10	102 28.5
48	Shaula	1.7	0 56	S 37 05.9	345 55.8	17 33	96 40.8
49	Rasalhague	2.1	0 58	N 12 33.9	345 34.3	17 35	96 19.3
50	Eltanin	2.4	1 19	N 51 29.4	340 07.2	17 57	90 52.2
51	Kaus Aust.......	2.0	1 47	S 34 23.1	333 17.3	18 24	84 02.3
52	Vega	0.1	1 59	N 38 46.7	330 03.2	18 37	80 48.2
53	Nunki	2.1	2 18	S 26 18.1	325 30.6	18 55	76 15.6
54	Altair..............	0.9	3 13	N 8 51.3	311 36.8	19 51	62 21.8
55	Peacock...........	2.1	3 48	S 56 44.9	302 56.1	20 25	53 41.1
56	Deneb	1.3	4 04	N 45 15.6	298 55.8	20 41	49 40.8
57	Enif	2.5	5 06	N 9 51.0	283 15.9	21 44	34 00.9
58	Al Na'ir	2.2	5 30	S 46 58.9	277 16.4	22 08	28 01.4
59	Fomalhaut	1.3	6 19	S 29 38.8	264 54.6	22 57	15 39.6
60	Markab	2.6	6 26	N 15 10.5	263 07.5	23 05	13 52.5

Stars Transit Corr Table

Date	Corr h m	Date	Corr h m
1	−0 00	17	−1 03
2	−0 04	18	−1 07
3	−0 08	19	−1 11
4	−0 12	20	−1 15
5	−0 16	21	−1 19
6	−0 20	22	−1 23
7	−0 24	23	−1 27
8	−0 28	24	−1 30
9	−0 31	25	−1 34
10	−0 35	26	−1 38
11	−0 39	27	−1 42
12	−0 43	28	−1 46
13	−0 47	29	−1 50
14	−0 51	30	−1 54
15	−0 55		
16	−0 59		

STAR'S TRANSIT

To find the approx time of transit of a star for any day of the month use above table. All corrections are subtractive. If the quantity taken from the table is greater than the time of transit for the first of the month, add 23h 56min to the time of transit before subtracting the correction.

Example: What is the time of meridian passage of Alioth (No 35) on June 26?

	h min
Transit on the 1st	20 13
Corr for the 26th	−01 38
Transit on the 26th	18 35

JUNE DIARY

1 04 Last Quarter
1 12 Saturn 7°S of Moon
5 13 Moon at apogee
6 05 Mars 2°S of Moon
8 03 Ceres in conjunction with Sun
9 08 New Moon
10 05 Venus 5°S of Pollux
11 00 Mercury 3°N of Moon
11 15 Juno stationary
12 12 Mercury stationary
12 13 Venus 7°N of Moon
16 20 First Quarter
19 16 Jupiter 3°N of Moon
21 07 Moon at perigee
21 15 Solstice
23 12 Full Moon
24 04 Saturn stationary
24 23 Neptune 4°S of Moon
25 05 Uranus 5°S of Moon
25 10 Mercury in inferior conjuction
28 21 Saturn 7°S of Moon
30 30 Last Quarter

Chapter 6

JUNE 1994 — SUN & ARIES — GMT

Wednesday, June 1

Time	SUN GHA	Dec	ARIES GHA
00	180 34.9	N21 59.4	249 15.0
02	210 34.7	22 00.1	279 20.0
04	240 34.5	22 00.8	309 24.9
06	270 34.4	22 01.5	339 29.8
08	300 34.2	22 02.2	9 34.8
10	330 34.0	22 02.9	39 39.7
12	0 33.8	22 03.6	69 44.6
14	30 33.6	22 04.2	99 49.5
16	60 33.4	22 04.9	129 54.5
18	90 33.2	22 05.6	159 59.4
20	120 33.0	22 06.2	190 04.3
22	150 32.8	N22 06.9	220 09.3

Thursday, June 2

Time	SUN GHA	Dec	ARIES GHA
00	180 32.6	N22 07.6	250 14.2
02	210 32.4	22 08.2	280 19.1
04	240 32.2	22 08.9	310 24.0
06	270 32.0	22 09.5	340 29.0
08	300 31.9	22 10.2	10 33.9
10	330 31.7	22 10.8	40 38.8
12	0 31.5	22 11.5	70 43.8
14	30 31.3	22 12.1	100 48.7
16	60 31.1	22 12.8	130 53.6
18	90 30.9	22 13.4	160 58.5
20	120 30.7	22 14.0	191 03.5
22	150 30.5	N22 14.7	221 08.4

Friday, June 3

Time	SUN GHA	Dec	ARIES GHA
00	180 30.3	N22 15.3	251 13.3
02	210 30.1	22 15.9	281 18.2
04	240 29.8	22 16.6	311 23.2
06	270 29.6	22 17.2	341 28.1
08	300 29.4	22 17.8	11 33.0
10	330 29.2	22 18.4	41 38.0
12	0 29.0	22 19.0	71 42.9
14	30 28.8	22 19.6	101 47.8
16	60 28.6	22 20.3	131 52.7
18	90 28.4	22 20.9	161 57.7
20	120 28.2	22 21.5	192 02.6
22	150 28.0	N22 22.1	222 07.5

Saturday, June 4

Time	SUN GHA	Dec	ARIES GHA
00	180 27.8	N22 22.7	252 12.5
02	210 27.6	22 23.3	282 17.4
04	240 27.4	22 23.8	312 22.3
06	270 27.1	22 24.4	342 27.2
08	300 26.9	22 25.0	12 32.2
10	330 26.7	22 25.6	42 37.1
12	0 26.5	22 26.2	72 42.0
14	30 26.3	22 26.8	102 47.0
16	60 26.1	22 27.3	132 51.9
18	90 25.9	22 27.9	162 56.8
20	120 25.6	22 28.5	193 01.7
22	150 25.4	N22 29.1	223 06.7

Sunday, June 5

Time	SUN GHA	Dec	ARIES GHA
00	180 25.2	N22 29.6	253 11.6
02	210 25.0	22 30.2	283 16.5
04	240 24.8	22 30.7	313 21.5
06	270 24.6	22 31.3	343 26.4
08	300 24.3	22 31.9	13 31.3
10	330 24.1	22 32.4	43 36.2
12	0 23.9	22 33.0	73 41.2
14	30 23.7	22 33.5	103 46.1
16	60 23.4	22 34.0	133 51.0
18	90 23.2	22 34.6	163 56.0
20	120 23.0	22 35.1	194 00.9
22	150 22.8	N22 35.7	224 05.8

Monday, June 6

Time	SUN GHA	Dec	ARIES GHA
00	180 22.6	N22 36.2	254 10.7
02	210 22.3	22 36.7	284 15.7
04	240 22.1	22 37.2	314 20.6
06	270 21.9	22 37.8	344 25.5
08	300 21.6	22 38.3	14 30.5
10	330 21.4	22 38.8	44 35.4
12	0 21.2	22 39.3	74 40.3
14	30 21.0	22 39.8	104 45.2
16	60 20.7	22 40.3	134 50.2
18	90 20.5	22 40.9	164 55.1
20	120 20.3	22 41.4	195 00.0
22	150 20.0	N22 41.9	225 04.9

Tuesday, June 7

Time	SUN GHA	Dec	ARIES GHA
00	180 19.8	N22 42.4	255 09.9
02	210 19.6	22 42.9	285 14.8
04	240 19.4	22 43.4	315 19.7
06	270 19.1	22 43.8	345 24.7
08	300 18.9	22 44.3	15 29.6
10	330 18.7	22 44.8	45 34.5
12	0 18.4	22 45.3	75 39.4
14	30 18.2	22 45.8	105 44.4
16	60 17.9	22 46.3	135 49.3
18	90 17.7	22 46.7	165 54.2
20	120 17.5	22 47.2	195 59.2
22	150 17.2	N22 47.7	226 04.1

Wednesday, June 8

Time	SUN GHA	Dec	ARIES GHA
00	180 17.0	N22 48.1	256 09.0
02	210 16.8	22 48.6	286 13.9
04	240 16.5	22 49.1	316 18.9
06	270 16.3	22 49.5	346 23.8
08	300 16.0	22 50.0	16 28.7
10	330 15.8	22 50.4	46 33.7
12	0 15.6	22 50.9	76 38.6
14	30 15.3	22 51.3	106 43.5
16	60 15.1	22 51.8	136 48.4
18	90 14.8	22 52.2	166 53.4
20	120 14.6	22 52.6	196 58.3
22	150 14.4	N22 53.1	227 03.2

Thursday, June 9

Time	SUN GHA	Dec	ARIES GHA
00	180 14.1	N22 53.5	257 08.2
02	210 13.9	22 53.9	287 13.1
04	240 13.6	22 54.4	317 18.0
06	270 13.4	22 54.8	347 22.9
08	300 13.1	22 55.2	17 27.9
10	330 12.9	22 55.6	47 32.8
12	0 12.6	22 56.0	77 37.7
14	30 12.4	22 56.5	107 42.7
16	60 12.2	22 56.9	137 47.6
18	90 11.9	22 57.3	167 52.5
20	120 11.7	22 57.7	197 57.4
22	150 11.4	N22 58.1	228 02.4

Friday, June 10

Time	SUN GHA	Dec	ARIES GHA
00	180 11.2	N22 58.5	258 07.3
02	210 10.9	22 58.9	288 12.2
04	240 10.7	22 59.3	318 17.1
06	270 10.4	22 59.7	348 22.1
08	300 10.2	23 00.0	18 27.0
10	330 09.9	23 00.4	48 31.9
12	0 09.7	23 00.8	78 36.9
14	30 09.4	23 01.2	108 41.8
16	60 09.2	23 01.6	138 46.7
18	90 08.9	23 01.9	168 51.6
20	120 08.7	23 02.3	198 56.6
22	150 08.4	N23 02.7	229 01.5

Saturday, June 11

Time	SUN GHA	Dec	ARIES GHA
00	180 08.1	N23 03.0	259 06.4
02	210 07.9	23 03.4	289 11.4
04	240 07.6	23 03.8	319 16.3
06	270 07.4	23 04.1	349 21.2
08	300 07.1	23 04.5	19 26.1
10	330 06.9	23 04.8	49 31.1
12	0 06.6	23 05.2	79 36.0
14	30 06.4	23 05.5	109 40.9
16	60 06.1	23 05.9	139 45.9
18	90 05.9	23 06.2	169 50.8
20	120 05.6	23 06.5	199 55.7
22	150 05.3	N23 06.9	230 00.6

Sunday, June 12

Time	SUN GHA	Dec	ARIES GHA
00	180 05.1	N23 07.2	260 05.6
02	210 04.8	23 07.5	290 10.5
04	240 04.6	23 07.9	320 15.4
06	270 04.3	23 08.2	350 20.4
08	300 04.1	23 08.5	20 25.3
10	330 03.8	23 08.8	50 30.2
12	0 03.5	23 09.1	80 35.1
14	30 03.3	23 09.4	110 40.1
16	60 03.0	23 09.8	140 45.0
18	90 02.8	23 10.1	170 49.9
20	120 02.5	23 10.4	200 54.9
22	150 02.2	N23 10.7	230 59.8

Monday, June 13

Time	SUN GHA	Dec	ARIES GHA
00	180 02.0	N23 11.0	261 04.7
02	210 01.7	23 11.3	291 09.6
04	240 01.4	23 11.5	321 14.6
06	270 01.2	23 11.8	351 19.5
08	300 00.9	23 12.1	21 24.4
10	330 00.7	23 12.4	51 29.3
12	0 00.4	23 12.7	81 34.3
14	30 00.1	23 13.0	111 39.2
16	59 59.9	23 13.2	141 44.1
18	89 59.6	23 13.5	171 49.1
20	119 59.3	23 13.8	201 54.0
22	149 59.1	N23 14.0	231 58.9

Tuesday, June 14

Time	SUN GHA	Dec	ARIES GHA
00	179 58.8	N23 14.3	262 03.8
02	209 58.6	23 14.6	292 08.8
04	239 58.3	23 14.8	322 13.7
06	269 58.0	23 15.1	352 18.6
08	299 57.8	23 15.3	22 23.6
10	329 57.5	23 15.6	52 28.5
12	359 57.2	23 15.8	82 33.4
14	29 57.0	23 16.1	112 38.3
16	59 56.7	23 16.3	142 43.3
18	89 56.4	23 16.5	172 48.2
20	119 56.2	23 16.8	202 53.1
22	149 55.9	N23 17.0	232 58.1

Wednesday, June 15

Time	SUN GHA	Dec	ARIES GHA
00	179 55.6	N23 17.2	263 03.0
02	209 55.4	23 17.5	293 07.9
04	239 55.1	23 17.7	323 12.8
06	269 54.8	23 17.9	353 17.8
08	299 54.6	23 18.1	23 22.7
10	329 54.3	23 18.3	53 27.6
12	359 54.0	23 18.6	83 32.6
14	29 53.8	23 18.8	113 37.5
16	59 53.5	23 19.0	143 42.4
18	89 53.2	23 19.2	173 47.3
20	119 53.0	23 19.4	203 52.3
22	149 52.7	N23 19.6	233 57.2

JUNE 1994 — SUN & ARIES — GMT

Thursday, June 16

Time	SUN GHA	Dec	ARIES GHA
00	179 52.4	N23 19.8	264 02.1
02	209 52.2	23 20.0	294 07.1
04	239 51.9	23 20.1	324 12.0
06	269 51.6	23 20.3	354 16.9
08	299 51.3	23 20.5	24 21.8
10	329 51.1	23 20.7	54 26.8
12	359 50.8	23 20.9	84 31.7
14	29 50.5	23 21.1	114 36.6
16	59 50.3	23 21.2	144 41.5
18	89 50.0	23 21.4	174 46.5
20	119 49.7	23 21.6	204 51.4
22	149 49.5	N23 21.7	234 56.3

Friday, June 17

Time	SUN GHA	Dec	ARIES GHA
00	179 49.2	N23 21.9	265 01.3
02	209 48.9	23 22.0	295 06.2
04	239 48.6	23 22.2	325 11.1
06	269 48.4	23 22.3	355 16.0
08	299 48.1	23 22.5	25 21.0
10	329 47.8	23 22.6	55 25.9
12	359 47.6	23 22.8	85 30.8
14	29 47.3	23 22.9	115 35.8
16	59 47.0	23 23.1	145 40.7
18	89 46.8	23 23.2	175 45.6
20	119 46.5	23 23.3	205 50.5
22	149 46.2	N23 23.5	235 55.5

Saturday, June 18

Time	SUN GHA	Dec	ARIES GHA
00	179 45.9	N23 23.6	266 00.4
02	209 45.7	23 23.7	296 05.3
04	239 45.4	23 23.8	326 10.3
06	269 45.1	23 23.9	356 15.2
08	299 44.9	23 24.1	26 20.1
10	329 44.6	23 24.2	56 25.0
12	359 44.3	23 24.3	86 30.0
14	29 44.0	23 24.4	116 34.9
16	59 43.8	23 24.5	146 39.8
18	89 43.5	23 24.6	176 44.8
20	119 43.2	23 24.7	206 49.7
22	149 43.0	N23 24.8	236 54.6

Sunday, June 19

Time	SUN GHA	Dec	ARIES GHA
00	179 42.7	N23 24.9	266 59.5
02	209 42.4	23 25.0	297 04.5
04	239 42.1	23 25.0	327 09.4
06	269 41.9	23 25.1	357 14.3
08	299 41.6	23 25.2	27 19.3
10	329 41.3	23 25.3	57 24.2
12	359 41.1	23 25.4	87 29.1
14	29 40.8	23 25.4	117 34.0
16	59 40.5	23 25.5	147 39.0
18	89 40.2	23 25.6	177 43.9
20	119 40.0	23 25.6	207 48.8
22	149 39.7	N23 25.7	237 53.7

Monday, June 20

Time	SUN GHA	Dec	ARIES GHA
00	179 39.4	N23 25.7	267 58.7
02	209 39.2	23 25.8	298 03.6
04	239 38.9	23 25.9	328 08.5
06	269 38.6	23 25.9	358 13.5
08	299 38.3	23 25.9	28 18.4
10	329 38.1	23 26.0	58 23.3
12	359 37.8	23 26.0	88 28.2
14	29 37.5	23 26.1	118 33.2
16	59 37.3	23 26.1	148 38.1
18	89 37.0	23 26.1	178 43.0
20	119 36.7	23 26.2	208 48.0
22	149 36.4	N23 26.2	238 52.9

Tuesday, June 21

Time	SUN GHA	Dec	ARIES GHA
00	179 36.2	N23 26.2	268 57.8
02	209 35.9	23 26.2	299 02.7
04	239 35.6	23 26.2	329 07.7
06	269 35.4	23 26.3	359 12.6
08	299 35.1	23 26.3	29 17.5
10	329 34.8	23 26.3	59 22.5
12	359 34.6	23 26.3	89 27.4
14	29 34.3	23 26.3	119 32.3
16	59 34.0	23 26.3	149 37.2
18	89 33.7	23 26.3	179 42.2
20	119 33.5	23 26.3	209 47.1
22	149 33.2	N23 26.3	239 52.0

Wednesday, June 22

Time	SUN GHA	Dec	ARIES GHA
00	179 32.9	N23 26.3	269 57.0
02	209 32.7	23 26.2	300 01.9
04	239 32.4	23 26.2	330 06.8
06	269 32.1	23 26.2	0 11.7
08	299 31.9	23 26.2	30 16.7
10	329 31.6	23 26.2	60 21.6
12	359 31.3	23 26.1	90 26.5
14	29 31.0	23 26.1	120 31.5
16	59 30.8	23 26.1	150 36.4
18	89 30.5	23 26.0	180 41.3
20	119 30.2	23 26.0	210 46.2
22	149 30.0	N23 25.9	240 51.2

Thursday, June 23

Time	SUN GHA	Dec	ARIES GHA
00	179 29.7	N23 25.9	270 56.1
02	209 29.4	23 25.9	301 01.0
04	239 29.2	23 25.8	331 05.9
06	269 28.9	23 25.7	1 10.9
08	299 28.6	23 25.7	31 15.8
10	329 28.4	23 25.6	61 20.7
12	359 28.1	23 25.6	91 25.7
14	29 27.8	23 25.5	121 30.6
16	59 27.6	23 25.5	151 35.5
18	89 27.3	23 25.4	181 40.4
20	119 27.0	23 25.3	211 45.4
22	149 26.8	N23 25.2	241 50.3

Friday, June 24

Time	SUN GHA	Dec	ARIES GHA
00	179 26.5	N23 25.1	271 55.2
02	209 26.2	23 25.0	302 00.2
04	239 26.0	23 25.0	332 05.1
06	269 25.7	23 24.9	2 10.0
08	299 25.4	23 24.8	32 14.9
10	329 25.2	23 24.7	62 19.9
12	359 24.9	23 24.6	92 24.8
14	29 24.6	23 24.5	122 29.7
16	59 24.4	23 24.4	152 34.7
18	89 24.1	23 24.3	182 39.6
20	119 23.8	23 24.2	212 44.5
22	149 23.6	N23 24.1	242 49.4

Saturday, June 25

Time	SUN GHA	Dec	ARIES GHA
00	179 23.3	N23 23.9	272 54.4
02	209 23.0	23 23.8	302 59.3
04	239 22.8	23 23.7	333 04.2
06	269 22.5	23 23.6	3 09.2
08	299 22.3	23 23.4	33 14.1
10	329 22.0	23 23.3	63 19.0
12	359 21.7	23 23.2	93 23.9
14	29 21.5	23 23.1	123 28.9
16	59 21.2	23 22.9	153 33.8
18	89 20.9	23 22.8	183 38.7
20	119 20.7	23 22.6	213 43.7
22	149 20.4	N23 22.5	243 48.6

Sunday, June 26

Time	SUN GHA	Dec	ARIES GHA
00	179 20.2	N23 22.3	273 53.5
02	209 19.9	23 22.2	303 58.4
04	239 19.6	23 22.0	334 03.4
06	269 19.4	23 21.9	4 08.3
08	299 19.1	23 21.7	34 13.2
10	329 18.8	23 21.5	64 18.1
12	359 18.6	23 21.4	94 23.1
14	29 18.3	23 21.2	124 28.0
16	59 18.1	23 21.0	154 32.9
18	89 17.8	23 20.9	184 37.9
20	119 17.5	23 20.7	214 42.8
22	149 17.3	N23 20.5	244 47.7

Monday, June 27

Time	SUN GHA	Dec	ARIES GHA
00	179 17.0	N23 20.3	274 52.6
02	209 16.8	23 20.1	304 57.6
04	239 16.5	23 20.0	335 02.5
06	269 16.3	23 19.8	5 07.4
08	299 16.0	23 19.6	35 12.4
10	329 15.7	23 19.4	65 17.3
12	359 15.5	23 19.2	95 22.2
14	29 15.2	23 19.0	125 27.1
16	59 15.0	23 18.8	155 32.1
18	89 14.7	23 18.5	185 37.0
20	119 14.4	23 18.3	215 41.9
22	149 14.2	N23 18.1	245 46.9

Tuesday, June 28

Time	SUN GHA	Dec	ARIES GHA
00	179 13.9	N23 17.9	275 51.8
02	209 13.7	23 17.7	305 56.7
04	239 13.4	23 17.5	336 01.6
06	269 13.2	23 17.2	6 06.6
08	299 12.9	23 17.0	36 11.5
10	329 12.7	23 16.8	66 16.4
12	359 12.4	23 16.5	96 21.4
14	29 12.2	23 16.3	126 26.3
16	59 11.9	23 16.1	156 31.2
18	89 11.6	23 15.8	186 36.1
20	119 11.4	23 15.6	216 41.1
22	149 11.1	N23 15.3	246 46.0

Wednesday, June 29

Time	SUN GHA	Dec	ARIES GHA
00	179 10.9	N23 15.1	276 50.9
02	209 10.6	23 14.8	306 55.9
04	239 10.4	23 14.6	337 00.8
06	269 10.1	23 14.3	7 05.7
08	299 09.9	23 14.0	37 10.6
10	329 09.6	23 13.8	67 15.6
12	359 09.4	23 13.5	97 20.5
14	29 09.1	23 13.2	127 25.4
16	59 08.9	23 13.0	157 30.4
18	89 08.6	23 12.7	187 35.3
20	119 08.4	23 12.4	217 40.2
22	149 08.1	N23 12.1	247 45.1

Thursday, June 30

Time	SUN GHA	Dec	ARIES GHA
00	179 07.9	N23 11.8	277 50.1
02	209 07.6	23 11.5	307 55.0
04	239 07.4	23 11.3	337 59.9
06	269 07.1	23 11.0	8 04.8
08	299 06.9	23 10.7	38 09.8
10	329 06.6	23 10.4	68 14.7
12	359 06.4	23 10.1	98 19.6
14	29 06.1	23 09.8	128 24.6
16	59 05.9	23 09.4	158 29.5
18	89 05.7	23 09.1	188 34.4
20	119 05.4	23 08.8	218 39.3
22	149 05.2	N23 08.5	248 44.3

Chapter 6

JUNE 1994 — PLANETS — 0h GMT

VENUS | JUPITER

Mer Pass h m	GHA ° '	Mean Var/hr 14°+	Dec ° '	Mean Var/hr '			GHA ° '	Mean Var/hr 15°+	Dec ° '	Mean Var/hr '	Mer Pass h m
14 21	144 51.1	59.2	N24 35.4	0.3	1	Wed	34 56.3	2.7	S12 20.0	0.1	21 36
14 23	144 32.1	59.2	N24 29.3	0.3	2	Thu	36 00.6	2.7	S12 18.5	0.1	21 32
14 24	144 13.3	59.2	N24 22.4	0.3	3	Fri	37 04.6	2.7	S12 17.1	0.1	21 28
14 25	143 54.7	59.2	N24 14.9	0.3	4	Sat	38 08.6	2.7	S12 15.7	0.1	21 24
14 26	143 36.3	59.2	N24 06.7	0.4	5	SUN	39 12.4	2.7	S12 14.3	0.1	21 19
14 28	143 18.2	59.3	N23 57.8	0.4	6	Mon	40 16.0	2.6	S12 13.0	0.1	21 15
14 29	143 00.3	59.3	N23 48.3	0.4	7	Tue	41 19.5	2.6	S12 11.8	0.1	21 11
14 30	142 42.7	59.3	N23 38.1	0.4	8	Wed	42 22.9	2.6	S12 10.6	0.0	21 07
14 31	142 25.4	59.3	N23 27.3	0.5	9	Thu	43 26.1	2.6	S12 09.5	0.0	21 03
14 32	142 08.4	59.3	N23 15.8	0.5	10	Fri	44 29.1	2.6	S12 08.4	0.0	20 58
14 33	141 51.7	59.3	N23 03.7	0.5	11	Sat	45 32.0	2.6	S12 07.3	0.0	20 54
14 34	141 35.3	59.3	N22 51.0	0.6	12	SUN	46 34.8	2.6	S12 06.4	0.0	20 50
14 35	141 19.2	59.3	N22 37.6	0.6	13	Mon	47 37.3	2.6	S12 05.5	0.0	20 46
14 36	141 03.4	59.4	N22 23.7	0.6	14	Tue	48 39.7	2.6	S12 04.6	0.0	20 42
14 37	140 48.0	59.4	N22 09.1	0.6	15	Wed	49 42.0	2.6	S12 03.8	0.0	20 38
14 38	140 32.9	59.4	N21 54.0	0.7	16	Thu	50 44.1	2.6	S12 03.0	0.0	20 34
14 39	140 18.2	59.4	N21 38.3	0.7	17	Fri	51 46.0	2.6	S12 02.4	0.0	20 29
14 40	140 03.9	59.4	N21 22.0	0.7	18	Sat	52 47.7	2.6	S12 01.7	0.0	20 25
14 41	139 49.9	59.4	N21 05.2	0.7	19	SUN	53 49.3	2.6	S12 01.2	0.0	20 21
14 42	139 36.3	59.4	N20 47.9	0.7	20	Mon	54 50.7	2.5	S12 00.7	0.0	20 17
14 43	139 23.1	59.5	N20 30.0	0.8	21	Tue	55 51.9	2.5	S12 00.2	0.0	20 13
14 44	139 10.3	59.5	N20 11.6	0.8	22	Wed	56 53.0	2.5	S11 59.8	0.0	20 09
14 45	138 57.8	59.5	N19 52.7	0.8	23	Thu	57 53.9	2.5	S11 59.5	0.0	20 05
14 45	138 45.8	59.5	N19 33.3	0.8	24	Fri	58 54.6	2.5	S11 59.2	0.0	20 01
14 46	138 34.1	59.5	N19 13.4	0.9	25	Sat	59 55.2	2.5	S11 59.0	0.0	19 57
14 47	138 22.9	59.5	N18 53.0	0.9	26	SUN	60 55.6	2.5	S11 58.9	0.0	19 53
14 48	138 12.0	59.6	N18 32.2	0.9	27	Mon	61 55.8	2.5	S11 58.8	0.0	19 49
14 48	138 01.6	59.6	N18 10.9	0.9	28	Tue	62 55.8	2.5	S11 58.8	0.0	19 45
14 49	137 51.5	59.6	N17 49.2	0.9	29	Wed	63 55.7	2.5	S11 58.8	0.0	19 41
14 50	137 41.8	59.6	N17 27.1	0.9	30	Thu	64 55.3	2.5	S11 58.9	0.0	19 37

VENUS, Av Mag –4.0
SHA June
5 250; 10 244; 15 238; 20 232; 25 226; 30 220.

JUPITER, Av Mag –2.3
SHA June
5 146; 10 146; 15 147; 20 147; 25 147; 30 147.

MARS | SATURN

Mer Pass h m	GHA ° '	Mean Var/hr 15°+	Dec ° '	Mean Var/hr '			GHA ° '	Mean Var/hr 15°+	Dec ° '	Mean Var/hr '	Mer Pass h m
09 38	215 17.2	0.7	N12 49.5	0.6	1	Wed	265 12.2	2.4	S 8 36.9	0.0	06 18
09 37	215 33.3	0.7	N13 04.7	0.6	2	Thu	266 09.2	2.4	S 8 36.3	0.0	06 14
09 36	215 49.3	0.7	N13 19.7	0.6	3	Fri	267 06.4	2.4	S 8 35.7	0.0	06 11
09 35	216 05.4	0.7	N13 34.6	0.6	4	Sat	268 03.6	2.4	S 8 35.2	0.0	06 07
09 34	216 21.3	0.7	N13 49.4	0.6	5	SUN	269 01.0	2.4	S 8 34.7	0.0	06 03
09 33	216 37.3	0.7	N14 04.0	0.6	6	Mon	269 58.4	2.4	S 8 34.3	0.0	05 59
09 32	216 53.2	0.7	N14 18.5	0.6	7	Tue	270 55.9	2.4	S 8 33.9	0.0	05 55
09 31	217 09.0	0.7	N14 32.8	0.6	8	Wed	271 53.5	2.4	S 8 33.5	0.0	05 51
09 30	217 24.8	0.7	N14 46.9	0.6	9	Thu	272 51.2	2.4	S 8 33.1	0.0	05 48
09 29	217 40.6	0.7	N15 00.9	0.6	10	Fri	273 49.0	2.4	S 8 32.9	0.0	05 44
09 28	217 56.4	0.7	N15 14.8	0.6	11	Sat	274 46.9	2.4	S 8 32.6	0.0	05 40
09 27	218 12.1	0.7	N15 28.5	0.6	12	SUN	275 44.8	2.4	S 8 32.4	0.0	05 36
09 26	218 27.8	0.7	N15 42.0	0.6	13	Mon	276 42.9	2.4	S 8 32.2	0.0	05 32
09 25	218 43.4	0.6	N15 55.4	0.5	14	Tue	277 41.0	2.4	S 8 32.0	0.0	05 28
09 24	218 59.0	0.6	N16 08.6	0.5	15	Wed	278 39.3	2.4	S 8 31.9	0.0	05 25
09 23	219 14.6	0.6	N16 21.6	0.5	16	Thu	279 37.6	2.4	S 8 31.9	0.0	05 21
09 22	219 30.1	0.6	N16 34.5	0.5	17	Fri	280 36.0	2.4	S 8 31.8	0.0	05 17
09 21	219 45.6	0.6	N16 47.2	0.5	18	Sat	281 34.6	2.4	S 8 31.8	0.0	05 13
09 20	220 01.1	0.6	N16 59.8	0.5	19	SUN	282 33.2	2.4	S 8 31.9	0.0	05 09
09 18	220 16.5	0.6	N17 12.1	0.5	20	Mon	283 31.9	2.4	S 8 32.0	0.0	05 05
09 17	220 31.9	0.6	N17 24.3	0.5	21	Tue	284 30.7	2.5	S 8 32.1	0.0	05 01
09 16	220 47.3	0.6	N17 36.3	0.5	22	Wed	285 29.6	2.5	S 8 32.2	0.0	04 57
09 15	221 02.6	0.6	N17 48.2	0.5	23	Thu	286 28.6	2.5	S 8 32.4	0.0	04 53
09 14	221 18.0	0.6	N17 59.8	0.5	24	Fri	287 27.6	2.5	S 8 32.7	0.0	04 49
09 13	221 33.2	0.6	N18 11.3	0.5	25	Sat	288 26.8	2.5	S 8 32.9	0.0	04 45
09 12	221 48.5	0.6	N18 22.6	0.5	26	SUN	289 26.1	2.5	S 8 33.3	0.0	04 41
09 11	222 03.7	0.6	N18 33.7	0.5	27	Mon	290 25.4	2.5	S 8 33.6	0.0	04 38
09 10	222 18.9	0.6	N18 44.6	0.5	28	Tue	291 24.9	2.5	S 8 34.0	0.0	04 34
09 09	222 34.0	0.6	N18 55.4	0.4	29	Wed	292 24.4	2.5	S 8 34.4	0.0	04 30
09 08	222 49.1	0.6	N19 05.9	0.4	30	Thu	293 24.1	2.5	S 8 34.9	0.0	04 26

MARS, Av Mag +1.2
SHA June
5 323; 10 320; 15 316; 20 312; 25 309; 30 305.

SATURN, Av Mag +1.0
SHA June
5 16; 10 16; 15 16; 20 16; 25 16; 30 16.

JUNE 1994   MOON

Day	GMT hr	GHA ° '	Mean Var/hr 14°+	Dec ° '	Mean Var/hr '
1 Wed	0	271 10.1	33.5	S 3 41.7	10.8
	6	358 30.7	33.6	S 2 36.7	10.9
	12	85 52.0	33.0	S 1 31.7	10.8
	18	173 15.6	34.0	S 0 26.7	10.8
2 Thu	0	260 39.5	34.1	N 0 37.9	10.7
	6	348 04.2	34.2	N 1 42.2	10.6
	12	75 29.4	34.3	N 2 45.9	10.5
	18	162 54.9	34.3	N 3 49.0	10.4
3 Fri	0	250 20.7	34.3	N 4 51.3	10.3
	6	337 46.4	34.3	N 5 52.7	10.0
	12	65 12.0	34.2	N 6 53.2	9.9
	18	152 37.2	34.1	N 7 52.4	9.7
4 Sat	0	240 02.0	34.1	N 8 50.5	9.4
	6	327 26.1	33.9	N 9 47.2	9.1
	12	54 49.5	33.7	N10 42.4	8.9
	18	142 12.0	33.6	N11 35.9	8.6
5 Sun	0	229 33.5	33.4	N12 27.8	8.3
	6	316 53.9	33.2	N13 17.8	7.9
	12	44 13.0	32.9	N14 05.8	7.7
	18	131 30.9	32.7	N14 51.7	7.2
6 Mon	0	218 47.4	32.5	N15 35.4	6.8
	6	306 02.5	32.3	N16 16.7	6.5
	12	33 16.2	32.0	N16 55.5	6.0
	18	120 28.3	31.8	N17 31.7	5.6
7 Tue	0	207 39.0	31.5	N18 05.2	5.0
	6	294 48.2	31.3	N18 35.8	4.5
	12	21 55.9	31.0	N19 03.4	4.0
	18	109 02.2	30.8	N19 27.9	3.5
8 Wed	0	196 07.1	30.6	N19 49.2	3.0
	6	283 10.8	30.4	N20 07.2	2.4
	12	10 13.2	30.2	N20 21.8	1.8
	18	97 14.6	30.0	N20 32.9	1.3
9 Thu	0	184 15.0	29.9	N20 40.5	0.6
	6	271 14.5	29.8	N20 44.4	0.0
	12	358 13.3	29.7	N20 44.7	0.6
	18	85 11.5	29.6	N20 41.2	1.3
10 Fri	0	172 09.4	29.6	N20 34.0	1.9
	6	259 06.9	29.5	N20 23.1	2.5
	12	346 04.2	29.6	N20 08.4	3.1
	18	73 01.6	29.6	N19 50.0	3.8
11 Sat	0	159 59.1	29.6	N19 28.0	4.4
	6	246 56.8	29.6	N19 02.3	5.0
	12	333 54.8	29.8	N18 33.0	5.5
	18	60 53.3	29.8	N18 00.2	6.0
12 Sun	0	147 52.4	29.9	N17 24.0	6.6
	6	234 51.9	30.0	N16 44.5	7.2
	12	321 52.1	30.1	N16 01.8	7.7
	18	48 53.0	30.2	N15 16.0	8.1
13 Mon	0	135 54.5	30.3	N14 27.3	8.6
	6	222 56.6	30.5	N13 35.7	9.1
	12	309 59.3	30.6	N12 41.4	9.5
	18	37 02.6	30.6	N11 44.7	9.9
14 Tue	0	124 06.4	30.7	N10 45.5	10.3
	6	211 10.6	30.7	N 9 44.1	10.6
	12	298 15.0	30.7	N 8 40.7	10.9
	18	25 19.7	30.8	N 7 35.4	11.1
15 Wed	0	112 24.4	30.7	N 6 28.5	11.4
	6	199 29.1	30.8	N 5 20.0	11.6
	12	286 33.5	30.7	N 4 10.2	11.9
	18	13 37.5	30.5	N 2 59.3	12.0
16 Thu	0	100 41.0	30.5	N 1 47.5	12.1
	6	187 43.8	30.3	N 0 35.0	12.2
	12	274 45.6	30.1	S 0 38.0	12.2
	18	1 46.4	29.9	S 1 51.3	12.2
17 Fri	0	88 45.9	29.7	S 3 04.5	12.2
	6	175 44.0	29.4	S 4 17.6	12.1
	12	262 40.4	29.1	S 5 30.2	11.9
	18	349 35.0	28.7	S 6 42.0	11.8
18 Sat	0	76 27.6	28.4	S 7 52.8	11.0
	6	163 18.2	28.0	S 9 02.3	11.3
	12	250 06.4	27.6	S 10 10.3	10.9
	18	336 52.3	27.2	S 11 16.3	10.6
19 Sun	0	63 35.7	26.7	S 12 20.2	10.2
	6	150 16.6	26.4	S 13 21.6	9.7
	12	236 54.8	25.9	S 14 20.2	9.2
	18	323 30.5	25.5	S 15 15.7	8.6
20 Mon	0	50 03.7	25.1	S 16 07.7	8.0
	6	136 34.3	24.7	S 16 56.1	7.3
	12	223 02.6	24.3	S 17 40.4	6.7
	18	309 28.7	23.9	S 18 20.5	5.8
21 Tue	0	35 52.8	23.7	S 18 56.1	5.1
	6	122 15.1	23.5	S 19 26.9	4.3
	12	208 36.0	23.3	S 19 52.7	3.4
	18	294 55.8	23.1	S 20 13.5	2.5
22 Wed	0	21 14.8	23.1	S 20 29.0	1.6
	6	107 33.4	23.1	S 20 39.2	0.8
	12	193 52.1	23.2	S 20 44.1	0.2
	18	280 11.1	23.3	S 20 43.6	1.0
23 Thu	0	6 31.0	23.6	S 20 37.8	1.9
	6	92 52.1	23.8	S 20 26.2	2.8
	12	179 14.8	24.1	S 20 10.6	3.6
	18	265 39.5	24.5	S 19 49.5	4.4
24 Fri	0	352 06.3	24.9	S 19 23.7	5.2
	6	78 35.7	25.4	S 18 53.3	5.9
	12	165 07.8	25.9	S 18 18.7	6.5
	18	251 42.8	26.4	S 17 40.1	7.2
25 Sat	0	338 20.9	26.9	S 16 57.7	7.7
	6	65 02.0	27.5	S 16 11.9	8.2
	12	151 46.4	28.0	S 15 22.9	8.6
	18	238 34.0	28.5	S 14 31.1	9.1
26 Sun	0	325 24.8	29.0	S 13 36.7	9.5
	6	52 18.7	29.5	S 12 40.0	9.8
	12	139 15.7	30.1	S 11 41.2	10.1
	18	226 15.6	30.5	S 10 40.7	10.3
27 Mon	0	313 18.3	31.0	S 9 38.8	10.6
	6	40 23.6	31.3	S 8 35.5	10.7
	12	127 31.5	31.7	S 7 31.3	10.9
	18	214 41.8	32.1	S 6 26.3	10.9
28 Tue	0	301 54.2	32.4	S 5 20.6	11.0
	6	29 08.6	32.7	S 4 14.6	11.1
	12	116 24.8	33.0	S 3 08.3	11.1
	18	203 42.6	33.2	S 2 02.1	11.1
29 Wed	0	291 01.8	33.5	S 0 55.9	11.0
	6	18 22.2	33.6	N 0 10.0	10.9
	12	105 43.6	33.7	N 1 15.5	10.8
	18	193 05.9	33.9	N 2 20.3	10.7
30 Thu	0	280 28.9	33.9	N 3 24.5	10.6
	6	7 52.3	34.0	N 4 27.9	10.3
	12	95 16.0	34.0	N 5 30.3	10.2
	18	182 39.8	34.0	N 6 31.7	10.0

Chapter 6

JULY 1994 — SUN & MOON — GMT

SUN

Yr	Mth	Week	Eq of Time 0h	Eq of Time 12h	Transit	Semi-diam	Lat 52°N Twi-light	Sun-rise	Sun-set	Twi-light	Lat	Corr Twi-light	Corr Sun-rise	Corr Sun-set	Corr Twi-light
			m s	m s	h m	′	h m	h m	h m	h m	°	h m	h m	h m	h m
182	1	Fri	+03 40	+03 46	12 04	15.8	02 56	03 44	20 23	21 11	N70	SAH	SAH	SAH	SAH
183	2	Sat	+03 52	+03 57	12 04	15.8	02 57	03 45	20 23	21 11	68	SAH	SAH	SAH	SAH
184	3	Sun	+04 03	+04 09	12 04	15.8	02 57	03 45	20 22	21 10	66	TAN	−2 21	+2 19	TAN
185	4	Mon	+04 14	+04 20	12 04	15.8	02 58	03 46	20 22	21 10	64	TAN	−1 42	+1 40	TAN
186	5	Tue	+04 25	+04 30	12 05	15.8	02 59	03 47	20 21	21 09	62	−2 21	−1 14	+1 14	+2 21
187	6	Wed	+04 36	+04 41	12 05	15.8	03 00	03 48	20 21	21 08	N60	−1 27	−0 54	+0 54	+1 27
188	7	Thu	+04 46	+04 51	12 05	15.8	03 01	03 49	20 20	21 07	58	−0 55	−0 37	+0 37	+0 56
189	8	Fri	+04 55	+05 00	12 05	15.8	03 03	03 50	20 20	21 07	56	−0 33	−0 22	+0 23	+0 34
190	9	Sat	+05 05	+05 09	12 05	15.8	03 04	03 51	20 19	21 06	54	−0 15	−0 10	+0 11	+0 15
191	10	Sun	+05 14	+05 18	12 05	15.8	03 05	03 52	20 18	21 05	50	+0 13	+0 10	−0 10	−0 13
192	11	Mon	+05 22	+05 27	12 05	15.8	03 06	03 53	20 17	21 04	N45	+0 39	+0 30	−0 30	−0 39
193	12	Tue	+05 31	+05 34	12 06	15.8	03 08	03 54	20 16	21 03	40	+0 59	+0 46	−0 46	−0 59
194	13	Wed	+05 38	+05 42	12 06	15.8	03 09	03 55	20 16	21 01	35	+1 16	+1 00	−0 59	−1 16
195	14	Thu	+05 45	+05 49	12 06	15.8	03 10	03 56	20 15	21 00	30	+1 30	+1 12	−1 11	−1 30
196	15	Fri	+05 52	+05 55	12 06	15.8	03 12	03 58	20 14	20 59	20	+1 53	+1 32	−1 31	−1 52
197	16	Sat	+05 58	+06 01	12 06	15.8	03 13	03 59	20 13	20 58	N10	+2 12	+1 46	−1 48	−2 11
198	17	Sun	+06 04	+06 06	12 06	15.8	03 15	04 00	20 11	20 56	0	+2 28	+2 05	−2 04	−2 27
199	18	Mon	+06 09	+06 11	12 06	15.8	03 16	04 01	20 10	20 55	S10	+2 43	+2 21	−2 19	−2 43
200	19	Tue	+06 13	+06 15	12 06	15.8	03 18	04 03	20 09	20 54	20	+2 59	+2 38	−2 36	−2 59
201	20	Wed	+06 17	+06 19	12 06	15.8	03 19	04 04	20 08	20 52	30	+3 15	+2 57	−2 54	−3 15
202	21	Thu	+06 21	+06 22	12 06	15.8	03 21	04 05	20 07	20 51	S35	+3 25	+3 08	−3 06	−3 25
203	22	Fri	+06 23	+06 25	12 06	15.8	03 23	04 07	20 05	20 49	40	+3 35	+3 21	−3 18	−3 35
204	23	Sat	+06 26	+06 27	12 06	15.8	03 24	04 08	20 04	20 47	45	+3 38	+3 36	−3 33	−3 47
205	24	Sun	+06 27	+06 28	12 06	15.8	03 26	04 09	20 03	20 46	S50	+4 02	+3 55	−3 51	−4 02
206	25	Mon	+06 28	+06 29	12 06	15.8	03 28	04 11	20 01	20 44					
207	26	Tue	+06 29	+06 29	12 06	15.8	03 29	04 12	20 00	20 42					
208	27	Wed	+06 29	+06 29	12 06	15.8	03 31	04 14	19 58	20 41					
209	28	Thu	+06 28	+06 28	12 06	15.8	03 33	04 15	19 57	20 39					
210	29	Fri	+06 27	+06 26	12 06	15.8	03 34	04 17	19 55	20 37					
211	30	Sat	+06 25	+06 24	12 06	15.8	03 36	04 18	19 54	20 35					
212	31	Sun	+06 23	+06 21	12 06	15.8	03 38	04 20	19 52	20 33					

NOTES
Lat corrections are for the middle of July. SAH = Sun above horizon. TAN = Twilight all night. **Equation of Time** is the excess of Mean Time over Apparent Time.

MOON

Yr	Mth	Week	Age	Transit Diff (Upper)	Semi-diam	Hor Par	Moon-rise (Lat 52°N)	Moon-set (Lat 52°N)
			days	h m m	′	′	h m	h m
182	1	Fri	22	06 10 44	14.8	54.4	23 43	13 12
183	2	Sat	23	06 54 44	14.8	54.2	− −	14 17
184	3	Sun	24	07 38 46	14.8	54.2	00 07	15 20
185	4	Mon	25	08 24 48	14.8	54.3	00 36	16 22
186	5	Tue	26	09 12 49	14.9	54.6	01 10	17 20
187	6	Wed	27	10 01 51	15.0	54.9	01 51	18 13
188	7	Thu	28	10 52 51	15.1	55.4	02 40	19 00
189	8	Fri	29	11 43 50	15.2	55.9	03 38	19 39
190	9	Sat	01	12 33 52	15.4	56.4	04 42	20 13
191	10	Sun	02	13 24 49	15.5	56.9	05 52	20 43
192	11	Mon	03	14 13 49	15.6	57.4	07 04	21 08
193	12	Tue	04	15 02 49	15.8	57.9	08 18	21 32
194	13	Wed	05	15 51 50	15.9	58.3	09 34	21 55
195	14	Thu	06	16 41 51	16.0	58.7	10 50	22 19
196	15	Fri	07	17 32 53	16.1	59.0	12 08	22 45
197	16	Sat	08	18 25 56	16.2	59.3	13 26	23 15
198	17	Sun	09	19 21 58	16.2	59.5	14 44	23 52
199	18	Mon	10	20 19 60	16.2	59.6	15 58	− −
200	19	Tue	11	21 19 59	16.2	59.6	17 05	00 37
201	20	Wed	12	22 18 58	16.2	59.4	18 02	01 32
202	21	Thu	13	23 16 55	16.1	59.0	18 49	02 37
203	22	Fri	14	24 11 _	15.9	58.5	19 26	03 49
204	23	Sat	15	00 11 51	15.8	57.9	19 56	05 04
205	24	Sun	16	01 02 49	15.6	57.2	20 22	06 18
206	25	Mon	17	01 51 46	15.4	56.5	20 44	07 31
207	26	Tue	18	02 37 45	15.2	55.8	21 05	08 42
208	27	Wed	19	03 22 43	15.1	55.3	21 26	09 50
209	28	Thu	20	04 05 44	14.9	54.8	21 47	10 57
210	29	Fri	21	04 49 44	14.8	54.4	22 11	12 02
211	30	Sat	22	05 33 45	14.8	54.3	22 38	13 07
212	31	Sun	23	06 18 47	14.8	54.3	23 09	14 09

Phases of the Moon

		d	h	m
●	New Moon	8	21	37
◐	First Quarter	16	01	12
○	Full Moon	22	20	16
◑	Last Quarter	30	12	40
	Apogee	3	05	
	Perigee	18	18	
	Apogee	30	23	

NOTES
For Latitude corrections to Moonrise and Moonset see page 706.

JULY 1994   STARS   0h GMT July 1

No	Name	Mag	Transit h m	Dec ° '	GHA ° '	RA h m	SHA ° '
	ARIES................		5 24		278 49.2		
1	Alpheratz 2.2		5 32	N 29 03.6	276 47.2	0 08	357 58.0
2	Ankaa............. 2.4		5 50	S 42 19.8	272 18.7	0 26	353 29.5
3	Schedar....... 2.5		6 04	N 56 30.3	268 45.8	0 40	349 56.6
4	Diphda 2.2		6 07	S 18 00.0	267 59.2	0 43	349 10.0
5	Achernar ,........ 0.6		7 01	S 57 15.5	254 26.5	1 38	335 37.3
6	POLARIS........... 2.1		7 50	N 89 14.1	242 16.1	2 26	323 26.9
7	Hamal............. 2.2		7 30	N 23 26.2	247 06.0	1 07	328 16.8
8	Acamar 3.1		8 21	S 40 19.4	234 18.5	2 58	315 29.3
9	Menkar 2.8		8 25	N 4 04.1	233 19.2	3 02	314 30.0
10	Mirfak.............. 1.9		8 47	N 49 50.3	227 50.1	3 24	309 00.9
11	Aldebaran 1.1		9 59	N 16 29.8	209 55.1	4 36	291 05.9
12	Rigel 0.3		10 37	S 8 12.5	200 15.2	5 14	281 26.0
13	Capella............. 0.2		10 39	N 45 59.4	199 45.0	5 16	280 55.8
14	Bellatrix........... 1.7		10 48	N 6 20.6	197 36.7	5 25	278 47.5
15	Elnath 1.8		10 49	N 28 36.1	197 20.1	5 26	278 30.9
16	Alnilam 1.8		10 59	S 1 12.3	194 50.2	5 36	276 01.0
17	Betelgeuse......0.1-1.2		11 18	N 7 24.3	190 06.1	5 55	271 16.9
18	Canopus ....–0.9		11 47	S 52 41.6	182 52.1	6 24	264 02.9
19	Sirius................–1.6		12 08	S 16 42.5	177 35.7	6 45	258 46.5
20	Adhara............. 1.6		12 21	S 28 57.9	174 13.2	6 58	255 24.0
21	Castor 1.6		12 57	N 31 54.0	165 15.6	7 34	246 26.4
22	Procyon 0.5		13 02	N 5 14.3	164 04.1	7 39	245 14.9
23	Pollux 1.2		13 08	N 28 02.3	162 34.6	7 45	243 45.4
24	Avior 1.7		13 45	S 59 29.7	153 13.6	8 22	234 24.4
25	Suhail 2.2		14 30	S 43 24.8	141 52.5	9 08	223 03.3
26	Miaplacidus.... 1.8		14 35	S 69 41.9	140 32.6	9 13	221 43.4
27	Alphard 2.2		14 50	S 8 38.2	136 59.5	9 27	218 10.3
28	Regulus............ 1.3		15 30	N 11 59.6	126 48.0	10 08	207 58.8
29	Dubhe 2.0		16 25	N 61 47.0	112 58.6	11 03	194 09.4
30	Denebola......... 2.2		17 11	N 14 36.2	101 37.4	11 49	182 48.2
31	Gienah 2.8		17 37	S 17 30.8	94 56.2	12 16	176 07.0
32	Acrux................ 1.1		17 48	S 63 04.5	92 14.5	12 26	173 25.3
33	Gacrux 1.6		17 53	S 57 05.3	91 06.0	12 31	172 16.8
34	Mimosa............. 1.5		18 09	S 59 39.9	86 57.9	12 47	168 08.7
35	Alioth............... 1.7		18 16	N 55 59.6	85 22.4	12 54	166 33.2
36	Spica................ 1.2		18 47	S 11 08.0	77 35.4	13 25	158 46.2
37	Alkaid 1.9		19 09	N 49 20.7	71 59.2	13 47	153 10.0
38	Hadar 0.9		19 25	S 60 21.1	67 57.1	14 03	149 07.9
39	Menkent.......... 2.3		19 28	S 36 20.8	67 13.4	14 06	148 24.2
40	Arcturus 0.2		19 37	N 19 12.8	64 57.8	14 15	146 08.6
41	Rigil Kent. 0.1		20 01	S 60 49.0	59 00.0	14 39	140 10.8
42	Zuben'ubi........ 2.9		20 12	S 16 01.2	56 10.2	14 51	137 21.0
43	Kochab............ 2.2		20 12	N 74 11.0	56 08.3	14 51	137 19.1
44	Alphecca......... 2.3		20 56	N 26 44.2	45 12.0	15 34	126 22.8
45	Antares............ 1.2		21 50	S 26 25.2	31 32.6	16 29	112 43.4
46	Atria 1.9		22 09	S 69 01.2	26 46.7	16 48	107 57.5
47	Sabik 2.6		22 31	S 15 43.0	21 17.7	17 10	102 28.5
48	Shaula.............. 1.7		22 54	S 37 06.0	15 30.0	17 33	96 40.8
49	Rasalhague 2.1		22 56	N 12 34.0	15 08.5	17 35	96 19.3
50	Eltanin 2.4		23 17	N 51 29.6	9 41.4	17 57	90 52.2
51	Kaus Aust........ 2.0		23 45	S 34 23.2	2 51.4	18 24	84 02.2
52	Vega 0.1		0 02	N 38 46.9	359 37.3	18 37	80 48.1
53	Nunki 2.1		0 20	S 26 18.1	355 04.7	18 55	76 15.5
54	Altair................ 0.9		1 15	N 8 51.4	341 10.9	19 51	62 21.7
55	Peacock........... 2.1		1 50	S 56 44.9	332 30.1	20 25	53 40.9
56	Deneb 1.3		2 06	N 45 15.7	328 29.9	20 41	49 40.7
57	Enif 2.5		3 08	N 9 51.1	312 49.9	21 44	34 00.7
58	Al Na'ir 2.2		3 32	S 46 58.9	306 50.3	22 08	28 01.1
59	Fomalhaut 1.3		4 21	S 29 38.8	294 28.5	22 57	15 39.3
60	Markab 2.6		4 29	N 15 10.6	292 41.4	23 05	13 52.2

Stars Transit Corr Table

Date	Corr	Date	Corr
	h m		h m
1	–0 00	17	–1 03
2	–0 04	18	–1 07
3	–0 08	19	–1 11
4	–0 12	20	–1 15
5	–0 16	21	–1 19
6	–0 20	22	–1 23
7	–0 24	23	–1 27
8	–0 28	24	–1 30
9	–0 31	25	–1 34
10	–0 35	26	–1 38
11	–0 39	27	–1 42
12	–0 43	28	–1 46
13	–0 47	29	–1 50
14	–0 51	30	–1 54
15	–0 55	31	–1 58
16	–0 59		

STAR'S TRANSIT

To find the approx time of transit of a star for any day of the month use above table. All corrections are subtractive. If the quantity taken from the table is greater than the time of transit for the first of the month, add 23h 56min to the time of transit before subtracting the correction.

Example: Find the time of transit of Kochab (No 43) on July 18.

	h min
Transit on the 1st	20 12
Corr for the 18th	–01 07
Transit on the 18th	19 05

JULY DIARY

2 16 Jupiter stationary
3 05 Moon at apogee
5 05 Mars 0.3°N of Moon
5 19 Earth at aphelion
6 20 Mercury stationary
7 13 Mercury 1.3°S of Moon
8 22 New Moon
10 17 Venus 1.1°N of Regulus
12 12 Venus 7°N of Moon
14 16 Neptune at opposition
16 01 First Quarter
16 23 Jupiter 3°N of Moon
17 04 Uranus at opposition
17 14 Mercury greatest elongation W(21°)
18 18 Moon at perigee
18 21 Mars 5°N of Aldebaran
22 07 Neptune 4°S of Moon
22 12 Uranus 5°S of Moon
22 12 Full Moon
26 04 Saturn 7°S of Moon
30 13 Last Quarter
30 23 Moon at apogee
31 07 Mercury 6°S of Pollux

Chapter 6

JULY 1994 — SUN & ARIES — GMT

Friday, July 1

Time	SUN GHA	Dec	ARIES GHA	Time
00	179 04.9	N23 08.2	278 49.2	00
02	209 04.7	23 07.9	308 54.1	02
04	239 04.4	23 07.5	338 59.1	04
06	269 04.2	23 07.2	9 04.0	06
08	299 03.9	23 06.9	39 08.9	08
10	329 03.7	23 06.5	69 13.8	10
12	359 03.5	23 06.2	99 18.8	12
14	29 03.2	23 05.9	129 23.7	14
16	59 03.0	23 05.5	159 28.6	16
18	89 02.7	23 05.2	189 33.6	18
20	119 02.5	23 04.8	219 38.5	20
22	149 02.2	N23 04.5	249 43.4	22

Saturday, July 2

Time	SUN GHA	Dec	ARIES GHA	Time
00	179 02.0	N23 04.1	279 48.3	00
02	209 01.8	23 03.8	309 53.3	02
04	239 01.5	23 03.4	339 58.2	04
06	269 01.3	23 03.1	10 03.1	06
08	299 01.1	23 02.7	40 08.1	08
10	329 00.8	23 02.3	70 13.0	10
12	359 00.6	23 02.0	100 17.9	12
14	29 00.3	23 01.6	130 22.8	14
16	59 00.1	23 01.2	160 27.8	16
18	88 59.9	23 00.8	190 32.7	18
20	118 59.6	23 00.5	220 37.6	20
22	148 59.4	N23 00.1	250 42.6	22

Sunday, July 3

Time	SUN GHA	Dec	ARIES GHA	Time
00	178 59.2	N22 59.7	280 47.5	00
02	208 58.9	22 59.3	310 52.4	02
04	238 58.7	22 58.9	340 57.3	04
06	268 58.5	22 58.5	11 02.3	06
08	298 58.2	22 58.1	41 07.2	08
10	328 58.0	22 57.7	71 12.1	10
12	358 57.8	22 57.3	101 17.0	12
14	28 57.5	22 56.9	131 22.0	14
16	58 57.3	22 56.5	161 26.9	16
18	88 57.1	22 56.1	191 31.8	18
20	118 56.8	22 55.7	221 36.8	20
22	148 56.6	N22 55.2	251 41.7	22

Monday, July 4

Time	SUN GHA	Dec	ARIES GHA	Time
00	178 56.4	N22 54.8	281 46.6	00
02	208 56.1	22 54.4	311 51.5	02
04	238 55.9	22 54.0	341 56.5	04
06	268 55.7	22 53.5	12 01.4	06
08	298 55.5	22 53.1	42 06.3	08
10	328 55.2	22 52.7	72 11.3	10
12	358 55.0	22 52.2	102 16.2	12
14	28 54.8	22 51.8	132 21.1	14
16	58 54.6	22 51.4	162 26.0	16
18	88 54.3	22 50.9	192 31.0	18
20	118 54.1	22 50.5	222 35.9	20
22	148 53.9	N22 50.0	252 40.8	22

Tuesday, July 5

Time	SUN GHA	Dec	ARIES GHA	Time
00	178 53.7	N22 49.6	282 45.8	00
02	208 53.5	22 49.1	312 50.7	02
04	238 53.2	22 48.6	342 55.6	04
06	268 53.0	22 48.2	13 00.5	06
08	298 52.8	22 47.7	43 05.5	08
10	328 52.6	22 47.3	73 10.4	10
12	358 52.4	22 46.8	103 15.3	12
14	28 52.1	22 46.3	133 20.3	14
16	58 51.9	22 45.8	163 25.2	16
18	88 51.7	22 45.4	193 30.1	18
20	118 51.5	22 44.9	223 35.0	20
22	148 51.3	N22 44.4	253 40.0	22

Wednesday, July 6

Time	SUN GHA	Dec	ARIES GHA	Time
00	178 51.1	N22 43.9	283 44.9	00
02	208 50.8	22 43.4	313 49.8	02
04	238 50.6	22 42.9	343 54.8	04
06	268 50.4	22 42.4	13 59.7	06
08	298 50.2	22 41.9	44 04.6	08
10	328 50.0	22 41.4	74 09.5	10
12	358 49.8	22 40.9	104 14.5	12
14	28 49.6	22 40.4	134 19.4	14
16	58 49.4	22 39.9	164 24.3	16
18	88 49.2	22 39.4	194 29.2	18
20	118 49.0	22 38.9	224 34.2	20
22	148 48.8	N22 38.4	254 39.1	22

Thursday, July 7

Time	SUN GHA	Dec	ARIES GHA	Time
00	178 48.5	N22 37.9	284 44.0	00
02	208 48.3	22 37.3	314 49.0	02
04	238 48.1	22 36.8	344 53.9	04
06	268 47.9	22 36.3	14 58.8	06
08	298 47.7	22 35.8	45 03.7	08
10	328 47.5	22 35.2	75 08.7	10
12	358 47.3	22 34.7	105 13.6	12
14	28 47.1	22 34.1	135 18.5	14
16	58 46.9	22 33.6	165 23.5	16
18	88 46.7	22 33.1	195 28.4	18
20	118 46.5	22 32.5	225 33.3	20
22	148 46.3	N22 32.0	255 38.2	22

Friday, July 8

Time	SUN GHA	Dec	ARIES GHA	Time
00	178 46.1	N22 31.4	285 43.2	00
02	208 45.9	22 30.9	315 48.1	02
04	238 45.7	22 30.3	345 53.0	04
06	268 45.5	22 29.7	15 58.0	06
08	298 45.3	22 29.2	46 02.9	08
10	328 45.1	22 28.6	76 07.8	10
12	358 44.9	22 28.0	106 12.7	12
14	28 44.7	22 27.5	136 17.7	14
16	58 44.5	22 26.9	166 22.6	16
18	88 44.3	22 26.3	196 27.5	18
20	118 44.1	22 25.7	226 32.5	20
22	148 43.9	N22 25.2	256 37.4	22

Saturday, July 9

Time	SUN GHA	Dec	ARIES GHA	Time
00	178 43.8	N22 24.6	286 42.3	00
02	208 43.6	22 24.0	316 47.2	02
04	238 43.4	22 23.4	346 52.2	04
06	268 43.2	22 22.8	16 57.1	06
08	298 43.0	22 22.2	47 02.0	08
10	328 42.8	22 21.6	77 07.0	10
12	358 42.6	22 21.0	107 11.9	12
14	28 42.4	22 20.4	137 16.8	14
16	58 42.2	22 19.8	167 21.7	16
18	88 42.1	22 19.2	197 26.7	18
20	118 41.9	22 18.6	227 31.6	20
22	148 41.7	N22 18.0	257 36.5	22

Sunday, July 10

Time	SUN GHA	Dec	ARIES GHA	Time
00	178 41.5	N22 17.4	287 41.4	00
02	208 41.3	22 16.7	317 46.4	02
04	238 41.1	22 16.1	347 51.3	04
06	268 41.0	22 15.5	17 56.2	06
08	298 40.8	22 14.9	48 01.2	08
10	328 40.6	22 14.2	78 06.1	10
12	358 40.4	22 13.6	108 11.0	12
14	28 40.2	22 13.0	138 15.9	14
16	58 40.1	22 12.3	168 20.9	16
18	88 39.9	22 11.7	198 25.8	18
20	118 39.7	22 11.0	228 30.7	20
22	148 39.5	N22 10.4	258 35.7	22

Monday, July 11

Time	SUN GHA	Dec	ARIES GHA	Time
00	178 39.4	N22 09.8	288 40.6	00
02	208 39.2	22 09.1	318 45.5	02
04	238 39.0	22 08.4	348 50.4	04
06	268 38.8	22 07.8	18 55.4	06
08	298 38.7	22 07.1	49 00.3	08
10	328 38.5	22 06.5	79 05.2	10
12	358 38.3	22 05.8	109 10.2	12
14	28 38.2	22 05.1	139 15.1	14
16	58 38.0	22 04.5	169 20.0	16
18	88 37.8	22 03.8	199 24.9	18
20	118 37.7	22 03.1	229 29.9	20
22	148 37.5	N22 02.4	259 34.8	22

Tuesday, July 12

Time	SUN GHA	Dec	ARIES GHA	Time
00	178 37.3	N22 01.8	289 39.7	00
02	208 37.2	22 01.1	319 44.7	02
04	238 37.0	22 00.4	349 49.6	04
06	268 36.8	21 59.7	19 54.5	06
08	298 36.7	21 59.0	49 59.4	08
10	328 36.5	21 58.3	80 04.3	10
12	358 36.4	21 57.6	110 09.3	12
14	28 36.2	21 56.9	140 14.2	14
16	58 36.0	21 56.2	170 19.2	16
18	88 35.9	21 55.5	200 24.1	18
20	118 35.7	21 54.8	230 29.0	20
22	148 35.6	N21 54.1	260 33.9	22

Wednesday, July 13

Time	SUN GHA	Dec	ARIES GHA	Time
00	178 35.4	N21 53.4	290 38.9	00
02	208 35.3	21 52.7	320 43.8	02
04	238 35.1	21 52.0	350 48.7	04
06	268 35.0	21 51.3	20 53.6	06
08	298 34.8	21 50.5	50 58.6	08
10	328 34.7	21 49.8	81 03.5	10
12	358 34.5	21 49.1	111 08.4	12
14	28 34.4	21 48.4	141 13.4	14
16	58 34.2	21 47.6	171 18.3	16
18	88 34.1	21 46.9	201 23.2	18
20	118 33.9	21 46.2	231 28.1	20
22	148 33.8	N21 45.4	261 33.1	22

Thursday, July 14

Time	SUN GHA	Dec	ARIES GHA	Time
00	178 33.6	N21 44.7	291 38.0	00
02	208 33.5	21 43.9	321 42.9	02
04	238 33.3	21 43.2	351 47.9	04
06	268 33.2	21 42.4	21 52.8	06
08	298 33.1	21 41.7	51 57.7	08
10	328 32.9	21 40.9	82 02.6	10
12	358 32.8	21 40.2	112 07.6	12
14	28 32.6	21 39.4	142 12.5	14
16	58 32.5	21 38.7	172 17.4	16
18	88 32.4	21 37.9	202 22.4	18
20	118 32.2	21 37.1	232 27.3	20
22	148 32.1	N21 36.4	262 32.2	22

Friday, July 15

Time	SUN GHA	Dec	ARIES GHA	Time
00	178 32.0	N21 35.6	292 37.1	00
02	208 31.8	21 34.8	322 42.1	02
04	238 31.7	21 34.0	352 47.0	04
06	268 31.6	21 33.2	22 51.9	06
08	298 31.4	21 32.5	52 56.8	08
10	328 31.3	21 31.7	83 01.8	10
12	358 31.2	21 30.9	113 06.7	12
14	28 31.1	21 30.1	143 11.6	14
16	58 30.9	21 29.3	173 16.6	16
18	88 30.8	21 28.5	203 21.5	18
20	118 30.7	21 27.7	233 26.4	20
22	148 30.6	N21 26.9	263 31.4	22

JULY 1994 — SUN & ARIES — GMT

Columns for each day: **Time | SUN GHA | Dec | ARIES GHA**

Saturday, July 16

Time	SUN GHA	Dec	ARIES GHA
00	178 30.4	N21 26.1	293 36.3
02	208 30.3	21 25.3	323 41.2
04	238 30.2	21 24.5	353 46.1
06	268 30.1	21 23.7	23 51.1
08	298 30.0	21 22.9	53 56.0
10	328 29.0	21 22.1	84 00.9
12	358 29.7	21 21.2	114 05.8
14	28 29.6	21 20.4	144 10.8
16	58 29.5	21 19.6	174 15.7
18	88 29.4	21 18.8	204 20.6
20	118 29.3	21 17.9	234 25.6
22	148 29.1	N21 17.1	264 30.5

Sunday, July 17

Time	SUN GHA	Dec	ARIES GHA
00	178 29.0	N21 16.3	294 35.4
02	208 28.9	21 15.4	324 40.3
04	238 28.8	21 14.6	354 45.3
06	268 28.7	21 13.8	24 50.2
08	298 28.6	21 12.9	54 55.1
10	328 28.5	21 12.1	85 00.1
12	358 28.4	21 11.2	115 05.0
14	28 28.3	21 10.4	145 09.9
16	58 28.2	21 09.5	175 14.8
18	88 28.1	21 08.7	205 19.8
20	118 28.0	21 07.8	235 24.7
22	148 27.9	N21 06.9	265 29.6

Monday, July 18

Time	SUN GHA	Dec	ARIES GHA
00	178 27.8	N21 06.1	295 34.6
02	208 27.7	21 05.2	325 39.5
04	238 27.6	21 04.3	355 44.4
06	268 27.5	21 03.5	25 49.3
08	298 27.4	21 02.6	55 54.3
10	328 27.3	21 01.7	85 59.2
12	358 27.2	21 00.9	116 04.1
14	28 27.1	21 00.0	146 09.1
16	58 27.0	20 59.1	176 14.0
18	88 26.9	20 58.2	206 18.9
20	118 26.8	20 57.3	236 23.8
22	148 26.7	N20 56.4	266 28.8

Tuesday, July 19

Time	SUN GHA	Dec	ARIES GHA
00	178 26.7	N20 55.5	296 33.7
02	208 26.6	20 54.6	326 38.6
04	238 26.5	20 53.7	356 43.6
06	268 26.4	20 52.8	26 48.5
08	298 26.3	20 51.9	56 53.4
10	328 26.2	20 51.0	86 58.3
12	358 26.1	20 50.1	117 03.3
14	28 26.1	20 49.2	147 08.2
16	58 26.0	20 48.3	177 13.1
18	88 25.9	20 47.4	207 18.1
20	118 25.8	20 46.5	237 23.0
22	148 25.7	N20 45.5	267 27.9

Wednesday, July 20

Time	SUN GHA	Dec	ARIES GHA
00	178 25.7	N20 44.6	297 32.8
02	208 25.6	20 43.7	327 37.8
04	238 25.5	20 42.8	357 42.7
06	268 25.4	20 41.8	27 47.6
08	298 25.4	20 40.9	57 52.5
10	328 25.3	20 40.0	87 57.5
12	358 25.2	20 39.0	118 02.4
14	28 25.2	20 38.1	148 07.3
16	58 25.1	20 37.2	178 12.3
18	88 25.0	20 36.2	208 17.2
20	118 25.0	20 35.3	238 22.1
22	148 24.9	N20 34.3	268 27.0

Thursday, July 21

Time	SUN GHA	Dec	ARIES GHA
00	178 24.8	N20 33.4	298 32.0
02	208 24.8	20 32.4	328 36.9
04	238 24.7	20 31.5	358 41.8
06	268 24.6	20 30.5	28 46.8
08	298 24.6	20 29.5	58 51.7
10	328 24.5	20 28.6	88 56.6
12	358 24.5	20 27.6	119 01.5
14	28 24.4	20 26.6	149 00.5
16	58 24.3	20 25.7	179 11.4
18	88 24.3	20 24.7	209 16.3
20	118 24.2	20 23.7	239 21.3
22	148 24.2	N20 22.8	269 26.2

Friday, July 22

Time	SUN GHA	Dec	ARIES GHA
00	178 24.1	N20 21.8	299 31.1
02	208 24.1	20 20.8	329 36.0
04	238 24.0	20 19.8	359 41.0
06	268 24.0	20 18.8	29 45.9
08	298 23.9	20 17.8	59 50.8
10	328 23.9	20 16.8	89 55.8
12	358 23.8	20 15.8	120 00.7
14	28 23.8	20 14.9	150 05.6
16	58 23.7	20 13.9	180 10.5
18	88 23.7	20 12.9	210 15.5
20	118 23.7	20 11.8	240 20.4
22	148 23.6	N20 10.8	270 25.3

Saturday, July 23

Time	SUN GHA	Dec	ARIES GHA
00	178 23.6	N20 09.8	300 30.3
02	208 23.5	20 08.8	330 35.2
04	238 23.5	20 07.8	0 40.1
06	268 23.5	20 06.8	30 45.0
08	298 23.4	20 05.8	60 50.0
10	328 23.4	20 04.8	90 54.9
12	358 23.3	20 03.7	120 59.8
14	28 23.3	20 02.7	151 04.7
16	58 23.3	20 01.7	181 09.7
18	88 23.2	20 00.7	211 14.6
20	118 23.2	19 59.6	241 19.5
22	148 23.2	N19 58.6	271 24.5

Sunday, July 24

Time	SUN GHA	Dec	ARIES GHA
00	178 23.2	N19 57.6	301 29.4
02	208 23.1	19 56.5	331 34.3
04	238 23.1	19 55.5	1 39.2
06	268 23.1	19 54.4	31 44.2
08	298 23.1	19 53.4	61 49.1
10	328 23.0	19 52.3	91 54.0
12	358 23.0	19 51.3	121 59.0
14	28 23.0	19 50.2	152 03.9
16	58 23.0	19 49.2	182 08.8
18	88 22.9	19 48.1	212 13.7
20	118 22.9	19 47.1	242 18.7
22	148 22.9	N19 46.0	272 23.6

Monday, July 25

Time	SUN GHA	Dec	ARIES GHA
00	178 22.9	N19 44.9	302 28.5
02	208 22.9	19 43.9	332 33.5
04	238 22.9	19 42.8	2 38.4
06	268 22.8	19 41.7	32 43.3
08	298 22.8	19 40.7	62 48.2
10	328 22.8	19 39.6	92 53.2
12	358 22.8	19 38.5	122 58.1
14	28 22.8	19 37.4	153 03.0
16	58 22.8	19 36.4	183 08.0
18	88 22.8	19 35.3	213 12.9
20	118 22.8	19 34.2	243 17.8
22	148 22.8	N19 33.1	273 22.7

Tuesday, July 26

Time	SUN GHA	Dec	ARIES GHA
00	178 22.8	N19 32.0	303 27.7
02	208 22.8	19 30.9	333 32.6
04	238 22.8	19 29.8	3 37.5
06	268 22.8	19 28.7	33 42.5
08	298 22.8	19 27.6	63 47.4
10	328 22.8	19 26.5	93 52.3
12	358 22.8	19 25.4	123 57.2
14	28 22.8	19 24.3	154 02.2
16	58 22.8	19 23.2	184 07.1
18	88 22.8	19 22.1	214 12.0
20	118 22.8	19 21.0	244 16.9
22	148 22.8	N19 19.9	274 21.9

Wednesday, July 27

Time	SUN GHA	Dec	ARIES GHA
00	178 22.8	N19 18.7	304 26.8
02	208 22.8	19 17.6	334 31.7
04	238 22.8	19 16.5	4 36.7
06	268 22.8	19 15.4	34 41.6
08	298 22.8	19 14.2	64 46.5
10	328 22.8	19 13.1	94 51.4
12	358 22.8	19 12.0	124 56.4
14	28 22.9	19 10.9	155 01.3
16	58 22.9	19 09.7	185 06.2
18	88 22.9	19 08.6	215 11.2
20	118 22.9	19 07.4	245 16.1
22	148 22.9	N19 06.3	275 21.0

Thursday, July 28

Time	SUN GHA	Dec	ARIES GHA
00	178 23.0	N19 05.2	305 25.9
02	208 23.0	19 04.0	335 30.9
04	238 23.0	19 02.9	5 35.8
06	268 23.0	19 01.7	35 40.7
08	298 23.0	19 00.6	65 45.7
10	328 23.1	18 59.4	95 50.6
12	358 23.1	18 58.2	125 55.5
14	28 23.1	18 57.1	156 00.4
16	58 23.1	18 55.9	186 05.4
18	88 23.2	18 54.8	216 10.3
20	118 23.2	18 53.6	246 15.2
22	148 23.2	N18 52.4	276 20.2

Friday, July 29

Time	SUN GHA	Dec	ARIES GHA
00	178 23.3	N18 51.3	306 25.1
02	208 23.3	18 50.1	336 30.0
04	238 23.3	18 48.9	6 34.9
06	268 23.4	18 47.7	36 39.9
08	298 23.4	18 46.5	66 44.8
10	328 23.4	18 45.4	96 49.7
12	358 23.5	18 44.2	126 54.7
14	28 23.5	18 43.0	156 59.6
16	58 23.6	18 41.8	187 04.5
18	88 23.6	18 40.6	217 09.4
20	118 23.6	18 39.4	247 14.4
22	148 23.7	N18 38.2	277 19.3

Saturday, July 30

Time	SUN GHA	Dec	ARIES GHA
00	178 23.7	N18 37.0	307 24.2
02	208 23.8	18 35.8	337 29.1
04	238 23.8	18 34.6	7 34.1
06	268 23.9	18 33.4	37 39.0
08	298 23.9	18 32.2	67 43.9
10	328 24.0	18 31.0	97 48.9
12	358 24.0	18 29.8	127 53.8
14	28 24.1	18 28.6	157 58.7
16	58 24.1	18 27.4	188 03.6
18	88 24.2	18 26.2	218 08.6
20	118 24.2	18 25.0	248 13.5
22	148 24.3	N18 23.7	278 18.4

Sunday, July 31

Time	SUN GHA	Dec	ARIES GHA
00	178 24.3	N18 22.5	308 23.4
02	208 24.4	18 21.3	338 28.3
04	238 24.4	18 20.1	8 33.2
06	268 24.5	18 18.8	38 38.1
08	298 24.3	18 17.6	68 43.1
10	328 24.6	18 16.4	98 48.0
12	358 24.7	18 15.1	128 52.9
14	28 24.7	18 13.9	158 57.9
16	58 24.8	18 12.7	189 02.8
18	88 24.9	18 11.4	219 07.7
20	118 24.9	18 10.2	249 12.6
22	148 25.0	N18 08.9	279 17.6

Chapter 6

JULY 1994 — PLANETS — 0h GMT

VENUS / JUPITER

Mer Pass h m	GHA ° '	Mean Var/hr 14°+	Dec ° '	Mean Var/hr '		Day	GHA ° '	Mean Var/hr 13°+	Dec ° '	Mean Var/hr '	Mer Pass h m
14 50	137 32.6	59.6	N17 04.5	1.0	1	Fri	65 54.9	2.5	S11 59.0	0.0	19 33
14 31	137 23.7	59.6	N16 41.6	1.0	2	Sat	66 54.2	2.5	S11 59.3	0.0	19 29
14 51	137 15.1	59.7	N16 18.2	1.0	3	SUN	67 53.4	2.5	S11 59.5	0.0	19 25
14 52	137 07.0	59.7	N15 54.5	1.0	4	Mon	68 52.4	2.5	S11 59.9	0.0	19 21
14 52	136 59.3	59.7	N15 30.3	1.0	5	Tue	69 51.2	2.4	S12 00.3	0.0	19 17
14 53	136 51.9	59.7	N15 05.8	1.0	6	Wed	70 49.8	2.4	S12 00.7	0.0	19 14
14 53	136 45.0	59.7	N14 41.0	1.0	7	Thu	71 48.3	2.4	S12 01.2	0.0	19 10
14 54	136 38.4	59.7	N14 15.9	1.1	8	Fri	72 46.6	2.4	S12 01.8	0.0	19 06
14 54	136 32.2	59.8	N13 50.4	1.1	9	Sat	73 44.7	2.4	S12 02.5	0.0	19 02
14 54	136 26.3	59.8	N13 24.6	1.1	10	SUN	74 42.7	2.4	S12 03.1	0.0	18 58
14 55	136 20.8	59.8	N12 58.5	1.1	11	Mon	75 40.5	2.4	S12 03.9	0.0	18 54
14 55	136 15.7	59.8	N12 32.2	1.1	12	Tue	76 38.1	2.4	S12 04.7	0.0	18 50
14 55	136 11.0	59.8	N12 05.5	1.1	13	Wed	77 35.5	2.4	S12 05.6	0.0	18 47
14 56	136 06.6	59.8	N11 38.6	1.1	14	Thu	78 32.8	2.4	S12 06.5	0.0	18 43
14 56	136 02.6	59.8	N11 11.5	1.1	15	Fri	79 29.9	2.4	S12 07.5	0.0	18 39
14 56	135 58.9	59.9	N10 44.1	1.1	16	Sat	80 26.8	2.4	S12 08.5	0.0	18 35
14 56	135 55.5	59.9	N10 16.5	1.2	17	SUN	81 23.6	2.4	S12 09.6	0.1	18 32
14 57	135 52.6	59.9	N 9 48.6	1.2	18	Mon	82 20.2	2.3	S12 10.8	0.1	18 28
14 57	135 49.9	59.9	N 9 20.6	1.2	19	Tue	83 16.6	2.3	S12 12.0	0.1	18 24
14 57	135 47.6	59.9	N 8 52.4	1.2	20	Wed	84 12.9	2.3	S12 13.3	0.1	18 20
14 57	135 45.6	59.9	N 8 24.0	1.2	21	Thu	85 09.0	2.3	S12 14.6	0.1	18 17
14 57	135 44.0	59.9	N 7 55.4	1.2	22	Fri	86 05.0	2.3	S12 16.0	0.1	18 13
14 57	135 42.6	15°	N 7 26.7	1.2	23	Sat	87 00.7	2.3	S12 17.4	0.1	18 09
14 57	135 41.6	0.0	N 6 57.8	1.2	24	SUN	87 56.4	2.3	S12 18.9	0.1	18 05
14 57	135 40.9	0.0	N 6 28.7	1.2	25	Mon	88 51.8	2.3	S12 20.4	0.1	18 02
14 57	135 40.5	0.0	N 5 59.6	1.2	26	Tue	89 47.1	2.3	S12 22.0	0.1	17 58
14 57	135 40.4	0.0	N 5 30.3	1.2	27	Wed	90 42.3	2.3	S12 23.6	0.1	17 54
14 57	135 40.6	0.0	N 5 01.0	1.2	28	Thu	91 37.3	2.3	S12 25.3	0.1	17 51
14 57	135 41.1	0.0	N 4 31.5	1.2	29	Fri	92 32.1	2.3	S12 27.1	0.1	17 47
14 57	135 41.9	0.0	N 4 01.9	1.2	30	Sat	93 26.8	2.3	S12 28.9	0.1	17 44
14 57	135 43.0	0.1	N 3 32.3	1.2	31	SUN	94 21.3	2.3	S12 30.7	0.1	17 40

VENUS, Av Mag –4.1
SHA July
5 214; 10 209; 15 203; 20 198; 25 193; 30 188.

JUPITER, Av Mag –2.1
SHA July
5 147; 10 147; 15 147; 20 147; 25 146; 30 146.

MARS / SATURN

Mer Pass h m	GHA ° '	Mean Var/hr 15°+	Dec ° '	Mean Var/hr '		Day	GHA ° '	Mean Var/hr 15°+	Dec ° '	Mean Var/hr '	Mer Pass h m
09 07	223 04.2	0.6	N19 16.3	0.4	1	Fri	294 23.8	2.5	S 8 35.4	0.0	04 22
09 06	223 19.3	0.6	N19 26.5	0.4	2	Sat	295 23.6	2.5	S 8 35.9	0.0	04 18
09 05	223 34.3	0.6	N19 36.4	0.4	3	SUN	296 23.5	2.5	S 8 36.5	0.0	04 14
09 04	223 49.3	0.6	N19 46.2	0.4	4	Mon	297 23.5	2.5	S 8 37.1	0.0	04 10
09 03	224 04.3	0.6	N19 55.8	0.4	5	Tue	298 23.6	2.5	S 8 37.7	0.0	04 06
09 02	224 19.3	0.6	N20 05.2	0.4	6	Wed	299 23.8	2.5	S 8 38.4	0.0	04 02
09 01	224 34.3	0.6	N20 14.4	0.4	7	Thu	300 24.1	2.5	S 8 39.1	0.0	03 58
09 00	224 49.3	0.6	N20 23.4	0.4	8	Fri	301 24.4	2.5	S 8 39.9	0.0	03 54
08 59	225 04.2	0.6	N20 32.3	0.4	9	Sat	302 24.9	2.5	S 8 40.6	0.0	03 50
08 58	225 19.1	0.6	N20 40.9	0.4	10	SUN	303 25.4	2.5	S 8 41.5	0.0	03 46
08 57	225 34.0	0.6	N20 49.3	0.3	11	Mon	304 26.0	2.5	S 8 42.3	0.0	03 42
08 56	225 49.0	0.6	N20 57.5	0.3	12	Tue	305 26.8	2.5	S 8 43.2	0.0	03 38
08 55	226 03.9	0.6	N21 05.5	0.3	13	Wed	306 27.6	2.5	S 8 44.1	0.0	03 34
08 54	226 18.8	0.6	N21 13.3	0.3	14	Thu	307 28.4	2.5	S 8 45.1	0.0	03 30
08 53	226 33.7	0.6	N21 20.9	0.3	15	Fri	308 29.4	2.5	S 8 46.1	0.0	03 25
08 52	226 48.6	0.6	N21 28.3	0.3	16	Sat	309 30.5	2.5	S 8 47.1	0.0	03 21
08 51	227 03.5	0.6	N21 35.5	0.3	17	SUN	310 31.6	2.6	S 8 48.1	0.0	03 17
08 50	227 18.5	0.6	N21 42.5	0.3	18	Mon	311 32.8	2.6	S 8 49.2	0.0	03 13
08 49	227 33.4	0.6	N21 49.3	0.3	19	Tue	312 34.1	2.6	S 8 50.3	0.1	03 09
08 48	227 48.4	0.6	N21 55.9	0.3	20	Wed	313 35.5	2.6	S 8 51.5	0.0	03 05
08 47	228 03.3	0.6	N22 02.3	0.3	21	Thu	314 37.0	2.6	S 8 52.6	0.1	03 01
08 46	228 18.3	0.6	N22 08.5	0.3	22	Fri	315 38.5	2.6	S 8 53.8	0.1	02 57
08 45	228 33.3	0.6	N22 14.5	0.2	23	Sat	316 40.1	2.6	S 8 55.1	0.1	02 53
08 44	228 48.3	0.6	N22 20.2	0.2	24	SUN	317 41.8	2.6	S 8 56.3	0.1	02 49
08 43	229 03.3	0.6	N22 25.8	0.2	25	Mon	318 43.6	2.6	S 8 57.6	0.1	02 45
08 42	229 18.3	0.6	N22 31.2	0.2	26	Tue	319 45.4	2.6	S 8 58.9	0.1	02 41
08 41	229 33.4	0.6	N22 36.3	0.2	27	Wed	320 47.3	2.6	S 9 00.3	0.1	02 36
08 40	229 48.5	0.6	N22 41.3	0.2	28	Thu	321 49.3	2.6	S 9 01.7	0.1	02 32
08 39	230 03.6	0.6	N22 46.0	0.2	29	Fri	322 51.3	2.6	S 9 03.0	0.1	02 28
08 38	230 18.7	0.6	N22 50.5	0.2	30	Sat	323 53.5	2.6	S 9 04.5	0.1	02 24
08 37	230 33.9	0.6	N22 54.9	0.2	31	SUN	324 55.7	2.6	S 9 05.9	0.1	02 20

MARS, Av Mag +1.2
SHA July
5 301; 10 298; 15 294; 20 290; 25 287; 30 283.

SATURN, Av Mag +0.8
SHA July
5 16; 10 16; 15 16; 20 16; 25 16; 30 16.

JULY 1994

MOON

Day	GMT hr	GHA ° '	Mean Var/hr 14°+	Dec ° '	Mean Var/hr '
1 Fri	0	270 03.6	33.9	N 7 31.9	9.8
	6	357 27.1	33.8	N 8 30.7	9.6
	12	84 50.3	33.8	N 9 28.2	9.3
	18	172 13.0	33.6	N10 24.1	9.1
2 Sat	0	259 33.8	33.5	N11 18.4	8.8
	6	346 56.2	33.4	N12 10.9	8.4
	12	74 16.4	33.2	N13 01.5	8.1
	18	161 35.7	32.9	N13 50.1	7.7
3 Sun	0	248 53.7	32.8	N14 36.7	7.4
	6	336 10.6	32.6	N15 21.0	7.0
	12	63 26.1	32.3	N16 03.0	6.5
	18	150 40.3	32.1	N16 42.5	6.1
4 Mon	0	237 53.0	31.9	N17 19.4	5.7
	6	325 04.2	31.6	N17 53.7	5.2
	12	52 14.0	31.4	N18 25.1	4.7
	18	139 22.2	31.1	N18 53.6	4.2
5 Tue	0	226 29.0	30.8	N19 19.0	3.7
	6	313 34.3	30.6	N19 41.3	3.1
	12	40 38.3	30.4	N20 00.3	2.5
	18	127 40.8	30.2	N20 16.0	2.0
6 Wed	0	214 42.2	30.0	N20 28.1	1.4
	6	301 42.3	29.8	N20 36.8	0.8
	12	28 41.4	29.7	N20 41.9	0.2
	18	115 39.5	29.5	N20 43.2	0.4
7 Thu	0	202 36.8	29.5	N20 40.9	1.1
	6	289 33.5	29.3	N20 34.7	1.7
	12	16 29.6	29.3	N20 24.8	2.3
	18	103 25.3	29.2	N20 11.1	2.9
8 Fri	0	190 20.8	29.2	N19 53.6	3.6
	6	277 16.1	29.3	N19 32.3	4.3
	12	4 11.5	29.2	N19 07.3	4.9
	18	91 07.1	29.4	N18 38.6	5.4
9 Sat	0	178 02.9	29.4	N18 06.2	6.0
	6	264 59.1	29.4	N17 30.3	6.6
	12	351 55.8	29.5	N16 51.0	7.1
	18	78 52.9	29.6	N16 08.4	7.6
10 Sun	0	165 50.7	29.7	N15 22.5	8.2
	6	252 49.2	29.9	N14 33.6	8.6
	12	339 48.2	30.0	N13 41.8	9.1
	18	66 47.9	30.1	N12 47.2	9.6
11 Mon	0	153 48.3	30.2	N11 50.0	9.9
	6	240 49.3	30.3	N10 50.3	10.4
	12	327 50.8	30.3	N 9 48.5	10.6
	18	54 52.7	30.4	N 8 44.5	11.0
12 Tue	0	141 55.1	30.4	N 7 38.8	11.3
	6	228 57.8	30.5	N 6 31.3	11.5
	12	316 00.6	30.5	N 5 22.5	11.7
	18	43 03.5	30.4	N 4 12.4	11.9
13 Wed	0	130 06.4	30.4	N 3 01.3	12.0
	6	217 09.0	30.3	N 1 49.4	12.1
	12	304 11.2	30.3	N 0 36.9	12.2
	18	31 13.0	30.2	S 0 35.9	12.2
14 Thu	0	118 14.0	30.0	S 1 48.8	12.1
	6	205 14.2	29.8	S 3 01.5	12.1
	12	292 13.4	29.7	S 4 13.9	12.0
	18	19 11.5	29.4	S 5 25.7	11.8
15 Fri	0	106 08.2	29.1	S 6 36.6	11.6
	6	193 03.4	28.9	S 7 46.4	11.4
	12	279 57.0	28.7	S 8 54.8	11.1
	18	6 48.8	28.3	S10 01.5	10.8
16 Sat	0	93 38.7	27.9	S11 06.3	10.4
	6	180 26.7	27.6	S12 09.0	10.0
	12	267 12.6	27.3	S13 09.2	9.6
	18	353 56.3	26.9	S14 06.7	9.1

Day	GMT hr	GHA ° '	Mean Var/hr 14°+	Dec ° '	Mean Var/hr '
17 Sun	0	80 37.9	26.5	S15 01.2	8.5
	6	167 17.3	26.1	S15 52.5	7.9
	12	253 54.6	25.8	S16 40.3	7.2
	18	340 29.9	25.5	S17 24.3	6.6
18 Mon	0	67 03.1	25.2	S18 04.3	5.9
	6	153 34.5	24.9	S18 40.2	5.2
	12	240 04.2	24.7	S19 11.7	4.4
	18	326 32.4	24.5	S19 38.5	3.6
19 Tue	0	52 59.4	24.3	S20 00.7	2.9
	6	139 25.4	24.2	S20 18.0	1.9
	12	225 50.7	24.2	S20 30.3	1.1
	18	312 15.7	24.2	S20 37.6	0.3
20 Wed	0	38 40.6	24.2	S20 39.8	0.5
	6	125 05.8	24.3	S20 37.0	1.4
	12	211 31.6	24.5	S20 29.2	2.2
	18	297 58.4	24.7	S20 16.4	3.0
21 Thu	0	24 26.4	25.0	S19 58.8	3.8
	6	110 56.0	25.2	S19 36.4	4.5
	12	197 27.4	25.6	S19 09.6	5.3
	18	284 00.9	26.0	S18 38.3	6.0
22 Fri	0	10 36.6	26.4	S18 03.0	6.6
	6	97 14.7	26.8	S17 23.7	7.2
	12	183 55.4	27.2	S16 40.8	7.8
	18	270 38.7	27.7	S15 54.5	8.3
23 Sat	0	357 24.7	28.2	S15 05.1	8.7
	6	84 13.6	28.6	S14 12.8	9.2
	12	171 05.1	29.1	S13 18.0	9.5
	18	257 59.4	29.6	S12 20.8	9.9
24 Sun	0	344 56.3	30.0	S11 21.5	10.2
	6	71 55.9	30.4	S10 20.5	10.4
	12	158 57.9	30.7	S 9 18.0	10.6
	18	246 02.4	31.2	S 8 14.2	10.8
25 Mon	0	333 09.1	31.5	S 7 09.3	10.9
	6	60 17.9	31.9	S 6 03.6	11.0
	12	147 28.7	32.1	S 4 57.4	11.2
	18	234 41.3	32.4	S 3 50.7	11.2
26 Tue	0	321 55.6	32.6	S 2 43.8	11.1
	6	49 11.3	32.9	S 1 37.0	11.1
	12	136 28.4	33.1	S 0 30.3	11.1
	18	223 46.7	33.2	N 0 36.0	11.0
27 Wed	0	311 05.9	33.3	N 1 41.9	10.9
	6	38 26.0	33.5	N 2 47.0	10.7
	12	125 46.7	33.5	N 3 51.4	10.5
	18	213 08.0	33.6	N 4 54.8	10.3
28 Thu	0	300 29.5	33.6	N 5 57.2	10.1
	6	27 51.2	33.6	N 6 58.4	9.9
	12	115 13.0	33.6	N 7 58.2	9.7
	18	202 34.6	33.5	N 8 56.6	9.5
29 Fri	0	289 55.9	33.5	N 9 53.5	9.1
	6	17 16.8	33.4	N10 48.6	8.9
	12	104 37.2	33.3	N11 42.0	8.6
	18	191 56.9	33.2	N12 33.5	8.2
30 Sat	0	279 15.8	33.0	N13 23.0	7.9
	6	6 33.8	32.9	N14 10.3	7.5
	12	93 50.8	32.7	N14 55.5	7.1
	18	181 06.7	32.4	N15 38.3	6.7
31 Sun	0	268 21.5	32.3	N16 18.7	6.3
	6	355 35.0	32.1	N16 56.5	5.8
	12	82 47.3	31.8	N17 31.6	5.3
	18	169 58.2	31.5	N18 04.0	4.9

Chapter 6

AUGUST 1994 — SUN & MOON — GMT

SUN

Day of Yr	Mth	Week	Equation of Time 0h	Equation of Time 12h	Transit	Semi-diam	Twi-light	Sun-rise	Sun-set	Twi-light	Lat	Twi-light	Sun-rise	Sun-set	Twi-light
			m s	m s	h m	′	h m	h m	h m	h m	°	h m	h m	h m	h m
213	1	Mon	+06 20	+06 18	12 06	15.8	03 40	04 21	19 50	20 32	N70	TAN	−1 50	+1 46	TAN
214	2	Tue	+06 16	+06 14	12 06	15.8	03 42	04 23	19 49	20 30	68	−2 28	−1 26	+1 23	+2 26
215	3	Wed	+06 12	+06 10	12 06	15.8	03 43	04 24	19 47	20 28	66	−1 48	−1 08	+1 06	+1 47
216	4	Thu	+06 07	+06 05	12 06	15.8	03 45	04 26	19 45	20 26	64	−1 21	−0 53	+0 51	+1 20
217	5	Fri	+06 02	+05 59	12 06	15.8	03 47	04 27	19 43	20 24	62	−1 01	−0 41	+0 39	+1 00
218	6	Sat	+05 56	+05 53	12 06	15.8	03 49	04 29	19 42	20 22	N60	−0 45	−0 30	+0 29	+0 44
219	7	Sun	+05 49	+05 46	12 06	15.8	03 51	04 31	19 40	20 20	58	−0 32	−0 21	+0 21	+0 30
220	8	Mon	+05 42	+05 38	12 06	15.8	03 52	04 32	19 38	20 17	56	−0 20	−0 13	+0 13	+0 18
221	9	Tue	+05 34	+05 30	12 06	15.8	03 54	04 34	19 36	20 15	54	−0 10	−0 06	+0 06	+0 09
222	10	Wed	+05 26	+05 22	12 05	15.8	03 56	04 35	19 34	20 13	50	+0 07	+0 06	−0 06	−0 04
223	11	Thu	+05 17	+05 12	12 05	15.8	03 58	04 37	19 32	20 11	N45	+0 23	+0 18	−0 18	−0 27
224	12	Fri	+05 07	+05 03	12 05	15.8	04 00	04 39	19 30	20 09	40	+0 36	+0 28	−0 28	−0 38
225	13	Sat	+04 57	+04 52	12 05	15.8	04 02	04 40	19 28	20 07	35	+0 47	+0 37	−0 37	−0 48
226	14	Sun	+04 47	+04 41	12 05	15.8	04 03	04 42	19 26	20 05	30	+0 57	+0 44	−0 45	−0 58
227	15	Mon	+04 35	+04 30	12 04	15.8	04 05	04 43	19 24	20 02	20	+1 12	+0 57	−0 57	−1 13
228	16	Tue	+04 24	+04 18	12 04	15.8	04 07	04 45	19 22	20 00	N10	+1 24	+1 09	−1 08	−1 25
229	17	Wed	+04 11	+04 05	12 04	15.8	04 09	04 47	19 20	19 58	0	+1 35	+1 19	−1 18	−1 35
230	18	Thu	+03 59	+03 52	12 04	15.8	04 11	04 48	19 18	19 56	S10	+1 44	+1 29	−1 28	−1 46
231	19	Fri	+03 45	+03 38	12 04	15.8	04 13	04 50	19 16	19 53	20	+1 54	+1 40	−1 39	−1 56
232	20	Sat	+03 31	+03 24	12 03	15.8	04 14	04 52	19 14	19 51	30	+2 05	+1 52	−1 51	−2 06
233	21	Sun	+03 17	+03 10	12 03	15.8	04 16	04 53	19 12	19 49	S35	+2 10	+2 00	−1 57	−2 11
234	22	Mon	+03 02	+02 55	12 03	15.8	04 18	04 55	19 10	19 47	40	+2 16	+2 07	−2 05	−2 17
235	23	Tue	+02 47	+02 39	12 03	15.8	04 20	04 56	19 08	19 44	45	+2 23	+2 17	−2 15	−2 24
236	24	Wed	+02 31	+02 23	12 02	15.8	04 22	04 58	19 06	19 42	S50	+2 30	+2 27	−2 26	−2 32
237	25	Thu	+02 15	+02 07	12 02	15.8	04 23	05 00	19 03	19 40					
238	26	Fri	+01 59	+01 50	12 02	15.9	04 25	05 01	19 01	19 37					
239	27	Sat	+01 42	+01 33	12 02	15.9	04 27	05 03	18 59	19 35					
240	28	Sun	+01 24	+01 15	12 01	15.9	04 29	05 05	18 57	19 33					
241	29	Mon	+01 07	+00 58	12 01	15.9	04 30	05 06	18 55	19 30					
242	30	Tue	+00 49	+00 39	12 01	15.9	04 32	05 08	18 52	19 28					
243	31	Wed	+00 30	+00 21	12 00	15.9	04 34	05 10	18 50	19 25					

Lat Corr to Sunrise, Sunset etc

NOTES

Lat corrections are for the middle of August. TAN = Twilight all night. **Equation of Time** is the excess of Mean Time over Apparent Time.

MOON

Day of Yr	Mth	Week	Age	Transit Diff (Upper)	Semi-diam	Hor Par	Moon-rise	Moon-set
			days	h m m	′	′	h m	h m
213	1	Mon	24	07 05 48	14.8	54.5	23 47	15 08
214	2	Tue	25	07 53 50	14.9	54.8	– –	16 03
215	3	Wed	26	08 43 51	15.1	55.3	00 33	16 53
216	4	Thu	27	09 34 51	15.2	55.8	01 26	17 36
217	5	Fri	28	10 25 51	15.4	56.5	02 28	18 12
218	6	Sat	29	11 16 51	15.6	57.1	03 36	18 44
219	7	Sun	00	12 07 50	15.7	57.7	04 48	19 12
220	8	Mon	01	12 57 50	15.9	58.3	06 03	19 37
221	9	Tue	02	13 47 50	16.0	58.7	07 20	20 01
222	10	Wed	03	14 37 52	16.1	59.0	08 37	20 25
223	11	Thu	04	15 29 53	16.1	59.2	09 56	20 51
224	12	Fri	05	16 22 55	16.2	59.3	11 15	21 20
225	13	Sat	06	17 17 57	16.2	59.3	12 32	21 54
226	14	Sun	07	18 14 58	16.1	59.2	13 47	22 36
227	15	Mon	08	19 12 58	16.1	59.1	14 55	23 27
228	16	Tue	09	20 10 57	16.0	58.8	15 55	– –
229	17	Wed	10	21 07 54	15.9	58.5	16 44	00 27
230	18	Thu	11	22 01 52	15.8	58.1	17 24	01 34
231	19	Fri	12	22 53 50	15.7	57.7	17 56	02 46
232	20	Sat	13	23 43 47	15.6	57.2	18 24	03 59
233	21	Sun	14	24 30 _	15.4	56.6	18 47	05 12
234	22	Mon	15	00 30 45	15.3	56.0	19 09	06 23
235	23	Tue	16	01 15 44	15.1	55.5	19 30	07 33
236	24	Wed	17	01 59 44	15.0	55.0	19 52	08 41
237	25	Thu	18	02 43 44	14.9	54.6	20 15	09 47
238	26	Fri	19	03 27 45	14.8	54.4	20 40	10 52
239	27	Sat	20	04 12 46	14.8	54.2	21 10	11 55
240	28	Sun	21	04 58 48	14.8	54.3	21 45	12 55
241	29	Mon	22	05 46 48	14.8	54.5	22 26	13 52
242	30	Tue	23	06 34 50	15.0	54.9	23 16	14 43
243	31	Wed	24	07 24 50	15.1	55.4	– –	15 28

Phases of the Moon

	d	h	m
● New Moon	7	08	45
◑ First Quarter	14	05	57
○ Full Moon	21	06	47
◐ Last Quarter	29	06	41
Perigee	12	23	
Apogee	27	18	

NOTES

For Latitude corrections to Moonrise and Moonset see page 706.

AUGUST 1994 — STARS — 0h GMT August 1

No	Name	Mag	Transit h m	Dec ° '	GHA ° '	RA h m	SHA ° '
	ARIES...............		3 22		309 22.5		
1	Alpheratz 2.2		3 30	N 29 03.7	307 20.3	0 08	357 57.8
2	Ankaa.............. 2.4		3 48	S 42 19.8	302 51.8	0 26	353 29.3
3	Schedar........... 2.5		4 02	N 56 30.4	299 18.7	0 40	349 56.2
4	Diphda 2.2		4 05	S 18 00.7	290 22.3	0 43	349 09.8
5	Achernar 0.6		4 59	S 57 15.5	284 59.5	1 38	335 37.0
6	POLARIS.......... 2.1		5 49	N 89 14.1	272 36.3	2 27	323 13.8
7	Hamal.............. 2.2		5 28	N 23 26.2	277 39.1	2 07	320 16.6
8	Acamar 3.1		6 20	S 40 19.3	264 51.5	2 58	315 29.0
9	Menkar 2.8		6 23	N 4 04.2	263 52.3	3 02	314 29.8
10	Mirfak 1.9		6 45	N 49 50.4	258 23.1	3 24	309 00.6
11	Aldebaran 1.1		7 57	N 16 29.9	240 28.2	4 36	291 05.7
12	Rigel 0.3		8 35	S 8 12.4	230 48.3	5 14	281 25.8
13	Capella............ 0.2		8 37	N 45 59.4	230 18.0	5 16	280 55.5
14	Bellatrix.......... 1.7		8 46	N 6 20.7	228 09.8	5 25	278 47.3
15	Elnath 1.8		8 47	N 28 36.1	227 53.1	5 26	278 30.6
16	Alnilam 1.8		8 57	S 1 12.3	225 23.4	5 36	276 00.9
17	Betelgeuse......0.1-1.2		9 16	N 7 24.4	220 39.3	5 55	271 16.8
18	Canopus .... −0.9		9 45	S 52 41.4	213 25.3	6 24	264 02.8
19	Sirius .... −1.6		10 06	S 16 42.5	208 08.9	6 45	258 46.4
20	Adhara............. 1.6		10 19	S 28 57.8	204 46.4	6 58	255 23.9
21	Castor 1.6		10 55	N 31 53.9	195 48.7	7 34	246 26.2
22	Procyon 0.5		11 00	N 5 14.3	194 37.3	7 39	245 14.8
23	Pollux.............. 1.2		11 06	N 28 02.3	193 07.8	7 45	243 45.3
24	Avior 1.7		11 43	S 59 29.5	183 46.9	8 22	234 24.4
25	Suhail 2.2		12 28	S 43 24.7	172 25.7	9 08	223 03.2
26	Miaplacidus.... 1.8		12 34	S 69 41.8	171 06.0	9 13	221 43.5
27	Alphard 2.2		12 48	S 8 38.1	167 32.8	9 27	218 10.3
28	Regulus............ 1.3		13 28	N 11 59.6	157 21.3	10 08	207 58.8
29	Dubhe 2.0		14 24	N 61 46.9	143 32.0	11 03	194 09.5
30	Denebola......... 2.2		15 09	N 14 36.2	132 10.8	11 49	182 48.3
31	Gienah 2.8		15 35	S 17 30.8	125 29.6	12 16	176 07.1
32	Acrux............... 1.1		15 46	S 63 04.4	122 48.0	12 26	173 25.5
33	Gacrux 1.6		15 51	S 57 05.2	121 39.5	12 31	172 17.0
34	Mimosa............ 1.5		16 07	S 59 39.8	117 31.4	12 47	168 08.9
35	Alioth 1.7		16 14	N 55 59.5	115 55.9	12 54	166 33.4
36	Spica................ 1.2		16 45	S 11 08.0	108 08.8	13 25	158 46.3
37	Alkaid 1.9		17 07	N 49 20.7	102 32.7	13 47	153 10.2
38	Hadar 0.9		17 23	S 60 21.1	98 30.6	14 03	149 08.1
39	Menkent 2.3		17 26	S 36 20.7	97 46.8	14 06	148 24.3
40	Arcturus 0.2		17 35	N 19 12.8	95 31.2	14 15	146 08.7
41	Rigil Kent. 0.1		17 59	S 60 49.0	89 33.6	14 39	140 11.1
42	Zuben'ubi....... 2.9		18 10	S 16 01.2	86 43.6	14 51	137 21.1
43	Kochab............. 2.2		18 10	N 74 11.0	86 42.2	14 51	137 19.7
44	Alphecca.......... 2.3		18 54	N 26 44.2	75 45.4	15 34	126 22.9
45	Antares............. 1.2		19 48	S 26 25.2	62 06.0	16 29	112 43.5
46	Atria 1.9		20 07	S 69 01.3	57 20.2	16 48	107 57.7
47	Sabik 2.6		20 29	S 15 43.0	51 51.1	17 10	102 28.6
48	Shaula 1.7		20 52	S 37 06.0	46 03.3	17 33	96 40.8
49	Rasalhague 2.1		20 54	N 12 34.1	45 41.9	17 35	96 19.4
50	Eltanin 2.4		21 16	N 51 29.7	40 14.9	17 57	90 52.4
51	Kaus Aust........ 2.0		21 43	S 34 23.2	33 24.7	18 24	84 02.2
52	Vega 0.1		21 56	N 38 47.0	30 10.7	18 37	80 48.2
53	Nunki 2.1		22 14	S 26 18.1	25 38.0	18 55	76 15.5
54	Altair................ 0.9		23 09	N 8 51.5	11 44.2	19 51	62 21.7
55	Peacock........... 2.1		23 44	S 56 45.0	3 03.3	20 25	53 40.8
56	Deneb 1.3		0 04	N 45 15.9	359 03.1	20 41	49 40.6
57	Enif 2.5		1 06	N 9 51.2	343 23.1	21 44	34 00.6
58	Al Na'ir 2.2		1 30	S 46 59.0	337 23.4	22 08	28 00.9
59	Fomalhaut 1.3		2 20	S 29 38.8	325 01.7	22 57	15 39.2
60	Markab 2.6		2 27	N 15 10.8	323 14.6	23 05	13 52.1

Stars Transit Corr Table

Date	Corr h m	Date	Corr h m
1	−0 00	17	−1 03
2	−0 04	18	−1 07
3	−0 08	19	−1 11
4	−0 12	20	−1 15
5	−0 16	21	−1 19
6	−0 20	22	−1 23
7	−0 24	23	−1 27
8	−0 28	24	−1 30
9	−0 31	25	−1 34
10	−0 35	26	−1 38
11	−0 39	27	−1 42
12	−0 43	28	−1 46
13	−0 47	29	−1 50
14	−0 51	30	−1 54
15	−0 55	31	−1 58
16	−0 59		

STAR'S TRANSIT

To find the approx time of transit of a star for any day of the month use above table. All corrections are subtractive. If the quantity taken from the table is greater than the time of transit for the first of the month, add 23h 56min to the time of transit before subtracting the correction.

Example: What is the time of transit of Al Na'ir (No 58) on August 26?

	h min
Transit on the 1st	01 30
	+23 56
	25 26
Corr for the 26th	−01 38
Transit on the 26th	23 48

AUGUST DIARY

3 04 Mars 3°N of Moon
7 09 New Moon
9 14 Pluto stationary
10 23 Venus 3°N of Moon
12 23 Moon at perigee
13 01 Mercury in superior conjunction
13 07 Jupiter 2°N of Moon
14 06 First Quarter
18 14 Neptune 4°S of Moon
18 18 Uranus 5°S of Moon
21 07 Full Moon
22 10 Saturn 7°S of Moon
24 23 Venus greatest elongation E(46°)
27 18 Moon at apogee
29 07 Last Quarter
31 04 Vesta 0.7°S of Moon
31 21 Venus 0.7°S of Spica

Chapter 6

AUGUST 1994 — SUN & ARIES — GMT

Monday, August 1

Time	SUN GHA	Dec	ARIES GHA
00	178 25.1	N18 07.7	309 22.5
02	208 25.1	18 06.5	339 27.4
04	238 25.2	18 05.2	9 32.4
06	268 25.3	18 04.0	39 37.3
08	298 25.4	18 02.7	69 42.2
10	328 25.4	18 01.4	99 47.1
12	358 25.5	18 00.2	129 52.1
14	28 25.6	17 58.9	159 57.0
16	58 25.7	17 57.7	190 01.9
18	88 25.7	17 56.4	220 06.9
20	118 25.8	17 55.1	250 11.8
22	148 25.9	N17 53.9	280 16.7

Tuesday, August 2

Time	SUN GHA	Dec	ARIES GHA
00	178 26.0	N17 52.6	310 21.6
02	208 26.1	17 51.3	340 26.6
04	238 26.1	17 50.0	10 31.5
06	268 26.2	17 48.8	40 36.4
08	298 26.3	17 47.5	70 41.3
10	328 26.4	17 46.2	100 46.3
12	358 26.5	17 44.9	130 51.2
14	28 26.6	17 43.6	160 56.1
16	58 26.7	17 42.3	191 01.1
18	88 26.8	17 41.1	221 06.0
20	118 26.8	17 39.8	251 10.9
22	148 26.9	N17 38.5	281 15.8

Wednesday, August 3

Time	SUN GHA	Dec	ARIES GHA
00	178 27.0	N17 37.2	311 20.8
02	208 27.1	17 35.9	341 25.7
04	238 27.2	17 34.6	11 30.6
06	268 27.3	17 33.3	41 35.6
08	298 27.4	17 32.0	71 40.5
10	328 27.5	17 30.7	101 45.4
12	358 27.6	17 29.4	131 50.3
14	28 27.7	17 28.1	161 55.3
16	58 27.8	17 26.8	192 00.2
18	88 27.9	17 25.4	222 05.1
20	118 28.0	17 24.1	252 10.1
22	148 28.1	N17 22.8	282 15.0

Thursday, August 4

Time	SUN GHA	Dec	ARIES GHA
00	178 28.2	N17 21.5	312 19.9
02	208 28.3	17 20.2	342 24.8
04	238 28.4	17 18.8	12 29.8
06	268 28.6	17 17.5	42 34.7
08	298 28.7	17 16.2	72 39.6
10	328 28.8	17 14.9	102 44.6
12	358 28.8	17 13.5	132 49.5
14	28 29.0	17 12.2	162 54.4
16	58 29.1	17 10.9	192 59.3
18	88 29.2	17 09.5	223 04.3
20	118 29.3	17 08.2	253 09.2
22	148 29.5	N17 06.9	283 14.1

Friday, August 5

Time	SUN GHA	Dec	ARIES GHA
00	178 29.6	N17 05.5	313 19.1
02	208 29.7	17 04.2	343 24.0
04	238 29.8	17 02.8	13 28.9
06	268 29.9	17 01.5	43 33.8
08	298 30.1	17 00.1	73 38.8
10	328 30.2	16 58.8	103 43.7
12	358 30.3	16 57.4	133 48.6
14	28 30.4	16 56.1	163 53.5
16	58 30.6	16 54.7	193 58.5
18	88 30.7	16 53.4	224 03.4
20	118 30.8	16 52.0	254 08.3
22	148 30.9	N16 50.6	284 13.3

Saturday, August 6

Time	SUN GHA	Dec	ARIES GHA
00	178 31.1	N16 49.3	314 18.2
02	208 31.2	16 47.9	344 23.1
04	238 31.3	16 46.5	14 28.0
06	268 31.5	16 45.2	44 33.0
08	298 31.6	16 43.8	74 37.9
10	328 31.7	16 42.4	104 42.8
12	358 31.9	16 41.0	134 47.8
14	28 32.0	16 39.7	164 52.7
16	58 32.2	16 38.3	194 57.6
18	88 32.3	16 36.9	225 02.5
20	118 32.4	16 35.5	255 07.5
22	148 32.6	N16 34.1	285 12.4

Sunday, August 7

Time	SUN GHA	Dec	ARIES GHA
00	178 32.7	N16 32.7	315 17.3
02	208 32.9	16 31.4	345 22.3
04	238 33.0	16 30.0	15 27.2
06	268 33.2	16 28.6	45 32.1
08	298 33.3	16 27.2	75 37.0
10	328 33.5	16 25.8	105 42.0
12	358 33.6	16 24.4	135 46.9
14	28 33.8	16 23.0	165 51.8
16	58 33.9	16 21.6	195 56.8
18	88 34.1	16 20.2	226 01.7
20	118 34.2	16 18.8	256 06.6
22	148 34.4	N16 17.4	286 11.5

Monday, August 8

Time	SUN GHA	Dec	ARIES GHA
00	178 34.5	N16 16.0	316 16.5
02	208 34.7	16 14.5	346 21.4
04	238 34.8	16 13.1	16 26.3
06	268 35.0	16 11.7	46 31.3
08	298 35.2	16 10.3	76 36.2
10	328 35.3	16 08.9	106 41.1
12	358 35.5	16 07.5	136 46.0
14	28 35.6	16 06.0	166 51.0
16	58 35.8	16 04.6	196 55.9
18	88 36.0	16 03.2	227 00.8
20	118 36.1	16 01.8	257 05.8
22	148 36.3	N16 00.3	287 10.7

Tuesday, August 9

Time	SUN GHA	Dec	ARIES GHA
00	178 36.5	N15 58.9	317 15.6
02	208 36.6	15 57.5	347 20.5
04	238 36.8	15 56.0	17 25.5
06	268 37.0	15 54.6	47 30.4
08	298 37.1	15 53.2	77 35.3
10	328 37.3	15 51.7	107 40.2
12	358 37.5	15 50.3	137 45.2
14	28 37.7	15 48.8	167 50.1
16	58 37.8	15 47.4	197 55.0
18	88 38.0	15 45.9	228 00.0
20	118 38.2	15 44.5	258 04.9
22	148 38.4	N15 43.0	288 09.8

Wednesday, August 10

Time	SUN GHA	Dec	ARIES GHA
00	178 38.6	N15 41.6	318 14.7
02	208 38.7	15 40.1	348 19.7
04	238 38.9	15 38.7	18 24.6
06	268 39.1	15 37.2	48 29.5
08	298 39.3	15 35.8	78 34.5
10	328 39.5	15 34.3	108 39.4
12	358 39.6	15 32.8	138 44.3
14	28 39.8	15 31.4	168 49.2
16	58 40.0	15 29.9	198 54.2
18	88 40.2	15 28.5	228 59.1
20	118 40.4	15 27.0	259 04.0
22	148 40.6	N15 25.5	289 09.0

Thursday, August 11

Time	SUN GHA	Dec	ARIES GHA
00	178 40.8	N15 24.0	319 13.9
02	208 41.0	15 22.6	349 18.8
04	238 41.2	15 21.1	19 23.7
06	268 41.4	15 19.6	49 28.7
08	298 41.6	15 18.1	79 33.6
10	328 41.8	15 16.7	109 38.5
12	358 42.0	15 15.2	139 43.5
14	28 42.2	15 13.7	169 48.4
16	58 42.4	15 12.2	199 53.3
18	88 42.6	15 10.7	229 58.2
20	118 42.8	15 09.2	260 03.2
22	148 43.0	N15 07.7	290 08.1

Friday, August 12

Time	SUN GHA	Dec	ARIES GHA
00	178 43.2	N15 06.2	320 13.0
02	208 43.4	15 04.7	350 18.0
04	238 43.6	15 03.2	20 22.9
06	268 43.8	15 01.7	50 27.8
08	298 44.0	15 00.2	80 32.7
10	328 44.2	14 58.7	110 37.7
12	358 44.4	14 57.2	140 42.6
14	28 44.6	14 55.7	170 47.5
16	58 44.8	14 54.2	200 52.4
18	88 45.1	14 52.7	230 57.4
20	118 45.3	14 51.2	261 02.3
22	148 45.5	N14 49.7	291 07.2

Saturday, August 13

Time	SUN GHA	Dec	ARIES GHA
00	178 45.7	N14 48.2	321 12.2
02	208 45.9	14 46.7	351 17.1
04	238 46.1	14 45.2	21 22.0
06	268 46.4	14 43.6	51 26.9
08	298 46.6	14 42.1	81 31.9
10	328 46.8	14 40.6	111 36.8
12	358 47.0	14 39.1	141 41.7
14	28 47.2	14 37.6	171 46.7
16	58 47.5	14 36.0	201 51.6
18	88 47.7	14 34.5	231 56.5
20	118 47.9	14 33.0	262 01.4
22	148 48.1	N14 31.4	292 06.4

Sunday, August 14

Time	SUN GHA	Dec	ARIES GHA
00	178 48.4	N14 29.9	322 11.3
02	208 48.6	14 28.4	352 16.2
04	238 48.8	14 26.8	22 21.2
06	268 49.1	14 25.3	52 26.1
08	298 49.3	14 23.8	82 31.0
10	328 49.5	14 22.2	112 35.9
12	358 49.8	14 20.7	142 40.9
14	28 50.0	14 19.1	172 45.8
16	58 50.2	14 17.6	202 50.7
18	88 50.5	14 16.1	232 55.7
20	118 50.7	14 14.5	263 00.6
22	148 50.9	N14 13.0	293 05.5

Monday, August 15

Time	SUN GHA	Dec	ARIES GHA
00	178 51.2	N14 11.4	323 10.4
02	208 51.4	14 09.9	353 15.4
04	238 51.7	14 08.3	23 20.3
06	268 51.9	14 06.7	53 25.2
08	298 52.2	14 05.2	83 30.2
10	328 52.4	14 03.6	113 35.1
12	358 52.6	14 02.1	143 40.0
14	28 52.9	14 00.5	173 44.9
16	58 53.1	13 58.9	203 49.9
18	88 53.4	13 57.4	233 54.8
20	118 53.6	13 55.8	263 59.7
22	148 53.9	N13 54.2	294 04.6

AUGUST 1994 — SUN & ARIES — GMT

Tuesday, August 16

Time	SUN GHA ° ′	SUN Dec ° ′	ARIES GHA ° ′
00	178 54.1	**N13 52.7**	324 09.6
02	208 54.4	**13 51.1**	354 14.5
04	238 54.6	**13 49.5**	24 19.4
06	268 54.0	**13 48.0**	54 24.4
08	298 55.1	**13 46.4**	84 29.3
10	328 55.4	**13 44.8**	114 34.2
12	358 55.7	**13 43.2**	144 39.1
14	28 55.9	**13 41.6**	174 44.1
16	58 56.2	**13 40.1**	204 49.0
18	88 56.4	**13 38.5**	234 53.9
20	118 56.7	**13 36.9**	264 58.9
22	148 57.0	**N13 35.3**	295 03.8

Wednesday, August 17

Time	SUN GHA ° ′	SUN Dec ° ′	ARIES GHA ° ′
00	178 57.2	**N13 33.7**	325 08.7
02	208 57.5	**13 32.1**	355 13.6
04	238 57.7	**13 30.5**	25 18.6
06	268 58.0	**13 28.9**	55 23.5
08	298 58.3	**13 27.4**	85 28.4
10	328 58.5	**13 25.8**	115 33.4
12	358 58.8	**13 24.2**	145 38.3
14	28 59.1	**13 22.6**	175 43.2
16	58 59.3	**13 21.0**	205 48.1
18	88 59.6	**13 19.4**	235 53.1
20	118 59.9	**13 17.8**	265 58.0
22	149 00.2	**N13 16.2**	296 02.9

Thursday, August 18

Time	SUN GHA ° ′	SUN Dec ° ′	ARIES GHA ° ′
00	179 00.4	**N13 14.6**	326 07.9
02	209 00.7	**13 12.9**	356 12.8
04	239 01.0	**13 11.3**	26 17.7
06	269 01.2	**13 09.7**	56 22.6
08	299 01.5	**13 08.1**	86 27.6
10	329 01.8	**13 06.5**	116 32.5
12	359 02.1	**13 04.9**	146 37.4
14	29 02.4	**13 03.3**	176 42.4
16	59 02.6	**13 01.7**	206 47.3
18	89 02.9	**13 00.0**	236 52.2
20	119 03.2	**12 58.4**	266 57.1
22	149 03.5	**N12 56.8**	297 02.1

Friday, August 19

Time	SUN GHA ° ′	SUN Dec ° ′	ARIES GHA ° ′
00	179 03.8	**N12 55.2**	327 07.0
02	209 04.1	**12 53.5**	357 11.9
04	239 04.3	**12 51.9**	27 16.8
06	269 04.6	**12 50.3**	57 21.8
08	299 04.9	**12 48.7**	87 26.7
10	329 05.2	**12 47.0**	117 31.6
12	359 05.5	**12 45.4**	147 36.6
14	29 05.8	**12 43.8**	177 41.5
16	59 06.1	**12 42.1**	207 46.4
18	89 06.4	**12 40.5**	237 51.3
20	119 06.6	**12 38.9**	267 56.3
22	149 06.9	**N12 37.2**	298 01.2

Saturday, August 20

Time	SUN GHA ° ′	SUN Dec ° ′	ARIES GHA ° ′
00	179 07.2	**N12 35.6**	328 06.1
02	209 07.5	**12 33.9**	358 11.1
04	239 07.8	**12 32.3**	28 16.0
06	269 08.1	**12 30.7**	58 20.9
08	299 08.4	**12 29.0**	88 25.8
10	329 08.7	**12 27.4**	118 30.8
12	359 09.0	**12 25.7**	148 35.7
14	29 09.3	**12 24.1**	178 40.6
16	59 09.6	**12 22.4**	208 45.6
18	89 09.9	**12 20.8**	238 50.5
20	119 10.2	**12 19.1**	268 55.4
22	149 10.5	**N12 17.5**	299 00.3

Sunday, August 21

Time	SUN GHA ° ′	SUN Dec ° ′	ARIES GHA ° ′
00	179 10.8	**N12 15.8**	329 05.3
02	209 11.1	**12 14.1**	359 10.2
04	239 11.4	**12 12.5**	29 15.1
06	269 11.7	**12 10.8**	59 20.1
08	299 12.0	**12 09.2**	89 25.0
10	329 12.4	**12 07.5**	119 29.9
12	359 12.7	**12 05.8**	149 34.8
14	29 13.0	**12 04.2**	179 39.8
16	59 13.3	**12 02.5**	209 44.7
18	89 13.6	**12 00.8**	239 49.6
20	119 13.9	**11 59.2**	269 54.6
22	149 14.2	**N11 57.5**	299 59.5

Monday, August 22

Time	SUN GHA ° ′	SUN Dec ° ′	ARIES GHA ° ′
00	179 14.5	**N11 55.8**	330 04.4
02	209 14.8	**11 54.2**	0 09.3
04	239 15.2	**11 52.5**	30 14.3
06	269 15.5	**11 50.8**	60 19.2
08	299 15.8	**11 49.1**	90 24.1
10	329 16.1	**11 47.5**	120 29.0
12	359 16.4	**11 45.8**	150 34.0
14	29 16.7	**11 44.1**	180 38.9
16	59 17.1	**11 42.4**	210 43.8
18	89 17.4	**11 40.7**	240 48.8
20	119 17.7	**11 39.0**	270 53.7
22	149 18.0	**N11 37.4**	300 58.6

Tuesday, August 23

Time	SUN GHA ° ′	SUN Dec ° ′	ARIES GHA ° ′
00	179 18.4	**N11 35.7**	331 03.5
02	209 18.7	**11 34.0**	1 08.5
04	239 19.0	**11 32.3**	31 13.4
06	269 19.3	**11 30.6**	61 18.3
08	299 19.6	**11 28.9**	91 23.3
10	329 20.0	**11 27.2**	121 28.2
12	359 20.3	**11 25.5**	151 33.1
14	29 20.6	**11 23.8**	181 38.0
16	59 21.0	**11 22.1**	211 43.0
18	89 21.3	**11 20.4**	241 47.9
20	119 21.6	**11 18.7**	271 52.8
22	149 21.9	**N11 17.0**	301 57.8

Wednesday, August 24

Time	SUN GHA ° ′	SUN Dec ° ′	ARIES GHA ° ′
00	179 22.3	**N11 15.3**	332 02.7
02	209 22.6	**11 13.6**	2 07.6
04	239 22.9	**11 11.9**	32 12.5
06	269 23.3	**11 10.2**	62 17.5
08	299 23.6	**11 08.5**	92 22.4
10	329 23.9	**11 06.8**	122 27.3
12	359 24.3	**11 05.1**	152 32.3
14	29 24.6	**11 03.4**	182 37.2
16	59 25.0	**11 01.7**	212 42.1
18	89 25.3	**10 59.9**	242 47.0
20	119 25.6	**10 58.2**	272 52.0
22	149 26.0	**N10 56.5**	302 56.9

Thursday, August 25

Time	SUN GHA ° ′	SUN Dec ° ′	ARIES GHA ° ′
00	179 26.3	**N10 54.8**	333 01.8
02	209 26.7	**10 53.1**	3 06.8
04	239 27.0	**10 51.4**	33 11.7
06	269 27.3	**10 49.6**	63 16.6
08	299 27.7	**10 47.9**	93 21.5
10	329 28.0	**10 46.2**	123 26.5
12	359 28.4	**10 44.5**	153 31.4
14	29 28.7	**10 42.7**	183 36.3
16	59 29.1	**10 41.0**	213 41.3
18	89 29.4	**10 39.3**	243 46.2
20	119 29.8	**10 37.6**	273 51.1
22	149 30.1	**N10 35.8**	303 56.0

Friday, August 26

Time	SUN GHA ° ′	SUN Dec ° ′	ARIES GHA ° ′	Time
00	179 30.5	**N10 34.1**	334 01.0	00
02	209 30.8	**10 32.4**	4 05.9	02
04	239 31.2	**10 30.6**	34 10.8	04
06	269 31.5	**10 28.9**	64 15.7	06
08	299 31.9	**10 27.2**	94 20.7	08
10	329 32.2	**10 25.4**	124 25.6	10
12	359 32.6	**10 23.7**	154 30.5	12
14	29 32.9	**10 21.9**	184 35.5	14
16	59 33.3	**10 20.2**	214 40.4	16
18	89 33.6	**10 18.5**	244 45.3	18
20	119 34.0	**10 16.7**	274 50.2	20
22	149 34.3	**N10 15.0**	304 55.2	22

Saturday, August 27

Time	SUN GHA ° ′	SUN Dec ° ′	ARIES GHA ° ′	Time
00	179 34.7	**N10 13.2**	335 00.1	00
02	209 35.0	**10 11.5**	5 05.0	02
04	239 35.4	**10 09.7**	35 10.0	04
06	269 35.8	**10 08.0**	65 14.9	06
08	299 36.1	**10 06.2**	95 19.8	08
10	329 36.5	**10 04.5**	125 24.7	10
12	359 36.8	**10 02.7**	155 29.7	12
14	29 37.2	**10 01.0**	185 34.6	14
16	59 37.6	**9 59.2**	215 39.5	16
18	89 37.9	**9 57.5**	245 44.5	18
20	119 38.3	**9 55.7**	275 49.4	20
22	149 38.7	**N9 54.0**	305 54.3	22

Sunday, August 28

Time	SUN GHA ° ′	SUN Dec ° ′	ARIES GHA ° ′	Time
00	179 39.0	**N9 52.2**	335 59.2	00
02	209 39.4	**9 50.4**	6 04.2	02
04	239 39.8	**9 48.7**	36 09.1	04
06	269 40.1	**9 46.9**	66 14.0	06
08	299 40.5	**9 45.1**	96 19.0	08
10	329 40.9	**9 43.4**	126 23.9	10
12	359 41.2	**9 41.6**	156 28.8	12
14	29 41.6	**9 39.9**	186 33.7	14
16	59 42.0	**9 38.1**	216 38.7	16
18	89 42.3	**9 36.3**	246 43.6	18
20	119 42.7	**9 34.5**	276 48.5	20
22	149 43.1	**N9 32.8**	306 53.5	22

Monday, August 29

Time	SUN GHA ° ′	SUN Dec ° ′	ARIES GHA ° ′	Time
00	179 43.4	**N9 31.0**	336 58.4	00
02	209 43.8	**9 29.2**	7 03.3	02
04	239 44.2	**9 27.5**	37 08.2	04
06	269 44.6	**9 25.7**	67 13.2	06
08	299 44.9	**9 23.9**	97 18.1	08
10	329 45.3	**9 22.1**	127 23.0	10
12	359 45.7	**9 20.4**	157 27.9	12
14	29 46.1	**9 18.6**	187 32.9	14
16	59 46.4	**9 16.8**	217 37.8	16
18	89 46.8	**9 15.0**	247 42.7	18
20	119 47.2	**9 13.2**	277 47.7	20
22	149 47.6	**N9 11.4**	307 52.6	22

Tuesday, August 30

Time	SUN GHA ° ′	SUN Dec ° ′	ARIES GHA ° ′	Time
00	179 47.9	**N9 09.7**	337 57.5	00
02	209 48.3	**9 07.9**	8 02.4	02
04	239 48.7	**9 06.1**	38 07.4	04
06	269 49.1	**9 04.3**	68 12.3	06
08	299 49.5	**9 02.5**	98 17.2	08
10	329 49.8	**9 00.7**	128 22.2	10
12	359 50.2	**8 58.9**	158 27.1	12
14	29 50.6	**8 57.1**	188 32.0	14
16	59 51.0	**8 55.4**	218 36.9	16
18	89 51.4	**8 53.6**	248 41.9	18
20	119 51.8	**8 51.8**	278 46.8	20
22	149 52.1	**N8 50.0**	308 51.7	22

Wednesday, August 31

Time	SUN GHA ° ′	SUN Dec ° ′	ARIES GHA ° ′	Time	SUN GHA ° ′	SUN Dec ° ′	ARIES GHA ° ′	Time	SUN GHA ° ′	SUN Dec ° ′	ARIES GHA ° ′	Time
00	179 52.5	**N8 48.2**	338 56.7	08	299 54.1	**N8 41.0**	99 16.4	16	59 55.6	**N8 33.8**	219 36.1	16
02	209 52.9	**8 46.4**	9 01.6	10	329 54.5	**8 39.2**	129 21.3	18	89 56.0	**8 32.0**	249 41.0	18
04	239 53.3	**8 44.6**	39 06.5	12	359 54.9	**8 37.4**	159 26.2	20	119 56.4	**8 30.2**	279 45.9	20
06	269 53.7	**N8 42.8**	69 11.4	14	29 55.2	**N8 35.6**	189 31.2	22	149 56.8	**N8 28.4**	309 50.9	22

Chapter 6

AUGUST 1994 — PLANETS — 0h GMT

VENUS / JUPITER

Mer Pass h m	GHA ° ′	Mean Var/hr 15°+	Dec ° ′	Mean Var/hr ′			GHA ° ′	Mean Var/hr 15°+	Dec ° ′	Mean Var/hr ′	Mer Pass h m
14 57	135 44.3	0.1	N 3 02.6	1.2	1	Mon	95 15.7	2.3	S12 32.6	0.1	17 36
14 57	135 45.9	0.1	N 2 32.8	1.2	2	Tue	96 10.0	2.3	S12 34.5	0.1	17 33
14 57	135 47.7	0.1	N 2 03.1	1.2	3	Wed	97 04.0	2.3	S12 36.5	0.1	17 29
14 57	135 49.9	0.1	N 1 33.2	1.2	4	Thu	97 58.0	2.2	S12 38.5	0.1	17 26
14 56	135 52.2	0.1	N 1 03.4	1.2	5	Fri	98 51.8	2.2	S12 40.6	0.1	17 22
14 56	135 54.9	0.1	N 0 33.5	1.2	6	Sat	99 45.4	2.2	S12 42.7	0.1	17 18
14 56	135 57.8	0.1	N 0 03.7	1.2	7	SUN	100 38.9	2.2	S12 44.8	0.1	17 15
14 56	136 00.9	0.1	S 0 26.2	1.2	8	Mon	101 32.3	2.2	S12 47.1	0.1	17 11
14 56	136 04.3	0.2	S 0 56.0	1.2	9	Tue	102 25.5	2.2	S12 49.3	0.1	17 08
14 55	136 08.0	0.2	S 1 25.8	1.2	10	Wed	103 18.6	2.2	S12 51.6	0.1	17 04
14 55	136 11.9	0.2	S 1 55.6	1.2	11	Thu	104 11.5	2.2	S12 53.9	0.1	17 01
14 55	136 16.1	0.2	S 2 25.3	1.2	12	Fri	105 04.3	2.2	S12 56.3	0.1	16 57
14 54	136 20.5	0.2	S 2 54.9	1.2	13	Sat	105 56.9	2.2	S12 58.7	0.1	16 54
14 54	136 25.1	0.2	S 3 24.5	1.2	14	SUN	106 49.5	2.2	S13 01.2	0.1	16 50
14 54	136 30.1	0.2	S 3 54.0	1.2	15	Mon	107 41.9	2.2	S13 03.6	0.1	16 47
14 53	136 35.3	0.2	S 4 23.4	1.2	16	Tue	108 34.1	2.2	S13 06.2	0.1	16 43
14 53	136 40.7	0.2	S 4 52.7	1.2	17	Wed	109 26.3	2.2	S13 08.7	0.1	16 40
14 53	136 46.4	0.3	S 5 21.9	1.2	18	Thu	110 18.3	2.2	S13 11.3	0.1	16 36
14 52	136 52.4	0.3	S 5 51.0	1.2	19	Fri	111 10.1	2.2	S13 14.0	0.1	16 33
14 52	136 58.7	0.3	S 6 19.9	1.2	20	Sat	112 01.9	2.2	S13 16.7	0.1	16 30
14 51	137 05.2	0.3	S 6 48.7	1.2	21	SUN	112 53.5	2.1	S13 19.4	0.1	16 26
14 51	137 12.0	0.3	S 7 17.4	1.2	22	Mon	113 45.0	2.1	S13 22.1	0.1	16 23
14 50	137 19.1	0.3	S 7 45.8	1.2	23	Tue	114 36.3	2.1	S13 24.9	0.1	16 19
14 50	137 26.5	0.3	S 8 14.1	1.2	24	Wed	115 27.6	2.1	S13 27.7	0.1	16 16
14 49	137 34.2	0.3	S 8 42.3	1.2	25	Thu	116 18.7	2.1	S13 30.5	0.1	16 12
14 49	137 42.2	0.3	S 9 10.2	1.2	26	Fri	117 09.7	2.1	S13 33.4	0.1	16 09
14 48	137 50.5	0.4	S 9 37.9	1.1	27	Sat	118 00.6	2.1	S13 36.3	0.1	16 06
14 48	137 59.1	0.4	S10 05.4	1.1	28	SUN	118 51.4	2.1	S13 39.3	0.1	16 02
14 47	138 08.0	0.4	S10 32.7	1.1	29	Mon	119 42.1	2.1	S13 42.2	0.1	15 59
14 46	138 17.3	0.4	S10 59.8	1.1	30	Tue	120 32.6	2.1	S13 45.2	0.1	15 56
14 46	138 26.9	0.4	S11 26.6	1.1	31	Wed	121 23.0	2.1	S13 48.2	0.1	15 52

VENUS, Av Mag –4.3
SHA August
5 183; 10 178; 15 173; 20 169; 25 165; 30 160.

JUPITER, Av Mag –1.9
SHA August
5 146; 10 145; 15 145; 20 144; 25 143; 30 143.

MARS / SATURN

Mer Pass h m	GHA ° ′	Mean Var/hr 15°+	Dec ° ′	Mean Var/hr ′			GHA ° ′	Mean Var/hr 15°+	Dec ° ′	Mean Var/hr ′	Mer Pass h m
08 36	230 49.1	0.6	N22 59.0	0.2	1	Mon	325 57.9	2.6	S 9 07.4	0.1	02 16
08 35	231 04.4	0.6	N23 02.9	0.2	2	Tue	327 00.2	2.6	S 9 08.9	0.1	02 12
08 34	231 19.7	0.6	N23 06.7	0.1	3	Wed	328 02.6	2.6	S 9 10.4	0.1	02 07
08 33	231 35.0	0.6	N23 10.2	0.1	4	Thu	329 05.1	2.6	S 9 11.9	0.1	02 03
08 32	231 50.4	0.6	N23 13.5	0.1	5	Fri	330 07.6	2.6	S 9 13.5	0.1	01 59
08 31	232 05.9	0.6	N23 16.6	0.1	6	Sat	331 10.1	2.6	S 9 15.0	0.1	01 55
08 30	232 21.4	0.6	N23 19.5	0.1	7	SUN	332 12.7	2.6	S 9 16.6	0.1	01 51
08 29	232 37.0	0.6	N23 22.2	0.1	8	Mon	333 15.4	2.6	S 9 18.2	0.1	01 47
08 28	232 52.6	0.7	N23 24.7	0.1	9	Tue	334 18.2	2.6	S 9 19.9	0.1	01 42
08 27	233 08.3	0.7	N23 27.0	0.1	10	Wed	335 20.9	2.6	S 9 21.5	0.1	01 38
08 26	233 24.1	0.7	N23 29.2	0.1	11	Thu	336 23.8	2.6	S 9 23.2	0.1	01 34
08 25	233 39.9	0.7	N23 31.1	0.1	12	Fri	337 26.6	2.6	S 9 24.8	0.1	01 30
08 24	233 55.8	0.7	N23 32.8	0.1	13	Sat	338 29.6	2.6	S 9 26.5	0.1	01 26
08 23	234 11.8	0.7	N23 34.3	0.1	14	SUN	339 32.5	2.6	S 9 28.2	0.1	01 22
08 22	234 27.9	0.7	N23 35.7	0.0	15	Mon	340 35.5	2.6	S 9 29.9	0.1	01 17
08 21	234 44.0	0.7	N23 36.8	0.0	16	Tue	341 38.6	2.6	S 9 31.7	0.1	01 13
08 20	235 00.2	0.7	N23 37.7	0.0	17	Wed	342 41.7	2.6	S 9 33.4	0.1	01 09
08 19	235 16.5	0.7	N23 38.5	0.0	18	Thu	343 44.8	2.6	S 9 35.1	0.1	01 05
08 17	235 33.0	0.7	N23 39.1	0.0	19	Fri	344 48.0	2.6	S 9 36.9	0.1	01 01
08 16	235 49.4	0.7	N23 39.4	0.0	20	Sat	345 51.1	2.6	S 9 38.7	0.1	00 56
08 15	236 06.0	0.7	N23 39.6	0.0	21	SUN	346 54.4	2.6	S 9 40.4	0.1	00 52
08 14	236 22.7	0.7	N23 39.6	0.0	22	Mon	347 57.6	2.6	S 9 42.2	0.1	00 48
08 13	236 39.5	0.7	N23 39.5	0.0	23	Tue	349 00.9	2.6	S 9 44.0	0.1	00 44
08 12	236 56.4	0.7	N23 39.1	0.0	24	Wed	350 04.2	2.6	S 9 45.8	0.1	00 40
08 11	237 13.3	0.7	N23 38.6	0.0	25	Thu	351 07.5	2.6	S 9 47.6	0.1	00 35
08 10	237 30.4	0.7	N23 37.8	0.0	26	Fri	352 10.8	2.6	S 9 49.3	0.1	00 31
08 08	237 47.6	0.7	N23 36.9	0.0	27	Sat	353 14.2	2.6	S 9 51.1	0.1	00 27
08 07	238 04.9	0.7	N23 35.9	0.1	28	SUN	354 17.6	2.6	S 9 52.9	0.1	00 23
08 06	238 22.3	0.7	N23 34.6	0.1	29	Mon	355 21.0	2.6	S 9 54.7	0.1	00 19
08 05	238 39.9	0.7	N23 33.2	0.1	30	Tue	356 24.4	2.6	S 9 56.5	0.1	00 14
08 04	238 57.5	0.7	N23 31.6	0.1	31	Wed	357 27.8	2.6	S 9 58.3	0.1	00 10

MARS, Av Mag +1.2
SHA August
5 279; 10 275; 15 271; 20 268; 25 264; 30 261.

SATURN, Av Mag +0.6
SHA August
5 17; 10 17; 15 17; 20 18; 25 18; 30 18.

AUGUST 1994 — MOON

Day	GMT hr	GHA ° '	Mean Var/hr 14°+	Dec ° '	Mean Var/hr '	Day	GMT hr	GHA ° '	Mean Var/hr 14°+	Dec ° '	Mean Var/hr '
1 Mon	0	257 07.6	31.7	N18 33.5	4.4	17 Wed	0	55 19.7	25.6	S 20 08.8	2.7
	6	344 16.0	31.1	N19 00.1	3.0		6	141 53.1	25.8	S 19 52.9	3.5
	12	71 22.8	30.9	N19 23.5	3.3		12	228 27.9	26.1	S 19 32.5	4.2
	18	158 28.3	30.7	N19 43.8	2.7		18	315 04.3	26.4	S 19 07.8	4.9
2 Tue	0	245 32.5	30.4	N20 00.8	2.2	18 Thu	0	41 42.4	26.7	S 18 39.0	5.5
	6	332 35.3	30.3	N20 14.5	1.7		6	128 22.5	27.1	S 18 06.1	6.2
	12	59 37.0	30.0	N20 24.7	1.1		12	215 04.6	27.4	S 17 30.4	6.8
	18	146 37.5	29.9	N20 31.4	0.5		18	301 48.9	27.8	S 16 49.1	7.3
3 Wed	0	233 36.9	29.7	N20 34.5	0.2	19 Fri	0	28 35.5	28.1	S 16 05.5	7.8
	6	320 35.4	29.6	N20 33.9	0.8		6	115 24.4	28.6	S 15 18.7	8.4
	12	47 33.0	29.4	N20 29.7	1.4		12	202 15.6	28.9	S 14 29.0	8.8
	18	134 29.8	29.4	N20 21.6	2.0		18	289 09.2	29.4	S 13 36.6	9.2
4 Thu	0	221 26.0	29.3	N20 09.9	2.6	20 Sat	0	16 05.0	29.8	S 12 41.8	9.6
	6	308 21.6	29.2	N19 54.3	3.3		6	103 03.2	30.1	S 11 44.8	9.9
	12	35 16.8	29.2	N19 34.9	3.9		12	190 03.6	30.5	S 10 45.9	10.2
	18	122 11.8	29.1	N19 11.8	4.5		18	277 06.2	30.8	S 9 45.2	10.4
5 Fri	0	209 06.5	29.1	N18 44.9	5.2	21 Sun	0	4 10.8	31.1	S 8 43.1	10.6
	6	296 01.2	29.1	N18 14.3	5.8		6	91 17.4	31.4	S 7 39.8	10.7
	12	22 56.0	29.1	N17 40.1	6.4		12	178 25.9	31.8	S 6 35.4	10.9
	18	109 50.8	29.1	N17 02.3	6.9		18	265 36.0	32.0	S 5 30.2	10.9
6 Sat	0	196 45.9	29.2	N16 21.1	7.5	22 Mon	0	352 47.8	32.2	S 4 24.5	11.0
	6	283 41.3	29.2	N15 36.4	8.0		6	80 01.1	32.5	S 3 18.3	11.1
	12	10 36.9	29.4	N14 48.5	8.5		12	167 15.7	32.6	S 2 12.0	11.0
	18	97 33.0	29.5	N13 57.6	9.0		18	254 31.5	32.8	S 1 05.7	11.1
7 Sun	0	184 29.4	29.5	N13 03.6	9.5	23 Tue	0	341 48.4	32.9	N 0 00.5	11.0
	6	271 26.2	29.5	N12 06.8	10.0		6	69 06.1	33.1	N 1 06.3	10.9
	12	358 23.5	29.6	N11 07.5	10.4		12	156 24.7	33.2	N 2 11.5	10.8
	18	85 21.0	29.6	N10 05.7	10.7		18	243 43.9	33.3	N 3 16.1	10.6
8 Mon	0	172 18.9	29.7	N 9 01.6	11.0	24 Wed	0	331 03.5	33.3	N 4 19.9	10.4
	6	259 17.1	29.7	N 7 55.5	11.3		6	58 23.5	33.4	N 5 22.6	10.3
	12	346 15.5	29.7	N 6 47.6	11.6		12	145 43.8	33.4	N 6 24.3	10.1
	18	73 14.0	29.8	N 5 38.2	11.8		18	233 04.1	33.4	N 7 24.6	9.8
9 Tue	0	160 12.6	29.7	N 4 27.4	12.0	25 Thu	0	320 24.4	33.3	N 8 23.6	9.6
	6	247 11.1	29.7	N 3 15.4	12.1		6	47 44.5	33.3	N 9 21.0	9.3
	12	334 09.4	29.6	N 2 02.7	12.2		12	135 04.3	33.2	N10 16.8	9.0
	18	61 07.4	29.6	N 0 49.3	12.2		18	222 23.7	33.1	N11 10.8	8.7
10 Wed	0	148 05.1	29.5	S 0 24.4	12.3	26 Fri	0	309 42.7	33.1	N12 02.9	8.3
	6	235 02.1	29.4	S 1 38.3	12.3		6	37 01.0	32.9	N12 53.1	8.0
	12	321 58.5	29.2	S 2 51.9	12.1		12	124 18.6	32.7	N13 41.1	7.6
	18	48 54.2	29.1	S 4 05.1	12.1		18	211 35.5	32.6	N14 26.9	7.2
11 Thu	0	135 48.8	28.9	S 5 17.5	11.9	27 Sat	0	298 51.5	32.5	N15 10.3	6.8
	6	222 42.5	28.8	S 6 29.0	11.7		6	26 06.5	32.3	N15 51.4	6.4
	12	309 34.9	28.5	S 7 39.2	11.4		12	113 20.6	32.1	N16 29.9	6.0
	18	36 26.1	28.3	S 8 47.9	11.1		18	200 33.7	32.0	N17 05.7	5.5
12 Fri	0	123 15.9	28.1	S 9 54.8	10.8	28 Sun	0	287 45.6	31.8	N17 38.9	5.0
	6	210 04.2	27.8	S 10 59.6	10.4		6	14 56.5	31.6	N18 09.2	4.6
	12	296 51.0	27.5	S 12 02.1	10.0		12	102 06.2	31.4	N18 36.6	4.0
	18	23 36.2	27.3	S 13 02.0	9.5		18	189 14.8	31.3	N19 01.0	3.5
13 Sat	0	110 19.7	27.0	S 13 59.1	8.9	29 Mon	0	276 22.3	31.1	N19 22.3	3.0
	6	197 01.6	26.7	S 14 53.1	8.4		6	3 28.7	30.9	N19 40.4	2.5
	12	283 41.8	26.5	S 15 43.7	7.9		12	90 33.9	30.7	N19 55.3	1.8
	18	10 20.5	26.2	S 16 30.8	7.2		18	177 38.2	30.5	N20 06.8	1.3
14 Sun	0	96 57.5	26.0	S 17 14.2	6.5	30 Tue	0	264 41.3	30.3	N20 14.9	0.8
	6	183 33.2	25.7	S 17 53.6	5.8		6	351 43.6	30.3	N20 19.6	0.1
	12	270 07.5	25.5	S 18 28.8	5.1		12	78 44.9	30.1	N20 20.8	0.5
	18	356 40.6	25.3	S 18 59.8	4.3		18	165 45.4	30.0	N20 18.4	1.1
15 Mon	0	83 12.7	25.2	S 19 26.2	3.6	31 Wed	0	252 45.1	29.8	N20 12.4	1.7
	6	169 44.0	25.1	S 19 48.2	2.8		6	339 44.1	29.7	N20 02.8	2.3
	12	256 14.7	25.1	S 20 05.4	2.0		12	66 42.5	29.6	N19 49.5	2.9
	18	342 44.9	25.1	S 20 17.9	1.2		18	153 40.4	29.6	N19 32.5	3.5
16 Tue	0	69 15.1	25.1	S 20 25.6	0.4						
	6	155 45.4	25.1	S 20 28.6	0.3						
	12	242 16.1	25.2	S 20 26.7	1.2						
	18	328 47.5	25.4	S 20 20.1	1.9						

Chapter 6

SEPTEMBER 1994 — SUN & MOON — GMT

SUN

Yr	Mth	Week	Eq. of Time 0h	Eq. of Time 12h	Transit	Semi-diam	Twilight	Sunrise	Sunset	Twilight	Lat	Twilight	Sunrise	Sunset	Twilight
			m s	m s	h m	′	h m	h m	h m	h m	°	h m	h m	h m	h m
244	1	Thu	+00 12	+00 02	12 00	15.9	04 36	05 11	18 48	19 23	N70	−0 53	−0 21	+0 20	+0 51
245	2	Fri	−00 07	−00 17	12 00	15.9	04 37	05 13	18 46	19 21	68	−0 42	−0 17	+0 16	+0 41
246	3	Sat	−00 27	−00 36	11 59	15.9	04 39	05 14	18 43	19 18	66	−0 34	−0 14	+0 13	+0 32
247	4	Sun	−00 46	−00 56	11 59	15.9	04 41	05 16	18 41	19 16	64	−0 27	−0 11	+0 10	+0 25
248	5	Mon	−01 06	−01 16	11 59	15.9	04 43	05 18	18 39	19 14	62	−0 20	−0 08	+0 08	+0 19
249	6	Tue	−01 26	−01 36	11 58	15.9	04 44	05 19	18 36	19 11	N60	−0 15	−0 06	+0 06	+0 15
250	7	Wed	−01 46	−01 56	11 58	15.9	04 46	05 21	18 34	19 09	58	−0 11	−0 04	+0 05	+0 10
251	8	Thu	−02 06	−02 16	11 58	15.9	04 48	05 23	18 32	19 06	56	−0 07	−0 02	+0 03	+0 07
252	9	Fri	−02 27	−02 37	11 57	15.9	04 50	05 24	18 29	19 04	54	−0 03	−0 01	+0 02	+0 03
253	10	Sat	−02 47	−02 58	11 57	15.9	04 51	05 26	18 27	19 02	50	+0 03	+0 02	−0 01	−0 03
254	11	Sun	−03 08	−03 19	11 57	15.9	04 53	05 27	18 25	18 59	N45	+0 09	+0 04	−0 03	−0 09
255	12	Mon	−03 29	−03 40	11 56	15.9	04 55	05 29	18 23	18 57	40	+0 12	+0 06	−0 06	−0 13
256	13	Tue	−03 51	−04 01	11 56	15.9	04 56	05 31	18 20	18 54	35	+0 16	+0 08	−0 08	−0 17
257	14	Wed	−04 12	−04 22	11 56	15.9	04 58	05 32	18 18	18 52	30	+0 20	+0 10	−0 09	−0 20
258	15	Thu	−04 33	−04 44	11 55	15.9	05 00	05 34	18 16	18 49	20	+0 24	+0 13	−0 12	−0 25
259	16	Fri	−04 54	−05 05	11 55	15.9	05 02	05 36	18 13	18 47	N10	+0 28	+0 16	−0 14	−0 28
260	17	Sat	−05 16	−05 27	11 55	15.9	05 03	05 37	18 11	18 45	0	+0 31	+0 18	−0 16	−0 31
261	18	Sun	−05 37	−05 48	11 54	15.9	05 05	05 39	18 08	18 42	S10	+0 33	+0 19	−0 17	−0 32
262	19	Mon	−05 59	−06 09	11 54	15.9	05 07	05 41	18 06	18 40	20	+0 33	+0 21	−0 19	−0 33
263	20	Tue	−06 20	−06 31	11 53	16.0	05 08	05 42	18 04	18 38	30	+0 34	+0 24	−0 20	−0 33
264	21	Wed	−06 42	−06 52	11 53	16.0	05 10	05 44	18 01	18 35	S35	+0 34	+0 26	−0 21	−0 32
265	22	Thu	−07 03	−07 13	11 53	16.0	05 12	05 45	17 59	18 33	40	+0 33	+0 27	−0 23	−0 32
266	23	Fri	−07 24	−07 35	11 52	16.0	05 13	05 47	17 57	18 30	45	+0 32	+0 28	−0 24	−0 31
267	24	Sat	−07 45	−07 56	11 52	16.0	05 15	05 49	17 54	18 28	S50	+0 31	+0 30	−0 26	−0 30
268	25	Sun	−08 06	−08 17	11 52	16.0	05 17	05 50	17 52	18 26					
269	26	Mon	−08 27	−08 37	11 51	16.0	05 18	05 52	17 50	18 23					
270	27	Tue	−08 47	−08 58	11 51	16.0	05 20	05 54	17 47	18 21					
271	28	Wed	−09 08	−09 18	11 51	16.0	05 22	05 55	17 45	18 19					
272	29	Thu	−09 28	−09 38	11 50	16.0	05 23	05 57	17 43	18 16					
273	30	Fri	−09 48	−09 58	11 50	16.0	05 25	05 59	17 40	18 14					

NOTES

Equation of Time changes its sign on the 1st. Lat corrections are for the middle of September. **Equation of Time** is the excess of Mean Time over Apparent Time.

MOON

Yr	Mth	Week	Age	Transit Diff (Upper)	Semi-diam	Hor Par	Moonrise	Moonset
			days	h m m	′	′	h m	h m
244	1	Thu	25	08 14 ₅₁	15.3	56.1	00 13	16 08
245	2	Fri	26	09 05 ₅₁	15.5	56.8	01 17	16 41
246	3	Sat	27	09 56 ₅₁	15.7	57.6	02 27	17 11
247	4	Sun	28	10 46 ₅₁	15.9	58.4	03 41	17 38
248	5	Mon	29	11 37 ₅₂	16.1	59.1	04 58	18 03
249	6	Tue	01	12 29 ₅₃	16.2	59.6	06 17	18 28
250	7	Wed	02	13 22 ₅₄	16.3	59.9	07 37	18 54
251	8	Thu	03	14 16 ₅₅	16.4	60.1	08 58	19 23
252	9	Fri	04	15 11 ₅₈	16.3	60.0	10 18	19 56
253	10	Sat	05	16 09 ₅₈	16.3	59.7	11 36	20 37
254	11	Sun	06	17 07 ₅₈	16.2	59.4	12 47	21 25
255	12	Mon	07	18 05 ₅₇	16.1	58.9	13 49	22 22
256	13	Tue	08	19 02 ₅₅	15.9	58.4	14 41	23 27
257	14	Wed	09	19 57 ₅₂	15.8	57.9	15 23	– –
258	15	Thu	10	20 49 ₄₉	15.6	57.4	15 58	00 36
259	16	Fri	11	21 38 ₄₇	15.5	56.9	16 26	01 47
260	17	Sat	12	22 25 ₄₅	15.4	56.4	16 51	02 59
261	18	Sun	13	23 10 ₄₅	15.2	55.9	17 13	04 09
262	19	Mon	14	23 55 ₄₃	15.1	55.4	17 35	05 18
263	20	Tue	15	24 38 ₋	15.0	55.0	17 56	06 26
264	21	Wed	16	00 38 ₄₅	14.9	54.7	18 19	07 33
265	22	Thu	17	01 23 ₄₄	14.8	54.4	18 43	08 38
266	23	Fri	18	02 07 ₄₆	14.8	54.2	19 11	09 42
267	24	Sat	19	02 53 ₄₇	14.7	54.1	19 44	10 43
268	25	Sun	20	03 40 ₄₇	14.8	54.2	20 23	11 41
269	26	Mon	21	04 27 ₄₉	14.8	54.4	21 09	12 34
270	27	Tue	22	05 16 ₄₉	14.9	54.8	22 02	13 21
271	28	Wed	23	06 05 ₄₉	15.1	55.4	23 01	14 02
272	29	Thu	24	06 54 ₅₀	15.3	56.1	– –	14 38
273	30	Fri	25	07 44 ₅₀	15.5	56.9	00 07	15 08

Phases of the Moon

		d	h	m
●	New Moon	5	18	33
◑	First Quarter	12	11	34
○	Full Moon	19	20	00
◐	Last Quarter	28	00	23
	Perigee	8	14	
	Apogee	24	12	

NOTES

For Latitude corrections to Moonrise and Moonset see page 706.

SEPTEMBER 1994   STARS   0h GMT September 1

No	Name	Mag	Transit h m	Dec ° '	GHA ° '	RA h m	SHA ° '
	ARIES................		1 20		339 55.8		
1	Alpheratz	2.2	1 28	N 29 03.8	337 53.5	0 08	357 57.7
2	Ankaa	2.4	1 46	S 42 19.9	333 24.9	0 26	353 29.1
3	Schedar..........	2.5	2 00	N 56 30.6	329 51.8	0 40	349 56.0
4	Diphda	2.2	2 03	S 18 00.7	329 05.5	0 43	349 09.7
5	Achernar	0.6	2 57	S 57 15.6	315 32.5	1 38	335 36.7
6	POLARIS	2.1	3 47	N 89 14.2	308 59.3	2 28	323 02.5
7	Hamal..............	2.2	3 27	N 23 26.3	308 12.2	2 07	328 16.4
8	Acamar	3.1	4 18	S 40 19.3	295 24.5	2 58	315 28.7
9	Menkar	2.8	4 22	N 4 04.3	294 25.4	3 02	314 29.6
10	Mirfak	1.9	4 43	N 49 50.4	288 56.1	3 24	309 00.3
11	Aldebaran	1.1	5 55	N 16 29.9	271 01.2	4 36	291 05.4
12	Rigel	0.3	6 34	S 8 12.3	261 21.3	5 14	281 25.5
13	Capella............	0.2	6 36	N 45 59.4	260 51.0	5 16	280 55.2
14	Bellatrix..........	1.7	6 44	N 6 20.7	258 42.9	5 25	278 47.1
15	Elnath	1.8	6 45	N 28 36.1	258 26.2	5 26	278 30.4
16	Alnilam...........	1.8	6 55	S 1 12.2	255 56.4	5 36	276 00.6
17	Betelgeuse 0.1-1.2		7 14	N 7 24.4	251 12.3	5 55	271 16.5
18	Canopus	–0.9	7 43	S 52 41.3	243 58.3	6 24	264 02.5
19	Sirius...............	–1.6	8 04	S 16 42.4	238 42.0	6 45	258 46.2
20	Adhara............	1.6	8 17	S 28 57.7	235 19.5	6 58	255 23.7
21	Castor	1.6	8 53	N 31 53.9	226 21.8	7 34	246 26.0
22	Procyon	0.5	8 58	N 5 14.3	225 10.4	7 39	245 14.6
23	Pollux	1.2	9 04	N 28 02.2	223 40.9	7 45	243 45.1
24	Avior	1.7	9 41	S 59 29.4	214 20.0	8 22	234 24.2
25	Suhail..............	2.2	10 26	S 43 24.6	202 58.9	9 08	223 03.1
26	Miaplacidus	1.8	10 32	S 69 41.6	201 39.1	9 13	221 43.3
27	Alphard	2.2	10 46	S 8 38.1	198 06.0	9 27	218 10.2
28	Regulus...........	1.3	11 26	N 11 59.6	187 54.5	10 08	207 58.7
29	Dubhe	2.0	12 22	N 61 46.7	174 05.3	11 03	194 09.5
30	Denebola........	2.2	13 07	N 14 36.1	162 44.1	11 49	182 48.3
31	Gienah	2.8	13 34	S 17 30.7	156 02.9	12 16	176 07.1
32	Acrux...............	1.1	13 44	S 63 04.3	153 21.5	12 26	173 25.7
33	Gacrux	1.6	13 49	S 57 05.1	152 12.9	12 31	172 17.1
34	Mimosa	1.5	14 05	S 59 39.7	148 04.8	12 47	168 09.0
35	Alioth..............	1.7	14 12	N 55 59.4	146 29.3	12 54	166 33.5
36	Spica...............	1.2	14 43	S 11 08.0	138 42.1	13 25	158 46.3
37	Alkaid	1.9	15 05	N 49 20.6	133 06.2	13 47	153 10.4
38	Hadar	0.9	15 21	S 60 21.0	129 04.2	14 03	149 08.4
39	Menkent.........	2.3	15 24	S 36 20.7	128 20.3	14 06	148 24.5
40	Arcturus..........	0.2	15 33	N 19 12.8	126 04.6	14 15	146 08.8
41	Rigil Kent.	0.1	15 57	S 60 48.9	120 07.1	14 39	140 11.3
42	Zuben'ubi.......	2.9	16 08	S 16 01.1	117 17.0	14 51	137 21.2
43	Kochab............	2.2	16 08	N 74 10.9	117 16.0	14 51	137 20.2
44	Alphecca.........	2.3	16 52	N 26 44.2	106 18.9	15 34	126 23.1
45	Antares...........	1.2	17 46	S 26 25.2	92 39.4	16 29	112 43.6
46	Atria	1.9	18 05	S 69 01.3	87 53.9	16 48	107 58.1
47	Sabik...............	2.6	18 27	S 15 43.0	82 24.5	17 10	102 28.7
48	Shaula.............	1.7	18 50	S 37 06.0	76 36.8	17 33	96 41.0
49	Rasalhague	2.1	18 52	N 12 34.1	76 15.3	17 35	96 19.5
50	Eltanin	2.4	19 14	N 51 29.8	70 48.4	17 56	90 52.6
51	Kaus Aust........	2.0	19 41	S 34 23.2	63 58.1	18 24	84 02.3
52	Vega	0.1	19 54	N 38 47.1	60 44.1	18 37	80 48.3
53	Nunki	2.1	20 12	S 26 18.1	56 11.4	18 55	76 15.6
54	Altair...............	0.9	21 07	N 8 51.5	42 17.5	19 51	62 21.7
55	Peacock...........	2.1	21 42	S 56 45.1	33 36.7	20 25	53 40.9
56	Deneb	1.3	21 58	N 45 16.0	29 36.5	20 41	49 40.7
57	Enif.................	2.5	23 00	N 9 51.3	13 56.4	21 44	34 00.6
58	Al Na'ir	2.2	23 24	S 46 59.1	7 56.7	22 08	28 00.9
59	Fomalhaut	1.3	0 18	S 29 38.8	355 34.9	22 57	15 39.1
60	Markab	2.6	0 25	N 15 10.8	353 47.8	23 05	13 52.0

Stars Transit Corr Table

Date	Corr h m	Date	Corr h m
1	–0 00	17	–1 03
2	–0 04	18	–1 07
3	–0 08	19	–1 11
4	–0 12	20	–1 15
5	–0 16	21	–1 19
6	–0 20	22	–1 23
7	–0 24	23	–1 27
8	–0 28	24	–1 30
9	–0 31	25	–1 34
10	–0 35	26	–1 38
11	–0 39	27	–1 42
12	–0 43	28	–1 46
13	–0 47	29	–1 50
14	–0 51	30	–1 54
15	–0 55		
16	–0 59		

STAR'S TRANSIT

To find the approx time of transit of a star for any day of the month use above table. All corrections are subtractive. If the quantity taken from the table is greater than the time of transit for the first of the month, add 23h 56min to the time of transit before subtracting the correction.

Example: What is the brightest star to cross the meridian between 1900h and 2000h on September 12?

	h min
Corr for 12th	–00 43

Corresponding time on the 1st is between 1943h and 2043h.
Answer: Vega (No 52) Mag 0.1, transit 1911h.

SEPTEMBER DIARY

1 03	Mars 4°N of Moon
1 17	Saturn at opposition
5 19	New Moon
7 09	Mercury 3°N of Moon
8 14	Moon at perigee
9 01	Venus 2°S of Moon
9 20	Jupiter 1.4°N of Moon
12 12	First Quarter
14 19	Neptune 4°S of Moon
14 23	Uranus 5°S of Moon
18 13	Saturn 7°S of Moon
19 20	Full Moon
21 13	Mercury 0.1°S of Spica
23 06	Equinox
24 12	Moon at apogee
24 15	Mars 6°S of Pollux
26 16	Mercury greatest elongation E(26°)
28 00	Last Quarter
28 03	Vesta 0.06°N of Moon
28 22	Venus greatest brilliancy
29 22	Mars 6°N of Moon

Chapter 6

SEPTEMBER 1994 — SUN & ARIES — GMT

Thursday, September 1

Time	SUN GHA	Dec	ARIES GHA
00	179 57.2	N8 26.6	339 55.8
02	209 57.6	8 24.7	10 00.7
04	239 58.0	8 22.9	40 05.7
06	269 58.4	8 21.1	70 10.6
08	299 58.8	8 19.3	100 15.5
10	329 59.2	8 17.5	130 20.4
12	359 59.6	8 15.7	160 25.4
14	29 59.9	8 13.9	190 30.3
16	60 00.3	8 12.1	220 35.2
18	90 00.7	8 10.2	250 40.1
20	120 01.1	8 08.4	280 45.1
22	150 01.5	N8 06.6	310 50.0

Friday, September 2

Time	SUN GHA	Dec	ARIES GHA
00	180 01.9	N8 04.8	340 54.9
02	210 02.3	8 03.0	10 59.9
04	240 02.7	8 01.2	41 04.8
06	270 03.1	7 59.3	71 09.7
08	300 03.5	7 57.5	101 14.6
10	330 03.9	7 55.7	131 19.6
12	0 04.3	7 53.9	161 24.5
14	30 04.7	7 52.0	191 29.4
16	60 05.1	7 50.2	221 34.4
18	90 05.5	7 48.4	251 39.3
20	120 05.9	7 46.6	281 44.2
22	150 06.3	N7 44.7	311 49.1

Saturday, September 3

Time	SUN GHA	Dec	ARIES GHA
00	180 06.7	N7 42.9	341 54.1
02	210 07.1	7 41.1	11 59.0
04	240 07.5	7 39.2	42 03.9
06	270 07.9	7 37.4	72 08.9
08	300 08.4	7 35.6	102 13.8
10	330 08.8	7 33.7	132 18.7
12	0 09.2	7 31.9	162 23.6
14	30 09.6	7 30.1	192 28.6
16	60 10.0	7 28.2	222 33.5
18	90 10.4	7 26.4	252 38.4
20	120 10.8	7 24.6	282 43.4
22	150 11.2	N7 22.7	312 48.3

Sunday, September 4

Time	SUN GHA	Dec	ARIES GHA
00	180 11.6	N7 20.9	342 53.2
02	210 12.0	7 19.0	12 58.1
04	240 12.4	7 17.2	43 03.1
06	270 12.8	7 15.4	73 08.0
08	300 13.2	7 13.5	103 12.9
10	330 13.7	7 11.7	133 17.9
12	0 14.1	7 09.8	163 22.8
14	30 14.5	7 08.0	193 27.7
16	60 14.9	7 06.1	223 32.6
18	90 15.3	7 04.3	253 37.6
20	120 15.7	7 02.4	283 42.5
22	150 16.1	N7 00.6	313 47.4

Monday, September 5

Time	SUN GHA	Dec	ARIES GHA
00	180 16.5	N6 58.7	343 52.3
02	210 16.9	6 56.9	13 57.3
04	240 17.4	6 55.0	44 02.2
06	270 17.8	6 53.2	74 07.1
08	300 18.2	6 51.3	104 12.1
10	330 18.6	6 49.5	134 17.0
12	0 19.0	6 47.6	164 21.9
14	30 19.4	6 45.8	194 26.8
16	60 19.9	6 43.9	224 31.8
18	90 20.3	6 42.1	254 36.7
20	120 20.7	6 40.2	284 41.6
22	150 21.1	N6 38.3	314 46.6

Tuesday, September 6

Time	SUN GHA	Dec	ARIES GHA
00	180 21.5	N6 36.5	344 51.5
02	210 21.9	6 34.6	14 56.4
04	240 22.4	6 32.8	45 01.3
06	270 22.8	6 30.9	75 06.3
08	300 23.2	6 29.0	105 11.2
10	330 23.6	6 27.2	135 16.1
12	0 24.0	6 25.3	165 21.1
14	30 24.5	6 23.5	195 26.0
16	60 24.9	6 21.6	225 30.9
18	90 25.3	6 19.7	255 35.8
20	120 25.7	6 17.9	285 40.8
22	150 26.1	N6 16.0	315 45.7

Wednesday, September 7

Time	SUN GHA	Dec	ARIES GHA
00	180 26.6	N6 14.1	345 50.6
02	210 27.0	6 12.3	15 55.6
04	240 27.4	6 10.4	46 00.5
06	270 27.8	6 08.5	76 05.4
08	300 28.3	6 06.7	106 10.3
10	330 28.7	6 04.8	136 15.3
12	0 29.1	6 02.9	166 20.2
14	30 29.5	6 01.0	196 25.1
16	60 30.0	5 59.2	226 30.1
18	90 30.4	5 57.3	256 35.0
20	120 30.8	5 55.4	286 39.9
22	150 31.2	N5 53.5	316 44.8

Thursday, September 8

Time	SUN GHA	Dec	ARIES GHA
00	180 31.7	N5 51.7	346 49.8
02	210 32.1	5 49.8	16 54.7
04	240 32.5	5 47.9	46 59.6
06	270 32.9	5 46.0	77 04.5
08	300 33.4	5 44.2	107 09.5
10	330 33.8	5 42.3	137 14.4
12	0 34.2	5 40.4	167 19.3
14	30 34.7	5 38.5	197 24.3
16	60 35.1	5 36.6	227 29.2
18	90 35.5	5 34.8	257 34.1
20	120 35.9	5 32.9	287 39.0
22	150 36.4	N5 31.0	317 44.0

Friday, September 9

Time	SUN GHA	Dec	ARIES GHA
00	180 36.8	N5 29.1	347 48.9
02	210 37.2	5 27.2	17 53.8
04	240 37.7	5 25.3	47 58.8
06	270 38.1	5 23.5	78 03.7
08	300 38.5	5 21.6	108 08.6
10	330 39.0	5 19.7	138 13.5
12	0 39.4	5 17.8	168 18.5
14	30 39.8	5 15.9	198 23.4
16	60 40.2	5 14.0	228 28.3
18	90 40.7	5 12.1	258 33.3
20	120 41.1	5 10.2	288 38.2
22	150 41.5	N5 08.3	318 43.1

Saturday, September 10

Time	SUN GHA	Dec	ARIES GHA
00	180 42.0	N5 06.5	348 48.0
02	210 42.4	5 04.6	18 53.0
04	240 42.8	5 02.7	48 57.9
06	270 43.3	5 00.8	79 02.8
08	300 43.7	4 58.9	109 07.8
10	330 44.2	4 57.0	139 12.7
12	0 44.6	4 55.1	169 17.6
14	30 45.0	4 53.2	199 22.5
16	60 45.5	4 51.3	229 27.5
18	90 45.9	4 49.4	259 32.4
20	120 46.3	4 47.5	289 37.3
22	150 46.8	N4 45.6	319 42.3

Sunday, September 11

Time	SUN GHA	Dec	ARIES GHA
00	180 47.2	N4 43.7	349 47.2
02	210 47.6	4 41.8	19 52.1
04	240 48.1	4 39.9	49 57.0
06	270 48.5	4 38.0	80 02.0
08	300 48.9	4 36.1	110 06.9
10	330 49.4	4 34.2	140 11.8
12	0 49.8	4 32.3	170 16.8
14	30 50.3	4 30.4	200 21.7
16	60 50.7	4 28.5	230 26.6
18	90 51.1	4 26.6	260 31.5
20	120 51.6	4 24.7	290 36.5
22	150 52.0	N4 22.8	320 41.4

Monday, September 12

Time	SUN GHA	Dec	ARIES GHA
00	180 52.5	N4 20.9	350 46.3
02	210 52.9	4 19.0	20 51.2
04	240 53.3	4 17.1	50 56.2
06	270 53.8	4 15.2	81 01.1
08	300 54.2	4 13.3	111 06.0
10	330 54.7	4 11.4	141 11.0
12	0 55.1	4 09.5	171 15.9
14	30 55.5	4 07.5	201 20.8
16	60 56.0	4 05.6	231 25.7
18	90 56.4	4 03.7	261 30.7
20	120 56.9	4 01.8	291 35.6
22	150 57.3	N3 59.9	321 40.5

Tuesday, September 13

Time	SUN GHA	Dec	ARIES GHA
00	180 57.7	N3 58.0	351 45.5
02	210 58.2	3 56.1	21 50.4
04	240 58.6	3 54.2	51 55.3
06	270 59.1	3 52.3	82 00.2
08	300 59.5	3 50.4	112 05.2
10	330 59.9	3 48.4	142 10.1
12	1 00.4	3 46.5	172 15.0
14	31 00.8	3 44.6	202 20.0
16	61 01.3	3 42.7	232 24.9
18	91 01.7	3 40.8	262 29.8
20	121 02.2	3 38.9	292 34.7
22	151 02.6	N3 37.0	322 39.7

Wednesday, September 14

Time	SUN GHA	Dec	ARIES GHA
00	181 03.0	N3 35.0	352 44.6
02	211 03.5	3 33.1	22 49.5
04	241 03.9	3 31.2	52 54.5
06	271 04.4	3 29.3	82 59.4
08	301 04.8	3 27.4	113 04.3
10	331 05.3	3 25.4	143 09.2
12	1 05.7	3 23.5	173 14.2
14	31 06.1	3 21.6	203 19.1
16	61 06.6	3 19.7	233 24.0
18	91 07.0	3 17.8	263 29.0
20	121 07.5	3 15.8	293 33.9
22	151 07.9	N3 13.9	323 38.8

Thursday, September 15

Time	SUN GHA	Dec	ARIES GHA
00	181 08.4	N3 12.0	353 43.7
02	211 08.8	3 10.1	23 48.7
04	241 09.3	3 08.2	53 53.6
06	271 09.7	3 06.2	83 58.5
08	301 10.2	3 04.3	114 03.4
10	331 10.6	3 02.4	144 08.4
12	1 11.0	3 00.5	174 13.3
14	31 11.5	2 58.5	204 18.2
16	61 11.9	2 56.6	234 23.2
18	91 12.4	2 54.7	264 28.1
20	121 12.8	2 52.8	294 33.0
22	151 13.3	N2 50.8	324 37.9

SEPTEMBER 1994 — SUN & ARIES — GMT

Friday, September 16

Time	SUN GHA	Dec	ARIES GHA
00	181 13.7	N2 48.9	354 42.9
02	211 14.2	2 47.0	24 47.8
04	241 14.6	2 45.1	54 52.7
06	271 15.1	2 43.1	84 57.7
08	301 15.5	2 41.2	115 02.6
10	331 15.9	2 39.3	115 07.5
12	1 16.4	2 37.4	175 12.4
14	31 16.8	2 35.4	205 17.4
16	61 17.3	2 33.5	235 22.3
18	91 17.7	2 31.6	265 27.2
20	121 18.2	2 29.6	295 32.2
22	151 18.6	N2 27.7	325 37.1

Saturday, September 17

Time	SUN GHA	Dec	ARIES GHA
00	181 19.1	N2 25.8	355 42.0
02	211 19.5	2 23.8	25 46.9
04	241 20.0	2 21.9	55 51.9
06	271 20.4	2 20.0	85 56.8
08	301 20.9	2 18.1	116 01.7
10	331 21.3	2 16.1	146 06.7
12	1 21.8	2 14.2	176 11.6
14	31 22.2	2 12.3	206 16.5
16	61 22.6	2 10.3	236 21.4
18	91 23.1	2 08.4	266 26.4
20	121 23.5	2 06.5	296 31.3
22	151 24.0	N2 04.5	326 36.2

Sunday, September 18

Time	SUN GHA	Dec	ARIES GHA
00	181 24.4	N2 02.6	356 41.2
02	211 24.9	2 00.7	26 46.1
04	241 25.3	1 58.7	56 51.0
06	271 25.8	1 56.8	86 55.9
08	301 26.2	1 54.8	117 00.9
10	331 26.7	1 52.9	147 05.8
12	1 27.1	1 51.0	177 10.7
14	31 27.6	1 49.0	207 15.6
16	61 28.0	1 47.1	237 20.6
18	91 28.5	1 45.2	267 25.5
20	121 28.9	1 43.2	297 30.4
22	151 29.3	N1 41.3	327 35.4

Monday, September 19

Time	SUN GHA	Dec	ARIES GHA
00	181 29.8	N1 39.4	357 40.3
02	211 30.2	1 37.4	27 45.2
04	241 30.7	1 35.5	57 50.1
06	271 31.1	1 33.5	87 55.1
08	301 31.6	1 31.6	118 00.0
10	331 32.0	1 29.7	148 04.9
12	1 32.5	1 27.7	178 09.9
14	31 32.9	1 25.8	208 14.8
16	61 33.4	1 23.9	238 19.7
18	91 33.8	1 21.9	268 24.6
20	121 34.3	1 20.0	298 29.6
22	151 34.7	N1 18.0	328 34.5

Tuesday, September 20

Time	SUN GHA	Dec	ARIES GHA
00	181 35.1	N1 16.1	358 39.4
02	211 35.6	1 14.2	28 44.4
04	241 36.0	1 12.2	58 49.3
06	271 36.5	1 10.3	88 54.2
08	301 36.9	1 08.3	118 59.1
10	331 37.4	1 06.4	149 04.1
12	1 37.8	1 04.4	179 09.0
14	31 38.3	1 02.5	209 13.9
16	61 38.7	1 00.6	239 18.9
18	91 39.2	0 58.6	269 23.8
20	121 39.6	0 56.7	299 28.7
22	151 40.0	N0 54.7	329 33.6

Wednesday, September 21

Time	SUN GHA	Dec	ARIES GHA
00	181 40.5	N0 52.8	359 38.6
02	211 40.9	0 50.9	29 43.5
04	241 41.4	0 48.9	59 48.4
06	271 41.8	0 47.0	89 53.4
08	301 42.3	0 45.0	119 58.3
10	331 42.7	0 43.1	150 03.2
12	1 43.2	0 41.1	180 08.1
14	31 43.6	0 39.2	210 13.1
16	61 44.0	0 37.2	240 18.0
18	91 44.5	0 35.3	270 22.9
20	121 44.9	0 33.4	300 27.9
22	151 45.4	N0 31.4	330 32.8

Thursday, September 22

Time	SUN GHA	Dec	ARIES GHA
00	181 45.8	N0 29.5	0 37.7
02	211 46.3	0 27.5	30 42.6
04	241 46.7	0 25.6	60 47.6
06	271 47.1	0 23.6	90 52.5
08	301 47.6	0 21.7	120 57.4
10	331 48.0	0 19.7	151 02.3
12	1 48.5	0 17.8	181 07.3
14	31 48.9	0 15.9	211 12.2
16	61 49.4	0 13.9	241 17.1
18	91 49.8	0 12.0	271 22.1
20	121 50.2	0 10.0	301 27.0
22	151 50.7	N0 08.1	331 31.9

Friday, September 23

Time	SUN GHA	Dec	ARIES GHA
00	181 51.1	N0 06.1	1 36.8
02	211 51.6	0 04.2	31 41.8
04	241 52.0	0 02.2	61 46.7
06	271 52.4	0 00.3	91 51.6
08	301 52.9	S0 01.7	121 56.6
10	331 53.3	0 03.6	152 01.5
12	1 53.8	0 05.5	182 06.4
14	31 54.2	0 07.5	212 11.3
16	61 54.6	0 09.4	242 16.3
18	91 55.1	0 11.4	272 21.2
20	121 55.5	0 13.3	302 26.1
22	151 56.0	S0 15.3	332 31.1

Saturday, September 24

Time	SUN GHA	Dec	ARIES GHA
00	181 56.4	S0 17.2	2 36.0
02	211 56.8	0 19.2	32 40.9
04	241 57.3	0 21.1	62 45.8
06	271 57.7	0 23.1	92 50.8
08	301 58.1	0 25.0	122 55.7
10	331 58.6	0 27.0	153 00.6
12	1 59.0	0 28.9	183 05.6
14	31 59.5	0 30.9	213 10.5
16	61 59.9	0 32.8	243 15.4
18	92 00.3	0 34.8	273 20.3
20	122 00.8	0 36.7	303 25.3
22	152 01.2	S0 38.6	333 30.2

Sunday, September 25

Time	SUN GHA	Dec	ARIES GHA
00	182 01.6	S0 40.6	3 35.1
02	212 02.1	0 42.5	33 40.1
04	242 02.5	0 44.5	63 45.0
06	272 02.9	0 46.4	93 49.9
08	302 03.4	0 48.4	123 54.8
10	332 03.8	0 50.3	153 59.8
12	2 04.2	0 52.3	184 04.7
14	32 04.7	0 54.2	214 09.6
16	62 05.1	0 56.2	244 14.5
18	92 05.5	0 58.1	274 19.5
20	122 06.0	1 00.1	304 24.4
22	152 06.4	S1 02.0	334 29.3

Monday, September 26

Time	SUN GHA	Dec	ARIES GHA
00	182 06.8	S1 04.0	4 34.3
02	212 07.3	1 05.9	34 39.2
04	242 07.7	1 07.9	64 44.1
06	272 08.1	1 09.8	94 49.0
08	302 08.5	1 11.8	124 54.0
10	332 09.0	1 13.7	154 58.9
12	2 09.4	1 15.6	185 03.8
14	32 09.8	1 17.6	215 08.8
16	62 10.3	1 19.5	245 13.7
18	92 10.7	1 21.5	275 18.6
20	122 11.1	1 23.4	305 23.5
22	152 11.5	S1 25.4	335 28.5

Tuesday, September 27

Time	SUN GHA	Dec	ARIES GHA
00	182 12.0	S1 27.3	5 33.4
02	212 12.4	1 29.3	35 38.3
04	242 12.8	1 31.2	65 43.3
06	272 13.2	1 33.2	95 48.2
08	302 13.7	1 35.1	125 53.1
10	332 14.1	1 37.1	155 58.0
12	2 14.5	1 39.0	186 03.0
14	32 14.9	1 41.0	216 07.9
16	62 15.4	1 42.9	246 12.8
18	92 15.8	1 44.8	276 17.8
20	122 16.2	1 46.8	306 22.7
22	152 16.6	S1 48.7	336 27.6

Wednesday, September 28

Time	SUN GHA	Dec	ARIES GHA
00	182 17.1	S1 50.7	6 32.5
02	212 17.5	1 52.6	36 37.5
04	242 17.9	1 54.6	66 42.4
06	272 18.3	1 56.5	96 47.3
08	302 18.7	1 58.5	126 52.3
10	332 19.2	2 00.4	156 57.2
12	2 19.6	2 02.4	187 02.1
14	32 20.0	2 04.3	217 07.0
16	62 20.4	2 06.3	247 12.0
18	92 20.8	2 08.2	277 16.9
20	122 21.3	2 10.1	307 21.8
22	152 21.7	S2 12.1	337 26.7

Thursday, September 29

Time	SUN GHA	Dec	ARIES GHA
00	182 22.1	S2 14.0	7 31.7
02	212 22.5	2 16.0	37 36.6
04	242 22.9	2 17.9	67 41.5
06	272 23.3	2 19.9	97 46.5
08	302 23.8	2 21.8	127 51.4
10	332 24.2	2 23.8	157 56.3
12	2 24.6	2 25.7	188 01.2
14	32 25.0	2 27.6	218 06.2
16	62 25.4	2 29.6	248 11.1
18	92 25.8	2 31.5	278 16.0
20	122 26.2	2 33.5	308 21.0
22	152 26.6	S2 35.4	338 25.9

Friday, September 30

Time	SUN GHA	Dec	ARIES GHA
00	182 27.1	S2 37.4	8 30.8
02	212 27.5	2 39.3	38 35.7
04	242 27.9	2 41.2	68 40.7
06	272 28.3	2 43.2	98 45.6
08	302 28.7	2 45.1	128 50.5
10	332 29.1	2 47.1	158 55.5
12	2 29.5	2 49.0	189 00.4
14	32 29.9	2 51.0	219 05.3
16	62 30.3	2 52.9	249 10.2
18	92 30.7	2 54.8	279 15.2
20	122 31.1	2 56.8	309 20.1
22	152 31.5	S2 58.7	339 25.0

Chapter 6

SEPTEMBER 1994 — PLANETS — 0h GMT

VENUS / JUPITER

Mer Pass h m	GHA ° '	Mean Var/hr 15°+	Dec ° '	Mean Var/hr '			GHA ° '	Mean Var/hr 15°+	Dec ° '	Mean Var/hr '	Mer Pass h m
14 45	138 36.9	0.4	S11 53.2	1.1	1	Thu	122 13.4	2.1	S13 51.3	0.1	15 49
14 44	138 47.3	0.4	S12 19.5	1.1	2	Fri	123 03.6	2.1	S13 54.4	0.1	15 46
14 44	138 58.1	0.5	S12 45.5	1.1	3	Sat	123 53.7	2.1	S13 57.5	0.1	15 42
14 43	139 09.2	0.5	S13 11.3	1.1	4	SUN	124 43.7	2.1	S14 00.6	0.1	15 39
14 42	139 20.8	0.5	S13 36.8	1.0	5	Mon	125 33.6	2.1	S14 03.7	0.1	15 36
14 41	139 32.9	0.5	S14 01.9	1.0	6	Tue	126 23.4	2.1	S14 06.9	0.1	15 32
14 40	139 45.4	0.5	S14 26.7	1.0	7	Wed	127 13.0	2.1	S14 10.1	0.1	15 29
14 40	139 58.4	0.6	S14 51.2	1.0	8	Thu	128 02.6	2.1	S14 13.3	0.1	15 26
14 39	140 11.9	0.6	S15 15.4	1.0	9	Fri	128 52.1	2.1	S14 16.6	0.1	15 22
14 38	140 26.0	0.6	S15 39.2	1.0	10	Sat	129 41.5	2.1	S14 19.8	0.1	15 19
14 37	140 40.6	0.6	S16 02.7	1.0	11	SUN	130 30.8	2.1	S14 23.1	0.1	15 16
14 36	140 55.9	0.7	S16 25.8	0.9	12	Mon	131 20.0	2.0	S14 26.4	0.1	15 13
14 35	141 11.7	0.7	S16 48.5	0.9	13	Tue	132 09.1	2.0	S14 29.7	0.1	15 09
14 33	141 28.3	0.7	S17 10.8	0.9	14	Wed	132 58.1	2.0	S14 33.1	0.1	15 06
14 32	141 45.6	0.8	S17 32.7	0.9	15	Thu	133 47.0	2.0	S14 36.4	0.1	15 03
14 31	142 03.6	0.8	S17 54.2	0.9	16	Fri	134 35.8	2.0	S14 39.8	0.1	15 00
14 30	142 22.4	0.8	S18 15.2	0.9	17	Sat	135 24.5	2.0	S14 43.2	0.1	14 56
14 28	142 42.0	0.9	S18 35.8	0.8	18	SUN	136 13.1	2.0	S14 46.6	0.1	14 53
14 27	143 02.5	0.9	S18 56.0	0.8	19	Mon	137 01.7	2.0	S14 50.0	0.1	14 50
14 26	143 23.9	0.9	S19 15.6	0.8	20	Tue	137 50.1	2.0	S14 53.4	0.1	14 47
14 24	143 46.2	1.0	S19 34.8	0.8	21	Wed	138 38.5	2.0	S14 56.9	0.1	14 43
14 22	144 09.6	1.0	S19 53.4	0.8	22	Thu	139 26.8	2.0	S15 00.3	0.1	14 40
14 21	144 34.0	1.1	S20 11.6	0.7	23	Fri	140 15.0	2.0	S15 03.8	0.1	14 37
14 19	144 59.5	1.1	S20 29.2	0.7	24	Sat	141 03.1	2.0	S15 07.3	0.1	14 34
14 17	145 26.2	1.2	S20 46.2	0.7	25	SUN	141 51.2	2.0	S15 10.8	0.1	14 31
14 15	145 54.1	1.2	S21 02.7	0.7	26	Mon	142 39.2	2.0	S15 14.3	0.1	14 27
14 13	146 23.3	1.3	S21 18.5	0.6	27	Tue	143 27.1	2.0	S15 17.8	0.1	14 24
14 11	146 53.8	1.3	S21 33.8	0.6	28	Wed	144 14.9	2.0	S15 21.3	0.1	14 21
14 09	147 25.7	1.4	S21 48.4	0.6	29	Thu	145 02.6	2.0	S15 24.8	0.2	14 18
14 07	147 59.0	1.4	S22 02.4	0.5	30	Fri	145 50.3	2.0	S15 28.4	0.1	14 15

VENUS, Av Mag −4.5
SHA September
5 155; 10 152; 15 148; 20 145; 25 142; 30 139.

JUPITER, Av Mag −1.8
SHA September
5 142; 10 141; 15 140; 20 139; 25 138; 30 137.

MARS / SATURN

Mer Pass h m	GHA ° '	Mean Var/hr 15°+	Dec ° '	Mean Var/hr '			GHA ° '	Mean Var/hr 15°+	Dec ° '	Mean Var/hr '	Mer Pass h m
08 03	239 15.3	0.7	N23 29.9	0.1	1	Thu	358 31.2	2.6	S10 00.1	0.1	00 06
08 01	239 33.2	0.8	N23 27.9	0.1	2	Fri	359 34.6	2.6	S10 01.9	0.1	00 02
08 00	239 51.2	0.8	N23 25.8	0.1	3	Sat	0 38.0	2.6	S10 03.7	0.1	23 53
07 59	240 09.4	0.8	N23 23.6	0.1	4	SUN	1 41.4	2.6	S10 05.4	0.1	23 49
07 58	240 27.7	0.8	N23 21.2	0.1	5	Mon	2 44.8	2.6	S10 07.2	0.1	23 45
07 57	240 46.1	0.8	N23 18.6	0.1	6	Tue	3 48.2	2.6	S10 09.0	0.1	23 41
07 55	241 04.7	0.8	N23 15.9	0.1	7	Wed	4 51.6	2.6	S10 10.7	0.1	23 36
07 54	241 23.4	0.8	N23 13.0	0.1	8	Thu	5 55.0	2.6	S10 12.4	0.1	23 32
07 53	241 42.3	0.8	N23 10.0	0.1	9	Fri	6 58.4	2.6	S10 14.2	0.1	23 28
07 51	242 01.3	0.8	N23 06.8	0.1	10	Sat	8 01.8	2.6	S10 15.9	0.1	23 24
07 50	242 20.4	0.8	N23 03.4	0.1	11	SUN	9 05.1	2.6	S10 17.6	0.1	23 20
07 49	242 39.7	0.8	N23 00.0	0.2	12	Mon	10 08.4	2.6	S10 19.3	0.1	23 15
07 48	242 59.2	0.8	N22 56.3	0.2	13	Tue	11 11.8	2.6	S10 21.0	0.1	23 11
07 46	243 18.8	0.8	N22 52.6	0.2	14	Wed	12 15.0	2.6	S10 22.6	0.1	23 07
07 45	243 38.6	0.8	N22 48.7	0.2	15	Thu	13 18.3	2.6	S10 24.3	0.1	23 03
07 44	243 58.5	0.8	N22 44.7	0.2	16	Fri	14 21.5	2.6	S10 25.9	0.1	22 59
07 42	244 18.6	0.8	N22 40.5	0.2	17	Sat	15 24.7	2.6	S10 27.6	0.1	22 54
07 41	244 38.8	0.9	N22 36.2	0.2	18	SUN	16 27.9	2.6	S10 29.2	0.1	22 50
07 40	244 59.3	0.9	N22 31.8	0.2	19	Mon	17 31.1	2.6	S10 30.7	0.1	22 46
07 38	245 19.8	0.9	N22 27.2	0.2	20	Tue	18 34.2	2.6	S10 32.3	0.1	22 42
07 37	245 40.6	0.9	N22 22.5	0.2	21	Wed	19 37.2	2.6	S10 33.8	0.1	22 38
07 35	246 01.5	0.9	N22 17.7	0.2	22	Thu	20 40.2	2.6	S10 35.4	0.1	22 33
07 34	246 22.6	0.9	N22 12.8	0.2	23	Fri	21 43.2	2.6	S10 36.9	0.1	22 29
07 33	246 43.9	0.9	N22 07.8	0.2	24	Sat	22 46.2	2.6	S10 38.3	0.1	22 25
07 31	247 05.3	0.9	N22 02.7	0.2	25	SUN	23 49.0	2.6	S10 39.8	0.1	22 21
07 30	247 26.9	0.9	N21 57.4	0.2	26	Mon	24 51.9	2.6	S10 41.2	0.1	22 17
07 28	247 48.7	0.9	N21 52.1	0.2	27	Tue	25 54.7	2.6	S10 42.6	0.1	22 12
07 27	248 10.7	0.9	N21 46.6	0.2	28	Wed	26 57.4	2.6	S10 44.0	0.1	22 08
07 25	248 32.8	0.9	N21 41.0	0.2	29	Thu	28 00.1	2.6	S10 45.3	0.1	22 04
07 24	248 55.2	0.9	N21 35.4	0.2	30	Fri	29 02.7	2.6	S10 46.7	0.1	22 00

MARS, Av Mag +1.1
SHA September
5 257; 10 253; 15 250; 20 247; 25 244; 30 240.

SATURN, Av Mag +0.5
SHA September
5 19; 10 19; 15 20; 20 20; 25 20; 30 21.

SEPTEMBER 1994   MOON

Day	GMT hr	GHA ° '	Mean Var/hr 14°+	Dec ° '	Mean Var/hr '	Day	GMT hr	GHA ° '	Mean Var/hr 14°+	Dec ° '	Mean Var/hr '
1 Thu	0	240 37.9	29.5	N 19 11.9	4.1	17 Sat	0	34 24.6	31.2	S 9 48.6	10.1
	6	327 34.0	29.5	N 18 47.6	4.7		6	121 31.8	31.6	S 8 48.4	10.3
	12	54 31.7	29.4	N 18 19.7	5.3		12	208 40.9	31.8	S 7 46.9	10.4
	18	141 28.2	29.4	N 17 48.1	5.9		18	295 51.5	32.1	S 6 44.3	10.6
2 Fri	0	228 24.6	29.4	N 17 13.1	6.5	18 Sun	0	23 03.7	32.3	S 5 40.5	10.7
	6	315 20.9	29.3	N 16 34.5	7.1		6	110 17.3	32.5	S 4 36.7	10.8
	12	42 17.0	29.4	N 15 52.5	7.6		12	197 32.1	32.7	S 3 32.1	10.8
	18	129 13.2	29.3	N 15 07.1	8.2		18	284 48.0	32.8	S 2 27.1	10.8
3 Sat	0	216 09.3	29.4	N 14 18.6	8.6	19 Mon	0	12 05.0	32.9	S 1 22.1	10.8
	6	303 05.5	29.3	N 13 26.9	9.2		6	99 22.8	33.1	S 0 17.0	10.8
	12	30 01.7	29.4	N 12 32.3	9.6		12	186 41.3	33.2	N 0 47.8	10.7
	18	116 57.8	29.3	N 11 34.8	10.1		18	274 00.4	33.3	N 1 52.2	10.6
4 Sun	0	203 53.9	29.3	N 10 34.7	10.5	20 Tue	0	1 20.0	33.3	N 2 56.0	10.5
	6	290 50.0	29.3	N 9 32.1	10.8		6	88 39.9	33.4	N 3 59.2	10.4
	12	17 45.9	29.3	N 8 27.2	11.2		12	176 00.0	33.4	N 5 01.5	10.2
	18	104 41.7	29.3	N 7 20.2	11.5		18	263 20.2	33.4	N 6 02.7	10.0
5 Mon	0	191 37.3	29.2	N 6 11.3	11.8	21 Wed	0	350 40.4	33.3	N 7 02.8	9.8
	6	278 32.5	29.2	N 5 00.8	12.0		6	78 00.5	33.3	N 8 01.6	9.5
	12	5 27.4	29.1	N 3 48.9	12.1		12	165 20.3	33.2	N 8 59.0	9.3
	18	92 21.8	29.0	N 2 35.9	12.4		18	252 39.8	33.2	N 9 54.8	8.9
6 Tue	0	179 15.5	28.8	N 1 22.0	12.4	22 Thu	0	339 58.9	33.1	N 10 48.9	8.7
	6	266 08.7	28.7	N 0 07.5	12.4		6	67 17.4	33.0	N 11 41.1	8.4
	12	353 01.0	28.6	S 1 07.3	12.5		12	154 35.4	32.9	N 12 31.4	8.0
	18	79 52.4	28.4	S 2 22.1	12.4		18	241 52.7	32.8	N 13 19.6	7.7
7 Wed	0	166 42.9	28.2	S 3 36.6	12.4	23 Fri	0	329 09.4	32.6	N 14 05.7	7.3
	6	253 32.3	28.0	S 4 50.5	12.1		6	56 25.2	32.5	N 14 49.4	6.8
	12	340 20.4	27.8	S 6 03.5	12.0		12	143 40.2	32.4	N 15 30.7	6.4
	18	67 07.4	27.5	S 7 15.4	11.7		18	230 54.4	32.2	N 16 09.6	6.0
8 Thu	0	153 53.0	27.3	S 8 25.7	11.3	24 Sat	0	318 07.7	32.0	N 16 45.8	5.5
	6	240 37.2	27.2	S 9 34.2	11.0		6	45 20.0	31.9	N 17 19.3	5.0
	12	327 19.9	26.8	S 10 40.5	10.6		12	132 31.5	31.8	N 17 50.0	4.6
	18	54 01.2	26.6	S 11 44.4	10.2		18	219 42.1	31.6	N 18 17.8	4.1
9 Fri	0	140 41.0	26.4	S 12 45.7	9.6	25 Sun	0	306 51.7	31.5	N 18 42.6	3.6
	6	227 19.4	26.1	S 13 43.9	9.1		6	34 00.5	31.3	N 19 04.4	3.1
	12	313 56.3	25.9	S 14 38.9	8.6		12	121 08.4	31.2	N 19 23.1	2.6
	18	40 31.8	25.7	S 15 30.3	7.9		18	208 15.5	31.0	N 19 38.6	2.0
10 Sat	0	127 06.0	25.5	S 16 18.1	7.2	26 Mon	0	295 21.8	30.9	N 19 50.8	1.5
	6	213 39.1	25.3	S 17 01.9	6.6		6	22 27.3	30.8	N 19 59.8	0.9
	12	300 11.1	25.2	S 17 41.5	5.8		12	109 32.1	30.7	N 20 05.4	0.3
	18	26 42.2	25.0	S 18 16.8	5.1		18	196 36.3	30.6	N 20 07.6	0.2
11 Sun	0	113 12.6	24.9	S 18 47.7	4.3	27 Tue	0	283 39.9	30.5	N 20 06.4	0.9
	6	199 42.5	24.9	S 19 14.0	3.5		6	10 42.9	30.4	N 20 01.7	1.4
	12	286 12.0	24.9	S 19 35.6	2.8		12	97 45.5	30.4	N 19 53.6	2.0
	18	12 41.6	24.9	S 19 52.5	1.9		18	184 47.6	30.3	N 19 41.9	2.6
12 Mon	0	99 11.2	25.1	S 20 04.6	1.1	28 Wed	0	271 49.4	30.2	N 19 26.8	3.1
	6	185 41.3	25.2	S 20 11.9	0.4		6	358 50.9	30.2	N 19 08.2	3.8
	12	272 12.1	25.3	S 20 14.5	0.4		12	85 52.1	30.2	N 18 46.1	4.3
	18	358 43.8	25.5	S 20 12.4	1.2		18	172 53.1	30.2	N 18 20.5	4.8
13 Tue	0	85 16.5	25.7	S 20 05.6	1.9	29 Thu	0	259 53.9	30.1	N 17 51.5	5.4
	6	171 50.7	25.9	S 19 54.2	2.7		6	346 54.5	30.1	N 17 19.1	6.1
	12	258 26.3	26.2	S 19 38.4	3.5		12	73 55.0	30.1	N 16 43.4	6.6
	18	345 03.7	26.5	S 19 18.3	4.1		18	160 55.4	30.1	N 16 04.3	7.1
14 Wed	0	71 42.9	26.9	S 18 54.0	4.8	30 Fri	0	247 55.6	30.0	N 15 22.1	7.6
	6	158 24.2	27.3	S 18 25.7	5.4		6	334 55.7	30.0	N 14 36.6	8.1
	12	245 07.6	27.6	S 17 53.7	6.0		12	61 55.7	29.9	N 13 48.2	8.6
	18	331 53.2	28.0	S 17 18.0	6.5		18	148 55.4	29.9	N 12 56.7	9.1
15 Thu	0	58 41.0	28.3	S 16 38.9	7.1						
	6	145 31.1	28.8	S 15 56.6	7.6						
	12	232 23.5	29.2	S 15 11.3	8.1						
	18	319 18.3	29.5	S 14 23.2	8.5						
16 Fri	0	46 15.3	29.9	S 13 32.5	8.9						
	6	133 14.4	30.2	S 12 39.5	9.2						
	12	220 15.8	30.6	S 11 44.4	9.5						
	18	307 19.2	30.9	S 10 47.4	9.8						

Chapter 6

OCTOBER 1994   SUN & MOON   GMT

SUN

Day of Yr	Mth	Week	Equation of Time 0h (m s)	Equation of Time 12h (m s)	Transit (h m)	Semi-diam (')	Lat 52°N Twilight (h m)	Lat 52°N Sunrise (h m)	Lat 52°N Sunset (h m)	Lat 52°N Twilight (h m)
274	1	Sat	-10 07	-10 17	11 50	16.0	05 27	06 00	17 38	18 12
275	2	Sun	-10 27	-10 36	11 49	16.0	05 28	06 02	17 36	18 09
276	3	Mon	-10 46	-10 55	11 49	16.0	05 30	06 04	17 34	18 07
277	4	Tue	-11 04	-11 13	11 49	16.0	05 32	06 05	17 31	18 05
278	5	Wed	-11 22	-11 31	11 48	16.0	05 33	06 07	17 29	18 03
279	6	Thu	-11 40	-11 49	11 48	16.0	05 35	06 09	17 27	18 00
280	7	Fri	-11 58	-12 07	11 48	16.0	05 37	06 10	17 24	17 58
281	8	Sat	-12 15	-12 24	11 48	16.0	05 38	06 12	17 22	17 56
282	9	Sun	-12 32	-12 40	11 47	16.0	05 40	06 14	17 20	17 54
283	10	Mon	-12 48	-12 56	11 47	16.0	05 42	06 16	17 18	17 51
284	11	Tue	-13 04	-13 12	11 47	16.0	05 43	06 17	17 15	17 49
285	12	Wed	-13 20	-13 27	11 47	16.1	05 45	06 19	17 13	17 47
286	13	Thu	-13 35	-13 42	11 46	16.1	05 47	06 21	17 11	17 45
287	14	Fri	-13 49	-13 56	11 46	16.1	05 48	06 22	17 09	17 43
288	15	Sat	-14 03	-14 10	11 46	16.1	05 50	06 24	17 07	17 41
289	16	Sun	-14 16	-14 23	11 46	16.1	05 52	06 26	17 04	17 39
290	17	Mon	-14 29	-14 36	11 45	16.1	05 53	06 28	17 02	17 36
291	18	Tue	-14 42	-14 48	11 45	16.1	05 55	06 29	17 00	17 34
292	19	Wed	-14 53	-14 59	11 45	16.1	05 57	06 31	16 58	17 32
293	20	Thu	-15 04	-15 10	11 45	16.1	05 58	06 33	16 56	17 30
294	21	Fri	-15 15	-15 20	11 45	16.1	06 00	06 35	16 54	17 28
295	22	Sat	-15 25	-15 29	11 45	16.1	06 02	06 36	16 52	17 26
296	23	Sun	-15 34	-15 38	11 44	16.1	06 04	06 38	16 50	17 24
297	24	Mon	-15 42	-15 46	11 44	16.1	06 05	06 40	16 48	17 22
298	25	Tue	-15 50	-15 53	11 44	16.1	06 07	06 42	16 46	17 20
299	26	Wed	-15 57	-16 00	11 44	16.1	06 09	06 44	16 44	17 19
300	27	Thu	-16 03	-16 06	11 44	16.1	06 10	06 45	16 42	17 17
301	28	Fri	-16 09	-16 11	11 44	16.1	06 12	06 47	16 40	17 15
302	29	Sat	-16 13	-16 15	11 44	16.1	06 14	06 49	16 38	17 13
303	30	Sun	-16 17	-16 19	11 44	16.1	06 15	06 51	16 36	17 11
304	31	Mon	-16 20	-16 21	11 44	16.1	06 17	06 53	16 34	17 09

Lat Corr to Sunrise, Sunset etc

Lat (°)	Twilight (h m)	Sunrise (h m)	Sunset (h m)	Twilight (h m)
N70	+0 19	+0 49	-0 51	-0 20
68	+0 16	+0 40	-0 41	-0 16
66	+0 13	+0 32	-0 33	-0 14
64	+0 10	+0 25	-0 27	-0 11
62	+0 08	+0 20	-0 21	-0 09
N60	+0 06	+0 14	-0 16	-0 07
58	+0 05	+0 10	-0 11	-0 05
56	+0 03	+0 06	-0 07	-0 04
54	+0 01	+0 03	-0 04	-0 02
50	-0 02	-0 03	+0 03	+0 01
N45	-0 05	-0 10	+0 09	+0 05
40	-0 08	-0 15	+0 14	+0 07
35	-0 11	-0 19	+0 19	+0 10
30	-0 14	-0 23	+0 23	+0 13
20	-0 18	-0 30	+0 30	+0 18
N10	-0 24	-0 36	+0 37	+0 23
0	-0 29	-0 42	+0 43	+0 29
S10	-0 36	-0 49	+0 49	+0 36
20	-0 43	-0 55	+0 57	+0 44
30	-0 53	-1 03	+1 05	+0 54
S35	-1 00	-1 08	+1 10	+1 00
40	-1 07	-1 13	+1 15	+1 08
45	-1 16	-1 19	+1 21	+1 16
S50	-1 27	-1 27	+1 28	+1 26

NOTES

Lat corrections are for the middle of October. **Equation of Time** is the excess of Mean Time over Apparent Time.

MOON

Day of Yr	Mth	Week	Age (days)	Transit Diff (Upper) (h m m)	Semi-diam (')	Hor Par (')	Lat 52°N Moonrise (h m)	Lat 52°N Moonset (h m)
274	1	Sat	26	08 34 50	15.8	57.8	01 18	15 36
275	2	Sun	27	09 24 51	16.0	58.7	02 32	16 02
276	3	Mon	28	10 15 53	16.2	59.6	03 49	16 27
277	4	Tue	29	11 08 54	16.4	60.2	05 09	16 53
278	5	Wed	00	12 02 57	16.5	60.7	06 31	17 21
279	6	Thu	01	12 59 59	16.6	60.9	07 54	17 54
280	7	Fri	02	13 58 60	16.6	60.8	09 16	18 33
281	8	Sat	03	14 58 60	16.5	60.4	10 32	19 20
282	9	Sun	04	15 58 59	16.3	59.8	11 40	20 16
283	10	Mon	05	16 57 56	16.1	59.1	12 37	21 19
284	11	Tue	06	17 53 53	15.9	58.4	13 23	22 28
285	12	Wed	07	18 46 49	15.7	57.7	14 00	23 39
286	13	Thu	08	19 35 48	15.5	57.0	14 30	– –
287	14	Fri	09	20 23 45	15.4	56.3	14 55	00 50
288	15	Sat	10	21 08 44	15.2	55.8	15 18	02 00
289	16	Sun	11	21 52 44	15.1	55.3	15 40	03 09
290	17	Mon	12	22 36 43	15.0	54.9	16 01	04 16
291	18	Tue	13	23 19 45	14.9	54.6	16 23	05 22
292	19	Wed	14	24 04 _	14.8	54.3	16 47	06 28
293	20	Thu	15	00 04 45	14.7	54.1	17 14	07 32
294	21	Fri	16	00 49 46	14.7	54.0	17 45	08 34
295	22	Sat	17	01 35 48	14.7	54.0	18 22	09 33
296	23	Sun	18	02 23 48	14.7	54.1	19 05	10 27
297	24	Mon	19	03 11 48	14.8	54.3	19 54	11 16
298	25	Tue	20	03 59 48	14.9	54.7	20 51	11 59
299	26	Wed	21	04 47 48	15.1	55.2	21 53	12 36
300	27	Thu	22	05 35 49	15.2	55.9	22 59	13 07
301	28	Fri	23	06 24 48	15.5	56.7	– –	13 36
302	29	Sat	24	07 12 49	15.7	57.7	00 10	14 01
303	30	Sun	25	08 01 51	16.0	58.6	01 23	14 26
304	31	Mon	26	08 52 52	16.2	59.6	02 40	14 51

Phases of the Moon

		d	h	m
●	New Moon	5	03	55
◐	First Quarter	11	19	17
○	Full Moon	19	12	18
◑	Last Quarter	27	16	44
	Perigee	6	14	
	Apogee	22	02	

NOTES

For Latitude corrections to Moonrise and Moonset see page 706.

OCTOBER 1994 — STARS — 0h GMT October 1

No	Name	Mag	Transit h m	Dec ° ′	GHA ° ′	RA h m	SHA ° ′
	ARIES.............		23 18		9 30.0		
1	Alpheratz	2.2	23 26	N 29 03.9	7 27.7	0 08	357 57.7
2	Ankaa	2.4	23 44	S 42 20.0	2 59.1	0 26	353 29.1
3	Schedar.............	2.5	0 02	N 56 30.7	359 26.0	0 40	349 56.0
4	Diphda	2.2	0 05	S 18 00.8	358 39.6	0 43	349 09.6
5	Achernar	0.6	0 59	S 57 15.7	345 06.6	1 38	335 36.6
6	POLARIS...........	2.1	1 50	N 89 14.4	332 25.1	2 20	322 55.1
7	Hamal	2.2	1 29	N 23 26.4	337 46.2	2 07	328 16.2
8	Acamar	3.1	2 20	S 40 19.4	324 58.6	2 58	315 28.6
9	Menkar	2.8	2 24	N 4 04.3	323 59.4	3 02	314 29.4
10	Mirfak	1.9	2 46	N 49 50.5	318 30.0	3 24	309 00.0
11	Aldebaran	1.1	3 57	N 16 29.9	300 35.2	4 36	291 05.2
12	Rigel	0.3	4 36	S 8 12.4	290 55.3	5 14	281 25.3
13	Capella.............	0.2	4 38	N 45 59.4	290 24.9	5 16	280 54.9
14	Bellatrix...........	1.7	4 46	N 6 20.7	288 16.9	5 25	278 46.9
15	Elnath	1.8	4 47	N 28 36.1	288 00.1	5 26	278 30.1
16	Alnilam	1.8	4 57	S 1 12.3	285 30.4	5 36	276 00.4
17	Betelgeuse 0.1-1.2		5 16	N 7 24.4	280 46.3	5 55	271 16.3
18	Canopus	–0.9	5 45	S 52 41.4	273 32.2	6 24	264 02.2
19	Sirius	–1.6	6 06	S 16 42.4	268 16.0	6 45	258 46.0
20	Adhara	1.6	6 19	S 28 57.7	264 53.5	6 58	255 23.5
21	Castor	1.6	6 55	N 31 53.8	255 55.8	7 34	246 25.8
22	Procyon	0.5	7 00	N 5 14.3	254 44.4	7 39	245 14.4
23	Pollux	1.2	7 06	N 28 02.2	253 14.9	7 45	243 44.9
24	Avior	1.7	7 43	S 59 29.4	243 53.8	8 22	234 23.8
25	Suhail	2.2	8 28	S 43 24.5	232 32.9	9 08	223 02.9
26	Miaplacidus	1.8	8 34	S 69 41.6	231 12.9	9 13	221 42.9
27	Alphard	2.2	8 48	S 8 38.1	227 40.0	9 27	218 10.0
28	Regulus............	1.3	9 29	N 11 59.5	217 28.6	10 08	207 58.6
29	Dubhe	2.0	10 24	N 61 46.5	203 39.3	11 03	194 09.3
30	Denebola.........	2.2	11 09	N 14 36.1	192 18.2	11 49	182 48.2
31	Gienah	2.8	11 36	S 17 30.7	185 37.0	12 16	176 07.0
32	Acrux...............	1.1	11 46	S 63 04.1	182 55.6	12 26	173 25.6
33	Gacrux	1.6	11 51	S 57 05.0	181 47.1	12 31	172 17.1
34	Mimosa............	1.5	12 07	S 59 39.6	177 39.0	12 47	168 09.0
35	Alioth..............	1.7	12 14	N 55 59.3	176 03.5	12 54	166 33.5
36	Spica................	1.2	12 45	S 11 08.0	168 16.4	13 25	158 46.4
37	Alkaid	1.9	13 07	N 49 20.4	162 40.4	13 47	153 10.4
38	Hadar	0.9	13 23	S 60 20.9	158 38.4	14 03	149 08.4
39	Menkent..........	2.3	13 26	S 36 20.6	157 54.5	14 06	148 24.5
40	Arcturus	0.2	13 35	N 19 12.7	155 38.8	14 15	146 08.8
41	Rigil Kent........	0.1	13 59	S 60 48.8	149 41.5	14 39	140 11.5
42	Zuben'ubi........	2.9	14 10	S 16 01.1	146 51.3	14 51	137 21.3
43	Kochab............	2.2	14 10	N 74 10.8	146 50.6	14 51	137 20.6
44	Alphecca..........	2.3	14 54	N 26 44.1	135 53.2	15 34	126 23.2
45	Antares............	1.2	15 48	S 26 25.2	122 13.7	16 29	112 43.7
46	Atria	1.9	16 07	S 69 01.2	117 28.5	16 48	107 58.5
47	Sabik	2.6	16 29	S 15 43.0	111 58.8	17 10	102 28.8
48	Shaula..............	1.7	16 52	S 37 06.0	106 11.1	17 33	96 41.1
49	Rasalhague	2.1	16 54	N 12 34.1	105 49.6	17 35	96 19.6
50	Eltanin.............	2.4	17 16	N 51 29.8	100 22.9	17 56	90 52.9
51	Kaus Aust.........	2.0	17 43	S 34 23.2	93 32.5	18 24	84 02.5
52	Vega	0.1	17 56	N 38 47.1	90 18.5	18 37	80 48.5
53	Nunki	2.1	18 14	S 26 18.1	85 45.7	18 55	76 15.7
54	Altair	0.9	19 09	N 8 51.6	71 51.9	19 51	62 21.9
55	Peacock...........	2.1	19 44	S 56 45.2	63 11.1	20 25	53 41.1
56	Deneb	1.3	20 00	N 45 16.1	59 10.9	20 41	49 40.9
57	Enif	2.5	21 02	N 9 51.3	43 30.7	21 44	34 00.7
58	Al Na'ir	2.2	21 26	S 46 59.2	37 31.0	22 08	28 01.0
59	Fomalhaut	1.3	22 16	S 29 38.9	25 09.1	22 57	15 39.1
60	Markab	2.6	22 23	N 15 10.9	23 22.0	23 05	13 52.0

Stars Transit Corr Table

Date	Corr h m	Date	Corr h m
1	–0 00	17	–1 03
2	–0 04	18	–1 07
3	–0 08	19	–1 11
4	–0 12	20	–1 15
5	–0 16	21	–1 19
6	–0 20	22	–1 23
7	–0 24	23	–1 27
8	–0 28	24	–1 30
9	–0 31	25	–1 34
10	–0 35	26	–1 38
11	–0 39	27	–1 42
12	–0 43	28	–1 46
13	–0 47	29	–1 50
14	–0 51	30	–1 54
15	–0 55	31	–1 58
16	–0 59		

STAR'S TRANSIT

To find the approx time of transit of a star for any day of the month use above table. All corrections are subtractive. If the quantity taken from the table is greater than the time of transit for the first of the month, add 23h 56min to the time of transit before subtracting the correction.

Example: It is 0130h on October 15. How soon will you be able to get a meridian altitude sight, and of which star?

	h min
Present time	01 30
Corr for the 15th	+00 55
Corresponding time on the 1st	02 25

Answer: 21 min, Mirfak (No 10).

OCTOBER DIARY

2 03	Uranus stationary
2 14	Neptune stationary
5 04	New Moon
6 14	Moon at perigee
6 18	Mercury 3°S of Moon
7 05	Pallas stationary
7 10	Venus 7°S of Moon
7 12	Jupiter 0.7°N of Moon
9 09	Mercury stationary
11 19	First Quarter
12 01	Neptune 4°S of Moon
12 04	Uranus 5°S of Moon
12 23	Venus stationary
15 16	Saturn 7°S of Moon
19 12	Full Moon
21 05	Mercury in inferior conjunction
22 02	Moon at apogee
25 19	Vesta 0.6°N of Moon
27 17	Last Quarter
28 13	Mars 7°N of Moon
29 17	Mercury stationary

Chapter 6

OCTOBER 1994 — SUN & ARIES — GMT

Time	SUN GHA	Dec	ARIES GHA	Time	SUN GHA	Dec	ARIES GHA	Time	SUN GHA	Dec	ARIES GHA	Time
Saturday, October 1				**Thursday, October 6**				**Tuesday, October 11**				
00	182 21.9	S3 00.7	9 30.0	00	182 55.2	S4 56.6	14 25.6	00	183 16.1	S6 51.0	19 21.3	00
02	212 32.3	3 02.6	39 34.9	02	212 55.6	4 58.5	44 30.6	02	213 16.4	6 52.9	49 26.3	02
04	242 32.8	3 04.5	69 39.8	04	242 55.9	5 00.5	74 35.5	04	243 16.8	6 54.8	79 31.2	04
06	272 33.2	3 06.5	99 44.7	06	272 56.3	5 02.4	104 40.4	06	273 17.1	6 56.7	109 36.1	06
08	302 33.6	3 08.4	129 49.7	08	302 56.7	5 04.3	134 45.4	08	303 17.4	6 58.6	139 41.1	08
10	332 34.0	3 10.4	159 54.6	10	332 57.0	5 06.2	164 50.3	10	333 17.7	7 00.5	169 46.0	10
12	2 34.4	3 12.3	189 59.5	12	2 57.4	5 08.1	194 55.2	12	3 18.1	7 02.4	199 50.9	12
14	32 34.8	3 14.2	220 04.5	14	32 57.8	5 10.1	225 00.1	14	33 18.4	7 04.3	229 55.8	14
16	62 35.2	3 16.2	250 09.4	16	62 58.1	5 12.0	255 05.1	16	63 18.7	7 06.1	260 00.8	16
18	92 35.6	3 18.1	280 14.3	18	92 58.5	5 13.9	285 10.0	18	93 19.0	7 08.0	290 05.7	18
20	122 36.0	3 20.1	310 19.2	20	122 58.9	5 15.8	315 14.9	20	123 19.4	7 09.9	320 10.6	20
22	152 36.4	S3 22.0	340 24.2	22	152 59.2	S5 17.7	345 19.9	22	153 19.7	S7 11.8	350 15.6	22
Sunday, October 2				**Friday, October 7**				**Wednesday, October 12**				
00	182 36.8	S3 23.9	10 29.1	00	182 59.6	S5 19.6	15 24.8	00	183 20.0	S7 13.7	20 20.5	00
02	212 37.2	3 25.9	40 34.0	02	212 59.9	5 21.6	45 29.7	02	213 20.3	7 15.6	50 25.4	02
04	242 37.6	3 27.8	70 38.9	04	243 00.3	5 23.5	75 34.6	04	243 20.6	7 17.4	80 30.3	04
06	272 38.0	3 29.7	100 43.9	06	273 00.7	5 25.4	105 39.6	06	273 20.9	7 19.3	110 35.3	06
08	302 38.3	3 31.7	130 48.8	08	303 01.0	5 27.3	135 44.5	08	303 21.3	7 21.2	140 40.2	08
10	332 38.7	3 33.6	160 53.7	10	333 01.4	5 29.2	165 49.4	10	333 21.6	7 23.1	170 45.1	10
12	2 39.1	3 35.6	190 58.7	12	3 01.7	5 31.1	195 54.4	12	3 21.9	7 24.9	200 50.0	12
14	32 39.5	3 37.5	221 03.6	14	33 02.1	5 33.0	225 59.3	14	33 22.2	7 26.8	230 55.0	14
16	62 39.9	3 39.4	251 08.5	16	63 02.4	5 35.0	256 04.2	16	63 22.5	7 28.7	260 59.9	16
18	92 40.3	3 41.4	281 13.4	18	93 02.8	5 36.9	286 09.1	18	93 22.8	7 30.6	291 04.8	18
20	122 40.7	3 43.3	311 18.4	20	123 03.2	5 38.8	316 14.1	20	123 23.1	7 32.5	321 09.8	20
22	152 41.1	S3 45.2	341 23.3	22	153 03.5	S5 40.7	346 19.0	22	153 23.4	S7 34.3	351 14.7	22
Monday, October 3				**Saturday, October 8**				**Thursday, October 13**				
00	182 41.5	S3 47.2	11 28.2	00	183 03.9	S5 42.6	16 23.9	00	183 23.7	S7 36.2	21 19.6	00
02	212 41.9	3 49.1	41 33.2	02	213 04.2	5 44.5	46 28.9	02	213 24.0	7 38.1	51 24.5	02
04	242 42.3	3 51.0	71 38.1	04	243 04.6	5 46.4	76 33.8	04	243 24.3	7 39.9	81 29.5	04
06	272 42.7	3 53.0	101 43.0	06	273 04.9	5 48.3	106 38.7	06	273 24.7	7 41.8	111 34.4	06
08	302 43.1	3 54.9	131 47.9	08	303 05.3	5 50.3	136 43.6	08	303 25.0	7 43.7	141 39.3	08
10	332 43.4	3 56.8	161 52.9	10	333 05.6	5 52.2	166 48.6	10	333 25.3	7 45.6	171 44.3	10
12	2 43.8	3 58.8	191 57.8	12	3 06.0	5 54.1	196 53.5	12	3 25.6	7 47.4	201 49.2	12
14	32 44.2	4 00.7	222 02.7	14	33 06.3	5 56.0	226 58.4	14	33 25.9	7 49.3	231 54.1	14
16	62 44.6	4 02.6	252 07.7	16	63 06.7	5 57.9	257 03.4	16	63 26.2	7 51.2	261 59.0	16
18	92 45.0	4 04.6	282 12.6	18	93 07.0	5 59.8	287 08.3	18	93 26.5	7 53.0	292 04.0	18
20	122 45.4	4 06.5	312 17.5	20	123 07.4	6 01.7	317 13.2	20	123 26.8	7 54.9	322 08.9	20
22	152 45.8	S4 08.4	342 22.4	22	153 07.7	S6 03.6	347 18.1	22	153 27.1	S7 56.7	352 13.8	22
Tuesday, October 4				**Sunday, October 9**				**Friday, October 14**				
00	182 46.2	S4 10.4	12 27.4	00	183 08.1	S6 05.5	17 23.1	00	183 27.3	S7 58.6	22 18.8	00
02	212 46.5	4 12.3	42 32.3	02	213 08.4	6 07.4	47 28.0	02	213 27.6	8 00.5	52 23.7	02
04	242 46.9	4 14.2	72 37.2	04	243 08.7	6 09.3	77 32.9	04	243 27.9	8 02.3	82 28.6	04
06	272 47.3	4 16.2	102 42.2	06	273 09.1	6 11.2	107 37.8	06	273 28.2	8 04.2	112 33.5	06
08	302 47.7	4 18.1	132 47.1	08	303 09.4	6 13.1	137 42.8	08	303 28.5	8 06.1	142 38.5	08
10	332 48.1	4 20.0	162 52.0	10	333 09.8	6 15.0	167 47.7	10	333 28.8	8 07.9	172 43.4	10
12	2 48.4	4 21.9	192 56.9	12	3 10.1	6 16.9	197 52.6	12	3 29.1	8 09.8	202 48.3	12
14	32 48.8	4 23.9	223 01.9	14	33 10.4	6 18.8	227 57.6	14	33 29.4	8 11.6	232 53.3	14
16	62 49.2	4 25.8	253 06.8	16	63 10.8	6 20.7	258 02.5	16	63 29.7	8 13.5	262 58.2	16
18	92 49.6	4 27.7	283 11.7	18	93 11.1	6 22.6	288 07.4	18	93 30.0	8 15.3	293 03.1	18
20	122 50.0	4 29.7	313 16.7	20	123 11.5	6 24.5	318 12.3	20	123 30.2	8 17.2	323 08.0	20
22	152 50.3	S4 31.6	343 21.6	22	153 11.8	S6 26.4	348 17.3	22	153 30.5	S8 19.0	353 13.0	22
Wednesday, October 5				**Monday, October 10**				**Saturday, October 15**				
00	182 50.7	S4 33.5	13 26.5	00	183 12.1	S6 28.3	18 22.2	00	183 30.8	S8 20.9	23 17.9	00
02	212 51.1	4 35.4	43 31.4	02	213 12.5	6 30.2	48 27.1	02	213 31.1	8 22.8	53 22.8	02
04	242 51.5	4 37.4	73 36.4	04	243 12.8	6 32.1	78 32.1	04	243 31.4	8 24.6	83 27.8	04
06	272 51.8	4 39.3	103 41.3	06	273 13.1	6 34.0	108 37.0	06	273 31.7	8 26.5	113 32.7	06
08	302 52.2	4 41.2	133 46.2	08	303 13.5	6 35.9	138 41.9	08	303 32.0	8 28.3	143 37.6	08
10	332 52.6	4 43.1	163 51.2	10	333 13.8	6 37.8	168 46.8	10	333 32.2	8 30.2	173 42.5	10
12	2 53.0	4 45.1	193 56.1	12	3 14.1	6 39.7	198 51.8	12	3 32.5	8 32.0	203 47.5	12
14	32 53.3	4 47.0	224 01.0	14	33 14.5	6 41.6	228 56.7	14	33 32.8	8 33.9	233 52.4	14
16	62 53.7	4 48.9	254 05.9	16	63 14.8	6 43.5	259 01.6	16	63 33.1	8 35.7	263 57.3	16
18	92 54.1	4 50.8	284 10.9	18	93 15.1	6 45.4	289 06.6	18	93 33.4	8 37.6	294 02.3	18
20	122 54.5	4 52.8	314 15.8	20	123 15.5	6 47.3	319 11.5	20	123 33.6	8 39.4	324 07.2	20
22	152 54.8	S4 54.7	344 20.7	22	153 15.8	S6 49.2	349 16.4	22	153 33.9	S8 41.3	354 12.1	22

OCTOBER 1994 — SUN & ARIES — GMT

Sunday, October 16

Time	SUN GHA	Dec	ARIES GHA
00	183 34.2	S8 43.1	24 17.0
02	213 34.5	8 44.9	54 22.0
04	243 34.7	8 46.8	84 26.0
06	273 35.0	8 48.6	114 31.8
08	303 35.3	8 50.5	144 36.7
10	333 35.5	8 52.3	174 41.7
12	3 35.8	8 54.1	204 46.6
14	33 36.1	8 56.0	234 51.5
16	63 36.3	8 57.8	264 56.5
18	93 36.6	8 59.7	295 01.4
20	123 36.9	9 01.5	325 06.3
22	153 37.1	S9 03.3	355 11.2

Monday, October 17

Time	SUN GHA	Dec	ARIES GHA
00	183 37.4	S9 05.2	25 16.2
02	213 37.7	9 07.0	55 21.1
04	243 37.9	9 08.8	85 26.0
06	273 38.2	9 10.7	115 31.0
08	303 38.4	9 12.5	145 35.9
10	333 38.7	9 14.3	175 40.8
12	3 38.9	9 16.1	205 45.7
14	33 39.2	9 18.0	235 50.7
16	63 39.5	9 19.8	265 55.6
18	93 39.7	9 21.6	296 00.5
20	123 40.0	9 23.4	326 05.5
22	153 40.2	S9 25.3	356 10.4

Tuesday, October 18

Time	SUN GHA	Dec	ARIES GHA
00	183 40.5	S9 27.1	26 15.3
02	213 40.7	9 28.9	56 20.2
04	243 41.0	9 30.7	86 25.2
06	273 41.2	9 32.6	116 30.1
08	303 41.4	9 34.4	146 35.0
10	333 41.7	9 36.2	176 40.0
12	3 41.9	9 38.0	206 44.9
14	33 42.2	9 39.8	236 49.8
16	63 42.4	9 41.6	266 54.7
18	93 42.7	9 43.5	296 59.7
20	123 42.9	9 45.3	327 04.6
22	153 43.1	S9 47.1	357 09.5

Wednesday, October 19

Time	SUN GHA	Dec	ARIES GHA
00	183 43.4	S9 48.9	27 14.5
02	213 43.6	9 50.7	57 19.4
04	243 43.8	9 52.5	87 24.3
06	273 44.1	9 54.3	117 29.2
08	303 44.3	9 56.1	147 34.2
10	333 44.5	9 57.9	177 39.1
12	3 44.8	9 59.7	207 44.0
14	33 45.0	10 01.5	237 48.9
16	63 45.2	10 03.3	267 53.9
18	93 45.5	10 05.1	297 58.8
20	123 45.7	10 06.9	328 03.7
22	153 45.9	S10 08.7	358 08.7

Thursday, October 20

Time	SUN GHA	Dec	ARIES GHA
00	183 46.1	S10 10.5	28 13.6
02	213 46.4	10 12.3	58 18.5
04	243 46.6	10 14.1	88 23.4
06	273 46.8	10 15.9	118 28.4
08	303 47.0	10 17.7	148 33.3
10	333 47.2	10 19.5	178 38.2
12	3 47.5	10 21.3	208 43.2
14	33 47.7	10 23.1	238 48.1
16	63 47.9	10 24.9	268 53.0
18	93 48.1	10 26.7	298 57.9
20	123 48.3	10 28.5	329 02.9
22	153 48.5	S10 30.3	359 07.8

Friday, October 21

Time	SUN GHA	Dec	ARIES GHA
00	183 48.7	S10 32.1	29 12.7
02	213 49.0	10 33.8	59 17.7
04	243 49.2	10 35.6	89 22.6
06	273 49.4	10 37.4	119 27.5
08	303 49.6	10 39.2	149 32.4
10	333 49.8	10 41.0	179 37.4
12	3 50.0	10 42.8	209 42.3
14	33 50.2	10 44.5	239 47.2
16	63 50.4	10 46.3	269 52.2
18	93 50.6	10 48.1	299 57.1
20	123 50.8	10 49.9	330 02.0
22	153 51.0	S10 51.6	0 06.9

Saturday, October 22

Time	SUN GHA	Dec	ARIES GHA
00	183 51.2	S10 53.4	30 11.9
02	213 51.4	10 55.2	60 16.8
04	243 51.6	10 57.0	90 21.7
06	273 51.8	10 58.7	120 26.7
08	303 52.0	11 00.5	150 31.6
10	333 52.2	11 02.3	180 36.5
12	3 52.3	11 04.0	210 41.4
14	33 52.5	11 05.8	240 46.4
16	63 52.7	11 07.6	270 51.3
18	93 52.9	11 09.3	300 56.2
20	123 53.1	11 11.1	331 01.2
22	153 53.3	S11 12.8	1 06.1

Sunday, October 23

Time	SUN GHA	Dec	ARIES GHA
00	183 53.5	S11 14.6	31 11.0
02	213 53.6	11 16.4	61 15.9
04	243 53.8	11 18.1	91 20.9
06	273 54.0	11 19.9	121 25.8
08	303 54.2	11 21.6	151 30.7
10	333 54.4	11 23.4	181 35.6
12	3 54.5	11 25.1	211 40.6
14	33 54.7	11 26.9	241 45.5
16	63 54.9	11 28.6	271 50.4
18	93 55.1	11 30.4	301 55.4
20	123 55.2	11 32.1	332 00.3
22	153 55.4	S11 33.9	2 05.2

Monday, October 24

Time	SUN GHA	Dec	ARIES GHA
00	183 55.6	S11 35.6	32 10.1
02	213 55.7	11 37.4	62 15.1
04	243 55.9	11 39.1	92 20.0
06	273 56.1	11 40.9	122 24.9
08	303 56.2	11 42.6	152 29.9
10	333 56.4	11 44.3	182 34.8
12	3 56.6	11 46.1	212 39.7
14	33 56.7	11 47.8	242 44.6
16	63 56.9	11 49.6	272 49.6
18	93 57.0	11 51.3	302 54.5
20	123 57.2	11 53.0	332 59.4
22	153 57.3	S11 54.8	3 04.4

Tuesday, October 25

Time	SUN GHA	Dec	ARIES GHA
00	183 57.5	S11 56.5	33 09.3
02	213 57.6	11 58.2	63 14.2
04	243 57.8	11 59.9	93 19.1
06	273 57.9	12 01.7	123 24.1
08	303 58.1	12 03.4	153 29.0
10	333 58.2	12 05.1	183 33.9
12	3 58.4	12 06.8	213 38.9
14	33 58.5	12 08.6	243 43.8
16	63 58.7	12 10.3	273 48.7
18	93 58.8	12 12.0	303 53.6
20	123 59.0	12 13.7	333 58.6
22	153 59.1	S12 15.4	4 03.5

Wednesday, October 26

Time	SUN GHA	Dec	ARIES GHA
00	183 59.2	S12 17.2	34 08.4
02	213 59.4	12 18.9	64 13.4
04	243 59.5	12 20.6	94 18.3
06	273 59.6	12 22.3	124 23.2
08	303 59.8	12 24.0	154 28.1
10	333 59.9	12 25.7	184 33.1
12	4 00.0	12 27.4	214 38.0
14	34 00.2	12 29.1	244 42.9
16	64 00.3	12 30.8	274 47.8
18	94 00.4	12 32.5	304 52.8
20	124 00.5	12 34.2	334 57.7
22	154 00.7	S12 35.9	5 02.6

Thursday, October 27

Time	SUN GHA	Dec	ARIES GHA
00	184 00.8	S12 37.6	35 07.6
02	214 00.9	12 39.3	65 12.5
04	244 01.0	12 41.0	95 17.4
06	274 01.1	12 42.7	125 22.3
08	304 01.3	12 44.4	155 27.3
10	334 01.4	12 46.1	185 32.2
12	4 01.5	12 47.8	215 37.1
14	34 01.6	12 49.5	245 42.1
16	64 01.7	12 51.2	275 47.0
18	94 01.8	12 52.9	305 51.9
20	124 01.9	12 54.6	335 56.8
22	154 02.0	S12 56.2	6 01.8

Friday, October 28

Time	SUN GHA	Dec	ARIES GHA
00	184 02.2	S12 57.9	36 06.7
02	214 02.3	12 59.6	66 11.6
04	244 02.4	13 01.3	96 16.6
06	274 02.5	13 03.0	126 21.5
08	304 02.6	13 04.6	156 26.4
10	334 02.7	13 06.3	186 31.3
12	4 02.8	13 08.0	216 36.3
14	34 02.9	13 09.7	246 41.2
16	64 03.0	13 11.3	276 46.1
18	94 03.0	13 13.0	306 51.1
20	124 03.1	13 14.7	336 56.0
22	154 03.2	S13 16.3	7 00.9

Saturday, October 29

Time	SUN GHA	Dec	ARIES GHA
00	184 03.3	S13 18.0	37 05.8
02	214 03.4	13 19.7	67 10.8
04	244 03.5	13 21.3	97 15.7
06	274 03.6	13 23.0	127 20.6
08	304 03.7	13 24.7	157 25.6
10	334 03.8	13 26.3	187 30.5
12	4 03.8	13 28.0	217 35.4
14	34 03.9	13 29.6	247 40.3
16	64 04.0	13 31.3	277 45.3
18	94 04.1	13 32.9	307 50.2
20	124 04.1	13 34.6	337 55.1
22	154 04.2	S13 36.2	8 00.0

Sunday, October 30

Time	SUN GHA	Dec	ARIES GHA
00	184 04.3	S13 37.9	38 05.0
02	214 04.4	13 39.5	68 09.9
04	244 04.4	13 41.2	98 14.8
06	274 04.5	13 42.8	128 19.8
08	304 04.6	13 44.5	158 24.7
10	334 04.6	13 46.1	188 29.6
12	4 04.7	13 47.7	218 34.5
14	34 04.8	13 49.4	248 39.5
16	64 04.9	13 51.0	278 44.4
18	94 04.9	13 52.7	308 49.3
20	124 05.0	13 54.3	338 54.3
22	154 05.0	S13 55.9	8 59.2

Monday, October 31

Time	SUN GHA	Dec	ARIES GHA
00	184 05.1	S13 57.5	39 04.1
02	214 05.1	13 59.2	69 09.0
04	244 05.2	14 00.8	99 14.0
06	274 05.2	S14 02.4	129 18.9
08	304 05.3	S14 04.1	159 23.8
10	334 05.3	14 05.7	189 28.8
12	4 05.4	14 07.3	219 33.7
14	34 05.4	S14 08.9	249 38.6
16	64 05.5	S14 10.5	279 43.5
18	94 05.5	14 12.1	309 48.5
20	124 05.6	14 13.8	339 53.4
22	154 05.6	S14 15.4	9 58.3

OCTOBER 1994 — PLANETS — 0h GMT

VENUS / JUPITER

Mer Pass h m	GHA ° '	Mean Var/hr 15°+	Dec ° '	Mean Var/hr '			GHA ° '	Mean Var/hr 15°+	Dec ° '	Mean Var/hr '	Mer Pass h m
14 04	148 33.8	1.5	S22 15.6	0.5	1	Sat	146 37.9	2.0	S15 31.9	0.1	14 12
14 02	149 10.2	1.6	S22 28.2	0.5	2	SUN	147 25.4	2.0	S15 35.5	0.1	14 08
13 59	149 48.3	1.7	S22 40.1	0.5	3	Mon	148 12.8	2.0	S15 39.0	0.1	14 05
13 57	150 28.0	1.7	S22 51.2	0.4	4	Tue	149 00.2	2.0	S15 42.6	0.2	14 02
13 54	151 09.6	1.8	S23 01.5	0.4	5	Wed	149 47.5	2.0	S15 46.2	0.1	13 59
13 51	151 52.9	1.9	S23 11.0	0.4	6	Thu	150 34.8	2.0	S15 49.7	0.1	13 56
13 48	152 38.3	2.0	S23 19.7	0.3	7	Fri	151 21.9	2.0	S15 53.3	0.2	13 53
13 44	153 25.5	2.1	S23 27.5	0.3	8	Sat	152 09.1	2.0	S15 56.9	0.1	13 50
13 41	154 14.9	2.1	S23 34.4	0.2	9	SUN	152 56.1	2.0	S16 00.5	0.1	13 46
13 38	155 06.3	2.2	S23 40.3	0.2	10	Mon	153 43.1	2.0	S16 04.0	0.1	13 43
13 34	156 00.0	2.3	S23 45.3	0.2	11	Tue	154 30.0	2.0	S16 07.6	0.2	13 40
13 30	156 55.8	2.4	S23 49.2	0.1	12	Wed	155 16.9	1.9	S16 11.2	0.1	13 37
13 26	157 54.0	2.5	S23 52.0	0.1	13	Thu	156 03.7	1.9	S16 14.8	0.2	13 34
13 22	158 54.4	2.6	S23 53.8	0.0	14	Fri	156 50.4	1.9	S16 18.4	0.1	13 31
13 18	159 57.2	2.7	S23 54.3	0.0	15	Sat	157 37.1	1.9	S16 22.0	0.1	13 28
13 13	161 02.3	2.8	S23 53.7	0.1	16	SUN	158 23.8	1.9	S16 25.5	0.1	13 25
13 09	162 09.7	2.9	S23 51.8	0.1	17	Mon	159 10.4	1.9	S16 29.1	0.2	13 22
13 04	163 19.5	3.0	S23 48.7	0.2	18	Tue	159 56.9	1.9	S16 32.7	0.1	13 18
12 59	164 31.6	3.1	S23 44.3	0.2	19	Wed	160 43.4	1.9	S16 36.3	0.1	13 15
12 54	165 46.0	3.2	S23 38.6	0.3	20	Thu	161 29.9	1.9	S16 39.8	0.2	13 12
12 49	167 02.5	3.3	S23 31.5	0.4	21	Fri	162 16.3	1.9	S16 43.4	0.1	13 09
12 44	168 21.2	3.4	S23 23.0	0.4	22	Sat	163 02.6	1.9	S16 46.9	0.1	13 06
12 38	169 41.9	3.4	S23 13.1	0.5	23	SUN	163 48.9	1.9	S16 50.5	0.1	13 03
12 33	171 04.5	3.5	S23 01.9	0.5	24	Mon	164 35.2	1.9	S16 54.0	0.1	13 00
12 27	172 28.9	3.6	S22 49.2	0.6	25	Tue	165 21.4	1.9	S16 57.6	0.1	12 57
12 21	173 54.9	3.6	S22 35.2	0.6	26	Wed	166 07.6	1.9	S17 01.1	0.1	12 54
12 16	175 22.3	3.7	S22 19.9	0.7	27	Thu	166 53.7	1.9	S17 04.6	0.1	12 51
12 10	176 50.9	3.7	S22 03.2	0.7	28	Fri	167 39.8	1.9	S17 08.2	0.1	12 48
12 04	178 20.7	3.8	S21 45.4	0.8	29	Sat	168 25.8	1.9	S17 11.7	0.1	12 45
11 58	179 51.2	3.8	S21 26.3	0.8	30	SUN	169 11.8	1.9	S17 15.2	0.1	12 42
11 52	181 22.4	3.8	S21 06.1	0.9	31	Mon	169 57.8	1.9	S17 18.7	0.1	12 39

VENUS, Av Mag –4.4
SHA October
5 138; 10 137; 15 137; 20 138; 25 139; 30 142.

JUPITER, Av Mag –1.7
SHA October
5 136; 10 135; 15 134; 20 133; 25 132; 30 131.

MARS / SATURN

Mer Pass h m	GHA ° '	Mean Var/hr 15°+	Dec ° '	Mean Var/hr '			GHA ° '	Mean Var/hr 15°+	Dec ° '	Mean Var/hr '	Mer Pass h m
07 22	249 17.7	0.9	N21 29.6	0.2	1	Sat	30 05.3	2.6	S10 48.0	0.1	21 56
07 21	249 40.4	1.0	N21 23.8	0.2	2	SUN	31 07.8	2.6	S10 49.2	0.1	21 52
07 19	250 03.3	1.0	N21 17.9	0.3	3	Mon	32 10.3	2.6	S10 50.5	0.1	21 48
07 18	250 26.4	1.0	N21 11.8	0.3	4	Tue	33 12.6	2.6	S10 51.7	0.1	21 43
07 16	250 49.7	1.0	N21 05.7	0.3	5	Wed	34 15.0	2.6	S10 52.9	0.0	21 39
07 15	251 13.3	1.0	N20 59.6	0.3	6	Thu	35 17.2	2.6	S10 54.0	0.0	21 35
07 13	251 37.0	1.0	N20 53.3	0.3	7	Fri	36 19.4	2.6	S10 55.1	0.0	21 31
07 11	252 00.9	1.0	N20 47.0	0.3	8	Sat	37 21.5	2.6	S10 56.2	0.0	21 27
07 10	252 25.0	1.0	N20 40.6	0.3	9	SUN	38 23.5	2.6	S10 57.3	0.0	21 23
07 08	252 49.4	1.0	N20 34.1	0.3	10	Mon	39 25.5	2.6	S10 58.3	0.0	21 19
07 07	253 14.0	1.0	N20 27.5	0.3	11	Tue	40 27.4	2.6	S10 59.3	0.0	21 15
07 05	253 38.8	1.0	N20 20.9	0.3	12	Wed	41 29.2	2.6	S11 00.3	0.0	21 10
07 03	254 03.8	1.1	N20 14.3	0.3	13	Thu	42 31.0	2.6	S11 01.2	0.0	21 06
07 02	254 29.0	1.1	N20 07.6	0.3	14	Fri	43 32.6	2.6	S11 02.1	0.0	21 02
07 00	254 54.4	1.1	N20 00.8	0.3	15	Sat	44 34.2	2.6	S11 02.9	0.0	20 58
06 58	255 20.0	1.1	N19 54.0	0.3	16	SUN	45 35.7	2.6	S11 03.8	0.0	20 54
06 56	255 45.9	1.1	N19 47.1	0.3	17	Mon	46 37.1	2.6	S11 04.5	0.0	20 50
06 55	256 12.0	1.1	N19 40.2	0.3	18	Tue	47 38.5	2.5	S11 05.3	0.0	20 46
06 53	256 38.3	1.1	N19 33.3	0.3	19	Wed	48 39.7	2.5	S11 06.0	0.0	20 42
06 51	257 04.8	1.1	N19 26.3	0.3	20	Thu	49 40.9	2.5	S11 06.7	0.0	20 38
06 49	257 31.6	1.1	N19 19.3	0.3	21	Fri	50 41.9	2.5	S11 07.3	0.0	20 34
06 48	257 58.6	1.1	N19 12.3	0.3	22	Sat	51 42.9	2.5	S11 07.9	0.0	20 30
06 46	258 25.8	1.1	N19 05.2	0.3	23	SUN	52 43.8	2.5	S11 08.5	0.0	20 26
06 44	258 53.3	1.2	N18 58.1	0.3	24	Mon	53 44.6	2.5	S11 09.0	0.0	20 22
06 42	259 21.0	1.2	N18 51.0	0.3	25	Tue	54 45.4	2.5	S11 09.5	0.0	20 18
06 40	259 48.9	1.2	N18 43.9	0.3	26	Wed	55 46.0	2.5	S11 10.0	0.0	20 14
06 38	260 17.1	1.2	N18 36.7	0.3	27	Thu	56 46.5	2.5	S11 10.4	0.0	20 10
06 36	260 45.6	1.2	N18 29.6	0.3	28	Fri	57 47.0	2.5	S11 10.8	0.0	20 06
06 35	261 14.2	1.2	N18 22.4	0.3	29	Sat	58 47.3	2.5	S11 11.1	0.0	20 01
06 33	261 43.2	1.2	N18 15.3	0.3	30	SUN	59 47.6	2.5	S11 11.4	0.0	19 57
06 31	262 12.4	1.2	N18 08.1	0.3	31	Mon	60 47.7	2.5	S11 11.7	0.0	19 54

MARS, Av Mag +0.9
SHA October
5 237; 10 234; 15 232; 20 229; 25 226; 30 224.

SATURN, Av Mag +0.7
SHA October
5 21; 10 21; 15 21; 20 21; 25 22; 30 22.

OCTOBER 1994 — MOON

Day	GMT hr	GHA ° ′	Mean Var/hr 14°+	Dec ° ′	Mean Var/hr ′
1 Sat	0	235 54.9	29.8	N12 02.4	9.6
	6	322 54.1	29.8	N11 05.4	9.9
	12	49 53.0	29.7	N10 06.9	10.4
	18	136 51.5	29.6	N 9 03.8	10.7
2 Sun	0	223 49.4	29.5	N 7 59.5	11.1
	6	310 46.8	29.4	N 6 55.1	11.1
	12	37 43.4	29.3	N 5 44.8	11.7
	18	124 39.3	29.2	N 4 34.8	12.0
3 Mon	0	211 34.3	29.0	N 3 23.4	12.2
	6	298 28.3	28.8	N 2 10.7	12.3
	12	25 21.1	28.6	N 0 57.1	12.4
	18	112 12.7	28.4	S 0 17.2	12.4
4 Tue	0	199 03.0	28.1	S 1 32.0	12.5
	6	285 51.8	27.9	S 2 46.8	12.4
	12	12 39.0	27.6	S 4 01.4	12.3
	18	99 24.6	27.3	S 5 15.5	12.2
5 Wed	0	186 08.4	27.0	S 6 28.8	12.0
	6	272 50.4	26.7	S 7 40.8	11.7
	12	359 30.6	26.4	S 8 51.3	11.4
	18	86 08.8	26.0	S 9 59.9	11.1
6 Thu	0	172 45.1	25.7	S 11 06.3	10.5
	6	259 19.5	25.4	S 12 10.1	10.1
	12	345 52.1	25.1	S 13 11.0	9.5
	18	72 22.8	24.9	S 14 08.7	9.0
7 Fri	0	158 51.9	24.6	S 15 02.8	8.3
	6	245 19.4	24.3	S 15 53.1	7.6
	12	331 45.5	24.1	S 16 39.4	6.9
	18	58 10.4	23.9	S 17 21.3	6.1
8 Sat	0	144 34.3	23.9	S 17 58.7	5.3
	6	230 57.5	23.8	S 18 31.4	4.5
	12	317 20.3	23.8	S 18 59.3	3.7
	18	43 42.9	23.8	S 19 22.2	3.0
9 Sun	0	130 05.6	23.9	S 19 40.2	2.0
	6	216 28.8	24.0	S 19 53.1	1.3
	12	302 52.7	24.1	S 20 00.9	0.4
	18	29 17.7	24.4	S 20 03.8	0.4
10 Mon	0	115 44.0	24.6	S 20 01.7	1.2
	6	202 11.9	25.0	S 19 54.9	2.0
	12	288 41.7	25.3	S 19 43.3	2.8
	18	15 13.5	25.7	S 19 27.1	3.5
11 Tue	0	101 47.6	26.1	S 19 06.6	4.2
	6	188 24.2	26.6	S 18 41.9	4.8
	12	275 03.2	27.0	S 18 13.2	5.4
	18	1 44.9	27.4	S 17 40.7	6.1
12 Wed	0	88 29.2	27.9	S 17 04.7	6.6
	6	175 16.3	28.3	S 16 25.4	7.1
	12	262 06.1	28.8	S 15 42.9	7.6
	18	348 58.7	29.2	S 14 57.6	8.1
13 Thu	0	75 53.8	29.6	S 14 09.6	8.4
	6	162 51.6	30.0	S 13 19.2	8.8
	12	249 51.8	30.5	S 12 26.5	9.2
	18	336 54.4	30.8	S 11 31.9	9.4
14 Fri	0	63 59.3	31.2	S 10 35.5	9.7
	6	151 06.4	31.6	S 9 37.6	9.9
	12	238 15.4	31.9	S 8 38.2	10.1
	18	325 26.3	32.2	S 7 37.7	10.2
15 Sat	0	52 39.0	32.4	S 6 36.1	10.4
	6	139 53.1	32.6	S 5 33.8	10.5
	12	227 08.7	32.8	S 4 30.8	10.6
	18	314 25.6	33.0	S 3 27.4	10.6
16 Sun	0	41 43.5	33.1	S 2 23.7	10.6
	6	129 02.4	33.3	S 1 19.8	10.7
	12	216 22.1	33.4	S 0 16.0	10.6
	18	303 42.4	33.5	N 0 47.7	10.5
17 Mon	0	31 03.3	33.5	N 1 51.0	10.4
	6	118 24.4	33.6	N 2 53.8	10.3
	12	205 45.8	33.6	N 3 56.0	10.2
	18	293 07.5	33.6	N 4 57.3	10.1
18 Tue	0	20 28.8	33.5	N 5 57.8	9.9
	6	107 50.1	33.5	N 6 57.2	9.7
	12	195 11.2	33.4	N 7 55.8	9.4
	18	282 31.8	33.4	N 8 52.1	9.2
19 Wed	0	9 52.1	33.2	N 9 47.4	8.9
	6	97 11.7	33.2	N10 41.1	8.6
	12	184 30.8	33.1	N11 33.1	8.3
	18	271 49.1	32.9	N12 23.1	8.0
20 Thu	0	359 06.7	32.8	N13 11.2	7.6
	6	86 23.5	32.7	N13 57.1	7.2
	12	173 39.4	32.5	N14 40.7	6.8
	18	260 54.4	32.4	N15 22.0	6.4
21 Fri	0	348 08.6	32.2	N16 00.9	6.0
	6	75 21.8	32.0	N16 37.1	5.6
	12	162 34.1	31.9	N17 10.7	5.1
	18	249 45.6	31.7	N17 41.5	4.6
22 Sat	0	336 56.1	31.6	N18 09.4	4.2
	6	64 05.9	31.5	N18 34.3	3.6
	12	151 14.8	31.3	N18 56.3	3.1
	18	238 23.0	31.3	N19 15.1	2.6
23 Sun	0	325 30.5	31.1	N19 30.8	2.0
	6	52 37.4	31.0	N19 43.2	1.5
	12	139 43.7	30.9	N19 52.4	1.0
	18	226 49.5	30.9	N19 58.2	0.4
24 Mon	0	313 54.9	30.8	N20 00.8	0.2
	6	41 00.0	30.8	N19 59.9	0.8
	12	128 04.8	30.8	N19 55.7	1.3
	18	215 09.4	30.7	N19 48.1	1.9
25 Tue	0	302 13.9	30.8	N19 37.2	2.4
	6	29 18.3	30.8	N19 22.8	3.0
	12	116 22.7	30.8	N19 05.1	3.5
	18	203 27.2	30.8	N18 44.1	4.1
26 Wed	0	290 31.7	30.7	N18 19.8	4.7
	6	17 36.3	30.7	N17 52.2	5.2
	12	104 41.0	30.8	N17 21.4	5.7
	18	191 45.9	30.8	N16 47.4	6.3
27 Thu	0	278 50.9	30.9	N16 10.4	6.7
	6	5 56.0	30.9	N15 30.3	7.2
	12	93 01.2	30.9	N14 47.2	7.7
	18	180 06.4	30.9	N14 01.3	8.2
28 Fri	0	267 11.6	30.8	N13 12.6	8.6
	6	354 16.9	30.8	N12 21.2	9.0
	12	81 21.7	30.8	N11 27.2	9.4
	18	168 26.4	30.7	N10 30.8	9.8
29 Sat	0	255 30.7	30.6	N 9 32.0	10.2
	6	342 34.6	30.5	N 8 30.9	10.5
	12	69 37.9	30.4	N 7 27.8	10.8
	18	156 40.4	30.3	N 6 22.8	11.2
30 Sun	0	243 42.2	30.1	N 5 16.0	11.5
	6	330 42.9	29.9	N 4 07.6	11.7
	12	57 42.5	29.7	N 2 57.8	11.9
	18	144 40.8	29.4	N 1 46.8	12.0
31 Mon	0	231 37.7	29.1	N 0 34.9	12.2
	6	318 33.0	28.9	S 0 37.7	12.2
	12	45 26.5	28.6	S 1 50.9	12.3
	18	132 18.1	28.3	S 3 04.2	12.2

Chapter 6

NOVEMBER 1994 — SUN & MOON — GMT

SUN

Day of Yr	Mth	Week	Equation of Time UH (m s)	12h (m s)	Transit (h m)	Semi-diam (′)	Lat 52°N Twi-light (h m)	Sun-rise (h m)	Sun-set (h m)	Twi-light (h m)	Lat Corr to Sunrise, Sunset etc Lat (°)	Twi-light (h m)	Sun-rise (h m)	Sun-set (h m)	Twi-light (h m)
305	1	Tue	−16 23	−16 23	11 44	16.1	06 19	06 54	16 32	17 08	N70	+1 27	+2 27	−2 27	−1 27
306	2	Wed	−16 24	−16 25	11 44	16.1	06 20	06 56	16 30	17 06	68	+1 09	+1 52	−1 52	−1 10
307	3	Thu	−16 25	−16 25	11 44	16.2	06 22	06 58	16 29	17 04	66	+0 56	+1 27	−1 26	−0 57
308	4	Fri	−16 25	−16 24	11 44	16.2	06 24	07 00	16 27	17 03	64	+0 44	+1 07	−0 07	−0 45
309	5	Sat	−16 24	−16 23	11 44	16.2	06 25	07 02	16 25	17 01	62	+0 34	+0 51	−0 51	−0 35
310	6	Sun	−16 22	−16 21	11 44	16.2	06 27	07 03	16 23	16 59	N60	+0 26	+0 38	−0 38	−0 26
311	7	Mon	−16 19	−16 18	11 44	16.2	06 29	07 05	16 22	16 58	58	+0 19	+0 26	−0 26	−0 18
312	8	Tue	−16 16	−16 14	11 44	16.2	06 30	07 07	16 20	16 56	56	+0 12	+0 17	−0 16	−0 12
313	9	Wed	−16 12	−16 10	11 44	16.2	06 32	07 09	16 18	16 55	54	+0 06	+0 08	−0 08	−0 06
314	10	Thu	−16 07	−16 04	11 44	16.2	06 34	07 11	16 17	16 53	50	−0 06	−0 07	+0 07	+0 06
315	11	Fri	−16 01	−15 58	11 44	16.2	06 35	07 12	16 15	16 52	N45	−0 17	−0 22	+0 22	+0 16
316	12	Sat	−15 54	−15 51	11 44	16.2	06 37	07 14	16 14	16 51	40	−0 26	−0 34	+0 34	+0 26
317	13	Sun	−15 47	−15 43	11 44	16.2	06 39	07 16	16 12	16 49	35	−0 34	−0 45	+0 45	+0 34
318	14	Mon	−15 39	−15 34	11 44	16.2	06 40	07 18	16 11	16 48	30	−0 42	−0 54	+0 54	+0 42
319	15	Tue	−15 29	−15 24	11 45	16.2	06 42	07 19	16 09	16 47	20	−0 56	−1 10	+1 10	+0 57
320	16	Wed	−15 19	−15 14	11 45	16.2	06 44	07 21	16 08	16 45	N10	−1 09	−1 24	+1 25	+1 10
321	17	Thu	−15 08	−15 03	11 45	16.2	06 45	07 23	16 07	16 44	0	−1 21	−1 37	+1 38	+1 22
322	18	Fri	−14 57	−14 51	11 45	16.2	06 47	07 25	16 05	16 43	S10	−1 36	−1 50	+1 51	+1 35
323	19	Sat	−14 44	−14 38	11 45	16.2	06 48	07 26	16 04	16 42	20	−1 52	−2 05	+2 06	+1 51
324	20	Sun	−14 31	−14 24	11 46	16.2	06 50	07 28	16 03	16 41	30	−2 10	−2 21	+2 23	+2 10
325	21	Mon	−14 17	−14 09	11 46	16.2	06 51	07 30	16 02	16 40	S35	−2 22	−2 31	+2 33	+2 22
326	22	Tue	−14 02	−13 54	11 46	16.2	06 53	07 31	16 00	16 39	40	−2 36	−2 42	+2 44	+2 36
327	23	Wed	−13 46	−13 38	11 46	16.2	06 54	07 33	15 59	16 38	45	−2 52	−2 55	+2 57	+2 53
328	24	Thu	−13 29	−13 21	11 47	16.2	06 56	07 35	15 58	16 37	S50	−3 14	−3 12	+3 13	+3 13
329	25	Fri	−13 12	−13 03	11 47	16.2	06 57	07 36	15 57	16 36					
330	26	Sat	−12 54	−12 44	11 47	16.2	06 59	07 38	15 56	16 35					
331	27	Sun	−12 35	−12 25	11 48	16.2	07 00	07 39	15 55	16 35					
332	28	Mon	−12 15	−12 05	11 48	16.2	07 02	07 41	15 55	16 34					
333	29	Tue	−11 55	−11 44	11 48	16.2	07 03	07 42	15 54	16 33					
334	30	Wed	−11 34	−11 23	11 49	16.2	07 04	07 44	15 53	16 33					

NOTES

Lat corrections are for the middle of November. **Equation of Time** is the excess of Mean Time over Apparent Time.

MOON

Day of Yr	Mth	Week	Age (days)	Transit Diff (Upper) (h m m)	Semi-diam (′)	Hor Par (′)	Lat 52°N Moon-rise (h m)	Moon-set (h m)	Phases of the Moon
305	1	Tue	27	09 44 56	16.5	60.4	03 59	15 17	
306	2	Wed	28	10 40 58	16.6	61.0	05 22	15 48	● New Moon d 3 h 13 m 35
307	3	Thu	29	11 38 62	16.7	61.3	06 45	16 23	◐ First Quarter 10 06 14
308	4	Fri	01	12 40 62	16.7	61.3	08 06	17 07	○ Full Moon 18 06 57
309	5	Sat	02	13 42 62	16.6	61.0	09 21	18 01	◑ Last Quarter 26 07 04
310	6	Sun	03	14 44 59	16.5	60.4	10 25	19 04	
311	7	Mon	04	15 43 56	16.2	59.6	11 18	20 14	
312	8	Tue	05	16 39 53	16.0	58.7	11 59	21 27	Perigee 4 00
313	9	Wed	06	17 32 48	15.7	57.8	12 32	22 40	Apogee 18 05
314	10	Thu	07	18 20 47	15.5	56.9	13 00	23 51	
315	11	Fri	08	19 07 44	15.3	56.2	13 24	– –	
316	12	Sat	09	19 51 43	15.1	55.5	13 46	01 00	
317	13	Sun	10	20 34 44	15.0	55.0	14 07	02 08	
318	14	Mon	11	21 18 43	14.9	54.6	14 28	03 14	
319	15	Tue	12	22 01 45	14.8	54.3	14 51	04 19	
320	16	Wed	13	22 46 46	14.7	54.1	15 17	05 23	
321	17	Thu	14	23 32 47	14.7	54.0	15 46	06 26	
322	18	Fri	15	24 19 _	14.7	54.0	16 21	07 26	
323	19	Sat	16	00 19 48	14.7	54.0	17 02	08 22	
324	20	Sun	17	01 07 48	14.8	54.2	17 50	09 13	
325	21	Mon	18	01 55 49	14.8	54.4	18 44	09 58	
326	22	Tue	19	02 44 48	14.9	54.8	19 44	10 37	
327	23	Wed	20	03 32 47	15.1	55.3	20 48	11 10	
328	24	Thu	21	04 19 47	15.2	55.8	21 56	11 38	
329	25	Fri	22	05 06 47	15.4	56.6	23 06	12 04	
330	26	Sat	23	05 53 48	15.6	57.4	– –	12 28	
331	27	Sun	24	06 41 50	15.9	58.3	00 18	12 52	
332	28	Mon	25	07 31 52	16.1	59.2	01 33	13 16	
333	29	Tue	26	08 23 55	16.4	60.0	02 52	13 43	
334	30	Wed	27	09 18 59	16.5	60.7	04 12	14 15	

NOTES

For Latitude corrections to Moonrise and Moonset see page 706.

NOVEMBER 1994   STARS   0h GMT November 1

No	Name	Mag	Transit h m	Dec ° ′	GHA ° ′	RA h m	SHA ° ′
	ARIES...............		21 16		40 03.3		
1	Alpheratz	2.2	21 24	N 29 04.0	38 01.0	0 08	357 57.7
2	Ankaa.............	2.4	21 42	S 42 20.1	33 32.5	0 26	353 29.2
3	Schedar............	2.5	21 56	N 56 30.9	29 59.3	0 40	349 56.0
4	Diphda............	2.2	22 00	S 18 00.8	29 12.9	0 43	349 09.6
5	Achernar	0.6	22 54	S 57 15.8	15 39.9	1 38	335 36.6
6	POLARIS.........	2.1	23 44	N 89 14.6	2 56.0	2 28	322 52.7
7	Hamal.............	2.2	23 23	N 23 26.4	8 19.5	2 07	328 16.2
8	Acamar	3.1	0 18	S 40 19.5	355 31.8	2 58	315 28.5
9	Menkar	2.8	0 22	N 4 04.2	354 32.6	3 02	314 29.3
10	Mirfak	1.9	0 44	N 49 50.6	349 03.2	3 24	308 59.9
11	Aldebaran	1.1	1 55	N 16 29.9	331 08.4	4 36	291 05.1
12	Rigel...............	0.3	2 34	S 8 12.4	321 28.5	5 14	281 25.2
13	Capella............	0.2	2 36	N 45 59.5	320 58.0	5 16	280 54.7
14	Bellatrix..........	1.7	2 44	N 6 20.7	318 50.0	5 25	278 46.7
15	Elnath	1.8	2 45	N 28 36.1	318 33.2	5 26	278 29.9
16	Alnilam	1.8	2 55	S 1 12.3	316 03.6	5 36	276 00.3
17	Betelgeuse......0.1-1.2		3 14	N 7 24.3	311 19.4	5 55	271 16.1
18	Canopus	−0.9	3 43	S 52 41.5	304 05.2	6 24	264 01.9
19	Sirius..............	−1.6	4 04	S 16 42.5	298 49.1	6 45	258 45.8
20	Adhara	1.6	4 18	S 28 57.8	295 26.5	6 58	255 23.2
21	Castor	1.6	4 53	N 31 53.8	286 28.8	7 34	246 25.5
22	Procyon	0.5	4 58	N 5 14.2	285 17.5	7 39	245 14.2
23	Pollux.............	1.2	5 04	N 28 02.1	283 47.9	7 45	243 44.6
24	Avior	1.7	5 41	S 59 29.4	274 26.8	8 22	234 23.5
25	Suhail.............	2.2	6 27	S 43 24.5	263 05.9	9 08	223 02.6
26	Miaplacidus	1.8	6 32	S 69 41.6	261 45.7	9 13	221 42.4
27	Alphard	2.2	6 46	S 8 38.2	258 13.1	9 27	218 09.8
28	Regulus...........	1.3	7 27	N 11 59.4	248 01.7	10 08	207 58.4
29	Dubhe	2.0	8 22	N 61 46.4	234 12.3	11 03	194 09.0
30	Denebola.........	2.2	9 07	N 14 36.0	222 51.4	11 49	182 48.1
31	Gienah	2.8	9 34	S 17 30.7	216 10.2	12 16	176 06.9
32	Acrux..............	1.1	9 44	S 63 04.0	213 28.7	12 26	173 25.4
33	Gacrux	1.6	9 49	S 57 04.9	212 20.2	12 31	172 16.9
34	Mimosa...........	1.5	10 06	S 59 39.5	208 12.1	12 47	168 08.8
35	Alioth	1.7	10 12	N 55 59.1	206 36.7	12 54	166 33.4
36	Spica...............	1.2	10 43	S 11 08.0	198 49.6	13 25	158 46.3
37	Alkaid	1.9	11 05	N 49 20.2	193 13.7	13 47	153 10.4
38	Hadar	0.9	11 21	S 60 20.7	189 11.6	14 03	149 08.3
39	Menkent	2.3	11 24	S 36 20.6	188 27.7	14 06	148 24.4
40	Arcturus	0.2	11 33	N 19 12.6	186 12.1	14 15	146 08.8
41	Rigil Kent.	0.1	11 57	S 60 48.7	180 14.7	14 39	140 11.4
42	Zuben'ubi	2.9	12 08	S 16 01.1	177 24.5	14 51	137 21.2
43	Kochab............	2.2	12 08	N 74 10.6	177 24.0	14 51	137 20.7
44	Alphecca..........	2.3	12 52	N 26 44.0	166 26.5	15 34	126 23.2
45	Antares...........	1.2	13 47	S 26 25.1	152 47.1	16 29	112 43.8
46	Atria	1.9	14 06	S 69 01.1	148 02.0	16 48	107 58.7
47	Sabik	2.6	14 27	S 15 43.0	142 32.2	17 10	102 28.9
48	Shaula	1.7	14 51	S 37 06.0	136 44.5	17 33	96 41.2
49	Rasalhague	2.1	14 52	N 12 34.0	136 23.0	17 35	96 19.7
50	Eltanin	2.4	15 14	N 51 29.7	130 56.4	17 56	90 53.1
51	Kaus Aust........	2.0	15 41	S 34 23.2	124 05.9	18 24	84 02.6
52	Vega	0.1	15 54	N 38 47.0	120 52.0	18 37	80 48.7
53	Nunki	2.1	16 12	S 26 18.1	116 19.1	18 55	76 15.8
54	Altair..............	0.9	17 08	N 8 51.5	102 25.3	19 51	62 22.0
55	Peacock...........	2.1	17 42	S 56 45.2	93 44.7	20 25	53 41.4
56	Deneb	1.3	17 58	N 45 16.1	89 44.4	20 41	49 41.1
57	Enif	2.5	19 01	N 9 51.3	74 04.1	21 44	34 00.8
58	Al Na'ir	2.2	19 25	S 46 59.2	68 04.5	22 08	28 01.2
59	Fomalhaut	1.3	20 14	S 29 39.0	55 42.5	22 57	15 39.2
60	Markab	2.6	20 21	N 15 10.9	53 55.4	23 05	13 52.1

Stars Transit Corr Table

Date	Corr h m	Date	Corr h m
1	−0 00	17	−1 03
2	−0 04	18	−1 07
3	−0 08	19	−1 11
4	−0 12	20	−1 15
5	−0 16	21	−1 19
6	−0 20	22	−1 23
7	−0 24	23	−1 27
8	−0 28	24	−1 30
9	−0 31	25	−1 34
10	−0 35	26	−1 38
11	−0 39	27	−1 42
12	−0 43	28	−1 46
13	−0 47	29	−1 50
14	−0 51	30	−1 54
15	−0 55		
16	−0 59		

STAR'S TRANSIT

To find the approx time of transit of a star for any day of the month use above table. All corrections are subtractive. If the quantity taken from the table is greater than the time of transit for the first of the month, add 23h 56min to the time of transit before subtracting the correction.

Example: What is the time of transit of Aldebaran (No 11) on November 16?

	h min
Transit on the 1st	01 55
Corr for the 16th	−00 59
Transit on the 16th	00 56

NOVEMBER DIARY

2 10	Mercury 4°N of Moon
2 23	Venus in inferior conjunction
3 14	New Moon (Eclipse)
4 00	Moon at perigee
6 01	Mercury greatest elongation W(19°)
9 21	Saturn stationary
10 06	First Quarter
11 21	Saturn 7°S of Moon
12 18	Mercury 5°N of Venus
17 20	Jupiter in conjunction with Sun
18 05	Moon at apogee
18 07	Full Moon (Penumbral Eclipse)
18 17	Juno in conjunction with Sun
20 13	Pluto in conjunction with Sun
21 16	Venus stationary
25 20	Mars 8°N of Moon
26 07	Last Quarter
30 14	Venus 2°N of Moon

Chapter 6

NOVEMBER 1994 — SUN & ARIES — GMT

Time	SUN GHA	Dec	ARIES GHA	Time	SUN GHA	Dec	ARIES GHA	Time	SUN GHA	Dec	ARIES GHA	Time
Tuesday, November 1				**Sunday, November 6**				**Friday, November 11**				
00	184 05.6	S14 17.0	40 03.3	00	184 05.5	S15 50.6	44 50.9	00	184 00.2	S17 17.6	49 54.6	00
02	214 05.7	14 18.5	70 08.2	02	214 05.4	15 52.1	75 03.9	02	214 00.1	17 19.0	79 59.6	02
04	244 05.7	14 20.2	100 13.1	04	244 05.4	15 53.6	105 08.8	04	244 00.0	17 20.4	110 04.5	04
06	274 05.8	14 21.8	130 18.0	06	274 05.4	15 55.1	135 13.7	06	273 59.8	17 21.8	140 09.4	06
08	304 05.8	14 23.4	160 23.0	08	304 05.3	15 56.6	165 18.7	08	303 59.7	17 23.2	170 14.4	08
10	334 05.8	14 25.0	190 27.9	10	334 05.3	15 58.1	195 23.6	10	333 59.6	17 24.6	200 19.3	10
12	4 05.9	14 26.6	220 32.8	12	4 05.2	15 59.6	225 28.5	12	3 59.4	17 26.0	230 24.2	12
14	34 05.9	14 28.2	250 37.8	14	34 05.1	16 01.1	255 33.4	14	33 59.3	17 27.3	260 29.1	14
16	64 05.9	14 29.8	280 42.7	16	64 05.1	16 02.6	285 38.4	16	63 59.1	17 28.7	290 34.1	16
18	94 05.9	14 31.4	310 47.6	18	94 05.0	16 04.1	315 43.3	18	93 59.0	17 30.1	320 39.0	18
20	124 06.0	14 33.0	340 52.5	20	124 05.0	16 05.6	345 48.2	20	123 58.8	17 31.5	350 43.9	20
22	154 06.0	S14 34.6	10 57.5	22	154 04.9	S16 07.1	15 53.2	22	153 58.7	S17 32.8	20 48.9	22
Wednesday, November 2				**Monday, November 7**				**Saturday, November 12**				
00	184 06.0	S14 36.2	41 02.4	00	184 04.9	S16 08.6	45 58.1	00	183 58.6	S17 34.2	50 53.8	00
02	214 06.0	14 37.8	71 07.3	02	214 04.8	16 10.1	76 03.0	02	213 58.4	17 35.6	80 58.7	02
04	244 06.0	14 39.4	101 12.3	04	244 04.7	16 11.5	106 07.9	04	243 58.3	17 36.9	111 03.6	04
06	274 06.1	14 41.0	131 17.2	06	274 04.7	16 13.0	136 12.9	06	273 58.1	17 38.3	141 08.6	06
08	304 06.1	14 42.5	161 22.1	08	304 04.6	16 14.5	166 17.8	08	303 58.0	17 39.6	171 13.5	08
10	334 06.1	14 44.1	191 27.0	10	334 04.6	16 16.0	196 22.7	10	333 57.8	17 41.0	201 18.4	10
12	4 06.1	14 45.7	221 32.0	12	4 04.5	16 17.4	226 27.7	12	3 57.6	17 42.4	231 23.4	12
14	34 06.1	14 47.3	251 36.9	14	34 04.4	16 18.9	256 32.6	14	33 57.5	17 43.7	261 28.3	14
16	64 06.2	14 48.9	281 41.8	16	64 04.3	16 20.4	286 37.5	16	63 57.3	17 45.1	291 33.2	16
18	94 06.2	14 50.4	311 46.7	18	94 04.2	16 21.9	316 42.4	18	93 57.2	17 46.4	321 38.1	18
20	124 06.2	14 52.0	341 51.7	20	124 04.2	16 23.4	346 47.4	20	123 57.0	17 47.8	351 43.1	20
22	154 06.2	S14 53.6	11 56.6	22	154 04.1	S16 24.8	16 52.3	22	153 56.8	S17 49.1	21 48.0	22
Thursday, November 3				**Tuesday, November 8**				**Sunday, November 13**				
00	184 06.2	S14 55.2	42 01.5	00	184 04.0	S16 26.3	46 57.2	00	183 56.7	S17 50.4	51 52.9	00
02	214 06.2	14 56.7	72 06.5	02	214 03.9	16 27.7	77 02.2	02	213 56.5	17 51.8	81 57.8	02
04	244 06.2	14 58.3	102 11.4	04	244 03.8	16 29.2	107 07.1	04	243 56.3	17 53.1	112 02.8	04
06	274 06.2	14 59.9	132 16.3	06	274 03.8	16 30.6	137 12.0	06	273 56.2	17 54.4	142 07.7	06
08	304 06.2	15 01.4	162 21.2	08	304 03.7	16 32.1	167 16.9	08	303 56.0	17 55.8	172 12.6	08
10	334 06.1	15 03.0	192 26.2	10	334 03.6	16 33.5	197 21.9	10	333 55.8	17 57.1	202 17.6	10
12	4 06.2	15 04.6	222 31.1	12	4 03.5	16 35.0	227 26.8	12	3 55.7	17 58.4	232 22.5	12
14	34 06.1	15 06.1	252 36.0	14	34 03.4	16 36.5	257 31.7	14	33 55.5	17 59.8	262 27.4	14
16	64 06.1	15 07.7	282 41.0	16	64 03.4	16 37.9	287 36.7	16	63 55.3	18 01.1	292 32.3	16
18	94 06.2	15 09.2	312 45.9	18	94 03.2	16 39.3	317 41.6	18	93 55.1	18 02.4	322 37.3	18
20	124 06.2	15 10.8	342 50.8	20	124 03.1	16 40.8	347 46.5	20	123 54.9	18 03.7	352 42.2	20
22	154 06.2	S15 12.3	12 55.7	22	154 03.0	S16 42.2	17 51.4	22	153 54.8	S18 05.1	22 47.1	22
Friday, November 4				**Wednesday, November 9**				**Monday, November 14**				
00	184 06.2	S15 13.9	43 00.7	00	184 03.0	S16 43.7	47 56.4	00	183 54.6	S18 06.4	52 52.1	00
02	214 06.2	15 15.4	73 05.6	02	214 02.9	16 45.1	78 01.3	02	213 54.4	18 07.7	82 57.0	02
04	244 06.1	15 17.0	103 10.5	04	244 02.8	16 46.5	108 06.2	04	243 54.2	18 09.0	113 01.9	04
06	274 06.1	15 18.5	133 15.5	06	274 02.7	16 48.0	138 11.2	06	273 54.0	18 10.3	143 06.8	06
08	304 06.1	15 20.1	163 20.4	08	304 02.6	16 49.4	168 16.1	08	303 53.8	18 11.6	173 11.8	08
10	334 06.1	15 21.6	193 25.3	10	334 02.5	16 50.8	198 21.0	10	333 53.7	18 12.9	203 16.7	10
12	4 06.1	15 23.2	223 30.2	12	4 02.3	16 52.3	228 25.9	12	3 53.5	18 14.2	233 21.6	12
14	34 06.1	15 24.7	253 35.2	14	34 02.2	16 53.7	258 30.9	14	33 53.3	18 15.5	263 26.6	14
16	64 06.0	15 26.2	283 40.1	16	64 02.1	16 55.1	288 35.8	16	63 53.1	18 16.8	293 31.5	16
18	94 06.0	15 27.8	313 45.0	18	94 02.0	16 56.5	318 40.7	18	93 52.9	18 18.1	323 36.4	18
20	124 06.0	15 29.3	343 50.0	20	124 01.9	16 58.0	348 45.6	20	123 52.7	18 19.4	353 41.3	20
22	154 06.0	S15 30.9	13 54.9	22	154 01.8	S16 59.4	18 50.6	22	153 52.5	S18 20.7	23 46.3	22
Saturday, November 5				**Thursday, November 10**				**Tuesday, November 15**				
00	184 05.9	S15 32.4	43 59.8	00	184 01.7	S17 00.8	48 55.5	00	183 52.3	S18 22.0	53 51.2	00
02	214 05.9	15 33.9	74 04.7	02	214 01.6	17 02.2	79 00.4	02	213 52.1	18 23.3	83 56.1	02
04	244 05.9	15 35.4	104 09.7	04	244 01.5	17 03.6	109 05.4	04	243 51.9	18 24.6	114 01.1	04
06	274 05.8	15 37.0	134 14.6	06	274 01.3	17 05.0	139 10.3	06	273 51.7	18 25.8	144 06.0	06
08	304 05.8	15 38.5	164 19.5	08	304 01.2	17 06.5	169 15.2	08	303 51.5	18 27.1	174 10.9	08
10	334 05.8	15 40.0	194 24.5	10	334 01.1	17 07.9	199 20.1	10	333 51.3	18 28.4	204 15.8	10
12	4 05.7	15 41.5	224 29.4	12	4 01.0	17 09.3	229 25.1	12	3 51.1	18 29.7	234 20.8	12
14	34 05.7	15 43.0	254 34.3	14	34 00.9	17 10.7	259 30.0	14	33 50.8	18 30.9	264 25.7	14
16	64 05.7	15 44.6	284 39.2	16	64 00.7	17 12.1	289 34.9	16	63 50.6	18 32.2	294 30.6	16
18	94 05.6	15 46.1	314 44.2	18	94 00.6	17 13.5	319 39.9	18	93 50.4	18 33.5	324 35.6	18
20	124 05.6	15 47.6	344 49.1	20	124 00.5	17 14.9	349 44.8	20	123 50.2	18 34.8	354 40.5	20
22	154 05.5	S15 49.1	14 54.0	22	154 00.4	S17 16.3	19 49.7	22	153 50.0	S18 36.0	24 45.4	22

NOVEMBER 1994 — SUN & ARIES — GMT

Left Panel

Time	SUN GHA	Dec	ARIES GHA
Wednesday, November 16			
00	183 49.8	S18 37.3	54 50.3
02	213 49.6	18 38.5	84 55.3
04	243 49.3	18 39.8	115 00.2
06	273 49.1	18 41.1	145 05.1
08	303 48.9	18 42.3	175 10.1
10	333 48.7	18 43.6	205 15.0
12	3 48.4	18 44.8	235 19.9
14	33 48.2	18 46.0	265 24.8
16	63 48.0	18 47.3	295 29.8
18	93 47.8	18 48.5	325 34.7
20	123 47.5	18 49.8	355 39.6
22	153 47.3	S18 51.0	25 44.5
Thursday, November 17			
00	183 47.1	S18 52.2	55 49.5
02	213 46.8	18 53.5	85 54.4
04	243 46.6	18 54.7	115 59.3
06	273 46.4	18 55.9	146 04.3
08	303 46.1	18 57.2	176 09.2
10	333 45.9	18 58.4	206 14.1
12	3 45.6	18 59.6	236 19.0
14	33 45.4	19 00.8	266 24.0
16	63 45.1	19 02.0	296 28.9
18	93 44.9	19 03.2	326 33.8
20	123 44.6	19 04.5	356 38.8
22	153 44.4	S19 05.7	26 43.7
Friday, November 18			
00	183 44.1	S19 06.9	56 48.6
02	213 43.9	19 08.1	86 53.5
04	243 43.6	19 09.3	116 58.5
06	273 43.4	19 10.5	147 03.4
08	303 43.1	19 11.7	177 08.3
10	333 42.9	19 12.9	207 13.3
12	3 42.6	19 14.1	237 18.2
14	33 42.3	19 15.2	267 23.1
16	63 42.1	19 16.4	297 28.0
18	93 41.8	19 17.6	327 33.0
20	123 41.5	19 18.8	357 37.9
22	153 41.3	S19 20.0	27 42.8
Saturday, November 19			
00	183 41.0	S19 21.2	57 47.8
02	213 40.7	19 22.3	87 52.7
04	243 40.5	19 23.5	117 57.6
06	273 40.2	19 24.7	148 02.5
08	303 39.9	19 25.8	178 07.5
10	333 39.6	19 27.0	208 12.4
12	3 39.4	19 28.2	238 17.3
14	33 39.1	19 29.3	268 22.3
16	63 38.8	19 30.5	298 27.2
18	93 38.5	19 31.6	328 32.1
20	123 38.2	19 32.8	358 37.0
22	153 38.0	S19 33.9	28 42.0
Sunday, November 20			
00	183 37.7	S19 35.1	58 46.9
02	213 37.4	19 36.2	88 51.8
04	243 37.1	19 37.4	118 56.7
06	273 36.8	19 38.5	149 01.7
08	303 36.5	19 39.7	179 06.6
10	333 36.2	19 40.8	209 11.5
12	3 35.9	19 41.9	239 16.5
14	33 35.6	19 43.1	269 21.4
16	63 35.3	19 44.2	299 26.3
18	93 35.0	19 45.3	329 31.2
20	123 34.7	19 46.4	359 36.2
22	153 34.4	S19 47.6	29 41.1

Middle Panel

Time	SUN GHA	Dec	ARIES GHA
Monday, November 21			
00	183 34.1	S19 48.7	59 46.0
02	213 33.8	19 49.8	89 51.0
04	243 33.5	19 50.9	119 55.9
06	273 33.2	19 52.0	150 00.8
08	303 32.9	19 53.1	180 05.7
10	333 32.6	19 54.2	210 10.7
12	3 32.3	19 55.3	240 15.6
14	33 32.0	19 56.4	270 20.5
16	63 31.6	19 57.5	300 25.5
18	93 31.3	19 58.6	330 30.4
20	123 31.0	19 59.7	0 35.3
22	153 30.7	S20 00.8	30 40.2
Tuesday, November 22			
00	183 30.4	S20 01.9	60 45.2
02	213 30.0	20 03.0	90 50.1
04	243 29.7	20 04.1	120 55.0
06	273 29.4	20 05.2	151 00.0
08	303 29.1	20 06.2	181 04.9
10	333 28.7	20 07.3	211 09.8
12	3 28.4	20 08.4	241 14.7
14	33 28.1	20 09.5	271 19.7
16	63 27.7	20 10.5	301 24.6
18	93 27.4	20 11.6	331 29.5
20	123 27.1	20 12.6	1 34.5
22	153 26.7	S20 13.7	31 39.4
Wednesday, November 23			
00	183 26.4	S20 14.8	61 44.3
02	213 26.1	20 15.8	91 49.2
04	243 25.7	20 16.9	121 54.2
06	273 25.4	20 17.9	151 59.1
08	303 25.0	20 19.0	182 04.0
10	333 24.7	20 20.0	212 09.0
12	3 24.4	20 21.1	242 13.9
14	33 24.0	20 22.1	272 18.8
16	63 23.7	20 23.1	302 23.7
18	93 23.3	20 24.2	332 28.7
20	123 23.0	20 25.2	2 33.6
22	153 22.6	S20 26.2	32 38.5
Thursday, November 24			
00	183 22.3	S20 27.2	62 43.4
02	213 21.9	20 28.3	92 48.4
04	243 21.5	20 29.3	122 53.3
06	273 21.2	20 30.3	152 58.2
08	303 20.8	20 31.3	183 03.2
10	333 20.5	20 32.3	213 08.1
12	3 20.1	20 33.4	243 13.0
14	33 19.7	20 34.4	273 17.9
16	63 19.4	20 35.4	303 22.9
18	93 19.0	20 36.4	333 27.8
20	123 18.6	20 37.4	3 32.7
22	153 18.3	S20 38.4	33 37.7
Friday, November 25			
00	183 17.9	S20 39.4	63 42.6
02	213 17.5	20 40.3	93 47.5
04	243 17.2	20 41.3	123 52.4
06	273 16.8	20 42.3	153 57.4
08	303 16.4	20 43.3	184 02.3
10	333 16.0	20 44.3	214 07.2
12	3 15.7	20 45.3	244 12.2
14	33 15.3	20 46.2	274 17.1
16	63 14.9	20 47.2	304 22.0
18	93 14.5	20 48.2	334 26.9
20	123 14.1	20 49.2	4 31.9
22	153 13.7	S20 50.1	34 36.8

Right Panel

Time	SUN GHA	Dec	ARIES GHA
Saturday, November 26			
00	183 13.4	S20 51.1	64 41.7
02	213 13.0	20 52.0	94 46.7
04	243 12.6	20 53.0	124 51.6
06	273 12.2	20 54.0	154 56.5
08	303 11.8	20 54.9	185 01.4
10	333 11.4	20 55.9	215 06.4
12	3 11.0	20 56.8	245 11.3
14	33 10.6	20 57.7	275 16.2
16	63 10.2	20 58.7	305 21.2
18	93 09.8	20 59.6	335 26.1
20	123 09.4	21 00.6	5 31.0
22	153 09.0	S21 01.5	35 35.9
Sunday, November 27			
00	183 08.6	S21 02.4	65 40.9
02	213 08.2	21 03.3	95 45.8
04	243 07.8	21 04.3	125 50.7
06	273 07.4	21 05.2	155 55.6
08	303 07.0	21 06.1	186 00.6
10	333 06.6	21 07.0	216 05.5
12	3 06.2	21 07.9	246 10.4
14	33 05.8	21 08.8	276 15.4
16	63 05.3	21 09.8	306 20.3
18	93 04.9	21 10.7	336 25.2
20	123 04.5	21 11.6	6 30.1
22	153 04.1	S21 12.5	36 35.1
Monday, November 28			
00	183 03.7	S21 13.4	66 40.0
02	213 03.3	21 14.2	96 44.9
04	243 02.8	21 15.1	126 49.9
06	273 02.4	21 16.0	156 54.8
08	303 02.0	21 16.9	186 59.7
10	333 01.6	21 17.8	217 04.6
12	3 01.2	21 18.7	247 09.6
14	33 00.7	21 19.6	277 14.5
16	63 00.3	21 20.4	307 19.4
18	92 59.9	21 21.3	337 24.4
20	122 59.4	21 22.2	7 29.3
22	152 59.0	S21 23.0	37 34.2
Tuesday, November 29			
00	182 58.6	S21 23.9	67 39.1
02	212 58.1	21 24.8	97 44.1
04	242 57.7	21 25.6	127 49.0
06	272 57.3	21 26.5	157 53.9
08	302 56.8	21 27.3	187 58.9
10	332 56.4	21 28.2	218 03.8
12	2 56.0	21 29.0	248 08.7
14	32 55.5	21 29.9	278 13.6
16	62 55.1	21 30.7	308 18.6
18	92 54.6	21 31.5	338 23.5
20	122 54.2	21 32.4	8 28.4
22	152 53.7	S21 33.2	38 33.4
Wednesday, November 30			
00	182 53.3	S21 34.0	68 38.3
02	212 52.8	21 34.9	98 43.2
04	242 52.4	21 35.7	128 48.1
06	272 51.9	21 36.5	158 53.1
08	302 51.5	21 37.3	188 58.0
10	332 51.0	21 38.1	219 02.9
12	2 50.6	21 38.9	249 07.9
14	32 50.1	21 39.8	279 12.8
16	62 49.7	21 40.6	309 17.7
18	92 49.2	21 41.4	339 22.6
20	122 48.8	21 42.2	9 27.6
22	152 48.3	S21 43.0	39 32.5

Chapter 6

NOVEMBER 1994   PLANETS   0h GMT

VENUS | JUPITER

Mer Pass h m	GHA ° '	Mean Var/hr 15°+	Dec ° '	Mean Var/hr '			GHA ° '	Mean Var/hr 15°+	Dec ° '	Mean Var/hr '	Mer Pass h m
11 45	182 53.9	3.8	320 45.0	0.9	1	Tue	170 43.8	1.9	S17 22.1	0.1	12 35
11 39	184 25.5	3.8	S20 22.9	1.0	2	Wed	171 29.7	1.9	S17 25.6	0.1	12 32
11 33	185 57.1	3.8	S20 00.1	1.0	3	Thu	172 15.6	1.9	S17 29.1	0.1	12 29
11 27	187 28.3	3.8	S19 36.6	1.0	4	Fri	173 01.4	1.9	S17 32.5	0.1	12 26
11 21	188 59.1	3.8	S19 12.6	1.0	5	Sat	173 47.2	1.9	S17 36.0	0.1	12 23
11 15	190 29.1	3.7	S18 48.2	1.0	6	SUN	174 33.0	1.9	S17 39.4	0.1	12 20
11 09	191 58.2	3.7	S18 23.6	1.0	7	Mon	175 18.8	1.9	S17 42.8	0.1	12 17
11 04	193 26.1	3.6	S17 58.8	1.0	8	Tue	176 04.5	1.9	S17 46.2	0.1	12 14
10 58	194 52.7	3.5	S17 34.0	1.0	9	Wed	176 50.2	1.9	S17 49.6	0.1	12 11
10 52	196 17.8	3.5	S17 09.3	1.0	10	Thu	177 35.9	1.9	S17 52.9	0.1	12 08
10 47	197 41.2	3.4	S16 45.0	1.0	11	Fri	178 21.6	1.9	S17 56.3	0.1	12 05
10 41	199 02.8	3.3	S16 21.0	1.0	12	Sat	179 07.3	1.9	S17 59.6	0.1	12 02
10 36	200 22.5	3.2	S15 57.6	0.9	13	SUN	179 52.9	1.9	S18 03.0	0.1	11 59
10 31	201 40.1	3.1	S15 34.8	0.9	14	Mon	180 38.5	1.9	S18 06.3	0.1	11 56
10 26	202 55.6	3.1	S15 12.7	0.9	15	Tue	181 24.1	1.9	S18 09.6	0.1	11 53
10 21	204 08.9	3.0	S14 51.5	0.8	16	Wed	182 09.7	1.9	S18 12.8	0.1	11 50
10 17	205 20.0	2.9	S14 31.2	0.8	17	Thu	182 55.3	1.9	S18 16.1	0.1	11 47
10 12	206 28.8	2.8	S14 11.9	0.8	18	Fri	183 40.8	1.9	S18 19.3	0.1	11 44
10 08	207 35.2	2.7	S13 53.6	0.7	19	Sat	184 26.4	1.9	S18 22.6	0.1	11 41
10 04	208 39.4	2.6	S13 36.4	0.7	20	SUN	185 11.9	1.9	S18 25.8	0.1	11 38
10 00	209 41.2	2.5	S13 20.3	0.6	21	Mon	185 57.4	1.9	S18 29.0	0.1	11 35
09 56	210 40.7	2.4	S13 05.3	0.6	22	Tue	186 43.0	1.9	S18 32.1	0.1	11 32
09 52	211 37.9	2.3	S12 51.6	0.5	23	Wed	187 28.5	1.9	S18 35.3	0.1	11 29
09 48	212 32.9	2.2	S12 39.0	0.5	24	Thu	188 14.0	1.9	S18 38.4	0.1	11 26
09 45	213 25.7	2.1	S12 27.6	0.4	25	Fri	188 59.5	1.9	S18 41.5	0.1	11 23
09 42	214 16.3	2.0	S12 17.4	0.4	26	Sat	189 45.0	1.9	S18 44.6	0.1	11 20
09 38	215 04.7	1.9	S12 08.4	0.3	27	SUN	190 30.5	1.9	S18 47.7	0.1	11 17
09 35	215 51.2	1.8	S12 00.5	0.3	28	Mon	191 16.0	1.9	S18 50.7	0.1	11 14
09 32	216 35.6	1.8	S11 53.7	0.2	29	Tue	192 01.6	1.9	S18 53.7	0.1	11 10
09 30	217 18.0	1.7	S11 48.1	0.2	30	Wed	192 47.1	1.9	S18 56.7	0.1	11 07

VENUS, Av Mag –4.3
SHA November
5 145; 10 147; 15 149; 20 150; 25 150; 30 149.

JUPITER, Av Mag –1.7
SHA November
5 130; 10 129; 15 128; 20 126; 25 125; 30 124.

MARS | SATURN

Mer Pass h m	GHA ° '	Mean Var/hr 15°+	Dec ° '	Mean Var/hr '			GHA ° '	Mean Var/hr 15°+	Dec ° '	Mean Var/hr '	Mer Pass h m
06 29	262 41.9	1.2	N18 01.0	0.3	1	Tue	61 47.8	2.5	S11 11.9	0.0	19 50
06 27	263 11.6	1.3	N17 53.9	0.3	2	Wed	62 47.7	2.5	S11 12.1	0.0	19 46
06 25	263 41.7	1.3	N17 46.8	0.3	3	Thu	63 47.6	2.5	S11 12.2	0.0	19 42
06 23	264 12.0	1.3	N17 39.7	0.3	4	Fri	64 47.4	2.5	S11 12.3	0.0	19 38
06 21	264 42.5	1.3	N17 32.6	0.3	5	Sat	65 47.0	2.5	S11 12.4	0.0	19 34
06 19	265 13.4	1.3	N17 25.6	0.3	6	SUN	66 46.6	2.5	S11 12.4	0.0	19 30
06 16	265 44.5	1.3	N17 18.5	0.3	7	Mon	67 46.1	2.5	S11 12.4	0.0	19 26
06 14	266 16.0	1.3	N17 11.6	0.3	8	Tue	68 45.5	2.5	S11 12.3	0.0	19 22
06 12	266 47.7	1.3	N17 04.6	0.3	9	Wed	69 44.7	2.5	S11 12.3	0.0	19 18
06 10	267 19.7	1.3	N16 57.7	0.3	10	Thu	70 43.9	2.5	S11 12.1	0.0	19 14
06 08	267 52.0	1.4	N16 50.9	0.3	11	Fri	71 43.0	2.5	S11 12.0	0.0	19 10
06 06	268 24.6	1.4	N16 44.0	0.3	12	Sat	72 42.0	2.5	S11 11.7	0.0	19 06
06 04	268 57.6	1.4	N16 37.3	0.3	13	SUN	73 40.9	2.4	S11 11.5	0.0	19 02
06 01	269 30.8	1.4	N16 30.6	0.3	14	Mon	74 39.6	2.4	S11 11.2	0.0	18 58
05 59	270 04.3	1.4	N16 23.9	0.3	15	Tue	75 38.3	2.4	S11 10.9	0.0	18 54
05 57	270 38.2	1.4	N16 17.4	0.3	16	Wed	76 36.9	2.4	S11 10.5	0.0	18 50
05 55	271 12.3	1.4	N16 10.9	0.3	17	Thu	77 35.4	2.4	S11 10.1	0.0	18 47
05 52	271 46.9	1.4	N16 04.4	0.3	18	Fri	78 33.8	2.4	S11 09.7	0.0	18 43
05 50	272 21.7	1.5	N15 58.1	0.3	19	Sat	79 32.1	2.4	S11 09.2	0.0	18 39
05 48	272 56.9	1.5	N15 51.8	0.3	20	SUN	80 30.2	2.4	S11 08.6	0.0	18 35
05 45	273 32.4	1.5	N15 45.6	0.3	21	Mon	81 28.3	2.4	S11 08.1	0.0	18 31
05 43	274 08.2	1.5	N15 39.5	0.3	22	Tue	82 26.3	2.4	S11 07.5	0.0	18 27
05 40	274 44.5	1.5	N15 33.5	0.2	23	Wed	83 24.2	2.4	S11 06.8	0.0	18 23
05 38	275 21.0	1.5	N15 27.6	0.2	24	Thu	84 22.0	2.4	S11 06.2	0.0	18 20
05 36	275 58.0	1.6	N15 21.8	0.2	25	Fri	85 19.7	2.4	S11 05.4	0.0	18 16
05 33	276 35.3	1.6	N15 16.2	0.2	26	Sat	86 17.3	2.4	S11 04.7	0.0	18 12
05 31	277 13.0	1.6	N15 10.6	0.2	27	SUN	87 14.8	2.4	S11 03.9	0.0	18 08
05 28	277 51.1	1.6	N15 05.1	0.2	28	Mon	88 12.2	2.4	S11 03.1	0.0	18 04
05 25	278 29.6	1.6	N14 59.8	0.2	29	Tue	89 09.5	2.4	S11 02.2	0.0	18 01
05 23	279 08.5	1.6	N14 54.6	0.2	30	Wed	90 06.7	2.4	S11 01.3	0.0	17 57

MARS, Av Mag +0.5
SHA November
5 221; 10 218; 15 216; 20 214; 25 212; 30 211.

SATURN, Av Mag +0.8
SHA November
5 22; 10 22; 15 22; 20 22; 25 22; 30 21.

NOVEMBER 1994 — MOON

Day	GMT hr	GHA ° '	Mean Var/hr 14°+	Dec ° '	Mean Var/hr '	Day	GMT hr	GHA ° '	Mean Var/hr 14°+	Dec ° '	Mean Var/hr '
1 Tue	0	219 07.7	27.9	S 4 17.5	12.1	17 Thu	0	17 53.1	32.4	N 15 21.0	6.4
	6	305 55.0	27.5	S 5 30.3	12.0		6	105 07.6	32.3	N 15 59.8	6.0
	12	32 40.1	27.1	S 6 42.5	11.8		12	192 21.0	32.0	N 16 36.1	5.5
	18	119 22.8	26.7	S 7 53.6	11.6		18	279 33.5	31.9	N 17 09.7	5.1
2 Wed	0	206 03.0	26.3	S 9 03.3	11.3	18 Fri	0	6 44.9	31.7	N 17 40.6	4.6
	6	292 40.6	25.8	S 10 11 3	10.9		6	93 55.3	31.6	N 18 08.7	4.1
	12	19 15.7	25.3	S 11 17.2	10.5		12	181 04.8	31.4	N 18 33.8	3.6
	18	105 48.2	25.0	S 12 20.7	10.0		18	268 13.4	31.3	N 18 55.0	3.1
3 Thu	0	192 18.1	24.6	S 13 21.3	9.5	19 Sat	0	355 21.1	31.2	N 19 14.8	2.6
	6	278 45.5	24.1	S 14 18.8	8.9		6	82 28.1	31.0	N 19 30.6	2.1
	12	Eclipse of the Sun					12	169 34.5	30.9	N 19 43.2	1.5
	18	91 33.5	23.5	S 16 02.8	7.6		18	256 40.3	30.9	N 19 52.5	1.0
4 Fri	0	177 54.3	23.2	S 16 48.7	6.9	20 Sun	0	343 45.6	30.8	N 19 58.5	0.4
	6	264 13.4	22.9	S 17 30.2	6.0		6	70 50.5	30.8	N 20 01.1	0.2
	12	350 31.0	22.7	S 18 06.9	5.2		12	157 55.1	30.7	N 20 00.4	0.8
	18	76 47.4	22.5	S 18 38.8	4.4		18	244 59.6	30.7	N 19 56.3	1.3
5 Sat	0	163 03.0	22.5	S 19 05.6	3.5	21 Mon	0	332 04.0	30.7	N 19 48.8	1.9
	6	249 18.1	22.5	S 19 27.1	2.6		6	59 08.4	30.7	N 19 37.9	2.4
	12	335 33.2	22.6	S 19 43.3	1.7		12	146 12.9	30.7	N 19 23.7	3.0
	18	61 48.7	22.7	S 19 54.2	0.8		18	233 17.6	30.8	N 19 06.1	3.5
6 Sun	0	148 04.9	22.9	S 19 59.7	0.0	22 Tue	0	320 22.6	30.9	N 18 45.3	4.0
	6	234 22.3	23.2	S 19 59.9	0.9		6	47 27.9	31.0	N 18 21.2	4.6
	12	320 41.1	23.4	S 19 54.8	1.7		12	134 33.6	31.0	N 17 53.9	5.1
	18	47 01.9	23.8	S 19 44.7	2.6		18	221 39.7	31.1	N 17 23.5	5.6
7 Mon	0	133 24.8	24.3	S 19 29.7	3.4	23 Wed	0	308 46.3	31.2	N 16 50.0	6.1
	6	219 50.2	24.8	S 19 09.9	4.1		6	35 53.3	31.3	N 16 13.6	6.6
	12	306 18.3	25.2	S 18 45.6	4.9		12	123 00.7	31.3	N 15 34.3	7.0
	18	32 49.3	25.7	S 18 16.9	5.5		18	210 08.6	31.4	N 14 52.1	7.5
8 Tue	0	119 23.4	26.3	S 17 44.3	6.1	24 Thu	0	297 16.9	31.5	N 14 07.3	8.0
	6	206 00.6	26.8	S 17 07.9	6.7		6	24 25.5	31.5	N 13 19.8	8.4
	12	292 41.0	27.3	S 16 27.9	7.2		12	111 34.4	31.6	N 12 29.9	8.8
	18	19 24.7	27.8	S 15 44.7	7.7		18	198 43.5	31.6	N 11 37.5	9.2
9 Wed	0	106 11.6	28.4	S 14 58.6	8.2	25 Fri	0	285 52.8	31.5	N 10 42.9	9.5
	6	193 01.7	28.9	S 14 09.7	8.6		6	13 02.0	31.5	N 9 46.0	9.9
	12	279 54.9	29.4	S 13 18.4	8.9		12	100 11.2	31.5	N 8 47.2	10.2
	18	6 51.2	29.9	S 12 24.9	9.2		18	187 20.1	31.5	N 7 46.4	10.4
10 Thu	0	93 50.3	30.4	S 11 29.5	9.6	26 Sat	0	274 28.7	31.3	N 6 43.9	10.7
	6	180 52.2	30.8	S 10 32.3	9.8		6	1 36.7	31.2	N 5 39.8	10.9
	12	267 56.7	31.2	S 9 33.6	10.0		12	88 44.1	31.1	N 4 34.1	11.1
	18	355 03.7	31.6	S 8 33.7	10.2		18	175 50.7	30.9	N 3 27.2	11.4
11 Fri	0	82 12.9	31.9	S 7 32.7	10.3	27 Sun	0	262 56.2	30.7	N 2 19.1	11.5
	6	169 24.2	32.2	S 6 30.8	10.4		6	350 00.6	30.5	N 1 10.1	11.7
	12	256 37.4	32.5	S 5 28.2	10.6		12	77 03.6	30.3	N 0 00.3	11.8
	18	343 52.4	32.8	S 4 25.1	10.6		18	164 05.1	29.9	S 1 10.1	11.8
12 Sat	0	71 08.9	33.0	S 3 21.6	10.6	28 Mon	0	251 04.8	29.6	S 2 20.8	11.8
	6	158 26.8	33.2	S 2 17.9	10.6		6	338 02.6	29.2	S 3 31.6	11.8
	12	245 45.9	33.3	S 1 14.2	10.6		12	64 58.4	28.9	S 4 42.3	11.7
	18	333 05.9	33.5	S 0 10.7	10.6		18	151 51.9	28.5	S 5 52.6	11.6
13 Sun	0	60 26.8	33.6	N 0 52.6	10.5	29 Tue	0	238 42.9	28.0	S 7 02.3	11.4
	6	147 48.3	33.7	N 1 55.5	10.4		6	325 31.4	27.6	S 8 11.0	11.2
	12	235 10.4	33.7	N 2 57.9	10.3		12	52 17.1	27.2	S 9 18.4	10.9
	18	322 32.7	33.8	N 3 59.6	10.1		18	139 00.0	26.6	S 10 24.3	10.6
14 Mon	0	49 55.2	33.7	N 5 00.4	10.0	30 Wed	0	225 40.0	26.2	S 11 28.2	10.3
	6	137 17.7	33.7	N 6 00.4	9.8		6	312 17.1	25.6	S 12 29.9	9.8
	12	224 40.1	33.6	N 6 59.2	9.6		12	38 51.1	25.1	S 13 29.0	9.3
	18	312 02.3	33.7	N 7 56.9	9.4		18	125 22.1	24.7	S 14 25.2	8.8
15 Tue	0	39 24.1	33.5	N 8 53.2	9.1						
	6	126 45.4	33.4	N 9 48.1	8.9						
	12	214 06.1	33.3	N 10 41.4	8.5						
	18	301 26.1	33.2	N 11 32.9	8.2						
16 Wed	0	28 45.3	33.0	N 12 22.7	7.9						
	6	116 03.7	32.9	N 13 10.5	7.6						
	12	203 21.1	32.7	N 13 56.3	7.2						
	18	290 37.6	32.6	N 14 39.8	6.9						

Chapter 6

DECEMBER 1994 — SUN & MOON — GMT

SUN

Yr	Mth	Week	Eq. of Time 0h	Eq. of Time 12h	Transit	Semi-diam	Twilight	Sunrise	Sunset	Twilight
			m s	m s	h m	′	h m	h m	h m	h m
335	1	Thu	−11 12	−11 01	11 49	16.2	07 06	07 45	15 52	16 32
336	2	Fri	−10 49	−10 38	11 49	16.2	07 07	07 47	15 52	16 31
337	3	Sat	−10 26	−10 14	11 50	16.3	07 08	07 48	15 51	16 31
338	4	Sun	−10 03	−09 50	11 50	16.3	07 09	07 49	15 51	16 31
339	5	Mon	−09 38	−09 26	11 51	16.3	07 11	07 51	15 50	16 30
340	6	Tue	−09 13	−09 01	11 51	16.3	07 12	07 52	15 50	16 30
341	7	Wed	−08 48	−08 35	11 51	16.3	07 13	07 53	15 49	16 30
342	8	Thu	−08 22	−08 09	11 52	16.3	07 14	07 54	15 49	16 29
343	9	Fri	−07 56	−07 42	11 52	16.3	07 15	07 56	15 49	16 29
344	10	Sat	−07 29	−07 15	11 53	16.3	07 16	07 57	15 49	16 29
345	11	Sun	−07 02	−06 48	11 53	16.3	07 17	07 58	15 48	16 29
346	12	Mon	−06 34	−06 20	11 54	16.3	07 18	07 59	15 48	16 29
347	13	Tue	−06 06	−05 52	11 54	16.3	07 19	08 00	15 48	16 29
348	14	Wed	−05 38	−05 24	11 55	16.3	07 20	08 01	15 48	16 29
349	15	Thu	−05 09	−04 55	11 55	16.3	07 21	08 02	15 49	16 29
350	16	Fri	−04 40	−04 26	11 56	16.3	07 21	08 02	15 49	16 30
351	17	Sat	−04 11	−03 57	11 56	16.3	07 22	08 03	15 49	16 30
352	18	Sun	−03 42	−03 27	11 57	16.3	07 23	08 04	15 49	16 30
353	19	Mon	−03 13	−02 58	11 57	16.3	07 24	08 05	15 49	16 30
354	20	Tue	−02 43	−02 28	11 58	16.3	07 24	08 05	15 50	16 31
355	21	Wed	−02 13	−01 59	11 58	16.3	07 25	08 06	15 50	16 31
356	22	Thu	−01 44	−01 29	11 59	16.3	07 25	08 06	15 51	16 32
357	23	Fri	−01 14	−00 59	11 59	16.3	07 26	08 07	15 51	16 32
358	24	Sat	−00 44	−00 29	12 00	16.3	07 26	08 07	15 52	16 33
359	25	Sun	−00 14	+00 01	12 00	16.3	07 26	08 07	15 53	16 34
360	26	Mon	+00 15	+00 30	12 01	16.3	07 27	08 08	15 53	16 34
361	27	Tue	+00 45	+01 00	12 01	16.3	07 27	08 08	15 54	16 35
362	28	Wed	+01 15	+01 30	12 01	16.3	07 27	08 08	15 55	16 36
363	29	Thu	+01 44	+01 59	12 02	16.3	07 27	08 08	15 56	16 37
364	30	Fri	+02 13	+02 28	12 02	16.3	07 28	08 08	15 57	16 38
365	31	Sat	+02 42	+02 57	12 03	16.3	07 28	08 08	15 58	16 38

Lat Corr to Sunrise, Sunset etc

Lat	Twilight	Sunrise	Sunset	Twilight
°	h m	h m	h m	h m
N70	+2 26	SBH	SBH	−2 26
68	+1 52	SBH	SBH	−1 52
66	+1 27	+2 25	−2 26	−1 27
64	+1 08	+1 44	−1 45	−1 08
62	+0 52	+1 16	−1 17	−0 52
N60	+0 38	+0 55	−0 56	−0 38
58	+0 27	+0 38	−0 39	−0 27
56	+0 17	+0 23	−0 24	−0 17
54	+0 08	+0 11	−0 11	−0 08
50	−0 08	−0 10	+0 10	+0 08
N45	−0 23	−0 30	+0 30	+0 23
40	−0 37	−0 47	+0 47	+0 37
35	−0 48	−1 01	+1 01	+0 48
30	−0 59	−1 13	+1 13	+0 59
20	−1 17	−1 34	+1 34	+1 18
N10	−1 34	−1 53	+1 53	+1 35
0	−1 51	−2 10	+2 10	+1 52
S10	−2 09	−2 27	+2 27	+2 10
20	−2 30	−2 46	+2 46	+2 31
30	−2 54	−3 08	+3 08	+2 15
S35	−3 09	−3 21	+3 21	+3 16
40	−3 27	−3 36	+3 36	+3 29
45	−3 49	−3 53	+3 54	+3 51
S50	−4 18	−4 16	+4 16	+4 20

NOTES

Equation of time changes its sign on the 25th. Lat corrections are for the middle of December. SBH = Sun below horizon. **Equation of Time** is the excess of Mean Time over Apparent Time.

MOON

Lat 52°N

Yr	Mth	Week	Age (days)	Transit Diff (Upper)	Diff	Semi-diam	Hor Par	Moonrise	Moonset
				h m	m	′	′	h m	h m
335	1	Thu	28	10 17	62	16.7	61.2	05 34	14 54
336	2	Fri	29	11 19	64	16.7	61.4	06 53	15 42
337	3	Sat	01	12 23	62	16.7	61.2	08 04	16 41
338	4	Sun	02	13 25	60	16.5	60.7	09 04	17 49
339	5	Mon	03	14 25	56	16.3	60.0	09 53	19 04
340	6	Tue	04	15 21	52	16.1	59.1	10 31	20 20
341	7	Wed	05	16 13	49	15.8	58.1	11 02	21 35
342	8	Thu	06	17 02	46	15.6	57.2	11 28	22 47
343	9	Fri	07	17 48	44	15.3	56.3	11 51	23 56
344	10	Sat	08	18 32	44	15.1	55.5	12 12	– –
345	11	Sun	09	19 16	43	15.0	54.9	12 34	01 04
346	12	Mon	10	19 59	45	14.8	54.5	12 56	02 10
347	13	Tue	11	20 44	45	14.8	54.2	13 21	03 14
348	14	Wed	12	21 29	47	14.7	54.0	13 49	04 18
349	15	Thu	13	22 16	48	14.7	54.0	14 21	05 19
350	16	Fri	14	23 04	48	14.7	54.1	15 00	06 17
351	17	Sat	15	23 52	49	14.8	54.2	15 45	07 10
352	18	Sun	16	24 41	_	14.8	54.5	16 38	07 57
353	19	Mon	17	00 41	48	14.9	54.8	17 36	08 38
354	20	Tue	18	01 29	48	15.0	55.1	18 40	09 13
355	21	Wed	19	02 17	47	15.1	55.6	19 46	09 43
356	22	Thu	20	03 04	47	15.3	56.1	20 55	10 10
357	23	Fri	21	03 51	47	15.4	56.7	22 06	10 34
358	24	Sat	22	04 38	47	15.6	57.3	23 18	10 57
359	25	Sun	23	05 25	50	15.8	58.0	– –	11 21
360	26	Mon	24	06 15	51	16.0	58.7	00 33	11 45
361	27	Tue	25	07 06	55	16.2	59.4	01 49	12 14
362	28	Wed	26	08 01	59	16.4	60.1	03 07	12 47
363	29	Thu	27	09 00	61	16.5	60.5	04 25	13 29
364	30	Fri	28	10 01	62	16.6	60.8	05 39	14 20
365	31	Sat	29	11 03	62	16.6	60.8	06 45	15 23

Phases of the Moon

	d	h	m
● New Moon	2	23	54
◐ First Quarter	9	21	06
○ Full Moon	18	02	17
◑ Last Quarter	25	19	06
Perigee	2	12	
Apogee	15	08	
Perigee	30	23	

NOTES

For Latitude corrections to Moonrise and Moonset see page 706.

DECEMBER 1994

STARS

0h GMT December 1

No	Name	Mag	Transit h m	Dec ° ′	GHA ° ′	RA h m	SHA ° ′
	ARIES..............		19 18		69 37.4		
1	Alpheratz	2.2	19 26	N29 04.0	67 35.2	0 08	357 57.8
2	Ankaa.............	2.4	19 44	S 42 20.2	63 06.7	0 26	353 29.3
3	Schedar..........	2.5	19 58	N56 30.9	59 33.6	0 40	349 56.2
4	Diphda	2.2	20 02	S 18 00.9	58 47.1	0 43	349 09.7
5	Achernar	0.6	20 56	S 57 16.0	45 14.2	1 38	335 36.8
6	POLARIS..........	2.1	21 46	N89 14.7	32 34.4	2 29	322 57.0
7	Hamal............	2.2	21 25	N23 26.4	37 53.6	2 07	328 16.2
8	Acamar	3.1	22 16	S 40 19.6	25 05.9	2 58	315 28.5
9	Menkar	2.8	22 20	N 4 04.2	24 06.7	3 02	314 29.3
10	Mirfak	1.9	22 42	N49 50.7	18 37.2	3 24	308 59.8
11	Aldebaran	1.1	23 53	N16 29.9	0 42.4	4 36	291 05.0
12	Rigel	0.3	0 36	S 8 12.5	351 02.5	5 14	281 25.1
13	Capella..........	0.2	0 38	N45 59.5	350 31.9	5 16	280 54.5
14	Bellatrix.........	1.7	0 46	N 6 20.6	348 24.0	5 25	278 46.6
15	Elnath	1.8	0 47	N28 36.1	348 07.2	5 26	278 29.8
16	Alnilam..........	1.8	0 57	S 1 12.4	345 37.5	5 36	276 00.1
17	Betelgeuse......0.1-1.2		1 16	N 7 24.3	340 53.4	5 55	271 16.0
18	Canopus	0.9	1 45	S 52 41.6	333 39.1	6 24	264 01.7
19	Sirius	1.6	2 06	S 16 42.6	328 23.0	6 45	258 45.6
20	Adhara...........	1.6	2 20	S 28 58.0	325 00.5	6 58	255 23.1
21	Castor	1.6	2 55	N31 53.8	316 02.7	7 34	246 25.3
22	Procyon	0.5	3 00	N 5 14.1	314 51.4	7 39	245 14.0
23	Pollux	1.2	3 06	N28 02.1	313 21.8	7 45	243 44.4
24	Avior	1.7	3 43	S 59 29.5	304 00.5	8 22	234 23.1
25	Suhail............	2.2	4 29	S 43 24.7	292 39.7	9 08	223 02.3
26	Miaplacidus	1.8	4 34	S 69 41.7	291 19.3	9 13	221 41.9
27	Alphard	2.2	4 48	S 8 38.3	287 46.9	9 27	218 09.5
28	Regulus..........	1.3	5 29	N11 59.3	277 35.6	10 08	207 58.2
29	Dubhe	2.0	6 24	N61 46.3	263 46.0	11 03	194 08.6
30	Denebola........	2.2	7 09	N14 35.9	252 25.2	11 49	182 47.8
31	Gienah	2.8	7 36	S 17 30.8	245 44.1	12 16	176 06.7
32	Acrux............	1.1	7 47	S 63 04.0	243 02.3	12 26	173 24.9
33	Gacrux	1.6	7 51	S 57 04.9	241 53.9	12 31	172 16.5
34	Mimosa..........	1.5	8 08	S 59 39.4	237 45.8	12 47	168 08.4
35	Alioth............	1.7	8 14	N55 58.9	236 10.5	12 54	166 33.1
36	Spica.............	1.2	8 45	S 11 08.1	228 23.5	13 25	158 46.1
37	Alkaid	1.9	9 07	N49 20.1	222 47.6	13 47	153 10.2
38	Hadar	0.9	9 23	S 60 20.7	218 45.4	14 03	149 08.0
39	Menkent........	2.3	9 26	S 36 20.5	218 01.6	14 06	148 24.2
40	Arcturus........	0.2	9 35	N19 12.4	215 46.0	14 15	146 08.6
41	Rigil Kent.......	0.1	9 59	S 60 48.6	209 48.5	14 39	140 11.1
42	Zuben'ubi.......	2.9	10 10	S 16 01.2	206 58.5	14 51	137 21.1
43	Kochab..........	2.2	10 10	N74 10.4	206 57.9	14 51	137 20.5
44	Alphecca........	2.3	10 54	N26 43.9	196 00.5	15 34	126 23.1
45	Antares.........	1.2	11 49	S 26 25.1	182 21.1	16 29	112 43.7
46	Atria	1.9	12 08	S 69 01.0	177 36.0	16 48	107 58.6
47	Sabik	2.6	12 30	S 15 43.0	172 06.2	17 10	102 28.8
48	Shaula...........	1.7	12 53	S 37 05.9	166 18.6	17 33	96 41.2
49	Rasalhague	2.1	12 54	N12 33.9	165 57.1	17 35	96 19.7
50	Eltanin	2.4	13 16	N51 29.5	160 30.5	17 56	90 53.1
51	Kaus Aust.......	2.0	13 43	S 34 23.1	153 40.0	18 24	84 02.6
52	Vega	0.1	13 56	N38 46.9	150 26.2	18 37	80 48.8
53	Nunki	2.1	14 14	S 26 18.1	145 53.3	18 55	76 15.9
54	Altair............	0.9	15 10	N 8 51.5	131 59.5	19 51	62 22.1
55	Peacock..........	2.1	15 44	S 56 45.1	123 18.9	20 25	53 41.5
56	Deneb	1.3	16 00	N45 16.1	119 18.6	20 41	49 41.2
57	Enif	2.5	17 03	N 9 51.3	103 38.3	21 44	34 00.9
58	Al Na'ir	2.2	17 27	S 46 59.2	97 38.7	22 08	28 01.3
59	Fomalhaut	1.3	18 16	S 29 39.0	85 16.7	22 57	15 39.3
60	Markab	2.6	18 23	N15 10.9	83 29.6	23 05	13 52.2

Stars Transit Corr Table

Date	Corr h m	Date	Corr h m
1	−0 00	17	−1 03
2	−0 04	18	−1 07
3	−0 08	19	−1 11
4	−0 12	20	−1 15
5	−0 16	21	−1 19
6	−0 20	22	−1 23
7	−0 24	23	−1 27
8	−0 28	24	−1 30
9	−0 31	25	−1 34
10	−0 35	26	−1 38
11	−0 39	27	−1 42
12	−0 43	28	−1 46
13	−0 47	29	−1 50
14	−0 51	30	−1 54
15	−0 55	31	−1 58
16	−0 59		

STAR'S TRANSIT
To find the approx time of transit of a star for any day of the month use above table. All corrections are subtractive. If the quantity taken from the table is greater than the time of transit for the first of the month, add 23h 56min to the time of transit before subtracting the correction.

Example: What time will Bellatrix (No 14) be on the meridian on December 9?

	h min
Transit on the 1st	00 46
Corr for 9th	−00 31
Transit on the 9th	00 15

DECEMBER DIARY

2 12 Moon at perigee
3 00 New Moon
5 19 Neptune 4°S of Moon
6 00 Uranus 6°S of Moon
8 08 Mars 2°N of Regulus
9 05 Saturn 7°S of Moon
9 11 Venus greatest brilliancy
9 21 First Quarter
14 03 Mercury in superior conjunction
15 08 Moon at apogee
18 02 Full Moon
22 02 Solstice
23 15 Mars 9°N of Moon
24 17 Ceres stationary
25 02 Vesta at opposition
25 19 Last Quarter
29 05 Venus 3°N of Moon
30 00 Jupiter 1.1°S of Moon
30 23 Moon at perigee

Chapter 6

DECEMBER 1994   SUN & ARIES   GMT

Thursday, December 1

Time	SUN GHA	Dec	ARIES GHA
00	182 47.8	S21 43.8	69 37.4
02	212 47.4	21 44.5	99 42.3
04	242 46.9	21 45.3	129 47.3
06	272 46.5	21 46.1	159 52.2
08	302 46.0	21 46.9	189 57.1
10	332 45.5	21 47.7	220 02.1
12	2 45.1	21 48.5	250 07.0
14	32 44.6	21 49.2	280 11.9
16	62 44.1	21 50.0	310 16.8
18	92 43.6	21 50.8	340 21.8
20	122 43.2	21 51.5	10 26.7
22	152 42.7	S21 52.3	40 31.6

Friday, December 2

Time	SUN GHA	Dec	ARIES GHA
00	182 42.2	S21 53.1	70 36.6
02	212 41.7	21 53.8	100 41.5
04	242 41.3	21 54.6	130 46.4
06	272 40.8	21 55.3	160 51.3
08	302 40.3	21 56.1	190 56.3
10	332 39.8	21 56.8	221 01.2
12	2 39.3	21 57.6	251 06.1
14	32 38.9	21 58.3	281 11.1
16	62 38.4	21 59.0	311 16.0
18	92 37.9	21 59.8	341 20.9
20	122 37.4	22 00.5	11 25.8
22	152 36.9	S22 01.2	41 30.8

Saturday, December 3

Time	SUN GHA	Dec	ARIES GHA
00	182 36.4	S22 02.0	71 35.7
02	212 35.9	22 02.7	101 40.6
04	242 35.5	22 03.4	131 45.6
06	272 35.0	22 04.1	161 50.5
08	302 34.5	22 04.8	191 55.4
10	332 34.0	22 05.5	222 00.3
12	2 33.5	22 06.2	252 05.3
14	32 33.0	22 06.9	282 10.2
16	62 32.5	22 07.6	312 15.1
18	92 32.0	22 08.3	342 20.1
20	122 31.5	22 09.0	12 25.0
22	152 31.0	S22 09.7	42 29.9

Sunday, December 4

Time	SUN GHA	Dec	ARIES GHA
00	182 30.5	S22 10.4	72 34.8
02	212 30.0	22 11.1	102 39.8
04	242 29.5	22 11.8	132 44.7
06	272 29.0	22 12.5	162 49.6
08	302 28.5	22 13.2	192 54.5
10	332 28.0	22 13.8	222 59.5
12	2 27.5	22 14.5	253 04.4
14	32 27.0	22 15.2	283 09.3
16	62 26.5	22 15.8	313 14.3
18	92 26.0	22 16.5	343 19.2
20	122 25.4	22 17.2	13 24.1
22	152 24.9	S22 17.8	43 29.0

Monday, December 5

Time	SUN GHA	Dec	ARIES GHA
00	182 24.4	S22 18.5	73 34.0
02	212 23.9	22 19.1	103 38.9
04	242 23.4	22 19.8	133 43.8
06	272 22.9	22 20.4	163 48.8
08	302 22.4	22 21.0	193 53.7
10	332 21.8	22 21.7	223 58.6
12	2 21.3	22 22.3	254 03.5
14	32 20.8	22 23.0	284 08.5
16	62 20.3	22 23.6	314 13.4
18	92 19.8	22 24.2	344 18.3
20	122 19.3	22 24.8	14 23.3
22	152 18.7	S22 25.4	44 28.2

Tuesday, December 6

Time	SUN GHA	Dec	ARIES GHA
00	182 18.2	S22 26.1	74 33.1
02	212 17.7	22 26.7	104 38.0
04	242 17.2	22 27.3	134 43.0
06	272 16.6	22 27.9	164 47.9
08	302 16.1	22 28.5	194 52.8
10	332 15.6	22 29.1	224 57.8
12	2 15.0	22 29.7	255 02.7
14	32 14.5	22 30.3	285 07.6
16	62 14.0	22 30.9	315 12.5
18	92 13.5	22 31.5	345 17.5
20	122 12.9	22 32.1	15 22.4
22	152 12.4	S22 32.7	45 27.3

Wednesday, December 7

Time	SUN GHA	Dec	ARIES GHA
00	182 11.9	S22 33.2	75 32.3
02	212 11.3	22 33.8	105 37.2
04	242 10.8	22 34.4	135 42.1
06	272 10.2	22 35.0	165 47.0
08	302 09.7	22 35.5	195 52.0
10	332 09.2	22 36.1	225 56.9
12	2 08.6	22 36.7	256 01.8
14	32 08.1	22 37.2	286 06.8
16	62 07.5	22 37.8	316 11.7
18	92 07.0	22 38.3	346 16.6
20	122 06.5	22 38.9	16 21.5
22	152 05.9	S22 39.4	46 26.5

Thursday, December 8

Time	SUN GHA	Dec	ARIES GHA
00	182 05.4	S22 40.0	76 31.4
02	212 04.8	22 40.5	106 36.3
04	242 04.3	22 41.0	136 41.2
06	272 03.7	22 41.6	166 46.2
08	302 03.2	22 42.1	196 51.1
10	332 02.6	22 42.6	226 56.0
12	2 02.1	22 43.2	257 01.0
14	32 01.5	22 43.7	287 05.9
16	62 01.0	22 44.2	317 10.8
18	92 00.4	22 44.7	347 15.7
20	121 59.9	22 45.2	17 20.7
22	151 59.3	S22 45.7	47 25.6

Friday, December 9

Time	SUN GHA	Dec	ARIES GHA
00	181 58.8	S22 46.2	77 30.5
02	211 58.2	22 46.7	107 35.5
04	241 57.7	22 47.3	137 40.4
06	271 57.1	22 47.7	167 45.3
08	301 56.6	22 48.2	197 50.2
10	331 56.0	22 48.7	227 55.2
12	1 55.4	22 49.2	258 00.1
14	31 54.9	22 49.7	288 05.0
16	61 54.3	22 50.2	318 10.0
18	91 53.8	22 50.7	348 14.9
20	121 53.2	22 51.1	18 19.8
22	151 52.6	S22 51.6	48 24.7

Saturday, December 10

Time	SUN GHA	Dec	ARIES GHA
00	181 52.1	S22 52.1	78 29.7
02	211 51.5	22 52.5	108 34.6
04	241 51.0	22 53.0	138 39.5
06	271 50.4	22 53.5	168 44.5
08	301 49.8	22 53.9	198 49.4
10	331 49.3	22 54.4	228 54.3
12	1 48.7	22 54.8	258 59.2
14	31 48.1	22 55.3	289 04.2
16	61 47.6	22 55.7	319 09.1
18	91 47.0	22 56.2	349 14.0
20	121 46.4	22 56.6	19 19.0
22	151 45.8	S22 57.0	49 23.9

Sunday, December 11

Time	SUN GHA	Dec	ARIES GHA
00	181 45.3	S22 57.5	79 28.8
02	211 44.7	22 57.9	109 33.7
04	241 44.1	22 58.3	139 38.7
06	271 43.6	22 58.7	169 43.6
08	301 43.0	22 59.2	199 48.5
10	331 42.4	22 59.6	229 53.4
12	1 41.8	23 00.0	259 58.4
14	31 41.3	23 00.4	290 03.3
16	61 40.7	23 00.8	320 08.2
18	91 40.1	23 01.2	350 13.2
20	121 39.5	23 01.6	20 18.1
22	151 38.9	S23 02.0	50 23.0

Monday, December 12

Time	SUN GHA	Dec	ARIES GHA
00	181 38.4	S23 02.4	80 27.9
02	211 37.8	23 02.8	110 32.9
04	241 37.2	23 03.2	140 37.8
06	271 36.6	23 03.6	170 42.7
08	301 36.0	23 03.9	200 47.7
10	331 35.5	23 04.3	230 52.6
12	1 34.9	23 04.7	260 57.5
14	31 34.3	23 05.1	291 02.4
16	61 33.7	23 05.4	321 07.4
18	91 33.1	23 05.8	351 12.3
20	121 32.6	23 06.2	21 17.2
22	151 32.0	S23 06.5	51 22.2

Tuesday, December 13

Time	SUN GHA	Dec	ARIES GHA
00	181 31.4	S23 06.9	81 27.1
02	211 30.8	23 07.2	111 32.0
04	241 30.2	23 07.6	141 36.9
06	271 29.6	23 07.9	171 41.9
08	301 29.0	23 08.3	201 46.8
10	331 28.4	23 08.6	231 51.7
12	1 27.9	23 08.9	261 56.7
14	31 27.3	23 09.3	292 01.6
16	61 26.7	23 09.6	322 06.5
18	91 26.1	23 09.9	352 11.4
20	121 25.5	23 10.3	22 16.4
22	151 24.9	S23 10.6	52 21.3

Wednesday, December 14

Time	SUN GHA	Dec	ARIES GHA
00	181 24.3	S23 10.9	82 26.2
02	211 23.7	23 11.2	112 31.2
04	241 23.1	23 11.5	142 36.1
06	271 22.5	23 11.8	172 41.0
08	301 21.9	23 12.1	202 45.9
10	331 21.3	23 12.4	232 50.9
12	1 20.7	23 12.7	262 55.8
14	31 20.2	23 13.0	293 00.7
16	61 19.6	23 13.3	323 05.7
18	91 19.0	23 13.6	353 10.6
20	121 18.4	23 13.9	23 15.5
22	151 17.8	S23 14.2	53 20.4

Thursday, December 15

Time	SUN GHA	Dec	ARIES GHA
00	181 17.2	S23 14.4	83 25.4
02	211 16.6	23 14.7	113 30.3
04	241 16.0	23 15.0	143 35.2
06	271 15.4	23 15.3	173 40.1
08	301 14.8	23 15.5	203 45.1
10	331 14.2	23 15.8	233 50.0
12	1 13.6	23 16.1	263 54.9
14	31 13.0	23 16.3	293 59.9
16	61 12.4	23 16.6	324 04.8
18	91 11.8	23 16.8	354 09.7
20	121 11.2	23 17.1	24 14.6
22	151 10.6	S23 17.3	54 19.6

DECEMBER 1994 — SUN & ARIES — GMT

Friday, December 16

Time	SUN GHA	Dec	ARIES GHA
00	181 10.0	S23 17.5	84 24.5
02	211 09.4	23 17.8	114 29.4
04	241 08.8	23 18.0	144 34.4
06	271 08.2	23 18.2	174 39.3
08	301 07.5	23 18.5	204 44.2
10	331 06.9	23 18.7	234 49.1
12	1 06.3	23 18.9	264 54.1
14	31 05.7	23 19.1	294 59.0
16	61 05.1	23 19.3	325 03.9
18	91 04.5	23 19.6	355 08.9
20	121 03.9	23 19.8	25 13.8
22	151 03.3	S23 20.0	55 18.7

Saturday, December 17

Time	SUN GHA	Dec	ARIES GHA
00	181 02.7	S23 20.2	85 23.6
02	211 02.1	23 20.4	115 28.6
04	241 01.5	23 20.6	145 33.5
06	271 00.9	23 20.7	175 38.4
08	301 00.3	23 20.9	205 43.4
10	330 59.7	23 21.1	235 48.3
12	0 59.0	23 21.3	265 53.2
14	30 58.4	23 21.5	295 58.1
16	60 57.8	23 21.7	326 03.1
18	90 57.2	23 21.8	356 08.0
20	120 56.6	23 22.0	26 12.9
22	150 56.0	S23 22.2	56 17.9

Sunday, December 18

Time	SUN GHA	Dec	ARIES GHA
00	180 55.4	S23 22.3	86 22.8
02	210 54.8	23 22.5	116 27.7
04	240 54.2	23 22.6	146 32.6
06	270 53.5	23 22.8	176 37.6
08	300 52.9	23 22.9	206 42.5
10	330 52.3	23 23.1	236 47.4
12	0 51.7	23 23.2	266 52.4
14	30 51.1	23 23.4	296 57.3
16	60 50.5	23 23.5	327 02.2
18	90 49.9	23 23.6	357 07.1
20	120 49.3	23 23.8	27 12.1
22	150 48.6	S23 23.9	57 17.0

Monday, December 19

Time	SUN GHA	Dec	ARIES GHA
00	180 48.0	S23 24.0	87 21.9
02	210 47.4	23 24.1	117 26.8
04	240 46.8	23 24.3	147 31.8
06	270 46.2	23 24.4	177 36.7
08	300 45.6	23 24.5	207 41.6
10	330 45.0	23 24.6	237 46.6
12	0 44.3	23 24.7	267 51.5
14	30 43.7	23 24.8	297 56.4
16	60 43.1	23 24.9	328 01.3
18	90 42.5	23 25.0	358 06.3
20	120 41.9	23 25.1	28 11.2
22	150 41.3	S23 25.2	58 16.1

Tuesday, December 20

Time	SUN GHA	Dec	ARIES GHA
00	180 40.6	S23 25.2	88 21.1
02	210 40.0	23 25.3	118 26.0
04	240 39.4	23 25.4	148 30.9
06	270 38.8	23 25.5	178 35.8
08	300 38.2	23 25.5	208 40.8
10	330 37.5	23 25.6	238 45.7
12	0 36.9	23 25.7	268 50.6
14	30 36.3	23 25.7	298 55.6
16	60 35.7	23 25.8	329 00.5
18	90 35.1	23 25.8	359 05.4
20	120 34.5	23 25.9	29 10.3
22	150 33.8	S23 25.9	59 15.3

Wednesday, December 21

Time	SUN GHA	Dec	ARIES GHA
00	180 33.2	S23 26.0	89 20.2
02	210 32.6	23 26.0	119 25.1
04	240 32.0	23 26.1	149 30.1
06	270 31.4	23 26.1	179 35.0
08	300 30.7	23 26.1	209 39.9
10	330 30.1	23 26.2	239 44.8
12	0 29.5	23 26.2	269 49.8
14	30 28.9	23 26.2	299 54.7
16	60 28.3	23 26.2	329 59.6
18	90 27.6	23 26.2	0 04.6
20	120 27.0	23 26.3	30 09.5
22	150 26.4	S23 26.3	60 14.4

Thursday, December 22

Time	SUN GHA	Dec	ARIES GHA
00	180 25.8	S23 26.3	90 19.3
02	210 25.2	23 26.3	120 24.3
04	240 24.5	23 26.3	150 29.2
06	270 23.9	23 26.3	180 34.1
08	300 23.3	23 26.3	210 39.0
10	330 22.7	23 26.2	240 44.0
12	0 22.1	23 26.2	270 48.9
14	30 21.4	23 26.2	300 53.8
16	60 20.8	23 26.2	330 58.8
18	90 20.2	23 26.2	1 03.7
20	120 19.6	23 26.1	31 08.6
22	150 18.9	S23 26.1	61 13.5

Friday, December 23

Time	SUN GHA	Dec	ARIES GHA
00	180 18.3	S23 26.1	91 18.5
02	210 17.7	23 26.0	121 23.4
04	240 17.1	23 26.0	151 28.3
06	270 16.5	23 26.0	181 33.3
08	300 15.8	23 25.9	211 38.2
10	330 15.2	23 25.9	241 43.1
12	0 14.6	23 25.8	271 48.0
14	30 14.0	23 25.8	301 53.0
16	60 13.4	23 25.7	331 57.9
18	90 12.7	23 25.6	2 02.8
20	120 12.1	23 25.6	32 07.8
22	150 11.5	S23 25.5	62 12.7

Saturday, December 24

Time	SUN GHA	Dec	ARIES GHA
00	180 10.9	S23 25.4	92 17.6
02	210 10.2	23 25.3	122 22.5
04	240 09.6	23 25.3	152 27.5
06	270 09.0	23 25.2	182 32.4
08	300 08.4	23 25.1	212 37.3
10	330 07.8	23 25.0	242 42.3
12	0 07.1	23 24.9	272 47.2
14	30 06.5	23 24.8	302 52.1
16	60 05.9	23 24.7	332 57.0
18	90 05.3	23 24.6	3 02.0
20	120 04.7	23 24.5	33 06.9
22	150 04.0	S23 24.4	63 11.8

Sunday, December 25

Time	SUN GHA	Dec	ARIES GHA
00	180 03.4	S23 24.3	93 16.8
02	210 02.8	23 24.2	123 21.7
04	240 02.2	23 24.1	153 26.6
06	270 01.6	23 23.9	183 31.5
08	300 00.9	23 23.8	213 36.5
10	330 00.3	23 23.7	243 41.4
12	359 59.7	23 23.5	273 46.3
14	29 59.1	23 23.4	303 51.3
16	59 58.5	23 23.3	333 56.2
18	89 57.8	23 23.1	4 01.1
20	119 57.2	23 23.0	34 06.0
22	149 56.6	S23 22.8	64 11.0

Monday, December 26

Time	SUN GHA	Dec	ARIES GHA
00	179 56.0	S23 22.7	94 15.9
02	209 55.4	23 22.5	124 20.8
04	239 54.7	23 22.4	154 25.7
06	269 54.1	23 22.2	184 30.7
08	299 53.5	23 22.0	214 35.6
10	329 52.9	23 21.9	244 40.5
12	359 52.3	23 21.7	274 45.5
14	29 51.8	23 21.5	304 50.4
16	59 51.0	23 21.4	334 55.3
18	89 50.4	23 21.2	5 00.2
20	119 49.8	23 21.0	35 05.2
22	149 49.2	S23 20.8	65 10.1

Tuesday, December 27

Time	SUN GHA	Dec	ARIES GHA
00	179 48.5	S23 20.6	95 15.0
02	209 47.9	23 20.4	125 20.0
04	239 47.3	23 20.2	155 24.9
06	269 46.7	23 20.0	185 29.8
08	299 46.1	23 19.8	215 34.7
10	329 45.5	23 19.6	245 39.7
12	359 44.8	23 19.4	275 44.6
14	29 44.2	23 19.2	305 49.5
16	59 43.6	23 19.0	335 54.5
18	89 43.0	23 18.8	5 59.4
20	119 42.4	23 18.5	36 04.3
22	149 41.8	S23 18.3	66 09.2

Wednesday, December 28

Time	SUN GHA	Dec	ARIES GHA
00	179 41.2	S23 18.1	96 14.2
02	209 40.5	23 17.8	126 19.1
04	239 39.9	23 17.6	156 24.0
06	269 39.3	23 17.4	186 29.0
08	299 38.7	23 17.1	216 33.9
10	329 38.1	23 16.9	246 38.8
12	359 37.5	23 16.6	276 43.7
14	29 36.9	23 16.4	306 48.7
16	59 36.2	23 16.1	336 53.6
18	89 35.6	23 15.9	6 58.5
20	119 35.0	23 15.6	37 03.5
22	149 34.4	S23 15.3	67 08.4

Thursday, December 29

Time	SUN GHA	Dec	ARIES GHA
00	179 33.8	S23 15.1	97 13.3
02	209 33.2	23 14.8	127 18.2
04	239 32.6	23 14.5	157 23.2
06	269 32.0	23 14.2	187 28.1
08	299 31.4	23 14.0	217 33.0
10	329 30.7	23 13.7	247 38.0
12	359 30.1	23 13.4	277 42.9
14	29 29.5	23 13.1	307 47.8
16	59 28.9	23 12.8	337 52.7
18	89 28.3	23 12.5	7 57.7
20	119 27.7	23 12.2	38 02.6
22	149 27.1	S23 11.9	68 07.5

Friday, December 30

Time	SUN GHA	Dec	ARIES GHA
00	179 26.5	S23 11.6	98 12.4
02	209 25.9	23 11.3	128 17.4
04	239 25.3	23 11.0	158 22.3
06	269 24.7	23 10.6	188 27.2
08	299 24.1	23 10.3	218 32.2
10	329 23.5	23 10.0	248 37.1
12	359 22.8	23 09.7	278 42.0
14	29 22.2	23 09.3	308 46.9
16	59 21.6	23 09.0	338 51.9
18	89 21.0	23 08.7	8 56.8
20	119 20.4	23 08.3	39 01.7
22	149 19.8	S23 08.0	69 06.7

Saturday, December 31

Time	SUN GHA	Dec	ARIES GHA
00	179 19.2	S23 07.6	99 11.6
02	209 18.6	23 07.3	129 16.5
04	239 18.0	23 06.9	159 21.4
06	269 17.4	S23 06.6	189 26.4
08	299 16.8	S23 06.2	219 31.3
10	329 16.2	23 05.9	249 36.2
12	359 15.6	23 05.5	279 41.2
14	29 15.0	S23 05.1	309 46.1
16	59 14.4	S23 04.8	339 51.0
18	89 13.8	23 04.4	9 55.9
20	119 13.2	23 04.0	40 00.9
22	149 12.6	S23 03.6	70 05.8

Chapter 6

DECEMBER 1994 — PLANETS — 0h GMT

VENUS / JUPITER

Mer Pass h m	GHA ° '	Mean Var/hr 15°+	Dec ° '	Mean Var/hr '		Day	JUPITER GHA ° '	Mean Var/hr 15°+	Dec ° '	Mean Var/hr '	Mer Pass h m
09 27	217 58.6	1.6	S11 43.5	0.1	1	Thu	193 32.6	1.9	S18 59.7	0.1	11 04
09 25	218 37.3	1.5	S11 40.0	0.1	2	Fri	194 18.1	1.9	S19 02.7	0.1	11 01
09 22	219 14.3	1.5	S11 37.5	0.1	3	Sat	195 03.7	1.9	S19 05.6	0.1	10 58
09 20	219 49.6	1.4	S11 36.0	0.0	4	SUN	195 49.2	1.9	S19 08.5	0.1	10 55
09 18	220 23.2	1.3	S11 35.4	0.0	5	Mon	196 34.8	1.9	S19 11.4	0.1	10 52
09 16	220 55.2	1.3	S11 35.8	0.1	6	Tue	197 20.4	1.9	S19 14.3	0.1	10 49
09 14	221 25.6	1.2	S11 37.0	0.1	7	Wed	198 06.0	1.9	S19 17.2	0.1	10 46
09 12	221 54.6	1.2	S11 39.1	0.1	8	Thu	198 51.6	1.9	S19 20.0	0.1	10 43
09 10	222 22.2	1.1	S11 42.0	0.1	9	Fri	199 37.2	1.9	S19 22.8	0.1	10 40
09 08	222 48.3	1.0	S11 45.6	0.2	10	Sat	200 22.9	1.9	S19 25.5	0.1	10 37
09 07	223 13.1	1.0	S11 50.0	0.2	11	SUN	201 08.5	1.9	S19 28.3	0.1	10 34
09 05	223 36.6	0.9	S11 55.1	0.2	12	Mon	201 54.2	1.9	S19 31.0	0.1	10 31
09 04	223 58.8	0.9	S12 00.9	0.3	13	Tue	202 40.0	1.9	S19 33.7	0.1	10 28
09 02	224 19.9	0.8	S12 07.3	0.3	14	Wed	203 25.7	1.9	S19 36.4	0.1	10 25
09 01	224 39.7	0.8	S12 14.3	0.3	15	Thu	204 11.5	1.9	S19 39.0	0.1	10 22
09 00	224 58.4	0.7	S12 21.8	0.3	16	Fri	204 57.3	1.9	S19 41.7	0.1	10 19
08 59	225 15.9	0.7	S12 29.9	0.4	17	Sat	205 43.1	1.9	S19 44.3	0.1	10 16
08 57	225 32.4	0.6	S12 38.5	0.4	18	SUN	206 29.0	1.9	S19 46.8	0.1	10 13
08 56	225 47.9	0.6	S12 47.6	0.4	19	Mon	207 14.9	1.9	S19 49.4	0.1	10 10
08 55	226 02.3	0.6	S12 57.1	0.4	20	Tue	208 00.8	1.9	S19 51.9	0.1	10 07
08 55	226 15.8	0.5	S13 06.9	0.4	21	Wed	208 46.8	1.9	S19 54.4	0.1	10 04
08 54	226 28.3	0.5	S13 17.2	0.4	22	Thu	209 32.8	1.9	S19 56.9	0.1	10 01
08 53	226 39.8	0.4	S13 27.8	0.5	23	Fri	210 18.8	1.9	S19 59.3	0.1	09 57
08 52	226 50.5	0.4	S13 38.7	0.5	24	Sat	211 04.9	1.9	S20 01.7	0.1	09 54
08 52	227 00.3	0.4	S13 49.9	0.5	25	SUN	211 51.0	1.9	S20 04.1	0.1	09 51
08 51	227 09.2	0.3	S14 01.4	0.5	26	Mon	212 37.2	1.9	S20 06.5	0.1	09 48
08 51	227 17.3	0.3	S14 13.1	0.5	27	Tue	213 23.4	1.9	S20 08.8	0.1	09 45
08 50	227 24.6	0.3	S14 25.0	0.5	28	Wed	214 09.7	1.9	S20 11.1	0.1	09 42
08 50	227 31.1	0.2	S14 37.0	0.5	29	Thu	214 56.0	1.9	S20 13.4	0.1	09 39
08 49	227 36.9	0.2	S14 49.2	0.5	30	Fri	215 42.4	1.9	S20 15.6	0.1	09 36
08 49	227 41.9	0.2	S15 01.5	0.5	31	Sat	216 28.8	1.9	S20 17.9	0.1	09 33

VENUS, Av Mag –4.6
SHA December
5 147; 10 144; 15 141; 20 138; 25 134; 30 129.

JUPITER, Av Mag –1.7
SHA December
5 123; 10 122; 15 121; 20 120; 25 119; 30 117.

MARS / SATURN

Mer Pass h m	GHA ° '	Mean Var/hr 15°+	Dec ° '	Mean Var/hr '		Day	SATURN GHA ° '	Mean Var/hr 15°+	Dec ° '	Mean Var/hr '	Mer Pass h m
05 20	279 47.8	1.7	N14 49.6	0.2	1	Thu	91 03.8	2.4	S11 00.4	0.0	17 53
05 18	280 27.6	1.7	N14 44.7	0.2	2	Fri	92 00.8	2.4	S10 59.4	0.0	17 49
05 15	281 07.7	1.7	N14 39.9	0.2	3	Sat	92 57.8	2.4	S10 58.4	0.0	17 45
05 12	281 48.3	1.7	N14 35.3	0.2	4	SUN	93 54.6	2.4	S10 57.3	0.0	17 42
05 09	282 29.4	1.7	N14 30.8	0.2	5	Mon	94 51.3	2.4	S10 56.2	0.0	17 38
05 07	283 10.9	1.7	N14 26.5	0.2	6	Tue	95 48.0	2.4	S10 55.1	0.0	17 34
05 04	283 52.8	1.8	N14 22.3	0.2	7	Wed	96 44.5	2.4	S10 53.9	0.1	17 30
05 01	284 35.2	1.8	N14 18.3	0.2	8	Thu	97 41.0	2.3	S10 52.7	0.1	17 27
04 58	285 18.1	1.8	N14 14.5	0.1	9	Fri	98 37.4	2.3	S10 51.5	0.1	17 23
04 55	286 01.5	1.8	N14 10.9	0.1	10	Sat	99 33.6	2.3	S10 50.3	0.1	17 19
04 52	286 45.3	1.8	N14 07.4	0.1	11	SUN	100 29.8	2.3	S10 49.0	0.1	17 15
04 49	287 29.7	1.9	N14 04.2	0.1	12	Mon	101 25.9	2.3	S10 47.6	0.1	17 12
04 46	288 14.6	1.9	N14 01.1	0.1	13	Tue	102 22.0	2.3	S10 46.3	0.1	17 08
04 43	289 00.0	1.9	N13 58.2	0.1	14	Wed	103 17.9	2.3	S10 44.9	0.1	17 04
04 40	289 45.9	1.9	N13 55.6	0.1	15	Thu	104 13.7	2.3	S10 43.4	0.1	17 00
04 37	290 32.3	2.0	N13 53.1	0.1	16	Fri	105 09.5	2.3	S10 42.0	0.1	16 57
04 34	291 19.3	2.0	N13 50.8	0.1	17	Sat	106 05.2	2.3	S10 40.5	0.1	16 53
04 31	292 06.9	2.0	N13 48.8	0.1	18	SUN	107 00.8	2.3	S10 38.9	0.1	16 49
04 28	292 55.0	2.0	N13 47.0	0.1	19	Mon	107 56.3	2.3	S10 37.4	0.1	16 46
04 24	293 43.7	2.1	N13 45.4	0.1	20	Tue	108 51.7	2.3	S10 35.8	0.1	16 42
04 21	294 33.0	2.1	N13 44.0	0.0	21	Wed	109 47.0	2.3	S10 34.1	0.1	16 38
04 18	295 22.9	2.1	N13 42.9	0.0	22	Thu	110 42.3	2.3	S10 32.5	0.1	16 35
04 15	296 13.4	2.1	N13 42.0	0.0	23	Fri	111 37.5	2.3	S10 30.8	0.1	16 31
04 11	297 04.6	2.2	N13 41.4	0.0	24	Sat	112 32.6	2.3	S10 29.1	0.1	16 27
04 08	297 56.3	2.2	N13 41.0	0.0	25	SUN	113 27.6	2.3	S10 27.3	0.1	16 24
04 04	298 48.7	2.2	N13 40.9	0.0	26	Mon	114 22.6	2.3	S10 25.6	0.1	16 20
04 01	299 41.8	2.2	N13 41.0	0.0	27	Tue	115 17.5	2.3	S10 23.7	0.1	16 16
03 57	300 35.5	2.3	N13 41.4	0.0	28	Wed	116 12.3	2.3	S10 21.9	0.1	16 13
03 53	301 29.9	2.3	N13 42.0	0.0	29	Thu	117 07.0	2.3	S10 20.1	0.1	16 09
03 50	302 25.1	2.3	N13 42.9	0.0	30	Fri	118 01.7	2.3	S10 18.2	0.1	16 05
03 46	303 20.9	2.4	N13 44.1	0.1	31	Sat	118 56.2	2.3	S10 16.2	0.1	16 02

MARS, Av Mag 0.0
SHA December
5 209; 10 208; 15 206; 20 205; 25 205; 30 204.

SATURN, Av Mag.+0.9
SHA December
5 21; 10 21; 15 21; 20 21; 25 20; 30 20.

DECEMBER 1994   MOON

Day	GMT hr	GHA ° ′	Mean Var/hr 14°+	Dec ° ′	Mean Var/hr ′	Day	GMT hr	GHA ° ′	Mean Var/hr 14°+	Dec ° ′	Mean Var/hr ′
1 Thu	0	211 50.2	24.2	S 15 18.0	8.2	17 Sat	0	13 40.0	30.8	N 19 53.0	1.0
	6	298 15.5	23.8	S 16 07.3	7.4		6	100 44.5	30.7	N 19 59.5	0.5
	12	24 39.1	23.4	S 16 52.6	6.7		12	187 48.6	30.6	N 20 02.7	0.1
	18	110 58.2	23.0	S 17 33.6	6.1		18	274 52.2	30.6	N 20 02.4	0.7
2 Fri	0	197 16.1	22.6	S 18 10.1	5.2	18 Sun	0	1 55.4	30.5	N 19 58.7	1.2
	6	283 32.0	22.4	S 18 41.8	4.4		6	88 58.5	30.5	N 19 51.6	1.8
	12	9 46.4	22.2	S 19 08.4	3.5		12	176 01.5	30.5	N 19 41.1	2.4
	18	95 59.6	22.1	S 19 29.8	2.6		18	263 04.6	30.5	N 19 27.2	2.9
3 Sat	0	182 12.0	22.0	S 19 45.8	1.7	19 Mon	0	350 07.7	30.6	N 19 09.9	3.5
	6	268 24.0	22.0	S 19 56.4	0.7		6	77 11.1	30.7	N 18 49.2	4.0
	12	354 36.1	22.1	S 20 01.5	0.1		12	164 14.9	30.7	N 18 25.2	4.5
	18	80 48.8	22.3	S 20 01.1	1.1		18	251 19.0	30.7	N 17 58.0	5.2
4 Sun	0	167 02.6	22.6	S 19 55.3	1.9	20 Tue	0	338 23.6	30.9	N 17 27.7	5.6
	6	253 17.7	22.8	S 19 44.1	2.8		6	65 28.8	31.0	N 16 54.2	6.1
	12	339 34.7	23.3	S 19 27.7	3.6		12	152 34.5	31.1	N 16 17.8	6.6
	18	65 53.9	23.6	S 19 06.3	4.4		18	239 40.9	31.2	N 15 38.4	7.0
5 Mon	0	152 15.7	24.1	S 18 40.1	5.2	21 Wed	0	326 47.9	31.3	N 14 56.3	7.5
	6	238 40.2	24.6	S 18 09.4	5.9		6	53 55.5	31.4	N 14 11.5	7.9
	12	325 07.8	25.1	S 17 34.4	6.5		12	141 03.7	31.4	N 13 24.1	8.4
	18	51 38.6	25.7	S 16 55.5	7.2		18	228 12.4	31.5	N 12 34.2	8.7
6 Tue	0	138 12.7	26.3	S 16 12.8	7.7	22 Thu	0	315 21.7	31.6	N 11 42.1	9.1
	6	224 50.2	26.9	S 15 26.8	8.2		6	42 31.4	31.6	N 10 47.7	9.5
	12	311 31.2	27.5	S 14 37.7	8.7		12	129 41.4	31.7	N 9 51.3	9.7
	18	38 15.5	28.0	S 13 45.9	9.1		18	216 51.8	31.8	N 8 53.0	10.0
7 Wed	0	125 03.3	28.5	S 12 51.6	9.5	23 Fri	0	304 02.3	31.7	N 7 52.9	10.3
	6	211 54.4	29.0	S 11 55.1	9.7		6	31 12.8	31.7	N 6 51.3	10.5
	12	298 48.7	29.6	S 10 56.7	10.0		12	118 23.3	31.7	N 5 48.1	10.7
	18	25 46.1	30.1	S 9 56.7	10.3		18	205 33.6	31.6	N 4 43.6	11.0
8 Thu	0	112 46.3	30.6	S 8 55.3	10.4	24 Sat	0	292 43.4	31.5	N 3 38.0	11.1
	6	199 49.4	31.0	S 7 52.9	10.6		6	19 52.8	31.4	N 2 31.5	11.3
	12	286 55.0	31.4	S 6 49.5	10.7		12	107 01.4	31.3	N 1 24.1	11.3
	18	14 03.0	31.7	S 5 45.4	10.8		18	194 09.2	31.1	N 0 16.1	11.4
9 Fri	0	101 13.3	32.1	S 4 40.9	10.8	25 Sun	0	281 15.9	30.9	S 0 52.4	11.4
	6	188 25.5	32.4	S 3 36.1	10.8		6	8 21.4	30.6	S 2 01.1	11.5
	12	275 39.6	32.6	S 2 31.1	10.8		12	95 25.5	30.4	S 3 09.8	11.4
	18	2 55.2	32.9	S 1 26.3	10.8		18	182 28.0	30.1	S 4 18.3	11.4
10 Sat	0	90 12.3	33.1	S 0 21.6	10.7	26 Mon	0	269 28.7	29.8	S 5 26.5	11.2
	6	177 30.6	33.2	N 0 42.7	10.6		6	356 27.5	29.4	S 6 34.1	11.1
	12	264 49.9	33.4	N 1 46.4	10.5		12	83 24.1	29.0	S 7 40.8	10.9
	18	352 10.1	33.4	N 2 49.5	10.4		18	170 18.5	28.7	S 8 46.4	10.7
11 Sun	0	79 30.9	33.5	N 3 51.9	10.2	27 Tue	0	257 10.4	28.1	S 9 50.6	10.4
	6	166 52.3	33.6	N 4 53.3	10.1		6	343 59.7	27.8	S 10 53.1	10.1
	12	254 13.9	33.6	N 5 53.7	9.9		12	70 46.3	27.2	S 11 53.8	9.7
	18	341 35.6	33.7	N 6 52.9	9.6		18	157 30.1	26.7	S 12 52.2	9.3
12 Mon	0	68 57.4	33.6	N 7 50.9	9.4	28 Wed	0	244 11.1	26.3	S 13 48.1	8.8
	6	156 19.0	33.5	N 8 47.5	9.2		6	330 49.1	25.8	S 14 41.3	8.3
	12	243 40.3	33.5	N 9 42.6	8.9		12	57 24.3	25.4	S 15 31.3	7.7
	18	331 01.2	33.4	N 10 36.0	8.6		18	143 56.6	24.9	S 16 17.9	7.1
13 Tue	0	58 21.5	33.3	N 11 27.8	8.3	29 Thu	0	230 26.1	24.4	S 17 00.8	6.4
	6	145 41.1	33.1	N 12 17.7	8.0		6	316 53.0	24.1	S 17 39.7	5.7
	12	233 00.0	33.0	N 13 05.7	7.6		12	43 17.4	23.6	S 18 14.4	5.0
	18	320 18.1	32.9	N 13 51.6	7.3		18	129 39.6	23.3	S 18 44.5	4.2
14 Wed	0	47 35.2	32.7	N 14 35.3	6.9	30 Fri	0	215 59.7	23.1	S 19 09.9	3.3
	6	134 51.3	32.5	N 15 16.7	6.5		6	302 18.1	22.9	S 19 30.4	2.4
	12	222 06.4	32.3	N 15 55.8	6.1		12	28 35.2	22.7	S 19 45.8	1.7
	18	309 20.4	32.2	N 16 32.4	5.6		18	114 51.4	22.6	S 19 56.0	0.7
15 Thu	0	36 33.4	32.0	N 17 06.3	5.2	31 Sat	0	201 06.9	22.6	S 20 00.8	0.2
	6	123 45.2	31.8	N 17 37.6	4.7		6	287 22.3	22.6	S 20 00.4	1.0
	12	210 56.0	31.6	N 18 06.0	4.2		12	13 38.0	22.7	S 19 54.6	2.0
	18	298 05.7	31.5	N 18 31.6	3.7		18	99 54.3	23.0	S 19 43.5	2.8
16 Fri	0	25 14.3	31.3	N 18 54.2	3.2						
	6	112 22.0	31.1	N 19 13.7	2.7						
	12	199 28.8	31.0	N 19 30.0	2.1						
	18	286 34.8	30.8	N 19 43.1	1.6						

Chapter 6

POLARIS (POLE STAR) TABLE, 1994

LHA Aries	Q	LHA Aries	Q	LHA Aries	Q	LHA Aries	Q	LHA Aries	Q	LHA Aries	Q	LHA Aries	Q	LHA Aries	Q
358 01	−36	84 22	−30	120 36	− 4	154 27	+22	229 20	+44	283 03	+18	316 29	− 8	354 11	−34
0 03	−37	86 02	−29	121 51	− 3	155 53	+23	234 12	+43	284 25	+17	317 46	− 9	356 0	−35
2 11	−38	87 39	−28	123 07	− 2	157 21	+24	238 01	+42	285 47	+16	319 03	−10	358 01	−36
4 27	−39	89 15	−27	124 22	− 1	158 50	+25	241 16	+41	287 07	+15	320 20	−11	0 03	−37
6 52	−40	90 48	−26	125 38	0	160 20	+26	244 10	+40	288 27	+14	321 37	−12	2 11	−38
9 28	−41	92 19	−25	126 54	+ 1	161 52	+27	246 48	+39	289 47	+13	322 55	−13	4 27	−39
12 19	−42	93 49	−24	128 09	+ 2	163 26	+28	249 15	+38	291 05	+12	324 14	−14	6 52	−40
15 32	−43	95 17	−23	129 25	+ 3	165 02	+29	251 32	+37	292 24	+11	325 33	−15	9 28	−41
19 18	−44	96 44	−22	130 40	+ 4	166 40	+30	253 41	+36	293 41	+10	326 53	−16	12 19	−42
24 07	−45	98 10	−21	131 56	+ 5	168 21	+31	255 45	+35	294 59	+ 9	328 13	−17	15 32	−43
32 53	−46	99 35	−20	133 12	+ 6	170 04	+32	257 43	+34	296 16	+ 8	329 34	−18	19 18	−44
40 24	−45	100 58	−19	134 28	+ 7	171 50	+33	259 37	+33	297 33	+ 7	330 56	−19	24 07	−45
49 10	−44	102 21	−18	135 44	+ 8	173 40	+34	261 27	+32	298 49	+ 6	332 19	−20	32 53	−46
53 59	−43	103 43	−17	137 01	+ 9	175 34	+35	263 13	+31	300 05	+ 5	333 42	−21	40 24	−45
57 45	−42	105 04	−16	138 18	+10	177 32	+36	264 56	+30	301 21	+ 4	335 07	−22	49 10	−44
60 58	−41	106 24	−15	139 36	+11	179 36	+37	266 37	+29	302 37	+ 3	336 33	−23	53 59	−43
63 49	−40	107 44	−14	140 53	+12	181 45	+38	268 15	+28	303 52	+ 2	338 00	−24	57 45	−42
66 25	−39	109 03	−13	142 12	+13	184 02	+39	269 51	+27	305 08	+ 1	339 28	−25	60 58	−41
68 50	−38	110 22	−12	143 30	+14	186 29	+40	271 25	+26	306 23	0	340 58	−26	63 49	−40
71 06	−37	111 40	−11	144 50	+15	189 07	+41	272 57	+25	307 39	− 1	342 29	−27	66 25	−39
73 14	−36	112 57	−10	146 10	+16	192 01	+42	274 27	+24	308 55	− 2	344 02	−28	68 50	−38
75 16	−35	114 14	− 9	147 30	+17	195 16	+43	275 56	+23	310 10	− 3	345 38	−29	71 06	−37
77 13	−34	115 31	− 8	148 52	+18	199 05	+44	277 24	+22	311 26	− 4	347 15	−30	73 14	−36
76 06	−33	116 48	− 7	150 14	+19	203 57	+45	278 50	+21	312 41	− 5	348 55	−31	75 16	−35
80 55	−32	118 04	− 6	151 37	+20	212 50	+46	280 16	+20	313 57	− 6	350 37	−32	77 13	−34
82 40	−31	119 20	− 5	153 01	+21	220 27	+45	281 40	+19	315 13	− 7	352 22	−33	79 06	−33
84 22		120 36		154 27		229 20		283 03		316 29		354 11		80 55	

NOTES. The table above can be used to find Latitude directly from an observation of Polaris (Mag 2.1, SHA 323°39′, Dec N 89°14.2′). Find LHA of Aries from the monthly pages, and apply correction Q to the True Altitude (corrected Sextant Altitude). In critical cases, use the higher value.

AZIMUTH OF POLARIS, 1994

LHA Aries	0°	30°	50°	55°	60°	65°	70°	LHA Aries	0°	30°	50°	55°	60°	65°	70°
0	0.5	0.5	0.7	0.8	0.9	1.1	1.4	180	359.5	359.5	359.3	359.2	359.1	359.0	358.7
10	0.3	0.4	0.5	0.6	0.7	0.8	1.0	190	359.7	359.6	359.5	359.4	359.3	359.2	359.0
20	0.2	0.3	0.3	0.4	0.4	0.5	0.7	200	359.8	359.8	359.7	359.6	359.6	359.5	359.4
30	0.1	0.1	0.1	0.2	0.2	0.2	0.3	210	359.9	359.9	359.9	359.8	359.8	359.8	359.8
40	0.0	359.9	359.9	359.9	359.9	359.9	359.9	220	0.0	0.1	0.1	0.1	0.1	0.1	0.1
50	359.8	359.8	359.7	359.7	359.6	359.6	359.5	230	0.2	0.2	0.3	0.3	0.4	0.4	0.5
60	359.7	359.6	359.5	359.5	359.4	359.3	359.1	240	0.3	0.3	0.5	0.5	0.6	0.7	0.9
70	359.6	359.5	359.3	359.3	359.1	359.0	359.7	250	0.4	0.5	0.6	0.7	0.8	1.0	1.2
80	359.5	359.4	359.2	359.1	358.9	358.7	358.4	260	0.5	0.6	0.8	0.9	1.0	1.2	1.5
90	359.4	359.3	359.0	358.9	358.8	358.5	358.2	270	0.6	0.7	0.9	1.1	1.2	1.4	1.7
100	359.3	359.2	358.9	358.8	358.6	358.4	358.0	280	0.7	0.8	1.0	1.2	1.3	1.6	2.0
110	359.3	359.2	358.9	358.7	358.5	358.3	357.8	290	0.7	0.8	1.1	1.3	1.4	1.7	2.1
120	359.2	359.1	358.8	358.7	358.5	358.2	357.8	300	0.8	0.9	1.2	1.3	1.5	1.8	2.2
130	359.2	359.1	358.8	358.7	358.5	358.2	357.8	310	0.8	0.9	1.2	1.3	1.5	1.8	2.2
140	359.2	359.1	358.9	358.7	358.5	358.3	357.9	320	0.7	0.9	1.2	1.3	1.5	1.8	2.2
150	359.3	359.2	358.9	358.8	358.6	358.4	358.0	330	0.7	0.8	1.1	1.2	1.4	1.7	2.1
160	359.4	359.3	359.0	358.9	358.7	358.5	358.2	340	0.6	0.7	1.0	1.1	1.3	1.5	1.9
170	359.4	359.4	359.1	359.0	358.9	358.7	358.4	350	0.6	0.6	0.9	1.0	1.1	1.3	1.7
180	359.5	359.5	359.3	359.2	359.1	359.0	358.7	360	0.5	0.5	0.7	0.8	0.9	1.1	1.4

When Cassiopeia is left (right), Polaris is west (east).

ARC INTO TIME CONVERSION TABLE

Arc °	Time h m	Arc °	Time h m	Arc °	Time h m	Arc °	Time h m	Arc °	Time h m	Arc °	Time h m	Arc '	Time m s	Arc "	Time s
0	0 0	60	4 0	120	8 0	180	12 0	240	16 0	300	20 0	0	0 0	0=0.0	0.00
1	0 4	61	4 4	121	8 4	181	12 4	241	16 4	301	20 4	1	0 4	1	0.07
2	0 8	62	4 8	122	8 8	182	12 8	242	16 8	302	20 8	2	0 8	2	0.13
3	0 12	63	4 12	123	8 12	183	12 12	243	16 12	303	20 12	3	0 12	3	0.20
4	0 16	64	4 16	124	8 16	184	12 16	244	16 16	304	20 16	4	0 16	4	0.27
5	0 20	65	4 20	125	8 20	185	12 20	245	16 20	305	20 20	5	0 20	5	0.33
6	0 24	66	4 24	126	8 24	186	12 24	246	16 24	306	20 24	6	0 24	6=0.1	0.40
7	0 28	67	4 28	127	8 28	187	12 28	247	16 28	307	20 28	7	0 28	7	0.47
8	0 32	68	4 32	128	8 32	188	12 32	248	16 32	308	20 32	8	0 32	8	0.53
9	0 36	69	4 36	129	8 36	189	12 36	249	16 36	309	20 36	9	0 36	9	0.60
10	0 40	70	4 40	130	8 40	190	12 40	250	16 40	310	20 40	10	0 40	10	0.67
11	0 44	71	4 44	131	8 44	191	12 44	251	16 44	311	20 44	11	0 44	11	0.73
12	0 48	72	4 48	132	8 48	192	12 48	252	16 48	312	20 48	12	0 48	12=0.2	0.80
13	0 52	73	4 52	133	8 52	193	12 52	253	16 52	313	20 52	13	0 52	13	0.87
14	0 56	74	4 56	134	8 56	194	12 56	254	16 56	314	20 56	14	0 56	14	0.93
15	1 0	75	5 0	135	9 0	195	13 0	255	17 0	315	21 0	15	1 0	15	1.00
16	1 4	76	5 4	136	9 4	196	13 4	256	17 4	316	21 4	16	1 4	16	1.07
17	1 8	77	5 8	137	9 8	197	13 8	257	17 8	317	21 8	17	1 8	17	1.13
18	1 12	78	5 12	138	9 12	198	13 12	258	17 12	318	21 12	18	1 12	18=0.3	1.20
19	1 16	79	5 16	139	9 16	199	13 16	259	17 16	319	21 16	19	1 16	19	1.27
20	1 20	80	5 20	140	9 20	200	13 20	260	17 20	320	21 20	20	1 20	20	1.33
21	1 24	81	5 24	141	9 24	201	13 24	261	17 24	321	21 24	21	1 24	21	1.40
22	1 28	82	5 28	142	9 28	202	13 28	262	17 28	322	21 28	22	1 28	22	1.47
23	1 32	83	5 32	143	9 32	203	13 32	263	17 32	323	21 32	23	1 32	23	1.53
24	1 36	84	5 36	144	9 36	204	13 36	264	17 36	324	21 36	24	1 36	24=0.4	1.60
25	1 40	85	5 40	145	9 40	205	13 40	265	17 40	325	21 40	25	1 40	25	1.67
26	1 44	86	5 44	146	9 44	206	13 44	266	17 44	326	21 44	26	1 44	26	1.73
27	1 48	87	5 48	147	9 48	207	13 48	267	17 48	327	21 48	27	1 48	27	1.80
28	1 52	88	5 52	148	9 52	208	13 52	268	17 52	328	21 52	28	1 52	28	1.87
29	1 56	89	5 56	149	9 56	209	13 56	269	17 56	329	21 56	29	1 56	29	1.93
30	2 0	90	6 0	150	10 0	210	14 0	270	18 0	330	22 0	30	2 0	30=0.5	2.00
31	2 4	91	6 4	151	10 4	211	14 4	271	18 4	331	22 4	31	2 4	31	2.07
32	2 8	92	6 8	152	10 8	212	14 8	272	18 8	332	22 8	32	2 8	32	2.13
33	2 12	93	6 12	153	10 12	213	14 12	273	18 12	333	22 12	33	2 12	33	2.20
34	2 16	94	6 16	154	10 16	214	14 16	274	18 16	334	22 16	34	2 16	34	2.27
35	2 20	95	6 20	155	10 20	215	14 20	275	18 20	335	22 20	35	2 20	35	2.33
36	2 24	96	6 24	156	10 24	216	14 24	276	18 24	336	22 24	36	2 24	36=0.6	2.40
37	2 28	97	6 28	157	10 28	217	14 28	277	18 28	337	22 28	37	2 28	37	2.47
38	2 32	98	6 32	158	10 32	218	14 32	278	18 32	338	22 32	38	2 32	38	2.53
39	2 36	99	6 36	159	10 36	219	14 36	279	18 36	339	22 36	39	2 36	39	2.60
40	2 40	100	6 40	160	10 40	220	14 40	280	18 40	340	22 40	40	2 40	40	2.67
41	2 44	101	6 44	161	10 44	221	14 44	281	18 44	341	22 44	41	2 44	41	2.73
42	2 48	102	6 48	162	10 48	222	14 48	282	18 48	342	22 48	42	2 48	42=0.7	2.80
43	2 52	103	6 52	163	10 52	223	14 52	283	18 52	343	22 52	43	2 52	43	2.87
44	2 56	104	6 56	164	10 56	224	14 56	284	18 56	344	22 56	44	2 56	44	2.93
45	3 0	105	7 0	165	11 0	225	15 0	285	19 0	345	23 0	45	3 0	45	3.00
46	3 4	106	7 4	166	11 4	226	15 4	286	19 4	346	23 4	46	3 4	46	3.07
47	3 8	107	7 8	167	11 8	227	15 8	287	19 8	347	23 8	47	3 8	47	3.13
48	3 12	108	7 12	168	11 12	228	15 12	288	19 12	348	23 12	48	3 12	48=0.8	3.20
49	3 16	109	7 16	169	11 16	229	15 16	289	19 16	349	23 16	49	3 16	49	3.27
50	3 20	110	7 20	170	11 20	230	15 20	290	19 20	350	23 20	50	3 20	50	3.33
51	3 24	111	7 24	171	11 24	231	15 24	291	19 24	351	23 24	51	3 24	51	3.40
52	3 28	112	7 28	172	11 28	232	15 28	292	19 28	352	23 28	52	3 28	52	3.47
53	3 32	113	7 32	173	11 32	233	15 32	293	19 32	353	23 32	53	3 32	53	3.53
54	3 36	114	7 36	174	11 36	234	15 36	294	19 36	354	23 36	54	3 36	54=0.9	3.60
55	3 40	115	7 40	175	11 40	235	15 40	295	19 40	355	23 40	55	3 40	55	3.67
56	3 44	116	7 44	176	11 44	236	15 44	296	19 44	356	23 44	56	3 44	56	3.73
57	3 48	117	7 48	177	11 48	237	15 48	297	19 48	357	23 48	57	3 48	57	3.80
58	3 52	118	7 52	178	11 52	238	15 52	298	19 52	358	23 52	58	3 52	58	3.87
59	3 56	119	7 56	179	11 56	239	15 56	299	19 56	359	23 56	59	3 56	59	3.93
60	4 00	120	8 00	180	12 00	240	16 00	300	20 00	360	24 00	60	4 00	60=1.0	4.00

Chapter 6

REFRACTION AND DIP TABLES

Mean Refraction Subtract				Dip of Sea Horizon Subtract			Sun's Parallax in Altitude Add	
App Alt ° ′	Refr ′	App Alt ° ′	Refr ′	HE ft	Dip ′	HE m	App Alt °	Parallax
0 00	34.9	10 00	5.3	2	1.5	0.6	0	0.15
10	32.8	10	5.2	3	1.8	0.9	5	0.15
20	30.9	20	5.1	4	2.0	1.2	10	0.14
30	29.1	30	5.0	5	2.2	1.5	15	0.14
40	27.4	40	5.0	6	2.4	1.8	20	0.14
50	25.8	50	4.9	7	2.6	2.1	25	0.13
1 00	24.4	11 00	4.8	8	2.8	2.4	30	0.12
10	23.1	10	4.7	9	2.9	2.7	40	0.11
20	21.9	20	4.7	10	3.1	3.0	50	0.10
30	20.9	30	4.6	11	3.3	3.4	60	0.08
40	19.9	40	4.5	12	3.4	3.7	70	0.06
50	19.0	50	4.5	13	3.5	4.0	80	0.03
2 00	18.1	12 00	4.4	14	3.7	4.3	90	0.00
10	17.4	10	4.4	15	3.8	4.6		
20	16.7	20	4.3	16	3.9	4.9		
30	16.0	30	4.2	17	4.0	5.2		
40	15.4	40	4.2	18	4.2	5.5		
50	14.8	50	4.1	19	4.3	5.8		
3 00	14.2	13 00	4.1	20	4.4	6.1		
10	13.7	10	4.0	22	4.6	6.7		
20	13.3	20	4.0	24	4.8	7.3		
30	12.8	30	3.9	26	5.0	7.9		
40	12.4	40	3.9	28	5.2	8.5		
50	12.0	50	3.8	30	5.4	9.1		
4 00	11.7	14 00	3.8	32	5.5	9.8		
10	11.3	20	3.7	34	5.7	10.4		
20	11.0	40	3.6	36	5.9	11.0		
30	10.7	15 00	3.5	38	6.0	11.6		
40	10.4	30	3.4	40	6.2	12.2		
50	10.1	16 00	3.3	42	6.4	12.8		
5 00	9.8	30	3.2	44	6.5	13.4		
10	9.5	17 00	3.1	46	6.7	14.0		
20	9.3	30	3.0	48	6.8	14.6		
30	9.0	18 00	2.9	50	6.9	15.2		
40	8.8	30	2.9	52	7.1	15.9		
50	8.6	19 00	2.8	54	7.2	16.5		
6 00	8.4	20 00	2.6	56	7.3	17.0		
10	8.2	21 00	2.5	58	7.5	17.7		
20	8.0	22 00	2.4	60	7.6	18.3		
30	7.8	23 00	2.3	65	7.9	19.8		
40	7.7	24 00	2.2	70	8.2	21.3		
50	7.5	26 00	2.0	80	8.8	24.4		
7 00	7.3	28 00	1.8	90	9.3	27.4		
10	7.2	30 00	1.7	100	9.8	30.5		
20	7.0	32 00	1.5	120	10.7	36.6		
30	6.9	34 00	1.4	140	11.6	42.7		
40	6.8	36 00	1.3	160	12.4	49.8		
50	6.6	38 00	1.2	180	13.2	54.9		
8 00	6.5	40 00	1.1	200	13.7	61.0		
10	6.4	43 00	1.0	220	14.5	67.1		
20	6.3	46 00	0.9	240	15.2	73.2		
30	6.1	50 00	0.8	260	15.8	79.3		
40	6.0	55 00	0.7	280	16.4	85.3		
50	5.9	60 00	0.6	300	17.0	91.4		
9 00	5.8	65 00	0.5	350	18.3	107		
10	5.7	70 00	0.4	400	19.6	122		
20	5.6	75 00	0.3	450	20.8	137		
30	5.5	80 00	0.2	500	21.9	152		
40	5.4	85 00	0.1					
50	5.4	90 00	0.0					

SUN ALTITUDE TOTAL CORRECTION TABLE (LOWER LIMB)

Always add

					Height of eye above sea level											
m	**0.9**	**1.8**	**2.4**	**3.0**	**3.7**	**4.3**	**4.9**	**5.5**	**6.0**	**7.6**	**9.0**	**12**	**15**	**18**	**21**	**24**
ft	**3**	**6**	**8**	**10**	**12**	**14**	**16**	**18**	**20**	**25**	**30**	**40**	**50**	**60**	**70**	**80**
°	'	'	'	'	'	'	'	'	'	'	'	'	'	'	'	'
9	8.6	8.0	7.6	7.0	6.9	6.6	6.4	6.2	5.9	5.4	4.0	4.1	3.4	2.7	2.1	1.5
10	9.1	8.5	8.1	7.9	7.5	7.2	7.0	6.7	6.6	6.0	5.5	4.7	3.5	3.3	2.7	2.1
11	9.6	9.0	8.6	8.3	8.0	7.7	7.4	7.2	7.0	6.4	6.0	5.2	4.4	3.7	3.1	2.5
12	10.0	9.4	9.0	8.7	8.4	8.1	7.8	7.6	7.4	6.8	6.4	5.6	4.8	4.1	3.5	2.9
13	10.3	9.7	9.3	9.0	8.7	8.4	8.2	7.9	7.7	7.2	6.7	5.9	5.2	4.5	3.9	3.3
14	10.6	10.0	9.6	9.3	9.0	8.7	8.5	8.2	8.0	7.5	7.0	6.2	5.5	4.8	4.2	3.6
15	10.9	10.2	9.9	9.5	9.2	9.0	8.7	8.5	8.2	7.7	7.2	6.4	5.7	5.0	4.4	3.8
16	11.1	10.5	10.1	9.7	9.5	9.2	8.9	8.7	8.5	7.9	7.5	6.7	5.9	5.2	4.6	4.1
17	11.3	10.7	10.3	10.0	9.7	9.4	9.1	8.9	8.7	8.2	7.7	6.9	6.1	5.5	4.9	4.3
18	11.5	10.8	10.5	10.1	9.9	9.6	9.3	9.1	8.9	8.3	7.9	7.0	6.3	5.6	5.0	4.5
19	11.6	11.0	10.6	10.3	10.0	9.7	9.5	9.2	9.0	8.5	8.0	7.2	6.5	5.8	5.2	4.6
20	11.8	11.2	10.8	10.4	10.2	9.9	9.6	9.4	9.2	8.6	8.2	7.4	6.6	5.9	5.3	4.8
21	11.9	11.3	10.9	10.6	10.3	10.0	9.8	9.5	9.3	8.8	8.3	7.5	6.8	6.1	5.5	4.9
22	12.0	11.4	11.0	10.7	10.4	10.1	9.9	9.7	9.4	8.9	8.4	7.6	6.9	6.2	5.6	5.0
23	12.1	11.5	11.1	10.8	10.5	10.2	10.0	9.8	9.5	9.0	8.5	7.7	7.0	6.3	5.7	5.1
24	12.2	11.6	11.2	10.9	10.6	10.3	10.1	9.9	9.6	9.1	8.6	7.8	7.1	6.4	5.8	5.2
25	12.3	11.7	11.3	11.0	10.7	10.4	10.2	10.0	9.7	9.2	8.7	7.9	7.2	6.5	5.9	5.3
26	12.4	11.8	11.4	11.1	10.8	10.5	10.3	10.1	9.8	9.3	8.8	8.0	7.3	6.6	6.0	5.4
27	12.5	11.9	11.5	11.2	10.9	10.6	10.4	10.1	9.9	9.4	8.9	8.1	7.4	6.7	6.1	5.5
28	12.6	12.0	11.6	11.3	11.0	10.7	10.4	10.2	10.0	9.5	9.0	8.2	7.4	6.8	6.2	5.6
30	12.7	12.1	11.7	11.4	11.1	10.8	10.6	10.4	10.1	9.6	9.1	8.3	7.6	6.9	6.3	5.7
32	12.9	12.2	11.9	11.5	11.2	11.0	10.7	10.5	10.2	9.7	9.3	8.4	7.7	7.0	6.4	5.8
34	13.0	12.3	12.0	11.6	11.3	11.1	10.8	10.6	10.3	9.8	9.4	8.5	7.8	7.1	6.5	5.9
36	13.1	12.4	12.1	11.7	11.4	11.2	10.9	10.7	10.4	9.9	9.5	8.6	7.9	7.2	6.6	6.0
38	13.2	12.5	12.1	11.8	11.5	11.2	11.0	10.8	10.5	10.0	9.5	8.7	8.0	7.3	6.7	6.1
40	13.3	12.6	12.2	11.9	11.6	11.3	11.1	10.8	10.6	10.1	9.6	8.8	8.1	7.4	6.8	6.2
42	13.4	12.7	12.3	12.0	11.7	11.4	11.2	10.9	10.7	10.2	9.7	8.9	8.2	7.5	6.9	6.3
44	13.4	12.7	12.4	12.0	11.7	11.5	11.2	11.0	10.7	10.2	9.8	8.9	8.2	7.5	6.9	6.3
46	13.5	12.8	12.4	12.1	11.8	11.5	11.3	11.0	10.8	10.3	9.8	9.0	8.3	7.6	7.0	6.4
48	13.6	12.9	12.5	12.2	11.9	11.6	11.3	11.1	10.9	10.4	9.9	9.1	8.3	7.7	7.1	6.4
50	13.6	12.9	12.5	12.2	11.9	11.6	11.4	11.1	10.9	10.4	9.9	9.1	8.4	7.7	7.1	6.5
52	13.6	13.0	12.6	12.3	12.0	11.7	11.4	11.2	11.0	10.5	10.0	9.2	8.4	7.8	7.2	6.5
54	13.7	13.0	12.6	12.3	12.0	11.7	11.5	11.3	11.0	10.5	10.0	9.2	8.5	7.8	7.2	6.6
56	13.7	13.1	12.7	12.4	12.1	11.8	11.5	11.3	11.1	10.6	10.1	9.3	8.5	7.9	7.3	6.7
58	13.8	13.1	12.7	12.4	12.1	11.8	11.6	11.3	11.1	10.6	10.1	9.3	8.6	7.9	7.3	6.8
60	13.8	13.1	12.8	12.4	12.1	11.9	11.6	11.4	11.1	10.6	10.2	9.3	8.6	7.9	7.3	6.8
62	13.9	13.2	12.8	12.5	12.2	11.9	11.7	11.4	11.2	10.7	10.2	9.4	8.7	8.0	7.4	6.8
64	13.9	13.2	12.8	12.5	12.2	11.9	11.7	11.5	11.2	10.7	10.2	9.4	8.7	8.0	7.4	6.9
66	14.0	13.2	12.9	12.5	12.3	12.0	11.7	11.5	11.3	10.7	10.3	9.5	8.7	8.1	7.5	7.0
70	14.1	13.3	12.9	12.6	12.3	12.0	11.8	11.6	11.3	10.8	10.3	9.5	8.8	8.1	7.5	7.0
80	14.2	13.5	13.1	12.8	12.5	12.2	11.9	11.7	11.5	11.0	10.5	9.7	8.9	8.3	7.7	7.1
90	14.3	13.6	13.2	12.9	12.6	12.3	12.1	11.9	11.6	11.1	10.6	9.8	9.1	8.4	7.8	7.2

Observed Altitude (row label, left margin)

MONTHLY CORRECTION

Jan	Feb	Mar	Apr	May	Jun	Jul	Aug	Sep	Oct	Nov	Dec
+0.3′	+0.2′	+0.1′	+0.0′	−0.1′	−0.2′	−0.2′	−0.2′	−0.1′	+0.1′	+0.2′	+0.3′

Note: This table combines the separate elements of the refraction, dip and parallax tables on the previous page, together with a correction for the Sun's semi-diameter, which changes monthly. It assumes that the observed altitude is that of the Sun's **lower limb**; if used to correct a sight of the upper limb, it will be necessary to subtract twice the Sun's semi-diameter (given on the monthly pages) from the observed altitude before entering the table.

Chapter 6

SUN, STAR AND ARIES GHA CORRECTION TABLES

Always add

	SUN α mins	SUN 1h+ α mins	SUN α secs	Date GMT	Corr for Date	α hours	STAR 1h+ α mins	STAR α mins	STAR α secs	
0	0 00.0	15 00.0	0.0	1st	0 00.0	0 00.0	15 02.5	0 00.0	0.0	0
1	0 15.0	15 15.0	0.3	2nd	0 59.1	15 02.5	15 17.5	0 15.0	0.3	1
2	0 30.0	15 30.0	0.5	3rd	1 58.2	30 04.9	15 32.6	0 30.1	0.5	2
3	0 45.0	15 45.0	0.8	4th	2 57.3	45 07.4	15 47.6	0 45.1	0.8	3
4	1 00.0	16 00.0	1.0	5th	3 56.5	60 09.9	16 02.7	1 00.2	1.0	4
5	1 15.0	16 15.0	1.3	6th	4 55.6	75 12.3	16 17.7	1 15.2	1.3	5
6	1 30.0	16 30.0	1.5	7th	5 54.8	90 14.8	16 32.7	1 30.2	1.5	6
7	1 45.0	16 45.0	1.8	8th	6 54.0	105 17.2	16 47.8	1 45.3	1.8	7
8	2 00.0	17 00.0	2.0	9th	7 53.1	120 19.7	17 02.8	2 00.3	2.0	8
9	2 15.0	17 15.0	2.3	10th	8 52.2	135 22.2	17 17.9	2 15.4	2.3	9
10	2 30.0	17 30.0	2.5	11th	9 51.4	150 24.6	17 32.9	2 30.4	2.5	10
11	2 45.0	17 45.0	2.8	12th	10 50.5	165 27.1	17 48.0	2 45.5	2.8	11
12	3 00.0	18 00.0	3.0	13th	11 49.6	180 29.6	18 03.0	3 00.5	3.0	12
13	3 15.0	18 15.0	3.3	14th	12 48.8	195 32.0	18 18.0	3 15.5	3.3	13
14	3 30.0	18 30.0	3.5	15th	13 48.0	210 34.5	18 33.1	3 30.6	3.5	14
15	3 45.0	18 45.0	3.8	16th	14 47.1	225 37.0	18 48.1	3 45.6	3.8	15
16	4 00.0	19 00.0	4.0	17th	15 46.2	240 39.4	19 03.2	4 00.7	4.0	16
17	4 15.0	19 15.0	4.3	18th	16 45.3	255 41.9	19 18.2	4 15.7	4.3	17
18	4 30.0	19 30.0	4.5	19th	17 44.5	270 44.4	19 33.2	4 30.7	4.5	18
19	4 45.0	19 45.0	4.8	20th	18 43.6	285 46.8	19 48.3	4 45.8	4.8	19
20	5 00.0	20 00.0	5.0	21st	19 42.7	300 49.3	20 03.3	5 00.8	5.0	20
21	5 15.0	20 15.0	5.3	22nd	20 41.9	315 51.7	20 18.4	5 15.9	5.3	21
22	5 30.0	20 30.0	5.5	23rd	21 41.0	330 54.2	20 33.4	5 30.9	5.5	22
23	5 45.0	20 45.0	5.8	24th	22 40.1	345 56.7	20 48.4	5 45.9	5.8	23
24	6 00.0	21 00.0	6.0	25th	23 39.3	360 59.1	21 03.5	6 01.0	6.0	24
25	6 15.0	21 15.0	6.3	26th	24 38.4		21 18.5	6 16.0	6.3	25
26	6 30.0	21 30.0	6.5	27th	25 37.6		21 33.6	6 31.1	6.5	26
27	6 45.0	21 45.0	6.8	28th	26 36.7		21 48.6	6 46.1	6.8	27
28	7 00.0	22 00.0	7.0	29th	27 35.8		22 03.6	7 01.1	7.0	28
29	7 15.0	22 15.0	7.3	30th	28 35.0		22 18.7	7 16.2	7.3	29
30	7 30.0	22 30.0	7.5	31st	29 34.1		22 33.7	7 31.2	7.5	30
31	7 45.0	22 45.0	7.8				22 48.8	7 46.3	7.8	31
32	8 00.0	23 00.0	8.0				23 03.8	8 01.3	8.0	32
33	8 15.0	23 15.0	8.3				23 18.9	8 16.4	8.3	33
34	8 30.0	23 30.0	8.5				23 33.9	8 31.4	8.5	34
35	8 45.0	23 45.0	8.8				23 48.9	8 46.4	8.8	35
36	9 00.0	24 00.0	9.0				24 04.0	9 01.5	9.0	36
37	9 15.0	24 15.0	9.3				24 19.0	9 16.5	9.3	37
38	9 30.0	24 30.0	9.5				24 34.1	9 31.6	9.5	38
39	9 45.0	24 45.0	9.8				24 49.1	9 46.6	9.8	39
40	10 00.0	25 00.0	10.0				25 04.1	10 01.6	10.0	40
41	10 15.0	25 15.0	10.3				25 19.2	10 16.7	10.3	41
42	10 30.0	25 30.0	10.5				25 34.2	10 31.7	10.5	42
43	10 45.0	25 45.0	10.8				25 49.3	10 46.8	10.8	43
44	11 00.0	26 00.0	11.0				26 04.3	11 01.8	11.0	44
45	11 15.0	26 15.0	11.3				26 19.3	11 16.8	11.3	45
46	11 30.0	26 30.0	11.5				26 34.4	11 31.9	11.5	46
47	11 45.0	26 45.0	11.8				26 49.4	11 46.9	11.8	47
48	12 00.0	27 00.0	12.0				27 04.5	12 02.0	12.0	48
49	12 15.0	27 15.0	12.3				27 19.5	12 17.0	12.3	49
50	12 30.0	27 30.0	12.5				27 34.6	12 32.1	12.5	50
51	12 45.0	27 45.0	12.8				27 49.6	12 47.1	12.8	51
52	13 00.0	28 00.0	13.0				28 04.6	13 02.1	13.0	52
53	13 15.0	28 15.0	13.3				28 19.7	13 17.2	13.3	53
54	13 30.0	28 30.0	13.5				28 34.7	13 32.2	13.5	54
55	13 45.0	28 45.0	13.8				28 49.8	13 47.3	13.8	55
56	14 00.0	29 00.0	14.0				29 04.8	14 02.3	14.0	56
57	14 15.0	29 15.0	14.3				29 19.8	14 17.3	14.3	57
58	14 30.0	29 30.0	14.5				29 34.9	14 32.4	14.5	58
59	14 45.0	29 45.0	14.8				29 49.9	14 47.4	14.8	59
60	15 00.0	30 00.0	15.0				30 04.9	15 02.5	15.0	60

Hours, minutes or seconds (α)

MOON ALTITUDE TOTAL CORRECTION TABLE

Add/subtract as indicated

Hor Par	Upper Limb — Add above line / Subtract below line								Lower Limb Add							
Observed Altitude	54'	55'	56'	57'	58'	59'	60'	61'	54'	55'	56'	57'	58'	59'	60'	61'
10	23.4	24.0	24.6	25.5	26.0	26.7	27.3	28.3	52.7	54.0	55.3	56.5	57.7	59.0	60.2	61.5
12	23.8	24.6	25.2	26.0	26.5	27.2	28.0	28.7	53.0	54.5	55.7	57.0	58.4	59.5	60.7	62.0
14	24.0	24.8	25.4	26.1	26.7	27.5	28.3	29.0	53.5	54.7	56.0	57.3	58.5	59.8	61.0	62.3
16	24.0	24.8	25.5	26.1	26.7	27.5	28.3	28.8	53.5	54.6	56.0	57.3	58.5	59.8	61.0	62.2
18	23.8	24.6	25.2	26.0	26.5	27.3	28.0	28.6	53.4	54.6	55.7	57.0	58.4	59.5	60.6	62.0
20	23.6	24.2	25.0	25.5	26.2	27.0	27.5	28.2	53.0	54.4	55.5	56.8	58.0	59.0	60.4	61.5
22	23.2	23.8	24.6	25.0	25.7	26.5	27.0	27.8	52.5	53.7	55.0	56.3	57.5	58.8	60.0	61.0
24	22.7	23.2	24.0	24.5	25.3	25.8	26.5	27.0	52.0	53.3	54.5	55.5	56.7	57.5	58.0	60.5
26	22.0	22.6	23.4	24.0	24.5	25.0	25.7	26.5	51.5	52.5	53.7	55.0	56.3	57.5	58.0	59.8
28	21.4	22.0	22.6	23.3	23.8	24.5	25.0	25.5	50.7	52.0	53.0	54.4	55.5	56.5	57.8	59.0
30	20.6	21.2	21.8	22.3	23.0	23.5	24.3	24.7	50.0	51.0	52.3	53.5	54.5	55.7	57.0	58.0
32	19.8	20.2	21.0	21.3	22.0	22.5	23.2	23.7	49.3	50.4	51.3	52.5	53.7	54.8	56.0	57.0
34	19.0	19.4	20.0	20.5	21.0	21.5	22.2	22.7	48.3	49.5	50.5	51.5	52.7	53.7	55.0	56.0
36	18.0	18.4	19.0	19.5	20.0	20.5	21.0	21.7	47.3	48.5	49.5	50.5	51.7	52.7	54.0	55.0
38	16.8	17.4	17.8	18.5	19.0	19.5	20.0	20.4	46.4	47.4	48.5	49.5	50.5	51.5	52.7	53.8
40	15.8	16.2	16.8	17.3	17.7	18.2	18.8	19.2	45.3	46.3	47.3	48.3	49.5	50.5	51.5	52.5
42	14.7	15.2	15.6	16.0	16.5	17.0	17.5	18.0	44.0	45.0	46.0	47.0	48.0	49.0	50.0	51.0
44	13.5	13.8	14.2	14.6	15.0	15.5	16.0	16.5	42.7	43.7	44.7	45.7	46.7	47.7	48.7	49.7
46	12.0	12.6	13.0	13.4	13.8	14.2	14.5	15.0	41.5	42.5	43.5	44.5	45.5	46.5	47.5	48.5
48	10.5	11.2	11.6	12.0	12.4	12.8	13.2	13.5	40.2	41.2	42.2	43.0	44.0	45.0	46.0	47.0
50	9.3	10.0	10.2	10.6	11.0	11.3	11.7	12.0	39.0	40.0	41.0	41.8	42.6	43.6	44.5	45.5
52	8.0	8.4	8.6	9.2	9.5	9.7	10.0	10.5	37.5	38.5	39.3	40.2	41.0	42.0	42.8	43.7
54	6.7	6.8	7.2	7.5	7.8	8.2	8.5	8.7	36.0	37.0	38.0	38.8	39.5	40.5	41.3	42.0
56	5.2	5.5	5.6	6.0	6.3	6.5	7.0	7.0	34.5	35.5	36.2	37.0	38.0	38.7	39.5	40.5
58	3.7	3.7	4.2	4.5	4.5	5.0	5.0	5.5	33.0	34.0	34.7	35.5	36.3	37.0	38.0	38.8
60	2.0	2.2	2.5	2.7	3.0	3.2	3.5	3.5	31.5	32.4	33.0	34.0	34.5	35.5	36.0	37.0
62	+0.5	+0.7	+1.0	+0.8	+1.2	+1.5	+1.5	+1.7	30.0	30.5	31.5	32.0	33.0	33.5	34.5	35.0
64	−1.2	−1.0	−1.0	−0.8	−0.6	−0.5	−0.3	−0.1	28.3	29.0	29.6	30.5	31.0	31.8	32.5	33.3
66	3.0	2.8	2.6	2.5	2.4	2.3	2.0	2.0	26.5	27.3	28.0	28.5	29.3	30.0	30.7	31.5
68	4.5	4.5	4.4	4.3	4.2	4.0	4.0	4.0	25.0	25.5	26.3	26.8	27.5	28.0	28.8	29.5
70	6.3	6.2	6.2	6.1	6.0	6.0	5.8	5.8	23.3	23.8	24.5	25.0	25.5	26.2	27.0	27.5
72	8.0	8.0	8.0	8.0	8.0	8.0	7.8	7.8	21.5	22.0	22.5	23.3	23.8	24.5	25.0	25.5
74	9.7	9.7	9.7	9.7	9.7	9.7	9.7	9.7	19.7	20.3	20.7	21.2	22.0	22.5	23.0	23.5
76	11.5	11.5	11.5	11.5	11.6	11.7	11.7	11.7	18.0	18.5	19.0	19.5	20.0	20.5	21.0	21.5
78	13.5	13.5	13.5	13.6	13.6	13.7	13.7	13.7	16.0	16.5	17.0	17.5	18.0	18.5	19.0	19.5
80	15.4	15.4	15.4	15.5	15.6	15.7	15.7	16.0	14.2	14.7	15.3	15.5	16.0	16.5	17.0	17.5
82	17.0	17.0	17.2	17.3	17.5	17.7	17.8	18.0	12.5	13.0	13.3	13.5	14.0	14.5	15.0	15.5
84	18.8	19.0	19.2	19.3	19.5	19.7	19.9	20.0	10.5	11.0	11.5	11.7	12.0	12.5	13.0	13.4
86	20.8	21.0	21.0	21.2	21.5	21.7	22.0	22.0	8.8	9.0	9.5	9.8	10.0	10.5	11.0	11.3
88	22.6	22.8	23.0	23.2	23.4	23.7	24.0	24.2	7.0	7.2	7.5	8.0	8.5	8.5	8.7	9.0
90																

HEIGHT OF EYE CORRECTION

Add

Height of eye (m)	0	1.5	3	4.6	6	7.6	9	10.7	12	14	15	17	18	20	21	23	24	26	30
Height of eye (ft)	0	5	10	15	20	25	30	35	40	45	50	55	60	65	70	75	80	85	100
Corr		9.8'	7.6'	6.7'	6.0'	5.5'	5.0'	4.5'	4.0'	3.5'	3.2'	3.0'	2.5'	2.3'	2.0'	1.7'	1.3'	1.0'	0.8'	0.0'

Chapter 6

Note: This table includes corrections for semi-diameter, parallax and refraction. The Horizontal Parallax figure required for the top line varies daily and can be found on the monthly pages.

STAR OR PLANET ALTITUDE TOTAL CORRECTION TABLE

Always subtract

Height of eye above sea level

Observed Altitude	m 1.5 / ft 5	3.0 / 10	4.6 / 15	6.0 / 20	7.6 / 25	9.0 / 30	10.7 / 35	12 / 40	13.7 / 45	15 / 50	16.8 / 55	18 / 60	21.3 / 70
9	8.0	8.9	9.6	10.3	10.7	11.2	11.6	12.0	12.4	12.8	13.1	13.5	14.1
10	7.4	8.4	9.1	9.7	10.2	10.6	11.1	11.5	11.8	12.2	12.5	12.9	13.5
11	7.0	7.9	8.6	9.2	9.7	10.2	10.6	11.0	11.4	11.8	12.0	12.4	13.0
12	6.6	7.5	8.2	8.8	9.3	9.8	10.2	10.6	11.0	11.4	11.6	12.0	12.6
13	6.2	7.2	7.9	8.4	9.0	9.4	9.9	10.3	10.6	11.0	11.3	11.6	12.3
14	5.9	6.9	7.6	8.1	8.6	9.2	9.6	10.0	10.3	10.7	11.0	11.3	12.0
15	5.7	6.6	7.3	7.9	8.4	8.9	9.3	9.7	10.1	10.4	10.8	11.1	11.7
16	5.5	6.4	7.1	7.7	8.2	8.7	9.1	9.5	9.9	10.2	10.5	10.9	11.5
17	5.3	6.2	6.9	7.5	8.0	8.5	8.9	9.3	9.7	10.0	10.3	10.7	11.3
18	5.1	6.0	6.7	7.3	7.8	8.3	8.7	9.1	9.5	9.8	10.2	10.5	11.1
19	4.9	5.8	6.5	7.1	7.6	8.1	8.5	8.9	9.3	9.7	10.0	10.3	11.0
20	4.8	5.7	6.4	7.0	7.5	8.0	8.4	8.8	9.2	9.6	9.9	10.2	10.8
25	4.2	5.1	5.8	6.4	6.9	7.4	7.8	8.2	8.6	9.0	9.3	9.6	10.2
30	3.8	4.7	5.4	6.0	6.5	7.0	7.4	7.8	8.2	8.6	8.9	9.2	9.8
35	3.5	4.4	5.1	5.7	6.3	6.7	7.2	7.6	7.9	8.3	8.6	8.9	9.5
40	3.3	4.2	4.9	5.5	6.0	6.5	6.9	7.3	7.7	8.1	8.4	8.7	9.3
50	3.0	3.9	4.6	5.2	5.7	6.2	6.6	7.0	7.4	7.7	8.1	8.4	9.0
60	2.7	3.6	4.4	4.9	5.5	5.9	6.4	6.8	7.1	7.5	7.8	8.1	8.8
70	2.5	3.4	4.1	4.7	5.3	5.7	6.2	6.6	6.9	7.3	7.6	7.9	8.6
80	2.3	3.3	4.0	4.6	5.1	5.5	6.0	6.4	6.7	7.1	7.4	7.8	8.4
90	2.2	3.1	3.8	4.4	4.9	5.4	5.8	6.2	6.6	6.9	7.3	7.6	8.2

Note: This table combines the corrections for refraction and dip included in the table on page 704, but not parallax or semi-diameter since these are of no significance in the case of star or planet sights.

MOON GHA CORRECTION TABLE (HOURS)

Always add

Var/hr	14°20'	14°20.5'	14°21'	14°21.5'	14°22'	14°22.5'	14°23'	14°23.5'	14°24'	14°24.5'	14°25'	14°25.5'
Hours	° '	° '	° '	° '	° '	° '	° '	° '	° '	° '	° '	° '
1	14 20.0	14 20.5	14 21.0	14 21.5	14 22.0	14 22.5	14 23.0	14 23.5	14 24.0	14 24.5	14 25.0	14 25.5
2	28 40.0	28 41.0	28 42.0	28 43.0	28 44.0	28 45.0	28 46.0	28 47.0	28 48.0	28 49.0	28 50.0	28 51.0
3	43 00.0	43 01.5	43 03.0	43 04.5	43 06.0	43 07.5	43 09.0	43 10.5	43 12.0	43 13.5	43 15.0	43 16.5
4	57 20.0	57 22.0	57 24.0	57 26.0	57 28.0	57 30.0	57 32.0	57 34.0	57 36.0	57 38.0	57 40.0	57 42.0
5	71 40.0	71 42.5	71 45.0	71 47.5	71 50.0	71 52.5	71 55.0	71 57.5	72 00.0	72 02.5	72 05.0	72 07.5

Var/hr	14°26'	14°26.5'	14°27'	14°27.5'	14°28'	14°28.5'	14°29'	14°29.5'	14°30'	14°30.5'	14°31'	14°31.5'
1	14 26.0	14 26.5	14 27.0	14 27.5	14 28.0	14°28.5	14 29.0	14 29.5	14 30.0	14 30.5	14 31.0	14 31.5
2	28 52.0	28 53.0	28 54.0	28 55.0	28 56.0	28 57.0	28 58.0	28 59.0	29 00.0	29 01.0	29 02.0	29 03.0
3	43 18.0	43 19.5	43 21.0	43 22.5	43 24.0	43 25.5	43 27.0	43 28.5	43 30.0	43 31.5	43 33.0	43 34.5
4	57 44.0	57 46.0	57 48.0	57 50.0	57 52.0	57 54.0	57 56.0	57 58.0	58 00.0	58 02.0	58 04.0	58 06.0
5	72 10.0	72 12.5	72 15.0	72 17.5	72 20.0	72 22.5	72 25.0	72 27.5	72 30.0	72 32.5	72 35.0	72 37.5

Var/hr	14°32'	14°32.5'	14°33'	14°33.5'	14°34'	14°34.5'	14°35'	14°35.5'	14°36'	14°36.5'	14°37'	14°37.5'
1	14 32.0	14 32.5	14 33.0	14 33.5	14 34.0	14 34.5	14 35.0	14 35.5	14 36.0	14 36.5	14 37.0	14 37.5
2	29 04.0	29 05.0	29 06.0	29 07.0	29 08.0	29 09.0	29 10.0	29 11.0	29 12.0	29 13.0	29 14.0	29 15.0
3	43 36.0	43 37.5	43 39.0	43 40.5	43 42.0	43 43.5	43 45.0	43 46.5	43 48.0	43 49.5	43 51.0	43 52.5
4	58 08.0	58 10.0	58 12.0	58 14.0	58 16.0	58 18.0	58 20.0	58 22.0	58 24.0	58 26.0	58 28.0	58 30.0
5	72 40.0	72 42.5	72 45.0	72 47.5	72 50.0	72 52.5	72 55.0	72 57.5	73 00.0	73 02.5	73 05.0	73 07.5

Note: Using the figure for variation per hour given in the monthly pages, the total GHA correction to be applied can be read off from this table and the Moon GHA Correction Table (Minutes) on the following page.

MOON GHA CORRECTION TABLE (MINUTES)

Var/hr	14°20'	14°21'	14°22'	14°23'	14°24'	14°25'	14°26'	14°27'	14°28'	Diff 1'	Sec	Corr
0	0 00.0	0 00.0	0 00.0	0 00.0	0 00.0	0 00.0	0 00.0	0 00.0	0 00.0	0.0	0	0.0
1	0 14.3	0 14.4	0 14.4	0 14.4	0 14.4	0 14.4	0 14.4	0 14.4	0 14.5	0.0	1	0.2
2	0 28.7	0 28.7	0 28.7	0 28.8	0 28.8	0 28.8	0 28.9	0 28.9	0 28.9	0.0	2	0.5
3	0 43.0	0 43.0	0 43.1	0 43.2	0 43.2	0 43.2	0 43.3	0 43.4	0 43.4	0.0	3	0.7
4	0 57.3	0 57.4	0 57.5	0 57.5	0 57.6	0 57.7	0 57.7	0 57.8	0 57.3	0.1	4	1.0
5	1 11.7	1 11.8	1 11.8	1 11.9	1 12.0	1 12.1	1 12.2	1 12.2	1 12.3	0.1	5	1.2
6	1 26.0	1 26.1	1 26.2	1 26.3	1 26.4	1 26.5	1 26.6	1 26.7	1 26.8	0.1	6	1.4
7	1 40.3	1 40.4	1 40.6	1 40.7	1 40.8	1 40.9	1 41.2	1 41.2	1 41.3	0.1	7	1.7
8	1 54.7	1 54.8	1 54.9	1 55.1	1 55.2	1 55.3	1 55.5	1 55.6	1 55.7	0.1	8	1.9
9	2 09.0	2 09.2	2 09.3	2 09.4	2 09.6	2 09.8	2 09.9	2 10.0	2 10.2	0.2	9	2.2
10	2 23.3	2 23.5	2 23.7	2 23.8	2 24.0	2 24.2	2 24.3	2 24.5	2 24.7	0.2	10	2.4
11	2 37.7	2 37.8	2 38.0	2 38.2	2 38.4	2 38.6	2 38.8	2 39.0	2 39.1	0.2	11	2.6
12	2 52.0	2 52.2	2 52.4	2 52.6	2 52.8	2 53.0	2 53.2	2 53.4	2 53.6	0.2	12	2.9
13	3 06.3	3 06.6	3 06.8	3 07.0	3 07.2	3 07.4	3 07.6	3 07.8	3 08.1	0.2	13	3.1
14	3 20.7	3 20.9	3 21.1	3 21.4	3 21.6	3 21.8	3 22.1	3 22.3	3 22.5	0.2	14	3.4
15	3 35.0	3 35.2	3 35.5	3 35.8	3 36.0	3 36.2	3 36.5	3 36.8	3 37.0	0.2	15	3.6
16	3 49.3	3 49.6	3 49.9	3 50.1	3 50.4	3 50.7	3 50.9	3 51.2	3 51.5	0.3	16	3.8
17	4 03.7	4 04.0	4 04.2	4 04.5	4 04.8	4 05.1	4 05.4	4 05.6	4 05.9	0.3	17	4.1
18	4 18.0	4 18.3	4 18.6	4 18.9	4 19.2	4 19.5	4 19.8	4 20.1	4 20.4	0.3	18	4.3
19	4 32.3	4 32.6	4 33.0	4 33.3	4 33.6	4 33.9	4 34.2	4 34.6	4 34.9	0.3	19	4.6
20	4 46.7	4 47.0	4 47.3	4 47.7	4 48.0	4 48.3	4 48.7	4 49.0	4 49.3	0.3	20	4.8
21	5 01.0	5 01.4	5 01.7	5 02.0	5 02.4	5 02.8	5 03.1	5 03.4	5 03.8	0.4	21	5.0
22	5 15.3	5 15.7	5 16.1	5 16.4	5 16.8	5 17.2	5 17.5	5 17.9	5 18.3	0.4	22	5.3
23	5 29.7	5 30.0	5 30.4	5 30.8	5 31.2	5 31.6	5 32.0	5 32.4	5 32.7	0.4	23	5.5
24	5 44.0	5 44.4	5 44.8	5 45.2	5 45.6	5 46.0	5 46.4	5 46.8	5 47.2	0.4	24	5.8
25	5 58.3	5 58.8	5 59.2	5 59.6	6 00.0	6 00.4	6 00.8	6 01.2	6 01.7	0.4	25	6.0
26	6 12.7	6 13.1	6 13.5	6 14.0	6 14.4	6 14.8	6 15.3	6 15.7	6 16.1	0.4	26	6.2
27	6 27.0	6 27.4	6 27.9	6 28.4	6 28.8	6 29.2	6 29.7	6 30.2	6 30.6	0.4	27	6.5
28	6 41.3	6 41.8	6 42.3	6 42.7	6 43.2	6 43.7	6 44.1	6 44.6	6 45.1	0.5	28	6.7
29	6 55.7	6 56.2	6 56.6	6 57.1	6 57.6	6 58.1	6 58.6	6 59.0	6 59.5	0.5	29	7.0
30	7 10.0	7 10.5	7 11.0	7 11.5	7 12.0	7 12.5	7 13.0	7 13.5	7 14.0	0.5	30	7.2
31	7 24.3	7 24.8	7 25.4	7 25.9	7 26.4	7 26.9	7 27.4	7 28.0	7 28.5	0.5	31	7.4
32	7 38.7	7 39.2	7 39.7	7 40.3	7 40.8	7 41.3	7 41.9	7 42.4	7 42.9	0.5	32	7.7
33	7 53.0	7 53.6	7 54.1	7 54.6	7 55.2	7 55.8	7 56.3	7 56.8	7 57.4	0.6	33	7.9
34	8 07.3	8 07.9	8 08.5	8 09.0	8 09.6	8 10.2	8 10.7	8 11.3	8 11.9	0.6	34	8.2
35	8 21.7	8 22.2	8 22.8	8 23.4	8 24.0	8 24.6	8 25.2	8 25.8	8 26.3	0.6	35	8.4
36	8 36.0	8 36.6	8 37.2	8 37.8	8 38.4	8 39.0	8 39.6	8 40.2	8 40.8	0.6	36	8.6
37	8 50.3	8 51.0	8 51.6	8 52.2	8 52.8	8 53.4	8 54.0	8 54.6	8 55.3	0.6	37	8.9
38	9 04.7	9 05.3	9 05.9	9 06.6	9 07.2	9 07.8	9 08.5	9 09.1	9 09.7	0.6	38	9.1
39	9 19.0	9 19.6	9 20.3	9 21.0	9 21.6	9 22.2	9 22.9	9 23.6	9 24.2	0.6	39	9.4
40	9 33.3	9 34.0	9 34.7	9 35.3	9 36.0	9 36.7	9 37.3	9 38.0	9 38.7	0.7	40	9.6
41	9 47.7	9 48.4	9 49.0	9 49.7	9 50.4	9 51.1	9 51.8	9 52.4	9 53.1	0.7	41	9.8
42	10 02.0	10 02.7	10 03.4	10 04.1	10 04.8	10 05.5	10 06.2	10 06.9	10 07.6	0.7	42	10.1
43	10 16.3	10 17.1	10 17.8	10 18.5	10 19.2	10 19.9	10 20.6	10 21.4	10 22.1	0.7	43	10.3
44	10 30.7	10 31.4	10 32.1	10 32.9	10 33.6	10 34.3	10 35.1	10 35.8	10 36.5	0.7	44	10.6
45	10 45.0	10 45.8	10 46.5	10 47.2	10 48.0	10 48.8	10 49.5	10 50.2	10 51.0	0.8	45	10.8
46	10 59.3	11 00.1	11 00.9	11 01.6	11 02.4	11 03.2	11 03.9	11 04.7	11 05.5	0.8	46	11.0
47	11 13.7	11 14.4	11 15.2	11 16.0	11 16.8	11 17.6	11 18.4	11 19.2	11 19.9	0.8	47	11.3
48	11 28.0	11 28.8	11 29.6	11 30.4	11 31.2	11 32.0	11 32.8	11 33.6	11 34.4	0.8	48	11.5
49	11 42.3	11 43.2	11 44.0	11 44.8	11 45.6	11 46.4	11 47.2	11 48.0	11 48.9	0.8	49	11.8
50	11 56.7	11 57.5	11 58.3	11 59.2	12 00.0	12 00.8	12 01.7	12 02.5	12 03.3	0.8	50	12.0
51	12 11.0	12 11.8	12 12.7	12 13.6	12 14.4	12 15.2	12 16.1	12 17.0	12 17.8	0.8	51	12.2
52	12 25.3	12 26.2	12 27.1	12 27.9	12 28.8	12 29.7	12 30.5	12 31.4	12 32.3	0.9	52	12.5
53	12 39.7	12 40.6	12 41.4	12 42.3	12 43.2	12 44.1	12 45.0	12 45.8	12 46.7	0.9	53	12.7
54	12 54.0	12 54.9	12 55.8	12 56.7	12 57.6	12 58.5	12 59.4	13 00.3	13 01.2	0.9	54	13.0
55	13 08.3	13 09.2	13 10.2	13 11.1	13 12.0	13 12.9	13 13.8	13 14.8	13 15.7	0.9	55	13.2
56	13 22.7	13 23.6	13 24.5	13 25.5	13 26.4	13 27.3	13 28.3	13 29.2	13 30.1	0.9	56	13.4
57	13 37.0	13 38.0	13 38.9	13 39.8	13 40.8	13 41.8	13 42.7	13 43.6	13 44.6	1.0	57	13.7
58	13 51.3	13 52.3	13 53.3	13 54.2	13 55.2	13 56.2	13 57.1	13 58.1	13 59.1	1.0	58	13.9
59	14 05.7	14 06.6	14 07.6	14 08.6	14 09.6	14 10.6	14 11.6	14 12.6	14 13.5	1.0	59	14.1
60	14 20.0	14 21.0	14 22.0	14 23.0	14 24.0	14 25.0	14 26.0	14 27.0	14 28.0	1.0	60	14.4

Minutes

Chapter 6

MOON GHA CORRECTION TABLE (MINUTES)

Var/hr	14°29'	14°30'	14°31'	14°32'	14°33'	14°34'	14°35'	14°36'	14°37'	Diff 1'	Sec	Corr
0	0 00.0	0 00.0	0 00.0	0 00.0	0 00.0	0 00.0	0 00.0	0 00.0	0 00.0	0.0	0	0.0
1	0 14.5	0 14.5	0 14.5	0 14.6	0 14.6	0 14.6	0 14.6	0 14.6	0 14.6	0.0	1	0.2
2	0 29.0	0 29.0	0 29.0	0 29.1	0 29.1	0 29.1	0 29.2	0 29.2	0 29.2	0.0	2	0.5
3	0 43.4	0 43.5	0 43.6	0 43.6	0 43.6	0 43.7	0 43.8	0 43.8	0 43.8	0.0	3	0.7
4	0 57.9	0 58.0	0 58.1	0 58.1	0 58.2	0 58.3	0 58.3	0 58.4	0 58.5	0.1	4	1.0
5	1 12.4	1 12.5	1 12.6	1 12.7	1 12.7	1 12.8	1 12.9	1 13.0	1 13.1	0.1	5	1.2
6	1 26.9	1 27.0	1 27.1	1 27.2	1 27.3	1 27.4	1 27.5	1 27.6	1 27.7	0.1	6	1.5
7	1 41.4	1 41.5	1 41.6	1 41.7	1 41.8	1 42.0	1 42.1	1 42.2	1 42.3	0.1	7	1.7
8	1 55.9	1 56.0	1 56.1	1 56.3	1 56.4	1 56.5	1 56.7	1 56.8	1 56.9	0.1	8	1.9
9	2 10.4	2 10.5	2 10.6	2 10.8	2 11.0	2 11.1	2 11.2	2 11.4	2 11.6	0.2	9	2.2
10	2 24.8	2 25.0	2 25.2	2 25.2	2 25.5	2 25.7	2 25.8	2 26.0	2 26.2	0.2	10	2.4
11	2 39.3	2 39.5	2 39.7	2 39.9	2 40.0	2 40.2	2 40.4	2 40.6	2 40.8	0.2	11	2.7
12	2 53.8	2 54.0	2 54.2	2 54.4	2 54.6	2 54.8	2 55.0	2 55.2	2 55.4	0.2	12	2.9
13	3 08.3	3 08.5	3 08.7	3 08.9	3 09.2	3 09.4	3 09.6	3 09.8	3 10.0	0.2	13	3.2
14	3 22.8	3 23.0	3 23.2	3 23.5	3 23.7	3 23.9	3 24.2	3 24.4	3 24.6	0.2	14	3.4
15	3 37.2	3 37.5	3 37.8	3 38.0	3 38.2	3 38.5	3 38.8	3 39.0	3 39.2	0.2	15	3.6
16	3 51.7	3 52.0	3 52.3	3 52.5	3 52.8	3 53.1	3 53.3	3 53.6	3 53.9	0.3	16	3.9
17	4 06.2	4 06.5	4 06.8	4 07.1	4 07.4	4 07.6	4 07.9	4 08.2	4 08.5	0.3	17	4.1
18	4 20.7	4 21.0	4 21.3	4 21.6	4 21.9	4 22.2	4 22.5	4 22.8	4 23.1	0.3	18	4.4
19	4 35.2	4 35.5	4 35.8	4 36.1	4 36.4	4 36.8	4 37.1	4 37.4	4 37.7	0.3	19	4.6
20	4 49.7	4 50.0	4 50.3	4 50.7	4 51.0	4 51.3	4 51.7	4 52.0	4 52.3	0.3	20	4.9
21	5 04.2	5 04.5	5 04.8	5 05.2	5 05.6	5 05.9	5 06.2	5 06.6	5 07.0	0.4	21	5.1
22	5 18.6	5 19.0	5 19.4	5 19.7	5 20.1	5 20.5	5 20.8	5 21.2	5 21.6	0.4	22	5.3
23	5 33.1	5 33.5	5 33.9	5 34.3	5 34.6	5 35.0	5 35.4	5 35.8	5 36.2	0.4	23	5.6
24	5 47.6	5 48.0	5 48.4	5 48.8	5 49.2	5 49.6	5 50.0	5 50.4	5 50.8	0.4	24	5.8
25	6 02.1	6 02.5	6 02.9	6 03.3	6 03.8	6 04.2	6 04.6	6 05.0	6 05.4	0.4	25	6.1
26	6 16.6	6 17.0	6 17.4	6 17.9	6 18.3	6 18.7	6 19.2	6 19.6	6 20.0	0.4	26	6.3
27	6 31.0	6 31.5	6 32.0	6 32.4	6 32.8	6 33.3	6 33.8	6 34.2	6 34.6	0.4	27	6.5
28	6 45.5	6 46.0	6 46.5	6 46.9	6 47.4	6 47.9	6 48.3	6 48.8	6 49.3	0.5	28	6.8
29	7 00.0	7 00.5	7 01.0	7 01.5	7 02.0	7 02.4	7 02.9	7 03.4	7 03.9	0.5	29	7.0
30	7 14.5	7 15.0	7 15.5	7 16.0	7 16.5	7 17.0	7 17.5	7 18.0	7 18.5	0.5	30	7.3
31	7 29.0	7 29.5	7 30.0	7 30.5	7 31.0	7 31.6	7 32.1	7 32.6	7 33.1	0.5	31	7.5
32	7 43.5	7 44.0	7 44.5	7 45.1	7 45.6	7 46.1	7 46.7	7 47.2	7 47.7	0.5	32	7.8
33	7 58.0	7 58.5	7 59.0	7 59.6	8 00.2	8 00.7	8 01.2	8 01.8	8 02.4	0.6	33	8.0
34	8 12.4	8 13.0	8 13.6	8 14.1	8 14.7	8 15.3	8 15.8	8 16.4	8 17.0	0.6	34	8.2
35	8 26.9	8 27.5	8 28.1	8 28.7	8 29.2	8 29.8	8 30.4	8 31.0	8 31.6	0.6	35	8.5
36	8 41.4	8 42.0	8 42.6	8 43.2	8 43.8	8 44.4	8 45.0	8 45.6	8 46.2	0.6	36	8.7
37	8 55.9	8 56.5	8 57.1	8 57.7	8 58.4	8 59.0	8 59.6	9 00.2	9 00.8	0.6	37	9.0
38	9 10.4	9 11.0	9 11.6	9 12.3	9 12.9	9 13.5	9 14.2	9 14.8	9 15.4	0.6	38	9.2
39	9 24.8	9 25.5	9 26.2	9 26.8	9 27.4	9 28.1	9 28.8	9 29.4	9 30.0	0.6	39	9.5
40	9 39.3	9 40.0	9 40.7	9 41.3	9 42.0	9 42.7	9 43.3	9 44.0	9 44.7	0.7	40	9.7
41	9 53.8	9 54.5	9 55.2	9 55.9	9 56.6	9 57.2	9 57.9	9 58.6	9 59.3	0.7	41	9.9
42	10 08.3	10 09.0	10 09.7	10 10.4	10 11.1	10 11.8	10 12.5	10 13.2	10 13.9	0.7	42	10.2
43	10 22.8	10 23.5	10 24.2	10 24.9	10 25.6	10 26.4	10 27.1	10 27.8	10 28.5	0.7	43	10.4
44	10 37.3	10 38.0	10 38.7	10 39.5	10 40.2	10 40.9	10 41.7	10 42.4	10 43.1	0.7	44	10.7
45	10 51.8	10 52.5	10 53.2	10 54.0	10 54.8	10 55.5	10 56.2	10 57.0	10 57.8	0.8	45	10.9
46	11 06.2	11 07.0	11 07.8	11 08.5	11 09.3	11 10.1	11 10.8	11 11.6	11 12.4	0.8	46	11.2
47	11 20.7	11 21.5	11 22.3	11 23.1	11 23.8	11 24.6	11 25.4	11 26.2	11 27.0	0.8	47	11.4
48	11 35.2	11 36.0	11 36.8	11 37.6	11 38.4	11 39.2	11 40.0	11 40.8	11 41.6	0.8	48	11.6
49	11 49.7	11 50.5	11 51.3	11 52.1	11 53.0	11 53.8	11 54.6	11 55.4	11 56.2	0.8	49	11.9
50	12 04.2	12 05.0	12 05.8	12 06.7	12 07.5	12 08.3	12 09.2	12 10.0	12 10.8	0.8	50	12.1
51	12 18.6	12 19.5	12 20.4	12 21.2	12 22.0	12 22.9	12 23.8	12 24.6	12 25.4	0.8	51	12.4
52	12 33.1	12 34.0	12 34.9	12 35.7	12 36.6	12 37.5	12 38.3	12 39.2	12 40.1	0.9	52	12.6
53	12 47.6	12 48.5	12 49.4	12 50.3	12 51.2	12 52.0	12 52.9	12 53.8	12 54.7	0.9	53	12.9
54	13 02.1	13 03.0	13 03.9	13 04.8	13 05.7	13 06.6	13 07.5	13 08.4	13 09.3	0.9	54	13.1
55	13 16.6	13 17.5	13 18.4	13 19.3	13 20.2	13 21.2	13 22.1	13 23.0	13 23.9	0.9	55	13.3
56	13 31.1	13 32.0	13 32.9	13 33.9	13 34.8	13 35.7	13 36.7	13 37.6	13 38.5	0.9	56	13.6
57	13 45.6	13 46.5	13 47.4	13 48.4	13 49.4	13 50.3	13 51.2	13 52.2	13 53.2	1.0	57	13.9
58	14 00.0	14 01.0	14 02.0	14 02.9	14 03.9	14 04.9	14 05.8	14 06.8	14 07.8	1.0	58	14.1
59	14 14.5	14 15.5	14 16.5	14 17.5	14 18.4	14 19.4	14 20.4	14 21.4	14 22.4	1.0	59	14.3
60	14 29.0	14 30.0	14 31.0	14 32.0	14 33.0	14 34.0	14 35.0	14 36.0	14 37.0	1.0	60	14.6

Minutes

MOON DECLINATION CORRECTION TABLE

Var/hr	0.0′	1.0′	2.0′	3.0′	4.0′	5.0′	6.0′	7.0′	8.0′	9.0′	10.0′	11.0′	12.0′	13.0′	14.0′	15.0′	16.0′	17.0′	18.0′
0	0.0	0.0	0.0	0.0	0.0	0.0	0.0	0.0	0.0	0.0	0.0	0.0	0.0	0.0	0.0	0.0	0.0	0.0	0.0
1	0.0	0.0	0.0	0.0	0.1	0.1	0.1	0.1	0.1	0.2	0.2	0.2	0.2	0.2	0.2	0.2	0.3	0.3	0.3
2	0.0	0.0	0.1	0.1	0.1	0.2	0.2	0.2	0.2	0.3	0.3	0.4	0.4	0.4	0.5	0.5	0.5	0.6	0.6
3	0.0	0.0	0.1	0.2	0.2	0.2	0.3	0.4	0.4	0.4	0.5	0.5	0.6	0.6	0.7	0.8	0.8	0.8	0.9
4	0.0	0.1	0.1	0.2	0.3	0.3	0.4	0.5	0.5	0.6	0.7	0.7	0.8	0.9	0.9	1.0	1.1	1.1	1.2
5	0.0	0.1	0.2	0.2	0.3	0.4	0.5	0.6	0.7	0.8	0.8	0.9	1.0	1.1	1.2	1.2	1.3	1.4	1.5
6	0.0	0.1	0.2	0.3	0.4	0.5	0.6	0.7	0.8	0.9	1.0	1.1	1.2	1.3	1.4	1.5	1.6	1.7	1.8
7	0.0	0.1	0.2	0.4	0.5	0.6	0.7	0.8	0.9	1.0	1.2	1.3	1.4	1.5	1.6	1.8	1.9	2.0	2.1
8	0.0	0.1	0.3	0.4	0.5	0.7	0.8	0.9	1.1	1.2	1.3	1.5	1.6	1.7	1.9	2.0	2.1	2.3	2.4
9	0.0	0.2	0.3	0.4	0.6	0.8	0.9	1.0	1.2	1.4	1.5	1.6	1.8	2.0	2.1	2.2	2.4	2.6	2.7
10	0.0	0.2	0.3	0.5	0.7	0.8	1.0	1.2	1.3	1.5	1.7	1.8	2.0	2.2	2.3	2.5	2.7	2.8	3.0
11	0.0	0.2	0.4	0.6	0.7	0.9	1.1	1.3	1.5	1.6	1.8	2.0	2.2	2.4	2.6	2.8	2.9	3.1	3.3
12	0.0	0.2	0.4	0.6	0.8	1.0	1.2	1.4	1.6	1.8	2.0	2.2	2.4	2.6	2.8	3.0	3.2	3.4	3.6
13	0.0	0.2	0.4	0.6	0.9	1.1	1.3	1.5	1.7	2.0	2.2	2.4	2.6	2.8	3.0	3.2	3.5	3.7	3.9
14	0.0	0.2	0.5	0.7	0.9	1.2	1.4	1.6	1.9	2.1	2.3	2.6	2.8	3.0	3.3	3.5	3.7	4.0	4.2
15	0.0	0.2	0.5	0.8	1.0	1.2	1.5	1.8	2.0	2.2	2.5	2.8	3.0	3.2	3.5	3.8	4.0	4.2	4.5
16	0.0	0.3	0.5	0.8	1.1	1.3	1.6	1.9	2.1	2.4	2.7	2.9	3.2	3.5	3.7	4.0	4.3	4.5	4.8
17	0.0	0.3	0.6	0.8	1.1	1.4	1.7	2.0	2.3	2.6	2.8	3.1	3.4	3.7	4.0	4.2	4.5	4.8	5.1
18	0.0	0.3	0.6	0.9	1.2	1.5	1.8	2.1	2.4	2.7	3.0	3.3	3.6	3.9	4.2	4.5	4.8	5.1	5.4
19	0.0	0.3	0.6	1.0	1.3	1.6	1.9	2.2	2.5	2.8	3.2	3.5	3.8	4.1	4.4	4.8	5.1	5.4	5.7
20	0.0	0.3	0.7	1.0	1.3	1.7	2.0	2.3	2.7	3.0	3.3	3.7	4.0	4.3	4.7	5.0	5.3	5.7	6.0
21	0.0	0.4	0.7	1.0	1.4	1.8	2.1	2.4	2.8	3.2	3.5	3.8	4.2	4.6	4.9	5.2	5.6	6.0	6.3
22	0.0	0.4	0.7	1.1	1.5	1.8	2.2	2.6	2.9	3.3	3.7	4.0	4.4	4.8	5.1	5.5	5.9	6.2	6.6
23	0.0	0.4	0.8	1.2	1.5	1.9	2.3	2.7	3.1	3.4	3.8	4.2	4.6	5.0	5.4	5.8	6.1	6.5	6.9
24	0.0	0.4	0.8	1.2	1.6	2.0	2.4	2.8	3.2	3.6	4.0	4.4	4.8	5.2	5.6	6.0	6.4	6.8	7.2
25	0.0	0.4	0.8	1.2	1.7	2.1	2.5	2.9	3.3	3.8	4.2	4.6	5.0	5.4	5.8	6.2	6.7	7.1	7.5
26	0.0	0.4	0.9	1.3	1.7	2.2	2.6	3.0	3.5	3.9	4.3	4.8	5.2	5.6	6.1	6.5	6.9	7.4	7.8
27	0.0	0.4	0.9	1.3	1.8	2.2	2.7	3.2	3.6	4.0	4.5	5.0	5.4	5.8	6.3	6.8	7.2	7.6	8.1
28	0.0	0.5	0.9	1.4	1.9	2.3	2.8	3.3	3.7	4.2	4.7	5.1	5.6	6.1	6.5	7.0	7.5	7.9	8.4
29	0.0	0.5	1.0	1.4	1.9	2.4	2.9	3.4	3.9	4.4	4.8	5.3	5.8	6.3	6.8	7.2	7.7	8.2	8.7
30	0.0	0.5	1.0	1.5	2.0	2.5	3.0	3.5	4.0	4.5	5.0	5.5	6.0	6.5	7.0	7.5	8.0	8.5	9.0
31	0.0	0.5	1.0	1.6	2.1	2.6	3.1	3.6	4.1	4.6	5.2	5.7	6.2	6.7	7.2	7.8	8.3	8.8	9.3
32	0.0	0.5	1.1	1.6	2.1	2.7	3.2	3.7	4.3	4.8	5.3	5.9	6.4	6.9	7.5	8.0	8.5	9.1	9.6
33	0.0	0.6	1.1	1.6	2.2	2.8	3.3	3.8	4.4	5.0	5.5	6.0	6.6	7.2	7.7	8.2	8.8	9.4	9.9
34	0.0	0.6	1.1	1.7	2.3	2.8	3.4	4.0	4.5	5.1	5.7	6.2	6.8	7.4	7.9	8.5	9.1	9.6	10.2
35	0.0	0.6	1.2	1.8	2.3	2.9	3.5	4.1	4.7	5.2	5.8	6.4	7.0	7.6	8.2	8.8	9.3	9.9	10.5
36	0.0	0.6	1.2	1.8	2.4	3.0	3.6	4.2	4.8	5.4	6.0	6.6	7.2	7.8	8.4	9.0	9.6	10.2	10.8
37	0.0	0.6	1.2	1.8	2.5	3.1	3.7	4.3	4.9	5.6	6.2	6.8	7.4	8.0	8.6	9.2	9.9	10.5	11.1
38	0.0	0.6	1.3	1.9	2.5	3.2	3.8	4.4	5.1	5.7	6.3	7.0	7.6	8.2	8.9	9.5	10.1	10.8	11.4
39	0.0	0.6	1.3	2.0	2.6	3.2	3.9	4.6	5.2	5.8	6.5	7.2	7.8	8.4	9.1	9.8	10.4	11.0	11.7
40	0.0	0.7	1.3	2.0	2.7	3.3	4.0	4.7	5.3	6.0	6.7	7.3	8.0	8.7	9.3	10.0	10.7	11.3	12.0
41	0.0	0.7	1.4	2.0	2.7	3.4	4.1	4.8	5.5	6.2	6.8	7.5	8.2	8.9	9.6	10.2	10.9	11.6	12.3
42	0.0	0.7	1.4	2.1	2.8	3.5	4.2	4.9	5.6	6.3	7.0	7.7	8.4	9.1	9.8	10.5	11.2	11.9	12.6
43	0.0	0.7	1.4	2.2	2.9	3.6	4.3	5.0	5.7	6.4	7.2	7.9	8.6	9.3	10.0	10.8	11.5	12.2	12.9
44	0.0	0.7	1.5	2.2	2.9	3.7	4.4	5.1	5.9	6.6	7.3	8.1	8.8	9.5	10.3	11.0	11.7	12.5	13.2
45	0.0	0.7	1.5	2.2	3.0	3.8	4.5	5.2	6.0	6.8	7.5	8.2	9.0	9.8	10.5	11.2	12.0	12.8	13.5
46	0.0	0.8	1.5	2.3	3.1	3.8	4.6	5.4	6.1	6.9	7.7	8.4	9.2	10.0	10.7	11.5	12.3	13.0	13.8
47	0.0	0.8	1.6	2.4	3.1	3.9	4.7	5.5	6.3	7.0	7.8	8.6	9.4	10.2	11.0	11.8	12.5	13.3	14.1
48	0.0	0.8	1.6	2.4	3.2	4.0	4.8	5.6	6.4	7.2	8.0	8.8	9.6	10.4	11.2	12.0	12.8	13.6	14.4
49	0.0	0.8	1.6	2.4	3.3	4.1	4.9	5.7	6.5	7.4	8.2	9.0	9.8	10.6	11.4	12.2	13.1	13.9	14.7
50	0.0	0.8	1.7	2.5	3.3	4.2	5.0	5.8	6.7	7.5	8.3	9.2	10.0	10.8	11.7	12.5	13.3	14.2	15.0
51	0.0	0.8	1.7	2.6	3.4	4.2	5.1	6.0	6.8	7.6	8.5	9.4	10.2	11.0	11.9	12.8	13.6	14.4	15.3
52	0.0	0.9	1.7	2.6	3.5	4.3	5.2	6.1	6.9	7.8	8.7	9.5	10.4	11.3	12.1	13.0	13.9	14.7	15.6
53	0.0	0.9	1.8	2.6	3.5	4.4	5.3	6.2	7.1	8.0	8.8	9.7	10.6	11.5	12.4	13.2	14.1	15.0	15.9
54	0.0	0.9	1.8	2.7	3.6	4.5	5.4	6.3	7.2	8.1	9.0	9.9	10.8	11.7	12.6	13.5	14.4	15.3	16.2
55	0.0	0.9	1.8	2.8	3.7	4.6	5.5	6.4	7.3	8.2	9.2	10.1	11.0	11.9	12.8	13.8	14.7	15.6	16.5
56	0.0	0.9	1.9	2.8	3.7	4.7	5.6	6.5	7.5	8.4	9.3	10.3	11.2	12.1	13.1	14.0	14.9	15.9	16.8
57	0.0	1.0	1.9	2.8	3.8	4.8	5.7	6.6	7.6	8.6	9.5	10.4	11.4	12.4	13.3	14.2	15.2	16.2	17.1
58	0.0	1.0	1.9	2.9	3.9	4.8	5.8	6.8	7.7	8.7	9.7	10.6	11.6	12.6	13.5	14.5	15.5	16.4	17.4
59	0.0	1.0	2.0	3.0	3.9	4.9	5.9	6.9	7.9	8.8	9.8	10.8	11.8	12.8	13.8	14.8	15.7	16.7	17.7
60	0.0	1.0	2.0	3.0	4.0	5.0	6.0	7.0	8.0	9.0	10.0	11.0	12.0	13.0	14.0	15.0	16.0	17.0	18.0

Minutes

Chapter 6

MOON MERIDIAN PASSAGE TRANSIT CORRECTION TABLE

Longitude E/W	Daily difference of Meridian Passage (Minutes) 39	42	45	48	51	54	57	60	63	66	69	
0°	0	0	0	0	0	0	0	0	0	0	0	0°
10°	1	1	1	1	1	1	2	2	2	2	2	10°
20°	2	2	2	3	3	3	3	3	3	4	4	20°
30°	3	3	4	4	4	4	5	5	5	5	6	30°
40°	4	5	5	5	6	6	6	7	7	7	8	40°
50°	5	6	6	7	7	7	8	8	9	9	10	50°
60°	6	7	7	8	8	9	9	10	10	11	11	60°
70°	8	8	9	9	10	10	11	12	12	13	13	70°
80°	9	9	10	11	11	12	13	13	14	15	15	80°
90°	10	10	11	12	13	13	14	15	16	16	17	90°
100°	11	12	12	13	14	15	16	17	17	18	19	100°
110°	12	13	14	15	16	16	17	18	19	20	21	110°
120°	13	14	15	16	17	18	19	20	21	22	23	120°
130°	14	15	16	17	18	19	21	22	23	24	25	130°
140°	15	16	17	19	20	21	22	23	24	26	27	140°
150°	16	17	19	20	21	22	24	25	26	27	29	150°
160°	17	19	20	21	23	24	25	27	28	29	31	160°
170°	18	20	21	23	24	25	27	28	30	31	33	170°
180°	19	21	22	24	25	27	28	30	31	33	34	180°

Apply correction in **minutes** to Time of Meridian Passage given in the monthly pages.
Add if Longitude is West; **Subtract** if Longitude is East.

MOON RISING AND SETTING TABLE

Latitude °N / Dec (N/S)	2°	4°	6°	8°	10°	12°	14°	16°	18°	20°	22°	24°	26°	28°	
24	6	14	20	27	34	41	48	57	65	74	84	93	105	117	**24**
26	6	13	19	25	32	39	46	54	62	70	80	89	100	112	**26**
28	6	12	18	24	30	37	44	51	58	66	75	84	95	106	**28**
30	5	12	17	22	29	35	41	48	55	62	71	79	90	101	**30**
32	5	11	16	21	27	32	38	45	51	58	67	74	84	94	**32**
34	5	10	15	20	26	31	36	43	48	55	63	71	79	89	**34**
36	5	9	14	19	24	29	34	40	46	52	58	66	73	83	**36**
38	4	8	13	17	22	26	31	36	41	47	53	60	67	75	**38**
40	4	7	11	15	19	23	27	32	37	42	47	54	60	68	**40**
41	4	7	10	14	18	21	26	30	34	39	44	50	57	64	**41**
42	3	6	9	13	16	20	24	28	32	36	41	46	53	60	**42**
43	3	6	9	12	15	18	22	25	29	33	38	43	49	55	**43**
44	3	5	8	11	14	17	20	23	26	30	34	39	44	50	**44**
45	2	5	7	10	12	15	18	20	23	27	31	35	40	45	**45**
46	2	4	6	8	11	13	15	18	20	24	27	31	35	40	**46**
47	2	3	5	7	9	11	13	15	17	20	23	26	30	34	**47**
48	1	3	4	6	7	9	11	12	14	16	19	21	24	28	**48**
49	1	2	3	4	6	7	8	9	11	13	14	16	19	22	**49**
50	1	2	2	3	4	5	6	6	7	9	10	11	13	15	**50**
50.5	1	1	1	2	3	3	4	5	5	7	7	9	10	11	**50.5**
51	0	1	1	1	2	2	3	3	4	4	5	6	7	8	**51**
51.5	0	0	1	1	1	1	1	2	2	2	3	3	3	4	**51.5**
52	0	0	0	0	0	0	0	0	0	0	0	0	0	0	**52**
52.5	0	0	1	1	1	1	1	2	2	2	3	3	3	4	**52.5**
53	0	1	1	1	2	3	3	3	4	4	5	6	7	8	**53**
53.5	1	1	2	2	3	4	4	5	7	7	8	9	11	13	**53.5**
54	1	2	2	3	4	5	6	7	8	10	11	13	15	17	**54**
54.5	1	2	3	4	5	6	8	9	11	12	14	16	19	22	**54.5**
55	1	3	4	5	6	8	9	11	13	15	17	20	23	27	**55**
55.5	1	3	4	6	8	9	11	13	15	18	20	23	27	33	**55.5**
56	2	3	5	7	9	11	13	15	18	20	24	27	32	38	**56**
56.5	2	4	6	8	10	12	15	17	20	23	27	31	37	44	**56.5**
57	2	4	7	9	11	14	17	20	23	26	31	35	42	51	**57**
57.5	2	5	7	10	13	15	19	22	25	30	34	40	47	57	**57.5**
58	3	5	8	11	14	17	21	24	28	33	38	45	53	65	**58**

All figures given are **minutes**, to be applied to the Moonrise/Moonset times on the monthly pages as follows:

From Latitude **24°N to 52°N** with Declination **N**: **Add** to Moonrise, **Subtract** from Moonset
From Latitude **24°N to 52°N** with Declination **S**: **Subtract** from Moonrise, **Add** to Moonset
From Latitude **52°N to 58°N** with Declination **N**: **Subtract** from Moonrise, **Add** to Moonset
From Latitude **52°N to 58°N** with Declination **S**: **Add** to Moonrise, **Subtract** from Moonset

PLANETS GHA CORRECTION TABLE (HOURS)

Always add

Var/hr	14°58.8'	14°59.0'	14°59.1'	14°59.3'	14°59.4'	14°59.6'	14°59.7'	14°59.9'	15°0.0'
	° '	° '	° '	° '	° '	° '	° '	° '	° '
0	0 00.0	0 00.0	0 00.0	0 00.0	0 00.0	0 00.0	0 00.0	0 00.0	0 00.0
1	14 58.8	14 59.0	14 59.1	14 59.3	14 59.4	14 59.6	14 59.7	14 59.9	15 00.0
2	29 57.6	29 58.0	29 58.2	29 58.6	29 58.8	29 59.2	29 59.4	29 59.8	30 00.0
3	44 56.4	44 57.0	44 57.3	44 57.9	44 58.2	44 58.8	44 59.1	44 59.7	45 00.0
4	59 55.2	59 56.0	59 56.4	59 57.2	59 57.6	59 58.4	59 58.8	59 59.6	60 00.0
5	74 54.0	74 55.0	74 55.5	74 56.5	74 57.0	74 58.0	74 58.5	74 59.5	75 00.0
6	89 52.8	89 54.0	89 54.6	89 55.8	89 56.4	89 57.6	89 58.2	89 59.4	90 00.0
7	104 51.6	104 53.0	104 53.7	104 55.1	104 55.8	104 57.2	104 57.9	104 59.3	105 00.0
8	119 50.4	119 52.0	119 52.8	119 54.4	119 55.2	119 56.8	119 57.6	119 59.2	120 00.0
9	134 49.2	134 51.0	134 51.9	134 53.7	134 54.6	134 56.4	134 57.3	134 59.1	135 00.0
10	149 48.0	149 50.0	149 51.0	149 53.0	149 54.0	149 56.0	149 57.0	149 59.0	150 00.0
11	164 46.8	164 49.0	164 50.1	164 52.3	164 53.4	164 55.6	164 56.7	164 58.9	165 00.0
12	179 45.6	179 48.0	179 49.2	179 51.6	179 52.8	179 55.2	179 56.4	179 58.8	180 00.0
13	194 44.4	194 47.0	194 48.3	194 50.9	194 52.2	194 54.8	194 56.1	194 58.7	195 00.0
14	209 43.2	209 46.0	209 47.4	209 50.2	209 51.6	209 54.4	209 55.8	209 58.6	210 00.0
15	224 42.0	224 45.0	224 46.5	224 49.5	224 51.0	224 54.0	224 55.5	224 58.5	225 00.0
16	239 40.8	239 44.0	239 45.6	239 48.8	239 50.4	239 53.6	239 55.2	239 58.4	240 00.0
17	254 39.6	254 43.0	254 44.7	254 48.1	254 49.8	254 53.2	254 54.9	254 58.3	255 00.0
18	269 38.4	269 42.0	269 43.8	269 47.4	269 49.2	269 52.8	269 54.6	269 58.2	270 00.0
19	284 37.2	284 41.0	284 42.9	284 46.7	284 48.6	284 52.4	284 54.3	284 58.1	285 00.0
20	299 36.0	299 40.0	299 42.0	299 46.0	299 48.0	299 52.0	299 54.0	299 58.0	300 00.0
21	314 34.8	314 39.0	314 41.1	314 45.3	314 47.4	314 51.6	314 53.7	314 57.9	315 00.0
22	329 33.6	329 38.0	329 40.2	329 44.6	329 46.8	329 51.2	329 53.4	329 57.8	330 00.0
23	344 32.4	344 37.0	344 39.3	344 43.7	344 46.2	344 50.8	344 53.1	344 57.7	345 00.0
24	359 31.2	359 36.0	359 38.4	359 43.2	359 45.6	359 50.4	359 52.8	359 57.6	0 00.0

(Hours)

Var/hr	15°00.2'	15°00.3'	15°00.5'	15°00.6'	15°00.8'	15°00.9'	15°01.1'	15°01.2'	15°01.4'
	° '	° '	° '	° '	° '	° '	° '	° '	° '
0	0 00.0	0 00.0	0 00.0	0 00.0	0 00.0	0 00.0	0 00.0	0 00.0	0 00.0
1	15 00.2	15 00.3	15 00.5	15 00.6	15 00.8	15 00.9	15 01.1	15 01.2	15 01.4
2	30 00.4	30 00.6	30 01.0	30 01.2	30 01.6	30 01.8	30 02.2	30 02.4	30 02.8
3	45 00.6	45 00.9	45 01.5	45 01.8	45 02.4	45 02.7	45 03.3	45 03.6	45 04.2
4	60 00.8	60 01.2	60 02.0	60 02.4	60 03.2	60 03.6	60 04.4	60 04.8	60 05.6
5	75 01.0	75 01.5	75 02.5	75 03.0	75 04.0	75 04.5	75 05.5	75 06.0	75 07.0
6	90 01.2	90 01.8	90 03.0	90 03.6	90 04.8	90 05.4	90 06.6	90 07.2	90 08.4
7	105 01.4	105 02.1	105 03.5	105 04.2	105 05.6	105 06.3	105 07.7	105 08.4	105 09.8
8	120 01.6	120 02.4	120 04.0	120 04.8	120 06.4	120 07.2	120 08.8	120 09.6	120 11.2
9	135 01.8	135 02.7	135 04.5	135 05.4	135 07.2	135 08.1	135 09.9	135 10.8	135 12.6
10	150 02.0	150 03.0	150 05.0	150 06.0	150 08.0	150 09.0	150 11.0	150 12.0	150 14.0
11	165 02.2	165 03.3	165 05.5	165 06.6	165 08.8	165 09.9	165 12.1	165 13.2	165 15.4
12	180 02.4	180 03.6	180 06.0	180 07.2	180 09.6	180 10.8	180 13.2	180 14.4	180 16.8
13	195 02.6	195 03.9	195 06.5	195 07.8	195 10.4	195 11.7	195 14.3	195 15.6	195 18.2
14	210 02.8	210 04.2	210 07.0	210 08.4	210 11.2	210 12.6	210 15.4	210 16.8	210 19.6
15	225 03.0	225 04.5	225 07.5	225 09.0	225 12.0	225 13.5	225 16.5	225 18.5	225 21.0
16	240 03.2	240 04.8	240 08.0	240 09.6	240 12.8	240 14.4	240 17.6	240 19.2	240 22.4
17	255 03.4	255 05.1	255 08.5	255 10.2	255 13.6	255 15.3	255 18.7	255 20.4	255 23.8
18	270 03.6	270 05.4	270 09.0	270 10.8	270 14.4	270 16.2	270 19.8	270 21.6	270 25.2
19	285 03.8	285 05.7	285 09.5	285 11.4	285 15.2	285 17.1	285 20.9	285 22.8	285 26.6
20	300 04.0	300 06.0	300 10.0	300 12.0	300 16.0	300 18.0	300 22.0	300 24.0	300 28.0
21	315 04.2	315 06.3	315 10.5	315 12.6	315 16.8	315 18.9	315 23.1	315 25.2	315 29.4
22	330 04.4	330 06.6	330 11.0	330 13.2	330 17.6	330 19.8	330 24.2	330 26.4	330 30.8
23	345 04.6	345 06.9	345 11.5	345 13.8	345 18.4	345 20.7	345 25.3	345 27.6	345 32.2
24	0 04.8	0 07.2	0 12.0	0 14.4	0 19.2	0 21.6	0 26.4	0 28.8	0 33.6

(Hours)

Chapter 6

PLANETS GHA CORRECTION TABLE (HOURS)

Always add

Var/hr	15°01.5′	15°01.7′	15°01.8′	15°02.0′	15°02.1′	15°02.3′	15°02.4′	15°02.6′	15°02.7′
	° ′	° ′	° ′	° ′	° ′	° ′	° ′	° ′	° ′
0	0 00.0	0 00.0	0 00.0	0 00.0	0 00.0	0 00.0	0 00.0	0 00.0	0 00.0
1	15 01.5	15 01.7	15 01.8	15 02.0	15 02.1	15 02.3	15 02.4	15 02.6	15 02.7
2	30 03.0	30 03.4	30 03.6	30 04.0	30 04.2	30 04.6	30 04.8	30 05.2	30 05.4
3	45 04.5	45 05.1	45 05.4	45 06.0	45 06.3	45 06.9	45 07.2	45 07.8	45 08.1
4	60 06.0	60 06.8	60 07.2	60 08.0	60 08.4	60 09.2	60 09.6	60 10.4	60 10.8
5	75 07.5	75 08.5	75 09.0	75 10.0	75 10.5	75 11.5	75 12.0	75 13.0	75 13.5
6	90 09.0	90 10.2	90 10.8	90 12.0	90 12.6	90 13.8	90 14.4	90 15.6	90 16.2
7	105 10.5	105 11.9	105 12.6	105 14.0	105.14.7	105 16.1	105 16.8	105 18.2	105 18.9
8	120 12.0	120 13.6	120 14.4	120 16.0	120 16.8	120 18.4	120 19.2	120 20.8	120 21.6
9	135 13.5	135 15.3	135 16.2	135 18.0	135 18.9	135 20.7	135 21.6	135 23.4	135 24.3
10	150 15.0	150 17.0	150 18.0	150 20.0	150 21.0	150 23.0	150 24.0	150 26.0	150 27.0
11	165 16.5	165 18.7	165 19.8	165 22.0	165 23.1	165 25.8	165 26.4	165 28.6	165 29.7
12	180 18.0	180 20.4	180 21.6	180 24.0	180 25.2	180 27.6	180 28.8	180 31.2	180 32.4
13	195 19.5	195 22.1	195 23.4	195 26.0	195 27.3	195 29.9	195 31.2	195 33.8	195 35.1
14	210 21.0	210 23.8	210 25.2	210 28.0	210 29.4	210 32.2	210 33.6	210 36.4	210 37.8
15	225 22.5	225 25.5	225 27.0	225 30.0	225 31.5	225 34.5	225 36.0	225 39.0	225 40.5
16	240 24.0	240 27.2	240 28.8	240 32.0	240 33.6	240 36.8	240 38.4	240 41.6	240 43.2
17	255 25.5	255 28.9	255 30.6	255 34.0	255 35.7	255 39.1	255 40.8	255 44.8	255 45.9
18	270 27.0	270 30.6	270 32.4	270 36.0	270 37.8	270 41.4	270 43.2	270 46.8	270 48.6
19	285 28.5	285 32.3	285 34.2	285 38.0	285 39.9	285 43.7	285 45.6	285 49.4	285 51.3
20	300 30.0	300 34.0	300 36.0	300 40.0	300 42.0	300 46.0	300 48.0	300 52.0	300 54.0
21	315 31.5	315 35.7	315 37.8	315 42.0	315 44.1	315 48.3	315 50.4	315 54.6	315 56.7
22	330 33.0	330 37.4	330 39.6	330 44.0	330 46.2	330 50.6	330 52.8	330 57.2	330 59.4
23	345 34.5	345 39.1	345 41.4	345 46.0	345 48.3	345 52.9	345 55.2	345 59.8	346 02.1
24	0 36.0	0 40.8	0 43..2	0 48.0	0 50.4	0 55.2	0 57.6	1 02.4	1 04.8

Var/hr	15°02.9′	15°03.0′	15°03.2′	15°03.3′	15°03.5′	15°03.6′	15°03.8′	15°03.9′	15°04.1′
	° ′	° ′	° ′	° ′	° ′	° ′	° ′	° ′	° ′
0	0 00.0	0 00.0	0 00.0	0 00.0	0 00.0	0 00.0	0 00.0	0 00.0	0 00.0
1	15 02.9	15 03.0	15 03.2	15 03.3	15 03.5	15 03.6	15 03.8	15 03.9	15 04.1
2	30 05.8	30 06.0	30 06.4	30 06.6	30 07.0	15 07.2	30 07.6	30 07.8	30 08.2
3	45 08.7	45 09.0	45 09.6	45 09.9	45 10.5	45 10.8	45 11.4	45 11.7	45 12.3
4	60 11.6	60 12.0	60 12.8	60 13.2	60 14.0	60 14.4	60 15.2	60 15.6	60 16.4
5	75 14.5	75 15.0	75 16.0	75 16.5	75 17.5	75 18.0	75 19.0	75 19.5	75 20.5
6	90 17.4	90 18.0	90 19.2	90 19.8	90 21.0	90 21.6	90 22.8	90 23.4	90 24.6
7	105 20.3	105 21.0	105 22.4	105 23.1	105 24.5	105 25.2	105 26.6	105 27.3	105 28.7
8	120 23.2	120 24.0	120 25.6	120 26.4	120 28.0	120 28.8	120 30.4	120 31.2	120 32.8
9	135 26.1	135 27.0	135 28.8	135 29.7	135 31.5	135 32.4	135 34.2	135 35.1	135 36.9
10	150 29.0	150 30.0	150 32.0	150 33.0	150 35.0	150 36.0	150 38.0	150 39.0	150 41.0
11	165 31.9	165 33.0	165 35.2	165 36.3	165 38.5	165 39.6	165 41.8	165 42.9	165 45.1
12	180 34.8	180 36.0	180 38.4	180 39.6	180 42.0	180 43.2	180 46.4	180 46.8	180 49.2
13	195 37.7	195 39.0	195 41.6	195 42.9	195 45.5	195 46.8	195 49.4	195 50.7	195 53.3
14	210 40.6	210 42.0	210 44.8	210 46.2	210 49.0	210 50.4	210 53.2	210 54.6	210 57.4
15	225 43.5	225 45.0	225 48.0	225 49.5	225 52.5	225 54.0	225 57.0	225 58.5	226 01.5
16	240 46.4	240 48.0	240 51.2	240 52.8	240 56.0	240 57.6	241 00.8	241 02.4	241 05.6
17	255 49.3	255 51.0	255 54.4	255 56.1	255 59.5	256 01.2	256 04.6	256 06.3	256 09.7
18	270 52.2	270 54.0	270 57.6	270 59.4	271 03.0	271 04.8	271 08.4	271 10.2	271 13.8
19	285 55.1	285 57.0	286 00.8	286 02.7	286 06.5	286 08.4	286 12.2	286 14.1	286 17.9
20	300 58.0	301 00.0	301 04.0	301 06.0	301 10.0	301 12.0	301 16.0	301 18.0	301 22.0
21	316 00.9	316 03.0	316 07.2	316 09.3	316 13.5	316 15.6	316 19.8	316 21.9	316 26.1
22	331 03.8	331 06.0	331 10.4	331 12.6	331 17.0	331 19.2	331 23.6	331 25.8	331 30.2
23	346 06.7	346 09.0	346 13.6	346 15.9	346 20.5	346 22.8	346 27.4	346 29.7	346 34.3
24	001 09.6	001 12.0	001 16.8	001 19.2	001 24.0	001 26.4	001 31.2	001 33.6	001 38.4

PLANETS GHA CORRECTION TABLE (MINUTES)

Always add

Var/hr	14°58.8′	14°59.4′	15°00.0′	15°00.6′	15°01.2′	15°01.8′	15°02.4′	15°03.0′	15°03.6′	Sec	′
0	0 00.0	0 00.0	0 00.0	0 00.0	0 00.0	0 00.0	0 00.0	0 00.0	0 00.0	0	0.0
1	0 15.0	0 15.0	0 15.0	0 15.0	0 15.0	0 15.0	0 15.0	0 15.0	0 15.1	1	0.3
2	0 30.0	0 30.0	0 30.0	0 30.0	0 30.0	0 30.1	0 30.1	0 30.1	0 30.1	2	0.5
3	0 44.9	0 45.0	0 45.0	0 45.0	0 45.1	0 45.1	0 45.1	0 45.1	0 45.2	3	0.8
4	0 59.9	1 00.0	1 00.0	1 00.0	1 00.1	1 00.1	1 00.2	1 00.2	1 00.2	4	1.0
5	1 14.9	1 14.9	1 15.0	1 15.0	1 15.1	1 15.2	1 15.2	1 15.2	1 15.3	5	1.3
6	1 29.9	1 29.9	1 30.0	1 30.1	1 30.1	1 30.2	1 30.2	1 30.3	1 30.4	6	1.5
7	1 44.9	1 44.9	1 45.0	1 45.1	1 45.1	1 45.2	1 45.3	1 45.3	1 45.4	7	1.8
8	1 59.8	1 59.9	2 00.0	2 00.1	2 00.2	2 00.2	2 00.3	2 00.4	2 00.5	8	2.0
9	2 14.8	2 14.9	2 15.0	2 15.1	2 15.2	2 15.3	2 15.4	2 15.4	2 15.5	9	2.3
10	2 29.8	2 29.9	2 30.0	2 30.1	2 30.2	2 30.3	2 30.4	2 30.5	2 30.6	10	2.5
11	2 44.8	2 44.9	2 45.0	2 45.1	2 45.2	2 45.3	2 45.4	2 45.5	2 45.7	11	2.8
12	2 59.8	2 59.9	3 00.0	3 00.1	3 00.2	3 00.4	3 00.5	3 00.6	3 00.7	12	3.0
13	3 14.7	3 14.9	3 15.0	3 15.1	3 15.3	3 15.4	3 15.5	3 15.6	3 15.8	13	3.3
14	3 29.7	3 29.9	3 30.0	3 30.1	3 30.3	3 30.4	3 30.6	3 30.7	3 30.8	14	3.5
15	3 44.7	3 44.8	3 45.0	3 45.2	3 45.3	3 45.4	3 45.6	3 45.7	3 45.9	15	3.8
16	3 59.7	3 59.8	4 00.0	4 00.2	4 00.3	4 00.5	4 00.6	4 00.8	4 01.0	16	4.0
17	4 14.7	4 14.8	4 15.0	4 15.2	4 15.3	4 15.5	4 15.7	4 15.8	4 16.0	17	4.3
18	4 29.6	4 29.8	4 30.0	4 30.2	4 30.4	4 30.5	4 30.7	4 30.9	4 31.1	18	4.5
19	4 44.6	4 44.8	4 45.0	4 45.2	4 45.4	4 45.6	4 45.8	4 45.9	4 46.1	19	4.8
20	4 59.6	4 59.8	5 00.0	5 00.2	5 00.4	5 00.6	5 00.8	5 01.0	5 01.2	20	5.0
21	5 14.6	5 14.8	5 15.0	5 15.2	5 15.4	5 15.6	5 15.8	5 16.0	5 16.3	21	5.3
22	5 29.6	5 29.8	5 30.0	5 30.2	5 30.4	5 30.7	5 30.9	5 31.1	5 31.3	22	5.5
23	5 44.5	5 44.8	5 45.0	5 45.2	5 45.5	5 45.7	5 45.9	5 46.1	5 46.4	23	5.8
24	5 59.5	5 59.8	6 00.0	6 00.2	6 00.5	6 00.7	6 01.0	6 01.2	6 01.4	24	6.0
25	6 14.5	6 14.8	6 15.0	6 15.2	6 15.5	6 15.7	6 16.0	6 16.2	6 16.5	25	6.3
26	6 29.5	6 29.7	6 30.0	6 30.3	6 30.5	6 30.8	6 31.0	6 31.3	6 31.6	26	6.5
27	6 04.5	6 44.7	6 45.0	6 45.3	6 45.5	6 45.8	6 46.1	6 46.3	6 46.6	27	6.8
28	6 59.4	6 59.7	7 00.0	7 00.3	7 00.6	7 00.8	7 01.1	7 01.4	7 01.7	28	7.0
29	7 14.4	7 14.7	7 15.0	7 15.3	7 15.6	7 15.9	7 16.2	7 16.4	7 16.7	29	7.3
30	7 29.4	7 29.7	7 30.0	7 30.3	7 30.6	7 30.9	7 31.2	7 31.5	7 31.8	30	7.5
31	7 44.4	7 44.7	7 45.0	7 45.3	7 45.6	7 45.9	7 46.2	7 46.5	7 46.9	31	7.8
32	7 59.4	7 59.7	8 00.0	8 00.3	8 00.6	8 01.0	8 01.3	8 01.6	8 01.9	32	8.0
33	8 14.3	8 14.7	8 15.0	8 15.3	8 15.7	8 16.0	8 16.3	8 16.6	8 17.0	33	8.3
34	8 29.3	8 29.7	8 30.0	8 30.3	8 30.7	8 31.0	8 31.4	8 31.7	8 32.0	34	8.5
35	8 44.3	8 44.6	8 45.0	8 45.5	8 45.7	8 46.0	8 46.4	8 46.7	8 47.1	35	8.8
36	8 59.3	8 59.6	9 00.0	9 00.4	9 00.7	9 01.1	9 01.4	9 01.8	9 02.2	36	9.0
37	9 14.3	9 14.6	9 15.0	9 15.4	9 15.7	9 16.1	9 16.5	9 16.8	9 17.2	37	9.3
38	9 29.2	9 29.6	9 30.0	9 30.4	9 30.8	9 31.1	9 31.5	9 31.9	9 32.3	38	9.5
39	9 44.2	9 44.6	9 45.0	9 45.4	9 45.8	9 46.2	9 46.6	9 46.9	9 47.3	39	9.8
40	9 59.2	9 59.6	10 00.0	10 00.4	10 00.8	10 01.2	10 01.6	10 02.0	10 02.4	40	10.0
41	10 14.2	10 14.6	10 15.0	10 15.4	10 15.8	10 16.2	10 16.6	10 17.0	10 17.5	41	10.3
42	10 29.2	10 29.6	10 30.0	10 30.4	10 30.8	10 31.3	10 31.7	10 32.1	10 32.5	42	10.5
43	10 44.1	10 44.6	10 45.0	10 45.4	10 45.9	10 46.3	10 46.7	10 47.1	10 47.6	43	10.8
44	10 59.1	10 59.6	11 00.0	11 00.4	11 00.9	11 01.3	11 01.8	11 02.2	11 02.6	44	11.0
45	11 14.1	11 14.6	11 15.0	11 15.4	11 15.9	11 16.3	11 16.8	11 17.2	11 17.7	45	11.3
46	11 29.1	11 29.5	11 30.0	11 30.5	11 30.9	11 31.4	11 31.8	11 32.3	11 32.8	46	11.5
47	11 44.1	11 44.5	11 45.0	11 45.5	11 45.9	11 46.4	11 46.9	11 47.3	11 47.8	47	11.8
48	11 59.0	11 59.5	12 00.0	12 00.5	12 01.0	12 01.4	12 01.9	12 02.4	12 02.9	48	12.0
49	12 14.0	12 14.5	12 15.0	12 15.5	12 15.9	12 16.5	12 17.0	12 17.4	12 17.9	49	12.3
50	12 29.0	12 29.5	12 30.0	12 30.5	12 31.0	12 31.5	12 32.0	12 32.5	12 33.0	50	12.5
51	12 44.0	12 44.5	12 45.0	12 45.5	12 46.0	12 46.5	12 47.0	12 47.5	12 48.1	51	12.8
52	12 59.0	12 59.5	13 00.0	13 00.5	13 01.0	13 01.6	13 02.1	13 02.6	13 03.1	52	13.1
53	13 13.9	13 14.5	13 15.0	13 15.5	13 16.1	13 16.6	13 17.1	13 17.6	13 18.2	53	13.3
54	13 28.9	13 29.5	13 30.0	13 30.5	13 31.1	13 31.6	13 32.2	13 32.7	13 33.2	54	13.5
55	13 43.9	13 44.4	13 45.0	13 45.6	13 46.1	13 46.6	13 47.2	13 47.7	13 48.3	55	13.8
56	13 58.9	13 59.4	14 00.0	14 00.6	14 01.1	14 01.7	17 02.2	14 02.8	14 03.4	56	14.0
57	14 13.9	14 14.4	14 15.0	14 15.6	14 16.1	14 16.7	14 17.3	14 17.8	14 18.4	57	14.3
58	14 28.8	14 29.4	14 30.0	14 30.6	14 31.2	14 31.7	14 32.3	14 32.9	14 33.5	58	14.5
59	14 43.8	14 44.4	14 45.0	14 45.6	14 46.2	14 46.8	14 47.4	14 47.9	14 48.5	59	14.8
60	14 58.8	14 59.4	15 00.0	15 00.6	15 01.2	15 01.8	15 02.4	15 03.0	15 03.6	60	15.0

Chapter 6

PLANETS DECLINATION CORRECTION TABLE

Var/hr	0.0′	0.1′	0.2′	0.3′	0.4′	0.5′	0.6′	0.7′	0.8′	0.9′	1.0	1.1′	1.2′	1.3′	1.4′	1.5′
h m	′	′	′	′	′	′	′	′	′	′	′	′	′	′	′	′
0 00	0.0	0.0	0.0	0.0	0.0	0.0	0.0	0.0	0.0	0.0	0.0	0.0	0.0	0.0	0.0	0.0
12	0.0	0.0	0.0	0.1	0.1	0.1	0.1	0.1	0.2	0.2	0.2	0.2	0.2	0.3	0.3	0.3
24	0.0	0.0	0.1	0.1	0.2	0.2	0.2	0.3	0.3	0.4	0.4	0.4	0.5	0.5	0.6	0.6
36	0.0	0.1	0.1	0.2	0.2	0.3	0.4	0.4	0.5	0.5	0.6	0.7	0.7	0.8	0.8	0.9
48	0.0	0.1	0.2	0.2	0.3	0.4	0.5	0.6	0.6	0.7	0.8	0.9	1.0	1.0	1.1	1.2
1 00	0.0	0.1	0.2	0.3	0.4	0.5	0.6	0.7	0.8	0.9	1.0	1.1	1.2	1.3	1.4	1.5
12	0.0	0.1	0.2	0.4	0.5	0.6	0.7	0.8	1.0	1.1	1.2	1.3	1.4	1.6	1.7	1.8
24	0.0	0.1	0.3	0.4	0.6	0.7	0.8	1.0	1.1	1.3	1.4	1.5	1.7	1.8	2.0	2.1
36	0.0	0.2	0.3	0.5	0.6	0.8	1.0	1.1	1.3	1.4	1.6	1.8	1.9	2.1	2.2	2.4
48	0.0	0.2	0.4	0.5	0.7	0.9	1.1	1.3	1.4	1.6	1.8	2.0	2.2	2.3	2.5	2.7
2 00	0.0	0.2	0.4	0.6	0.8	1.0	1.2	1.4	1.6	1.8	2.0	2.2	2.4	2.6	2.8	3.0
12	0.0	0.2	0.4	0.7	0.9	1.1	1.3	1.5	1.8	2.0	2.2	2.4	2.6	2.9	3.1	3.3
24	0.0	0.2	0.5	0.7	1.0	1.2	1.4	1.7	1.9	2.2	2.4	2.6	2.9	3.1	3.4	3.6
36	0.0	0.3	0.5	0.8	1.0	1.3	1.6	1.8	2.1	2.3	2.6	2.9	3.1	3.4	3.6	3.9
48	0.0	0.3	0.6	0.8	1.1	1.4	1.7	2.0	2.2	2.5	2.8	3.1	3.4	3.6	3.9	4.2
3 00	0.0	0.3	0.6	0.9	1.2	1.5	1.8	2.1	2.4	2.7	3.0	3.3	3.6	3.9	4.2	4.5
12	0.0	0.3	0.6	1.0	1.3	1.6	1.9	2.2	2.6	2.9	3.2	3.5	3.8	4.2	4.5	4.8
24	0.0	0.3	0.7	1.0	1.4	1.7	2.0	2.4	2.7	3.1	3.4	3.7	4.1	4.4	4.8	5.1
36	0.0	0.4	0.7	1.1	1.4	1.8	2.2	2.5	2.9	3.2	3.6	4.0	4.3	4.7	5.0	5.4
48	0.0	0.4	0.8	1.1	1.5	1.9	2.3	2.7	3.0	3.4	3.8	4.2	4.6	4.9	5.3	5.7
4 00	0.0	0.4	0.8	1.2	1.6	2.0	2.4	2.8	3.2	3.6	4.0	4.4	4.8	5.2	5.6	6.0
12	0.0	0.4	0.8	1.3	1.7	2.1	2.5	2.9	3.4	3.8	4.2	4.6	5.0	5.5	5.9	6.3
24	0.0	0.4	0.9	1.3	1.8	2.2	2.6	3.1	3.5	4.0	4.4	4.8	5.3	5.7	6.2	6.6
36	0.0	0.5	0.9	1.4	1.8	2.3	2.8	3.2	3.7	4.1	4.6	5.1	5.5	6.0	6.4	6.9
48	0.0	0.5	1.0	1.4	1.9	2.4	2.9	3.4	3.8	4.3	4.8	5.3	5.8	6.2	6.7	7.2
5 00	0.0	0.5	1.0	1.5	2.0	2.5	3.0	3.5	4.0	4.5	5.0	5.5	6.0	6.5	7.0	7.5
12	0.0	0.5	1.0	1.6	2.1	2.6	3.1	3.6	4.2	4.7	5.2	5.7	6.2	6.8	7.3	7.8
24	0.0	0.5	1.1	1.6	2.2	2.7	3.2	3.8	4.3	4.9	5.4	5.9	6.5	7.0	7.6	8.1
36	0.0	0.6	1.1	1.7	2.2	2.8	3.4	3.9	4.5	5.0	5.6	6.2	6.7	7.3	7.8	8.4
48	0.0	0.6	1.2	1.7	2.3	2.9	3.5	4.1	4.6	5.2	5.8	6.4	7.0	7.5	8.1	8.7
6 00	0.0	0.6	1.2	1.8	2.4	3.0	3.6	4.2	4.8	5.4	6.0	6.6	7.2	7.8	8.4	9.0
12	0.0	0.6	1.2	1.9	2.5	3.1	3.7	4.3	5.0	5.6	6.2	6.8	7.4	8.1	8.7	9.3
24	0.0	0.6	1.3	1.9	2.6	3.2	3.8	4.5	5.1	5.8	6.4	7.0	7.7	8.3	9.0	9.6
36	0.0	0.7	1.3	2.0	2.6	3.3	4.0	4.6	5.3	5.9	6.6	7.3	7.9	8.6	9.2	9.9
48	0.0	0.7	1.4	2.0	2.7	3.4	4.1	4.8	5.4	6.1	6.8	7.5	8.2	8.8	9.5	10.2
7 00	0.0	0.7	1.4	2.1	2.8	3.5	4.2	4.9	5.6	6.3	7.0	7.7	8.4	9.1	9.8	10.5
12	0.0	0.7	1.4	2.2	2.9	3.6	4.3	5.0	5.8	6.5	7.2	7.9	8.6	9.4	10.1	10.8
24	0.0	0.7	1.5	2.2	3.0	3.7	4.4	5.2	5.9	6.7	7.4	8.1	8.9	9.6	10.4	11.1
36	0.0	0.8	1.5	2.3	3.0	3.8	4.6	5.3	6.1	6.8	7.6	8.4	9.1	9.9	10.6	11.4
48	0.0	0.8	1.6	2.3	3.1	3.9	4.7	5.5	6.2	7.0	7.8	8.6	9.4	10.1	10.9	11.7
8 00	0.0	0.8	1.6	2.4	3.2	4.0	4.8	5.6	6.4	7.2	8.0	8.8	9.6	10.4	11.2	12.0
12	0.0	0.8	1.6	2.5	3.3	4.1	4.9	5.7	6.6	7.4	8.2	9.0	9.8	10.7	11.5	12.3
24	0.0	0.8	1.7	2.5	3.4	4.2	5.0	5.9	6.7	7.6	8.4	9.2	10.1	10.9	11.8	12.6
36	0.0	0.9	1.7	2.6	3.4	4.3	5.2	6.0	6.9	7.7	8.6	9.5	10.3	11.2	12.0	12.9
48	0.0	0.9	1.8	2.6	3.5	4.4	5.3	6.2	7.0	7.9	8.8	9.7	10.6	11.4	12.3	13.2
9 00	0.0	0.9	1.8	2.7	3.6	4.5	5.4	6.3	7.2	8.1	9.0	9.9	10.8	11.7	12.6	13.5
12	0.0	0.9	1.8	2.8	3.7	4.6	5.5	6.4	7.4	8.3	9.2	10.1	11.0	12.0	12.9	13.8
24	0.0	0.9	1.9	2.8	3.8	4.7	5.6	6.6	7.5	8.5	9.4	10.3	11.3	12.2	13.2	14.1
36	0.0	1.0	1.9	2.9	3.8	4.8	5.8	6.7	7.7	8.6	9.6	10.6	11.5	12.5	13.4	14.4
48	0.0	1.0	2.0	2.9	3.9	4.9	5.9	6.9	7.8	8.8	9.8	10.8	11.8	12.7	13.7	14.7
10 00	0.0	1.0	2.0	3.0	4.0	5.0	6.0	7.0	8.0	9.0	10.0	11.0	12.0	13.0	14.0	15.0
12	0.0	1.0	2.0	3.1	4.1	5.1	6.1	7.1	8.2	9.2	10.2	11.2	12.2	13.2	14.3	15.3
24	0.0	1.0	2.1	3.1	4.2	5.2	6.2	7.3	8.3	9.4	10.4	11.4	12.5	13.5	14.6	15.6
36	0.0	1.1	2.1	3.2	4.2	5.3	6.4	7.4	8.5	9.5	10.6	11.7	12.7	13.8	14.8	15.9
48	0.0	1.1	2.2	3.2	4.3	5.4	6.5	7.6	8.6	9.7	10.8	11.9	13.0	14.0	15.1	16.2
11 00	0.0	1.1	2.2	3.3	4.4	5.5	6.6	7.7	8.8	9.9	11.0	12.1	13.2	14.3	15.4	16.5
12	0.0	1.1	2.2	3.4	4.5	5.6	6.7	7.8	9.0	10.1	11.2	12.3	13.4	14.6	15.7	16.8
24	0.0	1.1	2.3	3.4	4.6	5.7	6.8	8.0	9.1	10.3	11.4	12.5	13.7	14.8	16.0	17.1
36	0.0	1.2	2.3	3.5	4.6	5.8	7.0	8.1	9.3	10.4	11.6	12.8	13.9	15.1	16.2	17.4
48	0.0	1.2	2.4	3.5	4.7	5.9	7.1	8.3	9.4	10.6	11.8	13.0	14.2	15.3	16.5	17.7
12 00	0.0	1.2	2.4	3.6	4.8	6.0	7.2	8.4	9.6	10.8	12.0	13.2	14.4	15.6	16.8	18.0

PLANETS DECLINATION CORRECTION TABLE

Var/hr	0.0'	0.1'	0.2'	0.3'	0.4'	0.5'	0.6'	0.7'	0.8'	0.9'	1.0'	1.1'	1.2'	1.3'	1.4'	1.5'
h m	'	'	'	'	'	'	'	'	'	'	'	'	'	'	'	'
12 00	0.0	1.2	2.4	3.6	4.8	6.0	7.2	8.4	9.6	10.8	12.0	13.2	14.4	15.6	16.8	18.0
12	0.0	1.2	2.4	3.7	4.9	6.1	7.3	8.5	9.8	11.0	12.2	13.4	14.6	15.9	17.1	18.3
24	0.0	1.2	2.5	3.7	5.0	6.2	7.4	8.7	9.9	11.2	12.4	13.6	14.9	16.1	17.4	18.6
36	0.0	1.3	2.5	3.8	5.0	6.3	7.6	8.8	10.1	11.3	12.6	13.9	15.1	16.4	17.6	18.9
48	0.0	1.3	2.6	3.8	5.1	6.4	7.7	9.0	10.2	11.5	12.8	14.1	15.4	16.6	17.9	19.2
13 00	0.0	1.3	2.6	3.9	5.2	6.5	7.8	9.1	10.4	11.7	13.0	14.3	15.6	16.9	18.2	19.5
12	0.0	1.3	2.6	4.0	5.3	6.6	7.9	9.2	10.6	11.9	13.2	14.5	15.9	17.2	18.5	19.8
24	0.0	1.3	2.7	4.0	5.4	6.7	8.0	9.4	10.7	12.1	13.4	14.7	16.1	17.4	18.8	20.1
36	0.0	1.4	2.7	4.1	5.4	6.8	8.2	9.5	10.9	12.2	13.6	15.0	16.3	17.7	19.0	20.4
48	0.0	1.4	2.8	4.1	5.5	6.9	8.3	9.7	11.0	12.4	13.8	15.2	16.6	17.9	19.3	20.7
14 00	0.0	1.4	2.8	4.2	5.6	7.0	8.4	9.8	11.2	12.6	14.0	15.4	16.8	18.2	19.6	21.0
12	0.0	1.4	2.8	4.3	5.7	7.1	8.5	9.9	11.4	12.8	14.2	15.6	17.0	18.5	19.9	21.3
24	0.0	1.4	2.9	4.3	5.8	7.2	8.6	10.1	11.5	13.0	14.4	15.8	17.3	18.7	20.2	21.6
36	0.0	1.5	2.9	4.4	5.8	7.3	8.8	10.2	11.7	13.1	14.6	16.1	17.5	19.0	20.4	21.9
48	0.0	1.5	3.0	4.4	5.9	7.4	8.9	10.4	11.8	13.3	14.8	16.3	17.8	19.2	20.7	22.2
15 00	0.0	1.5	3.0	4.5	6.0	7.5	9.0	10.5	12.0	13.5	15.0	16.5	18.0	19.5	21.0	22.5
12	0.0	1.5	3.0	4.6	6.1	7.6	9.1	10.6	12.2	13.7	15.2	16.7	18.2	19.8	21.3	22.8
24	0.0	1.5	3.1	4.6	6.2	7.7	9.2	10.8	12.3	13.9	15.4	16.9	18.5	20.0	21.6	23.1
36	0.0	1.6	3.1	4.7	6.2	7.8	9.4	10.9	12.5	14.0	15.6	17.2	18.7	20.3	21.8	23.4
48	0.0	1.6	3.2	4.7	6.3	7.9	9.5	11.1	12.6	14.2	15.8	17.4	19.0	20.5	22.1	23.7
16 00	0.0	1.6	3.2	4.8	6.4	8.0	9.6	11.2	12.8	14.4	16.0	17.6	19.2	20.8	22.4	24.0
12	0.0	1.6	3.2	4.9	6.5	8.1	9.7	11.3	13.0	14.6	16.2	17.8	19.4	21.1	22.7	24.3
24	0.0	1.6	3.3	4.9	6.6	8.2	9.8	11.5	13.1	14.8	16.4	18.0	19.7	21.3	23.0	24.6
36	0.0	1.7	3.3	5.0	6.6	8.3	10.0	11.6	13.3	14.9	16.6	18.3	19.9	21.6	23.2	24.9
48	0.0	1.7	3.4	5.0	6.7	8.4	10.1	11.8	13.4	15.1	16.8	18.5	20.2	21.8	23.5	25.2
17 00	0.0	1.7	3.4	5.1	6.8	8.5	10.2	11.9	13.6	15.3	17.0	18.7	20.4	22.1	23.8	25.5
12	0.0	1.7	3.4	5.2	6.9	8.6	10.3	12.0	13.8	15.5	17.2	18.9	20.6	22.4	24.1	25.8
24	0.0	1.7	3.5	5.2	7.0	8.7	10.4	12.2	13.9	15.7	17.4	19.1	20.9	22.6	24.4	26.1
36	0.0	1.8	3.5	5.3	7.0	8.8	10.6	12.3	14.1	15.8	17.6	19.4	21.1	22.9	24.6	26.4
48	0.0	1.8	3.6	5.3	7.1	8.9	10.7	12.5	14.2	16.0	17.8	19.6	21.4	23.1	24.9	26.7
18 00	0.0	1.8	3.6	5.4	7.2	9.0	10.8	12.6	14.4	16.2	18.0	19.8	21.6	23.4	25.2	27.0
12	0.0	1.8	3.6	5.5	7.3	9.1	10.9	12.7	14.6	16.4	18.2	20.0	21.8	23.7	25.5	27.3
24	0.0	1.8	3.7	5.5	7.4	9.2	11.0	12.9	14.7	16.6	18.4	20.2	22.1	23.9	25.8	27.6
36	0.0	1.9	3.7	5.6	7.4	9.3	11.2	13.0	14.9	16.7	18.6	20.5	22.3	24.2	26.0	27.9
48	0.0	1.9	3.8	5.6	7.5	9.4	11.3	13.2	15.0	16.9	18.8	20.7	22.6	24.4	26.3	28.2
19 00	0.0	1.9	3.8	5.7	7.6	9.5	11.4	13.3	15.2	17.1	19.0	20.9	22.8	24.7	26.6	28.5
12	0.0	1.9	3.8	5.8	7.7	9.6	11.5	13.4	15.4	17.3	19.2	21.1	23.0	25.0	26.9	28.8
24	0.0	1.9	3.9	5.8	7.8	9.7	11.6	13.6	15.5	17.5	19.4	21.3	23.3	25.2	27.2	29.1
36	0.0	2.0	3.9	5.9	7.8	9.8	11.8	13.7	15.7	17.6	19.6	21.6	23.5	25.5	27.4	29.4
48	0.0	2.0	4.0	5.9	7.9	9.9	11.9	13.9	15.8	17.8	19.8	21.8	23.8	25.7	27.7	29.7
20 00	0.0	2.0	4.0	6.0	8.0	10.0	12.0	14.0	16.0	18.0	20.0	22.0	24.0	26.0	28.0	30.0
12	0.0	2.0	4.0	6.1	8.1	10.1	12.1	14.1	16.2	18.2	20.2	22.2	24.2	26.3	28.3	30.3
24	0.0	2.0	4.1	6.1	8.2	10.2	12.2	14.3	16.3	18.4	20.4	22.4	24.5	26.5	28.6	30.6
36	0.0	2.1	4.1	6.2	8.2	10.3	12.4	14.4	16.5	18.5	20.6	22.7	24.7	26.8	28.8	30.9
48	0.0	2.1	4.2	6.2	8.3	10.4	12.5	14.6	16.6	18.7	20.8	22.9	25.0	27.0	29.1	31.2
21 00	0.0	2.1	4.2	6.3	8.4	10.5	12.6	14.7	16.8	18.9	21.0	23.1	25.2	27.3	29.4	31.5
12	0.0	2.1	4.2	6.4	8.5	10.6	12.7	14.8	17.0	19.1	21.2	23.3	25.4	27.6	29.7	31.8
24	0.0	2.1	4.3	6.4	8.6	10.7	12.8	15.0	17.1	19.3	21.4	23.5	25.7	27.8	30.0	32.1
36	0.0	2.2	4.3	6.5	8.6	10.8	13.0	15.1	17.3	19.4	21.6	23.8	25.9	28.1	30.2	32.4
48	0.0	2.2	4.4	6.5	8.7	10.9	13.1	15.3	17.4	19.6	21.8	24.0	26.2	28.3	30.5	32.7
22 00	0.0	2.2	4.4	6.6	8.8	11.0	13.2	15.4	17.6	19.8	22.0	24.2	26.4	28.6	30.8	33.0
12	0.0	2.2	4.4	6.7	8.9	11.1	13.3	15.5	17.8	20.0	22.2	24.4	26.6	28.9	31.1	33.3
24	0.0	2.2	4.5	6.7	9.0	11.2	13.4	15.7	17.9	20.2	22.4	24.6	26.9	29.1	31.4	33.6
36	0.0	2.3	4.5	6.8	9.0	11.3	13.6	15.8	18.1	20.3	22.6	24.9	27.1	29.4	31.6	33.9
48	0.0	2.3	4.6	6.8	9.1	11.4	13.7	16.0	18.2	20.5	22.8	25.1	27.4	29.6	31.9	34.2
23 00	0.0	2.3	4.6	6.9	9.2	11.5	13.8	16.1	18.4	20.7	23.0	25.3	27.6	29.9	32.2	34.5
12	0.0	2.3	4.6	7.0	9.3	11.6	13.9	16.2	18.6	20.9	23.2	25.5	27.8	30.2	32.5	34.8
24	0.0	2.3	4.7	7.0	9.4	11.7	14.0	16.4	18.7	21.1	23.4	25.7	28.1	30.4	32.8	35.1
36	0.0	2.4	4.7	7.1	9.4	11.8	14.2	16.5	18.9	21.2	23.6	26.0	28.3	30.7	33.0	35.4
48	0.0	2.4	4.8	7.1	9.5	11.9	14.3	16.7	19.0	21.4	23.8	26.2	28.6	30.9	33.3	35.7
24 00	0.0	2.4	4.8	7.2	9.6	12.0	14.4	16.8	19.2	21.6	24.0	26.4	28.8	31.2	33.6	36.0

Chapter 6

REED'S
NAUTICAL ALMANACS & COMPANIONS

1994

CARIBBEAN

The only almanac which covers the entire Caribbean basin including Bermuda, the Bahamas, Caribbean islands, the north coast of South America, Central America, Panama and Mexico. Contains 200 harbor chartlets, complete tide and celestial tables, coast pilot with aids to navigation, weather and communication information.   800 pages $29.95(US) Retail

NORTH AMERICAN: EAST COAST

Now in its 21st year of publication, it includes over 200 harbor chartlets, tide and current tables from Nova Scotia to the Bahamas, light and buoy lists, waypoints, radio and communication information, a complete nautical ephemeris and lots more

900 pages $29.95(US) Retail

NORTH AMERICAN: PACIFIC NORTHWEST

The only almanac to include US and Canadian Hydrographic information in a single volume, and covers from the head of the Columbia River to the Gulf of Alaska and Kodiak Island, including Puget Sound and the British Columbia coastline. More than 170 harbor charts, tide and current tables, nautical ephemeris, aids to navigation, communication and weather information.   900 pages $29.95(US) Retail

NORTHERN EUROPEAN

Our flagship almanac, now enjoying its 63rd year of publication. Its coverage ranges from Skagen, on the northern coast of Denmark, to the French-Spanish border and Biarritz. This extensive European coverage includes 450 chartlets and illustrations, 2000 ports and complete tidal information for each area.   1,200 pages $45.00(US) Retail

SOUTHERN EUROPEAN

A completely reorganized and updated version of our Mediterranean almanac, featuring the Atlantic-European coast and islands, as well as the complete coastline of one of the world's most popular cruising areas, the Mediterranean sea. This edition is an excellent reference book for those planning a transatlantic voyage including stopovers in the Azores and entry via Gibraltar to the Mediterranean.   800 pages $45.00(US) Retail

NAUTICAL COMPANION

The COMPANION is designed to complement the Caribbean, North American East Coast and Pacific Northwest REED'S ALMANACS, and is full of practical information for the cruising boater. It includes extensive chapters on seamanship, rules of the road, coastal passage making, signaling, first aid and more.   444 pages $19.95(US) Retail

NAUTICAL COMPANION (European edition)

An outstanding nautical reference with essential information on subjects similar to those included in our US COMPANION. Designed to complement our European editions.

450 pages $24.95(US) Retail

Call 1-800-995-4995 for your nearest dealer!

ABC TABLES

A + if hour angle is listed at top
− if hour angle is listed at bottom

LHA	1°/359°	2°/358°	3°/357°	4°/356°	5°/355°	6°/354°	7°/353°	8°/352°	9°/351°	10°/350°	11°/349°	12°/348°	13°/347°	14°/346°	15°/345°
0	0.00	.000	.000	.000	.000	.000	.000	.000	.000	.000	.000	.000	.000	.000	.000
3	3.00	1.50	1.00	.749	.599	.499	.427	.373	.331	.297	.270	.247	.227	.210	.196
6	6.02	3.01	2.01	1.50	1.20	1.00	.856	.748	.664	.596	.541	.494	.455	.422	.392
9	9.07	4.54	3.02	2.27	1.81	1.51	1.29	1.13	1.00	.898	.815	.745	.686	.635	.591
12	12.2	6.09	4.06	3.04	2.43	2.02	1.73	1.51	1.34	1.21	1.09	1.00	.921	.853	.793
15	15.4	7.67	5.11	3.83	3.06	2.55	2.18	1.91	1.69	1.52	1.38	1.26	1.16	1.07	1.00
18	18.6	9.30	6.20	4.65	3.71	3.09	2.65	2.31	2.05	1.84	1.67	1.53	1.41	1.30	1.21
21	22.0	11.0	7.32	5.49	4.39	3.65	3.13	2.73	2.42	2.18	1.97	1.81	1.66	1.54	1.43
24	25.5	12.7	8.50	6.37	5.09	4.24	3.63	3.17	2.81	2.53	2.29	2.09	1.93	1.79	1.66
27	29.2	14.6	9.72	7.29	5.82	4.85	4.15	3.63	3.22	2.89	2.62	2.40	2.21	2.04	1.90
30	33.1	16.5	11.0	8.26	6.60	5.49	4.70	4.11	3.65	3.27	2.97	2.72	2.50	2.32	2.15
33	37.2	18.6	12.4	9.29	7.42	6.18	5.29	4.62	4.10	3.68	3.34	3.06	2.81	2.61	2.42
36	41.6	20.8	13.9	10.4	8.30	6.91	5.92	5.17	4.59	4.12	3.74	3.42	3.15	2.91	2.71
38	44.8	22.4	14.9	11.2	8.93	7.43	6.36	5.56	4.93	4.43	4.02	3.68	3.38	3.13	2.92
40	48.1	24.0	16.0	12.0	9.59	7.98	6.83	5.97	5.30	4.76	4.32	3.95	3.63	3.37	3.13
42	51.6	25.8	17.2	12.9	10.3	8.57	7.33	6.41	5.69	5.11	4.63	4.24	3.90	3.61	3.36
44	55.3	27.7	18.4	13.8	11.0	9.19	7.86	6.87	6.10	5.48	4.97	4.54	4.18	3.87	3.60
46	59.3	29.7	19.8	14.8	11.8	9.85	8.43	7.37	6.54	5.87	5.33	4.87	4.49	4.15	3.86
48	63.6	31.8	21.2	15.9	12.7	10.6	9.05	7.90	7.01	6.30	5.71	5.23	4.81	4.45	4.14
50	68.3	34.1	22.7	17.0	13.6	11.3	9.71	8.48	7.52	6.76	6.13	5.61	5.16	4.78	4.45
52	73.3	36.7	24.4	18.3	14.6	12.2	10.4	9.11	8.08	7.26	6.58	6.02	5.55	5.13	4.78
54	78.9	39.4	26.3	19.7	15.7	13.1	11.2	9.79	8.69	7.81	7.08	6.48	5.96	5.52	5.14
56	84.9	42.5	28.3	21.2	16.9	14.1	12.1	10.5	9.36	8.41	7.63	6.97	6.42	5.95	5.53
58	91.7	45.8	30.5	22.9	18.3	15.2	13.0	11.4	10.1	9.08	8.23	7.53	6.93	6.42	5.97
60	99.2	49.6	33.0	24.8	19.8	16.5	14.1	12.3	10.9	9.82	8.91	8.15	7.50	6.95	6.46
62	108	53.9	35.9	26.9	21.5	17.9	15.3	13.4	11.9	10.7	9.68	8.85	8.15	7.54	7.02
64	117	58.7	39.1	29.3	23.4	19.5	16.7	14.6	12.9	11.6	10.5	9.65	8.88	8.22	7.65
66	129	64.3	42.9	32.1	25.7	21.4	18.3	16.0	14.2	12.7	11.6	10.6	9.72	9.01	8.38
LHA	179°/181°	178°/182°	177°/183°	176°/184°	175°/185°	174°/186°	173°/187°	172°/188°	171°/189°	170°/190°	169°/191°	168°/192°	167°/193°	166°/194°	165°/195°

Latitude (°N/S)

B − if Lat and Dec have same name
+ if Lat and Dec have different names

LHA	1°/359°	2°/358°	3°/357°	4°/356°	5°/355°	6°/354°	7°/353°	8°/352°	9°/351°	10°/350°	11°/349°	12°/348°	13°/347°	14°/346°	15°/345°
0	0.00	.000	.000	.000	.000	.000	.000	.000	.000	.000	.000	.000	.000	.000	.000
3	3.00	1.50	1.00	.751	.601	.501	.430	.377	.335	.302	.275	.252	.233	.217	.202
6	6.02	3.01	2.01	1.51	1.21	1.01	.862	.755	.672	.605	.551	.506	.467	.434	.406
9	9.08	4.54	3.03	2.7	1.82	1.52	1.30	1.14	1.01	.912	.830	.762	.704	.655	.612
12	12.2	6.09	4.06	3.05	2.44	2.03	1.74	1.53	1.36	1.22	1.11	1.02	.945	.879	.821
15	15.4	7.68	5.12	3.84	3.07	2.56	2.20	1.93	1.71	1.54	1.40	1.29	1.19	1.11	1.04
18	18.6	9.31	6.21	4.66	3.73	3.11	2.67	2.33	2.08	1.87	1.70	1.56	1.44	1.34	1.26
21	22.0	11.0	7.33	5.50	4.40	3.67	3.15	2.76	2.45	2.21	2.01	1.85	1.71	1.59	1.48
24	25.5	12.8	8.51	6.38	5.11	4.26	3.65	3.20	2.85	2.56	2.33	2.14	1.98	1.84	1.72
27	29.2	14.6	9.74	7.30	5.85	4.87	4.18	3.66	3.26	2.93	2.67	2.45	2.27	2.11	1.97
30	33.1	16.5	11.0	8.28	6.62	5.52	4.74	4.15	3.69	3.32	3.03	2.78	2.57	2.39	2.23
33	37.2	18.6	12.4	9.31	7.45	6.21	5.33	4.67	4.15	3.74	3.40	3.12	2.89	2.68	2.51
36	41.6	20.8	13.9	10.4	8.34	6.95	5.96	5.22	4.64	4.18	3.81	3.49	3.23	3.00	2.81
38	44.8	22.4	14.9	11.2	8.96	7.47	6.41	5.61	4.99	4.50	4.09	3.76	3.47	3.23	3.02
40	48.1	24.0	16.0	12.0	9.63	8.03	6.89	6.03	5.36	4.83	4.40	4.04	3.73	3.47	3.24
42	51.6	25.8	17.2	12.9	10.3	8.61	7.39	6.47	5.76	5.19	4.72	4.33	4.00	3.72	3.48
44	55.3	27.7	18.5	13.8	11.1	9.24	7.92	6.94	6.17	5.56	5.06	4.64	4.29	3.99	3.73
46	59.3	29.7	19.8	14.8	11.9	9.91	8.50	7.44	6.62	5.96	5.43	4.98	4.60	4.28	4.00
48	63.6	31.8	21.2	15.9	12.7	10.6	9.11	7.98	7.10	6.40	5.82	5.34	4.94	4.59	4.29
50	68.3	34.1	22.8	17.1	13.7	11.4	9.78	8.56	7.62	6.86	6.25	5.73	5.30	4.93	4.60
52	73.3	36.7	24.5	18.3	14.7	12.2	10.5	9.20	8.18	7.37	6.71	6.16	5.69	5.29	4.95
54	78.9	39.4	26.3	19.7	15.8	13.2	11.3	9.89	8.80	7.93	7.21	6.62	6.12	5.69	5.32
56	84.9	42.5	28.3	21.3	17.0	14.2	12.2	10.7	9.48	8.54	7.77	7.13	6.59	6.13	5.73
58	91.7	45.9	30.6	22.9	18.4	15.3	13.1	11.5	10.2	9.22	8.39	7.70	7.11	6.62	6.18
60	99.2	49.6	33.1	24.8	19.9	16.6	14.2	12.5	11.1	9.97	9.08	8.33	7.70	7.16	6.69
62	108	53.9	35.9	27.0	21.6	18.0	15.4	13.5	12.0	10.8	9.86	9.05	8.36	7.77	7.27
LHA	179°/181°	178°/182°	177°/183°	176°/184°	175°/185°	174°/186°	173°/187°	172°/188°	171°/189°	170°/190°	169°/191°	168°/192°	167°/193°	166°/194°	165°/195°

Declination (°N/S)

Chapter 6

ABC TABLES

A + if hour angle is listed at top
− if hour angle is listed at bottom

LHA	16° 344°	17° 343°	18° 342°	19° 341°	20° 340°	21° 339°	22° 338°	23° 337°	24° 336°	25° 335°	26° 334°	27° 333°	28° 332°	29° 331°	30° 330°
0	.000	.000	.000	.000	.000	.000	.000	.000	.000	.000	.000	.000	.000	.000	.000
3	.183	.171	.161	.152	.144	.137	.130	.123	.118	.112	.107	.103	.099	.095	.091
6	.367	.344	.323	.305	.289	.274	.260	.248	.236	.225	.215	.206	.198	.190	.182
9	.552	.518	.487	.460	.435	.413	.392	.373	.356	.340	.325	.311	.298	.286	.274
12	.741	.695	.654	.617	.584	.554	.526	.501	.477	.456	.436	.417	.400	.383	.368
15	.934	.876	.825	.778	.736	.698	.663	.631	.602	.575	.549	.526	.504	.483	.464
18	1.13	1.06	1.00	.944	.893	.846	.804	.765	.730	.697	.666	.638	.611	.586	.563
21	1.34	1.26	1.18	1.11	1.05	1.00	.950	.904	.862	.823	.787	.753	.722	.693	.665
24	1.55	1.46	1.37	1.29	1.22	1.16	1.10	1.05	1.00	.955	.913	.874	.837	.803	.771
27	1.78	1.67	1.57	1.48	1.40	1.33	1.26	1.20	1.14	1.09	1.04	1.00	.958	.919	.883
30	2.01	1.89	1.78	1.68	1.59	1.50	1.43	1.36	1.30	1.24	1.18	1.13	1.09	1.04	1.00
33	2.26	2.12	2.00	1.89	1.78	1.69	1.61	1.53	1.46	1.39	1.33	1.27	1.22	1.17	1.12
36	2.53	2.38	2.24	2.11	2.00	1.89	1.80	1.71	1.63	1.56	1.49	1.43	1.37	1.31	1.26
38	2.72	2.56	2.40	2.27	2.15	2.04	1.93	1.84	1.75	1.68	1.60	1.53	1.47	1.41	1.35
40	2.93	2.74	2.58	2.44	2.31	2.19	2.08	1.98	1.88	1.80	1.72	1.65	1.58	1.51	1.45
42	3.14	2.95	2.77	2.61	2.47	2.35	2.23	2.12	2.02	1.93	1.85	1.77	1.69	1.62	1.56
44	3.37	3.16	2.97	2.80	2.65	2.52	2.39	2.28	2.17	2.07	1.98	1.90	1.82	1.74	1.67
46	3.61	3.39	3.19	3.01	2.85	2.70	2.56	2.44	2.33	2.22	2.12	2.03	1.95	1.87	1.79
48	3.87	3.63	3.42	3.23	3.05	2.89	2.75	2.62	2.49	2.38	2.28	2.18	2.09	2.00	1.92
50	4.16	3.90	3.67	3.46	3.27	3.10	2.95	2.81	2.68	2.56	2.44	2.34	2.24	2.15	2.06
52	4.46	4.19	3.94	3.72	3.52	3.33	3.17	3.02	2.87	2.74	2.62	2.51	2.41	2.31	2.22
54	4.80	4.50	4.24	4.00	3.78	3.59	3.41	3.24	3.09	2.95	2.82	2.70	2.59	2.48	2.38
56	5.17	4.85	4.56	4.31	4.07	3.86	3.67	3.49	3.33	3.18	3.04	2.91	2.79	2.67	2.57
58	5.58	5.23	4.93	4.65	4.40	4.17	3.96	3.77	3.59	3.43	3.28	3.14	3.01	2.89	2.77
60	6.04	5.67	5.33	5.03	4.76	4.51	4.29	4.08	3.89	3.71	3.55	3.40	3.26	3.12	3.00
62	6.56	6.15	5.79	5.46	5.17	4.90	4.65	4.43	4.22	4.03	3.86	3.69	3.54	3.39	3.26
64	7.15	6.71	6.31	5.95	5.63	5.34	5.07	4.83	4.61	4.40	4.20	4.02	3.86	3.70	3.55
66	7.83	7.35	6.91	6.52	6.17	5.85	5.56	5.29	5.04	4.82	4.61	4.41	4.22	4.05	3.89
LHA	164° 196°	163° 197°	162° 198°	161° 199°	160° 200°	159° 201°	158° 202°	157° 203°	156° 204°	155° 205°	154° 206°	153° 207°	152° 208°	151° 209°	150° 210°

Left axis: Latitude (°N/S)

B − if Lat and Dec have same name
+ if Lat and Dec have different names

LHA	16° 344°	17° 343°	18° 342°	19° 341°	20° 340°	21° 339°	22° 338°	23° 337°	24° 336°	25° 335°	26° 334°	27° 333°	28° 332°	29° 331°	30° 330°
0	.000	.000	.000	.000	.000	.000	.000	.000	.000	.000	.000	.000	.000	.000	.000
3	.190	.179	.170	.161	.153	.146	.140	.134	.129	.124	.120	.115	.112	.108	.105
6	.381	.359	.340	.323	.307	.293	.281	.269	.258	.249	.240	.232	.224	.217	.210
9	.575	.542	.513	.486	.463	.442	.423	.405	.389	.375	.361	.349	.337	.327	.317
12	.771	.727	.688	.653	.621	.593	.567	.544	.523	.503	.485	.468	.453	.438	.425
15	.972	.916	.867	.823	.783	.748	.715	.686	.659	.634	.611	.590	.571	.553	.536
18	1.18	1.11	1.05	.998	.950	.907	.867	.832	.799	.769	.741	.716	.692	.670	.650
21	1.39	1.31	1.24	1.18	1.12	1.07	1.02	.982	.944	.908	.876	.846	.818	.792	.768
24	1.62	1.52	1.44	1.37	1.30	1.24	1.19	1.14	1.09	1.05	1.02	.981	.948	.918	.890
27	1.85	1.74	1.65	1.57	1.49	1.42	1.36	1.30	1.25	1.21	1.16	1.12	1.09	1.05	1.02
30	2.09	1.97	1.87	1.77	1.69	1.61	1.54	1.48	1.42	1.37	1.32	1.27	1.23	1.19	1.15
33	2.36	2.22	2.10	1.99	1.90	1.81	1.73	1.66	1.60	1.54	1.48	1.43	1.38	1.34	1.30
36	2.64	2.48	2.32	2.23	2.12	2.03	1.94	1.86	1.79	1.72	1.66	1.60	1.55	1.50	1.45
38	2.83	2.67	2.53	2.40	2.28	2.18	2.09	2.00	1.92	1.85	1.78	1.72	1.66	1.61	1.56
40	3.04	2.87	2.72	2.58	2.45	2.34	2.24	2.15	2.06	1.99	1.91	1.85	1.79-	1.73	1.68
42	3.27	3.08	2.91	2.77	2.63	2.51	2.40	2.30	2.21	2.13	2.05	1.98	1.92	1.86	1.80
44	3.50	3.30	3.13	2.97	2.82	2.69	2.58	2.47	2.37	2.29	2.20	2.13	2.06	1.99	1.93
46	3.76	3.54	3.35	3.18	3.03	2.89	2.76	2.65	2.55	2.45	2.36	2.28	2.21	2.14	2.07
48	4.03	3.80	3.59	3.41	3.25	3.10	2.96	2.84	2.73	2.63	2.53	2.45	2.37	2.29	2.22
50	4.32	4.08	3.86	3.66	3.48	3.33	3.18	3.05	2.93	2.82	2.72	2.63	2.54	2.46	2.38
52	4.64	4.38	4.14	3.93	3.74	3.57	3.42	3.28	3.15	3.03	2.92	2.82	2.73	2.64	2.56
54	4.99	4.71	4.45	4.23	4.02	3.84	3.67	3.52	3.38	3.26	3.14	3.03	2.93	2.84	2.75
56	5.38	5.07	4.80	4.55	4.33	4.14	3.96	3.79	3.65	3.51	3.38	3.27	3.16	3.06	2.97
58	5.81	5.47	5.18	4.92	4.68	4.47	4.27	4.10	3.93	3.79	3.65	3.53	3.41	3.30	3.20
60	6.28	5.92	5.61	5.32	5.06	4.83	4.62	4.43	4.26	4.10	3.95	3.82	3.69	3.57	3.46
62	6.82	6.43	6.09	5.78	5.50	5.25	5.02	4.81	4.62	4.45	4.29	4.14	4.01	3.88	3.76
LHA	164° 196°	163° 197°	162° 198°	161° 199°	160° 200°	159° 201°	158° 202°	157° 203°	156° 204°	155° 205°	154° 206°	153° 207°	152° 208°	151° 209°	150° 210°

Left axis: Declination (°N/S)

ABC TABLES

A
+ if hour angle is listed at top
− if hour angle is listed at bottom

LHA	32°/328°	34°/326°	36°/324°	38°/322°	40°/320°	42°/318°	44°/316°	46°/314°	48°/312°	50°/310°	52°/308°	54°/306°	56°/304°	58°/302°	60°/300°
0	.000	.000	.000	.000	.000	.000	.000	.000	.000	.000	.000	.000	.000	.000	.000
3	.084	.078	.072	.067	.062	.058	.054	.051	.047	.044	.041	.038	.035	.033	.030
6	.168	.156	.145	.135	.125	.117	.109	.101	.095	.088	.082	.076	.071	.066	.061
9	.253	.235	.218	.203	.189	.176	.164	.152	.143	.133	.124	.115	.107	.099	.091
12	.340	.315	.293	.272	.253	.236	.220	.205	.191	.170	.166	.154	.143	.133	.123
15	.429	.397	.369	.343	.319	.298	.277	.259	.241	.225	.209	.195	.181	.167	.155
18	.520	.482	.447	.416	.387	.361	.336	.314	.293	.273	.254	.236	.219	.203	.188
21	.614	.569	.528	.491	.457	.426	.398	.371	.346	.322	.300	.279	.259	.240	.222
24	.713	.660	.613	.570	.531	.494	.461	.430	.401	.374	.348	.323	.300	.278	.257
27	.815	.755	.701	.652	.607	.566	.528	.492	.459	.428	.398	.370	.344	.318	.294
30	.924	.856	.795	.739	.688	.641	.598	.558	.520	.484	.451	.419	.389	.361	.333
33	1.04	.963	.894	.831	.774	.721	.672	.627	.585	.545	.507	.472	.438	.406	.375
36	1.16	1.08	1.00	.930	.866	.807	.752	.702	.654	.610	.568	.528	.490	.454	.419
38	1.25	1.16	1.08	1.00	.931	.868	.809	.754	.703	.656	.610	.568	.527	.488	.451
40	1.34	1.24	1.15	1.07	1.00	.932	.869	.810	.756	.704	.656	.610	.566	.524	.484
42	1.44	1.33	1.24	1.15	1.07	1.00	.932	.870	.811	.756	.703	.654	.607	.563	.520
44	1.55	1.43	1.33	1.24	1.15	1.07	1.00	.932	.870	.810	.754	.702	.651	.603	.558
46	1.66	1.54	1.43	1.33	1.23	1.15	1.07	1.00	.932	.869	.809	.752	.698	.647	.598
48	1.78	1.65	1.53	1.42	1.32	1.23	1.15	1.07	1.00	.932	.868	.807	.749	.694	.641
50	1.91	1.77	1.64	1.53	1.42	1.32	1.23	1.15	1.07	1.00	.931	.866	.804	.745	.688
52	2.05	1.90	1.76	1.64	1.53	1.42	1.33	1.24	1.15	1.07	1.00	.930	.863	.800	.739
54	2.20	2.04	1.89	1.76	1.64	1.53	1.43	1.33	1.24	1.15	1.08	1.00	.928	.860	.795
56	2.37	2.20	2.04	1.90	1.77	1.65	1.54	1.43	1.33	1.24	1.16	1.08	1.00	.926	.856
58	2.56	2.37	2.20	2.05	1.91	1.78	1.66	1.55	1.44	1.34	1.25	1.16	1.08	1.00	.924
60	2.77	2.57	2.38	2.22	2.06	1.92	1.79	1.67	1.56	1.45	1.35	1.26	1.17	1.08	1.00
62	3.01	2.79	2.59	2.41	2.24	2.09	1.95	1.82	1.69	1.58	1.47	1.37	1.27	1.18	1.09
64	3.28	3.04	2.82	2.62	2.44	2.28	2.12	1.98	1.85	1.72	1.60	1.49	1.38	1.28	1.18
66	3.59	3.33	3.09	2.87	2.68	2.49	2.33	2.17	2.02	1.88	1.75	1.63	1.52	1.40	1.30
LHA	148°/212°	146°/214°	144°/216°	142°/218°	140°/220°	138°/222°	136°/224°	134°/226°	132°/228°	130°/230°	128°/232°	126°/234°	124°/236°	122°/238°	120°/240°

Latitude (°N/S)

B
− if Lat and Dec have same name
+ if Lat and Dec have different names

LHA	32°/328°	34°/326°	36°/324°	38°/322°	40°/320°	42°/318°	44°/316°	46°/314°	48°/312°	50°/310°	52°/308°	54°/306°	56°/304°	58°/302°	60°/300°
0	.000	.000	.000	.000	.000	.000	.000	.000	.000	.000	.000	.000	.000	.000	.000
3	.099	.094	.089	.085	.082	.078	.075	.073	.071	.068	.067	.065	.063	.062	.061
6	.198	.188	.179	.171	.164	.157	.151	.146	.141	.137	.133	.130	.127	.124	.121
9	.299	.283	.269	.257	.246	.237	.228	.220	.213	.207	.201	.196	.191	.187	.183
12	.401	.380	.362	.345	.331	.318	.306	.295	.286	.277	.270	.263	.256	.251	.245
15	.506	.479	.456	.435	.417	.400	.386	.372	.361	.350	.340	.331	.323	.316	.309
18	.613	.581	.553	.528	.505	.485	.468	.452	.437	.424	.412	.402	.392	.383	.375
21	.724	.686	.653	.623	.597	.574	.553	.534	.517	.501	.487	.474	.463	.453	.443
24	.840	.796	.757	.723	.693	.665	.641	.619	.599	.581	.565	.550	.537	.525	.514
27	.962	.911	.867	.828	.793	.761	.733	.708	.686	.665	.647	.630	.615	.601	.588
30	1.09	1.03	.982	.938	.899	.863	.831	.803	.777	.754	.733	.714	.696	.681	.667
33	1.23	1.16	1.11	1.05	1.01	.971	.935	.903	.874	.848	.824	.803	.783	.766	.750
36	1.37	1.30	1.24	1.18	1.13	1.09	1.05	1.01	.978	.948	.922	.898	.876	.857	.839
38	1.47	1.40	1.33	1.27	1.22	1.17	1.12	1.09	1.05	1.02	.991	.966	.942	.921	.902
40	1.58	1.50	1.43	1.36	1.31	1.25	1.21	1.17	1.13	1.10	1.06	1.04	1.01	.989	.969
42	1.70	1.61	1.53	1.46	1.40	1.35	1.30	1.25	1.21	1.18	1.14	1.11	1.09	1.06	1.04
44	1.82	1.73	1.64	1.57	1.50	1.44	1.39	1.34	1.30	1.26	1.23	1.19	1.16	1.14	1.12
46	1.95	1.85	1.76	1.68	1.61	1.55	1.49	1.44	1.39	1.35	1.31	1.28	1.25	1.22	1.20
48	2.10	1.99	1.89	1.80	1.73	1.66	1.60	1.54	1.49	1.45	1.41	1.37	1.34	1.31	1.28
50	2.25	2.13	2.03	1.94	1.85	1.78	1.72	1.66	1.60	1.56	1.51	1.47	1.44	1.41	1.38
52	2.42	2.29	2.18	2.08	1.99	1.91	1.84	1.78	1.72	1.67	1.62	1.58	1.54	1.51	1.48
54	2.60	2.46	2.34	2.24	2.14	2.06	1.98	1.91	1.85	1.80	1.75	1.70	1.66	1.62	1.59
56	2.80	2.65	2.52	2.41	2.31	2.22	2.13	2.06	2.00	1.94	1.88	1.83	1.79	1.75	1.71
58	3.02	2.86	2.72	2.60	2.49	2.39	2.30	2.22	2.15	2.09	2.03	1.98	1.93	1.89	1.85
60	3.27	3.10	2.95	2.81	2.69	2.59	2.49	2.41	2.33	2.26	2.20	2.14	2.09	2.04	2.00
62	3.55	3.36	3.20	3.05	2.93	2.81	2.71	2.61	2.53	2.46	2.39	2.32	2.27	2.22	2.17
LHA	148°/212°	146°/214°	144°/216°	142°/218°	140°/220°	138°/222°	136°/224°	134°/226°	132°/228°	130°/230°	128°/232°	126°/234°	124°/236°	122°/238°	120°/240°

Declination (°N/S)

Chapter 6

ABC TABLES

A + if hour angle is listed at top
     − if hour angle is listed at bottom

LHA	62° 298°	64° 296°	66° 294°	68° 292°	70° 290°	72° 288°	74° 286°	76° 284°	78° 282°	80° 280°	82° 278°	84° 276°	86° 274°	88° 272°	90° 270°
0	.000	.000	.000	.000	.000	.000	.000	.000	.000	.000	.000	.000	.000	.000	.000
3	.028	.026	.023	.021	.019	.017	.015	.013	.011	.009	.007	.006	.004	.002	.000
6	.056	.051	.047	.043	.038	.034	.030	.026	.022	.019	.015	.011	.007	.004	.000
9	.084	.077	.071	.064	.058	.051	.045	.039	.034	.028	.022	.017	.011	.006	.000
12	.113	.104	.095	.086	.077	.069	.061	.053	.045	.037	.030	.022	.015	.007	.000
15	.142	.131	.119	.108	.098	.087	.077	.067	.057	.047	.038	.028	.019	.009	.000
18	.173	.158	.145	.131	.118	.106	.093	.081	.069	.057	.046	.034	.023	.012	.000
21	.204	.187	.171	.155	.140	.125	.110	.096	.082	.068	.054	.040	.027	.013	.000
24	.237	.217	.198	.180	.162	.145	.128	.111	.095	.079	.063	.047	.031	.016	.000
27	.271	.249	.227	.206	.185	.166	.146	.127	.108	.090	.072	.054	.036	.018	.000
30	.307	.282	.257	.233	.210	.188	.166	.144	.123	.102	.081	.061	.040	.020	.000
33	.345	.317	.289	.262	.236	.211	.186	.162	.138	.115	.091	.068	.045	.023	.000
36	.386	.354	.323	.294	.264	.236	.208	.181	.154	.128	.102	.076	.051	.025	.000
38	.415	.381	.348	.316	.284	.254	.224	.195	.166	.138	.110	.082	.055	.027	.000
40	.446	.409	.374	.339	.305	.273	.241	.209	.178	.148	.118	.088	.059	.029	.000
42	.479	.439	.401	.364	.328	.293	.258	.224	.191	.159	.127	.095	.063	.031	.000
44	.513	.471	.430	.390	.351	.314	.277	.241	.205	.170	.136	.101	.068	.034	.000
46	.551	.505	.461	.418	.377	.336	.297	.258	.220	.183	.146	.109	.072	.036	.000
48	.591	.542	.494	.449	.404	.361	.318	.277	.236	.196	.156	.1147	.078	.039	.000
50	.634	.581	.531	.481	.434	.387	.342	.297	.253	.210	.167	.125	.083	.042	.000
52	.681	.624	.570	.517	.466	.416	.367	.319	.272	.226	.180	.135	.090	.045	.000
54	.732	.671	.613	.556	.501	.447	.395	.343	.293	.243	.193	.145	.096	.048	.000
56	.788	.723	.660	.559	.540	.482	.425	.370	.315	.261	.208	.156	.104	.052	.000
58	.851	.781	.713	.647	.582	.520	.459	.399	.340	.282	.225	.168	.112	.056	.000
60	.921	.845	.771	.700	.630	.563	.497	.432	.368	.305	.243	.182	.121	.060	.000
62	1.00	.917	.837	.760	.685	.611	.539	.469	.400	.332	.264	.198	.132	.066	.000
64	1.09	1.00	.913	.828	.746	.666	.588	.511	.436	.362	.288	.215	.143	.072	.000
66	1.19	1.10	1.00	.907	.817	.730	.644	.560	.477	.396	.316	.236	.157	.078	.000
LHA	118° 242°	116° 244°	114° 246°	112° 248°	110° 250°	108° 252°	106° 254°	104° 256°	102° 258°	100° 260°	98° 262°	96° 264°	94° 266°	92° 268°	90° 270°

Latitude (°N/S)

B − if Lat and Dec have same name
     + if Lat and Dec have different names

LHA	62° 298°	64° 296°	66° 294°	68° 292°	70° 290°	72° 288°	74° 286°	76° 284°	78° 282°	80° 280°	82° 278°	84° 276°	86° 274°	88° 272°	90° 270°
0	.000	.000	.000	.000	.000	.000	.000	.000	.000	.000	.000	.000	.000	.000	.000
3	.059	.058	.057	.057	.056	.055	.055	.054	.054	.053	.053	.053	.053	.052	.052
6	.119	.117	.115	.113	.112	.111	.109	.108	.107	.107	.106	.106	.105	.105	.105
9	.179	.176	.173	.171	.169	.167	.163	.162	.161	.161	.160	.159	.159	.158	.158
12	.241	.236	.233	.229	.226	.223	.221	.219	.217	.216	.215	.214	.213	.213	.213
15	.303	.298	.293	.289	.285	.282	.279	.276	.274	.272	.271	.269	.269	.268	.268
18	.368	.362	.356	.350	.346	.342	.338	.335	.332	.330	.328	.327	.326	.325	.325
21	.435	.427	.420	.414	.408	.404	.399	.396	.392	.390	.388	.386	.385	.384	.384
24	.504	.495	.487	.480	.474	.468	.463	.459	.455	.452	.450	.448	.446	.446	.445
27	.577	.567	.558	.550	.542	.536	.530	.525	.521	.517	.515	.512	.511	.510	.510
30	.654	.642	.632	.623	.614	.607	.601	.595	.590	.586	.583	.581	.579	.578	.577
33	.735	.723	.711	.700	.691	.683	.676	.669	.664	.659	.656	.653	.651	.650	.649
36	.823	.808	.795	.784	.773	.764	.756	.749	.743	.738	.734	.731	.728	.727	.727
38	.885	.869	.855	.843	.831	.821	.813	.805	.799	.793	.789	.786	.783	.782	.781
40	.950	.934	.919	.905	.893	.882	.873	.865	.858	.852	.847	.844	.841	.840	.839
42	1.02	1.00	.986	.971	.958	.947	.937	.928	.921	.914	.909	.905	.903	.901	.900
44	1.09	1.07	1.06	1.04	1.03	1.02	1.00	.995	.987	.981	.975	.971	.968	.966	.966
46	1.17	1.15	1.13	1.12	1.10	1.09	1.08	1.07	1.06	1.05	1.05	1.04	1.04	1.04	1.04
48	1.26	1.24	1.22	1.20	1.18	1.17	1.16	1.14	1.14	1.13	1.12	1.12	1.11	1.11	1.11
50	1.35	1.33	1.30	1.29	1.27	1.25	1.24	1.23	1.22	1.21	1.21	1.20	1.19	1.19	1.19
52	1.45	1.42	1.40	1.38	1.36	1.35	1.33	1.32	1.31	1.30	1.29	1.29	1.28	1.28	1.28
54	1.56	1.53	1.51	1.48	1.46	1.45	1.43	1.42	1.41	1.40	1.39	1.38	1.38	1.38	1.38
56	1.68	1.65	1.62	1.60	1.58	1.56	1.54	1.53	1.52	1.51	1.50	1.49	1.49	1.48	1.48
58	1.81	1.78	1.75	1.73	1.70	1.68	1.66	1.65	1.64	1.63	1.62	1.61	1.61	1.60	1.60
60	1.96	1.93	1.90	1.87	1.84	1.82	1.80	1.79	1.77	1.76	1.75	1.74	1.74	1.73	1.73
62	2.13	2.09	2.06	2.03	2.00	1.98	1.96	1.94	1.92	1.91	1.90	1.89	1.89	1.88	1.88
LHA	118° 242°	116° 244°	114° 246°	112° 248°	110° 250°	108° 252°	106° 254°	104° 256°	102° 258°	100° 260°	98° 262°	96° 264°	94° 266°	92° 268°	90° 270°

Declination (°N/S)

ABC TABLES

C = A±B

C Lat	.00	.05	.10	.15	.20	.25	.30	.35	.40	.45	.50	.55	.60	.70
0	90.0	87.1	84.3	81.5	70.7	76.0	73.3	70.7	68.2	65.8	63.4	61.2	59.0	55.0
10	90.0	87.2	84.4	81.6	78.9	76.2	73.3	71.0	68.5	66.1	63.8	61.6	59.4	55.4
20	90.0	87.3	84.6	81.8	87.0	76.8	74.3	71.8	69.4	67.1	64.8	62.7	60.6	56.7
24	90.0	87.4	84.8	82.2	79.0	77.1	74.7	72.3	69.9	67.7	65.5	63.5	61.3	57.4
28	90.0	87.5	85.0	82.5	80.0	77.6	75.2	72.8	70.5	68.3	66.2	64.1	62.1	58.3
30	90.0	87.5	85.1	82.6	80.2	77.8	75.4	73.1	70.9	68.7	66.6	64.5	62.5	58.8
32	90.0	87.6	85.2	82.8	80.4	78.0	75.7	73.5	71.3	69.1	67.0	65.0	63.0	59.3
34	90.0	87.6	85.3	82.9	80.6	78.3	75.9	73.8	71.7	69.5	67.5	65.5	63.6	59.9
36	90.0	87.7	85.4	83.1	80.8	78.6	76.4	74.2	72.1	70.0	68.0	66.0	64.1	60.5
38	90.0	87.7	85.5	83.3	81.0	78.9	76.7	74.6	72.5	70.5	68.5	66.6	64.7	61.1
40	90.0	87.8	85.6	83.4	81.3	79.2	77.1	75.0	73.0	71.0	69.0	67.2	65.3	61.8
42	90.0	87.9	85.7	83.6	81.5	79.5	77.4	75.4	73.4	71.5	69.6	67.8	66.0	62.5
44	90.0	87.9	85.9	83.8	81.8	79.8	77.8	75.9	73.9	72.1	70.2	68.4	66.7	63.3
46	90.0	88.0	86.0	84.1	82.1	80.1	78.2	76.3	74.5	72.6	70.8	69.1	67.4	64.1
48	90.0	88.1	86.2	84.3	82.4	80.5	78.6	76.8	75.0	73.2	71.5	69.8	68.1	64.9
50	90.0	88.2	86.3	84.5	82.7	80.9	79.1	77.3	75.6	73.9	72.2	70.5	68.9	65.8
52	90.0	88.2	86.5	84.7	83.0	81.2	79.5	77.8	76.2	74.5	72.9	71.3	69.7	66.7
54	90.0	88.3	86.6	85.0	83.3	81.6	80.0	78.4	76.8	75.2	73.6	72.1	70.6	67.6
56	90.0	88.4	86.8	85.2	83.6	82.0	80.5	78.9	77.4	75.9	74.4	72.9	71.5	68.6
58	90.0	88.5	87.0	85.5	84.0	82.5	81.0	79.5	78.0	76.6	75.2	73.8	72.4	69.6
60	90.0	88.6	87.1	85.7	84.3	82.9	81.5	80.1	78.7	77.3	76.0	74.6	73.3	70.7
62	90.0	88.7	87.3	86.0	84.6	83.3	82.0	80.7	79.4	78.1	76.8	75.5	74.3	71.8
64	90.0	88.7	87.5	86.2	85.0	83.7	82.5	81.3	80.1	78.8	77.6	76.4	75.3	72.9
66	90.0	88.8	87.7	86.5	85.3	84.2	83.0	81.9	80.8	79.6	78.5	77.4	76.3	74.1
68	90.0	88.9	87.9	86.8	85.7	84.6	83.6	82.5	81.5	80.4	79.4	78.4	77.3	75.3
	.00	.05	.10	.15	.20	.25	.30	.35	.40	.45	.50	.55	.60	.70

C Lat	.80	.90	1.00	1.10	1.20	1.40	1.60	1.80	2.00	2.20	2.40	2.60	2.80
0	51.3	48.0	45.0	42.3	39.8	35.5	32.0	29.1	26.6	24.4	22.6	21.0	19.7
10	51.8	48.4	45.4	42.7	40.2	36.0	32.4	29.4	26.9	24.8	22.9	21.3	19.9
20	53.1	49.8	46.8	44.1	41.6	37.2	33.6	30.6	28.0	25.8	23.9	22.3	20.8
24	53.8	50.6	47.6	44.9	42.4	38.0	34.4	31.3	28.7	26.5	24.5	22.8	21.4
28	54.8	51.5	48.6	45.8	43.3	39.0	35.3	32.2	29.55	27.2	25.3	23.5	22.0
30	55.3	52.1	49.1	46.4	43.9	39.5	35.8	32.7	30.0	27.7	25.7	23.9	22.4
32	55.8	52.6	49.7	47.0	44.5	40.1	36.4	33.2	30.5	28.2	26.2	24.4	22.8
34	56.4	53.3	50.3	47.6	45.1	40.7	37.0	33.8	31.1	28.7	26.7	24.9	23.3
36	57.1	53.9	51.0	48.3	45.8	41.4	37.7	34.5	31.7	29.3	27.3	25.4	23.8
38	57.8	54.7	51.8	49.1	46.6	42.2	38.4	35.2	32.4	30.0	27.9	26.0	24.4
40	58.5	55.4	52.5	49.9	47.4	43.0	39.2	36.0	33.1	30.7	28.5	26.7	25.0
42	59.3	56.3	53.4	50.7	48.3	43.9	40.1	36.8	33.9	31.5	29.3	27.4	25.7
44	60.1	57.1	54.3	51.6	49.2	44.8	41.0	37.7	34.8	32.3	30.1	28.1	26.4
46	60.9	58.0	55.2	52.6	50.2	45.8	42.0	38.7	35.7	33.2	31.0	29.0	27.2
48	61.8	58.9	56.2	53.6	51.2	46.9	43.0	39.7	36.8	34.2	31.9	29.9	28.1
50	62.8	60.0	57.3	54.7	52.4	48.0	44.2	40.8	37.9	35.3	33.0	30.9	29.1
52	63.8	61.0	58.4	55.9	53.5	49.2	45.4	42.1	39.1	36.4	34.1	32.0	30.1
54	64.8	62.1	59.6	57.1	54.8	50.6	46.8	43.4	40.4	37.7	35.3	33.2	31.3
56	65.9	63.3	60.8	58.4	56.1	51.9	48.2	44.8	41.8	39.1	36.7	34.5	32.6
58	67.0	64.5	62.1	59.8	57.5	53.4	49.7	46.4	43.4	40.6	38.2	36.0	34.0
60	68.2	65.8	63.4	61.2	59.0	55.0	51.3	48.0	45.0	42.3	39.8	37.6	35.5
62	69.4	67.1	64.9	62.7	60.6	56.7	53.1	49.8	46.8	44.1	41.6	39.3	37.3
64	70.7	68.5	66.3	64.3	62.3	58.5	55.0	51.7	48.8	46.0	43.5	41.3	39.2
66	72.0	69.9	67.9	65.9	64.0	60.3	56.9	53.8	50.9	48.2	45.7	43.4	41.3
68	73.3	71.4	69.5	67.6	65.8	62.3	59.1	56.0	53.2	50.5	48.0	45.8	43.6
	.80	.90	1.00	1.10	1.20	1.40	1.60	1.80	2.00	2.20	2.40	2.60	2.80

Naming the Azimuth: If answer is **+**, azimuth is **South** in North latitudes and **North** in South latitudes; if answer is **−**, azimuth is **North** in North latitudes and **South** in South latitudes.
If Hour Angle is **less than 180°**, azimuth is **West**; if **more than 180°**, azimuth is **East**.

Chapter 6

ABC TABLES

C = A±B

C	3.20	3.60	4.00	4.50	5.00	6.00	7.00	8.00	9.00	10.0	15.0	20.0	40.0
Lat °	°	°	°	'	°	°	°	°	°	°	°	°	°
0	17.4	15.5	14.0	12.5	11.3	9.5	8.1	7.1	6.3	5.7	3.8	2.9	1.4
10	17.6	15.8	14.2	12.7	11.5	9.6	8.3	7.2	6.4	5.8	3.9	2.9	1.5
20	18.4	16.5	14.9	13.3	12.0	10.1	8.6	7.6	6.7	6.1	4.1	3.0	1.5
24	18.9	16.9	15.3	13.7	12.3	10.3	8.9	7.8	6.9	6.2	4.2	3.1	1.6
28	19.5	17.5	15.8	14.1	12.8	10.7	9.2	8.1	7.2	6.5	4.3	3.2	1.6
30	19.8	17.8	16.1	14.4	13.0	10.9	9.4	8.2	7.3	6.6	4.4	3.3	1.7
32	20.2	18.1	16.4	14.7	13.3	11.1	9.6	8.4	7.5	6.7	4.5	3.4	1.7
34	20.7	18.5	16.8	15.0	13.6	11.4	9.8	8.6	7.6	6.9	4.6	3.5	1.7
36	21.1	19.0	17.2	15.4	13.9	11.6	10.0	8.8	7.8	7.0	4.7	3.5	1.8
38	21.6	19.4	17.6	15.8	14.2	11.9	10.3	9.0	8.0	7.2	4.8	3.6	1.8
40	22.2	19.9	18.1	16.2	14.6	12.3	10.6	9.3	8.3	7.4	5.0	3.7	1.9
42	22.8	20.5	18.6	16.7	15.1	12.6	10.9	9.5	8.5	7.7	5.1	3.8	1.9
44	23.5	21.1	19.2	17.2	15.5	13.0	11.2	9.9	8.8	7.9	5.3	4.0	2.0
46	24.2	21.8	19.8	17.8	16.1	13.5	11.6	10.2	9.1	8.2	5.5	4.1	2.1
48	25.0	22.5	20.5	18.4	16.6	14.0	12.1	10.6	9.4	8.5	5.7	4.3	2.1
50	25.9	23.4	21.3	19.1	17.3	14.5	12.5	11.0	9.8	8.8	5.9	4.4	2.2
52	26.9	24.3	22.1	19.9	18.0	15.1	13.1	11.5	10.2	9.2	6.2	4.6	2.3
54	28.0	25.3	23.1	20.7	18.8	15.8	13.7	12.0	10.7	9.7	6.5	4.9	2.4
56	29.2	26.4	24.1	21.7	19.7	16.6	14.3	12.6	11.2	10.1	6.8	5.1	2.6
58	30.5	27.7	25.3	22.8	20.7	17.5	15.1	13.3	11.8	10.7	7.2	5.4	2.7
60	32.0	29.1	26.6	24.0	21.8	18.4	15.9	14.0	12.5	11.3	7.6	5.7	2.9
62	33.6	30.6	28.0	25.3	23.1	19.6	16.9	14.9	13.3	12.0	8.1	6.1	3.0
64	35.5	32.4	29.7	26.9	24.5	20.8	18.1	15.9	14.2	12.9	8.6	6.5	3.3
66	37.6	34.3	31.6	28.7	26.2	22.3	19.4	17.1	15.3	13.8	9.3	7.0	3.5
68	39.8	36.6	33.7	30.7	28.1	24.0	20.9	18.5	16.5	14.9	10.1	7.6	3.8
	3.20	3.60	4.00	4.50	5.00	6.00	7.00	8.00	9.00	10.0	15.0	20.0	40.0

Naming the Azimuth: If answer is **+**, azimuth is **South** in North latitudes and **North** in South latitudes; if answer is **–**, azimuth is **North** in North latitudes and **South** in South latitudes. If Hour Angle is **less than 180°**, azimuth is **West**; if **more than 180°**, azimuth is **East**.

VERSINES

/	0° Log	Nat	1° Log	Nat	2° Log	Nat	3° Log	Nat	4° Log	Nat	5° Log	Nat	6° Log	Nat	/
0′	∞	0.0000	1827	0002	6.7847	0006	1369	0014	7.3867	0024	5804	0038	7.7386	0.0055	60
1	2.6264	0.0000	1971	0002	6.7919	0006	1417	0014	7.3903	0025	5833	0038	7.7410	0.0055	59
2	3.2285	0.0000	2110	0002	6.7991	0006	1465	0014	7.3939	0025	5862	0039	7.7434	0.0055	58
3	3.5807	0.0000	2251	0002	6.8062	0007	1512	0014	7.3975	0025	5890	0039	7.7458	0.0056	57
4	3.8305	0.0000	2388	0002	6.8132	0007	1560	0014	7.4010	0025	5919	0039	7.7482	0.0056	56
5	4.0244	0.0000	2522	0002	6.8202	0007	1607	0014	7.4046	0025	5947	0039	7.7506	0.0056	55
6	4.1827	0.0000	2655	0002	6.8271	0007	1653	0015	7.4081	0026	5976	0040	7.7530	0.0057	54
7	4.3166	0.0000	2786	0002	6.8340	0007	1700	0015	7.4116	0026	6004	0040	7.7553	0.0057	53
8	4.4326	0.0000	2914	0002	6.8408	0007	1746	0015	7.4151	0026	6032	0040	7.7577	0.0057	52
9	4.5349	0.0000	3041	0002	6.8476	0007	1792	0015	7.4186	0026	6060	0040	7.7601	0.0058	51
10	4.6264	0.0000	3166	0002	6.8543	0007	1838	0015	7.4221	0026	6089	0041	7.7624	0.0058	50
11	4.7092	0.0000	3289	0002	6.8609	0007	1884	0015	7.4256	0027	6116	0041	7.7647	0.0058	49
12	4.7848	0.0000	3411	0002	6.8675	0007	1929	0016	7.4290	0027	6144	0041	7.7671	0.0058	48
13	4.8543	0.0000	3531	0002	6.8741	0007	1974	0016	7.4325	0027	6172	0041	7.7694	0.0059	47
14	4.9187	0.0000	3649	0002	6.8806	0008	2019	0016	7.4359	0027	6200	0042	7.7717	0.0059	46
15	4.9786	0.0000	3765	0002	6.8870	0008	2064	0016	7.4393	0027	6227	0042	7.7741	0.0059	45
16	5.0347	0.0000	3880	0002	6.8934	0008	2108	0016	7.4427	0028	6255	0042	7.7764	0.0060	44
17	5.0873	0.0000	3994	0002	6.8998	0008	2152	0016	7.4461	0028	6282	0042	7.7787	0.0060	43
18	5.1370	0.0000	4106	0003	6.9061	0008	2196	0017	7.4495	0028	6310	0043	7.7810	0.0060	42
19	5.1839	0.0000	4217	0003	6.9124	0008	2240	0017	7.4528	0028	6337	0043	7.7833	0.0061	41
20	5.2285	0.0000	4326	0003	6.9186	0008	2284	0017	7.4562	0029	6364	0043	7.7855	0.0061	40
21	5.2709	0.0000	4434	0003	6.9248	0008	2327	0017	7.4595	0029	6391	0044	7.7878	0.0061	39
22	5.3113	0.0000	4540	0003	6.9309	0009	2370	0017	7.4628	0029	6418	0044	7.7901	0.0062	38
23	5.3499	0.0000	4646	0003	6.9370	0009	2413	0017	7.4661	0029	6445	0044	7.7924	0.0062	37
24	5.3868	0.0000	4750	0003	6.9431	0009	2456	0018	7.4694	0029	6472	0044	7.7946	0.0062	36
25	5.4223	0.0000	4852	0003	6.9491	0009	2498	0018	7.4727	0030	6499	0045	7.7969	0.0063	35
26	5.4564	0.0000	4954	0003	6.9551	0009	2540	0018	7.4760	0030	6525	0045	7.7991	0.0063	34
27	5.4891	0.0000	5054	0003	6.9610	0009	2582	0018	7.4792	0030	6552	0045	7.8014	0.0063	33
28	5.5207	0.0000	5154	0003	6.9669	0009	2624	0018	7.4825	0030	6578	0045	7.8036	0.0064	32
29	5.5512	0.0000	5252	0003	6.9727	0009	2666	0018	7.4857	0031	6605	0046	7.8059	0.0064	31
30	5.5807	0.0000	5349	0003	6.9785	0010	2707	0019	7.4889	0031	6631	0046	7.8081	0.0064	30
31	5.6091	0.0000	5445	0004	6.9843	0010	2749	0019	7.4921	0031	6657	0046	7.8103	0.0065	29
32	5.6367	0.0000	5540	0004	6.9900	0010	2790	0019	7.4953	0031	6684	0047	7.8125	0.0065	28
33	5.6634	0.0000	5634	0004	6.9957	0010	2830	0019	7.4985	0032	6710	0047	7.8147	0.0065	27
34	5.6894	0.0000	5727	0004	7.0014	0010	2871	0019	7.5017	0032	6736	0047	7.8169	0.0066	26
35	5.7146	0.0001	5818	0004	7.0070	0010	2912	0020	7.5049	0032	6762	0047	7.8191	0.0066	25
36	5.7390	0.0001	5909	0004	7.0126	0010	2952	0020	7.5080	0032	6788	0048	7.8213	0.0066	24
37	5.7628	0.0001	5999	0004	7.0181	0011	2992	0020	7.5111	0032	6813	0048	7.8235	0.0067	23
38	5.7860	0.0001	6088	0004	7.0237	0011	3032	0020	7.5143	0033	6839	0048	7.8257	0.0067	22
39	5.8085	0.0001	6177	0004	7.0291	0011	3072	0020	7.5174	0033	6865	0049	7.8279	0.0067	21
40	5.8305	0.0001	6264	0004	7.0346	0011	3111	0020	7.5205	0033	6890	0049	7.8301	0.0068	20
41	5.8520	0.0001	6350	0004	7.0400	0011	3151	0021	7.5236	0033	6916	0049	7.8322	0.0068	19
42	5.8729	0.0001	6436	0004	7.0454	0011	3190	0021	7.5267	0034	6941	0049	7.8344	0.0068	18
43	5.8934	0.0001	6521	0004	7.0507	0011	3229	0021	7.5297	0034	6967	0050	7.8365	0.0069	17
44	5.9133	0.0001	6605	0005	7.0560	0011	3268	0021	7.5328	0034	6992	0050	7.8387	0.0069	16
45	5.9328	0.0001	6688	0005	7.0613	0012	3306	0021	7.5359	0034	7017	0050	7.8408	0.0069	15
46	5.9519	0.0001	6770	0005	7.0666	0012	3345	0022	7.5389	0035	7042	0051	7.8430	0.0070	14
47	5.9706	0.0001	6852	0005	7.0718	0012	3383	0022	7.5419	0035	7067	0051	7.8451	0.0070	13
48	5.9889	0.0001	6932	0005	7.0770	0012	3421	0022	7.5450	0035	7092	0051	7.8472	0.0070	12
49	6.0068	0.0001	7012	0005	7.0821	0012	3459	0022	7.5480	0035	7117	0051	7.8494	0.0071	11
50	6.0244	0.0001	7092	0005	7.0872	0012	3497	0022	7.5510	0036	7142	0052	7.8515	0.0071	10
51	6.0416	0.0001	7170	0005	7.0923	0013	3535	0023	7.5539	0036	7167	0052	7.8536	0.0071	9
52	6.0584	0.0001	7248	0005	7.0974	0013	3572	0023	7.5569	0036	7191	0052	7.8557	0.0072	8
53	6.0750	0.0001	7325	0005	7.1024	0013	3610	0023	7.5599	0036	7216	0053	7.8578	0.0072	7
54	6.0912	0.0001	7402	0005	7.1074	0013	3647	0023	7.5629	0037	7240	0053	7.8599	0.0072	6
55	6.1071	0.0001	7478	0006	7.1124	0013	3684	0023	7.5658	0037	7265	0053	7.8620	0.0073	5
56	6.1228	0.0001	7553	0006	7.1174	0013	3721	0024	7.5687	0037	7289	0054	7.8641	0.0073	4
57	6.1382	0.0001	7628	0006	7.1223	0013	3757	0024	7.5717	0037	7314	0054	7.8662	0.0073	3
58	6.1533	0.0001	7701	0006	7.1272	0013	3794	0024	7.5746	0038	7338	0054	7.8682	0.0074	2
59	6.1681	0.0001	7775	0006	7.1320	0014	3830	0024	7.5775	0038	7362	0054	7.8703	0.0074	1
60	6.1827	0.0002	7847	0006	7.1369	0014	3867	0024	7.5804	0038	7386	0055	7.8724	0.0075	0
/	Log	Nat	Log	Nat	Log	Nat	Log	Nat	Log	Nat	Log	Nat	Log	Nat	/
	359°		358°		357°		356°		355°		354°		353°		

Chapter 6

VERSINES

′	7° Log	Nat	8° Log	Nat	9° Log	Nat	10° Log	Nat	11° Log	Nat	12° Log	Nat	13° Log	Nat	′
0	7.8724	0.0075	9882	0097	8.0903	0123	1816	0152	8.2642	0184	3395	0219	8.4087	0.0256	60
1	7.8744	0.0075	0000	0098	8.0919	0124	1831	0152	8.2655	0184	3407	0219	8.4099	0.0257	59
2	7.8765	0.0075	9918	0098	8.0935	0124	1845	0153	8.2668	0185	3419	0220	8.4110	0.0258	58
3	7.8786	0.0076	9936	0099	8.0951	0124	1859	0153	8.2681	0185	3431	0220	8.4121	0.0258	57
4	7.8806	0.0076	9954	0099	8.0967	0125	1874	0154	8.2694	0186	3443	0221	8.4132	0.0259	56
5	7.8826	0.0076	9972	0099	8.0983	0125	1888	0154	8.2707	0187	3455	0222	8.4143	0.0260	55
6	7.8847	0.0077	9990	0100	8.0999	0126	1902	0155	8.2720	0187	3467	0222	8.4154	0.0260	54
7	7.8867	0.0077	0008	0100	8.1015	0126	1917	0155	8.2733	0188	3479	0223	8.4165	0.0261	53
8	7.8887	0.0077	0025	0101	8.1031	0127	1931	0156	8.2746	0188	3491	0223	8.4176	0.0262	52
9	7.8908	0.0078	0043	0101	8.1046	0127	1945	0157	8.2759	0189	3502	0224	8.4187	0.0262	51
10	7.8928	0.0078	0061	0101	8.1062	0128	1959	0157	8.2772	0189	3514	0225	8.4198	0.0263	50
11	7.8948	0.0078	0078	0102	8.1078	0128	1974	0158	8.2785	0190	3526	0225	8.4209	0.0264	49
12	7.8968	0.0079	0096	0102	8.1094	0129	1988	0158	8.2798	0190	3538	0226	8.4220	0.0264	48
13	7.8988	0.0079	0114	0103	8.1109	0129	2002	0159	8.2811	0191	3550	0226	8.4230	0.0265	47
14	7.9008	0.0080	0131	0103	8.1125	0130	2016	0159	8.2824	0192	3562	0227	8.4241	0.0266	46
15	7.9028	0.0080	0149	0103	8.1141	0130	2030	0160	8.2836	0192	3573	0228	8.4252	0.0266	45
16	7.9048	0.0080	0166	0104	8.1156	0131	2044	0160	8.2849	0193	3585	0228	8.4263	0.0267	44
17	7.9068	0.0081	0184	0104	8.1172	0131	2058	0161	8.2862	0193	3597	0229	8.4274	0.0268	43
18	7.9088	0.0081	0201	0105	8.1187	0131	2072	0161	8.2875	0194	3609	0230	8.4285	0.0268	42
19	7.9108	0.0081	0219	0105	8.1203	0132	2086	0162	8.2887	0194	3620	0230	8.4296	0.0269	41
20	7.9127	0.0082	0236	0106	8.1218	0132	2100	0162	8.2900	0195	3632	0231	8.4306	0.0270	40
21	7.9147	0.0082	0253	0106	8.1234	0133	2114	0163	8.2913	0196	3644	0231	8.4317	0.0270	39
22	7.9167	0.0083	0271	0106	8.1249	0133	2128	0163	8.2926	0196	3655	0232	8.4328	0.0271	38
23	7.9186	0.0083	0288	0107	8.1265	0134	2142	0164	8.2938	0197	3667	0233	8.4339	0.0272	37
24	7.9206	0.0083	0305	0107	8.1280	0134	2156	0164	8.2951	0197	3679	0233	8.4350	0.0272	36
25	7.9225	0.0084	0322	0108	8.1295	0135	2170	0165	8.2964	0198	3690	0234	8.4360	0.0273	35
26	7.9245	0.0084	0339	0108	8.1311	0135	2184	0165	8.2976	0198	3702	0235	8.4371	0.0274	34
27	7.9264	0.0084	0357	0109	8.1326	0136	2198	0166	8.2989	0199	3714	0235	8.4382	0.0274	33
28	7.9284	0.0085	0374	0109	8.1341	0136	2211	0166	8.3001	0200	3725	0236	8.4392	0.0275	32
29	7.9303	0.0085	0391	0109	8.1357	0137	2225	0167	8.3014	0200	3737	0236	8.4403	0.0276	31
30	7.9322	0.0086	0408	0110	8.1372	0137	2239	0167	8.3027	0201	3748	0237	8.4414	0.0276	30
31	7.9342	0.0086	0425	0110	8.1387	0138	2253	0168	8.3039	0201	3760	0238	8.4424	0.0277	29
32	7.9361	0.0086	0442	0111	8.1402	0138	2266	0169	8.3052	0202	3771	0238	8.4435	0.0278	28
33	7.9380	0.0087	0459	0111	8.1417	0139	2280	0169	8.3064	0202	3783	0239	8.4446	0.0278	27
34	7.9399	0.0087	0475	0112	8.1432	0139	2294	0170	8.3077	0203	3794	0240	8.4456	0.0279	26
35	7.9418	0.0087	0492	0112	8.1447	0140	2307	0170	8.3089	0204	3806	0240	8.4467	0.0280	25
36	7.9437	0.0088	0509	0112	8.1463	0140	2321	0171	8.3102	0204	3817	0241	8.4478	0.0280	24
37	7.9456	0.0088	0526	0113	8.1478	0141	2335	0171	8.3114	0205	3829	0241	8.4488	0.0281	23
38	7.9475	0.0089	0543	0113	8.1493	0141	2348	0172	8.3126	0205	3840	0242	8.4499	0.0282	22
39	7.9494	0.0089	0559	0114	8.1508	0141	2362	0172	8.3139	0206	3851	0243	8.4509	0.0282	21
40	7.9513	0.0089	0576	0114	8.1522	0142	2375	0173	8.3151	0207	3863	0243	8.4520	0.0283	20
41	7.9532	0.0090	0593	0115	8.1537	0142	2389	0173	8.3164	0207	3874	0244	8.4530	0.0284	19
42	7.9551	0.0090	0609	0115	8.1552	0143	2402	0174	8.3176	0208	3886	0245	8.4541	0.0285	18
43	7.9569	0.0091	0626	0116	8.1567	0143	2416	0174	8.3188	0208	3897	0245	8.4551	0.0285	17
44	7.9588	0.0091	0642	0116	8.1582	0144	2429	0175	8.3200	0209	3908	0246	8.4562	0.0286	16
45	7.9607	0.0091	0659	0116	8.1597	0144	2443	0175	8.3213	0210	3920	0247	8.4572	0.0287	15
46	7.9625	0.0092	0675	0117	8.1612	0145	2456	0176	8.3225	0210	3931	0247	8.4583	0.0287	14
47	7.9644	0.0092	0692	0117	8.1626	0145	2469	0177	8.3237	0211	3942	0248	8.4593	0.0288	13
48	7.9662	0.0093	0708	0118	8.1641	0146	2483	0177	8.3250	0211	3953	0249	8.4604	0.0289	12
49	7.9681	0.0093	0725	0118	8.1656	0146	2496	0178	8.3262	0212	3965	0249	8.4614	0.0289	11
50	7.9699	0.0093	0741	0119	8.1671	0147	2510	0178	8.3274	0213	3976	0250	8.4625	0.0290	10
51	7.9718	0.0094	0757	0119	8.1685	0147	2523	0179	8.3286	0213	3987	0250	8.4635	0.0291	9
52	7.9736	0.0094	0774	0120	8.1700	0148	2536	0179	8.3298	0214	3998	0251	8.4645	0.0291	8
53	7.9755	0.0095	0790	0120	8.1715	0148	2549	0180	8.3310	0214	4010	0252	8.4656	0.0292	7
54	7.9773	0.0095	0806	0120	8.1729	0149	2563	0180	8.3323	0215	4021	0252	8.4666	0.0293	6
55	7.9791	0.0095	0823	0121	8.1744	0149	2576	0181	8.3335	0216	4032	0253	8.4677	0.0294	5
56	7.9809	0.0096	0839	0121	8.1758	0150	2589	0182	8.3347	0216	4043	0254	8.4687	0.0294	4
57	7.9828	0.0096	0855	0122	8.1773	0150	2602	0182	8.3359	0217	4054	0254	8.4697	0.0295	3
58	7.9846	0.0097	0871	0122	8.1787	0151	2615	0183	8.3371	0217	4065	0255	8.4708	0.0296	2
59	7.9864	0.0097	0887	0123	8.1802	0151	2629	0183	8.3383	0218	4076	0256	8.4718	0.0296	1
60	7.9882	0.0097	0903	0123	8.1816	0152	2642	0184	8.3395	0219	4087	0256	8.4728	0.0297	0
′	Log	Nat	Log	Nat	Log	Nat	Log	Nat	Log	Nat	Log	Nat	Log	Nat	′
	352°		351°		350°		349°		348°		347°		346°		

VERSINES

/	14°		15°		16°		17°		18°		19°		20°		/
	Log	Nat	Log	Nat	Log	Nat	Log	Nat	Log	Nat	Log	Nat	Log	Nat	
0	8.4728	0.0297	5324	0341	8.5881	0387	6404	0437	8.6897	0489	7362	0545	8.7804	0.0603	60
1	8.4738	0.0298	5334	0341	8.5890	0388	6413	0438	8.6905	0490	7370	0546	8.7811	0.0604	59
2	8.4749	0.0298	5343	0342	8.5899	0389	6421	0439	8.6913	0491	7378	0547	8.7818	0.0605	58
3	8.4758	0.0299	5353	0343	8.5908	0390	6430	0440	8.6921	0492	7385	0548	8.7825	0.0606	57
4	8.4769	0.0300	5363	0344	8.5917	0391	6438	0440	8.6929	0493	7393	0549	8.7832	0.0607	56
5	8.4779	0.0301	5372	0345	8.5926	0391	6447	0441	8.6937	0494	7400	0550	8.7839	0.0608	55
6	8.4790	0.0301	5382	0345	8.5935	0392	6455	0442	8.6945	0495	7408	0551	8.7847	0.0609	54
7	8.4800	0.0302	5391	0346	8.5944	0393	6463	0443	8.6953	0496	7415	0551	8.7854	0.0610	53
8	8.4810	0.0303	5401	0347	8.5953	0394	6472	0444	8.6961	0497	7423	0552	8.7861	0.0611	52
9	8.4820	0.0303	5410	0348	8.5962	0395	6480	0445	8.6968	0498	7430	0553	8.7868	0.0612	51
10	8.4830	0.0304	5420	0348	8.5971	0395	6488	0445	8.6976	0498	7438	0554	8.7875	0.0613	50
11	8.4841	0.0305	5429	0349	8.5980	0396	6497	0446	8.6984	0499	7445	0555	8.7882	0.0614	49
12	8.4851	0.0306	5439	0350	8.5989	0397	6505	0447	8.6992	0500	7453	0556	8.7889	0.0615	48
13	8.4861	0.0306	5448	0351	8.5997	0398	6514	0448	8.7000	0501	7460	0557	8.7896	0.0616	47
14	8.4871	0.0307	5458	0351	8.6006	0399	6522	0449	8.7008	0502	7468	0558	8.7903	0.0617	46
15	8.4881	0.0308	5467	0352	8.6015	0400	6530	0450	8.7016	0503	7475	0559	8.7910	0.0618	45
16	8.4891	0.0308	5476	0353	8.6024	0400	6539	0451	8.7024	0504	7482	0560	8.7918	0.0619	44
17	8.4901	0.0309	5486	0354	8.6033	0401	6547	0452	8.7031	0505	7490	0561	8.7925	0.0620	43
18	8.4911	0.0310	5495	0354	8.6042	0402	6555	0452	8.7039	0506	7497	0562	8.7932	0.0621	42
19	8.4921	0.0311	5505	0355	8.6051	0403	6563	0453	8.7047	0507	7505	0563	8.7939	0.0622	41
20	8.4932	0.0311	5514	0356	8.6059	0404	6572	0454	8.7055	0508	7512	0564	8.7946	0.0623	40
21	8.4942	0.0312	5523	0357	8.6068	0404	6580	0455	8.7063	0508	7520	0565	8.7953	0.0624	39
22	8.4952	0.0313	5533	0358	8.6077	0405	6588	0456	8.7071	0509	7527	0566	8.7960	0.0625	38
23	8.4962	0.0313	5542	0358	8.6086	0406	6597	0457	8.7078	0510	7534	0567	8.7967	0.0626	37
24	8.4972	0.0314	5552	0359	8.6094	0407	6605	0458	8.7086	0511	7542	0568	8.7974	0.0627	36
25	8.4982	0.0315	5561	0360	8.6103	0408	6613	0458	8.7094	0512	7549	0569	8.7981	0.0628	35
26	8.4992	0.0316	5570	0361	8.6112	0409	6621	0459	8.7102	0513	7557	0570	8.7988	0.0629	34
27	8.5002	0.0316	5579	0361	8.6121	0409	6630	0460	8.7110	0514	7564	0571	8.7995	0.0630	33
28	8.5012	0.0317	5589	0362	8.6129	0410	6638	0461	8.7117	0515	7571	0572	8.8002	0.0631	32
29	8.5021	0.0318	5598	0363	8.6138	0411	6646	0462	8.7125	0516	7579	0573	8.8009	0.0632	31
30	8.5031	0.0319	5607	0364	8.6147	0412	6654	0463	8.7133	0517	7586	0574	8.8016	0.0633	30
31	8.5041	0.0319	5617	0364	8.6156	0413	6662	0464	8.7141	0518	7593	0575	8.8023	0.0634	29
32	8.5051	0.0320	5626	0365	8.6164	0413	6671	0465	8.7148	0519	7601	0576	8.8030	0.0635	28
33	8.5061	0.0321	5635	0366	8.6173	0414	6679	0465	8.7156	0520	7608	0577	8.8037	0.0636	27
34	8.5071	0.0321	5644	0367	8.6182	0415	6687	0466	8.7164	0520	7615	0577	8.8044	0.0637	26
35	8.5081	0.0322	5654	0368	8.6190	0416	6695	0467	8.7172	0521	7623	0578	8.8051	0.0638	25
36	8.5091	0.0323	5663	0368	8.6199	0417	6703	0468	8.7179	0522	7630	0579	8.8058	0.0639	24
37	8.5101	0.0324	5672	0369	8.6208	0418	6711	0469	8.7187	0523	7637	0580	8.8065	0.0640	23
38	8.5110	0.0324	5681	0370	8.6216	0418	6720	0470	8.7195	0524	7645	0581	8.8072	0.0641	22
39	8.5120	0.0325	5691	0371	8.6225	0419	6728	0471	8.7202	0525	7652	0582	8.8079	0.0642	21
40	8.5130	0.0326	5700	0372	8.6234	0420	6736	0472	8.7210	0526	7659	0583	8.8086	0.0644	20
41	8.5140	0.0327	5709	0372	8.6242	0421	6744	0473	8.7218	0527	7666	0584	8.8092	0.0645	19
42	8.5150	0.0327	5718	0373	8.6251	0422	6752	0473	8.7225	0528	7674	0585	8.8099	0.0646	18
43	8.5160	0.0328	5727	0374	8.6259	0423	6760	0474	8.7233	0529	7681	0586	8.8106	0.0647	17
44	8.5169	0.0329	5736	0375	8.6268	0423	6768	0475	8.7241	0530	7688	0587	8.8113	0.0648	16
45	8.5179	0.0330	5745	0375	8.6277	0424	6776	0476	8.7248	0531	7696	0588	8.8120	0.0649	15
46	8.5189	0.0330	5755	0376	8.6285	0425	6785	0477	8.7256	0532	7703	0589	8.8127	0.0650	14
47	8.5199	0.0331	5764	0377	8.6294	0426	6793	0478	8.7264	0533	7710	0590	8.8134	0.0651	13
48	8.5208	0.0332	5773	0378	8.6302	0427	6801	0479	8.7271	0534	7717	0591	8.8141	0.0652	12
49	8.5218	0.0333	5782	0379	8.6311	0428	6809	0480	8.7279	0534	7725	0592	8.8148	0.0653	11
50	8.5228	0.0333	5791	0379	8.6319	0428	6817	0480	8.7287	0535	7732	0593	8.8155	0.0654	10
51	8.5237	0.0334	5800	0380	8.6328	0429	6825	0481	8.7294	0536	7739	0594	8.8161	0.0655	9
52	8.5247	0.0335	5809	0381	8.6336	0430	6833	0482	8.7302	0537	7746	0595	8.8168	0.0656	8
53	8.5257	0.0335	5818	0382	8.6345	0431	6841	0483	8.7309	0538	7753	0596	8.8175	0.0657	7
54	8.5266	0.0336	5827	0383	8.6353	0432	6849	0484	8.7317	0539	7761	0597	8.8182	0.0658	6
55	8.5276	0.0337	5836	0383	8.6362	0433	6857	0485	8.7325	0540	7768	0598	8.8189	0.0659	5
56	8.5286	0.0338	5845	0384	8.6370	0434	6865	0486	8.7332	0541	7775	0599	8.8196	0.0660	4
57	8.5295	0.0338	5854	0385	8.6379	0434	6873	0487	8.7340	0542	7782	0600	8.8202	0.0661	3
58	8.5305	0.0339	5863	0386	8.6387	0435	6881	0488	8.7347	0543	7789	0601	8.8209	0.0662	2
59	8.5315	0.0340	5872	0387	8.6396	0436	6889	0489	8.7355	0544	7797	0602	8.8216	0.0663	1
60	8.5324	0.0341	5881	0387	8.6404	0437	6897	0489	8.7362	0545	7804	0603	8.8223	0.0664	0
/	Log	Nat	Log	Nat	Log	Nat	Log	Nat	Log	Nat	Log	Nat	Log	Nat	/
	345°		344°		343°		342°		341°		340°		339°		

Chapter 6

VERSINES

′	21° Log	Nat	22° Log	Nat	23° Log	Nat	24° Log	Nat	25° Log	Nat	26° Log	Nat	27° Log	Nat	′
0	8.8223	0.0664	8622	0728	8.9003	0795	9368	0865	8.9717	0937	0052	1012	9.0374	0.1090	60
1	8.8230	0.0665	8629	0729	8.9010	0796	9374	0866	8.9723	0938	0058	1013	9.0379	0.1091	59
2	8.0237	0.0666	8635	0730	8.9016	0797	9380	0867	8.9728	0939	0063	1015	9.0385	0.1093	58
3	8.8243	0.0667	8642	0731	8.9022	0798	9386	0868	8.9734	0941	0068	1016	9.0390	0.1094	57
4	8.8250	0.0668	8648	0733	8.9028	0800	9392	0869	8.9740	0942	0074	1017	9.0395	0.1095	56
5	8.8257	0.0669	8655	0734	8.9034	0801	9398	0870	8.9745	0943	0079	1018	9.0400	0.1097	55
6	8.8264	0.0670	8661	0735	8.9041	0802	9403	0872	8.9751	0944	0085	1020	9.0406	0.1098	54
7	8.8271	0.0672	8668	0736	8.9047	0803	9409	0873	8.9757	0946	0090	1021	9.0411	0.1099	53
8	8.8277	0.0673	8674	0737	8.9053	0804	9415	0874	8.9762	0947	0096	1022	9.0416	0.1101	52
9	8.8284	0.0674	8681	0738	8.9059	0805	9421	0875	8.9768	0948	0101	1024	9.0421	0.1102	51
10	8.8291	0.0675	8687	0739	8.9065	0806	9427	0876	8.9774	0949	0107	1025	9.0426	0.1103	50
11	8.8298	0.0676	8693	0740	8.9071	0808	9433	0878	8.9779	0950	0112	1026	9.0432	0.1105	49
12	8.8304	0.0677	8700	0741	8.9078	0809	9439	0879	8.9785	0952	0117	1027	9.0437	0.1106	48
13	8.8311	0.0678	8706	0742	8.9084	0810	9445	0880	8.9791	0953	0123	1029	9.0442	0.1107	47
14	8.8318	0.0679	8713	0743	8.9090	0811	9451	0881	8.9796	0954	0128	1030	9.0447	0.1108	46
15	8.8325	0.0680	8719	0745	8.9096	0812	9457	0882	8.9802	0955	0134	1031	9.0453	0.1110	45
16	8.8331	0.0681	8726	0746	8.9102	0813	9462	0884	8.9808	0957	0139	1033	9.0458	0.1111	44
17	8.8338	0.0682	8732	0747	8.9108	0814	9468	0885	8.9813	0958	0145	1034	9.0463	0.1112	43
18	8.8345	0.0683	8738	0748	8.9114	0816	9474	0886	8.9819	0959	0150	1035	9.0468	0.1114	42
19	8.8351	0.0684	8745	0749	8.9121	0817	9480	0887	8.9825	0960	0155	1036	9.0473	0.1115	41
20	8.8358	0.0685	8751	0750	8.9127	0818	9486	0888	8.9830	0962	0161	1038	9.0479	0.1116	40
21	8.8365	0.0686	8758	0751	8.9133	0819	9492	0890	8.9836	0963	0166	1039	9.0484	0.1118	39
22	8.8372	0.0687	8764	0752	8.9139	0820	9498	0891	8.9841	0964	0172	1040	9.0489	0.1119	38
23	8.8378	0.0688	8770	0753	8.9145	0821	9503	0892	8.9847	0965	0177	1042	9.0494	0.1121	37
24	8.8385	0.0689	8777	0755	8.9151	0822	9509	0893	8.9853	0967	0182	1043	9.0499	0.1122	36
25	8.8392	0.0691	8783	0756	8.9157	0824	9515	0894	8.9858	0968	0188	1044	9.0505	0.1123	35
26	8.8398	0.0692	8790	0757	8.9163	0825	9521	0896	8.9864	0969	0193	1045	9.0510	0.1125	34
27	8.8405	0.0693	8796	0758	8.9169	0826	9527	0897	8.9869	0970	0198	1047	9.0515	0.1126	33
28	8.8412	0.0694	8802	0759	8.9175	0827	9533	0898	8.9875	0972	0204	1048	9.0520	0.1127	32
29	8.8418	0.0695	8809	0760	8.9182	0828	9538	0899	8.9881	0973	0209	1049	9.0525	0.1129	31
30	8.8425	0.0696	8815	0761	8.9188	0829	9544	0900	8.9886	0974	0215	1051	9.0530	0.1130	30
31	8.8432	0.0697	8821	0762	8.9194	0831	9550	0902	8.9892	0975	0220	1052	9.0536	0.1131	29
32	8.8438	0.0698	8828	0763	8.9200	0832	9556	0903	8.9897	0977	0225	1053	9.0541	0.1133	28
33	8.8445	0.0699	8834	0765	8.9206	0833	9562	0904	8.9903	0978	0231	1055	9.0546	0.1134	27
34	8.8452	0.0700	8840	0766	8.9212	0834	9568	0905	8.9909	0979	0236	1056	9.0551	0.1135	26
35	8.8458	0.0701	8847	0767	8.9218	0835	9573	0906	8.9914	0980	0241	1057	9.0556	0.1137	25
36	8.8465	0.0702	8853	0768	8.9224	0836	9579	0908	8.9920	0982	0247	1058	9.0561	0.1138	24
37	8.8471	0.0703	8859	0769	8.9230	0838	9585	0909	8.9925	0983	0252	1060	9.0566	0.1139	23
38	8.8478	0.0704	8866	0770	8.9236	0839	9591	0910	8.9931	0984	0257	1061	9.0572	0.1141	22
39	8.8485	0.0705	8872	0771	8.9242	0840	9596	0911	8.9936	0985	0263	1062	9.0577	0.1142	21
40	8.8491	0.0707	8878	0772	8.9248	0841	9602	0912	8.9942	0987	0268	1064	9.0582	0.1143	20
41	8.8498	0.0708	8885	0773	8.9254	0842	9608	0914	8.9947	0988	0273	1065	9.0587	0.1145	19
42	8.8504	0.0709	8891	0775	8.9260	0843	9614	0915	8.9953	0989	0279	1066	9.0592	0.1146	18
43	8.8511	0.0710	8897	0776	8.9266	0845	9620	0916	8.9959	0990	0284	1068	9.0597	0.1147	17
44	8.8518	0.0711	8903	0777	8.9272	0846	9625	0917	8.9964	0992	0289	1069	9.0602	0.1149	16
45	8.8524	0.0712	8910	0778	8.9278	0847	9631	0919	8.9970	0993	0295	1070	9.0607	0.1150	15
46	8.8531	0.0713	8916	0779	8.9284	0848	9637	0920	8.9975	0994	0300	1072	9.0613	0.1151	14
47	8.8537	0.0714	8922	0780	8.9290	0849	9643	0921	8.9981	0996	0305	1073	9.0618	0.1153	13
48	8.8544	0.0715	8929	0781	8.9296	0850	9648	0922	8.9986	0997	0311	1074	9.0623	0.1154	12
49	8.8550	0.0716	8935	0782	8.9302	0852	9654	0923	8.9992	0998	0316	1075	9.0628	0.1156	11
50	8.8557	0.0717	8941	0784	8.9308	0853	9660	0925	8.9997	0999	0321	1077	9.0633	0.1157	10
51	8.8564	0.0718	8947	0785	8.9314	0854	9666	0926	9.0003	1001	0327	1078	9.0638	0.1158	9
52	8.8570	0.0719	8954	0786	8.9320	0855	9671	0927	9.0008	1002	0332	1079	9.0643	0.1160	8
53	8.8577	0.0721	8960	0787	8.9326	0856	9677	0928	9.0014	1003	0337	1081	9.0648	0.1161	7
54	8.8583	0.0722	8966	0788	8.9332	0857	9683	0930	9.0019	1004	0342	1082	9.0653	0.1162	6
55	8.8590	0.0723	8972	0789	8.9338	0859	9688	0931	9.0025	1006	0348	1083	9.0658	0.1164	5
56	8.8596	0.0724	8979	0790	8.9344	0860	9694	0932	9.0030	1007	0353	1085	9.0664	0.1165	4
57	8.8603	0.0725	8985	0792	8.9350	0861	9700	0933	9.0036	1008	0358	1086	9.0669	0.1166	3
58	8.8609	0.0726	8991	0793	8.9356	0862	9706	0934	9.0041	1010	0363	1087	9.0674	0.1168	2
59	8.8616	0.0727	8997	0794	8.9362	0863	9711	0936	9.0047	1011	0369	1089	9.0679	0.1169	1
60	8.8622	0.0728	9003	0795	8.9368	0865	9717	0937	9.0052	1012	0374	1090	9.0684	0.1171	0
′	Log	Nat	Log	Nat	Log	Nat	Log	Nat	Log	Nat	Log	Nat	Log	Nat	′
	338°		337°		336°		335°		334°		333°		332°		

VERSINES

/	28° Log	Nat	29° Log	Nat	30° Log	Nat	31° Log	Nat	32° Log	Nat	33° Log	Nat	34° Log	Nat	/
0	9.0684	0.1171	0982	1254	9.1270	1340	1548	1428	9.1817	1520	2077	1613	9.2329	0.1710	60
1	9.0689	0.1172	0987	1255	9.1275	1341	1553	1430	9.1821	1521	2081	1615	9.2333	0.1711	59
2	9.0694	0.1173	0992	1257	9.1280	1343	1557	1431	9.1826	1523	2086	1616	9.2337	0.1713	58
3	9.0699	0.1175	0997	1258	9.1284	1344	1562	1433	9.1830	1524	2090	1618	9.2341	0.1715	57
4	9.0704	0.1176	1002	1259	9.1289	1346	1566	1434	9.1835	1526	2094	1620	9.2346	0.1716	56
5	9.0709	0.1177	1007	1261	9.1294	1347	1571	1436	9.1839	1527	2099	1621	9.2350	0.1718	55
6	9.0714	0.1179	1012	1262	9.1298	1348	1576	1437	9.1843	1529	2103	1623	9.2354	0.1719	54
7	9.0719	0.1180	1016	1264	9.1303	1350	1580	1439	9.1848	1530	2107	1624	9.2358	0.1721	53
8	9.0724	0.1181	1021	1265	9.1308	1351	1585	1440	9.1852	1532	2111	1626	9.2362	0.1723	52
9	9.0729	0.1183	1026	1267	9.1313	1353	1589	1442	9.1857	1533	2115	1628	9.2366	0.1724	51
10	9.0734	0.1184	1031	1268	9.1317	1354	1594	1443	9.1861	1535	2120	1629	9.2370	0.1726	50
11	9.0739	0.1186	1036	1269	9.1322	1356	1598	1445	9.1865	1537	2124	1631	9.2374	0.1728	49
12	9.0744	0.1187	1041	1271	9.1327	1357	1603	1446	9.1870	1538	2128	1632	9.2378	0.1729	48
13	9.0749	0.1188	1046	1272	9.1331	1359	1607	1448	9.1874	1540	2132	1634	9.2383	0.1731	47
14	9.0754	0.1190	1050	1274	9.1336	1360	1612	1449	9.1879	1541	2137	1636	9.2387	0.1732	46
15	9.0759	0.1191	1055	1275	9.1341	1362	1616	1451	9.1883	1543	2141	1637	9.2391	0.1734	45
16	9.0764	0.1192	1060	1276	9.1345	1363	1621	1452	9.1887	1544	2145	1639	9.2395	0.1736	44
17	9.0769	0.1194	1065	1278	9.1350	1365	1625	1454	9.1892	1546	2149	1640	9.2399	0.1737	43
18	9.0775	0.1195	1070	1279	9.1355	1366	1630	1455	9.1896	1547	2154	1642	9.2403	0.1739	42
19	9.0780	0.1197	1075	1281	9.1359	1368	1634	1457	9.1900	1549	2158	1644	9.2407	0.1741	41
20	9.0785	0.1198	1079	1282	9.1364	1369	1639	1458	9.1905	1550	2162	1645	9.2411	0.1742	40
21	9.0790	0.1199	1084	1284	9.1369	1370	1643	1460	9.1909	1552	2166	1647	9.2415	0.1744	39
22	9.0795	0.1201	1089	1285	9.1373	1372	1648	1461	9.1913	1554	2170	1648	9.2419	0.1746	38
23	9.0800	0.1202	1094	1286	9.1378	1373	1652	1463	9.1918	1555	2175	1650	9.2423	0.1747	37
24	9.0805	0.1204	1099	1288	9.1383	1375	1657	1464	9.1922	1557	2179	1652	9.2428	0.1749	36
25	9.0810	0.1205	1104	1289	9.1387	1376	1661	1466	9.1926	1558	2183	1653	9.2432	0.1751	35
26	9.0814	0.1206	1108	1291	9.1392	1378	1666	1468	9.1931	1560	2187	1655	9.2436	0.1752	34
27	9.0819	0.1208	1113	1292	9.1397	1379	1670	1469	9.1935	1561	2191	1656	9.2440	0.1754	33
28	9.0824	0.1209	1118	1294	9.1401	1381	1675	1471	9.1939	1563	2196	1658	9.2444	0.1755	32
29	9.0829	0.1210	1123	1295	9.1406	1382	1679	1472	9.1944	1565	2200	1660	9.2448	0.1757	31
30	9.0834	0.1212	1128	1296	9.1410	1384	1684	1474	9.1948	1566	2204	1661	9.2452	0.1759	30
31	9.0839	0.1213	1132	1298	9.1415	1385	1688	1475	9.1952	1568	2208	1663	9.2456	0.1760	29
32	9.0844	0.1215	1137	1299	9.1420	1387	1693	1477	9.1957	1569	2212	1664	9.2460	0.1762	28
33	9.0849	0.1216	1142	1301	9.1424	1388	1697	1478	9.1961	1571	2217	1666	9.2464	0.1764	27
34	9.0854	0.1217	1147	1302	9.1429	1390	1702	1480	9.1965	1572	2221	1668	9.2468	0.1765	26
35	9.0859	0.1219	1151	1304	9.1434	1391	1706	1481	9.1970	1574	2225	1669	9.2472	0.1767	25
36	9.0864	0.1220	1156	1305	9.1438	1393	1711	1483	9.1974	1575	2229	1671	9.2476	0.1769	24
37	9.0869	0.1222	1161	1306	9.1443	1394	1715	1484	9.1978	1577	2233	1672	9.2480	0.1770	23
38	9.0874	0.1223	1166	1308	9.1447	1396	1720	1486	9.1983	1579	2238	1674	9.2484	0.1772	22
39	9.0879	0.1224	1171	1309	9.1452	1397	1724	1487	9.1987	1580	2242	1676	9.2489	0.1774	21
40	9.0884	0.1226	1175	1311	9.1457	1399	1728	1489	9.1991	1582	2246	1677	9.2493	0.1775	20
41	9.0889	0.1227	1180	1312	9.1461	1400	1733	1490	9.1996	1583	2250	1679	9.2497	0.1777	19
42	9.0894	0.1229	1185	1314	9.1466	1401	1737	1492	9.2000	1585	2254	1680	9.2501	0.1779	18
43	9.0899	0.1230	1190	1315	9.1470	1403	1742	1493	9.2004	1586	2258	1682	9.2505	0.1780	17
44	9.0904	0.1231	1194	1317	9.1475	1404	1746	1495	9.2009	1588	2263	1684	9.2509	0.1782	16
45	9.0909	0.1233	1199	1318	9.1480	1406	1751	1496	9.2013	1590	2267	1685	9.2513	0.1784	15
46	9.0914	0.1234	1204	1319	9.1484	1407	1755	1498	9.2017	1591	2271	1687	9.2517	0.1785	14
47	9.0919	0.1236	1209	1321	9.1489	1409	1760	1500	9.2021	1593	2275	1689	9.2521	0.1787	13
48	9.0923	0.1237	1213	1322	9.1493	1410	1764	1501	9.2026	1594	2279	1690	9.2525	0.1789	12
49	9.0928	0.1238	1218	1324	9.1498	1412	1768	1503	9.2030	1596	2283	1692	9.2529	0.1790	11
50	9.0933	0.1240	1223	1325	9.1503	1413	1773	1504	9.2034	1597	2288	1693	9.2533	0.1792	10
51	9.0938	0.1241	1228	1327	9.1507	1415	1777	1506	9.2039	1599	2292	1695	9.2537	0.1793	9
52	9.0943	0.1243	1232	1328	9.1512	1416	1782	1507	9.2043	1601	2296	1697	9.2541	0.1795	8
53	9.0948	0.1244	1237	1330	9.1516	1418	1786	1509	9.2047	1602	2300	1698	9.2545	0.1797	7
54	9.0953	0.1245	1242	1331	9.1521	1419	1791	1510	9.2052	1604	2304	1700	9.2549	0.1798	6
55	9.0958	0.1247	1247	1332	9.1525	1421	1795	1512	9.2056	1605	2308	1701	9.2553	0.1800	5
56	9.0963	0.1248	1251	1334	9.1530	1422	1799	1513	9.2060	1607	2312	1703	9.2557	0.1802	4
57	9.0968	0.1250	1256	1335	9.1535	1424	1804	1515	9.2064	1609	2317	1705	9.2561	0.1803	3
58	9.0973	0.1251	1261	1337	9.1539	1425	1808	1516	9.2069	1610	2321	1706	9.2565	0.1805	2
59	9.0977	0.1252	1266	1338	9.1544	1427	1813	1518	9.2073	1612	2325	1708	9.2569	0.1807	1
60	9.0982	0.1254	1270	1340	9.1548	1428	1817	1520	9.2077	1613	2329	1710	9.2573	0.1808	0
/	Log	Nat	Log	Nat	Log	Nat	Log	Nat	Log	Nat	Log	Nat	Log	Nat	/
	331°		330°		329°		328°		327°		326°		325°		

Chapter 6

VERSINES

/	35° Log	Nat	36° Log	Nat	37° Log	Nat	38° Log	Nat	39° Log	Nat	40° Log	Nat	41° Log	Nat	/
0	9.2573	0.1808	2810	1910	9.3040	2014	3263	2120	9.3480	2229	3691	2340	9.3897	0.2453	60
1	9.2577	0.1810	2814	1912	9.3044	2015	3267	2122	9.3484	2230	3695	2341	9.3900	0.2455	59
2	9.2581	0.1812	2818	1913	9.3047	2017	3270	2123	9.3487	2232	3698	2343	9.3904	0.2457	58
3	9.2585	0.1813	2822	1915	9.3051	2019	3274	2125	9.3491	2234	3702	2345	9.3907	0.2459	57
4	9.2589	0.1815	2825	1917	9.3055	2021	3278	2127	9.3494	2236	3705	2347	9.3910	0.2461	56
5	9.2593	0.1817	2829	1918	9.3059	2022	3281	2129	9.3498	2238	3709	2349	9.3914	0.2462	55
6	9.2597	0.1819	2833	1920	9.3062	2024	3285	2131	9.3502	2240	3712	2351	9.3917	0.2464	54
7	9.2601	0.1820	2837	1922	9.3066	2026	3289	2132	9.3505	2241	3716	2353	9.3920	0.2466	53
8	9.2605	0.1822	2841	1924	9.3070	2028	3292	2134	9.3509	2243	3719	2355	9.3924	0.2468	52
9	9.2609	0.1824	2845	1925	9.3074	2029	3296	2136	9.3512	2245	3723	2356	9.3927	0.2470	51
10	9.2613	0.1825	2849	1927	9.3077	2031	3300	2138	9.3516	2247	3726	2358	9.3931	0.2472	50
11	9.2617	0.1827	2853	1929	9.3081	2033	3303	2140	9.3519	2249	3729	2360	9.3934	0.2474	49
12	9.2621	0.1829	2856	1930	9.3085	2035	3307	2141	9.3523	2251	3733	2362	9.3937	0.2476	48
13	9.2625	0.1830	2860	1932	9.3089	2036	3311	2143	9.3526	2252	3736	2364	9.3941	0.2478	47
14	9.2629	0.1832	2864	1934	9.3093	2038	3314	2145	9.3530	2254	3740	2366	9.3944	0.2480	46
15	9.2633	0.1834	2868	1936	9.3096	2040	3318	2147	9.3534	2256	3743	2368	9.3947	0.2482	45
16	9.2637	0.1835	2872	1937	9.3100	2042	3322	2149	9.3537	2258	3747	2370	9.3951	0.2484	44
17	9.2641	0.1837	2876	1939	9.3104	2044	3325	2150	9.3541	2260	3750	2371	9.3954	0.2485	43
18	9.2645	0.1839	2880	1941	9.3107	2045	3329	2152	9.3544	2262	3754	2373	9.3957	0.2487	42
19	9.2649	0.1840	2883	1942	9.3111	2047	3333	2154	9.3548	2263	3757	2375	9.3961	0.2489	41
20	9.2653	0.1842	2887	1944	9.3115	2049	3336	2156	9.3551	2265	3760	2377	9.3964	0.2491	40
21	9.2657	0.1844	2891	1946	9.3119	2051	3340	2158	9.3555	2267	3764	2379	9.3967	0.2493	39
22	9.2661	0.1845	2895	1948	9.3122	2052	3343	2159	9.3558	2269	3767	2381	9.3971	0.2495	38
23	9.2665	0.1847	2899	1949	9.3126	2054	3347	2161	9.3562	2271	3771	2383	9.3974	0.2497	37
24	9.2669	0.1849	2903	1951	9.3130	2056	3351	2163	9.3565	2273	3774	2385	9.3977	0.2499	36
25	9.2673	0.1850	2907	1953	9.3134	2058	3354	2165	9.3569	2275	3778	2387	9.3981	0.2501	35
26	9.2677	0.1852	2910	1955	9.3137	2059	3358	2167	9.3572	2276	3781	2388	9.3984	0.2503	34
27	9.2681	0.1854	2914	1956	9.3141	2061	3362	2168	9.3576	2278	3784	2390	9.3987	0.2505	33
28	9.2685	0.1855	2918	1958	9.3145	2063	3365	2170	9.3579	2280	3788	2392	9.3991	0.2507	32
29	9.2688	0.1857	2922	1960	9.3149	2065	3369	2172	9.3583	2282	3791	2394	9.3994	0.2509	31
30	9.2692	0.1859	2926	1961	9.3152	2066	3372	2174	9.3586	2284	3795	2396	9.3998	0.2510	30
31	9.2696	0.1861	2930	1963	9.3156	2068	3376	2176	9.3590	2286	3798	2398	9.4001	0.2512	29
32	9.2700	0.1862	2933	1965	9.3160	2070	3380	2178	9.3594	2287	3802	2400	9.4004	0.2514	28
33	9.2704	0.1864	2937	1967	9.3163	2072	3383	2179	9.3597	2289	3805	2402	9.4008	0.2516	27
34	9.2708	0.1866	2941	1968	9.3167	2074	3387	2181	9.3601	2291	3808	2404	9.4011	0.2518	26
35	9.2712	0.1867	2945	1970	9.3171	2075	3390	2183	9.3604	2293	3812	2405	9.4014	0.2520	25
36	9.2716	0.1869	2949	1972	9.3175	2077	3394	2185	9.3608	2295	3815	2407	9.4017	0.2522	24
37	9.2720	0.1871	2953	1974	9.3178	2079	3398	2187	9.3611	2297	3819	2409	9.4021	0.2524	23
38	9.2724	0.1872	2956	1975	9.3182	2081	3401	2188	9.3615	2299	3822	2411	9.4024	0.2526	22
39	9.2728	0.1874	2960	1977	9.3186	2082	3405	2190	9.3618	2300	3826	2413	9.4027	0.2528	21
40	9.2732	0.1876	2964	1979	9.3189	2084	3409	2192	9.3622	2302	3829	2415	9.4031	0.2530	20
41	9.2736	0.1877	2968	1981	9.3193	2086	3412	2194	9.3625	2304	3832	2417	9.4034	0.2532	19
42	9.2740	0.1879	2972	1982	9.3197	2088	3416	2196	9.3629	2306	3836	2419	9.4037	0.2534	18
43	9.2744	0.1881	2975	1984	9.3201	2090	3419	2198	9.3632	2308	3839	2421	9.4041	0.2536	17
44	9.2747	0.1883	2979	1986	9.3204	2091	3423	2199	9.3636	2310	3843	2422	9.4044	0.2537	16
45	9.2751	0.1884	2983	1987	9.3208	2093	3427	2201	9.3639	2312	3846	2424	9.4047	0.2539	15
46	9.2755	0.1886	2987	1989	9.3212	2095	3430	2203	9.3643	2313	3849	2426	9.4051	0.2541	14
47	9.2759	0.1888	2991	1991	9.3215	2097	3434	2205	9.3646	2315	3853	2428	9.4054	0.2543	13
48	9.2763	0.1889	2994	1993	9.3219	2098	3437	2207	9.3650	2317	3856	2430	9.4057	0.2545	12
49	9.2767	0.1891	2998	1994	9.3223	2100	3441	2208	9.3653	2319	3860	2432	9.4061	0.2547	11
50	9.2771	0.1893	3002	1996	9.3226	2102	3444	2210	9.3657	2321	3863	2434	9.4064	0.2549	10
51	9.2775	0.1894	3006	1998	9.3230	2104	3448	2212	9.3660	2323	3866	2436	9.4067	0.2551	9
52	9.2779	0.1896	3010	2000	9.3234	2106	3452	2214	9.3664	2325	3870	2438	9.4071	0.2553	8
53	9.2783	0.1898	3013	2001	9.3237	2107	3455	2216	9.3667	2326	3873	2440	9.4074	0.2555	7
54	9.2787	0.1900	3017	2003	9.3241	2109	3459	2218	9.3670	2328	3877	2441	9.4077	0.2557	6
55	9.2790	0.1901	3021	2005	9.3245	2111	3462	2219	9.3674	2330	3880	2443	9.4080	0.2559	5
56	9.2794	0.1903	3025	2007	9.3248	2113	3466	2221	9.3677	2332	3883	2445	9.4084	0.2561	4
57	9.2798	0.1905	3028	2008	9.3252	2115	3469	2223	9.3681	2334	3887	2447	9.4087	0.2563	3
58	9.2802	0.1906	3032	2010	9.3256	2116	3473	2225	9.3684	2336	3890	2449	9.4090	0.2565	2
59	9.2806	0.1908	3036	2012	9.3259	2118	3477	2227	9.3688	2338	3893	2451	9.4094	0.2567	1
60	9.2810	0.1910	3040	2014	9.3263	2120	3480	2229	9.3691	2340	3897	2453	9.4097	0.2569	0
/	Log	Nat	Log	Nat	Log	Nat	Log	Nat	Log	Nat	Log	Nat	Log	Nat	/
	324°		323°		322°		321°		320°		319°		318°		

VERSINES

/	42° Log	42° Nat	43° Log	43° Nat	44° Log	44° Nat	45° Log	45° Nat	46° Log	46° Nat	47° Log	47° Nat	48° Log	48° Nat	/
0	9.4097	0.2569	4292	2686	9.4482	2807	4667	2929	9.4848	3053	5024	3180	9.5197	0.3309	60
1	9.4100	0.2570	4295	2688	9.4485	2809	4670	2931	9.4851	3056	5027	3182	9.5199	0.3311	59
2	9.4103	0.2572	4298	2690	9.4488	2811	4673	2933	9.4854	3058	5030	3184	9.5202	0.3313	58
3	9.4107	0.2574	4301	2692	9.4491	2812	4676	2935	9.4857	3060	5033	3186	9.5205	0.3315	57
4	9.4110	0.2576	4305	2694	9.4494	2815	4679	2937	9.4860	3062	5036	3189	9.5208	0.3317	56
5	9.4113	0.2578	4308	2696	9.4497	2817	4682	2939	9.4863	3064	5039	3191	9.5211	0.3320	55
6	9.4117	0.2580	4311	2698	9.4501	2819	4685	2941	9.4866	3066	5042	3193	9.5214	0.3322	54
7	9.4120	0.2582	4314	2700	9.4504	2821	4688	2943	9.4869	3068	5045	3195	9.5216	0.3324	53
8	9.4123	0.2584	4317	2702	9.4507	2823	4691	2945	9.4872	3070	5048	3197	9.5219	0.3326	52
9	9.4126	0.2586	4321	2704	9.4510	2825	4694	2947	9.4875	3072	5050	3199	9.5222	0.3328	51
10	9.4130	0.2588	4324	2706	9.4513	2827	4698	2950	9.4878	3074	5053	3201	9.5225	0.3330	50
11	9.4133	0.2590	4327	2708	9.4516	2829	4701	2952	9.4881	3076	5056	3203	9.5228	0.3333	49
12	9.4136	0.2592	4330	2710	9.4519	2831	4704	2954	9.4883	3079	5059	3206	9.5231	0.3335	48
13	9.4140	0.2594	4333	2712	9.4522	2833	4707	2956	9.4886	3081	5062	3208	9.5233	0.3337	47
14	9.4143	0.2596	4337	2714	9.4525	2835	4710	2958	9.4889	3083	5065	3210	9.5236	0.3339	46
15	9.4146	0.2598	4340	2716	9.4529	2837	4713	2960	9.4892	3085	5068	3212	9.5239	0.3341	45
16	9.4149	0.2600	4343	2718	9.4532	2839	4716	2962	9.4895	3087	5071	3214	9.5242	0.3343	44
17	9.4153	0.2602	4346	2720	9.4535	2841	4719	2964	9.4898	3089	5074	3216	9.5245	0.3346	43
18	9.4156	0.2604	4349	2722	9.4538	2843	4722	2966	9.4901	3091	5076	3218	9.5247	0.3348	42
19	9.4159	0.2606	4352	2724	9.4541	2845	4725	2968	9.4904	3093	5079	3221	9.5250	0.3350	41
20	9.4162	0.2608	4356	2726	9.4544	2847	4728	2970	9.4907	3095	5082	3223	9.5253	0.3352	40
21	9.4166	0.2610	4359	2728	9.4547	2849	4731	2972	9.4910	3097	5085	3225	9.5256	0.3354	39
22	9.4169	0.2612	4362	2730	9.4550	2851	4734	2974	9.4913	3100	5088	3227	9.5259	0.3356	38
23	9.4172	0.2613	4365	2732	9.4553	2853	4737	2976	9.4916	3102	5091	3229	9.5262	0.3359	37
24	9.4175	0.2615	4368	2734	9.4556	2855	4740	2978	9.4919	3104	5094	3231	9.5264	0.3361	36
25	9.4179	0.2617	4372	2736	9.4560	2857	4743	2981	9.4922	3106	5097	3233	9.5267	0.3363	35
26	9.4182	0.2619	4375	2738	9.4563	2859	4746	2983	9.4925	3108	5099	3236	9.5270	0.3365	34
27	9.4185	0.2621	4378	2740	9.4566	2861	4749	2985	9.4928	3110	5102	3238	9.5273	0.3367	33
28	9.4188	0.2623	4381	2742	9.4569	2863	4752	2987	9.4931	3112	5105	3240	9.5276	0.3369	32
29	9.4192	0.2625	4384	2744	9.4572	2865	4755	2989	9.4934	3114	5108	3242	9.5278	0.3372	31
30	9.4195	0.2627	4387	2746	9.4575	2867	4758	2991	9.4937	3116	5111	3244	9.5281	0.3374	30
31	9.4198	0.2629	4391	2748	9.4578	2870	4761	2993	9.4940	3119	5114	3246	9.5284	0.3376	29
32	9.4201	0.2631	4394	2750	9.4581	2872	4764	2995	9.4942	3121	5117	3248	9.5287	0.3378	28
33	9.4205	0.2633	4397	2752	9.4584	2874	4767	2997	9.4945	3123	5120	3251	9.5290	0.3380	27
34	9.4208	0.2635	4400	2754	9.4587	2876	4770	2999	9.4948	3125	5122	3253	9.5292	0.3383	26
35	9.4211	0.2637	4403	2756	9.4590	2878	4773	3001	9.4951	3127	5125	3255	9.5295	0.3385	25
36	9.4214	0.2639	4406	2758	9.4594	2880	4776	3003	9.4954	3129	5128	3257	9.5298	0.3387	24
37	9.4218	0.2641	4410	2760	9.4597	2882	4779	3005	9.4957	3131	5131	3259	9.5301	0.3389	23
38	9.4221	0.2643	4413	2762	9.4600	2884	4782	3008	9.4960	3133	5134	3261	9.5304	0.3391	22
39	9.4224	0.2645	4416	2764	9.4603	2886	4785	3010	9.4963	3135	5137	3263	9.5306	0.3393	21
40	9.4227	0.2647	4419	2766	9.4606	2888	4788	3012	9.4966	3138	5140	3266	9.5309	0.3396	20
41	9.4231	0.2649	4422	2768	9.4609	2890	4791	3014	9.4969	3140	5142	3268	9.5312	0.3398	19
42	9.4234	0.2651	4425	2770	9.4612	2892	4794	3016	9.4972	3142	5145	3270	9.5315	0.3400	18
43	9.4237	0.2653	4428	2772	9.4615	2894	4797	3018	9.4975	3144	5148	3272	9.5318	0.3402	17
44	9.4240	0.2655	4432	2774	9.4618	2896	4800	3020	9.4978	3146	5151	3274	9.5320	0.3404	16
45	9.4244	0.2657	4435	2776	9.4621	2898	4803	3022	9.4981	3148	5154	3276	9.5323	0.3407	15
46	9.4247	0.2659	4438	2778	9.4624	2900	4806	3024	9.4984	3150	5157	3278	9.5326	0.3409	14
47	9.4250	0.2661	4441	2780	9.4627	2902	4809	3026	9.4986	3152	5160	3281	9.5329	0.3411	13
48	9.4253	0.2663	4444	2782	9.4630	2904	4812	3028	9.4989	3155	5162	3283	9.5331	0.3413	12
49	9.4256	0.2665	4447	2784	9.4633	2906	4815	3030	9.4992	3157	5165	3285	9.5334	0.3415	11
50	9.4260	0.2667	4450	2786	9.4637	2908	4818	3033	9.4995	3159	5168	3287	9.5337	0.3417	10
51	9.4263	0.2669	4454	2788	9.4640	2910	4821	3035	9.4998	3161	5171	3289	9.5340	0.3420	9
52	9.4266	0.2671	4457	2790	9.4643	2912	4824	3037	9.5001	3163	5174	3291	9.5343	0.3422	8
53	9.4269	0.2673	4460	2792	9.4646	2915	4827	3039	9.5004	3165	5177	3294	9.5345	0.3424	7
54	9.4273	0.2675	4463	2794	9.4649	2917	4830	3041	9.5007	3167	5180	3296	9.5348	0.3426	6
55	9.4276	0.2677	4466	2797	9.4652	2919	4833	3043	9.5010	3169	5182	3298	9.5351	0.3428	5
56	9.4279	0.2679	4469	2799	9.4655	2921	4836	3045	9.5013	3172	5185	3300	9.5354	0.3431	4
57	9.4282	0.2681	4472	2801	9.4658	2923	4839	3047	9.5016	3174	5188	3302	9.5357	0.3433	3
58	9.4285	0.2682	4476	2803	9.4661	2925	4842	3049	9.5018	3176	5191	3304	9.5359	0.3435	2
59	9.4289	0.2684	4479	2805	9.4664	2927	4845	3051	9.5021	3178	5194	3307	9.5362	0.3437	1
60	9.4292	0.2686	4482	2807	9.4667	2929	4848	3053	9.5024	3180	5197	3309	9.5365	0.3439	0

/	Log	Nat	Log	Nat	Log	Nat	Log	Nat	Log	Nat	Log	Nat	Log	Nat	/
	317°		316°		315°		314°		313°		312°		311°		

Chapter 6

VERSINES

/	49° Log	49° Nat	50° Log	50° Nat	51° Log	51° Nat	52° Log	52° Nat	53° Log	53° Nat	54° Log	54° Nat	55° Log	55° Nat	/
0	9.5365	0.3439	5529	3572	9.5690	3707	5847	3843	9.6001	3982	6151	4122	9.6298	0.4264	60
1	9.5368	0.3442	5532	3574	9.5693	3709	5850	3846	9.6003	3984	6154	4125	9.6301	0.4267	59
2	9.5370	0.3444	5535	3577	9.5695	3711	5852	3848	9.6006	3986	6156	4127	9.6303	0.4269	58
3	9.5373	0.3446	5537	3579	9.5698	3714	5855	3850	9.6008	3989	6159	4129	9.6306	0.4271	57
4	9.5376	0.3448	5540	3581	9.5701	3716	5857	3853	9.6011	3991	6161	4132	9.6308	0.4274	56
5	9.5379	0.3450	5543	3583	9.5703	3718	5860	3855	9.6014	3993	6164	4134	9.6311	0.4276	55
6	9.5381	0.3453	5546	3586	9.5706	3720	5863	3857	9.6016	3996	6166	4136	9.6313	0.4279	54
7	9.5384	0.3455	5548	3588	9.5709	3723	5865	3859	9.6019	3998	6169	4139	9.6315	0.4281	53
8	9.5387	0.3457	5551	3590	9.5711	3725	5868	3862	9.6021	4000	6171	4141	9.6318	0.4283	52
9	9.5390	0.3459	5554	3592	9.5714	3727	5870	3864	9.6024	4003	6174	4143	9.6320	0.4286	51
10	9.5393	0.3461	5556	3594	9.5716	3729	5873	3866	9.6026	4005	6176	4146	9.6323	0.4288	50
11	9.5395	0.3464	5559	3597	9.5719	3732	5876	3869	9.6029	4007	6178	4148	9.6325	0.4290	49
12	9.5398	0.3466	5562	3599	9.5722	3734	5878	3871	9.6031	4010	6181	4150	9.6327	0.4293	48
13	9.5401	0.3468	5564	3601	9.5724	3736	5881	3873	9.6034	4012	6183	4153	9.6330	0.4295	47
14	9.5404	0.3470	5567	3603	9.5727	3738	5883	3876	9.6036	4014	6186	4155	9.6332	0.4298	46
15	9.5406	0.3472	5570	3606	9.5730	3741	5886	3878	9.6039	4017	6188	4158	9.6335	0.4300	45
16	9.5409	0.3475	5572	3608	9.5732	3743	5888	3880	9.6041	4019	6191	4160	9.6337	0.4302	44
17	9.5412	0.3477	5575	3610	9.5735	3745	5891	3882	9.6044	4021	6193	4162	9.6340	0.4305	43
18	9.5415	0.3479	5578	3612	9.5738	3748	5894	3885	9.6046	4024	6196	4165	9.6342	0.4307	42
19	9.5417	0.3481	5581	3615	9.5740	3750	5896	3887	9.6049	4026	6198	4167	9.6344	0.4310	41
20	9.5420	0.3483	5583	3617	9.5743	3752	5899	3889	9.6051	4028	6201	4169	9.6347	0.4312	40
21	9.5423	0.3486	5586	3619	9.5745	3754	5901	3892	9.6054	4031	6203	4172	9.6349	0.4314	39
22	9.5426	0.3488	5589	3621	9.5748	3757	5904	3894	9.6056	4033	6206	4174	9.6352	0.4317	38
23	9.5428	0.3490	5591	3624	9.5751	3759	5906	3896	9.6059	4035	6208	4176	9.6354	0.4319	37
24	9.5431	0.3492	5594	3626	9.5753	3761	5909	3899	9.6061	4038	6210	4179	9.6356	0.4322	36
25	9.5434	0.3494	5597	3628	9.5756	3763	5912	3901	9.6064	4040	6213	4181	9.6359	0.4324	35
26	9.5437	0.3497	5599	3630	9.5759	3766	5914	3903	9.6066	4042	6215	4184	9.6361	0.4326	34
27	9.5439	0.3499	5602	3632	9.5761	3768	5917	3905	9.6069	4045	6218	4186	9.6364	0.4329	33
28	9.5442	0.3501	5605	3635	9.5764	3770	5919	3908	9.6071	4047	6220	4188	9.6366	0.4331	32
29	9.5445	0.3503	5607	3637	9.5766	3773	5922	3910	9.6074	4049	6223	4191	9.6368	0.4334	31
30	9.5448	0.3506	5610	3639	9.5769	3775	5924	3912	9.6076	4052	6225	4193	9.6371	0.4336	30
31	9.5450	0.3508	5613	3641	9.5772	3777	5927	3915	9.6079	4054	6228	4195	9.6373	0.4338	29
32	9.5453	0.3510	5615	3644	9.5774	3779	5930	3917	9.6081	4056	6230	4198	9.6376	0.4341	28
33	9.5456	0.3512	5618	3646	9.5777	3782	5932	3919	9.6084	4059	6233	4200	9.6378	0.4343	27
34	9.5458	0.3514	5621	3648	9.5779	3784	5935	3922	9.6086	4061	6235	4202	9.6380	0.4346	26
35	9.5461	0.3517	5623	3650	9.5782	3786	5937	3924	9.6089	4063	6237	4205	9.6383	0.4348	25
36	9.5464	0.3519	5626	3653	9.5785	3789	5940	3926	9.6091	4066	6240	4207	9.6385	0.4350	24
37	9.5467	0.3521	5629	3655	9.5787	3791	5942	3929	9.6094	4068	6242	4210	9.6388	0.4353	23
38	9.5469	0.3523	5631	3657	9.5790	3793	5945	3931	9.6096	4070	6245	4212	9.6390	0.4355	22
39	9.5472	0.3525	5634	3659	9.5793	3795	5947	3933	9.6099	4073	6247	4214	9.6392	0.4358	21
40	9.5475	0.3528	5637	3662	9.5795	3798	5950	3935	9.6101	4075	6250	4217	9.6395	0.4360	20
41	9.5478	0.3530	5639	3664	9.5798	3800	5953	3938	9.6104	4078	6252	4219	9.6397	0.4362	19
42	9.5480	0.3532	5642	3666	9.5800	3802	5955	3940	9.6106	4080	6255	4221	9.6400	0.4365	18
43	9.5483	0.3534	5645	3668	9.5803	3804	5958	3942	9.6109	4082	6257	4224	9.6402	0.4367	17
44	9.5486	0.3537	5647	3671	9.5806	3807	5960	3945	9.6111	4085	6259	4226	9.6404	0.4370	16
45	9.5489	0.3539	5650	3673	9.5808	3809	5963	3947	9.6114	4087	6262	4229	9.6407	0.4372	15
46	9.5491	0.3541	5653	3675	9.5811	3811	5965	3949	9.6116	4089	6264	4231	9.6409	0.4374	14
47	9.5494	0.3543	5655	3677	9.5813	3814	5968	3952	9.6119	4092	6267	4233	9.6412	0.4377	13
48	9.5497	0.3545	5658	3680	9.5816	3816	5970	3954	9.6121	4094	6269	4236	9.6414	0.4379	12
49	9.5499	0.3548	5661	3682	9.5819	3818	5973	3956	9.6124	4096	6272	4238	9.6416	0.4382	11
50	9.5502	0.3550	5663	3684	9.5821	3820	5975	3959	9.6126	4099	6274	4240	9.6419	0.4384	10
51	9.5505	0.3552	5666	3686	9.5824	3823	5978	3961	9.6129	4101	6277	4243	9.6421	0.4386	9
52	9.5508	0.3554	5669	3689	9.5826	3825	5981	3963	9.6131	4103	6279	4245	9.6423	0.4389	8
53	9.5510	0.3557	5671	3691	9.5829	3827	5983	3966	9.6134	4106	6281	4248	9.6426	0.4391	7
54	9.5513	0.3559	5674	3693	9.5832	3830	5986	3968	9.6136	4108	6284	4250	9.6428	0.4394	6
55	9.5516	0.3561	5677	3695	9.5834	3832	5988	3970	9.6139	4110	6286	4252	9.6431	0.4396	5
56	9.5518	0.3563	5679	3698	9.5837	3834	5991	3973	9.6141	4113	6289	4255	9.6433	0.4398	4
57	9.5521	0.3565	5682	3700	9.5839	3837	5993	3975	9.6144	4115	6291	4257	9.6435	0.4401	3
58	9.5524	0.3568	5685	3702	9.5842	3839	5996	3977	9.6146	4117	6294	4259	9.6438	0.4403	2
59	9.5527	0.3570	5687	3705	9.5845	3841	5998	3980	9.6149	4120	6296	4262	9.6440	0.4406	1
60	9.5529	0.3572	5690	3707	9.5847	3843	6001	3982	9.6151	4122	6298	4264	9.6442	0.4408	0
/	Log	Nat	Log	Nat	Log	Nat	Log	Nat	Log	Nat	Log	Nat	Log	Nat	/
	310°		309°		308°		307°		306°		305°		304°		

VERSINES

′	56° Log	Nat	57° Log	Nat	58° Log	Nat	59° Log	Nat	60° Log	Nat	61° Log	Nat	62° Log	Nat	′
0	9.6442	0.4408	6584	4554	9.6722	4701	6857	4850	9.6990	5000	7120	5152	9.7247	0.5305	60
1	9.6445	0.4410	6586	4556	9.6724	4703	6859	4852	9.6992	5003	7122	5154	9.7249	0.5308	59
2	9.6447	0.4413	6588	4559	9.6726	4706	6862	4855	9.6994	5005	7124	5157	9.7251	0.5310	58
3	9.6450	0.4415	6591	4561	9.6729	4708	6864	4857	9.6996	5008	7126	5160	9.7253	0.5313	57
4	9.6452	0.4418	6593	4563	9.6731	4711	6866	4860	9.6998	5010	7128	5162	9.7255	0.5316	56
5	9.6454	0.4420	6595	4566	9.6733	4713	6868	4862	9.7001	5013	7130	5165	9.7258	0.5318	55
6	9.6457	0.4423	6598	4568	9.6735	4716	6870	4865	9.7003	5015	7133	5167	9.7260	0.5321	54
7	9.6459	0.4425	6600	4571	9.6738	4718	6873	4867	9.7005	5018	7135	5170	9.7262	0.5323	53
8	9.6461	0.4427	6602	4573	9.6740	4721	6875	4870	9.7007	5020	7137	5172	9.7264	0.5326	52
9	9.6464	0.4430	6604	4576	9.6742	4723	6877	4872	9.7009	5023	7139	5175	9.7266	0.5328	51
10	9.6466	0.4432	6607	4578	9.6744	4725	6879	4875	9.7012	5025	7141	5177	9.7268	0.5331	50
11	9.6469	0.4435	6609	4580	9.6747	4728	6882	4877	9.7014	5028	7143	5180	9.7270	0.5334	49
12	9.6471	0.4437	6611	4583	9.6749	4730	6884	4880	9.7016	5030	7145	5182	9.7272	0.5336	48
13	9.6473	0.4439	6614	4585	9.6751	4733	6886	4882	9.7018	5033	7147	5185	9.7274	0.5339	47
14	9.6476	0.4442	6616	4588	9.6754	4735	6888	4885	9.7020	5035	7150	5188	9.7276	0.5341	46
15	9.6478	0.4444	6618	4590	9.6756	4738	6890	4887	9.7022	5038	7152	5190	9.7279	0.5344	45
16	9.6480	0.4447	6621	4593	9.6758	4740	6893	4890	9.7025	5040	7154	5193	9.7281	0.5346	44
17	9.6483	0.4449	6623	4595	9.6760	4743	6895	4892	9.7027	5043	7156	5195	9.7283	0.5349	43
18	9.6485	0.4452	6625	4598	9.6763	4745	6897	4895	9.7029	5045	7158	5198	9.7285	0.5352	42
19	9.6487	0.4454	6628	4600	9.6765	4748	6899	4897	9.7031	5048	7160	5200	9.7287	0.5354	41
20	9.6490	0.4456	6630	4602	9.6767	4750	6902	4900	9.7033	5050	7162	5203	9.7289	0.5357	40
21	9.6492	0.4459	6632	4605	9.6769	4753	6904	4902	9.7035	5053	7165	5205	9.7291	0.5359	39
22	9.6495	0.4461	6635	4607	9.6772	4755	6906	4905	9.7038	5056	7167	5208	9.7293	0.5362	38
23	9.6497	0.4464	6637	4610	9.6774	4758	6908	4907	9.7040	5058	7169	5211	9.7295	0.5364	37
24	9.6499	0.4466	6639	4612	9.6776	4760	6910	4910	9.7042	5061	7171	5213	9.7297	0.5367	36
25	9.6502	0.4469	6641	4615	9.6778	4763	6913	4912	9.7044	5063	7173	5216	9.7299	0.5370	35
26	9.6504	0.4471	6644	4617	9.6781	4765	6915	4915	9.7046	5066	7175	5218	9.7302	0.5372	34
27	9.6506	0.4473	6646	4620	9.6783	4768	6917	4917	9.7049	5068	7177	5221	9.7304	0.5375	33
28	9.6509	0.4476	6648	4622	9.6785	4770	6919	4920	9.7051	5071	7179	5223	9.7306	0.5377	32
29	9.6511	0.4478	6651	4625	9.6787	4773	6922	4922	9.7053	5073	7182	5226	9.7308	0.5380	31
30	9.6513	0.4481	6653	4627	9.6790	4775	6924	4925	9.7055	5076	7184	5228	9.7310	0.5383	30
31	9.6516	0.4483	6655	4629	9.6792	4777	6926	4927	9.7057	5078	7186	5231	9.7312	0.5385	29
32	9.6518	0.4485	6658	4632	9.6794	4780	6928	4930	9.7059	5081	7188	5234	9.7314	0.5388	28
33	9.6520	0.4488	6660	4634	9.6797	4782	6930	4932	9.7062	5083	7190	5236	9.7316	0.5390	27
34	9.6523	0.4490	6662	4637	9.6799	4785	6933	4935	9.7064	5086	7192	5239	9.7318	0.5393	26
35	9.6525	0.4493	6665	4639	9.6801	4787	6935	4937	9.7066	5088	7194	5241	9.7320	0.5395	25
36	9.6527	0.4495	6667	4642	9.6803	4790	6937	4940	9.7068	5091	7196	5244	9.7322	0.5398	24
37	9.6530	0.4498	6669	4644	9.6806	4792	6939	4942	9.7070	5093	7199	5246	9.7324	0.5401	23
38	9.6532	0.4500	6671	4647	9.6808	4795	6941	4945	9.7072	5096	7201	5249	9.7326	0.5403	22
39	9.6535	0.4502	6674	4649	9.6810	4797	6944	4947	9.7074	5099	7203	5251	9.7329	0.5406	21
40	9.6537	0.4505	6676	4652	9.6812	4800	6946	4950	9.7077	5101	7205	5254	9.7331	0.5408	20
41	9.6539	0.4507	6678	4654	9.6815	4802	6948	4952	9.7079	5104	7207	5257	9.7333	0.5411	19
42	9.6542	0.4510	6681	4656	9.6817	4805	6950	4955	9.7081	5106	7209	5259	9.7335	0.5414	18
43	9.6544	0.4512	6683	4659	9.6819	4807	6952	4957	9.7083	5109	7211	5262	9.7337	0.5416	17
44	9.6546	0.4515	6685	4661	9.6821	4810	6955	4960	9.7085	5111	7213	5264	9.7339	0.5419	16
45	9.6549	0.4517	6687	4664	9.6823	4812	6957	4962	9.7087	5114	7215	5267	9.7341	0.5421	15
46	9.6551	0.4520	6690	4666	9.6826	4815	6959	4965	9.7090	5116	7218	5269	9.7343	0.5424	14
47	9.6553	0.4522	6692	4669	9.6828	4817	6961	4967	9.7092	5119	7220	5272	9.7345	0.5426	13
48	9.6556	0.4524	6694	4671	9.6830	4820	6963	4970	9.7094	5121	7222	5274	9.7347	0.5429	12
49	9.6558	0.4527	6697	4674	9.6832	4822	6966	4972	9.7096	5124	7224	5277	9.7349	0.5432	11
50	9.6560	0.4529	6699	4676	9.6835	4825	6968	4975	9.7098	5126	7226	5280	9.7351	0.5434	10
51	9.6563	0.4532	6701	4679	9.6837	4827	6970	4977	9.7100	5129	7228	5282	9.7353	0.5437	9
52	9.6565	0.4534	6703	4681	9.6839	4830	6972	4980	9.7102	5132	7230	5285	9.7355	0.5439	8
53	9.6567	0.4537	6706	4684	9.6841	4832	6974	4982	9.7105	5134	7232	5287	9.7358	0.5442	7
54	9.6570	0.4539	6708	4686	9.6844	4835	6977	4985	9.7107	5137	7234	5290	9.7360	0.5445	6
55	9.6572	0.4541	6710	4688	9.6846	4837	6979	4987	9.7109	5139	7237	5292	9.7362	0.5447	5
56	9.6574	0.4544	6713	4691	9.6848	4840	6981	4990	9.7111	5142	7239	5295	9.7364	0.5450	4
57	9.6577	0.4546	6715	4693	9.6850	4842	6983	4992	9.7113	5144	7241	5298	9.7366	0.5452	3
58	9.6579	0.4549	6717	4696	9.6853	4845	6985	4995	9.7115	5147	7243	5300	9.7368	0.5455	2
59	9.6581	0.4551	6719	4698	9.6855	4847	6988	4997	9.7118	5149	7245	5303	9.7370	0.5458	1
60	9.6584	0.4554	6722	4701	9.6857	4850	6990	5000	9.7120	5152	7247	5305	9.7372	0.5460	0
′	Log	Nat	Log	Nat	Log	Nat	Log	Nat	Log	Nat	Log	Nat	Log	Nat	′
	303°		302°		301°		300°		299°		298°		297°		

Chapter 6

VERSINES

′	63° Log	Nat	64° Log	Nat	65° Log	Nat	66° Log	Nat	67° Log	Nat	68° Log	Nat	69° Log	Nat	′
0	9.7372	0.5460	7494	5616	9.7615	5774	7732	5932	9.7648	6093	7962	6254	9.8073	0.6416	60
4	9.7380	0.5470	7503	5627	9.7623	5784	7740	5943	9.7856	6103	7969	6265	9.8080	0.6427	56
8	0.7388	0.5481	7511	5637	9.7630	5795	7748	5954	9.7863	6114	7976	6276	9.8088	0.6438	52
12	9.7397	0.5491	7519	5648	9.7638	5805	7756	5965	9.7871	6125	7984	6286	9.8095	0.6449	48
16	9.7405	0.5502	7527	5658	9.7646	5816	7764	5975	9.7879	6136	7991	6297	9.8102	0.6460	44
20	9.7413	0.5512	7535	5669	9.7654	5827	7771	5986	9.7886	6146	7999	6308	9.8110	0.6471	40
24	9.7421	0.5522	7543	5679	9.7662	5837	7779	5997	9.7894	6157	8006	6319	9.8117	0.6482	36
28	9.7429	0.5533	7551	5690	9.7670	5848	7787	6007	9.7901	6168	8014	6330	9.8124	0.6492	32
32	9.7438	0.5543	7559	5700	9.7678	5858	7794	6018	9.7909	6179	8021	6340	9.8131	0.6503	28
36	9.7446	0.5554	7567	5711	9.7686	5869	7802	6029	9.7916	6189	8029	6351	9.8139	0.6514	24
40	9.7454	0.5564	7575	5721	9.7693	5880	7810	6039	9.7924	6200	8036	6362	9.8146	0.6525	20
44	9.7462	0.5575	7583	5732	9.7701	5890	7817	6050	9.7931	6211	8043	6373	9.8153	0.6536	16
48	9.7470	0.5585	7591	5742	9.7709	5901	7825	6061	9.7939	6222	8051	6384	9.8160	0.6547	12
52	9.7478	0.5595	7599	5753	9.7717	5911	7833	6071	9.7947	6232	8058	6395	9.8168	0.6558	8
56	9.7486	0.5606	7607	5763	9.7725	5922	7840	6082	9.7954	6243	8066	6405	9.8175	0.6569	4
60	9.7494	0.5616	7615	5774	9.7732	5933	7848	6093	9.7962	6254	8073	6416	9.8182	0.6580	0
	Log	Nat	Log	Nat	Log	Nat	Log	Nat	Log	Nat	Log	Nat	Log	Nat	
	296°		**295°**		**294°**		**293°**		**292°**		**291°**		**290°**		

′	70° Log	Nat	71° Log	Nat	72° Log	Nat	73° Log	Nat	74° Log	Nat	75° Log	Nat	76° Log	Nat	′
0	9.8182	0.6580	8289	6744	9.8395	6910	8498	7076	9.8600	7244	8699	7412	9.8797	0.7581	60
4	9.8189	0.6591	8296	6755	9.8402	6921	8505	7087	9.8606	7255	8706	7423	9.8804	0.7592	56
8	9.8197	0.6602	8304	6766	9.8409	6932	8512	7099	9.8613	7266	8712	7434	9.8810	0.7603	52
12	9.8204	0.6613	8311	6777	9.8416	6943	8519	7110	9.8620	7277	8719	7446	9.8817	0.7615	48
16	9.8211	0.6624	8318	6788	9.8422	6954	8525	7121	9.8626	7288	8726	7457	9.8823	0.7626	44
20	9.8218	0.6635	8325	6799	9.8429	6965	8532	7132	9.8633	7300	8732	7468	9.8829	0.7637	40
24	9.8225	0.6645	8332	6810	9.8436	6976	8539	7143	9.8640	7311	8739	7479	9.8836	0.7649	36
28	9.8232	0.6656	8339	6821	9.8443	6987	8546	7154	9.8646	7322	8745	7491	9.8842	0.7660	32
32	9.8240	0.6667	8346	6832	9.8450	6998	8552	7165	9.8653	7333	8752	7502	9.8849	0.7671	28
36	9.8247	0.6678	8353	6844	9.8457	7010	8559	7177	9.8660	7344	8758	7513	9.8855	0.7683	24
40	9.8254	0.6689	8360	6855	9.8464	7021	8566	7188	9.8666	7356	8765	7524	9.8861	0.7694	20
44	9.8261	0.6700	8367	6866	9.8471	7032	8573	7199	9.8673	7367	8771	7536	9.8868	0.7705	16
48	9.8268	0.6711	8374	6877	9.8478	7043	8579	7210	9.8679	7378	8778	7547	9.8874	0.7716	12
52	9.8275	0.6722	8381	6888	9.8484	7054	8586	7221	9.8686	7389	8784	7558	9.8881	0.7728	8
56	9.8282	0.6733	8388	6899	9.8491	7065	8593	7232	9.8693	7401	8791	7569	9.8887	0.7739	4
60	9.8289	0.6744	8395	6910	9.8498	7076	8600	7244	9.8699	7412	8797	7581	9.8893	0.7750	0
	Log	Nat	Log	Nat	Log	Nat	Log	Nat	Log	Nat	Log	Nat	Log	Nat	
	289°		**288°**		**287°**		**286°**		**285°**		**284°**		**283°**		

′	77° Log	Nat	78° Log	Nat	79° Log	Nat	80° Log	Nat	81° Log	Nat	82° Log	Nat	83° Log	Nat	′
0	9.8893	0.7750	8988	7921	9.9081	8092	9172	8264	9.9261	8436	9349	8608	9.9436	0.8781	60
4	9.8900	0.7762	8994	7932	9.9087	8103	9178	8275	9.9267	8447	9355	8620	9.9441	0.8793	56
8	9.8906	0.7773	9000	7944	9.9093	8115	9184	8286	9.9273	8459	9361	8631	9.9447	0.8804	52
12	9.8912	0.7785	9006	7955	9.9099	8126	9190	8298	9.9279	8470	9367	8643	9.9453	0.8816	48
16	9.8919	0.7796	9013	7966	9.9105	8138	9196	8309	9.9285	8482	9372	8654	9.9458	0.8828	44
20	9.8925	0.7807	9019	7978	9.9111	8149	9202	8321	9.9291	8493	9378	8666	9.9464	0.8839	40
24	9.8931	0.7819	9025	7989	9.9117	8160	9208	8332	9.9297	8505	9384	8677	9.9470	0.8851	36
28	9.8938	0.7830	9031	8001	9.9123	8172	9214	8344	9.9302	8516	9390	8689	9.9475	0.8862	32
32	9.8944	0.7841	9037	8012	9.9129	8183	9220	8355	9.9308	8528	9395	8701	9.9481	0.8874	28
36	9.8950	0.7853	9044	8023	9.9135	8195	9226	8367	9.9314	8539	9401	8712	9.9487	0.8885	24
40	9.8956	0.7864	9050	8035	9.9141	8206	9232	8378	9.9320	8551	9407	8724	9.9492	0.8897	20
44	9.8963	0.7875	9056	8046	9.9148	8218	9237	8390	9.9326	8562	9413	8735	9.9498	0.8908	16
48	9.8969	0.7887	9062	8058	9.9154	8229	9243	8401	9.9332	8574	9418	8747	9.9504	0.8920	12
52	9.8975	0.7898	9068	8069	9.9160	8241	9249	8413	9.9338	8585	9424	8758	9.9509	0.8932	8
56	9.8981	0.7910	9074	8080	9.9166	8252	9255	8424	9.9343	8597	9430	8770	9.9515	0.8943	4
60	9.8988	0.7921	9081	8092	9.9172	8264	9261	8436	9.9349	8608	9436	8781	9.9521	0.8955	0
′	Log	Nat	Log	Nat	Log	Nat	Log	Nat	Log	Nat	Log	Nat	Log	Nat	′
	282°		**281°**		**280°**		**279°**		**278°**		**277°**		**276°**		

VERSINES

/	84° Log	Nat	85° Log	Nat	86° Log	Nat	87° Log	Nat	88° Log	Nat	89° Log	Nat	90° Log	Nat	/
0	9.9521	0.8955	9604	9128	9.9686	9302	9767	9477	9.9846	9651	9924	9825	0.0000	1.0000	60
4	9.9526	0.8966	9609	9140	9.9691	9314	9772	9488	9.9851	9663	9929	9837	0.0005	1.0012	56
8	9.9532	0.8978	9615	9151	9.9697	9326	9777	9500	9.9856	9674	9934	9849	0.0010	1.0023	52
12	9.9537	0.8989	9620	9163	9.9702	9337	9782	9512	9.9861	9686	9939	9860	0.0015	1.0035	48
16	9.9543	0.9001	9626	9175	9.9708	9349	9788	9523	9.9867	9698	9944	9872	0.0020	1.0047	44
20	9.9548	0.9013	9631	9186	9.9713	9360	9793	9535	9.9872	9709	9949	9884	0.0025	1.0058	40
24	9.9554	0.9024	9637	9198	9.9718	9372	9798	9546	9.9877	9721	9954	9895	0.0030	1.0070	36
28	9.9560	0.9036	9642	9210	9.9724	9384	9804	9558	9.9882	9732	9959	9907	0.0035	1.0081	32
32	9.9565	0.9047	9648	9221	9.9729	9395	9809	9570	9.9887	9744	9964	9919	0.0040	1.0093	28
36	9.9571	0.9059	9653	9233	9.9734	9407	9814	9581	9.9893	9756	9970	9930	0.0045	1.0105	24
40	9.9576	0.9071	9659	9244	9.9740	9419	9819	9593	9.9898	9767	9975	9942	0.0050	1.0116	20
44	9.9582	0.9082	9664	9256	9.9745	9430	9825	9604	9.9903	9779	9980	9953	0.0055	1.0128	16
48	9.9587	0.9094	9670	9268	9.9751	9442	9830	9616	9.9908	9791	9985	9965	0.0060	1.0140	12
52	9.9593	0.9105	9675	9279	9.9756	9453	9835	9628	9.9913	9802	9990	9977	0.0065	1.0151	8
56	9.9598	0.9117	9681	9291	9.9761	9465	9840	9639	9.9918	9814	9995	9988	0.0070	1.0163	4
60	9.9604	0.9128	9686	9302	9.9767	9477	9846	9651	9.9924	9825	0000	0000	0.0075	1.0175	0

	Log	Nat	Log	Nat	Log	Nat	Log	Nat	Log	Nat	Log	Nat	Log	Nat	
	275°		274°		273°		272°		271°		270°		269°		

/	91° Log	Nat	92° Log	Nat	93° Log	Nat	94° Log	Nat	95° Log	Nat	96° Log	Nat	97° Log	Nat	/
0′	0.0075	1.0175	0149	0349	0.0222	0523	0293	0698	0.0363	0872	0432	1045	0.0499	1.1219	60
4	0.0080	1.0186	0154	0361	0.0226	0535	0298	0709	0.0368	0883	0436	1057	0.0504	1.1230	56
8	0.0085	1.0198	0159	0372	0.0231	0547	0302	0721	0.0372	0895	0441	1068	0.0508	1.1242	52
12	0.0090	1.0209	0164	0384	0.0236	0558	0307	0732	0.0377	0906	0445	1080	0.0513	1.1253	48
16	0.0095	1.0221	0168	0396	0.0241	0570	0312	0744	0.0381	0918	0450	1092	0.0517	1.1265	44
20	0.0100	1.0233	0173	0407	0.0245	0581	0316	0756	0.0386	0929	0454	1103	0.0522	1.1276	40
24	0.0105	1.0244	0178	0419	0.0250	0593	0321	0767	0.0391	0941	0459	1115	0.0526	1.1288	36
28	0.0110	1.0256	0183	0430	0.0255	0605	0326	0779	0.0395	0953	0463	1126	0.0531	1.1299	32
32	0.0115	1.0268	0188	0442	0.0260	0616	0330	0790	0.0400	0964	0468	1138	0.0535	1.1311	28
36	0.0120	1.0279	0193	0454	0.0264	0628	0335	0802	0.0404	0976	0473	1149	0.0539	1.1323	24
40	0.0125	1.0291	0197	0465	0.0269	0640	0340	0814	0.0409	0987	0477	1161	0.0544	1.1334	20
44	0.0129	1.0302	0202	0477	0.0274	0651	0344	0825	0.0414	0999	0481	1172	0.0548	1.1346	16
48	0.0134	1.0314	0207	0488	0.0279	0663	0349	0837	0.0418	1011	0486	1184	0.0553	1.1357	12
52	0.0139	1.0326	0212	0500	0.0283	0674	0354	0848	0.0423	1022	0490	1196	0.0557	1.1369	8
56	0.0144	1.0337	0217	0512	0.0288	0686	0358	0860	0.0427	1034	0495	1207	0.0562	1.1380	4
60	0.0149	1.0349	0222	0523	0.0293	0698	0363	0872	0.0432	1045	0499	1219	0.0566	1.1392	0

	Log	Nat	Log	Nat	Log	Nat	Log	Nat	Log	Nat	Log	Nat	Log	Nat	
	268°		267°		266°		265°		264°		263°		262°		

/	98° Log	Nat	99° Log	Nat	100° Log	Nat	101° Log	Nat	102° Log	Nat	103° Log	Nat	104° Log	Nat	/
0′	0.0566	1.1392	0631	1564	0.0695	1736	0758	1908	0.0820	2079	0881	2250	0.0941	1.2419	60
4	0.0570	1.1403	0636	1576	0.0700	1748	0763	1920	0.0824	2090	0885	2261	0.0945	1.2431	56
8	0.0575	1.1415	0640	1587	0.0704	1759	0767	1931	0.0829	2102	0889	2272	0.0949	1.2442	52
12	0.0579	1.1426	0644	1599	0.0708	1771	0771	1942	0.0833	2113	0893	2284	0.0953	1.2453	48
16	0.0583	1.1438	0648	1610	0.0712	1782	0775	1954	0.0837	2125	0897	2295	0.0957	1.2464	44
20	0.0588	1.1449	0653	1622	0.0717	1794	0779	1965	0.0841	2136	0901	2306	0.0961	1.2476	40
24	0.0592	1.1461	0657	1633	0.0721	1805	0783	1977	0.0845	2147	0905	2317	0.0965	1.2487	36
28	0.0597	1.1472	0661	1645	0.0725	1817	0787	1988	0.0849	2159	0909	2329	0.0968	1.2498	32
32	0.0601	1.1484	0666	1656	0.0729	1828	0792	1999	0.0853	2170	0913	2340	0.0972	1.2509	28
36	0.0605	1.1495	0670	1668	0.0733	1840	0796	2011	0.0857	2181	0917	2351	0.0976	1.2521	24
40	0.0610	1.1507	0674	1679	0.0738	1851	0800	2022	0.0861	2193	0921	2363	0.0980	1.2532	20
44	0.0614	1.1518	0678	1691	0.0742	1862	0804	2034	0.0865	2204	0925	2374	0.0984	1.2543	16
48	0.0618	1.1530	0683	1702	0.0746	1874	0808	2045	0.0869	2215	0929	2385	0.0988	1.2554	12
52	0.0623	1.1541	0687	1714	0.0750	1885	0812	2056	0.0873	2227	0933	2397	0.0992	1.2566	8
56	0.0627	1.1553	0691	1725	0.0754	1897	0816	2068	0.0877	2238	0937	2408	0.0996	1.2577	4
60	0.0631	1.1564	0695	1736	0.0758	1908	0820	2079	0.0881	2250	0941	2419	0.1000	1.2588	0

/	Log	Nat	Log	Nat	Log	Nat	Log	Nat	Log	Nat	Log	Nat	Log	Nat	/
	261°		260°		259°		258°		257°		256°		255°		

Chapter 6

VERSINES

′	105° Log	Nat	106° Log	Nat	107° Log	Nat	108° Log	Nat	109° Log	Nat	110° Log	Nat	111° Log	Nat	′
0	0.1000	1.2588	1057	2756	0.1114	2924	1169	3090	0.1224	3256	1278	3420	0.1330	1.3584	60
4	0.1004	1.2599	1061	2767	0.1118	2935	1173	3101	0.1228	3267	1281	3431	0.1334	1.3595	56
8	0.1007	1.2611	1065	2779	0.1121	2946	1177	3112	0.1231	3278	1285	3442	0.1337	1.3605	52
12	0.1011	1.2622	1069	2790	0.1125	2957	1180	3123	0.1235	3289	1288	3453	0.1341	1.3616	48
16	0.1015	1.2633	1072	2801	0.1129	2968	1184	3134	0.1238	3300	1292	3464	0.1344	1.3627	44
20	0.1019	1.2644	1076	2812	0.1133	2979	1188	3145	0.1242	3311	1295	3475	0.1347	1.3638	40
24	0.1023	1.2656	1080	2823	0.1136	2990	1191	3156	0.1246	3322	1299	3486	0.1351	1.3649	36
28	0.1027	1.2667	1084	2835	0.1140	3002	1195	3168	0.1249	3333	1302	3497	0.1354	1.3660	32
32	0.1031	1.2678	1088	2846	0.1144	3013	1199	3179	0.1253	3344	1306	3508	0.1358	1.3670	28
36	0.1034	1.2689	1091	2857	0.1147	3024	1202	3190	0.1256	3355	1309	3518	0.1361	1.3681	24
40	0.1038	1.2700	1095	2868	0.1151	3035	1206	3201	0.1260	3365	1313	3529	0.1365	1.3692	20
44	0.1042	1.2712	1099	2879	0.1155	3046	1210	3212	0.1263	3376	1316	3540	0.1368	1.3703	16
48	0.1046	1.2723	1103	2890	0.1158	3057	1213	3223	0.1267	3387	1320	3551	0.1372	1.3714	12
52	0.1050	1.2734	1106	2901	0.1162	3068	1217	3234	0.1271	3398	1323	3562	0.1375	1.3724	8
56	0.1053	1.2745	1110	2913	0.1166	3079	1220	3245	0.1274	3409	1327	3573	0.1378	1.3735	4
60	0.1057	1.2756	1114	2924	0.1169	3090	1224	3256	0.1278	3420	1330	3584	0.1382	1.3746	0
	Log	Nat	Log	Nat	Log	Nat	Log	Nat	Log	Nat	Log	Nat	Log	Nat	
	254°		253°		252°		251°		250°		249°		248°		

′	112° Log	Nat	113° Log	Nat	114° Log	Nat	115° Log	Nat	116° Log	Nat	117° Log	Nat	118° Log	Nat	′
0	0.1382	1.3746	1432	3907	0.1482	4067	1531	4226	0.1579	4384	1626	4540	0.1672	1.4695	60
4	0.1385	1.3757	1436	3918	0.1485	4078	1534	4237	0.1582	4394	1629	4550	0.1675	1.4705	56
8	0.1389	1.3768	1439	3929	0.1489	4089	1537	4247	0.1585	4405	1632	4561	0.1678	1.4715	52
12	0.1392	1.3778	1442	3939	0.1492	4099	1541	4258	0.1588	4415	1635	4571	0.1681	1.4726	48
16	0.1395	1.3789	1446	3950	0.1495	4110	1544	4268	0.1591	4425	1638	4581	0.1684	1.4736	44
20	0.1399	1.3800	1449	3961	0.1498	4120	1547	4279	0.1594	4436	1641	4592	0.1687	1.4746	40
24	0.1402	1.3811	1452	3971	0.1502	4131	1550	4289	0.1598	4446	1644	4602	0.1690	1.4756	36
28	0.1406	1.3821	1456	3982	0.1505	4142	1553	4300	0.1601	4457	1647	4612	0.1693	1.4766	32
32	0.1409	1.3832	1459	3993	0.1508	4152	1557	4310	0.1604	4467	1650	4623	0.1696	1.4777	28
36	0.1412	1.3843	1462	4003	0.1511	4163	1560	4321	0.1607	4478	1653	4633	0.1699	1.4787	24
40	0.1416	1.3854	1466	4014	0.1515	4173	1563	4331	0.1610	4488	1656	4643	0.1702	1.4797	20
44	0.1419	1.3864	1469	4025	0.1518	4184	1566	4342	0.1613	4498	1659	4654	0.1705	1.4807	16
48	0.1422	1.3875	1472	4035	0.1521	4195	1569	4352	0.1616	4509	1662	4664	0.1708	1.4818	12
52	0.1426	1.3886	1476	4046	0.1524	4205	1572	4363	0.1619	4519	1666	4674	0.1711	1.4828	8
56	0.1429	1.3897	1479	4057	0.1528	4216	1576	4373	0.1623	4530	1669	4684	0.1714	1.4838	4
60	0.1432	1.3907	1482	4067	0.1531	4226	1579	4384	0.1626	4540	1672	4695	0.1717	1.4848	0
	Log	Nat	Log	Nat	Log	Nat	Log	Nat	Log	Nat	Log	Nat	Log	Nat	
	247°		246°		245°		244°		243°		242°		241°		

′	119° Log	Nat	120° Log	Nat	121° Log	Nat	122° Log	Nat	123° Log	Nat	124° Log	Nat	125° Log	Nat	′
0	0.1717	1.4848	1761	5000	0.1804	5150	1847	5299	0.1888	5446	1929	5592	0.1969	1.5736	60
4	0.1720	1.4858	1764	5010	0.1807	5160	1849	5309	0.1891	5456	1932	5602	0.1972	1.5745	56
8	0.1723	1.4868	1767	5020	0.1810	5170	1852	5319	0.1894	5466	1934	5611	0.1974	1.5755	52
12	0.1726	1.4879	1770	5030	0.1813	5180	1855	5329	0.1896	5476	1937	5621	0.1977	1.5764	48
16	0.1729	1.4889	1773	5040	0.1816	5190	1858	5339	0.1899	5485	1940	5630	0.1979	1.5774	44
20	0.1732	1.4899	1775	5050	0.1818	5200	1861	5348	0.1902	5495	1942	5640	0.1982	1.5783	40
24	0.1734	1.4909	1778	5060	0.1821	5210	1863	5358	0.1905	5505	1945	5650	0.1985	1.5793	36
28	0.1737	1.4919	1781	5070	0.1824	5220	1866	5368	0.1907	5515	1948	5659	0.1987	1.5802	32
32	0.1740	1.4929	1784	5080	0.1827	5230	1869	5378	0.1910	5524	1950	5669	0.1990	1.5812	28
36	0.1743	1.4939	1787	5090	0.1830	5240	1872	5388	0.1913	5534	1953	5678	0.1992	1.5821	24
40	0.1746	1.4950	1790	5100	0.1833	5250	1875	5398	0.1916	5544	1956	5688	0.1995	1.5831	20
44	0.1749	1.4960	1793	5110	0.1835	5260	1877	5407	0.1918	5553	1958	5698	0.1998	1.5840	16
48	0.1752	1.4970	1796	5120	0.1838	5270	1880	5417	0.1921	5563	1961	5707	0.2000	1.5850	12
52	0.1755	1.4980	1799	5130	0.1841	5279	1883	5427	0.1924	5573	1964	5717	0.2003	1.5859	8
56	0.1758	1.4990	1801	5140	0.1844	5289	1886	5437	0.1926	5582	1966	5726	0.2005	1.5868	4
60	0.1761	1.5000	1804	5150	0.1847	5299	1888	5446	0.1929	5592	1969	5736	0.2008	1.5878	0
′	Log	Nat	Log	Nat	Log	Nat	Log	Nat	Log	Nat	Log	Nat	Log	Nat	′
	240°		239°		238°		237°		236°		235°		234°		

VERSINES

′	126° Log	Nat	127° Log	Nat	128° Log	Nat	129° Log	Nat	130° Log	Nat	131° Log	Nat	132° Log	Nat	′
0	0.2008	1.5878	2046	6018	0.2084	6157	2120	6293	0.2156	6428	2191	6561	0.2225	1.6691	60
6	0.2012	1.5892	2050	6032	0.2087	6170	2124	6307	0.2159	6441	2194	6574	0.2228	1.6704	54
12	0.2016	1.5906	2054	6046	0.2091	6184	2127	6320	0.2163	6455	2198	6587	0.2232	1.6717	48
18	0.2019	1.5920	2057	6060	0.2095	6198	2131	6334	0.2166	6468	2201	6600	0.2235	1.6730	42
24	0.2023	1.5934	2061	6074	0.2098	6211	2134	6347	0.2170	6481	2205	6613	0.2238	1.6743	36
30	0.2027	1.5948	2065	6088	0.2102	6225	2138	6361	0.2173	6494	2208	6626	0.2242	1.6756	30
36	0.2031	1.5962	2069	6101	0.2106	6239	2142	6374	0.2177	6508	2211	6639	0.2245	1.6769	24
42	0.2035	1.5976	2072	6115	0.2109	6252	2145	6388	0.2180	6521	2215	6652	0.2248	1.6782	18
48	0.2039	1.5990	2076	6129	0.2113	6266	2149	6401	0.2184	6534	2218	6665	0.2252	1.6794	12
54	0.2042	1.6004	2080	6143	0.2116	6280	2152	6414	0.2187	6547	2222	6678	0.2255	1.6807	6
60	0.2046	1.6018	2084	6157	0.2120	6293	2156	6428	0.2191	6561	2225	6691	0.2258	1.6820	0

Log	Nat	Log	Nat	Log	Nat	Log	Nat	Log	Nat	Log	Nat	Log	Nat
233°		232°		231°		230°		229°		228°		227°	

′	133° Log	Nat	134° Log	Nat	135° Log	Nat	136° Log	Nat	137° Log	Nat	138° Log	Nat	139° Log	Nat	′
0	0.2258	1.6820	2291	6947	0.2323	7071	2354	7193	0.2384	7314	2413	7431	0.2442	1.7547	60
6	0.2262	1.6833	2294	6959	0.2326	7083	2357	7206	0.2387	7325	2416	7443	0.2445	1.7559	54
12	0.2265	1.6845	2297	6972	0.2329	7096	2360	7218	0.2390	7337	2419	7455	0.2448	1.7570	48
18	0.2268	1.6858	2300	6984	0.2332	7108	2363	7230	0.2393	7349	2422	7466	0.2451	1.7581	42
24	0.2271	1.6871	2304	6997	0.2335	7120	2366	7242	0.2396	7361	2425	7478	0.2453	1.7593	36
30	0.2275	1.6884	2307	7009	0.2338	7133	2369	7254	0.2399	7373	2428	7490	0.2456	1.7604	30
36	0.2278	1.6896	2310	7022	0.2341	7145	2372	7266	0.2402	7385	2431	7501	0.2459	1.7615	24
42	0.2281	1.6909	2313	7034	0.2344	7157	2375	7278	0.2405	7396	2434	7513	0.2462	1.7627	18
48	0.2284	1.6921	2316	7046	0.2347	7169	2378	7290	0.2408	7408	2436	7524	0.2464	1.7638	12
54	0.2288	1.6934	2319	7059	0.2351	7181	2381	7302	0.2410	7420	2439	7536	0.2467	1.7649	6
60	0.2291	1.6947	2323	7071	0.2354	7193	2384	7314	0.2413	7431	2442	7547	0.2470	1.7660	0

Log	Nat	Log	Nat	Log	Nat	Log	Nat	Log	Nat	Log	Nat	Log	Nat
226°		225°		224°		223°		222°		221°		220°	

′	140° Log	Nat	141° Log	Nat	142° Log	Nat	143° Log	Nat	144° Log	Nat	145° Log	Nat	146° Log	Nat	′
0	0.2470	1.7660	2497	7771	0.2524	7880	2549	7986	0.2574	8090	2599	8192	0.2622	1.8290	60
6	0.2473	1.7672	2500	7782	0.2526	7891	2552	7997	0.2577	8100	2601	8202	0.2625	1.8300	54
12	0.2476	1.7683	2503	7793	0.2529	7902	2554	8007	0.2579	8111	2603	8211	0.2627	1.8310	48
18	0.2478	1.7694	2505	7804	0.2531	7912	2557	8018	0.2582	8121	2606	8221	0.2629	1.8320	42
24	0.2481	1.7705	2508	7815	0.2534	7923	2560	8028	0.2584	8131	2608	8231	0.2631	1.8329	36
30	0.2484	1.7716	2511	7826	0.2537	7934	2562	8039	0.2587	8141	2611	8241	0.2634	1.8339	30
36	0.2486	1.7727	2513	7837	0.2539	7944	2565	8049	0.2589	8151	2613	8251	0.2636	1.8348	24
42	0.2489	1.7738	2516	7848	0.2542	7955	2567	8059	0.2591	8161	2615	8261	0.2638	1.8358	18
48	0.2492	1.7749	2518	7859	0.2544	7965	2569	8070	0.2594	8171	2618	8271	0.2641	1.8368	12
54	0.2495	1.7760	2521	7869	0.2547	7976	2572	8080	0.2596	8181	2620	8281	0.2643	1.8377	6
60	0.2497	1.7771	2524	7880	0.2549	7986	2574	8090	0.2599	8192	2622	8290	0.2645	1.8387	0

Log	Nat	Log	Nat	Log	Nat	Log	Nat	Log	Nat	Log	Nat	Log	Nat
219°		218°		217°		216°		215°		214°		213°	

0	147° Log	Nat	148° Log	Nat	149° Log	Nat	150° Log	Nat	151° Log	Nat	152° Log	Nat	153° Log	Nat	
0	0.2645	1.8387	2667	8480	0.2689	8572	2709	8660	0.2729	8746	2748	8829	0.2767	1.8910	60
6	0.2647	1.8396	2669	8490	0.2691	8581	2711	8669	0.2731	8755	2750	8838	0.2769	1.8918	54
12	0.2650	1.8406	2671	8499	0.2693	8590	2713	8678	0.2733	8763	2752	8846	0.2771	1.8926	48
18	0.2652	1.8415	2674	8508	0.2695	8599	2715	8686	0.2735	8771	2754	8854	0.2772	1.8934	42
24	0.2654	1.8425	2676	8517	0.2697	8607	2717	8695	0.2737	8780	2756	8862	0.2774	1.8942	36
30	0.2656	1.8434	2678	8526	0.2699	8616	2719	8704	0.2739	8788	2758	8870	0.2776	1.8949	30
36	0.2658	1.8443	2680	8536	0.2701	8625	2721	8712	0.2741	8796	2760	8878	0.2778	1.8957	24
42	0.2661	1.8453	2682	8545	0.2703	8634	2723	8721	0.2743	8805	2761	8886	0.2779	1.8965	18
48	0.2663	1.8462	2684	8554	0.2705	8643	2725	8729	0.2745	8813	2763	8894	0.2781	1.8973	12
54	0.2665	1.8471	2686	8563	0.2707	8652	2727	8738	0.2746	8821	2765	8902	0.2783	1.8980	6
60	0.2667	1.8480	2689	8572	0.2709	8660	2729	8746	0.2748	8829	2767	8910	0.2785	1.8988	0

′	Log	Nat	Log	Nat	Log	Nat	Log	Nat	Log	Nat	Log	Nat	Log	Nat	′
	212°		211°		210°		209°		208°		207°		206°		

Chapter 6

VERSINES

′	154° Log	Nat	155° Log	Nat	156° Log	Nat	157° Log	Nat	158° Log	Nat	159° Log	Nat	160° Log	Nat	′
0	0.2785	1.8988	2802	9063	0.2818	9135	2834	9205	0.2849	9272	2864	9336	0.2877	1.9397	60
6	0.2787	1.8996	2804	9070	0.2820	9143	2836	9212	0.2851	9279	2865	9342	0.2879	1.9403	54
12	0.2788	1.9003	2805	9078	0.2822	9150	2837	9219	0.2852	9285	2866	9348	0.2880	1.9409	48
18	0.2790	1.9011	2807	9085	0.2823	9157	2839	9225	0.2854	9291	2868	9354	0.2881	1.9415	42
24	0.2792	1.9018	2809	9092	0.2825	9164	2840	9232	0.2855	9298	2869	9361	0.2883	1.9421	36
30	0.2793	1.9026	2810	9100	0.2826	9171	2842	9239	0.2857	9304	2871	9367	0.2884	1.9426	30
36	0.2795	1.9033	2812	9107	0.2828	9178	2843	9245	0.2858	9311	2872	9373	0.2885	1.9432	24
42	0.2797	1.9041	2814	9114	0.2829	9184	2845	9252	0.2859	9317	2873	9379	0.2887	1.9438	18
48	0.2799	1.9048	2815	9121	0.2831	9191	2846	9259	0.2861	9323	2875	9385	0.2888	1.9444	12
54	0.2800	1.9056	2817	9128	0.2833	9198	2848	9265	0.2862	9330	2876	9391	0.2889	1.9449	6
60	0.2802	1.9063	2818	9135	0.2834	9205	2849	9272	0.2864	9336	2877	9397	0.2890	1.9455	0

	Log	Nat	Log	Nat	Log	Nat	Log	Nat	Log	Nat	Log	Nat	Log	Nat	
	205°		204°		203°		202°		201°		200°		199°		

′	161° Log	Nat	162° Log	Nat	163° Log	Nat	164° Log	Nat	165° Log	Nat	166° Log	Nat	167° Log	Nat	′
0	0.2890	1.9455	2903	9511	0.2914	9563	2925	9613	0.2936	9659	2945	9703	0.2954	1.9744	60
6	0.2892	1.9461	2904	9516	0.2915	9568	2926	9617	0.2937	9664	2946	9707	0.2955	1.9748	54
12	0.2893	1.9466	2905	9521	0.2917	9573	2927	9622	0.2938	9668	2947	9711	0.2956	1.9751	48
18	0.2894	1.9472	2906	9527	0.2918	9578	2929	9627	0.2939	9673	2948	9715	0.2957	1.9755	42
24	0.2895	1.9478	2907	9532	0.2919	9583	2930	9632	0.2940	9677	2949	9720	0.2958	1.9759	36
30	0.2897	1.9483	2909	9537	0.2920	9588	2931	9636	0.2941	9681	2950	9724	0.2959	1.9763	30
36	0.2898	1.9489	2910	9542	0.2921	9593	2932	9641	0.2942	9686	2951	9728	0.2959	1.9767	24
42	0.2899	1.9494	2911	9548	0.2922	9598	2933	9646	0.2942	9690	2952	9732	0.2960	1.9770	18
48	0.2900	1.9500	2912	9553	0.2923	9603	2934	9650	0.2943	9694	2953	9736	0.2961	1.9774	12
54	0.2901	1.9505	2913	9558	0.2924	9608	2935	9655	0.2944	9699	2953	9740	0.2962	1.9778	6
60	0.2903	1.9511	2914	9563	0.2925	9613	2936	9659	0.2945	9703	2954	9744	0.2963	1.9781	0

	Log	Nat	Log	Nat	Log	Nat	Log	Nat	Log	Nat	Log	Nat	Log	Nat	
	198°		197°		196°		195°		194°		193°		192°		

′	168° Log	Nat	169° Log	Nat	170° Log	Nat	171° Log	Nat	172° Log	Nat	173° Log	Nat	174° Log	Nat	′
0	0.2963	1.9781	2970	9816	0.2977	9848	2983	9877	0.2989	9903	2994	9925	0.2998	1.9945	60
6	0.2963	1.9785	2971	9820	0.2978	9851	2984	9880	0.2990	9905	2995	9928	0.2999	1.9947	54
12	0.2964	1.9789	2972	9823	0.2978	9854	2985	9882	0.2990	9907	2995	9930	0.2999	1.9949	48
18	0.2965	1.9792	2972	9826	0.2979	9857	2985	9885	0.2991	9910	2995	9932	0.3000	1.9951	42
24	0.2966	1.9796	2973	9829	0.2980	9860	2986	9888	0.2991	9912	2996	9934	0.3000	1.9952	36
30	0.2966	1.9799	2974	9833	0.2980	9863	2986	9890	0.2992	9914	2996	9936	0.3000	1.9954	30
36	0.2967	1.9803	2974	9836	0.2981	9866	2987	9893	0.2992	9917	2997	9938	0.3001	1.9956	24
42	0.2968	1.9806	2975	9839	0.2982	9869	2987	9895	0.2993	9919	2997	9940	0.3001	1.9957	18
48	0.2969	1.9810	2976	9842	0.2982	9871	2988	9898	0.2993	9921	2998	9942	0.3001	1.9959	12
54	0.2969	1.9813	2977	9845	0.2983	9874	2989	9900	0.2994	9923	2998	9943	0.3002	1.9960	6
60	0.2970	1.9816	2977	9848	0.2983	9877	2989	9903	0.2994	9925	2998	9945	0.3002	1.9962	0

	Log	Nat	Log	Nat	Log	Nat	Log	Nat	Log	Nat	Log	Nat	Log	Nat	
	191°		190°		189°		188°		187°		186°		185°		

′	175° Log	Nat	176° Log	Nat	177° Log	Nat	178° Log	Nat	179° Log	Nat	′
0	0.3002	1.9962	3005	9976	0.3007	9986	3009	9994	0.3010	9998	60
6	0.3002	1.9963	3005	9977	0.3008	9987	3009	9995	0.3010	9999	54
12	0.3003	1.9965	3006	9978	0.3008	9988	3009	9995	0.3010	9999	48
18	0.3003	1.9966	3006	9979	0.3008	9989	3009	9996	0.3010	9999	42
24	0.3003	1.9968	3006	9980	0.3008	9990	3009	9996	0.3010	9999	36
30	0.3004	1.9969	3006	9981	0.3008	9990	3010	9997	0.3010	0000	30
36	0.3004	1.9971	3006	9982	0.3008	9991	3010	9997	0.3010	0000	24
42	0.3004	1.9972	3007	9983	0.3009	9992	3010	9997	0.3010	0000	18
48	0.3004	1.9973	3007	9984	0.3009	9993	3010	9998	0.3010	0000	12
54	0.3005	1.9974	3007	9985	0.3009	9993	3010	9998	0.3010	0000	6
60	0.3005	1.9976	3007	9986	0.3009	9994	3010	9998	0.3010	0000	0

′	Log	Nat	Log	Nat	Log	Nat	Log	Nat	Log	Nat	′
	184°		183°		182°		181°		180°		

Versine = 1–cosine = twice the haversine.

Hav ZD = hav P × cos L × cos D + hav (L-D)

Vers ZD = vers P × cos L × cos D + vers (L-D)

Where Lat and Dec have the same name, subtract the lesser from the greater. Where the names are different, add the two together.

LOG COSINES

	0°	1°	2°	3°	4°	5°	6°	7°	8°	9°	10°	11°	12°	13°	14°	
0	0.0000	9999	9997	9994	9989	9.9983	9976	9968	9958	9.9946	9934	9919	9904	9887	9.9869	60
1	0.0000	9999	9997	9994	9989	9.9983	9976	9967	9957	9.9946	9933	9919	9904	9887	9.9869	59
2	0.0000	9999	9997	9994	9989	9.9983	9976	9967	9957	9.9946	9933	9919	9904	9887	9.9868	58
3	0.0000	9999	9997	9994	9989	9.9983	9976	9967	9957	9.9946	9933	9919	9903	9886	9.9868	57
4	0.0000	9999	9997	9994	9989	9.9983	9976	9967	9957	9.9945	9933	9918	9903	9886	9.9868	56
5	0.0000	9999	9997	9994	9989	9.9983	9976	9967	9957	9.9945	9932	9918	9903	9886	9.9867	55
6	0.0000	9999	9997	9994	9989	9.9983	9975	9967	9956	9.9945	9932	9918	9902	9885	9.9867	54
7	0.0000	9999	9997	9994	9989	9.9983	9975	9966	9956	9.9945	9932	9917	9902	9885	9.9867	53
8	0.0000	9999	9997	9994	9989	9.9983	9975	9966	9956	9.9945	9932	9917	9902	9885	9.9867	52
9	0.0000	9999	9997	9993	9989	9.9982	9975	9966	9956	9.9944	9931	9917	9902	9885	9.9866	51
10	0.0000	9999	9997	9993	9989	9.9982	9975	9966	9956	9.9944	9931	9917	9901	9884	9.9866	50
11	0.0000	9999	9997	9993	9988	9.9982	9975	9966	9956	9.9944	9931	9917	9901	9884	9.9866	49
12	0.0000	9999	9997	9993	9988	9.9982	9975	9966	9955	9.9944	9931	9916	9901	9884	9.9865	48
13	0.0000	9999	9997	9993	9988	9.9982	9974	9965	9955	9.9944	9931	9916	9901	9883	9.9865	47
14	0.0000	9999	9997	9993	9988	9.9982	9974	9965	9955	9.9943	9930	9916	9900	9883	9.9865	46
15	0.0000	9999	9997	9993	9988	9.9982	9974	9965	9955	9.9943	9930	9916	9900	9883	9.9864	45
16	0.0000	9999	9997	9993	9988	9.9982	9974	9965	9955	9.9943	9930	9915	9900	9883	9.9864	44
17	0.0000	9999	9997	9993	9988	9.9982	9974	9965	9954	9.9943	9930	9915	9899	9882	9.9864	43
18	0.0000	9999	9996	9993	9988	9.9981	9974	9965	9954	9.9943	9929	9915	9899	9882	9.9863	42
19	0.0000	9999	9996	9993	9988	9.9981	9974	9964	9954	9.9942	9929	9915	9899	9882	9.9863	41
20	0.0000	9999	9996	9993	9988	9.9981	9973	9964	9954	9.9942	9929	9914	9899	9881	9.9863	40
21	0.0000	9999	9996	9993	9987	9.9981	9973	9964	9954	9.9942	9929	9914	9898	9881	9.9862	39
22	0.0000	9999	9996	9992	9987	9.9981	9973	9964	9954	9.9942	9929	9914	9898	9881	9.9862	38
23	0.0000	9999	9996	9992	9987	9.9981	9973	9964	9953	9.9941	9928	9913	9897	9880	9.9862	37
24	0.0000	9999	9996	9992	9987	9.9981	9973	9964	9953	9.9941	9928	9913	9897	9880	9.9861	36
25	0.0000	9999	9996	9992	9987	9.9981	9973	9964	9953	9.9941	9928	9913	9897	9880	9.9861	35
26	0.0000	9999	9996	9992	9987	9.9980	9973	9963	9953	9.9941	9928	9913	9897	9880	9.9861	34
27	0.0000	9999	9996	9992	9987	9.9980	9972	9963	9953	9.9941	9927	9913	9897	9879	9.9860	33
28	0.0000	9999	9996	9992	9987	9.9980	9972	9963	9952	9.9940	9927	9912	9896	9879	9.9860	32
29	0.0000	9999	9996	9992	9987	9.9980	9972	9963	9952	9.9940	9927	9912	9896	9879	9.9860	31
30	0.0000	9999	9996	9992	9987	9.9980	9972	9963	9952	9.9940	9927	9912	9896	9878	9.9859	30
31	0.0000	9998	9996	9992	9986	9.9980	9972	9963	9952	9.9940	9926	9911	9895	9878	9.9859	29
32	0.0000	9998	9996	9992	9986	9.9980	9972	9962	9952	9.9940	9926	9911	9895	9878	9.9859	28
33	0.0000	9998	9996	9992	9986	9.9980	9972	9962	9951	9.9939	9926	9911	9895	9877	9.9858	27
34	0.0000	9998	9996	9992	9986	9.9979	9971	9962	9951	9.9939	9926	9911	9894	9877	9.9858	26
35	0.0000	9998	9996	9992	9986	9.9979	9971	9962	9951	9.9939	9925	9911	9894	9877	9.9858	25
36	0.0000	9998	9996	9991	9986	9.9979	9971	9962	9951	9.9939	9925	9910	9894	9876	9.9857	24
37	0.0000	9998	9995	9991	9986	9.9979	9971	9962	9951	9.9939	9925	9910	9894	9876	9.9857	23
38	0.0000	9998	9995	9991	9986	9.9979	9971	9961	9951	9.9938	9925	9910	9893	9876	9.9857	22
39	0.0000	9998	9995	9991	9986	9.9979	9971	9961	9950	9.9938	9925	9910	9893	9876	9.9856	21
40	0.0000	9998	9995	9991	9986	9.9979	9971	9961	9950	9.9938	9924	9909	9893	9875	9.9856	20
41	0.0000	9998	9995	9991	9985	9.9979	9970	9961	9950	9.9938	9924	9909	9893	9875	9.9856	19
42	0.0000	9998	9995	9991	9985	9.9978	9970	9961	9950	9.9937	9924	9909	9892	9875	9.9855	18
43	0.0000	9998	9995	9991	9985	9.9978	9970	9960	9950	9.9937	9924	9909	9892	9874	9.9855	17
44	0.0000	9998	9995	9991	9985	9.9978	9970	9960	9949	9.9937	9923	9908	9892	9874	9.9855	16
45	0.0000	9998	9995	9991	9985	9.9978	9970	9960	9949	9.9937	9923	9908	9892	9874	9.9854	15
46	0.0000	9998	9995	9991	9985	9.9978	9970	9960	9949	9.9937	9923	9908	9891	9873	9.9854	14
47	0.0000	9998	9995	9991	9985	9.9978	9969	9960	9949	9.9936	9923	9908	9891	9873	9.9854	13
48	0.0000	9998	9995	9990	9985	9.9978	9969	9960	9949	9.9936	9922	9907	9891	9873	9.9853	12
49	0.0000	9998	9995	9990	9985	9.9978	9969	9959	9948	9.9936	9922	9907	9890	9872	9.9853	11
50	0.0000	9998	9995	9990	9985	9.9977	9969	9959	9948	9.9936	9922	9907	9890	9872	9.9853	10
51	0.0000	9998	9995	9990	9984	9.9977	9969	9959	9948	9.9936	9922	9906	9890	9872	9.9852	9
52	0.0000	9998	9995	9990	9984	9.9977	9969	9959	9948	9.9935	9921	9906	9890	9872	9.9852	8
53	9.9999	9998	9994	9990	9984	9.9977	9969	9959	9948	9.9935	9921	9906	9889	9871	9.9852	7
54	9.9999	9998	9994	9990	9984	9.9977	9968	9959	9947	9.9935	9921	9906	9889	9871	9.9851	6
55	9.9999	9998	9994	9990	9984	9.9977	9968	9958	9947	9.9935	9921	9905	9889	9871	9.9851	5
56	9.9999	9998	9994	9990	9984	9.9977	9968	9958	9947	9.9934	9920	9905	9888	9870	9.9851	4
57	9.9999	9997	9994	9990	9984	9.9977	9968	9958	9947	9.9934	9920	9905	9888	9870	9.9850	3
58	9.9999	9997	9994	9990	9984	9.9976	9968	9958	9946	9.9934	9920	9905	9888	9870	9.9850	2
59	9.9999	9997	9994	9989	9984	9.9976	9968	9958	9946	9.9934	9919	9904	9887	9869	9.9850	1
60	9.9999	9997	9994	9989	9983	9.9976	9968	9958	9946	9.9934	9919	9904	9887	9869	9.9849	0
	89°	88°	87°	86°	85°	84°	83°	82°	81°	80°	79°	78°	77°	76°	75°	

LOG SINES

Chapter 6

LOG COSINES

	15°	16°	17°	18°	19°	20°	21°	22°	23°	24°	25°	26°	27°	28°	29°	
0	9.9849	9828	9806	9782	9757	9.9730	9702	9672	9640	9.9607	9573	9537	9499	9459	9.9410	60
1	9.9849	9828	9806	9782	9756	9.9729	9701	9671	9640	9.9607	9572	9536	9498	9459	9.9417	59
2	9.9849	9828	9805	9781	9756	9.9729	9701	9671	9639	9.9606	9572	9535	9498	9458	9.9417	58
3	9.9848	9827	9805	9781	9755	9.9728	9700	9670	9639	9.9606	9571	9535	9497	9457	9.9416	57
4	9.9848	9827	9804	9780	9755	9.9728	9700	9670	9638	9.9605	9570	9534	9496	9457	9.9415	56
5	9.9848	9827	9804	9780	9755	9.9728	9699	9669	9638	9.9604	9570	9534	9496	9456	9.9415	55
6	9.9847	9826	9804	9780	9754	9.9727	9699	9669	9637	9.9604	9569	9533	9495	9455	9.9414	54
7	9.9847	9826	9803	9779	9754	9.9727	9698	9668	9636	9.9603	9569	9532	9494	9455	9.9413	53
8	9.9847	9826	9803	9779	9753	9.9726	9698	9668	9636	9.9603	9568	9532	9494	9454	9.9413	52
9	9.9846	9825	9802	9778	9753	9.9726	9697	9667	9635	9.9602	9567	9531	9493	9453	9.9412	51
10	9.9846	9825	9802	9778	9752	9.9725	9697	9667	9635	9.9602	9567	9530	9492	9453	9.9411	50
11	9.9846	9824	9802	9778	9752	9.9725	9696	9666	9634	9.9601	9566	9530	9492	9452	9.9410	49
12	9.9845	9824	9801	9777	9751	9.9724	9696	9666	9634	9.9601	9566	9529	9491	9451	9.9410	48
13	9.9845	9824	9801	9777	9751	9.9724	9695	9665	9633	9.9600	9565	9529	9490	9451	9.9409	47
14	9.9845	9823	9801	9776	9751	9.9723	9695	9664	9633	9.9599	9564	9528	9490	9450	9.9408	46
15	9.9844	9823	9800	9776	9750	9.9723	9694	9664	9632	9.9599	9564	9527	9489	9449	9.9408	45
16	9.9844	9823	9800	9775	9750	9.9722	9694	9663	9632	9.9598	9563	9527	9488	9449	9.9407	44
17	9.9844	9822	9799	9775	9749	9.9722	9693	9663	9631	9.9598	9563	9526	9488	9448	9.9406	43
18	9.9843	9822	9799	9775	9749	9.9722	9693	9662	9631	9.9597	9562	9525	9487	9447	9.9406	42
19	9.9843	9821	9799	9774	9748	9.9721	9692	9662	9630	9.9597	9561	9525	9486	9447	9.9405	41
20	9.9843	9821	9798	9774	9748	9.9721	9692	9661	9629	9.9596	9561	9524	9486	9446	9.9404	40
21	9.9842	9821	9798	9773	9747	9.9720	9691	9661	9629	9.9595	9560	9524	9485	9445	9.9403	39
22	9.9842	9820	9797	9773	9747	9.9720	9691	9660	9628	9.9595	9560	9523	9485	9444	9.9403	38
23	9.9842	9820	9797	9773	9747	9.9719	9690	9660	9628	9.9594	9559	9522	9484	9444	9.9402	37
24	9.9841	9820	9797	9772	9746	9.9719	9690	9659	9627	9.9594	9558	9522	9483	9443	9.9401	36
25	9.9841	9819	9796	9772	9746	9.9718	9689	9659	9627	9.9593	9558	9521	9483	9442	9.9401	35
26	9.9841	9819	9796	9771	9745	9.9718	9689	9658	9626	9.9593	9557	9520	9482	9442	9.9400	34
27	9.9840	9818	9795	9771	9745	9.9717	9688	9658	9626	9.9592	9557	9520	9481	9441	9.9399	33
28	9.9840	9818	9795	9770	9744	9.9717	9688	9657	9625	9.9591	9556	9519	9481	9440	9.9398	32
29	9.9839	9818	9795	9770	9744	9.9716	9687	9657	9625	9.9591	9555	9519	9480	9440	9.9398	31
30	9.9839	9817	9794	9770	9743	9.9716	9687	9656	9624	9.9590	9555	9518	9479	9439	9.9397	30
31	9.9839	9817	9794	9769	9743	9.9715	9686	9656	9623	9.9590	9554	9517	9479	9438	9.9396	29
32	9.9838	9817	9793	9769	9743	9.9715	9686	9655	9623	9.9589	9554	9517	9478	9438	9.9396	28
33	9.9838	9816	9793	9768	9742	9.9714	9685	9655	9622	9.9589	9553	9516	9477	9437	9.9395	27
34	9.9838	9816	9793	9768	9742	9.9714	9685	9654	9622	9.9588	9552	9515	9477	9436	9.9394	26
35	9.9837	9815	9792	9767	9741	9.9714	9684	9654	9621	9.9587	9552	9515	9476	9436	9.9393	25
36	9.9837	9815	9792	9767	9741	9.9713	9684	9653	9621	9.9587	9551	9514	9475	9435	9.9393	24
37	9.9837	9815	9791	9767	9740	9.9713	9683	9652	9620	9.9586	9551	9513	9475	9434	9.9392	23
38	9.9836	9814	9791	9766	9740	9.9712	9683	9652	9620	9.9586	9550	9513	9474	9433	9.9391	22
39	9.9836	9814	9791	9766	9739	9.9712	9682	9651	9619	9.9585	9549	9512	9473	9433	9.9391	21
40	9.9836	9814	9790	9765	9739	9.9711	9682	9651	9618	9.9584	9549	9512	9473	9432	9.9390	20
41	9.9835	9813	9790	9765	9739	9.9711	9681	9650	9618	9.9584	9548	9511	9472	9431	9.9389	19
42	9.9835	9813	9789	9764	9738	9.9710	9681	9650	9617	9.9583	9548	9510	9471	9431	9.9388	18
43	9.9835	9812	9789	9764	9738	9.9710	9680	9649	9617	9.9583	9547	9510	9471	9430	9.9388	17
44	9.9834	9812	9789	9764	9737	9.9709	9680	9649	9616	9.9582	9546	9509	9470	9429	9.9387	16
45	9.9834	9812	9788	9763	9737	9.9709	9679	9648	9616	9.9582	9546	9508	9469	9429	9.9386	15
46	9.9833	9811	9788	9763	9736	9.9708	9679	9648	9615	9.9581	9545	9508	9469	9428	9.9385	14
47	9.9833	9811	9787	9762	9736	9.9708	9678	9647	9615	9.9580	9545	9507	9468	9427	9.9385	13
48	9.9833	9811	9787	9762	9735	9.9707	9678	9647	9614	9.9580	9544	9506	9467	9427	9.9384	12
49	9.9832	9810	9787	9761	9735	9.9707	9677	9646	9613	9.9579	9543	9506	9467	9426	9.9383	11
50	9.9832	9810	9786	9761	9734	9.9706	9677	9646	9613	9.9579	9543	9505	9466	9425	9.9383	10
51	9.9832	9809	9786	9761	9734	9.9706	9676	9645	9612	9.9578	9542	9505	9465	9424	9.9382	9
52	9.9831	9809	9785	9760	9734	9.9705	9676	9645	9612	9.9577	9542	9504	9465	9424	9.9381	8
53	9.9831	9809	9785	9760	9733	9.9705	9675	9644	9611	9.9577	9541	9503	9464	9423	9.9380	7
54	9.9831	9808	9785	9759	9733	9.9704	9675	9643	9611	9.9576	9540	9503	9463	9422	9.9380	6
55	9.9830	9808	9784	9759	9732	9.9704	9674	9643	9610	9.9576	9540	9502	9463	9422	9.9379	5
56	9.9830	9808	9784	9758	9732	9.9703	9674	9642	9610	9.9575	9539	9501	9462	9421	9.9378	4
57	9.9830	9807	9783	9758	9731	9.9703	9673	9642	9609	9.9575	9538	9501	9461	9420	9.9377	3
58	9.9829	9807	9783	9758	9731	9.9702	9673	9641	9608	9.9574	9538	9500	9461	9420	9.9377	2
59	9.9829	9806	9782	9757	9730	9.9702	9672	9641	9608	9.9573	9537	9499	9460	9419	9.9376	1
60	9.9828	9806	9782	9757	9730	9.9702	9672	9640	9607	9.9573	9537	9499	9459	9418	9.9375	0
	74°	73°	72°	71°	70°	69°	68°	67°	66°	65°	64°	63°	62°	61°	60°	

LOG SINES

LOG COSINES

	30°	31°	32°	33°	34°	35°	36°	37°	38°	39°	40°	41°	42°	43°	44°	
0	9.9375	9331	9284	9236	9186	9.9134	9080	9023	8965	9.8905	8843	8778	8711	8641	9.8569	60
1	9.9375	9330	9283	9235	9185	9.9133	9079	9023	8964	9.8904	8841	8777	8710	8640	9.8568	59
2	9.9374	9329	9283	9234	9184	9.9132	9078	9022	8963	9.8903	8840	8776	8708	8639	9.8567	58
3	9.9373	9328	9282	9233	9183	9.9131	9077	9021	8962	9.8902	8839	8775	8707	8638	9.8566	57
4	9.9372	9328	9281	9233	9182	9.9130	9076	9020	8961	9.8901	8838	8773	8706	8637	9.8564	56
5	9.9372	9327	9280	9232	9181	9.9129	9075	9019	8960	9.8900	8837	8772	8705	8635	9.8563	55
6	9.9371	9326	9279	9231	9181	9.9128	9074	9018	8959	9.8899	8836	8771	8704	8634	9.8562	54
7	9.9370	9325	9278	9230	9180	9.9127	9073	9017	8958	9.8898	8835	8770	8703	8633	9.8561	53
8	9.9369	9325	9278	9229	9179	9.9127	9072	9016	8957	9.8897	8834	8769	8702	8632	9.8560	52
9	9.9369	9324	9277	9229	9178	9.9126	9071	9015	8956	9.8896	8833	8768	8700	8631	9.8558	51
10	9.9368	9323	9276	9228	9177	9.9125	9070	9014	8955	9.8895	8832	8767	8699	8629	9.8557	50
11	9.9367	9322	9275	9227	9176	9.9124	9069	9013	8954	9.8894	8831	8766	8698	8628	9.8556	49
12	9.9367	9322	9275	9226	9175	9.9123	9069	9012	8953	9.8893	8830	8765	8697	8627	9.8555	48
13	9.9366	9321	9274	9225	9175	9.9122	9068	9011	8952	9.8892	8829	8763	8696	8626	9.8553	47
14	9.9365	9320	9273	9224	9174	9.9121	9067	9010	8951	9.8891	8828	8762	8694	8625	9.8552	46
15	9.9364	9319	9272	9224	9173	9.9120	9066	9009	8950	9.8890	8827	8761	8694	8624	9.8551	45
16	9.9364	9318	9272	9223	9172	9.9119	9065	9008	8949	9.8889	8825	8760	8692	8622	9.8550	44
17	9.9363	9318	9271	9222	9171	9.9119	9064	9007	8948	9.8888	8824	8759	8691	8621	9.8549	43
18	9.9362	9317	9270	9221	9170	9.9118	9063	9006	8947	9.8887	8823	8758	8690	8620	9.8547	42
19	9.9361	9316	9269	9220	9169	9.9117	9062	9005	8946	9.8885	8822	8757	8689	8619	9.8546	41
20	9.9361	9315	9268	9219	9169	9.9116	9061	9004	8945	9.8884	8821	8756	8688	8618	9.8545	40
21	9.9360	9315	9268	9219	9168	9.9115	9060	9003	8944	9.8883	8820	8755	8687	8616	9.8544	39
22	9.9359	9314	9267	9218	9167	9.9114	9059	9002	8943	9.8882	8819	8753	8686	8614	9.8542	38
23	9.9358	9313	9266	9217	9166	9.9113	9058	9001	8942	9.8881	8818	8752	8684	8613	9.8541	37
24	9.9358	9312	9265	9216	9165	9.9112	9057	9000	8941	9.8880	8817	8751	8683	8613	9.8540	36
25	9.9357	9312	9264	9215	9164	9.9111	9056	9000	8940	9.8879	8816	8750	8682	8612	9.8539	35
26	9.9356	9311	9264	9214	9163	9.9110	9056	8999	8939	9.8878	8815	8749	8681	8610	9.8537	34
27	9.9355	9310	9263	9214	9163	9.9110	9055	8998	8938	9.8877	8814	8748	8680	8609	9.8536	33
28	9.9355	9309	9262	9213	9162	9.9109	9054	8997	8937	9.8876	8813	8747	8679	8608	9.8535	32
29	9.9354	9308	9261	9212	9161	9.9108	9053	8996	8936	9.8875	8812	8746	8677	8607	9.8534	31
30	9.9353	9308	9260	9211	9160	9.9107	9052	8995	8935	9.8874	8810	8745	8676	8606	9.8532	30
31	9.9352	9307	9259	9210	9159	9.9106	9051	8994	8934	9.8873	8809	8743	8675	8604	9.8531	29
32	9.9352	9306	9259	9209	9158	9.9105	9050	8993	8933	9.8872	8808	8742	8674	8603	9.8530	28
33	9.9351	9305	9258	9209	9157	9.9104	9049	8992	8932	9.8871	8807	8741	8673	8602	9.8529	27
34	9.9350	9305	9257	9208	9156	9.9103	9048	8991	8931	9.8870	8806	8740	8672	8600	9.8527	26
35	9.9349	9304	9256	9207	9156	9.9102	9047	8990	8930	9.8869	8805	8739	8671	8600	9.8526	25
36	9.9349	9303	9255	9206	9155	9.9101	9046	8989	8929	9.8868	8804	8738	8669	8598	9.8525	24
37	9.9348	9302	9255	9205	9154	9.9101	9045	8988	8928	9.8867	8803	8737	8668	8597	9.8524	23
38	9.9347	9301	9254	9204	9153	9.9100	9044	8987	8927	9.8866	8802	8736	8667	8595	9.8522	22
39	9.9346	9301	9253	9204	9152	9.9099	9043	8986	8926	9.8865	8801	8734	8666	8595	9.8521	21
40	9.9346	9300	9252	9203	9151	9.9098	9042	8985	8925	9.8864	8800	8733	8665	8594	9.8520	20
41	9.9345	9299	9251	9202	9150	9.9097	9041	8984	8924	9.8863	8799	8732	8664	8592	9.8519	19
42	9.9344	9298	9251	9201	9149	9.9096	9041	8983	8923	9.8862	8797	8731	8662	8591	9.8517	18
43	9.9343	9298	9250	9200	9149	9.9095	9040	8982	8922	9.8860	8796	8730	8661	8590	9.8516	17
44	9.9343	9297	9249	9199	9148	9.9094	9039	8981	8921	9.8859	8795	8729	8660	8589	9.8515	16
45	9.9342	9296	9248	9198	9147	9.9093	9038	8980	8920	9.8858	8794	8728	8659	8588	9.8514	15
46	9.9341	9295	9247	9198	9146	9.9092	9037	8979	8919	9.8857	8793	8727	8657	8585	9.8512	14
47	9.9340	9294	9247	9197	9145	9.9091	9036	8978	8918	9.8856	8792	8725	8657	8585	9.8511	13
48	9.9340	9294	9246	9196	9144	9.9091	9035	8977	8917	9.8855	8791	8724	8655	8584	9.8510	12
49	9.9339	9293	9245	9195	9143	9.9090	9034	8976	8916	9.8854	8790	8723	8654	8582	9.8509	11
50	9.9338	9292	9244	9194	9142	9.9089	9033	8975	8915	9.8853	8789	8722	8653	8582	9.8507	10
51	9.9337	9291	9243	9193	9142	9.9088	9032	8974	8914	9.8852	8788	8721	8652	8580	9.8506	9
52	9.9337	9291	9242	9193	9141	9.9087	9031	8973	8913	9.8851	8787	8720	8651	8579	9.8505	8
53	9.9336	9290	9242	9192	9140	9.9086	9030	8972	8912	9.8850	8785	8719	8650	8577	9.8504	7
54	9.9335	9289	9241	9191	9139	9.9085	9029	8971	8911	9.8849	8784	8718	8648	8577	9.8502	6
55	9.9334	9288	9240	9190	9138	9.9084	9028	8970	8910	9.8848	8783	8716	8647	8575	9.8501	5
56	9.9334	9287	9239	9189	9137	9.9083	9027	8969	8909	9.8847	8782	8715	8646	8574	9.8500	4
57	9.9333	9287	9238	9188	9136	9.9082	9026	8968	8908	9.8846	8781	8714	8645	8572	9.8499	3
58	9.9332	9286	9238	9187	9135	9.9081	9025	8967	8907	9.8845	8780	8713	8644	8572	9.8497	2
59	9.9331	9285	9237	9187	9135	9.9080	9024	8966	8906	9.8844	8779	8712	8642	8571	9.8496	1
60	9.9331	9284	9236	9186	9134	9.9080	9023	8965	8905	9.8843	8778	8711	8641	8569	9.8495	0
	59°	58°	57°	56°	55°	54°	53°	52°	51°	50°	49°	48°	47°	46°	45°	

LOG SINES

Chapter 6

LOG COSINES

	45°	46°	47°	48°	49°	50°	51°	52°	53°	54°	55°	56°	57°	58°	59°	
0	9.8495	8418	8338	8255	8169	9.8081	7989	7893	7795	9.7692	7586	7476	7361	7242	9.7118	60
1	9.8494	8416	8336	8254	8168	9.8079	7987	7892	7793	9.7690	7584	7474	7359	7240	9.7116	59
2	9.8492	8415	8335	8252	8167	9.8078	7986	7890	7791	9.7689	7582	7472	7357	7238	9.7114	58
3	9.8491	8414	8334	8251	8165	9.8076	7984	7889	7790	9.7687	7580	7470	7355	7236	9.7112	57
4	9.8490	8412	8332	8249	8164	9.8075	7982	7887	7788	9.7685	7579	7468	7353	7234	9.7110	56
5	9.8489	8411	8331	8248	8162	9.8073	7981	7885	7786	9.7683	7577	7466	7351	7232	9.7108	55
6	9.8487	8410	8330	8247	8161	9.8072	7979	7884	7785	9.7682	7575	7464	7349	7230	9.7106	54
7	9.8486	8409	8328	8245	8159	9.8070	7978	7882	7783	9.7680	7573	7462	7347	7228	9.7104	53
8	9.8485	8407	8327	8244	8158	9.8069	7976	7880	7781	9.7678	7571	7461	7345	7226	9.7102	52
9	9.8483	8406	8326	8242	8156	9.8067	7975	7879	7780	9.7676	7570	7459	7344	7224	9.7099	51
10	9.8482	8405	8324	8241	8155	9.8066	7973	7877	7778	9.7675	7568	7457	7342	7222	9.7097	50
11	9.8481	8403	8323	8240	8153	9.8064	7972	7876	7776	9.7673	7566	7455	7340	7220	9.7095	49
12	9.8480	8402	8322	8238	8152	9.8063	7970	7874	7774	9.7671	7564	7453	7338	7218	9.7093	48
13	9.8478	8401	8320	8237	8150	9.8061	7968	7872	7773	9.7669	7562	7451	7336	7216	9.7091	47
14	9.8477	8399	8319	8235	8149	9.8060	7967	7871	7771	9.7668	7561	7449	7334	7214	9.7089	46
15	9.8476	8398	8317	8234	8148	9.8058	7965	7869	7769	9.7666	7559	7447	7332	7212	9.7087	45
16	9.8475	8397	8316	8233	8146	9.8056	7964	7867	7768	9.7664	7557	7445	7330	7210	9.7085	44
17	9.8473	8395	8315	8231	8145	9.8055	7962	7866	7766	9.7662	7555	7444	7328	7208	9.7082	43
18	9.8472	8394	8313	8230	8143	9.8053	7960	7864	7764	9.7661	7553	7442	7326	7205	9.7080	42
19	9.8471	8393	8312	8228	8142	9.8052	7959	7863	7763	9.7659	7551	7440	7324	7203	9.7078	41
20	9.8469	8391	8311	8227	8140	9.8050	7957	7861	7761	9.7657	7550	7438	7322	7201	9.7076	40
21	9.8468	8390	8309	8225	8139	9.8049	7956	7859	7759	9.7655	7548	7436	7320	7199	9.7074	39
22	9.8467	8389	8308	8224	8137	9.8047	7954	7858	7758	9.7654	7546	7434	7318	7197	9.7072	38
23	9.8466	8387	8306	8223	8136	9.8046	7953	7856	7756	9.7652	7544	7432	7316	7195	9.7070	37
24	9.8464	8386	8305	8221	8134	9.8044	7951	7854	7754	9.7650	7542	7430	7314	7193	9.7068	36
25	9.8463	8385	8304	8220	8133	9.8043	7949	7853	7752	9.7648	7540	7428	7312	7191	9.7065	35
26	9.8462	8383	8302	8218	8131	9.8041	7948	7851	7751	9.7647	7539	7427	7310	7189	9.7063	34
27	9.8460	8382	8301	8217	8130	9.8040	7946	7849	7749	9.7645	7537	7425	7308	7187	9.7061	33
28	9.8459	8381	8300	8215	8128	9.8038	7945	7848	7747	9.7643	7535	7423	7306	7185	9.7059	32
29	9.8458	8379	8298	8214	8127	9.8037	7943	7846	7746	9.7641	7533	7421	7304	7183	9.7057	31
30	9.8457	8378	8297	8213	8125	9.8035	7941	7844	7744	9.7640	7531	7419	7302	7181	9.7055	30
31	9.8455	8377	8295	8211	8124	9.8034	7940	7843	7742	9.7638	7529	7417	7300	7179	9.7053	29
32	9.8454	8375	8294	8210	8122	9.8032	7938	7841	7740	9.7636	7528	7415	7298	7177	9.7050	28
33	9.8453	8374	8293	8208	8121	9.8031	7937	7840	7739	9.7634	7526	7413	7296	7175	9.7048	27
34	9.8451	8373	8291	8207	8120	9.8029	7935	7838	7737	9.7632	7524	7411	7294	7173	9.7046	26
35	9.8450	8371	8290	8205	8118	9.8027	7934	7836	7735	9.7631	7522	7409	7292	7171	9.7044	25
36	9.8449	8370	8289	8204	8117	9.8026	7932	7835	7734	9.7629	7520	7407	7290	7168	9.7042	24
37	9.8448	8369	8287	8203	8115	9.8024	7930	7833	7732	9.7627	7518	7406	7288	7166	9.7040	23
38	9.8446	8367	8286	8201	8114	9.8023	7929	7831	7730	9.7625	7517	7404	7286	7164	9.7037	22
39	9.8445	8366	8284	8200	8112	9.8021	7927	7830	7728	9.7624	7515	7402	7284	7162	9.7035	21
40	9.8444	8365	8283	8198	8111	9.8020	7926	7828	7727	9.7622	7513	7400	7282	7160	9.7033	20
41	9.8442	8363	8282	8197	8109	9.8018	7924	7826	7725	9.7620	7511	7398	7280	7158	9.7031	19
42	9.8441	8362	8280	8195	8108	9.8017	7922	7825	7723	9.7618	7509	7396	7278	7156	9.7029	18
43	9.8440	8361	8279	8194	8106	9.8015	7921	7823	7722	9.7616	7507	7394	7276	7154	9.7027	17
44	9.8439	8359	8277	8193	8105	9.8014	7919	7821	7720	9.7615	7505	7392	7274	7152	9.7025	16
45	9.8437	8358	8276	8191	8103	9.8012	7918	7820	7718	9.7613	7504	7390	7272	7150	9.7022	15
46	9.8436	8357	8275	8190	8102	9.8010	7916	7818	7716	9.7611	7502	7388	7270	7148	9.7020	14
47	9.8435	8355	8273	8188	8100	9.8009	7914	7816	7715	9.7609	7500	7386	7268	7146	9.7018	13
48	9.8433	8354	8272	8187	8099	9.8007	7913	7815	7713	9.7607	7498	7384	7266	7144	9.7016	12
49	9.8432	8353	8270	8185	8097	9.8006	7911	7813	7711	9.7606	7496	7382	7264	7141	9.7014	11
50	9.8431	8351	8269	8184	8096	9.8004	7910	7811	7710	9.7604	7494	7380	7262	7139	9.7012	10
51	9.8429	8350	8268	8182	8094	9.8003	7908	7810	7708	9.7602	7492	7379	7260	7137	9.7009	9
52	9.8428	8349	8266	8181	8093	9.8001	7906	7808	7706	9.7600	7491	7377	7258	7135	9.7007	8
53	9.8427	8347	8265	8180	8091	9.8000	7905	7806	7704	9.7599	7489	7375	7256	7133	9.7005	7
54	9.8426	8346	8264	8178	8090	9.7998	7903	7805	7703	9.7597	7487	7373	7254	7131	9.7003	6
55	9.8424	8345	8262	8177	8088	9.7997	7901	7803	7701	9.7595	7485	7371	7252	7129	9.7001	5
56	9.8423	8343	8261	8175	8087	9.7995	7900	7801	7699	9.7593	7483	7369	7250	7127	9.6998	4
57	9.8422	8342	8259	8174	8085	9.7993	7898	7800	7697	9.7591	7481	7367	7248	7125	9.6996	3
58	9.8420	8341	8258	8172	8084	9.7992	7897	7798	7696	9.7590	7479	7365	7246	7123	9.6994	2
59	9.8419	8339	8257	8171	8082	9.7990	7895	7796	7694	9.7588	7477	7363	7244	7120	9.6992	1
60	9.8418	8338	8255	8169	8081	9.7989	7893	7795	7692	9.7586	7476	7361	7242	7118	9.6990	0
	44°	43°	42°	41°	40°	39°	38°	37°	36°	35°	34°	33°	32°	31°	30°	

LOG SINES

LOG COSINES

	60°	61°	62°	63°	64°	65°	66°	67°	68°	69°	70°	71°	72°	73°	74°	
0	9.6990	6856	6716	6570	6418	9.6259	6093	5919	5736	9.5543	5341	5126	4900	4659	9.4403	60
1	9.6988	6853	6714	6568	6416	9.6257	6090	5916	5733	9.5540	5337	5123	4896	4655	9.4399	59
2	9.6985	6851	6711	6566	6413	9.6254	6087	5913	5729	9.5537	5334	5119	4892	4651	9.4395	58
3	9.6983	6849	6709	6563	6411	9.6251	6085	5910	5726	9.5533	5330	5115	4888	4647	9.4390	57
4	9.6981	6847	6707	6561	6408	9.6249	6082	5907	5723	9.5530	5327	5112	4884	4643	9.4386	56
5	9.6979	6844	6704	6558	6405	9.6246	6079	5904	5720	9.5527	5323	5108	4880	4639	9.4381	55
6	9.6977	6842	6702	6556	6403	9.6243	6076	5901	5717	9.5524	5320	5104	4876	4634	9.4377	54
7	9.6974	6840	6699	6553	6400	9.6240	6073	5898	5714	9.5520	5316	5101	4873	4630	9.4372	53
8	9.6972	6837	6697	6551	6398	9.6238	6070	5895	5711	9.5517	5313	5097	4869	4626	9.4368	52
9	9.6970	6835	6695	6548	6395	9.6235	6068	5892	5708	9.5514	5309	5093	4865	4622	9.4364	51
10	9.6968	6833	6692	6546	6392	9.6232	6065	5889	5704	9.5510	5306	5090	4861	4618	9.4359	50
11	9.6966	6831	6690	6543	6390	9.6230	6062	5886	5701	9.5507	5302	5086	4857	4614	9.4355	49
12	9.6963	6828	6688	6541	6387	9.6227	6059	5883	5698	9.5504	5299	5082	4853	4609	9.4350	48
13	9.6961	6826	6685	6538	6385	9.6224	6056	5880	5695	9.5500	5295	5078	4849	4605	9.4346	47
14	9.6959	6824	6683	6536	6382	9.6221	6053	5877	5692	9.5497	5292	5075	4845	4601	9.4341	46
15	9.6957	6821	6680	6533	6379	9.6219	6050	5874	5689	9.5494	5288	5071	4841	4597	9.4337	45
16	9.6955	6819	6678	6531	6377	9.6216	6047	5871	5685	9.5490	5285	5067	4837	4593	9.4332	44
17	9.6952	6817	6675	6528	6374	9.6213	6045	5868	5682	9.5487	5281	5064	4833	4588	9.4328	43
18	9.6950	6814	6673	6526	6371	9.6210	6042	5865	5679	9.5484	5278	5060	4829	4584	9.4323	42
19	9.6948	6812	6671	6523	6369	9.6208	6039	5862	5676	9.5480	5274	5056	4825	4580	9.4319	41
20	9.6946	6810	6668	6521	6366	9.6205	6036	5859	5673	9.5477	5270	5052	4821	4576	9.4314	40
21	9.6943	6808	6666	6518	6364	9.6202	6033	5856	5670	9.5474	5267	5049	4817	4572	9.4310	39
22	9.6941	6805	6663	6515	6361	9.6199	6030	5853	5666	9.5470	5263	5045	4813	4567	9.4305	38
23	9.6939	6803	6661	6513	6358	9.6197	6027	5850	5663	9.5467	5260	5041	4809	4563	9.4301	37
24	9.6937	6801	6659	6510	6356	9.6194	6024	5847	5660	9.5463	5256	5037	4805	4559	9.4296	36
25	9.6935	6798	6656	6508	6353	9.6191	6021	5844	5657	9.5460	5253	5034	4801	4555	9.4292	35
26	9.6932	6796	6654	6505	6350	9.6188	6019	5841	5654	9.5457	5249	5030	4797	4550	9.4287	34
27	9.6930	6794	6651	6503	6348	9.6186	6016	5838	5650	9.5453	5246	5026	4793	4546	9.4283	33
28	9.6928	6791	6649	6500	6345	9.6183	6013	5834	5647	9.5450	5242	5022	4789	4542	9.4278	32
29	9.6926	6789	6646	6498	6342	9.6180	6010	5831	5644	9.5447	5239	5019	4785	4538	9.4274	31
30	9.6923	6787	6644	6495	6340	9.6177	6007	5828	5641	9.5443	5235	5015	4781	4533	9.4269	30
31	9.6921	6784	6642	6493	6337	9.6175	6004	5825	5638	9.5440	5231	5011	4777	4529	9.4264	29
32	9.6919	6782	6639	6490	6335	9.6172	6001	5822	5634	9.5437	5228	5007	4773	4525	9.4260	28
33	9.6917	6780	6637	6488	6332	9.6169	5998	5819	5631	9.5433	5224	5003	4769	4521	9.4255	27
34	9.6914	6777	6634	6485	6329	9.6166	5995	5816	5628	9.5430	5221	5000	4765	4516	9.4251	26
35	9.6912	6775	6632	6483	6327	9.6163	5992	5813	5625	9.5426	5217	4996	4761	4512	9.4246	25
36	9.6910	6773	6629	6480	6324	9.6161	5990	5810	5621	9.5423	5213	4992	4757	4508	9.4242	24
37	9.6908	6770	6627	6477	6321	9.6158	5987	5807	5618	9.5420	5210	4988	4753	4503	9.4237	23
38	9.6905	6768	6625	6475	6319	9.6155	5984	5804	5615	9.5416	5206	4984	4749	4499	9.4232	22
39	9.6903	6766	6622	6472	6316	9.6152	5981	5801	5612	9.5413	5203	4981	4745	4495	9.4228	21
40	9.6901	6763	6620	6470	6313	9.6149	5978	5798	5609	9.5409	5199	4977	4741	4491	9.4223	20
41	9.6899	6761	6617	6467	6311	9.6147	5975	5795	5605	9.5406	5196	4973	4737	4486	9.4219	19
42	9.6896	6759	6615	6465	6308	9.6144	5972	5792	5602	9.5403	5192	4969	4733	4482	9.4214	18
43	9.6894	6756	6612	6462	6305	9.6141	5969	5789	5599	9.5399	5188	4965	4729	4478	9.4209	17
44	9.6892	6754	6610	6460	6303	9.6138	5966	5785	5596	9.5396	5185	4962	4725	4473	9.4205	16
45	9.6890	6752	6607	6457	6300	9.6135	5963	5782	5592	9.5392	5181	4958	4721	4469	9.4200	15
46	9.6887	6749	6605	6454	6297	9.6133	5960	5779	5589	9.5389	5177	4954	4717	4465	9.4195	14
47	9.6885	6747	6603	6452	6295	9.6130	5957	5776	5586	9.5385	5174	4950	4713	4460	9.4191	13
48	9.6883	6744	6600	6449	6292	9.6127	5954	5773	5583	9.5382	5170	4946	4709	4456	9.4186	12
49	9.6881	6742	6598	6447	6289	9.6124	5951	5770	5579	9.5379	5167	4942	4705	4452	9.4182	11
50	9.6878	6740	6595	6444	6286	9.6121	5948	5767	5576	9.5375	5163	4939	4700	4447	9.4177	10
51	9.6876	6737	6593	6442	6284	9.6119	5945	5764	5573	9.5372	5159	4935	4696	4443	9.4172	9
52	9.6874	6735	6590	6439	6281	9.6116	5943	5761	5570	9.5368	5156	4931	4692	4438	9.4168	8
53	9.6872	6733	6588	6437	6278	9.6113	5940	5758	5566	9.5365	5152	4927	4688	4434	9.4163	7
54	9.6869	6730	6585	6434	6276	9.6110	5937	5754	5563	9.5361	5148	4923	4684	4430	9.4158	6
55	9.6867	6728	6583	6431	6273	9.6107	5934	5751	5560	9.5358	5145	4919	4680	4425	9.4153	5
56	9.6865	6726	6580	6429	6270	9.6104	5931	5748	5556	9.5354	5141	4915	4676	4421	9.4149	4
57	9.6863	6723	6578	6426	6268	9.6102	5928	5745	5553	9.5351	5137	4911	4672	4417	9.4144	3
58	9.6860	6721	6575	6424	6265	9.6099	5925	5742	5550	9.5347	5134	4908	4668	4412	9.4139	2
59	9.6858	6718	6573	6421	6262	9.6096	5922	5739	5547	9.5344	5130	4904	4663	4408	9.4135	1
60	9.6856	6716	6570	6418	6259	9.6093	5919	5736	5543	9.5341	5126	4900	4659	4403	9.4130	0
	29°	28°	27°	26°	25°	24°	23°	22°	21°	20°	19°	18°	17°	16°	15°	

LOG SINES

Chapter 6

LOG COSINES

	75°	76°	77°	78°	79°	80°	81°	82°	83°	84°	85°	86°	87°	88°	89°	
0	9.4130	3837	3521	3179	2806	9.2397	1943	1436	0859	9.0192	0597	1564	2812	4572	8.2415	60
1	9.4125	3832	3515	3173	2799	9.2390	1935	1427	0849	9.0180	0012	1582	2836	4608	8.2346	59
2	9.4121	3827	3510	3167	2793	9.2382	1927	1418	0838	9.0168	0626	1600	2860	4645	8.2272	58
3	9.4116	3822	3504	3161	2700	9.2375	1919	1409	0828	9.0156	0641	1619	2885	4682	8.2196	57
4	9.4111	3816	3499	3155	2780	9.2368	1911	1399	0818	9.0144	0655	1637	2910	4719	8.2119	56
5	9.4106	3811	3493	3149	2773	9.2361	1903	1390	0807	9.0132	0670	1655	2934	4757	8.2041	55
6	9.4102	3806	3488	3143	2767	9.2354	1895	1381	0797	9.0120	0685	1674	2959	4794	8.1961	54
7	9.4097	3801	3482	3137	2760	9.2346	1887	1372	0786	9.0107	0699	1693	2984	4833	8.1880	53
8	9.4092	3796	3477	3131	2754	9.2339	1879	1363	0776	9.0095	0714	1711	3009	4871	8.1798	54
9	9.4087	3791	3471	3125	2747	9.2332	1871	1354	0765	9.0083	0729	1730	3035	4910	8.1713	51
10	9.4083	3786	3466	3119	2740	9.2324	1863	1345	0755	9.0070	0744	1749	3060	4950	8.1627	50
11	9.4078	3781	3460	3113	2734	9.2317	1855	1336	0744	9.0058	0759	1768	3086	4989	8.1539	49
12	9.4073	3775	3455	3107	2727	9.2310	1847	1326	0734	9.0046	0774	1787	3111	5029	8.1450	48
13	9.4068	3770	3449	3101	2721	9.2303	1838	1317	0723	9.0033	0789	1806	3137	5070	8.1359	47
14	9.4063	3765	3444	3095	2714	9.2295	1830	1308	0712	9.0021	0804	1825	3163	5110	8.1265	46
15	9.4059	3760	3438	3089	2707	9.2288	1822	1299	0702	9.0008	0819	1844	3190	5152	8.1170	45
16	9.4054	3755	3432	3083	2701	9.2281	1814	1289	0691	8.9996	0834	1863	3216	5193	8.1072	44
17	9.4049	3750	3427	3077	2694	9.2273	1806	1280	0680	8.9983	0850	1883	3242	5235	8.0972	43
18	9.4044	3745	3421	3070	2687	9.2266	1797	1271	0670	8.9970	0865	1902	3269	5277	8.0870	42
19	9.4039	3739	3416	3064	2681	9.2258	1789	1261	0659	8.9958	0881	1922	3296	5320	8.0765	41
20	9.4035	3734	3410	3058	2674	9.2251	1781	1252	0648	8.9945	0896	1941	3323	5363	8.0658	40
21	9.4030	3729	3404	3052	2667	9.2244	1772	1242	0637	8.9932	0911	1961	3350	5407	8.0548	39
22	9.4025	3724	3399	3046	2661	9.2236	1764	1233	0626	8.9919	0927	1981	3378	5451	8.0436	38
23	9.4020	3719	3393	3040	2654	9.2229	1756	1224	0616	8.9907	0943	2001	3405	5496	8.0320	37
24	9.4015	3713	3387	3034	2647	9.2221	1747	1214	0605	8.9894	0958	2021	3433	5541	8.0201	36
25	9.4010	3708	3382	3027	2640	9.2214	1739	1205	0594	8.9881	0974	2041	3461	5586	8.0078	35
26	9.4006	3703	3376	3021	2634	9.2206	1731	1195	0583	8.9868	0990	2061	3489	5632	7.9953	34
27	9.4001	3698	3370	3015	2627	9.2199	1722	1186	0572	8.9855	1006	2082	3517	5678	7.9823	33
28	9.3996	3692	3365	3009	2620	9.2191	1714	1176	0561	8.9842	1022	2102	3546	5725	7.9689	32
29	9.3991	3687	3359	3003	2613	9.2184	1705	1167	0550	8.9829	1038	2123	3574	5773	7.9551	31
30	9.3986	3682	3353	2997	2606	9.2176	1697	1157	0539	8.9816	1054	2143	3603	5821	7.9409	30
31	9.3981	3677	3348	2990	2600	9.2169	1689	1147	0527	8.9803	1070	2164	3632	5869	7.9262	29
32	9.3976	3671	3342	2984	2593	9.2161	1680	1138	0516	8.9789	1086	2185	3661	5918	7.9109	28
33	9.3971	3666	3336	2978	2586	9.2153	1672	1128	0505	8.9776	1102	2206	3691	5968	7.8952	27
34	9.3966	3661	3331	2972	2579	9.2146	1663	1118	0494	8.9763	1118	2227	3721	6018	7.8788	26
35	9.3962	3655	3325	2965	2572	9.2138	1655	1109	0483	8.9750	1135	2248	3750	6069	7.8617	25
36	9.3957	3650	3319	2959	2565	9.2131	1646	1099	0472	8.9736	1151	2269	3780	6120	7.8440	24
37	9.3952	3645	3313	2953	2558	9.2123	1637	1089	0460	8.9723	1167	2290	3811	6172	7.8255	23
38	9.3947	3640	3308	2947	2551	9.2115	1629	1080	0449	8.9710	1184	2312	3841	6225	7.8062	22
39	9.3942	3634	3302	2940	2545	9.2108	1620	1070	0438	8.9696	1201	2333	3872	6278	7.7860	21
40	9.3937	3629	3296	2934	2538	9.2100	1612	1060	0426	8.9683	1217	2355	3903	6332	7.7649	20
41	9.3932	3624	3290	2928	2531	9.2092	1603	1050	0415	8.9669	1234	2377	3934	6387	7.7426	19
42	9.3927	3618	3284	2921	2524	9.2085	1594	1040	0403	8.9655	1251	2398	3965	6442	7.7191	18
43	9.3922	3613	3279	2915	2517	9.2077	1586	1030	0392	8.9642	1267	2420	3997	6498	7.6943	17
44	9.3917	3608	3273	2909	2510	9.2069	1577	1020	0380	8.9628	1284	2443	4028	6555	7.6680	16
45	9.3912	3602	3267	2902	2503	9.2061	1568	1011	0369	8.9614	1301	2465	4061	6612	7.6399	15
46	9.3907	3597	3261	2896	2496	9.2054	1560	1001	0357	8.9601	1318	2487	4093	6671	7.6100	14
47	9.3902	3591	3255	2890	2489	9.2046	1551	0991	0346	8.9587	1335	2509	4125	6730	7.5778	13
48	9.3897	3586	3250	2883	2482	9.2038	1542	0981	0334	8.9573	1353	2532	4158	6790	7.5431	12
49	9.3892	3581	3244	2877	2475	9.2030	1533	0971	0323	8.9559	1370	2555	4191	6850	7.5053	11
50	9.3887	3575	3238	2870	2468	9.2022	1525	0961	0311	8.9545	1387	2577	4224	6912	7.4639	10
51	9.3882	3570	3232	2864	2461	9.2015	1516	0951	0299	8.9531	1405	2600	4258	6975	7.4182	9
52	9.3877	3564	3226	2858	2454	9.2007	1507	0940	0287	8.9517	1422	2623	4292	7038	7.3671	8
53	9.3872	3559	3220	2851	2447	9.1999	1498	0930	0276	8.9503	1440	2646	4326	7102	7.3091	7
54	9.3867	3554	3214	2845	2439	9.1991	1489	0920	0264	8.9489	1457	2670	4360	7168	7.2422	6
55	9.3862	3548	3208	2838	2432	9.1983	1480	0910	0252	8.9475	1475	2693	4395	7234	7.1631	5
56	9.3857	3543	3202	2832	2425	9.1975	1471	0900	0240	8.9460	1492	2717	4429	7301	7.0663	4
57	9.3852	3537	3197	2825	2418	9.1967	1462	0890	0228	8.9446	1510	2740	4465	7370	6.9415	3
58	9.3847	3532	3191	2819	2411	9.1959	1453	0879	0216	8.9432	1528	2764	4500	7439	6.7657	2
59	9.3842	3526	3185	2812	2404	9.1951	1445	0869	0204	8.9417	1546	2788	4536	7510	6.4657	1
60	9.3837	3521	3179	2806	2397	9.1943	1436	0859	0192	8.9403	1564	2812	4572	7581	4.1228	0
	14°	13°	12°	11°	10°	9°	8°	7°	6°	5°	4°	3°	2°	1°	0°	

LOG SINES

MULTILANGUAGE GLOSSARY

Appendices

MULTILANGUAGE GLOSSARY

Translations are given under the following headings:

ENGLISH	FRENCH	SPANISH	DUTCH
1 PROHIBITIONS	Interdictions	Prohibiciones	Verbouwen
2 TYPES OF VESSEL	Types du bateau	Typos de barco	Scheepstypen
3 PARTS OF VESSEL	Parties du bateau	Partes del barco	Scheeps onderdelen
4 MASTS & SPARS	Mâts	Mástiles y palos	Masten
5 RIGGING	Gréement	Aparejo	Tuigage
6 SAILS	Voilure	Velas	Zeilen
7 BELOW DECK	Cabine	Alcázar	Onderdeks
8 NAVIGATION EQUIPMENT	Equipement de navigation	Equipo de navigación	Navigatie uitrusting
9 ENGINES	Moteurs	Motores	Motoren
10 ENGINE ACCESSORIES	Accessoires moteur	Máquina accesorio	Onderdelen van motoren
11 ELECTRICS	Electricité	Electricidad	Elektriciteit
12 FUEL, ETC	Combusitibles	Gazolina	Div brandstoffen
13 METALS	Métaux	Metales	Metalen
14 LIGHTS	Lumières	Luz	Lichten
15 SHIP'S PAPERS	Papiers du bateau	Papeles del barco	Scheepspapieren
16 TOOLS	Outils	Herramientas	Gereedschap
17 CHANDLERY	Ship chandler	Pertrechos	Scheepsbehoeften
18 FOOD	Nourriture	Comida	Proviand
19 SHOPS AND PLACES ASHORE	Boutiques et endroio divers	Tiendas y sitios en tierra	Winkels & plaatsen aan land
20 IN HARBOR	Au port	En el puerto	In de haven
21 FIRST AID	Premiers secours	Primero socorro	Eerste hulp bij ongelukken

1 PROHIBITIONS

Prohibited area	Zone interdite	Zona prohibida	Verboden gebied
Anchoring prohibited	Defense de mouiller	Fondeadero prohibido	Verboden ankerplaats
Mooring prohibited	Accostage interdite	Amarradero prohibido	Verboden aan te leggen

2 TYPES OF VESSEL
PRIVATE

Sloop	Sloop	Balandra	Sleep
Cutter	Cotre	Cúter	Kotter
Ketch	Ketch	Queche	Kits
Yawl	Yawl	Yola	Yaw
Schooner	Goélette	Goleta	Schoener
Motor sailer	Bateau mixte	Moto-velero	Motorzeiljacht
Dinghy	Youyou, prame	Balandro	Jol, bijboot
Launch	Chaloupe	Lancha	Barkas
Motor boat	Bateau a moteur	Motora, bote a motor	Motorboot
Lifeboat	Bateau, canot de sauvetage	Bote salvadidas	Reddingboot

ENGLISH	FRENCH	SPANISH	DUTCH
		COMMERCIAL	
Trawler	Chalutier	Pesquero	Stoomtreiler
Tanker	Bateau-citerne	Petrolero	Tankschip
Merchantman	Navire marchand	Buque mercante	Koopvaardijschip
Ferry	Transbordeur, bac	Transbordador	Pont, veerboot
Tug	Remorqueur	Remolcador	Sleepboot

3 PARTS OF VESSEL

Stem	Étrave	Roda	Voorsteven
Stern	Poupe	Popa	Achtersteven
Forecastle (fo'c's'le)	Gaillard d'avant	Castillo de proa	Vooronder
Fore peak	Pic avant	Pique de proa	Voorpiek
Cabin	Cabine	Camarote	Kajuit
Chain locker	Puits à chaines	Caja de cadenas	Kettingbak
Heads	Toilette	Retrete	W.C.
Galley	Cuisine	Cocina	Kombuis
Chartroom	Salle des cartes	Caseta de derrota	Kaartenkamer
Bunk	Couchette	Litera	Kooi
Pipe cot	Cadre	Catre	Pijkooi
Engine room	Chambre des machines	Cámara de máquinas	Motorruim
Locker	Coffre	Taquilla	Kastje
Bulkhead	Cloison	Mamparo	Schot
Hatch	Écoutille	Escotilla	Luik
Cockpit	Cockpit	Cabina	Kuip
Sail locker	Soute à voiles	Panol de velas	Zeilkooi
Freshwater tank	Reservoir d'eau douce	Tanque de agua potable	Drinkwatertank
Rudder	Gouvernail	Timón	Roer
Propeller	Hélice	Hélice	Schroef
Bilges	Cale	Sentina	Kim
Keel	Quille	Quilla	Kiel
Gunwhale	Plat-bord	Borda, regala	Dolboord
Rubbing strake	Bourrelet de défense	Verduguillo	Berghout
Tiller	Barre	Cana	Helmstok
Stanchions	Chandelier	Candelero	Scepters
Bilge pump	Pompe de cale	Bombas de achique de sentina	Lenspomp
Pulpit	Balcon avant	Pülpito	Preekstoel
Pushpit	Balcon arrière	Púlpito de popa	Hekstoel

4 MASTS AND SPARS

Mast	Mât	Palo	Mast
Foremast	Mât de misaine	Trinquete	Fokkemast
Mizzen mast	Mât d'artimon	Palo mesana	Bezaansmast
Boom	Bôme	Botavara	Giek
Bowsprit	Beaupré	Baupres	Boegspriet
Bumpkin	Bout-dehors	Pescante amura trinquette	Papegaaistok
Spinnaker boom	Tangon de spi	Tangon del espinaquer	Nagel-of spinnakerboom
Gaff	Corne	Pico (de vela cangreja)	Gaffel
Spreaders	Barres de flèche	Crucetas	Dwarszaling
Jumper struts	Guignol	Contrete	Knikstagen

Appendices

ENGLISH	FRENCH	SPANISH	DUTCH
Truck	Pomme	Tope (galleta)	Top
Slide	Coulisseau	Corredera	Slede
Roller reefing	Bôme à rouleau	Rizo de catalina	Patentrif
Worm gear	Vis sans fin	Husillo	Worm en wormwiel
Solid	Massif	Macizo	Massief
Hollow	Creux	Hueco	Hol
Derrick	Grue	Pluma de carga	Dirk of Kraanlijn

5 RIGGING

STANDING

Forestay	Étai avant, étai de trinquette	Estay de proa	Voorstag
Aft stay	Étai arriere	Stay de popa	Achterstag
Shrouds	Haubans	Obenques	Want
Stay	Étai	Estay	Stag
Bob stay	Sous-barbe	Barbiquejo	Waterstag
Backstay	Galhauban	Brandal	Pakstagen
Guy	Retenue	Retenida (Cabo de retenida viento)	Bulletalie

RUNNING

Halyard	Drisse	Driza	Val
Foresail halyard	Drisse de misaine	Driza de trinquetilla	Voorzeil val
Throat halyard	Attache de drisse	Driza de boca	Klauwval
Peak halyard	Drisse de pic	Driza de pico	Piekeval
Burgee halyard	Drisse de guidon	Driza de grimpola	Clubstandaardval
Topping lift	Balancine	Amantillo	Dirk
Main sheet	Écoute de grand voile	Escota mayor	Grootschoot
Foresail sheet	Écoute de Misaine	Trinquetilla (escota de)	Voorzeil of Fokkeschoot
Boom Vary	Hale-bas de bôme	Trapa	Neerhouder
Rope	Cordage	Cabulleria	Touw
Single block	Poule simple	Motón de una cajera	Eenschijfsblok
Double block	Poulie double	Motón de dos cajeras	Tweeschijfsblok
Sheave	Réa	Roldana	Schijf
Shackle	Manille	Grillete	Sluiting
Pin	Goupille	Perno, cabilla	Bout
"D" shackle	Manille Droite	Grillete en D	Harpsluiting
Snap shackle	Manille rapide	Grillete de escape	Patentsluiting

6 SAILS

Mainsail	Grand voile	Vela mayor	Grootzeil
Foresail	Voile de misaine	Vela trinquete	Voorzeil
Jib	Foc	Foque	Fok
Storm jib	Tourmetin	Foque de capa	Stormfok
Trysail	Voile de cape	Vela de cangrejo	Stormzeil
Genoa	Génois	Foque génova	Genua
Spinnaker	Spinnaker	Espinaquer (foque balón)	Spinnaker
Topsail	Flèche	Gavia	Topzeil
Mizzen sail	Artimon	Mesana	Druil of bezaan
Lugsail	Boile de fortune	Vela al tercio	Emmerzeil

ENGLISH	FRENCH	SPANISH	DUTCH
		PARTS OF SAIL	
Head	Point de drisse	Puno de driza	Top
Tack	Point d'amure	Puno de amura	Hals
Clew	Point d'écoute	Puno de escota	Schoothoorn
Luff	Guidant	Gratil	Voorlijk
Leech	Chute arrière	Apagapenol	Achterlijk
Foot	Bordure	Pujamen	Onderlijk
Roach	Rond échancrure	Alunamiento	Gilling
Peak	Pic	Pico	Piek
Throat	Gorge	Puno de driza	Klauw
Batten pocket	Étui, gaine de latte	Bolsa del sable	Zeillatzak
Batten	Latte	Enjaretado	Zeillat
Cringle	Anneau, patte de bouline	Garruncho de cabo	Grommer
Seam	Couture	Costura	Naad
Sailbag	Sac à voile	Saco de vela	Zeilzak

7 BELOW DECK

ENGLISH	FRENCH	SPANISH	DUTCH
Toilet	Toilette	Retretes	W.C.
Toilet paper	Papier hygiénique	Papel higiénico	Toilet-papier
Towel	Serviette	Toalla	Handdoek
Soap	Savon	Jabón	Zeep
Cabin	Cabine	Camarote	Kajuit
Mattress	Matelas	Colchón	Matras
Sleeping bag	Sac de couchage	Saco de dormir	Slaapzak
Sheet	Drap	Sábana	Laken
Blanket	Couverture	Manta	Wollen deken
Galley	Cuisine	Cocina	Kombuis
Cooker	Cuisinière	Fogón	Kookpan
Frying pan	Poêle à frire	Sartén	Braadpan
Saucepan	Casserole	Cacerola	Steelpan of Stoofpanl
Kettle	Bouilloire	Caldero	Ketel
Tea pot	Théière	Tetera	Theepot
Coffee pot	Cafetière	Cafetera	Koffiepot
Knives	Couteaux	Cuchillos	Messen
Forks	Fourchettes	Tenedores	Vorken
Spoons	Cuillères	Cucharas	Lepels
Can opener	Ouvre-boites	Abrelatas	Blikopener
Corkscrew	Tire-bouchon	Sacacorchos	Kurketrekker
Matches	Allumettes	Cerillas	Lucifers
Dishwashing liquid	Détergent	Detergente	Afwasmiddel

8 NAVIGATION EQUIPMENT

ENGLISH	FRENCH	SPANISH	DUTCH
Chart table	Table à cartes	Planero	Kaartentafel
Chart	Carte marine	Carta Náutica	Zeekaarta
Parallel ruler	Règles parallèles	Regla de paralelas	Parallel Liniaal
Protractor	Rapporteur	Transportador	Gradenboog
Pencil	Crayon	Lápiz	Potlood
Eraser	Gomme	Goma	Vlakgom
Dividers	Pointes sèches	Compas de puntas	Verdeelpasser
Binoculars	Jumelles	Gemelos	Kijker
Compass	Compas	Compás	Kompas
Hand bearing compass	Compas de relèvement	Alidada	Handpeilkompas
Depth sounder	Echosondeur	Sondador acústico	Echolood
Radio receiver	Poste récepteur	Receptor de radio	Radio-ontvangtoestel

Appendices

ENGLISH	FRENCH	SPANISH	DUTCH
Direction finding radio	Récepteur goniométrique	Radio goniómetro	Radiopeiltoestel
Patent log	Loch enregistreur	Coredera de patente	Patent log
Sextant	Sextant	Sextante	Sextant

9 ENGINES

Gas engine	Moteur à essence	Motor de gasolina	Benzinemotor
Diesel engine	Moteur diesel	Motor diesel	Dieselmotor
Two-stroke	À deuxtemps	Dos tiempos	Tweetakt
Four-stroke	À quartre temps	Cuatro tiempos	Viertakt
Exhaust pipe	Tuyau déchappement	Tubo de escape	Uitlaatpijp
Gearbox	Boîte de vitesse	Caja de engranajes	Versnelligsbak
Gear lever	Levier des vitesses	Palanca de cambio	Versnellingshendel
Throttle	Accélérateur	Estrangulador	Manette
Clutch	Embrayage	Embrague	Koppeling
Stern tube	Tube d'étambot, arbre	Bocina	Schroefaskoker
Fuel pump	Pompe à combustible	Bomba de alimentación	Brandstofpomp
Carburetor	Carburateur	Carburado	Carburateur
Fuel tank	Réservoir de combustible	Tanque de combustible	Brandstoftank

10 ENGINE ACCESSORIES

Cylinder head	Culasse	Culata	Cilinderkop
Jointing compound	Pâte à joint	Junta de culata	Vloeibare pakking
Nut	Ecrou	Tuerca	Moer
Bolt	Boulon	Perno	Bout
Washer	Rondelle	Arandela	Ring
Split pin	Coupille fendue	Pasador abierto	Splitpen
Asbestos tape	Ruban d'amiante	Cinta de amianto	Asbestband
Copper pipe	Tuyau de cuivre	Tubo de cobre	Koperpijp
Plastic pipe	Tuyau de plastique	Tubo de plastico	Plastikpijp

11 ELECTRICS

Voltage	Tension	Voltaje	Spanning
Amp	Ampères	Amperio	Ampère
Spark plug	Bougie	Bujia	Bougie
Dynamo	Dynamo	Dinamo	Dynamo
Magneto	Magnéto	Magneto	Magneet
Dynamo belt	Courroi de dynamo	Correa de dinamo	Dynamo-riem
Battery	Accumulateur	Bateria	Accu
Contact breaker	Interrupteur	Disyuntor	Contactonderbreker
Fuse box	Boîte à fusibles	Caja de fusibles	Zekeringskast
Switch	Commutateur	Interruptor	Schakelaar
Bulb	Ampoule	Bombilla	Lampje
Copper wire	File de cuivre	Cable de cobre	Koperdraad
Distilled water	Eau distillée	Agua destilada	Gedistilleerd water
Solder	Soudure	Soldadura	Soldeer
Flux	Flux	Flux	Smeltmiddel
Insulating tape	Ruban isolant	Cinta aislante	Isolatieband

ENGLISH	FRENCH	SPANISH	DUTCH

12 FUEL, ETC

ENGLISH	FRENCH	SPANISH	DUTCH
Gasoline	Essence	Gasolina	Benzine
Kerosene	Pétrole lampant	Petroleo	Petroleum
Diesel oil	Gas-oil	Gasoil	Dieselolie
Alcohol	Alcool à brûler	Alcool desnaturalizado	Spiritus
Lubricating oil	Huile	Aceite de lubricación	Smeerolie
Two-stroke oil	Huile deux temps	Aceite de motor 2 tiempos	Tweetaktolie
Penetrating oil	Huile penetrante, dégrippant	Aceite penetrante	Kruipolie
Grease	Graisse	Grasa	Vet

13 METALS

ENGLISH	FRENCH	SPANISH	DUTCH
Galvanised iron	Fer galvanisé	Hierro galvanizado	Gegalvaniseerd ljzer
Stainless steel	Acier inoxydable	Acero inoxidable	Roestvrij staal
Iron	Fer	Hierro	Ijzer
Steel	Acier	Acero	Staal
Copper	Cuivre	Cobre	Koper
Brass	Laiton	Latón	Messing
Aluminum	Aluminium	Aluminio	Aluminium
Bronze	Bronze	Bronce	Brons

14 LIGHTS

ENGLISH	FRENCH	SPANISH	DUTCH
Navigation lights	Feux de bord	Luces de navegación	Navigatie lichten
Mast head light	Fue de téte de mât	Luz del tope de proa	Toplicht
Spreader light	Feu de barre de flèche	Luz de verga	Zalinglicht
Port light	Feu de babord	Luz de babor	Bakboordlicht
Starboard light	Feu de tribord	Luz de estribor	Stuurboordlicht
Stern light	Feu arrière	Luz de alcance	Heklicht
Cabin lamp	Lampe de cabine	Lámpera de camarote	Kajuitlamp
Lamp glass	Verre de lampe	Lámpara de cristal	Lampeglas
Wick	Mèche	Mecha (para engrase)	Kous

15 SHIP'S PAPERS

ENGLISH	FRENCH	SPANISH	DUTCH
Certificate of Registry	Acte de francisation	Patente de Navegación	Zeebrief
Pratique	Libre-pratique	Plática	Verlof tot ontscheping
Ship's Log	Livre de bord	Cuaderno de bitácora	Journaal
Insurance certificate	Certificat d'assurance	Poliza de seguro	Verzekeringsbewijs
Passport	Passeport	Passaporte	Paspoort
Customs clearance	Dédouanement	Despacho de aduana	Bewijs van inklaring door douane

16 TOOLS

ENGLISH	FRENCH	SPANISH	DUTCH
Hammer	Marteau	Martillo	Hamer
Wood chisel	Ciseau à bois	Formón	Beitel
Cold chisel	Ciseau à froid	Cortafrio	Koubeitel
Screwdriver	Tournevis	Destornillador	Schroevedraaier
Spanner	Clé	Llave para tuercas	Sleutel
Adjustable spanner	Clé anglaise	Llave adjustable	Verstelbare sleutel
Saw	Scie	Sierra	Zaag
Hacksaw	Scie à métaux	Sierra para metal	IJzerzaag
Hand drill	Chignolle à main	Taladro de mano	Handboor

Appendices

ENGLISH	FRENCH	SPANISH	DUTCH
File	Lime	Lima	Vijl
Wire cutters	Pinces coupantes	Cortador de alambre	Draadschaar
Pliers	Pinces	Alicates	Buigtang
Wrench	Tourne-à-gauche	Llave de boca	Waterpomptang

17 CHANDLERY

Burgee	Guidon	Grimpola	Clubstandaard
Ensign	Pavillon	Pabellón	Natie vlag
Courtesy flag	Fanion de courtoisie	Pabellón extranjero	Vreemde natievlag
Q flag	Pavillon Q	Bandera Q	Quarantaine Vlag
Signal flag	Pavillon (alphabetique)	Bandera de senales	Seinvlag
Anchor	Ancre	Ancla	Anker
Anchor chain	Chaîne d'ancre	Cadena del ancla	Ankerketting
Rope	Cordage	Cabulleria	Touw
Hawser	Cable d'acier	Estacha, amarra	Staaldraad
Synthetic rope	Cordage synthétique	Cabullería sintetica	Synthetisch touw
Nylon rope	Cordage de nylon	Cabullería de nylon	Nylon touw
Dacron	Cordage de Tergal	Cabullería de terylene	Terylene touw
Hemp rope	Cordage de chanvre	Cabullería de canamo	Henneptouw
Fender	Defense	Defensa	Stootkussen
Lifebuoy	Bouée sauvetage	Guindola	Redding boei
Cleat	Taquet	Cornamusa	Klamp
Winch	Winch	Chigre	Lier
Boat hook	Gaffe	Bichero	Pikhaak
Oar	Aviron	Remo	Riem
Fair lead	Chaumard	Guía	Verhaalkam
Eye bolt	Piton de filière	Cáncamo	Oogbout
Paint	Peinture	Pintura	Verf
Varnish	Vernis	Barniz	Lak
Sandpaper	Papier de verre	Papel de lija	Schuurpapier
Foghorn	Corne de brume	Bocina de niebla	Misthoorn

18 FOOD

Cheese	Fromage	Queso	Kaas
Butter	Beurre	Mantequilla	Boter
Bread	Pain	Pan	Brood
Milk	Lait	Leche	Melk
Jam	Confiture	Compota	Jam
Marmalade	Confiture d'oranges	Marmelada	Marmelade
Mustard	Moutarde	Mostaza	Mosterd
Salt	Sel	Sal	Zout
Pepper	Poivre	Pimienta	Peper
Vinegar	Vinaigre	Vinagre	Azijn
Meat	Viande	Carne	Vlees
Fish	Poisson	Pescado	Vis
Fruit	Fruits	Frutas	Fruit
Vegetables	Légumes	Legumbres	Groenten
Sausages	Saucisses	Embutidos	Worstjes
Ham	Jambon	Jamón	Ham
Beef	Boeuf	Carne de vaca	Rundvlees
Pork	Porc	Carne de cerdo	Varkensvlees
Lamb	Mouton	Carne de cernero	Schapenvlees
Bacon	Lard fumé	Tocino	Spek
Eggs	Oeufs	Huevos	Eieren
Fresh water	Eau douce	Agua dulce	Zoetwater

ENGLISH	FRENCH	SPANISH	DUTCH

19 SHOPS AND PLACES ASHORE

ENGLISH	FRENCH	SPANISH	DUTCH
Grocer	Épicier	Tendero de Comestibles	Kruidenier
Greengrocer	Marchand de légumes	Verdulero	Groente handelaar
Butcher	Boucher	Carnicero	Slager
Baker	Boulanger	Panadero	Bakker
Fishmonger	Quincaillerie	Ferretero	IJzerwaronwinkel
Supermarket	Supermarché	Supermercado	Supermarkt
Market	Marché	Mercado	Markt
Yacht chandler	Fournisseur de marine	Almacén de efectos navales	Scheepsleverancier
Sailmaker	Voilier	Velero	Zeilmakeri
Garage	Garage	Garaje	Garage
Railway station	Gare	Estación	Station
Bus	Autobus	Autobus	Bus
Post Office	Poste	Correos	Postkantoor
Bank	Banque	Banco	Bank
Pharmacist	Pharmacien	Farmaceútico	Apotheek
Hospital	Hôpital	Hospital	Ziekenhuis
Doctor	Médecin	Medico	Dokter
Dentist	Dentiste	Dentista	Tandarts

20 IN HARBOR

ENGLISH	FRENCH	SPANISH	DUTCH
Harbor	Bassin	Puerto	Haven
Yacht harbor	Bassin pour yachts	Puerto de yates	Jachthaven
Fishing harbor	Port de pêche	Puerto pesquero	Vissershaven
Harbor master	Capitaine de port	Capitan de puerto	Havenmeester
Harbor master's office	Bureau de Capitaine de port	Comandacia de puerto	Havenkantoor
Immigration officer	Agent du service de l'immigration	Oficial de inmigración	Immigratie beamte
Customs office	Bureau de douane	Aduana	Douanekantoor
Prohibited area	Zone interdite	Zona prohibida	Verboden gebied
Anchoring prohibited	Défense de mouiller	Fondeadero prohibido	Verboden ankerplaats
Mooring prohibited	Accostage interdit	Amarradero prohibido	Verboden aan te leggen
Lock	Écluse	Esclusa	Sluis
Canal	Canal	Canal	Kanaal
Mooring place	Point d'accostage	Amarradero	Aanlegplaats
Movable bridge	Pont mobile	Puente móvil	Beweegbare brug
Swing bridge	Pont tourant	Puente giratorio	Draaibrug
Lifting bridge	Pont basculant	Puente levadizo	Hefbrug
Ferry	Bac	Transbordador	Veer
Harbor steps	Éscalier du quai	Escala Real	Haventrappen

21 FIRST AID

ENGLISH	FRENCH	SPANISH	DUTCH
Bandage	Bandage	Venda	Verband
Lint	Pansement	Hilacha	Verbandgaas
Bandaid	Pansement adhésif	Esparadrapo	Kleefpleister
Scissors	Ciseaux	Tijeras	Schaar
Safety pin	Épingle de sûreté	Imperidibles	Veiligheidsspeld
Tweezers	Pince à échardes	Pinzas	Pincet
Thermometer	Thermométre	Termómetro	Thermometer
Disinfectant	Désinfectant	Desinfectante	Desinfecterend-middel
Aspirin tablets	Aspirine	Pastillas de aspirina	Aspirine
Laxative	Laxatif	Laxante	Laxeermiddel

Appendices

ENGLISH	FRENCH	SPANISH	DUTCH
Indigestion tablets	Pillules contre l'indigestion	Pastillas laxantes	Laxeertabletten
Antiseptic cream	Onguent antiseptique	Pomada antiséptica	Antiseptische zalf
Anti-seasickness pills	Remède contre le mal de mer	Pildoras contra el mareo	Pillen tegen zeeziekte
Calamine lotion	Lotion a la calamine	Locion de calamina	Anti-jeuk middel
Wound dressing	Pansement stérilisé	Botiquin para heridas	Noodverband
Stomach upset	Mal à l'estomac	Corte de digestion	Last van de maag

CHART TERMS

1 LIGHT CHARACTERISTICS

F.	Fixe	f.	v.
Oc.	Occ.	Oc.	O.
Iso	Iso	Iso./Isof.	Iso.
Fl.	É	D.	S.
Q	Scint	Ct.	Fl.
IQ	Scint. dis.	Gp. Ct.	Int. Fl.
Al.	Alt.	Alt.	Alt.
Oc.(..)	… Occ.	Gp. Oc. Gr. Oc.	GO.
Fl.(..)	… É	Gp. D.	GS.
Mo	-	Mo	-
FFl	Fixe É	F.D.	V & S
FFl.(..)	Fixe .. É	F. Gp. D./Gp. DyF.	V & GS

2 COMPASS POINTS

North (N) South (S)	Nord (N) Sud (S)	Norte (N) Sur (S)	Noord (N) Zuid (Z)
East (E) West (W)	Est (E) Ouest (O)	Este, Leste (E) Oeste (W)	Oost (O) West (W))
North East (NE)	Nordé (NE)	Nordeste (NE)	Noord-oost (NO)
North-North East (NNE)	Nord-Nordé (NNE)	Nornordeste (NNE)	Noord-noord-oost (NNO)
North by East	Nord quart Nordé	Norte cuarta al Este (N4NE)	Noord ten oosten (N-t-O)

3 COLORS

Black	Noir (n)	Negro (n)	Zwart (Z)
Red	Rouge (r)	Rojo (r)	Rood (R)
Green	Vert (v)	Verde (v)	Groen (Gn)
Yellow	Jaune (j)	Amarillo (am)	Geel (Gl)
White	Blanc (b)	Blanco (b)	Wit (w)
Orange	Orange (org)	Naranja	Oranje (or)
Blue	Bleu (bl)	Azul (az)	Blauw (B)
Brown	Brun	Pardo (p)	Bruin
Violet	Violet (vio)	Violeta	Violet (Vi)

4 RADIO AND AURAL AIDS

Radiobeacon	Radiophare	Radiofaro	Radiobaken
Diaphone	Diaphone	Diafono	Diafoon
Horn	Nautophone	Nautofono	Nautofoon
Siren	Siène	Sirena	Mistsirene
Reed	Trompette	Bocina	Mistfluit
Explosive	Explosion	Explosivo	Knalsignaal
Bell	Cloche	Campana	Mistklok
Gong	Gong	Gong	Mistgong
Whistle	Sifflet	Silbato	Mistfluit

ENGLISH	FRENCH	SPANISH	DUTCH
5 STRUCTURE OR FLOAT			
Dolphin	Duc d'Albe	Dague de Alba	Ducdalf
Light	Feu	Luz	Licht
Lighthouse	Phare	Faro	Lichttoren
Light vessel	Bateau feu	Faro flotanto	Lichtschip
Light float	Feu flottant	Luzflotante	Lichtvlot
Beacon	Balise	Baliza	Baken
Column	Colonne	Columna	Lantaarnpaal
Dwelling	Maison	Cora	Huis
Framework Tower	Pylone	Armazon	Traliemast
House	Bâtiment	Casa	Huis
Hut	Cabane	Caseta	Huisje
Mast	Mât	Mastil	Mast
Post	Poteau	Poste	Lantaarnpaal
Tower	Tour	Torre	Toren
Mooring buoy	Boueé de corps-mort	Boya de amarre muerto	Meerboei
Buoy	Bouée	Boya	Ton
6 TYPE OF MARKING			
Band	Bande	Fajas horizontales	Horizontaal gestreept
Stripe	Raie	Fajas verticales	Vertikaal gestreept
Chequered	à damier	Damero	Geblokt
Top mark	Voyant	Marea de Tope	Topteken
7 SHAPE			
Round	Circulaire	Redondo	Rond
Conical	Conique	Conico	Kegelvormig
Diamond	Losange	Rombo	Ruitvormig
Square	Carré	Cuadrangular	Vierkant
Triangle	Triangle	Triangulo	Driehoek
8 DESCRIPTION			
Destroyed	Détruit	Destruido	Vernield
Occasional	Feu occasionnel	Ocasional	Facultatief
Temporary	Temporaire	Temporal	Tijdelijk
Extinguished	Éteint	Apagada	Gedoofd
9 TIDE			
High Water	Pleine mer	Pleamar	Hoog water
Low Water	Basse mer	Bajamar	Lagg watery
Flood	Marée montante	Entrante	Vloed
Ebb	Marée decandante	Vaciante	Eb
Stand	Étale	Margen	Stil water
Range	Amplitude	Repunte	Verval
Spring tide	Vive eau	Marea viva	Springtij
Neap tide	Morte eau	Aguas Muertas	Doodtij
Sea level	Niveau	Nivel	Waterstand
Mean	Moyen	Media	Gemiddeld
Current	Courant	Corriente	Stroomt
10 CHART DANGERS			
Sunken rock	Roche subergée	Roca siempre cubierta	Blinde klip
Wreck	Épave	Naufragio (Nauf)	Wrak
Shoal	Haut fond (Ht. Fd.)	Bajo (Bo)	Droogte, ondiepte (Dre.)
Obstruction	Obstruction (Obs.)	Obstrución (Obston.)	Belemmering van de vaart, hindernis (Obstr.)

Appendices

ENGLISH	FRENCH	SPANISH	DUTCH
Overfalls	Remous et clapotis	Escarceos, hileros	Waterrafel
Dries	Assèche	Que vela en bajmar	Droogvallend
Isolated Danger	Danger isolé	Peligro aislado	Losliggend gevaar

11 WEATHER

ENGLISH	FRENCH	SPANISH	DUTCH
Weather Forecast	Prévions météo	Previsión meteorologica	Weersvoorspelling
Gale	Coup de vent	Duro	Storm
Squall	Grain	Turbonada	Bui
Fog	Brouillard	Niebla	Mist
Mist	Brume légere ou mouillée	Neblina	Nevel

12 DIMENSIONS

ENGLISH	FRENCH	SPANISH	DUTCH
Height	Tirant d'air	Altura	Doorvaarthoogte
Width	Largeur, de large	Ancho, anchura	Breedte
Depth	Profondeur	Fondo, profundidad	Diepte
Draft	Tirant d'eau	Calado	Diepgang

SIMPLE FORM OF SALVAGE AGREEMENT

"No Cure — No Pay"
(Incorporating Lloyd's Open Form)

DATE:_____

It is Hereby Agreed Between_____

for and on behalf of the Owners of the _____
(Hereinafter called "the Owners")

And_____ for and on behalf of _____
(Hereinafter called "the Contractor")

1) That the Contractor will use his best endeavors to salve the _____
and take her into_____
or such other place as may hereinafter be agreed, or if no place is named or agreed, to a place of
safety.

2) That the services shall be rendered by the Contractor and accepted by the owner as salvage
services upon the principal of "No cure — No pay", subject to the terms, conditions and provisions (including those relating to Arbitration and the providing of security) of the current Standard Form of Salvage Agreement approved and published by the Council of Lloyd's of London
and known as Lloyd's Open Form.

3) In the event of success, the Contractor's remuneration shall be $_____, or if no sum
be mutually agreed between the parties or entered herein, same shall be fixed by arbitration in
London in the manner prescribed in Lloyd's Open Form.

4) The Owners, their servants and agents, shall cooperate fully with the Contractor in and about
the salvage including obtaining entry to the place named in Clause 1 hereof or the place of safety. The Contractor may make reasonable use of the vessel's machinery, gear, equipment, anchors,
chains, stores and other appurtenances during, and for the purpose of the services, free of
expense, but shall not unnecessarily damage, abandon or sacrifice the same, or any property, the
subject of this Agreement.

For and on behalf of the Owners of property to be salved

_____

For and on behalf of the Contractor

_____

Note: Full copies of the Lloyd's Open Form Salvage Agreement can be obtained from the Salvage Arbitration Branch, Lloyd's of London, One Lime Street, London EC3M 7HA, Telephone:
(071) 623 7100, extension 5849, who should be notified of the services only when no agreement
can be reached as to remuneration.

Appendices

REED'S NAUTICAL COMPANION

Table of Contents

To get your **REED'S NAUTICAL COMPANION,** call 1-800-995-4995 and ask for the **REED'S** dealer nearest you!

INDEX

Index

Index

Index

Index

REED'S NAUTICAL ALMANAC

Index

Index

Index

Index

Notes

Notes

Notes

Notes

Notes